PREFACE

THIS is the first instalment of *The Oxford History of the Laws of England*, which will eventually comprise a dozen volumes prepared by different authors. The idea was floated by Professor Brian Simpson in 1986. It was refined in discussions between Professor Simpson, Professor Milsom, and myself, and the present scheme was accepted by Oxford University Press in 1987. The authors were commissioned over the next decade. Perhaps if the work had been undertaken in the 1880s rather than the 1980s it would have been completed in ten years; but the distractions of modern academic life, not to mention the supervening removal of the older public records from the centre of the metropolis, have delayed even the start well beyond a decade. And we begin, as it were, in the middle—with the period which seems to mark a fundamental transition between the medieval legal world and the more familiar; the period of intellectual revolution, of print and humanism, of Renaissance, Reformation, and Reception. The year 1483 has been chosen as the notional starting-point, rather than the year of Bosworth, by reason of the importance of the property legislation of 1483–4.

As the general editor of the series, I was the first to begin writing; and I have been able to borrow shamelessly from my own earlier work. So it is not surprising that this is one of the first two volumes to be published. In an ideal world it would have been better if the volumes had all appeared in chronological sequence, since law develops in a cumulative fashion and the contents of each volume necessarily depend on what has gone before. That has turned out not to be practicable, and so I have had to make assumptions about what will be treated in volumes which are yet to appear. Some important topics—such as the basic principles of feudal land law and the scheme of real actions—are given scant treatment here, on the footing that the core learning was largely inherited from an earlier period. Other topics are taken up at a rather advanced stage for a volume which for a while will have no immediate precursors. Much of this work lacks precursors in a historiographical sense as well, and therefore rests heavily on unpublished and unfamiliar sources. Reliance on so much previously unused material has made it necessary to provide more substantial footnotes than would have been acceptable in a work of synthesis. The account of legal institutions might also seem out of proportion, to a modern legal eye, since it has come to occupy as much space as the treatment of substantive law; but this is more than justified by the complexity of the legal system, which was still a system of jurisdiction and procedure and professional culture as much as it was a body of abstract jurisprudence. Canon law has been excluded, since it is the subject of a separate volume by Professor R. H. Helmholz; but it has been necessary to say something, from the common-law point of view, about the relations between ecclesiastical and secular jurisdiction.

It would have been a great advantage if the various questions of social, economic, constitutional, and political history which impinge directly upon some of the legal changes traced here could have been resolved with precision before this book went to press. Yet it would have been unrealistic to await such a miracle. The various layers of historical reality which should support our understanding of the legal past are no easier to uncover than the arcana of the law itself, and—for this period at any rate—hard information is still on many points unobtainable. It so happens that our voluminous legal records, and our reports of legal discussions, if properly understood, tell us a good deal about the England which existed outside the courts. Perhaps, indeed, the legal history of the period will throw as much light on other aspects of history as general histories have been able to cast upon the law. But for the time being the aims are better kept separate. This is not a constitutional history of England or a social history. The focus of this book, and of this series, is the intellectual and institutional framework within which the lawyers' opinions were formed and their arguments devised, the processes of litigation managed and recorded, and the legislative changes achieved. Some of the concerns are fundamentally jurisprudential; a few are inescapably technical. But they should not on that account be dismissed as historically insignificant, or as matters purely for the specialist, since they illuminate almost every aspect of English life and thought. I hope that most of the chapters will be reasonably accessible to readers who are not already experts in legal history.

Despite the generous length of time allowed by the publisher, it has been difficult to let go of this volume. A project of so broad a nature can never be finished, since every journey to the Public Record Office leads to further modifications. But completeness is unattainable, and doubtless undesirable. The object is to describe the main characteristics of English law and legal institutions in the early Tudor period, and to identify and explain the principal changes which occurred in the course of that period, rather than to provide an encylcopaedia digesting every jot and tittle of law and procedure, which would require several volumes.

So many colleagues and students have influenced my work, directly or indirectly, that I dare not embark on a list of particular acknowledgements for fear of accidental omission. I hope they will accept a general tender of gratitude, duly pleaded with an *uncore prist*.

J.H.B.

1 December 2002

The Oxford History of the Laws of England

THE OXFORD HISTORY OF THE LAWS OF ENGLAND

General Editor: Sir John Baker, Q.C., LL.D., F.B.A., Downing Professor of the Laws of England, and Fellow of St Catharine's College, Cambridge

The Oxford History of the Laws of England will provide a detailed survey of the development of English law and its institutions from the earliest times until the twentieth century, drawing heavily upon recent research using unpublished materials.

The Oxford History of the Laws of England

VOLUME VI
1483–1558

Sir John Baker

OXFORD
UNIVERSITY PRESS

OXFORD
UNIVERSITY PRESS

Great Clarendon Street, Oxford OX2 6DP

Oxford University Press is a department of the University of Oxford.
It furthers the University's objective of excellence in research, scholarship,
and education by publishing worldwide in

Oxford New York

Auckland Cape Town Dar es Salaam Hong Kong Karachi
Kuala Lumpur Madrid Melbourne Mexico City Nairobi
New Delhi Shanghai Taipei Toronto

With offices in

Argentina Austria Brazil Chile Czech Republic France Greece
Guatemala Hungary Italy Japan Poland Portugal Singapore
South Korea Switzerland Thailand Turkey Ukraine Vietnam

Oxford is a registered trade mark of Oxford University Press
in the UK and in certain other countries

Published in the United States
by Oxford University Press Inc., New York

British Library Cataloguing in Publication Data

Data available

Library of Congress Cataloging in Publication Data

Data available

ISBN 978–0–19–825817–9

3 5 7 9 10 8 6 4

Typeset by Newgen Imaging Systems (P) Ltd., Chennai, India
Printed in Great Britain
on acid-free paper by
CPI Antony Rowe,
Chippenham, Wiltshire

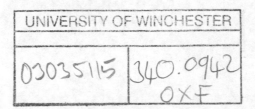

SUMMARY CONTENTS

IX. THE LAW OF TORTS

X. THE LAW OF CONTRACT

CONTENTS

IV. CIVIL PROCEDURE AND PLEADING

V. THE LEGAL PROFESSION AND ITS LEARNING

VI. CRIMINAL LAW AND PROCEDURE

VII. PERSONS

VIII. THE LAW OF PROPERTY

ABBREVIATIONS

Printed law reports, other than those referred to above, are cited according to the usual legal conventions. The abbreviations may be found in D. Raistrick, *Index to Legal Citations and Abbreviations* (2nd edn, 1993); or *Osborn's Concise Law Dictionary*, 2nd edn by S. Bone (2001); texts may be found in the *English Reports* reprint. Statutes are cited by regnal year and chapter; texts may be found in *SR*.

abr.	abridged
Adgore's reading	Reading by Gregory Adgore in the Inner Temple, *c.*1489, on uses, tr. from CUL MS. Hh.3.10, ff. 19–28
adm.	admitted
A.-G.	Attorney-General
AJLH	*American Journal of Legal History*
Alnwick Castle MS.	Manuscript belonging to the duke of Northumberland, Alnwick Castle, Northumberland
Ames Fdn	Ames Foundation
APC	*Acts of the Privy Council,* new series, ed. J. R. Dasent (1890–1907), 32 vols. Vols 1–6 (1890–3) cover the period 1542 to 1558
app.	appointed
Att.-Gen.	Attorney-General
B.	Baron of the Exchequer
B. & M.	J. H. Baker and S. F. C. Milsom, *Sources of English Legal History: Private Law to 1750* (1986; corrected repr. 1999)
Baker, *IELH*	J. H. Baker, *An Introduction to English Legal History* (4th edn, 2002)
Baker, *Readers and Readings*	J. H. Baker, *Readers and Readings in the Inns of Court and Chancery* (13 Selden Soc. Suppl. Ser.; 2001)
Baker, *Serjeants at Law*	J. H. Baker, *The Order of Serjeants at Law* (5 Selden Soc. Suppl. Ser.; 1984)
BBLI	*The Records of the Honorable Society of Lincoln's Inn: The Black Books,* i, ed. W. P. Baildon (1897)
Benl.	*Les Reports de Gulielme Benloe,* ed. J. Rowe (1689). The reports are by William Bendlowes (d. 1584) of Lincoln's Inn, serjeant at law from 1555
BIHR	*Bulletin of the Institute of Historical Research*
BL	British Library
Bl. Comm.	W. Blackstone, *Commentaries on the Laws of England* (1765–9), 4 vols
Bodl. Lib.	Bodleian Library, Oxford

Bracton	*Bracton on the Laws and Customs of England*, ed. G. E. Woodbine, reissued with a translation by S. E. Thorne (1968–77), 4 vols. Cited by volume and page
Brooke Abr.	R. Brooke, *La Graunde Abridgement* (1573)
C.	Chancellor
C1	PRO, Chancery, files of bills and pleadings (Early Chancery Proceedings)
C4	PRO, Chancery, supplementary files
C24	PRO, Chancery, depositions
C33	PRO, Chancery, decree and order books
C38	PRO, Chancery, masters' reports
C43	PRO, Chancery, common-law proceedings (Rolls Chapel Series, Hen. VII onwards)
C44	PRO, Chancery, common-law proceedings (Tower Series, ending Ric. III)
C49	PRO, *Placita Cancellariae* (cases of privilege)
C66	PRO, Chancery, patent rolls
C67	PRO, Chancery, pardon rolls
C78	PRO, Chancery, decree rolls
C193	PRO, Chancery, Crown Office miscellaneous books
C244	PRO, Chancery, filed writs of *corpus cum causa*
C261	PRO, Chancery, filed injunctions
Caryll	*The Reports of John Caryll* (ed. J. H. Baker, 109–10 Selden Soc. 1999), 2 vols: cited as 1 or 2 Caryll
Caryll (Jun.)	Reports of cases (*c.*1527–37) by John Caryll (d. 1566), son of Serjeant Caryll, and a bencher of the Inner Temple, interspersed with Inner Temple material, pr. in 121 Selden Soc. 366–416
c.a.v.	*curia advisari vult*
CB	Chief Baron of the Exchequer
CCR	*Calendar of Close Rolls*
CELMC	J. H. Baker, *Catalogue of English Legal Manuscripts in Cambridge University Library* (Woodbridge, 1996)
CFR	*Calendar of Fine Rolls*
Chaloner	Reports of cases (*c.*1515–19) by Robert Chaloner (d. 1555) of Gray's Inn, pr. in 121 Selden Soc. 278–89
CHES	PRO, records of the County Palatine of Chester
Cholmeley	Reports of three cases (1544) by Randle Cholmeley (d. 1563) of Lincoln's Inn, pr. in 121 Selden Soc. 450–68
Chr. Yelverton's reports	Unprinted reports of cases (1556–62) by Christopher Yelverton (d. 1612), of Gray's Inn, later justice of the King's Bench: BL MS. Hargrave 388, ff. 243v–255v

CIPM	*Calendar of Inquisitions Post Mortem*
CITR	*The Inner Temple: its early history as illustrated by its records, 1558-1603,* ed. F. A. Inderwick (1896); reckoned as the first volume in the series *Calendar of Inner Temple Records*
CJCP	Chief Justice of the Common Pleas
CJKB	Chief Justice of the King's Bench
CLJ	*Cambridge Law Journal*
CLRO	Corporation of London Record Office, Guildhall
CLT	J. H. Baker, *The Common Law Tradition: lawyers, books and the law* (2001). Collected papers
Co. Ent.	E. Coke, *Booke of Entries* (1614)
Co. Inst.	E. Coke, *Institutes of the Laws of England* (1628–44), four parts, the first of which is Co. Litt
Co. Litt.	E. Coke, commentary on Litt. (q.v.), being the first part (1628) of Co. Inst. (q.v.)
CP 25	PRO, Common Pleas, feet of fines
CP 40	PRO, Common Pleas, plea rolls
CP 45	PRO, Common Pleas, prothonotaries' remembrance rolls
CP 50	PRO, Common Pleas, writs of covenant (for final concords)
CP 52	PRO, Common Pleas, writ files
CP 60	PRO, Common Pleas, docket rolls
CPMR	*Calendar of Plea and Memoranda Rolls Preserved among the Archives of the City of London,* ed. A. H. Thomas and P. E. Jones (1926–61), 6 vols covering the period 1323–1482
CPR	*Calendar of Patent Rolls*
Crown Office entries	Unprinted book of entries from the Crown side of the King's Bench, *c.*1465–95, with sixteenth-century additions, marked on the cover 'Oli: Cook E. iiii <& Hen. vii>', PRO, KB 15/42
CSC	Comparative Studies in Anglo-American and Continental Legal History (1985–)
CSPD	*Calendar of State Papers (Domestic)*
CUL	Cambridge University Library
Dal.	*Les Reports des divers Special Cases... colligees par Gulielme Dalison,* ed. J. Rowe (1689)
Dalison's reports	Unprinted reports of cases by William Dalison (1552–8), justice of the Queen's Bench: BL MS. Harley 5141
Derbs. Record Office	Derbyshire Record Office, Matlock, Derbyshire

Diversite de Courtz	Anon., *Diversite de Courtz et lour Jurisdictions* (1526); or later edns as cited
DKR	*Reports of the Deputy Keeper of Public Records*
DL	PRO, records of the duchy of Lancaster
DNB	*Dictionary of National Biography*. The *New DNB* is due for publication in 2004
Doctor and Student, ed. Plucknett and Barton	*St German's Doctor and Student*, ed. T. F. T. Plucknett and J. L. Barton (91 Selden Soc.; 1974)
Dudley's reading (1496)	Reading by Edmund Dudley in Gray's Inn, Lent 1496, on Westminster II, c. 25, tr. from CUL MS. Hh. 3.10, ff. 59–96v
DURH	PRO, records of the county palatine of Durham
Dyer	J. Dyer, *Ascuns Novel Cases* (1585/6; tr. by J. Vaillant, 1794). Translations here were made by the author from the 1671 edn
E12	PRO, Exchequer, order and rule books of the Exchequer of Pleas
E13	PRO, Exchequer, plea rolls of the Exchequer of Pleas
E111	PRO, Exchequer, bills and pleadings on the equity side
E159	PRO, Exchequer, remembrance rolls of the king's remembrancer
E315	PRO, records of the Court of General Surveyors
E338	PRO, records of the Court of First Fruits
E368	PRO, Exchequer, remembrance rolls of the lord treasurer's remembrancer
Econ. Hist. Rev.	*Economic History Review*
EHR	*English Historical Review*
ELJ	*Ecclesiastical Law Journal*
ELMUSA	J. H. Baker, *English Legal Manuscripts in the United States of America* (1985, 1990), 2 pts
Elton, *Studies*	G. R. Elton, *Studies in Tudor and Stuart Politics and Government* (Cambridge, 1974–83), 3 vols. Collected papers
Fitz. Abr.	A. Fitzherbert, *La Graunde Abridgement* (1577 edn). The 1st edn was printed without title in 1514–16
Fitz. J.P.	A. Fitzherbert, *The Newe Boke of Justices of the Peas* (1538; facsimile repr. 1969, 1972)
FNB	A. Fitzherbert, *La Novel Natura Brevium* (1635 edn). The 1st edn was printed in 1534
Gell's reports	Unprinted reports of cases by Anthony Gell (d. 1583), bencher of the Inner Temple, in 2 vols: (i) (mostly 1542–55) Library of Congress, Law MS. 15; (ii) (mostly 1557–62) Derbs. Record Office, Hopton Hall deposit
GI	Gray's Inn library, London

Hall's Chronicle	*Hall's Chronicle*: *containing the history of England . . . to the end of the reign of Henry the Eighth*, ed. H. Ellis (1809). The author, Edward Hall or Halle (d. 1547), was a bencher of Gray's Inn
Hall's reading	Reading by Edward Hall in Gray's Inn, Lent 1541, on the peace of the Church, tr. from BL MS. Hargrave 92, ff. 57–62v
Hare	Reports of cases (*c.*1516–45) attributable to Sir Nicholas Hare (d. 1557), of the Inner Temple, pr. in 120 Selden Soc. 84–8
HCA	PRO, records of the High Court of Admiralty
HCJ	*Journals of the House of Commons*
HEHL	H. E. Huntington Library, San Marino, Calif.
Hesketh's reading	Reading by Richard Hesketh in Gray's Inn (*c.*1506/8), on the *Carta de Foresta*, tr. from BL MS. Lansdowne 1145
Hil.	Hilary term
HLJ	*Journals of the House of Lords*
HLS	Harvard Law School library, Cambridge, Mass.
HMC	Historical Manuscripts Commission
Holdsworth, *HEL*	W. S. Holdsworth, *History of English Law* (1903–66), 16 vols
HPHC 1509–58	*The History of Parliament*: *The House of Commons 1509–1558*, ed. S. T. Bindoff (1982), 3 vols
HPHC 1558–1603	*The History of Parliament*: *The House of Commons 1558–1603*, ed. P. W. Hasler (1981), 3 vols
HSCL	C. H. S. Fifoot, *History and Sources of the Common Law* (1949)
IJ	The Irish Jurist
IND	PRO, index series
IT	Inner Temple library, London
J.	Justice
J. Ass.	Justice of Assize
JCP	Justice of the Common Pleas
Jenour's entries	Unprinted book of entries compiled by John Jenour (d. 1542), second prothonotary of the Common Pleas: Library of Congress (MSS Division), MS. Phillipps 26752
JHB MS.	Manuscript belonging to the author
JJ	Justices
JKB	Justice of the King's Bench
JLH	*Journal of Legal History*
Jnl	*Journal*
JP	Justice of the Peace
JSPTL	*Journal of the Society of Public Teachers of Law*

KB 8	PRO, King's Bench, *baga de secretis*
KB 9	PRO, King's Bench, indictment files
KB 27	PRO, King's Bench, plea rolls
KB 29	PRO, King's Bench, Crown Office controlment rolls
KB 136	PRO, King's Bench, writ files (*Anglia* Series)
KB 146	PRO, King's Bench, files (*Panella* Series)
KB 147	PRO, King's Bench, bill files (*Bille Communes*)
KB 148	PRO, King's Bench, bill files (*Bille*)
KB 150	PRO, King's Bench, warrants of attorney
KB 167	PRO, King's Bench, secondary's remembrance rolls
Keil.	*Relationes quorundam Casuum Selectorum ex Libris Roberti Keilwey*, ed. J. Croke (1602). The reports of cases and moots were actually by John Caryll (d. 1523), serjeant at law; where texts are now pr. in Caryll (q.v.) or *Moots* (q.v.), only the Selden Soc. reference is given
K.Sjt	King's Serjeant
LHR	*Law and History Review*
LI	Lincoln's Inn library, London
li. lo.	imparlance (*licencia loquendi*)
Lib. Ass.	*Liber Assisarum*
Lisle Letters, ed. Byrne	*The Lisle Letters*, ed. M. S. Byrne (Chicago, 1981), 6 vols
Litt.	T. Littleton, *Tenures Novelli* [1481]; numerous subsequent edns; repr. in Co. Litt. (q.v.)
LK	Lord Keeper of the Great Seal
LP	*Letters and Papers of the Reign of Henry VIII*, ed. J. S. Brewer and others (1862–1932), 21 vols in 33. Includes a calendar of the state papers and patent rolls for the reign. Unless otherwise stated, references are to the item numbers, not the pages
LPCL	J. H. Baker, *The Legal Profession and the Common Law: historical essays* (1986). Collected papers
LQR	*Law Quarterly Review*
Lucas's entries	Unprinted book of King's Bench entries (temp. Hen. VII and Hen. VIII) compiled by John Lucas (d. 1525), filazer of the court: Library of Congress (MSS Division), MS. Phillipps 11910
m.	membrane
Marow, *Reading*, ed. Putnam	B. H. Putnam, *Early Treatises on Justices of the Peace* (7 Oxford Studies in Social and Legal History, Oxford; 1924), 286–414, being an edition of Thomas Marow's reading in the Inner Temple (Lent 1503) on Westminster I, c. 1, *de pace*

Maycote's entries	Unprinted book of King's Bench entries (mostly 1490s to 1520s) compiled by Robert Maycote (d. 1533), clerk of the papers in that court: Library of Congress (MSS Division), MS. Phillipps 9071
Mich.	Michaelmas term
Milsom, *HFCL*	S. F. C. Milsom, *Historical Foundations of the Common Law* (2nd edn, 1981)
Moots	*Readings and Moots at the Inns of Court in the Fifteenth Century*, ii, Moots and Readers' Cases, ed. J. H. Baker (105 Selden Soc.; 1989)
MR	Master of the Rolls
MT	Middle Temple library, London
MT 12	Middle Temple archives, records of New Inn
MTR	*Middle Temple Records: Minutes of Parliament*, i (1501–1603), ed. C. A. Hopwood (1904)
n.	note
NfRO	Norfolk Record Office, Norwich
OED	*Oxford English Dictionary*
op. se	*optulit se*
Ord.	Order (of court)
Pas.	Easter term
PBGI	*Pension Book of Gray's Inn*, i, ed. R. J. Fletcher (1901)
PCC	Prerogative Court of Canterbury. See PROB 11
PCY	Prerogative Court of York, will registers now in the Borthwick Institute, York
Perk.	J. Perkins, *Perutilis Tractatus Magistri Johannis Parkins Interioris Templi Socii* (1528); or later edns (with section numbers)
Pilkington Narrative	*The Narrative of Robert Pilkington*, manuscript in North Yorkshire Record Office, Northallerton, partly pr. in HMC, *Report on Manuscripts in Various Collections*, ii (1903), 28–56
PL	PRO, records of the county palatine of Lancaster
Plowd.	*Les Comentaries, ou Reports de Edmund Plowden* (1571, being the first part). Translations here were made by the author from the 1613 edn
Plucknett, *CHCL*	T. F. T. Plucknett, *Concise History of the Common Law* (5th edn, 1956)
Plumpton Letters	*The Plumpton Letters and Papers*, ed. J. Kirby (8 Camden 5th ser., Cambridge; 1996)
Pollard	Reports of cases by Richard Pollard (d. 1542), bencher of the Middle Temple, pr. 121 Selden Soc. 246–77
Port	*The Notebook of Sir John Port*, ed. J. H. Baker (102 Selden Soc.; 1986)
pr.	printed
PRO	Public Record Office, Kew, Surrey

PROB 11	PRO, Prerogative Court of Canterbury, registers of wills
Rast. Ent.	W. Rastell, *A Colleccion of Entrees* (1566), with references to the 1670 edn in brackets. Compiled by William Rastell (d. 1565), justice of the Queen's Bench
Readers and Readings	J. H. Baker, *Readers and Readings in the Inns of Court and Chancery* (13 Selden Soc. Suppl. Ser.; 2001)
repr.	reprinted
REQ	PRO, records of the Court of Requests
RHD	*Revue Historique de Droit Français et Étranger*
RP	*Rotuli Parliamentorum ut et Petitiones in Parliamento* [1783], 6 vols
RS	Rolls Series
St German, *Doctor and Student*	see *Doctor and Student*
St German, *Little Treatise*, ed. Guy	C. St German, *A Litle Treatise concerning Writs of Subpena* [*c*.1531], pr. in J. Guy, *Christopher St German on Chancery and Statute* (1985), at 106–26
SBEL	A. K. R. Kiralfy, *Source Book of English Law* (1957)
SC	PRO, Special Collections
Selden Soc.	Selden Society
SfRO	Suffolk Record Office, Ipswich branch
S.-G.	Solicitor-General
SHCL	S. F. C. Milsom, *Studies in the History of the Common Law* (1985). Collected papers
Shakelady's precedents	Collection of precedents of writs (mostly *c*.1550–60) by Rowland Shakelady, cursitor of the Chancery: BL MS. Harley 1856
sig.	signature (of printed book)
sjt	serjeant at law
Sol.-Gen.	Solicitor-General
SP	PRO, State Papers series
Spelman	*The Reports of Sir John Spelman*, ed. J. H. Baker (93 Selden Soc; 1977)
Spelman's reading	*John Spelman's Reading on Quo Warranto delivered in Gray's Inn (Lent, 1519)*, ed. J. H. Baker (113 Selden Soc.; 1997)
sp. mod.	spelling modernized
SR	*Statutes of the Realm* (Record Commission, 1810–28), 12 vols. Quotations here are rendered into modern spelling
Sta. P. C.	W. Staunford, *Les Plees del Coron* (1557)
STAC	PRO, records of the Court of Star Chamber
Starkey, *Dialogue*	*Thomas Starkey: a dialogue between Pole and Lupset*, ed. T. F. Mayer (37 Camden Soc., 4th ser.; 1989)

STC²	A. W. Pollard and G. R. Redgrave, *A Short-title Catalogue of Books printed in England 1475–1640*, 2nd edn by W. A. Jackson, F. S. Ferguson, and K. Pantzer (1976–91), 3 vols
St. Tr.	W. Cobbett, T. B. Howell, and T. J. Howell (eds), *A Complete Collection of State Trials* (1809–26), 33 vols, of which the first covers the period of this volume
Stubbe's entries	Unprinted book of Common Pleas entries (temp. Hen. VIII) by Edward Stubbe (d. 1533), chief prothonotary: BL MS. Add. 24078
temp.	in the time of (*tempore*)
tr.	translated
Treherne's reading	Reading by George Treherne, in Lincoln's Inn (autumn 1520), on the *Carta de Foresta*, tr. (unless otherwise stated) from the French text in CUL MS. Dd.3.39
TRHS	*Transactions of the Royal Historical Society*
Trin.	Trinity term
Tudor Royal Proclamations	*Tudor Royal Proclamations*, ed. P. L. Hughes and J. F. Larkin, vols i (1485–1553) and ii (1553–87) (New Haven, 1964–9)
VCH	Victoria County History of England and Wales
Venetian Relation	*A Relation, or rather a True Account of the Island of England about the Year 1500*, ed. C. A. Sneyd (37 Camden Soc.; 1847); tr. from Italian
WARD	PRO, records of the Court of Wards and Liveries
Wm Yelv.	Reports of cases (1526–40) attributable to William Yelverton (d. 1586), bencher of Gray's Inn, pr. 121 Selden Soc. 290–365
YCA	York City Archives, York
Yelverton's reports	see Chr. Yelverton's reports; Wm Yelv.
Yorke	Reports of cases (mostly *c.*1520–35) by Roger Yorke (d. 1536), bencher of Gray's Inn, sjt 1531, pr. in 120 Selden Soc. 89–245

TABLE OF CASES

I. YEAR BOOKS

Note that named year-book cases are included in Part II of the Table (Named Cases), with cross-references from this part.

II. NAMED CASES

TABLE OF STATUTES

Part I

ENGLISH LAW AND
THE RENAISSANCE

1

English Law and the Renaissance

THE period between the accession of Richard III and the death of Mary I witnessed many striking changes in English society and culture: in economic conditions and the distribution of wealth, in the state of religion and the Church, in intellectual attitudes and scholarly enquiries, in literature and in the fine arts. There was nothing peculiarly English about this tide of change, which flowed across the Continent as well and is usually attributed to the new spirit of humanist rationalism which pervaded all Europe in the wake of the Renaissance. The whole universe came under questioning examination, from the heavens and the furthest reaches of the earth to the structure and physiology of tiny living creatures. The age of discovery was also the age of the Reformation and of the Scientific Revolution, each of which altered the ways in which intellectuals thought about the world and man's place in it. Nor did the new quest for rational understanding stop with God and the natural world; simultaneous advances were made in the humane sciences, such as history, philology, economics, and politics. Could the law of man possibly be immune from this new spirit?

Anyone who approaches the history of the common law during this age of intellectual revolution has to confront the rather surprising fact that the law of England seems on the surface hardly to have changed at all. The essential features of the law, and of the constitution, were settled long before the battle of Bosworth and were recognizably the same when Elizabeth I was crowned three-quarters of a century later. This anomaly struck Maitland as one of the great puzzles of English legal history, especially since the legal systems of continental Europe had proved to be as susceptible to humanist influence as other institutions. How, he asked, in an age when 'old creeds of many kinds were crumbling and all knowledge was being transfigured', could the medieval law of the year books survive and persist with such vigour that Coke in 1602 was able to describe Littleton's *Tenures* (written in the mid-fifteenth century) as 'the most perfect and absolute work that ever was written in any human science'?[1] How, in an age when 'Roman

---

[1] F. W. Maitland, *English Law and the Renaissance* (1901), 3–5. Maitland cited Coke's introductory letter to *La Dixme part des Reports* (1614) and the preface to Co. Litt., but the passage first occurs (in French) in *Le Second Part des Reportes* (1602), fo. 67.

law was driving German law out of Germany', could this medieval learning—written in 'queer old French'—stand its ground and fend off the competition from elegant Romanism?[2]

ENGLISH LAW AND THE RECEPTION

Maitland's discussion of the problem, in his scintillating Rede Lecture at Cambridge in 1901, has proved controversial, and most of his major assumptions have turned out, after a century's further research, to be mistaken. Nevertheless, the subject-matter of the lecture is so fundamental, and the influence of Maitland's questions on the concerns of subsequent historians has been so profound, that it ought to be tackled at the outset. Of course, the mistaken assumptions did not result from any lack of perceptiveness on Maitland's part, but from the state of the available evidence in 1901. He was well aware of the deficiencies of current knowledge, and therefore—as was appropriate to the occasion—attacked his subject with a broad brush, using vivid colours, and with due warnings that most of the detail would need further attention later. Several of his suggestions were made by allusion and nuance rather than direct assertion. As a result of overlooking the gradations of uncertainty in the lecture, a number of undercurrent themes were isolated by subsequent writers, usually as propositions to be criticized, where Maitland's own position was deliberately tentative.[3] But Maitland certainly made the assumption that the common law was in serious difficulties at the beginning of the sixteenth century, and that 'the continuity of English legal history was seriously threatened' by current Romanizing trends. Intellectuals were attacking the language and content of English law as barbarous, and praising the Civil law as refined and humane. Moreover, Schröder and other contemporary German historians had given Maitland to understand that the effect of the 'Reception' there had been either to drive out native law or at least to force it into 'humble forms and obscure corners'. Could not the English conciliar courts have done for English law what the Reichskammergericht had done for Germany? And there was also the political dimension. Was there not 'pleasant reading in the Byzantine Code for a king who wished to be monarch in church as well as state: pleasanter reading than could be found in our ancient English law-books'?[4]

---

[2] Maitland had first posed these questions in 1898, in a review of Baildon's edition of the first volume of *The Black Books of Lincoln's Inn*: 13 *EHR* 576-8.

[3] There is a useful commentary on some of these cross-purposes by D. Jenkins, 'English Law and the Renaissance Eighty Years On: in defence of Maitland' (1981) 2 *JLH* 107-42.

[4] *English Law and the Renaissance*, 14. For Henry VIII's claim to be an 'emperor' see W. Ullmann, 'This Realm of England is an Empire' (1979) 30 *Jnl Eccles. Hist.* 175-203; and below, 55, 246-7.

Given these premises, the stubborn continuity of English law seemed doubly remarkable. Maitland's answer to his own question was that England alone had, in the inns of court, schools of national law. No continental university could boast lecture-courses in municipal law, let alone such a galaxy of lecturers as the societies which produced (among many others) Littleton, Fortescue, and More. And it was this system of education which explained the feat of survival, for it was a system ideally suited to 'toughen and harden a traditional body of law'.[5]

Holdsworth was the first to re-examine Maitland's thesis in detail. He agreed that the continuity of English law was a remarkable phenomenon which demanded explanation, but he concluded that Maitland had over-emphasized the real danger of a reception of Roman law. There was a factual basis for all the individual arguments about the state of the common law: the decline of business (though this had been exaggerated), the defects in jurisprudence and administration, and the cessation of the year books. The supremacy of the common law was in consequence 'in very serious danger'. But Holdsworth thought it inconceivable that Parliament would have assented to a project to subvert the common law. There was no evidence that Roman law was widely felt to have been superior in practice, or that it would have helped the king's policies.[6]

The latter conclusion has been supported by later writers.[7] Henry VII and Henry VIII achieved what they wanted without recourse to alien jurisprudence. A well-received lecture in the inns of court on the prerogative, or on *Quo Warranto*, or uses, was a better qualification for royal service than years spent lecturing on the pandects or decretals in the universities. Under Henry VII, common-law trained ministers such as Empson, Dudley, and Lovell,[8] carried the royal interests as far as any Civilian would have dared. Henry VIII advanced common lawyers for the first time to the offices of master of the rolls and master of requests, and, after Cardinal Wolsey, appointed first a bencher of Lincoln's Inn (Sir Thomas More) and then a serjeant at law (Sir Thomas Audley) as lord chancellor. He filled his revenue courts with benchers and barristers. He continued to suppress the court of the Constable and Marshal, a court of Civil law, and in 1536 Parliament introduced common law criminal procedure in Admiralty cases. Moreover, no one ever produced a practical project for introducing substantive Roman law into England. A vague suggestion thrown out by a young clergyman, Thomas Starkey, recently a law student at Padua and enthusiastic about continental learning but with no

---

[5] *English Law and the Renaissance*, 24–8. [6] Holdsworth, *HEL*, iv. 252–93.

[7] S. E. Thorne, 'English Law and the Renaissance' (1966) repr. in *Essays in English Legal History* (1985), 187–95; F. W. Ives, *The Common Lawyers in pre-Reformation England* (1983), 189–91; G. R. Elton, 'The Common Law in Danger' in *F. W. Maitland* (1985), 79–88.

[8] All three were benchers, and had therefore lectured on the common law. Sir Richard Empson was of the Middle Temple, Edmund Dudley of Gray's Inn, and Sir Thomas Lovell of Lincoln's Inn.

deep knowledge of English law, is not the same thing.[9] It is true that Richard Morison, another Oxford cleric who read law at Padua,[10] did attempt an outline scheme for the codification of English law in Latin. But he did not suggest any reception of legal doctrine, only the reduction of the common law to a Roman method. As he put it, an English tailor could make an English gown from Italian velvet,[11] though it would have been more a case of making an Italian gown from English broadcloth. John Hales, a friend of Morison who likewise advocated a form of codification—that the laws be 'digested and gathered together as the Civil laws be'—regarded the substance of the existing law as better suited to the English than any other. He said there were some (unnamed) who wanted to introduce Roman law, but warned that 'if they had any wit they might soon perceive that changing of laws is very pernicious to a common weal and breedeth many scabs'.[12] Now, Morison and Hales are the only writers known to have penned more than a few words on the possibility of reforming English law after the Roman example. Neither of them was a lawyer,[13] and they were seduced by the popular fallacy that a code would reduce legal wrangling and litigation. No practical case was made. The introduction of some kind of order into the common and statute law was a more modest proposal which might and indeed did win some support from practising common lawyers.[14] But most of the latter would probably have agreed with the sentiments of Thomas Williams, who as reader of the Inner Temple in Lent 1558 defended the common law against the criticism 'by some persons of late days' that it was 'not a certain law digested into great volumes, like the Civil law'. Williams pointed out that Civilians did not despise the law of nature because it was unwritten, and asserted that in practice the common law was as certain and expeditious as any other, adding the confident challenge, 'whether it be so dilatory and tedious as the Civil law, in processes of appeal, I shall submit to the judgment of those that have had experience of both'.[15] Whether or not Williams's assessment

---

[9] Thorne, 'English Law and the Renaissance', 438–9; G. R. Elton, 'Reform by Statute: Thomas Starkey's *Dialogue* and Thomas Cromwell's policy' in *Studies*, ii. 246–7. There is now a modern edition of Starkey: *Thomas Starkey: a dialogue between Pole and Lupset*, ed. T. F. Mayer (37 Camden Soc., 4th ser., 1989). See also T. F. Mayer, *Thomas Starkey and the Commonweal: humanist politics and religion in the reign of Henry VIII* (1989).

[10] For the English law students at Padua, and their influence, see J. Woolfson, *Padua and the Tudors: English students in Italy 1485–1603* (1998), 39–72.

[11] R. Morison, *A Perswasion to the Kyng that the Law of his Realme shulde be in Latin* [c.1536]. BL Royal MS. 18 A. 50 (presentation copy with royal arms and HR monogram); BL Cotton MS. Faustina C. II, ff. 5–22 (corrected draft). See also Elton, *Studies*, ii. 247–50; below, 26–7.

[12] Hales, *An Oration in Commendation of the Laws of England* [c.1540] Royal MS., fo. 21.

[13] Morison was remarkably ignorant, suggesting that some of the law was written in Italian and some in Greek: *Perswasion*, fo. 6v.   [14] See below, 27–8, 502.

[15] Reading on 35 Hen. VIII, c. 6, pr. as *The Excellency and Praeheminence of the Law of England asserted in a learned Reading* (1680), at 9, 11.

was correct, it is unrealistic to think that anyone in the early Tudor period could have produced the 'great volumes' which a digest of the whole of English law would certainly have required. Even if they had, codification was not the same as Reception.

Not only has the practicability of a Reception been questioned, but so also has the assumption that the common law was so weakened by inherent defects that either replacement or substantial displacement could have been sensibly contemplated. Holdsworth himself made random samplings of the plea rolls which indicated that, despite a temporary falling-off in business, there was no such dramatic decline as might be gathered from Maitland's anecdotal references.[16] In fact there was, from the 1530s, a very significant steady growth in the business of both common-law benches. As for Maitland's remarks about the 'ominous event' of 1535, the 'dramatically appropriate' cessation of the year books 'when the Henrician terror is at its height',[17] Holdsworth's response was that this was not as significant as it would have been if the year books had been official publications. The decline could be explained, according to Holdsworth, by the appearance of the printed abridgments of Statham and Fitzherbert. This was an unconvincing response on its face, because the printing of abridgments of old cases could hardly explain a cessation of new reports. A. F. Pollard and Plucknett challenged the significance of the date more directly by pointing out that it was tied up with the history of law publishing rather than with the use made of law reports in the 1530s, since the year books were not printed contemporaneously with their contents and their printing did not decline after 1530.[18] But neither Holdsworth nor Plucknett, let alone Maitland, knew about the manuscript reports of the early Tudor period. We now know that the reporting tradition continued unabated, and that there were probably more lawyers keeping reports in this period than at any time since Edward II. There was no 'event' in 1535 at all, ominous or otherwise; the decision to end the printed year books in that year was made much later, and it was made by printers rather than lawyers or ministers.[19]

Then there is the problem of the Chancery and the conciliar courts. These tribunals bore some resemblance both to the imperial chamber court in Frankfurt

16 Elton, *Maitland*, points out that Holdsworth may have underestimated the decline in King's Bench business. On the other hand, Holdsworth misrepresented the state of Common Pleas business by unaccountably selecting a plague term for analysis: the roll for Mich. 1525 (CP 40/1048B) has the writ of common adjournment on m. 1d. See further below, ch. 5.

17 *English Law and the Renaissance*, 21–2, 77 n. 49. By 'terror', Maitland seems to be referring specifically to the execution of More: see p. 21.

18 A. F. Pollard, *Wolsey* (1929), 68; T. F. T. Plucknett, 'The Place of the Legal Profession in the History of English Law' (1932) 48 *LQR* 328 at 329–30.

19 See below, 473. The only known manuscript of the year book for 1535 continues into the 1540s with no change of style.

and to the Court of Session in Edinburgh, each of which was the scene of a Reception. They already followed a Romano-canonical form of written procedure, and some of their judges and masters were doctors of law. The reality of a jurisdictional threat from these tribunals has been generally accepted, and it is an established fact that their business increased dramatically in the early Tudor period. The increase began at a time when the common-law business was at a low ebb, around the time of Wolsey's chancellorship,[20] and this may explain contemporary fears of a jurisdictional revolution. Yet the new courts had limited capacities, and were more expensive than the common law.[21] By the end of Henry VIII's reign the work of the two common-law benches was increasing at least at the same rate as that of the Chancery and Star Chamber, and probably faster. In any case, the benches handled ten times more cases than the newer courts. There seems, therefore, to be no direct relationship between the fortunes of the two kinds of court when viewed across a longer span of time. Even more to the point, there is little evidence that the extraordinary tribunals ever tried to apply rules of Civil or canon law.[22] The odd quotation of a learned maxim by a canonist chancellor is unsurprising, since even a common-law judge might on occasion display his erudition with a Latin tag; but the use of learned texts and glosses would have been unthinkable in a court of conscience, especially in a court where those familiar with such learning had no rights of audience. Even if these courts were seen to pose a threat, for a short time, to the old courts of common law, they did not threaten the common-law system itself, because they had become in a sense an integral part of it, serviced by the very same profession. Indeed, it was Maitland who elsewhere argued that they helped to save English law from Romanism by pushing the regular courts into making desirable changes.[23] A century later the conciliar courts could be swept away without creating a gap in English jurisprudence. The Chancery would live on; but its jurisprudence was a gloss upon, not an alternative to, the common law.

All these criticisms are directed at Maitland's arguments rather than his principal question and its answer. If there was no real danger of a Reception of Roman law in England, the initial question simply becomes more insistent than Maitland realized: why was the English experience so different from that of continental countries? Why was there no fight for survival in the face of a trend which a few hundred miles from Westminster seemed irresistible? It is in the context of these questions that the most serious challenge has come to Maitland's thesis, though it has arisen from the work of continental scholars who did not have Maitland in mind. Maitland had assumed that the effect of the Reception on the

[20] Note the legend reported by David Lloyd, below, 156.
[21] Below, 124.   [22] See further below, 179–82.
[23] 'Outline of English Legal History, 560–1600' in *Collected Papers*, ii. 416–96, at 495–6.

Continent was to sweep away the older customary forms of national law to make way for Roman law. But this, perhaps his most basic assumption, is not borne out by what is now thought in fact to have occurred.[24]

Maitland's view of the Reception was based chiefly on recent research in Germany, but it has since become evident that Germany's experience was untypical.[25] Germany had not previously had a national system of law, and in the area where the Reichskammergericht had greatest sway the procedure for disposing of cases before *schöffen* had not required the kind of distinguishing between fact and law which causes legal development. The introduction of a new royal court, with learned judges, meant that detailed questions of law were being raised formally for the first time; and, in the absence of a pre-existing body of legal rules to provide the answers, it was almost inevitable that the judges should have done the rationalizing with Romanist concepts and language, in much the same way as the author of *Bracton* had flirted with Roman terminology in thirteenth-century England. The Reception may therefore have had more to do with a shift towards the declaration of rules by courts than with an adoption of classical learning on its own merits; and this is a shift which is directly parallelled in England. In those parts of Germany where some indigenous principles of law were already committed to writing, as in the *Sachsenspiegel*, the Romanizing was much slower.[26] It seems also that Romanizing, when it took place, did not necessarily mean 'driving German law out of Germany', as Maitland assumed: 'It was not Roman Law as such which established itself, but the jurists and their professional, that is, rational, approach to law.'[27] Roman law in any case made allowance for local custom;[28] and much of the law of property everywhere in Europe was embodied

[24] The principal conclusions which follow were first advanced in 1978 in *The Reports of Sir John Spelman*, vol. ii (94 Selden Soc.), introd., ch. 1. They were enlarged upon in a special Ford lecture at Oxford in 1984, printed as 'English Law and the Renaissance' (1985) 44 *CLJ* 46–61; repr. *LPCL*, 461–76.

[25] There is now an extensive literature on the Reception, most of which is consistent with the interpretation here. See Holdsworth, *HEL*, iv. 217–93; H. Coing, *Die Rezeption des römischen Rechts in Frankfurt am Main* (1939); H. Krause, *Kaiserrecht und Rezeption* (1952); F. Wieacker, *Privatrechtsgeschichte der Neuzeit* (2nd edn, 1967; tr. English by J. A. Weir, 1995), pt ii (and bibliography); H. Coing, *Römisches Recht in Deutschland* (1964); W. Kunkel, 'The Reception of Roman Law in Germany: an interpretation', in *Pre-Reformation Germany*, ed. E. Strauss (1972), 263–81; G. Dahm, 'On the Reception of Roman and Italian Law in Germany', ibid. 282–315; P. Bender, *Die Rezeption des römischen Rechts im Urteil der deutschen Rechtswissenschaft* (1979); Jenkins, 'English Law and the Renaissance', 117–19; S. Rowan, *Ulrich Zasius: a jurist of the German Renaissance* (1987), 6–10; G. Strauss, *Law, Resistance and the State: the opposition to Roman Law in Reformation Germany* (1986), especially at 56–95 ('Reception: the new law in Germany'); R. Feenstra, 'The Development of European Private Law: a Romanist watershed?' in *The Civilian Tradition and Scots Law*, ed. D. L. C. Miller and R. Zimmermann (1997), 103–15; P. Stein, *Roman Law in European Legal History* (1999), 88–92; O. F. Robinson, T. D. Fergus, and W. M. Gordon, *European Legal History* (3rd edn, 2000), ch. 11.

[26] Jenkins, 'English Law and the Renaissance', 119.

[27] Kunkel, 'The Reception of Roman Law in Germany', at 276.

[28] See the comments in this connection by Feenstra, 'Development of European Private Law', at 105.

in feudal customs which no rational person could possibly have wished to replace with the laws of ancient Rome. Even in the Reichskammergericht, primacy was given to feudal and municipal customs. And where royal codification occurred, in the Roman manner, an effort was made to incorporate and restate existing Germanic customs rather than to replace them. The essence of the German Reception was not, therefore, a replacement of medieval with classical law, but a wave of procedural and professional changes which brought about an increasingly scientific approach to decision-making, confining lay judges to questions of fact and turning more cases into questions of law for learned tribunals.

If we then turn to France and Italy, where there had already been a partial reception of Roman legal method in an earlier period, we find that the new interest in Roman law took root on an academic rather than a practical plane.[29] The leading humanist jurists of the sixteenth century, beginning with Guillaume Budé (1468–1540) in France and Andrea Alciato (1492–1550) in Italy, were first and foremost historians and philologists. Their sense of anachronism showed them that the original meaning of Justinian's code had been perverted through centuries of sophisticated glossing, and that the *Corpus Juris* itself was a perversion of classical Roman law. From their discoveries there arose the new science of legal history. But, just as Renaissance philology was to kill Latin as a useful international language by restricting it to the forms of its infancy, so humanist jurisprudence removed Roman law from the land of the living and rendered it about as useful to practising lawyers as the study of Greek coins would have been to bankers. Indeed, it was remarked in 1560 that an advocate equipped only with the Roman rules of property would be understood about as well in a French court of law as he would among the American savages.[30] Yet, if the legal humanists of Europe had no more direct impact on the living law than the now almost forgotten Civilians of Oxford and Cambridge had in England, the methods which they pioneered could be applied to customary law as well as Roman law. And so, while the legal historians strove to discover for its own sake the pristine purity of classical Roman law, the professors of contemporary French law (such as

---

[29] H. D. Hazeltine, 'The Renaissance and the Laws of Europe' in *Cambridge Legal Essays* (1926), 139–71; P. Koschaker, *Europa und das römische Recht* (1947; 4th edn, 1966); L. C. Stevens, 'The Contribution of French Jurists to the Humanism of the Renaissance' (1953) 1 *Studies in the Renaissance* 92–105; D. Maffei, *Gli Inizi dell'Umanesimo Giuridico* (1956); G. Kisch, 'Humanistic Jurisprudence' (1961) 8 *Studies in the Renaissance* 71–87; M. P. Gilmore, *Humanists and Jurists* (1963); C. C. Turpin, 'The Reception of Roman Law' (1968) 3 *Irish Jurist* (new ser.) 162–74; D. R. Kelley, *Foundations of Modern Historical Scholarship* (1970); W. Vogt, *Franciscus Duarenus 1509–59* (1971); R. C. Van Caenegem, 'The "Reception of Roman Law": a meeting of northern and Mediterranean traditions' (1972) 1 *Medievalia Lovaniensia* 195–204; D. J. Osler, 'Budaeus and Roman Law' (1985) 13 *Ius Commune* 195–212; P. Stein, 'Legal Humanism and Legal Science' (1986) 54 *RHD* 297–306; J. M. Kelly, *A Short History of Western Legal Theory* (1992), ch. 5; Robinson *et al.*, *European Legal History*, ch. 10.

[30] F. Hotman, cited by P. Stein, *The Character and Influence of the Roman Civil Law* (1988), 97.

Charles Dumoulin) were seeking to purify national customary law by scraping off the encrustations of scholastic Romanism. There was, in fact, a nationalistic legal tendency rather than a casting aside of national law to make way for Justinian or a transnational *jus commune*.[31]

Finally, we come to Scotland. The Court of Session, reformed in 1532, may have been the imperial chamber court of the king of Scotland, but was it 'the scene of a Reception', as Maitland tentatively suggested,[32] in any stronger sense than elsewhere? Like the English Chancery and Star Chamber it followed a Roman procedural model, though unlike them it was subject to the further Civilian influences of a new-fledged body of advocates trained in university law schools. Nevertheless, its judges acknowledged that their duty was to apply the existing law of Scotland, whether statutory or customary. As in England, they could have recourse to Roman law only if a case arose in which the Scots custom could not be discovered. This was more likely to occur than in England, given the paucity of written sources from before 1532; but it is quite certain that the question never arose of displacing native Scots law with Roman.[33] The prime influence of the new learning in Scotland, as in France, was to encourage new philological and historical approaches to the national law.[34] In so far as there was a reception at all, it was a reception of juristic system and rationality rather than of substantive Roman law.[35]

These newer interpretations of the effect of Renaissance humanism on the living law of continental Europe and Scotland show that the contrast with the English experience is not nearly as sharp as it seemed to Maitland in 1901. Perhaps, indeed, it has been toned down so far that it no longer calls for explanation. For, once we draw aside the net curtain inscribed 'Reception', and shelve for a moment the abstract tomes of the humanist jurists, we find that at ground level the changes taking place on the Continent had more in common with those in England than was once imaginable. All across Europe, not excluding England and Scotland, there was a tendency to move away from the more or less arbitrary resolution of disputes by laymen towards the treatment of disputes as legal problems set before professional judges in central royal courts. It was accompanied, from Italy to

---

[31] See also D. Osler, 'The Myth of European Legal History' (1997) 16 *Rechtshistorische Jnl* 393–410.

[32] *English Law and the Renaissance*, 20. He confessed privately to Neilson, 'I was oppressed by my ignorance of Scotland': *Letters of F. W. Maitland*, ii, ed. P. Zutshi (1995), no. 216, at 169.

[33] P. Stein, 'The Influence of Roman Law on the Law of Scotland' (1963) 8 *Juridical Review* (new ser.) 205 at 215–16; repr. in *The Character and Influence of the Roman Civil Law*, 319 at 329–30; W. D. H. Sellar, 'Scots Law: Mixed from the very Beginning? A Tale of Two Receptions' (2000) 4 *Edinburgh Law Rev.* 3–18.

[34] J. W. Cairns, T. D. Fergus, and H. L. MacQueen, 'Legal Humanism in Renaissance Scotland' (1990) 11 *JLH* 40–69, esp. at 41–2. There was, however, a tendency for law students to apply themselves to Civil law rather than Scots law, a trend condemned by Sir John Skene (d. 1617): ibid. 53. See also the essays in *The Civil Law Tradition in Scotland*, ed. R. L. Evans-Jones (Stair Soc., 1995); *The Civilian Tradition and Scots Law*, ed. Miller and Zimmermann (1997).   [35] Sellar, 'A Tale of Two Receptions', at 14–15.

Germany, and indeed to Scotland, by an explosion of reported case-law.[36] And that is particularly worthy of remark. A Reception which made judges into juridical authorities, and spawned law reports, has more than a little in common with the English legal tradition and does not look especially Roman.

If all this new evidence has undermined Maitland's question, it has nevertheless underlined his answer. The almost completely effective resistance to Romanizing influences in the common-law system was surely a result of the one circumstance which was undeniably unique to England. The lawyers who dominated the lower house of the legislature, much of the nation's bureaucracy, and nearly all the courts of law, were trained in advanced schools of municipal law and not in the university law faculties. Had the early Tudor authorities insisted upon an academical law degree before call to the Bar, that might indeed have revolutionized the history of English law and achieved what books alone could not. Henry VIII was quite capable of interfering with law schools when it suited him,[37] and an opportunity for effecting a reformation of legal education might have been taken when the freehold title to three of the inns of court came to the Crown at the dissolution of the monasteries and the fourth almost fell in by a different course.[38] But the Crown had nothing to gain from radical interference. The inns of court and chancery were already a well established and expanding university, far larger than the two university law faculties combined, and home not only to lawyers and serious law students but to the sons of a considerable part of the landed gentry of England. In their sophisticated learning exercises they had nurtured their own methodology, even their own dialect, and however bizarre these may have seemed to a young university graduate they were thoroughly entrenched as part of the English way of life. There could be no Reception here: 'Law schools make tough law'.[39]

The continuity of common-law language and logic does not, however, betoken immunity to change. Legal continuity is often an illusion, enabling radical changes to be effected without anything much appearing to have happened. One of Coke's achievements, in a slightly later generation, would be to blur the lines between old and new so effectively that lawyers were prevented for centuries from seeing that most of their law took the shape they knew in

[36] See *Handbuch der Quellen und Literatur des neueren europäischen Privatrechtsgeschichte*, ed. H. Coing, ii, pt 2 (1976), 1113–445; G. Gorla and L. Moccia, 'A Revisiting of the Comparison between Continental Law and English Law' (1981) 2 *JLH* 143–56; J. H. Baker (ed.), *Judicial Records, Law Reports, and the Growth of Case Law* (5 CSC; 1989); and below, 51–2.

[37] He suppressed the faculties of canon law at Oxford and Cambridge around this time. See also below, 472, 681, for an example of pressure placed on the inns of court.

[38] This may have been the occasion for the 1539 report on the state of the inns: R. M. Fisher, 'Thomas Cromwell, the Dissolution of the Monasteries, and the Inns of Court' (1977) 14 *JSPTL* 103–17.

[39] Maitland, *English Law and the Renaissance*, 25.

the sixteenth century. The illusion was compounded by the vagaries of legal publishing.[40] The law printers created a canonical series of medieval year books but passed over most of the case-law of Henry VIII's reign; they published student primers, but tacitly sanctioned a chasm in legal literature between the old oral tradition of readings and moots—which they left unprinted—and the newer written tradition of Staunford, Lambarde, and Coke. Change was not yet the stuff of legal publishing. The press gave students cheap copies of standard matter which they would otherwise have had to transcribe by hand. But current problems, unless the government was moved to stir a public debate on a major controversy, were for the classroom, the dinner table, and the private notebook, rather than the bookstalls. In our quest to dispel the illusion, the unpublished sources come into their own, including the vast formal records of litigation. The plea rolls of the central courts survive almost completely intact, and there are numerous available series of records for other courts of all descriptions. For most of the stories related in this volume, the plea rolls are a prime source, augmented by such theoretical explanations as can be gleaned from manuscript reports and the meagre literature. Taken in combination, these show that English law was undergoing something of a transformation, a process which in a rapidly changing world provided additional insurance against more drastic change imposed from without.

THE EARLY-MODERN LEGAL TRANSFORMATION

Since this transformation was not, at any rate in England, a result of the Reception, some other approach to an explanation is needed. There is no reason why it should necessarily be a wholly insular explanation. Immunity to Romanization does not mean that English law must have been impervious to the more general intellectual attitudes represented by the term 'humanism', nor that it should have been insensitive to social and economic factors which were not peculiarly local. What is difficult, and probably futile, is to seek a single explanation of a more specific kind.

One possible approach to the task of explanation, which would have the advantage of solving the problem of chronological coincidence, might be to attribute the changes to outstanding legal personalities, to individuals who took an interest—or, if we are inclined to cynicism, had an interest—in reform. Several leading changes, for instance, occurred under the chief justiceship (1495–1525) of Sir John Fyneux, whose son-in-law John Roper had a personal financial interest in the success of the King's Bench.[41] Judicial cooperation was essential in effecting

---

[40] Cf. below, 29–30.   [41] See below, 148–9.

profitable reforms in the law; and the internecine conflicts between the common law courts, which begin in our period, show how reform of the common law, and resistance to it, can be associated with identifiable groups of judges. If we include among our influential personalities such Crown servants as Thomas Wolsey, Thomas Cromwell, and Thomas Audley, the same approach could be extended to programmes of administrative and legislative reform.[42] It would be dangerous, however, to attribute our transformation solely to the genius or avarice of prominent individuals. Great men of the law are seldom lone thinkers, because the common law does not change by sudden invention, and legal ideas cannot flourish without broad professional acceptance. That certain characters played an important role, by seizing the moment, is obvious; but the agenda was not within any one person's control.

If the major changes in the land law are taken as an example, we find a number of disparate factors at work. The legislation concerning uses and wills most obviously had a revenue purpose, and it is easy to account for the statutory changes in political terms;[43] yet, while politics may explain the timing and some of the details, it is clear that the thinking behind the legislation was part of a much broader movement, rooted in the rise of feoffments to uses in the fifteenth century and the manifold legal problems to which they had given rise. Similarly, although the immediate impetus for the initial Reformation legislation may have been Henry VIII's concerns for the royal succession, it would be manifestly wrong to ignore the international intellectual context and equally wrong to overlook the English legal background extending back into the fourteenth century.

Other reforms in the land law can be explained in the context of social change. Uses had become popular in order to achieve greater freedom of disposition, and this was doubtless as important to the landowner as the evasion of feudal dues. Disputes over the legal status of the beneficiary under a use are matched by disputes over the status of the tenant for years and the copyholder, beneficial occupiers who likewise (but for different historical reasons) lacked freehold status yet were in need of legal protection. All came under the wing of the common law in our period, without recourse to legislation, and part of the explanation must be that the social position and expectations of such tenants had changed to the point where they could not be ignored. The perfection of the common recovery at the beginning of our period was also presumably a result of social pressure on lawyers, in this instance to enable the reframing of

---

[42] See e.g. G. R. Elton, *Reform and Renewal: Thomas Cromwell and the common weal* (1973). Cromwell was a member of Gray's Inn, but did not become a bencher.

[43] See e.g. J. B. Hurstfield, 'The Revival of Feudalism in early Tudor England' (1952) 37 *History* 131–45.

entails to suit changing family circumstances, or their barring with a view to creating uses.

If we then turn from the law of property to contract and tort, we find other large changes which are far less amenable to explanation in terms of external forces, political or social.[44] The establishment of *assumpsit* for money opened up a new commercial jurisdiction in the King's Bench, and marked the beginning of the modern law of contract. As far as we can tell, merchants and other creditors already had similar remedies in urban courts, and what we are witnessing here is not so much a substantive change of thought as a belated acceptance of such remedies by the central courts.[45] It would be tempting to find an explanation in terms of expanding mercantilism, and growing credit transactions. And yet the development of *assumpsit* seems to be part and parcel of the development of actions on the case, matched term by term with the development of actions for defamation—certainly not the preserve of merchants—and later in our period by actions for conversion, which seem most often to be for the benefit of personal representatives. There may also here be a subtext of jurisdictional readjustment, not only between central and local but also between lay and spiritual courts.

All in all, it seems that neither the king, nor the nobility, nor the gentry, nor the merchants, nor the lawyers, hold the magic key to the problem. Nor can all the developments be accounted for in terms of individual genius, political will, or the accidents of social and economic change. We are driven back on to the remarkable coincidence of so many diverse legal changes in the very period which saw the greatest impact of humanism on English culture. Here at least we might look for some unifying theme. Were the key figures in our story in effect applied humanists, who consciously or unconsciously followed the new spirit of rational enquiry not only in identifying the problems thrown up by rapid social change but also in finding suitable devices for tackling them?

A vague question cannot expect a precise answer. But we should, before proceeding to the details of our transformation, dwell a little upon the broader theme, and enquire whether any of the characteristic manifestations of the humanist intelligence are discernible in English legal development.

HUMANIST INFLUENCES ON ENGLISH LAW

The fact that most English lawyers received their legal education in the inns of court rather than in the universities does not in itself preclude the possibility of

---

[44] See also 94 Selden Soc. 48.
[45] It was not, however, a simple transfer of jurisdiction: below, 157–8.

humanist influence on the common law.[46] Even in the universities, the new trends were more likely to influence the teaching of Arts than of Law. We know next to nothing about the character of the English university law schools in the period before Sir Thomas Smith, though it is a fair inference from surviving books and book-lists that they were not much interested in legal humanism.[47] How many common lawyers read Arts at university is beyond discovery, since it was rare to remain in residence long enough to graduate, and the nominal rolls of the colleges and halls have generally not survived. In any case, the intellectual life of secular England was centred on the inns of court as much as on the universities. Sir Thomas More and Sir Thomas Elyot were benchers of their inns, well acquainted with both private practice and public office, and both sons of common-law judges. Christopher St German was a barrister, though more occupied in legal publishing than in practising law or holding office. The so-called 'More circle', the Rastells, the Ropers, the Stubbes, and the Heywoods, were closely involved with the common law, its administration, and (in the case of the Rastells) its printed literature.[48] With the exception of St German, however, none of our lawyer intellectuals has left substantial juristic writings. Most of them would have found the Latin of the plea rolls as accessible as the elegance of antiquity, and some would have written the court-hand more readily than the italic. Here, then, we encounter a terminological problem. We should be distorting contemporary understanding to identify more than two or three of our lawyers as 'humanists' at all.[49] It is true that direct resort to the classics became sufficiently fashionable to affect the rhetoric even of common-law judges,[50] though there is little display of classical knowledge in the law reports[51] before the 1550s.[52] But a passing acquaintance with Roman history hardly makes humanists, and we shall do best to avoid using the term anachronistically. On the other hand, Renaissance humanism is sometimes

---

[46] For academic influence on common lawyers see further below, 447-9.

[47] A. Wijffels, 'Law Books at Cambridge 1500-1640' in *The Life of the Law*, ed. P. Birks (1993), 59-87, at 68.

[48] See P. Hogrefe, *The Sir Thomas More Circle* (1959); *The Life and Times of Sir Thomas Elyot* (1967). See the pedigree in 94 Selden Soc. 56-7. For Rastell see below, 495.

[49] For a warning against liberal uses of the term, see A. Fox, 'Facts and Fallacies: interpreting English humanism' in A. Fox and J. A. Guy, *Reassessing the Henrician Age: humanism, politics and reformation, 1500-50* (1986), 9-33. Even St German is there rejected as a humanist (pp. 16-17).

[50] See the speeches to new serjeants in Baker, *Serjeants at Law*, 280-302. The 1521 speech cites Aristotle, Virgil, Valerius Maximus, and Justinian. There are more numerous classical allusions in Mountagu CJ's speech of 1540: below, 448.

[51] An early example is in *Rollesley v. Toft* (1495) 1 Caryll 285, where Serjeant Kebell traces sanctuary back to Romulus. This had a legal point, since it suggested that sanctuary was not of papal origin: cf. 2 Caryll 712 (1519). See further below, 547.

[52] There does then seem to be a change, though it may have more to do with the tastes of Dyer and Plowden (the reporters) than with a revolution in advocacy. See e.g. *Reniger v. Fogassa* (1550) Plowd. 1 at 18v, *per* Pollard sjt (story from Roman history, 'as I have read in books...');

characterized as a set of ideals rather than a particular brand of scholarship or set of ideas,[53] and ideals are more difficult to monopolize.

It has been observed that the English humanists were characteristically men of affairs rather than speculative scholars, applied rather than pure humanists,[54] and certainly not 'legal humanists' in the special sense attributed to that term by historians of humanist culture on the Continent. Yet there are certain attitudes of thought commonly associated with humanists which were shared by intelligent contemporaries who could not in strictness be so classified. Perhaps, indeed, too much concentration on 'humanism' has distracted attention from these innominate currents of thought which owe no direct debt to classicism but profoundly affected perceptions of society[55] and the natural world. The most appropriate historical question, therefore, is not whether English law was influenced by humanist scholarship in a narrow technical sense—which manifestly it was not—but whether there were any tendencies in English legal thought and law reform, in the period under scrutiny, which can be particularly linked with the ideals commonly associated with humanism, or at least with the rationalist spirit of the age of Renaissance.[56]

The answer is not unqualified, since there is a deep conservative element in the common law which often conspires to deny or conceal any sense of movement. We search our legal sources in vain for any direct allusion to the new learning,[57] and it may reasonably be supposed that this silence reflects some measure of genuine indifference to external influences. Nevertheless we may identify six trends or tendencies which, however subliminal or tentative, seem to represent the new spirit, and which also have continental parallels in the same period. They are: first, a historical understanding of legal development, informed by a newly discovered awareness of anachronism; second, a concern with the structure, form, language, and relative authority of legal sources in the first age of printing; third, a rational approach to law and law reform, often associated with the utilitarian ideal of the

---

Throckmorton v. *Tracy* (1556) Plowd. 145 at 161v, *per* Saunders J. (Cicero); *Hunt* v. *Ellisdon* (1557) Dyer at 154a (Ausonius). There are more examples after 1558 in Dyer and Plowden. For Dyer's classical learning, acquired at Oxford in the 1520s, see 109 Selden Soc., pp. xxi–xxii.

[53] See e.g. D. Kelley, *Renaissance Humanism* (1991).

[54] D. Bush, *The Renaissance and English Humanism* (1939); Elton, *Studies*, ii. 236–58.

[55] Cf. J. Thirsk, *Economic Policy and Projects* (1978), 31–2.

[56] Recent comment on the influence of humanism on English lawyers has focused on the period after 1560: e.g. D. R. Kelley, 'History, English Law and the Renaissance' (1974) 65 *Past & Present* 24–51 (and comment by C. Brooks and K. Sharpe in vol. 72, pp. 133–42); A. B. Ferguson, *Clio Unbound: perception of the social and cultural past in Renaissance England* (1979), 259–311; C. P. Rodgers, 'Humanism, History and the Common Law' (1985) 6 *JLH* 129–56. For comparable tendencies in Scotland (during the same slightly later period) see Cairns *et al.*, 'Legal Humanism in Renaissance Scotland'. The key figure there, Thomas Craig of Riccarton (1538–1608), may legitimately be classifiable as a humanist himself.

[57] For an accusation of being a 'heretic and of the new learning' (1535) see below, 791. No doubt this was not a reference to humanism.

'common weal'; fourth, a new confidence in the role of legislation as a means of advancing the common weal and removing 'mischiefs'; fifth, an enhanced interest in the equitable approach to the diversity of individual cases; and last, but certainly not least, a new-found judicial positivism which laid emphasis on the reasoned decisions of courts as a primary source of law. Each of these tendencies merits a brief excursion.

LEGAL HISTORY AND THE SENSE OF CHANGE

At the beginning of our period, if the year books are a safe guide, common lawyers had an anachronistic view of legal history. Here and there, in fact, we find a remark which suggests considerable historical naivety. For example, Serjeant Catesby remarked in 1470, and without contradiction, that the common law had been in existence since the creation of the world.[58] Likewise Sir John Fortescue, who a few years earlier had written that the common law was not merely the best in the world but the oldest: older than Normans, Danes, Saxons, or even Romans.[59] By the last quarter of the century, however, not everyone accepted this simple creed. Morgan Kydwelly, lecturing in the Inner Temple in 1483, maintained that originally the law was founded on Civil law, but that William the Conqueror, after conferring with the wise men of England and Normandy, chose the law of England instead.[60] This statement seems to imply that between Romans and Normans there was already a law of England for William to choose. It would hardly have been a wild assumption that Roman law must once have held sway in a land under Roman dominion,[61] but the obscurity of Kydwelly's remark rests in the hiatus which he leaves between the Romans and the time of William I. His mention of William is perhaps the most significant part of the statement. There was a growing tendency to attribute parts of English law to the Conqueror,[62] albeit without any sense of the 'Norman yoke' implications to which such theories would give rise during and after the sixteenth century.[63] There were sensible

---

[58] Pas. 10 Edw. IV, fo. 4, pl. 9.

[59] J. Fortescue, *De Laudibus Legum Angliae*, ed. S. B. Chrimes (1942), ch. 17.

[60] CUL MS. Ee.5.18, fo. 28. Kydwelly dated this event in the fourth year of William I.

[61] Cf. Robert Sheffield's assertion in the Inner Temple, ten years after Kydwelly, that in the time of Julius Caesar all common pleas and pleas of the Crown were held at the Tower of London before the constable: *Moots*, 284 (1493). There was a legend that Casear had built the Tower, though it was denied by Vergil (*c*.1511): *Polydore Vergil's English History*, ed. H. Ellis (Camden Soc.; 1846), 40.

[62] See, especially, Polydore Vergil, *Anglica Historia* (1534), 151–2; (1546 edn), 154–5; Port 135, no. 99 (laws of Alfred continued until the Conquest); Starkey, *Dialogue between Pole and Lupset*, ed. Mayer, 77, 82, 129. Villeinage was attributed to the Norman conquest by J. Fitzherbert, *The Boke of Surveyeng* (1523), fo. xxiv.

[63] *Polydore Vergil's English History*, ed. Ellis, 292, says that the Normans took away the common laws introduced by King Edward; this was written *c*.1511. An even stronger account of William's

reasons for attributing the common-law system of tenures to the Conquest, but it did not follow that Anglo-Saxon law must have been supplanted entirely by the law of Normandy, or even by new Anglo-Norman legislation, and no one seems to have made such a sweeping claim. The Anglo-Saxon laws were still not wholly forgotten, and it was clear from them that certain institutions—such as counties and hundreds—had existed before the Normans.[64] The principal advance represented by Kydwelly's remark, so far as it can be understood intelligibly, is that he seems to have achieved some sense of historical relativity.

In the early Tudor period we begin to find more sophisticated accounts of the origins and continuity of the legal system, principally derived from the history of Geoffrey of Monmouth and its derivatives. These histories circulated very widely in manuscript, and some were printed at an early date.[65] They traced the history of Britain back to the legendary King Brut, a royal refugee from Troy, who founded London and established laws. The legend was familiar enough to Fortescue, who even traced the English constitutional monarchy to the ancient Trojan immigrants.[66] John Port, probably reporting an Inner Temple reading of the 1490s, noted that Brut had introduced laws from Greece; that these had been altered by King Alfred, who interpolated some Civil and canon law into 'the old laws of this realm'; and that Alfred's laws had continued until the Norman conquest, though what then happened he does not state.[67] The Brut legend was still being taught in the Inner Temple nearly twenty years later, when Edward Hales added—on what authority is unclear—that Brut established the first royal court, the Court of Marshalsea.[68] Although its historical basis had been questioned even in the fifteenth century, the legend became entrenched under the early Tudors because of the supposed connection between the Welsh dynasty and the ancient Britons.[69] Its explanation for the origin of a separate government in Wales remained the accepted constitutional theory throughout our period.[70]

A more elaborate historical discourse on the same theme is to be found in John Hales's reading of 1514 in Gray's Inn.[71] His statutory text concerned the hindering

high-handedness in abrogating the good old laws is found in *Grafton's Chronicle* [1568] (1809 edn), i. 160.

[64] Anon. reading on Gloucester, c. 8, HLS MS. 13, p. 261; Anon. reading on Westminster II, c. 13, BL MS. Hargrave 87, fo. 372v (King Alfred made division into tenths and hundreds). Cf. Pas. 12 Hen. VII, fo. 17, pl. 1, per Fyneux CJ; Richard Littleton's reading (Inner Temple, 1493) Port 119; these are less chronologically specific.

[65] e.g. Caxton's *Chronicle of England* (1480; repr. 1973). For other historical sources available in Tudor times, see A. Gransden, *Historical Writing in England*, ii (1982).

[66] *De Laudibus*, ed. Chrimes, 32–3; *The Governance of England*, ed. C. Plummer (1885), 112 (and note on 185–6). [67] Port 135, no. 99.

[68] CUL MS. Fe.3.46, fo. 66v. [69] T. D. Kendrick, *British Antiquity* (1950), 34–5.

[70] *Bulkeley* v. *Thomas* (1555) Plowd. 118 at 129v, per Brooke CJ (tripartite division of Brut's kingdom).

[71] Reading on Westminster II, c. 39: GI MS. 25, fo. 290 (tr.). This was not the John Hales (d. 1572) who wrote the *Oration*, but the future baron of the Exchequer (1522–39), who was perhaps the former's father.

of justice, and he decided to open with a lecture in praise of the law and its antiquity. He began by saying that the law should be honoured, because it was founded on the law of God. At one time there was no law but the law of Moses, which applied *inter electos Dei*; the ten commandments were still part of the law of England, being enforced partly by the spiritual law and partly by the temporal law.[72] This was probably intended as a jurisprudential rather than a historical statement, since the main body of law was thought to have descended from pre-Christian times. It was appropriate to remind the audience of the law's relationship to the law of God before tracing its ultimate origins to the heathen laws of the ancient Britons or of Greece. After this preamble, Hales could safely launch into history:

The law should also be praised for its antiquity, which is proved by the *Gestes Romanorum*.[73] When Brut was reigning in this land and died, he had two sons who were in dispute as to which of them should be king; and it was decided by the wise men of the realm that the elder should have the realm and be king, and they said that it was so used in Troy.[74] That law continues until the present day, but in no other land: for the Saxons divided their lands, and therefore the men of Kent still do so. Also Dunvallo, who was king seven centuries before the Incarnation, made a law that if anyone took [sanctuary in] a church he should have the protection thereof,[75] which law continues here to this day but in no other country in the world. Later, when the king of England called Lucius was baptised and christened, he asked the pope to inform him what laws he might use in order to pursue his faith and the law of God; and the pope wrote him a letter saying that there was the law anciently used and also his law (which he sent him), and he commanded him to take from them what he and his council thought fit, and to make law thereof; and so it was done.[76] Afterwards, when Hengist conquered this realm again, he still used all the old laws;

[72] Cf. Hales, *Oration*, fo. 17v.

[73] Presumably a slip for the *Gesta Regum Britanniae* or some similarly titled version of Monmouth, a version of which was printed in Paris in 1508. None of the versions now in print, however, exactly bears out Hales's assertions. For Monmouth's treatment of legal history, cf. J. S. P. Tatlock, *The Legendary History of Britain* (1950), 278–83.

[74] Monmouth says that on Brut's death his realm was divided between his three sons (as Britain, Scotland, and Wales). On Dunvallo's death, however, the three kingdoms of England, Wales, and Cornwall all went to the eldest son according to the custom of Troy: *The Historia Regum Britanniae of Geoffrey of Monmouth*, ed. R. E. Jones (1929), 276; *Gesta Regum Britanniae*, ed. N. Wright (1991), 32–3.

[75] *Historia*, ed. Jones, 275; *Gesta*, ed. Wright, 52. In the longer *Historia*, he and his son are said to have introduced laws called the *Leges Molmutinae*, 'quae usque ad hoc tempus inter Anglos celebrantur' (p. 282). These, said Monmouth, were translated by Gildas from British into Latin, and by Alfred from Latin into English.

[76] This is more than can be found in Monmouth; but Hales's version is borne out by the forged letter of Eleutherius, which was in existence by the fourteenth century, and mentions the selection of laws from the Civil and canon laws: BL Cotton MS. Claudius D. II, fo. 33; printed in *Munimenta Gildhallae Londoniensis... Liber Custumarum*, ed. H. T. Riley, pt ii (RS, 1860), 632. The story was still current temp. Eliz. I: anon., 'Causes denforcer lauthoritie del comen ley dengliterre', BL MS. Harley 4990, ff. 57–79v. See also below, 22.

and when new causes arose, he ordained new laws by his council.[77] That law so continued until St Edward was king; he took a book and extracted all the laws therein, and they were called the Law of St Edward.[78] This continued until the Conquest, and down to the present day; and when new mischiefs were found, new laws were made, as is done today by statutes.

Hales proceeded to explain the origin of sheriffs, who were the main subject of his text. Before the Conquest, counties belonged to earls, who appointed reeves to hold courts and keep rule in them; William the Conqueror appointed royal sheriffs after seizing most of the counties into his own hands, and called them *vicecomites*.[79] Serjeant Broke intervened to say that, although Hales's explanation was correct, he was not sure that he had placed it in the right period since *vicecomites* were mentioned in the *Leges Edwardi*. Hales went on to state that the annual election of sheriffs by the king began under Henry III, and that the qualifications and procedure for election were introduced by statutes of Edward II and Edward III. Later in the lecture, when speaking of ecclesiastical jurisdiction, he alluded to the clash between Henry II and Becket; everyone presumably knew the background to Becket's martyrdom, and its connection with benefit of clergy.[80] Elsewhere, Hales pointed out that the enacting words in thirteenth-century statutes sometimes only mentioned the king; but this historical observation must have been equally commonplace to lawyers bred on the *Statuta Antiqua*.

If we feel tempted to be harsh on Hales for some of his interpretations of legal history, we must remember that he had few books on which to rely and could hardly be expected to be wiser than the received historians of his time. No doubt much of his earlier history is based on a mixture of etymology, *ex post facto* rationalization, and guesswork, but the lecture clearly indicates a desire to know why things were as they were, a genuine attempt to make coherent sense of all the available historical accounts, and a ready awareness of historical change. Hales's account is substantially more sophisticated than Fortescue's or Catesby's, in that it does not represent the common law as immutable. Indeed, part of the character of the law, as Hales saw it, was that it had always been possible to remedy mischiefs while yet retaining the same body of law. This approach was not lost on the government either, since Thomas Cromwell saw the value of historical arguments in justifying imperial England's independence from Rome.[81] However, the mutability of the law was hardly a new discovery.

[77] This is a remarkable slip. Monmouth represented Hengist as a heathen enemy who adhered to uncivilized customs. Hales perhaps intended only a general reference to the Saxons.

[78] Cf. *Polydore Vergil's English History*, ed. Ellis, 292, where Edward is said to have made the common laws by choosing from and rationalizing the older laws.

[79] Cf. Vergil, *Anglica Historia* (1546), 154.

[80] Cf. John Caryll's reading (Inner Temple, 1510) CUL MS. Ee.3.46, fo. 50v; below, 531.

[81] See Elton, *Reform and Renewal*, 13–16; J. Guy, 'The Crown and the Intellectual Origins of the Henrician Revolution' in *Reassessing the Henrician Age*, ed. Fox and Guy, 151–78; and below, 246, 652.

It had been part of the routine training in the inns of court, for at least a generation before Hales, to show how statutes had remedied defects in the common law, and to that extent the readings had long inculcated a historical approach. A reader was expected to explain the 'remedy' by identifying the 'mischief' before the statute, and this necessarily involved placing the statute in a historical context.[82] This was done intelligently, given the sources available, albeit the mischief was often identified from the terms of the statute alone.[83] An early Tudor judge might even recognize that a remedy such as novel disseisin, while part of the common law, was nevertheless an innovation—his explanation being that in the twelfth century the law could be changed without Parliament.[84] Port and Hales were thus making use of popular histories to extend the legal technique of historical explanation back into a more remote past. Yet this further speculation about prehistoric origins, however fanciful it now seems,[85] could be said to betoken a new kind of interest in history as history, an interest which was to flower in the Elizabethan society of antiquaries at the end of the century.

Lawyers were prominent among the sceptics who questioned the Trojan Brut legend long before another lawyer, John Selden, published his more famous refutation in 1610.[86] An anonymous reader on Magna Carta in the early 1530s remarked that:[87]

although the laws of this realm had continued in this island many years before this statute was made, some of which laws were made by Lucius sometime king of this realm, some by Canutus, some by St Edward the Confessor,[88] some by William Conqueror, and some by others, yet were the same laws so out of use [by 1215] that there were almost none of the said ancient laws of this realm put in ure . . .

This must have been fairly obvious to anyone who read thirteenth-century sources, and lawyers still did so. It was natural for lawyers to adopt a critical

The statute restraining appeals to the pope began with reference to 'divers sundry old authentick histories and chronicles': 24 Hen. VIII, c. 12.

[82] George Ferrers, the translator of the statutes, also observed that 'by searching the great extremities of the common laws before the making of statutes, and the remedies provided by them, a good student shall soon attain to a perfect judgment': *The Great Charter* [1534] (1542 edn), sig. ╬ii.

[83] Egerton complained in the 1560s that readers often simply presumed the common law to have been the opposite of the statute: *Discourse upon the Exposicion of Statutes*, ed. S. E. Thorne (1942), 141–2.   [84] Dictum attributed to Townshend J. (1490) 1 Caryll 41, pl. 42.

[85] A particularly fanciful Elizabethan account of English legal history, beginning with Brut and attributing the Mercian laws to 'a woman of excellent learning' called Marcia, is in BL MS. Add. 4317.

[86] They included John Rastell and Sir Thomas Elyot: Kendrick, *British Antiquity*, 41, 109.

[87] BL MS. Harley 4990, ff. 146v–147 (sp. mod.).

[88] Cf. a reading of similar date on the *Carta de Foresta*, Nottingham Univ Lib., Middleton MS. L18b, ff. 61–65v, which says of the laws of St Edward: '(tr.) which was and still is the very root and the original of all the laws of England'.

approach to historical questions; they were regularly required by their profession to investigate historical evidence for practical purposes, and they knew that legends were not evidence. But their more speculative interest in origins and development was no doubt stirred by the humanist spirit. A similar historical inspiration may have lain behind the partial rehabilitation of *Glanvill* and *Bracton* at the same period. It is not fully known to what extent Bractonian scholarship had declined in the fourteenth century, though it is clear that new copies had ceased to be made before 1400, and we are firmly told by Fitzherbert that *Bracton* had never been held an authority.[89] By the early Tudor period, however, *Bracton* was certainly being read and quoted,[90] especially in the inns of court,[91] with the result that even the benchers of the Inner Temple sometimes found themselves debating points first stirred by the jurists of ancient Rome.[92] *Hengham,*[93] *Britton,*[94] and the *Mirror of Justices,*[95] were still known to some. And *Glanvill* was revered as the first book on English law[96]—though manuscripts were so relatively rare that, when an Inner Templar tried to recover a copy he had lent out, he thought it worth asking for the king's assistance on the grounds that its

[89] Fitz. Abr., *Garde*, pl. 71. Fitzherbert attributed this view to a case of 1457, though it does not appear in the printed text: see D. E. C. Yale, 'Some later Uses of Bracton' in *On the Laws and Customs of England*, ed. Arnold *et al.*, at 384–5. An anonymous reader temp. Hen. VIII (BL MS. Hargrave 87, fo. 374) pointed out that *Bracton* 'nest my ley en plusours poyntes'.

[90] e.g. *Gylys* v. *Walterkyn* (1486) Hil. 1 Hen. VII, fo. 6, pl. 3, *per* Calow; *Say* v. *Doket* (1495) Mich. 10 Hen. VII, fo. 6, pl. 12, *per* Kebell sjt; *Harecourt* v. *Spycer* (1521) Trin. 13 Hen. VIII, fo. 16, pl. 1 (119 Selden Soc. 83–4), *per* Shelley sjt; *Re Lady E. S.* (*c.*1530/5) Wm Yelv. 292, no. 2, *per* Shelley J.; *Colthirst* v. *Bejushin* (1550) Plowd. 1 at 29, *per* Saunders sjt; *Throckmerton* v. *Tracy* (1556) Plowd. 145 at 159v, *per* Dyer J. (who showed his manuscript to Plowden), and 160v, *per* Staunford J.; *Basset's Case* (1556) Dyer 136a at 137a; *Duke of Norfolk's Case* (1557) Dyer 138a at 138b. Earlier references are very uncommon.

[91] Early examples are: William Catesby's reading on Magna Carta, c. 35 (Inner Temple, temp. Edw. IV) CUL MS. Ee.5.22, fo. 50v; Thomas Frowyk's reading on Prerogativa Regis (Inner Temple, 1495) CUL MS. Mm.6.58, ff. 1, 9; anon. reading, perhaps Richard Littleton's (Inner Temple, *c.*1493) Port 120 (*Bracton* or *Britton*); Edmund Dudley's reading (Gray's Inn, 1496) CUL MS. Hh.3.10, fo. 59v; anon., CUL MS. Ee.5.19, fo. 113; *Moots*, p. lxxi n. 363. Hales began his reading of 1514 (above) with Bracton's statement that it behoves a kingdom to have both *arma* and *leges*. There are many examples temp. Hen. VIII.

[92] e.g. the case put at Francis Mountford's reading (1527) of a man who throws a ball which accidentally strikes a barber's hand while his razor is at a customer's throat: BL MS. Hargrave 87, fo. 177. This case was discussed by Mela, Proculus, and Ulpian, recorded in D.9.2.11, and transmitted to the inns of court through *Bracton*, fo. 136b.

[93] *Moots*, 284. Frowyk mentioned *Hengham* and *Bracton* as examples of 'treatises': reading on Prerogativa Regis (Inner Temple, 1495) CUL MS. Mm.6.58, ff. 1, 9.

[94] Nicholas Tichborne cited *Bracton, Glanvill* and *Britton* in his Inner Temple reading (1509) CUL MS. Ee.3.46, ff. 24–33v. William Conyngesby (Inner Temple, 1526) also cited *Glanvill*: BL MS. Hargrave 87, fo. 399. In 1536 Fitzherbert J. said *Britton* was 'bone authority' (Dyer 13b); but cf. *Wimbish* v. *Tailbois* (1550) Plowd. 38v at 58, *per* Mountagu CJ (tr. 'I have no great respect for [Britton], for his book contains many errors').

[95] *Reniger* v. *Fogassa* (1550) Plowd. 1 at 8, cited by Bradshaw A.-G.

[96] See Kydwelly's reading (Inner Temple, 1483) CUL MS. Ee.5.18, fo. 28. There are citations in *Lord Windsor* v. *St John* (1554) Dyer 98a; *Warren* v. *Lee* (1555) Dyer 126b at 127b.

disappearance would be a great loss to the king and his realm.[97] *Britton* was printed in about 1540, followed by *Glanvill* in 1555 and *Bracton* in 1569. Numerous quotations from all three were printed by Staunford in his *Plees del Coron* (1557), and his colleague Dyer also liked to cite them whenever possible.[98]

It would, however, be mistaken to see in this minor 'gothic revival' a parallel with the Roman legal history of the humanists, let alone an indirect means of absorbing substantive Roman law in early-English guise.[99] The old English law books were not deployed to undermine the teaching of the inns of court, nor even to reconstruct the law of the twelfth and thirteenth centuries for its own sake, but were chiefly cited by way of ornament in support of orthodox propositions. At best they might provide arguments when new questions arose. But this ornamental scholarship did not threaten any breach with legal tradition or method among the common lawyers. English law was rooted in the past, and lawyers had taken a professional interest in the past—albeit not as history—long before the rise of antiquarianism in the sixteenth century. Even the new kind of historical learning could be taken as bolstering the Fortescue thesis that the English common law was the best in the world: there had already been a partial reception of Greek and Roman law, long before the Norman conquest, and English law had advanced in its own way since then by adjusting to new situations as they arose. This image of the slow perfection of the common law by trial and error, including even the trial of foreign ideas when occasion arose, was a persuasive antidote to Reception of a more revolutionary kind.

ORDER AND SYSTEM IN THE SOURCES OF LAW

The common law did not, of course, find its Tribonian, and to the uninitiated its apparent lack of coherence and system made it less perfect than the Civil law. Certainly no one could characterize the sources of the common law of the sixteenth century as orderly or elegant, any more than were the sources of customary law in other European countries. There was, moreover, a school of lawyers—and they have their descendants today—for whom it was almost a point of honour to reject fine letters and 'academic' learning, even to the point of denying the value of elegant Latin. Richard Morison was irritated by lawyers who could not draft documents in Latin, 'but are forced to draw it first in their French, and after to cause their clerks to turn it into Latin':[100]

Good letters be so abhorred among this sort of lawyers that when they perceive any young man given to good learning, desirous therewith to have the knowledge of the laws, they will

---

[97] Letter of John Lucas: *LP*, iv. 6125.   [98] 109 Selden Soc., pp. xxviii–xxix.
[99] *Pace* Holdsworth, *HEL*, iv. 286.   [100] *Perswasion*, ff. 9v–10 (sp. mod.).

earnestly persuade him to forget and leave his old study, as though good letters and the law could not agree in one person.

He suggested that lawyers be compelled to learn Latin, presumably meaning classical Latin, a suggestion adopted by the committee which reported in 1539 on the inns of court,[101] but not adopted by the profession until centuries later—when Latin had ceased to have any vocational use. His further suggestion that the law itself be translated into Latin was rather less practicable. It was not impossible to write law reports in Latin, as an unknown reporter of 1485–8 demonstrated,[102] but the result was unfamiliar and obscure since the terminology of common-law discourse was peculiarly Anglo-French with no convenient Latin equivalent. Nor was there much point in trying to purify the language of conveyancing,[103] or of the plea rolls. The classical tongue could not always accommodate a millennium of social change, as the courts discovered when they sought the advice of philologists.[104] Conveyances and plea rolls alike achieved a high degree of precision—too high for some tastes—and aesthetic considerations had to give way to the eminent suitability of law Latin for its special purpose.

The principal linguistic tendency in England was towards the vernacular, and this accorded even better with the views of humanists such as Starkey, who argued that the law and the scriptures should be 'written in the common tongue' so that everyone might understand them.[105] Law French, for the new intellectuals, represented a barbarous relic of Norman tyranny, severing English law decisively from the liberal arts.[106] Rastell argued that French had served a purpose when English was 'homely and rude' and lacking in vocabulary; but 'now of late days' the language had been transformed, 'by reason that divers famous clerks and learned men had translated and made many noble works into our English tongue, whereby there was much more plenty and abundance of English used than there was in times past, and by reason thereof our vulgar tongue so amplified and

---

[101] Report by Denton, Bacon, and Cary, pr. in E. Waterhous, *Fortescutus Illustratus* (1663), at, 540–1. It was also urged by Starkey, *Dialogue between Pole and Lupset*, ed. Mayer, 128, with the more practical end of encouraging lawyers to read Roman law.

[102] Mich. 2 Ric. III, pl. 1–32; Hil. 1 Hen. VII, pl. 26–9; Pas. 1 Hen. VII, pl. 4–16; Pas. 3 Hen. VII, pl. 1–5, 9–10; Trin. 3 Hen. VII, pl. 1–4. These 60 cases are substantially in Latin, with occasional lapses into law French.

[103] Note the obscure slander complained of in 1554, that the plaintiff had stolen some deeds 'and caused them to be translated out of French into Latin, and out of Latin into English': *Scullard* v. *Benbery* (1554) CP 40/1158, m.724.

[104] Hil. 9 Hen. VII, fo. 16, pl. 8, where masters of grammar were sent for and could not tell the court the correct Latin for 'fine gold'. Cf. the citation of rules of grammar in *Bolde* v. *Molyneux* (1536) Dyer 15b, *per* Shelley J. (meaning of *tunc*); *Bulkeley* v. *Thomas* (1555) Plowd. 118 at 125v (meaning of *licet*); *Hunt* v. *Ellisdon* (1557) Dyer at 154a (relation of *quaelibet*).

[105] Starkey, *Dialogue between Pole and Lupset*, ed. Mayer, 82 (sp. mod.).

[106] ibid. 82, 129; T. Elyot, *The Book named the Governor*, ed. S. E. Lehmberg (1962), 51–4.

sufficient of itself to expound many laws or ordinances'.[107] Parliamentary statutes from 1485 were entirely in English—Rastell praised Henry VII for this reason as 'worthy to be called the second Solomon'—and over the next fifty years a very high standard of draftsmanship was achieved. At the same time translations of student books were made,[108] though they did not appear in print until the six-teenth century: the medieval abridgment of statutes in 1519, and the old and new *Tenures* in the 1520s, all undertaken by Rastell,[109] followed in the 1530s by the old *Natura Brevium* and a translation by George Ferrers of the full texts of the medieval statutes.[110] Rastell also provided the 'young beginners which intend to be students of the law' with a dictionary of legal terminology, a little guide which—though embellished with a Latin title—consisted of parallel French and English text.[111] Rastell's efforts had a long-term effect in promoting the use of English for legal purposes,[112] but for the time being the glossary served only to emphasize the continued primacy of law French. The idiosyncratic form of Rastell's own French may indicate an amateurish attempt to assimilate it to the language of contemporary France. Yet, he was no philologist, or he would have sought his model in the Anglo-French of earlier centuries; and if men such as Rastell cared so little for legal philology we cannot take too seriously the aesthetic objections to the language of the common law. If linguistic purity be the test, it must be admitted that the common law on the whole failed it. But the truth is that any attempt to translate the common law into classical Latin, or contemporary French, would have led to uncertainty and confusion. Language was not seriously on the agenda.

Codification, on the other hand, was on the agenda of those outside the common law who wished to reform its condition. As we have seen, Starkey and Morison advocated it in the 1530s, and their proposal was not the first.[113] But carrying it into effect was another matter. Starkey's interesting treatise was virtually unknown until 1878, and Morison's proposals cannot have been widely

---

[107] *The Abbreviacion of Statutes translated out of French into English by John Rastell* (1519), 'Prohemium Johannis Rastell' (sp. mod.). For Rastell's promotion of legal English see J. H. Baker, 'John Rastell and the Terms of the Law' (forthcoming); and below, n. 112.

[108] A translation from the 1480s of Littleton and the *Natura Brevium*, with the French in parallel texts, is to be found in CUL MS. Ee.1.2. A mid-fifteenth century translation of the statutes from Ric. II to 23 Hen. VI is in CUL MS. Ff.3.1.

[109] Below, 495.   [110] 94 Selden Soc. 30.

[111] *Exposiciones Terminorum Legum Anglorum* (*c*.1523/5), prol., sig. A2. A few years later Rastell pub-lished an edition in French alone. It is to be noted that another student book, Perkins's *Profitable Book* (so called from 1555), was launched in 1528 with a Latin title and a French text: *Perutilis Tractatus Magistri Johannis Parkins Interioris Templi Socii* (1528).

[112] See further R. J. Ross, 'The Commoning of the Common Law: the Renaissance debate over printing English law, 1520–1640' (1998) 146 *Univ. Pennsylvania Law Rev.* 323–461, esp. at 329–42.

[113] Above, 6, 24. See also 94 Selden Soc. 31.

canvassed. Morison himself went so far as to produce a specimen code on tenures, in Latin, but it was distinctly inferior to Littleton and was not calculated to encourage professional support.[114] The author of an elementary introduction to the law in English, written at the same period, also called for some 'expert and learned man' to benefit the community by setting forth 'the whole course of the laws used in this realm'.[115] This was not to be, either in the sixteenth century or in any succeeding century, because codes and case-law do not sit well together: a code may inhibit legal development or prove irrelevant to emergent concerns. To the common-law mind, the lack of codification was not a defect at all.[116] The real problem with case-law was that of access to the ever growing body of reports. Here the alphabet provided interim assistance. Experiments with current alphabetical reporting ultimately failed,[117] because they did not coincide with the invention of the loose-leaf book; but the alphabetical digest or abridgment of year-book cases had been invented just before our period and reached its high point with the printed abridgments of Fitzherbert (completed by 1514) and Brooke (completed by 1558).[118] The same treatment was accorded to the statutes in 1557.[119] Lawyers began at the same time to augment these 'grand' abridgments with their own private alphabetical abridgments or commonplace books.

By gathering together the authorities on particular topics, the abridgments had the further beneficial effect of paving the way for the scientific analysis of discrete branches of the law. The principal fruit in our period was *Les Plees del Coron* (1557), written by Sir William Staunford, justice of the Common Pleas. Inspired to systematize the large collection of cases under the title *Corone* in Fitzherbert's abridgment, and assisted by previous systematic compilations for justices of the peace,[120] Staunford brought the body of the criminal law into some kind of analytical order. He expressed the hope that others would digest the whole of the common law in the same fashion, using the titles in Fitzherbert as their guide.[121] But criminal law was more amenable to systematization than most branches of the common law, since it consisted of a fairly uniform procedure, a few general principles, and a list of crimes. Staunford's general challenge was not taken up in our period.

---

[114] BL Royal MS. 11 A. XVI. Elton described it as 'a kind of elevated undergraduate essay': see *Studies*, ii. 247–9. For the impracticability of these proposals, see also S. E. Thorne, 'English Law and the Renaissance' (1966), reprinted in *Essays in English Legal History*, at 188–91.

[115] *Institutions in the Lawes of Englande* [1538?]: see 94 Selden Soc. 31. The 1540 edition has a prologue signed by Richard Taverner, though his authorship of the book has been doubted.

[116] See this argued by Thomas Williams in the Inner Temple in 1558: Holdsworth, *HEL*, iv. 260–1.

[117] 94 Selden Soc. 32, 173–4.   [118] Below, 480–2, 501.

[119] W. Rastell, *A Colleccion of all the Statutes* (1557).   [120] See below, 504.

[121] W. Staunford, *An Exposition of the Kinges Prerogative* [1548] (1st edn, 1567), preface (quoted below, 502–3). See also Elyot, *The Governour*, ff. 55, 59.

Ease of reference was in practice a more important achievement than the imposition of an elegant but artificial scheme which might have stifled development. Here again, therefore, and with a good pragmatic excuse, the common law might only merit a low mark in the achievement of superficial elegance. But we are looking for new tendencies rather than outward appearances. And, as with some of our other tendencies, the spirit of the times may be seen working beneath the surface. This is particularly true in the treatment of texts. The change in the character of legislative texts was accompanied by a subtle change in the principles of interpretation,[122] and was followed (though perhaps not until later in the century) by a more rigorous textual analysis of variant versions of the older statutes.[123] At the same time we see the beginnings of year-book hermeneutics. It was important to know whether a case had been formally decided,[124] and if so whether extempore or by 'good advice',[125] whether it was antiquated,[126] how far the report was borne out by the record,[127] and above all which was the most reliable reading of the available texts.[128] Not all judges and counsel were so careful with texts which supported their own arguments,[129] but a growing awareness of textual problems is nevertheless evident in the texts themselves. By the 1550s even textbooks were subject to textual comparison, and the judges would sometimes declare the new printed versions deficient.[130] This is not to say that the general level of textual scholarship was that of Alciato or Budé; nor was it in the law courts

---

[122] See below, 78-9.   [123] For examples from the time of Dyer CJ, see 109 Selden Soc., p. lxi.

[124] Below, 388-9 (examples of cases argued or agreed but not adjudged).

[125] *Byflete* v. *White* (1493) 1 Caryll 167 at 169 (tr. 'Keble said that this case . . . was adjudged to be good law recently in Wilmer's case, in the time of the present king; and he showed a copy of the record thereof. The court said that that case was adjudged by good advice, and so they thought that case was good law.').

[126] *Abbot of Hyde* v. *Benger* (1493) 1 Caryll 178 at 180 ('Jay: . . . your case . . . is an aged precedent. Show us such a case adjudged in modern reports. Kebell: no one could do that, because the case has simply not arisen in recent times . . .'); 94 Selden Soc. 162; *Moots*, 281.

[127] e.g. *Anon.* (1531) Brooke Abr., *Executours*, pl. 22 (Fitzherbert J. reported that a case of 34 Hen. VI was contrary to the record 'and therefore misreported', and ordered the book to be amended); *Bellengeham's Case* (1537) Dyer 34a (case of 22 Edw. IV found to be contrary to the record); *Woodland* v. *Mantell* (1553) Plowd. 94 at 95v (tr. 'the record of the said case in 5 Hen. VII was searched and looked at by some of the justices, as I heard'); *Anon.* (1554) Dyer 97b (case of 33 Hen. VI traced in record); *Norwood* v. *Norwood and Rede* (1557) Plowd. 180v at 182v (tr. 'the justices ordered the record of the said case in 12 Hen. VIII to be searched and shown to them').

[128] *Anon.* (1536) Dyer 13a (two versions of a case of 19 Edw. III); *Barrington* v. *Potter* (1553) Dyer 82a (two Edw. I manuscripts compared by Dyer CJ). Cf. *Bishop of Carlisle* v. *Smith* (1556) Dyer 129a (two manuscript registers compared with the print).

[129] A notable example occurs in *Core* v. *May* (1536) Dyer 22b, where Fitzjames CJ stated that *Orwell* v. *Mortoft* (1505) was ruled and adjudged. This is not supported by the record: B. & M. 245, 408.

[130] e.g. *Wimbish* v. *Tailbois* (1550) Plowd. 38v at 58 (praise for early edns of Littleton, 'in which the recent additions are omitted'). For Dyer's condemnation of the 1529 edn of the *Natura Brevium* by William Owen, because of his interpolations, see 109 Selden Soc., p. xxix n. 78; below, 500.

of Italy or France. But England and its lawyers were not immune to the currents of contemporary scholarship.

THE ADVENT OF PRINTING[131]

One of the most obvious changes in the outward appearances of scholarship was that caused by the introduction of printing, a craft which from the very beginning was deployed to meet the needs of lawyers and law students.[132] The use of printing to make knowledge accessible was favoured by the humanists, and there was some explicit reference in our period to the desirability of opening the law to public access.[133] Printers such as John Rastell harnessed this sentiment to business acumen by publishing a few elementary legal works in English;[134] but this made little impact on the advanced learning of the legal profession or the scientific development of the law. The principal innovation affecting the form of the law itself was that standard texts of legislation were made freely available, and this coincided with a more literal approach to legislative interpretation and an abandonment of the greater flexibility which had prevailed in the days of corrupt manuscripts.[135] The publication of the year books—though gradual and haphazard, one year at a time—made possible a standard means of reference, and this in itself encouraged explicit citation where previously arguments had typically rested on principle and vague references to 'our books'.[136] Students also were major beneficiaries of the press, since they could now buy Littleton, the *Natura Brevium*, and a few other student primers,[137] for a few pence. Another advantage of the new medium was to give wider access to some relative rarities, such as *Glanvill*, and obscure or unique year books. But it did not yet attract many major authors. And, more seriously, the printing of law books led subconsciously to the introduction of a *de facto* canon of legal literature, and a diminution in the status of manuscript texts.[138] A good law library in 1558 still consisted more of manuscript than of printed material, and yet for most lawyers the core of acceptable authority was coming to be seen in terms of printed books. Authorities were texts available to all, and indeed—like scripture—well known to all in the same words frozen in type. This might have been beneficial if the press had exercised high standards of selection and editorial attention; but in reality the printing of

---

[131] See further below, 494–507.   [132] See below, 494.   [133] See above, 25–6.

[134] See above, 26; below, 495.   [135] Below, 76–7.   [136] Below, 487.

[137] The list was not long. The principal additions were Perkins's *Perutilis Tractatus* or *Profitable Book* (1528), Fitzherbert's *Novel Natura Brevium* (1534), and Staunford's *Les Plees del Coron* (1557). Unlike Littleton, these were written for the press and printed in their authors' lifetimes.

[138] See D. Ibbetson, 'Legal Printing and Legal Doctrine' (2000) 35 *Irish Jurist* 345–54; below, 506.

materials other than statutes was piecemeal, erratic, and virtually free from scholarly editorial control. At the same time that the English legal profession acquired a love of footnotes and citations, lawyers in general all but abandoned the proper evaluation of legal materials to a series of unlearned printers who enjoyed the monopoly of law publishing. Worst of all, current law was virtually unprovided for,[139] so that, while the printing of case-law was concentrated on year books from an earlier period, the circulation of current law reports for a generation or two fell into decline and confusion.[140] The great changes in the common law of our period cannot, therefore, be linked to the printing press. On the contrary, in this first century of printing the policy of law publishers was backward-looking and its chief effect on the study and practice of the law was restrictive and narrowly conservative.

INDIVIDUALISM AND THE 'COMMON WEAL'

A frequently discussed ethical and political concept associated with sixteenth-century England was the principle that the 'common weal', or public good, should be advanced and that the 'singular commodity' or private advantage of individuals should if necessary give way to it. 'The end of the laws is the preservation of the common wealth.'[141] This notion has been interpreted not as precocious socialism but as the result of a conservative reaction—borne up by humanist philosophy—against the new capitalism which threatened to undermine the social order.[142] Elyot argued that the *res publica* was not to be equated with the *res plebeia*, for the promotion of the commonalty alone would also destroy social order.[143] The commonwealth ideal is most prominent in political and economic literature, where its prime association is with disparity of income and concern for the indigent;[144] but it also percolated in a more general form into jurisprudence.

[139] Above, 13. The one major exception was the genre of controversial literature associated with Christopher St German: below, 244–5, 502.

[140] For the illusory cessation of year books in 1535, which resulted from changes in circulation rather than a decline in reporting, see above, 7; below, 473.

[141] Hales, *Oration* (1540/2), fo. 46v.

[142] A. B. Ferguson, 'Renaissance Realism in the "Commonwealth" Literature of early Tudor England' (1955) 16 *Jnl History of Ideas* at 298.   [143] Elyot, *The Governour*, fo. 1.

[144] J. W. Allen, 'The Very and True Commonweal' in *A History of Political Thought in the Sixteenth Century* (1928), 134–56; A. B. Ferguson, 'The Tudor Commonwealth and the Sense of Change' (1963) 3 *Jnl British Studies*, pt i, 11–35; *The Articulate Citizen and the English Renaissance* (1965); W. R. D. Jones, *The Tudor Commonwealth 1529–59* (1970); *The Tree of Commonwealth 1450–1793* (2000); Elton, *Reform and Renewal*, 5–7; J. J. Scarisbrick, 'Cardinal Wolsey and the Common Weal' in *Wealth and Power in Tudor England*, ed. Ives (1978) 45–67; J. Thirsk, *Economic Policy and Projects* (1978), 1–50; J. C. K. Cornwall, 'The Common Weal', in *Wealth and Society in Early Sixteenth Century England* (1988), 154–97; T. F. Mayer, *Thomas Starkey and the Commonweal* (1989); P. A. Fideler and T. F. Mayer (eds), *Political Thought and the Tudor Commonwealth* (1992).

According to some radicals, the very existence of common lawyers was against the common weal, because they supported strife for personal profit.[145] In More's Utopia there were few laws and no lawyers. But Utopia was not reality. More was not an anarchist, and his friend John Rastell devoted several pages to an eloquent demonstration that the essence of a true commonwealth lay in its good laws:[146] 'a good reasonable common law maketh a good common peace and a common wealth among a great commonalty of people'.[147] Since laws required lawyers, to ensure that they were properly enforced, it followed that lawyers were also necessary to a commonwealth.[148] A more practical goal than the abolition of strife was to ensure that laws promoted the common weal,[149] and this required some principles for determining when private interest ought to give way to the public good. Generally speaking, the common law had long favoured individualism, and we shall see that steps were taken in the early Tudor period to advance the liberties of the individual both against the claims of lords and against the government.[150] Nevertheless, there were traces of a countervailing doctrine which permitted private rights of property occasionally to be overridden in the public interest, and by the time of Edward IV cases of this kind were being justified in terms of the 'common weal' (res publica).[151] For example, the protection of commerce in fairs and markets was so important that private property could be taken away by a sale in market overt,[152] and an otherwise lawful distress was forbidden in respect of goods brought there.[153] Even an uninvited entry on another's land could be justified in exceptional circumstances of public necessity: to defend the realm,[154] or to pull down houses to prevent the spread of fire.[155] Since the common law

---

[145] Henry Brinklow's, Complaynt of Roderick Mors [c.1542], ed. J. M. Cowper (1874), 21; Starkey, Dialogue between Pole and Lupset, ed. Mayer, 79–80, 127.

[146] Liber Assisarum [1514], prologue. Cf. Hales, Oration (1540/2), in the passage quoted on the opposite page.

[147] J. Rastell, Exposiciones Terminorum Legum Anglorum (c.1523), prohemium (sp. mod.).

[148] In addressing a call of new serjeants, a chief justice of the same period concluded that lawyers were necessary to a 'publique weal'. Law was a necessity, and law was 'dumb and dead' without ministers to put it into practice: Baker, Serjeants at Law, 280.

[149] This was also a principle of statutory interpretation: Wimbish v. Tailbois (1550) Plowd. 38v at 54, 59v; Partridge v. Straunge (1553) Plowd. 77v at 82, per Saunders sjt (quoted below, 78).

[150] See below, ch. 3.

[151] For examples temp. Edw. IV and later, see 94 Selden Soc. 34 n. 5; N. Doe, Fundamental Authority in Medieval English Law (1990), 71.

[152] Rollesley v. Toft (1495) 1 Caryll 285 at 286; St German, Doctor and Student, 146. The doctrine had been settled by the mid-fifteenth century: below, 738 n. 82.

[153] Mich. 7 Hen. VII, fo. 2, pl. 1 (things not distrainable in a market or fair, or an inn, 'pur le prejudice de common weal').

[154] Mich. 8 Edw. IV, fo. 23, pl. 41; Cuny v. Brugewode (1506) Trin. 21 Hen. VII, fo. 27, pl. 5, per Kingsmill J. (tr. '…these are things justifiable and lawful for maintenance of the common weal'); Malyverer v. Spynke (1537) Dyer 36b, §40, per Knightley sjt.

[155] Harecourt v. Spycer (1521) Trin. 13 Hen. VIII, fo. 16, pl. 1 (119 Selden Soc. 84), per Shelley sjt; Malyverer v. Spynke (1537) Dyer 36b, §40, per Knightley sjt.

apparently did not allow an uninvited entry in order to assist the absent landowner himself in an emergency,[156] let alone simply to improve his neighbour's position,[157] this rarely invoked principle did genuinely depend on the protection of the common interest as against the private. It is possible that the principle of necessity also excused the jettisoning of cargo from a ship, to save life during a storm.[158]

The common-weal principle appeared in different guise in the notion that jurisdictional franchises, though a form of property, were enjoyed only upon condition that the incumbent public duties be discharged satisfactorily for the good of the common weal,[159] and that it was impossible to make a valid claim to a liberty or custom which would prejudice the common weal, such as a prescriptive right to enclose, or to clip current coin.[160] In the latter case there was no property interest at all, but in the former the property was lost, by forfeiture, if the owner abused his liberty. However, this was a very special kind of property coupled with the performance of a public duty, and was therefore analogous to a freehold office, which could likewise be taken away for abuse.

These limited cases hardly support Serjeant Shelley's broad generalization that one could do something for the good of the common weal without being liable to an action.[161] It is true that St German's student went so far as to say that 'the general grounds of the law of England heed more what is good for many than what is good for one singular person only'.[162] However, what the student had in mind seems rather to have been the notion that hard cases make bad law, that clear general rules are more in the public interest than individual exceptions grounded on hardship. This more abstract common-weal approach was directly opposed to equity, in which context we shall return to it.[163]

Our more specific common-law doctrine favouring the common weal was little used in legal argument, and when a particular application of it was tested it was found wanting, precisely because it was not a universal principle and did not

---

[156] *Cuny v. Brugewode* (1506–7) Trin. 21 Hen. VII, fo. 27, pl. 5; 2 Caryll 542; CP 40/978, m. 449; B. & M. 316 (entry to save grain from cattle). But cf. *Alyn v. Facy* (1541) CP 40/1111, m. 616 (pleads entry to put out fire in plaintiff's house; replication *de injuria*).

[157] e.g. *Pender v. Beche* (1506) KB 27/981, m. 63 (error from Canterbury piepowder court; defendant entered plaintiff's shop after two years' absence and, finding his stock of cloth damaged by moths, sold the cloth and kept the money for the plaintiff; demurrer; judgment for plaintiff; reversed on a technical ground).

[158] See the discussions in *Reniger v. Fogassa* (1550) Plowd. 1. A plea to this effect was pleaded without demurrer in *Spencer v. Kent* (1540) CP 40/1106, m. 426 (*assumpsit* against the carrier; plaintiff traverses the danger).

[159] Dudley's reading (Gray's Inn, c.1486) 113 Selden Soc. 66; Spelman's reading (Gray's Inn, 1519) 113 Selden Soc. 66, 101; GI MS. 25, fo. 288v, *per* Fyneux CJ.

[160] Spelman's reading (Gray's Inn, 1519) 113 Selden Soc. 78.

[161] *Harecourt v. Spycer* (1521) Trin. 13 Hen. VIII, fo. 16, pl. 1 (119 Selden Soc. 84; 94 Selden Soc. 35).

[162] *Doctor and Student*, ed. Plucknett and Barton, 79   [163] See below, 41.

weigh heavily in the balance against legitimate private property. The test came in relation to the fundamental question, what is 'property' for legal purposes? Were there any limits to what an individual could own? The premise of the conservative 'common weal' approach seems to have been that it was in the interest of the common weal to protect private property in objects of value, but that a matter only of private pleasure should not affect legal relationships. Thus, a grant of a profit à prendre could not be freely countermanded, whereas a grant of a mere pleasure could.[164] And a thing of pleasure could not constitute consideration to raise a use.[165] According to Edmund Dudley, an assize of novel disseisin would lie for a profit but not for a matter of pleasure, such as hunting rights, or a grant of all herons and hawks on a piece of land.[166] And a thing 'only of commodity or pleasure' could not be taken in execution.[167] Then again, an easement or profit in the enjoyment of real property was protected by the law, but not mere interference with comfort or peace of mind by a bad neighbour or by the reasonable pursuit of industry.[168] It was arguable that the reason why a use without consideration was not legally protected was that it was a matter purely of pleasure,[169] and a similar notion that something of legal value should have a price underlay the emergent requirement of consideration in *assumpsit*.[170] The principle came to the test in the more surprising proposition that property could not subsist in things kept only for amusement or sport, such as hunting dogs, hawks, or peacocks, nor perhaps in other things which brought no measurable profit. The notion persisted in the criminal law, in favour of life, at least until 1553, when a judge took the astounding position that diamonds could not be stolen because they were of no intrinsic value.[171] Doubts had stirred in the private law by 1519, when it was argued at Spelman's reading in Gray's Inn that a grant of a court without amercements was not good, because it had no value, but Broke J. retorted that it was profitable in the eyes of God to do justice; Broke J. added that an advowson was valuable for a similar reason, though it brought no financial profit.[172] The Common Pleas firmly rejected the doctrine the following year, on the grounds that comfort and good health were valuable. Even a singing bird could be said to

---

[164] *Duchess of Norfolk* v. *Wiseman* (1498) Trin. 12 Hen. VII, fo. 25, pl. 5; Hil. 13 Hen. VII, fo. 13, pl. 2; KB 27/945, m. 62. Cf. Spelman 17, 161. [165] Yorke 136, no. 127.

[166] Reading in Gray's Inn (1496) CUL MS. Hh.3.10, at ff. 61v–62 ('quar il nest forsque plesure'). On the other hand, it would lie on a grant of all strawberries or hurtleberries in a particular wood, or of so many bushels of roses in my garden. [167] Port 147, §19.

[168] Privacy was not regarded as valuable, though it could be protected by immemorial local custom: Spelman 17, *per* Fyneux CJ (1512).

[169] *Gervys* v. *Cooke* (1522) Mich. 14 Hen. VIII, fo. 7, pl. 5 (119 Selden Soc. 115), *per* Fitzherbert J.

[170] See below, 862–4.

[171] Dalison's reports, BL MS. Harley 5141, fo. 12 (1553), *per* Hales J. Likewise peacocks: Mich. 18 Hen. VIII, fo. 2, pl. 11. See further below, 564–5.

[172] BL MS. Hargrave 5265, fo. 119 (quoted in 94 Selden Soc. 36).

refresh the spirits which cause bodily health, and therefore to have a legal value. It was difficult to draw a workable distinction between a singing bird and a valuable musical instrument, or between a hunting-dog and a park or chase (which was a well-established property right separate from the land). The conclusion was that trespass could be brought for a bloodhound,[173] as no doubt it could for diamonds and other *jocalia*. Not long afterwards an action of detinue was brought in London for a 'whistling linnet... of great pleasure', said to be worth 20 marks.[174] And damages could be recovered for hunting wild animals, because 'it is necessary for every man of ability to have pleasures'.[175] By 1539 the distinction between pleasure and profit was sufficiently discredited to be denied in an act of Parliament which made it felony to steal the king's hawks or their eggs. Perhaps the king himself had been affronted by mention of legal scruples on the point. At any rate, the Commons did not give their assent gracefully.[176] And there seems a touch of petulance in the assertion in the preamble that every landowner ought 'in equity' to have the profits of his property 'as well in things of high pleasure as in things commonly valuable... and in especial of and in things of pleasure'.[177]

All in all, the doctrine that the common weal is to be favoured before private interest bore little or no fruit in the sixteenth-century common law. It was a way of explaining some rare cases, but not a source of new answers or successful forensic arguments. The courts were not best placed to weigh private against public interest; and there was far more scope for the advancement of the common weal through parliamentary legislation, to which we now turn.

THE ROLE OF LEGISLATION

Even a cursory glance at the statute-books will show that, while the outward forms of legislation may have remained more or less the same between the reigns of Richard III and Elizabeth I, a transformation occurred both in the volume and in the range of parliamentary enactments, especially during and after the reign of Henry VIII. Different specific explanations may be put forward for particular pieces of legislation, and several examples will be discussed in their proper contexts later in this volume. Yet it is also possible, in viewing the output as a whole,

---

[173] *Fyloll* v. *Assheleygh* (1520) Trin. 12 Hen. VIII, fo. 4, pl. 3 (119 Selden Soc. 14); CP 40/1027, m. 433; discussed in 94 Selden Soc. 35–6; 17 CSC 50–4. Followed on demurrer in *Cary* v. *Braye* (1527) CP 40/1055, m. 430d (greyhound); and in *Anon.* (1544) Gell's reports, I, Trin. 36 Hen. VIII, fo. 44. Cf. *Crowe* v. *Barley* (1549) CP 40/1142, m. 308d (goshawk; demurrer to defendant's plea that he found it).

[174] *Goldwyn* v. *Wulberde* (c.1536) C1/803/29. The plaintiff lost the action in the Sheriffs' Court, but complained in Chancery that the defendant had pleaded *Non detinet* untruthfully.

[175] *Anon.* (1529/30) Keil. 202v, pl. 1; Caryll (Jun.) 410, no. 105, at 411, *per* Broke J.

[176] *Lisle Letters*, ed. Byrne, v. 557 (report on 28 June that 'they are scant agreed' on the measure).

[177] 31 Hen. VIII, c. 12.

to see running through it a new confidence in the power of the sovereign to advance the good of the common weal by means of carefully planned legal change. Such policies are evident in much of Henry VIII's legislation, especially during the rule of Thomas Cromwell. Humanists such as Starkey identified the roots of the nation's supposed poverty as underpopulation of the countryside, the decay of towns, idleness at all levels, and a desire to live beyond one's means. When necessities such as grain were exported in return for luxurious trifles such as fine wines and silks, it was obvious that pleasure had got the better of industry and profit.[178] However wrong this analysis may have been, it does seem to have influenced the legislative programme. Prolonged and concerted efforts were now made to redress the perceived causes of decline with measures relating to the plight of agriculture, enclosures,[179] the condition of towns, the regulation of industry and apprenticeship, wage and price control, the surveillance of imports and exports, the treatment of vagrancy and the poor,[180] and the prohibition of excess in diet, apparel, and unlawful gaming.[181] In the absence of a police force, provision was made for some of the paternalistic measures to be enforced by common informers,[182] though Sir Thomas More considered that this device had been relatively ineffective.[183] In its struggle to control the economy, Parliament was persuaded to meddle not only with human society but also with the natural environment, as in the solemn and detailed scheme for annihilating choughs, rooks, and crows (in order to protect tillage),[184] or that to improve the breeding of horses,[185] and apparently contemplated even a human population policy.[186]

[178] This is one of the central themes of Starkey's *Dialogue between Pole and Lupset*. See also 94 Selden Soc. 47. [179] Below, 650.

[180] Below, 96–9.

[181] Holdsworth, *HEL*, iv. 294–407; Jones, *The Tudor Commonwealth 1529–1559*, 184–5; Elton, 'Reform by Statute' in *Studies*, ii. 236–58; *English Law in the Sixteenth Century: reform in an age of change* (Selden Soc. lecture, 1979).

[182] e.g., to take but one example, the series of very detailed and regularly revised acts of apparel: 1 Hen. VIII, c. 14; 6 Hen. VIII, c. 1; 7 Hen. VIII, c. 6; 24 Hen. VIII, c. 13; 1 & 2 Phil. & Mar., c. 2. Actions of debt for the penalty, shared between the informer and the king, were regularly brought in the Common Pleas, probably with a view to compromise (judgments are not found): e.g. *Blathe* v. *Alynson* (1516) CP 40/1016, m. 666 (satin doublet); *Payne* v. *Aprice* (1517) CP 40/1019, m. 332 (gentleman using gown guarded with black velvet in Westminster Hall); *Gun* v. *Marlyng* (1521) CP 40/1032A, m. 27 (sim.); *Wodderuff* v. *Wright* (1531) CP 40/1068, m. 457 (satin doublet); *Hill* v. *Morgan* (1536) CP 40/1090, m. 546; *Hyll* v. *Forest* (1536) CP 40/1090, m. 552 (surgeon using velvet coif and gown welted with velvet); *Ap Robert* v. *Ap John* (1541) CP 40/1110, m. 316; *Forkynson* v. *Jones* (1544) CP 40/1121, m. 534 (velvet coif and satin doublet); *Legh* v. *Forman* (1557) CP 40/1169, m. 434d (velvet coif); *Chamberleyn* v. *Stanton*, ibid., m. 646 (sim.); *Jackson* v. *Sadler*, ibid., m. 653 (satin nightcap); *Staples* v. *Hall* (1557) CP 40/1170, m. 1207 (velvet night-cap). The same is true of similar regulatory measures. See further below, 163–4.

[183] *The Debellation of Salem and Bizance*, ed. J. Guy et al. (1987), 143. [184] 24 Hen. VIII, c. 10.

[185] 27 Hen. VIII, c. 6; 32 Hen. VIII, c. 13. Elton, *Studies*, ii. 252, indicated that this was a concern of Starkey's. For the general context see P. Edwards, *The Horse Trade of Tudor and Stuart England* (1988), ch. 1. [186] *LP*, ix. 725 (ii).

The Reformation Parliament exhibited a different kind of self-confidence when it finally established the legislative supremacy of the king in Parliament over its only serious rival, the supposedly catholic Church.[187] Parliament was obviously subordinate to the law of God, and that was never in question; a statute contrary to the law of God would in theory be void. But how the Church should be governed on earth, and who should interpret the laws of God, were at least partly matters of human law. There were medieval precedents for parliamentary legislation which purported to override the canon law,[188] though these had not been universally accepted by canonists and there was still an element of doubt about the scope of parliamentary competence in the spiritual sphere.[189] The conviction and execution of Sir Thomas More, who at his trial challenged the validity of the legislation under which he was condemned,[190] finally and terribly put an end to the question as far as English law was concerned. When Mary I restored the authority of the pope, and the mass, it was thought necessary, or at least prudent, to do it by act of Parliament and to repeal the Henrician and Edwardian legislation, though a Common Pleas judge was imprisoned for daring to declare that the old law remained in force until the repeal.[191]

The sovereignty of Parliament in temporal matters was less controversial, though it had in the past been wielded with caution. At the dawn of the century a foreign visitor had commented on English conservatism with the remark that, 'if the king should propose to change any old established rule, it would seem to every Englishman as if his life were taken from him'.[192] No one could have made such a comment forty years later, when an Englishman who ventured to question some of the sweeping changes wrought since 1500 was liable in fact to have his life taken from him.[193] The statutes of Henry VIII pressed against the very limits of legislative capability: entailing the Crown with remainders,[194] new treasons of appalling width,[195]

---

[187] See G. R. Elton, *England under the Tudors* (3rd edn, 1991), 160–2, 165–70; *The Tudor Constitution* (2nd edn, 1982), 236–40; *Studies*, ii. 55–7; S. E. Lehmberg, *The Reformation Parliament 1529–36* (1970); below, 244. Elton pointed out that the supremacy in the Church was monarchical, claimed directly under God rather than through Parliament, but that it required parliamentary legislation to give it an enforceable form.

[188] e.g. 45 Edw. III, c. 3 (*sylva caedua*), discussed at length in St German, *Doctor and Student*, 300–14. In 1393 Parliament had declared that the king had no earthly sovereign but was subject immediately to God in all things touching the regality of the Crown: 16 Ric. II, c. 5. See further below, 238–44.

[189] See *Prior of Castleacre* v. *Dean of Westminster* (1503) Hil. 21 Hen. VII (misdated), fo. 2, pl. 1, *per* Palmes sjt (tr. 'no temporal act [of Parliament] may cause a temporal man to have spiritual jurisdiction'); the argument was accepted by Frowyk CJ but not by Vavasour J.

[190] For what is known of the trial see J. D. M. Derrett, 'Neglected Versions of the Contemporary Account of the Trial of Sir Thomas More' (1960) 33 *BIHR* 202–23; 'The Trial of Sir Thomas More' (1964) 79 *EHR* 449–77.   [191] See below, 251, 419.

[192] *Venetian Relation*, 37.   [193] 94 Selden Soc. 45.

[194] 25 Hen. VIII, c. 22; 28 Hen. VIII, c. 7; 35 Hen. VIII, c. 1.

[195] See I. D. Thornley, 'The Treason Legislation of Henry VIII' (1917) 11 *TRHS* (3rd ser.) 87–123; G. R. Elton, 'The Law of Treason in the Early Reformation' (1968) 11 *Historical Jnl* 211–36.

fictional liveries of seisin,[196] even boiling in oil.[197] Perhaps most arrogantly of all, the legislature thought itself competent in 1539 to abolish diversity of theological opinions, with the possibility of death by burning for those who did not think as they were told.[198] If Parliament could override common law, it could as easily override immemorial custom. On the eve of the Reformation Parliament, Sir John More (Sir Thomas's father) had denied that Parliament could alter immemorial local customs such as gavelkind; but within twelve years it had been done.[199] And Parliament was certainly no longer thought to be legally fettered by reason or conscience; if it offended either, no lesser tribunal could set things right.[200]

A case can be made for saying that the new confidence in the capacity of Parliament first manifested itself in the reigns of Richard III and Henry VII, when it produced legislation of greater conceptual importance than anything in the previous century.[201] But the most dramatic achievements were those of the reign of Henry VIII. Henry exalted Parliament by goading it into new feats of sovereignty; and Parliament, in return, magnified Henry. Together they assumed a legislative sovereignty which they exercised with prodigious industry. The 677 statutes which they passed occupied almost as much space as the whole statute-book had done in 1509, and some individual enactments were of unprecedented length and complexity. This torrent of legislation was a reflection of the intellectual climate of Renaissance Europe, which expected the good ruler to exercise his supreme will to improve the common weal. The new approach was accompanied by a change in the style of legislation, which was cast in such detailed and precise language, and with such extensive and explicit preambles, that the judges were plainly being warned not to indulge in the kind of creative exegesis which they had bestowed on medieval legislation. At the same time we find a newer approach to the interpretation of statutes which gave weight to the intention of the lawgiver.[202] This subtle change may not have had much effect in practice, but it had a Romanesque flavour.

Yet all this impressive legislative activity did not fundamentally alter the character of English jurisprudence. The constitution remained the same. The new

---

[196] 27 Hen. VIII, c. 10; below, 672.   [197] 22 Hen. VIII, c. 9; below, 539.

[198] An Act abolishing Diversity in Opinions, 31 Hen. VIII, c. 14 (*SR*, iii. 739), which made it heresy merely to 'hold' opinions contrary to those declared by the act to be true. Failing to read the act in church was also punishable: *Draycot* v. *Broke* (1540) E159/319, Trin. 32 Hen. VIII, m. 24 (information against curate of Bunbury, Cheshire, who pleads that he did read it).

[199] *Marmyon* v. *Baldwyn* (1527) 120 Selden Soc. 61 at 69; 31 Hen. VIII, c. 3; 94 Selden Soc. 44–5. Although he gave gavelkind as an example, More J. evidently thought all local customs were unalterable by statute. See further below, 81 n. 192.

[200] St German, *Little Treatise*, ed. Guy, 117; Co. Inst. iv. 37 (judicial resolution temp. Hen. VIII). Cf. *Anon.* (1535) Mich. 27 Hen. VIII, fo. 24, pl. 1 (tr. 'no reason, but only by force of the statute').

[201] It is noteworthy that the readers in the inns of court during our period hardly ever lectured on statutes between Edward I and Richard III: below, 464. The first statute of Richard (1 Ric. III, c. 1), concerning uses, occasioned endless legal debate, both in the courts and in the inns of court.

[202] See below, 78–9.

leges were not the will of the *princeps* alone, but a compromise between the ruler, his peers, and his commons, in Parliament assembled. And, in social and legal terms, the underlying legislative policy was conservative. There was no attempt to establish a new Utopia, no systematic overhaul of the legal system, no threats to the supremacy of the common law, no project for its codification. There were few attempts to rethink legal concepts. The most legally imaginative measures were those embodied in the Statutes of Uses and Wills, which had the object of resurrecting and protecting fiscal feudalism; but the policy behind the draftsman's ingenuity was not innovation so much as restoration of the king's feudal rights, along with primogeniture and the dynastic spirit. The boldest legislation was that which reformed the Church, removing it from Roman sovereignty and remedying the abuses of sanctuary and benefit of clergy. To a few minds this encroachment on the spiritual sphere was so shocking that it were better to die than accept it. And yet here again, the ends—at least as presented on behalf of the lawmaker— were essentially conservative: to free the Church from foreign influences which were associated more with political expediency and greed than Christian values, to stop churches from harbouring murderers and thieves, to restore capital punishment for murder and serious felonies, to end the abuses of monasticism, and to return vast tracts of rich monastic land to the world. To be sure, the king had motives which were not entirely altruistic, but—as in the case of uses—the legislative programme was rendered intellectually acceptable by its claim to work a restoration of something good from the past, by removing subsequent corruptions and perversions, rather than a root and branch reconstruction. There was no reference in scripture to a system of judicial appeals to the pope, and even Thomas More could hardly deny that it was man-made; the issue could therefore be presented as one of human rather than of natural law, whether the spiritual courts had forfeited their jurisdictional franchise by abuse.[203] Opinions still differ as to the true extent of the abuses in the Church and its courts. But the principal sources of complaint were certainly familiar to the king's subjects and their lawyers long before the Reformation Parliament met, and the intellectual background to even the most sweeping legislative reforms must be traced in the law courts rather than the royal court.[204]

Part of Cromwell's genius lay in his ability to harness existing grievances to remedies which advantaged the king, and for our present purpose it matters little whether Henry VIII genuinely favoured the conservatism affected by his legislation or whether his advisers were translating more radical intentions into a palatable form. The results might have been politically and theologically radical, but

[203] Cf. below, 244–5.
[204] For the common law background to the Statute of Uses see below, 654–60. And for the common law background to the Reformation legislation, see below, 237–44.

they were legally conservative. The king might, for instance, have achieved his material ends more directly by introducing a secular divorce law and an income tax, institutions which we have come to take for granted since the nineteenth century; but, even if such innovations were thinkable in the early Tudor period, they were not seriously pursued.[205] Henry preferred to settle for what—if frustrating obstacles were removed—the law already gave him.

Lesser legislation which affected the work of the courts was typically concerned with smoothing away operational defects rather than with substantive law.[206] That these reforms were important enough is shown by the fact that readers in the inns of court began to turn their attention in our period from the great legislation of the thirteenth century to the most recent statutes of Henry VIII. It must have been a considerable struggle after the 1530s for the lawyer to keep up to date. Much ingenuity would have to be expended on the effects of the property legislation, especially those which were unforeseen by the draftsman, and much litigation would be occasioned by the complexities of title to monastic and manorial land. The unsettling effect of these legal adjustments may have contributed to the demise of 'common learning', in the late medieval sense of a corpus of received legal wisdom, and to the rise of the dispositive judicial decision.[207] Certainly the accessibility of written law in printed form was to give statutes an undue prominence in English history; for historians of later generations, commenting on the law of the early Tudor period, would understandably devote most of their attentions to the great constitutional statutes which established the Church of England and its liturgy. However, the statutory reforms of the law were moderate and modest; their aim was to perfect a common-law system of procedure and thought which was in essence taken for granted, the *lex terrae* of Magna Carta. And, from the legal point of view, some of the largest changes in the character of English law during the first half of the sixteenth century were not attributable to Parliament at all. The reformation of the common law, unlike that of the English Church, was not imposed from without by the king in Parliament. It was largely an internal revolution, only partly planned, and it reflected in a less direct manner than legislation the law's response to the needs of the times; but revolution it may fairly be called.

EQUITY AND CONSCIENCE

This internal revolution, as we shall see, occurred at a time of increasing litigiousness, a phenomenon which probably had economic rather than intellectual

205 See further below, 66–8.
206 See 94 Selden Soc. 46. Most of the reforms will be considered below.
207 For this phenomenon see below, ch. 21, 467–72, 486–9.

causes but which put pressure on the central courts to improve the remedies available to potential plaintiffs. One of the large questions of policy which this raised was touched on in Maitland's Rede lecture, though Maitland was unaware of the boom in litigation. Would the common-law courts themselves respond to the needs of plaintiffs, or would the solution be found in a jurisdictional movement towards the Chancery and conciliar courts? Would equity, in particular, be seen as the principal resource in establishing new remedies? Equity was another dominant and fruitful theme in the writings of sixteenth-century humanist jurists,[208] though only in England was equity channelled into specialist tribunals.

There was nothing new about the idea of *aequitas*, which had passed from the Digest into the canon law and the medieval Civil law, and from Aquinas into moral theology and the curriculum of the universities. Two somewhat different meanings had emerged in medieval times, both of which were distinguished by the fourteenth-century Italian jurists Lucas of Penna and Marsilius of Padua.[209] In one sense it was the source and spirit of all law, an abstract concept of justice. In the other it was a criterion for interpreting written law according to the true meaning of the lawmaker, on the basis that words were an imperfect vehicle for expressing legislative intention in detail.

Both forms of equity were to be found in medieval English law.[210] In the first sense it was known to English lawyers under the name of 'reason', or rightwiseness, the sense of right and wrong which inspired and explained all legal doctrine, preserved consistency, and prevented absurdities.[211] It was not to be confused with private reasoning, for if a judge's own reasoning conflicted with established reason he had to give way.[212] The second kind of equity was used, by that name, in the interpretation of statutes. It gave the judges the same freedom in expounding legislation as they enjoyed when declaring the common law.[213] But neither kind of equity had much in common with the classical English notion of equity, as it developed from the fifteenth century onwards, which involved the relaxation

---

[208] See e.g. G. Kisch, 'Summum Ius Summa Iniuria' in *Aequitas und Bona Fides* (1955), 195–211; *Erasmus unde die Jurisprudenz seiner Zeit* (1960); 'Melanchthons Epieikeia-Aequitaslehre' in *Melanchthons Rechts- und Sozial-lehre* (1967), at 168–84.

[209] W. Ullmann, *The Medieval Idea of Law* (1946), 41–4; A. Gewirth (ed.), *Marsilius of Padua* (1951), ii. 37–44, 58, 190.

[210] See S. E. Thorne, 'The Equity of a Statute and Heydon's Case' (1936) 31 *Illinois Law Rev.* 202–16 (repr. in *Essays in English Legal History*, 155–70); J. L. Barton, 'Equity in the Medieval Common Law' in *Equity in the World's Legal Systems*, ed. R. A. Newman (1973), 139–55.

[211] For 'reason' see 94 Selden Soc. 37 n. 3; Doe, *Fundamental Authority*, ch. 5.

[212] Cf. Mich. 26 Hen. VIII, fo. 8, pl. 5 (tr. 'Shelley [J]. My opinion is against everyone on this point, for it is against reason as it seems to me. And Norwich [CJ] said that if our books were not so it would be hard to prove by reason').

[213] For the 'equity of the statute' see Doe, *Fundamental Authority*, 104–6. For statutory interpretation generally see further below, 76–81.

of known but unwritten general rules of law to meet the exigencies of justice or conscience in particular cases.

This English form of equity required a judicial procedure for delving into the individual circumstances which might require its application, a task for which jury trial was ill equipped. The medieval common law shut out a good many facts from judicial consideration, especially in personal actions, leaving the variable facts of particular cases to the jury, who embodied their decision in an inscrutable general verdict. Not only did this inhibit the refinement of many branches of the law, but it could also work hardship in those individual cases where a more sophisticated body of principle might have permitted exceptions. The general attitude of the common-law judges, however, seems to have favoured simplicity and certainty. They set a high value on legal clarity and regarded exceptions made in hard cases as contrary to the public interest in having legal rules which were simple and absolute. It was better to suffer a 'mischief' in an individual case than the 'inconvenience' which would follow from admitting exceptions in hard cases.[214] On this view, the judges were not usually concerned with conscience or personal weakness. If a sane adult failed to take reasonable precautions to protect his own interests, it was his 'folly'; and the law did not protect fools by bending the rules for them.[215] The stock example was that of the debtor who did not ensure that his bond was cancelled when he paid up; he would obviously suffer a grave mischief by being sued on the bond for a second payment, but it was the result of his own foolishness and the law would not be set aside for his benefit. To make an exception would subvert the legal rule which made written evidence incontestable in such circumstances.[216] Of course, no one thought debtors morally obliged to pay

[214] e.g. *Hoper* v. *Abbot of St Albans* (1490) Pas. 5 Hen. VII, fo. 25, pl. 7, *per* Vavasour J. (tr. 'The law will rather suffer such a mischief than inconvenience...'); *Waller* v. *Debenham* (1493) 1 Caryll 125 at 129, *per* Fairfax J.; *Re Lady E. S.* (*c.*1530/5) Wm Yelv. 292 at 293, *per* Fitzherbert J. ('as our learning says, it is better to suffer a mischief than an inconvenience'); *Gawen* v. *Hussee* (1537) Dyer 38a at 40b ('that injury shall be sooner suffered than an inconvenience'); *Waberley* v. *Cockerel* (1541) Dyer 51a; tr. B. & M. 258 ('It is nevertheless better to suffer a mischief to one man than an inconvenience to many, which would subvert the law'); Hales, *Oration*, fo. 43; St German, *Little Treatise*, ed. Guy, 117. This principle may be traced back to the fourteenth century at least: see 94 Selden Soc. *38* n. 1; Doe, *Fundamental Authority*, 155–74.

[215] For references to irremediable harm caused by one's own foolishness (*folie*), see e.g. *Anon.* (1494) Pas. 9 Hen. VII, fo. 24, pl. 10; *Harald* v. *Tyrell* (1496) Mich. 12 Hen. VII, fo. 5, pl. 3, *per* Bryan CJ; *Anon.* (1497) Mich. 13 Hen. VII, fo. 9, pl. 4; *Anon.* (1507) Spelman 30, pl. 10, *per* Fyneux CJ; *Sherborne* v. *Anon.* (1522) Spelman 18, pl. 3; *Anon.* (152/4) Port 79, no. 4; *Pope* v. *See* (1534) Spelman 215, *per* Luke J.; *Note* (n.d.) Spelman 123; *Moots*, 107, 111, 127, 146, 193, 204, 215, 221, 233, 242, 257, 260, 267, 305 (see index on p. 365).

[216] *Anon.* (1482) Pas. 22 Edw. IV. fo. 6, pl. 18, *per* Huse CJ; *Donne* v. *Cornwall* (1486) Pas. 1 Hen. VII, fo. 14, pl. 2; B. & M. 255; *Rede* v. *Capel* (1492) Pas. 7 Hen. VII, fo. 12, pl. 2, *per* Moreton C.; *Waberley* v. *Cockerel* (1541) Dyer 51a, B. & M. 258; St German, *Doctor and Student*, ed. Plucknett and Barton, 77, 79; *Replication of a Serjeant*, ed. Guy, 99–100; St German, *Little Treatise*, ed. Guy, 110–12; Hales, *Oration*, ff. 43–4.

twice if they failed to obtain a sealed receipt. It was simply the unfortunate result of a rigid rule of evidence which was thought in general to do more good than harm.[217] The burden of the undisclosed facts weighed upon the consciences of the parties, but not upon a court constrained by its rules of evidence to remain blindfold.

The detailed consideration of particular circumstances, which in England came to adopt the name 'equity', was more suited to the Court of Chancery than the common-law courts because the Chancery in exercising its bill jurisdiction behaved much more like a jury than a court of law. The Chancery was free from the procedural formalities of due process which circumscribed the regular courts. It could collect written evidence in detail by means of deposition and interrogation, and its decisions on the evidence—more akin to verdicts than judgments— bound the parties concerned but no one else. It could therefore depart from general rules without causing 'inconvenience', because its judgments were not of record and operated solely *in personam*.[218] The chancellor came not to destroy the law,[219] but to fulfil it by ordering what conscience demanded. In doing so, he did not thwart the common law, because the law did not forbid the conscientious result.[220] And the chancellor, like the Almighty, would look after the foolish, at any rate if someone else sought to take advantage of them: for instance, he was prepared to stop the unconscionable use of uncancelled bonds.[221]

This was the legal context in which St German set out for his readers the learning about equity to be found in Aristotle and Gerson.[222] It was because the regular courts of common law could not always give effect to the finest principles

---

[217] See *Anon.* (1482) Pas. 22 Edw. IV, fo. 6, pl. 18, where Huse CJ argued that the same policy should even prevent relief in Chancery: 'it is a lesser evil to make him pay again what he has paid through negligence than to disprove a matter of specialty by two proofs in the Chancery' (tr.). Cf. St German, *Little Treatise*, ed. Guy, 111.

[218] *Rede* v. *Capel* (1492) Pas. 7 Hen. VII, fo. 11, pl. 2, *per* Kebell sjt; St German, *Doctor and Student*, ed. Plucknett and Barton, 105. See also Milsom, *HFCL* (2nd edn), 84–6, 88–93; D. E. C. Yale, 8 *Irish Jurist* (new ser.) 332–3.

[219] *Diversite de Courtz* (1530), sig. A6 (tr. 'It was then said by the chancellor, that he shall not have remedy in this matter; for if it were remedied, then every record would be examined before him, and so thereby the common law destroyed'); St German, *Doctor and Student*, 105 ('the lord chancellor must order his conscience after the rules and grounds of the law of the realm'); *Little Treatise*, ed. Guy, 123 (sim.). The biblical allusion is from F. W. Maitland, *Equity* (1909), 17.

[220] See St German, *Little Treatise*, ed. Guy, 115–19, 123–4; Guy, *St German on Chancery and Statute*, 19–21, 83–8, 91–2. St German held that where the law denied a remedy in order to prevent an inconvenience, Chancery would also deny a remedy: *Little Treatise*, 117.

[221] *Rede* v. *Capel* (1492) Pas. 7 Hen. VII, fo. 12, pl. 2, *per* Moreton C. (argument against protecting fools does not hold in conscience); Fitz. Abr., *Subpena*, pl. 7, correcting Pas. 8 Edw. IV, fo. 4, pl. 11, *per* Stillingfleet C. ('*Deus est procurator fatuorum*'). Cf. Guy, *Public Career of Sir Thomas More*, 66–7.

[222] This is discussed by Z. Rueger, 'Gerson's Concept of Equity and Christopher St Germain' (1982) 3 *Hist. Pol. Thought* 1–30; Guy, *St German on Chancery and Statute*, 72–5; 'Law, Equity and Conscience in Henrician Juristic Thought' in *Reassessing the Henrician Age*, ed. Fox and Guy, 179–98; G. Behrens,

of law, since by custom they were obliged to follow an inflexible system of pleading and proof, that there had to be an alternative procedure and another court to give relief where conscience required it. St German did not, however, associate equity exclusively with the Chancery, and it was no part of his purpose to defend the Chancery jurisdiction against the courts of law. Equity could sometimes help in a court of law, and the Chancery acting as a court of conscience was not challenging the law but administering the law on a different plane. Thus, for St German, the common law operated on two different levels. In its usual understanding it was the system 'grounded upon the customs and maxims and the general rules of the law, and according to the process as is used in the King's Bench, Common Place, and such other courts of record as be commonly taken for courts of the common law'. But there was also the common law 'grounded upon the law of reason and the law of God' which the common-law judges applied when sitting as assistants in Chancery or when acting as arbitrators.[223] These two aspects of the common law were not mutually inconsistent. In the case of the uncancelled bond:[224]

the judges of the common law know as judges by the grounds of the law that the payment sufficiently dischargeth the debt in reason and conscience, as the Chancery doth, but yet they may not by the maxims and customs of the law openly admit the only payment [i.e. without a deed] for a sufficient plea before them: not for that they think it not sufficient in reason and conscience to discharge the debt, but for that they may not break the grounds and principles of old time used in the courts where the action is taken. But the common law pretendeth not that that maxim stretcheth to all courts, nor to the whole common law.

Admittedly, this cautious view of the relationship between the common law and conscience was not universally accepted. *Doctor and Student* provoked in one writer of the 1530s a somewhat exaggerated reaction, perhaps feigned,[225] called *The Replication of a Serjeant at the Laws of England*.[226] It was a reaction not so much against the philosophy of conscience as against the support which the enforcement of one man's view of conscience lent to the despotic tendency of the Chancery. St German had presented conscience as an objective ideal implanted in

'An Early Tudor Debate on the Relation between Law and Equity' (1998) 19 *JLH* 143–61. For the rather different context of St German's real theme, see below, 502.

[223] St German, *Little Treatise*, ed. Guy, 124–5. Cf. a similar passage on p. 110.

[224] ibid. 111 (sp. mod.).

[225] It has been suggested that the *Replication* was also written by St German, as a device to introduce a refutation penned with more convincing moderation (his *Little Treatise concerning Writs of Subpoena*). Yet it has close similarities to Audley's reading on uses: below, 666. For the date and authorship see D. E. C. Yale, 'St German's Little Treatise concerning Writs of Subpoena' (1975) 10 *Irish Jurist* 324; Guy, *St German on Chancery and Statute*, 56–62.

[226] BL MS. Harley 829, ff. 53–59v (St German's copy); four other copies are known. There is a modern edition by J. Guy in *Christopher St German on Chancery and Statute* (6 Selden Soc. Suppl. Series; 1985), 99–105, which supersedes that in *Law Tracts*, ed. F. Hargrave (1787), 321–31.

man by the mysterious workings of synderesis; but the fictitious serjeant at law in the *Replication,* apparently still smarting from Wolsey's chancellorship and as yet unsure of More,[227] took a more realistic view of the vagaries of human nature. The choice in practice was not between crude, tough law and absolute justice, but between the certainty of a known rule and the uncertainty of an arbitrary decision by a single judge in conscience:[228]

The common weal of every realm is to have a good law, so that the subjects of the realm may be justified by the same, and the more plain and open that the law is, and the more knowledge and understanding that the subject hath of the same, the better it is for the common weal of the realm. And the more uncertain that the law is in any realm, the less and the worse it is for the common weal of the realm. And if the subjects of the realm shall be compelled to leave the law of the realm and to be ordered by the discretion of one man, what thing may be more unknown or more uncertain?

If a chancellor was unlearned (like Cardinal Wolsey), his jurisdiction arrogated questions of law to a layman,[229] the very anathema which the entire system of common law pleading had been designed to avoid. If the law was reason, rather than the whim of the justices, conscience might be seen as its antithesis: the whim of the judge instead of reason. And conscience had the same dangerous propensities as the commonwealth ideal; for 'some men thinketh that if he lack money and another hath too much that he may take part of his with conscience, and so divers men divers consciences'.[230] Although Sir Thomas More, as Wolsey's successor, was careful to denounce arbitrariness, the partial alienation of the common-law judges from the ethos of equity during Wolsey's tenure of the great seal was to have lasting consequences for English law by ensuring that equity and law would continue to run in separate channels.

The 'serjeant' in the *Replication* gave the impression that he did not see any place for conscience in the legal system at all: 'these two laws, one being contrary to the other, cannot stand together, but one of them must stand as void'.[231] This apparent misunderstanding of St German may explain the emergence of the newer English sense of the terms 'law' and 'equity' as representing the comple-mentary jurisdictions of two law courts. The need to enquire as far into the facts of individual cases as justice required was universal, but in practice it had to be balanced against 'inconvenience'. Some facts could never be proved, and then

227 For the chancellors see below, 175–9.
228 *Replication of a Serjeant,* ed. Guy, 101 (sp. mod.).
229 The 'serjeant' attributed the misdoings of the Chancery to chancellors who were 'spiritual men', not learned in the laws of the realm: *Replication of a Serjeant,* ed. Guy, 101–2. This obviously points a deliberate contrast with More.
230 *Replication of a Serjeant,* ed. Guy, 101. The student retorted that he had overlooked the difference between a scrupulous and an erroneous conscience: St German, *Little Treatise,* ed. Guy, 123.
231 *Replication of a Serjeant,* ed. Guy, 100.

the 'court of conscience'[232] was the party's own soul. In the realms of human justice, what was permitted to be proved depended on the procedure of the court.
Here again, it could be argued that some matters were best left to the party's
conscience. No system of human justice could deal with every question of
conscience, but differences in procedure could result in some courts delving further into such questions than others. When, in 1489, Cardinal Moreton remarked
that no one should leave the Court of Chancery without a remedy, Serjeant
Fyneux retorted:[233]

Sir, if no one should leave without a remedy, there would be no need for anyone to be
confessed. However, sir, the law of the land [serves] for many matters; many matters are to
be sued here which are not remediable at common law; and some matters are in conscience
between a man and his confessor, as is this [present case].

Some might have regarded the procedures of the common-law courts as being so
rigid that conscience did not belong within their ambit at all.[234] A more balanced
view was that conscience and equity permeated all justice.[235] Even common-law
judges enjoyed a measure of discretion, and Fyneux CJ once observed that
'whoso[ever] taketh from a justice the order of his discretion taketh surely from
him more than half his office'.[236] In addressing a call of serjeants in 1521, Fyneux CJ
(or possibly Brudenell CJ) expounded the text *Diligite justiciam* from the Book of
Wisdom; serjeants, he said, should be men of good conscience, not 'too strait, too
rigorous, too extreme in executing the laws', nor too slack or remiss, but following
a middle course, and they should 'temper the rigour of the law with a discreet
mercy'.[237] Another chief justice, addressing the same theme a few years later,
argued that a 'singular good and upright conscience' was necessary in the administration of the law, because 'great learning and knowledge without good conscience...can not but fall to outrage of wrong'. Lawyers should seek a balance
between the rigour of the law and the 'intent and equity of the law', as their
discretion should require in the interests of justice: 'for, as the wise man saith,
sometimes *extremum jus* is *summa injuria* (that is to say, that extreme right is

---

[232] St German, *Doctor and Student*, ed. Plucknett and Barton, 131, uses this term as equivalent to
forum conscientiae.

[233] *Anon.* (1489) Hil. 4 Hen. VII, fo. 5, pl. 8 (tr.). Cf. St German, *Little Treatise*, ed. Guy, 115–19, on
cases where a man has a right in conscience but shall have no *subpoena.*

[234] Fitzjames CJ (d. 1538) is reputed to have said that the 'Two main principles that guide human
nature are conscience and law; by the one we are obliged in reference to another world, by the latter in
relation to this': seventeenth-century biographical notice in BL MS. Sloane 1523, fo. 31.

[235] See Doe, 'Conscience in the Common Law', in *Fundamental Authority*, 132–54.

[236] Quoted by Sir Thomas More, *Debellation of Salem and Bizance*, ed. J. Guy and others, 164, lines
4–7 (sp. mod.). Fitzherbert J. once equated the law with judicial discretion: *Re Lady E. S.* (c.1530/5) Wm
Yelv. 292 at 293. See also *Partridge v. Straunge* (1553) Plowd. 77v at 83v, *per* Saunders sjt (tr. 'You judges
have a private knowledge and a judicial knowledge, and from your private knowledge you may not
judge; but you may use your discretion').   [237] Baker, *Serjeants at Law*, 280, 286, 287 (sp. mod.).

extreme wrong)'.[238] It is not clear from these vague exhortations exactly how the balance was to be achieved, and this was the essence of the debate over law and equity during this period. Some of the business traditionally associated with the Chancery could be handled just as well, if differently, by the courts of law: as in the case of uses, which passed from one side of Westminster Hall to the other during our period. In 1530 the line was not finally drawn across the hall, and if the judges complained of interference from the Chancery[239] it was at least arguable that it resulted from their own failure to develop procedures which advanced equity.

Sir Thomas More certainly responded in those terms when the judges, in about 1530, complained that he had continued Wolsey's practice of issuing common injunctions to inhibit proceedings in their courts. The story is best told in the words of More's son-in-law and biographer, William Roper, who was chief clerk of the King's Bench at the time of the episode:[240]

[More] invited all the judges to dine with him in the Council Chamber at Westminster: where, after dinner, when he had broken with them what complaints he had heard of his injunctions, and moreover shewed them both the number and causes of every one of them, in order, so plainly that, upon full debating of those matters, they were all forced to confess that they, in like case, could have done no otherwise themselves, then offered he this unto them: that if the justices of every court (unto whom the reformation of the rigour of the law, by reason of their office, most especially appertained) would, upon reasonable considerations, by their own discretions (as they were, he thought, in conscience bound) mitigate and reform the rigour of the law themselves, there should from thenceforth by him no more injunctions be granted.

It is not apparent whether More's 'offer' was genuine, or whether the legal impossibility of its acceptance was already beyond serious question. Nevertheless, by declining the invitation the judges finally settled the role of the Court of Chancery for the next three hundred years as a separate court of equity. Although some judges might still pay lip-service to the principle that conscience was the basis of all law,[241] by 1566 it would be an indictable offence to say that the King's Bench was a court of conscience.[242] The best way of reconciling the two philosophies was through the new terminology of equity, and distinguishing the vague kind of equity which underlay all law from the special form of equity administered by the Chancery.[243] The distinction would have made some sense even at the beginning

---

[238] ibid. 289, 293 (sp. mod.). The 'wise man' is Cicero.   [239] See below, 174–5.

[240] Roper, *Lyfe of Moore*, ed. Hitchcock (1935), 44–5 (sp. mod.). More was chancellor from 1529 to 1533.

[241] e.g. *Anon.* (1550) Brooke Abr., *Estates*, pl. 78 (tr. 'conscience is *aequum et bonum*, which is the basis of every law'). Note also Serjeant Saunders's remark (in the Common Pleas) that it is the office of a judge to execute justice according to his conscience: *Anon.* (1544) Gell's reports, I, 36 Hen. VIII, fo. 36. As to the force of 'equity and reason' see a divided court in *Taverner's Case* (1543) Dyer 56a.

[242] *R. v. Walsh* (1566) CUL MS. Dd.3.87(7), fo. 21.

[243] Audley referred in a letter of 1535 to 'equity' in Chancery: *Lisle Letters*, ed. Byrne, ii. 634, no. 489.

of our period, but after the meeting between More and the judges it became crystallized. John Hales, writing in about 1540, could see the distinction clearly, treating the former brand of equity as the equal treatment which the common law itself favoured:[244]

There be two manner of equities: the one is called arithmetic, the other geometric. Arithmetic equity is the matter and ground of all laws positive, which hath respect and helpeth the thing that happeneth commonly and regardeth not the diversity of men's natures nor the divers circumstances, but supposeth all men to be of one nature... And this equity I think no man understanding it but will say that our laws be grounded upon, and this is the material cause that the Civilians call *aequum et bonum*... Equity geometric is an amendment or correction of the laws in that part that lacketh by reason of the generality, that is to say, sometimes adding to the law where it lacketh or diminishing where it is too rigorous, according to the nature of the person and the circumstances of the matter, which every man lightly perceiveth not... Equity geometric will help in another court, that is to say in the Chancery, the circumstances [being] examined.

The reason why the judges declined to exercise 'geometric' equity may simply have been the strong professional tradition which abhorred the 'inconvenience' of departing from certain rules. More later confided to Roper a more subtle reason for their response: 'I perceive son,' he said, 'why they like not so to do, for they see that they may by the verdict of the jury cast off all quarrels from themselves upon them, which they account their chief defence'.[245] The judges sought refuge from the agony of decision—and the perils of undue influence—by umpiring the ancient game strictly according to the rules, and by refusing to meddle with questions of fact. The procedures protected them to such an extent that they could 'sometimes give judgment against their own knowledge, and also against the truth, and yet no default to be in them, as it is in all trials'.[246] Conscience belonged to the realms of fact rather than law, for whereas judges were sworn to do justice according to law,[247] jurors were charged to give a true verdict according to their conscience.[248] More wrote elsewhere that judges were perfectly capable of trying facts, and that many people would rather trust them than a jury, since they were less susceptible to local pressures: 'but the judges be so wise men, that for the avoiding of obloquy they will not be put in the trust'.[249] Anyone who exercised a jurisdiction in

---

[244] *Oration*, ff. 42–43 (sp. mod.).

[245] Roper, *Lyfe of More*, ed. Hitchcock, 45 (sp. mod.). Cf. Trin. 10 Hen. VII, fo. 25, pl. 2, *per* Bryan CJ (tr. [to amend a plea contrary to the facts] 'would be wholly against equity', because the judges were not concerned with facts).

[246] St German, *Little Treatise*, ed. Guy, 124 (sp. mod.). He said that this did not apply in capital cases.

[247] So in fact was the chancellor. Guy notes that the oath administered to More as chancellor was to do right according to the laws and usages of the realm: *St German on Chancery and Statute*, 91–2, citing C54/398. St German was unaware of this; *Little Treatise*, ed. Guy, 122.

[248] *Diversite de Courtz* (1533), sig. C2v. Cf. Doe, 'Conscience and Jurors', in *Fundamental Authority*, 146–8.

[249] *Debellation of Salem and Bizance*, ed. J. Guy and others, 131, lines 30–5 (sp. mod.).

conscience, whether as a juror or as a chancellor, had to accept the burden of weighing up the evidence and deciding the facts to the best of his ability, and so it is not surprising that the judges took advantage of the 'common order and long continued law' (as More termed it) which excused them from this task. Wolsey's chancellorship had shown that a court of equity could be subject to the same limitations imposed by human frailty as the jury, and recent memories may have helped persuade the judges to remain aloof from factual investigations of their own. Moreover, experience was beginning to show that some kinds of litigation—such as commercial cases from the city—were best tried by jury, while others were more suited to the Chancery procedure for unravelling documentary evidence.

What perhaps no one could see at the time, or only those few with the insight of Sir Thomas More, was that English jurisprudence would ultimately derive more benefit from the 'equitable' development of the common law, and from the reduction of Chancery equity into a species of case-law, than from the unpredictable kind of justice which followed the chancellor's individual and considerably overworked conscience. Yet we can now see that the former process had already begun. Just as equity, in its specialist sense, was becoming the sole prerogative of the Chancery and its analogues,[250] so the common law was developing procedures which enabled it to embark upon the increasingly detailed consideration of the facts of particular cases.

JUDICIAL POSITIVISM

The proposition that legal development consists in the increasingly detailed consideration of facts[251] has the converse implication that legal development is retarded by the inability of courts to consider material variations of fact. The consequences of the older common-law tradition of ignoring special cases, in the interests of clarity, were not only the rise of a separate equitable jurisdiction but also that large areas of law remained substantially undeveloped at the beginning of our period. The law of real property is an exception, because it had been subjected to very detailed analysis and discussion over the previous three centuries. But questions of personal property, of contract and tort, and of criminal law, were largely left to the good sense of juries whose decisions were final and inscrutable. Even the land law was affected by the same retarding tendency, since most property suits by the beginning of our period ended in a broad general issue of fact for a jury rather than a point of law.[252]

---

[250] For other courts of equity see below, 169, 191, 223–4, 281, 288, 294, 296.

[251] S. F. C. Milsom, 'Law and Fact in Legal Development' (1967) 17 *Univ. Toronto Law Jnl* 1; repr. *SHCL*, 171.   [252] See below, 720–2. It had not always been so.

The later year-book period is also characterized by a certain inconclusiveness in the legal system viewed as a mechanism for developing the law. The prime function of courts is to settle disputes between litigants. Although we have come to regard it as an important secondary function to refine the law, case by case, there is no inherent reason why all courts in all periods should have conceived it as part of their function to do so. In the late-medieval period, the notion that people should live within a framework of relatively simple law, free from subtle distinctions known only to erudite lawyers—the notion that the law would rather suffer a mischief than an inconvenience—was deeply engrained and led the judges to discourage fights, except in the interlocutory stages of litigation, over nice points of law. If a legal doubt was raised formally by demurrer, and the answer was not obvious to the court, we see a distinct reluctance to give judgment. The court would first adjourn for advisement, perhaps for many terms in succession; if the parties persisted, the judges might consult their brethren across the hall, by sending the puisne judge with a copy of the record;[253] if doubts remained, the judges might be assembled for a confabulation in Serjeants' Inn or even a full-scale public moot in the Exchequer Chamber. But if, after all that, they still had qualms, they often did nothing. Judicial indecision on a point of law was not seen as a dereliction of duty, as it would be today, because it encouraged and helped the parties to settle their differences—or induced the plaintiff to give up—when the merits were in balance. And, if the parties settled or abandoned the dispute, the courts were relieved from the embarrassment of having to settle the legal doubt. Of course, such an approach was less favourable to weaker parties where bargaining power was unequal, especially if they were plaintiffs; but such considerations belonged rather to courts of conscience than courts of law.[254]

The role of the late-medieval judges could be characterized as having as much in common with that of sports referees as with the proactive role of the modern English judiciary. The game of chess has been played continuously since the year-book period, under much the same laws, and yet there is still no great body of referee-jurisprudence for chess enthusiasts. Nor is there any room for equity in

---

[253] See *Lewys* v. *Cam* (1531) Spelman 124 ('he went to the Common Bench with a marshal before him and a clerk after him with the record'); *Anon.* (1542) Gell's reports, I, 34 Hen. VIII, fo. 12. See also 94 Selden Soc. 62 n. 7.

[254] Hence the Council, more concerned with fact than law, was urged by Henry VII to be decisive. In *c*.1491 it was ordered that if the Council was 'in divers opinions' in a case it should be adjourned until the next meeting, and then the majority should prevail: M. M. Condon, 'An Anachronism with Intent? Henry VII's Council Ordinance of 1491/2' in *Kings and Nobles in the later Middle Ages*, ed. R. A. Griffiths and J. Sherborne (1986), 246, art. 13 (sp. mod.). A similar provision was made for the Council in the Marches in 1525: BL MS. Harley 6068, fo. 27v. Nevertheless, it is doubtful whether the Council or the Chancery were in practice so decisive.

administering the rigid laws of the game. What players expect is a challenging contest played according to simple rules which do not need to change over the centuries, and referees (if they are needed at all) are there to ensure that the rules are observed. The same may be supposed of most late-medieval litigants, if we allow for the fact that the rules of litigation were infinitely more complex than those of chess. They were expected to pursue the formalized strife of litigation according to rules which could not be bent to suit special cases. They did not want the judges to change or improve the rules, but to oversee the strict procedures and to ensure fair play. No one looked to litigation as a means of creating or refining legal doctrine, any more than one would watch or play chess in the expectation that new and more sophisticated rules of chess will emerge as more games are played. The later year books, in consequence, are not particularly concerned with judicial decisions. The judicial indecision could be just as interesting to the reporter; and in any case the books served primarily as guides to the science and technique of pleading, illustrating what should be done in court in the context of principles which seem to have been absorbed into the legal consciousness else-where than in court. In fact, one would learn more doctrine in the halls of the inns of court than in the courts of Westminster Hall. This is not to say that the judges were passive or inert. The courts were recognized as repositories of learning, and the dicta of judges in real cases—whether in helping parties to frame their pleadings or making interlocutory rulings—were certainly treated as evidence of the law. But it would be misleading to characterize the substantive common law as case-law in the modern sense, because the system was not designed to produce as a matter of routine the appropriate kind of judgment. Reason and inherited wisdom were still more important as sources of law than the mere existence of precedent.[255] Yet, with the exception of judgments upon demurrer or writs of error, and purely procedural matters,[256] reasoned final judgments were seldom called for.[257] The judges made their input while the game was being played, not when it had ended.

A prominent feature of the Tudor transformation of the common law was the eclipse of this late-medieval approach to litigation. Litigants were no longer uni-versally content merely that their disputes should be resolved; many of them wanted judicial decisions on points of substance, with reasons. Courts were therefore

---

[255] LPCL, 472–3; Doe, Fundamental Authority, 130–1; below, 467–72 (common learning).

[256] The most formal, since they were enrolled, were judgments to abate a writ (below, 324) or to order a repleader after a jeofail (below, 346). In other cases the rolls show the procedural outcome but do not reveal that it resulted from a judicial decision.

[257] The 'judgment' was usually entered up in chambers following the result of the trial, and (being in such cases automatic) it was unaccompanied by reasons. The decision which really disposed of the case was that of the jury.

increasingly asked to decide points of law, and they in turn showed themselves more and more willing to accept the invitation, with the result that their decisions in test-cases were coming to be seen as the prime authorities on which the common law was based. If questions were to be put to courts they had to be removed from juries, and this was mostly effected by means of demurrers, special verdicts, and motions in arrest of judgment. All these procedures existed before the sixteenth century, but they had been limited in scope and had not contributed in a major way to doctrinal development. By the time of Elizabeth I, on the other hand, it was only decisions in such cases that deserved full reporting for the purposes of precedent.[258] By the end of the century, moreover, the final judicial decision will have become so important that majority-rule will be tolerated as a matter of routine in order to achieve it.[259]

The procedural changes were accompanied by a major expansion of central jurisdiction, partly facilitated by increased use of the action on the case. This was the common lawyers' counterpart to the bill in Chancery. It set out the facts on which the plaintiff relied, unfettered by forms, and could be used both to fill gaps between the older remedies and also to supplant them when their procedures were found less welcome. Even before 1500 it had been hailed as a way of minimizing the need for resort to Chancery,[260] and later in the sixteenth century it could properly be described as the equitable remedy of the common law.[261] During the first half of the sixteenth century the action on the case provided the means for parol contracts in general to be enforced, provided there was some recompense, gave new remedies for defamation and conversion, and extended the remedies for fraud and nuisance. We see the King's Bench emerging as a commercial court, and in its infinitely variable bills on the case we catch new glimpses of trade, of maritime adventures, and of the insurance and exchange markets.[262] By somewhat different means, the common law also began for the first time to take cognizance of uses and copyholds, and to expound the law which governed them. The result of these procedural developments was a great deal of novel substantive law.

The declaratory authority of the superior courts was as much a product of the intellectual climate of the times as of any factor peculiar to the realm of England. It coincided chronologically with the new self-confidence of the high court of Parliament as lawgiver, and of the high court of Chancery as a forum in equity,

---

[258] This is explicitly stated in the preface to Plowd. (1571).

[259] *LPCL*, 166–9, 474–5. Cf. *Anon.* (1558) Chr. Yelverton's reports, ff. 246v–247 (tr. 'held clearly by the lord Dyer [CJ] and Mr Weston [J.] . . . but Browne [J.] was absent and therefore judgment was deferred until etc.').

[260] Pas. 21 Edw. IV, fo. 23, pl. 6, *per* Fairfax J; 14 Hen. VII, Fitz. Abr., *Accion sur le Cas*, pl. 45 (repr. in Mich. 21 Hen. VII, fo. 41, pl. 66; tr. B. & M. 401), *per* Fyneux CJ.

[261] E. Hake, *Epiekeia*, ed. D. E. C. Yale (1953), 106–7.   [262] See below, 158, 859.

which we have already noticed. It was also paralleled on the Continent, where it was similarly associated with a recourse to learned royal courts and a decline of older methods of dispute-resolution which had laid no emphasis on the authoritative settlement of legal principle. In point of detail, the English story is obviously very different; and so, come to that, are the individual stories of each continental jurisdiction. But the universal tendency to develop *la jurisprudence* through judicial decision-making affords rather striking parellels. It is marked by the publication of a growing body of secular *decisiones*, beginning with the appearance in 1490 of Guy Pape's reports of the decisions of the Parlement of Dauphiné (1444–87), and reaching Italy with Matteo d'Afflitto's reports from the Sacro Regio Consiglio of Naples in the 1490s (printed in 1508). The sixteenth century brought a torrent of similar reports, spreading northwards to Germany, the low countries, and Scotland.[263] Contrary to the Civil law tradition which gave no authority to courts, the royal judges in these continental courts were seen as having lawmaking powers. They were regarded as a new manifestation of regal power: according to the Neapolitan lawyers, the decisions of the Royal Council had the force of law (*vis legis*) because the Council represented the king's person.[264] The same reasoning gave royal councils the power to administer equity, which (as in the Court of Session in Scotland) was not jurisdictionally separated from law. We have already seen how the effect known as 'the Reception' had less to do with substantive rules than with the manner in which royal judges educated in Roman law exercised their new-found authority; that it was a reception of the techniques and reasoning processes of learned lawyers rather than a reception of ancient Roman law in its own right; and that it came about—at least in some jurisdictions—by removing the resolution of disputes from laymen or by reviewing lay decisions. In that sense, we might dare say that the English superior courts experienced a Reception as well: but it was a Reception of Holborn law, and Temple law, rather than Roman law. And so we return to Maitland's original difficulty, which seems, in the light of all the subsequent research, to have been founded on false premises. There is no longer such a deep mystery to be explained, since English law was sailing with the jurisprudential tide, not against it. The tough law of the inns of court, however impervious to direct foreign influence, was indeed susceptible to new ways of thinking about the legal process and to development by the courts.

---

[263] See *LPCL*, 469–70; J. H. Baker (ed.), *Judicial Records, Law Reports, and the Growth of Case Law* (5 CSC; 1989), and the works cited ibid. 6–7 n. 4.   [264] *LPCL*, 471.

Part II

THE CONSTITUTION

2

General Features of the Constitution

Of general constitutional principles there is little to be found in Tudor legal sources. It is true that the king's prerogatives were a favourite topic for lectures in the inns of court,[1] and were the subject of a treatise by William Staunford written in 1548,[2] but these were prerogative rights—the droits of the Crown—as enumerated in the pseudo-statute Prerogativa Regis, and more or less unrelated to the later constitutional concept of the royal prerogative.[3] The prerogative in the latter sense—the governmental authority of the Crown—was extensive but already qualified by the conventions of a limited monarchy. It was a commonplace among lawyers that the king was head of the body politic or common weal (*caput reipublicae*[4]),[5] or even the 'supreme head' of an empire,[6] and the lords and commons were the members or limbs.[7] King Henry VIII himself said to the commons in 1542, 'We be informed by our judges that we at no time stand so highly in our estate royal as in the time of Parliament, wherein we as head and you as members

---

[1] The principal surviving readings are those of Thomas Frowyk (1495), Robert Constable (1495), John Spelman (1521), and George Willoughby (1549). At least six others are known: Baker, *Readers and Readings*, p. lii. See also M. McGlynn, 'The King and the Law: Prerogativa Regis in early Tudor England', Ph.D. thesis (University of Toronto, 1997); *The Royal Prerogative and the Learning of the Inns of Court* (forthcoming in 2003).

[2] *An Exposition of the Kinges Prerogative* [preface dated 6 Nov. 1548] (pr. 1567). A near contemporary version, which belonged to Sir Robert Catlyn, is now Alnwick Castle MS. 475, ff. 136–171v. Another (lacking the first three folios) is in Bodl. Lib. MS. Ashmole 1149(4).

[3] For prerogative wardship and primer seisin see below, 653, 662, 672. For droits of the admiralty see below, 211–12.

[4] Serjeant Broke uses the Latin term in 113 Selden Soc. 169 (1519). Cf. 4 Co. Rep. 124 ('[Rex] est caput et salus reipublicae').

[5] e.g. *Anon.* (1534) 121 Selden Soc. 431, no. 6, *per* Shelley J. ('the king is a body politic and is the head of all the common weal'). Cf. *Anon.* (1550) BL MS. Hargrave 4, fo. 112v (tr. 'head of the realm').

[6] See the preambles to 24 Hen. VIII, c. 12; 26 Hen. VIII, c. 1; and the passage of 1547 quoted below, 179; W. Ullmann, 'This Realm of England is an Empire' (1979) 30 *Jnl Eccles. Hist.* 175–203 (who points out that the term was in use before 1530); J. Guy, 'The Crown and the Intellectual Origins of the Henrician Revolution' in *Reassessing the Henrician Age*, ed. Fox and Guy (1986), 151–78; S. J. Gunn, 'Empire' in *Early Tudor Government* (1995), ch. 4.

[7] See e.g. Spelman's reading (1519) 113 Selden Soc. 76, 119, 169; *Duke of Buckingham's Case* (1521) Port 124–5, 119 Selden Soc. 57, *per* Fyneux CJ; Hynde's reading (1527) BL MS. Add. 35939, fo. 275v, *per* Broke CB.

are conjoined and knit together into one body politic'.[8] This consciously anthropomorphic representation of the state—sometimes elaborated with the law as the sinews,[9] or the heart,[10] and the judges as the eyes[11]—derived from the political notion that the king and his subjects were mutually supportive and could not function without each other. In the same vein, Fyneux CJ was reputed to have said that 'The prince's prerogative and the subject's privilege are solid felicities together and but empty notions asunder'.[12] England had long been a constitutional monarchy, the king being subject to the law, and legislative sovereignty belonging to the king in Parliament rather than the king alone.[13] Parliament was for this purpose also viewed as a body politic,[14] a corporation with the king as head and the peers and commons as members.[15] There was nothing new in any of this. But rhetoric can easily obscure changes in political reality. The Tudor kings devoted themselves to strengthening the monarchy, the *imperium*,[16] and centralizing its power,[17] in ways which have been seen as posing a threat to the constitutional balance and the rule of law. The real extent of that threat has been the subject of much debate

---

[8] *Ferrers' Case* (1542) pr. from Holinshed in G. R. Elton, *Tudor Constitution* (2nd edn, 1982), 277.

[9] *Duke of Buckingham's Case* (1521) Port 125, *per* Fyneux CJ; reading on Magna Carta (1530s) BL MS. Harley 4990, fo. 146; cf. J. Ponet, *A Shorte Treatise of Politike Power* (1556), sig. cviii.

[10] Reading on Magna Carta (1530s) BL MS. Harley 4990, fo. 146.

[11] Warham C. said in 1510 that the judges were the eyes of the commonwealth and the lawyers its tongues: *HLJ*, i. 3a. Cf. William Staunford's reading (1545) BL MS. Hargrave 92, fo. 86 (public good as the eye).

[12] BL MS. Sloane 1523, fo. 27 (seventeenth-century biography, the sources of which are not stated).

[13] See St German, *Doctor and Student*, ed. Plucknett and Barton, 327, where the king in Parliament is referred to as the 'high sovereign over the people' (sp. mod.).

[14] The king alone was likewise a corporation, or 'body politic', so that a general reference to 'the king' in legislation extended to his successors: *Hill* v. *Grange* (1556) Plowd. 164 at 176v, 177v.

[15] *King's College, Cambridge* v. *Hekker* (1522) Mich. 14 Hen. VIII, fo. 3, pl. 2 (119 Selden Soc. 101), *per* Fyneux CJ (tr. 'the king, lords, and commons, in Parliament are a corporation'); anonymous reading on forest law (1530s?) BL MS. Hargrave 88, fo. 88v (sp. mod. 'the king and his Parliament are a body incorporate to make laws and ordinances for the well governing of the realm'); *Courteney and Tomyewe (executors of Skewes)* v. *Chamond* (1545) Dyer 59b at 60a.

[16] Several historians have attached significance to Henry VII's use of the closed or arched imperial crown on his coinage from 1487. But the closed crown had been used on the great seal of Edward IV, and is also shown on formal portraits of that king and of Richard III (e.g. in the transept windows of Canterbury cathedral, and in the Rous roll). There is some evidence of its use as early as 1399. See P. Grierson, 'The Origins of the English Sovereign and the Symbolism of the Closed Crown' (1964) 33 *British Numismatic Jnl* 118 at 127–34; S. B. Chrimes, *Henry VII* (1972), 225; Gunn, *Early Tudor Government*, 164; D. Hoak, 'The Iconography of the Crown Imperial' in *Tudor Political Culture*, ed. D. Hoak (1995), 54–103.

[17] The classic study of the Tudor state is Elton, *The Tudor Constitution*. Elton saw the period of Thomas Cromwell's ministry (1529–40) as marking an administrative revolution: *The Tudor Revolution in Government* (1953). This thesis has been qualified or controverted by several writers. For general accounts of the subject see P. Williams, *The Tudor Regime* (1979); J. Guy, *Tudor England* (1988); S. J. Gunn, *Early Tudor Government 1485–1558* (1995). See also *Revolution Reassessed: revisions in the history of Tudor government and administration*, ed. C. Coleman and D. R. Starkey (1986).

among historians and will be returned to presently. But first something must be said of the Crown itself and of the legal issues concerning the royal succession.

THE DEVOLUTION OF THE CROWN[18]

The legacy of the royal dynastic struggles of the fifteenth century was a constant fear, throughout the Tudor period, that the stability of the realm might again be rocked by contention for the throne. As Henry VII formally acknowledged, monarchy rests ultimately on *de facto* power.[19] Yet claims to the throne had always been made in hereditary terms, and, even if the rules governing the descent of the Crown—and how far they could be altered by kings and parliaments—were not matters decided in courts, or debated openly in the inns of court, the royal succession was nevertheless a matter of law in so far as the king was deemed to be subject to the law. Succession problems were usually debated in legal terms, and in accordance with the common-law canons of inheritance.

Richard, duke of York, father of the two kings Edward IV and Richard III, was descended from Edward III, and his right to the Crown had been accepted by the House of Lords shortly before his death in 1460. The law officers had been unwilling to become involved in that hearing, the outcome of which was a political compromise (or 'act of accord') rather than a legal judgment.[20] The settlement was that Henry VI would be allowed to continue to rule, but that the York line would succeed him. Only months later, after Richard was slain at the battle of Wakefield, his son Edward nevertheless deposed Henry VI and assumed the throne. By the time of Edward IV's own death in April 1483, Henry VI and his issue had died, and Edward's young son Edward became king—with his uncle, Richard, duke of Gloucester, as guardian. However, a rumour was resurrected that Edward IV had been illegitimate, and in June an assembly of lords and commons asked Richard to accept the throne himself as legitimate heir, which he did. Since the lords and commons had been summoned in the name of Edward V they were not, on their own showing, a lawful Parliament; and so one of the first acts of Richard III's Parliament in 1484 was formally to establish his title, by bastardizing the issue of Edward IV on the pretext that his marriage to Elizabeth Woodville was void for

---

[18] A valuable survey is provided by M. Levine, *Tudor Dynastic Problems 1460–1571* (1973).

[19] 11 Hen. VII, c. 1. On this statute see K. Eising, *Aspekte des englischen 'de facto'-Gesetzes vom 14. Oktober 1495* (1995).

[20] The importance of this act in the development of parliamentary sovereignty has been a matter of dispute: see W. H. Dunham and C. T. Wood, 'The Right to Rule in England: depositions and the kingdom's authority 1327–1485' (1976) 81 *Amer. Hist. Rev.* 748–52; J. W. McKenna, 'The Myth of Parliamentary Sovereignty in Late-Medieval England' (1979) 94 *EHR* 481 at 494–6. See also S. B. Chrimes, *English Constitutional Ideas in the Fifteenth Century* (1936), 23, 26–31.

precontract, and declaring that the Crown belonged to Richard in tail.[21] The issue of Richard's elder brother, the duke of Clarence, were deemed to be excluded by reason of his attainder for treason in 1478.[22] Any doubts about the bastardization of Prince Edward and his younger brother Richard were ended when they mysteriously disappeared, presumed murdered, in the summer or autumn of 1483. Then Richard III's only son, Edward, prince of Wales, died in 1484. After Richard's own death at the battle of Bosworth in 1485, there was therefore another difficulty over the succession. The victor of Bosworth, Henry Tudor, was descended from Edward III through John Beaufort, earl of Somerset, the illegitimate son of John of Gaunt. Beaufort had been legitimized by the pope and by act of Parliament, though Henry IV's patent of confirmation had purported to bar his descendants from the throne. The hereditary claim was open to other objections; but victory in a trial by battle had given Henry VII an alternative title by judgment of God.[23] Henry summoned a Parliament, and the judges were asked to consider the effect of his previous attainder for treason. If the attainder incapacitated him in law, he could not lawfully summon Parliament and therefore there was no Parliament to reverse the attainder. The question was somewhat academic, since if the king was not king the judges appointed by him were not judges either. But the vicious circle was avoided by the judges' ruling that the attainder was automatically discharged by the king's taking upon himself the kingdom.[24]

Early in 1486, it having been decided that Henry VII should marry Elizabeth of York, the only surviving child of Edward IV, it was resolved to reverse Richard III's act which bastardized her. On the advice of the judges, the act of 1484 was removed from the record and care taken not to recite its contents in the act of revocation.[25] Another act of the same Parliament confirmed the Crown to Henry and the heirs of his body,[26] though it was held by the judges that this did not effect a resumption of franchises and liberties for any of his subjects.[27] The judges' ruling acknowledged the authority of a *de facto* king in making grants.[28] On the other

[21] *RP*, vi. 240-2. The marriage was also attributed to witchcraft and sorcery.

[22] Levine, *Tudor Dynastic Problems*, 30, points out that this common-law rule had not always been applied to the Crown. But it had legal plausibility.

[23] This was Henry VII's own claim in addressing parliament: *RP*, vi. 268 ('per verum Dei judicium in tribuendo sibi victoriam de inimico suo in campo'). Cf. Elton, *England under the Tudors*, 19 ('a Tudor kind of divine right').

[24] Mich. 1 Hen. VII, fo. 4, pl. 5. It was also asked how Sir Thomas Lovell could be speaker, since he was also attainted: 'to which there was no answer' (tr.).

[25] Hil. 1 Hen. VII, fo. 5, pl. 1; *RP*, vi. 289. It was also necessary to obtain a papal dispensation from the impediment by reason of kindred and affinity: Chrimes, *Henry VII*, 65-6, 330-1.

[26] *RP*, vi. 268-70; *SR*, ii. 499. The exclusion of collateral heirs could have led to problems on failure of issue, but perhaps it was thought best to extinguish all such claims once and for all.

[27] Hil. 1 Hen. VII, ff. 12-13, pl. 25. The question was put to all the judges by Alcock C.

[28] Cf. the decision of all the judges in 1483 that grants of non-judicial offices made by Edward IV remained valid after the accession of Richard III: Mich. 1 Ric. III, fo. 4, pl. 3.

hand, Richard III and his supporters were at the same time attainted of treason.[29] In legal records thereafter Richard III was always referred to as 'the lord Richard, lately *de facto* but not *de jure* king of England',[30] though his *de facto* reign was recognized for legal purposes,[31] and the acts of his one and only Parliament remained valid. By another act of his first Parliament, Henry VII resumed all the lands that Henry VI had possessed in 1455, intermediate grants by the Yorkists being annulled.[32]

The accession of the Tudors was generally accepted as a fait accompli, and the only serious threats to Henry VII's legitimacy came from the impostures of Lambert Simnel, pretending to be a son of George, duke of Clarence, and Perkin Warbeck, pretending to be the missing Prince Richard of York. Simnel was actually crowned in Dublin in 1487, as King Edward VI, but his supporters were defeated at the battle of Stoke and it seemed politic to pardon Simnel himself, a weak figure who lived on in obscurity until 1525. Warbeck was more persistent in his campaign to be recognized as King Richard IV and consequently less fortunate in his fate. He was convicted under martial law, being an alien, and executed in 1499.[33]

Henry VII's eldest son Arthur predeceased his father in 1502, so that on the king's death in 1509 the Crown came to his second and only surviving son Henry. Since King Henry VIII united the red rose and the white, as the immediate heir of both Lancaster and York, the principal threat to stability now came from Edward Stafford, duke of Buckingham, a descendant of Edward III by two lines, who had been suggested as a possible king if the issue of Henry VII died out.[34] The threat was removed by Buckingham's attainder and execution in 1521. In 1538, Henry Courteney, marquess of Exeter, son of Edward IV's daughter Katherine, was also removed from the world after he became involved in a papal plot to overthrow the king. However, the succession was thrown into confusion in a completely different way by Henry's own matrimonial vicissitudes.

---

[29] *RP*, vi. 275–8.

[30] This may explain the statute 11 Hen. VII, c. 1, which reassured Henry VII's subjects that if they supported the king 'for the time being', and the king was overthrown, they would not be guilty of treason. It probably was not intended to protect Richard III's supporters, as is sometimes supposed. Although it is ambiguous whether the phrase 'from henceforth' refers to the support given or to the liability to conviction, any ambiguity argues against retrospective intentions. Nor did it help the supporters of Lady Jane Grey in 1553.   [31] See *Anon.* (1491) 1 Caryll 54–5.

[32] *RP*, vi. 336.

[33] *Perkin Warbeck's Case* (1499) below, 216–17, 616. He had been recognized as the legitimate duke of York by Charles VIII of France and the Emperor Maximilian.

[34] When Buckingham claimed the office of lord high constable in 1514, the attorney-general noted that his hereditary claim was 'very dangerous to the king': 2 Caryll 647. But this alluded to the fact that Buckingham was sole heir to the Bohuns: below, 218.

The divorce from Queen Katherine seemed to carry the corollary that the Princess Mary (later Queen Mary I) was illegitimate,[35] and his divorce from Queen Anne likewise bastardized Elizabeth (later Queen Elizabeth I). On each occasion the new line of succession was settled by act of Parliament.[36] The second act directed the devolution of the Crown to children as yet unborn, and there-fore—to provide for the possibility that there might in the event be no legitimate royal issue—the king was given power to adjust the succession by letters patent or last will, and to appoint a council of regency in the event that his heir apparent was under age. Anyone who questioned this remarkable departure from precedent was to be guilty of high treason. Robert Aske, and other protestors involved in the Pilgrimage of Grace, were brave enough to attack it as a dangerous novelty, their chief concern being that Henry might devise the Crown to James V of Scotland, grandson of his sister Margaret. On that point, at least, they were heeded. In 1537 the king's Council agreed that it would be better to include the king's two daugh-ters in the line of succession, though illegitimate, than have it go in remainder to a foreigner. Concern diminished when Prince Edward was born later in 1537; but by the 1540s it seemed unlikely that the king would have any other male heir than the sickly prince and it seemed expedient to make further provision for the possib-ility that he would not survive.[37] In 1544 the king obtained a new act of succes-sion settling the Crown in remainder after Prince Edward—and any unborn future issue—upon the two princesses in turn, subject to any conditions which the king might impose by will, with power to appoint a further remainder by will.[38] This was another unprecedented act of parliamentary sovereignty, replac-ing such rules of law as there were by what was in effect a family settlement which altered the ordinary course of descent and overrode the disabilities of bastardy. Henry made his last will at the end of 1546, imposing conditions on the princesses that they should not marry without the consent of the council of regency, and appointing remainders for breach of these conditions to the heirs of the body respectively of Frances and Eleanor, the daughters of Henry's younger sister Mary by Charles Brandon, duke of Suffolk.[39] The Brandon children were the next in line under the common-law rules of inheritance, because the descendants of Mary's elder sister Margaret were aliens born in Scotland. There is some doubt whether

[35] She was, however, arguably legitimate in the canon law by reason of her parents' good faith in the validity of the marriage at the time of birth.

[36] 25 Hen. VIII, c. 22 (to issue of Anne and then of any later wives); 28 Hen. VIII, c. 7 (to issue of Jane and then of any later wives). The first statute did not explicitly declare Mary illegitimate, though she was excluded from the succession. The second statute explicitly declared both daughters illegitimate.

[37] For the foregoing see Levine, *Tudor Dynastic Problems*, 68–71, 157–8.

[38] 35 Hen. VIII, c. 1; confirmed by 1 Eliz. I, c. 3.

[39] Rymer, *Foedera* ed. G. Holmes and R. Sanderson (1727–35), xv. 112–14; pr. in Levine, *Tudor Dynastic Problems*, 163–4.

the will was signed by the king's hand, as the statute required,[40] but the point was not taken at the time. Henry's only son succeeded shortly afterwards as King Edward VI, as he would have done had there been no statute.

Difficulties nevertheless arose on Edward's death in 1553. The 1544 statute was still in force; but Edward, advised by the duke of Northumberland, had purported to make a further alteration to the succession by his own last will alone, without the sanction of Parliament. Edward's will, authenticated by the sign manual and great seal,[41] limited the Crown to Lady Jane Grey—eldest daughter of the Frances Brandon mentioned in his father's will, and her husband Henry Grey, duke of Suffolk—thereby passing over the princesses Mary and Elizabeth.[42] That was consistent with the common law, since the princesses remained illegitimate by statute. And minority did not invalidate the king's will, since a king in his politic capacity was never under age.[43] But the 'devise' was contrary to the statute of 1544, and, when it was proposed in Council, Mountagu CJ requested that it be referred to the whole judiciary for their opinion. After a day in conference at Ely House, in June 1553, the judges advised the Privy Council that not only was the scheme invalid in law but that it would be a statutory treason to support it. They were nevertheless persuaded by the Council to draft and countersign the will on promise of pardons.[44] Edward died on 6 July 1553 and Lady Jane was proclaimed queen in London on 10 July; but Mary's statutory right prevailed and she was proclaimed queen on 19 July.[45] Jane suffered execution for treason;[46] and Mountagu CJ, for all that he had tried to prevent the crisis, was deprived of his office.

The first Parliament of Mary I legitimized her by declaring lawful her father's marriage to Katherine of Aragon, and for good measure declared in a separate statute that she had the same powers as a king and that the word 'king' in any

[40] Plowden said the will was kept by the lord treasurer in a black velvet bag, and that when it was inspected by some privy councillors in 1566 it was found to be signed with the stamp and not with the sign manual. But the matter is still in dispute. See 109 Selden Soc., p. l n. 33.

[41] It is sometimes referred to as a patent, but it did not contain the usual words *fieri fecimus patentes* and was not enrolled on the patent rolls.

[42] Two legal reasons were given for their exclusion: they were bastards, and they were of the half-blood. Both facts would have prevented inheritance under the common-law rules; but those defects had been overridden by the statute of 1544.

[43] See *Bunye* v. *Stubley* (1557–62) KB 27/1181, m. 156; Plowd. 212; Dyer's report in 109 Selden Soc. 30. The case, which arose from a duchy lease by Edward VI, occasioned discussion of the 'king's two bodies'.

[44] See 109 Selden Soc., p. xlvii; HMC, *Manuscripts of Lord Montagu of Beaulieu*, 4–5; Levine, *Tudor Dynastic Problems*, 82–3 n. 21; W. K. Jordan, *Edward VI* (1970), 516–20. Hales J. alone refused to sign and offered 'his head in his hand sooner than be forced to subscribe': R. Wingfield, *Vita Mariae Reginae*, ed. D. McCulloch (29 Camden Soc., 4th ser.; 1984), 200.

[45] Dyer's note, 109 Selden Soc. 6, no. 8. Dyer referred to Jane's accession as a 'usurpation by colour of the last will' of Edward VI, even though he had signed the instrument himself as a king's serjeant.

[46] Her husband was executed on the same day: Dyer's note, 109 Selden Soc. 10; KB 8/23. Like Anne Boleyn, she was allowed the illicit but merciful favour of beheading.

statute extended to a queen.[47] The latter point doubtless addressed a real doubt. There had not been a queen regnant of England before;[48] there were those who opposed government by females as contrary to the law of nature;[49] and indeed the first Tudor king had succeeded to the throne while his mother, through whom he claimed royal descent, was still living. Even if the 1544 act had already disposed of those objections, the point of statutory construction might still have threatened trouble. But the enactment was equally important in another way because of the queen's marriage with King Philip of Spain in 1554. Philip became titular king of England in right of his wife, and the government was thereafter carried on in the somewhat outlandish joint names of the king and queen of England, France, Naples, Jerusalem, and Ireland, princes of Spain and Sicily, archdukes of Austria, dukes of Milan, Burgundy, and Brabant, and counts of Hapsburg, Flanders, and Tyrol.[50] The union was nevertheless in name only, the kingdom of England remaining a distinct entity. To his annoyance, Philip was not even crowned.[51] Parliament declared that the queen should be considered a femme sole, with the same sovereignty and prerogatives that she had before marriage, without any right or title accruing to the king as tenant by the curtesy; and she was empowered to exercise her royal authority by her sole sign manual. The king was explicitly forbidden to introduce any innovations in English law or to appoint aliens to office.[52] In 1554 the judges were asked to decide whether the title 'supreme head in earth of the Church of England', which Parliament had 'annexed and united to the imperial Crown',[53] was still a necessary part of the queen's style, it having been omitted from the writs of summons to Parliament. By a bare majority, and with

[47] 1 Mar. I, sess. 2, c. 1; sess. 3, c. 1. Some light was thrown on the origin of the second measure by William Fletewoode of the Middle Temple: see J. Loach, *Parliament and the Crown in the Reign of Mary Tudor* (1986), 96–7; J. D. Alsop, 'The Act for the Queen's Regal Power 1554' (1994) 13 *Parliamentary History* 261–76.

[48] A queen consort had nevertheless acted in the recent past as regent. In 1513, when Henry VIII was in France, Queen Katherine was appointed 'ruler and governor of England' (*rectrix et gubernatrix Angliae*), and writs and patents were issued in that name and style: *Hale's Prerogatives of the King*, ed. Yale (92 Selden Soc.; 1975), 101, 103.

[49] It is noticeable that the literature on this subject appears to begin in 1554, prompted by a reaction against Mary's papism: see M. Levine, 'The Place of Women in Tudor Government' in *Tudor Rule and Revolution*, ed. Guth and McKenna (1982), 109–23. But it was not a purely protestant viewpoint: see e.g. Plowd. 305 (1565).

[50] See the proclamation of the new style in *Tudor Royal Proclamations*, ii. 45, no. 414; 110 Selden Soc. 401; *CPR 1553-4*, p. 503; KB 27/1178, m. 20.

[51] It was proposed in 1555 but proved too controversial to be effected.

[52] 1 Mar. I, sess. 3, c. 2. The provision that patents themselves should be signed by the queen was probably an error, since it was (and still is) the practice only to sign the warrant for the great seal. This was corrected by 1 & 2 Phil. & Mar., c. 1. See also 1 & 2 Phil. & Mar., c. 10 (Philip to govern the realm during the minority of any issue between him and the queen).

[53] 26 Hen. VIII, c. 1; clarified by 35 Hen. VIII, c. 3. The title was used in the proclamation of the queen's style soon after her accession: *Tudor Royal Proclamations*, ii. 12, no. 393.5.

misgivings, it was ruled that the title was an addition to the royal name but not indispensably part of it, and it could therefore be omitted from writs without affecting their validity.[54] The Parliament, when it met, promptly repealed the Henrician statutes.[55]

THE RULE OF LAW[56]

We may now return to the question how far the authority of the early Tudor monarchs, and their ministers, was contained within constitutional boundaries. No one questions that England by the time of Henry VII was a limited monarchy, so that government had to be conducted according to legal forms and procedures. The king could not change the law or break it. Everyone, including the king, was subject to the law; and new law could only be made by Parliament. The theory was dramatically proclaimed on the accession of Henry VIII, when the unlawful activities of his father's ministers Empson and Dudley were roundly condemned, the ministers executed, and the injustices to some extent remedied.[57] As the judges advised Henry VIII in 1532, the king could not use his subjects contrary to the law, for instance by imprisoning them without trial.[58] Moreover, men trained in the common law permeated the machinery of government at every level, and their cast of mind influenced its mode of operation.[59] But the historical debate concerns the reality behind the legal forms. The use of Parliament is not inconsistent with arbitrariness, if the king could be sure of having his way. And the rule of law is little more than a figure of speech where a government can achieve any legislative change it wishes, or procure any judicial decision which suits its purposes. What really matters, then, is not the mere existence of Parliament but its character, its independence in the face of royal pressure, its representativeness and responsiveness to the world outside, and the willingness of governments to listen to argument and opposition. Likewise, the effectiveness of the common law, as a control on executive power, is related to the degree of independence of the judiciary from the government.

---

[54] Dyer 98a; Dalison's reports, BL MS. Harley 5141, fo. 19; Dal. 14, pl. 4. Dyer said the question was raised again in 1559 and decided the same way.   [55] 1 & 2 Phil. & Mar., c. 8.

[56] For the classic debate see W. H. Dunham, 'Regal Power and the Rule of Law: a Tudor paradox' (1964) 3 *Jnl British Studies* 24–56; J. Hurstfield, 'Was there a Tudor Despotism after all?' (1967) 17 *TRHS* (5th ser.) 83–108; G. R. Elton, 'The Rule of Law in Renaissance England' in *Tudor Men and Institutions*, ed. A. J. Slavin (1972), 265–94, repr. in *Studies*, i. 260–84; G. W. Bernard, 'The Tyranny of Henry VIII' in *Authority and Consent in Tudor England*, ed. G. W. Bernard and S. J. Gunn (2002), 113–29. See also W. S. Holdsworth, 'The Prerogative in the Sixteenth Century' (1921) 21 *Columbia Law Rev.* 554–71.

[57] See below, 194–5 (conciliar activities), 582–3 (supposed treason); 1 Hen. VIII, c. 12 (untrue inquisitions procured by Empson and Dudley).

[58] *Serjeant Browne's Case* (1532) Spelman 183, 184 (misdated 1540). Emergencies were another matter: note the occasional use of martial law in times of commotion, below, 217–18.

[59] Gunn, *Early Tudor Government*, 15, 206; above, 5.

In seeking an answer to our question, attention has often been focused on Henry VIII's Statute of Proclamations (1539), which empowered the king to issue proclamations with the advice of his Council, and enacted that such proclamations should be 'obeyed, observed, and kept, as though they were made by act of Parliament'.[60] On the face of it, this might seem to have given the government power to legislate without reference to Parliament, albeit a power which could be revoked or overridden by later statutes—as happened only eight years later when the act was repealed. It certainly raised fears at the time, and was long debated in Parliament. However, the primary intention of the act as passed seems to have been to give statutory confirmation to the long-standing practice of issuing proclamations in certain well-defined areas of government, chiefly in reinforcement of parliamentary enactments,[61] but also in the exercise of acknowledged prerogative powers,[62] and it is known that the statute was promoted as a consequence of the judges' qualms about the validity of some recent proclamations which were not warranted by any parent legislation.[63] Resort to Parliament in this instance was intended to cure a legal doubt, in deference to the judges, and in that sense was consonant with rule by law. Yet it would have undermined the constitution if it had given the king an unbridled unilateral power to legislate. More significant, however, than the general provision mentioned above was the explicit qualification in the statute itself that it did not authorize proclamations made to the prejudice of any person's life, liberty, or property, or in breach of any laws or customs currently in force. Practice after 1539 shows that proclamations continued to be used to support statutes rather than to replace them.[64] Although the 1539 act was repealed in 1547, the repeal made no difference to the range of proclamations issued by Edward VI, whose ministers did not scruple to threaten penal slavery in the galleys by proclamation without explicit statutory sanction.[65] And probably

---

[60] 31 Hen. VIII, c. 8; pr. Elton, *Tudor Constitution*, 27–30; repealed by 1 Edw. VI, c. 12. Cf. the various experiments with delegated legislation, below, 82–3.

[61] See Chrimes, *Henry VII*, 175–7.

[62] e.g. declarations of war and peace, alliances, provisions for defence of the realm, or alterations in the coinage. These remain to this day matters of royal prerogative to be dealt with by proclamation rather than statute. It was in this context that Fitzjames CJ and the judges advised Cromwell in 1531 that the export of bullion could be stopped by proclamation alone: see Elton, *Reform and Renewal*, 117–18; *Tudor Constitution*, 22, 26–7; *Studies*, i. 273 (dated 1535); *LP*, viii. 1042 (dated 1535).

[63] *Letters of Stephen Gardiner*, ed. J. A. Muller (1933), 391. Cf. *LP*, viii. 411.

[64] E. R. Adair, 'The Statute of Proclamations' (1917) 32 *EHR* 34–46; G. R. Elton, 'Henry VIII's Act of Proclamations' (1960) 75 *EHR* 208–22; 'The Rule of Law', 271–4; 'Government by Edict' (1965) 8 *Historical Jnl* 266–71; R. W. Heinze, *The Proclamations of the Tudor Kings* (1976), chs 6–7; M. L. Bush, 'The Act of Proclamations: a reinterpretation' (1983) 27 *AJLH* 33–53; J. Loach, *Parliament under the Tudors* (1991), 9–12. However, they occasionally went further: Holdsworth, *HEL*, iv. 101, 296; P. L. Hughes and J. F. Larkin, *Tudor Royal Proclamations* (1964–9), i, pp. xxix–xxx; Elton, 'Government by Edict', 270–1.

[65] For spreading seditious rumours: *Tudor Royal Proclamations*, i. 456, no. 329 ('every such author or maker of such false tale or news shall be committed into the galley, there to row in chains as a

the repeal made no difference to the judges' assertion in 1555 that 'no proclamation by itself may make a law which was not law before, but may only confirm and ratify an old law, and not change it'.[66] Staunford J., a former queen's serjeant, even held that it was unlawful to debase the coinage by proclamation, since that would prejudice the queen's subjects. Alterations in the currency had always been made by proclamation, but Staunford J. was referring to the drastic debasement of 1551, which—by decision of the Privy Council rather than Parliament—had halved the value of money [67] and thrown the law of debt into some confusion.[68]

Historians have also drawn attention, in discussing the rule of law, to the dispensing power of the Crown, whereby the operation of a statute could in some circumstances be set aside.[69] However, the power could only be used to waive revenue due to the Crown, or to dispense with a public duty, or a punishment, or to create a new tenure,[70] not to diminish the private rights of another subject or to sanction a wrong which was *malum in se*.[71] Nor could the king alter the law by charter or letters patent;[72] and his power to grant temporary exemption from its operation by writs of protection was heavily circumscribed by the judges.[73] According to a king's serjeant, 'the king may not grant that justice shall not be done, for justice binds the king himself'.[74] It was conceded that the king could grant exemption from jury service,[75] or from being made a serjeant at law—even though every such exemption was to a slight extent against the common good— on the footing that no individual was prejudiced by such a grant. Admittedly

slave . . . to the example and terror of all other'). Plucknett suggested that this could have been justified under the statute of *scandalum magnatum* (12 Ric. II, c. 11), which left the punishment open: *Taswell-Langmead's Constitutional History* (11th edn, 1960), 239 n. 60.

[66] BL MS. Add. 24845, fo. 31; Dal. 20, pl. 10 (tr.). The reporter added, 'Nevertheless various precedents were shown out of the Exchequer to the contrary, but the justices had no regard to them: *quod nota bene*'.

[67] ibid.; *Tudor Royal Proclamations*, i. 518–19, no. 372 (shillings, introduced in 1549, reduced in value from 12*d.* to 9*d.*, and groats from 4*d.* to 3*d.*); ibid. 529–30, no. 379 (shillings further reduced to 6*d.*, groats to 2*d.*, pennies to ½*d.*). Later in the year new (debased) coins were introduced with the old values: ibid. 535, no. 382.

[68] For the effect of the 1551 debasement on contracts see *Barrington* v. *Potter* (1553) CP 40/1152, m. 726 (undetermined demurrer); reported in Dyer 81b; *Anon.* (1553) Dyer 82b–83a.

[69] See e.g. Elton, 'The Rule of Law', 274–7.

[70] The king was not bound by *Quia Emptores*: *Case of Barking Abbey* (1495) Pas. 10 Hen. VII, fo. 23, pl. 26. For waiver of *Quia Emptores* by the Crown, see Mich. 27 Hen. VIII, fo. 26, pl. 5; *Lord North's Case* (1555) 109 Selden Soc. 14.

[71] Mich. 3 Hen. VII, fo. 15, pl. 30; Mich. 11 Hen. VII, fo. 11, pl. 35, *per* Fyneux CJ; *Note* (*c.*1530) Caryll (Jun.) 385, no. 32, *per* Bromley (in the Inner Temple); 109 Selden Soc., pp. li–liii.

[72] *Anon.* (1486) Mich. 2 Hen. VII, fo. 6, pl. 20 (inconclusive discussion of dispensations by clause of *non obstante*); 64 Selden Soc. 126 (shorter version in Latin); *Anon.* (1493) 1 Caryll 144–5, pl. 129; *Anon.* (*c.*1535/9) Wm Yelv. 330, no. 36 (king cannot grant land to be held by customary tenure, or change the customs of a city); *Anon.* (1544) Bro. Abr., *Denizen*, pl. 9 (tr. 'for he may not alter his law by his letters patent or otherwise unless by Parliament'); *Chafyn* v. *Lord Sturton* (1553) Dyer 94a at 94b. On the same principle, a pardon could not prejudice a suitor: below, 240 n. 62.

[73] Below, 94–5.   [74] *Marmyon* v. *Baldwyn* (1527) 120 Selden Soc. 61 at 62.

[75] e.g. *Sir John Rainsford's Case* (1513) Rast. Ent. 116 (117v).

justice would be obstructed if such grants were made to everyone; but the answer was that the king would not do anything so generally prejudicial.[76] The extent to which the king could grant licences of exemption from regulatory legislation, such as statutes governing exports and imports, also raised occasional questions; but the proper answer depended on the interpretation of the statute in question.[77]

These traditional test-cases, then, were red herrings. Yet there were undoubtedly other cases in the Tudor period where the government acted despotically. No doubt it could put considerable pressure on members of Parliament; and it could also make its influence felt in legal proceedings. In *Lord Dacre's Case* (1534) the judges were somehow persuaded to overturn the common learning on uses and to declare that uses of land could not be left by will. This volte-face, for which the judges were promised the king's 'good thanks', conveniently enabled Thomas Cromwell to drive the Statute of Uses through Parliament without opposition.[78] The government, having been defeated in the House of Commons upon an earlier bill, had here proceeded to undermine the opposition by securing a dramatic change in the common-law. By 1535 Parliament was only too willing to give the king all he asked, the quid pro quo being the preservation of existing titles in the aftermath of this startling judgment. Soon afterwards, in *Sir John Melton's Case* (1535), Cromwell managed to effect a change in the law by act of Parliament while the suit was pending, so as to defeat Melton's bold claim to the Lucy inheritance— which the king wished to preserve for the Percy family.[79] In this second case, however, the judges were less inclined to assist the Crown, and that is why a retrospective statute was promoted to put the matter beyond dispute. Retrospective legislation, of which this was not the only instance,[80] affords one of the clearest examples of conflict between legal formality and the spirit of the rule of law.

We may never get to the bottom of what happened behind the scenes in these cases of 1534–5. Both could be made to support an argument that Henry VIII's government under Cromwell was essentially autocratic, in the sense that, although the outward forms of law were strictly observed, both the judges and the legislature were in practice amenable to the king's will. Nevertheless, assuming that they were unusual cases, they could also be taken as indicating a commitment to the law in quite a conservative sense. Henry could have achieved the revenue purposes

---

[76] Caryll (Jun.) 376, no. 16.

[77] See *Case of the Waterford Merchants* (1484–5) Mich. 2 Ric. III, fo. 11, pl. 26; 64 Selden Soc. 94; Mich. 1 Hen. VII, fo. 2, pl. 2; *Anon.* (1542) Dyer 52a (whether the king could dispense with a statute not yet made); *Att.-Gen.* v. *Richards* (1542) Dyer 54a; *Anon.* (1553) Dyer 92a; Gell's reports, I, unfol.; *Anon.* (1559) Gell's reports, II, ff. 74v–75. See also *Anon.* (undated) Spelman 152, pl. 19.   [78] Below, 418, 669.

[79] See 'Sir John Melton's Case (1535): Cockermouth Castle and the three silver luces' (1996) 55 *CLJ* 249–64, repr. in *CLT*, 363–80.

[80] Note also the cases of Richard Roose (1531) below, 539 (poisoning); Sir John Shelton (1540) below, 681 (tax avoidance); and Sir Edmund Knyvet (1541), below, 590 (fighting in king's palace).

of the Statute of Uses by replacing feudal revenue with some new kind of regular taxation. But that, even if already thinkable, was too bold a step.[81] One of the first enactments of Richard III had condemned in strong terms the imposition of arbitrary taxes such as benevolences, and forbidden them for the future.[82] Regular parliamentary taxation to support the government seems to have been scarcely more acceptable in political theory.[83] Rather than introduce a new tax regime, the solution was to legislate against tax avoidance. The king's policy, or Cromwell's, was in this case not to innovate but to restore the ancient feudal revenue to which the Crown was entitled at common law, a source of regular income which had been severely reduced as a result of uses. That is a far cry from despotism as generally understood. In Melton's case the object of the government was to protect an ancient and important inheritance from passing to a remote relative for technical breach of a medieval heraldic stipulation which seems to have had no parallel—a result which would have seemed bizarre to most observers, then or since. Even if we turn to larger policy issues, it is possible to draw a similar conclusion. In an imaginary Utopia, Henry might have introduced, through Parliament, a modern divorce law. But that was unthinkable for a Defender of the Faith; and in any case he had no grounds for divorce in the modern sense. He wanted a decree of nullity under existing canon law, a divorce to which the better opinion of contemporary canonists held him entitled; and this required an ecclesiastical jurisdiction independent of a pope known to side with Aragon. The result was revolutionary in respect to ecclesiastical polity, but it was achieved without secularizing divorce, without altering the jurisdiction of the Church courts, without modifying the rules of canon law (except in relation to the jurisdiction of

---

[81] Apart from feudal incidents and customs duties, the principal kind of taxation was still the ad hoc parliamentary grant of a subsidy, or of a tenth and fifteenth. These grants were supposedly emergency measures, usually for military purposes. Indeed, Dyer said that, whereas customs were due by the common law, subsidies were granted for the defence of merchants upon the sea: Dyer 44a, §24 (1539). See also the preamble to 1 Mar. I, sess. 2, c. 18 (defence of realm and safeguard of seas). They were, however, increasing in frequency to the point of becoming routine; and by the 1550s the subsidy acts were the most complex statutes on the book.

[82] 1 Ric. III, c. 2. It was perhaps because of the statute that Wolsey's 'amicable grant' of 1525 was condemned as contrary to law: Hall's Chronicle, 696.

[83] According to Elton, Thomas Cromwell did indeed promote the idea that parliamentary taxation could be raised for ordinary peaceful purposes; but the thesis has proved very controversial. See G. R. Elton, 'Taxation for War and Peace in Early-Tudor England' (1975) repr. in Studies, iii. 216–33; G. L. Harriss, 'Thomas Cromwell's New Principle of Taxation' (1978) 93 EHR 721–38; 'Theory and Practice in Royal Taxation: some observations' (1982) 97 EHR 811–19; J. D. Alsop, 'The Theory and Practice of Tudor Taxation' (1982) 97 EHR 1–30; 'Innovation in Tudor Taxation' (1984) 99 EHR 83–93; G. W. Bernard, War, Taxation and Rebellion in Early Tudor England (1986); R. Schofield, 'Taxation and the Political Limits of the Tudor State' in Law and Government under the Tudors, ed. C. Cross et al. (1988), 227–55; M. Bush, 'Tax Reform and Rebellion in early Tudor England' (1991) 76 History 379–400; R. W. Hoyle, 'Crown, Parliament and Taxation in Sixteenth-Century England' (1994) 109 EHR 1174–96; Gunn, Early Tudor Government, 131–41.

the pope), and without separating the Church of England from the catholic and apostolic church.

Strong kings could be cruel, and Henry VIII undoubtedly abused the courts with some of his prosecutions for treason. In high matters of state the judges seem to have lacked the power or the will to ensure a balanced trial, at any rate by the standards of later times. Yet even in that context they were by no means always compliant.[84] As it was, the law required a public hearing, with a clear accusation, evidence given on oath, an opportunity to challenge the evidence and present a defence, and a sworn jury of twelve each satisfied in his conscience that the charge was true. To have done more would have required judicial interference with the process of prosecution, and with the examination of witnesses, to an extent not yet contemplated as possible. If the judges threatened to be too difficult they could in any case be bypassed by an act of attainder: Thomas Cromwell, who arranged some of Henry's state trials in the 1530s, was himself condemned by Parliament without trial in 1540.[85] Be that as it may, particular aberrations from higher standards do not disprove the prevalence and acceptance of a rule of law. There was already a judicial tradition of independence, and there were cases in which the judges gave opinions against the Crown.[86] Indeed, Mountagu and Baldwin CJJ are said to have advised against Cromwell's attainder on the grounds that 'it was a dangerous question, and that the High Court of Parliament ought to give examples to inferior courts for proceeding according to justice'.[87] Henry's determination always to act within legal forms may have been disingenuous but it was of some consequence in shaping attitudes. Since the rule of law is incapable of precise definition, the question of its prevalence in a particular age is one of degree and opinion. Of the general attitude of the early Tudor age there seems no room for doubt. Whatever lapses and failures may have occurred from time to time at moments of

[84] See below, 413–20. In 1533 Chapuys, the ambassador, noted the judges' unwillingness to sanction a prosecution of Elizabeth Barton, but added, 'It is to be feared, however, that they will do that which the king desires, as they did when they condemned the cardinal [Wolsey] for having received his legateship': *LP*, vi. 1445. (Wolsey was in fact condemned on his own formal confession for misuse of the legatine authority, not merely for accepting it, and so the judges had little option but to give judgment: Port 57; Spelman 190; below, 245.)

[85] For the growing practice of using this device to avoid trials see S. E. Lehmberg, 'Parliamentary Attainder in the Reign of Henry VIII, 1536–47' (1975) 18 *Historical Jnl* 675–702; W. Stacy, 'Richard Roose and the Use of Parliamentary Attainder in the Reign of Henry VIII' (1986) 29 *Historical Jnl* 1–15. Before Lord Seymour was attainted in 1549, he was given an opportunity to answer articles in Council and the 'lawers' were asked to confirm that the charges amounted to treason: *APC*, ii. 248 at 258–60.

[86] See below, 417, 419.

[87] Co. Inst., iv. 37. Coke's informant was Sir Thomas Gawdy, who reported that Henry VIII had commanded him to attend the chief justices for their opinions. Coke does not say the point arose from Cromwell's attainder, but this seems likely: K. Pickthorn, *Early Tudor Government* (1934), ii. 431–4; J. W. Gough, *Fundamental Law in English Constitutional History* (1955), 43. Gawdy was a young member of the Inner Temple in 1540, but probably not yet a barrister.

crisis, 'Tudor thinking and practice on the law subordinated everybody, the king included, to the rule of law'.[88]

Maintenance and retaining

The rule of law was not threatened solely by the king's government. A constant source of complaint and concern throughout the period was the abuse of power and influence by dominant individuals for private purposes. We might even deduce—not only from the volume of complaints, but from the frequent official acknowledgment of the underlying cause by those in authority—that this was in practice a more serious threat to the uniform enforcement of the law than occasional high-handedness by the central government. Abuses might involve positive conduct, as in the case of forcible entries,[89] or negative, as where sheriffs failed to execute writs, or justices of the peace—the only effective police authority—declined to enforce the law against their supporters. Other forms of abuse may be classified under the heading of improper influence. The temptation for powerful men to influence juries, sheriffs, and even the judiciary, was considerable.[90] As the year books show us, the means adopted might be blatant, as when Lord Cobham tried to distract Fitzherbert J. in open court so that he could not hear counsel.[91] But covert influence was the more pervasive problem with the jury system and accounts for the importance attached to the law of challenges.[92] Moreover, a great man could secure a permanent basis of local influence by retaining supporters with fees, badges, or liveries of clothing in his colours.

None of this was new to Tudor England. According to Richard III's Parliament, there had since the 1460s been unmitigated chaos, crime, and a complete breakdown of law and order, 'so that this land was ruled by self-will and pleasure, fear and dread, all manner of equity and laws laid apart and despised'.[93] This was rhetorical exaggeration; and the extent to which the system of justice had in fact been frustrated during the dynastic troubles remains in controversy. But it was certainly perceived by both Richard III and Henry VII, at the time of their accession,[94] that lack of good law-enforcement was one of the principal problems confronting the government.[95] In addressing his first Parliament, Henry VII enjoined the lords and commons, and especially the justices of the peace, to ensure that crimes were punished and vagabonds chastised; while a little later the members of

---

[88] Elton, 'The Rule of Law', at 277. This was also the opinion of Holdsworth, 'The Prerogative in the Sixteenth Century', at 555–6; *HEL*, v. 201.   [89] See below, 722–3.

[90] See below, 352.   [91] Trin. 27 Hen. VIII, fo. 20, pl. 10.   [92] Below, 355–61.

[93] *RP*, vi. 240.

[94] Again, this was not new, since the same concerns had been addressed by Edward IV.

[95] Note also the reflections of Edmund Dudley: D. M. Brodie, 'Edmund Dudley: minister of Henry VII' (1932) 15 *TRHS* (4th ser.) at 140–1.

both houses were given an oath not to receive or give assistance to felons, to retain men by indenture, to give liveries or badges contrary to law, to cause maintenance, embracery, riot, or unlawful assembly, or to hinder the king's writs.[96] The judges, who were assembled at the Blackfriars to discuss this measure, expressed some scepticism about the effectiveness of a mere oath, which had been tried before.[97]

But how these statutes should be enforced, that was the question. And the chief justice said that the law would never be well enforced until all the lords spiritual and temporal were of one firm resolve (*confirment*)—for the love and dread which they had towards God or the king, or both together—to enforce it effectively. For when the king, on his side, and the lords on their side, were willing to do this, and did so, everyone else would do it easily: and, if they would not, they should be so chastised and punished that everyone would heed the warning. For he said that in Edward IV's time, when he was attorney-general,[98] all the lords were sworn to keep the statutes... and he saw that within an hour, when they were still in the Star Chamber, several of the lords made retainers by oath and did other things which were directly contrary to their said sureties and oaths. Thus oaths and sureties are to no effect unless the lords have the will (*ils sont en le purpos*) as aforesaid. And he said he had told this to the king himself.

It may have been in consequence of Huse CJ's opinion that in the following session a new statutory body was appointed to examine and punish maintenance, the giving of liveries and badges, retaining, misbehaviour by sheriffs and jurors,[99] riots, and unlawful assemblies,[100] by which means 'the policy and good rule of the realm is almost subdued'.[101] Jurors who concealed such offences were to be punished by the justices of the peace. A year later, justices of the peace themselves were ordered to perform their duty of enforcement on pain of punishment by the assize judges.[102] Steps were taken simultaneously to prevent the evasion of the statutes against maintenance and oppression through the use of collusive informer actions.[103]

Indentured retaining does seem to have ended with Henry VII, but informal retainers—usually effected by giving liveries of uniform clothing (in 'livery colours') and heraldic badges or cognizances (*signa*)[104]—remained common. In

---

[96] *RP*, vi. 278, 287. See also *Tudor Royal Proclamations*, i. 3, no. 1 (1485) and 14, no. 13 (1487).

[97] Mich. 1 Hen. VII, fo. 3, pl. 3 (tr.).   [98] 1471-8.   [99] See further below, 332-3, 364-9.

[100] For riot and unlawful assembly see 11 Hen. VII, c. 7; below, 590-2.

[101] 3 Hen. VII, c. 1. This is the so-called act 'pro camera stellata'. It did not in terms confer any jurisdiction on the Council, though the matters mentioned were subsumed in its jurisdiction: below, 196, 198. See also 3 Hen. VII, c. 12, against giving liveries to the king's officers or tenants.

[102] 4 Hen. VII, c. 12; reinforced by *Tudor Royal Proclamations*, i. 18, no. 17; supplemented by 19 Hen. VII, c. 14. See also *Tudor Royal Proclamations*, i. 55, no. 50 (prohibiting retainers, liveries, and badges in Kent, 1502).

[103] A recovery of the penalty by an accomplice—though by agreement not enforced—would bar genuine proceedings: see 4 Hen. VII, c. 20.

[104] Indictments were usually for giving silver badges, whereas excavated examples are mostly of pewter, presumably made for social inferiors.

1511 lords raising forces for the war in France were forbidden to retain or give badges to other than their own tenants, servants, and officials,[105] but for which they would presumably have done so. The government's position was ambivalent, because in times of trouble it relied on great men to produce retinues for the king's service.[106] It is therefore not too surprising that, despite the regular commencement of proceedings to punish the various statutory offences, both by indictment and by common-informer actions,[107] their apparent result was slight.[108] Many were brought against the recipients rather than the givers,[109] and after the 1504 statute some were brought against people for the quite different offence of using badges and liveries to which they were not entitled, presumably to give themselves some kind of benefit.[110] Since the statutory machinery of 1487 was difficult to operate,[111] enforcement was itself subject to local goodwill, and indeed to the effectiveness of the rule of law. Although the justices of the peace were supposed to be the prime movers in enforcing the law, doubts existed as to the extent of their authority.[112] And the scope of the various statutes caused legal difficulties, since some did not refer to receiving, as opposed to giving.[113] In 1490 the judges were divided on whether it was an offence merely to receive liveries without wearing them. Serjeant Wode argued that it was, because it was within the mischief of retaining: 'when someone gives liveries he shall have a large company at his command, whereby men will not dare to enforce the law upon any of them; and if someone takes a livery and does not use the livery he is still named his man'.[114]

---

[105] *Tudor Royal Proclamations*, i. 84, no. 62. See also ibid. 124, no. 77 (1514). An alternative strategy was to retain men in the king's name with the badge of a rose: see D. Luckett, 'Crown Office and Licensed Retinues in the Reign of Henry VII' in *Rulers and Ruled in Late Medieval England* (1995), 223–38.

[106] See e.g. the signet letters to raise forces in *LP*, xi. 562, 580, 688(4).

[107] An example of the latter is *Pekham v. Hastynges and others* (1490) KB 27/916, m. 74 (giving and receiving the Hastings livery of green medley, contrary to 8 Edw. IV, c. 2). There was an ongoing feud between Piers Pekham and Sir Ralph Hastings.

[108] See Chrimes, *Henry VII*, 190–1; R. C. E. Hayes, '"Ancient Indictments" for the North of England, 1461–1509' in *The North of England in the Age of Richard III*, ed. A. J. Pollard (1996), 19 at 36–7.

[109] e.g. *R. v. Dorant* (1498) KB 27/948, Rex m. 3d (using gown and Bourgchier knot of earl of Essex); *R. v. Hylton* (1499) KB 27/950, Rex m. 8d (using livery gown of Sir John Turvervyle); *Att.-Gen. v. Woode* (1499) KB 27/952, Rex m. 7d (using glove and falcon of Lord Grey of Wilton); *Bowntayn v. Camfeld* (1506) KB 27/980, Rex m. 3d (using silver portcullis of Lady Margaret Beaufort). All were discharged.

[110] e.g. 19 Hen. VII, c. 14; Hayes, '"Ancient Indictments" for the North of England', 19 at 37; and cf. *R. v. Lewisham* (1508) 2 Caryll 576 (falsely calling himself a servant of Sir Matthew Browne).

[111] The judges held in 1493 that the membership of the tribunal had to conform strictly with the statute: Pas. 8 Hen. VII, fo. 13, pl. 7; 75 Selden Soc. 60–1.

[112] *R. v. Newark* (1508) KB 27/986, m. 4d (discharged because JPs have no jurisdiction); *R. v. Frank* (1508) KB 27/987, Rex 12 (using Percy crescent; indictment quashed because JPs not shown to have jurisdiction; and cf. sim. in KB 27/977, Rex m. 10d; KB 27/978, Rex m. 7).

[113] See *R. v. Dorant* (1498) KB 27/948, Rex m. 3d (recipient discharged because no allegation that the earl gave him the badge or livery); *R. v. Hylton* (1499) KB 27/950, Rex m. 8d (sim.); *R. v. Webster* (1506) KB 27/978, Rex m. 2d (recipients discharged because the statute did not warrant punishment for receiving or using liveries). [114] Mich. 6 Hen. VII, fo. 12, pl. 13, at fo. 13.

The main stream of prosecutions for giving liveries seems to end in 1516, when Lord Burgavenny and a number of other peers were at Wolsey's instance indicted in the King's Bench.[115] Threats of prosecution may thereafter have been a sufficient deterrent; and the Star Chamber—standing as it did above local influence—may also have helped to change the culture. Liveries and badges seem to have gone out of general use during Henry VIII's reign,[116] though retaining nevertheless remained a politically sensitive matter. The assize judges were instructed in 1518 to look into retaining and maintenance and report to the Council;[117] some Star Chamber proceedings followed in 1519.[118] In 1524 commissions were appointed to hear complaints of maintenance and oppression in the north.[119] Retaining featured in the indictment of the duke of Buckingham for treason in 1521,[120] and in the charges against Lord Seymour in 1549.[121] And it was a sufficiently serious charge to enable the marquess of Exeter to recover £3,000 damages in 1533 for a false accusation that he had retained a great number of men contrary to law.[122] The ambiguous nature of private retaining could only be removed by the establishment of a public militia, which was to some extent achieved with the introduction of lords lieutenant[123] and improvements in the county muster system in the middle of the sixteenth century.[124] Yet it is evident from the records of the

[115] *Hall's Chronicle*, 585; A. F. Pollard, *Wolsey* (1929), 75–6; J. A. Guy, *The Cardinal's Court* (1977), 31; *Att.-Gen. v. Lord Burgavenny* (1516) KB 29/148, mm. 17d, 18d; KB 27/1020, Rex m. 25 (pardon pleaded); *Att.-Gen. v. Earl of Arundel* (1516) KB 27/1021, Rex m. 3 (retaining and giving silver-gilt badges of the oak-leaf and the white horse; imparlance); *Att.-Gen. v. Lord Hastings and others* (1516) KB 29/148, m. 16 (issue); *Att.-Gen. v. Marquess of Dorset* (1516) KB 29/148, mm. 16d, 43 (issue). Burgavenny had been prosecuted in the previous reign: W. H. Dunham, *Lord Hastings' Indentured Retainers* (1955), 103–05.

[116] Note, however, that in 1535 the lord warden of the cinque ports found it necessary to forbid the use of cognizances other than his own or the king's: *Lisle Letters*, ed. Byrne, ii. 481, no. 386.

[117] Guy, *The Cardinal's Court*, 33.   [118] *Hall's Chronicle*, 599.

[119] *Tudor Royal Proclamations*, i. 143–4, nos. 98–9 (issued to duke of Norfolk, Swillington A.-G., Port S.-G., and others).

[120] 119 Selden Soc. 65; and see Guy, *The Cardinal's Court*, 74 (pardon of the recipient, Sir William Bulmer).

[121] *R. v. Lord Seymour* (1549) 2 & 3 Edw. VI, c. 18; 1 St. Tr. 483 at 488 (retaining around 10,000 young men).

[122] *Marquess of Exeter v. Coryngton* (1534) KB 27/1091, m. 39. The accusation had cost him his place in the privy chamber.

[123] See G. S. Thomson, *Lords Lieutenants in the Sixteenth Century* (1923); Holdsworth, *HEL*, iv. 76. The regular system began under Edward VI and Mary, albeit on an ad hoc basis; but there were earlier antecedents in the commissions of array. In William Porter's Crown Office precedent book, C193/142, fo. 92v, the earl of Surrey's commission in the North (1512) is marked in a later hand as a 'lieutenancy'. A muster proclamation of 1545 refers to 'his majesty's lieutenant in [northern] parts': *Tudor Royal Proclamations*, i. 354, no. 252. See also 3 & 4 Edw. VI, c. 5, s. 13 (ad hoc lieutenants of counties, for suppression of rebellion).

[124] Musters were originally made under the prerogative (e.g. by proclamations of 1513, 1522, 1532, and 1545) but were put on a statutory basis in 1558: 4 & 5 Phil. & Mar., cc. 2–3 (penalties for neglecting to attend musters and for corruptly granting exemptions).

King's Bench and Star Chamber that the other impediments to the rule of law noted at the beginning of Henry VII's reign had not been wholly removed by the middle of the sixteenth century.

PARLIAMENT[125]

Parliaments were summoned, when occasion arose and sometimes with considerable intervals,[126] by the king (or queen regnant) on the advice of the Council. Peers were summoned on the hereditary principle, and it was coming to be accepted that one attendance upon summons conferred a hereditary right to be summoned in future—though in practice peers were sometimes excluded from the summons on grounds of incapacity, and in any case perhaps only half actually attended.[127] The bishops were summoned as full members, but by virtue of their temporalities and not as a separate estate of the realm:[128] an act of Parliament could be validly passed without any of them being present.[129] Thirty-one mitred abbots were entitled to be summoned to the upper house, until the dissolution of the monasteries,[130] though it is not clear that they played a significant role in Tudor times.

The commons' house was enlarged as a result of the recognition of new boroughs entitled to send representatives, including twenty-four Welsh constituencies in 1542 and a number of rotten boroughs under Edward VI. While the number of members elected in the reign of Henry VII remained constant at around 296, by 1558 it had risen to 398.[131] Elections were conducted by the sheriffs, who returned the results in a sealed indenture. They were commonly determined by acclamation or show of hands, without counting; but the principle was that the majority should prevail.[132] It was said that the returns were incontestable, so that if someone was returned who had not been elected, or who was unqualified, he nevertheless became the sitting member and his consent to an act of Parliament was valid. The remedy for an elected candidate who was not returned was said to be an action on the case against

---

[125] See Elton, 'Parliament' in *Tudor Constitution*, 233–326; Loach, *Parliament under the Tudors*.

[126] The total sitting time in the entire 75-year period covered by this volume was only about 320 weeks: Elton, *Tudor Constitution*, 233.

[127] Chrimes, *Henry VII*, 137–41; Loach, *Parliament under the Tudors*, 21–4.

[128] The bishops had claimed to be a third estate as late as the 1480s: Elton, *Studies*, ii. 33.

[129] *Dr Standish's Case* (1515) 2 Caryll 683 at 690; L. O. Pike, *Constitutional Position of the House of Lords* (1894), 326–7.

[130] It was only from this point that the temporal lords began to outnumber the spiritual: Elton, *Tudor Constitution*, 247.

[131] J. C. Wedgwood, *History of Parliament: biographies of the members of the Commons House 1439-1509* (1936), pp. vi–viii; S. T. Bindoff, *The History of Parliament: the House of Commons 1509-58* (1982), i. 4.

[132] See *Bulkeley v. Thomas* (1554) Plowd. 118 at 126, *per* Saunders J., and 128v, *per* Brooke CJ (adding, tr. 'I was elected in London by raising of hands, but I could not say how many there were in number who raised their hands').

the sheriff.[133] In practice actions were more commonly brought on the statute of 1445 which made sheriffs liable to actions of debt for making false returns.[134] Such actions were known in the fifteenth century;[135] and they were common in the time of Edward VI and Mary I,[136] no doubt as a result of widespread interference with elections in obedience to royal letters of recommendation.[137]

Most parliaments were held at Westminster, and their procedures were becoming regularized.[138] The lords met in the White Chamber,[139] under the presidency of the lord chancellor or lord keeper (even if he was not a bishop or peer), and attended by the judges and law officers,[140] who still played an active role as legal advisers.[141] The commons met in the chapter house or refectory of Westminster Abbey until 1549, when they acquired St Stephen's Chapel within the palace. They were presided over by an elected speaker, who was always an eminent lawyer of the rank of bencher, and they had a separate clerk.[142] Bills proposing legislation could be introduced in either house and usually received three readings in each, the principal debate taking place on the second reading. They were no longer drawn as petitions but were verbatim texts of proposed statutes, many of them emanating from the government. They could be referred to a committee, especially if redrafting was

---

[133] *Anon.* (1558) BL MS. Harley 1624, fo. 76; MS. Hargrave 4, fo. 135v ('in the parliament house', referring to boroughs); John Kitchin's reading (Gray's Inn, 1564) BL MS. Lansdowne 1134, fo. 47.

[134] 23 Hen. VI, c. 14.

[135] e.g. *Radclyff* v. *Wyngfeld* (1483) CP 40/883, m. 408 (Norfolk, 1483; see comment by R. Virgoe, 60 *BIHR* 24); *Corbet* v. *Talbot* (1487) CP 40/902, m. 404, pr. in *Intrationum Liber* (1510), fo. 126v; Rast. Ent. 410 (446) (Shropshire, 1485; noted in Plowd. 126, 129). Note also *Belknappe* v. *Barkeley* (1512) CP 40/1001, m. 617 (Warwickshire, 1512; recovers £100 penalty and £30 costs).

[136] e.g. *Gunter* v. *Welshe* (1548) CP 40/1137, m. 424 (Monmouth 1547); *Godwyn* v. *Sydnam* (1549) CP 40/1143, m. 518 (Lyme, 1547); *Roger Bodenham* v. *Scudamore* (1554) CP 40/1157, m. 414 (Herefordshire, 1553); *Lee* v. *Mitton* (1554) CP 40/1159, m. 519 (Shrewsbury, 1553); *Channon* v. *Moghan* (1555) CP 40/1161, m. 528 (Grampound, 1553); *Chapell* v. *Moghan*, ibid., m. 621 (same); *John Fytz* v. *Egecombe*, ibid., m. 652 (Tavistock, 1553); *Mayhewe* v. *Egecombe*, ibid., m. 653 (same); *Bulkeley* v. *Thomas* (1554-5) KB 27/1176, m. 287; Plowd. 118 (Anglesey, 1553; error from Common Pleas); *Edward Fytz* v. *Egecombe* (1556) CP 40/1165, m. 546 (Tavistock, 1553); *Collyns* v. *Egecombe* (1556) ibid., m. 658 (Tavistock, 1553). All these disputes related to western parts of the country, from Wales and its borders down to Cornwall. They were unknown to the principal historian of the Marian Parliaments: Loach, *Parliament and the Crown in the Reign of Mary Tudor*, 24, who mentioned two other cases (Staffordshire, 1553; Gloucester, 1555).

[137] For 'management' of (interference with) elections, see Holdsworth, *HEL*, iv. 94-6; Elton, *Tudor Constitution*, 292-3; Loach, *Parliament and the Crown in the Reign of Mary Tudor*, 28-31; *Parliament under the Tudors*, 25-34. There was nothing new about this in the 1550s.

[138] Elton, *Tudor Constitution*, 249-54; Loach, *Parliament under the Tudors*, 43-53.

[139] The expression House of Lords is not found until the 1540s: Elton, *Tudor Constitution*, 246. Cf. ibid. 276 ('Upper House' in 1542). Since the lords sat in the Parliament chamber, only the commons were at first seen as meeting in a distinct 'house'.

[140] Summoned for this purpose by writs of assistance were the common-law judges, the master of the rolls, the king's serjeants at law, and the attorney- and solicitor-general. Masters in chancery could also attend as assistants, without writ.   [141] See also below, 79.

[142] The journals of the House of Commons did not, however, begin until 1547.

required, but this was not essential.[143] If necessary a bill was put to the vote, and a majority sufficed to carry it.[144] Until as late as 1504, the king occasionally amended statutes without reference back to the two houses; but the practice was abandoned by Henry VIII, so that bills only became law with the full concurrence of king, lords, and commons.[145] These internal procedures were nevertheless no concern of the courts, which would accept as validly made any properly recorded act of Parliament which recited the assent of the lords and commons and the royal assent.[146] Indeed, the courts were obliged to accept an exemplification of a statute under the great seal, even if it was factually inaccurate, so long as it appeared on its face to be a statute.[147]

These rules as to authenticity were applications of the principle of estoppel by record. The High Court of Parliament may have been 'nothing but a court',[148] but it was superior to the regular courts of law, and therefore no other court could recognize or remedy latent errors in its record.[149] On the same principle, the courts could not question a parliamentary attainder obtained contrary to natural justice.[150] The doctrine also explains why, for legal purposes, all acts of Parliament were deemed to take effect from the first day of the session.[151] Since the parliament roll did not record the day on which each statute was passed, in fiction of law 'the whole parliament is but one day'.[152] However, according to Fitzjames CJ, if there was a different commencement date mentioned within an act the rule did not apply.[153]

[143] For a suggestion that it may have been usual practice by the 1530s see Lehmberg, *Reformation Parliament*, 240.

[144] As late as 1550, Thomas Stanley in his Gray's Inn reading thought it worth asserting that a majority decision would suffice: BL MS. Hargrave 199, fo. 62. In the House of Lords the votes were counted, but in the Commons 'the assent is tried by the voices sounding all at one time': *Bulkeley* v. *Thomas* (1554) Plowd. 118 at 126, *per* Saunders J.

[145] Elton, *Studies*, ii. 56–7; *Partridge* v. *Straunge* (1553) Plowd. 78v at 79v (where it is said that the royal assent was usually given on the last day of the parliament).

[146] Trin. 11 Hen. VII, fo. 27, pl. 10, *per* Danvers and Vavasour JJ. Cf. *Pilkington's Case* (1455) Pas. 33 Hen. VI, fo. 17, pl. 8. Note also *Duke of Norfolk's Case* (1553) Dyer 93a; Dal. 19, 20 (query as to royal assent given by commission which appeared to be stamped rather than signed). But the court would not accept an act which did not purport to have the assent of the commons: Mich. 4 Hen. VII, fo. 18, pl. 11; *King's College, Cambridge* v. *Wylmot* (1492) Trin. 7 Hen. VII, fo. 14, pl. 1, *per* Kebell sjt.

[147] *King's College, Cambridge* v. *Wylmot* (1492) Trin. 7 Hen. VII, fo. 14, pl. 1; CP 40/921, m. 255; *Duke of Norfolk's Case* (1555) BL MS. Add. 24845, fo. 28v; Dal. 19, 20. In the first case the main question was whether a grant by the king in Parliament, with the assent of the lords and commons, was an act of Parliament.

[148] *Wimbish* v. *Tailboys* (1550) Plowd. 38 at 59, *per* Mountagu CJ ('nest que un court').

[149] As to whether there were legal restrictions on the legislative competence of Parliament see below, 80.

[150] Co. Inst. iv. 37 (opinion of the judges in the 1530s, related to Coke by Sir Thomas Gawdy).

[151] The rule may be traced back to *Pilkington's Case* (1455) Pas. 33 Hen. VI, fo. 18, pl. 8, *per* Faux; but cf. *Selected Historical Essays of F. W. Maitland*, ed. H. M. Cam (1957), 236. It stood until 1793: 33 Geo. III, c. 13.

[152] Cf. the fiction that a whole assize session took place on one day, since the record mentioned only the commencement: below, 260.

[153] Yorke 117, no. 82 (1530s), *per* Fitzjames CJ (tr. 'the whole parliament is but one day, and the last day shall have relation to the first day of the parliament in all acts which are done unless the

When parliaments were prorogued to a later date,[154] this was a matter of record, and therefore the relation-rule applied separately to each session in which statutes were passed.[155] Where, therefore, a statute was passed in the third session of a parliament against shooting with crossbows, someone who had used a crossbow between the second and third sessions was not caught by the statute.[156] Statutes could be passed in different sessions if the royal assent was given before prorogation, and they were complete statutes even though the Parliament had not yet been dissolved.[157] For the purposes of judicial notice, a distinction was taken between general and particular statutes; the latter, which applied only to particular people or places, had to be pleaded, but the former did not.[158] It was not the same distinction as that later made between public and private statutes, but depended on the particularity of the subject-matter.[159]

Legislation and its interpretation

Attention has already been drawn to significant changes in the character and scope of legislation during the early Tudor period, and to the achievement by Parliament of more or less unqualified sovereignty.[160] Moreover, as a result of concurrent changes in procedure, parliamentary legislation was 'no longer the Government's reply to vaguely worded complaints, but rather the deliberate adoption of specific proposals embodied in specific texts'.[161] Since proposed legislation now began its parliamentary life as a draft statute, the exact wording could be debated, and amended,[162] usually with the benefit of the combined legal expertise of judges, law officers, and legally qualified members of the lower house. As a

day is comprised within the act when the act should commence, for then this act shall not have relation').

[154] For notes by the clerk of the Crown on prorogation (1519) see C193/142, ff. 41–44. In 1554, the first Parliament of Mary I was adjourned from Oxford without anyone appearing there, which was not strictly a prorogation: 109 Selden Soc., pp. lv, 11.

[155] *Anon.* (1541) Brooke Abr., *Parlement*, pl. 86; *Relation*, pl. 35 (tr. 'every such session is a parliament in itself'); *Myners* v. *Plaine* (1550) BL MS. Hargrave 4, fo. 112 at 113, *per* Brooke; *Partridge* v. *Straunge* (1553) Plowd. 77v at 79v, *per* Hales J.; Dalison's reports, BL MS. Harley 5141, fo. 9v; MS. Add. 24845, fo. 17, *per* Hales J. Cf. *Anon.* (1550) HLS MS. 5048, fo. 149; *Whitton* v. *Marine* (1553) Dyer 95a.

[156] *Myners* v. *Plaine* (1550) BL MS. Hargrave 4, fo. 112 at 113, *per* Brooke.

[157] Walter Hendley's reading (Gray's Inn, 1530) BL MS. Hargrave 88, fo. 4. Hendley had chosen to read on such a statute (21 Hen. VIII, c. 3).

[158] *Anon.* (1534) Trin. 26 Hen. VIII, fo. 7, pl. 34, *per* Fitzherbert J.; *Anon.* (1544) Gell's reports, I, Mich. 36 Hen. VIII, fo. 23v; *Dean and Chapter of Bristol* v. *Clerke* (1553) Dyer 83 at 85; *Partridge* v. *Straunge* (1553) Plowd. 77 at 84. Cf. *Heydon* v. *Ibgrave* (1556) Dyer 129b (general act not shown to jury because not pleaded).

[159] See *Dyve* v. *Maningham* (1550) Plowd. 62 at 65; Wm Yelv. 343, *per* Mountagu CJ, following *Lord Say's Case* (1473) Pas. 13 Edw. IV, fo. 8, pl. 4.   [160] Above, 36–7.

[161] T. F. T. Plucknett, 'Ellesmere on Statutes' (1944) 60 *LQR* 242 at 248.

[162] This was formally recognized in the mid-sixteenth century, when bills were no longer presented on parchment but on paper, and only engrossed after the second reading.

consequence, the finished product could be regarded as textually more significant than the mere record of a decision to grant a petition. The use of printing for all statutes, from the very beginning of our period,[163] further emphasized the weight of the *ipsissima verba* of the text. Draftsmen recognized this, taking increasingly elaborate care to furnish bills with preambles setting out their objects, and to ensure that they provided for every contingency in the operative provisions, piling clause upon clause and qualifying them with provisos, savings, and exceptions.[164] The new form of legislation reflected very well the new humanist approach to law-making.[165] It would result in a more literal approach to the statutory text, and the eventual eclipse—in a later period—of the medieval notion of the equity of a statute. Already in the first half of the sixteenth century, Fyneux CJ was an advocate of strict literal construction wherever it could be sensibly achieved.[166] But the two approaches to statutory interpretation were in tension,[167] and Fyneux CJ himself recommended construction according to the mind of the makers where the words of a statute were 'difficult'.[168]

Strict or narrow interpretation had become the rule for statutes which were deemed to be 'negative': that is penal, or in derogation of common right, or in abridgment of the common law.[169] On the other hand, statutes which were 'affirmative' or beneficial, which 'enlarged' the common law or remedied a mischief at common law,

---

[163] Below, 505–6.

[164] See S. E. Lehmberg, 'Early Tudor Parliamentary Procedure: provisos in the legislation of the Reformation Parliament' (1970) 85 *EHR* 1–11.   [165] Above, 34–9.

[166] See Yorke 114, no. 73 ('Note by the lord Fyneux [CJ] that a statute must be construed and taken according to the letter, so far as may be', though he proceeded to list three alternative approaches); Spelman's reading (1519), 145, *per* Broke sjt and Fyneux CJ ('all acts of Parliament that are plain shall be so taken and construed'). Cf. p. 169, *per* Broke sjt ('all old statutes shall be construed according to the wording unless they have been otherwise put into practice'). Cf. Fyneux CJ's remarks at Petit's reading (1518) LI MS. Misc. 486(1), fo. 12v (tr. 'those who are expositors of a statute must have three things ... the letter ... experience how the statute was taken before this time ... [and] common reason').

[167] See 'Construction del estatutez' (notes collected *c.*1520–30) in Yorke 114–19; *A Discourse upon the Exposicion and Understandinge of Statutes*, ed. S. E. Thorne (1942); *Reports from the Lost Notebooks of Sir James Dyer*, ed. J. H. Baker, 109 Selden Soc., introd., pp. lix–lxi. The *Discourse* was probably written by Thomas Egerton in the 1560s: Plucknett, 'Ellesmere on Statutes' (1944) 60 *LQR* 242.

[168] *Anon.* (1516) Chaloner 278, no. 1. He said there were three relevant factors in construing statutes: (i) the words; (ii) if the words are difficult, 'the mind of those who made it'; (iii) previous interpretation by 'wise men'. These should be combined with 'good reason'. There is an almost identical anonymous exposition on fo. 20v of the Chaloner manuscript (GI MS. 25) (in a Gray's Inn reading *c.*1520/5), which adds as a fourth principle that one should seek out the mischief.

[169] John Scott's treatise on tenures (1493), ff. 20–25 (tr. 'the common principle of the law upon the construction of the letter of the statutes' is that negative words are taken *stricte in re*); Richard Littleton's reading (1493) 102 Selden Soc. 83; Port 115, no. 60, and 116, no. 63; Hil. 14 Hen. VII, fo. 13, pl. 2, *per* Bryan CJ; *Digby's Case* (1499) ibid., fo. 18, pl. 7, *per* Vavasour J.; *Toft's Case* (1506) Hil. 21 Hen. VII, fo. 17, pl. 28, *per* Rede CJ; Mich. 21 Hen. VII, fo. 36, pl. 45, *per* Elyot sjt (tr. 'every penal statute shall be taken strictly'); *Anon.* (1507) 2 Caryll 572, pl. 413; Yorke 114, no. 74; 116, no. 79; 117, no. 81; *Discourse upon Statutes*, introd., 48–51.

were to be taken broadly, by the equity.[170] Thus a statute passed to remedy a particular case of some identified mischief could be extended to other cases within the same mischief.[171] The distinction probably had a canonical origin.[172] However, since most statutes effected some change in the law, the distinction between 'abridgment' and 'enlargement' was difficult to apply and required a view to be taken of the general beneficence or otherwise of the underlying legislative policy.[173] If elevated to the status of a rule, it was seen to be hedged around with numerous qualifications, not the least of which was that some statutes were both beneficial and penal, depending on one's point of view. Any guiding principle of this kind therefore had to give way to overriding legislative policy or intention. Serjeant Saunders pointed out the difficulty in a well-known speech of 1553:[174]

although the statute [32 Hen. VIII, c. 9] gives a punishment, yet, given that it is so beneficial to the public weal, things outside the letter thereof shall be taken by the equity thereof. And the words within it are so obscure that, by the same reason, they shall be expounded more strongly in favour of the public weal. For words, which are nothing but vibrations in the air, are not the statute but only the image of the statute. And the life of the statute rests in the minds of the expositors of the words, who are the makers of the statutes; and if they are dispersed—so that their minds cannot be known—then those who may approach closest to their minds shall construe the words, and those are the sages of the law whose wits are exercised in the study of such matters... Thus the efficacy of statutes is not solely in the wording of the statutes but in the intent of the statutes, which ought always to be greatly weighed, and the words ought to be bent thereto; and upon like reason a penal statute shall be extended by the equity if the intent of the makers thereof may be so perceived.

[170] John Scott's treatise on tenures (1493), fo. 28 (tr. 'another common principle in the law', that affirmative and beneficial statutes construed by the equity); Mich. 14 Hen. VII, fo. 9, pl. 19, per Fyneux CJ (statute for the 'common profit of the realm'); and ff. 17–18, pl. 7; moot in Gray's Inn (c.1500) BL MS. Harley 5103, fo. 59, per Broke (statute which remedies a mischief); Anon. (1508) 2 Caryll 590–1, pl. 432; Yorke 114, no. 74; 116, no. 80. Beneficial statutes were those which 'enlarged' the common law or introduced a new remedy: Port 115, no. 60.

[171] Hil. 14 Hen. VII, fo. 14, pl. 2, per Fyneux CJ; Digby's Case (1499) ibid., ff. 17–18, pl. 7, per Conyngesby and Kebell sjts.

[172] In 1428 Paston sjt—following a bachelor of law, who 'argued much in Latin'—stated it in the form of a Latin maxim which he attributed to 'the clerk': 'lex beneficialis rei consimili remedium praestat, odiosa autem casu quo efficitur ulterius non extendit': Mich. 7 Hen. VI, fo. 11, pl. 16. See also Discourse, ed. Thorne, introd., 48–50.

[173] So said Shelley J. in Marmyon v. Baldwyn (1527) 120 Selden Soc. 61 at 63 (tr. 'a statute is always taken as it has been applied, and is not taken strictly [even] if it is penal. For no statute is more penal than the praemunire, and yet no statute has been more largely construed. Thus the intention of the makers [is paramount]').

[174] Partridge v. Straunge (1553) Plowd. 77v at 82 (tr.). Cf. his similar argument in Reniger v. Fogassa (1550) Plowd. 1 at 10 (tr. 'although the statute is penal, still it shall be taken according to common reason and common intendment, and according to the minds of the makers'). See also Wimbish v. Tailbois (1550) Plowd. 38v at 46v, 53v–54, 59v.

An increasingly common solution was therefore to propose that statutes should be interpreted according to the will or intention of the makers.[175] As Shelley J. put it, 'the sense and intent of the makers of any statute, and the *mens statuti*, should alone lead a judge to an upright judgment in construction of any statute'.[176] Reference was also sometimes made to the 'intention of the statute',[177] or to the 'intention of Parliament',[178] which presumably meant the same thing. But how was such an intention to be ascertained?

There might be inside information about recent statutes, during the parliament in which they were made,[179] or even after the makers were 'dispersed'. A bencher of Gray's Inn in the 1530s might very well claim to have discussed a statute with 'all the makers';[180] but he was himself a member of the parliament which passed it. Judges possessed similar insights into recent legislation, by reason of their attendance on the House of Lords and their participation in the legislative process. This gave special authority to contemporary judicial exposition, whether ancient or modern.[181] For outsiders, however, and for later generations,[182] the intention of the makers could only be a kind of fiction, a constructive intention to be gathered from the wording, and especially from the preamble which purported to explain it: for, 'if a statute recites the intention, this statute may not be construed otherwise than according to the intention as recited'.[183] Legislative

---

[175] 94 Selden Soc. 45; Trin. 4 Hen. VII, fo. 11, pl. 6, *per* Jay sjt (tr. 'we must go to the minds of the makers of the same act'); Hil. 14 Hen. VII, fo. 18, pl. 7; Hil. 21 Hen. VII, fo. 17, pl. 28; *Earl of Bridgewater's Case* (1541) Dyer 48b; *Anon.* (c.1545/50) Wm Yelv. 357–8, no. 95, *per* Mountagu CJ; *Reniger* v. *Fogassa* (1550) Plowd. 1 at 5v, 12v, 17–18; *Wimbish* v. *Tailboys* (1550) Plowd. 38 at 57v, *per* Mountagu CJ (tr. 'if the terms and letter of any statute are obscure and difficult to be perceived, we ought to resort to the intent of the makers'; 'ambiguous words have always been expounded according to the intent of the makers').

[176] Recalled by Dyer CJ as a 'good lesson' learned in the Common Pleas when he was a student (c.1532/42): 109 Selden Soc., p. lx. Cf. the 1527 passage cited above.

[177] e.g. Mich. 10 Hen. VI, fo. 8, pl. 30; *Lord Beauchamp* v. *Croft* (1497) 1 Caryll 349 at 353, 354.

[178] *Argall* v. *Smith* (1561) 109 Selden Soc. 59; and see Dyer 203b.

[179] Yorke 114, no. 73, *per* Fyneux CJ (statutes usually to be construed literally, but 'if not by the letter, then during the parliament according to the construction of those who made the statute'); reading in Gray's Inn (c.1520/5) GI MS. 25, fo. 20v (tr. 'if a statute is obscure, and the parliament continues, it shall be construed according to the intent of the makers'). Cf. *Discourse*, ed. Thorne, 151–2 (sp. mod., 'so, in our days, have those that were the penners and devisers of statutes been the greatest light for exposition of statutes').

[180] BL MS. Hargrave 253, fo. 9 (tr. 'Note that Wroth said that he had communicated with all the makers of this statute [21 Hen. VIII, c. 13], who said...'). This is Robert Wroth (d. 1535), MP for Middlesex 1529.

[181] See Port 115, no. 59 (undated note, probably 1490s), which may refer principally to old statutes: cf. Serjeant Broke's remarks at Spelman's reading (1519), 159 (next note). This was old doctrine: see *Discourse*, ed. Thorne, 151–2.

[182] Serjeant Broke said the doctrine only applied to current statutes, since 'in the case of old statutes no one can know the intention of the makers': Spelman's reading (1519), 159.

[183] Port 115, no. 59. Dyer CJ said in *Stowell* v. *Lord Zouche* (1565) Plowd. 353v at 369 (tr.) that the preamble was 'a key to open the minds of the makers of the act, and the mischiefs which they intended to remedy'.

intention is a fiction in any case, since a collective body does not have a mind: 'so many statute-makers, so many minds'.[184] It was a way of justifying the equitable or common-sense approach to statutory language rather than a genuine exercise in uncovering relevant factual information. The seemingly new, purposive method of interpretation was therefore really no different from 'equity',[185] which was still very frequently mentioned in arguments reported by Plowden in the 1550s. Objective or presumptive intention was different in kind from real or subjective intention. Indeed, the presumption that Parliament would not intend anything unreasonable came close to giving the courts an objective reviewing power.[186] And reasons of general policy might still weigh with the court, regardless of 'intention', as was made dramatically explicit when Dyer J. advocated the restrictive interpretation of a statute on the grounds that it was 'too harsh and cruel against women, who have no voice in Parliament'.[187]

Occasionally it was noted that a statute had received an interpretation clean contrary to its express words.[188] Could a statute ever be interpreted so as to deprive it of any effect at all? The point was open to debate. The common law might not be superior to Parliament, but it could nevertheless be seen as anterior to Parliament, and it was not absurd to suggest that the rules for the interpretation of statutes were rules of common law.[189] On the other hand, according to Serjeant Pollard in 1550, 'a denial of the text is absolutely contrary to the rules of the common law'.[190] In the 1520s the question arose at a moot in Gray's Inn whether Parliament could sanction the grant of land on condition that it should not escheat, and the case provoked a broad discussion of what would later be called judicial review of legislation. Several opinions were expressed that, although Parliament could make new law, it could not enact something repugnant, absurd, or contrary to law and reason.[191] This included, for at least some of the disputants, a statute removing a piece of land from all human ownership

---

[184] *Discourse*, ed. Thorne, 151 (sp. mod.).

[185] See *Dod* v. *Chyttynden* (1502) 2 Caryll 407 ('the tenant at sufferance was construed to be within this statute by the equity, for he is within the intention of the makers of the statute').

[186] See *Partridge* v. *Straunge* (1553) Plowd. 77v at 80v, *per* Morgan sjt; *Fulmerston* v. *Steward* (1554) Plowd. 102 at 109v; below, 81.   [187] *Villers* v. *Beamont* (1557) Dyer 146a at 148a.

[188] See. e.g. Yorke 116, no. 78 ('so that this statute is construed directly contrary to the words of the statute'); Gray's Inn reading (*c.*1536) BL MS. Hargrave 253, fo. 5v (tr. 'The reader said that a statute is sometimes taken contrary to the words'); *Dutton* v. *Manley* (1544) Cholmeley 462 at 468 ('Sometimes the words of a statute are void...'); *Fulmerston* v. *Steward* (1554) Plowd. 102 at 109v (tr. 'the judges who were our predecessors have sometimes expounded words [of statutes] clean contrary to the text, and have sometimes taken things by the equity of a text contrary to the text'). Cf. *Discourse*, ed. Thorne, 161–70.

[189] *Reniger* v. *Fogassa* (1550) Plowd. 1 at 17, *per* Pollard sjt; *Wimbish* v. *Tailbois* (1550) Plowd. 38v at 47, *per* Saunders sjt.   [190] ibid. at 17v (speaking of penal statutes).

[191] BL MS. Add. 35939, fo. 269 (*c.*1526/9). The date is fixed by the presence of Broke CB and Christopher Hales as solicitor-general.

('absurd'), a statutory feoffment of land without the right to take the income ('repugnant'), or a statutory grant of land in fee on terms that it should not descend to heirs ('against law and reason').[192] These opinions are remarkably close to Coke's in the next century[193]—for holding which he has been universally accused of innovation—and it is unfortunate that our brief report of the moot does not spell out any underlying theory. With hindsight the opinions appear to have challenged the reach of parliamentary sovereignty; but they were perhaps understood at the time in terms of the impossibility of doing the impossible. Parliament could not make the impossible happen, and factual impossibility might seem to shade into legal impossibility with notions such as ownerless land. That may also have been Coke's position, in the different context of a statute contrary to natural justice, for it was in a sense impossible to be a judge in one's own cause: one could reach a decision, and it might even be a fair decision, but it could never be the decision of an independent judge. Another explanation of the opinions could be sought in the presumption that, whatever the words, Parliament cannot have intended something contrary to reason.[194] It is possible, however, that some lawyers had a more sweeping conception of the limitations on parliamentary competence. At a reading in Gray's Inn during the same period it was said, probably by Fyneux CJ, that a statute had to serve the king and the common weal or else it was no statute; and he put these requirements on the same level as the several assents of king, lords, and commons.[195] However, if there was any broader notion that Parliament was incompetent to change basic principles of law, it did not survive the Reformation Parliament.[196] Even the Chancery could afford no relief from a statute made against reason and conscience.[197]

---

[192] It was also suggested, in the same period, that Parliament could not alter immemorial local customs: *Marmyon* v. *Baldwyn* (1527) 120 Selden Soc. 61 at 69, *per* More J.; above, 37. But this may also have been a point of interpretation. The city claimed, through its recorder, that 'they ought not by reason of any statute made contrary to the liberties and customs of the aforesaid city alter or infringe its liberties or free customs used from ancient time unless express mention is made thereof in the aforesaid statute'). See also *Dutton* v. *Manley* (1544) Cholmeley 462 at 467, *per* Saunders sjt ('there are some customs which are directly against . . . statute law and yet they are good').

[193] *Dr Bonham's Case* (1610) 8 Co. Rep. 114.

[194] See *Fulmerston* v. *Steward* (1554) Plowd. 102 at 109v (tr. 'the judges have taken it to be against reason . . . and thus they have expounded [the statute] contrary to the text to make it agree with reason'), 110 (tr. 'which exposition is contrary to the text, inasmuch as the text is contrary to reason . . . and they would not take that to be the intent of the makers of the statute').

[195] GI MS. 25, fo. 20v (tr. 'To a statute five things are requisite, or else it is not a statute: (i) that it serve the king; (ii) that it be for the common weal; (iii) the king's assent; (iv) the assent of the lords; (iv) the assent of the commons'). There follows an exposition of statutory exposition identical with that of Fyneux CJ (above).   [196] See above, 36.

[197] St German, *Little Treatise*, ed. Guy, 116; above, 37. St German held that a statute against the law of God, or the law of reason, would be void: *Doctor and Student*, ed. Plucknett and Barton, 41, 113, 158, 331. But this was a matter of abstract theory in the absence of any higher jurisdiction.

Delegated legislation[198]

The statute of 1539 which empowered the king to legislate by proclamation acknowledged the constitutional principle that a power to make or alter law must derive from Parliament rather than from the king alone or from the king in Council.[199] It is true that a power to make bye-laws could be claimed by prescription or royal grant,[200] and was enjoyed by all or most courts leet and municipal corporations, though it was exercised in limited spheres and rested largely on local consent.[201] Bye-laws could restrict the personal freedom of those who were subject to them, and they were enforceable by local courts, but—like proclamations—they were doubtless seen as regulating conduct within the existing boundaries of the law rather than as changing the law itself. Colleges, craft guilds, and companies also had statute-making powers granted to them by the Crown, but again these were seen as powers of self-regulation under the law rather than as authority to make or change law. In 1504, Parliament gave formal expression to this distinction by enacting that no ordinances should be made by guilds in derogation of the king's prerogative or 'against the common profit of the people', but that 'the same acts or ordinances' should be submitted for judicial approval.[202] The statute is poorly drawn, since the phrase 'same acts or ordinances' refers grammatically to ordinances which were against the prerogative or common profit, and that would seem to introduce a statutory power to make such ordinances subject to judicial approval. But that seems improbable, and the intention was doubtless the reverse—namely that all ordinances should be submitted for approval to ensure that they were not unlawful.[203]

In an age of greatly increased legislative activity there was a desire for some legislative powers to be conferred on the central government; and such powers were especially required for use when Parliament was not in session. Parliament could settle the principle, leaving the details to the government. There were already precedents for the king to do things by parliamentary authority, as when letters patent were made *auctoritate parliamenti*; in such cases the king acted in his own name, without the lords and commons, yet with their prior

---

[198] See P. R. Roberts, 'The "Henry VIII Clause": delegated legislation and the Tudor principality of Wales' in *Legal Record and Historical Reality*, ed. T. G. Watkin (1989), 37–49.

[199] 31 Hen. VIII, c. 8; above, 64. The judges had opined in 1531 that proclamations made by the king on the advice of his Council 'should be of as good effect as any law made by Parliament': in Elton, *Tudor Constitution*, 27 (letter from Cromwell, redated 1531); *Studies*, i. 273 (dated 1535). But they were apparently referring to the exercise of acknowledged prerogative powers: above, 64 n. 62.

[200] Holdsworth, *HEL*, iv. 100.

[201] It was said that bye-laws could not be made to bind outsiders: below, 302.

[202] 19 Hen. VII, c. 7; pr. Elton, *Tudor Constitution*, 34; and see below, 165 n. 50. It was also enacted that they should not restrain members from suing in the king's courts.

[203] This was the later judicial interpretation: *Case of the Tailors of Ipswich* (1614) 11 Co. Rep. 53.

authorization.[204] The next step was for a parliamentary statute to delegate limited powers of legislation to the king.[205] An example may be found in 1504, when Henry VII was given the power to annul acts of attainder by letters patent.[206] But it was the Reformation Parliament which established delegated legislation in its widest forms. In 1531 commissioners of sewers were empowered to make perpetual 'laws and statutes' within the scope of their commissions, provided they were certified into Chancery and given the royal assent.[207] In 1532–4 we find instances of powers to bring a statute into operation, in whole or in part, or to inhibit its operation.[208] In 1534 the king was authorized to appoint commissioners with power to decide which canons and constitutions of the Church should continue in force, and their decisions were to have the force of law once confirmed by the king under the great seal.[209] Two years later, as we have seen, the king was empowered to alter the royal succession by patent or last will, such appointment to be as effective as if the Crown had been given 'by the full and immediate authority' of Parliament.[210] At the same time it was provided that the king's successor should have power to repeal any statutes passed while he was under the age of 24.[211] And in 1543 the Laws in Wales Act empowered the king to 'change, add, alter, order, minish, and reform, all manner of things afore rehearsed, as to his most excellent wisdom and discretion shall be thought convenient; and also to make laws and ordinances for the common wealth and good quiet of his said dominion of Wales . . .'.[212] These measures—together with the Statute of Proclamations, already noticed[213]—conferred large powers on the Crown, and yet in doing so they consistently emphasized that the lawmaking authority did not rest in the king alone but derived from Parliament.

[204] This was remarked upon in the Inner Temple in the 1490s: Port 135, pl. 98.

[205] See, generally, Dunham, 'Regal Power and the Rule of Law', at 31–2.

[206] 19 Hen. VII, c. 28; pr. Elton, *Tudor Constitution*, 23–4. The statute only applied to attainders between 1484 and the date of enactment.

[207] 23 Hen. VIII, c. 5, ss. 12, 14. This clarified the lawmaking power introduced in 1427, which was thought not to extend beyond the duration of each commission. The need for the royal assent was removed in 1571: 13 Eliz. I, c. 9. A similar power was given to commissioners for rebuilding castles in 1555: 2 & 3 Phil. & Mar., c. 1, ss. 3–7.

[208] 23 Hen. VIII, c. 20; pr. Elton, *Tudor Constitution*, 352 (and see the confirmation recited in 25 Hen. VIII, c. 20); 25 Hen. VIII, c. 21.

[209] Act for the Submission of the Clergy 1534, 25 Hen. VIII, c. 19; below, 248. The commissioners were not in the event appointed. Cf. the similar fate of the commission to investigate Welsh law (1536), where the power of final decision was given to the Council: below, 106.

[210] 28 Hen. VIII, c. 7, ss. 9–10; above, 60.

[211] 28 Hen. VIII, c. 17; replaced by 1 Edw. VI, c. 11. The power was exercisable by letters patent with proclamations; but it never took effect.

[212] 34 & 35 Hen. VIII, c. 26; Roberts, 'The "Henry VIII Clause"'; below, 106. The wording was not in fact new but was borrowed from that of the so-called Statute of Rhuddlan 1284 (*SR*, i. 55). The 1536 statute for Wales had given the king a power of partial suspension or revocation: see also *Tudor Royal Proclamations*, i. 253–4, no. 173.   [213] 31 Hen. VIII, c. 8; above, 64.

Parliamentary privilege

The members of both houses of Parliament were entitled to certain privileges in connection with legal proceedings in the courts. Peers charged with capital offences could claim to be tried by their peers rather than by a common jury;[214] and in civil cases, at any rate by the middle of the sixteenth century, they were entitled to challenge the array if no knights were empanelled.[215] These were not strictly parliamentary privileges, confined to the periods of sitting, but permanent privileges attaching to their nobility. While Parliament was in session, they additionally enjoyed exemption from arrest and civil suit.[216] There was also said to be a privilege of appearing by attorney in cases where personal attendance in court was normally required.[217] None of these privileges belonged to the wives of peers,[218] or the sons of dukes, marquesses, and earls, whose titles of 'lady' and 'lord' were purely a matter of courtesy.[219] There was no noble caste, for legal purposes, in England.[220]

Members of the lower house obviously had no permanent status analogous to that of peers, since their status ended with each parliament, but they—and their household servants[221]—enjoyed the same privilege of exemption from arrest and imprisonment during a parliamentary session, and this privilege occasioned several legal arguments in the sixteenth century. The first question was whether the privilege applied to someone who was already in execution for debt before the parliament began. George Ferrers MP was released in such a case in 1542, through the intervention of the serjeant at arms, and the sheriffs of London were committed to the Tower for two days for breach of privilege. Both the liberation of Ferrers and the imprisonment for contempt, by the sole authority of the House of Commons, were new manifestations of power by that house. Moreover, according to Dyer, the proceedings were against the advice of the 'sages of the law' because they appeared to deprive the debtor of his debt.[222] An attempt to amend the law

---

[214] Below, 520.   [215] Below, 354.

[216] M. A. R. Graves, 'Freedom of Peers from Arrest' (1977) 21 *AJLH* 1–14. An example of a writ of privilege is CP 40/1018, m. 411 (Lord Darcy, 1517).

[217] *Ferrers v. Abbot of St Albans* (1500) Trin. 15 Hen. VII, fo. 9, pl. 12; KB 27/959, m. 40 (privilege not allowed in *praemunire*); *R. v. Lord de Clifford* (1505) CP 40/973, m. 518 (privilege recited for attorney to appear in ravishment of ward).

[218] With the exception of trial by peers, which was extended to peers' wives by statute: below, 520 n. 96. A peer's widow who married a commoner lost her status: below, 619.

[219] Richard Hesketh's reading (*c.*1508), fo. 66v; George Treherne's reading (1520) BL MS. Stowe 414, fo. 76v; *Duchess of Suffolk v. Bishop of Exeter* (1557) Owen 82, *per* Bendlowes sjt (duke's son need not be named 'lord' in writ); below, 520.   [220] See further below, 597–8.

[221] e.g. *Pays v. Seth* (1473) KB 27/849, m. 103 (privilege for 'serviens familiaris' of Richard Boughton MP); *Roo v. Wadeluff* (1486) CP 40/895, m. 104 (sim. for servant of Sir John Savage MP).

[222] *Ferrers' Case* (1542) Dyer 275a (with incorrect roll reference); Moo. 57, pl. 163, and Dal. 58, pl. 7, *per* Dyer CJ (1564); *HPHC 1509–58*, ii. 130–1; Elton, *Tudor Constitution*, 261–2, 275–7. For a consequential contract case see below, 870–1.

by statute in the 1542 session nevertheless failed. The question was reopened in the next session, when William Trewynnard MP was released from imprisonment for debt by the sheriff of Cornwall, in obedience to a writ of privilege from Parliament.[223] Trewynnard's creditors then sued the sheriff for the debt, as for an escape, and the sheriff demurred. No judgment was entered, but according to Dyer the court ruled in favour of the sheriff. Although the effect was to recognize the privilege, the court made it clear that the privilege did not operate to extinguish the debt; it was merely temporary, to enable the member to attend Parliament, and when the session was ended the creditors could renew the process.[224] The temporary nature of the privilege was confirmed in 1555 when Star Chamber proceedings against Gabriel Pleydell MP were stayed by writ of privilege, Pleydell being bound over to appear in court once Parliament was dissolved. The recognizance was complained of as a breach of privilege, but Portman and Broke CJJ and the queen's serjeants advised that it was not; and the Star Chamber gave judgment against Pleydell after the dissolution.[225]

Parliamentary privilege in the modern sense, notably freedom of speech in debate, seems to have been first clearly formulated in the Tudor period.[226] Although some speakers of the House of Commons, such as Thomas Moyle in 1542, formally claimed freedom of speech only for themselves as representatives of the commons, in the same way that speakers claimed the privilege of access to the king on behalf of the commons, it was nevertheless well understood by the time of Henry VIII that the commons also claimed a wider privilege for all members in respect of their deliberations.[227] Parliament itself was jealous of this privilege, and in 1512 Richard Strode MP obtained an act of Parliament to annul proceedings against him in the Stannaries arising from his speeches in the lower house.[228] In practice the privilege of free speech seems generally to have been acknowledged by the Crown as well.[229]

---

[223] Reported anonymously in Gell's reports, I, 36 Hen. VIII, fo. 39.

[224] *Courteney and Tomyewe (executors of Skewes) v. Chamond* (1545) KB 27/1134, m. 39; Dyer 59b; *HPHC 1509–58*, iii. 485 (and references there); 109 Selden Soc., pp. lvii, 3; J. Hatsell, *Precedents of Proceedings in the House of Commons* (1818 edn), i. 59–65; and cf. C78/1/36 (*Trewynnard v. Skewes*). The deceased creditor was John Skewes or Skewys (d. 1544), bencher of Lincoln's Inn.

[225] *Knight v. Pleydell ('Pleadall')* (1555) BL MS. Harley 2143, fo. 3 (from lost register); *HPHC 1509–58*, ii. 111; Hatsell, *Precedents*, i. 74–5.   [226] Elton, *Tudor Constitution*, 260–1, 266.

[227] This wider privilege, for every member to 'discharge his conscience, and boldly ... to declare his advice' without fear of royal displeasure, was eloquently claimed by Sir Thomas More as speaker in 1523: ibid. 270 (quoting from Roper's *Life of More*). See also Holdsworth, *HEL*, iv. 91.

[228] *Strode's Case* (1512) *HPHC 1509–58*, iii. 399–400; 4 Hen. VIII, c. 8.

[229] For an unusual exception see Loach, *Parliament and the Crown in the Reign of Mary Tudor*, 42, 139 (imprisonment of member in Tower for blockading the House of Commons and forcing a vote). See also Bernard, 'The Tyranny of Henry VIII', 117–18.

3

Freedom, the State, and the Individual[1]

IF a medieval Englishman were asked what it meant to be free, his answer would most probably have been given in terms of freedom from villeinage. Freedom was, first and foremost, the antithesis of private servility. In the Tudor period, however, as villeinage disappeared,[2] Englishmen may have begun to think about their freedom more expansively as including freedom from arbitrary governmental restraint, and to connect it with the fine-sounding words in chapter 29 of Magna Carta. The connection between Magna Carta and freedom from restraint would soon become embedded in popular constitutional thought, and yet its ancient words were being cast in a new role. Although the very uncertainty of its broad phrases was to be its strength in Tudor and Stuart times, in the fifteenth century chapter 29 was not taken as a guarantee of personal liberty. Indeed, readers in the mid-fifteenth-century inns of court had taken the words as narrowly as could be: 'peers' meant lords of Parliament, and 'judgment of his peers' referred only to trials of peers for felony; 'take' meant arrest by writ of *capias*; and, most perversely of all, 'right and justice' (at the end of the chapter) meant writs of right and *justicies*.[3] There was nothing yet in the way of broad principle. Moreover, no remedy was laid down by the statute for dealing with infringements. The 1368 statute of due process, mentioned by some of the readers on Magna Carta, merely provided that whatever was done contrary to these enactments should be void; but a mere declaration of nullity was no remedy for someone who was currently being deprived of liberty, and it gave no redress for harm already suffered. The remedy most discussed by the readers was the common-law action of false imprisonment, to which we shall turn in a moment. It was occasionally debated, however, whether a special action might be founded on the legislation itself.[4] By the beginning of the sixteenth century such actions are indeed found in the plea rolls,

---

[1] For this section see J. H. Baker, 'Personal Liberty under the Common Law 1200–1600' in *The Origins of Modern Freedom in the West*, ed. R. W. Davis (1995), 178–202, repr. in *CLT*, 319–47; introd. to *Cases from the lost Notebooks of Sir James Dyer*, i (109 Selden Soc.; 1994), pp. lxxvi–lxxxv.

[2] See below, 598–607.   [3] Baker, 'Personal Liberty', at 335–6.

[4] CUL MS. Ii.5.43, fo. 40v; Derbyshire Record Office, MS. D3287, unfol. Both texts refer to a controversy on the question. St German queried whether an action would lie on Magna Carta in respect of a Chancery suit: *A Little Treatise*, ed. Guy, 121.

chiefly in respect of coercion to appear in irregular lawsuits before individual royal councillors or conciliar committees. There is no reported example, and so we do not know the nature of any underlying debates, but the actions—always against the opposing party rather than the offending councillor or minister—were sometimes successful.[5] It is particularly noteworthy that some of the indictments found against Empson and Dudley in 1509 alleged infringements of Magna Carta.[6] The great charter was growing new teeth.

FALSE IMPRISONMENT

Freedom from unwarranted restraints on liberty was to some extent protected by the ordinary law of trespass. False imprisonment was an actionable wrong, and the action lay not only against the person who first laid hands on the prisoner but also against the servant who turned the key and the gaoler who kept the key.[7] If an imprisonent was proved, the defendant—whatever his status—had to justify it under some rule of law which gave him a power of arrest or detention. It was therefore a common remedy against a public official, such as a sheriff, bailiff, or constable, alleged to have exceeded or abused his authority. Most of the actions in the rolls, which are numerous, arose from arrests on suspicion of felony. But the action had wider uses as well. For example, it could be used in jurisdictional disputes, as in challenging the power of bishops to imprison offending clergy,[8] or in the case of 1495 (known to Coke and Dyer) where it was used to question the scope of ecclesiastical jurisdiction over defamation.[9]

Arrest for felony was not a prerogative of the government or of public officials, because, as was said in 1499, 'everyone is an officer of the law to arrest felons'.[10] But no one could arrest without cause. The law was well settled by 1500 that in order to justify an arrest it was necessary to show that a felony had actually been committed, and that the defendant suspected the plaintiff of having committed it; it was not necessary to show that the plaintiff had in fact committed it.[11] It was

---

[5] See 94 Selden Soc. 72–3; below, 192–3. The earliest precedent so far discovered is from 1501. The actions were framed either on Magna Carta or on one of the statutes of due process.

[6] These were indictments for misdemeanour and were never tried: below, 582.

[7] It was held in *Whele's Case* (1483) Hil. 22 Edw. IV, fo. 45, pl. 9, that a servant who has the key to a prison, and knows someone is inside, is chargeable with the imprisonment, and that imprisonment even for one hour is actionable. See also Co. Inst. ii. 52–5, 186–7, 482.

[8] See 1 Hen. VII, c. 4, empowering ordinaries to imprison clerks and religious men for 'fleshly incontinency' without being liable to actions of false imprisonment.

[9] *Warner* v. *Hudson* (1495) CP 40/934, m. 327; Hil. 10 Hen. VII, fo. 17, pl. 17; Co. Inst. ii. 55; Co. Inst. iii. 42.

[10] Case at Greene's reading (Inner Temple, 1499) *Moots*, 300; differently reported in Port 163, no. 65. Cf. fifteenth-century reading on Magna Carta, Library of Congress Law MS. 139, p. 34 (tr. 'without mainour the bailiff or constable or known officer shall arrest, and no other man').

[11] Hil. 7 Hen. IV, fo. 35, pl. 3, *per* Gascoigne CJ; *Anon.* (1487) Pas. 2 Hen. VII, fo. 15, pl. 1; *Wynslowe* v. *Cleypole* (1489) Mich. 5 Hen. VII, fo. 4, pl. 10; CP 40/910, m. 340; *Waller* v. *Debenham* (1493) 1 Caryll

common to plead a cause of suspicion, such as 'common rumour and repute' (*communis vox et fama*),[12] or circumstantial evidence,[13] but arguably it was unnecessary to do so.[14] In the case of non-felonious wrongs, arrest without writ was generally permitted only to prevent a breach of the peace or its continuance,[15] and therefore the offender had to be released once the trouble was over,[16] unless he refused to give surety to keep the peace.[17] There was an exception in the case of a serious assault which might result in death, in which case the offender could be detained until it became apparent whether the victim would live.[18] There was also a power to arrest suspicious persons found outdoors in the night until they found surety for their good behaviour,[19] and there seem to have been other cases in which offenders could be set briefly in the stocks to make an example of them.[20] In these cases the power of arrest was usually said to be exercisable only by a constable or other officer of justice,[21] though it was said in 1488 that 'everyone may arrest common nightwalkers, because it is for the common good'.[22] The only other regular form of arrest was by a sheriff or bailiff executing a writ of *capias*.

125 at 128; *Warner* v. *Hudson* (1494) Hil. 10 Hen. VII, fo. 17, pl. 17; CP 40/934, m. 327; J. Rastell, *Exposiciones Terminorum* [*c.*1523], sig. A7, and (1527 edn), fo. 11; *Anon.* (1535) Trin. 27 Hen. VIII, fo. 23, pl. 22, *per* Fitzherbert J.

12 Mich. 5 Hen. VII, fo. 4, pl. 10. Cf. Pas. 2 Hen. VII, fo. 15, pl. 1, where it is suggested that common repute was an insufficient cause of arrest without personal knowledge of the grounds for suspicion.

13 e.g. *Freman* v. *Wylde* (1528) KB 27/1069, m. 111; *Anon.* (1535) Trin. 27 Hen. VIII, fo. 23, pl. 22 (stolen goods in plaintiff's possession). Or simply that the plaintiff was vagrant: *Fraunceys* v. *Warner* (1528) KB 27/1069, m. 64d; *Anon.* (1554) Gell's reports, I, Pas. 1 & 2 Phil. & Mar., fo. 10.

14 *Cooche* v. *Davys* (1523–4) Spelman 134, 214; CP 40/1039, m. 540.

15 e.g. *Fyssher* v. *Burnham* (1489) Mich. 5 Hen. VII, fo. 6, pl. 12; KB 27/913, m. 37d; Fitz. J.P. 48v (constable justifies imprisonment for one hour for breach of peace); *Pycher* v. *Boner* (1511) CP 40/995, m. 488 (constable justifies imprisonment for affray); *Flemyng* v. *Howles* (1513) CP 40/1002, m. 342 (justifies imprisonment for affray, by command of JP).

16 Mich. 22 Edw. IV, fo. 35, pl. 16; *Anon.* (1546/7) Brooke Abr., *Faux Imprisonment*, pl. 6.

17 FNB 48v–49; *Stanclyff* v. *Turton* (1520) KB 27/1034, m. 36; *Cumberford* v. *Aleyn* (1520) CP 40/1029, m. 614 (demurrer).

18 Pas. 10 Hen. VII, fo. 20, pl. 8, *per* Kebell sjt; Fitz. J. P. 49. Precedents: *Ex parte Hancoke* (1511) KB 29/143, m. 16 (returned to *habeas corpus*); *Ex parte Annesley* (1514) KB 29/146, m. 15 (sim.); *Wykes* v. *Grey* (1518) KB 27/1026, m. 60; *Cryspyn* v. *Ryder* (1556) CP 40/1168, m. 1200; *Cryspyn* v. *Mychell* (1557) CP 40/1169, m. 649.

19 Mich. 13 Hen. VII, fo. 10, pl. 10 (tr. 'all the justices said that it is permissible for every constable to arrest suspect persons who go in the night, and sleep in the day, or who keep suspicious company').

20 e.g. *Miles* v. *Cryppys* (1510) KB 27/997, m. 103d (prostitution); *Hudson* v. *Penyngton* (1517) CP 40/1018, m. 444d (keeping a bawdy house); *Fynche* v. *Harman* (1519) KB 27/1031, m. 80 (barratry, breach of the peace, and seditious words); *Freman* v. *Hode* (1523) CP 40/1038, m. 536 (raising the hue and cry at midnight without reasonable cause).

21 For the power of justices of the peace to issue warrants see below, 270.

22 Mich. 4 Hen. VII, fo. 18, pl. 12, *per* Huse CJ and Fairfax J.; but cf. Hil. 4 Hen. VII, fo. 2, pl. 2, *per* Kebell sjt (must be official watchmen). In Mich. 13 Hen. VII, fo. 10, pl. 10, the judges said the constables could require neighbours to assist them.

Arrest or detention outside the ordinary rules of law was sometimes defended by alleging local custom. But the courts showed considerable hostility towards customs which impinged upon liberty. Thus, in 1481, Bryan CJ held that a mayor could not prescribe to imprison an affrayer until he found surety to keep the peace. Even the Common Pleas could not do that, and such a power could not rest on usage.[23] Yet this was, as we have seen, a power claimed by constables and justices. The following year, a defendant in false imprisonment pleaded a custom for the mayor of a borough to arrest anyone on suspicion of felony and imprison them for three days in the town gaol before taking them to the nearest king's gaol. Bryan CJ retorted: 'You cannot have this prescription, for it is completely against common right and all reason', in that it did not allow for any means of release within the three days, or for bail, and if one could prescribe for three days (as in this case) another might prescribe for three weeks or three years. The case was adjourned without known result.[24] Four years later, two defendants pleaded a custom of London for parish beadles to arrest people found in adultery, take them to the sheriffs' counter,[25] and leave them there in custody. Bryan CJ was against the plea because they had not said how long they left the plaintiff in the counter; but the judges were divided as to whether the prescription was in principle good, the main doubt being that adultery was a 'spiritual' matter beyond the cognizance of the temporal authorities.[26] No judgment was given, but as in the other cases there is clearly a sense that liberty ought not to be eroded on the basis of mere local usage.[27] A fortiori, a private person ought not to use imprisonment as a means of preventing a civil trespass.[28]

The action of false imprisonment was long established and in daily use; but it was nevertheless an imperfect guarantee of freedom from restraint. For one thing, it was retrospective. It could only be brought after the event, by someone who had

[23] Mich. 21 Edw. IV, fo. 67, pl. 48.

[24] Hil. 22 Edw. IV, fo. 43, pl. 4. Cf. 27 Edw. III, Lib. Ass. fo. 27, where the countess of Warwick claimed a franchise to imprison in her castle for three days and three nights before delivering to the king's gaol; the case was left undetermined.   [25] A city prison: below, 284.

[26] Gylys v. Walterkyn (1486) Hil. 1 Hen. VII, fo. 6, pl. 3; CP 40/893, m. 244.

[27] For local customs see also Gylmyn v. Staneley (1512) KB 27/1005, m. 79 (custom of York to imprison for forty days for breach of peace); Stretche v. Busshe (1521) CP 40/1033, m. 157 (custom of Tewkesbury to imprison for affray); Waldyeve v. Woodshawe (1523) CP 40/1040, m. 458 (custom of Tamworth to arrest for affray; demurrer); Vowell v. Hurste (1527) CP 40/1052, m. 728 (custom of Exeter to imprison for keeping a bawdy house; demurrer); Macotte v. Benett (1527) ibid., m. 627 (custom of Exeter to imprison for contempt of mayor); Vowell v. Hurste (No. 2) (1527) CP 40/1054, m. 537d (custom of Exeter to imprison women of ill repute). Cf. Letheley v. Adyson (1529–30) CP 40/1063, m. 402 (plea justifying arrest by mayor for scandalous words impugning the immemorial right of Chichester to take market rolls, held bad on demurrer).

[28] There was doubt even as to the sweeping terms of 21 Edw. I, De Malefactoribus in Parcis: see Broun v. Seger, Vesek v. Segar (1514–16) CP 40/1006, mm. 352, 455 (servant of countess of Devon justifies for hunting in park; demurrer, but no judgment); Colvyle v. Warner (1531) CP 40/1071, m. 510 (bishop of London's park-keeper justifies imprisonment of plaintiffs until they agreed not to hunt again; demurrer, but no judgment).

regained sufficient freedom to be able to launch an action, against someone whom it was practicable to sue; and it lay to recover monetary compensation, not liberty itself. The rule that an action could not be brought against the Crown was not a serious drawback, in so far as the king did not personally lock up his subjects. There was always an agent who made the arrest or kept the keys, and was therefore liable to suit. But where an arrest was ordered on high by the king's Council, or by a justice of the peace, or some other authority closely associated with governmental power, the efficacy of a common-law action which required the cooperation of the sheriff was necessarily limited. The worst case was someone kept so closely and for so long that there was no practicable recourse to justice. Before the development of *habeas corpus*, the only practicable solution was to petition the king's Council itself. And we find that, at any rate by early Tudor times, the Star Chamber could be sensitive to complaints of injustice committed by others. Sir Thomas Egerton at the end of the sixteenth century collected the following three precedents (1488, 1520, and 1529) from the early registers, now lost:[29]

December in the year 4 Hen. VII, Pilkington fined in ten marks and imprisoned in the Fleet for imprisoning a poor man. 13 February, 11 Hen. VIII, Sir John Townley to the Fleet for attaching one who had a cause here against him. 27 May, 22 Hen. VIII, ten pounds awarded to Bennet Tracy for wrongful imprisonment three quarters of a year in the castle of Jersey by Sir Hugh Vaughan.

Not long after these cases, Spelman reported that of Sir Humphrey Browne, a king's serjeant at law incarcerated in the Fleet in 1532, apparently on the king's orders, for offences against the Crown. After his release, Browne complained to the Star Chamber, and the legality of his imprisonment was discussed. Although no resolution in favour of liberty was arrived at, the case is of great interest as showing that the serjeant placed reliance on chapter 29 of Magna Carta in making out his case.[30] Bishop Gardiner must have been thinking in similar terms when he protested in 1548 that his imprisonment, without bail or any accusation being made, was contrary to law and deprived him of the inheritance of an Englishman.[31]

HABEAS CORPUS

Under the Tudors a more effective remedy against arbitrary imprisonment was developed in the form of the writ of *habeas corpus*. In the variety known as *corpus cum causa*, the remedy seems to have been pioneered by the Chancery, where its main

---

[29] HEHL MS. EL 2652, unfol. (sp. mod.).

[30] Spelman 184 (misdated). The apparatus in 93 Selden Soc. 184 confuses two incidents when Browne was in disgrace, the second being in 1540. For the date of the first case see *LP*, vi. 1635. Magna Carta, c. 29, seems also to have been relied upon in the earlier case of Sir Robert Sheffield: below, 93.

[31] *Letters of Gardiner*, 439–40.

purpose was to secure the review of inferior jurisdictions,[32] but in that context it could be used to challenge the grounds of an imprisonment, for instance where bail was wrongly refused.[33] Already in the fifteenth century we may find examples of *corpus cum causa* being used to challenge an unwarranted imprisonment other than by a court.[34] The King's Bench form of the writ, the classic *habeas corpus ad subjiciendum*,[35] was designed primarily for the removal from place to place of defendants on criminal charges;[36] but since it had to be returned 'together with the day and cause of detention' the court was able to review the justifications for imprisonment and to release prisoners if not satisfied, or to grant bail. The Common Pleas had a similar writ at its disposal,[37] though most known examples are writs of privilege— that is, where the party was a litigant or official of the court itself.

In the absence of privilege, the King's Bench writ does not seem to have been generally used to question causes of detention before the sixteenth century.[38] There is an example in the year books for 1499, where it was used to challenge a rearrest by the bailiff of a franchise, and the court said it was 'in their discretion to ask other men to inform them why [the party] should not be released on mainprise' and to grant bail.[39] In the time of Henry VIII there are several examples of *habeas corpus* being used to challenge causes of imprisonment, even in matters of state. For example, in 1511 a servant who had been arrested for some rambling words which were barely seditious, let alone treasonable, was discharged by the King's Bench on a writ of *habeas corpus*,[40] and a few years later a Welshman

[32] See below, 188.

[33] e.g. *Godard v. Mayor and sheriffs of London* (1500/01) C1/240/26; *Hoggekyn v. same* (1500/01) C1/241/51.

[34] e.g. *Ex parte Cornewe* (1475) C244/120/58 (arrest 'by special command of the king himself', tr.); *Scotteswell v. Keeper of Bedford Gaol* (c.1485) C1/78/79 (imprisonment without known cause). Cf. *Lordwyn v. Thymbilby* (1510) C1/330/2 (alleged villeins seek *subpoena* against lord of manor, who has them under close arrest, to bring them into court).

[35] The operative words were 'have the body of N. before us to undergo and receive what our court should then and there order'. A variant was the *habeas corpus ad standum recto*.

[36] e.g. for a gaol delivery: see KB 29/140, m. 18 (*habeas corpus ad subjiciendum* to bailiff of Westminster to produce all his prisoners with the causes of their detention, 1509). Most returns in the early Tudor period are that the applicant was arrested and detained for suspicion of felony.

[37] See 109 Selden Soc. 54 (fifteenth-century precedent collected by Dyer from Jenour). There is little evidence of its use. For writs returnable before Common Pleas judges at their houses, see *Ex parte Yngoldesby* (1551) CP 40/1147A, m. 754; *Ex parte Restwold* (1551) CP 40/1147B, m. 133; *Ex parte Warde* (1558) CP 40/1174, m. 710.

[38] Cf. *Kayser's Case* (1465) KB 27/818, m. 143d; cited in Dyer's reports, 109 Selden Soc. 108, in Catlyn CJ's precedent book, Alnwick Castle MS. 475, fo. 30, and in Co. Inst. ii. 55; iii. 42. But this was a writ of privilege. The Elizabethan cases cited in Co. Inst. ii. 55, from Dyer's unpublished reports, were also cases of privilege.

[39] *Ex parte Broke* (1496) 1 Caryll 296; Mich. 13 Hen. VII, fo. 1, pl. 1 (misdated); KB 27/936, m. 39d (rearrest by bailiff of Westminster on a *capias ad satisfaciendum*).

[40] *R. v. Prior of Dunstable*, ex parte *Hope* (1511) KB 29/143, m. 10. He said (sp. mod.) that his master had been committed to the Tower 'and he said and if he had killed the king he would say no more

arrested by the marshal of the household as a vagabond was similarly discharged.[41] Then again, in 1518, one Thomas Aprice—detained by command of Cardinal Wolsey—was released by *habeas corpus* in the King's Bench because the attorney-general would not support the detention.[42] The precedent was collected over forty years later by Dyer CJ, when marshalling authorities on the scope of the remedy.[43] Aprice was probably implicated in the feud between Wolsey and Sir Robert Sheffield, a bencher of the Inner Temple, formerly speaker of the Commons and recorder of London, a dispute which was known to Coke.[44] Sheffield had been accused by Wolsey of harbouring two murderers, Milner and 'Rice' (presumably the same as Aprice, or Ap Rhys), though he claimed the accusation was motivated by malice.[45] Sheffield's protestation is credible, since he had become leader of the anti-clerical faction in the Commons and Wolsey's political opponent.[46] In one outburst he had even come close to accusing Wolsey of treason.[47] However, despite obtaining a pardon—which Wolsey forced him to cut up—he did not benefit from his own *habeas corpus*, minuted in the same roll as Aprice's, which is returned 'by command of the king alone'.[48] He died in the Tower the same year. Another of Dyer CJ's precedents was from 1546, when John Hogges and Thomas Heyth, after being committed to the Tower 'by order of the king's Council', were removed into the King's Bench by *habeas corpus* and committed to the marshal there.[49] They seem to have been common criminals. At any rate, they were sentenced to death the same term for receiving a thief.[50] But that was not the cause stated in the return, and—as Dyer CJ noted—the legal significance of these precedents was that they established the authority of the King's Bench to examine the cause of imprisonment of any prisoner in the realm, even if committed by the Council, and to commit, bail, or enlarge him as they thought expedient.

words to them'. Cf. *Ex parte Fory* (1512) KB 29/144, m. 17d (sp. mod. 'If the king of England were dead I know one of the lords shall be king'; bailed, absconded, and outlawed).

[41] *R. v. Marshal of Household*, ex parte *Ap Morgan* (1516) KB 29/148, m. 26.

[42] KB 29/150, m. 34 (Mich. 1518). There are many other examples of *habeas corpus* in the controlment rolls (KB 29), but they are difficult to evaluate in the absence of reports.

[43] 109 Selden Soc. 77.

[44] Co. Inst. ii. 55 refers to an indictment for imprisonment contrary to Magna Carta; but the reference given there is wrong.

[45] SP 1/16/140–4; *LP*, ii. II. 3951; KB 27/1021, Rex m. 10 (indictments as accessory to murder by Milner; pardoned, 1516). Some further details of this feud, from unarranged Star Chamber material in PRO, STAC 10/4/2, are given in J. A. Guy, *The Cardinal's Court* (1977), 76–8.

[46] *History of Parliament 1509-58*, iii. 305. For Sheffield's role in the dispute over benefit of clergy, see below, 538.   [47] A. F. Pollard, *Wolsey* (1929), 74.

[48] *Ex parte Sheffield* (Trin. 1518) KB 29/150, m. 18 (tr. 'committed by command of the lord king alone, and this is the cause and no other'; recommitted to the Tower).

[49] KB 29/179, m. 13 (Pas. 1546).

[50] KB 29/179, m. 4d (convicted as accessories to William Hynde of Southwark); *LP*, xxi. I. 1166(18) (pardon for Heyth, 7 June 1546).

In the same period we find a prisoner released because he had been arrested merely for slander,[51] and others because no indictments were found against them.[52] Dyer CJ also recalled how, when he was a student, the judges of the Common Pleas had disallowed a general return of a committal to the Tower by the mighty Thomas Cromwell as a member of the Council.[53] There was probably not yet a broad principle outlawing general returns, since there are other examples in the King's Bench where they were upheld—maybe in cases where the court knew of criminal proceedings against the applicants.[54] But the courts had found an effective means of curbing arbitrary power, whether exercised by ministers of the Crown or by any other person exercising an authority or jurisdiction which deprived a subject of his liberty.[55]

WRITS OF PROTECTION

The common law had long recognized the power of the Crown to place a person temporarily outside the reach of the courts by means of a writ of protection, the ordinary form of which was for persons on military or government service outside the realm.[56] It was available only for one year,[57] could not be issued for someone already in custody in a prior suit,[58] and could not extend to a cause of action arising after its date of issue.[59] It was unclear how far it was available for

---

[51] *Ex parte Hope* (1511) KB 29/143, m. 10. He had accused Sir Hugh Turbervile of treason.

[52] *Ex parte Mores* (1517) KB 29/149, m. 13d (arrest in Westminster Hall on suspicion of felony); *Ex parte Gardyner* (1518) KB 29/150, m. 32 (accused of sedition). In both cases there was an inquest *de gestu et fama* which found 'nothing but good' of the prisoner.

[53] *Ex parte Hynde* (1576-7) 4 Leon. 21; BL MS. Hargrave 373, fo. 226, and other manuscript reports; 94 Selden Soc. 74.

[54] e.g. *Ex parte Justice* (1513) KB 29/145, m. 14 (arrest '(tr.) at the lord king's command by Master Mewtys'; hanged later in the term); *Ex parte Page* (1515) KB 29/147, m. 23d (arrest '(tr.) by command of the lord king'); *Ex parte Eton* (1517) KB 29/149, m. 26 (committed to safe custody by Wolsey's command; then arraigned for felony); *Ex parte Aleyn* (1517) ibid., m. 26 (committal by Wolsey and other lords of the Council; then arraigned for felony).

[55] e.g. by ecclesiastical courts: *Ex parte Lawles* (1529) Port 66; KB 27/1071, m. 67 (delivery from ecclesiastical prison before absolution); *R. v. Smyth* (1534) Spelman 52, 169 (clerk attaint removed from ecclesiastical prison to establish effect of pardon). But the procedure was not appropriate where a regular review procedure existed: below, 215 (Admiralty).

[56] There were various statutory restrictions: 13 Ric. II, stat. 1, c. 16.

[57] Hil. 39 Hen. VI, fo. 38, pl. 3. In 1510 a bill was introduced in the Lords forbidding the issue of protections unless they were expressly limited to one year: HLJ, i. 7a. See also HLJ, i. 16, 26.

[58] J. Rastell, *Exposiciones Terminorum* [c.1523], sig. F3; *Thurland's Case* (1558) Dyer 162b; Dal. 23, pl. 2. In *Barker* v. *Deyson* (1529) CP 40/1061, m. 616, a protection was disallowed on demurrer in an action of debt on a judgment; but it was pleaded for only one of several defendants.

[59] Rastell, *Exposiciones Terminorum* [c.1523], sig. F3.

those still within the realm,[60] though there is some evidence that those with protections wore distinctive armbands in England.[61] Notwithstanding all the safeguards, the procedure was open to abuse if the cause was fictitious. But in such a case the other party could challenge the fact of overseas service,[62] and could have the protection annulled by *innotescimus*, as was done in the major dispute between Thomas Hunston MP and the bishop of Ely in 1484.[63] The courts did not allow protections readily, and their production often resulted in adjournments for advisement.[64] Particularly open to abuse was the prerogative writ of protection. Its established form was the protection *quia indebitatus nobis*, used to protect the king's debtors from losing their assets to creditors until the king's debts had been satisfied.[65] This was supposed to be used only to delay execution, not to stop an action.[66] In early Tudor times, however, the practice arose of issuing more sweeping protections under the great seal, without any cause shown, 'by reason of our royal prerogative, which we will not have disputed'. It is not yet clear how or why this started. The recipients seem usually to have been London tradesmen, though presumably the writs could not have been obtained without court favour.[67] In 1495,[68] and again in 1515,[69] the Common Pleas adjudged such protections to be invalid, and indeed in the latter case the sheriff was fined for obeying the prerogative writ and disobeying the judicial writ which it purported to overtake. The practice thereafter went into decline, but was to be revived in the early years of Elizabeth I and was not finally eliminated until the end of the century.

---

[60] *Re Lady E. S.* (*c*.1530/5) Wm Yelv. 292, no. 2, *per* Fitzherbert J. For the main point in this case—whether a protection lay for a woman—see below, 618.

[61] *Weston* v. *Graunt* (1539) CP 40/1103, m. 332 (sp. mod. 'W. hath gotten a protection and hath a ring about his arm, and by reason of the same what goods so ever he hath of any man he will never pay them').

[62] e.g. *Norton* v. *Bromley* (1531) CP 40/1071, mm. 410d, 414d (plaintiff alleges that defendant is living in London, and his protection is disallowed).

[63] *Hunston* v. *Bishop of Ely, Tymperley, and others* (1484-5) Mich. 2 Ric. III, fo. 13, pl. 35; KB 27/893, m. 91. William Tymperley obtained a protection on grounds of service in Calais (C244/135/32), but it was annulled on proof that he remained in Gravesend. Another protection was obtained on 12 Feb. 1485, but it apparently lapsed on the death of Richard III. In the end the plaintiff was nonsuited.

[64] e.g. *Fitzherbert* v. *Alman* (1499-1501) KB 27/955, m. 39 (protection dated 24 Nov. 1499, because in Calais; no judgment); *Scrope* v. *Earl of Surrey* (1513-15) CP 40/1004, m. 444 (allowed, but a *rescire facias* granted); *Boureman* v. *Levyns* (1555) KB 27/1175, m. 109 (allowed a term later). In *Bryan* v. *Sandys* (1512) CP 40/998, m. 130, Sir William Sandys 'of London' was not allowed a protection granted to Sir William Sandys 'nuper de Vyne'.

[65] FNB 28B; *Stringfellow* v. *Brownesoppe* (1549) Dyer 67b; *Polsted* v. *Cockerell* (1551) CP 40/1147A, m. 737. See 109 Selden Soc., pp. lxxxiv–lxxxv.   [66] 25 Edw. III, stat. 5, c. 19.

[67] In the 1515 case, below, the recipient (a London fishmonger) was described in the protection as a groom of the king's chamber. The 1495 protection was for a London vintner. A form of prerogative protection for a London draper (temp. Hen. VIII) may be found in Bodl. Lib. MS. Rawlinson C.339, fo. 43v.

[68] *Devvkke* v. *Halman* (1495) CP 40/934, m. 124; 109 Selden Soc. 153.

[69] *Isaac* v. *Camden* (1515) CP 40/1010, m. 66d; Rast. Ent. 316 (335v); 109 Selden Soc. 152. The writ he produced was only for one year, though Camden had a patent of protection for four: *LP*, i. 3324(15).

PURVEYANCE AND PRE-EMPTION

The prerogative power of the Crown to requisition provisions for the king's household and armed forces had long been regarded as an arbitrary infringement of private property, and was a source of continuous grievance, not least because the Crown could set favourable prices and pay at its own convenience. Despite numerous parliamentary attempts to control it, purveyance remained a significant source of royal income throughout the Tudor period. A Crown Office precedent book from the beginning of the sixteenth century contains numerous examples of commissions to take provisions for the king's household, navy, and army. These show that purveyance was not limited to consumables, such as victuals, fodder, fuel, and their transport, but included raw materials (such as timber, or even parchment for the central courts) and also specialized labour (such as carpenters and shipwrights to repair ships).[70] The commissions always specified that payment should be reasonable, but there was no regular means of admeasurement in the courts. The system was obviously open to abuse, and even a lord chancellor (Wolsey) was accused of taking provisions for himself under colour of purveyance for the household.[71] In 1549 most forms of purveyance were abolished, save with the consent of the supplier and an agreed price, and an attempt was made to shift the burden of supporting the royal household from poorer farmers on to sheep-owners and clothiers; but this proved controversial and the legislation was not renewed.[72] Attempts were then made under Mary I to impose tighter restrictions on commissions of purveyance—which were thenceforth to be in English—and to regulate the process of seizure.[73] But the institution continued into the reign of Elizabeth I and was not finally abolished until 1660.

THE POOR

Though rarely troubling the central courts, the social problems caused by poverty and unemployment were a constant concern to local and central government throughout the period and resulted in several pieces of legislation designed to prevent the idle from being a burden upon the community.[74] The poor were a substantial section of the population, though there was no legal definition of poverty

---

[70] William Porter's precedent book, C193/142, ff. 81–98.

[71] Articles against Wolsey (1529) Co. Inst. iii. 93, nos. 33, 35.

[72] 2 & 3 Edw. VI, c. 3. See the useful summary in Gunn, *Early Tudor Government*, 130–1, and the sources cited there. For an attempt to enforce the statute see *Davers* v. *Wodhowse* (1551) CP 40/1148, m. 734.

[73] 2 & 3 Phil. & Mar., c. 6.

[74] For a general survey see P. Slack, *Poverty and Policy in Tudor and Stuart England* (1988); and his *The English Poor Law 1531-1782* (1990), which is mainly concerned with later periods. For the Tudor period see also Holdsworth, *HEL*, iv. 387–402.

and it was an elastic concept.[75] No one questioned the moral duty to support the aged and helpless, and it was recognized by Parliament in 1536 that paupers who lacked means through misfortune rather than choice ought not to be compelled to beg for their living.[76] The poor were also entitled to free writs and legal assistance.[77] On the other hand, much of the begging which disturbed Tudor England was perceived as a sign of unwillingness to work, and it was often aggravated by fraudulent misrepresentation on the part of those who 'delight to live in idleness'. Idleness was therefore a social evil to be eradicated by legal coercion. Indeed, a proclamation of 1511 referred to it as 'the mother and cause of all vices'.[78] The problem was hardly new, and had been addressed in rather vague terms by a number of fourteenth-century statutes which gave regulatory powers to the justices of the peace. In 1493 an attempt was made by proclamation to clarify and enforce the principal statute of 1383, and the new law was put into statutory form in 1495.[79] Vagabonds and idle persons were to be set in the stocks for three days and nights with only bread and water for sustenance, and every beggar who was unable to work was to return to the hundred where he last lived. University scholars and mariners—who had no wages to support them on the road—were not to be exempt from this punishment unless they had begging licences from their superiors. The punishment was later modified to one day and night in the stocks before being sent away, with three days and nights for anyone who came back.[80] The theory may have seemed clear enough to the king's councillors; but it had never proved easy to eradicate poverty by penal sanctions. The 1495 statute and 1511 proclamation produced no lasting effect, and the situation worsened considerably during the great dearth of the 1520s. There were still complaints that 'long suffering of idleness and vice unpunished' was leading to an increase in crime.[81] Yet by this time, although it was still the prevailing belief that most poverty was attributable to wilful idleness, there was a growing perception that the

---

[75] Huse CJ seems to have regarded the poor as those who were not gentlemen: *Fitzwater's Case* (1493) Pas. 8 Hen. VII, fo. 12, pl. 4 (tr. 'the church is in common for everyone, and so it is unreasonable that one should have a pew and two should stand... but it seems that the [bishop] will ordain a suitable place for gentlemen, and other suitable places for the poor'). Obviously this was not meant as an exhaustive analysis of society.

[76] 27 Hen. VIII, c. 25 (below). St German held that it would be contrary to the law of God to forbid the giving of alms generally: *Doctor and Student*, ed. Plucknett and Barton, 41, 101.

[77] See 11 Hen. VII, c. 12 (poor plaintiffs to have writs without payment, and to be assigned learned counsel and attorneys to act without reward); 23 Hen. VIII, c. 14 (pauper plaintiffs who fail to prosecute may be punished corporally in lieu of an award of costs); below, 146 n. 9, 378 n. 30 (no fees), 185 (free writs), 194, 203, 430 (free counsel). Such suits leave little trace in plea rolls, though there is a rare example of a bill *in forma pauperis* in (1539) KB 27/1113, m. 29d (action for 30s.).

[78] *Tudor Royal Proclamations*, i. 89, no. 63; cf. ibid. 191, no. 128 ('idleness, mother and root of all vices', 1530). This measure had been ordered by the Star Chamber: BL MS. Lansdowne 639, fo. 40v.

[79] 7 Ric. II, c. 5; *Tudor Royal Proclamations*, i. 33, no. 30; 11 Hen. VII, c. 2.

[80] 19 Hen. VII, c. 12.   [81] *Tudor Royal Proclamations*, i. 174, no. 118 (1527); 191, no. 128 (1530).

situation had deteriorated as a result of economic forces.[82] Moreover, to the humanist mind, poverty itself was a social evil which could be eliminated by good policy. Among those with policies to suggest was Christopher St German, taking inspiration from the poor-relief schemes in a number of European cities. In his influential parliamentary draft of 1531 he suggested a scheme of public works to provide employment for the poor, with funding both from charity and from rates, to be accompanied by heavier penalties for wilful vagrancy.[83]

The outcome of these concerns was the more elaborate statutory scheme of 1531, which nevertheless ignored the economic causes and concentrated on the evil of wilful poverty and its eradication.[84] Justices of the peace were empowered to grant begging licences to aged and impotent persons,[85] but anyone who begged without licence was to be punished with whipping or the stocks.[86] Punishment was introduced for physiognomists, palmists, and other fortune-tellers, since their activities were deemed to be a form of begging.[87] Able vagrants were to be sworn to return to their place of birth, or of last permanent abode, in order to be put to work. Apart from the concession that some poor people had no option but to beg for their living, so that control was more sensible than prohibition, there was still no hint of organized poor relief. St German's proposed job-creation scheme was not to be. Five years later, however, a more humanitarian—though short-lived—additional measure was introduced,[88] implementing some of St German's ideas.[89] Alms were to be collected by local authorities to support the aged, poor, and impotent persons who lived in their areas or were born there; and the clergy were to exhort their parishioners to give generously. Vagabonds returning to their places of origin were to be given food and drink at ten-mile intervals on the way. Indiscriminate doles were forbidden. Children between the ages of 5 and 14 who lived in idleness and were caught begging were to be found employment and put

---

[82] See the discussion (c.1530) in Starkey, *Dialogue*, ed. Mayer, 60–2.

[83] *St German on Chancery and Statute*, ed. Guy, 133–5, discussed at 29–30. This document (SP 6/7, pp. 55–74) was attributed by Elton to Cromwell's advisers, slightly later in the 1530s (*Reform and Renewal*, 73–4); but it is full of corrections in St German's hand and Guy has convincingly assigned it to him.

[84] 22 Hen. VIII, c. 12; continued by 28 Hen. VIII, c. 6; 37 Hen. VIII, c. 23; revived by 3 & 4 Edw. VI, c. 16; 5 & 6 Edw. VI, c. 2 (with provisions for collection of a poor rate); 2 & 3 Phil. & Mar., c. 5. It was finally repealed by 14 Eliz. I, c. 5, which nevertheless retained some of its essential features.

[85] The statute is ambiguous as to whether age was an indispensable requirement.

[86] The option of whipping had been first introduced by proclamation in 1530: *Tudor Royal Proclamations*, i. 191–3, no. 128.

[87] Cf. the legislation of the same year against gypsies, below, 615. See also 1 Hen. VIII, c. 9 ('mummers' liable to three months' imprisonment); *Tudor Royal Proclamations*, i. 352, no. 250 ('common players' treated as ruffians and vagabonds, 1545); 5 & 6 Edw. VI, c. 21 (wandering tinkers and pedlars).

[88] 27 Hen. VIII, c. 25.

[89] For a report to Cromwell on similar lines in 1535/6 see BL MS. Royal 18 C. VI; G. R. Elton, 'An Early Tudor Poor Law' (1953) 6 *Econ. Hist. Rev.* (2nd ser.) 55–67, repr. in *Studies*, ii. 137–54.

in service, with whipping as a punishment for refusal.[90] But humane compassion did not extend to the voluntarily idle. The provisions for sending 'valiant' beggars and sturdy vagabonds back to their places of origin, to find work, were reinforced with the new sanction that anyone who continued his roguish ways was to have 'the upper part of the gristle of his right ear cut clean off', and if after that he was found wandering in idleness he was to suffer death as a felon.

The 1536 act lapsed and was not renewed; but the 1531 scheme endured until 1572, apart from two years at the beginning of Edward VI's reign when a more draconian experiment was attempted. The experiment was introduced by a statute of 1547, under which every able person loitering or wandering about without seeking employment, or who left his employment in order to be idle, was to be deemed a vagabond, branded on the breast with a V, and adjudged a 'slave' for two years to any master offering him work. The master was obliged to feed him only on bread, water, and scraps ('refuse of meat'), and could force him to work 'by beating, chaining, or otherwise'. A slave who ran away was liable to become a slave for life, whereupon he was branded with an S. Other escaping vagabonds could be made slaves to cities and boroughs, in order to labour on road improvements and other public works. Slavery was apparently to be a new form of property; and masters were given the power to sell or lease their slaves.[91] This ill-judged attempt to introduce the Roman law of slavery into English law was a concrete example of Protector Somerset's reputed fondness for the Civil law.[92] But renaissance has its limits. The scheme met with little or no public support, and proved an utter failure. Only two years later it was repealed *tout court*.[93]

[90] In case this proved unpopular, anyone who refused to impose the punishment was liable to be put in the stocks.

[91] 1 Edw. VI, c. 3; repealed by 3 & 4 Edw. VI, c. 16, which revived the statute of 1530. Cf. Henry VIII's scheme, two years earlier, for impressing vagabonds into galley-service: *Tudor Royal Proclamations*, i. 352, no. 250 (1545).   [92] For the common lawyers' complaints of this in 1547 see below, 179–81.

[93] See C. S. L. Davies, 'Slavery and Protector Somerset: the Vagrancy Act of 1547' (1966) 19 *Econ. Hist. Rev.* (2nd ser.) 533–49.

4

The King's Dominions outside the Realm

ENGLISH law was not confined to England, though it did not run throughout the king's dominions, some of which were not subject to the common law or to the jurisdiction of the English courts. Some notice needs now to be taken of these other jurisdictions, albeit necessarily in outline. Although Henry VII was declared to have inherited 'the realms of England and of France... and all other seignories to the king belonging beyond the sea',[1] neither in 1485 nor in 1558 did the 'empire'[2] extend very far beyond the English shores and borders. Scotland was not yet included, even in name, and the Scots were treated as aliens or even as alien enemies.[3] The new world had been discovered, and voyages were made in Henry VII's time to Newfoundland under authority of letters patent which authorized the explorers to take possession of unoccupied territory in the king's name, make statutes, and appoint governors.[4] Voyages were also made to Iceland,[5] while regular trading with Africa began in the 1550s. But nothing was in fact annexed to the Crown.[6] The dominions of the Tudor kings extended no further north than Berwick and no further west than Ireland.

WALES[7]

The dominion or country of Wales consisted, until the 1530s, of the principality and the marcher lordships. The principality, strictly so called, consisted of the five westward counties which since the reign of Edward I had belonged to the princes

---

[1] *RP*, vi. 270.   [2] For the use of this phrase see above, 55 n. 6.

[3] Below, 616–17, 786. Berwick was in English control, and was represented in Parliament, but was outside the realm (e.g. for the purposes of writs of protection: Spelman 189, no. 2).

[4] See *CPR 1494–1509*, pp. 224 (1501), 320 (1506); below, 623 n. 235.

[5] *Smyth* v. *Hylton* (1528) CP 40/1058A, m. 635 (*assumpsit* against surety, alleging that principal had been to Iceland and returned; confessed).

[6] The law printer John Rastell had set out to annex Newfoundland in 1517, but the sailors had mutinied in Ireland and he had proceeded no further: *Rastell* v. *Thetford* (1522–3) KB 27/1042, m. 60; A. W. Reed, *Early Tudor Drama* (1926), 189–201 (based on REQ 3/192); J. A. Williamson, *The Voyages of the Cabots and the Discovery of North America under Henry VII and Henry VIII* (1929), ch. 6; below, 214. For the Russia Company of 1555 see below, 623.

[7] See generally T. J. Pierce, 'The Law of Wales: the last phase' (1963) *Trans. Honorable Soc. of Cymmrodorion* 7–32; R. R. Davies, 'The Twilight of Welsh Law 1284-1536' (1966) 51 *History* 143–64;

of Wales by a special kind of interrupted inheritance sanctioned by Parliament.[8] When there was no prince of Wales, the principality revested in the Crown without merging or losing its separate identity. The Crown appointed non-lawyers as justices (or chief justices) of north and south Wales, with power to hold great and petty sessions in the royal counties, having the powers of justices in eyre; but their jurisdiction had fallen into decay by Tudor times.[9] The marcher lordships were situated to the east of the principality, along the border with England. They were numerous,[10] and were in several ownership,[11] each with its own courts and customs.[12] In south Wales and Denbigh the lords kept up their right to hold eyres, but chiefly so that they could collect fines in return for not doing so. When the eyres (or 'great sessions') actually sat, they exercised a jurisdiction in felony and personal actions.[13]

Though annexed to the English Crown in the time of Edward I, these various territories were not part of the realm of England,[14] and they lay outside the original jurisdiction of the courts at Westminster.[15] They had their own courts, administering local custom, and it was not clear that they were subject to the surveillance of the King's Bench.[16] Even treason committed in Wales could not be

J. Goronwy Edwards, *The Principality of Wales 1267–1967: a study in constitutional history* (1969); R. A. Griffiths, 'Wales and the Marches' in *Fifteenth Century England 1399–1509*, ed. S. B. Chrimes and others (2nd edn, 1995), 145–72. Hale's work is still useful: *Prerogatives of the King*, ed. D. E. C. Yale (92 Selden Soc.; 1976), 21–32.

[8] The counties were Anglesey, Caernarvon, and Merioneth (in the north), Cardigan and Carmarthen (in the south). The duchy of Cornwall followed the same descent: *Chafyn v. Lord Sturton* (1553–4) Dyer 94a; CP 40/1155, m. 303; CP 40/1157, m. 114 (demurrer).

[9] Little is known of it for want of records.

[10] See T. B. Pugh, *The Marcher Lordships of South Wales 1415–1536: select documents* (1963).

[11] Some of them were in the king's hands before 1485. Bromfield and Yale (in the north) came to the Crown upon the attainder of Sir William Stanley in 1495 and were retained by the Crown until 1617. Few important lordships remained in private hands after the attainder of the duke of Buckingham in 1521.

[12] For a particular example see A. C. Reeves, 'The Great Sessions in the Lordship of Newport 1503' (1975) 26 *Bulletin of the Board of Celtic Studies* 323–41.

[13] Pugh, *Marcher Lordships*, 118–32, prints a roll of the 'Sessio Magni Itineris' at Brecon in 1503. He describes it as an assize roll, but it is *coram justiciariis itinerantibus*.

[14] See Thomas Frowyk's reading (Inner Temple, 1495) 113 Selden Soc. 38; *Bulkley v. Thomas* (1554) Plowd. 120v at 121v (tr. 'although Wales was for a long time under the rule of the kings of England, yet it was not part of the realm of England, nor were the people there bound by English law'); T. G. Watkin, 'Legal Cultures in Mediaeval Wales' in *Legal Wales*, ed. T. G. Watkin (2001), 21–39, at 21–3. Cf. the reading in BL MS. Harley 4990, fo. 161v, which treats Welshmen as *liberi homines* within Magna Carta on the ground that Wales was part of England at the time of the charter. Note also *Re Lady E. S.* (*c*.1530/5) Wm Yelv. 292, where Englefield J. treats Wales as being within the realm.

[15] See *Moots*, 128 (recovery of land in Wales utterly void); *Vernon v. Lodelowe* (1501) KB 27/961, m. 26 (error upon an assize of 20 Hen. VI on the ground that the king's writ does not run in the Marches); *Bulkley v. Thomas* (1554) Plowd. 120v at 121v (last note).

[16] See Mich. 21 Hen. VII, fo. 33, pl. 32 (no writ of error from Wales or Calais); *Re Earl of Derby* (1522) 2 Caryll 731 at 732, *per* Brudenell CJ (writ of error lies to Ireland or Wales).

tried in England.[17] However, it was said that litigation concerning real property in Wales could be pursued in England if there would otherwise be a failure of justice: for instance, if a marcher lord was party.[18] On the same principle, since a marcher lord could not send a writ to a bishop in another lordship, *quare impedit* could if necessary be brought in the Common Pleas for a church in Wales, the action being laid in the next adjacent English county.[19]

Although the old courts in Wales followed either Welsh or local custom, there was a noticeable tendency towards Anglicization in the early Tudor period. The marcher lords of Gower, for instance, held occasional eyres,[20] biannual 'head-shires', and monthly county courts to hear pleas of the Crown (which were laid as being against the lord's peace) together with all actions real and personal.[21] The felony jurisdiction seems to have been much the same as in England, both grand and petty juries being in use. The civil actions were modelled on those of the common law, including actions on the case, and by 1534 the common recovery was in use.[22] Under Henry VII English law was extended to parts of Wales by the royal prerogative when inhabitants of particular lordships were, by letters patent, granted common-law rights and freed from local customs, gavelkind[23] was replaced by primogeniture, and the control of intestate succession transferred from the escheator to the ordinary.[24]

Further Anglicization occurred, at any rate on the borders, through the activities of the Council in the Marches of Wales.[25] Founded in 1473 as the prince of Wales's council,[26] it was chiefly concerned with public order. It disappeared between 1483 and 1490, when it was revived upon the creation of Prince Arthur as

[17] *Dolbyn* v. *Ap Tudor* (1531–2) Spelman 156; KB 27/1083, m. 66 (abstr. 94 Selden Soc. 340); and see STAC 2/12; SP 46/3/5, ff. 20–21 (murder of recorder of Denbigh). Cf. *Clayton* v. *Traver* (1520) KB 27/1036, m. 35 (pr. 120 Selden Soc. 37); reported in 120 Selden Soc. 36 (appeal of murder committed at Oswestry in principality of North Wales; plea to jurisdiction; undetermined demurrer).

[18] Hale, *Prerogatives of the King*, ed. Yale, 28, citing fourteenth-century precedents; Mich. 21 Hen. VII, fo. 34, pl. 32, *per* Fyneux CJ; *Anon.* (1569) Dyer's reports, 109 Selden Soc. 172, no. 235.

[19] e.g. *Owen* v. *Stradlyng* (1530–1) Spelman 196; CP 40/1068, m. 530; *R.* v. *Stradlyng* (1532) CP 40/1074, m. 416 (special imparlance): actions in Herefordshire for the church of Narberth, now in Pembrokeshire.

[20] T. B. Pugh and W. R. B. Robinson, *Sessions in Eyre in a Marcher Lordship: a dispute between the earl of Worcester and his tenants in Gower and Kilvey in 1524* (1957).

[21] *Lloyd* v. *Cradock* (1524) SC 2/16/190–196 (right to hold eyre upheld in Council); Pugh, *Marcher Lordships*, 4–6.

[22] See W. R. B. Robinson, 'The County Court of the Englishry of Gower 1498–1500: a preliminary study' (1995–6) 29 *National Library of Wales Jnl* 357–89, at 365–73.

[23] Partibility of land among all the sons seems to have been the general custom in Wales.

[24] For the marcher lordship of Chirk (1506) see *CPR 1494–1509*, pp. 464–5. See further J. B. Smith, 'Crown and Community: the principality of Wales in the Reign of Henry Tudor' (1966) 3 *Welsh History Rev.* 145–71.

[25] C. A. J. Skeel, *The Council in the Marches of Wales* (1904); P. H. Williams, *The Council in the Marches of Wales under Elizabeth* (1958) (also discussing the earlier history); Elton, *Tudor Constitution*, 202–3; R. Horrox, *Richard III* (1989), 205–12; Gunn, *Early Tudor Government*, 67–70; Griffiths, 'Wales and the Marches', 158–65; below, 206–7.

[26] The prince's council also served as the duchy council for Cornwall. For Cornish petitions in the 1470s and 1480s see SC 8/E.1326, 1338–1359.

prince of Wales. Although it is said to have lapsed again on Arthur's death, there does not seem to have been a significant break in the legal arrangements, however irregularly they may have operated. Its authority extended to the four English border counties, and groups of non-residents common to these counties were appointed continuously to the commissions of the peace between the 1490s and the end of our period. A council was certainly functioning under the presidency of William Smith, bishop of Lincoln, at the time of Prince Arthur's death in 1502, and perhaps for some years thereafter.[27] It was revived in 1518,[28] then reconstituted and enlarged with fresh instructions in 1525 as Princess Mary's Council.[29] The new Council had extensive civil and criminal jurisdiction,[30] and was attended by lawyer members, including the assize judges of the Oxford circuit and some of the Welsh judges.[31] It may in practice have been more active in the border counties of England than in Wales, but it nevertheless marked the beginning of the process of extending English law to the latter.

Notwithstanding these arrangements, disorders in Wales remained a concern of the government and came to a head after Rhys ap Griffith's treasonable uprising in 1529, followed by the decision of 1534 that treason in Wales was not triable in the King's Bench.[32] The chief explanation for their prevalence was the fragmentation of authority there. There was also said to be a misconception that, because the Welsh spoke a different language, they were not equal to English subjects.[33]

[27] CPR 1494–1509, p. 295 (special commission of oyer and terminer to the bishop, as president of the Council in the Principality, and to seven others who were presumably members, 1502). The members (including the bishop until his death in 1514) appear on the commissions of the peace for the four border counties. See also Guy, 47 BIHR 295 (Welsh case at a joint session of the king's Council and the prince's council in the prince's council chamber, 1508); M. M. Condon, 'Ruling Elites in the Reign of Henry VII' in Patronage, Pedigree and Power in Late Medieval England, ed. C. Ross (1979), 116, 137 n. 35; Smith, 'Crown and Community', 160–1.

[28] LP, i. 4141, 4528 (special commission of the peace for Wales, the border counties, and the Marches, 1518); Grynys v. Hille (1518) CP 40/1021B, m. 335 (deposition in the Marches put in evidence; demurrer to the evidence); Elton, The Tudor Constitution, 202; Guy, The Cardinal's Court, 48 (mentioned in 1519 and 1521).

[29] See W. R. B. Robinson, 'Princess Mary's Itinerary in the Marches of Wales, 1525–27' (1998) 71 BIHR 233–52. The 1525 and 1526 instructions, probably drafted by Wolsey, survive in a number of later copies: ibid. 236 n. 19. The princess (aged 9 in 1525) only remained in the marches for two years.

[30] It included a commission of oyer and terminer, another 'for administration of justice and detention of causes, griefs and complaints to be made between party and party', a quo warranto jurisdiction, and the survey of crown lands: Instructions (1525) BL MS. Harley 6068, fo. 22v.

[31] e.g. the lawyer members in 1525–7 were Sir John Port (appointed JKB in 1525) and Serjeant Rudhale, assize JJ on the Oxford circuit; John Salter and George Bromley, deputy JJ of North Wales and Chester respectively; Richard Hassall (sol.-gen. for Wales) and Thomas Audley, the princess's learned counsel: BL MS. Harley 6068, ff. 22, 32v; Rudhale's membership is deduced from the commissions of the peace. All six were or had been members of the Inner Temple. Bromley and Salter were seated in Shropshire, Hassall in Cheshire (Port's native county), Rudhale in Herefordshire.

[32] Dolbyn v. Ap Tudor (1531–4) above. The mischief was recited in 27 Hen. VIII, c. 26, s. 3.

[33] Preamble to 27 Hen. VIII, c. 26.

The bold solution, evidently Cromwell's, was to abolish the remains of Welsh law, and bring Wales effectively under the English system of justice. The principal statute, passed in 1536,[34] has been referred to as an act of union. It recited that, 'Albeit the dominion, principality, and country of Wales justly and righteously is and ever hath been incorporated, annexed, united and subject to and under the imperial crown of England', nevertheless discords had arisen there as a result of the differences of laws and language. The act then declared, in the first section, that Wales should

be, stand, and continue for ever from henceforth incorporated, united, and annexed to and with [the king's] realm of England; and that all and singular person and persons, born and to be born in the said principality, country, or dominion of Wales, shall have, enjoy, and inherit all and singular freedoms, liberties, rights, privileges, and laws within this his realm and other the king's dominions as other the king's subjects naturally born within the same have, enjoy, and inherit.

It will be noted that this language did not purport to effect a union of what was already united, nor did it in terms make Wales part of the realm of England; but the words of subjection in the preamble ('subject to and under') were removed in the body of the act, and the Welsh were given the same status and rights as English subjects within England as well as Wales—including, by a later section of the act, representation in Parliament.

The second section of the statute abrogated Welsh customs of inheritance, and provided that in future all inheritable property in Wales should descend according to English law, without division or partition. It then enacted, more generally,

that the laws, ordinances, and statutes of this realm of England, for ever,[35] and none other laws, ordinances, ne statutes ... shall be had, used, practised, and executed in the said country or dominion of Wales, and every part thereof, in like manner, form, and order as they be and shall be had, used, practised, and executed in this realm, and in such like manner and form as hereafter by this Act shall be further established and ordained.

Although this section did not explicitly abolish local customs, which if reasonable were generally recognized by English law,[36] a clear intention was expressed in the preamble to 'extirp all and singular the sinister usages and customs differing from the laws of this realm', and the only local customs expressly saved—by a later

---

[34] Laws in Wales Act 1536, 27 Hen. VIII, c. 26. See W. L. Williams, 'The Union of England and Wales' (1907-8) *Trans. Honourable Soc. of Cymmrodorion* 47-117; P. Roberts, 'The English Crown, the Principality of Wales and the Council in the Marches 1534-1641' in *The British Problem c.1534-1707*, ed. B. Bradshaw and J. Morrill (1996), 118-47.

[35] As to whether this extended to earlier statutes see *Bulkeley* v. *Thomas* (1554) Plowd. 118

[36] The application of the English doctrine of local custom to Wales was acknowledged in *Anon.* (1579) Dyer 363 (custom of Denbigh town as to alienations of land by married women).

proviso—were those used in the three counties of North Wales. The absence of explicit words of abolition was connected with the provision for a law commission to 'enquire and search out, by all ways and means that they can, all and singular laws, usages, and customs used within the said dominion and country of Wales' and to report to the king's Council, so that a decision could be taken as to which of them should be allowed to stand.[37] There is no evidence that this enquiry was ever carried out, and therefore the statute was assumed to have abolished all the laws and customs which were not saved by the proviso for North Wales.[38] Any remaining Welsh tenures were converted into common-law tenures in 1543.[39]

The statute of 1536 proceeded to divide the marcher lordships and towns between the existing Welsh counties and the five newly created counties of Monmouth (which was placed under English jurisdiction), Brecknock, Radnor, Montgomery, and Denbigh.[40] Commissions were to be appointed to divide these new counties into hundreds. Although the liberties of the marcher lords were preserved,[41] the 'shiring' process brought their territories under the jurisdiction of sheriffs and justices appointed by the Crown, thereby greatly curtailing their autonomy.[42] Moreover, under contemporaneous legislation, lords lost their power to appoint their own justices.[43] All court proceedings were thenceforth to be in English, and no Welsh-speaker was to hold public office in England or Wales 'unless he or they use and exercise the English speech or language'.[44]

The Great Sessions for Wales

The 1536 legislation concentrated on criminal jurisdiction, which had been the government's chief concern. Although it incidentally established the inferior civil

[37] The statute expressly provided that the new counties of Brecknock, Radnor, Montgomery, and Denbigh should be subject to English law and such Welsh laws and customs as were approved by the Council. But in the cases of Glamorgan, Carmarthen, and Cardigan the statute provided that justice should be administered according to English law 'and after no Welsh laws'. The reason for this distinction is not made clear.

[38] Cf. the precedent of the proposed commission to examine the canon laws (1534), which likewise failed to function, leaving the transitional provision in permanent effect: below, 248–9.

[39] 34 & 35 Hen. VIII, c. 26, s. 36 (s. 91 in *Statutes at Large*).

[40] Some adjustments were later required: 28 Hen. VIII, c. 3. For lordships annexed to English border counties see *Tudor Royal Proclamations*, i. 250, no. 172.

[41] These were confirmed and clarified by 1 & 2 Phil. & Mar., c. 15.

[42] A separate statute authorized the appointment of justices of the peace in Wales and Chester: 27 Hen. VIII, c. 5. (This apparently grew from an independent proposal from John Puleston and others concerning the northern counties: Roberts, 'The "Henry VIII Clause"', 43.) Note also some preliminary measures in 1534: 26 Hen. VIII, cc. 4, 5, 11, 12; Lehmberg, *The Reformation Parliament* (1970), 209–10.

[43] 27 Hen. VIII, c. 24, which also abolished liberties to grant pardons for treason and felony. The act extended to England, Wales, and the marches of Wales.

[44] See, on this, P. R. Roberts, 'The Welsh Language, English Law and Tudor Legislation' (1989) *Trans. Hon. Soc. of Cymmrodorion* 19–75.

jurisdiction of counties and hundreds, there was as yet nothing in Wales corresponding to the central courts of common law at Westminster,[45] or their palatinate counterparts at Chester. The act did, perhaps as an afterthought, empower the king to erect such new courts of record as should be thought sufficient and convenient; but the implementation of that further stage of the reform was put off until about 1540, when a scheme was devised for a new system of superior courts in Wales.[46] Apart from the proposal for a chancellor and great seal for Wales, which was dropped,[47] the scheme was substantially adopted in 1541 and embodied in royal 'ordinances', which were approved by Parliament in 1543.[48] Instead of a chancery court there was to continue to be, as 'accustomed and used', a President and Council in the Dominion and Principality of Wales, with power to hear and determine causes assigned to them by the king. In each of the twelve[49] shires there were to be two six-day judicial sessions a year, known as the king's Great Sessions for Wales. For this purpose, the dominion was divided into four circuits, each of which was to have a 'person learned in the laws of England' as presiding justice.[50] These judges of the Great Sessions were in the event appointed from the benchers of the inns of court,[51] and began to wear robes identical in pattern to those of the judges in Westminster Hall but without the miniver facings.[52] They were empowered to hear all pleas of the Crown, assizes, and all real and personal actions, in as ample a manner as the King's Bench and Common Pleas in England. Real actions, and personal actions above 40s., were to be commenced by original writ sealed by one of the four 'original seals for justice' kept by the respective chamberlains. Other personal actions were to be commenced by bill. The courts were courts of

[45] The only territory brought under Westminster jurisdiction was that of the marcher lordships annexed to Monmouthshire.

[46] 'A Breviat of the Effectes devized for Wales' (c.1540/1) BL Cotton MS. Vitellius C.1, ff. 39–43; ed. P. R. Roberts (26 Camden Misc.; 1975), 31–47.

[47] The chancellor's jurisdiction would have supplanted the Council in the Marches. The 1536 act had erected a Chancery and Exchequer each for north and south Wales, but these were for revenue rather than judicial purposes. Nevertheless a great seal, or chancellor's seal, for Wales is said to have been made in 1548: APC, ii. 187, 218.

[48] 34 & 35 Hen. VIII, c. 26. The ordinances were issued earlier, under the royal prerogative and under the powers contained in the 1536 act: Roberts, 'The "Henry VIII Clause"', 46–7. The first justices had been appointed by patent on 28 June 1542, though plea rolls survive from August and September 1541.

[49] The statute made clear that, in addition, the town of Haverfordwest should continue to be a county in itself.

[50] In 1576 the number of justices in each circuit was increased to two (18 Eliz. I, c. 18), one of them becoming a chief justice.

[51] The first appointments were Nicholas Hare, John Pakington, and David Broke (all of the Inner Temple), and Thomas Holt (Middle Temple). See W. R. Williams, The History of the Great Sessions in Wales 1542–1830 (1899).

[52] See the brass of Thomas Holt (d. 1546), first justice of the North Wales circuit, at Aston, Warwickshire: 70 Trans. Monumental Brass Soc. 197. Oil paintings of slightly later date show that the robes were scarlet with black facings.

record, and in each circuit there were prothonotaries responsible for keeping plea rolls.[53] Writs of error lay from these courts, as from English courts of record, to the King's Bench. This system remained in place—together with an equity juris-diction acquired somewhat later[54]—until Wales was brought under the English court system in 1830.

IRELAND[55]

Ireland was the principal overseas dominion of the Crown, and long beset with problems of governance. Its constitutional relationship with England at the begin-ning of the Tudor period was similar to that of Wales, in that the lordship of Ireland was said in 1537 to depend and belong to the imperial Crown of England,[56] as 'the king's proper dominion of England, and united, knit and belonging to the imperial Crown of the same realm'.[57] Unlike Wales, however, it was governed by English law. Ireland was, indeed, the first common-law country outside England. It was stated by the justices in 1488 that Ireland was like a limb of England (*quasi membrum Angliae*) and used its laws;[58] while Peter Dillon, a bencher of Gray's Inn, went so far as to tell a fellow member of the inn in 1516 that Ireland and England were 'all one' because their laws were the same.[59] The Anglo-Irish—unlike, with rare exceptions, the Welsh—had long sent students to the inns of court and chancery, so that its future judges and practitioners were directly exposed to English legal learning;[60] and by 1541 there was a sufficient legal community in

[53] For the rolls (now held by the National Library of Wales) see E. J. Sherrington, 'The Plea-Rolls of the Courts of Great Sessions 1541–75' (1964) 13 *National Library of Wales Jnl* 363–73; K. O. Fox, 'An Edited Calendar of the First Brecknockshire Plea Roll of the Courts of the King's Great Sessions in Wales, July 1542' (1965) 14 id. 469–84; G. Parry, *A Guide to the Records of the Great Sessions in Wales* (1995).

[54] Parry, *Guide*, pp. viii–x, suggests there may have been an equity jurisdiction from the beginning, citing a bill of complaint of 1546 subscribed with an order to issue a subpoena. But this looks like a Chancery bill, signed by John Croke (a six clerk). The Carmarthen circuit judge was David Broke, not Croke.

[55] Little is known of the legal administration in Ireland for want of records, but a good deal has been written on Tudor governance there. See generally K. Nicholls, *Land, Law and Society in Sixteenth Century Ireland* (1976); B. Bradshaw, *The Irish Constitutional Revolution in the Sixteenth Century* (1979); S. G. Ellis, *Reform and Revival: English government in Ireland 1470–1534* (RHS, 1986); *Tudor Frontiers and Noble Power: the making of the British state* (1995).

[56] *Statutes at Large, passed in the Parliaments held in Ireland* (1786) i. 76, 90 (28 Hen. VIII, Ir., c. 2 and c. 5).

[57] ibid. i. 91 (c. 6). This claim was repeated in paraphrase at i. 156, in c. 19 ('the king's land of Ireland is his proper dominion, and a member appending and rightfully belonging to the imperial crown of the said realm of England and united to the same').

[58] Trin. 3 Hen. VII, fo. 10, pl. 3 (tr. from Latin).

[59] LI MS. Misc. 486, unfol. (tr. 'Note that Dyllon said to me that Ireland and England shall be (*serront*) [treated as] all one; the same law is used in both places etc.').

[60] See P. Brand, 'Irish Law Students and Lawyers in Late Medieval England' (2000) 32 *Irish Historical Studies* 161–73. Occasional attempts were made by the inns to exclude or restrict the number of Irish

Dublin for it to acquire its own professional society, known as the King's Inn (later the King's Inns).[61] Ireland was therefore, by reason of the identity of law and legal institutions, more closely allied to England juridically than Wales was before the Henrician union. From such little evidence as survives, it appears that the Dublin courts proceeded in much the same way as the courts at Westminster or in the English palatinates, with a professional bench and bar.[62] By way of contrast with Wales, writs of error did run from the two benches in Dublin to the King's Bench in England.[63] If an issue of fact arose in such proceedings, it was tried in the nearest English county.[64]

However, two important qualifications should be made to Dillon's broad proposition. One is that Ireland had its own Parliament,[65] and it was arguable that English statutes did not automatically apply there. This was debated in the case of the Waterford merchants in 1484,[66] where the principal question was whether an Irish seaport town was bound by an English shipping statute. All the justices in the Exchequer Chamber held that, since Ireland had its own Parliament which could make and change laws, it was not bound by a statute made in England, where it was not represented; but they added the important proviso that this applied only to matters touching land in Ireland, because the Irish were the king's subjects and were bound like other subjects—including the inhabitants of Calais and Gascony. The following year, however, Huse CJ, who had been absent from the previous discussion, asserted categorically that English statutes did bind in Ireland: 'which was not much denied by the other justices'.[67] It is not clear whether a final decision was reached. But it may have been partly with this uncertainty in mind that the Irish

students, but their presence was fairly continuous. Dillon was exceptional in staying to become a bencher. Little is known about him.

[61] It seems never to have been intended, however, that the Dublin society should have educational functions or degrees. See C. Kenny, *King's Inns and the Kingdom of Ireland* (1992).

[62] There are no Irish law reports from this period. The rolls have been destroyed, though some stray examples remain, such as those removed to England by writs of error. See also S. G. Ellis, 'The Common Bench Plea Roll of 19 Edw. IV' (1984) 31 *Analecta Hibernica* 21 60.

[63] FNB 24C; *Diversite de Courtz*, sig. A3; e.g. *Barnwell* v. *Barnewell* (1517) KB 140/54/1 (original record under seal of Irish King's Bench); *Blakny* v. *Welsly* (1532) KB 27/1085, m. 82; *Russell* v. *Lord Houth* (1539) KB 27/1110, m. 69 (assize in Dublin; writ to Gerald Aylmer CJ of Chief Place; judgment reversed); *Barnewell* v. *Rochford* (1545) KB 27/1134, m. 35 (assize in Dublin; writ to CJ of Chief Place); 108 Selden Soc. 52. Earlier precedents are collected in Hale, *Prerogatives of the King*, ed. Yale, 37.

[64] *Barnewell* v. *Rochford* (1545) KB 27/1134, m. 35 (issue tried in Shropshire).

[65] For its legislation see *Statutes at Large, passed in the Parliaments held in Ireland* (1786) vol. i; D. B. Quinn ed., 'The Bills and Statutes of the Irish Parliaments of Henry VII and Henry VIII' (10 *Analecta Hibernica*; 1941).

[66] Mich. 2 Ric. III, fo. 11, pl. 26; *Select Cases in the Exchequer Chamber*, ed. M. Hemmant (64 Selden Soc.; 1948), 94, pl. 28. Cf. *Pilkington's Case* (1455) Pas. 33 Hen. VI, fo. 17, pl. 8, where Serjeant Portington asserted that a revenue statute did not extend to Ireland because the Irish were not represented in the English Parliament; but there was disagreement as to whether Ireland was separate (*severe*) from England.   [67] Mich. 1 Hen. VII, fo. 3, pl. 2 (tr.).

Parliament in 1495 was made to enact that 'all statutes late made' in England, 'concerning and belonging to the common and public weal of the same', were to apply in Ireland.[68] The statute was to cause trouble, and the word 'late' was to be ignored; but it confirmed, perhaps contrary to the intention of its promoters, the thinking that English statutes did not apply automatically. The same Irish statute—the Statute of Drogheda, commonly known as Poynings' Law, from the name of the lord deputy, Sir Edward Poynings—declared that no parliament should in future be held in Ireland without the assent of the king's Council in England, which had to be informed of the acts which it was proposed to make. Ireland was not to be a law unto itself. In the 1530s an English lawyer would even maintain that the Irish were not *liberi homines* for the purposes of Magna Carta, because Ireland was not part of England.[69]

The second qualification is that the law which Dillon perceived as being the same as in England was in reality confined within the pale around Dublin. Beyond the pale, among the 'wild Irish'—as the English called them[70]—Irish customs held sway and royal authority was difficult to enforce. There were marcher lordships and counties palatine, but little is known of their legal operation and it is doubtful how far the Anglo-Irish gentry who controlled them understood the local customs.[71] It has been said that the Gaelic chieftancies or lordships in the western half of Ireland were until 1534 more or less independent sovereign states subject to the old Gaelic law.[72] On the other hand, some places had fully fledged courts on the English model—for instance, the county of Wexford had a chancellor, justice, treasurer, sheriff, coroner, and justices of the peace—but the courts were said to be ineffective 'in default of learned men'.[73] The lawyers preferred to stay in Dublin.

Attempts were made under Henry VIII to assert greater control over justice in Ireland, in pursuance of Cromwell's policy of imposing one law upon his master's empire. More regular assizes were held, and after 1534 the maintenance of a standing army in Ireland made practicable enforcement more possible. In 1541 Henry VIII, to please the Irish, assumed the title of king of Ireland;[74] and a recent commentary on

---

[68] *Statutes at Large, passed in the Parliaments held in Ireland* (1786) i. 56 (10 Hen. VII, Ir., c. 4).

[69] BL MS. Harley 4990, fo. 161v. He distinguished the Welsh on the grounds that Wales had (as he supposed) been part of England at the time of Magna Carta.

[70] e.g. *R. v. Ap Griffith* (1531) Spelman 47; speech to new serjeants (1540) BL MS. Harley 361, fo. 80, *per* Mountagu CJ, pr. Baker, *Serjeants at Law*, 302 (sp. mod., 'the wild Irish and such other which liveth more like beasts than men').

[71] See D. B. Quinn, 'Anglo-Irish Local Government 1485–1534' (1939) 1 *Irish Historical Studies* 354–81, at 360, 363.

[72] N. Patterson, 'Gaelic Law and the Tudor Conquest of Ireland' (1991) 27 *Irish Historical Studies* 193–215; and see E. Lennon, *Sixteenth Century Ireland* (1995), 57–64.

[73] Quinn, 'Anglo-Irish Local Government', 376–7.

[74] *Statutes at Large, passed in the Parliaments held in Ireland* (1786) i. 176 (33 Hen. VIII, Ir., c. 1). The new title had to be used in England as well as Ireland: see the proclamation of January 1542 enrolled

this measure concluded that it was designed to extend the Crown's sovereign jurisdiction throughout the land by conciliation rather than force, and 'to affirm the sovereign nature of the constitutional bond between the English crown and Ireland with a view to having that sovereignty acknowledged among the Irishry'.[75] However, it did not directly affect the Irish legal system or the legal relationship with England.

ISLE OF MAN

The Isle of Man—formerly part of Norway—had long been annexed to the English Crown, and since 1405 the lordship had belonged to the Stanley family, who throughout the Tudor period were earls of Derby.[76] It was not parcel of the realm of England, and for this reason a Chancery inquisition concerning the island, upon the death of the twelfth earl in 1521, was held void for want of jurisdiction. The judges on that occasion likened its status to that of Calais or Tournai.[77] Little is yet known of early Manx law,[78] though it is said in the year books for 1520 that 'in the Isle of Man if someone takes a horse or an ox it is not felony, because he cannot abscond with it, whereas if he takes a capon or a pig he shall be hanged'.[79]

FRANCE

The king of England still used the title of king of France, and bore the French royal arms quartering those of England, but for the greater part possession no longer went with the bare title. The only remaining French territories in English hands at the beginning of the Tudor period were the Channel Islands and Calais. There was never any suggestion that English law should operate in any of these places, and so they require only a brief notice in a history of the laws of England.

The Channel Islands were the only portion of the duchy of Normandy remaining in the possession and under the governance of the king of England,[80] and by long continuance it was the custom of Normandy which—together with local

---

in the English King's Bench, *Tudor Royal Proclamations*, i. 307, no. 208; KB 27/1122, Rex m. 1. Henry was also styled supreme head of the Church of Ireland.

[75] Bradshaw, *Irish Constitutional Revolution of the Sixteenth Century*, 233.

[76] See *Handbook of British Chronology* (3rd edn), 65–6.

[77] *Re Earl of Derby* (1522) 2 Caryll 731–2.

[78] Some court records are preserved from the early Tudor period (the *Libri placitorum* from 1496): 15 *JLH* 125 n. 3.

[79] *Fyloll* v. *Assheleygh* (1520) Trin. 12 Hen. VIII, fo. 3, pl. 3, at fo. 5 (119 Selden Soc. 18), *per* Brudenell CJ. The same custom is mentioned in *Marmyon* v. *Baldwyn* (1527) 120 Selden Soc. 61 at 63, *per* Shelley J.

[80] See F. de L. Bois, *A Constitutional History of Jersey* (1970); A. J. Eagleston, *The Channel Islands under Tudor Government 1485–1642* (1949); T. Thornton, 'The English King's French Islands: Jersey and Guernsey in English politics and administration, 1485-1642' in *Authority and Consent in Tudor England*, ed. G. W. Bernard and S. J. Gunn (2002), 197–217.

customs—applied there. Although English judges had gone to the islands on eyre in the fourteenth century,[81] and the King's Bench had once exercised some super-intendence,[82] since a decision of 1368 writs of error were no longer taken to the King's Bench. By the end of Henry VII's reign, however, cases could be pursued in the king's Council in England as the nearest representative of the duchy council.[83]

The fortified town and marches of Calais in Picardy had been conquered by Edward III in 1347. The territory had its own courts, including a flourishing staple court which followed the law merchant. Apart from administrative regulations,[84] and ecclesiastical jurisdiction,[85] no attempt was made to impose English law in Calais,[86] its own laws being confirmed by Parliament. Writs of error did not there-fore, in principle, lie to reverse judgments given there.[87] Nevertheless, judgments in Calais could be questioned in the English Chancery,[88] and occasional attempts were made to bring writs of error against the mayor and aldermen in the King's Bench.[89] In 1506 the King's Bench even heard a dispute about tolls in the marches of Calais and, after taking advisement as to how it should be tried, ordered a jury to be summoned from Kent as the next adjacent county.[90] A legislative nexus was created when, in 1536, Parliament passed a lengthy statute to improve the admin-istration of Calais.[91] By the same statute, and perhaps as a necessary corollary to

[81] There is even a report surviving of a session in Guernsey in Keil. 138, pl. 3.

[82] See Co. Inst. iv. 286; Hale, *Prerogatives of the King*, ed. Yale, 41.

[83] See J. H. Smith, *Appeals to the Privy Council from the American Plantations* (1950), 11–12. Cases were heard both in the Star Chamber and in the Chancery: see Thornton, 'The English King's French Islands', 205.

[84] Commissions of sewers were issuable to Calais, and apparently followed English law: see 4 Hen. VII, c. 1; *Lisle Letters*, ed. Byrne, i. 289, no. 276. Note also the ordinances for the county of Guisnes made by Sir William Fitzwilliam, John Hales B., Christopher Hales, S.-G., and William Brewode, in 1525: BL Cotton MS. Faustina E. VII, ff. 40–74.

[85] This was subject to Canterbury. See *Lisle Letters*, ed. Byrne, ii. 74, no. 143 (Cranmer asks Lisle to hear testamentary case according to equity, 1534).

[86] *Ex parte the Freemen of Marck and Oye* (1506) Mich. 21 Hen. VII, fo. 31, pl. 17 (tr. 'their law is Civil law there'); Hale, *Prerogatives of the King*, ed. Yale, 42.

[87] See Mich. 21 Hen. VII, fo. 33, pl. 32, *per* Brudenell sjt (error does not lie to Wales or Calais); *Re Earl of Derby* (1522) 2 Caryll 731 at 732, *per* Brudenell CJ (error does not lie to Calais). Cf. *Ex parte the Freemen of Marck and Oye* (1506) Mich. 21 Hen. VII, fo. 31, pl. 17, where the King's Bench held the contrary.

[88] e.g. *Merricokke* v. *Williamson* (1493) C244/142/22 (detinue); *Robyns* v. *Andrewes* (1497) C47/24/16/7–8 (debt for £340); *Lynne* v. *Baker* (1497) ibid. 9–10 (debt for £8. 13s. 4d.); *Dalton* v. *Pays* (1527) ibid. 11–14 (debt for £40); *Bryan's Case* (1537) noted in *Lisle Letters*, ed. Byrne, iv. 253–4.

[89] e.g. *Palder* v. *Whetyll* (probably temp. Hen. VIII) Bodl. Lib. MS. Rawl. C.339, ff. 22v–23 (writ of error to mayor and aldermen of Calais to remove a record *coram nobis ubicumque fuerimus*); *Bereworth* v. *Wollar* (1551) KB 27/1158, m. 171 (error to mayor and aldermen of Calais in case of debt; English record includes depositions; no error assigned).

[90] *R.* v. *Mayor and Aldermen of Calais ex parte the Freemen of Marck and Oye* (1506) KB 27/981, m. 70; Mich. 21 Hen. VII, fo. 31, pl. 17.

[91] 27 Hen. VIII, c. 63; Lehmberg, *Reformation Parliament*, 239–40. For Viscount Lisle's papers as deputy of Calais around this time see *Lisle Letters*, ed. Byrne.

parliamentary interference, provision was made for Calais to send two burgesses to the English Parliament.[92] However, this limited form of union did not affect the ordinary law in Calais, or the constitutional relationship between Calais and the English Crown.[93]

Henry VIII's imperial ambitions in France had led him much earlier in his reign to seek to emulate the famous deeds of Edward III and Henry V. His principal victory—though it was expensive and of brief consequence—was the capture of Tournai in 1513.[94] The town was surrendered to him as king of France, and occupied by him in right of his kingdom of France until it was returned to François I under the treaty of London (1519). During this short rule Henry issued coins from the Tournai mint and used a seal with the title 'king of France and England'. The constitutional position of Tournai was similar to that of the Channel Islands and Calais,[95] in that no change was made to the local constitution or court system and French law continued to operate. But since appeals had customarily gone to the Parlement of Paris, which was outside the king's control, a substitute appellate procedure had to be provided. A new court was therefore established in 1514, by an ordinance made in the time of Parliament but not by act of Parliament, to exercise the same jurisdiction as the Parlement of Paris.[96] At the same time, Parliament provided for the registration of Tournai contracts so that they could be enforced there or in England.[97]

A similarly precarious foothold was obtained in Boulogne at the end of Henry VIII's reign in 1544,[98] but it was given up in 1550. The lilies of France were to linger in the royal arms until 1800; but the loss of Calais in 1557 finally ended the territorial ambitions of the English monarchs on the French mainland.

[92] *HPHC 1509–58*, i. 284.

[93] See D. Grummitt, ' "One of the mooste pryncipall treasours belongyng to his Realme of Englande": Calais and the Crown, c.1450–1558' in *The English Experience of France, c.1450–1558*, ed. D. Grummitt (2002), 46–62.

[94] C. S. L. Davies, 'Tournai and the English Crown 1513–19' (1998) 41 *Historical Jnl* 1–26, which contains important corrections to the previous literature. Davies doubts whether Tournai ever sent a member to Parliament, as suggested in *HPHC 1509–58*, i. 285. See further 'Tournai MPs at Westminster?' (2001) 20 *Parliamentary History* 233–5.

[95] See *Re Earl of Derby* (1522) 2 Caryll 731 at 732, *per* Brudenell CJ.

[96] Rymer, *Foedera*, xiii. 519–20. It was to include four learned lawyers, presumably local graduates in Civil law.   [97] 5 Hen. VIII, c. 1.

[98] Somewhat inconsistently with the king's asserted title, the French who opposed him were treated as enemy aliens who could be enslaved: *Anon.* (1544/5) Brooke Abr., *Propertie*, pl. 38.

Part III

THE COURTS

5

Introduction: Jurisdictional Movements

To understand the transformation of English law in the early Tudor period it is first necessary to understand the role of the courts and their relationships with each other. Fluctuations in the fortunes of the central courts have been the subject of debate since Maitland painted his gloomy picture of a declining common law in the middle of Henry VIII's reign,[1] and this for a number of reasons. Patterns of litigation are of interest to social and economic historians, because of what they tell us about prosperity, the network of credit, social stability, rivalry and disorder, and changes in personal relations. Jurisdictional shifts are also of legal interest, because sometimes an apparent change in the substantive law turns out to be little more than a diversion of pre-existing business from one kind of court to another.[2] The changes have nevertheless proved to be remarkably difficult to trace with acceptable accuracy, and the failure to solve this difficulty remains one of the outstanding problems concerning the legal history of the period.[3] To begin with, the records of the major courts are so voluminous that exact counting is almost unendurably tedious; it is not merely a matter of counting entries, because if one is to avoid double counting it is necessary to note the stage of each case and the names of the parties as well.[4] Besides this, counting cases is not enough for the purposes of studying jurisdictional movement, because attention needs also to be paid to the subject-matter of the litigation and to the amounts in suit. Perhaps the most serious problem of all, since there is no obvious remedy, is that the records of local courts have not survived uniformly. Given that there must have been over twelve thousand local courts, each with its own rolls, the scale of the evidential problem is considerable.[5] It is not implausible

---

[1] See above, 4, 7; M. Blatcher, 'The Great Depression', in *The Court of King's Bench 1450–1550* (1978), 10–33; E. W. Ives, *The Common Lawyers in pre-Reformation England* (1983), 199–207, 212–16; C. W. Brooks, 'The Increase in Litigation', in *Pettyfoggers and Vipers of the Commonwealth* (1986), 48–74.

[2] Milsom, *Historical Foundations*, 244–5, 314–15, 340–3.

[3] The same problem faces social historians: see C. Carpenter, 'The Use of Legal Records' in *Locality and Polity: a study of Warwickshire landed society 1401–1499* (1992), 705–9.

[4] It is necessary also to distinguish multiple entries in the same suit from multiple suits between the same parties, which is a fairly common phemomenon.

[5] Brooks estimates that there were over 12,000 manorial courts alone: *Pettyfoggers and Vipers*, 306 n. 21.

to suppose that the survival of court records was often related to the fortunes of the court in later times, and that surviving records are therefore not necessarily typical: indeed, they may be skewed towards the untypical. Certainly it cannot be assumed that a true nationwide picture is to be obtained simply by multiplying the average figures in surviving records by the total number of courts which must have been operating within the period.

A second complicating factor is the common practice of pursuing litigation in several courts at once, or by multiple suits in succession. A substantial proportion of bills in Chancery and Star Chamber, for instance, mention litigation already pending in other central or local courts; and in these cases the Chancery or Star Chamber litigation is self-evidently a net addition to the total volume of litigation rather than a transfer of business from elsewhere. The same is true of the common-law courts. It was not unusual for the same dispute to be pursued by cross-actions or successive actions in the two benches,[6] or even in the same court,[7] and in some cases we find a lawsuit surfacing in both benches, the Chancery, and the Star Chamber as well.[8] Even if such cases are not a large proportion of the whole, they certainly throw into doubt some of the traditional thinking about competition between the central courts.

The relationship between central and local courts is equally problematic. While local courts in general possessed the advantage of cheapness,[9] and speed, they must have seemed in several respects less advantageous to plaintiffs than the courts at Westminster. Some local courts were seriously hampered by jurisdictional limits,[10] which were continuously eroded by inflation; their process was less

[6] For examples in print see *Abbot of St Mary Graces* v. *Bullesdon* (1494–1502) Port 46; *Stepney* v. *Cressey* (1529–32) Spelman 187. Cf. *Bishop of London* v. *Kellett* (1533–5) Spelman 137 (in King's Bench); CP 40/1084, m. 328. A single suit might also spread into the other bench by means of error or attaint.

[7] e.g. *Browne* v. *Abbot of Waltham* (1512–23) Spelman 32 (detinue and trespass); *Prior of St Neots* v. *Wolley* (1528) Spelman 74 (covenant and *secta ad molendinum*); *Wadham* v. *Rogers* (1528–30) Spelman 81 (*quare impedit*, debt on a bond, and forgery). An example of cross-actions of trespass, with pleadings raising the same title, and mutual demurrers, is *Roupe* v. *Gaverok* (1552) CP 40/1149, m. 509; *Gaverok* v. *Roupe*, ibid., m. 513. For cross-actions of different forms see e.g. the dispute over chantry land in *Walkeleyn* v. *Lendall* (1552) CP 40/1150, m. 617 (avowry for rent; demurrer); *Lendall* v. *Walkeleyn* (1552) CP 40/1154, m. 721 (debt for rent).

[8] Two notorious examples are *Fortescue* v. *Stonor* (1497–1532) Spelman 106; *Millys* v. *Guldeford* (1506–35) Spelman 167; 110 Selden Soc. 383–4. Cf. *Marke* v. *Eweader* (1519–23) Spelman 156 (three actions in both benches, error, and a Chancery suit); *Gresley* v. *Saunders* (1522–3) Spelman 22 (cross-actions in the benches, and a Chancery suit); *Zouche* v. *Cornwall* (1522–30) Spelman 207; C261/9/71 (two actions in the Common Pleas, an assize of novel disseisin, and suits in Chancery and the Star Chamber).

[9] In a city court, the attorney's fee might be as little as 8*d.* (under half that of the Common Pleas attorney): see the 18 bills of costs (*c.*1498) bound at the end of the Sheriffs' Court book in York City Archives, E25a.

[10] e.g. hundred courts: below, 301–2. It was arguable that the central courts should presume a 40*s.* limit even for a borough court, so that it was necessary to allege a charter or prescription to support a more extensive jurisdiction: see *Welbroke* v. *Gilberte* (1525) KB 27/1055, m. 30 (error from mayor and

effective, especially since it could not reach defendants outside the precincts; and there was always the worry that a recovery might be upset by proceedings in one of the central courts. There was also a constitutional aspect to the matter. It has been suggested by constitutional historians that it was conscious royal policy under the Tudors to suppress jurisdictional and other franchises in order to emphasize the king's authority;[11] but this may be reading too much into the evidence of particular cases. The king was often described as 'the head of justice',[12] and all jurisdiction was already deemed to derive from him,[13] even if it was in the hands of subjects. Inferior jurisdiction had long been subject to control by means of *quo warranto* or, in individual cases, by writs of error (for courts of record) and writs of false judgment (for courts not of record). In so far as local jurisdiction was still wanted, and used, few serious changes were made in the Tudor period. Certainly courts of piepowder had once been seen as a grievance, and were clamped down upon by legislation and other means in the later fifteenth century.[14] But they continued to flourish; and, in any case, there is no comparable legislation dealing with other local courts from which a general policy might be deduced. The judges in the Star Chamber had discussed, at the very beginning of Henry VIII's reign, the 'suppression of inferior courts which were not courts of record ratified', but they almost certainly had novel sub-conciliar tribunals rather than local courts in mind.[15] In 1535 measures were taken by Parliament to modify jurisdictional franchises, for instance by requiring that writs in the palatine courts issue in the king's name, and it has been argued that these enactments 'in general extended the operation of the royal justice . . . to all England'.[16] However, the impact of such measures on jurisdiction was minimal. Though they were no doubt of symbolic importance in marking the political power of the central government, they were not meant to and did not in practice affect the working of the palatinate or lesser franchisal courts. In fact, almost the only direct effect of Cromwell's administrative reforms on the jurisdiction of the central courts was to bring Monmouth into England.[17]

bailiffs of Great Totnes; first error assigned on this ground). However, there are many precedents which contradict this position.

[11] H. M. Cam, *Liberties and Communities* (1944), 215–18; Elton, *The Tudor Constitution*, 32, 155–6. Cam's examples are not so much of rival jurisdiction as of exemption from justice: in sanctuaries (cf. below, 546–51) and in Wales (cf. above, 105–8).

[12] e.g. Spelman's reading (1519), 147, *per* Fyneux CJ; *Marmyon* v. *Baldwyn* (1527) 120 Selden Soc. 61 at 69, *per* Conyngesby J.; *The Serjeants' Case* (1531) Wm Yelv. 294 at 309, *per* Audley sjt; *Diversite de Courtz* (1533), sig. A2; Inner Temple moot (1530s) Caryll (Jun.) 376, no. 16.

[13] This is stated as a historical fact in Port 119 (probably Richard Littleton's reading, 1493), where it is said that the king was once the sole judge.

[14] See below, 314.   [15] BL MS. Lansdowne 639, fo. 28; below, 194.

[16] Elton, *England under the Tudors*, 175–8, at 176. The principal statute referred to is 27 Hen. VIII, c. 24.

[17] 27 Hen. VIII, c. 26, s. 4. The Common Pleas had a filazer for Monmouth from Hil. 1542.

It is true that legislation was not the only means of control. The work of local courts could be seriously hindered by the zealous use of *quo warranto* proceedings at common law, and Edmund Dudley's lecture in Gray's Inn on the Statute of *Quo Warranto*, early in Henry VII's reign,[18] set out the principles on which courts could be forfeited by disuse or abuse. The subject was taken up by other readers; and there was a revival of *quo warranto* proceedings soon after 1509, increased vigour under Wolsey,[19] and continuing activity beyond the middle of the century.[20] Nevertheless, few of the cases concerned jurisdictional franchises in isolation from other privileges,[21] and it seems clear that the main purpose of the campaign cannot have been to suppress inferior jurisdictions.[22] Most of these suits arose in reality from local or private disputes, and the king's law officers were taking advantage of them for fiscal rather than political reasons. The same disputes might equally well have been pursued by means of actions on the case,[23] and some of them were in fact pursued under both procedures.[24] A more telling piece of evidence is that, when the Crown had the opportunity to suppress the many jurisdictional franchises exercised by religious houses, which would have been extinguished on their surrender or confiscation at the time of the Dissolution, deliberate steps were taken—again, it may be supposed, for fiscal reasons—to

[18] 'Lectura secundum Dudley. Prima lectura...Lectura Dudley', CUL MS. Hh.3.10, ff. 1–18v. His second reading was in 1496, and the usual interval between readings was seven to ten years, so the probable date is *c*.1486. The same statute was lectured upon by Robert Constable (Lincoln's Inn, 1494), William Marshall (ibid., 1516), and John Spelman (Gray's Inn, 1519).

[19] See especially *Att.-Gen.* v. *Trelawney* (1516–29) KB 29/148, m. 38d (information in nature of *quo warranto* for using jurisdictional privileges; continued throughout Wolsey's chancellorship). At least four cases in the Middlesex *quo warranto* proceedings of 1519 were concerned with jurisdiction: see Chaloner 282–5, nos. 9–13.

[20] The cases are found every term in the Rex portion of the plea rolls (KB 27).

[21] See H. Garrett-Goodyear, 'The Tudor Revival of *Quo Warranto*', in *On the Laws and Customs of England*, ed. Arnold *et al.*, 231–95. Only four cases before 1540 concerned civil pleas: ibid. 274, 275, 279, 288. Four further cases in 1543–6 all concerned town courts: ibid. 292 (Reading, 1543; Winchester, Ipswich, 1544), 294 (Saltash, 1546). For wider aspects of the policy see also S. G. Ellis, 'The Destruction of the Liberties: some further evidence' (1981) 54 *BIHR* 150–61 (mainly concerning liberties in Ireland).

[22] Cf. Elton, *England under the Tudors*, 14–15, where the problems caused by jurisdictional franchises are perhaps over-emphasized. An early example which does suggest government hostility is the Star Chamber order of 1512 that the liberties (unspecified) claimed by the men of Denbigh, under a charter of Hen. VII, be challenged by *quo warranto*: BL MS. Lansdowne 639, ff. 42v–43.

[23] e.g. *Ryngeley* v. *Somer* (1525) E159/304, Hil. m. 15 (dispute between mayor and bailiff over hundred court of Sandwich). The usual context of actions on the case for infringing jurisdictional franchises was the profitable view of frankpledge: e.g. *Prior of Christchurch, Canterbury* v. *Bendysshe* (1503–8) KB 27/966, m. 74 (94 Selden Soc. 261); KB 27/987, m. 57d; Spelman 8; *Dean and Canons of Windsor* v. *Gurney* (1511) KB 27/1000, m. 56d; *Newdegate* v. *Prior of St John's* (1517) CP 40/1018, m. 451d; CP 40/1022, m. 885; CP 40/1028, m. 540 (demurrer).

[24] Serjeant Newdegate's claim (last note) was also ventilated in the Middlesex *quo warranto* session of 1519: Chaloner 283–4, nos. 10, 12.

preserve them by legislation.[25] In the case of boroughs, many new charters were issued which clarified or strengthened the jurisdiction of borough courts in personal actions.[26] Thus, whatever it was that the Council discussed in 1509, it seems that the government never adopted a policy of suppressing inferior local jurisdictions within our period. As we shall see, some—if not most—local courts shared in the general boom in litigation in the sixteenth century.

The jurisdictional story is confused by a general decline in litigation in the middle of our period, before the boom came, reaching its low point in the 1520s and 1530s.[27] It has been supposed by some writers that this decline bears out Maitland's thesis that the common law was for a time in serious trouble.[28] But it now seems more likely that this temporary phenomenon was not the result of redistributing work between courts, or of defects in the common law suddenly driving plaintiffs away, but rather a reflection of dearth, war, and economic depression.[29] It was, in most jurisdictions, followed by an enormous surge in litigation which more than compensated for the decline.

It is now clear beyond argument that in the long term—between the beginning and the end of our period—the work-load of all the central courts increased dramatically, especially in the 1540s and 1550s. Indeed, such was the resurgence at Westminster that in 1545 it was necessary to issue a commission of purveyance to gather sheepskins and pelts to make parchment for the Chancery and Common Pleas.[30] Most writers have assumed a centripetal movement bringing this business to Westminster from elsewhere,[31] though more recent research renders this questionable. Some small part of the gain may have been at the expense of spiritual jurisdiction: for instance, actions for defamation and actions concerning the administration of estates.[32] However, most of the increase seems to be accounted for by actions to recover debts. While it is true that this coincides with an abandonment of contract jurisdiction by the ecclesiastical courts, there is too great a disparity between the sums of money typically in dispute in the two jurisdictions to indicate a direct transfer of business.[33] In any case, the Church courts seem to have enjoyed a boom in their overall level of business at the same time as the secular courts.[34] The London business, much of it commercial, which soars to prominence

---

[25] 32 Hen. VIII, c. 20.

[26] See R. Tittler, 'The Incorporation of Boroughs, 1540-58' (1977) 62 *History* 24–42.

[27] Blatcher, *Court of King's Bench*, 10–35; Ives, *Common Lawyers in pre-Reformation England*, 200–7.

[28] Blatcher, *Court of King's Bench*, 10–14, 24–33; J. A. Guy, *The Public Career of Sir Thomas More* (1980), 38–49.

[29] Brooks, *Pettyfoggers and Vipers*, 81–4. On the other hand, similar factors do not seem to have held back the tide of litigation in the 1550s.

[30] Copy in John Hales's precedent book, BL MS. Add. 38136, fo. 86v (19 Nov. 1545).

[31] e.g. the present writer in 94 Selden Soc. 51–3. A note of caution appears in Blatcher, *Court of King's Bench*, 155–6.   [32] See 94 Selden Soc. 53.

[33] R. H. Helmholz, 'Assumpsit and *Fidei Laesio*' (1975) 91 LQR 406–32.   [34] Below, 252–3.

in the two benches in the 1540s and 1550s, may possibly have been lured away from the city courts; but since their records have disappeared this remains a matter for conjecture. Most other urban courts whose records survive seem to have experienced their own increase in jurisdiction at the same period, especially in debt cases,[35] and this appears to have happened in rural courts as well.[36] However, the evidence is defective. We cannot know what happened in courts which either disappeared or declined so seriously that their records were not preserved, and we cannot even tell whether the decline or disappearance of local courts in this period was more typical than the boom we see in the rolls we still have.

In so far as we can make out a national pattern, however, it now seems to be of a general increase in litigation by 1550 in all the courts which remained in existence. There was also a large increase in the sums of money being claimed, often exceeding the rate of inflation. Whereas in the time of Henry VII and Henry VIII the average sum recovered in actions of debt in the central courts was between £10 and £20,[37] by the 1550s three-figure sums were quite common,[38] and in 1555 we find an action for £2,000 on a bond.[39] There could be a number of reasons for these changing fortunes.[40] Gains in some courts may have been achieved at the expense of other jurisdictions, albeit to an extent which can no longer be measured. Other gains represent new forms of litigation, such as disputes over monastic land, uses, and copyhold; but these do not account for more than a fraction of the new business. It seems unlikely that procedural improvements can have been primarily responsible for stirring litigants into action, especially given that the fortunes of the most progressive court, the King's Bench, were matched in courts which made few if any changes.[41] The increase in debt litigation in local as well as central courts

[35] See W. A. Champion, 'Litigation in the Boroughs' (1994) 15 *JLH* 201–22; below, 311.

[36] e.g. J. H. Baker, 'Personal Actions in the High Court of Battle Abbey' (1992) repr. in *CLT*, 263 at 284.

[37] In 1486 an action on a bond for 1,000 marks caused a considerable stir: *Whalley* v. *Leke* (1486–7) Mich. 2 Hen. VII, fo. 2, pl. 3; Pas. 2 Hen. VII, fo. 17, pl. 3.

[38] e.g. from two sample terms, *Moreany* v. *Basyng* (1551) KB 27/1157, m. 40 (£120 damages in *assumpsit*); *Fox* v. *Antony* (1551) ibid., m. 139 (£100 damages for libelling a merchant venturer); *Seymour* v. *Cruche* (1551) KB 27/1158, m. 95 (£1,000 debt recovered on a recognizance to perform covenants). Note also *Saxcy* v. *Hudson* (1553) KB 27/1167, m. 145 (£852 damages recovered on informal factoring agreement); *Madyson* v. *Heygate* (1555) KB 27/1175, m. 105 (£400 penalty recovered in debt on a bond); *Heydon* v. *Weston* (1555) KB 27/1176, m. 158 (£1,000 damages recovered by confession in case for words); *Cornewell* v. *Colwych*, ibid., m. 126d (£500 penalty); *Founte* v. *Cranech* (1556) KB 27/1178, m. 167 (£620 penalty); *Earl of Pembroke* v. *Recorde* (1556) KB 27/1180, m. 36 (£1,000 damages for libel). The 3,000 marks recovered by writ of inquiry in *Marquess of Exeter* v. *Coryton* (1533) CP 40/1077, m. 504 (*scandalum magnatum*) were exceptional.

[39] *Boureman* v. *Levyns* (1555) KB 27/1175, m. 109. The defendant was discharged by a protection *quia moraturus* in Calais. The highest award of damages noticed before 1558 is £2,000: previous note. Cf. *Compton* v. *Yorke* (1526) CP 40/1051, m. 455 (£2,100 recovered by confession on bond relating to customs).

[40] Cf. Brooks, 'The Causes of the Increase in Litigation', in *Pettyfoggers and Vipers*, 75–111. This is concerned mainly with the period after 1560, but the arguments are equally applicable to the previous two or three decades and have been followed here.

[41] Brooks, *Pettyfoggers and Vipers*, 86–9. Cf. Ives, *Common Lawyers in pre-Reformation England*, 212–16.

doubtless reflected a growing reliance on credit and loans at all levels of society,[42] and the need to call in debts promptly in times of inflation,[43] though it should be borne in mind that debt actions are by no means solely concerned with monetary transactions and outstanding bills.[44] The larger sums claimed in debt actions are chiefly attributable to the higher penalties exacted in bonds, doubtless in consequence of the same influences but perhaps rendered more palatable to obligors by the knowledge that relief was obtainable in Chancery.[45] At the same time, a combination of drastic price rises,[46] a steady increase in population to at least the pre-Black Death level,[47] an active land market, and 'the dilution of a predominantly agricultural economy by the infiltration of commercial capital',[48] destabilized the economy in ways which engendered disputes over resources.

Amongst its many effects, inflation also reduced the cost of litigation at the critical moment.[49] The standard fee of an attorney at Westminster remained fixed at 20*d.* a term throughout our period,[50] and counsel were generally paid a standard fee of 3*s.* 4*d.*—or 6*s.* 8*d.* for a serjeant—for each piece of work.[51] The court officers' fees

[42] Brooks, *Pettyfoggers and Vipers*, 95–6; M. McIntosh, 'Money Lending on the Periphery of London' (1988) 20 *Albion* 557–71, at 564–7; C. Muldrew, *The Economy of Obligation: the culture of credit and social relations in early modern England* (1998). For pawnbroking, see below, 745–6.

[43] It was held in *Anon.* (1524) Spelman 87–8 (debt for grain) that the plaintiff could not recover damages to compensate for inflation between the contract and its performance. Cf. *Duodo* v. *White* (1528–9) CP 40/1058A, m. 457 (debt for 600 quarters of grain price £300; pleads tender and no one came to receive it, so he sold to persons unknown, and the price doubled from 6*s.* 8*d.* to 13*s.* 4*d.* a quarter between 1525 and 1528; demurrer). See also *Anon.* (1553) Dyer 82b, 83a (two cases as to whether debtor bears loss of debasement).

[44] A high proportion of debt cases were actions on bonds, and these were used to secure all kinds of transactions: see below, 819–20. [45] Below, 822–4.

[46] See 94 Selden Soc. 47 n. 1; C. G. A. Clay, 'The Movement of Prices', in *Economic Expansion and Social Change: England 1500–1700* (1984), i. 29–51; Cornwall, *Wealth and Society in Early Sixteeenth Century England*, 154–97.

[47] This seems now to be generally accepted, though the figures are a matter of debate: see D. C. Coleman, *The Economy of England 1450–1750* (1977), ch. 2; J. Hatcher, *Plague, Population and the English Economy 1348–1530* (1977); B. M. S. Campbell, 'The Population of Early Tudor England' (1981) 7 *Jnl Historical Geography* 145–54. It does, however, seem that the temporary slump in litigation occurred after the population had begun to increase: see Blatcher, *Court of King's Bench*, 21–2.

[48] S. E. Thorne, 'Tudor Social Transformation and Legal Change' (1951), repr. in *Essays in English Legal History*, 197–210 (quotation from p. 198). Thorne was, however, writing about the century 1540-1640.

[49] See Brooks, *Pettyfoggers and Vipers*, 101–7, for further detail (mostly from a slightly later period).

[50] This is shown by actions for fees: e.g. *Denne* v. *Soule* (1492) CP 40/921, m. 216; *Denne* v. *Furbysshour* (1494) CP 40/928, m. 367; *Grote* v. *Steyk* (1496) CP 40/935, m. 379; *Polstede* v. *Norbirgge* (1506) CP 40/977, m. 454d; *Flemyng* v. *Vowell* (1528) CP 40/1028A, m. 441d; *Dyon* v. *Ganne* (1537) CP 40/1095, m. 539d; *Waller* v. *Mynsterchamber* (1546) CP 40/1130, m. 648; *Nasshe* v. *Jeffrays* (1547) CP 40/1134., m. 333; *Gold* v. *Clarke*, ibid., m. 898; *Grey* v. *Irby* (1548) CP 40/1137, m. 425; *Predyaux* v. *Doble* (1558) CP 40/1176(1), m. 745. Likewise in the King's Bench: *Narrative of Robert Pylkington*, 38 (1496); *Ayer* v. *Stonard* (1543) KB 27/1126, m. 113.

[51] *Pilkington Narrative*, 38 (1496); *LPCL*, 105; Ives, *Common Lawyers*, 293–305. Likewise in the conciliar courts: Guy, *The Cardinal's Court*, 114. There were, however, annuities, gifts, loans, and other benefits, which counsel could obtain besides the standard fee, and there is some evidence of fee inflation in the sixteenth century: *LPCL*, 106–8; Ives, *Common Lawyers*, 305–6; below, 431–5.

were in the same range. A debt action in the central courts might be managed in the 1540s and 1550s for a total of 30s. or 40s.,[52] much the same as in the previous century,[53] and a defendant's costs in the 1530s were usually taxed at around 30s. also.[54] This was considerably more than was needed to sue in local courts,[55] but it had become smaller in proportion to the larger debts being claimed. Even an attorney actively engaged by a nobleman might incur less than £50 in costs over a period of thirty years, as appears from an action brought against the executor of the duke of Suffolk in respect of numerous suits pursued between 1514 and 1542.[56] Chancery litigation was more expensive than the common law,[57] chiefly because of the cost of taking written evidence,[58] but the burden may have been similarly moderated by inflation. Despite recurrent complaints about fees, therefore, the retainer of lawyers came within the reach of more people, and the legal profession itself began an expansion which continued until the Civil War.[59]

[52] e.g. *Ayer* v. *Stonard* (1543) KB 27/1126, m. 113 (*assumpsit* by attorney for 46s. 8d. spent on a *qui tam* debt action in 1532, including his own fee); *Forman* v. *Fotherbye* (1556) CP 40/1168, m. 523 (debt by attorney for 30s. 6d. spent on a debt action in 1552, including his own fee, adding a fictitious loan— later remitted—to bring the total above 40s.).

[53] For some high fifteenth-century figures for costs, see Ives, *Common Lawyers*, 320. In *Burgh* v. *Blount* (1504) CP 40/969, m. 455, an attorney claimed 32s. 6d. costs, in addition to 30s. for his fee for three years, for pursuing a debt action as far as the *habeas corpora juratores*.

[54] See below, 381.

[55] The scale of costs in the borough court of Canterbury in 1505 showed that only 2d. or 4d. was paid to the town clerk for each common step: precedent book of C. Levyns, BL MS. Stowe 856, fo. 5.

[56] *Barne* v. *Marquess of Winchester* (1560) CP 40/1189, m. 280 (debt for £9. 18s. 5d. residue of a bill of £45. 9s. 10d. due to Ralph Caldwall, the deceased attorney; the bill of costs fills three membranes).

[57] Note Leonard Smyth's remark in 1533 that 'all thing that is done in the Chancery is very chargeable': *Lisle Letters*, ed. Byrne, i. 654, no. 97 (though this was in the context of letters patent).

[58] e.g. *Homwode* v. *Homwode* (1506) CP 40/975, m. 349, where the plaintiff claimed £3. 13s. 4d. laid out in Chancery: 6s. 8d. a year for an attorney (i.e. a six clerk), 26s. 8d. a year for a serjeant at law, 13s. 4d. to two counsel, 2s. for a copy of the bill, 4s. for a copy of the answer and rejoinder (apparently settled by the counsel), 2s. for a copy of the replication, 6s. to the examiner of the court for examining three witnesses, 17s. to the same for a copy of their depositions, and 44s. for the expenses of the witnesses. For the Star Chamber see Guy, *The Cardinal's Court*, 114–15.

[59] For the legal profession in general see below, 421–44.

6

The Court of Common Pleas

THE Common Pleas,[1] usually known to contemporaries as the Bench (*curia domini regis de Banco*) or 'Common Place',[2] though inferior to the King's Bench in the sense that its judgments were subject to review there by writ of error,[3] was the pre-eminent court of law and had by far the largest share of all common-law business throughout our period. Its constitution and business therefore deserve a more detailed scrutiny than is possible for other courts.[4]

At the beginning of the reign of Henry VII there were five judges assigned to the court, including the chief justice, though one of the puisne justices (Starkey) was also chief baron of the Exchequer and was probably not counted on the regular strength.[5] The normal complement of puisnes was three, and despite major fluctuations in the workload this was to remain the case for over three hundred years after 1487.[6] It was not necessary for all the judges to sit in banc, however, and on occasion we hear in the reports of one judge sitting alone.[7] By the mid-sixteenth century the fees and allowances paid by the Crown were £161. 13s. 1d. for the chief justice and £128. 6s. 5d. for each of the puisnes, besides the £20 payable for going on assize.[8] The judges' remuneration was charged on the

[1] The more familiar title is used for convenience, though it is rare before the end of our period: e.g. *Laurence* v. *Reynoldes* (1556) CP 40/1167, m. 740 ('attornatus curie...de communibus placitis').

[2] This name is used on the brasses of Danvers J. (d. 1504) and Englefield J. (d. 1537): 94 Selden Soc. 370 n. 11, 373 n. 4. Cf. *Billyngford* v. *Songer* (1542) KB 27/1122, m. 10 ('curia domini regis de Banco vocata le comon place').   [3] See below, 403.

[4] The only previous study (Hastings, *Common Pleas*) concentrated on the reign of Edward IV.

[5] Starkey died in 1486 and was not replaced in the Common Pleas. Nele died in June 1486 and was not replaced until December (by Haugh), so that in Michaelmas term there were only two puisnes. When Catesby died in Jan. 1487, he was replaced within a week.

[6] For Dyer CJ's unsuccessful attempt to increase the number in 1579 see 109 Selden Soc., p. xxviii.

[7] *LPCL*, 166. Note e.g. *Anon.* (1481) Pas. 21 Edw. IV, fo. 31, pl. 26, *per* Bryan CJ (tr. 'now none of my fellows are here except me, in whom the entire authority resides'); Mich. 21 Edw. IV, fo. 53, pl. 18; *Anon.* (1497) 1 Caryll 341 at 345. However, the single judge was cautious about giving judgment: *Anon.* (1482) Hil. 21 Edw. IV, fo. 79, pl. 24 (Choke J. sitting alone held writ bad but nothing was done); Mich. 10 Hen. VII, fo. 8, pl. 15 (case adjourned because Huse CJ alone); Hil. 26 Hen. VIII, fo. 9, pl. 1 (Fitzherbert J. would not give judgment till his fellows came).

[8] *Cases from the lost Notebooks of Sir James Dyer*, 109 Selden Soc. 11. Thomas Jakes (PRO, IND 17180, fo. 3) gives the figures in 1506 as £141. 17s. 1¼d. for the chief justice, and £108. 10s. 5¼d. for the puisnes. The increase of £20 was authorized in 1545: *LP*, xx. II. 910(40). The puisnes of both benches received a

petty customs until 1539, when it was converted into a charge on the first fruits and tenths.[9]

At the beginning of our period the court was presided over by Sir Thomas Bryan, whose tenure of the chief justiceship (1471–1500) was the longest ever. His personality is dominant in the year books, but his influence was staid rather than innovative.[10] For instance, he did not favour the current movement to find a means of barring entails, and he approved of what were later called 'perpetuity clauses'.[11] He was also opposed to the circumvention of wager of law by means of actions on the case, the issue later to provide the main source of contention between the two benches. Thus, in a period when the King's Bench under Huse and Fyneux was developing new remedies and becoming a rival court for common pleas, Bryan's judicial conservatism set the Common Pleas on a course which by the end of the sixteenth century would seem distinctly reactionary. With the exception of Thomas Frowyk, whose promising tenure (1502–6) was cut short by early death, there seems to have been little obvious distinction among the chief justices over the next forty years or so, and puisnes such as Anthony Fitzherbert (1526–38) and William Shelley (1526–48) probably carried more weight in the profession by virtue of their learning. During these dim years—and the darkness is partly caused by the paucity of surviving Common Pleas reports[12]—the court suffered from the slump which affected most courts.

The court revived somewhat under Sir Edward Mountagu, who presided from 1545 until the accession of Queen Mary, who refused to reappoint him.[13] He is credited with having tried to bring some King's Bench innovations with him when he was translated from that court.[14] Certainly he had presided over the King's Bench during the time when its fortunes revived and its commercial jurisdiction began to flourish, though it is difficult to assess how far this was his personal achievement. He did not stay long enough to convert the Common Pleas from its conservative mood, though it managed to enjoy a similar boom during his presidency and seems to have accepted some innovations, such as the wider use of special verdicts,[15] and the awakening of the dormant action of ejectment,[16] which bore fruit after our period. In the early 1550s, the plea rolls for the first time

---

further increase in 1556 which brought them within a few pounds of the chief: J. Sainty, *The Judges of England 1272–1990* (1993), 20, 58.

[9] 94 Selden Soc. 352. The customs accounts in E356 record the payments. Stray judges' receipts in E101/209–210 (1518–19, 1520–1, 1526–7, 1528–9) show that they were usually paid a year in arrears. In 1499, Bryan CJ had to sue the chief butler of England for his fees: E13/178, m. 59d (imparlance).

[10] He did, however, favour the protection of copyholders when this was not generally accepted: below, 647 n. 130.   [11] See below, 699.

[12] There were nevertheless more reports in manuscript than was until recently known, and these are now being printed by the Selden Society (vols 120–1).   [13] Above, 61.

[14] See B. & M. 450; below, 873.   [15] Below, 401–2.   [16] Below, 636–7, 724.

began routinely to contain over 1,000 membranes a term, putting the clerks in a quandary as to the correct way of painting in the numbers.[17] The business continued to increase until long after the end of our period.

OFFICERS AND MINISTERS OF THE COURT[18]

The court was staffed by over fifty permanent officials, most of whom had their set places in the court in Westminster Hall but kept their offices in the inns of court.[19] The nominal chief clerk was the custos brevium, appointed by the Crown, whose position was lucrative but not legally influential. The duties were performed by deputy,[20] since the principal office was conferred as a favour rather than an employment; the last holder in our period was William Cecil. The other major Crown appointment was that of the chirographer, who was responsible for the noting and engrossing of final concords and filing the records relating to fines.[21] The clerk of the outlawries was an under-clerk of the attorney-general who occupied a few rotulets in his own name until 1530,[22] when the name of the clerk disappeared and was replaced by that of the attorney-general himself; the principal use of these membranes after 1530 was to record recognizances protecting the king's interest when common recoveries were suffered. In 1541 a new officer, called the clerk of the king's process, was appointed to assist the attorney-general in issuing process and enrolling recognizances; the office was granted by the Crown, but seems to have subsumed that of clerk of the outlawries.[23] The clerk thereafter

---

[17] They were unwilling at first to use an M. In Mich. 1551 (CP 40/1148) they started using DD, but in Trin. 1553 (CP 40/1155) we find x^c. It did not occur to them to split these enormous bundles into two: a measure belatedly adopted in 1994 in preparation for the move to Kew.

[18] For most of the offices (with lists) see 94 Selden Soc. 367–8, 374–82.

[19] e.g. the chief prothonotary kept an office in Lincoln's Inn gateway from 1518 until 1557/9, when it moved to the new buildings in the Middle Temple: Black Books, i. 198, 216, 244; MTR, i. 123. In 1544, the chirographer, the custos brevium, and the filazer for London, all kept their offices in the Inner Temple: CITR, i. 133, 138.

[20] For the duties see below, 137. For mention of the deputy see Hastings, Common Pleas, 134 (John Elryngton, 1482); CP 40/980, mm. 343, 403d (Walter Luke, 1507); CP 40/1012, m. 526d (Henry Joye, 1515). Thomas Danby, mentioned as custos brevium in 1484 (Mich. 2 Ric. III, fo. 10, pl. 22), must also have been the deputy.

[21] See Hastings, Common Pleas, 137–9. In 1540 the prothonotaries made an unsuccessful attempt to take over this business, because they feared that a bill then before Parliament would lead to the use of fines instead of recoveries: LP, xvi. 690. When error was brought to reverse a fine, a certiorari went to the chirographer to search for the writ of covenant: Seyntyll v. Smart (1554) KB 27/1171, m. 174; below, 404 n. 131.

[22] The last clerk of the outlawries named in the rolls is Anthony Poney (1528–30). The rolls thereafter bear the name of Christopher Hales, A.-G. (cf. next note).

[23] The first occupant was John Bowes (1541–51), who had previously acted as clerk to the attorney-general: LP, xvii. 1056(55); CP 40/1111, m. 1 (occupies rolls in own name). The patent mentions that Thomas Scott had performed the duties as clerk to Christopher Hales, A.-G. (1529–36).

signed rotulets in his own name. Two further Crown officers were added under Henry VIII, neither of whom encroached on existing offices: the clerk of the recognizances (1532), who recorded debts secured by recognizances in the nature of statutes staple,[24] and the even more obscure office of receiver of the debts levied in the court by reason of fines and recoveries (1536).[25]

Also holding office under the Crown, but as a grand serjeanty in fee tail, was the warden of the Fleet prison, who was in addition keeper of the palace. As keeper of the palace, he was responsible for the state of Westminster Hall, where his duties included having it strewn with rushes to subdue the dust,[26] and his privileges including letting the shops and booths along the sides.[27] As keeper of the prison, he was also gaoler to the Exchequer, Chancery, Star Chamber, and perhaps the Duchy Council of Lancaster.[28] He was nevertheless regarded as an officer belonging to the Common Pleas and within its privilege.[29] The office was the subject of a number of disputes. Under the terms of compromise of the litigation in *Babington* v. *Venour* (1465), when the office was settled on Elizabeth Venour in tail, with remainder to Robert Babington in tail, the wardenship belonged to members of the Babington family until 1558,[30] when it was sold for £4,000.[31] But the prison was sometimes leased,[32] and the office was actually performed by a deputy, known as the lieutenant;[33] it is probably the lieutenant who is usually intended when the warden of the Fleet is mentioned.[34] Henry VII occasioned a further dispute by attempting to sever the keepership of the palace, and of certain places within the

---

[24] Established by 23 Hen. VIII, c. 6, s. 4; below, 707. He did not occupy any rolls in the CP 40 series.

[25] *LP*, xi. 519(22), granted to James Morice, a courtier.

[26] *LP*, vii. 1204 (1534); 5 *Univ. Toronto Law Jnl* at 384 n. 8 (1571).

[27] Pas. 12 Hen. VII, fo. 15, pl. 1, *per* Conyngesby sjt. The stallholders paid 6s. 8d. per annum for every 10 feet occupied: *Lord Dynham* v. *Carvenell* (1489) CP 40/910, m. 608; *Babyngton* v. *Davys* (1557) CP 40/1169, m. 746. William Porter's precedents include a proclamation for all persons holding booths and stalls in the hall to remove them on pain of forfeiture, by order of the king's Council: C193/142, ff. 108v–109 (1504/21, probably in preparation for a state occasion).

[28] *Wingfield's Case* (1481) Mich. 21 Edw. IV, fo. 71, pl. 55; *Warden of the Fleet* v. *Constable of Hertford Castle* (1564) Dyer 204a; 109 Selden Soc. 88 (duties attach to the courts rather than the places).

[29] Baker, *Serjeants at Law*, 45 n. 8, 47 n. 7. He had extensive ceremonial duties when new serjeants were created.

[30] The first remainderman to take possession was William Babington (son of Robert), and from him it descended to his son Richard, on Richard's death to his brother Edward, and on Edward's death to his son Thomas: *Babyngton* v. *Davys* (1557) CP 40/1169, m. 746.

[31] C. H. Williams, 'A 15th-Century Lawsuit' (1924) 40 *LQR* 354; M. Bassett, 'The Fleet Prison in the Middle Ages' (1944) 5 *Univ. Toronto Law Jnl* 383–402.

[32] e.g. *Huse* v. *Babyngton* (1514) KB 27/1013, m. 66 (mentions lease to William Villers for seven years from 1512).

[33] Humphrey Catesby was 'locumtenens prisone de Flete' in 1488 (C244/139/40–1). Edmund Hasylwode, 'locumtenens custodis prisone de Flete' in 1520 (KB 27/1037, m. 38), sued by bill of privilege as warden in 1524 (CP 40/1045, m. 108d).

[34] e.g. John Haselwood described himself in a bill in Chancery as warden of the Fleet: *Hasylwood* v. *Broke* (1530) C1/640/30. An Edward Haselwood was 'warden' in 1506: Bassett, 'The Fleet Prison', 392.

Hall (such as 'purgatory'), from the hereditary wardenship. The keepership was granted to a courtier for life in 1485 by letters patent,[35] and the surviving trustees of the Venour settlement brought an assize of novel disseisin to test the title.[36] The assize was stopped *rege inconsulto*, and the immediate outcome is unknown,[37] though the warden continued to exercise the office of keeper of the palace. Then in 1519 the whole title was pleaded in the King's Bench upon a *quo warranto*, again with no known outcome.[38] A further challenge was made by the Crown, in the 1530s, to the warden's claim to return and execute all judicial writs issued within the palace while the courts were sitting.[39] Yet another dispute in 1557 turned on whether some of the places in the palace, mentioned above, were by custom excluded from the privileges of the warden.[40]

The most important officers, by virtue of their technical knowledge and influence, and volume of business, were the three prothonotaries,[41] who were responsible for the enrolment of most of the records of litigation after issue joined,[42] including anything which raised a point of law, all common recoveries, and all bills of privilege against officers. They were repositories of technical learning, often consulted by the court,[43] and by its inferior officers.[44] The second prothonotary was appointed by the custos brevium, having perhaps once been his under-clerk; the first and third were appointed by the chief justice. Their positions were not hierarchical, for although the chief prothonotary had the sole right to enrol occasional memoranda relating to the court's own constitution and discipline,[45]

[35] *CPR 1485–94*, p. 22 (grant to Anthony Kene, 21 Sept. 1485); unenrolled patent recited in *Lord Dynham* v. *Carvanell* (next note; grant to Peter Carvanell, 4 Oct. 1485, reciting the grant to Kene). The first patent included the keeping of 'Paradise' and 'Hell', though the plea refers only to Purgatory ('purgatore infra aulam'), a house beneath the Exchequer called 'le Puttans house ou turre', and a house called 'le Grenelates' (i.e. Green Lattice).   [36] *Lord Dynham* v. *Carvenell* (1489) CP 40/910, m. 608.

[37] This may be the case referred to in *Att.-Gen.* v. *Babyngton* (1519) Chaloner 285 at 288, *per* Fyneux CJ (tr. 'in the time of Henry VII it was doubted whether the house of the Fleet was appendant to the office or the office to the house, or whether all was given at one time').

[38] *Att.-Gen.* v. *William Babyington* (1519) Chaloner 285, no. 14. The claim, as reported, was to a house and garden and certain rent, the office of keeping the prisoners in the Fleet, and the return of all judicial writs issued within the palace while the justices were sitting. The report ends with an adjournment for the warden to reframe his claim.

[39] *Att.-Gen.* v. *William Babyngton* (1532–4) KB 29/164, m. 48d; KB 27/1092, Rex m. 7; *Att.-Gen.* v. *Thomas Babyngton* (1537–8) KB 29/170, mm. 24, 35; KB 27/1106, Rex m. 7.

[40] *Babyngton* v. *Davys* (1557) CP 40/1169, m. 746 (assize; title set out at length); *Babyngton* v. *Evererde*, ibid., m. 748 (sim.). The first assize concerned the Green Lattice.

[41] For the first known oath of a prothonotary (1518) see Rast. Ent. 407 (442v), from Stubbe's entries.

[42] The filazers could continue to record cases after the general issue was joined, and occasionally enrolled other issues, but their share of business proceeding to judgment was small.

[43] See below, 359, 451–2.

[44] An attorney accused of misconduct in 1512 reported an interview with 'Mr Mordaunt' (chief prothonotary), when he sought his advice: *Re Robert Jenour* (1512) CP 40/1001, m. 720d.

[45] e.g. judicial patents, writs of adjournment, surrenders of filazerships, and enquiries into official misconduct.

the contentious business was shared as between equals at the discretion of the instructing attorneys. The chief justice also appointed the clerk of the warrants and estreats, the clerk of the treasury (or clerk of Hell), the keeper of the seal,[46] the clerk of the essoins,[47] the clerk of acknowledgments of fines and recoveries,[48] and all the exigenters and filazers. The custos brevium nominated the clerk of the juries,[49] who was responsible for issuing writs of *distringas juratores* and *habeas corpora*, and for enrolling continuances against juries.[50] These officers were mostly appointed for life,[51] and could only be removed for misbehaviour.[52] They were entitled to the privilege of suing in the court by attachment, and were conversely liable to be sued by bill of privilege rather than by writ.[53]

There were four exigenters (*exigendarii*), each responsible for issuing and enrolling the process leading to outlawry in their assigned groups of counties. The most valuable of the exigenterships was that for London, Middlesex, Sussex, Kent, Dorset, Somerset, Devon, Cambridgeshire, Huntingdonshire, Bristol, and Exeter; by the mid-1550s the London outlawries alone fill hundreds of rotulets each year. The exigenter for Yorkshire and other northern counties was also *ex officio* filazer for Northumberland, Westmorland, Cumberland, and Newcastle, and clerk of the king's silver for the whole of England.[54] There were in all thirteen filazers (*filaciarii*), who shared the counties between them according to a customary division which was unaltered throughout our period,[55] save that in 1542 a fourteenth filazer was appointed with responsibility for Monmouthshire.[56] The filazers issued writs of mesne process

---

[46] The seal was considered to be in the chief justice's custody, and he received one seventh part of the fees for its use, notionally to defray the cost of parchment: see BL MS. Add. 383136, ff. 31v–32v, 74v, 82v (accounts relating to the keeper of the seal and John Hales, clerk of the hanaper, 1547–52); E101/277/2 (accounts, with Mountagu CJ's autograph receipts given to the keeper of the seal in the 1550s); 109 Selden Soc., p. xxvi.

[47] His office had been eroded by the disuse of essoins. See Hastings, *Common Pleas*, 150; below, 331. He kept separate essoin rolls (CP 21) and did not enter his business in the CP 40 bundles.

[48] He was the chief justice's own clerk rather than the court's, but the appointment was nevertheless for life. The office is mentioned in 1546, when debt was brought on an alleged lease made (with Baldwin CJ's consent) in 1542, reserving a rent of £8: *Welche v. Smyth* (1546) CP 40/1128, m. 432d.

[49] Although the custos brevium had the right of presentation, even in this case the chief justice had the admission: see CP 40/843, m. 494 (1472); 109 Selden Soc. 55.

[50] The duties are summarized in *Countess of Devonshire v. Stepneth* (1526) CP 40/1049, m. 656 (action on the case for negligence in making out an insufficient writ, having been paid 6d. in Holborn).

[51] The clerk of the treasury, however, originally held at the will of the chief justice: below, 134. George Rolle (d. 1552) was given life tenure by act of Parliament: 14 & 15 Hen. VIII, c. 35; below, 139.

[52] Enrolled judgments of removal are few: e.g. *Re Cheker, clerk of the juries* (1469) CP 40/833, m. 328d; 109 Selden Soc. 54–5; *Re Elryngton, clerk of the juries* (1500) CP 40/954, m. 101.

[53] Baker, *Serjeants at Law*, 45–6.

[54] Memorandum of admission of John Fowke, 24 May 1519: CP 40/1024, m. 110.

[55] Hastings (*Common Pleas*, 50, 106, 151) did not realize that some of the rolls belonged to exigenters, and drew the mistaken conclusion that the county-division was not established in the 1480s.

[56] This office was held until Elizabeth's reign by John Lennard, the second prothonotary.

over their own names, filed both the original and judicial writs for their counties and transmitted them to the custos brevium for composite filing at each return-day, and sometimes handled routine cases down to judgment. They were not allowed to issue process of outlawry, which belonged exclusively to the exigenters.

The clerk of the warrants and estreats had three functions.[57] The first was to file and enrol the warrants of attorney which were required every time an attorney acted in litigation, for which he received a fee of 4d. or 8d. depending on the type of warrant.[58] Second, he had to look through the plea rolls at the end of every term and estreat the fines and amercements, which were sent to the Exchequer on separate membranes.[59] But his most valuable work by the end of the period, especially after the Statute of Enrolments 1536,[60] was to enrol deeds and recognizances, since this carried a fee of 2s. or 4s. for each entry.

It can hardly be doubted that when Mountagu CJ was translated from the King's Bench in 1545, the Common Pleas brought him more profit, by reason of the extensive patronage belonging to the chief justice.[61] It was, of course, pure chance which of the offices would fall in during a particular chief justice's period of office, but there were enough offices for vacancies to occur regularly. Mountagu, for example, was able to appoint a prothonotary (John Poley, 1552), an exigenter (John Campynett, 1548, who also acted as Mountagu's associate at the Guildhall), the filazer for London and Middlesex (John Mychell, 1552)—whose office was the most valuable of all the filazerships—and eight other filazers.[62] The offices could be used as a means of advancing members of the chief justice's family: for instance, Sir Robert Rede appointed two of his sons in law to be filazers.[63] There is no direct evidence that chief justices ever actually sold the offices, either for cash or for a share of the proceeds, though the exception of the chief justices of the two benches from the legislation of 1552 which prohibited the sale of offices[64] strongly suggests that it was sometimes done. On the rare occasions when admissions were recorded on the rolls, it was always in connection with a

[57] Hastings (*Common Pleas*, 107–8) erred in supposing that he was also keeper of the treasury (as to whom see below, 137–9).

[58] The rolls are bound at the end of each CP 40 bundle. The fees were noted by Thomas Jakes in 1506: 'Feoda pertinentia officio clerici warrantium et extractorum de Communi Banco', PRO, IND 17180, fo. 2; Hastings, *Common Pleas*, 257.

[59] Hastings, *Common Pleas*, 43, 55, 148–9. The rolls are mostly in E101/112; but there are some rotulets for 14–16 Hen. VII in E101/123/26. The estreats in E101/112/9 (1530–1) consist entirely of fines *pro licencia concordandi* and issues against defaulting juries.   [60] For which see below, 675–6.

[61] He was also entitled to a share of the sealing fees, which he did not have in the King's Bench: above, 130 n. 46; Blatcher, *King's Bench*, 17.   [62] Signatures of rolls in CP 40/1126–1155.

[63] Thomas Willoughby (d. 1545), who married Bridget Rede, was appointed filazer of London etc. in 1513; he was later JCP. Edward Wotton (d. 1551), who married Dorothy Rede, was appointed filazer of Suffolk in 1513 and of London etc. in 1517. Rede's eldest daughter Jane married John Caryll (d. 1523) when he was third prothonotary (1493–1510).   [64] 5 & 6 Edw. VI, c. 16.

surrender and admittance: the present holder surrendered his office to the chief justice to the use of the new officer, who was then admitted by the chief justice and sworn.[65] Such entries doubtless indicate sales of office from one holder to another,[66] but since the new officer was admitted for his own life the chief justice's consent was more than just formally necessary. Towards the end of our period the signatures at the foot of the filazers' rotulets occasionally reveal very short tenures,[67] and these may also indicate increasing commerce in offices.[68] It is possible that the filazerships were being farmed on short terms to rent-paying tenants,[69] or that *locum tenentes* were being admitted by the chief justice while a suitable long-term arrangement was sought.[70] However, the farming or assignment of offices without official sanction was improper. This is confirmed by an assize of novel disseisin brought in 1555 for the filazership of Hampshire and Wiltshire. It was brought by Nicholas Vaus against the three officers who occupied rotulets in succession to him, and the choice of an assize—which no one thought to question—shows that the clerkships of the courts, when granted for life, were regarded as freehold property.[71] The plaintiff alleged that he was admitted and sworn in 1542, and was seised by the receipt of 3*d.* paid to him for a *capias*; the place where he had sat, 'next to the post at the higher end of the court', was put in view.[72]

[65] Only five examples have been noted (all filazerships): CP 40/1048A, m. 1 (1525); CP 40/1049, m. 1 (1526); CP 40/1090, m. 511 (1535); CP 40/1091, m. 508d (1536); CP 40/1110, m. 1 (1541).

[66] There is a documented example of the assignment of an exigentership in 1507: *Astell* v. *Leeke* (1510) CP 40/990, m. 336; 94 Selden Soc. *380–1* (debt on a bond to secure Astell's admission; the issue is obscure, because the rolls show that Astell succeeded Leeke in Trin. 1507 as agreed). And there is an action arising from the sale of the clerkship of the essoins in 1525: *Radclyf* v. *Pyne* (1528) CP 40/1059, m. 130 (debt 'pro officio clericatu essoniorum').

[67] e.g. the filazership for Derbs., Leics., Notts., and Warw. had three occupants in 1539 (Maynard, Hil. to Trin. 1539; Grey in Trin. 1539 jointly with Maynard, and in Mich. 1539 jointly with Dyon; and Dyon, Mich. 1539 to 25 June 1541, when he surrendered to the use of Chalfount). The filazership for Essex and Herts. had five occupants between 1540 and 1550 (Hert 1538–41; Aleyn 1542–4; Amps 1545–6; Kympton 1546–50; Parker 1550–7), as did that for Northants., Shropshire, and Staffs. (Spurlyng 1537–41; Welche 1541; Wolcote 1541–7; Gawdy 1547–9; Pake 1549–54).

[68] e.g. it is known that Amps's filazership (last note) was the subject of a contract of sale, though Amps died before the sale could take effect: *Potter* v. *Amps* (1546/7) C1/1150/97–98. In 1536, John Bosse (who never signed rolls) surrendered a filazership to the use of Richard Bydwell (CP 40/1091, m. 508d); he was described by Baldwin CJ in 1545 as his trusty friend (PROB 11/30, fo. 303v), and was here presumably acting as Baldwin's nominee.

[69] Cf. above, 130 n. 48, for evidence of a lease of another freehold office with leave of the chief justice.

[70] In 1546 William Welche sued by attachment of privilege as 'one of the filazers' (*Welche* v. *Smyth* (1546) CP 40/1128, m. 432d), though he was not then occupying rolls in his own name. However, he appears in the rolls as filazer for Northants. etc. in Hil. 1541 only, and as filazer for Kent etc. in Mich. 1545 only. He may therefore have farmed one or both of these offices.

[71] This was established before our period: *Ingram* v. *Holme* (1468) CP 40/829, m. 139 (assize for clerkship of the essoins); Baker, *Serjeants at Law*, 45 n. 7.

[72] Cf. Edmund Dudley's reading (Gray's Inn, 1496) CUL MS. Hh.3.10, fo. 74, where it is said that in an assize for an office in the Common Pleas or King's Bench a view is not taken.

But it appeared in evidence that he had farmed his office from year to year without leave of the court, and had been personally absent for two years, for which offence he had been removed by Mountagu CJ. No record had been made of the removal, but it was nevertheless held to have been effective and the assize found for the defendants.[73] The words 'without leave of the court' clearly imply that offices could properly be farmed out if such leave was obtained.

The prerogative of the chief justice was absolute in relation to nomination, though the judges of the court could disallow the presentation if they felt the nominee unsuitable. This was established in 1557, when Brooke CJ named his wife's brother, Thomas Gateacre of the Middle Temple, as chief prothonotary; the judges rejected Gateacre as unfit, but Brooke's second nominee William Wheteley was allowed to take office despite the puisnes' preference for another candidate.[74] The nature of the privilege came to a head in a serious dispute concerning the major offices in 1558–60, occasioned by court interference with the chief justice's prerogatives.[75] The situation arose because of the unfortunate coincidence that three of the offices—those of third prothonotary, exigenter of London, and clerk of Hell—were vacant after the death of Sir Robert Brooke (chief justice for most of Mary's reign) on 6 September 1558.[76] The Crown, acting apparently on ministerial rather than legal advice, took the view that the appointments devolved *sede vacante* on the Crown and promptly filled the offices by letters patent. The prothonotaryship was conferred on Richard Cupper, already secondary of the court and suitably qualified.[77] At his earnest entreaty, he was allowed by the court to keep the office provided that he surrendered the patent and received his admission from the chief justice. This decision was made with the approval of all the justices and serjeants, and the attorney-general.[78]

The clerkship of Hell caused considerably more trouble. Although no mention was made of it, there had been a precedent for royal interference with the

---

[73] *Vaus v. Jefferne, Lynton, and Keble* (1554–5) CP 40/1162, m. 955; Dyer 114b; Chr. Yelverton's reports, fo. 240v. The succession (as shown in the rolls) was: Nicholas Vaus 1542–9, William Jefferne 1549–50, Bartholomew Lynton 1550–2, John Keble 1552–8. Vaus was also an attorney, and a member of the Middle Temple.

[74] Latin memorandum pr. Dyer 150b; BL Cotton MS. Nero C.I, fo. 42v; Rast. Ent. (1670 edn), fo. 443. The preferred candidate was John Byll of Lincoln's Inn, an attorney.

[75] *Cases from the Lost Notebooks of Sir James Dyer*, 109 Selden Soc., pp. lxxvii, 23–5, 54–7; Dyer 175a; *Scrogges v. Coleshill* (1560) CP 40/1189, m. 1097; 94 Selden Soc. *376, 378, 380*.

[76] Thomas Hemmyng (exigenter of London 1527–58) died before Brooke CJ on 1 Aug.; John Poley (third prothonotary 1552–8) died after Brooke on 26 Sept. The clerk of the treasury has not been identified. [77] Cupper was also a six clerk in Chancery: C1/1157/11–14 (c.1544/7).

[78] The outcome was complicated by the fact that Brooke CJ had in his lifetime appointed Richard Lone, the son of Prothonotary Jenour's sister. Cupper (d. 1566) signed the rolls until 1562, when Lone took over, but Lone's dockets begin in 1558: 94 Selden Soc. *378*.

clerkship of the treasury back in 1506, when (on the death of Frowyk CJ) the previous holder was dismissed by royal writ and the office was given to someone who was said to have bought the office for 300 marks from the king; nevertheless, Rede CJ succeeded in establishing the principle that the clerk should hold office under him and not by virtue of the royal grant.[79] In 1558 the office was conferred on William Smythe, one of the clerks of the Privy Council, apparently through influence at court. Smythe was supported by some privy councillors in resisting pressure from the judges to resign, and his case had to be referred to a judicial committee including the three chief justices and the attorney-general. The committee resolved that the clerkship was an inseparable incident of the office of chief justice, who was personally responsible for the treasury, that the clerk was the chief justice's personal servant, removable at will,[80] and accordingly that no appointment could be made by the Crown. Smythe had to make way for Dyer CJ's nephew George Farwell.[81]

The greatest contention of all arose in relation to the valuable exigentership for London, which had been granted to one Robert Coleshill, a protégé of the earl of Bedford. Coleshill was a soldier, with no experience of the office, and the judges were adamant that non-experts could not hold such important positions. The judges therefore decided at a meeting in Serjeants' Inn to eject Coleshill, whereupon Browne CJ appointed his nephew Alexander Scrogges.[82] The earl of Bedford and Lord Dudley then procured a special commission to hear and determine the matter, with power to imprison Scrogges if he refused to answer. Scrogges demurred to Coleshill's bill, was committed to the Fleet by the commissioners in June 1560, released by *habeas corpus* in November, rearrested and put in close custody, and only after another five weeks in prison released by Lord Keeper Bacon. The outcome was that Scrogges kept his office, but had to pay 200 marks to Coleshill, who surrendered his patent in February 1561.[83] This was a substantial victory for the Common Pleas, and particularly its new chief justice (Dyer CJ), in protecting the patronage of his office against outside interference.

---

[79] Notes written by Thomas Jakes (the dismissed officer) in PRO, IND 17180, fo. 5. Jakes consoled himself by marrying Lady Frowyk, and continued in his office as clerk of the warrants. According to him, the sale of the clerkship of Hell to his successor (John Kyrton) had been managed by Alderman Stephen Jenyns, Kyrton's brother in law.

[80] This must refer to the common-law position, which had been altered by the act of 14 & 15 Hen. VIII, c. 35.

[81] See the succession set out in *CPR 1580–2*, p. 167, no. 1235. Dyer was not appointed CJCP until Jan. 1559, so it seems that if Browne CJ made an appointment in Nov. 1558 it was treated (despite the statute of 1522) as having lapsed on his removal from office. Farwell's tenure ended with Dyer CJ's death in 1582.

[82] Scrogges was the son of Browne's sister Jane: see Browne's will (1567) PROB 11/49, fo. 153.

[83] *CPR 1557–8*, p. 460.

Of the inferior officers little is known. No doubt most of the clerks mentioned above had under-clerks,[84] or secondaries,[85] and perhaps writing clerks as well.[86] Some of these may have practised independently as attorneys. For instance, John Fytz, who described himself in 1541 as 'one of the clerks of William Johnson, one of the exigenters',[87] was also an attorney, and a member of the Inner Temple. By 1558 there was a 'secondary of the Common Pleas', who was presumably the chief pro-thonotary's secondary.[88] Even the more lowly ministerial officials, such as the criers,[89] the doorkeeper,[90] and the keeper of the ink,[91] were entitled to the same privilege in litigation as the higher officers. The keeper of the ink or some other minor official received payment for daily putting out the cloth or cloths,[92] the cushions for the judges, and mats for the officers in court,[93] though the duty of finding these items probably belonged to the under-sheriff of Middlesex.[94] The common vouchee was also presumably in attendance when recoveries were

[84] Each prothonotary was allowed two under-clerks by Ord. Trin. 35 Hen. VI (Hastings, *Common Pleas*, 29). See also Hastings, *Common Pleas*, 147 (under-clerks of filazers), 258 (under-clerk of the warrants).

[85] The clerk of Hell had a secondary: 109 Selden Soc. 23. This may have been the same office as under-clerk of the treasury: CP 40/1060, m. 406d (attachment of privilege for John Wichehalfe by that title, 1528).

[86] A note in 1482 distinguished 'he who wrote the roll' from the prothonotary's clerk: Pas. 22 Edw. IV, fo. 3, pl. 12.   [87] CP 40/1111, m. 834 (tr.).

[88] *CPR 1557–8*, p. 460 (Cupper confirmed in office of secondary, and second clerk of the treasury, on appointment as prothonotary). For the chief prothonotary's secondary at a later period (1637) see Baker, *Serjeants at Law*, 383.

[89] There were three criers besides the chief crier: Baker, *Serjeants at Law*, 45, 276–7. The appointment belonged to the Bilney family by inheritance: *Anon.* (1530) 121 Selden Soc. 417 at 420. The office of chief crier was reckoned to be as valuable as those of the custos brevium and prothonotaries: Jakes's memoranda, IND 17180, fo. 1. An attachment of privilege for 'unus proclamatorum' is noted in 1560: CP 40/1189, rolls of warrants, m. 29.

[90] CP 40/832, m. 438 (attachment of privilege for John Boteler, *ostiarius*, 1469).

[91] CP 40/950, m. 121d (attachment of privilege for John Palmer, *custos encausti*, 1499); CP 40/1189, rolls of warrants, m. 29 (likewise for Alexander Welhed, *clericus incausti*, 1560). In 1521 he is called 'the bearer of the inkpot': Baker, *Serjeants at Law*, 276.

[92] It is not clear whether this refers to the cloth on the table, or a cloth of estate behind the judges. The reference to a linen cloth (n. 94, below) does not readily fit either use.

[93] This may be gathered from the notes of appropriations of fines paid into court. CP 40/1043, m. 103 (20d. paid to widow of William Bexley for daily every term taking up and putting down the cloth and cushions for the justices—'pro levatione et depositione panni et pulvinarum pro justiciariis domini regis hic quotidie quolibet termino'—and 'lez mattes' for the officers, 1524); CP 40/1044, m. 606 (6s. 8d. paid to Bexley 'pro lez mattez preparandis' for the prothonotaries, filazers, exigenters, and other ministers of the Bench attendant upon their offices in court, 1524); CP 40/1058A, m. 103d (5s. 8d. paid to William Utterworth for his fee 'pro cotidiana impositione pannorum pro justiciariis hic et pro lez mattez pro officiariis hic ordinatis', 1528); CP 40/1095, m. 342d (fine paid to John Wolriche for arrears of wages for keeping the cloths and ink, 1537).

[94] CP 40/1041, m. 117 (10s. paid to William Colyns 'pro lez mattez et aliis necessariis hic in curia factis quando idem Willelmus fuit subvicecomes Midd.', 1523). Cf. CP 40/925, m. 139 (fine paid to one of criers for repairing the linen cloth in the Bench, 1493).

suffered at bar, and he may have had other duties in court.[95] He is identifiable in a record of 1538 as one of four 'yeomen' of London giving mainprize for an outlaw; we can identify two of the others as the keeper of the ink and the keeper of the treasury, and so it may be guessed that all four were minor officials whose presence was available in court.[96]

The establishment of the court was completed by the attorneys. They were the largest group of officers by far, numbering over 130 in 1480 and growing to at least 200 by 1550.[97] There is no surviving record of their admission, though their names can be found in the rolls and files of the clerk of the warrants. The attorneys were officers of the court, sworn in court[98] and subject to its disciplinary control,[99] and within its privilege for the purposes of their own litigation.[100] Unlike the clerks, however, they did not have freehold offices which could be put in view and protected by novel disseisin.

Discipline over officers was generally exercised on the occasion of ad hoc complaints of misbehaviour or neglect, but a procedure existed for summoning a grand jury of officers and attorneys to present felonies, erasures, deceits, and other offences committed in the court.[101] Such a jury was occasionally summoned in the time of Henry VIII, by means of a *venire facias* to the keeper of the palace; it would probably have been charged by the chief justice, though the earliest text of a charge so far discovered is from 1567.[102]

The serjeants at law were ministers of a different kind, since they possessed an 'estate and degree' and were brethren of the judges.[103] Indeed, by taking the coif a serjeant automatically vacated any clerical office in the court.[104] The serjeants shared with the other ministers the privilege of suing by attachment.[105] However,

[95] In later times he was the bag-bearer. Hastings, *Common Pleas*, 122, says he was one of the criers, but cites no evidence.

[96] CP 40/1096, mm. 326, 326d, 328d (John Thornecroft [unidentified]; Nicholas Webster [common vouchee]; John Wolryche [keeper of the ink]; William May [keeper of the treasury]).

[97] For the earlier figure see J. H. Baker, 'The Attorneys and Officers of the Common Law in 1480' (1980) 1 *JLH* 182–203. Sample counts of names in the warrants (CP 40) at five-yearly intervals show between 120 and 150 in the early sixteenth century, but around 200 by mid-century. There were, however, more attorneys than appear in the warrants for any particular year.

[98] See below, 438–9.   [99] See below, 439–40.

[100] Baker, *Serjeants at Law*, 46. Their servants were also privileged: *Chapeleyn* v. *Carter* (1500) KB 27/954, m. 34). In *Kyngeston* v. *Dryland* (1505) CP 40/973, m. 418d, an attorney boldly pleaded a custom for attorneys to be sued in debt and trespass by writ rather than by bill; the plaintiff rightly demurred, though no judgment is entered.

[101] e.g. CP 40/1063, m. 1 (16 sworn, Mich. 1529) and m. 616d (interim findings as to alteration of outlawry kept in treasury); CP 40/1095, m. 419d (19 sworn, Mich. 1537); CP 40/1122, m. 682 (15 sworn, Trin. 1544).

[102] *Cases from the Lost Notebooks of Sir James Dyer*, 109 Selden Soc. 132; *Praxis Utriusque Banci* (1674), 42–51.   [103] For serjeants see below, 421–4.

[104] *Conyngesby* v. *Caryll* (1510) KB 27/997, m. 111 (pleads that by becoming a serjeant he vacated *ipso facto* the office of prothonotary). Such circumstances were, however, very rare.

[105] e.g. CP 40/939, m. 154d (Conyngesby, 1497); CP 40/957, m. 345 (idem, 1501); CP 40/1048A, m. 520 (Englefield, 1525); CP 40/1062, m. 538d (Browne, 1529).

unlike attorneys, they were not liable to be sued by bill of privilege.[106] Whether the chief justice and other justices played a part in the nomination of new serjeants, and might claim a reward (as in later times) for their favour, is not recorded in this period.

THE RECORDS OF THE COURT[107]

Two officers of the court bore responsibility for keeping its records—the custos brevium and the clerk of Hell—and the relationship between their roles is not obvious from their titles. Although the custos brevium was officially styled 'the keeper of the lord king's writs and rolls for the Common Bench', and the deputy custos brevium may have been known as 'keeper of the records',[108] the records for which he was responsible were the files rather than the plea rolls. It was the custos brevium to whom the King's Bench sent writs of *certiorari* when searches were to be made for writs, and it was his duty to make the current and recent files available to the court and its officers. They were not, it seems, kept in Westminster Palace.[109] Only when no longer current were they brought to the Palace and deposited in the treasury ('Hell'). Most of the files still survive. The principal writ files (CP 52) were made up for the custos brevium at each return-day, and contain original and judicial writs, jury panels (returned to writs of *venire facias* or subsequent process against juries, with the posteas), and posteas.[110] The writs of covenant used in levying fines (CP 50), and the feet and notes of fines (CP 25, 26), were filed separately by the chirographer's office.[111]

The principal record was the series of plea rolls (CP 40), which contain the authentic record of every step in litigation from the issue of first process down to the execution of judgment. The plea rolls were officially in the custody of the chief justice, and it was to him that writs of error were directed to send the record to the King's Bench, and writs of *certiorari* in respect of entries on the roll.[112] As we have seen, the chief justice himself appointed the clerk of Hell to look after them. The official style of the clerk included the phrase 'keeper of the records (*custos recordorum*) of the Common Bench',[113] and it seems certain that it was he and his under-clerk who had the prime responsibility for the records rather than the custos brevium. There are references to the office in the time of Henry VI,

---

[106] *Paston* v. *Jenney* (1471) Baker, *Serjeants at Law*, 47–8.   [107] See 94 Selden Soc. *100–3, 381–2*.

[108] John Elryngton, who was deputy custos brevium by 1482, was so described on his tomb at Hackney: J. Weever, *Ancient Funeral Monuments* (1767 edn), 306.

[109] In 1481 they were kept in St Bartholomew's church: Pas. 21 Edw. IV, fo. 27, pl. 21.

[110] They are made up in county order, beginning with Cumberland and Westmorland.

[111] The surviving files of concords of fines (CP 24) do not begin until 1559.

[112] e.g. *Archer* v. *Hawe* (1519) KB 27/1031, m. 87; 109 Selden Soc. 86.

[113] *LP*, i. 438(1), m. 7 (pardon for Thomas Jakes, late clerk of Hell, 1509); CP 40/1039, m. 505d (attachment of privilege for George Rolle, 1523).

but the first identified holder is Leonard Knyght (d. 1500), who acted under Bryan CJ.[114]

The individual membranes or rotulets (*rotuli*) were kept by the prothonotaries, exigenters, and filazers, who brought them in to be bound up within seven or eight days after the end of every term, together with the less numerous rotulets of the attorney-general (and later the clerk of the king's process), the clerk of the king's silver, and the clerk of the juries. The task of binding them up belonged to the clerk of the essoins, who received a termly fee from the chief justice for performing this duty.[115] They were partly arranged in a customary sequence, the officers having one roll each at the beginning of the bundle, and the prothonotaries having batches of membranes (twenty each) at numbers 101–60, 301–60, 401–60, and so forth;[116] most of the other membranes were added in irregularly sized batches in no particular order. The bound membranes were then numbered in uniquely strange roman numerals, applied with a brush. At the end of each bundle, separately numbered in ink, were the rotulets containing deeds and recognizances, followed (with a third sequence of numbers) by the enrolled warrants of attorney; these last two batches of membranes were signed by the clerk of the warrants. After their delivery to the clerk of the treasury, the officers' clerks were allowed free access to them to enter continuances and judgments.[117]

The first membrane of each term's plea rolls bears the name of the chief justice—or the senior puisne justice, when the chief justiceship was vacant—indicating that they were his rolls. Moreover, on the death of a chief justice it was the practice to send a writ to his personal representatives to hand over the records to his successor.[118] Apart from current documents, such as acknowledgments of fines taken on circuit,[119] this was probably a mere formality. In reality the rolls were already an enormous archive, stored in a dank cellar beneath

---

[114] CP 40/906, m. 128d (fine paid to him for 'repairs of the chests and other necessaries belonging to his office', 1488); CP 40/919, m. 115 (fine paid to him to mend the chests and to repair the doors and windows of the house where the records are supposed to be kept, 1492); PRO, IND 17180, fo. 5 (mentioned in 1505 as a former clerk).

[115] Ord. Mich. 23 Hen. VII, IND 17180, fo. 9; Hastings, *Common Pleas*, 259. The order confirms what it declares to have been the previous practice: the rolls were sent to the clerk of the essoins via the clerk of estreats, who kept them for two days to estreat the fines and amercments. In BL MS. Add. 63643, m. 3d (Richard Colnett's remembrance), is a receipt for Colnett's 25 exigent rolls of Trin. 1537 signed by Andrew Bernard, who was clerk of the essoins (bill of privilege, 25 June 1555, in CP 40/1164, m. 701).

[116] In the latter part of each bundle the order might be abandoned, and the prothonotaries' additional rolls mixed up with the rest.

[117] Ord. Mich. 23 Hen. VII, IND 17180, fo. 9. In *Burgh* v. *Blount* (1504) CP 40/969, m. 455, an attorney's bill of costs included a sum 'for continuation of the plea by the roll in Hell' ('pro continuatione placiti predicti per rotulum in inferni').

[118] 109 Selden Soc., p. xxvi n. 45; Hastings, *Common Pleas*, 143–4. The writ to the executors of Rede CJ is pr. in Rast. Ent. 386 (420v), from Stubbe's entries.

[119] See Dyer CJ's note in 110 Selden Soc. 233–4.

the Exchequer—or in the subterranean passage linking the Exchequer and the Common Pleas—officially known by the misleadingly grand name of king's treasure house, or treasury of the Common Bench, but better known since the fourteenth century as 'Hell'.[120] The place was ill ventilated and dark, the floor was bare earth, and the constant dampness occasionally gave way to flooding when the spring tides brought the Thames into Westminster Hall. When Brudenell CJ took office in 1520, some of the coffers standing on the ground had rotted, and the rodents were beginning to gnaw at the parchment.[121] He was disturbed by what he found, and took some steps to set things right. He appointed a new clerk of Hell, George Rolle, who was given life tenure by act of Parliament in 1522;[122] and it was Rolle's deputy, William May, who seems to have been active in improving conditions.[123] Brudenell's scheme for renovating the treasury is found in a bill of costs enrolled in the plea roll for Michaelmas term 1520.[124] A tiled floor was to be provided, raised on timber joists; two 'great presses' were to be made; a new free-stone window, barred with iron, was to be cut; and the roof was to be plastered. The scheme was implemented in part by allocating money received from fines to the repair account.[125] Money from the same source was allocated in 1521 for repairing the plea rolls of Henry V and Henry VI.[126] Nevertheless, Hell continued to earn its name, and the problems identified by Brudenell CJ were still troubling Dyer CJ fifty years later.

The clerk of Hell controlled access to the records, for which he was entitled to charge fees; and, unless the searcher knew the number of the roll he wished to inspect, the clerk could charge a search fee which was not fixed by the rules of court. Historical research without fee was permitted only to the officers and attorneys, 'for the assurances of their matters'.[127] Searching the rolls has always been tiresome, in the absence of indexes, and contemporaries had to rely on memory, on private notes, on books of entries, and on the experience of the senior officers. There are two kinds of parchment rolls besides the plea rolls which were once

[120] 94 Selden Soc. *102* n. 1. For Paradise, Hell, and Purgatory see above, 129 n. 35 For their location see Hastings, *Common Pleas*, 143–4; H. M. Colvin (ed.), *The History of the King's Works*, i (1963), 543.

[121] 94 Selden Soc. *102*. In *Nichols v. Haywood* (1545) Dyer 59a, the court had to consider the consequences of a deed allegedly having been eaten by mice while in its custody.

[122] 14 & 15 Hen. VIII, c. 35; 94 Selden Soc. *381*. He is described in CP 40/1063, m. 616d (1529) as *clericus thesaurarii*.   [123] He is mentioned in the plea rolls between 1521 and 1536, cited below.

[124] CP 40/1030, m. 2; extract pr. 94 Selden Soc. *102*.

[125] e.g. CP 40/1033, mm. 110d, 601d (Trin. 1521); CP 40/1032B, m. 130d (Mich. 1521); CP 40/1043, m. 103 (thirteen glass quarries put into the Treasury window, Pas. 1524); CP 40/1044, m. 505 (mending the covering of the rolls—'pro emendatione cooperture rotulorum domini regis in loco Thezaurarii de Banco hic existentium'—and other necessaries, Trin. 1524); CP 40/1045, m. 558 (Mich. 1524); CP 40/1077, m. 351 (Pas. 1533); CP 40/1078, m. 526d (Trin. 1533); CP 40/1090, m. 442d (Trin. 1536).

[126] CP 40/1033, m. 614d (13s. 4d. paid for twelve 'forelles' to bind the rolls, and for food and drink for a workman for six weeks).   [127] Hastings, *Common Pleas*, 252, 253.

incorrectly regarded by the Public Record Office as indexes or reference aids. Each of the three prothonotaries kept rolls of both kinds. There are therefore three distinct series in each category, none of them reflecting the whole business of the court. The so-called 'docket rolls', the earliest of which is John Muscote's for the first term of Henry VIII,[128] are essentially accounts of business done for named attorneys. They were kept for the purpose of calculating debts due to the prothonotaries from their attorney-clients, the debts being drawn out of the dockets into 'pye books' which have not survived.[129] Occasionally a prothonotary,[130] or more usually his personal representatives, would put the outstanding debts in suit.[131] When the executors of John Jenour (d. 1542) issued writs against fifty attorneys in 1545, many of them were sued by surname only—with windows left for the forenames to be added—because the dockets and pyes did not give full names.[132] The other supplementary rolls, also known to contemporaries as dockets (or 'doggets'), are best distinguished by their alternative title of remembrance rolls (CP 45). The earliest surviving remembrance is Jenour's for Easter term 1524.[133] These rolls contain memoranda of draft pleas and the rules given in particular cases, and are useful as providing a means of going beyond the plea roll into the day to day progress of litigation.[134] Both kinds of docket were compiled for contemporary administrative purposes, and not to ease the search for precedents.

Although only prothonotaries' remembrances have survived in the archives of the court—and those with many gaps—it is known that filazers and exigenters kept them as well.[135] But there was no need to preserve such things because they were not technically records, and (as the court said in 1484) at the end of every term the docket 'died'.[136] There may also have been a rudimentary library in the

---

[128] CP 60/1 (formerly IND 1, and before that CP 19/1). Muscote was second prothonotary 1498–1512.

[129] 94 Selden Soc. 101.

[130] e.g. *Reymond* v. *Chamber et al.* (1547) CP 40/1132, m. 449 (debt against fourteen attorneys, all but four of them for 40s.).

[131] e.g. *Osberne (executrix of Muscote)* v. *Skrymshawe* (1521) CP 40/1032B (declaration setting out the custom of the court for prothonotaries to receive fees from attorneys, laying a retainer in 1500); *same* v. *Fitz* (1522) CP 40/1036, m. 409d (sim., laying a retainer in 1498); *same* v. *Treheyron* (1522) ibid., m. 475 (sim.). See further below, 340.

[132] *Heigham and Jenour (executors of Jenour)* v. *Bere et al.* (1545) CP 40/1125, mm. 551, 554d (debt for 40s. each).   [133] CP 45/1.

[134] See below, 342–3.

[135] *Anon.* (*c.*1510) 120 Selden Soc. 8, no. 1 (tr. 'he appeared by attorney upon the filazer's remembrance, and the filazer nevertheless made out a *capias*...'). Three exigenters' remembrance rotulets for Trin. 1537 have survived: BL MS. Add. 63643. A stray filazer's remembrance roll of 1581 is now in Minnesota: *ELMUSA*, ii. 291, no. 1190.

[136] *Barret* v. *Lokyngton* (1484–5) Mich. 2 Ric. III, fo. 11, pl. 24 ('termino finito ille doket moritur', referring to the docket of the clerk of the juries); entered in KB 27/895, m. 29 (*certiorari* to custos brevium to search for *distringas juratores*; no mention of docket). Cf. *Anon.* (1482) Pas. 22 Edw. IV, fo. 3, pl. 12 (recourse to docket of prothonotary's clerk where plea roll erased).

treasury. At any rate, we know that in 1524 the court ordered the purchase of a book of new statutes, to be kept there 'with the intention that the justices here may inspect the statutes contained in the same book at convenient times'.[137] But there was still no thought of providing books for use in court.[138]

THE BUSINESS OF THE COURT

The jurisdiction of the court was formally unchanged throughout the period. It still had a monopoly over the real actions, though by the sixteenth century the only real actions regularly encountered were partition, formedon, and the fictional forms of writs of entry.[139] Some mixed actions, such as *quare impedit* and waste, were also within its exclusive jurisdiction. In addition it had a monopoly of false judgment, to review proceedings in local courts which were not of record. It used *corpus cum causa* to remove London cases where one of the parties was a litigant in the Common Pleas, and these removals became very frequent towards the end of the period. Most other actions were shared with the King's Bench: trespass, including actions on the case, and replevin had long been shared, while debt, detinue, and covenant, had been brought within the compass of the latter by means of its bill procedure. The vast majority of actions throughout the period were writs of debt, followed some way behind by trespass *quare clausum fregit*.

The sheer volume of business in the rolls has made exact quantification unachievable. Hastings counted the entries in Michaelmas term 1482 as including 4,412 debt cases and 1,252 trespass, with a total of over 6,000. Nearly 700 of these cases reached issue or imparlance during the term.[140] These figures give a sense of the extent of business, though they are open to the objection that they include double or multiple entries in the same cases. The double-counting is most serious in relation to entries before appearance, at which stage the same case might appear two or three times in the same term. But her figure of 700 for appearances is also misleading, since some of the imparlances would have been in cases which reached issue later. Thus, even if it is assumed that the business was evenly distributed between all four terms, the total number of cases reaching the stage of an appearance in one year would have been well under 2,800. A figure of 1,600 has been suggested, though it can only be a matter of informed guesswork.[141]

---

[137] CP 40/1044, m. 302 (fines totalling 6s. 8d. paid 'quo quodam libro novorum statutorum in loco Thesaurarii hujus curie remanendo ad intentionem quod justiciarii hic statuta in eodem libro contento respicere possunt quolibet tempore oportuno'). [138] See below, 487.

[139] i.e. writs of entry in the *post* for common recoveries (below, 694) and writs of entry in the *quibus* for freeing villeins (below, 605).

[140] CP 40/882; Hastings, *Common Pleas*, 26–7, 190. [141] Brooks, *Pettyfoggers and Vipers*, 51.

Only between 5 and 10 per cent of cases proceeded as far as judgment. In the four terms of 1494, the number of judgments entered for the plaintiff was 103. Of these, 70 were in actions of debt, mostly (53) on bonds, 29 in trespass and forcible entry, and one each in waste, replevin, rescue, and case. Sixty-four per cent of the judgments in debt followed a confession or failure to answer. The average size of debt recovered was around £15,[142] the average damages in trespass around £6.[143]

Some later figures were produced by Holdsworth, who counted 4,410 entries in Trinity term 1525; 7,718 in Michaelmas term 1557; and 6,840 in Trinity term 1558.[144] Assuming that he and Hastings were both using the same method, these figures suggest a modest increase, following a dip in the 1520s. It is, however, not wholly clear in either case what was being counted or whether allowance was made for multiple entries in the same suit. On the other hand, the practice of grouping debt actions in batches on the filazers' rotulets means that what appears to be a single entry may sometimes represent several discrete actions brought by the same plaintiff.[145]

A full count of entries in the prothonotaries' rotulets for the year 1535 reveals that 1,001 cases were pleaded to issue (of which 126 ended in a recorded judgment) and that there were in addition 283 judgments by default.[146] This suggests that the total volume of contested litigation may have decreased slightly since the 1480s. Although the total number of judgments entered for the plaintiff (409) shows a dramatic fourfold increase over the 1494 figure, this must be because a higher proportion of cases were now proceeding to judgment. It is more difficult to assess the number of actions commenced in 1535. It could in theory be done precisely by counting the number of original writs in the files, but these have curled up in a way which makes counting very difficult. Another approach is to analyse the filazers' rotulets, where mesne process was entered. The membranes kept by Geoffrey Chamber, filazer for London, in Hilary term 1535, contain 588 entries, of which 332 end with a *sicut prius capias*. The latter figure may be a safer indication of the number of actions commenced—albeit perhaps commenced in a previous term—and if we assume the same density of entries on the membranes of the other filazers, we obtain a rough figure of between 2,500 and 3,000 new suits in the

---

[142] Not counting damages for the withholding of the debt, or costs.

[143] CP 40/927–930. A similar count was made for 1495, though the rolls for Trin. 1495 (CP 40/933) were unavailable for inspection. A total of 188 judgments was obtained for the seven terms of 1494 and 1495, of which 130 were in debt; 84 of them were by confession or default.

[144] *HEL*, iv. 255. His low figure of 984 for Mich. 1525 is explained by an adjournment of the term for plague.

[145] Yorke 98, pl. 33; 153, no. 172. Extreme examples are actions by the inns of court and chancery against hundreds of members for dues, combined in one long entry. The writ files, however, show that in these cases there was a separate writ for each defendant.

[146] CP 40/1084 (182 issue, 72 default); CP 40/1085 (290 issue, 82 default); CP 40/1086 (261 issue, 49 default); CP 40/1087 (275 issue, 80 default).

term, or over 10,000 for the year.[147] The analysis of Chamber's membranes for Hilary term 1535 by forms of action shows that as many as 560 (95 per cent) of the 588 actions entered are for debt, with only 14 for trespass; but London may well be untypical in this regard, and debt cases may have been more amenable to settlement than others. If we count only cases proceeding as far as issue or judgment, the total number of debt cases in all the filazers' and prothonotaries' membranes for the year 1535 was 783 (61 per cent of the cases reaching that stage), and the average debt recovered was £19. The number of trespass cases reaching the same stage was 523 (25 per cent), of which 48 (4 per cent of the total) were actions on the case.

Between 1535 and 1555 the number of membranes normally enrolled each term increased by around 50 to 70 per cent, and since the entering practices did not visibly change in the interim it may be supposed that this increase resulted from a boom in litigation. The relative sizes of the bundles point, very roughly, to a doubling between 1482 and 1555 in the number of cases commenced each year. The figures for sealing fees corroborate the conclusion that the business of the court more or less doubled between 1490 and 1560.[148]

---

[147] CP 40/1084. Chamber used 34 rolls, and the total number of filazers' rolls is 277. The exigenters need not be counted, since the actions on their rolls would all have been on a filazers' roll first. There are a few cases on the prothonotaries' rolls (e.g. in real actions) which have no previous entry on a filazer's roll, but the total is not very significant. There are 1,555 filazers' rolls in the whole year, and 1,005 prothonotaries' rolls.   [148] Brooks, *Pettyfoggers and Vipers*, 51.

7

The Court of King's Bench

THE most innovative court in our period was the King's Bench, especially during the fifty years covered by the three chief justiceships of Sir John Fyneux (1495–1525), Sir John Fitzjames (1526–38), and Sir Edward Mountagu (1539–45). In the more turbulent period which followed the death of Henry VIII, there were five chief justices in ten years, none of them exerting such a demonstrable influence on the court or the law.

The court was smaller, in terms of clerical personnel, than the Common Pleas, and throughout our period it had a much smaller work-load. It also began with a smaller judicial establishment, for until 1522 the full court consisted of only three judges. In that year, Fitzjames was added as a third puisne judge, but he was appointed chief baron of the Exchequer the next day and was apparently never paid as a King's Bench judge. The purpose of the appointment may simply have been to overcome doubts as to the qualifications of the chief baron to undertake certain kinds of business. In 1525, however, John Port became a permanent third puisne, and four judges—as in the Common Pleas—remained the normal establishment for the next three hundred years.[1] The judges were paid the same wages and fees as those of the Common Pleas, except that the chief justice received a considerably larger sum than any other judge,[2] reflecting his special position as 'chief justice of England'[3] or (as he was sometimes now called) 'lord chief justice of England'.[4] By custom, the

---

[1] For the period 1485–1547 see 94 Selden Soc. 358–60. For the remainder see Sainty, *Judges of England*, 9–10, 19, 29.

[2] Sainty, *Judges of England*, 4, 20. The chief justice received £168. 10s. at the beginning of the period (Blatcher, *King's Bench*, 39) and £198. 6s. 5d. by 1556, when it was increased to £224. 19s. 9d. (cf. 109 Selden Soc. 11). In 1506 it was said to be £188. 10s. 5¼d.: Jakes, 'Feoda justiciariorum de ambobus locis', IND 17180, fo. 3. £20 of that probably represents the assize fee. The principal fee was raised by £30 in 1545: *LP*, xii. II. 910(40).

[3] This informal title was recognized before our period: *Paston v. Jenney* (1471) 64 Selden Soc. 189. It was used on the brass of Billyng CJ's wife Mary (1499) in St Margaret's Church, Westminster: Weever, *Ancient Funeral Monuments* (1767 edn), 270. Markham, Billyng, and Fyneux CJJ were each described in windows formerly in Gray's Inn hall as: 'Judex Anglie supremus': BL MS. Harley 1042, ff. 30v, 54v. The title was recognized by Parliament in 34 & 35 Hen. VIII, c. 26, s. 5. Other examples are *Anon.* (1508) 2 Caryll 584, pl. 427; Fitz. J.P. 48 (1538); *LP*, xx. II. 910(40) (patent of 1545); *Anon.* (c.1544/5) Wm Yelv. 360, no. 99 ('Mountagwe, cheffe justyce dengleterre'); BL MS. Harley 1624, fo. 72 ('Saunders, chief justice de Engleterre', 1558).

[4] This form is used in the will of Lady Huse (d. 1503/4), widow of Huse CJ (d. 1495): PCC 22 Holgrave; BL MS. Stowe 542, fo. 76v; and on the monumental inscription at Wroxeter, Salop., for Bromley CJ ('lord chyffe justes of englond', 1555);

senior puisne was known as the secondary justice, and he sometimes pronounced the judgments of the court.[5]

OFFICERS OF THE COURT

The clerical staff consisted of the king's coroner and attorney in the King's Bench,[6] known informally as the clerk of the Crown; the chief clerk (or prothonotary[7]); the custos brevium (who was also clerk of the warrants); and thirteen filazers.[8] There were no exigenters. Apart from the clerk of the Crown, who was appointed by letters patent, all the clerical offices were in the gift of the chief justice for the time being when they fell vacant. The chief clerk appointed the secondary of the King's Bench office, one or two under-clerks, and the clerk of the papers. The secondary is an elusive figure, who begins to appear in the plea rolls in the middle of the sixteenth century when *damna clericorum* are noted as having been 'paid to the secondary',[9] though the office may date from the fifteenth century.[10] The secondary's remembrance rolls begin in 1552, and show that he was principally responsible for entering satisfactions of judgments.[11] The clerk of the Crown appointed his own under-clerk, sometimes called 'one of the clerks of the Crown',[12] but known in later times as the secondary of the Crown Office. The prisoners of the court were the ultimate responsibility of the earl marshal of England, whose patent, enrolled in the King's Bench when he was sworn in,[13] empowered him to appoint the marshal or under-marshal of the King's Bench prison—also known as the Marshalsea[14]—to discharge the duty

---

[5] e.g. 1 Caryll 50, 54, 56 (judgment given by secondary judge *ex assensu curiae*); 93 Selden Soc., p. xiii n. 9.

[6] Cf. the king's attorney-general, who had been the corresponding officer in the Common Pleas, and still remained an officer there rather than in the King's Bench.

[7] The Ropers favoured this designation (94 Selden Soc. 363 nn. 13–14), though the official title remained *capitalis clericus*.

[8] For the filazers see C. A. F. Meekings and J. H. Baker, 'Clerks of the King's Bench 1399–1547', in *Legal Records and the Historian*, ed. Baker, 128–39. For the other officers see 94 Selden Soc. 352–7, 361–7.

[9] These entries are common in the 1550s but do not give names. An interesting example is *Hepworth v. Oxley* (1554) KB 27/1170, m. 145 (plaintiff recovers £15. 6s. 8d. '(tr.), whereof 15s. 4d. for *damna clericorum*, which the secondary remits with the consent of the officer because the plaintiff is admitted by the court *in forma pauperis*').

[10] In 94 Selden Soc. 364–5, the earliest known secondary was said to be John Lucas (d. 1525). But he may have been preceded by John Fisher, described in 1498 as 'prothonotary next [to] Master Roper': Ives, *Common Lawyers in pre-Reformation England*, 124.

[11] KB 167/1–2 (rolls of Francis Sandbach, Hil. 1552 to Mich. 1581).

[12] *CITR*, i. 462; 94 Selden Soc. 354 (Thomas Blake, 1523).

[13] e.g. KB 27/1065, Rex m. 12 (duke of Suffolk sworn, 20 Nov. 1527). The patents were also enrolled in the Exchequer: e.g. E159/289, Mich. m. 7 (earl of Surrey, 1510). They included an express power to appoint marshals of the King's Bench, Exchequer, Steward's Court, and Household: *CPR 1485–94*, p. 74.

[14] Cf. 19 Hen. VII, c. 10, s. 4, where the King's Bench prison and Marshalsea seem to be different; but the latter probably means the Marshalsea of the Household. The word originally denoted the

of keeping them.[15] However, the history of this office is obscured, as in earlier periods, by the fact that the Crown also appointed marshals of the King's Bench.[16] The court also had an usher (or doorkeeper) and crier, appointed by letters patent and probably discharging the duties by deputy.[17] The officers had the like privilege as those of the other bench to sue in their own court by attachment of privilege, and they were suable by bill because of their duty of attendance. They were subject to removal for negligence.[18] There is some evidence relating to the sale and transfer of offices,[19] but none revealing the kind of dispute which beset the mid-Tudor Common Pleas.

The work of the chief clerk corresponded to that of a prothonotary in the Common Pleas, but his exclusive responsibility for cases commenced by bill gave him an ever-increasing share of the official business.[20] By the middle of the sixteenth century, the filazers were faring very badly. It was not uncommon for two or three of them to share a membrane, and some filazers had no enrolled business in a particular term at all. We know from a note written by the clerk of the papers in 1532 that they all had their set places in court;[21] but it may be doubted whether they had any particular reason to attend for most of the time. The clerk of the papers himself had no known counterpart in the Common Pleas, but it seems that he was in effect one of the under-clerks of the chief clerk responsible for filing paper pleadings and other documents.[22] The Crown side of the court was managed by the clerks of the Crown, who handled all proceedings on indictment, criminal informations,

marshalcy rather than a place; but in the King's Bench rolls the marshal is *marescallus marescalcie domini regis.*

[15] e.g. Crown Office entries, fo. 150 (Sir Gilbert Debenham appointed deputy marshal by duke of Norfolk, 1484); ibid., fo. 181 (Thomas Brandon appointed by Marquess Berkeley, *vice* William Brandon, 1491); KB 27/1079, Rex m. 5 (Gawain Carewe, appointed by duke of Suffolk, 1531). The servants of Sir William Carrant, 'knight marshal' of the Marshalsea in 1540s, wore liveries of ginger-coloured broadcloth: C1/1109/18. In 1558, Sir William Fitzwilliam is mentioned as under-marshal: KB 27/1186, m. 158 (*submarescallus Marescalcie*); CP 40/1174, m. 522 (writ of privilege as *submarescallus noster in curia nostra*).

[16] e.g. *LP*, i. 31 (Sir Thomas Brandon reappointed, 1509; cf. previous note); ibid., no. 17 (Charles Brandon appointed, 1510); *LP*, ii. I. 510 (Sir Henry Sharneburne appointed to succeed Sir Thomas Brandon, 1515).

[17] Blatcher, *King's Bench*, 35–6; *CPR 1485–94*, p. 14 (Robert Harding appointed, 1485); KB 27/957, m. 1 (James Rede appointed, 1500); *CPR 1494–1509*, p. 516 (John Williams appointed, *vice* Rede, 1507); KB 27/1055, m. 33 (Robert Webbe and Thomas Brightman appointed, *vice* Williams, 1523); *Brightman v. Vaus* (1537) KB 27/1103, m. 73 (sues for defamation, reciting his patent as usher and crier); *CPR 1555–7*, p. 122 (John Skynner appointed, 1556). The last patent mentions the previous holders as John Williams, William Burditt, Robert Webbe, and Thomas Brightman.

[18] e.g. *Re Philip Wharton* (1502) KB 27/964, m.34d (filazer removed for prolonged absence without leave, despite warning).

[19] Blatcher, *King's Bench*, 40 n. 30; KB 27/957, m. 1 (John Gogh surrenders filazership to Fyneux CJ to the use of John Holme, 1500).   [20] For the increase in bill litigation see below, 154–6.

[21] 'Sessio filaciariorum in curia domini regis coram ipso rege' in Maycote's entries, ff. 142v–143; 94 Selden Soc. *354–5.*   [22] For the 'papers' see below, 338–42 (pleadings), 357 (pedigrees for challenges).

and process against outlaws. They did not deal with appeals of felony, which belonged to the chief clerk, unless and until the appeal was discontinued, in which case the king's coroner and attorney took over the prosecution in the king's name.

Most of the attorneys practising in the King's Bench[23] were either Common Pleas attorneys or filazers of the King's Bench, but there are enough names not falling into either category to show that the court also had a small cadre of attorneys of its own.[24] However, unlike their counterparts in the Common Pleas—which had rolls of admission, now lost—the attorneys allowed by the King's Bench were not admitted 'of record' and had no legal duty of attendance. For this reason it was held in 1486 that attorneys could not be sued in this court by bill of privilege.[25] Moreover, when a Common Pleas attorney was sued in the King's Bench by writ in 1535, he pleaded that by custom he could only be sued in the former, and by bill.[26] In certain circumstances now obscure the attorneys and clerks were entitled to presents of gloves from litigants.[27]

To a far greater extent than in the other central courts, the plea side of the King's Bench became in the early Tudor period something of a family business.[28] The root of the relationships was Sir John Fyneux, whose long tenure of the chief justiceship has already been noticed. In 1498 he appointed his son-in-law John Roper (d. 1524) as chief clerk,[29] perhaps as part of a marriage settlement for Jane Fyneux.[30] What financial arrangements were made between John Roper and Fyneux is not known, though Roper remarked in his will that 'the attaining of the office was to me no little charge'. In 1518, Roper obtained Fyneux's consent for a resettlement of the office on himself and his son William (d. 1578), in jointure, and the Roper dynasty remained chief clerks until they were bought out in 1616. One of Roper's daughters married Sir Edward Mountagu (d. 1557), whom we have noted as the second influential chief justice of the early Tudor period, and the other married first John Pilbarough (d. 1548), baron of the Exchequer, and secondly Leonard Sandell (d. 1570), who became a filazer under Mountagu and rose to be clerk of the Crown

[23] As in the case of the Common Pleas, their names may be discovered from the warrants enrolled with the plea rolls. The files of warrants of attorney survive in KB 150.

[24] It is possible that some or even all of these were under-clerks in the office.

[25] Hil. 1 Hen. VII, fo. 12, pl. 17 (tr. 'Note that if an attorney is sued by bill in the King's Bench, the bill shall abate; for no attorney is there of record, nor is his attendance necessary; but it is otherwise in the Common Bench...').   [26] Frognall v. Hawes (1535) KB 27/1096, m. 30d.

[27] Pilkington Narrative, 53 (c.1500); Maycote's entries, fo. 143 ('Divisio sive participatio cirothecarum in curia domini regis coram ipso rege. Memorandum quod integrum feodum cirothecarum consistat in [no more written]').

[28] For what follows see 94 Selden Soc. 55–7; Blatcher, King's Bench, 150; Ives, Common Lawyers in pre-Reformation England, 384–7.

[29] Roper succeeded John Bray between Hil. and Pas. 1498: 94 Selden Soc. 363. Roper is the spelling later adopted by the family, and is used by DNB, though John always signed his rolls as 'Rooper'.

[30] Another Jane Fyneux, apparently her half-sister, married Anthony Sonde, grandson of the Reynold Sonde who was chief clerk 1468–91.

in the court under Elizabeth. William Roper's marriage with Sir Thomas More's daughter Margaret brought the Ropers into the family circle of the Mores and Rastells, and through the Rastells with Richard Heywode (who became joint chief clerk with William Roper in 1548) and Edward Stubbe (chief prothonotary of the Common Pleas from 1518 to 1533). Fyneux and Roper were settled in Kent, and other Kentish lawyers were brought into the group. John Lucas (d. 1525), a protégé of either Fyneux or John Roper, was appointed by the former as a filazer in 1503; he later became secondary of the King's Bench and one of the wealthiest clerks in the court. Robert Maycote (d. 1533), who married Lucas's widow or daughter, was clerk of the papers.[31] And Henry See (d. 1537) was custos brevium. The two Ropers, Sir Thomas More and his father, William Rastell, Heywode, Stubbe, Maycote, Lucas, and See, were also linked by their common membership of Lincoln's Inn. That the links were real enough is shown by the fact that when William Rastell compiled his *Collection of Entrees* he was able to make use of books owned by Stubbe (whose son married his niece), Sir John More (his maternal grandfather), and John Lucas.[32] The extended family was very well placed to encourage and supervise the reforms which were to take place in the King's Bench during the early Tudor period.

THE RECORDS OF THE COURT

The principal records of the King's Bench were the plea rolls (KB 27), which are similar in appearance to those of the Common Pleas. Each term's bundle is arranged in four parts with separately numbered sequences of membranes: the plea rolls properly so called, or rolls of the plea side (kept by the chief clerk and the filazers); the rolls of estreats of fines and amercements (kept by the clerk of the estreats); the 'Rex rolls' of the Crown side (kept by the clerk of the Crown); and the rolls of warrants of attorney (kept by the clerk of the warrants).

The so-called docket rolls (or *Remembrancia*) of the King's Bench are in effect repertory rolls of the chief clerk's business as enrolled on the plea rolls, and are still of some use as indexes to the rolls.[33] They are not equivalent to the Common Pleas remembrance rolls, which contain rules.[34] The clerk of the Crown kept a different series of docket rolls—now known as the controlment rolls (KB 29)[35]

---

[31] For Lucas and Maycote see 94 Selden Soc. 364–5; PCC 38 Alen (will of Elizabeth Roper). Their books of entries both survive in the Library of Congress.   [32] See below, 345–6.

[33] They are in the class IND 1, and begin in the time of Ric. II (IND 1/1322). They are headed *Remembr*[*ancia*], followed by the name of the chief clerk.

[34] The surviving King's Bench rule books begin in 1603 (KB 125/1).

[35] These are arranged in yearly bundles. Within each term there are three sections: (i) memoranda of business begun that term, 'per bagam de secretis'; (ii) memoranda of other proceedings in court; (iii) special writs, such as *supersedeas* and *habeas corpus*. Like the plea rolls, they are annotated with subsequent proceedings, sometimes extending over several years.

—which are more nearly equivalent to those of the prothonotaries in the other bench, and minute the Crown business in more detail than the Rex rolls. It seems highly likely that remembrance rolls of some kind were also kept on the plea side, but all that now remain are the remembrances of the secondary (KB 167) from the very end of the period.[36]

Besides the rolls, there was an elaborate filing system of growing complexity. Until recently the files were inaccessible, having centuries ago been thrown together with other unsorted material in sacks; but they have now been almost completely sorted.[37] The principal files on the Crown side are the *Indictamenta* (KB 9), and (after 1500) the so-called *Baga de Secretis* series (KB 8),[38] which includes the records of state trials. On the plea side, the series called *Anglia* (KB 136) consists of writ-files corresponding closely to those of the Common Pleas, except in that they do not include process against juries or posteas. These latter were filed separately in the *Panella* series (KB 146), which in the fifteenth and early sixteenth centuries also included bills and proceedings thereon. As the bill jurisdiction grew in the sixteenth century, the associated documents were removed from the *Panella* and several new series of files were created to accommodate them. The most important were the *Bille Communes* (KB 148) and *Bille* (KB 147), which were in turn subdivided in 1549.

There can be no confusion over the responsibility for the records, because in the King's Bench there was only one officer, appointed by and responsible to the chief justice. The custos brevium was known in the fifteenth century as the keeper of the rolls (*custos rotulorum*) but by 1532 had adopted the more compendious title of 'keeper of the writs, records, pleas, writings, and muniments'.[39] The 'writings and muniments' may refer to his additional responsiblity, throughout the period, of serving as clerk of the warrants; but this office did not, as in the Common Pleas, include the privilege of enrolling deeds, which belonged to the chief clerk. John Payne, an attorney who held the office from 1540, obtained a private act of Parliament in 1543 securing his position as clerk of the treasury and clerk of the warrants for life.[40] It seems probable that the clerk of the warrants also acted as clerk of estreats, receiving a small payment from the Crown for this work.[41] The clerk could charge fees for access to the records in his keeping.[42]

[36] The first of these are the rolls of Francis Sandbache (d. 1581), who may be identified as secondary: 94 Selden Soc. 366.

[37] C. A. F. Meekings, 'King's Bench Files', in *Legal Records and the Historian*, ed. Baker, 97–139.

[38] As the controlment rolls demonstrate, the contemporary *baga de secretis* included the routine cases as well.

[39] 94 Selden Soc. 366–7; to which should be added the private statute 34 Hen. VIII, c. vii.

[40] 94 Selden Soc. 367; 34 Hen. VIII, c. vii; copied in Catlyn's precedent book, Alnwick Castle MS. 475, fo. 207. He died in 1573 and was buried in St Clement Danes.

[41] Blatcher, *King's Bench*, 41 n. 36 (Richard Pynfold), 43 n. 43 (John Gogh). Pynfold and Gogh were both keepers of the records: 94 Selden Soc. 366.

[42] John Husee was charged as much as 12*d.* per file for searching the files for an appeal in 1537: *Lisle Letters*, ed. Byrne, iv. 267.

As in the case of the Common Pleas, there is some slender evidence of the beginnings of a court library in this period. In 1533, a filazer donated to the office a copy of the *Liber Intrationum* (1510), though it does not seem to have remained there for very long.[43]

BILLS OF MIDDLESEX AND COMMON PLEAS

In 1483, Morgan Kydwelly defined the jurisdiction of the King's Bench as including all pleas touching the king, such as treason, murder, felony, trespass, maintenance, and conspiracy, writs of right brought by the king himself, writs of error, and also 'debt, detinue, account, and such like, by bill against someone in the custody of the marshal'.[44] He should have added replevin, ravishment of ward,[45] assizes,[46] statutory actions (such as *praemunire*), and the various forms of supervisory jurisdiction on the Crown side such as *habeas corpus*,[47] *quo warranto*,[48] and prohibition.[49] The Crown side of the court was largely criminal, though it also dealt with traverses of inquisitions transmitted from the Chancery,[50] and other occasional revenue business,[51] and in theory (though very rarely) actions by the king.[52]

By 'trespass', Kydwelly would have meant indictments for misdemeanour as well as civil actions of trespass *vi et armis*, which had always been clearly within the jurisdiction; the civil action was of direct concern to the king because of the allegation of a breach of the king's peace and the possibility of a fine to the king if the defendant was found guilty. It was not so obvious whether actions on the case were 'common pleas' for the purposes of chapter 11 of Magna Carta, and therefore excluded. Some of the readers on Magna Carta took the view that actions on the case, or at least some of them, were indeed outside the proper jurisdiction of the

[43] CUL, Syn. 3.51.3 (inscribed 'Anno Domini 1533 ... Memorandum quod Johannes Percyvall gent. donavit hunc librum officine domini Roperi armigeri prothonotarii domini regis in curia domini regis coram ipso rege ex mera et spontanea voluntate sua qu[...] ob zelum quem officine antedicte gessit'). It later belonged to Sir William Staunford JCP (d. 1558).

[44] Reading in the Inner Temple (1483) CUL MS. Ee.5.18, ff. 28v–29. Cf. *Note* (1529) Port 61, pl. 6; *Diversite de Courtz* (1533), sig. A3.

[45] e.g. *Danvers v. Pole* (1485) Mich. 2 Ric. III, fo. 13, pl. 37; KB 27/894, m. 66.

[46] e.g. *Wyndesore v. Albery* (1516) KB 27/1020, m. 88 (novel disseisin). These are very uncommon.

[47] See above, 91.

[48] See above, 119. The old method of proceeding by a special eyre commission (last used in 1521) was replaced by the less cumbersome information in the nature of *quo warranto*, the first example being *Att.-Gen. v. Abbot of Glastonbury* (1512) KB 27/964, Rex m. 134. See H. Garrett-Goodyear, 'The Tudor Revival of *Quo Warranto*' in *On the Laws and Customs of England*, ed. Arnold *et al.*, 232, 239–41.

[49] See below, 212–15 (to the Admiralty), 239, 250–1 (to spiritual courts).   [50] See below, 171–3.

[51] e.g. *Att.-Gen. v. Prior of Norwich, ex parte John* (1487) KB 27/905, Rex m. 10 (*de corodio habendo*). Corodies were more usually dealt with by the Exchequer: below, 162 n. 27.

[52] e.g. *Att.-Gen. v. Wise* (1557) Dyer 145a; 109 Selden Soc. 219; KB 29/189, mm. 71, 72d (debt against receiver in Ireland upon arrears of his account). The king usually brought debt and other actions in the Common Pleas.

King's Bench.[53] But their distinctions were too refined and inconclusive to deter the judges and officers of the court from accepting a profitable new line of work. It may be that *assumpsit* was first accommodated on the basis that it was a form of deceit, which the commentators accepted as being proper for the King's Bench; but any scruples seem to have disappeared in practice and no formal jurisdictional objection is found to any species of action on the case being brought in the King's Bench by writ.[54] Even Fitzherbert, a conservative Common Pleas judge, conceded that all actions on the case could be brought in the King's Bench, because in his view all writs on the case were supposed to allege a trespass against the king's peace.[55]

Any possible jurisdictional dispute over case was rendered almost academic by the development of the bill procedure mentioned by Kydwelly. The origins of this procedure lie in the earlier part of the fifteenth century and need not be traced here.[56] It was to be the principal attraction of the King's Bench, without which it might have disappeared altogether as a court of civil jurisdiction, but as a result of which it became the most creative of all the common-law courts in the sixteenth century. The procedure worked in two stages. First, the plaintiff sued his adversary by a 'bill of Middlesex', alleging a fictional trespass *vi et armis*—usually the breaking of a close at Westminster or (after 1540) at Hendon[57]—upon which the defendant could be arrested and bailed. The defendant was then, even though in reality at large on bail,[58] a prisoner of the marshal of the Marshalsea and within the privilege of the court. This meant, by ancient custom, that the defendant could now be sued by another bill in respect of any personal action, even if it would otherwise be of a kind falling within the category of common pleas. Debt, detinue, covenant, and account, were thus brought within the King's Bench jurisdiction, notwithstanding Magna Carta, and any remaining difficulties about actions on the case were for the same reason dispelled. But at the same time it gave a plaintiff the positive advantages of being able to sue without purchasing an original writ from the Chancery,[59] of an expeditious first process, and of not having to disclose the true

---

[53] e.g. *Anon.* (fifteenth cent.) HLS MS. 13, p. 411 (tr. 'Trespass is a common plea and the plea may as well be returned in the Common Bench as in the King's Bench, and this is because the writ is *contra pacem*... but if it is not *vi et armis*, it may only be returned in the Common Bench'); Edward Hales (Inner Temple, 1512) CUL MS. Ee.3.46, fo. 67v (King's Bench may only hear actions where the king is to have a fine). See also *Diversite de Courtz* (1532 edn), quoted at 94 Selden Soc. 58 (some actions on the case may be brought in the King's Bench, others not).   [54] See 94 Selden Soc. 58–9.

[55] FNB 86H, 92E (1534).

[56] M. Blatcher, 'Touching the Writ of Latitat: an Act "of no great moment"', in *Elizabethan Government and Society*, ed. S. T. Bindoff *et al.* (1961), 188–212; Blatcher, *King's Bench*, 111–37; C. A. F. Meekings, 'King's Bench Files', in *Legal Records and the Historian*, ed. Baker (1978), at 105–9; Meekings, 'A King's Bench Bill Formulary' (1985) 6 *JLH* 86–104.

[57] See Meekings, 'King's Bench Files', at 106.

[58] The effect of bail was confirmed in *Anon.* (1505) Mich. 21 Hen. VII, fo. 33, pl. 26, *per* Tremaile J.

[59] This was not necessarily cheaper than a writ. In an action of debt in 1532, the plaintiff paid 3*s.* 4*d.* for drawing the declaration (bill) and 3*s.* 5*d.* for the *latitat: Ayer v. Stonard* (1543) KB 27/1126, m. 113.

case against the defendant until he was in custody. These attractions led to use of the bill even in cases which were within the regular jurisdiction of the court, such as actions of trespass *vi et armis*, appeals of felony,[60] and informations on the statute of *praemunire*.[61] The King's Bench had in effect acquired its own counterpart to the subpoena, and this may have played its part in warding off what was seen as competition from the Chancery.[62] The advantage of the fictional procedure seems to have been recognized by Parliament in 1531, when it studiously omitted trespass *quare clausum fregit* from the new legislation which made a plaintiff liable to costs if he discontinued an action.[63]

The device of the bill of Middlesex had one potential drawback. The fictional trespass had to be laid in Middlesex, the county in which the King's Bench now invariably sat, in order to justify the use of an original bill.[64] This meant that the precept to attach the defendant, and the first *capias*, had to be issued to the sheriff of Middlesex, who in most cases would be unable to serve it. The regular procedure in such cases, in both benches, was for the sheriff to return that the defendant was 'Not found' (*Non est inventus*) and for the filazer then to issue a form of *capias* known as a *latitat* to the sheriff of the county where the defendant was reported to be available. This first step was obviously a waste of time and money, but the clerks managed to minimize the problem. In the first place, it was not necessary to use two filazers; and no doubt the country filazers were anxious not to see all their business pass to the filazer for Middlesex and London. The suit was therefore handled, down to the arrest, by the filazer of the county to whom it was intended to issue the *latitat*,[65] and it may be supposed that he had an understanding with the office of the sheriff of Middlesex to avoid wasted costs where no real search was required. The court also took the view that bill procedure was not tied to the return-days which governed procedure by writ,[66] and so the precept, the Middlesex *capias*, and the *latitat*, could all be issued in prompt succession.[67] Then, between 1539 and 1542 a more drastic saving was effected.

Even in 1623, an original writ of debt cost only 1s. 4d. (unless the debt exceeded £40), and each judicial writ 1s. 1d. But a writ needed to be sent to the sheriff and returned.

[60] *Salmon* v. *Mando* (1532) Spelman 155.

[61] *Att.-Gen.* v. *Wolsey* (1529) Spelman 190; *Att.-Gen.* v. *Bishop of Norwich* (1534) Spelman 192 (advantage of bill explicitly mentioned).

[62] For awareness of an element of competition between the King's Bench and Chancery at the end of the fifteenth century, see below, 174.

[63] 23 Hen. VIII, c. 15; below, 378–9. Miss Blatcher (*King's Bench*, 130, 142) overlooked this vital omission and drew a mistaken conclusion.

[64] i.e. the bill which put the defendant in custody. The second bill, containing the true cause of action, was justified by reason of the privilege over prisoners.   [65] Meekings, 'King's Bench Files', 106.

[66] See *Salmon* v. *Mando* (1532) Spelman 155 ('upon a bill the court may give what day they wish').

[67] See the precedent in 94 Selden Soc. 242–3 (bill dated 20 Nov. 1522; precept to attach the defendant to appear on 24 Nov.; *capias* to appear on 27 Nov.; *latitat* to appear on 26 Jan., when a bill of trespass on the case was preferred).

The fictional bill and initial process directed to the sheriff of Middlesex came to be omitted from the roll, so that the return of *Non est inventus* and the precept for the *latitat* became the first entry. At the same time, it became unnecessary for the impotent first precept to pass the seal.[68] The initial rigmarole was still observed, after a fashion, but it had become a purely bureaucratic routine of depositing pieces of parchment in the burgeoning files.[69] In reality, if not in theory, the first process was now the *latitat* and the procedural drawback had been virtually circumvented. The statistics suggest that this refinement was more important than the original fiction in drawing suitors. The court gained immeasurably, albeit at the expense of the filazers—since bills against prisoners were within the exclusive province of the chief clerk's office and that office consequently managed to engross the whole business.

Soon after this development, in the time of Lyster CJ, there was a skirmish preliminary to the Elizabethan battle over the legal propriety of the new procedure. It was complained in Parliament that fines were being lost on original writs of debt, that the King's Bench was assuming a jurisdiction to which it was not in law entitled, and that it was 'a great absurdity and contrary to the order of all laws' for someone to be arrested for something he had not done. The complainant proposed that bills of Middlesex should be forbidden where the suit was for more than £40, and that the *latitat* should only be allowed where the true cause of action was set out.[70] The first suggestion was never acted on, while the second had to wait till 1661. Whatever absurdity there was in the fictional trespass in Middlesex, the new bill procedure had already proved irresistible, and the King's Bench had effectively become a second court of common pleas.

EFFECT OF THE BILL PROCEDURE ON BUSINESS

It is not known who the complainant was, though the reference to the loss of fines on originals suggests that it was someone from the Chancery rather than the Common Pleas. Before 1558, the Chancery would take the matter into its own hands by assuming the power to restrain a *latitat* by injunction until the plaintiff had settled with the Chancery for the lost fine.[71] But the Common Pleas were also losers, and they were not entirely complacent about the loss. There is some slight evidence of disgruntlement as early as 1498, when the under-sheriff of Middlesex was committed for contempt in arresting a Common Pleas defendant in

---

[68] Blatcher, *King's Bench*, 130–1.

[69] In 1550, the *latitats* were removed into a separate series of files, called *Non sunt inventi* (KB 153).

[70] SP 46/162, pp. 146–9 (*c*.1549), quoted at 94 Selden Soc. 59; discussed in Blatcher, *King's Bench*, 103–7.

[71] W. J. Jones, *The Elizabethan Court of Chancery* (1967), 453–4; N. G. Jones, 'The Bill of Middlesex and the Chancery 1556–1608' (2002) 22 *JLH* 1–20.

Westminster Hall. The under-sheriff, George Godeman, who was also a filazer of the King's Bench, had arrested the party upon a bill of Middlesex, shortly after the party had appeared in the Common Pleas, 'upon the rising of the court'. Godeman was closely questioned by the latter court. The bill of Middlesex had been sued out by the same plaintiff against the same defendant for a trespass in Middlesex, 'with the intention that he might be forced to answer in the custody of the marshal to other bills to be brought against him afterwards'.[72] Since the Common Pleas suit was for a trespass *vi et armis* (in Worcestershire), it may be that the purpose here was not so much to circumvent Magna Carta by bringing a personal action as to transfer the dispute to the superior court. The Common Pleas attorney was examined, and said that the bill of Middlesex was not sued out by him. After an adjournment, presumably to visit the King's Bench, Godeman defiantly said that he would rather submit to the grace of the court than release the prisoner: an answer which Mordaunt, the chief prothonotary, recorded as having being made 'with no reasonable cause shown'. This is perhaps the only record in which the veil is lifted and the King's Bench fiction laid bare. Although the sequel to the incident is unknown, the sense of disapproval is manifest.[73]

Well might the Common Pleas judges and officers have felt disquieted by the developments at the upper end of the hall; and yet the fact is that their work-load far surpassed that of the King's Bench until long after 1558. The encroachment cannot therefore have been sufficiently serious during this period to excite real antagonism between the courts. Moreover, the Common Pleas had the means at its disposal to introduce its own bill procedure, though it would have required a writ of trespass rather than a bill to effect the initial arrest.[74] But it did not retaliate in this way until a later period. The attitude was still one of aloof conservatism, grounded in a secure flow of business which the King's Bench did not possess.

Whether or not it is a mere coincidence that the Godeman incident occurred in 1498, it was certainly symbolic of the new order which began earlier that very year with the appointment of John Roper as chief clerk. Though not responsible for inventing the bill procedure, and though the dramatic growth in business occurred in the time of his son and grandsons, the foundations of future development seem to have been laid during the years when John Roper was chief clerk and his father-in-law was chief justice. By 1503 the volume of litigation by bill of

---

[72] The precise words are: 'ad intentionem quod idem Henricus cogi potuisset respondere in custodia marescalli super aliis billis versus ipsum postea impetrandis et prosequendis'.

[73] *Ardern* v. *Hadersiche* (1499) CP 40/946, m. 526 (*capias utlagatum* upon an outlawry in 1496).

[74] There is a statement in the year books that a bill could not be brought against a prisoner in the Fleet: Trin. 11 Edw. IV, fo. 3, pl. 4; Blatcher, *King's Bench*, 140. But sixteenth-century practice seems to have allowed it: e.g. CP 40/1045, m. 559d.

Middlesex was already such that these 'common bills' were removed into a separate series of files, and it was around 1520 that the extant *Bille* files—for the bills of custody—seem to have become a regular series. Shortly before their deaths, the tax returns of 1523 show that Fyneux and Roper were each worth more in goods than any other judge or lawyer in the land.[75] Blatcher seems to have regarded them as conspirators in a story of greed and chicanery. But that is an unduly severe judgment. They made themselves wealthy by improving remedies for litigants and cheapening litigation, rather than by extortion, and although fictions might offend the sense of fair play it is undeniable that the raison d'être of chapter 11 of Magna Carta had been lost once the King's Bench settled down in Westminster Hall and that the innovation was generally beneficial to the public.

Exact quantification of the changes in business is even more difficult than in the case of the Common Pleas, because the plea rolls seem to be a very imperfect record of the total business once bill procedure began to flourish.[76] This defect is shared by the docket rolls, which only record business entered on the plea rolls. Estimates based on the income from sealing fees—the details of which were returned to the hanaper—are likewise unreliable, since the seal seems increasingly to have been evaded in the initial stages of the bill procedure. The hanaper evidence shows a much more marked decline and recovery than the docket evidence. Nevertheless, both kinds of evidence reveal a somewhat similar story which must be an approximation to the truth.[77] There was a steady decline towards the 1490s, followed by an increase corresponding roughly with the Fyneux–Roper period. By 1500 there were about 500 suits a year in advanced stages. As with the Common Pleas there was then a temporary decline in the years around 1530,[78] but by 1550 the business had at least fully recovered and probably exceeded the highest levels in the previous hundred years. By 1558 the business was about 60 to 90 per cent higher than in 1500, and was about to increase very rapidly indeed. The rate of growth, it should be noted, was as yet no faster than that of the Common Pleas. The success of the new procedures had lain not in overtaking the Common Pleas but in capturing a fair share of the growing debt business which came to Westminster, business which Magna Carta had once seemed to guarantee exclusively to the other court.

---

[75] *CITR*, i. 464 (Fyneux assessed at 1,000 marks), 466 (Roper at £500).

[76] Many bills were not enrolled at all: Blatcher, *King's Bench*, 134–5.

[77] Blatcher, *King's Bench*, 10–21; Ives, *Common Lawyers in pre-Reformation England*, 199–207; Brooks, *Pettyfoggers and Vipers*, 49–52.

[78] D. Lloyd, *State-Worthies* (1670), 116, says, 'The same day that there was no cause to be tried in the Chancery in Sir Thomas More's time [1529–32], there were but three in the King's Bench, in Sir John FitzJames his time [1526–39]: the reason whereof some imagine was Cardinal Wolsey's extraordinary power... others know it was the judge's integrity, who was too honest to allow... delays and obstructions'. But no dramatic change is evidenced by the plea rolls.

SUBSTANTIVE LAW REFORM

The innovations which occurred in the King's Bench during the first half of the sixteenth century were not confined to the establishment of bill procedure. There were also, beginning in the time of Fyneux CJ,[79] numerous developments in the substantive remedies available, and these changes were to have an even longer-lasting impact on the common law. These remedies have been almost universally regarded as beneficial to the individual, and provide another argument for the defence of Fyneux CJ and his successor against charges of abusing their judicial position for personal gain.

On the Crown side, Fyneux CJ was actively concerned with the removal of abuses related to sanctuary and benefit of clergy, a conflict of some significance in the story of the break with Rome. His arguments persuaded king and Parliament.[80] His reputed opposition to the machinations of Empson and Dudley is borne out by his having allowed actions based on Magna Carta for parties treated unconstitutionally in the name of the Council.[81] His court sanctioned a new remedy whereby villeins could claim their freedom,[82] and also pioneered the use of *habeas corpus*.[83] In the field of property law, he favoured the protection of the leaseholder by means of ejectment, an action which was to take a new lease of life at the end of our period.[84] But the widest range of remedies came with actions on the case. The decision that *assumpsit* lay to recover damages for failing to perform a promised service, without proof of physical harm, was announced by Fyneux CJ in Gray's Inn in 1499 and never again judicially questioned.[85] Fyneux CJ doubted whether the action could also be used to recover contract-debts, thereby avoiding wager of law, which allowed debtors to swear themselves out of liability.[86] But in 1520 his court sanctioned its use against a deceased debtor's executors, who until that time had been immune in the absence of a document under seal.[87] In an *assumpsit* action which he brought himself in 1517 he sought to push the remedy further, relying on a purely consensual theory of contractual liability which was not to become orthodox for another generation.[88] In admitting the new action on the case for slander, which had previously belonged exclusively to the Church courts, it is not clear which of the benches took the lead, but the King's Bench was certainly in at the beginning.[89]

The wave of innovation did not stop with Fyneux CJ's death in 1525.[90] In the 1530s we notice the first actions of trover and conversion,[91] and in the late 1530s

---

[79] Note, however, his initial caution: below, 781 (against actions for defamation, 1497), 855 (against *assumpsit* for debt, 1505).   [80] See below, 538, 547–9.

[81] See below, 192–3.   [82] See below, 603–5.   [83] See above, 92–3.   [84] See below, 635–8.

[85] See below, 844–7.

[86] The demurrers remained undetermined during his last years: see below, 833–7.   [87] See below, 856.

[88] See below, 845–6.   [89] See below, 783.

[90] For a table of innovations see 94 Selden Soc. 60–1.   [91] See below, 806.

and early 1540s we find *assumpsit* extended into the commercial sphere with actions to enforce contracts of marine insurance, bills of exchange, freight, and partnership.[92] The new torts of inducing a breach of contract, enticement, and malicious prosecution, make their appearance in the same short period. It was in the King's Bench that the consideration clause in *assumpsit*, which led to the doctrine of consideration, was developed in the 1540s. Hardly any of these innovations were copied in the Common Pleas during the same period. The result was that, in its sittings out of term at the Guildhall,[93] the King's Bench started to become the principal court for commercial and personal actions which it was to remain until the time of Mansfield and beyond.

[92] See below, 859.
[93] The Guildhall was used for trials of London issues after 1518: below, 285 n. 75.

8

The Court of Exchequer

THE Court of Exchequer was in our period a relatively small jurisdiction concerned chiefly with royal revenue. It nevertheless had a judicial and clerical staff comparable in size to that of the King's Bench, a fact which is explained by the various non-judicial functions which the court performed in relation to the revenue. This duality of function reached to the highest offices, since the lord treasurer[1] and the chancellor of the Exchequer both had judicial authority while being first and foremost ministers of the Crown and administrators.

Most of the regular judicial business fell to the chief baron and barons, who held court in the chamber of the Exchequer just outside Westminster Hall. After 1478, when the number of junior barons was reduced to three, the complement of the court consisted of four judges, and so it remained throughout our period,[2] save that in 1549 a 'cursitor baron' was added with special accountancy duties.[3] Until 1526 the chief baron was also given a puisne judgeship in one of the benches,[4] either to augment his income or to clear some doubt as to his judicial powers. Unlike the judgeships in the benches, the offices of junior baron were specific numbered offices, so that when John Hales was promoted from third baron to second baron on the death of William Wotton in 1526, he received a new patent and was sworn in again before the lord chancellor,[5] and yet the fourth baron at the time (William Elys) did not move into his place.

It became a complaint in the 1530s that the third and fourth barons were usually learned in the law rather than in accountancy and the course of the Exchequer,[6] and this may have been the reason for appointing a cursitor baron in 1549. Nevertheless, the junior barons were regarded as inferior in rank to the

---

[1] He is sometimes mentioned as being present in court, or as having given instructions in suits on the Crown side: e.g. *Fox* v. *Rodrigus* (1540) E159/319, Pas. 32 Hen. VIII, m. 13 (demurrer to information; judgment for the defendant in the presence of the lord treasurer).

[2] See lists of the chief barons and barons in 94 Selden Soc. 382–4 (1509–47); Sainty, *Judges of England*, 94–5, 119–22.

[3] The only holder in our period was Edward Saxilby of the Inner Temple, formerly an attorney of the court, appointed in 1549: Sainty, *Judges of England*, 137–8.　　　　[4] Sainty, *Judges of England*, 89.

[5] E159/307, Pas., m. 29d; 94 Selden Soc. 383; Sainty, *Judges of England*, 103. The numbering system began to break down after 1547.

[6] S. Jack and R. S. Schofield (eds), 'Four Early Tudor Financial Memoranda' (1963) 36 *BIHR* 189–206, at 197, 202–3.

judges of the benches, and (if lawyers) were drawn from the ranks of benchers in the inns of court and not from the serjeants at law. They were accordingly less well remunerated than the justices,[7] and they could not augment their incomes by going on circuit, a role for which they had no statutory qualification. In 1511, perhaps mindful of the limited rewards of the office, the king made a remarkable grant to Robert Blagge appointing him as third baron of the Exchequer but confirming his former office of remembrancer, which he continued to hold for four years before it was granted to his son Barnaby. The judges later held the 1511 patent void; a judge cannot at the same time be a clerk in his own court.[8]

The Exchequer had a large staff of departmental officials, most of whom were not concerned with contentious litigation.[9] The principal legal officials were the two remembrancers (one 'on the side of the king', the other 'on the side of the lord treasurer'[10]), whose duties included the recovery of revenues due to the Crown, and the clerk of the pleas,[11] who managed the private litigation. The remembrancers were often benchers of the inns of court, and were commonly promoted in due course to be barons of the Exchequer.[12] The clerk of the pleas had less to do, and was of lower professional status, but was generally a member of an inn of court. The administrative officers, such as the clerk of the pipe, the clerks of the parcels, and the foreign opposer, were also usually men of court.[13] All the principal officers had secondaries and under-clerks, some of whose names can be recovered from the rolls.[14] There is some evidence of offices being bought and sold, though little is known of their value.[15] In addition there was the hereditary office of chief usher of the Exchequer, which belonged throughout our period to the Billesby family, save that during a minority (1539–47) the duties were performed by attorneys of the court as deputies.[16]

[7] Sainty, *Judges of England*, 106 (£46. 13s. 4d. a year until 1556, when a £20 increase was granted). The chief baron received £100 a year throughout the period: ibid. 90.

[8] *Re Barnaby Blagge* (1524) Spelman 150; Dyer 197b.

[9] For lists see J. Sainty, *Officers of the Exchequer* (1983). Some idea of their duties may be gleaned from the list of fees settled in 1447, printed as *The Ordinaunce . . . to be observed in the kynges Eschequier, by the Offycers and Clerkes of the Same* [c.1533].

[10] From 1505 the lord treasurer's remembrancer was also appointed by the king: Sainty, *Officers of the Exchequer*, 50, 54.   [11] He was appointed by the chancellor of the Exchequer: ibid. 92–7.

[12] Of the sixteen junior barons appointed by Henry VIII, three (Blagge, Walshe, and Fortescue) were formerly king's remembrancers, and two (Denny and Smith) lord treasurer's remembrancers.

[13] e.g. Walter Roudon, who was clerk of the parcels (1480–91) before his call to the bar of Lincoln's Inn, where he was later treasurer: *LPCL*, 86–9.

[14] e.g. John Fitzherbert, king's remembrancer, had at least five clerks in 9–10 Hen. VII: E13/176, mm. 27, 32d, 42, 44d (William Barowe, Robert Blagge, Thomas Pole, and Robert Randolf); E13/177, mm. 2, 29d (John Copwode).

[15] e.g. Thomas Sacheverell, dismissed in 1524 from the office of summoner, was sued in 1527 by the foreign opposer for not performing a covenant to sell the office: *Pymme v. Sacheverell* (1527) CP 40/1056, m. 441 (demurrer to plea of arbitration); Sainty, *Officers of the Exchequer*, 102.

[16] Dyer 213b; Sainty, *Officers of the Exchequer*, 145–6. The deputies were Robert Lister and James Lord.

The Exchequer had its own attorneys as well, to the number of a dozen or more, the most active of whom did not practise in the benches.[17] It seems at first sight surprising that the slender business of the court should have supported so many attorneys, but the explanation is that the plea-side business was only a small part of their work. The principal lists of attorneys are not the sparse rolls of warrants in the plea rolls but those at the beginning of the *Communia* of both remembrancers, which recorded the appearances of sheriffs, escheators, and bailiffs of franchises, by their named attorneys. The names here include attorneys who appeared for private clients as well, but it is not certain that all of them were lawyers and it may reasonably be supposed that their most important work was assisting with the complex, forbidding, and increasingly archaic accounting procedures of the revenue side. In 1550 two 'attorneys in the office of the clerk of the pleas', one of them of considerable standing, were barred from practice on grounds of long absence from the court.[18] This remarkable judgment is of interest not only as recognizing a duty of attendance but also as showing that the attorneys in question were regarded as belonging to the clerk's office;[19] it may therefore be conjectured that (as in later times) there were attorneys similarly appropriated to the other principal offices.[20] However, some of the attorneys were also under-clerks in the offices,[21] and some names appear in the rolls of more than one office. Whatever the precise professional arrangements, the personnel of the court clearly lived in a relatively closed world, united by its specialist expertise.

THE REVENUE SIDE

The court had three 'sides'. What may be called the revenue or Crown side was chiefly controlled by the king's remembrancer and his clerks, the business being

---

[17] They may already have had exclusive rights on the plea side: R. M. Ball, 'Exchequer of Pleas, Bills and Writs' (1988) 9 *JLH* 308–23, at 315.

[18] *Re Ralph and Thomas Rathebowne* (4 Nov. 1550) E13/232, m. 3d.

[19] Note also the description of Humphrey Hatton in 1552 as 'one of the attorneys in the office of the clerk of the pleas' in E13/235, m. 4 (tr.). In the same roll (mm. 26–27) Thomas Browne sues for slander as one of the clerks of the treasurer's remembrancer, but counts on his income as an attorney.

[20] According to the treatise by Peter Osborne (d. 1592), printed in 1658 under the intials T[homas] F[anshawe], there were attorneys and clerks assigned to the offices of the king's remembrancer, the clerk of the pipe, and the clerk of the pleas (pp. 95–7 of the 1658 edition). In 1642 there were four attorneys (or clerks) in the pleas office, and eight in the king's remembrancer's office: L. Squibb, *A Book of all the Several Officers of the Court of Exchequer*, ed. W. H. Bryson (Camden Misc.; 1975), 98, 112.

[21] In the 1530s it was said that until recently no one meddled with Exchequer records unless he was a sworn clerk in one of the offices, but now there were one or two under-clerks in every office: 'Early Tudor Financial Memoranda', ed. Jack and Schofield, 198.

enrolled in the 'Recorda' section of the *Communia* rolls kept by his office (E159). Its main preoccupation was the recovery of occasional sums of money due to the Crown,[22] especially upon penal informations, but it also managed the recovery of land and feudal dues following an inquisition of office returned in the Exchequer,[23] distraints to do homage and fealty,[24] failures to undertake knighthood,[25] the collection of subsidies and other forms of taxation,[26] and occasionally the enforcement of other royal interests.[27] Much of the business concerned the customs revenue. The usual method of initiating proceedings of this nature was by information,[28] either by the attorney-general or by a common person 'who sues as well for the lord king as for himself' (*qui tam pro seipso quam pro domino rege sequitur*).[29] The defendant could plead a traverse or a justification, usually with a protestation that the information was insufficient in law. The disappearance of most cases from the rolls before judgment may indicate compounding; and occasionally a defendant, having traversed the information, would be recorded as offering a fine to save expense without having to withdraw his plea.[30]

Sometimes an information was laid against a named person for concealment, rescue, or non-payment of revenue.[31] But this was not essential. An information commonly alleged simply that certain goods had been seized for non-payment of

[22] e.g. *Att.-Gen.* v. *Lord North* (1558) Dyer 161a (liability of chancellor of Augmentations).

[23] e.g. *Att.-Gen.* v. *Ralegh* (1522) Spelman 24 (intrusion); *Att.-Gen.* v. *Haberdashers of London* (1522) Spelman 165 (mortmain); *Worseley* v. *Regem* (1522) Spelman 146, 171 (petition of grace); *Att.-Gen.* v. *Skrimshire* (1552) Dyer 73a (intrusion). It was said *c.*1530 that inquisitions *virtute officii* were returned in the Exchequer and traversed there, whereas inquisitions *virtute brevis* were returned in the Chancery and traversed there, even though they were also estreated into the Exchequer: Yorke 211, no. 323 (agreed by the judges in Serjeants' Inn). See also *Att.-Gen.* v. *Edgecombe* (1515–19) 2 Caryll 728, pl. 522.

[24] There are many routine entries in the *Communia*, but cases could be contentious: e.g. Spelman 154, pl. 2 (dean and canons discharged because corporation cannot do homage).

[25] A whole roll (E159/279) is devoted to over 100 such cases in 1501.

[26] e.g. *Att.-Gen.* v. *Abbot of Shrewsbury* (1485) Mich. 2 Ric. III, fo. 4, pl. 9; 64 Selden Soc. 102 (tenths; referred to all the judges in the Exchequer Chamber).

[27] e.g. the recovery of deodand: *Banyard (deputy almoner)* v. *Bosom* (1510) E159/289, Mich. mm. 27, 33d (grisly accident with '*machina vocata* a crane'). Or corodies: *Att.-Gen.* v. *Abbot of Pipewell* (1522) Spelman 43. Or the collection of a 'mounter' from the representatives of a deceased bishop: e.g. E159/304, Pas. m. 9 (bishop of Bath and Wells, 1525); 109 Selden Soc. 2 (bishop of Bath and Wells, 1542).

[28] There is a file of original informations, from Hen. VII to Phil. & Mar., in E148/1.

[29] There is a brief discussion of informations in Anthony Fitzherbert's reading in Gray's Inn on Beaupleader (LI MS. Maynard 3, ff. 36–37). He distinguishes those brought solely for the king by the attorney-general, e.g. for intrusion, and those where a party suing *qui tam* was to have part of the penalty. The same distinction is made in *Anon.* (1549) Wm Yelv. 350, no. 75, *per* Hales J., who says that the second kind of information required an oath.

[30] e.g. *Talwerth* v. *Helman* (1545) E159/324, Pas. 37 Hen. VIII, m. 44 (traverses the keeping of bloodhounds, but to avoid expense '*petit se ex gracia curie ad rationabilem finem cum domino rege in premissis faciendam admitti*'). Cf. the similar King's Bench procedure, below, 522.

[31] e.g. *Anon.* (1487) 64 Selden Soc. 131, pl. 139; *Harrys* v. *Hochster* (1522) Spelman 154; *Anon.* (1538) Dyer 43b; *Att.-Gen.* v. *Richards* (1542) Dyer 54a; *Att.-Gen.* v. *Donatt* (1561) 109 Selden Soc. 49–53.

customs duties; a proclamation was then made for anyone to show why the goods should not be forfeited, and the usual result was an uncontested judgment of forfeiture, with a share going to the informant. The owner could nevertheless come and claim the property and justify or traverse any revenue offence.[32] Such cases could raise interesting questions of law.[33] In a case of 1523, where a bale of cloves was seized at Plymouth as unmerchantable, Charles V ('king of the Romans, emperor-elect') was permitted to claim property through his attorney on the ground that the goods had been shipwrecked on a voyage from Flanders to Antwerp, and salvaged by mariners, and were being taken back to Flanders rather than unloaded in England; the plea was confessed by the attorney-general.[34]

Until the middle of Henry VIII's reign the rolls are dominated by cases concerning the customs and other regular forms of revenue, and the king's property interests.[35] There were also a relatively small number of informations for breaches of penal statutes,[36] such as (to take but one example) the statute of 1511 prohibiting the practice of medicine or surgery without an episcopal licence.[37] These could be brought by the attorney-general,[38] but were most commonly brought by informers. A wide range of statutes were enforced by this means, from those of the fourteenth century[39] to the most recent.[40] From the 1530s informations

---

[32] e.g. *Re forty bales of Toulouse woad, Cok and Myrable* v. *Van Beyson* (1515) KB 27/1020, m. 32 (jury finds for king; error). In 1545 the Privy Council imprisoned William Rigges for extortion as an Exchequer informer in such a case: *APC 1542–7*, p. 193.

[33] e.g. *Re a quantity of broadcloth, Leyghton* v. *Bonvixi* (1531) KB 27/1080, m. 63 (pleads import licence; judgment for king on demurrer; error); *Re thirty tuns of ale, Grey* v. *Cleydon* (1545) E159/324, Pas. 37 Hen. VIII, m. 2 (justifies under proclamation concerning the victualling of Boulogne; demurrer by att.-gen.).

[34] *Re a bale of cloves* (1523) E159/302, Pas. 15 Hen. VIII, m. 11.

[35] The following account is based chiefly on sampling at five-year intervals. References to E159 are all to the *Communia* ('Recorda' section).

[36] Examples in the reports are: *Caldecote* v. *Daveson* (1522) Spelman 157 (importing wine in a foreign ship, contrary to 4 Hen. VII, c. 10); *Croxton* v. *Baghrawgh* (1529) Port 61 (exporting cloth contrary to 7 Edw. IV, c. 3).

[37] 3 Hen. VIII, c. 11; e.g. *Harryson* v. *Breten* (1520) E159/299, Mich. m. 16 (Chelmsford, Essex); *Leke* v. *Pendylton* (1535) E159/314, Mich. m. 16 (Mansfield, Notts.); *Ryx* v. *Poynter* (1545) E159/324, Pas. m. 72 (West Dereham, Norf.); *Clerke* v. *Gyle* (1545) E159/324, Mich. m. 53 (Bishopsgate; pleads the statute 34 & 35 Hen. VIII, c. 8, and that he was a specialist in herbs, roots, and waters, *absque hoc* that he practised medicine).

[38] e.g. *Att.-Gen.* v. *Lye* (1520) E159/299, Mich. m. 5 (shooting with a cross-bow, contrary to 6 Hen. VIII, c. 2); *Att.-Gen.* v. *Muschamp* (1542) Dyer 53a (buying a pretended title, contrary to 32 Hen. VIII, c. 9); *Att.-Gen.* v. *Hunt* (1545) E159/324, Mich. 32 Hen. VIII, m. 32 (usury, contrary to 11 Hen. VII, c. 8).

[39] e.g. *Lyon* v. *Smyth* (1510) E159/289, Pas. m. 21; *Swyllyngton* v. *Hamkyn* (1530) E159/309, Pas. m. 20; *same* v. *Simon* (1530) Trin. m. 10 (making horse-bread contrary to 13 Ric. II, c. 8). Cf. *Shyrdwyn* v. *Kelsey* (1526) KB 27/1059, m. 11 (*qui tam* action on same statute)

[40] e.g. in 1550 (E159/329, Trin. 4 Edw. VI) there are numerous informations on 3 & 4 Edw. VI, c. 19 (for buying cattle outside markets and fairs) and c. 21 (for selling butter and cheese in gross).

upon statutes represent an ever growing proportion of the total business,[41] and in the same period more and more statutes were passed with provision for enforcement by informers. The first major wave of informations—other than for customs offences—seems to have been occasioned by the statute of 1523 restraining the employment of alien craftsmen.[42] Even more widely used, from the mid-1530s, was the statute of 1529 against non-residence and the taking of farms by spiritual persons,[43] which simultaneously occasioned a stream of debt actions in the Common Pleas[44] and thereby raised problems of double jeopardy.[45] Occasional lesser purges are indicated by batches of informations for the same statutory offence, sometimes laid by the same person.[46] Thus, in Hilary term 1535 there are eleven informations against silversmiths, apparently brought in connection with the assay (or trial of the pyx) held in the Star Chamber,[47] and in Hilary term 1541 eight informations for selling wine at excessive prices in Hertfordshire.[48]

The Exchequer procedure was different from that used in the King's Bench and Common Pleas to enforce the same statutes. In the two benches the informer brought an action of debt *qui tam* (both for himself and for the king), by original writ, and counted on the breach of statute; the proceedings were continued throughout by the informer.[49] In the Exchequer an information was laid upon

[41] See also M. W. Beresford, 'The Common Informer, the Penal Statutes and Economic Regulation' (1958) 10 *Econ. Hist. Rev.* (2nd ser.) 221–37, at 223–4 (table based on Mich. 1519, Mich. 1529, and all Mich. terms after 1543).

[42] 14 & 15 Hen. VIII, c. 2; enrolled in E159/304, Mich. m. 3 (1525). An early example is *Johnson* v. *Goscon* (1525) E159/304, Pas. m. 2 (Flemish cordwainers in the Strand). There are more than a dozen examples in 1530 (all against joiners, cordwainers, and cappers): E159/309, Pas. m. 13; Trin. mm. 1, 3, 6–15. In Trinity term 1540 alone there are ten such informations: E159/319, Trin. 32 Hen. VIII, mm. 19, 27–29, 36, 40–44 (Whelpley, informant). See further below, 614.

[43] 21 Hen. VIII, c. 13. There are seven examples in Pas. 1535: E159/314, Pas. 27 Hen. VIII, mm. 7–8, 10–13, 17. (Two allege non-residence, the rest having farms.)

[44] CP 40/1085(2), mm. 101, 112, 311, 404, 406.

[45] At least one of the debt actions was between the same parties as an Exchequer suit, but for a different breach of the statute: *Dey* v. *Marche* (1535) ibid., m. 311 (for having a farm); E159/314, Pas. 27 Hen. VIII, m. 7–8 (for buying and selling). In *Todde* v. *Harryson* (1535) E159/314, Trin. 27 Hen. VIII, m. 17, the defendant pleaded that an action of debt was pending in the Common Pleas on the same alleged non-residence.

[46] Some of the informers were minor officials, but some were private individuals. For the career of one informer (George Whelplay) in 1538–43, see G. R. Elton, *Star Chamber Stories* (1958), 78–113. In about 1534 there was a proposal to replace private informers by 'serjeants of the common weal', but nothing came of it: T. F. T. Plucknett, 'Some Proposed Legislation of Henry VIII' (1936) 19 *TRHS* (4th ser.) 119 at 125–33.

[47] E159/313, Hil. 26 Hen. VIII, mm. 10–16 (John Wall, informant). There is one more in Easter term (m. 7d). They came unstuck because of uncertainty as to the effect of the statutory general pardon (enrolled on m. 19).   [48] E159/319, Hil. 32 Hen. VIII, mm. 23–30 (three informers involved).

[49] The following examples are limited to the statutes referred to in the previous notes. Physicians and surgeons: Rast. Ent. 426 (463v); *Walsh* v. *Alyson* (1516) KB 27/1020, m. 33 (pleads he was specialist pox-curer and not a surgeon); *Rosse* v. *Parons* (1516) CP 40/1016, m. 554 (alien practising physic in

oath, whereupon the accused was summoned and pleadings were exchanged with the attorney-general,[50] who was an officer of this court as well as of the Common Pleas. This distinction was recognized in the penal statutes themselves, which usually speak of enforcement by action or information, and in 1559 the Common Pleas construed this language to give them a parallel jurisdiction over informations.[51] The converse proposition, that the Exchequer could hear actions of debt upon penal statutes, was opposed in the same year on the grounds that the court could not hear common pleas.[52] Doubtless the Exchequer procedure was on balance the better of the two, and the number of suits begun by information in our period was considerable:[53] in 1535, for example, there were fifty-nine informations for statutory offences and eight for non-payment of revenue (not counting the proclamation procedure), while by 1557 there might be over one hundred informations in a single term.[54] Even so, the great age of the common informer was yet to dawn.[55]

A certain amount of Crown business was also handled by the lord treasurer's remembrancer, and recorded in his *Communia* rolls (E368). Most of it arose from the recovery of the king's feudal incidents from tenants in chief, in the form of distraints to do homage and fealty, sometimes accompanied with the command to show 'how and by what title' the tenant had entered, so that it could be recorded; respites of homage and fealty;[56] and proceedings arising from inquisitions of office (mostly judgments of ousterlemain). There are also claims made upon

London; pleads he was created MD and duly admitted to practise in London); *Taillour* v. *Grene* (1521) KB 27/1039 m. 64d (dispute over Oxford MB taken without due examination); *Bouton* v. *Sevell* (1530) KB 27/1075 m. 80 (surgery); *Wheler* v. *Poyntour* (1539) CP 40/1100, m. 312 (surgery in Norfolk). Crossbows: *Nevell* v. *Bastweke* (1537) CP 40/1095, m. 737 (on 25 Hen. VIII, c. 17); *Chatterton* v. *Stamford* (1555) CP 40/1161, m. 750 (on 6 Hen. VIII, c. 2). Pretended titles: *Playne* v. *Moynynges* (1542) CP 40/1112, m. 440; *Hampton* v. *Ansley* (1543) 1116, m. 457; *Ayre* v. *Chaworth* (1544) CP 40/1121, mm. 459, 724 (claims £1,500 and £1,000); *Baryngton* v. *Frank* (1556) CP 40/1166, m. 552 (issue); *Notte* v. *Evett* (1557) CP 40/1169, m. 458 (claims £1,000). Usury: below, 834–5.

[50] For a specimen entry see *Venables* v. *Wardens of the Mystery of Founders* (1505) 16 Selden Soc. 279–83 (for making bye-laws contrary to 19 Hen. VII, c. 7). In *Cockys* v. *Raynold* (1535) KB 27/1096, m. 21, it was held not to be error that the informer was not mentioned in the attorney-general's replication.

[51] *Anon.* (1559) Gell's reports, II, ff. 60v–61; 109 Selden Soc., p. xxvii.

[52] *Stradling* v. *Morgan* (1560) Plowd. 199 at 207–9. This is probably the point also in *Anon.* (1549) Wm Yelv. 349, no. 75.

[53] According to D. J. Guth, 'Enforcing Late-Medieval Law', in *Legal Records and the Historian*, ed. Baker, 80 at 86, there were 1,806 prosecutions in the Exchequer for statutory offences in the reign of Henry VII, but 75% of them were for customs offences.

[54] Beresford, 'The Common Informer', 227 (analysis of Mich. 1557). Customs offences were still the largest single category, about 42% of the total.

[55] D. R. Lidington counted 18,760 Exchequer informations between 1558 and 1571, of which 13,000 were on penal statutes: 'The Enforcement of Penal Statutes at the Court of Exchequer', Ph.D. dissertation (Cambridge, 1988), 41; 'Mesne Process in Penal Actions at the Elizabethan Exchequer' (1984) 5 *JLH* 33–8, at 33. See also Beresford, 'The Common Informer', 223–4.

[56] By respiting homage and fealty, the heir could avoid the fees payable to the lord chamberlain: as to which see Constable's reading on *Prerogativa Regis* (1495), ed. Thorne, 63.

accounts, and other accounting matters. Most of this routine business was non-contentious, or at least does not appear on the rolls in a litigious form; but occasionally an entry contains pleading to issue.[57]

THE PLEA SIDE

The 'plea side' of the court—sometimes called by historians the Exchequer of Pleas—was concerned with private litigation, and was controlled by the clerk of the pleas and his under-clerks. There were four main jurisdictional categories of suit. First there were actions brought against sheriffs or bailiffs of franchises at the time of their accounting. Their position as accountants with the king brought them within the jurisdiction for the purposes of personal actions by strangers, and although some of the actions related to their official duties[58] there was no need for the cause of action to relate directly to their accounts or indeed to their office at all.[59] Second, there were actions by and against the barons and officials of the Exchequer, and their servants. Actions by plaintiffs with privilege—the larger category—were usually commenced by writ, while those against persons within the privilege were usually by bill. Most of the officers and clerks who used the privilege are known from extrinsic sources to have occupied the offices claimed, but the availability of the privilege to ill-defined 'servants' had always laid it open to potential abuse. It is not known for certain whether the servant was a wholly fictional concept in this period, though there are certainly instances which raise doubts.[60] Third, a bill could be brought against a defendant 'present in court', probably meaning that he was in custody at someone else's suit,[61] or that he had been removed from an inferior court by *corpus cum causa*.[62] This could have given

---

[57] e.g. in a sample year chosen at random: *Re Dolben* (1535) E368/309, Pas. 27 Hen. VIII, m. 1 (traverse to an inquisition finding lunacy).

[58] e.g. *Johnson v. Kytson* (1535) E13/214, m. 6 (debt on escape from Ludgate; verdict for plaintiff); *Scudamore v. Croft* (1535) ibid., m. 11 (debt for expenses of knight of shire); *Talbott v. Ferrers* (1535) ibid., m 11d (sim.); *Mynours v. Turke and Yorke* (1549–51) Dyer 66a; Brooke Abr., *Escape*, pl. 45; E12/1, fo. 21v (debt on escape from Ludgate); *Platte v. Aylyfe* (1551) Plowd. 35; E12/1, ff. 24v, 35, 38 (debt on escape from Ludgate).

[59] In *Vivaldi v. Pargetour* (1523) KB 27/1049, m. 74, a sheriff of London tried to reverse an Exchequer judgment against him on the ground that the record did not state whether the jurisdiction in debt was founded on prescription or statute; but this seems a rather desperate argument.

[60] e.g. E13/174, m. 17 (Thomas Boote, servant of one of the auditors, *alias* of Calais, soldier, 1490); *Thrower v. Whetstone* (1555) Dyer 118b, 119b (citizen and wax-chandler of London, keeper of Ludgate prison, and servant of Cholmeley CB).

[61] For bills against Exchequer prisoners in the custody of the warden of the Fleet, see Ball, 'Exchequer of Pleas', 314.

[62] e.g. *Dymock v. Damport* (1550) E13/232, m. 6 (tr. 'present here in court the same day in his own person'); *Bishop of Bath v. Sergeant* (1550) ibid., m. 9 (sim.). Cf. *Fenell v. Nowyngton* (1550) ibid., m. 8d (tr. 'present here in court the same day by virtue of a writ of *corpus cum causa*'); *Laundys v. Hatcher* (1552) E13/235, m. 37 (sim.). Such entries are very common.

the court the same means of expanding its jurisdiction as the King's Bench, but the opportunity was not taken.

The fourth and legally the most interesting category comprised *quominus* suits. The principle of *quominus* was that someone who owed money to the king, at least if he did so as a regular accountant in the Exchequer, could bring personal actions there against his own debtors so that he might be the better enabled to pay the king. Even though chapter 11 of Magna Carta was generally thought to prohibit the Exchequer as well as the King's Bench from hearing common pleas,[63] it was permissible to bring a writ containing a *quominus* clause, which stated that the plaintiff was less able to pay the king because of the outstanding debt or damages.[64] Writs of this kind account for a substantial proportion of the business of the plea side in the early Tudor period. The plaintiff was required to indicate his status as a Crown accountant, and the usual practice by the time of Henry VII[65] was for him to allege that he was a farmer of royal property.[66] It is well known that in later times—certainly by 1660—the *quominus* allegation would become a fiction, or at any rate a disingenuous device for transferring business to the Exchequer. The great advantage of bringing debt in the Exchequer was that wager of law was not allowed in *quominus*,[67] and this in turn meant that the action could be brought against executors without a deed.[68] There was therefore good reason for creditors to bring such actions in the Exchequer if they possibly could, and there is a hint in 1496 that Edmund Dudley had 'practised' this remedy.[69] It is difficult to prove how far, if at all, the allegation was fictitious, but the strong predominance of debt on a bond, the small proportion of actions against executors, and the lack of a noticeable increase in the case-load, all suggest that the fiction was

[63] The matter was publicly debated in *Stradling* v. *Morgan* (1558–60) E12/1, fo. 93v (commenced Hil. 1558); Plowd. 199 at 207–9, where Saunders CB challenged the orthodox position espoused by two of the junior barons.

[64] The procedure was not confined to debt: e.g. *Butler* v. *Ardeson* (1522) E13/200, m. 22 (libel); *Garroway* v. *Thomas* (*c*.1560) cit. Plowd. 208 (ejectment).

[65] It is noticed by Kebell in the Inner Temple (*c*.1490) 105 Selden Soc. 127.

[66] Not necessarily land: e.g. *Butler* v. *Ardeson* (1522) E13/200, m. 22 (farmer of king's exchange). Occasionally a plaintiff alleged that he was *debitor domini regis* in some other way: e.g. E13/233, m. 10d (Richard Musgrave, debtor to the king for various sums owed by his father, as contained in the pipe roll, 1551).

[67] Fitz. Abr., *Ley*, pl. 66 (1421); John Hales, reading in Gray's Inn (1514) GI MS. 25, fo. 292v; *Anon.* (1543) Brooke Abr., *Ley*, pl. 102; *Quominus*, pl. 5.

[68] Trin. 11 Hen. VII, fo. 26, pl. 9 (cf. next note); Trin. 27 Hen. VIII, fo. 23, pl. 21, *per* Knightley sjt. In the 1535 report, Fitzherbert J. denied that it was the course of the Exchequer, but there was an example that very term: *Algar* v. *Bavessor* (Trin. 1535) E13/214, m. 12 (*nil debet per patriam*).

[69] Bodl. Lib. MS. Rawlinson C.705, fo. 55v; 94 Selden Soc. 63 n. 4 (tr. '. . . practised by Dudley and in common use'). The same text occurs in the year book, Trin. 11 Hen. VII, fo. 26, pl. 9, except that Dudley is there 'Davers'. Danvers is less likely, since he had been a Common Pleas judge since 1488; moreover the manuscript passage has a Gray's Inn context.

not yet in common use.[70] This is also borne out by the particularity with which the debt to the king had to to be set out, at any rate until the mid-1550s, and by the fact that its legal adequacy could be contested.[71] Quite apart from the possibility of challenge, there must have been a risk that a party who took advantage of a false claim to privilege would lay himself open to an action for deceit in another court.[72] In any case, the special advantages of being able to sue executors and avoid wager of law lost much of their significance after 1520, when the same remedies could be achieved by bringing *assumpsit* in the King's Bench.[73] The Exchequer would in due course follow the King's Bench and allow *assumpsit* in the same situations.[74]

The clerk of the pleas enrolled the plea-side business on the plea rolls (E13). The enrolling system was different from that used in the benches in that the rotulets—which are unsigned—apparently all belonged to the one clerk, who made a practice of continuing entries from one membrane to another. The result makes search rather inconvenient, because a case which occupies more than one roll may continue on a blank space several rolls distant, and sometimes on two or three blank spaces. The same rolls were also used in the early sixteenth century in the manner of docket rolls, rules of court being noted in the margins. No parchment was wasted. In 1549, however, paper was deployed with bureaucratic good sense to remove the rules and other remembrances into paper rule-books (E12). These are the first examples of rule-books surviving from any of the common-law courts. Typical rules found in the 1550s are:

a day is given... to show the court why the said defendant's plea is insufficient in law, and if the plaintiff says nothing he is to reply to the plea[75]

the plaintiff has a day either to reply or to show the causes of demurrer... and if he does not do so let a nonsuit be entered[76]

the defendant has a day to make his plea perfect and sufficient in law... and if he does not, let a demurrer in law be entered[77]

---

[70] The possibility of fiction was nevertheless acknowledged in Elizabeth I's time: 94 Selden Soc. 63 n. 5.

[71] For a question relating to the title shown see *Anon.* (1558) Dyer 174a. The general *debitor regis* form began around 1554: Ball, 'Exchequer of Pleas', 317.

[72] Thus in *Burele* v. *Lomelyn* (1510) KB 27/995, m. 67, a litigant recovered £27 damages against an adversary who had stopped a suit in London by falsely claiming to be an accountant in the Exchequer.

[73] See below, 856. There was nevertheless the uncertainty, for country plaintiffs, that the suits might come before a Common Pleas judge at the assizes.

[74] e.g. *Fennell* v. *Newyngton* (1550) E13/232, mm. 8d, 7d (for price of goods sold; judgment for the plaintiff); *Jennyns* v. *Rayman* (1551) E13/233, m. 19 (against executors; count only).

[75] e.g. *Dowtty* v. *Knyvett* (1552) E12/1, fo. 38.   [76] e.g. *Broke* v. *Watkys* (1558) E12/1, fo. 99v.

[77] e.g. *Bishop of Coventry* v. *Sneyde* (1551) E12/1, fo. 18; *Langrave* v. *Calverley* (1551) ibid., fo. 22v; *Platt* v. *Aylyff* (1552) ibid., fo. 24, reported in Plowd. 35 (a demurrer was entered, but then a plea *puis darrein continuance*: fo. 35). The formula is thereafter very common.

the defendant has a day...to show here in court why the same court should not give judgment in the foregoing[78]

a day is given to the plaintiff...to show why judgment should not be entered for the defendant [following a verdict for the defendant at the assizes].[79]

Here we see very clearly the demurrer procedure in its practical operation, and
rules *nisi* which could be discharged or made absolute following either a motion
in court or appropriate action out of court. The system would look essentially the
same on the eve of reform in the nineteenth century.

The range of actions in the Exchequer of Pleas was similar to that in the
benches,[80] with debt predominant, followed by trespass and case in second place.
But the amount of litigation on the plea side remained very slight throughout our
period. In 1535, a year chosen at random, there were only twenty-nine suits in all
categories, all but five of them for debt.[81]

THE EQUITY SIDE

The third branch of Exchequer jurisdiction was the nascent 'equity side' of the
court, which was in existence by the 1540s and possibly earlier.[82] The origin of this
jurisdiction, which in scope and in the manner of its exercise closely paralleled
that of the English side of the Chancery,[83] is obscure. In later times the decrees
were pronounced by the lord treasurer, or in his absence the chancellor of the
Exchequer, suggesting an analogy with the Chancery, though the barons were also
involved in the proceedings. The basis of the jurisdiction seems to have been an
extension of the *quominus* principle so that the king's debtors could make equitable claims to money which would help them discharge their duties to the king.
There seems also to have been a power to allow equitable defences on the revenue
side.[84] What remains unclear is why this jurisdiction began in the early Tudor
period, and also why the business belonged to the king's remembrancer's office
rather than the clerk of the pleas. The relatively few cases in our period are known
chiefly from the files of bills and pleadings (E111), though a damaged decree book
survives from the end of Mary I's reign.[85]

[78] e.g. *Platt* v. *Aylyff* (1552) E12/1, fo. 38 (a plea having been entered previously: last note).
[79] *Tytley* v. *Port* (1555) E12/1, fo. 70v.   [80] As in the King's Bench, real actions were excluded.
[81] E13/213 (Hil.); E13/214 (Pas. to Mich.). Analysis shows that eleven were against sheriffs or bailiffs,
nine were *quominus*, seven were brought by officials, and two were against officials.
[82] What follows is based on W. H. Bryson, *The Equity Side of the Exchequer* (1975). Bryson discusses
eight cases before 1530 preserved in E111 but concludes that they cannot safely be connected with the
equity jurisdiction of the Exchequer.   [83] See below, 173.
[84] *Lord North's Case* (1558–61) Dyer 161a (defendant relieved upon an information on a bond, 'on
account of equity and good conscience').
[85] E111/56, continued (from 1559) in E123/2. Bryson says (p. 152) that decrees were later enrolled by
the king's remembrancer in E159; sampling of these rolls did not reveal any examples temp. Hen. VIII.

ERROR FROM THE EXCHEQUER

Proceedings in error from the Exchequer were supposed to be heard, in accordance with a statute of 1357, before the lord chancellor and lord treasurer sitting in the Council Chamber near the Exchequer, with the assistance of common-law justices.[86] The statute was taken to require the personal presence of both high officers of state, and it was doubtless because of the practical difficulty of achieving this that thoughts turned to reform.[87] A bill was submitted to Parliament in 1515 suggesting that parties might bring error in the King's Bench instead,[88] and the proposal was adopted in the form of a small amendment to the statute of 1515 governing the general surveyors, further amended in 1523.[89] This jurisdiction was quite regularly invoked in the time of Henry VIII,[90] but it probably did not survive the repeal of the 1523 act in 1541.

[86] 31 Edw. III, stat. 1, c. 12. The proceedings were recorded on the Exchequer plea rolls: e.g. *Platte* v. *Aylyfe* (1551) E13/234, mm. 3–5, 6d–7, 9; cf. Plowd. 35.

[87] See *The Case of the Steelyard Merchants* (1491) Hil. 6 Hen. VII, fo. 15, pl. 9; 64 Selden Soc. 158, pl. 46. Three writs of error were brought and discontinued for want of the presence of both officers. The same point is mentioned in Pas. 8 Hen. VII, fo. 13, pl. 7.

[88] *HLJ*, i. 31 mentions a bill for reforming errors in the Exchequer in 1515. Cf. 36 *BIHR* 194, where 'errors' is misunderstood to mean administrative defects and it is supposed that the proposal was dropped.

[89] 7 Hen. VIII, c. 7, s. 32; 14 & 15 Hen. VIII, c. 15, ss. 26, 38; below, 225. The statutes were recited in the writs of error.

[90] e.g. *Cok* v. *Speryng* (1516) KB 27/1020, m. 32 (information); *Prior of Caldwell* v. *Mayor of Cambridge* (1516) KB 27/1021, m. 36 (annuity payable from farm of town); *Lovell* v. *Halys* (1518) KB 27/1029, m. 37 (debt on bond to treasurer of household); *Vivaldi* v. *Pargetour* (1523–5) KB 27/1049, m. 74 (debt against sheriff of London); *Croxton* v. *Baghrawgh* (1529) KB 27/1073, m. 31; Port 61 (information); *Leyghton* v. *Bonvixi* (1531) KB 27/1080, m. 63 (error *coram nobis*; information); *Darrell* v. *Shaa* (1534–47) KB 27/1092, m. 33; KB 27/1094, mm. 39, 65 (information); *Cockys* v. *Raynold* (1535) KB 27/1096, m. 21 (information; judgment affirmed); *Fuller* v. *Pole* (1541) KB 27/1118, m. 28 (debt by *quominus; certiorari* to the barons to search for warrants of attorney; judgment affirmed).

9

The Court of Chancery

To move across Westminster Hall from the King's Bench to the Chancery was to enter a different juridical world, and it is a world which we see less sharply for want of complete records. Although the Court of Chancery was a superior royal court with ever increasing business, and power even to inhibit proceedings in the two benches, it was not a court of record in the sense of a court which kept a full and legally incontrovertible parchment record of its proceedings. Indeed, for most of our period there was no continuous record of any kind. This is on the face of it rather surprising, since the Chancery was the original bureaucratic department of state, and was still in early modern times one of the principal branches of the central bureaucracy, keeping some of its more formal administrative records on parchment rolls.[1] The Chancery was also closely connected with the business of the common law through its responsibility for issuing original writs, the work of the cursitors' department.[2] However, the chancellor's judicial business before our period was only a relatively small part of the departmental work-load, and the court had never been designed as the place of constant resort which it was rapidly becoming. Its informality was part of its strength, but it has made its history the more elusive.

THE COMMON-LAW SIDE

The jurisdiction which derived directly from the departmental work of the Chancery, or from the privilege of its officers and their servants to be sued only in Chancery,[3] was the closest in character to that of the common-law courts.[4] The principal business consisted of matters relating to the king's feudal revenue, mostly traverses to inquisitions *post mortem* found under a writ of *diem clausit extremum*,[5] and the occasional petition of right or monstrans de droit.[6] A monstrans de droit enabled a finding to be confessed and avoided, whereas a traverse could only be

---

[1] For the range of its records see *Guide to the Contents of the Public Record Office*, ed. M. S. Giuseppi, i (1963), 7–44.   [2] See below, 325.

[3] For this privilege see below, 186.

[4] The fullest account of this jurisdiction relates to a slightly later period: W. J. Jones, 'An Introduction to the Petty Bag Proceedings in the Reign of Elizabeth I' (1963) 51 *California Law Rev.* 882–905.

[5] Cf. the Exchequer jurisdiction over inquisitions, above, 162, 165.

[6] e.g. *Lord Ormonde* v. *Regem* (1485–9) 1 Caryll 12; Pas. 4 Hen. VII, fo. 7, pl. 6; 64 Selden Soc. 138 (enrolled in the Exchequer); *Conyngesby and Mallom* v. *Regem* (1509) C43/2/35, 37; 2 Caryll 595; *West*

used to challenge a finding which was factually incorrect. A petition was required where the king was entitled by record, such as an act of attainder, unless the party also relied on a record.[7] Other miscellaneous business on this side included the enforcement of recognizances and statutes staple,[8] *scire facias* to show cause why letters patent should not be revoked,[9] and personal actions involving Chancery clerks. This was common-law business, and the procedure was conducted formally in Latin.[10] Indeed, in respect of such business the court was said to be a court of record from which a writ of error lay to Parliament.[11] Here, at least, one might have expected plea rolls to be kept, as on the plea side of the Exchequer. But no such rolls have survived, and it is unlikely that any ever existed. The chancellor applied the common law.[12] Contentious common-law questions were generally referred to the judges as assistants to the court,[13] while any issue of fact was transmitted to the King's Bench so that it could be tried at nisi prius.[14] The proceedings were then enrolled on the rolls of the King's Bench—the *Rex* rolls for traverses,[15] and the

v. *Regem* (1526) C43/2/39; *Blyaunt* v. *Regem* (1515) KB 27/1016, Rex m. 14 (issue tried at assizes; judgment for supplicant); Rast. Ent. 423–5 (461–3).

[7] In addition to the reported cases in the last note, see *Re Lord Greystoke* (1488) Hil. 3 Hen. VII, fo. 2, pl. 10; 64 Selden Soc. 131.

[8] e.g. *Duplege* v. *Debenham* (1485–99) Mich. 2 Ric. III, fo. 7, pl. 14; 64 Selden Soc. 75; Mich. 15 Hen. VII, fo. 14, pl. 6; *Vowell* v. *Couper* (1489) KB 27/906, m. 54 (issue sent for trial). See also Jones in 51 *California Law Rev.* at 893–7.

[9] e.g. *Bladsmyth* v. *Legh* (1503) *CCR 1500–9*, no. 363; *Hunt* v. *Coffin* (1518) Dyer 197b (second of two patents granting same park revoked by Wolsey C.); *Re Toly* (1522) ibid. (auditor of royal lands dismissed for not performing office); *Re Blagge* (1524) above, 160; *Re Eston* (1534) Dyer 198a (serjeant at arms dismissed for absence); *Penwarren* v. *Thomas* (1537) ibid. (two patents of same office); *R.* v. *Burgesses of Launceston* (1558) KB 27/1185, m. 23 (patent granting market); *Throgmorton's Case* (1557) Chr. Yelverton's reports, fo. 247 (custody of park). The records of the cases in Dyer are found in Catlyn's precedent book, Alnwick Castle MS. 475, fo. 174.

[10] A petition of right was presented in Latin ('Supplicat humillime vestre celsitudini regie vester fidelis subditus...'), unlike a petition or bill on the English side.

[11] *Diversite de Courtz* (1533), sig. A5 (some uncertainty is indicated by the word *dicitur*).

[12] *Rosse* v. *Pope* (1551) Plowd. 72 (tr. 'he ought to adjudge in this case according to the course of the common law...but upon matters depending before him by bill he may adjudge according to conscience'); this was an *audita querela* upon a recognizance.

[13] If an important case, in the Exchequer Chamber: e.g. *Duplege* v. *Debenham* (1485), above n. 8; *Re Benstede* (1486–92) Trin. 1 Hen. VII, fo. 27, pl. 5; Spelman 161; *Re Higford* (1487) Hil. 2 Hen. VII, fo. 12, pl. 14; Trin. 2 Hen. VII, fo. 17, pl. 3; 64 Selden Soc. 127; *Re Lord Greystoke* (1488) Hil. 3 Hen. VII, fo. 2, pl. 10; 64 Selden Soc. 131; *CPR 1485–94*, p. 285; *Re Lord Dacre of the South* (1535) Spelman 228; C43/2/32; Bean, *The Decline of English Feudalism*, 275–81; below, 670. But sometimes judges attended in Chancery: *Re Lady Mountagu* (1486) Pas. 1 Hen. VII, fo. 14, pl. 1 (three judges); *Re De la Warr* (1495) Mich. 10 Hen. VII, fo. 10, pl. 24 (two chief justices); *Rosse* v. *Pope* (1551) Plowd. 72 (Portman and Hales JJ).

[14] e.g. *Spynell* v. *Taillour* (1484) Mich. 2 Ric. III, fo. 12, pl. 30; 64 Selden Soc. 96; KB 27/895, m. 56 (bill against servant of clerk of Crown); n. 16, below. The procedure is referred to in the statute 27 Hen. VIII, c. 27, s. 10.

[15] e.g. *Re Stoner* (1496) 64 Selden Soc. 101; 94 Selden Soc. 106; KB 27/938, Rex m. 4; *Anon.* (1506) Mich. 21 Hen. VII, fo. 35, pl. 44; *Re Langforth* (1523) Spelman 212, pl. 2; *Re West* (1532) ibid., pl. 1. The

plea rolls for actions of privilege[16] or actions to enforce statutes staple[17]—and although no doubt the result was certified to the Chancery for final decree[18] and execution, it is said that the record remained in the King's Bench.[19] In matters not requiring a trial, a record was supposed to remain in Chancery.[20] The meaning of this seems to be that the Chancery kept pleadings on file unless and until they were sent to the King's Bench.[21] No decree rolls have been found for the Latin side, but a permanent record could always be achieved by entering decrees on the patent or close rolls.[22]

The common-law business was controlled by the three clerks of the petty bag, who were appointed by and answerable to the master of the rolls.[23] Some files of pleadings in common-law cases are preserved from the time of Henry VII onwards (C43).

THE ENGLISH SIDE

Far more litigation was conducted on what was later known as the 'English side' of the court, so called because the proceedings were commenced by English bill (or petition) and continued by English pleadings. In the 1480s, the jurisdiction was barely a century old, but it had become a routine feature of the legal system and it has been estimated that over 500 suits a year were commenced in the time

lengthy King's Bench record in *Re Langforth* was also enrolled in the Exchequer: E159/304, Hil. m. 27 (10 mm).

[16] e.g. *Spynell* v. *Taillour* (1485) KB 27/895, m. 56 (debt against servant of clerk of Crown); Mich. 2 Ric. III, fo. 12, pl. 30; 64 Selden Soc. 96; *Ayssh* v. *Aport* (1499) KB 27/950, m. 29 (forcible entry against servant of Warham MR); *Studde* v. *Adamson* (1510) KB 27/997, m. 27 (debt by servant of MR); *Waren* v. *Maruffo* (1511) KB 27/999, m. 62 (debt by Chancery clerk); *Wheler* v. *Berley* (1516) KB 27/1020, m. 70d (trespass by a cursitor); *Somer* v. *Fynche* (1530) KB 27/1076, m. 60 (*assumpsit* against lord chancellor's servant); *Chamber* v. *Claxston* (1551) KB 27/1158, m. 96 (*assumpsit* against a cursitor); *Claxston* v. *Baspole* (1552) KB 27/1163, m. 122 (*assumpsit* by same cursitor, described as servant of MR).

[17] e.g. *Vowell* v. *Couper* (1489) KB 27/906, m. 54 (issue as to authenticity of receipt given by testator). Cases are quite common in the 1550s.

[18] *Anon.* (1506) Mich. 21 Hen. VII, fo. 35, pl. 44, *per* Fyneux CJ (tr. 'When the traverse is tendered in Chancery, they have no power to try it there; and when it is tried here, we are but justices of nisi prius in effect and cannot give judgment, but send it back to the Chancery').

[19] This is explicitly stated in Constable's reading on *Prerogativa Regis* (1495), 84; *Anon.* (1497) Port 29. Cf. *Claxton's Case* (1554) Dalison's reports, BL MS. Harley 5141, fo. 19v (even if only a transcript is sent to the King's Bench, the proceedings continue there).

[20] It is said in *Anon.* (1497) Port 29, that where an inquisition was enforced through the Exchequer, the record remained in Chancery and what was sent to the Exchequer was merely a transcript.

[21] C44/33 is a thin file of 'Placita in Cancellaria' containing privilege suits from the fifteenth century. The latest item is *Wheler* v. *Hans* (1485) C44/33/7, which is enrolled in KB 27/896, m. 22d; the King's Bench process against the jury is not recorded in the Chancery file.

[22] e.g. *Re Bensted, Att.-Gen.* v. *Suy* (1486–92) Trin. 1 Hen. VII, fo. 27, pl. 51 Spelman 161; CPR 1485–91, p. 387; *Bladsmyth* v. *Legh* (1503) CCR 1500–9, no. 363.

[23] Cf. *LP*, xiii. II. 638 (nomination by Hales MR sent to Cromwell, 1537).

of Henry VII.[24] The Chancery was in this aspect of its work a 'court of con-science'.[25] Since the theoretical basis of its jurisdiction was that a party sometimes required a remedy in conscience where none was available at common law, it was requisite that a plaintiff show not only a cause of action in conscience but also the absence of a remedy at law. Nevertheless, even if in theory the jurisdiction in con-science was exclusive and could not conflict with the common law, in practice it was perceived by the 1480s as presenting the two benches with a form of jurisdic-tional competition. As early as 1481, Fairfax J. advised counsel in the King's Bench that if they paid more attention to actions on the case, the Chancery would not be used so often.[26] And in 1499, when Fyneux CJ announced the final official accept-ance of *assumpsit* for nonfeasance, he added the telling comment that a plaintiff who brought an action on his case was relieved of the need to sue in Chancery.[27] Prohibition was not used against the Chancery; but the common law could be protected by offensive action, since it was considered that an action would lie in the King's Bench on the statutes of due process for unlawful vexation in Chancery in respect of a matter properly determinable at law.[28]

The Chancery was not similarly reticent about interfering with the processes of law, and its practice of issuing common injunctions to restrain suits at common law unless and until the matter in the Chancery petition was determined[29]—though sometimes necessary to bring about a conscionable result—brought the Chancery into more direct conflict with the courts of law. Indeed, there had been a conflict with the King's Bench as early as 1482, when Huse CJ had offered to release a prisoner by *habeas corpus* where an injunction was issued to stay judg-ment after verdict.[30] On occasion the Chancery would even grant an injunction to

[24] For general surveys see N. Pronay, 'The Chancellor, the Chancery and the Council at the End of the Fifteenth Century' in *British Government and Administration*, ed. H. Hearder and H. R. Loyn (1974), 87–103; F. Metzger, 'The Last Phase of the Medieval Chancery' in *Law-Making and Law-Makers in British History*, ed. A. Harding (1980), 79–89; J. A. Guy, 'The Development of Equitable Jurisdiction 1450–1550' in *Law, Litigants and the Legal Profession*, ed. A. H. Manchester and E. W. Ives (1983), 80–6; T. S. Haskett, 'The Medieval English Court of Chancery' (1996) 14 *LHR* 245–313 (for the period 1417–1532).

[25] *Diversite de Courtz* (1533), sig. A5 (tr. 'in this court a man shall have remedy for matters for which he had no remedy at common law, and it is called in common speech [*en le bouche des gentz*] the court of conscience'); 94 Selden Soc. *75* n. 6. For conscience see above, 39, 48.

[26] *Sarger's Case* (1481) B. & M. 513 at 515 ('I advise you who are pleaders that if we pay more atten-tion to these actions on the case, and maintain the jurisdiction of this and other courts, subpoenas would not be used as often as they are at present').

[27] Fitz. Abr., *Action sur le Case*, pl. 45; B. & M. 401 ('I shall have an action on my case and need not sue out a subpoena').

[28] John Hales's reading in Gray's Inn (1514) GI MS. 25, fo. 292v (tr. in 94 Selden Soc. *75*); St German, *Little Treatise*, ed. Guy, 121. An example of such an action is *Fitzherbert v. Wellys* (1516) KB 27/1020, m. 83d (on 42 Edw. III, c. 3); C1/590/6.

[29] The wording of the common injunctions filed in C261/9 (1524–8) is: 'donec et quousque materia... plenarie fuerit discussa et determinata vel aliter licenciam inde habueris'.

[30] *Russel's Case* (1482) Mich. 22 Edw. IV, fo. 37, pl. 21; Brooke Abr., *Consciens*, pl. 16.

stay execution of a judgment already given at common law,[31] and this must have been a leading cause of the friction which led to the celebrated meeting between More and the judges.[32] St German considered the practice to be contrary to the statute of Henry IV which protected judgments from impeachment,[33] and it was certainly open to legal challenge: for instance, in a case of 1532 before More C., the defendant objected that long before the injunction was issued he had obtained judgment by default at common law, and prayed that the injunction be dissolved.[34] The outcome is unrecorded, but the case does not stand alone[35] and it seems from the pleadings that injunctions were granted *ex parte* before the merits were argued. On the other hand, it is said to have been ruled by More or one of his predecessors that the chancellor would give no remedy after judgment, 'for then every record would be examined before him and the common law would be thereby destroyed'.[36]

There is no evidence of any serious friction during the long chancellorships of Cardinal Moreton (1485–1500) and Archbishop Warham (1503–15), who were both trained as canonists, although the latter was once accused of giving judgment against the opinion of all the justices of England, 'without the advice of any judge', in a case on the Latin side.[37] Relationships with the legal profession seem to have soured when the great seal was held by Cardinal Wolsey (1515–29), who had no legal training of any kind: no doctor of the law, bewailed Skelton, 'nor of none other saw'.[38] Soon after his appointment, an Italian diplomat observed his arbitrary tendencies: his will was law, *Hoc volo, sic jubeo*.[39] Opinions still differ as to Wolsey's judicial qualities,[40] and it is difficult to achieve an objective view of

---

[31] The common form of injunction before the end of our period was framed so as to include a stay of execution if judgment had been given at law: E. G. Henderson, 18 *AJLH* at 306.   [32] Above, 46.

[33] 4 Hen. IV, c. 23; *Doctor and Student*, ed. Plucknett and Barton, 107; *Little Treatise*, ed. Guy, 90, 119–20; 94 Selden Soc. 74. This was the issue which provoked the row between Coke and Ellesmere in 1615–16.   [34] *Drewys* v. *Pryst* (1532) C1/626/25–6.

[35] Examples temp. Wolsey C. are *Sole's Case* (1527) C261/9/51; *Wolrich's Case* (1528) C261/9/67; *Zouche* v. *Cornwall* (1528) C261/9/71; *Praty* v. *Bowyer* (undated), C4/19; Guy, *St German on Chancery and Statute*, 68. Examples temp. Audley C. are: *Farley* v. *Knyght*, C1/787/26 (judgment already affirmed on a writ of error); *Fosse's Case*, C1/797/58–59 (verdict and judgment before subpoena granted). For the 1540s and 1550s, and complaints temp. Wriothesley C., see below, 179.

[36] *Diversite de Courtz* (1530), sig. A6.

[37] *Conyngesby and Mallom* v. *Regem* (1509) 2 Caryll 605. This was a petition of right, not a matter of equity, but Warham C. was intent on undoing some mischief committed by Empson and Dudley.

[38] *The Complete Poems of John Skelton*, ed. P. Henderson (2nd edn, 1948), 323. Skelton painted a disagreeable portrait of an arrogant bully who would not give others a chance to speak: in the Star Chamber, 'clapping his rod on the board, no man dare speak a word' (ibid. 313–14, 318).

[39] *Calendar of State Papers (Venetian) 1509–19*, p. 500; Pollard, *Wolsey*, 97.

[40] For assessments of his chancellorship see F. Metzger, 'Das Englische Kanzleigericht unter Kardinal Wolsey', Ph.D. thesis (1976); Guy, *Public Career of More*, 37–49; *Thomas More* (2000), 127–32; Pollard, *Wolsey*, ch. 3. See also P. Gwyn, *The King's Cardinal* (1990), 101–43.

particular conflicts which are not objectively documented.[41] Moreover, it is difficult to separate the different spheres of Wolsey's authority, and unclear whether he himself kept them separate. Certainly he made a habit of sending distinguished lawyers to prison,[42] and there is ample testimony from contemporaries that he was apt to treat counsel with an arrogant hauteur born of his unwillingness to grapple with the finer points of law they were arguing.[43] His desire to seem to be a great judge, and to improve access to justice, led him to encourage plaintiffs without always paying due regard to the interests of defendants.[44] And his arbitrary habits may have encouraged the development of *habeas corpus* by the King's Bench.[45] In 1523, Spelman tells us that none of the serjeants would argue a revenue case in the Exchequer Chamber 'for displeasure at the great cardinal of York',[46] though this may allude to his recent parliamentary conduct over the subsidy rather than his judicial behaviour. In 1526 he committed Serjeant Roo and Thomas Moyle to prison for a play in Gray's Inn which—though written twenty years earlier—he conceived as containing a satirical attack on his government.[47] And there can be no mistaking the reference to Wolsey's Chancery in Thomas Audley's reading in the Inner Temple in the same year. The certainty of the land law, he lamented, had been destroyed by uncertainty, since title had come to depend on the whim (*arbitrement*) of the judge in conscience.[48] The signatories of the Lords' articles against Wolsey on his fall (in 1529), including Sir Thomas More, Fitzjames CJ, and Fitzherbert J., complained that he had 'examined divers and many matters in the Chancery after judgment thereof given at the common law' and in other ways hindered justice and hampered the judges with injunctions, in subversion of the law.[49] No doubt these complaints are

[41] Guy argues that Wolsey's demerits were exaggerated by the recusant writers who sought to glorify More.

[42] There were two celebrated instances in 1518, when he threatened to teach Serjeant Pygot and Sir Andrew Windsor 'the new law of the Star Chamber': Pollard, *Wolsey*, 75. For the case of Sir Robert Sheffield the same year see above, 93. For the imprisonment of David Broke (later chief baron) in 1526 see *Hasylwood* v. *Broke* (1530) C1/640/30 (warden of the Fleet seeks injunction to stop Broke's action of false imprisonment, commenced after Wolsey's fall).

[43] See 94 Selden Soc. *77–8*. Cf. Ives, *Common Lawyers in pre-Reformation England*, 219, where a defence is offered.   [44] See Guy, *The Cardinal's Court*, 81; *Public Career of More*, 89.

[45] See above, 93.

[46] Spelman 169 ('lez serjaunz ne fueront retaine de counsell et pur ceo ilz ne voilent argue pur displesure de le graund cardinall de Yorke').

[47] *Hall's Chronicle*, 719; and see R. M. Fisher, 69 *Archiv für Reformationsgeschichte* (1978), 293–8. Roo had written the play at the end of Henry VII's reign. Moyle was not a student but an 'ancient' barrister who became a bencher in 1533 and was knighted (as speaker of the Commons) in 1542.

[48] 94 Selden Soc. *79, 198*; B. & M. 103 at 104; below, 666.

[49] *LP*, iv. 6075; 1 St. Tr. 376. What Coke referred to as Wolsey's 'indictment' (Co. Inst. ii. 626, referring to his attempted subjugation of England and its people to 'the imperial laws, commonly called the Civil laws') is a recital of Wolsey's offences in the indictment of the dean of arches for favouring his papal legacy: *Att.-Gen.* v. *Ligham* (1531) KB 27/1080, Rex m. 14 (and against other judges, mm. 16–20). The passage is not in Wolsey's indictment as printed in 102 Selden Soc. 58.

one-sided, if not positively unfair.[50] Legal practitioners flourished in Wolsey's Chancery,[51] and it is impossible to discover their collective opinion of its efficacy. It is arguable that Wolsey's very haughtiness placed him at a salutary distance from influential lawyers and enabled him to deal the more firmly with abuses of procedure. At least he was able to remind the men of law that they were not above the law. But the price paid for a one-man supreme court with proactive tendencies was a growing impression that the chancellor himself was above or indifferent to law. One of the king's serjeants recorded Wolsey's fall with undisguised satisfaction: a man of great pomp and riches, he noted, deposed from office 'for his great iniquity'.[52] Whatever the final judgment on Wolsey as chancellor, it seems right to conclude that his tenure of the office provoked a division in the profession over the proper functioning of a court of conscience in the legal system.

No doubt More's acceptance of the seal had been expected by many lawyers to inaugurate a new regime in Chancery.[53] He was a bencher of Lincoln's Inn, with extensive experience in practice, administration, and judicial work, both in the city of London and as chancellor of the duchy.[54] His judicial impartiality was legendary, and there seems no reason to doubt the hagiographies in this respect.[55] Unfortunately, very little evidence survives for reconstructing More's views about the proper exercise of a jurisdiction in conscience. However, it appears from a passage in his answer to Luther, written in the 1520s, that he had given careful thought to the balance between law and conscience and had concluded firmly against the evil of judicial arbitrariness:[56]

If you take away laws and leave everything free to the judges... they will rule as their own nature leads and order whatever pleases them, in which case the people will in no wise be more free but worse off and in a condition of slavery, since instead of settled and certain laws they will have to submit to uncertain whims changing from day to day. And this is bound to happen even under the best judges, for the people will still complain and mutter against them...

---

[50] Guy, *Public Career of More*, 125, describes More's signature of the document as an 'act of hypocrisy', since he himself continued Wolsey's practices.

[51] Guy, *Public Career of More*, 40–1.

[52] Spelman, 38, 190. The remark does not necessarily allude to the Chancery: his legatine jurisdiction (below, 245) was a greater bone of contention. For another common lawyer's view of his pride and unpopularity, see *Hall's Chronicle*, 567, 583, 593, 696, 773–4.

[53] For More's chancellorship see J. A. Guy, 'Thomas More as Successor to Wolsey' (1977) 52 *Thought: Fordham University Qly* 272–92; *Public Career of More*, 35–93; *Thomas More* (2000), ch. 7. For some of what follows see also 94 Selden Soc. 80–2.

[54] For his legal career before 1529 see G. R. Elton, 'Thomas More, Councillor (1517–29)' (1972), repr. in *Studies*, i. 129–54; Guy, *Public Career of More*, 1–33. For what little is known of his views on law see also G. B. Wegemer, *Thomas More on Statesmanship* (1996).

[55] For a balanced assessment see Guy, *Public Career of More*, 80–93.

[56] *Responsio ad Lutherum*, ed. J. M. Headley (1969), 276–9 (retranslated above).

More can hardly have written those words without calling Wolsey to mind, and he can hardly have sat in Chancery himself without recollecting them. We have seen how the very same distaste for arbitrariness provoked a scathing attack on the Chancery in the early 1530s—the *Replication* (to *Doctor and Student*) by an anonymous critic styling himself a serjeant at law—which in turn produced an eloquent defence of the court from St German.[57] It has been suggested that the 'serjeant' was none other than Thomas Audley,[58] but whoever he was it may be supposed that he represented a point of view genuinely held at that time. Internal references to unlearned chancellors who trusted to their own 'wit and wisdom' rather than to objective standards point unmistakably at Wolsey. The question was whether More would give the same grounds for complaint. The 'serjeant' seemed to think that the very existence of an equitable jurisdiction was a cause for complaint, at any rate when it took the form of direct interference with the common law: the lord chancellor was made a 'judge in every matter' and the law was becoming so uncertain that no man could be sure of his land.[59] But that was an extreme position, containing either an element of parody or an explosion of pent-up frustration with an unpredictable tribunal. It was fully answered by St German in his *Little Treatise concerning Writs of Subpoena*, written during More's tenure of office as a rejoinder to the 'serjeant'. And it was certainly not More's own position, for we learn from the story of his meeting with the judges that he firmly believed in the need for the injunctive power and continued to exercise it.[60] That the complaints subsided thereafter is perhaps attributable to the manner in which the jurisdiction was now exercised. Good conscience was not arbitrary.[61]

If More was a success as chancellor, it may well be because he reintroduced into the court a lawyer's view of justice and resisted the temptation to confuse the conscience of the court with his own idiosyncratic notions of fairness. Doubtless his increasing political isolation also gave him more time for judicature than had been available to Wolsey; even his home in Chelsea provided no haven from the burdens of a keen judicial conscience.[62] On the other hand, the legend that he was the only chancellor to have succeeded in wiping out the backlog of cases in the court seems to have no basis in fact. His brief tenure of office was not long enough for him to make a significant impact on the Chancery, though he can be shown to have improved the procedures for enforcing decrees.[63]

---

[57] See above, 43–4.

[58] Guy, *Public Career of More*, 45. However, Guy later concluded that St German could have written the treatise himself: above, 43 n. 225.   [59] *Replication of a Serjeant*, ed. Guy, 105.

[60] See above, 46. It is not so clear whether he thought it proper to exercise it after judgment had been given at law.

[61] See *Little Treatise*, ed. Guy, 123 (sp. mod. 'the conscience that the chancellor is bound to follow is that conscience which is grounded upon the law of God, and the law of reason, and upon the law of the realm...').   [62] For suits heard at Chelsea see Guy, *Public Career of More*, 72, 82, 92.

[63] Guy, *Public Career of More*, 91; *Thomas More*, 137. He also made a rule allowing defendants to appear by attorney.

There is even less to say, in the present state of knowledge, about the chancellors who came between More and the beginning of Sir Nicholas Bacon's long and distinguished tenure in 1559.[64] Audley was the first serjeant at law to receive the great seal since the time of Edward III, and his conservative views—certainly resembling those attributed to the 'serjeant' in the *Replication*—enabled him with some semblance of good conscience to do the king's bidding in relation to uses.[65] There is little doubt that he was firmly under the influence of Cromwell and was not expected to show the kind of independence which had brought his two predecessors to their untimely ends. From the point of view of legal administration, the positive advantage of such a chancellor was that any remaining irritation between the courts was removed. After ten years of common-law chancellors, the exasperation evinced by the *Replication* seems to have become spent. There was no longer any question of curtailing the ever-growing jurisdiction of the Chancery.

INFLUENCE OF THE CIVILIANS

The irritation was to be briefly revived under Lord Wriothesley (1544–7), though the episode of his removal in 1547 was coloured by political considerations matching those surrounding Wolsey's fall.[66] The crisis arose shortly after the accession of Edward VI, who had continued Wriothesley (now earl of Southampton) in office as chancellor. Wriothesley was accused of arbitrariness, and of illegal conduct in appointing four civilians to hear causes in Chancery, thereby—it was said—discouraging the study of the common law. The complaints were similar to those of 1529, but they were now given an anti-civilian twist. Indeed, the petition to the lord protector and Council was couched in terms of high constitutional principle, the rule of law, and the independence of the common law from foreign influence:[67]

...whereas the imperial Crown of this realm of England, and the whole estate of the same, have been always from the beginning a realm imperial, having a law of itself called the common laws of the realm of England...now of late these common laws of this realm, partly by injunctions, as well before verdicts, judgments, and executions as after, and partly by writs of subpoena issuing out of the king's Court of Chancery, hath been not only stayed of their direct course but also many times altered and violated by reason of decrees made in the said Court of Chancery, most grounded upon the law civil and upon matter

[64] Jones, *The Elizabethan Court of Chancery*, 28–30; S. E. Lehmberg, 'Sir Thomas Audley: a soul as black as marble?' in *Tudor Men and Institutions*, ed. A. J. Slavin (1972), 1–31; 94 Selden Soc. 82–3.

[65] See below, 666–7, 670–1.

[66] A. F. Pollard, *England under Protector Somerset* (1900), 31–3; A. J. Slavin, 'The Fall of Lord Chancellor Wriothesley' (1975) 7 *Albion* 265 86; D. Loades, *John Dudley, Duke of Northumberland* (1996), at 92–4.

[67] *APC 1547–50*, pp. 48–50 (sp. mod.); repr. in Maitland, *English Law and the Renaissance*, 79–80.

depending in the conscience and discretion of the hearers thereof, who—being civilians and not learned in the common laws, setting aside the said common laws—determine the weighty causes of this realm according either to the said law civil or to their own conscience: which law civil is to the subjects of this realm unknown, and they not be bounden nor inheritable to the same law, and which judgments and decrees grounded upon conscience are not grounded nor made upon any rule certain or law written.

The case was referred to Richard Rich and six other common lawyers for their opinion; and on 28 February they signed an opinion to the effect that Wriothesley, by issuing a commission without warrant, had 'by the common law forfeit his office of chancellor' and incurred such penalty as the king should impose.[68] The effect of this remarkable opinion was that dismissal was unnecessary. Since the chancellorship was conditional upon lawful conduct, it had become vacant for breach of the condition.

Although the opinion was doubtless guided by political exigency, the government did not have to manufacture the allegations which produced the result: as in Wolsey's case, it was simply a matter of tapping an existing stream of discontent. Of course, that discontent would not have led to an official enquiry in 1547 had there not been a desire to remove Wriothesley from office. But our present interest is less with the politics than with the incidental light which the episode throws on the Chancery at the end of Henry VIII's reign. For Maitland it was further evidence that, by the middle of the century, 'the life our ancient law was by no means lusty'.[69] How far, though, was the supposed civilian threat a real one?

The relationship between the Chancery and the Romano-canonical legal tradition has been a matter of some disagreement among historians. Since most of the fifteenth-century chancellors were trained canonists, it has sometimes been assumed that the Chancery was in some sense a court of canon law.[70] It cannot be denied that the written procedure, as developed since the late fourteenth century, had a Romano-canonical inspiration; and its guardians—the masters of the court—were predominantly civilian throughout our period. To suppose from this procedural circumstance that the court could have applied substantive canon law is, however, to suppose a feat which was hardly possible. For one thing, Chancery procedure was a thoroughly English version of the Roman procedural tradition, as may be seen from the phraseology of the pleadings themselves.[71] In any case procedure was a servant rather than a master; the court was not bound by any

[68] The original opinion, signed by Richard 'Ryche', Roger Cholmeley, John Baker, Thomas Moyle, John Caryll, John Gosnold, and Robert Keylwey, is BL MS. Harley 284, fo. 9. The signatories were all in the Crown employ, but did not include the king's serjeants or the king's attorney and solicitor. There is a related rough draft in BL MS. Harley 249, ff. 16–17v.   [69] *English Law and the Renaissance*, 22.
[70] See W. T. Barbour, *History of Contract in Early English Equity* (1914), 167–8; J. L. Barton, *Roman Law in England* (1971), 67–71; Simpson, *Rise of Assumpsit*, 400–2.
[71] J. P. Dawson, *A History of Lay Judges* (1960), 149.

artificial rules of pleading or procedure.[72] More to the point, the court did not regard itself as applying substantive rules of law either. In so far as it had to take notice of law, it was necessarily the law of the land—the law about land and commerce—which was noticed.[73] No doubt, so long as the chancellors were canonists, their attitudes towards questions of conscience must have been influenced in a general way by their professional training; they were entitled to collect abstract wisdom wherever they could find it. But had they shown any inclination to apply principles of canon law, or to listen to submissions based on canonical texts, it would have been essential to allow rights of audience to the doctors of law. This never happened. Since the fifteenth century, Chancery pleadings had usually been drawn by serjeants or benchers of the inns of court, and cases were argued at the bar by men of the same profession.[74] A writer of the 1540s flatly denied that the equity of the Chancery had any connection with the Civil law.[75]

The complaint to Somerset asserted that interference with the common law by civilians,[76] acting either on unknown principles of Roman law or on no principles at all, was undermining the law to such an extent that 'few have or do regard to take pains of the profound and sincere knowledge of the [common] law, by reason whereof there are now very few, and it is to be doubted that within few years there shall not be sufficient of learned men within this realm to serve the king in that faculty'. This was a serious piece of rhetorical exaggeration, since the evidence of the inns of court records shows that the common lawyers were increasing in numbers at this period. The underlying grouse was really that professional pride had been wounded by indifference, that legal learning was not taken sufficiently seriously. It was, in effect, the anonymous serjeant's grouse resurfacing in a slightly new, nationalist guise. The petitioners did not descend into detail, and the principal gravamen of their complaint—the commission issued to civilians—was far from straightforward, since similar commissions had been issued before Wriothesley's time. In any case, the Rich Commission achieved little in practice beyond the transfer of the great seal to Rich himself. Rich was said by his fellow bencher Robert Brooke to have been the first chancellor who was an apprentice of the court,

---

[72] St German, *Little Treatise*, ed. Guy, 121, 123.

[73] Cf. *Anon.* (1464) Pas. 4 Edw. IV, fo. 8, pl. 9, *per* Catesby sjt (tr. 'The law of the Chancery is the common law of the land'). For the notion that equity follows the law of the land see Guy, *St German on Chancery and Statute*, 19–21, 83–8, 91–2.

[74] Below, 427. See also J. H. Baker, 'Lawyers Practising in Chancery 1474–86' (1983) 4 *JLH* 54–76.

[75] Hales, *Oration* (1540/2), fo. 43 (sp. mod. 'Because most of the masters thereof be civilians some will say that our laws be tempered by the Civil, which is not so, for in the Civil laws as far as I have heard or seen there is as few equities as be in ours').

[76] This complaint was not necessarily confined to the Chancery: note Somerset's unsuccessful attempt to introduce slavery into English law in 1547, above, 99.

meaning a practitioner below the degree of the coif.[77] But of his own short chancellorship (1547–51) next to nothing is known, save for the fact that towards the end of it the lord treasurer declared the king's pleasure that the Star Chamber and Chancery should desist from holding pleas 'to the derogation of the common law'.[78]

For most of the 1550s, the great seal was entrusted to bishops, only one of whom (Gardiner) had any legal training, and that Roman.[79] This circumstance likewise is of more political than legal significance; but it does show that the conclusions of the Rich Commission were not taken very seriously. Not only did the inns of court survive these very diverse appointments, but the benchers and barristers continued to furnish the bar of the court to the exclusion of civilians. The petition itself proves that the Chancery was not seen as a court of canon law. Moreover, it does not appear from the records that the Chancery at the accession of Elizabeth I was substantially different, in jurisdiction or procedure, from the Chancery under More.

THE MASTERS AND CLERKS

The Chancery was always in essence a one-man court, since the final responsibility for its decisions rested solely with the chancellor. But it is obvious that a conscientious chancellor, with many duties besides those of sitting in Chancery, could not hear all the cases himself. The increase in business, even by the start of our period, necessitated delegation and reliance on written evidence. Here the masters in Chancery found a new role. Though originally styled *clerici*, or clerks of the first form,[80] they were also members or ministers of the court who sat on the bench beside the chancellor,[81] and to whom the chancellor could delegate interlocutory procedural and investigative functions. They did not, however, formally participate in making decrees and could not on their own authority determine cases in the chancellor's absence. The masters were not, therefore, the equivalent of puisne justices, and indeed they had no direct parallel in the common-law courts. They received no wages from the Crown, but only a modest allowance in lieu of a livery of robes.[82] They are best regarded as assistants to

---

[77] Brooke Abr., *Statute Merchant*, pl. 42 (1544). More was a bencher of Lincoln's Inn, but had left the practising bar by the time of his appointment.

[78] HEHL MS. EL 2652, fo. 17 (pr. in Guy, *The Star Chamber*, 57). Guy thought the mischief was probably interference with title to land: see also Guy, *Tudor England*, 26–7.

[79] Thomas Goodrich DD (Cantab.), bishop of Ely (1551–3); Stephen Gardiner LL D (Cantab.), bishop of Winchester (1553–5); and Nicholas Heath DD (Cantab.), archbishop of York (1556–8).

[80] See e.g. *CPR 1476–85*, p. 445 ('clerks of the first form of Chancery called masters of Chancery', 1484).

[81] IT MS. Misc. 188 (a miniature painting of the court, *c*.1460, which shows the master of the rolls and four masters in ordinary sitting with the chancellor).

[82] *LP*, ii. II. 3153 (1517); vii. 1204 (1534). In the 1540s, the masters in ordinary received £3 in summer and £3. 14*s*. in winter, the MR receiving £1 more: John Hales's memoranda, BL MS. Add. 38136, ff. 83v–84. The supernumerary masters received nothing.

the chancellor, by whom they were appointed. At the beginning of our period, the masterships had recently been taken over almost entirely by doctors of law: the last stronghold of the clergy in the secular legal system, they nevertheless represented an innovation, the older tradition being to employ non-graduate clerics bred up in the department.[83]

The master of the rolls, who was nominally keeper of the records of the Chancery, was alone appointed by the Crown and had a pre-eminence over the other masters. By 1500 he was already developing a judicial role, the extent of which is unclear.[84] Sir Thomas Cromwell (MR 1534–6) was doubtless a special case, since he was concurrently the king's principal secretary of state, but he certainly sat in court and expressed opinions there.[85] Nevertheless, the judicial role of the master of the rolls was clearly subordinate to the chancellor. A rather cryptic story was told of Sir Christopher Hales (MR 1536–41) that 'He, resting at the side bar in Westminster after the Lord Audley, Lord Chancellor, had gone up to sit, and being sent to that it was not his place *sedente curia*, answered that he wist well enough where his place was'.[86] How far the master of the rolls could dispose of cases on his own authority is not, and probably was not, clear; but it became the practice in the time of Henry VIII to issue commissions to the master of the rolls and a small number of other masters to hear and determine causes in Chancery in the absence of the chancellor.[87] Such commissions removed any doubt for current purposes, though they served to preserve the doubt in the long term.

Corresponding to the attorneys and filazers of the benches were the six clerks, who are indeed sometimes referred to in Chancery records as 'attorneys'.[88] They were appointed by the master of the rolls, and used to wear his livery.[89] According to Wriothesley's orders of 1545, they were supposed to stand in court, three on each side of the bars, and not speak unless spoken to.[90] But they were sometimes formally consulted by the court as a body, being the collective repositories of technical knowledge concerning Chancery practice.[91] The clerks took it in turns for a

[83] Pronay, 'The Chancellor, the Chancery and the Council', 91.

[84] See *Ayshecum* v. *Boughan* (1501) *CCR 1500–9*, no. 48 (recognizance to appear before Warham MR at the Rolls in a debt case). For the master of the rolls' judicial role on the Latin side, see *Re Lady Mountague* (1486) Pas. 1 Hen. VII, fo. 14, pl. 1; *Re Bensted* (1486) Trin. 1 Hen. VII, fo. 27, pl. 5.

[85] *Lord Dacre's Case* (1535) Spelman 228–30; below, 669–70; *Docwra's Case* (1535) below, 190.

[86] Recollection of old Mr Valence of Lincoln's Inn, quoted in BL MS. Lansdowne 163, fo. 98v; *Orders of the High Court of Chancery*, ed. G. W. Sanders (1845), i. I. 17.

[87] e.g. *LP*, iv. 5666 (with numerous others, including judges, June 1529); xix. II. 527(24) (with other masters, 1544).

[88] e.g. in *CCR* (where they occur as attorneys for sheriffs), and in C33 (where they are named as attorneys for litigants). It was possible for attorneys of the Common Pleas to solicit causes in Chancery, but they could not act as attorneys there: 4 *JLH* 56.

[89] BL MS. Lansdowne 163, fo. 99; Sanders, *Orders*, i. I. 17.

[90] Ord. 9 May 1545; Sanders, *Orders*, i. I. 19.   [91] *Stathum* v. *Denton* (1536) Spelman 23, 24.

year at a time to make up the files on the English side, and another of the clerks by turns acted as riding clerk with the duty of attending the chancellor outside the court and assisting at sealings. In 1549, Thomas Powle, already clerk of the Crown in Chancery and comptroller of the hanaper, made an agreement with his fellow clerks that he would act permanently as riding clerk.[92] It was one of the six clerks also who acted as clerk of the enrolments.[93]

In 1523 an act of Parliament abrogated the custom that the six clerks should remain unmarried on pain of losing office. Holdsworth misunderstood the act as showing that the six clerks were all in Holy Orders before that time.[94] But the six clerks named in the act must have been laymen or the provision would have been in vain, and in any case the sense of the act is that the custom had long since become outdated, especially since a similar custom was no longer observed by the cursitors. In fact, the six clerks seem by the time of Henry VII at the latest to have become an entirely lay body. As yet there is no complete list of their names, but the names in abbreviated form are commonly noted at the top left-hand corner of filed answers.[95] Several were members of the inns of court and chancery—especially Clifford's Inn, which adjoined the Rolls, or (less commonly) Lincoln's Inn, which faced it.[96] For instance, Christopher Hanyngton (d. 1490), who was a six clerk from the 1460s until his death, was a gentleman of Clifford's Inn until 1482, when he migrated to Lincoln's Inn.[97] However, it seems probable that in the time of Henry VII the six clerks had not only an office but also some kind of unincorporated society with a common table, for in 1501 they were given money to purchase a silver salt with the donor's arms.[98] The rule against marrying also seems to hint at some kind of communal existence. All we know for certain is that before 1530 they acquired a tenancy from Nocton Priory of some premises in Chancery Lane called Harflew Inn or Harflete Inn,[99] where they kept

[92] Ord. 22 June 1557; Sanders, *Orders*, i. I. 16–19; Jones, *Elizabethan Court of Chancery*, 128–34.

[93] John Croke was appointed in 1534, and was succeeded in 1540 by Richard Snowe: *LP*, vii. 922(6).

[94] 14 & 15 Hen. VIII, c. 8; *HEL*, i. 421 n. 3.

[95] Five of the six clerks in 1507 are known, and they seem all to have been lay: *CCR 1500–9*, nos. 73, 76, 138, 800, 827, 879 (John Gawsein, William Nanson, Michael Poynant, John Studde and John Trevethen); *LP*, i, no. 438(1), at pp. 219 (Studde), 262 (Trevethen). All five were in office by 1501: annotations on answers in C1/238–239 (Gaws', Nan', Poy', St', and Tre'). The sixth in 1507 was probably Ralph Pexsall.

[96] It is known that at least five (Christopher Hanyngton, William Hede, William Jeffson, Ralph Pexsall, and Henry Wyncote) were members of Clifford's Inn. Others (e.g. Walter Berecok, William Nanson, and John Sutton) were members of Lincoln's Inn. Clifford's Inn was patronized by cursitors as well (e.g. John Baron: *CPR 1553–4*, p. 448).

[97] *CPR 1461–8*, p. 458 (attorney in 1467); *CPR 1468–76*, nos. 160, 389 (gentleman in 1468); *CPR 1485–1509*, no. 486 (attorney in 1490); *BBLI*, i. 73 (adm. from Clifford's Inn); CUL MS. Mm. 5.2 (his copy of Littleton).   [98] *CCR 1500–9*, no. 76 (bequest by Lady Hill).

[99] The inn belonged temp. Hen. VI to a master in Chancery, Nicholas Wymbyssh (d. 1461), who granted it in 1454 to Nocton Priory. It was later let to one Andrew Harflete: E. V. Williams, *Early Holborn*

commons.[100] When the duke of Suffolk granted them the freehold after the dissolution of the priory, they were incorporated by charter and private act of Parliament so that the inn would belong to them in perpetual succession.[101]

There were a number of other clerks attached to the court.[102] In the metropolis, evidence was taken down in writing by an official examiner, using interrogatories settled by the parties,[103] and by the 1540s the work had increased sufficiently to require the appointment of a second examiner.[104] The examiners also recorded evidence *in perpetuam rei memoriam*, where a witness was in danger of dying, for potential future use.[105] The clerks of the alms discharged the chancellor's statutory duty of providing free original writs and writs of subpoena for paupers; they were in consequence poor themselves, but the position was regarded as a form of training before a more remunerative appointment was obtained.[106] Finally, there were the registers, who from at least the 1530s recorded the acts of the court.[107]

The clerk of the hanaper, an administrative officer concerned with the finances of the Chancery, had duties in connection with the court's material supplies. For instance, he was responsible for parchment and wax, and for the court fittings and trimmings, which in 1534 included green say hangings on the wall of the court behind the chancellor and two cushions with the royal arms within a garter.[108] The notary, or prothonotary, unlike his namesakes in the other courts, was not involved with judicial work but with diplomatic business.

(1927), ii. §1439–41; P. W. Chandler, 'A Short History of the Site of the Law Society's Hall' in *Handbook of the Law Society* (1938), at 94–6. Later in the sixteenth century it was called Kederminster's Inn, supposedly after a member (John Kederminster) who assisted with the purchase of the freehold.

[100] According to a recollection in BL MS. Lansdowne 163, fo. 99 (Sanders, *Orders*, i. I. 17), they began their hall and commons about the middle of Hen. VIII's reign. Certainly they were tenants by 1530: *LP*, v. 47(1).

[101] Pat. 31 Hen. VIII, pt vii, m. 12; 31 Hen. VIII, c. 27 (not printed); *LP*, xiv. I. 403; *LPCL*, 52 n. 22. The statute recites that they were already in occupation. Cf. *R. v. Middelmowre* (1539) KB 9/541/81 (indictment for breaking the chamber of Richard Welles 'in quodam loco vocato Harfleuen alias dicto the Syx Clerkes In').

[102] Besides, that is, the departmental officials, such as the clerk of the Crown and the cursitors. The clerk of the Crown had a deputy by the 1550s: see A. F. Pollard, 57 *EHR* 333.

[103] 4 *JLH* 56 (George Kyrkham, examiner in 1506). Some examples from the 1530s and 1540s survive in C24, with the name of Henry Polsted (of the Inner Temple, d. 1555) as examiner. They are written in English, on large sheets of paper folded in two (now often split along the fold). Most sets of depositions have with them a sheet of interrogatories.

[104] Sanders, *Orders*, i. I. 8, 10; Dawson, *History of Lay Judges*, 151–2; Jones, *Elizabethan Court of Chancery*, 135–6.

[105] *Anon.* (1526) Yorke 202, no. 299 (perpetuation ordered upon a bill brought for the purpose). There are two examples (one dated 1544) in C24/1, and a precedent of a commission for the same purpose in John Hales's book, BL MS. Add. 38136, fo. 15v (c.1535/45). The procedure was formalized by an order of 12 Nov. 1556, Sanders, *Orders*, i. I. 14–15.

[106] 11 Hen. VII, c. 12; Sanders, *Orders*, i. I. 11; Jones, *Elizabethan Court of Chancery*, 166. For proceedings *in forma pauperis*, see ibid. 323–8.   [107] Below, 187.

[108] Cromwell's accounts, *LP*, vii. 1204.

The officers and clerks were privileged from being sued in other courts, including the Common Pleas,[109] but in a 'notable' decision of 1510 it was held that this privilege did not avail in the King's Bench.[110] The privilege extended to the officers' servants, but it seems that this rule was abused by issuing writs of privilege as favours; at any rate, claims to privilege by 'servants' were frequently contested.[111]

THE RECORDS OF THE COURT

The Chancery on its English side was not a court of record,[112] and for the period before Henry VIII the only archives to survive are the files assembled by the six clerks. The principal surviving files are those which contain the bills and pleadings (C1, C4). Occasionally an interlocutory order or final decree is endorsed (in Latin) on the bill, but no continuous record of decrees has survived before the 1530s, when the decree rolls begin (C78). The absence of earlier decree books is something of a mystery, since the Council had decree books from 1486 at the latest,[113] and the old Latin ordinances of the Chancery referred to the existence of two notaries (*tabelliones*) whose function was to write down the acts of the court.[114] The explanation is probably that the Chancery followed the canonistic practice of supplying on request an authenticated notarial copy of its judgments to the parties, without regularly keeping a copy for itself. Such a decree could, if a party so desired, be enrolled on the patent roll.[115] A precedent from 1503/4 of an

[109] e.g. *Coker v. Kydwelly* (1488) CP 40/904, m. 137 (writ of privilege for Morgan Kydwelly as servant of William MR; Kydwelly was a bencher of the Inner Temple). Cf. *Anon.* (1537) Dyer 33b. For privilege pleaded in the Mayor's Court of London, see *Ernley's Case* (1492) 105 Selden Soc. 259. See also Sanders, *Orders*, i. I. 20–4.

[110] *Bothe v. Kyrkeham* (1509–10) KB 27/993, m. 35d (judgment on demurrer); contd (1511) KB 27/999, m. 71; record copied in Catlyn's precedent book, Alnwick Castle MS. 475, ff. 2, 58–60v, as 'Notable presydent pur jurisdiction de Banco Regis versus curiam Cancellarie'. Cf. *Cowper v. Caundyche* (1526) KB 27/1061, m. 70d (privilege pleaded by Richard Cavendish as servant of Wolsey C.).

[111] e.g. *Power v. Bailly* (1482) CP 40/882, m. 135 (vicar of South Mimms); *Hert v. Danvers* (1485) CP 40/891, m. 314 (gentleman); *Reynold's Case* (1491) CP 40/916, m. 353d (cooper); *Everard's Case* (1500) CP 40/951, m. 464 (gentleman); *Sayer v. Forest* (1539) CP 40/1101, m. 404 (butcher); *Morys v. Turnour* (1551) CP 40/1148, mm. 742, 744 (yeoman). This was not a new phenomenon: cf. *Remston's Case* (1442) Mich. 21 Hen. VI, fo. 20, pl. 40; *Grove v. Okebourne* (1449) CP 40/752, m. 516 (parson); *Beton v. Sutton* (1451) CP 40/761, m. 122 (goldsmith).

[112] John Hales, reading in Gray's Inn (1514) GI MS. 25, fo. 292v (tr. 94 Selden Soc. 75). Archbishop Rotherham C. said in 1482 that 'we find record in the Chancery' of subpoenas against feoffees of trust: Pas. 22 Edw. IV, fo. 6, pl. 18 (tr.). It is not clear what kind of record this might have been.

[113] See below, 192.

[114] 'Renovatio Ordinationum', Sanders, *Orders*, i. I. 7c; G. Spence, *Jurisdiction of the Chancery* (1846), i. 366. The orders appear to date from 1388, amended temp. Hen. V: *CELMC*, 266–7. Cf. M. Beilby, 'The Profits of Expertise' in *Profit, Piety and the Professions in Later Medieval England*, ed. M. Hicks (1990), at 78, 88 (who suggests a date as late as the sixteenth century).

[115] e.g. *Colyns v. Sauvey* (1495–6) CPR 1485–94, p. 75 (suit concerning detinue of deeds, and uses).

exemplified Chancery decree seems to confirm the absence of a central record: the instrument recites the subpoena, and the filed pleadings (in the form of an '*inspeximus... in filaciis*'), but the decree itself is set out without an *inspeximus*.[116] Even when decree rolls began to be kept in the late 1530s, they were not a continuous record, and far less complete than the plea rolls of the common-law courts. Evidently not all decrees were enrolled, and those that were seem to have been entered at the instance of the parties rather than the court itself; they are not in strict chronological order, and some date from several years before the enrolment.[117] At the end of our period, some sixty to seventy decrees a year were being enrolled,[118] perhaps 6 per cent of all cases commenced, and in the time of Edward VI the language of the decrees changed from Latin to English.

The first surviving paper book of decrees and orders dates from 1545, when Wriothesley was chancellor, though it seems likely that there were once earlier volumes. The decree books (C33) were in two series, known as A and B, which overlap and duplicate each other. The reason seems to be that there were originally two clerks or 'registers', one appointed by the chancellor and the other by the master of the rolls, though the dual record system continued after the clerical offices were combined in 1548.[119]

The beginning of these records coincides also with what seems to be an improved system for preserving the working files. The old series of files (C1) contains only bills and pleadings. From 1534 there are files of depositions taken before examiners (C24),[120] and from 1544 files of masters' reports (C38). But the surviving archive of the Court of Chancery before Elizabeth I is nothing like as extensive or intricate as that for the two benches.

BUSINESS OF THE COURT

It is natural to assume that a court of conscience built its fortunes upon equity in its later traditional sense, and indeed it has often been assumed that the rise of the English side of the Chancery was connected with the increase of uses. Some calculations suggest that over 40 per cent of cases in the later fifteenth-century

[116] Bodl. Lib. MS. Rawlinson C.339, fo. 44 (copy in a Chancery precedent-book). The chancellor is named as William Warham, bishop of London. Cf. conciliar decrees, below, 196.

[117] The earliest decrees in the rolls are from 1534, but they were entered several years later: e.g. C78/2/56 (follows decree of 1543). The rolls probably began to be written in the late 1530s.

[118] A calendar of all the entries from Hen. VIII to Mary I was published in 160 List & Index Soc. (1979). There are 392 decrees temp. Edw. VI and 397 temp. Mar.

[119] Jones, *Elizabethan Court of Chancery*, 143–6. Ralph Standyshe was appointed in 1548 as 'register and keeper of the registers or decree books in Chancery': CPR 1548–9, p. 3.

[120] In our period only the town depositions (taken by examiners) survive; the files of country depositions (taken by commission) begin temp. Eliz.

Chancery concerned uses.[121] Recent studies have nevertheless thrown some doubt upon the traditional picture. Analysis of a single, perhaps untypical, bundle of 202 bills from around 1480–3 reveals that only 12 per cent of the cases concerned uses, with perhaps another 12 per cent concerning real property in some way, while over 50 per cent concerned commercial matters and another 15 per cent concerned aliens. Two-thirds of the cases emanated from towns.[122] This discovery led to the suggestion that the clerks—faced with 'extreme poverty'[123]—became involved with city merchants by lending their names to moneylending transactions in such a way that they could be enrolled on the close rolls and made enforceable in Chancery, and that this profitable connection with the city led in turn to an influx of mercantile business.[124] Certainly there was a growing proportion of petitions to remove cases from municipal courts by writs of *habeas corpus cum causa* or *certiorari*,[125] a jurisdiction which extended not only to provincial towns but even to Calais.[126] The procedure was chiefly used in contract cases, but sometimes it also brought actions in tort into the Chancery.[127] In these suits, the plaintiff was not usually seeking equitable relief in the later sense, though it is difficult to make out from the bills alone what the disputes were really about. The plaintiff had to allege some ground for interference, such as the fear of an unfair trial because an insider-defendant was better known to potential jurors; but it is usually impossible in particular cases to tell whether that was the true gist of the matter, or merely a pretext for removing the case or trying to arrest its progress. The same difficulty besets all attempts to analyse Chancery business by using the files of bills, and explains the radically different calculations which different observers have made. The core of a Chancery dispute is often just as hidden by jurisdictional fictions, or side issues, as in a court of law. Nevertheless, the work of the Chancery does appear to have undergone a shift of emphasis in the first half of the sixteenth century, and this may be due in part to the development of better commercial remedies in the King's Bench.[128] By 1530, between a half and

[121] Haskett, 'Medieval English Court of Chancery', 298–300, whose figures appear to show that uses featured in 46% (72% of 64%) of the 1,500 cases analysed from the period 1475–85. There is an extraordinary variation between samples, which may have something to do with the vagaries of record-keeping; but it has also to be recognized that all analyses are subjective, since they depend on the way that cases are categorized.

[122] Pronay, 'The Chancellor, the Chancery and the Council', 92–4 (based on C1/59).

[123] See the clerks' petition to Moreton C., pr. 94 Selden Soc. 76.

[124] Pronay, 'The Chancellor, the Chancery and the Council', 95–6.

[125] The former was used where the Chancery plaintiff was in local custody. For a study of this jurisdiction in 1470 see P. M. Barnes, 'The Chancery corpus cum causa file, 10–11 Edw. IV' in *Medieval Legal Records edited in Memory of C. A. F. Meekings* (1978), 430–76.   [126] See above, 112.

[127] e.g. *Povy's Case* (temp. Warham C.) C1/348/39 (tricked out of £10 with false dice); *Bradwey v. Starkey* (1529/33) C1/747/29 (defamation). These were both actions in the sheriffs' court, London, and a *certiorari* was prayed.   [128] See above, 158; below, 859.

two-thirds of the cases again concerned landed property.[129] Uses were prominent,[130] though not dominant,[131] and it is significant that the Statute of Uses 1535 did not, by turning most uses into legal estates,[132] cause a noticeable collapse in Chancery litigation. The property suits were mostly framed as actions for the withholding of title-deeds, and it has been plausibly supposed that the issue in many of them was not equitable but legal title.[133] That alone would account for their survival after 1535.[134] Notwithstanding the resurgence of property cases, contract suits continued to account for a substantial proportion of the business, principally in cases of debt removed from London and other urban jurisdictions.[135]

Plaintiffs in Chancery did not have to state in their bills the decretal relief which they were ultimately seeking, but only the initial relief: almost invariably a writ of subpoena to summon the defendant, and sometimes a writ of common injunction to stop the prosecution of a suit in a superior court, or (where the parties were in suit in an inferior court) a writ of *certiorari* or *corpus cum causa*. They were not normally able to seek monetary awards,[136] as they were in most common-law actions, and it was this limitation which eventually drove mercantile plaintiffs into the King's Bench. The types of relief available by the latter part of our period included not only the specific performance of contracts, the discovery of title-deeds and other forms of evidence, and the cancellation of instruments, but also orders to give possession of land,[137] or to quiet

[129] Guy, *Public Career of More*, 39, 50. Metzger favoured the higher figure, but Guy's calculation shows around 50% under both Wolsey and More. The discrepancy arises largely from the 'miscellaneous' category, which clearly includes some property cases (e.g. where forgery of deeds is alleged). (A radical difference in categorization also explains Haskett's figures of only 16% for real property cases in 1515–18, and 26% in 1529–32: 'Medieval English Court of Chancery', 301.)

[130] Guy, *Public Career of More*, 53, estimates that as many as two-thirds of the real property cases temp. More C. may have involved uses in some way.

[131] Haskett, 'Medieval English Court of Chancery', 298, 301, indicates a decline in uses business from 72% to 10% of all real property cases between 1475 and 1532, and says uses represented only 2.6% (10% of 26%) of all cases in 1529–32. These figures cannot be reconciled with Guy's, except on the basis that Haskett must have classified some uses cases under other headings. See also Guy, *St German on Chancery and Statute*, 76. [132] See below, 672.

[133] E. G. Henderson, 'Legal Rights to Land in the Early Chancery' (1982) 26 *AJLH* 97–122; Guy, 'The Development of Equitable Jurisdiction 1450–1550', 84; *Public Career of More*, 51–2. The technical justification for allowing suits for discovery of title-deeds is given in St German, *Little Treatise*, ed. Guy, 108.

[134] Henderson, 'Legal Rights to Land in the Early Chancery', at 110, refers to Chancery pleadings in which the execution of uses by the statute is mentioned.

[135] Guy, *Public Career of More*, 65–79. For relief against penal bonds see E. G. Henderson, 'Relief from Bonds in the English Chancery: mid-sixteenth century' (1974) 18 *AJLH* 298–306.

[136] Cf. the orders to pay debt and damages noted in Guy, *Public Career of More*, 68, 76: *Heton* v. *Farmer* (1529) ibid. 68; *Parnell* v. *Vaughan* (1531) ibid. 76.

[137] e.g. *Carpenter* v. *Roo* (1520) C1/395/13–21, *Bradley* v. *Hall* (c.1536) C1/604/21–24. By the 1550s such decrees were common, and Henderson noted 100 temp. Edw. VI: 26 *AJLH* 98, 103. The same end could be achieved by means of a commission: *Boles* v. *Walley* (1559) Cary 38.

possession,[138] and some more unusual remedies such as *ne exeat regno* (to prevent a party leaving the jurisdiction without leave).[139] A decree was never final, in that it could always be reopened if fresh matter in conscience could be shown. The reason was that a decree did not bind the right, but was a judgment *in personam* based on the requirements of conscience, which might change with circumstances.[140] In 1535 Serjeant Densill challenged this doctrine on the grounds that 'if every decree which is made here might be reversed in the same court, there would be incessant confusion in all causes'; but he was cut short by Cromwell MR, who 'interrupted him and said, speak no more of the authority of this court'.[141]

Although it is impossible to calculate how much business was finally disposed of by Chancery decree, the number of suits commenced may be gauged from the number of bills in the files. It has been calculated that the volume increased steadily from little more than 500 a year in the time of Henry VII to just over 1,000 by the 1550s.[142] Although there was no intermediate decline corresponding to that in the two benches, the net gain over seventy years was almost exactly in proportion to that of the common-law courts. Contrary to earlier speculation, therefore, the growth of Chancery jurisdiction appears not in the end to have been at the expense of the courts of law, though the threat may have seemed serious for a time. It had little to do with competition between courts, and little to do with the personalities of particular chancellors, but was a result of the general increase in litigation—a boom which affected the Chancery before it affected the other courts. Particularly worthy of note is that, by the 1550s, when Maitland thought the common law was in deep trouble, the case-load of the Chancery was still only a tenth of that of the Common Pleas.

---

[138] e.g. *Faller v. Fetiplace* (1521) C1/407/2–11; *Huddeswell v. Huddeswell* (1530) C244/173/37b; *Norwich v. Burwell* (1530) C1/548/32. The last two cases are discussed in Guy, *Public Career of More*, 54–6.

[139] *De Swigo v. Van Affren* (1557) in Monro, *Acta Cancellariae*, 335.

[140] *Docwra's Case* (1535) Trin. 27 Hen. VIII, fo. 15, pl. 6, *per* Knightley sjt.   [141] ibid. at fo. 16.

[142] Brooks, *Pettyfoggers and Vipers*, 54–5, 85–8. An average of 535 bills a year were filed in the time of Wolsey C. increasing to 912 under More C.: Guy, *Public Career of More*, 38, 50. (Cf. Pronay, 'The Chancellor, the Chancery and the Council', 89, who reckons there were 770 a year under Wolsey.)

10

The Council and Conciliar Courts

THE development of the English side of the Chancery under the Tudors was matched very closely by that of conciliar jurisdiction in general.[1] Indeed, the judicial sides of the Council and Chancery seem to have shared a common origin in the fourteenth century. When the Chancery became a distinct tribunal, belonging to the chancellor alone, the councillors at large were left with a less easily definable role in hearing petitions which combined private with public wrongs. The Council followed a procedure closely similar to that of the Chancery, and distributed 'equitable' remedies—in the sense of remedies not available at law. Like the Chancery, it was not supposed to interfere in matters belonging solely to the common law. And yet it was not thought or spoken of as a court of conscience. It was a court which could intervene to redress imbalances between litigants resulting from power, undue influence, or criminal misconduct, and in doing so could incidentally punish all forms of misbehaviour falling short of felony. An attempt to codify its procedure in 1491 provided simply that 'all bills that comprehendeth matters determinable at the common law shall be remitted there to be determined, but if so be that [i.e. unless] the discretion of the Council feel too great might on that one side and unmight on the tother, or else other cause reasonable that shall move them'.[2]

From near the beginning of our period the judicial business of the Council was being recorded in a series of act books, which were treated as records for the purposes of *certiorari*,[3] and in 1540 the formal separation of what had become the

---

[1] There is now a considerable literature for this period. Besides works on more specific topics mentioned below, see A. F. Pollard, 'Council, Star Chamber and Privy Council under the Tudors' (1922–4) 37 *EHR* 337–60, 516–39; 38 *EHR* 42–60; Elton, 'The Privy Council' in *Tudor Revolution in Government*, 316–69; 'The Council' and 'The Conciliar Courts' in *The Tudor Constitution*, 88–116, 163–217; *Studies*, i. 294–9, 303–38; C. G. Bayne and W. H. Dunham, *Select Cases in the Council of Henry VII* (75 Selden Soc.; 1958); J. A. Guy, 'Wolsey, the Council and the Council Courts' (1976) 91 *EHR* 481–505; *The Cardinal's Court* (1977); *The Court of Star Chamber and its Records to the reign of Elizabeth I* (1985); 'The Privy Council: revolution or evolution?' in *Revolution Reassessed*, ed. C. Coleman and D. Starkey (1986), 59–85.

[2] Draft ordinance of 1491/2 (sp. mod.) in M. M. Condon, 'An Anachronism with Intent? Henry VII's Council Ordinance of 1491/2' in *Kings and Nobles in the Later Middle Ages*, ed. R. A. Griffiths and J. Sherborne (1986), 245, art. 4. This was drawn up to govern conciliar procedure while the king was abroad in France.

[3] e.g. *CPR 1494–1509*, p. 461 (clerk of the Council certifies that he has searched the acts and decrees of the Council in the Star Chamber for 1505 and found the decree sought); *LP*, i. 133(43); 16 Selden Soc.

Court of Star Chamber from the Privy Council was reflected in a fission of clerical offices and register-books. During the same period we find experiments with sub-conciliar tribunals, the principal outcome of which was the Court of Requests. This period of innovation and expansion in conciliar jurisdiction Is rather better documented than in the case of the Chancery, whose decrees are not regularly preserved before 1534. Although the earliest registers of the Privy Council date from 1540,[4] the act books of the Council attendant survive from 1493, and the acts and decrees of the Council in the Star Chamber from 1486 onwards can to some extent be reconstructed from the numerous extracts made in the Elizabethan and Jacobean periods from the act books which are now missing.[5]

The informality of conciliar proceedings, though part of their attraction for plaintiffs, was open to the same objections as were voiced against the Chancery.[6] In particular, the duty of attendance from day to day (in person or by counsel) at varying locations, enforced by heavy bonds,[7] could place an intolerable burden on defendants. The procedure often resembled a form of compulsory arbitration. Arbitration was not in itself objectionable. Indeed, it was very widely used by voluntary submission. But in this case it was imposed on one of the parties and displaced his legal rights, because the Council had assumed the same power as the Chancery to inhibit related proceedings in the regular courts by means of injunctions.[8] Such a procedure was arguably contrary to the medieval statutes of due process, some of which were explicitly directed against interference with the course of the common law by extraordinary processes. Already under Henry VII it was a source of complaint,[9] and from around 1501 there began a stream of actions in the King's Bench and Common Pleas founded on Magna Carta and the various statutes of due process, to recover damages against opponents who had sued the plaintiffs by subpoena and made them appear before particular councillors. The actions hardly ever mention a court or institution by name,[10] and it is

---

187–9 (decree of 1508 in Latin but certified in English). Note also *CPR 1494–1509*, p. 388 (exemplification of decree of 1504).

[4] See below, 201.   [5] Bayne and Dunham, *Select Cases*, p. xliii; Guy, *Court of Star Chamber*, 30–5.

[6] For what follows in this paragraph see further 94 Selden Soc. 70–4.

[7] e.g. *R. v. Lord Clifford* (1508) CP 40/983, m. 406 (undertaking to appear in Star Chamber); *Lawmplewe v. Bewley* (1516) CP 40/1016, m. 539 (bond to pay costs in Requests, 1514).

[8] Bayne and Dunham, *Select Cases*, 19, 25, 49, 50.

[9] This may be the explanation of 'the bill concernyng pryve sealis' in the parliament of 11 Hen. VII, which did not pass: C49/42, no. 2.

[10] The Council is mentioned in *Abbot of Bury v. Adams* (1514–17) KB 27/1011, m. 33d (action on Magna Carta for suit in Council by bill; defendant justifies suit for annuity, and subpoena issued by archbishop of Canterbury and other councillors; demurrer); *Mylde v. Sympson* (1514) KB 27/1013, m. 40d (bill of debt); *Brandon v. Jenny* (1515) KB 27/1016, m. 62d (bill of trespass for taking a ward); *Butler v. Fuller* (1523) KB 27/1048, m. 75 (bill of detinue).

probable that the attack was directed primarily against the practice of informal delegation of suits to particular members of the Council.[11]

There is some debate as to whether delegation or commission are the correct terms to apply to the phenomenon of hearings by small groups of councillors, or individuals, inasmuch as the concept of the king's Council seems to have been sufficiently amorphous to permit of it functioning in several places at once and in bodies of varying composition.[12] It was, for instance, perfectly possible for suits to be sent back and forth between different branches of the Council.[13] But the terms are not too misleading if they indicate merely that all modes of proceeding depended on the approval of, and were subject to the supervision of, the whole Council.[14] The best-known sub-conciliar tribunal under Henry VII was the Council Learned in the Law (or the 'Learned Council', as it was called), a body of four or so common lawyers which met from at least 1499 until 1509.[15] It is known because of the chance survival among the records of the duchy of Lancaster of two act books (DL 5/2, 5/4) which record its activities in some detail.[16] The business is part fiscal, part regulatory, and part private litigation, the latter categories being of the same character as the business of the whole Council. Parties could be summoned by privy seal to appear before the Learned Council,[17] which occasionally made a final decree,[18] but

[11] 94 Selden Soc. 72–3. Several cases can be shown to arise from proceedings on the requests side: below, 205 n. 112. For an account of a feud conducted in sub-conciliar tribunals see A. Cameron, 'A Nottinghamshire Quarrel in the Reign of Henry VII' (1972) 45 BIHR 27–32.

[12] For this reason, Chrimes (Henry VII, 147) took the view that the Council Learned should not be called a committee.

[13] e.g. REQ 1/3, fo. 105 (defendant dismissed in 1504 from further appearance 'before the lord king's Council wherever [it might be]'—coram consilio domini regis ubicumque etc.—because the cause was determined 'before the Council at Westminster in the Star Chamber'—coram consilio apud Westmonasterium in Camera Stellata), fo. 208 (case remitted to Star Chamber for determination, 1505), fo. 212v (defendant remitted to appear before Council Learned, 1505); Case of the Dean and Canons of Ottery St Mary (1508) 54 EHR 440–1 (case remitted by whole Council to Council Learned, then referred to commissioners, and finally determined in Star Chamber).

[14] The councillors were a defined body, since they had to be sworn: the memorandum of admission of Cuthbert Tunstall (1509) recorded that he took the customary oath for councillors (BL MS. Lansdowne 639, fo. 28). For the swearing of councillors see Condon, 'An Anachronism with Intent?', 231–2. It is not clear whether the judges and law officers who attended the Council were sworn councillors or merely attendants.

[15] R. Somerville, 'Henry VII's "Council Learned in the Law"' (1939) 54 EHR 427–42; 75 Selden Soc., pp. xxv–xxviii; Chrimes, Henry VII, 149–52; M. Condon, 'Ruling Elites in the Reign of Henry VII' in Patronage, Pedigree and Power in Late medieval England, ed. C. Ross (1979), 109 at 131–2, 133–4.

[16] The books overlap in date and may have been kept by the clerks of different members. DL 5/4 seems to have been kept by a clerk of Richard Empson.

[17] The books themselves use this name, apparently to distinguish it from the whole Council (DL 5/2, fo. 53, mentions an order by the 'hoole counsell'). Cf. REQ 1/3, fo. 212v (order to appear coram consilio jurisperitorum, 1505), the Latin confirms that the 'counsel' of DL 5/2 denotes a council

[18] e.g. DL 5/2, fo. 69v (Hil. 1505): order by Sir John Husee, James Hobart, Richard Empson, and Thomas Lucas, for restoration of possession.

the general absence of decrees and the preponderance of process and evidence-gathering shows that the Council Learned acted chiefly as an interlocutory tribunal to which cases were only occasionally referred for determination. Its domination by Empson and Dudley, and its sudden disappearance in 1509,[19] suggest strongly that it was one of the forms of conciliar activity complained of in the last decade of Henry VII's reign; and this no doubt because of its keen involvement in the relentless pursuit of revenue.[20]

It is known that an attempt was made, soon after the accession of Henry VIII, to curtail the extraordinary jurisdictions, possibly at the instance of the judges. On 5 November 1509, a discussion took place in the Star Chamber 'concerning dissolution of commissions of oyer and terminer and fordoing of petty courts, for the ease of the subject', and the matter was referred to the king. Nine days later, in the presence of Fyneux and Rede CJJ and other judges and common lawyers, there was further consideration of the proposal 'for suppression of inferior courts which were not of record ratified, and of commissions of oyer and terminer, and all to sue in the king's courts at Westminster, and those that are poor to have counsel assigned to them without paying money, and persons heretofore imprisoned to be bailed'.[21] Although these references are less than explicit, they can hardly refer to established local courts, and the combination of grievances suggests the sub-conciliar tribunals such as the Council Learned and the committees to hear the requests of paupers. The difficulty of interpretation is compounded by the fact that commissions of oyer and terminer had been used in the summer of 1509 for hearing complaints about councillors acting without due process of law;[22] and so it may be that the judges were attacking an irregular means of redress, which was open to political manipulation, as a remedy partaking of the disease. The general concern with informal conciliar jurisdiction is confirmed by a different version of the November council minute, which reads, '... all such by-courts which be of no record shall be fordone and that every man from thenceforth may resort to such courts and judges as they did before such offices were occupied'.[23] The proposals for abolition were defeated,

---

[19] Cf. Elton, *Studies*, i. 91 n. 5, where it is suggested on rather weak evidence that it continued into the next reign.

[20] For this theme see J. P. Cooper, 'Henry VII's Last Years Reconsidered' (1959) 2 *Historical Jnl* 103–29; criticized by G. R. Elton, 'Henry VII: a restatement' (1961) 4 *Historical Jnl* 1–29 (repr. in *Studies*, i, 66–99); criticism partially retracted in *Studies*, i, 97 n., as a result of C. J. Harrison, 'The Petition of Edmund Dudley' (1972) 87 *EHR* 82–99.

[21] Hudson's extracts from the lost Star Chamber register, BL MS. Lansdowne 639, fo. 28.

[22] *George Chancey's Case* (1509) Catlyn's precedent book, Alnwick Castle MS. 475, fo. 24 (copy of bill, in French, against Chancey for suing a false bill before Sir Robert Sheffield, contrary to 42 Edw. III, c. 3; the bill, addressed to Lord Dacre and other commissioners, is dated 17 Aug. 1509); and cf. *Southworth* v. *Smyth* (1510) KB 27/996, m. 65 (error to commissioners at the Guildhall in a suit complaining of conciliar proceedings). For the commissions see below, 264.

[23] HEHL MS. EL 2655, ff. 7, 8 (pr. B. Wolffe, *The Crown Lands 1461 to 1536* (1970), 162–3). For its interpretation see also Cooper, 'Henry VII's Last Years', at 121–3; Elton, *Studies*, i. 91; Guy, 'Wolsey and the Council Courts', at 481; *The Cardinal's Court*, 24–5; above, 119.

but only at the new king's personal insistence.[24] As a consequence, the due-process actions continued to be used, and in 1511 a party recovered as much as £32 in damages in respect of a suit before Empson.[25] Indeed, some of the complaints were now made in the form of criminal prosecutions.[26] Most of the actions, however, did not lead as far as judgment, and it is doubtful whether they had any direct effect on conciliar experimentation. They were even challenged by demurrer, albeit without recorded result;[27] but the petering out of the actions around 1524[28] perhaps owes less to doubts about their legal basis than to the regularization of the jurisdictions under Wolsey, which removed for a time the principal causes of complaint.

THE STAR CHAMBER

At the beginning of our period the Star Chamber was primarily the name of a room rather than of an institution. The *camera stellata* was a chamber in the palace of Westminster,[29] decorated with gilded stars set on an azure ceiling,[30] where the king's councillors met to transact both judicial and administrative business. The Council which sat there in term-time and the 'Council attendant' which followed the king on his progresses were essentially parts of the same body functioning in different locations. The two parts could function concurrently, or they could unite in the king's presence at Westminster.[31] Doubtless the central manifestation of the Council was the more formal, and the more suited to complex legal investigations. The movable branch was more appropriate for dealing with the requests of poor

---

[24] *HLJ*, i. 5–7; Elton, *Studies*, i. 94.   [25] *Speccote* v. *Fry* (1511) KB 27/1000, m. 37.

[26] e.g. *R.* v. *Phillip* (1511) KB 27/999, Rex m. 5 (false suit by privy seal before Sir Robert Sheffield; according to the pardon, the prosecution was founded on Magna Carta).

[27] *Fetiplace* v. *Field* (1509) KB 27/993, m. 78; *Abbot of Bury* v. *Adams* (1514–17) KB 27/1011, m. 33d; *Butler* v. *Fuller* (1523) KB 27/1048, m. 75.

[28] Late examples are *Pomerey* v. *Bucland* (1524) KB 27/1050, m. 47; *Saunders* v. *Broke* (1524) CP 40/1044, m. 280 (suit by bill in 1521 for an assault; compelled by signet to appear before three councillors at Colchester, and then from day to day at Westminster; *latitat*). A still later precedent (founded on Magna Carta) arose from a Chancery suit before More C.: *Parnell* v. *Vaughan* (1533) KB 27/1082, m. 37.

[29] It was rebuilt between 1456 and 1461: *The History of the King's Works*, ed. H. M. Colvin, i (1963), 546. There was an 'inner Star Chamber' adjoining, which could be used for private meetings, occasionally of a legal character: e.g. Mich. 2 Ric. III, fo. 9, pl. 22; 64 Selden Soc. 86 (question put by the king himself concerning the erasure of process, 1485); 2 Caryll 710 (meeting to discuss sanctuaries before Wolsey C., Fyneux CJ, Brudenell J., and various lords, 1519). For early Elizabethan references see 109 Selden Soc., p. xlv.

[30] Guy, *Court of Star Chamber*, 1. By 1570, however, the principal feature was a single, large gilded star: *History of the King's Works*, ed. Colvin, iv. II (1982), 296.

[31] A. F. Pollard, 'The Star Chamber' (1922) 37 *EHR* 516 at, 531–2. Cf. 19 Hen. VII, c. 14, which explicitly distinguishes cases 'before the chancellor . . . in the Star Chamber' and 'before the king and his council attending upon his most royal person' (1504). Occasionally there was an especially grand manifestation called the Great Council: see P. J. Holmes, 'The Great Council in the Reign of Henry VII' (1986) 101 *EHR* 840–62; 'The Last Tudor Great Councils' (1990) 33 *Historical Jnl* 1–22.

people or matters of local government.[32] Yet there was but one Council; there were no rigid jurisdictional divisions between its various manifestations, and cases could be transferred from one place to another.[33] Indeed, the central place—the starred chamber—could be used even for sittings of the Court of Chancery.[34]

The Star Chamber had been used for judicial purposes since the mid-fourteenth century, and so there is no need to seek a statutory origin for a court of that name in the Tudor period. Indeed, it was already sometimes used as the name of a court before 1485.[35] The so-called 'Star Chamber Act' of 1487[36] did not mention—or affect the jurisdiction of—the Council in the Star Chamber, but empowered a smaller body, effectively a sub-set of the Council, to deal with various forms of disorder and overbearing.[37] The full Council had a long-standing jurisdiction in civil and criminal causes,[38] usually in combination, and, although decree books do not seem to have been kept before 1486,[39] formal decrees were made before then.[40] Indeed, examples of exemplified decrees survive from 1475[41] and 1482.[42] The Council also dealt with important fiscal questions, before the establishment of the statutory revenue courts.[43] A massive influx of business after 1515 has been attributed to Wolsey's encouragement of suitors to make use of his

[32] These forms of business themselves bifurcated in the sixteenth century into the Court of Requests (below, 203) and the residuary legal work of the Privy Council (below, 201). The former became fixed at Westminster, but the latter was attendant on the king.   [33] See above, 193.

[34] As on 10 Feb. 1511, when Westminster Hall was in use for the triumphs after the birth of Prince Henry: BL MS. Lansdowne 639, fo. 40.

[35] e.g. Wingfield's Case (1481) Mich. 21 Edw. IV, fo. 71, pl. 55 (warden of the Fleet said to be an officer of the Star Chamber as well as the Chancery, Common Pleas, and Exchequer).

[36] 3 Hen. VII, c. 1. (The marginal title Pro camera stellata was added later.) The court could only operate if the statutory requirements as to membership were strictly observed: Anon. (1493) Pas. 8 Hen. VII, fo. 13, pl. 7.

[37] Pollard, 'The Star Chamber', 520–8; C. H. Williams, 'The So-Called Star Chamber Act' (1930) 15 History 129–35; C. G. Bayne, 75 Selden Soc., pp. xlix–lxxii; Guy, The Cardinal's Court, 19–20; M. Stuckey, 'A Consideration of the Emergence and Exercise of Judicial Functions in the Star Chamber' (1933) 19 Monash Law Rev. 117 at 131–5; above, 70. A similar tribunal was set up by 11 Hen. VII, c. 25.

[38] For its early involvement in criminal prosecutions which might be continued at common law, see Condon, 'Ruling Elites', 129–30. This investigative role continued throughout our period.

[39] Above, 192.   [40] Cf. Chancery decrees, above, 186.

[41] Stanley v. Haryngton (1475) C49/53, no. 4, dated 20 Jan. 1475. The decree, concerning a wardship of land which was partly entailed, was made by the king 'with the advice of our councill and diverse of our judges and other councill learned in law'. The document is written in English in an informal hand, without a seal, but bears the sign manual ('R E'). It later became possible to obtain Chancery exemplifications of conciliar decrees under the great seal: e.g. Case of the City of York (1517) in Porter's precedent book, C193/142, fo. 125v.

[42] Whele v. Fortescue (1482) E28/93, 26 June 1482, pr. in J. F. Baldwin, The King's Council in England during the Middle Ages (1913), 433–4; and in 35 Selden Soc. 117–18. The plaintiff was a King's Bench filazer, accused of being an enemy alien (a Scot): cf. Whele v. Reynold (1483) Hil. 22 Edw. IV, fo. 45, pl. 9; KB 27/885, m. 34d.

[43] e.g. Duke of Buckingham v. Bishop of Winchester (1515) 2 Caryll 670 ('at Baynard's Castle in London, in the presence of all the king's Council, lords and others, and also in the presence of the

tribunal instead of the older courts.[44] By Michaelmas term 1517 it was necessary for the Council to set aside two days a week (Wednesdays and Fridays) 'for reformation of misorders and other enormities in the king's several courts', presumably meaning judicial business in general; and this arrangement remained in place until the court was abolished in 1641.[45] Nevertheless, despite the growth in its activity, the business of the Star Chamber never reached anything like the same level as that of the Chancery. Between 1529 and 1547 it is thought to have heard an average of 150 suits a year, and the work-load remained much the same throughout the 1550s.[46]

The legal business of the Council in the Star Chamber may be reconstructed from the files of bills, pleadings, and proofs, which survive from 1485 onwards (STAC 1–4, 10),[47] augmented by surviving extracts from the lost decree books. Much of the business overlapped with the Chancery, and no very precise division between the two jurisdictions can be made, save that plaintiffs in Star Chamber usually emphasized the use of force or the abuse of authority rather than equity and good conscience. The Star Chamber was not a court of equity in the substantive sense, though its procedure gave it that ability to delve into facts and provide remedies which may be accounted equitable in a wider sense. Relative poverty may also have been a factor; as many as a third of the plaintiffs in Wolsey's time were yeomen, husbandmen, or men of lesser rank.[48] The types of business transacted during Wolsey's chancellorship (1515–29) have been very thoroughly analysed,[49] and they are all foreshadowed in the earlier records.[50] The court existed primarily for the benefit of private litigants seeking some form of relief, though plaintiffs frequently alleged misdemeanours which could be punished as criminal offences at the same time. In punishing offences it did not confine itself to fines and imprisonment, but in appropriate cases ordered the party to undergo public humiliation by wearing papers,[51] standing in the

---

greater part of all the justices of England...'). This was an attempt to recover £1,000 paid to Hen. VII for the duke's special livery.

[44] Guy, *The Cardinal's Court*, 23–40.

[45] BL MS. Lansdowne 639, fo. 54v; Guy, *The Cardinal's Court*, 37–8; *Court of Star Chamber*, 5–6. In 1191 it had been suggested that the Council meet twice a week in term time for hearing bills; Guy, 'An Anachronism with Intent', 245, art. 3. Cf. BL MS. Lansdowne 639, fo. 48v, which says the lords were to sit in Chancery on Wednesdays and Fridays.   [46] Guy, *Court of Star Chamber*, 9.

[47] The records are fully discussed in Guy, *Court of Star Chamber*, 19–29, 67–77. The STAC class includes, by error, some material belonging to other courts.

[48] Guy, *The Cardinal's Court*, 109. The proportion of gentlemen or above was slightly lower, the remaining third being clergy, merchants, officials, and professional people.

[49] Guy, *The Cardinal's Court*, 51–117.

[50] See samples in *Select Cases before the King's Council in the Star Chamber*, ed. I. S. Leadam, i (16 Selden Soc.; 1903); ii (25 Selden Soc.; 1911).

[51] e.g. in 1517 John Caunton was ordered to wear papers in Westminster Hall and to do penance in Cheapside and at the assizes for perjury: BL MS. Lansdowne 639, ff. 48v–49. In *Vernon v. Sharpe*

pillory,[52] or riding at the horse's tail,[53] or even the permanent humiliation of losing ears.[54] We first hear of such punishments in the time of Wolsey, and they may have resulted from his policy of giving the Star Chamber more power, though we have no complete records from an earlier period for comparison.[55]

The largest single subject-matter of litigation, as in most of the central courts, was real property. In the majority of property cases plaintiffs alleged some form of disorder, ranging from riot and forcible entry to assault, though a careful study of the pleadings shows that the true issue was normally title. A second large field of jurisdiction was the alleged perversion of justice, by corruption, maintenance, champerty, perjury,[56] subornation, embracery, and other abuses of legal procedure. Under this heading may also be placed proceedings against juries for false acquittals,[57] a form of control which seems to have been encouraged under Wolsey.[58] A third category consisted of complaints of corruption or extortion by royal or franchisal officers. The Council did not hesitate to punish justices of the peace,[59] and in unusual circumstances—where politics permitted—it could discipline a master of the rolls[60] or even a lord chancellor.[61] Municipal and trade disputes, and disputes between corporations,[62] constitute a fourth. But there were a substantial number of miscellaneous cases falling outside these categories, including a few in

(c.1539/45) Wm Yelv. 332, no. 41, a perjurer was ordered to stand in the pillory in Palace Yard 'with a paper set upon his head inscribed in large letters "For wilful perjury" etc.', and this was noted as a normal punishment at the discretion of the lord chancellor.

[52] e.g. *Snow's Case* (1536) 110 Selden Soc. 338; last note.

[53] For the entry of a judgment to do penance at the horse's tail, with papers, and the form of the warrant to execute the judgment, see *Midlemore's Case* (1519) in William Porter's precedent book, C193/142, fo. 46.

[54] e.g. *Dunkell's Case* (1519) HEHL MS. EL 2655, fo. 14v; *Vowles' Case* (1537) 110 Selden Soc. 344. For corporal punishments see further 110 Selden Soc. 337–41, 344–5.

[55] Guy, *The Cardinal's Court*, 117, attributes the development of corporal punishments to Wolsey.

[56] See also the temporary statutory measures in 11 Hen. VII, c. 25; 12 Hen. VII, c. 2 (expired).

[57] See below, 373 (examples from 1498 onwards).

[58] Four cases in the register for 1516–17 are noted in HEHL MS. EL 2652, fo. 10v; BL MS. Lansdowne 639, fo. 45.

[59] BL MS. Harley 2143, ff. 3v–4; Dyer 135a–b (Anglesea justices fined for holding sessions in wrong place, 1556). In 1526 Wolsey ordered all the JPs in the country to attend the Star Chamber: *Tudor Royal Proclamations*, i. 153, no. 109.

[60] *Att.-Gen.* v. *Beaumont* (1552) BL MS. Harley 2143, fo. 7; *HPHC 1509–58*, i. 405–6. In the same year it accepted the resignation of Lord Paget as chancellor of the duchy, for misconduct: MS. Harley 2143, fo. 6v. The following year the vice-treasurer of Ireland (Andrew Wise) was removed: ibid., fo. 7; 109 Selden Soc. 219 n. 2.   [61] See the case of Wriothesley, above, 179.

[62] e.g. universities and colleges: *Mayor of Cambridge* v. *University of Cambridge* (1496) REQ 1/1, ff. 158, 175; *University of Oxford* v. *Mayor of Oxford* (1520) STAC 2/25/63; Guy, *The Cardinal's Court*, 67; *Heynes* v. *President of Queens' College, Cambridge* (1526) HEHL MS. EL 2652, fo. 7v; Guy, *The Cardinal's Court*, 38; *Mayor of Cambridge* v. *University of Cambridge* (1534) discussed in Elton, *Star Chamber Stories*, ch. 2. Cf. below, 202 n. 87 (Privy Council).

contract and tort, and even tithe disputes.[63] The court was occasionally used for Crown prosecutions for misdemeanour, brought by the attorney-general,[64] and informations by the king's almoner for deodands or suicides' goods.[65] The extent of the Crown business is obscured by the availability of a procedure of oral accusation, with no information filed, which was certainly used for prosecutions by the beginning of Mary I's reign.[66] Finally, from the 1520s, there are informations brought by common informers, for breaches of proclamation.[67]

The history of the jurisdiction in the middle of the sixteenth century has still not been fully explored, but forays into the records suggest that accusations of criminal conduct were becoming de rigueur. The punishments were becoming more inventive, including from the 1540s branding in the cheek with letters,[68] and even a sentence 'to be in the king's galleys for ever as a slave'.[69] Nevertheless, the court was still essentially a civil court and it had not abandoned its jurisdiction to decree possession of land.[70] Indeed, it was asserted later in the century that 'The lords of the Star Chamber did in Edward VI's time and Queen Mary's time for the most part determine of all titles'.[71]

The de facto president of the Star Chamber was the lord chancellor, rather than the president of the Council, and a chancellor such as Wolsey exercised tremendous personal influence on its proceedings. Most of the members of the Council were not lawyers, but it was usual for the two chief justices to attend; other common lawyers were sworn as members of the Council to assist in its legal work, and the puisne judges could be summoned when their advice was

---

[63] For a well-documented instance from Hayes, Midd., see Elton, Star Chamber Stories, 174–220. Two earlier examples are given in Guy, The Cardinal's Court, 163 n. 141.

[64] Only three or four instances are known under Henry VII, and only nine in the time of Wolsey: Guy, The Cardinal's Court, 18–19, 72–8. For a collection of later cases (1535–56) see 110 Selden Soc. 338–41, 344–5. The Council had no jurisdiction over treason or felony.

[65] Guy, Court of Star Chamber, 91 n. 7, notes groups of such cases in the files (e.g. STAC 2/1/100–29). Dyer reports such a case in 1558: Dyer 160b (suicide).

[66] Anon. (1553) BL MS. Harley 2143, fo. 2; cf. 109 Selden Soc., pp. lxxxviii–lxxxix (temp. Eliz.). For the use of informations by the attorney-general see Guy, Star Chamber, 91 n. 5.

[67] See Elton, Star Chamber Stories, 94. Only two cases have been found before 1530: Guy, The Cardinal's Court, 70.

[68] Stephenson's Case (1545) HEHL MS. EL 2652, fo. 14; 110 Selden Soc. 339 (clergyman branded F A in the cheek, for False Accuser). The precedent was followed in Veer's Case (1556) 109 Selden Soc. 136, 110 Selden Soc. 340. Note also Coryton v. Roberte (1547) CP 40/1134, m. 120 (action for saying 'Peter Coryton is forsworn and shall be marked by the Council with a F on the one cheek and a P upon the other cheek for his false perjury').

[69] Grymeston's Case (1549) HEHL MS. EL 2652, fo. 14; 109 Selden Soc. 135 n. 3.

[70] Guy, Court of Star Chamber, 40–1, 55–9; Horsman v. Inhabitants of Silk Willoughby and Rosse v. Lord Dacre (1553) BL MS. Harley 5143, fo. 1. For earlier decrees relating to land see Tempest v. Tempest (1495) in Select Cases, ed. Bayne and Dunham, 50 (to avoid possession); Bowett's Case, ibid (to quiet possession); Fitzherbert v. Mering (1510) BL MS. Lansdowne 639, fo. 3.

[71] BL MS. Harley 2143, fo. 1v (sp. mod.), citing a number of cases from the 1550s.

needed.[72] In 1491 it was provided, in a draft ordinance codifying the procedure of the Council:[73]

Forasmuch as it is likely that many matters shall be treated before the Council the which toucheth the king's prerogative and freehold on that one part, and other of his subjects on the tother, in the which matters the Council is not learned to keep the king's right and the parties' both without th'advice of the king's justices which be learned both in his prerogative and common law, that in all such matters the king's judges shall be called thereto, and their advice with their names also to be entered of record what and how they determine and advise them.

The clerical staff consisted of the clerk of the Council and—from the beginning of Henry VIII's reign—an assistant clerk of the Council in the Star Chamber.[74] In 1532 a clerk of the process was added to the secretariat, with the result that the issuing of process was finally separated from the Chancery.[75] Until Wolsey's time it seems there were no attorneys specially belonging to the court, but from the 1520s there were two official attorneyships in the Star Chamber, with the monopoly of representation there;[76] their existence, however, did not preclude other attorneys from soliciting causes in the Star Chamber, for instance by preferring bills of complaint for their clients.[77] As in Chancery, the counsel—at any rate, those who signed their names on pleadings—were the serjeants at law, the benchers of the inns of court, and perhaps a few utter barristers.

Given the strong legal presence in the Star Chamber, and the interesting questions of law which must have arisen, it may seem surprising that so few cases were reported before the reign of Elizabeth I. Doubtless the main reason, as with the Chancery, is that cases turned so much on their individual facts that general principles beyond the obvious were difficult to discern. Even later in the century, when collections of Star Chamber reports begin, they read more like news reports than technical law reports. Another reason may have been that few if any lawyers from outside the Council were in the habit of attendance in this period, and that we are therefore dependent on reports by judges or law officers.[78]

THE PRIVY COUNCIL

The Privy Council originated in the 'inner ring' of councillors who attended the king in person, instead of sitting in the Star Chamber at Westminster, and whose

---

[72] For the importance of the legal element temp. Hen. VII, see Condon, 'An Anachronism with Intent?', 242–4.   [73] ibid. 246–7, art. 14 (sp. mod.).
[74] For the succession to both offices see Guy, *Court of Star Chamber*, 11.   [75] ibid. 14–15.
[76] ibid. 16; *The Cardinal's Court*, 112–13. Only five are known in our period.
[77] e.g. *Nasshe* v. *Jeffrays* (1547) CP 40/1134, m. 333 (attorney of Common Pleas sues *inter alia* for costs of bill in Star Chamber).
[78] e.g. *Re Dudley and Empson* (1509) Spelman 175; *Pauncefote* v. *Savage* (1519) Port 41; 2 Caryll 704; *Case of the Earl of Northumberland's Servant* (1532) Spelman 184; *Serjeant Browne's Case* (1532) Spelman

primary role was therefore to advise the king on matters of state and hold the reins of government.[79] There had been a council attendant under Henry VII and in the early years of Henry VIII, but the 'inner ring' had disappeared when Wolsey concentrated conciliar authority in the Star Chamber and reserved matters of foreign policy to the king and himself. In the 1530s, however, the council attendant reappeared and grew in importance, and between 1533 and 1538 the junior clerk of the council—who was appointed to attend on the king's person—came to be known as the clerk of the Privy Council.[80] In August 1540 the junior clerk was replaced by a clerk to the Privy Council (William Paget), equal in standing to the clerk of the Council in the Star Chamber, and the former began to keep a separate register.[81] It is from this date that the Privy Council is generally reckoned to have attained a distinct existence. Although both bodies were manifestations of the primordial council, and the same privy councillors also sat in the Star Chamber, there was now a formal as well as a functional difference between the types of session. The Star Chamber met only in the law terms, on particular days of the week, and followed set procedures. The Privy Council followed the king,[82] at all times of year, and did not follow the formalities of law. Numerous recognizances are registered in the books whereby parties, having been summoned by letter, bound themselves to attend hearings and submit to the award of the Council. This suggests arbitration rather than the process of law, and it may even be a fair generalization to say that the Privy Council did not 'ordinarily' act as a court at all, but as a board of arbitration.[83]

The Privy Council was primarily an instrument of government rather than of judicature, and usually sat without the judges being present. This administrative bifurcation left the Star Chamber with the bulk of the judicial business. But there was no constitutional demarcation, and the Privy Council retained the authority

---

183–4; Withers v. Isham (1552) Dyer 71b; Case of the Borough of Islington (1554) Dyer 100a; Lowe v. Sumpter (1556) Dyer in 109 Selden Soc. 15; Dalaber v. Lyster (1557) Dyer 141b; Tichborne v. Eyre (1558) Dyer in 109 Selden Soc. 22; Anon. (1558) Dalison's reports, BL MS. Harley 5141, fo. 35 (going armed in Westminster Hall).

[79] For what follows see Elton, Tudor Revolution in Government, 316–69; 'The Council' in The Tudor Constitution, 199–212; Studies, i. 308–38; Guy, 'Privy Council', 59–85.

[80] Elton, Tudor Revolution, 335, 441–2. The clerk in question (Thomas Derby) was said to have the office which was formerly Richard Eden's, so it was not new.

[81] The first volume (PC 2/1), extending from 1540 to 1543, was printed in two instalments: Proceedings and Ordinances of the Privy Council of England, ed. H. Nicolas, vii (1837), from 1540 to 1542; and the rest in Acts of the Privy Council of England, ed. J. R. Dasent, i (1890), 1–157. The second volume (1543–5) is missing. The third (1545–7) is BL MS. Sloane 5476, printed in APC, i. 158–568.

[82] Occasionally, when the king was far from London, a branch of the Privy Council was maintained simultaneously at Westminster; but this was now distinct from the Council in the Star Chamber.

[83] D. E. Hoak, The King's Council in the Reign of Edward VI (1976), 221, 225–6, commenting on Elton, The Tudor Constitution, 103–4.

to hear private suits and punish misdemeanours.[84] Thus, we find in the first register a number of property disputes,[85] disputes about public offices,[86] jurisdictional disputes between corporations and civic authorities,[87] commercial cases involving aliens,[88] and even a suit by a wife for maintenance.[89] It is probable that far more suits of this kind were entertained than are mentioned in the registers, and that they were recorded in separate books.[90] There were also a number of complaints against high officers of state, the usual outcome of which was that the complainant was punished for slander.[91] During the king's progress in 1541 towards Yorkshire and back, the Council heard various complaints on the way about local officials and problems with local government. Towards the mid-1540s there was also a substantial prize jurisdiction.

The Privy Council took a particular interest in criminal investigation, especially in matters touching treason, public order, or misdemeanours of a kind which were currently troubling the government.[92] The board would itself punish for misdemeanours, usually by imprisonment or pillory, or it would bind over an offender to behave in the future.[93] By imposing punishments it was certainly acting coercively as a court, even if it did not follow the common law. The jurisdiction was not confined to the lowly, for in 1543 the Privy Council sent the earl of Surrey to prison for wandering around London at night and breaking windows with stones.[94] In the case of treason or felony, however, the board could only

---

[84] For such business in the time of Edward VI see Hoak, *King's Council*, 222–30.

[85] e.g. *Lee* v. *Bowland* (1540) in *Proceedings*, ed. Nicolas, 52–5 (decree for quiet possession, enforced by bonds); *Augustine* v. *Denys* (1541) ibid. 121, 123 (decree for defendant); *Oldney* v. *Lucy* (1541) ibid. 214, 218 (settled); *Poyntz* v. *Higges* (1542) in *APC 1542–7*, p. 9; *Halleswell* v. *Stroode* (1543) ibid. 157 (decree for possession). Cf. *Tailboys* v. *Wimbushe* (1550), in *APC 1550–52*, pp. 48, 83–4, which was also litigated in the Common Pleas: Plowd. 38v.

[86] e.g. *Aprice* v. *Fox* (1540) in *Proceedings*, ed. Nicolas, 31, 35 (contention between secretary and clerk of council in the Marches); *Beseley* v. *Savill* (1542) in *APC 1542–7*, p. 5 (clerkship of the castle at York).

[87] e.g. *Borough of Southwark* v. *City of London* (1541) in *Proceedings*, ed. Nicolas, 191; *Case of the Mayor of Calais* (1542) in *APC 1542–7*, p. 43; *University of Oxford* v. *Mayor of Oxford* (1543) ibid. 137–8; and cf. *same* v. *same* (1546) ibid. 365, 521; *University of Cambridge* v. *Mayor of Cambridge* (1546) ibid. 546; *City of London* v. *Lord Admiral* (1547), discussed in Hoak, *King's Council*, 224–5.

[88] e.g. *Neretti* v. *Bowyer* (1542) in *APC 1542–7*, pp. 38, 42 (sale of woad; broker sentenced to have his ears nailed to the pillory); *Fremont* v. *Thrower* (1542–3) ibid. 10, 40, 49, 68, 76, 78, 101 (escape of debtor from Ludgate prison).   [89] *Bulmer* v. *Bulmer* (1542) in *APC 1542–7*, pp. 48, 81, 82, 89, 98.

[90] Hoak, *King's Council*, 222. Even in the earlier registers, most suits are not mentioned beyond the initial recognizance.

[91] e.g. *Chaundeler* v. *Wryothesley* (1540) in *Proceedings*, ed. Nicolas, 101–2; *Hillary* v. *Riche* (1541) ibid. 169; *Brathwayt* v. *Morrys* (1541) ibid. 179; and cf. *Skill* v. *Petre* (1545) in *APC 1542–7*, p. 246.

[92] This is recognized by 33 Hen. VIII, c. 23. For general instructions to JPs see Holdsworth, *HEL*, iv. 72 n. 8.

[93] e.g. *Proceedings*, ed. Nicolas, 38 (John Heron bound over to refrain from necromancy, astronomy, or calculations), 94 (vicar of Calne bound over because he had failed to erase the name of Thomas Becket in one of his books), 293 (Pigott bound over to deliver up books and scrolls containing prophecies).

[94] *APC 1542–7*, pp. 104–5. He was also charged with eating meat during Lent.

conduct the preliminary investigation and decide whether a prosecution should be launched.[95]

After about 1550 the Privy Council was too engrossed in affairs of state to busy itself with suitors, and in truth there was no need for it to maintain an interest in litigation except in special cases. The policy was therefore adopted of hearing private suits only on Sunday afternoons.[96] Supplicants were generally referred to the Star Chamber or Requests, leaving it to the discretion of a master of requests when to bring a case before the board.[97]

REQUESTS

One of the acknowledged functions of the fifteenth-century Council attendant was to hear petitions from those, especially poor persons, who came to the king in person seeking justice. Procedure was expeditious, and could be wholly oral. The Council had a special responsibility for the poor, and a draft ordinance of 1491 not only required the poorest suitors' causes to be heard first but charged the king's serjeants with the duty of representing paupers without fee, on pain of losing their office.[98] However, these cases were not thought of sufficient importance to justify the attention of all the councillors, and so they were usually delegated to a few individuals,[99] among whom the king's almoner and the dean of the chapel royal were often included.[100] In 1483 John Harrington was appointed second clerk of the Council in recognition of his services in keeping, registering, and expediting the bills, requests, and supplications of poor persons,[101] which indicates that this business was already regarded as a distinct feature of conciliar activity. Indeed, there is evidence of an unsuccessful attempt in 1485 to abolish what was actually called a Court of Requests.[102] From 1493 the business of the itinerant Council began to be recorded in separate act books, which survive as a continuous series (REQ 1) quite distinct from the books of the Star Chamber and Privy Council. The survival of the act books and of the files (REQ 2, 3) from the same period makes this one of the best documented of the English bill jurisdictions, though the

[95] e.g. *Proceedings*, ed. Nicolas, 90–2 (consideration of a 'book' of evidence against Lord Leonard Grey, 1540). Grey was tried and convicted on indictment the following year: 109 Selden Soc. 2. See also J. H. Langbein, *Prosecuting Crime in the Renaissance* (1974), 80–1; J. Bellamy, *The Tudor Law of Treason* (1979), 121–2; Spelman 48, 60; 102 Selden Soc., p. xviii n. 57.

[96] Rules of 1550, BL MS. Egerton 2603, fo. 33; Hoak, *King's Council*, 273.

[97] Hoak, *King's Council*, 222.   [98] See Condon, 'An Anachronism with Intent?', 236, 247, art. 15.

[99] Cf. ibid., art. 8–9, which provided for a *quorum* of four councillors and prohibited the expedition of suits by bill other than 'in the place ordained'.

[100] Cf. the account of a rather heavier case before the Council attendant in *Aynesworth v. Pilkington* (1493) in *Pilkington Narrative*, 32–3. Evidence was heard orally.

[101] *CPR 1476–85*, p. 413.

[102] A. F. Pollard, 56 *EHR* at 301. The special use of the word 'requests' may have come from France.

material still awaits its historian. A small selection of suits has been printed,[103] and these are enough to show that litigation was by no means confined to paupers.[104] The jurisdiction was threatened by the proposed reforms of 1509, which included a scheme to enable poor people to have free counsel to use the regular courts of common law.[105]

Major changes in the requests jurisdiction were made by Wolsey C., who wished to develop it as a means of relieving the Star Chamber from the burden of dealing with small suits.[106] This object required a stationary court, in addition to the group of councillors following the king, and various experiments were made in 1517, 1518, and 1520, in establishing 'under-courts' to sit at Westminster—usually in the White Hall—while two councillors were appointed to follow the king and hear requests in the old way. The new sedentary tribunal, which kept to the law terms, was called the Court of Requests[107] and had a continuous history thereafter until the Civil War. But the experiment was not immediately successful, since the councillors responsible found themselves unable to dispose of the increasing number of suits and many were left undetermined. In 1543, an order was made that suits brought by gentlemen (other than members of the royal household[108]) were to be remitted to the common law or to Chancery, to prevent the hindering of poor men's causes,[109] though it is doubtful whether it proved possible to enforce it.

The business of the court had no discrete character of its own. It was indistinguishable from that of the Star Chamber, and overlapped with that of the Chancery and the benches, as is made plain by the redistribution under Wolsey. As in all these courts, questions of real property predominated. A tendency to reopen matters in the Requests after judgment elsewhere—a bone of contention in the case of the Chancery[110]—was stopped by the court itself in 1543.[111] Although proceedings before the requests side of the Council had long been the

---

[103] *Select Cases in the Court of Requests 1497–1569*, ed. I. S. Leadam (12 Selden Soc.; 1898). See also J. Caesar, *The Ancient State, Authoritie and Proceedings of the Court of Requests*, ed. L. M. Hill (1975), which is a compilation from the 1590s using earlier material.

[104] e.g. *Lacy v. Sayvel* (1497) 12 Selden Soc. 1; *Powtrell v. Babington* (1495) REQ 1/1, fo. 121; Caesar, *Court of Requests*, ed. Hill, 42; *Rouclif v. Plompton* (1503) REQ 1/3, fo. 92v. By Wolsey's time, few plaintiffs were really poor: Guy, *The Cardinal's Court*, 41, 154.

[105] Above, 194; *HLJ*, i. 6, 7.   [106] Guy, *The Cardinal's Court*, 38–45.

[107] The act books use the style 'the king's honorable Council in his Court of Requests' from 20 May 1531: REQ 1/5, fo. 127v. Cf. ibid., fo. 43v (names of councillors appointed for hearing poor men's causes, 1528/9; there is no mention of a court by name). But the 'king's court of Requests' is mentioned (in Latin) in *Lawmplewe v. Bewley* (1516) CP 40/1016, m. 539 (held before dean of chapel royal and other councillors).

[108] These had the privilege of suing in Council, because of their duty of attendance on the king's court, but after 1540 were encouraged to use the Requests: Guy, *Court of Star Chamber*, 10.

[109] BL MS. Lansdowne 125, fo. 170; 12 Selden Soc., p. lxxxv, Ord. 3.   [110] See above, 174–8.

[111] BL MS. Lansdowne 125, fo. 172; 12 Selden Soc., p. lxxxvii, Ord. 10. Any such suits were to be dismissed, with costs for the defendant.

subject of occasional actions on the statutes of due process,[112] dissatisfaction grew after 1521 when Dr John Stokesley was appointed to dispatch routine business by himself in the White Hall, as a kind of master of requests. His handling of questions of common law, in which he was not trained, gave rise to complaints,[113] and Wolsey had to appoint a committee of common-law judges and serjeants to investigate what he had done 'and to make report whether they be allowable or not'.[114] The result was that Stokesley was removed, and it was probably then or soon afterwards that common lawyers began to play a greater part in the hearing of requests business.[115] It became the practice to pay a stipend of £100 to an established barrister to take on the responsibility of managing the business, and there was a continuous succession of these stipendiary councillors from at least 1530.[116] By 1541 they had acquired the title 'master of requests', and by 1546 there were two masters in ordinary.[117] Common lawyers continued to occupy both positions into the 1550s,[118] providing a contrast with the Chancery where the masterships were still mostly given to Civilians.

One distinct advantage which the requests procedure shared with the Chancery, though not usually with the Council at large,[119] was that litigants could (with leave) attend by attorney and counsel without being personally present

[112] *Bartram* v. *Barowe* (1506) KB 27/981, m. 104d; Bayne and Dunham, *Select Cases*, p. xxvii; *Younghusband* v. *Prior of Tynemouth* (1510) CP 40/991, m. 529; *Pole* v. *Bagworth* (1515) KB 27/1017, m. 58; Caesar, *Court of Requests*, ed. Hill, 91; *Lawmplewe* v. *Bewley* (1516) CP 40/1016, m. 539 (proceedings and decree set out in detail in plea); *Boys* v. *Cokke* (1517) KB 27/1022, m. 60 (process before the dean of the chapel royal and almoner at Greenwich).

[113] For actions on Magna Carta and 42 Edw. III, c. 3, in respect of proceedings before him, see *Butler* v. *Fuller* (1523) KB 27/1048, m. 75 (demurrer); *Pomerey* v. *Bucland* (1523) KB 27/1050, m. 47. And see Catlyn's precedent book, Alnwick Castle MS. 475, fo. 95 (copy of *habeas corpus* for John Newman, committed to the Fleet by Stokesley, 8 July 1522).

[114] Hudson, *Star Chamber Extracts*, fo. 56v; Guy, *The Cardinal's Court*, 44–5. For further trouble under Edward VI see M. L. Bush, 'Protector Somerset and Requests' (1974) 17 *Historical Jnl* 451–64.

[115] William Ellis B. performed a special role for most of the 1520s: Guy, *The Cardinal's Court*, 39.

[116] The succession temp. Hen. VIII was: William Sulyard (1530), bencher of Lincoln's Inn; Nicholas Hare (1537), bencher of the Inner Temple; Robert Southwell (1540), bencher of the Middle Temple; Robert Dacres (1542), barrister of the Inner Temple. For slender evidence that Christopher St German may have served in this capacity in 1529 see REQ 1/5, fo. 43v ('Sulyard' and 'Saint Jermyne' listed as members of the court, 1529); 12 Selden Soc., p. cv; Guy, *St German on Chancery and Statute*, 14–15. The annuity of £100 granted to Thomas More in 1518 may be an earlier precedent.

[117] Guy, 'The Privy Council', 83. Two extraordinary masters were added in 1562.

[118] There is no adequate list, because the patents for the stipend make no mention of any office: *LP*, iv. III. 6751(12); xiii. I. 1008(38); xv. 436(56); *CPR Edw. VI*, iii. 307; iv. 50. Appointed in the early 1550s were John Cock (1550) and John Lucas (1551) of the Inner Temple, and John Throgmorton (1553) of the Middle Temple.

[119] The act books of the Council Learned (DL 5/2, 4) contain occasional admissions of attorneys and counsel, but the numbers are very few. A defendant in Council even complained in 1494 that the lord president refused to allow him learned counsel: *Aynesworth* v. *Pilkington* (1494) in *Pilkington Narrative*, 36.

beyond the first appearance.[120] Since the clerks when recording admissions by attorney usually added the names of counsel, and very often the inns of both attorneys and counsel, more is known about the lawyers retained in this court than in any other. It seems that members of the inns of court and chancery were generally allowed in either capacity. Most of the counsel were benchers or established barristers, or occasionally even serjeants.[121] Most of the attorneys were men who practised in other courts, but it seems that there were two who specialized in Requests business and who may been formally recognized as attorneys of the court.[122] There is no sign of Civilians.

PROVINCIAL COUNCILS

In addition to the king's principal Council there were, for most of the Tudor period, two provincial councils which provided conciliar justice in the more remote north and west parts of the country in the name of 'the king's council'.[123] These councils were not derived out of the central Council but were created under the royal prerogative with separate presidents and membership. They were, however, governed by instructions approved by the central Council, and business could be transferred in both directions. The jurisdictional foundation was therefore the same as the Council and Chancery, and the business was of the same character, though it was augmented by commissions of oyer and terminer which gave members of the councils a jurisdiction over capital offences.

The Council in the North[124] originated in the time of Edward IV when the government of the north was placed in the hands of Richard, duke of Gloucester, who as Richard III continued the council under the presidency of the earl of Lincoln. The instructions issued to the earl in 1484 show that it met at least once a quarter in York and dealt with disorder, forcible entry, and other 'debates' in the north parts. It met less regularly in the time of Henry VII, but in the last decade of the reign it met from time to time at York under Archbishop Savage, and it was revived in 1525 as the duke of Richmond's council. The Council in the Marches of

[120] The practice was embodied in an order of 1543: BL MS. Lansdowne 125, fo. 171; 12 Selden Soc., p. lxxxvi, Ord. 7.

[121] e.g. in 1531 George Willoughby esq. was represented by Serjeants Audley and Willoughby, and by Richard Heydon of Lincoln's Inn: REQ 1/5, fo. 156v.

[122] In REQ 1/3 (1502–7) there are 81 appearances by Richard Turnour, and 16 by William Wilkyns (to 1504). In REQ 1/5 (1523–33), there are 46 appearances by William Dobson, and 15 by Simon Sampson (from 1530).

[123] See Elton, The Tudor Constitution, 199–203. In addition, a council in the West was established in 1539, for political reasons, but abandoned the following year: J. A. Youings, 'The Council in the West' (1960) 10 TRHS (5th ser.) 41–60.

[124] R. R. Reid, The King's Council in the North (1921); F. W. Brooks, The Council of the North (1966); Elton, The Tudor Constitution, 199–202; Gunn, Early Tudor Government, 66–7.

Wales had a similarly discontinuous history, beginning before Wales was brought into the English legal system, with an authority extending to the four English border counties.[125] It was revived in 1518 and given increased authority in 1525, when it was seen in part as a court of requests, with special provision for hearing the suits of paupers.[126] On the reorganization of Welsh judicature in 1543 it was preserved and remodelled by statute as the Council in the Principality of Wales and the Marches.[127]

The main reason for resurrecting or revitalizing these bodies in Wolsey's time was to enable the devolution of business from the Star Chamber, which was becoming overloaded.[128] They enjoyed some popularity as providing a forum for those who could not afford a sojourn in Westminster, and the northern rebels of 1536 included among their demands the suggestion that no one living north of the Trent should be required to appear in person upon a subpoena except at York.[129] By the middle of the century both jurisdictions were flourishing and thereby achieving their aim of decentralizing the administration of conciliar and equitable jurisdiction. Though possessing conciliar authority, the provincial councils did not send injunctions to the central courts, but they exercised a parallel supervisory jurisdiction over local courts within their purview.[130]

The prince of Wales's council for the duchy of Cornwall, and the learned councils of the queens consort, though once supposed to have had an equitable jurisdiction, were really administrative bodies rather than courts of judicature.[131] The latter, presided over by the queen's chancellor, and attended by her attorney- and solicitor-general and finance officers, occasionally summoned tenants and heard them by their counsel in connection with the administration of the queen's property.[132]

---

[125] See above, 103–4. The English counties within its purview were Gloucestershire, Herefordshire, Shropshire, and Worcestershire.

[126] Instructions (1525) BL MS. Harley 6068, ff. 25v (committee of at least four to hear poor men's causes), 28 (men learned in the law to be sworn to assist the poor gratis).

[127] 34 & 35 Hen. VIII, c. 26, s. 3; above, 107.

[128] Pollard, 'Council under the Tudors', 37 EHR at 359–60; Guy, The Cardinal's Court, 47–8.

[129] Reid, King's Council in the North, 142. In 1543 the Council of the North was given power to stop Chancery subpoenas by injunction if directed to northern residents.

[130] These are sometimes mentioned in the records of the recipient courts: e.g. Spurriour v. Preston (1531) KB 27/1081, m. 39 (York mayor's court; respited before the Council at York by order of the bishop of Durham; this was assigned in error as a discontinuance); Mylner v. Hayns (1550) KB 27/1153, m. 93 (Bridgnorth town court; letter from Council in Marches to 'minister indifferent justice' to the plaintiff); Dyer v. Gryff (1552) KB 27/1161, m. 142 (Monmouth town court; letters from Council in Marches to stay proceedings, followed by procedendo).

[131] There was a court of record for the 'king's fee' of Trematon, within the duchy: Symon v. Molton (1557) KB 27/1184, m. 191 (writ of error directed to the steward of the court in an action on the case). For the prince of Wales's council in the principality of Wales see above, 103.

[132] D. L. Hamilton, 'The Learned Councils of the Tudor Queens Consort' in State, Sovereigns and Society in Early Modern England, ed. C. Carlton et al. (1998), 87–101.

11

Admiralty Courts and
Courts Martial

T HERE were other superior extraordinary courts which did not derive their
authority from the Council. The family relationship between the courts of the
admiral and of the constable and marshal was symbolized in 1482 by the appointment of Robert Rydon as the king's promoter of all civil and criminal causes
before the king's judges of the constableship and admiralty of England.[1] The
connection was that these were the only secular courts which purported, or were
indeed permitted, to follow the Civil law, and the judges were usually either
graduates in Civil law or at least proctors trained in Civilian practice.[2] The Latin
procedure, with libels and positions, resembled more closely that of the Church
courts than the English bill procedure of the Chancery. The substantive law seems
to have been chiefly derived from the customs of merchants and the law of the
sea,[3] or (in the other court) the customs of chivalry and of arms, though by the
end of the sixteenth century the Civilians will have contrived to effect a reception
of juristic Roman law. Very little is yet known about the practitioners in these
courts before Elizabethan times, but since there were Civilian judges, and a distinct profession of proctors in Admiralty,[4] it may be conjectured that there were
also Civilian advocates.

Although these were not strictly conciliar courts, they were closely associated
with the Council and Chancery. William Lacy LLB, appointed judge of the
Admiralty in 1483, became clerk of the Council under Richard III.[5] Robert Rydon
LL B (d. 1509), the promoter under Edward IV, became clerk of the Council in 1492[6]

---

[1] *CPR 1476-85*, p. 343. He was succeeded the following year by William Biller, a notary: ibid. 411.
Rydon was assessor to the vice-constable in 1485: Rymer, *Foedera*, v. iii. 163.

[2] Although a doctorate was later usual, William Lacy LL B was appointed chief judge in Admiralty
in 1483: *CPR 1476-85*, p. 346. His successor, Robert Rydon, was an LL B in 1490: *CPR 1485-94*, p. 350.
Anthony Hussey, president of the Admiralty Court *c.*1536-47, was a notary public and proctor: *HPHC
1509-8*, ii. 420; 6 Selden Soc. 44 (proctor in Admiralty, 1536).

[3] See *Austen c. Castelyn* (1541) 6 Selden Soc. 106, 107, where the articles refer to the law maritime and
civil, and custom.

[4] Anthony Hussey was a proctor until the time of his becoming judge of the court: note 2, above.
The name of Kidd appears several times as a proctor *c.*1537: HCA 24/1/63, 66, 68, 70.

[5] *CPR 1476-85*, pp. 346, 461.   [6] Guy, *Court of Star Chamber*, 11.

and was concurrently judge of the Admiralty.[7] Dr John Tregonwell (d. 1565), judge of the Admiralty from 1526 to 1542, and commissary of the earl marshal,[8] was also a master in Chancery and a master of Requests.[9] These judges, and the lord admiral himself, were usually members of the Council. But the interrelationship was not in the case of maritime causes merely a function of the versatility of the Civilians. Both the Chancery and the Council exercised a concurrent jurisdiction over cases concerning foreign merchants,[10] and the Privy Council continued to investigate cases of piracy throughout the sixteenth century. Indeed, it has been plausibly supposed that until the end of the fifteenth century the primary maritime jurisdiction was perceived as resting with the Chancery and Council, the Admiralty being an ancillary tribunal subject to the survey of the former.[11]

THE HIGH COURT OF ADMIRALTY

The High Court of Admiralty, so called to distinguish it from local courts of admiralty, did not formally derive its authority from the Council but from the royal prerogative and ancient custom. Local courts of admiralty, or vice-admiralty, which existed in a number of maritime towns,[12] likewise derived their authority from the royal prerogative (through charters) or prescription, and some of them were independent of the lord high admiral.[13] The cinque ports were also exempt from the lord admiral's jurisdiction.[14] The king conferred juridical authority upon the

[7] He is described as commissary and lieutenant of the admiral in 1490 (*CPR 1485–94*, p. 350), as vice-admiral of England in 1499 (*CPR 1494–1509*, p. 180), and as commissary or deputy in 1502 (ibid. 290). These are synonyms for the president of the court.

[8] According to the title recited in 6 Selden Soc. 41 (1535).

[9] 12 Selden Soc., p. cxvi; A. B. Emden, *Biographical Register of the University of Oxford 1501–40*, pp. 575–6. Before he was reappointed judge of the Admiralty in 1540 (*LP*, xv. 492), Hussey was sitting as his deputy. In 1537 Tregonwell and Hussey are both described as judges of the Admiralty: *Lisle Letters*, ed. Byrne, v. 733.

[10] e.g. *The Carrier's Case* (1473) Pas. 13 Edw. IV, fo. 9, pl. 5; 64 Selden Soc. 30; *Case of the Spanish Merchants* (1485) Mich. 2 Ric. III, fo. 2, pl. 4; 64 Selden Soc. 73 (Chancery jurisdiction acknowledged in Star Chamber).

[11] Baldwin, *King's Council in England*, 274–5. The Chancery sometimes removed Admiralty cases by *certiorari*, and appeals lay to delegates appointed in Chancery under the great seal: below, 215.

[12] See R. G. Marsden, *Select Pleas in the Court of Admiralty*, ii (11 Selden Soc.; 1897), p. xx; 'The Vice-Admirals of the Coast' (1907) 22 *EHR* 468–77, at 472. The most important was Bristol: *CPR 1494–1509*, p. 155 (commission to exercise the office of admiralty in Bristol, in accordance with its charters, 1498); *LP*, i. 485(40) (similar commission, 1510); *Fleete* v. *Seymour* (1554) KB 27/1172, m. 162, 164 (prohibition). Southampton had a similar jurisdiction: e.g. *Yoxale* v. *Serra* (1485) C244/136/119 (£110 debt claimed before the mayor and admiral). For a record of the admiralty court of Dunwich (1498) see BL Add. Ch. 40733; and for one in Chester (1544) see BL Add. Ch. 50247. The Dunwich roll mentions fines for offences committed at fairs 'juxta littoram maris'.

[13] There were frequent disputes with the lord admiral over these claims: e.g. 6 Selden Soc., p. lxxvi; *Wellys* v. *Felton* (1539) ibid. 78, 203 (Yarmouth); 11 Selden Soc., pp. xix–xx (Tynemouth); *APC 1542–7*, p. 254 (Hull).   [14] Below, 318.

admiral by letters patent under the great seal, and the admiral in turn appointed a professional commissary-general to act as judge of the court. There was also, by Henry VIII's reign, a 'deputy', 'president', or 'steward', who presided in the absence of the commissary-general.[15] The sessions were usually held in Southwark.

Although the medieval Court of Admiralty remains obscure for want of records, the court is well documented by the middle of Henry VIII's reign. Files of libels are preserved from 1519 onwards (HCA 24), act books from 1524 (HCA 3), and depositions from 1536 (HCA 13). These records were kept by the register (*registrarius*), an official appointed for life by the admiral when a vacancy occurred.[16] Extracts from these sources are in print, and reveal a court active in the maritime commercial world, a court apparently enjoying a rapid increase in its fortunes.[17] The principal business was commercial—contracts made abroad, bills of exchange drawn or payable abroad, agencies abroad, charterparties, marine insurance,[18] freight, and other matters relating to the carriage of goods by sea. Other matters dealt with were the ownership and sale of ships, torts committed at sea or overseas,[19] spoil and piracy, and the discipline and remuneration of mariners. Salvage, average, and prize claims were not yet common.[20] Appeals were heard from some local admiralty courts, for instance those of the vice-admiral of Calais and the steward of Harwich.[21] A small number of suits were in the form of contempt proceedings to protect the jurisdiction against suits in local courts.[22]

The court was also used to enforce the droits of Admiralty, those perquisites of the sea which belonged to the Crown by virtue of its prerogative, half of which were taken by the lord admiral.[23] These included unclaimed

[15] Anthony Hussey was called 'president' in 1538 (6 Selden Soc. 61, 64, 67), when he was surrogate to Dr Tregonwell ('commissary and official principal': ibid. 41), but he continued the title when he became chief judge (ibid. 116, 131). He was also called *subdelegatus* in 1537 (HCA 24/1/64d) and 'warden or steward' (*custos sive senescallus*) in 1541 (6 Selden Soc. 102). Cf. the title of vice-admiral in this context: Marsden in 22 *EHR* at 473–4.

[16] *Hunt* v. *Elesdon* (1557–8) CP 40/1170, m. 148; Dyer 149a, 152b (assize for the office of register); *Hunt* v. *Eston* (1557) CP 40/1169, m. 1056 (action on the case concerning the records; pleads dismissal of Hunt). The office was granted jointly in 1536 to Richard Watkyns (d. 1550), described as the king's prothonotary and formerly the sole officer, and Roger Hunt, notary public, his servant.

[17] Marsden, *Select Pleas in the Court of Admiralty*, i (6 Selden Soc.; 1894), p. lvii. For the distribution of types of business in the middle of Henry VIII's reign, see the table ibid., p. lxxxiii. See also A. A. Ruddock, 'The Earliest Records of the High Court of Admiralty, 1515–58' (1949) 22 *BIHR* 139–51.

[18] According to Marsden, the first case was *Cavalicant* c. *Maynard* (1550) HCA 24/18/132.

[19] e.g. *Colmer* c. *Anthony* (1544) 6 Selden Soc. 130 (damages recovered for false imprisonment at Middleburgh in Zealand).

[20] Marsden, *Select Pleas*, i, pp. lxx, lxxii, says there was only one case of salvage and one of general average in the time of Hen. VIII. The Privy Council dealt with a good many prize cases during the war with France in the mid-1540s. [21] 11 Selden Soc., p. lxv (1537, 1538).

[22] e.g. *Jewell* c. *Norman* (1530) 6 Selden Soc., pp. lxxvi, 37, 200 (suit in city of London on a contract made in Bilbao; suit in Admiralty for contempt removed to Chancery by *certiorari*).

[23] Marsden, *Select Pleas*, ii, pp. xxiv–xxvi.

wreck,[24] flotsam, jetsam, lagan, and royal fish,[25] where these did not belong to franchise-owners by patent or prescription. The nature of these rights was fully expounded in the inns of court by the readers on *Prerogativa Regis*, c. 11,[26] and on Westminster I, c. 4.[27]

The criminal jurisdiction in Admiralty, which was principally concerned with piracy and murder committed on the sea or in waters within the limits of the admiral's authority, was exercised through commissions of oyer and terminer. Commissions were at first issued ad hoc, and named the offenders to be tried,[28] but as the jurisdiction increased in the time of Henry VIII it became the practice to issue general commissions. The system was regularized by statute in 1535 and 1536,[29] and records of the proceedings survive from 1537 (HCA 1). The principal purpose of the 1536 act was to alter the mode of the trial from 'the course of the Civil laws' to 'the common course of the laws of the land used for felonies'. And the motive for introducing jury trial, according to the preamble, was that it was difficult to obtain the necessary proof required by the Civil law without resorting to 'torture or pains'; juries, it seems, were more easily persuaded of guilt. Commissions were henceforward to be issued to the lord admiral and his judges, and three or four 'substantial persons'; special provision was made for the cinque ports. The venue problem was solved by the provision that both the grand and trial juries were to be drawn from the county limited in the commission.

Throughout its history the court had been beset by prohibitions, and Admiralty litigants were attacked by actions for damages founded on the Admiralty statutes,[30] or on the Statute of Winchester,[31] or on common law.[32] Admiralty litigation was

[24] For suggestions for prohibitions in case of wreck, see *Mayhowe* v. *Leyson* (1552) KB 27/1161, m. 144 (wreck claimed by men of Yarmouth); *Newman* v. *Coke* (1554) KB 27/1170, m. 179; *Flete* v. *Harryson* (1554) KB 27/1172, m. 91.

[25] For disputes over porpoises see *Devonshire Justices* v. *Lord Admiral* (1518/29) 25 Selden Soc. 122 (in the Star Chamber); *Cordell* v. *Turnebull* (1557) KB 27/1183, m. 177 (prohibition to Admiralty commissary in the North Parts).

[26] Robert Constable's reading in Lincoln's Inn (1495) 113 Selden Soc. 32–35; Thomas Frowyk's reading in the Inner Temple (1495) ibid. 36–40; John Spelman's reading in Gray's Inn (1521) ibid. 40–42.

[27] Thomas Kebell's reading in the Inner Temple (1486 or earlier) 113 Selden Soc. 27–30; anon., ibid. 30–2.

[28] e.g. *CPR 1485–94*, p. 475 (1493); *CPR 1494–1509*, p. 290 (1502); 108 Selden Soc., p. cxli (1515).

[29] 27 Hen. VIII, c. 4; 28 Hen. VIII, c. 15. For a full discussion of this legislation, see Prichard and Yale, 108 Selden Soc., pp. cxxxvii–cxlvi. Eleven pirates were tried at the Guildhall in 1537: *Lisle Letters*, ed. Byrne, 293.

[30] 13 Ric. II, c. 5; 15 Ric. II, c. 3; 2 Hen. IV, c. 11. For fifteenth-century examples see Dyer 159b; Rast. Ent. 24 (from Lucas); Co. Inst. iv. 138; CP 40/865, m. 440; *Barwell qui tam etc.* v. *Cely* (1492) KB 27/923, m. 51d; KB 27/929, m. 33d; *Barwell qui tam etc.* v. *Raweson* (1492) KB 27/929, m. 70. A form of prohibition, where suit was brought on a contract made in London, is in print: *Kyrkby* c. *Barfote* (1527) 6 Selden Soc. 27, 172. See also *Parry* c. *Melhuysshe* (1549) 11 Selden Soc. 9.

[31] For an example of an action of *praemunire* see Rast. Ent. 24. The reference given is incorrect (not KB 27/932, m. 32).

[32] See *Anon.* (1529/30) Wm Yelv. 322, no. 21 (trespass lies against judge and officials of the Admiralty for executing a precept *coram non judice*); *Fermor* v. *Stone* (1531) KB 27/1081, m. 7 (action on the case

also vulnerable to writs of *supersedeas* or prohibition from the Chancery[33] and Exchequer.[34] The flow of actions and prohibitions increased in the time of Henry VIII,[35] though since few of them have a final conclusion enrolled in the plea rolls it is not to be assumed that they were necessarily effective. There was no quarrel with the legitimate jurisdiction of the Admiralty in respect of matters arising on the high seas, and there was only occasional controversy over inland waterways.[36] The problem was that litigants had not unnaturally been tempted to bring in other maritime causes of action, such as contracts of affreightment made in London. This extension was contrary to statute,[37] though in respect of contracts made overseas the matter had been confused in 1525 by the grant of a patent to the duke of Richmond as lord high admiral conferring jurisdiction over such contracts *non obstante* the legislation.[38] If the Admiralty could not hear contract cases arising overseas there might be a failure of justice, and it was suggested that this justified jurisdiction over transmarine contracts,[39] though the common lawyers were willing enough to come to the rescue by allowing such contracts to be laid fictitiously in England.[40] The main source of complaint, however, seems to have been the practice of suing on cismarine contracts. A party claimed in the Common Pleas in 1508 that the Admiralty had a prescriptive right to entertain

for causing the attachment of a ship in which the plaintiff had undertaken to carry a hundred pilgrims to Compostella, so that he lost profit; action discontinued).

[33] *Snodham* v. *Prowe* (1516) Bodl. Lib. MS. Rawlinson C.339, fo. 291 (in a Chancery precedent book); *Barker* c. *Maynard* (1531) 11 Selden Soc., p. xlii (and below); *Warner* c. *Wheler* (1544) 11 Selden Soc., p. xlviii; Co. Inst. iv. 139. See also 6 Selden Soc. 49; 11 Selden Soc., pp. xliv–xlv.

[34] *Chapilion* v. *Byrd* (1528) 6 Selden Soc., pp. lxxiv, 30–4; and cf. 11 Selden Soc., p. xlv. The Exchequer frequently considered seizures of ships and cargoes for customs offences. The present case involved wines imported in a foreign vessel.

[35] 6 Selden Soc., pp. lxxiv–lxxix; 94 Selden Soc. 73 n. 4. Rast. Ent. 24v prints the form of a prohibition to the Admiralty signed by Fyneux CJ. There are numerous entries of suggestions for prohibitions in the King's Bench rolls (KB 27) in the 1540s and 1550s. A Common Pleas example is *Masheroder* v. *Wynn* (1557) CP 40/1171, m. 709; Benl. 57.

[36] *Gold qui tam etc.* v. *Bowes* (1524) CP 40/1045, m. 140 (action on statutes of 13 Ric. II and 2 Hen. IV in respect of a contract made on the River Thames at Billingsgate; cf. injunction in C261/9/20); *Spycer* v. *Cleyton* (1548) KB 27/1145, m. 105 (suggestion for a prohibition; fishing in a river in Suffolk which was a creek within the body of the county); 11 Selden Soc. 3 (prohibition printed in full from Admiralty file). Cf. *Melhuysshe* v. *Parry* (1549) KB 27/1151, m. 62; 11 Selden Soc. 9 (detinue of blocks of tin freighted on the Thames). [37] 13 Ric. II, c. 5; 15 Ric. II, c. 3; 2 Hen. IV, c. 11.

[38] This gave rise to a dispute lasting until the seventeenth century: M. J. Prichard and D. E. C. Yale, *Hale and Fleetwood on Admiralty Jurisdiction* (108 Selden Soc.; 1993), p. lxxxii.

[39] Morgan Kydwelly's reading in the Inner Temple (1483) CUL MS. Ee.5.18, fo. 31v, distinguishes transmarine and cismarine causes.

[40] Brooke Abr., *Faites*, pl. 95 (temp. Hen. VIII: Caen in Kent); *Anon.* (Hil. 1558) BL MS. Harley 1624, fo. 78v; MS. Hargrave 4, fo. 137v (charter to carry wine from Bordeaux to London or Antwerp; consignee appoints Antwerp; venue laid at Antwerp in the county of Northampton). For earlier precedents see *Hale on the Admiralty*, 108 Selden Soc. 47–8. Cf. *Draymews* v. *Bailly* (1502) C1/239/17 (suit in Chancery because no remedy at law on bill drawn in Bruges).

pleas on contracts of affreightment in respect of ships which were located within the jurisdiction, but the ensuing demurrer was not decided.[41]

A way of evading attack was to omit all mention in the libel of the place where the contract was made, and in one case this apparently defeated a prohibition.[42] Plaintiffs in Admiralty also resorted to the brazen fictional allegation that a cismarine contract had been made on the high seas. This device was already in use in the 1520s, but the legal problem in attacking it was whether the King's Bench could take judicial notice that an allegation of a contract made at sea, however improbable, was fictitious. The question was raised by demurrer in 1522 by John Rastell, whose ill-fated expedition to Newfoundland had resulted in an action for £60 freight against him and his ship (the *Frances Rastell*) before the lieutenant of the lord admiral. The plaintiff in Admiralty relied on a written charterparty to hire the *Barbara*, alleging that the contract was made upon the high seas. Rastell brought an action on the statutes, claiming damages, and the defendant demurred; but no judgment was ever entered. If the high-seas allegation was true, there was no breach of statute. But how could the common-law court know that it was not true?[43] The solution was to allow the plaintiff seeking a prohibition to aver that the contract was made in London or within a county.[44] By 1555 it was also possible to recover damages on the statutes for a false jurisdictional allegation.[45] But no accord over this issue was reached in Tudor times. In 1558 it vexed the King's Bench to the point that the chief justice actually ordered the attachment of the judge in Admiralty.[46]

The Admiralty was far from stunted by these checks. Although the volume of statutory actions and suggestions for prohibitions indicates a climate favourable to such complainants, it is not clear from the rolls how far success was achieved. The King's Bench rolls, if they record prohibitions at all, do not usually indicate

[41] *Hamond qui tam etc. v. Bough* (1516–17) CP 40/1016, m. 664. This was an action on the statutes of Ric. II and Hen. IV in respect of a suit in 1508 on a covenant made in London to demise the *Elizabeth*, in London bound for Bordeaux.

[42] *Crane v. Bell* (1546), below. This was a promise to indemnify against the Spanish for salvage. A prohibition was sought on the grounds that the promise was made at Dartford, but a consultation was granted.

[43] *Rastell qui tam etc. v. Thetford* (1522–3) KB 27/1042, m. 60. The defendant, a merchant tailor, had sued in Admiralty as proctor (*procurator in rem suam*) to the ship-owner (the earl of Surrey, lord high admiral), who had ceded his action to him. For Rastell's voyage see above, 101 n. 6.

[44] *Gold qui tam etc. v. Bowes* (1524) CP 40/1045, m. 140 (alleges contract made at Billingsgate *super aquam infra libertatem civitatis*); cf. C261/9 (injunction against Gold, 12 Nov. 1524); *Anon.* (1539) Brooke Abr., *Prohibition*, pl. 17; *Andrew v. Gamble* (1552) KB 27/1160, m. 201 (interference with ferry at Gravesend); *Playstowe v. Whyskyn* (1553) KB 271168, m. 124 (suggestion for prohibition alleging contract made at Rochester *infra corpus comitatus*); *Fleete v. Cox* (1554) KB 27/1172, m. 156 (suggestion alleging that bond made in London *infra corpus civitatis*); *Fleete v. Seymour*, ibid., mm. 162, 164; *Tyrrell v. Robertes* (1556) KB 27/1177, m. 1⦁ (suggestion that contract for affreightment to Spain made in county of Somerset).

[45] *Swanton v. Gyllett* (1555) KB 27/1174, m. 180 (trespass to fishing nets on a boat at Tilbury Hope, alleged to be within the county of Essex; awarded £10, doubled to £20 by the statute).

[46] *Crane c. Wyntropp* (1558) 11 Selden Soc. 23; *APC 1558–70*, p. 12. Cf. *Wyntrop v. Combes* (1558) KB 27/1188, m. 148 (complaint of proceedings to recover a debt upon an Admiralty recognizance).

whether a consultation was granted.[47] And inconclusive actions for damages may conceal a complex deadlock. For example, the King's Bench record of an action in 1533 on the statutes of 13 Ric. II and 2 Hen. IV ends with an issue of fact—whether or not the contract was made on the sea—but no verdict. The case had begun in the town court of Dartmouth, and the Admiralty suit was brought to inhibit the local proceedings for contempt. The Admiralty records show that there had previously been a Chancery *supersedeas*, a King's Bench prohibition, followed by a consultation, and finally an appeal on the question of jurisdiction.[48] The outcome is unknown, but there is no evidence here that the King's Bench was interfering in a hostile manner. There is even some evidence that the Common Pleas in 1558 took steps to deter unfounded attacks on the Admiralty, both by requiring those who sought prohibitions to enter into a bond that the surmise was true and by perusing statutory actions with a sceptical punctiliousness.[49] But the boundaries were drawn. And the common-law courts had meanwhile ensured that their own remedies were effective to bring within their purview all contracts relating to the carriage of goods by sea,[50] and even marine insurance.[51]

An attempt by the King's Bench in 1542 to subject the Admiralty to review by means of *habeas corpus* was defeated on the grounds that a proper appellate machinery was already in existence.[52] The proper course was to appeal to delegates appointed ad hoc by letters patent,[53] a system which provided the model for the ecclesiastical Delegates after the break with Rome.[54]

[47] e.g. *Crane* v. *Bell* (1546) KB 27/1139, m. 126; Co. Inst. iv. 139. Only the Admiralty records show that a consultation was granted in this case: *Bell* c. *Crane*, 6 Selden Soc., pp. lxxviii, 129; 11 Selden Soc., p. xlviii.

[48] *Gylbert qui tam etc.* v. *Barker* (1533) KB 27/1089, m. 85; *Barker* c. *Maynard* (1531) HCA 24/1/73; 11 Selden Soc., p. xlii.

[49] *Bilota qui tam etc.* v. *Poyntell* (1558) CP 40/1173, m. 831 (demurrer to declaration; abstr. in Catlyn's precedent book, Alnwick Castle MS. 475, fo. 85); Dyer 159b; Benl. 58, 64; BL MS. Harley 1624, ff. 60–62 (referred to arbitration); *Anon.* (1558) BL MS. Harley 1624, fo. 66; MS. Hargrave 4, fo. 123.

[50] e.g. *Anon.* (1495) Pas. 10 Hen. VII, fo. 22, pl. 21; Hil. 11 Hen. VII, fo. 16, pl. 13 (debt on bond for carriage of goods from Norway to Lynn); *Rede* v. *Manyard* (1519) CP 40/1023(2), m. 191 (debt for freight of wine carried from Bordeaux to London); *Sygyns* v. *Lyster* (1523) CP 40/1038, m. 447 (debt for freight to Bordeaux); *Palmer* v. *Robson* (1530) CP 40/1065, m. 344 (*assumpsit* on contract for carriage by sea); *Spert* v. *Parker* (1536) CP 40/1089, m. 527 (debt on charterparty for voyage to Cadiz); *Borne* v. *Grene* (1538) CP 40/1097, m. 419d (*assumpsit* on contract for carriage by sea); *Sabyn* v. *Toly* (1541) KB 2/1121, m. 111 (*assumpsit* for freight); *Guybon* v. *Firmuge* (1542) CP 40/1114, m. 627 (*assumpsit* to buy a ship); *Browne* v. *Wodlefe* (1546) CP 40/1130, m. 413 (debt on bond to pay freight, average, porterage, lighterage, wharfage, and hoopage); *Closter* v. *Cannesby* (1550) KB 27/1154, m. 126 (*assumpsit* for freight).

[51] *Mayne* v. *De Gozi* (1538) KB 27/1107 m. 37 (*assumpsit* to insure goods shipped from London to Rouen). This was twelve years before the first known Admiralty case.

[52] *Dolphin* c. *Shutford* (1542) 11 Selden Soc., pp. xlvi–xlvii.

[53] e.g. *Folkes* c. *Fenkyll* (1478) CPR 1476–85, p. 102 (judgment for £700 debt and £700 damages); *Hawkyns* c. *Heron* (1490) CPR 1485–94, p. 350; *More's Case* (1511) LP, i. 969(4) (an appeal on grounds of want of jurisdiction). Other examples may be found back to the fourteenth century.

[54] 25 Hen. VIII, c. 19 ('like as in case of appeal from the admiral's court').

THE COURT OF THE CONSTABLE AND MARSHAL

It is very doubtful whether the court of the lord high constable and marshal of England, as established in the fourteenth century, survived as a recognized institution into the early Tudor period. The original role of trying cases concerning the supply of the army had become obsolete, and appeals of treason were rare.[55] Moreover, the strengthening of the College of Arms after its incorporation by Richard III[56] had the effect of steering disputes over armorial bearings towards the kings of arms. Although a dispute over a coat of arms might still be heard in the 1490s before the lord high constable, the result was registered with the kings of arms rather than drawn up as a definitive sentence of the court of chivalry.[57]

A special manifestation of the authority of the constable and marshal, which had been used after the battle of Tewkesbury in 1471, was by commission to execute martial law following an armed conflict within the realm. There were a few instances of this in our period,[58] following major uprisings. The first was a commission issued in 1497—after the battle of Blackheath—to the lord treasurer, the knight-marshal, another knight, and the clerk of the Council, as commissioners (*commissarii*) to exercise the office of constable and marshal and to try Lord Audley summarily, by evidence and proofs, according to the laws and customs used before the constable and marshal.[59] Audley was sentenced to death in the White Hall, without benefit of trial by peers. This seems a rather remarkable infringement of the rule of law,[60] and seems from the next case to have been so viewed at the time. The second commission went to the knight-marshal and Sir Robert Clifford to execute the office of constable and marshal in respect of those who had levied war in Devon and Cornwall, meaning principally Perkin Warbeck, the Flemish pretender who had landed in Cornwall claiming the Crown as a son

---

[55] G. D. Squibb, *The High Court of Chivalry* (1959), 29.

[56] *CPR 1477–85*, p. 422. It was reincorporated in 1555: *CPR 1555–7*, p. 31. The purpose of these incorporations was to enable the college to acquire property in perpetuity rather than to enlarge the powers of the officers of arms, but they coincided with increasing visitatorial activity. See A. R. Wagner, *Heralds of England* (1967), ch. 3.

[57] *Ashton c. Legh* (1496) Squibb, *Court of Chivalry*, 29–30; *The Visitation of Lancashire 1533* (110 Chetham Soc.; 1882), 161. The dispute between the kings of arms themselves which was argued before the earl marshal in the 1520s (Squibb, 131–2) seems even less like litigation before a court.

[58] Cf. a case in 1482 where four knights and four civilians were put in commission: *CPR 1476–85*, p. 317. The 1482 patent uses the terms vice-constable and vice-marshal, though the latter was usually known as the knight-marshal. Another example of a vice-constable occurs in 1485: Rymer, *Foedera*, v. III. 163. Henry VII's first proclamation (25 Aug. 1485) ordered the peace to be kept on pain of death: *Tudor Royal Proclamations*, i. 3, no. 1.

[59] *CPR 1494–1509*, p. 115; L. W. Vernon Harcourt, *His Grace the Steward and Trial of Peers* (1907), 44–5.

[60] It was arguably contrary to the Treason Act, 25 Edw. III, stat. 5, c. 2: see *Hale on the Admiralty*, 108 Selden Soc. 44–5.

of Edward IV and proclaimed himself King Richard IV.[61] The better accounts of this case make it clear that the justification for issuing such a commission was that, as an alien enemy, Warbeck could not be indicted for treason at common law, and had therefore to be tried by martial law. After preliminary hearings in the Star Chamber, the commissioners sat in the White Hall in 1499 and conducted a trial 'by proofs'. Warbeck was convicted and sentenced to death as an enemy, rather than as a traitor.[62] However, when the earl of Warwick was tried a week later for aiding Warbeck, it was upon a common-law indictment and by his peers,[63] an evident indication that the 1497 precedent had been rejected. A further martial law commission was issued in 1500 to Sir Thomas Darcy alone to deal with Warbeck's adherents, but the outcome is unknown.[64] The third judgment in the time of Henry VII is found in 1502, when Thomas Tyrell was convicted in the White Hall for treason at Guisnes in Picardy.[65] The procedure was used by Henry VIII after the Lincolnshire rebellion in 1536, when the king proclaimed 'we will withdraw the eye of our mercy and clemency' from rioters who refused to disperse, 'and proceed against them with all our royal power, force, and minions of war which we now have in readiness, and destroy them, their wives, and children, with fire and sword'.[66] The following year seventy-four prisoners were condemned to death by the knight-marshal without jury trial.[67] After the Western rebellion in 1549, Edward VI threatened enclosure rioters with 'pain of death presently to be suffered and executed by the authority and order of law martial, wherein no delay or deferring of time shall be permitted or suffered',[68] appointing lords lieutenant to execute this policy;[69] and Mary I—without any legal sanction—once tried to extend this system so as to enable death sentences to be passed on undesirables in general without having to indict them for a known felony or run the risk of acquittal by jury.[70] In the summer of 1553, following the proclamation of Queen Jane, there was for three days in the west country 'nothing else but martial law to hang and draw'; but this may refer to a lawless chaos, a brief opportunity for local

[61] See above, 59.

[62] *Perkin Warbeck's Case* (1499) Port 125; 1 Caryll 383; James Hobart's report, 109 Selden Soc. 206; below, 616.　　　　　　　　　　　　　　[63] *R. v. Earl of Warwick* (1499) Port 125; KB 8/2.

[64] *CPR 1494–1509*, p. 202.　　　[65] *CPR 1494–1509*, p. 506 (pardoned).

[66] *Tudor Royal Proclamations*, i. 245, no. 168. See also Bernard, 'The Tyranny of Henry VIII', 122.

[67] *LP*, xii. 1. 498 (and cf. p. 468, where the expression 'martial law' is used). Some forms of law were used, because Robert Bowes (a member of Lincoln's Inn and of the Council in the North, later master of the rolls, d. 1555) was employed as attorney for the Crown. The previous year two were hanged at Windsor under martial law for treason 'in the rage of horley borley': *Hall's Chronicle*, 823.

[68] *Tudor Royal Proclamations*, i. 476, no. 341.　　　[69] For lieutenants see above, 72.

[70] See L. Boynton, 'The Tudor Provost-Marshal' (1962) 77 *EHR* 437–55; J. V. Capua, 'The Early History of Martial Law in England' (1977) 36 *CLJ* 152–73; Bellamy, *The Tudor Law of Treason*, 230–1. The provost-marshal seems at first to have been the executive officer of the knight-marshal, who was appointed by the earl marshal; but after 1549 he was appointed by the lord lieutenant.

gentry to settle old scores, rather than summary legal proceedings.[71] Mary I also claimed a power to impress mariners for the navy on pain of death.[72]

Somewhat different arrangements were made when the army went on active service. For example, in 1513, when the expedition set out against the king of Scots, the earl of Shrewsbury was commissioned as lieutenant general of the army with powers to make orders, to hear and determine criminal causes, contracts and disputes, and to impose punishments including death and mutilation; and later in the same year Sir Thomas Lovell, a common-law member of the king's Council, was given a commission as deputy to the marshal of England to hear and determine criminal causes in the absence of the earl of Surrey, and to pass sentence of death.[73]

These ad hoc commissions, though they sometimes mentioned the customary authority of the constable and marshal (as a synonym for martial law), have no direct bearing on the fate of the court of chivalry properly so called.[74] In Tyrell's case, the last permanent[75] lord high constable—the earl of Derby (d. 1504)—was one of the commissioners, but usually the constable was not named. The desuetude of the constable and marshal's court proper was confirmed by the decision of Henry VIII to leave the office of constable vacant. At the beginning of the reign the duke of Buckingham laid claim to the constableship as a grand serjeanty, by descent from Humphrey de Bohun, a claim which—as the attorney-general secretly confided to Serjeant Caryll—was 'a dangerous thing for our lord the king'. The petition was referred to the Star Chamber, where written pleadings were exchanged with the attorney-general and the duke given leave to proceed.[76] The case does not seem to have been openly argued until 1514, when the judges reported in favour of the duke;[77] but it was never finally decided. Buckingham was executed for treason in 1521, and the office has remained unfilled ever since.

---

[71] *Blake* v. *Coppe* (1554) CP 40/1158, m. 834 (action for saying, on 30 July 1553, sp. mod. 'I trust hereafter we shall have a merry world, for the martial law is now past, and that Roger Blake had in times past sought my death but (thanks be to God) it lieth not in his power, but now I trust to see his head off within short time...'; defendant admits saying, 'I trust the martial law is now at an end—a right queen, God save her grace, Queen Mary is proclaimed in Gloucester—for within these three days was nothing else but the martial law to hang and draw; I trust to God he that threatened us here with the martial law when the Lady Jane was proclaimed queen shall first be hanged himself').

[72] *Tudor Royal Proclamations*, ii. 91, no. 444 (1558).

[73] The commissions are copied in William Porter's precedent book, C193/142, ff. 98v–101.

[74] Cf. Harcourt, *Trial of Peers*, 397–8, where he says Audley was tried 'in a court of chivalry before special commissioners'.

[75] The duke of Buckingham was appointed, for the day of the coronation only, in 1509.

[76] Hudson's extracts from the lost register, BL MS. Lansdowne 639, ff. 34v (duke to put claim in writing, 19 June 1510), 35v (bill put in, 21 June; attorney-general puts in answer, 2 July), 35v (duke given leave to proceed, 8 July).

[77] 2 Caryll 645 (abstracted in Dyer 285b); Staffs. Record Office, MS. D1721/1/11, ff. 133–150. See comment in J. H. Round, *Peerage and Pedigree* (1910), i. 147–66; C. Rawcliffe, *The Staffords* (1978), 37–9.

The permanent vacancy left the Crown with an uncontrolled discretion as to when or whether the ancient jurisdiction could be exercised.[78] That may have been one of the reasons behind a proposal in the 1530s to introduce a Court of Centeners, to hear suits concerning the army; but the court was also in part to be concerned with military revenue—diverted from the monasteries—and administration. The idea was not taken up by Cromwell.[79]

[78] See *Sir Francis Drake's Case* (1582), in Coke's notebook (*LPCL*, 202).
[79] Elton, *Reform and Renewal*, 140.

12

The New Revenue Courts[1]

ALTHOUGH the Exchequer provided what might be termed a common-law system of revenue collection, with a court which has already been described, it was by the Tudor period regarded as cumbrous and archaic. Its elaborate and dilatory accounting procedures, with arcane Latin forms and wooden tallies, proved frustrating to kings or ministers who wished to raise and spend large sums of money as need arose, and from the time of Edward IV much of the revenue of the Crown was diverted to the King's Chamber, where it came under the control of the treasurer of the Chamber and the regular scrutiny of the king himself.[2] The new fiscal system was pioneered in the Duchy Chamber of Lancaster at the end of Edward IV's reign, when Richard Empson was attorney-general of the duchy, and it included improving the feudal revenues of the Crown.[3] There is some evidence that Richard III wished to replace the Exchequer entirely by a new revenue department based on the Duchy Chamber, which had become an effective board of finance operating independently of the Exchequer and combining modern methods of management with legal expertise.[4] His vision, however, was not achieved for another fifty years.

Some steps were taken under Henry VII to organize the non-Exchequer revenue without establishing new courts. Management of the Chamber revenue was further strengthened, and the line between public and private royal finances was more or less removed.[5] Commissions were appointed to investigate shortfalls in certain forms of revenue and organize its collection. The Council Learned—shortly before it came to an end in 1509—tried to extend the methods of the

---

[1] What follows is based heavily on W. C. Richardson, *Tudor Chamber Administration 1485–1547* (1952); H. E. Bell, *An Introduction to the History and Records of the Court of Wards and Liveries* (1953), Elton, *The Tudor Revolution in Government; The Tudor Constitution*, 129–34; Wolffe, *The Crown Lands 1461 to 1536*. The anonymous typescript notes in the PRO standard lists are invaluable guides to the records of the courts.

[2] Wolffe, *The Crown Lands*, 51–65. The Exchequer kept responsibility for the farms of counties and towns, the customs revenue, much of the feudal revenue, and miscellaneous casual revenue: see above, 161.

[3] R. Somerville, *History of the Duchy of Lancaster*, i (1953), 243–6; J. M. W. Bean, *The Decline of English Feudalism, 1215–1540* (1968), 238–40.

[4] F. Dietz, *English Government Finance 1485–1558* (1921), 65.

[5] See D. Grummitt, 'Henry VII, Chamber Finance and the "New Monarchy": some new evidence' (1999) 72 *BIHR* 229–43.

Duchy Chamber to the supervision of the king's Chamber revenue, apparently while Sir Reynold Bray (chancellor of the Duchy) was its leading member.[6] In the same decade, a master of the wards was appointed (1503), with a staff of officials to manage revenues from the sale of wardships, and a surveyor of the king's prerogative (1508) with similar functions in relation to a wider field of revenue.[7] From these administrative expedients emerged the new system which came to be embodied in the statutory revenue courts of Henry VIII.

The disadvantages of the prerogative system which developed under Henry VII were that it was excessively informal, that it required the king's personal vigilance in routine financial management, that on a demise of the Crown it left officials in a state of uncertainty about their accounts,[8] that it caused a confusing overlap with the parallel procedures of the Exchequer,[9] and that it was dependent on existing judicial institutions for its enforcement. For instance, the infamous bonds exacted by Empson, Dudley, and their associates,[10] had to be enforced through the Common Pleas. Many stale bonds from their time were still in suit in the 1520s, though after 1509 it was worth challenging them on grounds of duress;[11] that such defences existed against the Crown speaks well of the common law, but it could be seen as another shortcoming of an informal revenue system. The new system of revenue courts as planned by Thomas Cromwell was intended to strike a balance between the lax informality of Henry VII's methods and the archaic formality of the Exchequer. As torrents of new-found royal revenue threatened to bring both of the old revenue systems to the point of collapse in the middle years of Henry VIII, Cromwell devised the expedient of establishing new courts to

[6] Somerville, 'Henry VII's "Council Learned in the Law"' 427 at 434–5; Bell, *Court of Wards and Liveries*, 4–5, 12.

[7] W. C. Richardson, 'The Surveyor of the King's Prerogative' (1941) 56 *EHR* 52–75; *Tudor Chamber Administration*, 166–75, 192–214.

[8] This seems to have been the main reason for the statute 3 Hen. VIII, c. 23 (below). A good example of lingering trouble is *Curteys* v. *Lynom* (1500) CP 40/952, m. 381 (action by keeper of wardrobe to Ric. III against the same king's solicitor-general).

[9] See e.g. M. R. Horowitz, 'An Early Tudor Teller's Book' (1981) 96 *EHR* 103–16. Fines for refusing knighthood in 1501–3 were pursued both through the Exchequer (above, 162 n. 25) and through the Council Learned (DL 5/2, fo. 33v).

[10] For the use of bonds and recognizances under Henry VII see Dietz, *English Government Finance*, 33–50; Brodie, 'Edmund Dudley: minister of Henry VII' 133–61 at 149; Somerville, 54 *EHR* at 435–6; Richardson, *Tudor Chamber Administration*, 141–58; J. R. Lander, 'Bonds, Coercion, and Fear: Henry VII and the peerage' in *Florilegium Historiale*, ed. J. F. Rowe and W. H. Stockdale (1971), 327–67; Harrison, 'The Petition of Edmund Dudley', 82–99; Chrimes, *Henry VII*, 212–16; M. R. Horowitz, 'Richard Empson, Minister of Henry VII' (1982) 55 *BIHR* 35–49. BL MS. Lansdowne 127 is a notebook of Dudley's concerning bonds given to him.

[11] e.g. five such pleas in 1516: CP 40/1016, mm. 632, 633, 635, 638, 681. These were bonds made to Dudley personally, but the king now claimed them as forfeited for treason. In Trin. 1512 there are at least 19 actions on bonds forfeited by Empson or Dudley: CP 40/1000, mm. 341, 342, 346, 347, 349d, 351, 352, 355d, 358d, 360, 477–481, 483.

handle both the new income and any associated legal problems, in an efficient and more bureaucratic manner. There is little doubt that the model was still the Duchy Chamber, since the same titles were adopted for the statutory officials, and the statutes in some places expressly link the new tribunals to the procedure of that body.

Although these new institutions were called 'courts'—and with reason, for they had significant powers of judicature over the areas within their competence—their functions were more administrative than judicial, and the legislative draftsmen gave little detailed attention to the ancillary judicial systems. The institutions have been very fully examined by historians of Tudor government and financial administration, and for present purposes it is necessary only to give a brief account of them from the judicial point of view. But we should begin with the older court on which they were modelled.

THE COURT OF DUCHY CHAMBER

The duchy of Lancaster, which belonged to the Crown,[12] owned land all over England and provided the king with a considerable part of his revenue. The council of the duchy, presided over by its chancellor, therefore had a nationwide jurisdiction, unlike the Chancery court of the county palatine of Lancaster, which was a court of equity for Lancashire alone.[13] It usually met at Westminster in a room within the Exchequer of Receipt called the Duchy Chamber, and (as in the case of the Star Chamber) the name of the room came to be used for the name of the court. In the time of Henry VIII meetings were also held in the Savoy, where the duchy had an office.

The council of the duchy was in origin primarily an administrative body—like that of the duchy of Cornwall, which did not have a judicial side—charged with surveying its property and revenues and making management decisions. Occasional legal questions might be referred to arbitration[14] or remitted to the common law, though the duchy council assumed in the fifteenth century the authority to make decrees itself. Most plaints were brought before the court by duchy farmers, feodaries, or king's counsel, but there were also disputes between tenants of the duchy. Already in Bray's time the court was sufficiently judicial in nature to be attended by counsel and for a decision to be reported.[15]

---

12 The king's title was confirmed by *RP*, vi. 272 (1485).

13 The difference is explained in R. Somerville, 'The Duchy of Lancaster Council and the Court of Duchy Chamber' (1940) 23 *TRHS* (4th ser.) 159–77. For the palatinate see below, 294.

14 e.g. *Trafford v. Asshton* (1488) REQ 5/3, fo. 42 (referred to Thomas Babington and William Huntley, 'lerned men'—they were barristers of the Inner Temple); *Abbot of Chester v. Hesketh* (1505) ibid., fo. 245v (referred to Frowyk CJ).

15 BL MS. Hargrave 87, fo. 140 (case before Bray as chancellor of the duchy, reported by Thomas Babington of the Inner Temple).

The jurisdiction as to title may have been based at first on the parties' submission to bonds, making it analogous to arbitration.[16] But before the end of Henry VII's reign we see the full judicial machinery in place. Thus, in 1505 the court heard a dispute concerning land at Great Waltham, in Essex, belonging to the abbot of Westminster as appurtenant to the free chapel of Pleshey, late parcel of the duchy. The suit was brought against the tenant in possession, who was summoned by privy seal and pleaded to issue; the court heard witnesses and examined depositions before making a decree nisi for the abbot to have possession.[17]

In the time of Henry VIII the judicial business grew dramatically, and there are files of English bills, pleadings, and depositions resembling those of the Chancery and conciliar courts.[18] The court was always staffed by eminent common lawyers, who in cases of difficulty would call upon the judges for assistance.[19] There is no full account of its judicial work, but it is clear from the law reports that it was not confined to revenue business. Indeed, it possessed the same range of jurisdiction in respect of duchy lands and tenants as the Star Chamber.[20] Although it was later said to be a court of equity and not of common law,[21] it seems also to have exercised a jurisdiction corresponding to that of the Latin side of the Chancery within the county palatine of Lancaster.[22] What made the court an attractive model for revenue reformers was not the general civil jurisdiction, which seems scarcely distinguishable from that of the other English-bill courts, but the use made of an informal conciliar procedure in the garnering and improvement of royal revenue from widely dispersed lands. This revenue system, though centred judicially on the Duchy Chamber, was managed through an elaborate network of local receivers and surveyors answerable to the general receivers who prepared the accounts for the duchy chancellor and Council.

[16] These were enforceable elsewhere: e.g. *R.* v. *Leigh* (1508) CP 40/983, m. 353 (debt on recognizance to appear before Bray in the Duchy Chamber).

[17] *Hervy* v. *Whether* (1504–5) DL 5/3, ff. 234v, 247v, 251, 254. The court also began around this date formally to allow appearance by attorneys and counsel (in the parties' absence): e.g. *Cutte* v. *Cheyne* (1504) ibid., fo. 242v (the plaintiff 'ponit loco suo W. Heydon jun., he to call upon Mr Broke of Greyse Inne').

[18] DL 1 (bills and pleadings), DL 3 (depositions). The act books (DL 5) begin in 1478, but at first contain mainly administrative memoranda.

[19] e.g. Mich. 22 Edw. IV, fo. 60, pl. 17 (case put in the Exchequer Chamber by the attorney of the duchy); *Case of the Duchy of Lancaster* (1559–62) 109 Selden Soc. 30–1; Dyer 209b; Plowd. 212v; BL MS. Add. 24845, fo. 36v. Both cases raised the question whether the prerogative extended to grants and leases made by the king as duke rather than as king.

[20] See the account of its business when More was chancellor of the duchy (1525–9) in Guy, *Public Career of More*, 27–9. Note also *Anon.* (1514/15) Spelman 158 (a case of riot argued in the Duchy Chamber by two serjeants).   [21] Co. Inst. iv. 206.

[22] *Re Bidlowe* (1535) Hil. 26 Hen. VIII, fo. 9, pl. 3 (Fitzherbert J. present).

THE COURT OF GENERAL SURVEYORS

A similar system of local receivers for non-duchy revenue was established in the fifteenth century, and since part of the royal policy was to circumvent the Exchequer they were made accountable to the King's Chamber and to groups of councillors known as general surveyors.[23] The surveyors acted in concert, and the board of surveyors has been called a court of audit;[24] but it was not a court of law, and the status of the accounts was thrown into doubt by the death of Henry VII. The new king placed the supervision of the receivers' accounts on a more regular footing in 1511, when he appointed Sir Robert Southwell and a baron of the Exchequer (Bartholomew Westby), by commission under the privy seal, as general surveyors and improvers (*supervisores et appruatores*) of Crown lands.[25] The commission was given a statutory foundation later in the year, and made subject to the Exchequer; the statutory powers of 1511 were later continued by a series of increasingly elaborate temporary statutes culminating in a perpetuating statute of 1536.[26] The general surveyors at this stage still did not constitute a court of record,[27] though they had the power to summon officials to sessions in the Prince's Chamber at Westminster in relation to their accounts.[28] Suits against accountants, and any questions of law, were to be referred to the Exchequer. In 1523 it was further enacted that if any demurrer in law or plea was not accepted by the surveyors, they were to make up a record and certify it to the barons of the Exchequer, who were to decide the matter and remand the tenor of the record to the surveyors.[29] No such proceedings have been found, although the provisions of this legislation did occasion a demurrer in the Common Pleas in 1553.[30]

[23] Wolffe, *The Crown Lands*, 66–75. See also ibid. 147–61 (extracts from E315/263, a docket book of the surveyors, 1505–8).

[24] See J. A. Guy, 'A Conciliar Court of Audit at Work in the Last Months of the Reign of Henry VII' (1976) 47 *BIHR* 289–95. Cf. Richardson, *Tudor Chamber Administration*, 461–2; Wolffe, *The Crown Lands*, 147–61.

[25] Commission dated 6 Feb. 1511, pr. *SR*, iii. 72. See also Wolffe, *The Crown Lands*, 77–9. Later surveyors were appointed by patent: e.g. *LP*, ii. 3710 (Daunce, Blagge, and Westby, 1518).

[26] 3 Hen. VIII, c. 23; 7 Hen. VIII, c. 10; 6 Hen. VIII, c. 24; 7 Hen. VIII, c. 7; 14 & 15 Hen. VIII, c. 15; 27 Hen. VIII, c. 62. The 1511 statute has only 13 sections, while the 1523 statute has 38.

[27] Nevertheless, in 1515 it was enacted that writs of error were to lie from the proceedings of the surveyors to the King's Bench: 7 Hen. VIII, c. 7, s. 32; 14 & 15 Hen. VIII, c. 15, ss. 26, 38.

[28] Wolffe, *The Crown Lands*, 76–88. See also ibid. 183–97 (extracts from E315/313A, a docket book of the surveyors 1514–37).

[29] 14 & 15 Hen. VIII, c. 15, s. 10. The previous statutes did not mention this procedure, or what should be done in the case of a plea in bar.

[30] *Daunce v. Lord Paget* (1553) CP 40/1155, m. 621 (ejectment for the manor of Marlow; defendant relies on a lease by the surveyors in 1515, and the plaintiff on a lease in 1529 warranted by a bill signed by the then surveyors without any warrant signed by the king).

The general surveyors thus already possessed many of the attributes of a court before 1541, when they were reconstituted as a court of record to be known as the Court of the General Surveyors of the King's Lands.[31] The immediate model for this court was the Court of Augmentations, to be considered presently, and the wording of the legislation followed closely that of the 1536 act creating the latter. In neither case was much thought given to judicial procedure, but the court was clearly meant to proceed judicially when appropriate: it was given a seal for its process to summon parties to account, a power to make and enforce recognizances, and a clerk to register its acts and decrees. It was no longer necessary for disputes to be transmitted to the Exchequer for determination.[32] One volume of decrees survives (for 1542–6),[33] together with a minute-book for the same period, and some bills, informations, pleadings, and depositions.[34] The decree books contain enrolled deeds, summonses to pay debts or show title, and plaints by individual accountants (for instance, about rent or disputed offices). In 1547, the court was amalgamated with the Court of Augmentations.[35]

THE COURT OF THE FIRST FRUITS AND TENTH

Following the break with the papacy, Parliament in 1534 assigned to the king the first fruits of every spiritual promotion and a yearly tenth of the income of all livings.[36] Different procedures were established for the collection of the two new branches of revenue. The tenth was to be collected by bishops, and the collection enforced through the Exchequer, as in the case of an occasional subsidy. Commissioners were appointed to value benefices, make composition agreements for first fruits, and take bonds for payment of the compositions. These bonds were to have the force of statutes staple, and were therefore to be enforced in Chancery. The first treasurer in practice took charge of other forms of income which had previously been handled by Cromwell, including lands of attainted persons and of the suppressed religious houses before the establishment of the Court of Augmentations.[37]

[31] 33 Hen. VIII, c. 39. See also Richardson, *Tudor Chamber Administration*, 362–74. A new building was erected towards the south end of Westminster Hall in 1542 to house the Surveyors and First Fruits offices: *History of the King's Works*, ed. Colvin, iv. I. 289.

[32] This seems to be the point of s. 37, which gave all the new courts power to hear and determine suits for debts and all related suits, excepting capital offences and freehold title.

[33] E315/106; fully calendared by E. H. Rhodes, 'Calendar of Decrees of the Court of General Surveyors 34 to 38 Hen. 8' (1869) 30 *DKR* 166–96.

[34] E315/313b (minute or court book); E315/19–23, 108–33 (bills etc., mixed with similar matter from the Augmentations).   [35] See below, 228.

[36] 26 Hen. VIII, c. 3. See Richardson, *Tudor Chamber Administration*, 333–45. For the effect on a pre-1536 composition with the ordinary see *Anon.* (1536/7) Caryll 399, no. 67.

[37] Elton, *Tudor Revolution in Government*, 190–203.

Six years later, following the precedent set in creating the Court of Augmentations, this revenue was secured by the erection of a new court of record, independent of the Exchequer and Chancery, called the Court of the First Fruits and Tenth.[38] This was given a chancellor, treasurer, attorney, solicitor, and auditors, though no explicit provisions were made concerning litigation. A process book survives,[39] but little is known of the jurisdiction before its merger in the Exchequer in 1553.[40] Separate plea rolls were then kept by the remembrancer of the first fruits in the Exchequer, recording suits against incumbents in contested cases for failing to compound, for failing to pay compositions, and for failing to pay the tenth.[41]

The payment of first fruits was temporarily stopped in 1554; when the first fruits were revived by Elizabeth I, the separate court was not revived as well.[42]

THE COURT OF AUGMENTATIONS[43]

The most difficult of all the revenue problems was occasioned by the dissolution of the monasteries.[44] It was not merely that the Crown acquired a new stream of revenue. It had taken over going concerns, some of them very large, with leases and contracts still running; and the administration of the new property alone required a large financial department. The original department was established in 1536, when the small monasteries were dissolved. The legislation, doubtless planned by Cromwell, but possibly drafted by Audley or Rich, was to provide a model for three further financial courts soon afterwards.[45]

The department was to be a court of record called the Court of the Augmentations of the Revenues of the King's Crown, and was to have its own great and privy seals, a chancellor, treasurer, attorney, solicitor, auditors, receivers, and other officers.[46] It was to have within its survey not only the lands of the dissolved monasteries but also all other lands acquired by the king. The oath of the chancellor of the Augmentations—to 'minister equal justice to rich and poor'—clearly contemplated judicial functions, and the legislation provided that he should have power to award such process under the court's privy seal as was used in the Duchy Chamber in connection with the king's title to any premises within

---

[38] 32 Hen. VIII, c. 45. Tenth is here in the singular, since it was a recurrent tenth—unlike the occasional tenths granted by Parliament. But the plural is found in 7 Edw. VI, c. 2.

[39] E338/1 (1543–7).   [40] 1 Mar. I, sess. 2, c. 10.

[41] For the records see P. Carter, 'The Records of the Court of First Fruits and Tenths 1540–1554' (1994) 21 *Archives* 57–66.   [42] 2 & 3 Phil. & Mar., c. 4 (confirming a patent of 1554); 1 Eliz. I, c. 4.

[43] See W. C. Richardson, *History of the Court of Augmentations 1536–54* (1961).

[44] See also below, ch. 37.

[45] The Surveyors and First Fruits (above), and the Wards (below).

[46] 27 Hen. VIII, c. 27. A substantial new building was erected next to the Exchequer in 1537 to house the Augmentations: *History of the King's Works*, ed. Colvin, iv. II. 288–9.

the survey of the court. If an issue of fact was joined, it was to be sent to the King's Bench for trial in the same way as issues from the Chancery. Beyond that, the act was silent as to the form of judicial proceedings. The language is of supervision and government rather than of judicature.

In practice the court exercised judicial functions from the beginning,[47] and Dyer reports a case which was argued in the presence of the master of the rolls in 1539.[48] The jurisdiction was chiefly in debt, but included other personal actions relating to monastic lands.[49] The jurisdiction extended to alienated lands, provided the Crown still retained the reversion; but that it was not exclusive of the common law is evident from the frequent litigation in the Common Pleas over monastic land, in which grants by the Court of Augmentations were sometimes pleaded.[50] The court was not supposed to adjudicate upon title to land, but like other English-bill jurisdictions it seems to have done so in effect: a court which can issue writs of possession and enjoin the plaintiff from suing further at law comes as near as may be to exercising a jurisdiction over title.[51] It also permitted litigants to sue on the *quominus* principle, borrowed from the Exchequer.[52] Despite the statutory provision for issues to be sent for trial at common law, the court could try cases in the 'equitable' manner by the use of depositions,[53] and used commissions to hear and determine. The court appointed a common-law judge as assistant.[54]

The main weakness of Cromwell's elaborate scheme was its diversity. There was no need for so many courts operating in parallel, and between 1547 and 1553 there was some consolidation. In 1547, the Court of Surveyors and the Court of Augmentations were dissolved and reconstituted by letters patent of Henry VIII— confirmed by Parliament in 1553—as the Court of Augmentations and Revenues of the King's Crown.[55] Under the Edwardian statute of 1553, the officers of the

[47] Decree and order books survive from 1536 (E315/91-105). Original decrees are in E321/44-5. Bills, informations, and pleadings are in E321/1-43 (over 3,000 documents).

[48] *Parry v. Harbert* (1539) Dyer 45b (concerning the construction of a will).

[49] The jurisdiction is discussed at length, but with surprisingly little legal information, in Richardson, *Court of Augmentations*, 371-425. An informative introduction is F. A. Youings, *Dissolution of the Monasteries (1970)*, 98-100.

[50] e.g. *Willughby v. Welstede* (1542) CP 40/1112, m. 508 (trespass; defendant pleads lease of abbey land by Court of Augmentations; demurrer to reply alleging earlier grant of freehold); *Ireland v. Poyner* (1548) CP 40/1138, m. 393 (waste; count on assignment of monastic woods; demurrer to plea alleging lease from abbot and decree of Court of Augmentations); below, 714.

[51] Richardson, *Court of Augmentations*, 394-5.

[52] Richardson, *Court of Augmentations*, 400. For *quominus* in the Exchequer see above, 167.

[53] This may be what Richardson meant when he said it was a court of equity rather than of law. Youings (*Dissolution of the Monasteries*, 99-100) takes issue on this point. For the overlap with Chancery and conciliar jurisdiction, see Richardson, *Court of Augmentations*, 394-5.

[54] Mountagu CJ was appointed in 1544, and Hales J. served from 1550 to 1552: Richardson, *Court of Augmentations*, 388, 391.

[55] Patent of 1547 pr. in Elton, *Tudor Revolution*, 224-9; 7 Edw. VI, c. 2; 1 Mar. I, stat. 2, c. 10.

court were forbidden to hear causes save where the king was the sole party against the subject, a provision intended to stop private *quominus* suits.[56] By a Marian statute passed later in 1553, the queen was given power to alter, unite, or dissolve any of the statutory revenue courts, and this power was promptly exercised to unite the new Court of Augmentations and Revenues with the Exchequer,[57] the functions being placed temporarily into commission while the old offices were wound up.[58] Thereafter the Augmentations was merely a department of the Exchequer, with no separate judicial functions.

THE COURT OF WARDS AND LIVERIES

Although the Court of Wards was the last of the revenue courts to be established by statute, its administrative origins belong with the reforms of Henry VII.[59] Henry and his advisers had sought to maximize their revenue from wardships, even—as Parliament acknowledged in 1510—to the extent of procuring false inquisitions *post mortem*.[60] In order to implement this policy it became necessary to appoint officials to manage the revenue. As a limited experiment, in 1499, the bishop of Carlisle was appointed surveyor of the wards and marriages in Yorkshire, Cumberland, and Westmorland; and then in 1503 Sir John Hussey was appointed surveyor (or master) of the wards throughout England, with a receiver-general and a network of receivers in each county. From 1529 there was also a surveyor of the liveries.[61] The funds from wardships and liveries were at the same time diverted from the Exchequer into the Chamber. After the appointment of a master of the wards, the quasi-judicial business of the surveyors increased, and the Venetian ambassador spoke of a 'court' of wards as early as 1519.[62] From 1528 there were regular judicial sittings, and the office assumed most of the powers of the

---

[56] 7 Edw. VI, c. 2, s. 4; re-enacted in 1 Mar. I, stat. 2, c. 10, s. 3.

[57] 1 Mar. I, stat. 2, c. 10; patents of 23 and 24 Jan. 1554 (enrolled on the Close Rolls) extr. in Elton, *The Tudor Constitution*, 144–7. Dyer CJ pointed out in 1562 that the patent for dissolving the court and then the next day uniting it with the Exchequer was 'quasi absurdum et impossibile': Dyer 216a.

[58] *CPR 1553–4*, p. 300 (17 Oct. 1553).

[59] What follows is based largely upon Bell, *Court of Wards and Liveries*. See also Richardson, *Tudor Chamber Administration*, 282–304, 345–61.

[60] 1 Hen. VIII, c. 8 and c. 12. The nature of the abuses is hinted at in c. 8, which required a verdict of twelve substantial jurors for any 'office' (i.e. inquisition *post mortem*), that the escheator should sit in an open place and permit anyone to give evidence, and that the Chancery should receive and file adverse inquisitions.

[61] For the office of the liveries see Richardson, *Tudor Chamber Administration*, 296–304. In 1550 there was a dispute between John Hynde JCP (appointed by Hen. VIII) and Robert Keilwey (appointed by Edw. VI), and the fee was divided between them: *APC*, ii. 386. The 'liveries' here referred to were the liveries of possession of land to the heirs of tenants in chief.

[62] Bell, *Court of Wards and Liveries*, 10.

later statutory court.[63] The office acquired an attorney to handle the legal proceedings,[64] and a clerk, but the administration was confused by the overlap with
the work of the Chancery and Exchequer.

In the later 1530s the revenue from wardships and liveries rose dramatically, as
a result both of the Statute of Uses 1536[65] and of the practice of the Court of
Augmentations when granting freeholds in former monastic land to convert
tenures to knight-service, which rendered all such land potentially subject to
wardship.[66] This was doubtless the occasion for the legislation of 1540 which
placed the court on a statutory footing, once again following the successful model
of the Court of Augmentations.[67]

The new court of 1540 was to be called the Court of the King's Wards. It was to
have the same process against accountants as the Duchy, with power to summon
wards and former wards to answer for instrusions. The Exchequer was no longer
to meddle with matters within the survey of the new court. The staff of the new
court was much as it had been before the statute. The master of the wards was to
be its president, with the standard oath of office to administer justice equally to
rich and poor; the other principal members (or 'council') were the receiver-
general, the attorney-general of the wards, and the auditors. The following year, by
another statute, the office of the liveries was united to the court, and its name
changed to the King's Court of his Wards and Liveries. The surveyor of the liveries
was thereupon made the second officer of the court, with a judicial oath of office
like that of the master.[68] The surveyor and the attorney were always distinguished
lawyers.[69] Some pleadings and decrees survive from the first twenty years of the
statutory tribunal,[70] though the decree books have been lost.[71]

The Court of Wards was extremely successful in its first twenty years, increasing its revenue from £4,434 in 1542 to £20,290 in 1559.[72] It was to be the longest

[63] Richardson, *Tudor Chamber Administration*, 286; Bell, *Court of Wards and Liveries*, 11-12. There is
a list of pleadings in this period (IND 10218). The appearance books from 1535 to 1541 survive in Bodl.
Lib. MSS. A.150, A.396.

[64] Bell, *Court of Wards and Liveries*, 12, lists the first attorneys as Henry See (of Lincoln's Inn) and
William Portman (of the Middle Temple).

[65] 27 Hen. VIII, c. 10; below, 672.   [66] Bell, *Court of Wards and Liveries*, 14.

[67] 32 Hen. VIII, c. 46.   [68] 33 Hen. VIII, c. 22.

[69] The surveyors in our period were John Hynde, serjeant at law (JCP 1545), 1540-7; Robert Keilwey,
bencher of the Inner Temple, 1547-81. The attorneys were Thomas Polsted, barrister of the Inner
Temple, 1540-1; John Sewster, bencher of the Middle Temple, 1541-6; Richard Goodrich, ancient of
Gray's Inn, 1546-7; Nicholas Bacon, bencher of Gray's Inn, 1547-61.

[70] WARD 3 contains depositions from then onwards. WARD 15 has some pleadings temp. Hen. VIII.
WARD 13 has pleadings from Edw. VI onwards.

[71] WARD 1 contains some original decrees temp. Hen. VIII, and WARD 9/103 has some decrees
temp. Mar. I, though the surviving decree books do not begin until the 1570s. There was at least one
earlier volume, from which extracts were made by John Hare: *CELMC*, 9-10.

[72] Bell, *Court of Wards and Liveries*, 47-8.

lived of the new statutory courts, and it was certainly the most important in legal terms. Already before the reign of Elizabeth I it had become the practice to consult the common-law judges in cases of difficulty,[73] and several cases were reported.[74] Moreover, decrees could be made with recorded reasons.[75] However, the legal history of the court remains to be written.[76]

[73] See e.g. *Re Townsend* (1554) Plowd. 111 (Portman and Saunders JJ); *Jane Tyrrel's Case* (1557) Dyer 155a (tr. 'all the judges of the Common Bench and Saunders CJ'); below, 685; *Puttenham* v. *Duncombe* (1558) Dyer 157b (tr. 'all the justices of either bench'); *Randal's Case* (1558) Dyer 158b (tr. 'all the counsellors of the court and the judges thought...'); *Lord Powis's Case* (1559) Dyer 170a (tr. 'the resolution was by the judges...'); 109 Selden Soc., p. lxxxvii.

[74] The first case reported by Dyer is *Whorwood* v. *Lord Lisle* (1546) Dyer 61b.

[75] e.g. *Re Townsend* (1554) Plowd. 111 at 115.

[76] For some observations on its judicial work in a later period see Bell, *Court of Wards and Liveries*, 87–111; Baker, 'The Court of Wards and Liveries' (temp. Dyer CJ), 109 Selden Soc., pp. lxxxvi–lxxxviii.

13

Ecclesiastical Courts

THE complex legal system of the Church will be the subject of a more detailed description in another volume,[1] but it needs to be noticed here both because of the pervasiveness of the jurisdiction and because of the changing relationship between the spiritual and temporal courts in the early Tudor period.[2]

By far the larger and more important of the two English provinces was that of Canterbury,[3] which had three superior courts, one for appeals, one for probate causes, and the third for audience causes. The appellate court of Canterbury was the Court of Arches, which sat in London, though very few of its records have survived and what is known of its working has to be pieced together from occasional references, from *praemunire* cases in the King's Bench rolls, and from documents copied into precedent books. The Prerogative Court of Canterbury exercised a jurisdiction over the probate of wills and administration of estates of those who left goods worth £5 in more than one diocese.[4] The archbishop also had a provincial Audience Court, and a stray volume of its *acta* survives from 1521–3.[5] At that time all three courts had the same judge, the dean of Arches.[6] York likewise had three provincial courts with similar functions: the Chancery Court for appeals, the Exchequer Court for probate, and a Court of Audience.[7] In each diocese, including the dioceses of Canterbury and York, there was a consistory court presided over by the bishop's official principal,[8] and very often an audience

---

[1] By R. H. Helmholz (vol. i in the series). The present volume was written before vol. i was available.

[2] The following account of the courts relies heavily on C. Donahue (ed.), *The Records of the Medieval Ecclesiastical Courts. Part II: England* (CSC 7, 1994); R. Houlbrooke, 'The Decline of Ecclesiastical Jurisdiction under the Tudors' in *Continuity and Change*, ed. R. O'Day and F. Heal (1976), 239–57; *Church Courts and People during the English Reformation 1520–70* (1979).

[3] Donahue, *Records*, 83–9.

[4] C. Kitching, 'The Prerogative Court of Canterbury from Warham to Whitgift' in *Continuity and Change*, ed. O'Day and Heal, 191–214. For prohibition to the master of the Prerogative Court see *Brandon v. Powes* (1554) KB 27/1172, m. 33.

[5] At Peterborough: Donahue, *Records*, 92. For later proceedings before the same auditor of causes (John Cocks LL D) see 102 Selden Soc. 68. There is a reference to proceedings before 'Master T. Peckinham' (probably William Pykenham DCL), auditor of causes in the Court of Audience, in *Sonde v. Pekham* (1484) Mich. 2 Ric. III, fo. 22, pl. 51; cf. KB 27/892, m. 54 (not named in record).

[6] John Cocks LL D: last note; Kitching, 'The Prerogative Court', 199–200.

[7] Donahue, *Records*, 109–11; C. I. A. Ritchie, *The Ecclesiastical Courts of York* (1956).

[8] The titles varied: in *Rawlyn v. Fowye* (1508) KB 27/988, m. 61d, Thomas Coke LL B is described as president of the bishop of Exeter's consistory court and dean.

court presided over by the bishop's chancellor, who might well be the same person. Each archdeaconry had a court, usually presided over by the bishop's legally trained commissary rather than the archdeacon himself. There were also peculiars and exempt monastic jurisdictions.[9] In London there was in addition a busy Commissary Court, which sat several days a week in St Paul's Cathedral, with disciplinary and probate jurisdiction in the city of London and the deaneries of Middlesex and Barking. This court was distinct from, though its jurisdiction over-lapped with, the archdeaconry courts of London and Middlesex.[10] Thirteen London parishes were peculiars subject to the archbishop of Canterbury rather than the bishop of London, and cases from them were heard before the dean of the peculiars.

The bishops' courts heard civil suits 'at the instance' of a party, chiefly concerning the law of marriage and succession to personal property, and criminal suits 'ex officio judicis', such as accusations of sexual impropriety, breaking sabbaths and fasts,[11] gluttony and drunkenness, quarrelling, causing a disturbance in a church or churchyard, striking a cleric, or non-residence by a beneficed cleric.[12] The line between 'civil' and 'criminal' was not precise, because the instance jurisdiction extended to wrongs such as defamation and breach of faith,[13] where the suit was promoted by the individual who had been wronged but the object was punishment rather than civil redress. A flexible range of punishments included offering a candle inscribed with the penitent's offence,[14] fasting,[15] saying paternosters and hail-maries,[16] doing penance in a white shirt and holding a candle,[17] imprisonment,[18] temporary suspension from the Church, or ultimately a sentence of excommunication pronounced with bell, book, and burning candle.[19] Heresy was punishable with death by burning, but the sentence could only be carried out by the temporal authorities on receipt of a writ *de haeretico*

[9] e.g. in Sussex there were no less than nine different ecclesiastical jurisdictions: S. Lander, 'Church Courts and the Reformation in the Diocese of Chichester 1500–58' in *Continuity and Change*, ed. O'Day and Heal, at 216–17.

[10] For the London courts see R. Wunderli, *London Church Courts and Society on the Eve of the Reformation* (1981).

[11] B. L. Woodcock, *Medieval Ecclesiastical Courts in the Diocese of Canterbury* (1952), 81, mentions the cases of Luke Pancake, cited in 1520 for shaving his own beard on a Sunday, and of one Robertson, cited in 1528 for eating bread and butter on a Friday.

[12] The range of business is well illustrated by M. Bowker (ed.), *An Episcopal Court Book for the Diocese of Lincoln 1514–1520* (61 Lincoln Record Soc.; 1967).

[13] These could also be prosecuted *ex officio*. Houlbrooke, *Church Courts*, 38, says most cases could be commenced either way.   [14] Bowker, *Court Book of Lincoln*, 32.

[15] ibid. 54, 136, 138.   [16] ibid. 54, 133.

[17] *Myxbery v. Parker* (1518) KB 27/1029 m. 30 (dispute over oblations).

[18] See 1 Hen. VII, c. 4 (bishops' courts empowered to imprison clerks for 'fleshly incontinency' without being liable to an action for false imprisonment).

[19] *Middelmore v. Abbot of Bordsley* (1513) KB 27/1009 m. 28 (mentioned in action of *praemunire*).

comburendo.[20] The episcopal courts also heard disputes as to tithes and church repairs, and tried issues sent from the common-law courts, the commonest of which was bastardy.[21] Disciplinary criminal jurisdiction, and sometimes probate jurisdiction, was shared with the courts of archdeacons and their officials,[22] and with the courts of bishops' commissaries for certain archdeaconries or for peculiars which were exempt from archidiaconal jurisdiction. The balance of jurisdiction between these lesser courts and the two kinds of episcopal court varied in practice from one diocese to another.[23]

The Court of Arches was the professional focus for the practising 'doctors of the Arches', also known as the 'advocates of the court of Canterbury'.[24] By the fifteenth century these advocates formed a distinct body regulated by the court, and seem in practice to have been holders of a doctorate in law from Oxford or Cambridge, though this was not legally necessary. Before 1500 they had established a society in London, soon afterwards known as Doctors' Commons, which during our period occupied a home in Paternoster Row, near St Paul's.[25] Doctors' Commons was a private society serving the convenience of its members. Membership was not the equivalent of a licence to practise: some members were not practitioners, and some practitioners were not members. But it had a public aspect, because the doctors, like the serjeants, engaged in legal discussion at their common table.[26] Little is known of the advocates at York, except that they do not seem to have kept commons or to have been invariably doctors of law. Corresponding to the attorneys of the secular courts were the proctors,[27] some of whom practised as notaries public,[28] or even as

---

[20] For precedents see William Porter's precedent book (*c*.1520) C193/142, ff. 14v–15; FNB 269C. In 1533 the chancellor of Worcester was fined for exhuming and burning the body of William Tracy, gentleman, for supposed heresy in his last will: *Hall's Chronicle*, 796–7.

[21] For bastardy issues in villeinage cases see below, 605. An example of 'Never joined in lawful matrimony' is *Tuchet v. Lord Audley* (1558) CP 40/1176(1), m. 438 (marriage certified by guardian of spiritualties of bishop of Bristol, *sede vacante*).

[22] In *Cressy v. Incent* (1516) KB 27/1019, m. 36, the defendant pleaded a prescriptive right by the *lex canonica et ecclesiastica* for the official of the archdeacon of St Albans to cite parties before him.

[23] Donahue, *Records*, 23–5.

[24] There were at least nine 'advocates of the court of Canterbury' buried in the Greyfriars, London, including from our period John Charnock (d. 1485) and James Hulton (d. 1490): John Stow's notes, BL MS. Harley 544, ff. 50v–55v.

[25] G. D. Squibb, *Doctors' Commons* (1977), 1–22. In 1496 the proctors of Cambridge University paid for a dinner 'apud Pater Noster Row cum doctoribus de arcubus': ibid. 6. The doctors left the Paternoster Row premises in 1568; the house was destroyed in the Great Fire.

[26] See *Bulkeley v. Thomas* (1554) Plowd. 118 at 126 (question propounded to the doctors of the Arches at their table).

[27] Like attorneys, proctors took a term fee of 3s. 4d. as against the advocates' 6s. 8d.: Kitching, 'The Prerogative Court', 210, 214.

[28] e.g. C1/239/21 (John Dunnyng, notary and general proctor of the Court of Arches, 1501); CP 40/972, m. 422 (William Goldsmyth, 'notarius puplicus curieque Cantuariensis procuratorum generalium unus', 1505); next note. A formulary compiled by Nicholas Collys (*c*.1480–1520), notary public and proctor of Canterbury, is in Corpus Christi College, Cambridge, MS. 170.

common-law attorneys.[29] In 1558 a litigant at York sought the counsel of several civilians including Reynold Beesley LL B, who was also an attorney of the Common Pleas, clerk of the county court, vice-admiral in the northern parts, and recorder of Scarborough;[30] but this was an unusual case of pluralism. Notaries were the ecclesiastical counterparts of scriveners, their primary work being to prepare and authenticate documents.[31] Their admission and control belonged ultimately to the pope, by whom it was usually delegated to bishops;[32] in 1533 the authority was transferred by statute to the archbishop of Canterbury, who exercised it through the master of the Faculties.[33] There was also a body of registrars and 'scribes' (scribae)—some of them serving dioceses, and some serving individual archdeaconries[34]—who were typically laymen.[35] These offices were in the nature of freehold, and could apparently be leased to deputies.[36] The judges of the various courts, known as officials and commissaries, were usually chosen from the ranks of the advocates; most, but not all, were—until 1545[37]—ordained.[38]

[29] e.g. Robert Mareys of Thavies Inn, attorney of the Common Pleas, and proctor of the Arches: CP 40/942, m. 408 (attorney in 1497); CP 40/951, m. 443 (notary and proctor in 1500); CP 40/977, m. 529d (sued by Thavies Inn, 1506).

[30] Wyllson v. Tompson (1558) CP 40/1174, m. 1029; HPHC 1509–58, i. 425. For Beesley see below, 438 n.9. The leading counsel at the conference was Richard Farley LL D (Cantab.).

[31] See N. L. Ramsay, 'Scriveners and Notaries as Intermediaries in Later Medieval England' in Enterprise and Individuals in Fifteenth-Century England, ed. J. I. Kermode (1991), 118–31. Notaries often practised as scriveners as well.

[32] The title 'notarius papalis' is found in 1507: CP 40/982, m. 512 (William Crawme, public notary of Northampton). The Holy Roman Emperor also claimed a power of appointment, and an imperial notary is found in England as late as 1495: Ramsay, 'Scriveners and Notaries', 124.

[33] 25 Hen. VIII, c. 21; W. Hooper, 'The Court of Faculties' (1910) 25 EHR 670–86.

[34] e.g. Thomas Elyot of Exeter, who claimed the addition 'esquire' as well as 'gentleman', was a notary public and registrar of the archdeaconry of Exeter in 1495: C67/55, m. 8 (pardon roll). Alexander Mather of Norwich, notary, was joint registrar of the archdeaconry of Suffolk in the mid-1540s: C1/1146/14. See also Cantrell v. Coraunt (1542) CP 40/1115, m. 434 (dispute between two 'gentlemen', in an action on the case, for the office of registrar of the archdeaconry of Norwich, which the plaintiff claims by grant from the bishop in 1528); Taylor v. Marshall (1556) CP 40/1168, m. 714 (assize for office of registrar to archdeaconry of Lincoln).

[35] There was a monument in the Greyfriars, London, to Nicholas Parker (d. 1484), registrar and keeper of the records of the court of Canterbury, and his two wives: BL MS. Harley 544, fo. 54. Henry Trewonwall, registrar of Canterbury before 1507, had a son John (probably the eminent civilian Sir John Tregonwell): CP 40/980, m. 406. Anthony Huse (d. 1560), registrar of Canterbury, was an 'esquire': J. Stow, Survey of London, ed. J. Strype (1720), I. iii. 176 (monumental inscription in St Martin's Ludgate). Thomas Argall (d. 1563), registrar of Canterbury in 1532, was 'of London, gentleman' and also registrar of the First Fruits: CP 40/1074, m. 316; Kitching, 'The Prerogative Court', 202. A Richard Watkyns, gentleman, was registrar to the bishop of Llandaff in the 1540s: C1/1123/83.

[36] See George v. Potkyn (1501) CP 40/957, mm. 313, 319; Potkyn v. George (1501) C1/244/88 (registrarship of Norwich consistory court leased to a notary).

[37] 37 Hen. VIII, c. 17, which recited that provincial legislation had prohibited lay or married men from exercising ecclesiastical jurisdiction.

[38] In 1500 John Walter, 'gentleman', as chancellor of Pembroke heard a complaint of witchcraft (an attempt to destroy John Morgan, bishop of St David's by hiring a woman 'practized in wychecraft' and using wax images): Bishop of St David's v. Mayor and Sheriffs of Bristol (1500) C1/267/41.

RELATIONSHIP WITH THE COMMON-LAW COURTS

In his Gray's Inn reading of 1514, John Hales said that the temporal and spiritual jurisdictions were like two swords, each of which should give assistance to the other.[39] He was alluding to a remark of Thomas à Becket, who had been martyred for defending the legal privileges of the Church in England and was by Hales's time the most popular of English saints. New serjeants at law created in Henry VIII's reign processed to the London shrine of St Thomas in Cheapside to perform their devotions, and in Gray's Inn chapel there was (until 1539) a portrait 'gloriously painted' of the same saint.[40] In the same vein, Shelley J. declared in 1533 that 'the temporal law and the spiritual law concur, and the one is not opposed to the other, but each of them helps the other'.[41]

Yet it must have been apparent even at the beginning of the sixteenth century that the peace between the two jurisdictions was nearing crisis. Popular dislike of the Church courts had arisen from extortion by officials, particularly in connection with the probate of wills,[42] from the meddlesome prying into private lives which supported prosecutions for sin, and from the uncertainty of litigation in courts which had a seemingly endless tier of appeals leading eventually to Rome.[43] The spiritual jurisdictions had even fallen out among themselves over the profits of probate, and in 1510–13 there had been a wasteful contest at Rome over the extent of the Canterbury prerogative jurisdiction.[44] The common-law courts had also begun to exercise a vigilant control over the worldly exercise of spiritual power. Aid might be refused to the spiritual arm in arresting excommunicates or executing heretics if the proceedings were not legally justifiable, or if there was undue interference by the pope, who was not an officer to whom the court could write.[45] If the king's jurisdiction overlapped the spiritual sphere, this could be justified by immemorial usage, for—as a doctor of law once told Bryan CJ—the kingly person was united with the priesthood.[46] The uncertainties of litigation

---

[39] GI MS. 25, fo. 292. Cf. 24 Hen. VIII, c. 12, preamble. The ultimate source of the metaphor seems to be Luke 22: 38.

[40] Baker, *Serjeants at Law*, 101, 274; W. Dugdale, *Origines Juridiciales* (3rd edn, 1680), 284.

[41] *Carvanell* v. *Mower* (1533) 121 Selden Soc. 425 at 428.

[42] e.g. Sir Henry Guldeford complained in Parliament in 1529 that Wolsey had forced him to pay £1,000 for the probate of Sir William Compton's will: *Hall's Chronicle*, 765.

[43] See Starkey, *Dialogue*, ed. Mayer, 83, 132–3. For a testamentary case taken to Rome by both parties and lasting sixteen years, see below, 240 n. 66.

[44] J. B. Sheppard (ed.), *Literae Cantuarienses* (RS, 1889), iii. 416–40; M. J. Kelly, 'Canterbury Jurisdiction and Influence during the Episcopate of William Warham 1503–32', Ph.D. diss. (Cambridge, 1963).

[45] 94 Selden Soc. 64–5. See also *Dean of Windsor's Case* (1506) Hil. 21 Hen. VII, fo. 6, pl. 5.

[46] *Warner* v. *Hudson* (1495) Hil. 10 Hen. VII, fo. 18, pl. 17, per Bryan CJ (tr. 'a wise doctor of law once said to [me] that priests and clerks may be impleaded at common law well enough by reason of usage, for he said *quod rex est persona mixta*, that is, *persona unita cum sacerdotibus* of Holy Church, in which case the king may maintain his jurisdiction by prescription').

in the Church courts were well illustrated at the beginning of our period by the lengthy testamentary dispute involving Reynold Sonde (d. 1491), chief clerk of the King's Bench, in which two groups of papal delegates reached conflicting decisions and the King's Bench had to try to find a solution.[47] In the course of the dispute, John Vavasour, king's serjeant, argued that a decision by papal delegates 'shall not prejudice anyone at common law'.[48] Huse CJ remarked diplomatically at a later stage of the case that he would not meddle with the authority of the bishop of Rome, but pointed out the procedural difficulty that the court could not write to him or join him as a party in *quare impedit*. In 1486, however, when Dr Alcock C. had asked the judges in the Parliament Chamber about the effect of a papal threat of excommunication, the same chief justice recollected that the pope's word had not always been taken as law in England:[49]

in the time of Edward I the pope sent letters to the said king that he should make peace with Scotland, which was held of him, and that he should submit the matter to him; and the king by advice of his council wrote to the pope that there was no one above him in the temporalty but that he was immediate to God...And the bishop of London[50] said that in the time of Henry VI, when the pope sent letters which were in derogation of the king, and the [lords] spiritual durst not discuss them, he saw Humphrey duke of Gloucester take the letters and cast them in the fire, and they were burned.

It thus seems that the judges were not alone in being wary of papal intrusion in temporal matters; and 'temporal' matters, by the custom of England, included the patronage of benefices and the imprisonment of excommunicates. What was true of the pope was also true of the English episcopacy at large. For, according to Thomas Kebell, in his Inner Temple reading of 1485, there was no synodical power to override English law: 'if all the prelates were to make a provincial constitution it would be void, for they cannot change the law of the land'.[51] Thus, at the very beginning of Henry VII's reign, the lines were being drawn for the legal battle to come.

The courts of common law accepted that the spiritual courts had an exclusive jurisdiction in certain areas, and this had indeed been confirmed by medieval legislation. Issues of marriage and bastardy were regularly referred to the ecclesiastical courts for determination, and their certificates were conclusive.[52] On the

---

[47] *Sonde* v. *Pekham* (1484–5) Mich. 2 Ric. III, fo. 4, pl. 8 (trespass); fo. 22, pl. 51; KB 27/892, m. 55 (verdict for plaintiff); (1488–9) Trin. 4 Hen. VII, fo. 13, pl. 12; KB 27/909, m. 76 (debt; judgment for plaintiff on demurrer). Cf. (1484) Mich. 2 Ric. III, fo. 17, pl. 45; KB 27/892, m. 54 (*praemunire*); ibid., m. 55d (detinue; entry vacated). The cases arose from the will of Robert Strongbon.

[48] Mich. 2 Ric. III, fo. 22, pl. 51 (tr. 'such a judgment of the court of Rome shall not prejudice anyone at common law, for if an excommunication is certified here that such and such a person is excommunicated in the court of Rome, or for something which belongs to the court of Rome, this shall be no disablement here').   [49] *Case of the Florentine Merchants* (1486) Hil. 1 Hen. VII, fo. 10, pl. 10 (tr.).

[50] Thomas Kempe, bishop of London 1450–89.   [51] BL MS. Hargrave 87, fo. 304v (tr.).

[52] For marriage and bigamy see Port 128 and below, 533–4; for bastardy see below, 605.

other hand, questions of canon law could intrude into common-law proceedings,[53] especially in the testamentary sphere, and principles of ecclesiastical law could even be pleaded.[54] Some elementary principles were well enough known to be noticed by the judges; but if necessary the royal judges would take direct advice from doctors of law to inform themselves.[55] The main jurisdictional disputes arose in areas where there seemed to be an overlap of jurisdiction between the spiritual and the lay courts. These were not, by and large, disputes between the Church and the Crown, though after the death of Henry VII it was alleged that the late king's ministers had used threats of *praemunire* as one of their many devices for extorting money.[56] Most of the suits were brought by private litigants anxious either to stop proceedings against them or to recover compensation. The procedures used for challenging ecclesiastical jurisdiction were not new, and in most of the cases no final outcome is recorded in the plea rolls. Nevertheless, it is evident from the sheer number of such cases in the early Tudor period that the King's Bench was perceived as being favourably inclined, in the forty years prior to the break with Roman jurisdiction, towards requests for control or restraint of the ecclesiastical courts.

The principal means of control and attack were the writ of prohibition and actions of *praemunire* founded either on the Statute of Praemunire 1364 or (more usually) on the Statute of Winchester 1393. Prohibitions remain something of a mystery in the decades before the Reformation, since few were entered on the plea rolls of the benches,[57] or in the records of the ecclesiastical courts

---

[53] See St German, *Doctor and Student*, ed. Plucknett and Barton, 41–5.

[54] e.g. *Shelley* v. *Penyngton* (1492) KB 27/925, m. 87d; 1 Caryll 98 at 101 (*jus canonicum* as to spousals); *Prior of Folkestone* v. *Cleybroke* (1494) CP 40/926, m. 464; 1 Caryll 270 at 271 (*lex ecclesiastica* as to citation, deprivation, and tuitory appeals); *Clyff* v. *Morgan* (1512) CP 40/999, m. 389 (*lex ecclesiastica* as to compensation of executors, pleaded by protestation); *Cressy* v. *Incent* (1516) KB 27/1019, m. 36; below, 240 n. 66 (*lex canonica et ecclesiastica* as to citation and assignment of terms).

[55] e.g. *Purre* v. *Grene* (1491) CP 40/911, m. 378; Hil. 6 Hen. VII, fo. 14, pl. 2; Pas. 10 Hen. VII, fo. 19, pl. 7; Mich. 11 Hen. VII, fo. 8, pl. 30; Trin. 11 Hen. VII, fo. 26, pl. 10 (the later reports probably misdated). The question here concerned the procedure for uniting two spiritual foundations (Wanborough chapel and Magdalen College, Oxford), and Bryan CJ reported that he had changed his mind after speaking with the doctors of law. Note also *Bohun* v. *Broughton* (1455) Mich. 34 Hen. VI, fo. 11, pl. 22 (two doctors present at the bar).

[56] *Hare* v. *Hobart* (1514) C1/319/48; C1/321/28 (official of the bishop of Norwich complains that an information of *praemunire* was laid before James Hobart as recorder of Norwich; Hobart caused Erneley A.-G. to prefer an information in the King's Bench; then Lucas S.-G. and Empson compelled Dr Hare to appear in the Duchy Chamber and to defend the King's Bench suit for two years, saying that he would be discharged if he paid the king 100 marks); a commission issued to the prior of Norwich, John Spelman, and others, to examine witnesses, but the outcome is unknown. See also R. L. Storey, *Diocesan Administration in 15th Century England* (1972), 30–2; Houlbrooke, 'The Decline of Ecclesiastical Jurisdiction', 240–1.

[57] There is a marked increase in the 1540s. Occasionally a prohibition was issued on the Crown side of the King's Bench: e.g. *Awbrey's Case* (1515) KB 29/147, m. 36d (below, 243 n. 91). But it is likely that most prohibitions before the 1540s issued from the Chancery.

themselves,[58] and it is difficult to assess their practical impact. They were hindered by procedural obstacles. It had become the general practice to frame libels in ecclesiastical courts so as not to disclose the cause of action in detail,[59] which cast the burden onto the applicant to surmise the true cause, the surmise being then issuable through the process of 'consultation'.[60] On the other hand, actions of *praemunire* were brought in considerable numbers in the King's Bench between the 1490s and the early 1530s, the defendants being not only the oppos-ing parties but sometimes the judges, notaries, and scriveners as well. Some con-sidered such actions to be more restricted in scope than prohibition,[61] but this is hardly borne out by the records. Actions on the statute had the advantage of being *qui tam* actions which could not be stopped by the purchase of a pardon,[62] and they were wide-ranging in scope. According to Shelley J., 'no statute is more penal than the *praemunire*, and yet no statute has been more largely construed'.[63] Challenges to spiritual jurisdiction could also be made by means of writs of false imprisonment,[64] trespass to chattels,[65] actions to enforce statutes,[66] or even actions on the case.[67] The wave of activity resulted in an angry reaction from some of the bishops, especially the bishop of Norwich, James Goldwell, a canon-ist who had been incensed by Sir James Hobart's interfering activities as recorder of Norwich.[68] Continuing high feelings lay behind the outrageous case of

[58] R. H. Helmholz, *Canon Law and the Law of England* (1987), 81–2, 84. According to Woodcock, *Medieval Ecclesiastical Courts*, 108, there are no cases in the Canterbury diocesan act books between 1454 and 1535. Houlbrooke, 'The Decline of Ecclesiastical Jurisdiction', 254, says none were recorded by the consistory court of Norwich between 1519 and 1551.

[59] As to this, see Helmholz, *Canon Law and the Law of England*, 73.

[60] *Abbot of St Albans' Case* (1482) Trin. 22 Edw. IV, fo. 20, pl. 47; *Anon.* (1499) Port 17–18; *Anon.* (1557/8) BL MS. Hargrave 4, fo. 127. Cf. the similar problem in Admiralty: above, 214.

[61] *Anon.* (1532/3) Brooke Abr., *Premunire*, pl. 16.

[62] The effect of a pardon was raised inconclusively by demurrer in *Amys* v. *Peele* (1519–33) KB 27/1032, m. 64 (advisement for fourteen years); but apparently decided in *Prior of Sheen* v. *Swillington* (1532) KB 27/1082, m. 38; Spelman 191.

[63] *Marmyon* v. *Baldwyn* (1527) 120 Selden Soc. 61 at 63.

[64] *Warner* v. *Hudson* (1495–97) Hil. 10 Hen. VII, fo. 17, pl. 17; CP 40/934, m. 327 (judgment for plaintiff).

[65] *Playfote* v. *John Cokkys LL D, chancellor of Canterbury, and Thomas Argall, registrar* (1532) CP 40/1074, m. 316; KB 27/1089, m. 38 (error); CP 40/1079, m. 455 (costs); Dyer 32a. This was a challenge to the jurisdiction of the court of Canterbury to sequester the chattels of a deceased person whose executors refused the administration.

[66] *Cressy* v. *Incent* (1516) KB 27/1019, m. 36 (bill founded on 2 Hen. V, stat. 1, c. 3, for denying a copy of the libel; defendant official of St Albans pleads the canonical procedure for assigning terms). This was the beginning of a lengthy testamentary dispute, with appeals to Rome by both parties: see *Stepney* v. *Cressey* (1532) Spelman 187.

[67] *Knap* v. *Prior of St Bartholomew's, Smithfield* (1511) KB 27/998, m. 8d (infringement of mayor of London's jurisdiction over orphans); *Awldwyn* v. *Aleyn* (1527) KB 27/1064, m. 35 (citing plaintiff for defamation in respect of proceedings at a view of frankpledge).

[68] Houlbrooke, 'The Decline of Ecclesiastical Jurisdiction', 241–2; *Church Courts*, 9; and note *Hare* v. *Hobart* (1514), above, 239 n. 56. Houlbrooke suggested that the foundation of Doctors' Commons may have been motivated by a desire to unite in fending off the attacks.

Richard Hunne,[69] a prominent London merchant who was murdered in the bishop of London's prison in 1514 while awaiting trial for heresy.[70] The real complaint against Hunne was that he had threatened to bring a *praemunire* against the parish priest who had demanded his child's winding-sheet as a mortuary.[71] Hunne's seemingly unanswerable objection was that his baby had not, in his brief lifetime, owned the winding-sheet. It is easy to understand the popular disrespect earned by a Church hierarchy which fought such a case, and with such pertinacity, whether or not its officials murdered the complainant in the process. The incident dominated the Parliament of 1515 and had a profound effect on lay opinion for at least a generation.[72]

THE JURISDICTIONAL BOUNDARY

Actions of *praemunire* were sometimes used to challenge abuses of authority in the purely spiritual sphere, for instance in suing to Rome before all domestic remedies were exhausted,[73] or in obtaining bulls from Rome to interfere by way of provision with rights of patronage or office,[74] or with religious houses,[75] and this—so it was said—even if the bulls were not put into execution.[76] But the usual ground of complaint was that a spiritual court in England had entertained a cause of action which belonged to the common law. For instance, contract cases were said to be outside the scope of the Church courts because spiritual men had no understanding of commerce and might not know when a contract was binding.[77]

---

[69] S. F. C. Milsom, 'Richard Hunne's "Praemunire"' (1961) 76 *EHR* 80–2, repr. in *SHCL*, 145–7. For the Hunne affair see P. Vergil, *Anglica Historia*, ed. Hay (1950), 228–31; *Hall's Chronicle*, 573–80; J. Davis, 'The Authorities for the Case of Richard Hunne (1514-15)' (1915) 30 *EHR* 477–88; Pollard, *Wolsey*, 31–42; A. Ogle, *The Tragedy of the Lollards' Tower* (1949); J. A. F. Thomson, *The Later Lollards 1414–1520* (1965), 162–71; R. J. Schoeck, 'Common Law and Canon Law' in *St Thomas More: Action and Contemplation*, ed. R. S. Sylvester (1972), 23–42, 50; J. D. M. Derrett, 'The Affairs of Richard Hunne and Friar Standish'(1979) in *Complete Works of More*, ix. 213–46; Houlbrooke, *Church Courts*, 9–10. For the sequel see below, 538.

[70] The coroner's jury indicted the chancellor of London, Dr Horsey, for the murder, though he was never tried and the facts were disputed.   [71] For mortuaries see below, 243.

[72] One of the first measures of the Reformation Parliament in 1529 was to restrict mortuaries and to vindicate Hunne's position regarding children: 21 Hen. VIII, c. 6. When a mercer was shot dead in Cheapside in 1537, Londoners suspected the clergy and drew a parallel with Hunne's case: *Hall's Chronicle*, 824.   [73] *Anon.* (1526) Yorke 234, no. 398; 94 Selden Soc. 68.

[74] e.g. *Bishop of St Davids and Denby* v. *Walter* (1493-7) KB 27/928, m. 64; KB 27/930, m. 64 (archdeaconry of St Davids; defendant pleads excommunication of clerk collated by bishop; demurrer).

[75] e.g. *Prior of Bath* v. *Prior of Exeter* (1505) KB 27/974, m. 69 (bull annulling an appropriation); *Hychynson* v. *Machell* (1512) KB 27/1005, m. 109 (bull concerning land claimed by prioress); *Prior of St Bartholomew's, Smithfield,* v. *Aleyn* (1516) KB 27/1020, m. 98 (interference with keeping of hospital during vacancy in mastership); *Abbot of St Mary Graces* v. *Palmer* (1518) KB 27/1028, m. 71; extr. in Maycote, *Entries*, fo. 41 (dispensation for monk to hold benefice); *Abbess of Polesworth* v. *Rydermyster* (1522) KB 27/1043, m. 81 (bulls of acquittance).

[76] Yorke 234, no. 399 (*c.*1532), *per* Fitzherbert and Spelman JJ.

[77] John Hales's reading (Gray's Inn, 1514) GI MS. 25, fo. 292; 94 Selden Soc. 65.

There was a permissible *ex officio* jurisdiction to punish 'breach of faith' (*laesio fidei*),[78] but it was not supposed to be used for temporal purposes such as the recovery of money.[79] The objection was not confined to simple contracts[80] and debts upon bonds,[81] but could extend to monetary claims or actions of detinue against executors in connection with the administration of estates[82]—whether or not the common law provided an alternative remedy[83]—and even to money-claims founded on ecclesiastical causes such as oblations,[84] pensions and annuities,[85] and compositions for tithes.[86] A similar objection was made to suits where the prime object was to persuade the defendant to make reparation for a tort.[87] The largest single category of *praemunire* actions concerned suits for defamation in respect of temporal matters,[88] and by the 1530s the courts were willing to construe words in their worst sense for this purpose.[89] Complaints of assault in a church, or of taking church goods, could also

[78] See also R. H. Helmholz, '*Assumpsit* and *Fidei Laesio*' (1975) 91 *LQR* 406–32; repr. in *Canon Law and the Law of England*, 263–89.

[79] Prohibition would therefore lie: *Anon.* (1480) Mich. 20 Edw. IV, fo. 10, pl. 9; *Abbot of St Albans Case* (1482) Trin. 22 Edw. IV, fo. 20, pl. 47; Yorke 234, no. 400, at 235; Brooke Abr., *Prohibition*, pl. 14. However, a reader on Magna Carta in the 1530s argued that suit would lie in the spiritual court for money promised with a daughter on marriage: BL MS. Harley 4990, fo. 158.

[80] For simple contracts see Trin. 12 Hen. VII, fo. 24, pl. 2, *per* Fyneux CJ; Hil. 13 Hen. VII, fo. 16, pl. 16; *Constable* v. *Holme* (1495) KB 27/934, m. 26 (prohibition); *Pierce* v. *Richardson* (1498) KB 27/949, m. 84; *Somer* v. *Perot* (1499) KB 27/950, m. 63 (unspecified debt to churchwardens); *Pere* v. *Sad* (1501) KB 27/960, m. 77; *Gilbart* v. *Spersalt* (1503) KB 27/968, m. 72; *Gilbard* v. *Bean* (1504) KB 27/971, m. 37; *Cagell* v. *Stanley* (1505) KB 27/977, m. 23; *Stykberd* v. *England* (1520) KB 27/1036, m. 86; *Anon.* (1532) Brooke Abr., *Premunire*, pl. 16.

[81] *Mylne* v. *Barfote* (1504) KB 27/970, m. 24 (commissary of Cambridge); *Cruge* v. *Powell* (1522) KB 27/1044, m. 75 (chancellor of Oxford). These were both in university courts, and in the former the jurisdiction was defended by a special plea. Sir William Capell was later indicted for maintaining Barfote: KB 27/986, Rex m. 7d.

[82] *Sonde* v. *Pekham* (1484) Mich. 2 Ric. III, fo. 17, pl. 45; KB 27/892, m. 54 (above, 238); *Poyntz* v. *Blunt* (1503) KB 27/969, m. 63d; *Savyll* v. *Boughton* (1506) KB 27/978, m. 26; *Noreys* v. *Portas* (1510) KB 27/995, m. 27; *Anon.* (1532) Spelman 187, pl. 5 (prohibition); Brooke Abr., *Premunire*, pl. 16; *Anon.* (1533) Spelman 188, pl. 7 (similar); Brooke Abr., *Premunire*, pl. 16; Yorke 234, no. 400.

[83] St German, *Doctor and Student*, ed. Plucknett and Barton, 232–3.

[84] e.g. the dispute between the vicar of Thame and his parishioners: *Hewys* v. *Parker* (1518) KB 27/1028, m. 70 (detinue); *Myxbery* v. *Parker* (1518) KB 27/1029, m. 30 (*praemunire*); *Parker* v. *Hewes* (1518) ibid., m. 88 (account); *Parker* v. *Mixbury* (1519) KB 27/1033, m. 59 (trespass).

[85] *Hamond* v. *Somnour* (1492) KB 27/925, m. 29; *Abbot of Reading* v. *Shirwode* (1497) KB 27/942, m. 59; *Prior of Shulbred* v. *Prior of Lewes* (1501) KB 27/960, m. 71d; *Bunse* v. *Elwyn* (1511) KB 27/1000, m. 21; *Bak* v. *Wellys* (1511) ibid., m. 26d; *Maltson* v. *Huske* (1545) KB 27/1135, m. 122 (prohibition).

[86] *Anon.* (undated) Spelman 42; *Anon.* (1553) Dyer 49, §49. Cf. St German, *Doctor and Student*, ed. Plucknett and Barton, 314. For post-Reformation cases, see below, 249–51.

[87] e.g. *Bromflete* v. *Snowe* (1484) KB 27/892, m. 27 (false imprisonment); *Clerk* v. *Stevyn* (1526) KB 27/1059, m. 21; Yorke 233, no. 397 (forgery).

[88] 94 Selden Soc. 67 n. 2; below, 781. These were nearly all accusations of temporal crime. In *Reynolds* v. *Horwood* (1505) KB 27/975, m. 26, the accusation was said to be of oppression, but the defendant justified on the ground that it was an accusation of heresy. Prohibition also was available for temporal slander: *Anon.* (1482) Mich. 22 Edw. IV, fo. 29, pl. 9; *Anon.* (1498) 1 Caryll 382.

[89] See *Marsshe* v. *Bele* (1530) Spelman 187; Co. Inst. ii. 493 (false knave); cf. Spelman 238 (perhaps the same case). Marsshe counterclaimed at common law for 'false thief': KB 27/1072, m. 67d.

be claimed as belonging to the common law,[90] as could homicide in a church.[91] Assault on a cleric was acknowledged to be within the spiritual jurisdiction, but not if the cleric was wearing lay dress or if the other party pleaded self-defence or consent (for instance, to wrestling).[92] Real property was plainly within the common-law jurisdiction, and this arguably prevented suits in the spiritual courts in respect of advowsons,[93] wills of land (or uses of land) or legacies charged on land,[94] spiritual duties arising from tenure,[95] disputes over land belonging to chapels,[96] spoliation of glebe land,[97] dilapidations,[98] and leases of rectories or vicarages.[99] Tithes of timber or minerals (being deemed part of the freehold), and annuities claimed in lieu of tithes by prescription or composition (being a kind of debt), were long-standing areas of controversy;[100] yet, according to Brooke, the spiritual jurisdiction could only be questioned here by prohibition and not by *praemunire*.[101] Mortuary—the customary right claimed by some parsons to take the second-best beast or chattel of a deceased parishioner, or a sum of money instead—was likewise contentious, not merely because of Hunne's case, but because the prescriptive nature of a claim to mortuary arguably brought it within the common law;[102] nevertheless in 1529

---

[90] 94 Selden Soc. 67 n. 3–4.

[91] e.g. *Awbrey's Case* (1515) KB 29/147, m. 36d (writ to the bishop of London concerning an altercation over a pew which had resulted in the death of Gregory Lovell, esquire, in Hardington church, Middlesex; bishop returns that he was only concerned with the ownership of the pew, which belonged to the *lex ecclesiastica*).   [92] *Note* (undated, perhaps from a moot) Port 114, pl. 57.

[93] *Abbot of Malmesbury* v. *Harys* (1530) KB 27/1074, m. 22; *Bussy* v. *Marshall* (1530) KB 27/1076, m. 26; *Pygot* v. *Grene* (1530) KB 27/1077, m. 65; *Hunt* v. *Savage* (1531) KB 27/1078, m. 64. These cases were, however, connected with Wolsey's legatine authority. An earlier example is *Prior of Bridgewater* v. *Snowe* (1485) KB 27/894, m. 37 (hospital).

[94] *Noreys* v. *Portas* (1510) KB 27/995, m. 37; *Anon.* (1527) Wm Yelv. 361 at 363; *Note* (*c.*1530) Caryll (Jun.) 382, no. 25, *per* Audley (in the Inner Temple); *Wales' Case* (1530) Spelman 187; *Paschal* v. *Keterich* (1557) Dyer 151b; Benl. 60; BL MS. Hargrave 4, fo. 127. See also *Rolfe* v. *Hampden* (1542) Dyer 53b (will of land may be proved by witnesses without probate); *Anon.* (1545/6) Brooke Abr., *Testament*, pl. 20 (executors not needed for a valid will of land at common law).

[95] *Pateshale* v. *Wodyngton* (1501) KB 27/961, m. 38 (duty to render holy loaf); *Amys* v. *Peele* (1519) KB 27/1032, m. 64 (duty to find candles before image of St Anne of Chilham).

[96] *Sympson* v. *Fell* (1507) KB 27/1007, m. 32; *Fynamore* v. *Chambre* (1519) KB 27/1030, m. 20 (chantry).

[97] *Prior* v. *Callawey* (1499–1505) KB 27/953, m. 67d; KB 27/976, m. 26.

[98] *Anon.* (1522) Spelman 186, pl. 1.

[99] *Hunt* v. *Prowde* (1502) KB 27/963, m. 34; Maycote's entries, fo. 10, *Amyas* v. *Wodorove* (1504) KB 27/971, m. 67; *Dalton* v. *Hutton* (1504) KB 27/973, m. 35d; *Rawlyn* v. *Fowye* (1508) KB 27/988, m. 61d. Cf. *Wynnall* v. *Lawrans* (1498) KB 27/948, m. 34; Maycote's entries, fo. 18 (title to vicarage land); *Rede* v. *Hare* (1503) KB 27/966, m. 34d (lease of unspecified messuage and land).

[100] 94 Selden Soc. 66 n. 7; *Anon.* (1499) Port 17; St German, *Doctor and Student*, ed. Plucknett and Barton, 312–13; FNB 53E, G; *Anon.* (1539) Brooke Abr., *Prohibition*, pl. 17. See also below, 250–1.

[101] *Anon.* (1532) Brooke Abr., *Prohibition*, pl. 16. The reason given is that the nature of the action belongs to the spiritual court, but not the particular form, though this distinction is hardly borne out by the other cases cited above.

[102] St German, *Doctor and Student*, ed. Plucknett and Barton, 317–19. For the celebrated Hunne case see above, 241. Note also *Perys* v. *Grene* (1517) KB 27/1024, m. 86 (with long plea justifying the ecclesiastical jurisdiction).

Parliament appeared to acknowledge that mortuaries or corpse-presents were recoverable in the spiritual courts.[103] Attempts were also made to challenge spiritual jurisdiction over hospitals[104] and schools, though with what degree of success is uncertain.[105] Although the majority of *praemunire* cases have no recorded outcome, it is evident from the records of the Church courts that all this litigation made a noticeable impact on their business, particularly in reducing the number of actions for breach of faith.[106]

THE BREAK WITH ROME

After the murder of Richard Hunne in 1514 and the persecution of Dr Standish in 1515,[107] lay confidence in the clerical establishment and its legal system reached a low ebb.[108] In both cases the clergy were seen to be insulating themselves against secular responsibility even for murder, and it was their haughty disregard for common-law standards of justice rather than questions of speculative theology which caused a rift with some of the common lawyers. Wolsey's arrogance as papal legate (1518–29) deepened the rift and, according to Edward Hall of Gray's Inn, so infected the rest of the clergy 'that no man durst once reprove anything in them for fear to be called heretic, and then they would make him smoke or bear a faggot'.[109] Heresy prosecutions were a major bone of contention. Despite the horrific nature of the penalty for heresy, the spiritual courts did not use juries, it was not always clear what the accusation was, and little or no opportunity was given to present a defence. Much of Christopher St German's pamphlet debate with Sir Thomas More was concentrated upon the unfairness of heresy trials.[110] While More felt the need to defend the Church—right or wrong—not only in relation to heresy proceedings in general but even in the matter of Richard Hunne, a very different and more humane position was taken by other prominent lawyers such as St German, Hall, and Serjeant Caryll. By the 1530s it could be seriously argued by lawyers that the spiritual jurisdiction had become intolerable.

---

[103] 21 Hen. VIII, c. 6.

[104] *Ferrers* v. *Abbot of St Albans* (1501) KB 27/959, m. 40; reported on another point in Trin. 15 Hen. VII, fo. 9, pl. 12. Cf. *Prior of St Bartholomew's, Smithfield,* v. *Aleyn* (1516) KB 27/1020, m. 98 (complaint of papal interference with hospital).

[105] *Tatersale* v. *Incent* (1516) KB 27/1019, m. 61d (St Albans grammar school). Cf. FNB 40L.

[106] Houlbrooke, 'The Decline of Ecclesiastical Jurisdiction', 240; Helmholz, '*Assumpsit* and *Fidei Laesio*', 406–32; 'Contracts and the Canon Law', in *Towards a General Law of Contract,* ed. J. Barton (8 CSC; 1990), at 59.   [107] Above, 241; below, 538.

[108] See Pollard, *Wolsey,* 26–58; Elton, *England under the Tudors,* 102–9.

[109] *Hall's Chronicle,* 593. Se also Vergil, *Anglica Historia,* ed. Hay (1951), 256–61. Bearing a faggot was a form of penance calculated to remind the penitent of the ultimate punishment for persistence.

[110] This problem did not end in the 1530s. Hall recorded that in 1540 three learned divines were burned for heresy without any formal accusation or opportunity to present their case (*Hall's Chronicle,* 840), and an ignorant boy of 15 was burned shortly afterwards (ibid. 841).

Quite apart from the cruelty and intolerance shown to conscientious dissenters, the clergy were accused of bias in cases concerning their own privileges, especially in criminal matters, and of hypocrisy in punishing poor laymen for sexual offences while ignoring worse scandals among their own kind.[111] Their powers to make laws were not derived immediately from God, and so it was maintained that if they made laws to the detriment of the king's prerogative or abused their jurisdiction they should lose it, just as any franchise-owner lost his jurisdiction by abuse. Indeed, if the jurisdiction were transferred to the king's courts, 'we should shortly have more divines than lawyers, where now it is clean contrary'.[112]

Whatever other factors led to the final break with papal jurisdiction in 1533, there seems little doubt that the torrent of actions of *praemunire* played a part in helping to prepare the legal ground for a more ambitious jurisdictional challenge. In 1529 the attorney-general prosecuted Cardinal Wolsey, papal legate *a latere* and archbishop of York, for *praemunire* upon the Statute of Winchester for abusing his legatine jurisdiction.[113] The particular abuses relied on by the prosecution were the filling of a benefice in the patronage of the prior of Lewes, and the usurpation of a probate jurisdiction in respect of testators dying outside Wolsey's own diocese.[114] These were, it will be noted, wrongs not against laymen but against the traditional legal constitution of the Church in England. Wolsey's high-handedness had alienated not only the common lawyers, but also many of the clergy, from the remote and seemingly arbitrary Roman authority which supported it; and the role of the common law was to give legal form to their natural reaction. The King's Bench proceedings of 1529 moved the jurisdictional debate further than ever before, because Wolsey was not a subordinate ecclesiastical judge stepping out of line but a papal legate relying expressly on papal authority to act outside the usual course. They demonstrated that an authority derived directly from the pope did not itself protect an archbishop against judgment in a lay court for breaking English law. The fallen cardinal was doubtless eager to avoid a public trial in which he was unlikely to prevail, and was sentenced on his own confession. His conviction cost him not only his position but all his worldly property and—perhaps

---

[111] 'Certen Considerations why the Spirituell Jurisdiction wold be abrogatt and repelled or at the leest reformed' (c.1534) BL Cotton MS. Cleopatra F.II, fo. 242v.

[112] 'Certen Considerations', fo. 250 (sp. mod.). See also *A Treatise concerynge the Division betwene the Spiritualtie and the Temporaltie* [1530]; *A Treatyse concerninge the Power of the Clergye and the Lawes of the Realme* [1530]; *A Treatise concernynge divers of the Constitucyons Provynciall and Legatines* [1535]. Most of these have been attributed to St German.

[113] In terms he was also charged with merely accepting the legatine jurisdiction: see the helpful comments on the indictment in Ogle, *Thugedy of the Lollards' Tower*, 216–20.

[114] *Att.-Gen.* v. *Wolsey* (1529) Spelman 190; Port 57; KB 27/1073, m. 18 (pr. 102 Selden Soc. 58–61). Guy regards the charges as 'fabricated': *Thomas More* (2000), 127.

equally hurtful to him—the dissolution of his college at Oxford.[115] It also 'shook the edifice of clerical privilege to its foundations'.[116]

The disgrace of Wolsey encouraged a number of parties to commence actions of *praemunire* in respect of similar abuses of the papal legacy, and within a year there were at least seven such suits pending.[117] Then, in 1530–1, the attorney-general commenced several further prosecutions, this time against the bishop of Norwich and other bishops and clergy.[118] The effect was to enlarge the scope of *praemunire* still further, so as to include any support given to the bull for the legacy, even in respect of spiritual matters: it was held to be an 'entire' bull, and therefore any support given to it, in whatever way, incurred the penalties of the statute.[119] These proceedings directly paved the way for the 'submission of the clergy' immediately before the break with Rome.[120] The jurisdictional revolution was, of course, completed by Parliament and not by the King's Bench. Nevertheless, it is evident that the initial attack on papal authority, and the perceived excesses of ecclesiastical jurisdiction, was launched under the common law; and it is conversely significant that the stream of private *praemunire* suits virtually dried up around 1532. It may be true that Parliament would not have taken the final step in 1533 had it not been for the impasse into which the king's matrimonial litigation had fallen. Yet the story of *praemunire*, and the widespread acceptance among the clergy themselves of the initial break, shows that the jurisdictional story owes as much to law, and the common desire to be ruled by law, as to the politics of the moment, the reformation of religion, or the impatience of a strong-willed king. There was nothing new or protestant about the notion that a king was answerable directly to God, and that the Crown was not subordinate to any extra-territorial jurisdiction such as that of the pope.[121] It was a view which Wolsey himself had once supported.[122] And the king's law had long set the boundaries of the spiritual jurisdiction, a power defensible under canon law: *rex est persona unita cum sacerdotibus.*[123]

The eloquently phrased preamble to the Act for the Restraint of Appeals 1533, after observing that 'by divers sundry old authentick histories and chronicles it is manifestly declared and expressed that this realm of England is an

---

[115] For the legal reasons see *LP*, iv. III. 6579.

[116] A. G. Dickens, *The English Reformation* (2nd edn, 1989), 124.   [117] 94 Selden Soc. 69.

[118] *Att.-Gen.* v. *Nix and others* (1530) KB 27/1077, Rex m. 27 et seq.; 94 Selden Soc. 69. Nix (or Nykke) was prosecuted again in 1534, convicted on his own confession, and pardoned: Spelman 192; Port 75; KB 27/1091, Rex m. 13 (noted in 102 Selden Soc. 75–6).

[119] *Att.-Gen.* v. *Baker and others* (1531) Spelman 190; KB 27/1080, Rex mm. 16–20.

[120] 94 Selden Soc. 69–70; J. A. Guy, 'Henry VIII and the Praemunire Manoeuvres 1530–31' (1982) 97 *EHR* 481–503. See also M. J. Kelly, 'The Submission of the Clergy' (1965) 15 *TRHS* (5th ser.) 97–119.

[121] Statute of Praemunire, 16 Ric. II, c. 5. This statute, however, asserted the king's supremacy only in matters 'touching the regality of his crown'.

[122] Ullmann, 'This Realm of England is an Empire', 175 at 186–7.   [123] Above, 237 n. 46.

empire ... governed by one supreme head and king', and that legislation had been passed by many former parliaments to preserve the king's imperial jurisdiction 'from the annoyance as well of the see of Rome as from the authority of other foreign potentates', pointed out how:

divers and sundry inconveniences and dangers, not provided for plainly by the said former acts, statutes, and ordinances, have arisen and sprung by reason of appeals sued out of this realm to the see of Rome in causes testamentary, causes of matrimony and divorces, right of tithes, oblations, and obventions, not only to the great inquietation, vexation, trouble, costs, and charges, of the king's highness and many of his subjects and resiants of this his realm, but also to the great delay and let to the true and speedy determination of the said causes, for so much as the parties appealing to the said Court of Rome most commonly do the same for the delay of justice.

It was therefore enacted that causes belonging to the spiritual jurisdiction should be finally adjudged and determined in the spiritual courts within the king's jurisdiction and not elsewhere, notwithstanding any inhibition, appeal, or other impediment 'from the see of Rome or any other foreign courts or potentates of the world'.[124] The following year it was enacted that appeals from the provincial courts should lie to the king in Chancery, and would be heard by ad hoc commissioners appointed 'like as in case of appeal from the Admiral's Court'; these commissioners came to be known as the Delegates.[125] Thomas à Becket was to be solemnly removed from the calendar; far from being a martyr, he was now branded a rebel and a traitor, a stubborn champion of the pope's usurped jurisdiction and a maintainer of the enormities of the clergy.[126] Yet no change was made in the jurisdiction of the existing courts within England. *Praemunire* was not wholly retired, and Audley once told the bishops that it would 'ever hang over your heads' to prevent them encroaching upon common-law rights,[127] though in fact prohibition was to be the usual mechanism for jurisdictional control thereafter.

[124] 24 Hen. VIII, c. 12; 25 Hen. VIII, c. 19. The former statute, probably by careless drafting, applied only to the kinds of cause mentioned in the quotation; but the defect was cured by the second. For the drafting history of the former see G. R. Elton, 'The Evolution of a Reformation Statute' (1949) 64 *EHR* 174–97, repr. *Studies*, ii. 82–106; G. Nicholson, 'The Act of Appeals and the English Reformation' in *Law and Government under the Tudors*, ed. C. Cross et al. (1988), 19–30.

[125] See G. I. O. Duncan, *The High Court of Delegates* (1971).

[126] *Tudor Royal Proclamations*, i. 275–6, no. 186 (1538). Even his death was now attributed to a brawl rather than an assassination. For the virtual reinstatement of the Provisions of Clarendon in 1531 see below, 540.

[127] *Letters of Stephen Gardiner*, 392–3. It might still be used in connection with local constitutional wrangles within the Church: e.g. *Goodman* v. *Meryck* (1550) KB 27/1156, mm. 59, 89 (controversy over the deanery of Wells; cf. lengthy sequel in 109 Selden Soc. 8); *Grene* v. *Yonge* (1553) KB 27/1167, m. 106 (visitation by bishop of St Davids and appeal to official of Canterbury; demurrer to declaration; removed into Parliament under Mary I).

Some thought was given at this time to fusion of the two systems of law, and an edition of the provincial canons translated into English was printed by Robert Redman in 1534, presumably reflecting an active lay interest in the texts.[128] Following a conference between the Lords and Commons in March of the same year,[129] the king was empowered to appoint a commission of sixteen members of Parliament and sixteen clergy to edit and abridge the 'constitutions, ordinances and canons provincial or synodal', and to recommend the abrogation of those which should no longer be followed. Until this task was carried out, the old canon law was to continue in force except in so far as it was contrary to the law of the realm or the king's prerogative.[130] The 1534 act did not mention codification, though the decisions of the commissioners required the royal assent and it is generally assumed that the revision was to take the form of a code. A Latin draft was soon produced by a working committee of canonists,[131] but it was couched in very broad terms, did not squarely tackle the problem of jurisdictional boundaries, and did not provide an adequate basis for agreement with the common lawyers.[132] On the lay side, some radical new solutions were put forward by Richard Pollard and others, which would have transferred the *ex officio* penal jurisdiction, probate, and defamation, to the lay courts; but these failed to win the king's support.[133] After these initial efforts, the matter seems to have been laid aside for fifteen years and no commission was ever appointed under the 1534 act, though shortly before his death Henry VIII turned again to the project and asked to see the old draft.[134]

[128] *Constitutions provincialles, and of Otho, and Octhobone, translated in to Englyshe* (1534): Beale T.410. It was taken from Lyndwood's *Provinciale*, but omitted the gloss. There is a modern reprint entitled *Provinciale: the text of the canons therein contained*, ed. J. V. Bullard and H. C. Bell (1929). The translator acknowledged an unnamed patron, tentatively identified as Cromwell, or perhaps Cranmer: D. MacCulloch, *Thomas Cranmer* (1996), 119–20.

[129] *LP*, vii. 399; pr. in Lehmberg, *Reformation Parliament*, 193. The appointment of a canon law commission had first been suggested in 1532: *LP*, vi. 276(2); Lehmberg, *Reformation Parliament*, 149–50.

[130] Submission of the Clergy 1534, 25 Hen. VIII, c. 19; renewed by 27 Hen. VIII, c. 15 (and mentioned in c. 20); 35 Hen. VIII, c. 16.

[131] 'Ecclesiastical laws devised in King Henry VIII's Days', BL MS. Add. 48040, ff. 13–104v; pr. and tr. G. Bray, *Tudor Church Reform* (2000), 1–143; and see F. D. Logan, 'The Henrician Canons' (1974) 47 *BIHR* 99–103. The principal contents are: crimes and punishments; clergy and benefices; marriage; tithes and revenue; administration of estates; appeals. Dr Gwent and Dr Edward Carne were working on a draft in 1535: *LP*, ix. 549, 690; S. E. Lehmberg, 81 *EHR* at 229–31. Dr Thomas Thyrleby, Dr John Oliver, and others, were responsible for some 'articles', which may refer to the same enterprise: *LP*, ix. 119; next note. Dr William Petre was also involved: F. G. Emmison, *Tudor Secretary* (1961), 104; Lehmberg, 81 *EHR* 229. See further Bray, *Tudor Church Reform*, pp. xv–xli.

[132] Vagueness on jurisdictional issues was the main reason given by Richard Pollard for not accepting the 'articles' proposed by Drs Thyrleby, Oliver, and others: *LP*, ix. 119 (18 Aug. 1535). The common lawyers working with Pollard were Thomas Rushton, Thomas Polsted, and Anthony Bury. (Polsted is believed to have opposed the 1534 legislation in the Commons: *HPHC 1509–58*, iii. 127.)

[133] *LP*, ix. 119, 1071; Houlbrooke, 'The Decline of Ecclesiastical Jurisdiction', 243–4; Elton, *Reform and Renewal*, 130–5.

[134] Letter from Cranmer to Henry VIII, *LP*, xxi. I. 109 (referring to the 'book' made 'in times past').

In 1551, Parliament renewed the authority to appoint a commission of thirty-two, charging them 'to peruse and examine the ecclesiastical laws of long time here used, and to gather, order, and compile such laws ecclesiastical as shall be thought by His Majesty in Council and them or the more part of them convenient to be used, practised, and set forth within this his realm and other dominions'.[135] This time a code was clearly contemplated.[136] It was to be published by royal proclamation, and its contents were to be 'only taken, reputed, practised, and put in ure for the king's ecclesiastical laws of this realm and no other'. In November 1551, a sub-committee of eight was appointed to do the preparatory work, and the following February the full commission of thirty-two—under the chairmanship of Archbishop Thomas Cranmer—was at last appointed by letters patent.[137] A draft code was duly produced,[138] but it was 'scornfully sabotaged' by the duke of Northumberland in March 1553,[139] just before the accession of Mary I,[140] and was never afterwards approved by Parliament or Convocation. As a result of inertia, therefore, the transitional provision of 1534 lengthened into permanence. There was to be no reformation of the spiritual courts or the substantive canon law,[141] apart from the statute qualifying lay doctors of law for judicial office,[142] and some modifications made in the law of tithes by a statute of 1549.[143]

Tithes soon became the new jurisdictional battleground,[144] partly because they were becoming myred in complexity as a result of the numerous grants made to and by lay impropriators after the dissolution of the monasteries,[145] and the practice of

---

[135] 3 & 4 Edw. VI, c. 11.   [136] The same form of words was used in the 1544 act: 35 Hen. VIII, c. 16.

[137] APC, iii. 382, 410, 471; CPR 1550–3, pp. 114, 354. The common lawyers were Bromley and Hales JJ, Robert Brooke and William Staunford (created serjeants in Oct. 1552), John Caryll, John Gosnold, Richard Goodrick, and John Lucas. At least half of them were probably Roman Catholics. See further Bray, Tudor Church Reform, pp. xli–lxxvi.

[138] It was published as Reformatio Legum (1571; new edn by E. Cardwell, 1850; tr. Bray, Tudor Church Reform, 145–743). It went much further than the 1535 draft and would, for instance, have made adultery, desertion, and cruelty grounds for divorce a vinculo: Bray edn, 266–71. (The 1571 publication may explain the strange case of Martin Harburgh in 1574: Dyer's reports, 110 Selden Soc. 299.)

[139] CSP Spanish 1553, p. 33; quotation from MacCulloch, Thomas Cranmer, 533. See also J. Ridley, Cranmer (1962), 330–42.

[140] The enabling legislation was, however, repealed by 1 & 2 Phil. & Mar., c. 8.

[141] The reforms in benefit of clergy were more important, but these began before the Reformation and were effectively changes in secular criminal law: below, 536–40.

[142] 37 Hen. VIII, c. 17; above, 236. The new provision only applied to judges who were doctors of Civil law 'in any university'.

[143] 2 & 3 Edw. VI, c. 13. The first full exposition of the statute seems to be Robert Mounson's reading (Lincoln's Inn, 1565) BL MS. Harley 5265, ff. 27–56; CUL MS. Dd.11.87, ff. 136–150v.

[144] Cases of testamentary or intestate succession are still occasionally encountered: e.g. Habrehall v. Tunkyns (1542) KB 27/1122, m. 112; Sandes v. Sandes (1544) KB 27/1133, m. 136; Paschal v. Keterich (1557) Benl. 60, pl. 104 (legacy charged on profits of land); Brandon v. Powes (1554) KB 27/1172, m. 33. Other types of case are rare: e.g. Moris v. Wakerfylde (1558) KB 27/1186, m. 155 (dispute concerning 'paling' of a ground in London).   [145] For some legal consequences of the dissolution see below, 713–15.

leasing tithes to lay farmers,[146] and partly because of a popular reluctance or inability to pay full tithes even to the clergy in a period of dearth,[147] or to pay new forms of tithe resulting from changes in husbandry, an even greater reluctance to pay tithes to farmers or lay impropriators,[148] and the widespread practice of accepting fixed monetary payments in lieu of tithes.[149] Between 1530 and 1550 there was a massive increase in tithe suits in the ecclesiastical courts,[150] and this is reflected in the rise of prohibition cases in the King's Bench in the middle decades of the century.[151] In their 'suggestions'—the enrolled informations on which prohibitions were granted[152]—plaintiffs relied on the statute of 1371 concerning coppice wood (*sylva caedua*);[153] the statute of dissolution of 1539, which preserved the exempt status of such abbey lands as had been exempt from yielding tithes when in mortmain;[154] the various provisions of the statute of 1549[155]—including the seven-year exemption of lands recently converted to husbandry from barren heath and waste ground;[156] and also the old common-law principle that a prescription or

[146] Lay impropriators and farmers were enabled to sue for tithes in the ecclesiastical courts by 32 Hen. VIII, c. 7.

[147] This was recognized by Parliament in 1536, which improved the remedies for enforcement: 27 Hen. VIII, c. 20.   [148] See Houlbrooke, 'The Decline of Ecclesiastical Jurisdiction', 246.

[149] Partly as a result of enclosures: see E. Kerridge, *Agrarian Problems in the Sixteenth Century and After* (1969), 108–9 (referring to a slightly later period).

[150] Houlbrooke, 'The Decline of Ecclesiastical Jursidiction', 246; *Church Courts*, 117–50. In the diocese of Winchester, Houlbrooke reckoned a tenfold increase between the 1520s and the 1560s: *Church Courts*, 146. There was a similar increase in York: J. S. Purvis (ed.), *Select Sixteenth Century Causes in Tithe from the York Diocesan Registry* (1949), p. viii.

[151] Prohibitions in the Common Pleas are rare but not unknown: e.g. *Radyshe v. Aldworth* (1557) CP 40/1169, m. 1074 (tithes).

[152] A suggestion was entered in the form 'Remember that P gives the lord king's court to understand that...' ('Memorandum quod P dat curie domini regis intelligi quod...'), as in the case of an information. It was distinguished by the marginal annotation *Anglia*, rather than the name of a county.

[153] 45 Edw. III, c. 3; above, 36. See e.g. *Anon.* (1539) Brooke Abr., *Prohibition*, pl. 17; *Case of the Vicar of Stansted Mountfitchet* (1541) 121 Selden Soc. 445, no. 24; *Bennet v. Triplett* (1542) KB 27/1122, m. 113; *Vernon v. Fox* (1558) KB 27/1185, m. 35. Twenty similar cases were noted in 1542–57.

[154] 31 Hen. VIII, c. 13. These disputes come to the fore under Mary. See e.g. *Dolman v. Dawes* (1554) KB 27/1172, m. 29; KB 27/1179, m. 20; *Andrewe v. Bassett* (1556) KB 27/1180, m. 85 (attachment in KB 27/1185, m. 108); *Rogers v. Bassett*, ibid., m. 86 (attachment in KB 27/1185, m. 88); *Courtenay and others v. Robert* (1557) KB 27/1182, mm. 27, 114, 118, 119; *Roose v. Duke*, ibid., m. 118; *Thorowgood v. Rayner*, ibid., m. 129; *Pate v. Atkyns* (1557) KB 27/1184, m. 93; *Ap Rychardes v. Herbert* (1558) KB 27/1185, m. 73; *Mode v. Shyrke* (1558) KB 27/1186, m. 37; *Randall v. Tayler*, ibid., m. 81.

[155] 2 & 3 Edw. VI, c. 13. See e.g. *Honywood v. Beke* (1552) KB 27/1161, m. 23; *Walman v. Hunte* (1552) KB 27/1164, m. 150; *Smythe v. Denton*, ibid., m. 151; *Doys v. Master*, ibid., m. 161; *Smythe v. Master*, ibid., m. 168; *Whyte v. Master*, ibid., m. 169; *Gryphyn v. Master*, ibid., m. 170 (these last five cases all concerning the rectory of Aldington, Kent); *Heynes v. Harman* (1558) KB 27/1186, m. 33; *Chapman v. Fytche*, ibid., m. 39. Ten similar cases were noted in 1553–7.

[156] *Pelles v. Saunderson* (1558–9) KB 27/1186, m. 161; Dyer 170b (mentions a special verdict not enrolled); *Hyckmans v. Aston* (1558) KB 27/1187, m. 128; *Tunkes v. Aston*, ibid., m. 129. For disputes arising from this section see also Houlbrooke, *Church Courts*, 127–8.

composition to pay an annuity or portion in lieu of tithes removed the matter from the purview of the spiritual courts.[157]

The 1549 act introduced a procedural change of an unusual kind in the common-law courts, apparently intended to restrict the undue use of prohibitions. After 1549 a prohibition could not be granted without production of a copy of the libel used in the spiritual court,[158] and then if the plaintiff did not prove his suggestion by at least two witnesses, within six months, a consultation was to be granted with double costs and damages.[159] As a precaution against this heavy sanction, the King's Bench rolls in such cases routinely minuted the names, ages, and evidence, of the witnesses called to prove the suggestion. Such detail is never found elsewhere in the common-law rolls, even in demurrers to the evidence.

CONTINUITY

With the accession of a Roman Catholic queen in 1553 the legal position was unsettled, and a respected judge was incarcerated at the beginning of the reign for daring to assert that the previous legislation remained in force until it was repealed.[160] The following year Parliament did repeal the Henrician legislation, so that the realm might be brought once more under the obedience of the apostolic see.[161] Cardinal Pole, as papal legate *a latere*, thereupon issued a dispensation, confirmed by Parliament, ratifying all proceedings which had taken place in the ecclesiastical courts in the interim. It is doubtful whether the act of repeal had much practical effect on the workings of ecclesiastical justice, save in matters of discipline and heresy.[162] As an act of ecclesiological politics, however, it was obviously intended to herald a complete return to the status quo. The very act of appointing a legate *a latere* was a gesture of reactionary triumphalism, a refusal even to recognize

[157] See e.g. *Anon.* (1544) Gell's Reports, I, Mich. 36 Hen. VIII, fo. 25v (composition for tithes of fish); *Maltson* v. *Huske* (1545) KB 27/1135, m. 122; *Gybbons* v. *Carre* (1550) KB 27/1154, m. 128; *Hungerford* v. *Nanseglose* (1552) KB 27/1163, m. 120; *Hygdon's Case* (1553) KB 27/1165, m. 121, reported in Dyer 79a; *Wood* v. *Blakewall* (1558) KB 27/1187, m. 110; *Mawe* v. *Lewes*, ibid., 111; *Thackwrey* v. *Mawde* (1558) KB 27/1188, m. 69; *Langfelley* v. *Mawde*, ibid., m. 82; *Jaxon* v. *Lame*, ibid., m. 144. Twenty-one similar cases were noted in 1554–7.

[158] For the previous practice see Hil. 13 Hen. VII, fo. 16, pl. 16, Port 115, pl. 50. A special prohibition could be used to secure a copy of the libel: Rast. Ent. 450 (491); *Anon.* (1533) Spelman 188.

[159] 2 & 3 Edw. VI, c. 13. An example of a judgment for the defendant where the plaintiff failed to prove his suggestion is *Ferrers* v. *Lysley* (1554) KB 27/1170, m. 146.

[160] Sir James Hales, who took his own life in 1554: below, 419.

[161] 1 & 2 Phil. & Mar., c. 8. The statute was not to affect any royal prerogative or jurisdiction as it was before the year 20 Hen. VIII.

[162] It was also asserted that the bishops appointed in the time of Edward VI had not been properly consecrated: Brooke Abr., *Leases*, pl. 68. For this question, which continued to be debated into the 1560s and has remained an issue with the Roman curia in relation to the validity of Anglican orders, see also 109 Selden Soc., pp. lxvii–lxviii.

the genuineness of the problems which had been cited to justify the Henrician measures, or the legitimacy of the principles which had been deployed in striking down Wolsey's lawless legatine power. Papal authority was only supreme if it could be used arbitrarily: the law of England therefore had to give way.

In reasserting the sovereign authority of the papacy to the point of extremity, the new regime also chose to show itself capable of even more cruelty than Henry's, and set about burning heretics with a repulsive enthusiasm.[163] Although the policy did not have the wholehearted support of the local magistrates and sheriffs responsible for its execution, it was pursued with increasing relentlessness towards the end of the reign.[164] Nothing could have been better calculated to destroy the papal cause in England. Indeed, the government itself perceived that it was supplying protestantism with a stream of martyrs, and latterly strove to arrange burnings out of the public gaze, forbidding attendance by the impressionable young. Not only in retrospect, therefore, did the consequence of this brief taste of Roman justice fail to surprise. The Act of Repeal was itself repealed promptly after Mary's death, and the 'bondage' of foreign power permanently cast aside.[165]

The great theological and ecclesiological conflicts which underlay these changes of regime are beside our present concerns, for a striking feature of the Henrician Reformation in England is the very limited effect which it had on the ecclesiastical legal system. Not only did the English courts remain in being as they were before the 1530s, but the medieval learning which they applied remained substantially in place as well.[166] The same advocates and proctors continued in practice under Henry VIII, Edward VI, and Mary, their business seemingly immune from the theological turmoil around them.[167] Moreover, calculations of the numbers of cases in two specimen dioceses show that after the spiritual courts had experienced a decline in business between the 1500s and 1530s they enjoyed in some places an increase to two or three times the starting level by the middle of the century.[168]

[163] G. Alexander, 'Bonner and the Marian Persecutions' in *The English Reformation Revised*, ed. C. Haigh (1987), 157–75; T. F. Mayer, *Cardinal Pole* (2000), 279–80; Dyer's reports, 109 Selden Soc. 13 (1555).

[164] See D. M. Loades, 'The Enforcement of the Reaction 1553–8' (1965) 16 *Jnl Eccles. Hist.* 54–66; *The Oxford Martyrs* (1970); C. Haigh, *Reformation and Resistance in Tudor Lancashire* (1975), ch. 12. In 1557 a sheriff (Sir John Butler) was fined for reprieving a woman, and the following year another sheriff (Sir Richard Pexall) was imprisoned for respiting execution on a heretic who recanted at the stake: *APC*, vi. 144; 109 Selden Soc., p. lxxiv.

[165] 1 Eliz. I, c. 1 ('by reason of which Act of Repeal your said humble subjects were eftsoons brought under an usurped foreign power and authority, and do yet remain in that bondage, to the intolerable charges of your loving subjects').

[166] R. H. Helmholz, *Roman Canon Law in Reformation England* (1990).

[167] R. H. Helmholz, 'Ecclesiastical Lawyers and the English Reformation' (1995) 3 *ELJ* 360–70.

[168] Houlbrooke, *Church Courts*, esp. 273–4 (figures from Norwich and Winchester). In Chichester the recovery did not occur in the 1550s: Lander, 'Church Courts and the Reformation', 230–1. Helmholz places the main recovery in the reign of Elizabeth: 3 *ELJ* 361. For the decline see also Woodcock, *Medieval Ecclesiastical Courts*, 84.

The decline preceded the break with Rome,[169] and the recovery followed it. Although the categories of business were not constant throughout this period, the overall figures suggest that the ecclesiastical courts may have been subject to the same economic or demographic influences as all the others.

[169] Wunderli (*London Church Courts*, 19–23) attributes the decline in London between 1490 and 1516 chiefly to the plague. There are no London records after 1516 to provide a comparison.

14

Commissions

THE judicial system, particularly in relation to criminal proceedings, was still heavily dependent on commissions. The general eyre had been defunct since the fourteenth century, though one or two special eyres were commissioned for *quo warranto* enquiries[1] and the enforcement of forest law.[2] In the eyre held at Lynn in 1521, which was adjourned to Middlesex in 1522, it was even possible to bring private suits by bill.[3] But the eyre was an anachronism, and even in the case of *quo warranto* the government law officers soon found ways to avoid its pitfalls,[4] so that the jurisdiction effectively passed to the King's Bench.[5] On the other hand, commissions of assize, oyer and terminer, and general gaol delivery, and the standing commissions of the peace in each county, represented a continuing, indispensable routine.

ASSIZES

The circuit system was well established before our period, and underwent no substantial change.[6] The six circuits were visited twice a year by two commissioners, appointed from among the justices of one of the benches—who almost all went on circuit—and the other serjeants, the chief baron, and the attorney-general.[7]

---

[1] e.g. the Middlesex eyre of 1519, adjourned into the King's Bench: 120 Selden Soc. 43, no. 27; Chaloner 282–8; BL MS. Add. 25168, fo. 559 (writ and claims). And the eyre held at Bishops Lynn (soon to become Kings Lynn), Norfolk, in 1521: Spelman 199; Porter's precedent book, C193/142, fo. 128v (copy of commission and summons). The jurisdiction was discussed in *R.* v. *Savage* (1519) 2 Caryll 699 at 703.

[2] e.g. the New Forest eyre of 1488: see *A Calendar of New Forest Documents*, ed. D. J. Stagg (Hants. Record Series 5; 1983).

[3] See *Abbot of Sawtrey* v. *Bullyngbroke* (1534) KB 27/1092, m. 34 (attaint upon a verdict in forcible entry before Sir Robert Drury and other justices in eyre at Lynn on 20 Aug. 1521).

[4] By informations in the nature of *quo warranto*: above, 151 n. 48.

[5] Garrett-Goodyear, 'The Tudor Revival of *Quo Warranto*', 231–95. The King's Bench was for this purpose said to be 'higher than justices in eyre': *Att.-Gen.* v. *Babington* (1519) Chaloner 285 at 288, *per* Fyneux CJ. Cf. *R.* v. *Savage* (1519) 2 Caryll 699 at 703.

[6] The principal change was the addition of Monmouth to the Oxford circuit upon its becoming an English county in 1535 (27 Hen. VIII, c. 26). A table of the circuits in 1504/5, with a list of the gaols in each county, is in BL MS. Add. 35205, m. 1 (wrapper). There is a similar list (*c.*1519/20) in William Porter's precedent book, C193/142, fo. 18.

[7] The coif was the usual statutory qualification: 14 Edw. III, stat. 5, c. 16. The words 'serjeant le roy' were nevertheless taken by the equity to include serjeants other than king's serjeants, and also

They may have been given a special oath: at any rate, when Serjeant Rede was sent on assize in 1488, he was sworn to do all that belonged to a king's serjeant to do on his circuit (*in progressu suo*).[8] In order to avoid local bias, justices were not supposed to ride circuit in the county where they lived, though an attempt to reinforce this by legislation failed in 1510 and the law was not clarified until 1541.[9] The Chancery issued, for each circuit, a commission of assize and a commission of general gaol delivery, each extending to all the counties and county-towns comprised in the circuit.[10] In addition, the assize judges were usually included in the commissions of the peace for each county,[11] and they occasionally received ad hoc comissions of oyer and terminer as well. From 1537, general commissions of oyer and terminer were also made out for each circuit; these were issued to a group of justices of the peace, with the assize judges as the *quorum*.[12]

The commission of assize empowered the justices not only to take petty assizes but also the verdicts of juries at nisi prius. As justices of nisi prius the assize judges conducted civil trials in cases emanating from the central courts, and occasional criminal trials in appeals or indictments from the King's Bench,[13] but they had no power to give judgment.[14] They could record a nonsuit or a plea pleaded 'after the last continuance', but in the latter case they had to send the record back to Westminster for repleading to a new issue.[15] Likewise, if an appellor was nonsuited at nisi prius, the justices could not arraign the appellee upon the declaration—as they could in the King's Bench, or when the appeal was commenced before justices of gaol delivery—because the nisi prius authority did not extend to this.[16]

(it seems) the attorney-general. For their remuneration (increased in 1556) see 109 Selden Soc. 11. For a list of commissioners from 1483 to 1513, see Ives, *Common Lawyers in pre-Reformation England*, 68–73.

[8] Memorandum dated 17 July 1488 in Bodl. Lib. MS. Rawlinson C.339, fo. 179v (Chancery precedent book).

[9] *HLJ*, i. 5b (tr. 'The bill for justices of assize and commissioners of gaol delivery, being read, was sent back to the Commons for amendment, because the Lords were minded to insert in the bill not only those who lived in such places but also those who were born there'), 6b, 7a. For the old law see 8 Ric. II, c. 2. The reform came in 33 Hen. VIII, c. 24.

[10] Mostly enrolled on the patent rolls and calendared in *CPR* and (temp. Hen. VIII) in *LP*. The calendars do not identify the gaol delivery commissions as relating to the 'assizes', since that term is not in the patents and is not so generally used in our period. For examples of general and special commissions of gaol delivery, see Porter's precedent book, C193/142, ff. 19–22.

[11] *Burneby* v. *Holywell* (1494) Mich. 9 Hen. VII, fo. 8, pl. 5, at fo. 9.

[12] A. Bevan, 'The Henrician Assizes and the Enforcement of the Reformation' in *The Political Context of Law*, ed. R. Eales and D. Sullivan (1987), 61–76. Bevan has shown how this change was obscured in the sight of historians by a series of misunderstandings.

[13] e.g. *Anon.* (1495) Pas. 10 Hen. VII, fo. 20, pl. 8; *Gawen's Case* (1535) Spelman 166 (held that a nisi prius *cum proviso* could be awarded at the prayer of an appellee); *Reade* v. *Rochforth* (1555–6) Dyer 120b, 131b; KB 27/1164, m. 159 (power of justices of nisi prius to award damages to an acquitted appellee).

[14] Unless by statute, as in the case of *quare impedit*: *Henslow* v. *Keble* (1552) Dyer 76b; *Poyner* v. *Chorleton* (1556) Dyer 135a.   [15] *Anon.* (1495) Pas. 10 Hen. VII, fo. 21, pl. 17.

[16] *Anon.* (1482) Trin. 22 Edw. IV, fo. 19, pl. 44; Brooke Abr., *Nisi Prius*, pl. 28.

Under the commission of the peace, and by virtue of a statute of 1429, the assize judges had the power to award restitution of land which had been the subject of a forcible entry.[17] And by a statute of 1530 they also had the power to award restitution of stolen goods.[18] Their powers in criminal cases derived from the two commissions of gaol delivery and of the peace[19]—and from 1537 the general oyer and terminer—which between them enabled the assize judges to try prisoners on indictment, or by way of appeal of felony,[20] for all manner of offences, and to issue process against prisoners indicted before them who were not yet in custody. Unlike the civil jurisdiction of the assize judges, this criminal jurisdiction was exercisable without reference to the central courts; the cases were commenced, tried, and disposed of on circuit. The principal difference between the two commissions was that justices of oyer and terminer were empowered to try only those prisoners who were indicted before them,[21] whereas justices of gaol delivery could only try prisoners already in gaol, whether indicted before themselves or elsewhere.[22] Because of the difference, and the mutual support which they gave each other, a commission of oyer and terminer did not impliedly rescind a commission of gaol delivery in the same place.[23] The commission of the peace included an oyer and terminer jurisdiction, which was exercised at quarter sessions as well as assizes, but it did not extend to treason. The reason for introducing the general oyer and terminer commission in 1537 was to enable indictments for treason to be both found and tried at assizes, a change which proved necessary after difficulties were encountered with some of the prosecutions under the Reformation treason legislation.[24]

[17] 8 Hen. VI, c. 9; Port 79–80; *Note* (1555) 110 Selden Soc. 405 (Derby assizes). This jurisdiction was excercised by virtue of the commission of the peace only: *Anon.* (1510) 2 Caryll 605 at 606 (not by commission of oyer and terminer); 110 Selden Soc. 412, 414. See also D. W. Sutherland, *The Assize of Novel Disseisin* (1973), 175.

[18] 21 Hen. VIII, c. 11; *Note* (1555) 110 Selden Soc. 407; *Note* (1557) ibid. 414. This did not extend to special commissioners of oyer and terminer: *Anon.* (1557) Dal. 25, pl. 8.

[19] The assize judges for the time being were usually included in the commissions of the peace, though these were not always up to date in that respect.

[20] For the jurisdiction over appeals, see 3 Hen. VII, c. 2 (appeals of death); *Note* (1554) 110 Selden Soc. 400; Dyer 99a (appeals of robbery).

[21] *Anon.* (1555/6) Brooke Abr., *Commissions*, pl. 24. This was apparently because the words 'to enquire, hear and determine' were construed conjunctively.

[22] See *Anon.* (1500) Pas. 16 Hen. VII, fo. 5, pl. 1, *per* Kebell sjt (tr. 'if someone is indicted of felony before justices of peace, and then outlawed thereof, taken, and put in prison, and then the justices of gaol delivery come into the county, they shall award execution against this prisoner'). Cf. Yorke 203, no. 301; *Penyngton* v. *Hunte* (1544) Cholmeley 454 at 457, *per* Bradshaw S.-G., and 458–9, *per* Hales sjt.

[23] *Burneby* v. *Holywell* (1494) Mich. 9 Hen. VII, fo. 8, pl. 5, at fo. 9; 3 Mar. I, Brooke Abr., *Commissions*, pl. 24. On the other hand, a commission impliedly rescinded any former commission of the same type still in being (e.g. successive commissions of the peace): below, 267 n. 103.

[24] Bevan, 'The Henrician Assizes', 67, 72–4. Note also 33 Hen. VIII, c. 23 (trial outside the county of persons vehemently suspected of treason after enquiry by committee of Council).

The formal procedure at the assizes is set out in a manual produced around 1518, apparently on the Western circuit.[25] The proceedings commenced with the crier's proclamation for silence: 'The king's justices [straitly charge and] command that every man keep silence and hear the king's commission[s] openly read.'[26] Then the clerk of assize read out verbatim the patents of assize and association, in Latin ('Henricus...'), and broke open and read the writs of admittance and *si non omnes*.[27] After that he called on the sheriff to return his precept and on bailiffs to answer to their names. The crier was then directed to make proclamation for essoins, assizes, and nisi prius records, to be put in 'this forenoon, or else none shall be received.' Parties were formally demanded, with the warning that if they failed to appear they would lose by default; and the assizes were arraigned.

It would seem from the manual that all this was done before the gaol delivery began, though it may be that, as in later times, the judges sometimes separated to conduct the two types of business simultaneously.[28] Certainly it would have been more expeditious for the grand jury to be sworn in as soon as possible, so that they could begin their deliberations. At any rate, a separate proclamation was made for silence before the commission of gaol delivery was read, suggesting that it was a separate event.[29] There followed a proclamation for attendance of the justices of the peace and coroners; next the grand jurors were called, sworn by the marshal, and charged by one of the assize judges; and then a further proclamation was made for records of indictments to be brought in for the grand jury to consider.

The arraignment of prisoners began with the 'suspects', meaning those against whom no indictment had been found. They were 'delivered by proclamation', which was in the following form:

(A.B., of such a place, hold up thy hand.) Four men and the reeve of the township of B., come forth and shew why A.B., prisoner at the bar, was taken at your town for suspicion of felony, or else the township shall be amerced. The prisoner standeth at his deliverance.

[25] *Modus Tenendi Curiam coram Justiciariis ad Assisas* (*c*.1518) in JHB MS. 39, ff. 29–39 (quotations with sp. mod.); also in Newberry Library, Chicago, Case MS. fK 545.3575, ff. 26–35v. The earlier precedents mention Elyot and Pollard JJ (justices on the Western circuit) in Lent 1518. The clerk of assize at that time was Thomas Elyot.

[26] The words in brackets occur in the slightly later form on fo. 6 of the first manuscript. The same wording was used until recent times.

[27] The manual reads (tr.): 'then he must break [the] two close commissions and read them, and also that which is patent'. The later form (last note) identifies them. For the *si non omnes* see *Penyngton* v. *Hunte* (1544) Cholmeley 454 at 461, *per* Baldwin CJ.

[28] It has been suggested that the separation did not begin until the second half of the century: 109 Selden Soc., p. xciv. In March 1559, Serjeant Bendlowes rode the Midland circuit alone because Dyer CJ had to attend parliament: 110 Selden Soc. 420.

[29] It is marked by a new heading, *Modus Tenendi Curiam ad Gaolam Deliberandam*. This seems to be intended as part of the same manual, and the commission begins 'Henricus', though it includes some notes made on the Midland circuit in 1543–4. It may be compared with the *Modus Intrandi Deliberationem Gaole* (temp. Edw. VI) in Bodl. Lib. MS. è Mus. 57, ff. 88–89, which follows an account of criminal procedure at the sessions, without an assize section.

If there be any man that will inform the king's justices, the king's serjeant, or the king's attorney, of any treasons, murders, felonies, trespasses, or other misdemeanours committed and done by [A.B.], prisoner at the bar, come forth and he shall be heard. The prisoner standeth at his deliverance.[30]

Then the court proceeded with the arraignment of those who had been appealed or indicted,[31] the clerk arranging with the under-sheriff for the panels of trial jurors in waiting to be produced. Here we may leave the manual for the present.

Little is known in detail of the conduct of trials at assizes.[32] The judges sat with the justices of the peace when trying the criminal calendar,[33] but it is likely that the nisi prius business was dealt with by the judges alone. Probably they sat together.[34] Apart from the proclamation for records of nisi prius to be 'put in' on the morning of the first day, and some precedents of posteas, the manual is silent on the formal conduct of this category of business. Counsel certainly attended the nisi prius 'side',[35] and in cases of difficulty they might be senior members of the Bar. This is evident from demurrers to the evidence, the only records which give the names of counsel; those named are nearly always serjeants, or benchers of the inns of court.[36] What the system lacked, at the beginning of the sixteenth century, was any formal means of ensuring uniformity in the application of the law. But by the end of our period the judges had taken some steps to coordinate their work by reserving questions for discussion by the assembled assize judges in term-time.[37]

---

[30] This main proclamation, which is close to the classical form, is not in the Newberry Lib. MS., but is given in *Modus Intrandi Deliberationem Gaole* (temp. Edw. VI) Bodl. Lib. MS. è Mus. 57, fo. 89 (*bis*). There follows, in the latter, the oath given to the prisoner before discharge, for his allegiance and good bearing.

[31] It was said to be the practice in the 1530s for those indicted at the gaol delivery to be arraigned on the same day: Yorke 203, no. 301.

[32] For civil trials see below, 361–9; for criminal trials see below, 516–20.

[33] Bevan, 'The Henrician Assizes', 64–5. Other examples may be found in actions on the case for defamation or conspiracy, where convictions at assizes are recited in detail.

[34] See *Anon.* (1561) Chr. Yelverton's reports, fo. 231v (trespass case at the assizes before Catlyn CJ and Browne J.); cf. *Anon.* (1561/2) ibid., fo. 253v (tr. 'at Bedford assizes... held clearly by Browne [J.], my lord Catlyn being sick and absent...') and ibid. (tr. 'at Northampton assizes... held by my lord Dyer [CJ] and Bendlowes...').

[35] For evidence from the early part of Elizabeth I's reign, see 109 Selden Soc., p. xcv.

[36] Distant counties may have been less well served. William Clayton (of Lincoln's Inn), who practised at Shrewsbury assizes, does not seem to have been a bencher, though he was appointed serjeant in the county palatine of Chester in 1524: *Browne* v. *Elmer* (1519) CP 40/1023, m. 124d; *Master of St John's Hospital, Shrewsbury* v. *Ap Owen* (1524) CP 40/1043, m. 303; P. Turner, 'List of Officers of the County Palatine of Chester' (1870) 31 *DKR* at 185. His opponents were William Rudhale and Thomas Mataton, benchers of the Inner and Middle Temple respectively. In *Whytney* v. *Gough* (1556) CP 40/1166, m. 140, an utter barrister (James Boyle of the Middle Temple) appeared at Hereford assizes; but his opponent, Richard Seybourne, was a bencher of the Inner Temple.   [37] See below, 526–8.

Since the business of an assize session was rarely transacted in a single day, it was usual to adjourn the commission overnight, though all the proceedings were recorded in the postea as having occurred on the first day.[38] If any jurors were still deliberating, they were kept in strict custody, but could attend the judges privately to give a 'privy verdict' and thereby obtain leave to eat and drink.[39] The judges were also permitted to adjourn a petty assize to any location in the event of a demurrer or a doubt arising from the pleading or the verdict.[40] The usual venue for an adjourned assize was one of the benches at Westminster,[41] one of the Serjeants' Inns,[42] or the Exchequer Chamber,[43] but an adjournment could be made to the Whitefriars[44] or even to the chief justice's private house.[45] After judgment, the record could be removed into one of the benches by *certiorari*.[46] In the event of plague, the judges could adjourn the nisi prius to a more salubrious part of the county and take the juries there. They could not in strictness move the general gaol delivery,[47] but since the assize judges were also on the commission of the peace they could by virtue of that commission try the prisoners elsewhere in

[38] *Saunders* v. *Freman* (1561) CP 40/1189, m. 1321 (next note). According to Spelman 155 (*Jour*, pl. 1), this was the case even when a verdict was given by a jury carted into another county. The plea rolls do not, therefore, enable us to establish the precise duration of assize sittings.

[39] See *Saunders* v. *Freman* (1561) CP 40/1189, m. 1321 (jurors at Northampton Castle charged on 8 July, and at about 8 p.m. in the absence of the parties gave a privy verdict at the inn where Dyer CJ and Serjeant Bendlowes were staying; the court resumed at 8 a.m.). For privy verdicts see below, 370.

[40] Brooke Abr., *Verdit*, pl. 28; Port 126–7.

[41] For an adjournment to the King's Bench, see *Stokes* v. *Somersall* (1558) 110 Selden Soc. 418.

[42] *Maunde* v. *Staunton* (1525) KB 27/1056, m. 31 (to Serjeants' Inn, Fleet Street); *Stonor* v. *Fortescue* (1528) CP 40/1059, m. 152 (to the Exchequer Chamber, then to Serjeants' Inn, Chancery Lane); *Wymbysshe* v. *Taylboys* (1544) CP 40/1123, m. 702 (to Serjeants' Inn, Chancery Lane, then to the Common Pleas); *Villers* v. *Beamonte* (1556) CP 40/1166, m. 516 (to Serjeants' Inn, Fleet Street, and a week later to the Common Pleas); *Taylor* v. *Marshall* (1556) CP 40/1168, m. 724 (to the Exchequer Chamber, then to the 'Hospitium Justiciariorum' in Fleet Street); *Ellys* v. *Rokeby* (1557) CP 40/1169, m. 1077 (to the Justices' Inn).

[43] *Burneby* v. *Holywell* (1494–1500) Mich. 9 Hen. VII, fo. 8, pl. 5; Trin. 16 Hen. VII, fo. 11, pl. 5 (misdated); CP 40/929, m. 333; *Mathewe* v. *Phillipp* (1506–8) CP 40/978, m. 338; *Bulstrode* v. *Broughton* (1516–19) CP 40/1015, m. 509 (demurrer); *Stonor* v. *Fortescue* (1528), previous note; *Seymour* v. *Cheffins* (undated) Yorke 198, no. 285; *Earl of Arundel* v. *Lord Windsor* (1549) Dyer 65a.

[44] *Fabyan* v. *Fyncham* (1502) CP 40/959, m. 413 (to Westminster, then to the Whitefriars at 1 p.m., then to the Common Pleas). The Whitefriars adjoined Serjeants' Inn, Fleet Street.

[45] *Colt* v. *Thorp* (1490–6) CP 40/912, m. 295 (adjourned from Chelmsford assizes to the parish of St Sepulchre's, London, doubtless Bryan CJ's house there, and then to the Common Pleas). Bryan CJ's house in St Sepulchre's is mentioned in the same plea roll, rot. warr. 1.

[46] e.g. *Penington's Case* (1495) Mich. 11 Hen. VII, fo. 5, pl. 21; *Anon.* (1500) Pas. 15 Hen. VII, fo. 5, pl. 1; *Duke of Somerset* v. *Lord Audley* (1549) CP 40/1139, m. 519.

[47] As to adjournment see Yorke 94, no. 20 (of a special gaol delivery: 'there the justices must deliver all those who are in the first calendar, and if they have insufficient time to do so they may adjourn these sessions to another day certain . . . and so from day to day'); *R.* v. *Lord Dacre and Greystock* (1534) Caryll (Jun.) 415 at 416 ('like the commission of the justices of gaol delivery, where the common course is to adjourn their sessions to another day').

the county than the town where the gaol was situated.[48] It was said that if a jury could not reach agreement before the judges were due to move on in their progress, they could order the jurors to be taken with them in a cart into another county; but since the record was supposed to omit all mention of such mechanisms it is impossible to know whether it was ever done in our period.[49] No doubt the mere threat was useful enough. Although the gaol delivery commission was determined when the justices completed the calendar and left, it was usual for the justices to make consequential orders—for instance warrants or respites of execution—between then and the issue of the next commission.[50]

The assize judges fulfilled an important role not only in the legal system but also by acting in effect as intermediaries between the central government and county government. They were supposed to exercise a superintendence over the local magistrates, who were bound to attend the assizes,[51] and in charging grand juries they could intimate to the county the current concerns of the court. Wolsey and Cromwell both made good use of this chain of control. In 1518, the Star Chamber ordered the assize judges to provide 'a true report of the misdemeanours in their several circuits, that is to say who be retainers of oppressors or maintainers of wrongful causes or otherwise misbehaved persons in their said several circuits'.[52] And Cromwell's papers show how the judges kept in written touch with the secretary of state concerning Crown business.[53] For instance, in 1535 Jenney J. wrote from York assizes for advice as to whether certain words were treasonable; and the outcome in this case was new legislation to close a loophole.[54] The registers of the Privy Council from the 1540s and 1550s show that the government continued to maintain an active channel of communication with the assize judges.

Each circuit had a clerk or clerks of assize. The clerk was 'associated' with the judges in the commission, and a writ of association was sent to the judges to inform them of his identity, though in practice the clerkship was continuous from year to year.[55] The right of nomination to the office belonged to the senior judge who happened to be in commission when a vacancy occurred. Most of the clerks

---

[48] *Anon.* (1529) Spelman 155.

[49] ibid.; Brooke Abr., *Enquestes*, pl. 65; and see Richard Littleton's comment at Marow's first reading (Inner Temple, 1497) Port 127.

[50] Yorke 93, no. 14; *Note* (1561) Dyer 205a (said to be custom of realm).

[51] See *Tudor Royal Proclamations*, i. 19 (1489); Fitz. J. P. 5v–6v; Bevan, 'The Henrician Assizes', 65; above, 258.   [52] BL MS. Lansdowne 639, fo. 54v (sp. mod.).

[53] See 102 Selden Soc., pp. xvii–xviii; below, 415–16.

[54] SP 1/95, fo. 38; 28 Hen. VIII, c. 10; Bevan, 'The Henrician Assizes', 71.

[55] Many associations temp. Hen. VIII are calendared in *LP* as commissions of assize; the associate is identifiable as not being a serjeant at law. Associations temp. Hen. VII (but not Ric. III) are in *CPR*. For the writ of association see *Prior of St Mary Overy* v. *Culpeper* (1523) Spelman 109; *Penyngton* v. *Hunte* (1544) Cholmeley 454.

of assize in our period were officers of the central courts, as prothonotaries,[56] filazers, or attorneys, many of them with a local base in one of the counties on the circuit.[57] But it had already become an accepted practice to appoint relatives, a practice which would continue until the twentieth century. There are three known instances in our period.[58] Elyot J. appointed his son Thomas as clerk of assize on the western circuit in 1510, though he was still under age, and notwithstanding a purported settlement of the office by Humphrey Conyngesby in 1495 when he took the coif.[59] Brudenell J. did the like for his son Robert on the Oxford circuit in 1511. Robert Brudenell was succeeded by his brother Thomas (a filazer of the Common Pleas) in 1526, when his father was no longer on the circuit, perhaps by consent of the then assize judges;[60] a few years later, however, Port J. appointed his eldest son John to the same office.[61]

Marshals were also appointed by each of the assize judges. Little is known of them or their duties, save that of swearing in juries,[62] though we do know that in the 1530s the Norfolk attorney Robert Howson apparently attended his master Spelman J. on the northern circuit.[63] The clerks and marshals were remunerated by fees from litigants, including a substantial proportion of any sum of money levied by execution.[64]

The clerks of assize probably kept the records in their own houses or inns, and although there may have been in the time of Henry VII a central repository in

---

[56] Between 1498 and 1510 all three prothonotaries were clerks of assize: Mordaunt (chief prothonotary) on the Norfolk circuit, Muscote (second) on the Home, and Caryll (third) on the Western. Two of them (Mordaunt and Caryll) had succeeded clerks who were their predecessors in the office of prothonotary. By the 1520s, however, none of the prothonotaries were clerks of assize. None of the King's Bench chief clerks acted in our period, though some King's Bench filazers did.

[57] Parliament confirmed in 1541 that associates were not subject to the rule that a justice could not take assizes in the counties where he lived: 33 Hen. VIII, c. 24. However, the statute forbade clerks of assize to act as counsel on their circuits 'otherwise than to that office only appertaineth'.

[58] Cf. 93 Selden Soc., p. xvii (Cromwell persuades Spelman J. to appoint Anthony Browne rather than a relative as clerk of assize on the Home circuit in 1538).

[59] The agreement was that John Caryll should have the office on trust to surrender it to Conyngesby if he became a serjeant, which he did in 1510: C1/292/59. Elyot answered that it was a corrupt bargain, because the office belonged to the justices of assize and had been granted to him by Elyot and Pollard JJ.

[60] The grant may have been jointly to Robert and Thomas, who were both associated in the commission for Lent 1526, but it must have been the expectation that Thomas would succeed, as indeed he did before the summer circuit.   [61] 102 Selden Soc., p. xvii. Patents of association in LP.

[62] Mentioned in the manual, above, 258; it remained the practice in modern times.

[63] Marshal at York: C1/839/29 (temp. Audley). Clerk to Serjeant Spelman in 1523: Derbs. Record Office, MS. D185B/54A. Of Staple Inn and Narborough, Norfolk: CP 40/1052, m. 490 (sued for dues, 1526). Spelman lived at Narboorugh.

[64] In Leghe v. Foxe (c.1535) C1/839/29, it was complained that James Foxe (clerk of assize) and the two marshals of the justices of assize in Yorks. had claimed one third of a £66 debt for which they levied execution.

St Bride's church, Fleet Street,[65] there was no permanent archival system and in consequence virtually all the assize records for our period have been lost. Only the nisi prius business is fully recorded, since the clerk had to return the result of the trial—or its failure to take place—to the court at Westminster.[66] The clerk himself could return the postea even if both assize judges died before the term, as happened on the Home circuit in 1558.[67] The assize rolls, containing assizes of novel disseisin and mort d'ancestor, were supposed to be transmitted to the Treasury 'every second year', but few of the original rolls have survived.[68] Nor have the gaol delivery rolls survived, though a small proportion of individual cases were removed into the King's Bench and may be found in the Rex rolls. Where the justices sat under two concurrent commissions, the records of cases falling under both jurisdictions could be made up under either authority.[69]

OYER AND TERMINER

Before the introduction of the general circuit commissions of oyer and terminer, general commissions of oyer and terminer were occasionally issued for particular reasons: for instance, in 1495, after the discovery of the Warbeck conspiracy, in 1509, on the demise of the Crown,[70] and in 1518, when Wolsey was suppressing local disorders;[71] but otherwise commissions of this kind were issued ad hoc for particular places or to deal with particular individuals.

Special commissions of oyer and terminer could be issued in the wake of particular outbreaks of disorder, or in preparation for state trials to be held in Westminster Hall. In the case of noblemen, the lord chancellor or some other senior peer was appointed to act as lord high steward and preside over the trial by peers;[72] there was a separate commission of oyer and terminer for the purpose of charging the grand jury which found the indictment,[73] and the appointment of lord high steward was always temporary (*pro hac vice tantum*). In other cases, the

---

[65] See *Narrative of Robert Pylkington*, 53 (search for record kept there, c.1500). Cf. ibid. 54, where it is said that the clerk of assize at Derby kept certain records with him.

[66] For posteas see below, 371.

[67] *Note* (1558) Dyer 163a–b, §54. Morgan JKB (d. 19 Aug.) and Prideaux sjt (d. 29 Sept.) had been judges on the summer circuit.

[68] 11 Hen. IV, c. 3; *Anon.* (1500) Pas. 15 Hen. VII, fo. 5, pl. 1, *per* Mordaunt sjt. If the assize was adjourned into the Common Pleas, the record was transcribed onto the plea rolls (CP 40), where a number of them may be found. A stray original roll is *Wandesford* v. *Elleryngton* (1488) KB 138/106 (enrolled in CP 40/905, m. 114; error proceedings in KB 27/913, m. 63; 1 Caryll 42).

[69] *Burneby* v. *Holywell* (1494) Mich. 9 Hen. VII, fo. 8, pl. 5, at fo. 9.

[70] But revoked by order of the Council in 1509, all undetermined causes being transferred to the King's Bench and Common Pleas: *LP*, i. 257(85).   [71] Bevan, 'The Henrician Assizes', 68–9.

[72] For trial by peers see below, 520.   [73] e.g. *R.* v. *Duke of Buckingham* (1521) Port 124; KB 8/5.

commissioners were usually a combination of peers and common-law judges, though in practice the higher-ranking commissioners did not always sit and the charge to the jury would be given by the chief justice. The difference between the recorded form and the reality is well illustrated by a comparison of two state trials which were held in June 1535 by virtue of similar commissions of oyer and terminer addressed to the chancellor (Sir Thomas Audley), the dukes of Norfolk and Suffolk, several other peers, and the judges. The Carthusian priors were tried on 11 June before the chief justice of the King's Bench and the chief baron of the Exchequer, 'and neither the chancellor nor the others were then present, for the prisoners were of little reputation'; but a week later Sir Thomas More was tried before Audley and numerous noblemen in the commission, judgment being pronounced by the chancellor.[74] The clerk for such special proceedings—including trials of peers—was the clerk of the Crown in the King's Bench, who preserved the records in the *Baga de Secretis*.[75]

By virtue of the power to hear and determine trespasses, justices of oyer and terminer assumed a civil jurisdiction in cases of trespass *vi et armis*. Little is known of this aspect of their work, a few instances of which are found in the plea rolls for the earlier years of Henry VIII's reign.[76] The cases in 1509–10 arose from the special commissions of 1509 which were intended to redress grievances suffered under the previous regime. In the event the commissions had given rise principally to civil litigation, and the Council decided to revoke them on grounds of inconvenience and expense.[77] Nevertheless, further instances are found in 1516, when plague compelled the adjournment of the central courts into the country,[78] and likewise in the summer of 1518.[79] One of the advantages for plaintiffs was that they could have a jury summoned immediately at the assizes,[80] without

[74] Spelman 57, 58.

[75] KB 8. For a full calendar see F. Palgrave, 'Inventory and Calendar of the Baga de Secretis' (1842) 3 *DKR*, app. ii, 210–68; (1843) 4 *DKR*, app. ii, 213–97.

[76] e.g. *Dowdeney* v. *Whitmore* (1510) KB 27/997, m. 36 (verdict and judgment before Grevill J. and other commissioners at Exeter); *Corpson* v. *Bate* (1510) ibid., m. 60 (general issue pleaded before Botiller J. and other commissioners at Aylesbury; removed in banc).

[77] Cooper, 'Henry VII's Last Years', 117–24; Elton, *Studies*, i. 87–91; Guy, *The Cardinal's Court* (1977), 24–5. Commissions to hear and determine individual cases continued to be used by consent: BL MS. Harley 2143, fo. 2v.

[78] When the courts were adjourned to Oxford, in April 1516, the proclamation of adjournment announced that the king had deputed justices in every shire to hear and determine causes: Porter's precedent book, C193/142, ff. 35–36.

[79] e.g. on the Midland circuit: *Thurland* v. *Godley* (1518) CP 40/1022, m. 529 (verdict and judgment before Brudenell J. and others at Nottingham); *Walker* v. *Robynson* (1519) KB 27/1030, m. 26 (bill of defamation before same commissioners at Derby, removed into King's Bench by *certiorari*; judgment there after trial at nisi prius); reported in 120 Selden Soc. 49. Both the Easter and Trinity terms were adjourned for plague: CP 40/1021A, m. 185; CP 40/1021B, m. 1.

[80] In *Thurland* v. *Godley* (last note) the *venire facias* ordered a jury for the following day, with a 100s. qualification. They found for the defendant.

going through the nisi prius procedure; but the corresponding inconvenience to potential jurors probably explains why it did not become standard practice.

A particular species of oyer and terminer—with extensive powers—was contained in the commissions of sewers, which empowered any six commissioners (with a *quorum*) to hold enquiry by jury into liability for damage, to assess rates for carrying out repairs, to impose punishments, and to hear and determine all suits concerning the premises,[81] 'doing therein as to our justices appertaineth after the laws and statutes of the realm'.[82] Under Henry VIII new qualifications were laid down for the commissioners, who after 1514 were to be worth £20 a year or 'justice of *quorum* learned'.[83] In 1531 the qualification was altered to 40 marks in land, or £100 in goods in a town, unless the commissioner was a barrister;[84] and a judicial oath of office was introduced. Even after these reforms, interested parties might still attempt to have their own lawyers put into the commission.[85] Surviving records are fragmentary.[86]

COMMISSIONS OF THE PEACE[87]

In every county a group of justices of the peace was appointed by commission under the great seal, charged with a wide variety of functions. They were not only royal judges but also the principal form of local government, an important link between the central government and the shires.[88] Marow, in his reading on justices of the peace, devoted a day's lecture to expounding the legal distinction between keepers (or 'conservators') of the peace, and justices of the peace,[89]

---

[81] 6 Hen. VI, c. 5; renewed by 4 Hen. VII, c. 1; perpetuated by 6 Hen. VIII, c. 10; commission revised and tr. into English in 23 Hen. VIII, c. 5; perpetuated by 3 & 4 Edw. VI, c. 8. For the form of commission in 1516 see Porter's precedent book, C193/142, ff. 32–33. See also H. G. Richardson, 'The Early History of the Commissions of Sewers' (1919) 34 *EHR* 385–93.

[82] Wording of the commission, before and after 1531. However, the statute 23 Hen. VIII, c. 5 provided that suits should be determined according to the laws and customs of Romney Marsh: apparently a careless abridgment of the wording of previous legislation.   [83] 6 Hen. VIII, c. 10.

[84] 23 Hen. VIII, c. 5, s. 7. This seems to be the first public recognition of barristers.

[85] *Lisle Letters*, ed. Byrne, ii. 654, no. 507 (1535).

[86] e.g. KB 29/146, m. 39 (presentments at a 'Sessio Sewariarum' in Berks., 1508).

[87] The fullest contemporary discussion of the law relating to justices of the peace is Thomas Marow's reading (Inner Temple, 1503) on Westminster I, c. 1, pr. in Putnam, *Early Treatises*, 289–413 (cited below as Marow, *Reading*). (In deference to the convention of not reading on more recent statutes, Marow took as his text a statute passed before justices of the peace were introduced.) There were also two important practice manuals: the anonymous *Boke of Justices of Peas* (*c*.1505), and Sir Anthony Fitzherbert's *The Newe Boke of Justices of the Peas* (1538).

[88] By the 1550s they were expected to report monthly to the Privy Council: *Acts of the Privy Council*, ed. J. R. Dasent, v. 161.

[89] Marow, *Reading*, 301–6; and ensuing discussion reported in Port 156, *per* Frowyk CJ. Cf. *R. v. Warcop* (1533) Spelman 99 (JPs do not have power of oyer and terminer unless expressly mentioned in their commission). For examples of commissions of the peace *c*.1506, see Porter's precedent book, C193/142, ff. 24–26.

though it is doubtful whether this had much practical application by his time since the regular commissions of the peace included both an executive authority to 'keep' the peace and a judicial authority to hear and determine cases. The justices also possessed numerous statutory powers,[90] both judicial and administrative, which were constantly being added to in the sixteenth century.[91]

The commission, as used in the 1530s and 1540s,[92] contained three charges each indicated by the operative word *assignavimus*. The first charge was executive: that the justices should jointly and severally keep, and cause to be kept, the king's peace and various statutes and ordinances, should punish those who offended against the statutes, and should cause all those who threatened others to find surety for their good behaviour. The second charge was to enquire, by the oath of good and lawful men,[93] into all felonies and misdemeanours—including a long list of specific statutory offences—committed in their county, and also to inspect all indictments found before them or before the justices of Edward IV, Edward V, Richard III or Henry VII, and to make and continue process against the persons indicted until they appeared or were outlawed. And the third charge was judicial: that the justices, or any two or more of them (with the *quorum* clause[94]), might hear and determine all the offences aforementioned, with proviso that if any case of difficulty arose upon the decision and determination of 'such extortions'— meaning all the said offences[95]—they should not proceed to judgment except in the presence of a justice of one of the benches, or of the assize judges. The commission ended with commands to attend to their various duties, to order the sheriff to cause good and lawful men to come before them at appointed days and places to enquire into the truth concerning the premises,[96] and for one of the justices by name (the *custos rotulorum*[97]) to have the various writs, precepts, processes, and indictments brought before his fellows at the same day and place. It was the third charge, together with the three final commands, which enabled the justices to hold their judicial sessions, where they might try and give judgment in criminal cases as justices of oyer and terminer. The second charge enabled them to receive

[90] A statute could confer jurisdiction on all justices of the peace, even in matters not expressly mentioned in the commission: Marow's reading (1503), as reported in Port 156, *per* Frowyk CJ.

[91] See Holdsworth, *HEL*, iv. 137–45. Holdsworth described them as 'the men of all work in the Tudor scheme of local government': ibid. 137.

[92] Fitz. J. P. 1–3v (datable from the king's style as supreme head to 1534/8); same form temp. Edw. VI summarized in *CPR 1547–8*, p. 80 (1547).   [93] i.e. the grand jury or juries.

[94] i.e. that a specified number of those named in the *quorum* ('of whom') clause must be present.

[95] Fitz. J. P. 6. According to Fitzherbert, the proceedings were not invalidated by the proviso if the justices omitted to reserve such a problem for the assize judges.

[96] i.e. to summon the panels from which trial juries were drawn.

[97] There is a discussion of his relationship to the other JPs in Mich. 2 Hen. VII, fo. 1, pl. 2 (1486). Marow said he was only responsible for the quarter sessions records, and was not even entitled to custody of the commission: *Reading*, 411–12.

indictments and issue process thereon. Although this was directed to 'you and any of you' (*vos et quoscumque vestrum*), this also required the presence of at least two justices, since *vos et quos* were both plural.[98] It will be noted that the commission did not include a power of gaol delivery, and therefore the justices of the peace could not deliver suspects by proclamation.[99] The judicial authority was generally exercised in county quarter sessions, though in the 1540s there was a short-lived experiment with county divisions which anticipated the later petty sessions.[100]

Although commissions of the peace were regularly reissued in common form, each was technically a new authority, so that the central courts would not take notice that justices of the peace were always justices of oyer and terminer.[101] In reality, however, they were a permanent institution; and new commissions were issued only for the purpose of effecting changes in composition.[102] Each commission remained in force until a new commission was issued, which always impliedly superseded the previous one;[103] if a name was omitted from the new commission, that had the effect of removing the person from office.[104] In some places, the power of appointing justices was delegated—usually to a corporation—by royal charter.[105] New justices were given an oath of office, which included the hallowed promise to 'do equal right both to rich and poor'.[106]

There have been a number of analyses of the membership of peace commissions in particular counties,[107] though they usually underestimate the legally trained element, doubtless because of the difficulty in identifying lawyers. Despite earlier attempts to limit the commissions to a handful of active justices,[108] the

[98] Fitz. J. P. 5v. Cf. Mich. 14 Hen. VII, fo. 8, pl. 19, *per* Constable sjt.

[99] This is confirmed by a note in Yorke 203, no. 301 (early 1530s).

[100] 33 Hen. VIII, c. 10 (repealed by 37 Hen. VIII, c. 7); F. A. Youngs, 'Towards Petty Sessions: Tudor JPs and the divisions of counties' in *Tudor Rule and Revolution*, ed. D. J. Guth and J. W. McKenna (1982), 201–16.   [101] *Anon.* (1482) Pas. 22 Edw. IV, fo. 12, pl. 33; *R. v. Warcop* (1533) Spelman 99.

[102] A new commission was needed to add even a single name, since the Statute of Cambridge 1388 (12 Ric. II, c. 10) forbade the addition of justices by writ of association.

[103] Mich. 20 Hen. VII, fo. 6, pl. 16, *per* Pigot and Broke; *Penyngton v. Hunte* (1544) Cholmeley 454 at 459, *per* Hales sjt, and 461, *per* Baldwin CJ; 2 & 3 Phil. & Mar., c. 18 (principle not to apply to city or town commissions).   [104] Marow, *Reading*, ed. Putnam, 311–12.

[105] See *Abbot of St Albans v. Fortescue and others* (1496) CP 40/935, m. 337 (action on the case for holding the sessions at Chipping Barnet, being an infringement of plaintiff's privilege granted by charters of Edw. IV and Hen. VII; imparlance).

[106] An oath to put statutes in execution 'without favour' was required by the statute 13 Ric. II, stat. 1, c. 7. At the beginning of the sixteenth century, justices were sworn to 'do egall right to the pore and to the riche': Porter's precedent book, C193/142, fo. 29. The classic form was printed in Fitz. J. P. 16v (1538).

[107] See M. L. Zell, 'Early Tudor Justices of the Peace at Work' (1978) 93 *Archaeologia Cantiana* 125–43, at 126–32 (Kent); J. R. Lander, *English Justices of the Peace 1461–1509* (1989), ch. 2, and 49 n. 3.

[108] The Statute of Cambridge 1388 (12 Ric. II, c. 10), limiting the number of justices to six (besides the two assize judges), was explained away in early Tudor times as not rendering void the acts of a greater number, because it was a 'general negative': Port 116. Marow held the effect to be merely that the supernumerary justices could not receive wages: *Reading*, ed. Putnam, 360.

commissions grew in the early Tudor period to include numerous non-resident privy councillors and state officials, besides the assize judges, while in the western and northern counties the members of the provincial councils were also added. The only formal qualification for appointment was £20 a year in land, though this did not extend to 'discreet persons learned in the law':[109] a formal acknowledgement of the need for legal expertise. Perhaps more than half the resident justices were members of the inns of court, though that does not mean they were lawyers.[110] There was certainly a substantial cadre of lawyers in every commission, since the judges, serjeants at law, and most of the benchers of the inns of court, were active justices in their own counties, and it was usual to include a few lesser members of the profession. The *quorum* was dominated by the legal element, and such information as has been gleaned about the attendance of justices at sessions—derived from payment claims[111]—shows that the lawyers' actual influence was even stronger than a bare analysis of the nominal membership reveals.[112]

The clerical work was handled in each county by the clerk of the peace and clerk of the Crown, usually if not invariably the same person.[113] Their respective duties are set out in an assize brought in 1519 for both clerkships in the county of Worcester. The clerk or clerks sat at the feet of the justices of the peace, and had the duty of reading out commissions, writs, indictments, and other records, the clerk of the Crown taking the principal place at Crown sittings. The clerk of the Crown, who was in effect the king's attorney at the sessions,[114] was responsible for making a record of criminal cases, with a fee of 2s. from every prisoner acquitted of felony and a similar fee from every surety when a prisoner for felony was bailed or mainprised. The clerk of the peace, who may in that capacity have been regarded as clerk to the *custos rotulorum*,[115] wrote out petitions and plaints for surety to keep the peace, and for contempt or trespass against the statutes of

---

[109] 18 Hen. VI, c. 11; discussed in Marow, *Reading*, ed. Putnam, 314–21.   [110] Below, 461–2.

[111] Lander, *English Justices of the Peace 1461–1509*, 58–78. The claims are not wholly reliable as evidence, since not all justices who attended were necessarily paid.

[112] Lander, *English Justices of the Peace 1461–1509*, 64–73; Zell, 'Early Tudor Justices of the Peace', 140–1. Lander underestimated the number of lawyers among those identified as frequent attenders: e.g. taking Norfolk alone (pp. 70–1), John Fyncham JP (d. 1496) was an eminent counsel, 'legis peritus' (CP 40/857, m. 320; CP 40/878, m. 426; KB 27/908, m. 21) and probably a bencher of the Middle Temple; Thomas Gygges JP (d. 1497) was a bencher of Lincoln's Inn; and William Elys JP (d. 1534), 'an otherwise obscure local gentleman' (p. 71), was a barrister of Lincoln's Inn (later a bencher and a baron of the Exchequer).

[113] e.g. John Southcote of the Middle Temple was for over thirty years clerk of the peace and clerk of the Crown for Devon, and he also served as sheriff's clerk to successive sheriffs: *LP*, iv. II. 3622(17) (appointed 1526); *Southcote v. Tothill* (1555) CP 40/1164, m. 1361; *Kyrke v. Southcote* (1556) CP 40/1165, m. 742; *Totthyll v. Southcott*, ibid., m. 743 (sued for holding latter office beyond a year); CP 40/1166, m. 850 (denies clerkship under third sheriff). For the sheriff's clerk see also below, 301.

[114] This expression is used of the clerk of the peace in Mich. 2 Hen. VII, fo. 1, pl. 2 (1486).

[115] Marow, *Reading*, ed. Putnam, 363 (tr. 'if the clerk of peace makes default at the sessions, he shall not be amerced for it, for he is not an officer of the court, but is only the clerk of the *custos rotulorum*').

labourers, received and entered recognizances, and wrote the precepts thereupon. He claimed a fee of 2s. for his attendance, 2s. for a recognizance to keep the peace, and 1s. for writing plaints, petitions, and precepts.[116] After 1536, the clerk had the additional statutory duty of keeping records of deeds enrolled in the county under the Statute of Enrolments.[117] He also had the responsibility—presumably as clerk of the Crown—for drawing the bills of indictment to be considered at the quarter sessions,[118] and our few surviving precedent books of indictments were probably made by or for clerks of the peace.[119] Unlike the clerk of assize, the clerk of the Crown was not associated with the justices in the commission; but to remedy any practical problems which this caused, the patent of appointment might make him a permanent justice of oyer and terminer and gaol delivery in the county where he held office.[120]

The offices were until 1545 in the gift of the Crown,[121] and if granted for life were regarded as saleable.[122] However, in that year it was enacted by Parliament that the office of clerk of the peace—presumably now a compendious term including the clerkship of the Crown—should be in the gift of the *custos rotulorum*, who should thereafter be appointed by bill under the sign manual. This measure was presented as a device to stop the granting of offices as a favour to unsuitable and untrained persons, for whom patents were obtained without the king's personal knowledge.[123] No doubt it was really concerned with the control of patronage. But the

Cf. ibid. 412 (tr. 'none of the justices of the peace ought to write in the sessions rolls, but only the *custos rotulorum* and his clerks').

[116] *Rudhale* v. *Salwey* (1519–20) CP 40/1025, m. 560. John Rudhale claimed to have been appointed by patent of 22 Hen. VII, which is not in *CPR*.   [117] 27 Hen. VIII, c. 16; below, 676.

[118] See *Salwey* v. *Abbot of Pershore* (1539) CP 40/1102, m. 324 (*assumpsit* to pay fees for drawing indictments against 120 persons indicted for trespass at Worcester and Pershore sessions, and he claimed £20). For Richard Salwey see above, n. 116.

[119] e.g. BL MS. Add. 42077 (Kent, temp. Hen. VII, with some additions from the Home circuit in the 1530s); Kent Archives Office, MS. U4, U419 (two fragments of one book, Kent, c.1545), tr. by R. E. A. Poole in *A Kentish Miscellany*, ed. F. Hull (21 Kent Records; 1979), at 138–57; MS. in the possession of Meyer Boswell Books, noted in *ELMUSA*, ii. 1182 (c.1538/47); CUL MS. Dd.9.56, ff. 1–9v (Dorset, temp. Edw. VI). In 1549, John Randall recovered damages for taking two books of precedents, one of them containing '(tr.) all manner of indictments and matters concerning the office of clerk of the peace', and a copy of FNB, from his house near Newgate: KB 27/1149, m. 80.

[120] e.g. *LP*, iv. II. 3622(17) (appointment of John Southcote, Devon, 1526).

[121] They could be granted in reversion: e.g. that granted to John Jaques in the 1540s: C1/1134/39–40.

[122] *Spenser* v. *Boleyn* (1538–9) KB 27/1110, m. 71 (deceit for procuring surrender of patent of Hen. VII; pleads sale; demurrer). Leonard Spencer was clerk of the peace in Norfolk and Suffolk from 1506 to 1533, when he surrendered to the use of Sir James Boleyn and James Hawe: *CPR 1494–1509*, p. 495; *LP*, vi. 300(12). Several other appointments were made by patent in 1506, apparently a conscious revival: Putnam, *Early Treatises*, 103.

[123] 37 Hen. VIII, c. 1. Appointments of the *custos rotulorum* were formerly by patent: e.g. *LP*, i. 1732(36) (Walter Rowdon, 1513); Rowdon succeeded William Grevill (d. 1513), who had continued to hold the office after becoming JCP, since he remained a JP.

use of signed bills of appointment ceased under Edward VI, and the appointment of the *custos rotulorum* was restored to the lord chancellor in 1549.[124]

By virtue of the first charge in the commission—*ad pacem nostram conservandam*—individual justices had the power to take recognizances to keep the peace,[125] a power which Marow denied to most other courts. Marow also held that it was good authority for a keeper of the peace to make an arrest in person.[126] Since both these powers were executive, they did not belong to judges as such.[127] Keeping order on the streets was primarily the function of the constables,[128] but the justices had a statutory role in preventing or suppressing public disorder,[129] and dealing with forcible entries,[130] and they also became involved in extrajudicial criminal investigations.[131] This last seems to have been a new development, since in 1481 Bryan CJ had doubted the authority of justices of the peace to ask questions or take informations out of the sessions,[132] and in the next generation it was held that a justice could not issue a warrant of arrest except for an offence committed in his own presence.[133] We learn from defences to actions of conspiracy in the time of Henry VIII that informants might approach a justice privately about their suspicions,[134] though in most cases reports of crime were said to have

[124] 3 & 4 Edw. VI, c. 1. The act recited that the appointment had belonged to the lord chancellor long before 1545.

[125] Discussed in Marow, *Reading*, ed. Putnam, 321–30; Fitz. J. P. 6v–9v. W. O. Williams (*Cal. Caernarvonshire Quarter Sessions Records 1541–58*, p. cviii) says this was the main business out of sessions, and that individual JPs rarely made committals.   [126] Marow, *Reading*, ed. Putnam, 304.

[127] Cf. *Note* (*c.*1530) Caryll (Jun.) 390, no. 47, where it is suggested that JPs had the same protection as judges for executive acts done within their statutory authority but without factual warrant.

[128] See the discussion in Marow, *Reading*, ed. Putnam, 335–7 (tr. 'How this breach of the peace may be pacified').

[129] 13 Hen. IV, c.7; Marow, *Reading*, ed. Putnam, 338–47; *Anon.* (*c.*1514) Spelman 158. See *Sir Thomas Grene's Case* (1498) Mich. 14 Hen. VII, fo. 7, pl. 19 (false imprisonment; pleads riot, and arrest by command of single JP); *Staynclyff* v. *Turton* (1520) KB 27/1034, m. 36 (false imprisonment; pleads that plaintiff disturbed the peace in the presence of two 'conservators' of the peace, who ordered him to keep the peace in the king's name and then arrested him for refusing to do so).

[130] 8 Hen. VI, c. 9; Marow, *Reading*, ed. Putnam, 348–58; Zell, 'Early Tudor Justices of the Peace', 134–5.

[131] Marow said that a justice could arrest someone through his own servant, and keep him for a short time in his own home, which implies an individual police role: *Reading*, ed. Putnam, 337, citing 5 Hen. IV, c. 10. Cf. *Lutterell's Case* (undated) Spelman 159.

[132] *Anon.* (1481) Mich. 21 Edw. IV, fo. 67, pl. 49, *per* Bryan CJ (but questioned by Choke J.). Serjeant Catesby argued that '(tr.) when a man comes to [a JP or JPs] before the sessions, and shows how he has been robbed by such and such a person, and shows the suspiciousness of the act and the circumstances, the justices may ask him various questions, and thereupon he is bound to inform the [grand] jury.'

[133] *Sir Thomas Grene's Case* (1498) YB Mich. 14 Hen. VII, fo. 7, pl. 19; *Anon.* (*c.*1500) 2 Caryll 388; *Hyll* v. *Gylle* (1523) Hil. 14 Hen. VIII, fo. 16, pl. 3 (119 Selden Soc. 142); CP 40/1037, m. 551; *Walsshe* v. *Owtred* (1529) CP 40/1061, m. 705 (justification by virtue of warrant held bad on demurrer).

[134] e.g. *Leynes* v. *Cordell* (1525) KB 27/1055, m. 69 (theft of wethers in Middlesex; defendants reported their suspicion to Robert Wroth JP, who ordered them to attend the sessions where they informed the grand jury).

been made directly to the justices assembled in their sessions.[135] By the 1550s, investigations before individual justices were commonplace.[136]

QUARTER SESSIONS OF THE PEACE

The jurisdiction of the justices as commissioners of oyer and terminer was defined both by the wording of their commission and by the numerous statutes which enlarged their judicial powers.[137] The extent of the standard-form commission was not beyond doubt in this period. Although it mentioned a very extensive list of offences, it did not include treason or murder, and Fitzherbert concluded that, since treason and murder did not come under the general heading of 'felonies', they were outside the justices' jurisdiction and could not be included by implication.[138] That seems to have been the orthodox position with respect to high treason.[139] There was, however, a contrary view that murder was included in felony.[140] Indictments for murder were in practice taken at the sessions,[141] and the matter was put beyond doubt by the courts in 1553,[142] though in the absence of sessions rolls we cannot be sure how many of these indictments were tried at the sessions and how many

[135] e.g. *Tomson* v. *Fulleluff* (1510) KB 27/995, m. 35 (JPs order defendants to cause a bill of the felony to be made for the grand jury); *Horsyngton* v. *Dounton* (1512) CP 40/997, m. 450 (gave evidence to grand jury at quarter sessions; demurrer); *Markewyke* v. *Alee* (1516) KB 27/1019, m. 32; *Speyghte* v. *Uncle* (1516) KB 27/1020 m. 64; *Pethyll* v. *Atwyll* (1518) CP 40/1020B, m. 439; *Cornysshe* v. *Goodeve* (1519) KB 27/1033, m. 72; *Penyngton* v. *Gyldon* (1522) KB 27/1045, m. 61 (counsel advised informant to show the matter at the next sessions, which he did on oath); *Forty* v. *Forme* (1533) KB 27/1087, m. 74; *Walker* v. *Collyns* (1534) CP 40/1081, m. 444.

[136] See further below, 515. Note the defamation action of *Raynesforde* v. *Symmes* (1551) KB 27/1158, m. 122 (JP scandalously accused of threatening to burn off the fingernails of suspects with iron tongues).

[137] Fitz. J. P. 4; Yorke 110–13.

[138] Fitz. J. P. 19. According to Fitzherbert, the sessions could arraign someone indicted of murder 'as for felony': i.e. he could be tried upon it for manslaughter only.

[139] See G. R. Elton, *Policy and Police* (1972), 298–300. Note, however, *R.* v. *Wulnall* (1532) NfRO, C/S3/1, m. 42k (petty treason in clipping coin; pleads Guilty at county quarter sessions); *R.* v. *With* (1550) NfRO, C/S3/3 (treasonable assembly and making proclamations in the 1549 rebellion; withdraws plea of Not guilty, confesses, and has 'judgment' at county quarter sessions); *R.* v. *Ledeham* (1550) ibid. (petty treason in coining false shillings; found Not guilty).

[140] *Boke of Justices*, sig. A5v (murder included in charge). Putnam went so far as to accuse Fitzherbert of a 'serious mistake': *Early Treatises*, 38–9, 198–200 (attributing the error to Statham); 'Sixteenth Century Treatises', 7 *Univ. Toronto Law Jnl* 140.

[141] See e.g. *Anon.* (1488) Pas. 3 Hen. VII, fo. 5, pl. 2 (indictment for murder at Rutland sessions); *Sibill* v. *Nele* (1498) Mich. 14 Hen. VII, fo. 2, pl. 7, *per* Fyneux CJ; *R.* v. *Weston* (1536) 94 Selden Soc. 297 (indictment for murder at Oxford sessions); *R.* v. *Moris ap Eliza* (1551) *Cal. Caernarvonshire Quarter Sessions Records 1541-58*, pp. lxxx–lxxxi (trial for murder at Caernarvon sessions); Dalison's reports (1553) BL MS. Harley 5141, fo. 10v (says it was the 'experience'); Rast. Ent. 362 (385v), pl. 12. Three indictments for murder were found at Norfolk quarter sessions in 1532–3: NfRO, C/S3/1, mm. 39f, 45c, 77c.

[142] *R.* v. *Duckler* (King's Bench, Pas. 1551) Dyer 69a (tr. 'contrary to the opinion of Mr Fitzherbert'); *Anon.* (Serjeants' Inn, Hil. 1553) Dalison's reports, BL MS. Harley 5141, fo. 10v (tr. 'notwithstanding the opinion of Fitzherbert').

transmitted to the assizes. The phrase 'trespasses and other misdeeds' (*transgressiones et alia malefacta*) was wide enough to include all lesser offences against individuals, whether or not specifically mentioned, even including (in Fitzherbert's view) non-forcible trespasses of the kind for which actions upon the case lay.[143] Such evidence as we have from the Norfolk quarter sessions indicates that accusations of non-forcible wrongs to individuals were usually coupled with trespass to land.[144] On the other hand, it was held that this jurisdiction did not extend to nuisances against the general public, because such offences were not 'trespasses'.[145]

There are very few county quarter sessions records surviving for the period before 1549,[146] though specimen records may be found in the King's Bench rolls.[147] Although theft was probably the commonest offence presented at county sessions,[148] and occasionally other felonies (such as rape and arson) were met with, the range of non-capital offences was wide indeed, and extended to many areas of economic and social regulation. The justices were still active in the enforcement of the fourteenth-century labour legislation,[149] which enabled them to curb excessive wages or unduly long dinner-breaks,[150] and punish bad workmanship.[151] Other offences punishable at the sessions included regrating and forestalling,[152] giving alms to unauthorized beggars,[153] harbouring idle and suspect persons,[154] playing unlawful games such as

---

[143] Fitz. J. P. 11.

[144] e.g. *R.* v. *Smyth* (1533) n. 160, below (trespass to land and eavesdropping); *R.* v. *Miller* (1539) NfRO, C/S3/2 (trespass to house and leaving a baby girl there 'to the grave disquiet and nuisance' of the owner); *R.* v. *Wigmore* (1539) ibid. (trespass to house and defamation in saying, *inter alia* (sp. mod.), 'Thou art a[s] strong whore as any is in the stews'). For trespass to land see below, 273.

[145] *R.* v. *Cooke* (1491) KB 27/918, Rex m.3d (indictment for non-repair of bridge quashed because JPs have no jurisdiction to take indictment for common nuisance); *Anon.* (1526) 120 Selden Soc. 57, pl. 43; Yorke 159, no. 184; William Saunders's reading (Middle Temple, 1533) 121 Selden Soc. 267.

[146] i.e. when the Middlesex records begin. Cf. *Calendar of the Caernarvonshire Quarter Sessions Records 1541-58*, ed. W. O. Williams (1956). A few odd files of county indictments survive, e.g. NfRO, C/S3/1-2 (1532-3, 1539-40). City and borough sessions records survive in greater quantity.

[147] See e.g. Hayes, ' "Ancient Indictments" for the North of England, 1461-1509', 19 at 27-8.

[148] This observation is based on several hundred Norfolk indictments in NfRO, C/S3/1-3 (1532-50).

[149] J. Whittle, *The Development of Agrarian Capitalism: land and labour in Norfolk 1440-1580* (2000), 276-304.

[150] *Boke of Justices*, sig. H4; Fitz. J. P. 67-8; 7 Hen. VIII, c. 5. Also refusal to work, departure from service, or procuring a departure from service, contrary to the Statute of Labourers: *Kent Records*, xxi. 156; numerous examples in NfRO, C/S3/1-3 (Norfolk quarter sessions).

[151] e.g. in the 1520s the York city sessions fined 28 cordwainers for making shoes deceitfully and insufficiently from sheepskin, calfskin, and horse-skin contrary to statute, and to the common nuisance: city chamberlains' accounts, YCA, CC 2, fo. 140v. And in 1550 several Norfolk tanners were indicted for selling falsely tanned hides: NfRO, C/S3/3 (Quarter Sessions file).

[152] e.g. NfRO, C/S3/1, mm. 21b (regrating), 37 (forestalling). Cf. courts leet, below, 302.

[153] *Boke of Justices*, sig. B3; Fitz. J. P. 83v.

[154] 19 Hen. VII, c. 12; *Kent Records*, xxi. 156-7 (vagabonds pretending to have knowledge of physiognomy and palmistry); *R.* v. *Bungey* (1550) NfRO, C/S3/3 (supporting vagabonds, whores, and other idle

football,[155] or cards and dice,[156] keeping houses of ill repute,[157] keeping hand-guns,[158] poaching,[159] eavesdropping,[160] practising surgery without a licence,[161] and selling beef derived from mad cows 'contrary to the custom of the realm'.[162] Despite the legal doubts about their jurisdiction over nuisance, justices in practice punished public nuisances, such as blocking the highway or diverting a common watercourse,[163] creating health hazards and other dangers, or failing to maintain public amenities such as bridges, or stocks for restraining offenders.[164] By virtue of the word *transgressiones* in the commission, even a simple trespass to land was indictable at the sessions; and such cases seem to have been fairly common, even without aggravation by riot or forcible entry.[165] The justices had a statutory authority to enquire into heresy and related offences, but any

persons of bad conversation, and keeping bad rule in his house). Cf. 22 Hen. VIII, c. 10, concerning gypsies ('egyptians').

[155] *Boke of Justices*, sig. B2v; Fitz. J. P. 68; 12 Ric. II, c. 6. BL MS. Add. 42077 contains on fo. 22 an indictment of 1485 for playing quoits ('coytyng') contary to the custom of the realm prohibiting unlawful games, namely football and hand-throwing (*illicita joca videlicet pila pedalis et manualis disculatio*). Cf. fo. 15v (indictment in 1480 against footballers riotously claiming a piece of land as a common playing ground, and chanting threats).

[156] R. v. *Rede* (1501) 3 *DKR*, app. ii, 225 (dice; outlawry in Lincs.); *Kent Records*, xxi. 140–1 (cards, dice, and bowls); R. v. *Avyson* (1533) NfRO, C/S3/1, m. 83a (cards and dice); *Cal. Caernarvonshire Quarter Sessions Records 1541–58*, pp. 40, 41, 88, 152 (cards and dice); R. v. *Skynner* (1550) NfRO, C/S3/3 (dice, painted cards, and bowls, played for large sums of money).

[157] e.g. R. v. *Bastard* (1533) NfRO, C/S3/1, m. 67c (gaming house); R. v. *Smyth* (1539) NfRO, C/S3/2 (keeping 'blind alehouses' where he maintained ill-governed persons who disturbed the neighbours); R. v. *Power* (1539) ibid. (frequenting other 'blind alehouses'); R. v. *Rynger et uxorem* (1539) ibid. (keeping a brothel to the grave disquiet of their neighbours).

[158] Fitz. J. P. 68; 14 & 15 Hen. VIII, c. 7; 25 Hen. VIII, c. 17; 33 Hen. VIII, c. 6. Cf. 6 Hen. VIII, c. 13 (which only mentions common informers).

[159] e.g. R. v. *Newale* (1532) NfRO, C/S3/1, m. 32a (taking pheasants in warren); R. v. *Senowe* (1539) NfRO, C/S3/2 (hunting coneys in warren). Cf. R. v. *Thacker* (1550) NfRO, C/S3/3 (clergyman indicted for keeping nets and engines for taking pheasants, which were 'gentlemen's game', not having £10 per annum).

[160] e.g. R. v. *Smyth* (1533) NfRO, C/S3/1, m. 68l (trespass to land at night and listening like an eaves-dropper—*noctanter in similitudine unius le evisdripper ascultavit*—and recounting everything he heard to others).

[161] e.g. R. v. *Monman* (1544) KB 27/1133, Rex m. 1 ('egiptianus' indicted in Hunts. for practising surgery by undertaking to cure someone of colic and the stone, against the peace and against the statute of 3 Hen. VIII, c. 11).

[162] BL MS. Add. 42077, fo. 8v (buying, butchering, and selling meat from a mad cow—*vacca furiosa*—knowing it to be mad and unfit for human consumption, contrary to the custom of the realm; undated). As to unwholesome victual, see also *Boke of Justices*, sig. B5; *Kent Records*, xxi. 141–2 (putrid slaughtered pig). [163] e.g. *Kent Records*, xxi. 148–9, nos. 27–8.

[164] *Boke of Justices*, sig. B6 and K5 (presentment against abbot whose customary duty it was to find them). Cf. R. v. *Cooke* (1491) KB 27/918, Rex m. 3d (above, 272 n. 145).

[165] e.g. at Norfolk quarter sessions in 1532–3: NfRO, C/S3/1, mm. 14e (taking reeds), 15 (breaking close), 50j (depasturing), 63g (destroying hedges), 72e (breaking close and assault); and note also 68g (pound breach). Cf. *Kent Records*, xxi. 147, nos. 23–4 (depasturing animals and trampling grass). Cases of forcible entry are found in similar numbers in the Norfolk files.

presentment had to be certified to the bishop for trial.[166] Thus, at Canterbury sessions in 1536, several men were presented for speaking words 'against the worshipping of saints', including the assertion that the images in the church were 'but mammets and puppets' and that 'Our Lady neither other saint is of power to help any man'.[167] The defendants were in consequence cited before the archbishop of Canterbury (Cranmer), but the outcome is unknown.

The manner of conducting the quarter sessions emerges into view in our period through a few manuals for the guidance of the clerk of the peace,[168] the earliest of which was compiled in Suffolk, perhaps by John Higham, clerk of the peace from 1497 to 1506.[169] These manuals are, not surprisingly, more concerned with form than with substance; but the forms are more helpful than the bare records in reconstructing what happened in court. Before the day, the clerk made out a precept (or writ of attendance) in the name of one or two of the justices of the peace,[170] directing the sheriff to summon twenty-four men from every hundred and borough, and to warn the coroners, stewards, constables, and hundred-bailiffs, to attend. When the session opened, the clerk wrote the caption in his book, with the place and date, and directed the crier to make the general proclamation: 'Oyez. Oyez. All manner of men which have ado here before these justices of the peace of the shire of Suffolk come forth and [they] shall be heard.' No mention is made of any reading of the commission, as at the assizes, and it seems probable that a commission of the peace was only publicly read once, when it was newly received.[171] The next step, according to our guide, was to call upon the sheriff and officers to appear and return their precepts. Appearances were then

---

[166] 2 Hen. V, c. 7; reaffirmed by 25 Hen. VIII, c. 12; repealed by 1 Edw. VI, c. 12. For examples see G. R. Elton, *Policy and Police* (1967), 40, 102.

[167] Precedent book of C. Levyns, BL MS. Stowe 850, ff. 45–46 (sessions before the mayor and alderman, and the recorder, John Hales, 8 June 1536). A third man (fo. 46) was even less respectful to the wooden image of Our Lady, saying that '(sp. mod.) her arse is worm eaten and that he would as lief kiss his shoe as Our Lady's feet or any other relic in Christ Church or elsewhere'. Another was accused merely of eating eggs and butter in Lent.

[168] Cf. *Regule atque Ordines nonnulle Observande tam in Sessione Pacis quam in Sessione Gaole Deliberationis* (Bucks., temp. Edw. VI) Bodl. Lib. MS. è Mus. 57, ff. 87v–89; *The Manner and Order of Keeping the Quarter Cessions* (Sussex, temp. Eliz.) BL MS. Harley 1591, ff. 6–10. There is a slightly earlier formulary in BL MS. Harley 773, noted in *Proceedings before Justices of the Peace in the 14th and 15th Centuries*, ed. B. H. Putnam (1938), p. xcviii.

[169] *La Forme d'Office dun Clerk de Peas*, BL MS. Harley 1777, ff. 33v–48 (quotations with sp. mod.); excerpted in Putnam, *Early Treatises*, 53–4; further noted by her in 7 *Univ. Toronto Law Jnl* at 138–40; also in London Guildhall Lib. MS. 3035, ff. 59–64; Derbs. Record Office MS. D2440; Oslo/London, The Schøyen Collection, MS. 1641. The name of Sir Robert Drury (JP Suffolk 1488–1535) occurs in the precedents, which range in date from 1494 to 1501.

[170] The precedent is in Drury's name alone, but Marow says the precept should be made by at least two, 'and not under the name of the *custos rotulorum* only': *Reading*, ed. Putnam, 362, 363.

[171] Marow said that reading the commission in the sessions was necessary to give notice of the changes of composition which it effected: *Reading*, ed. Putnam, 311. The Elizabethan manual in BL MS. Harley 1591, fo. 6, does include the reading of the commission.

recorded, and the clerk checked the record of the previous sessions to see whether anyone had been bound over to appear; if any of these did not appear, after proclamation, he made out the appropriate process returnable at the next sessions. He also read the returns of the precepts, and took the appropriate action against defaulters. Then the crier was instructed to call in by name the grand jurors (the jurors of enquiry for the body of the county), the coroner, the franchise-bailiffs and constables, and then three or four 'petty inquests of various hundreds'. After this, the jury of presentment was sworn in the following form:[172]

Good men which have appeared here, stand to the bar that ye may be sworn. [*To the first 'chief constable'*:] Hold your hand upon the Book, and say after me: This hear ye, justices, that I shall duly enquire and true presentment make of all such points and articles where-with I shall be lawfully charged in the king's behalf, and for no cause let but the sooth say, and the king's counsel, my fellows' and mine own well and truly hold and keep, as far as I can; so help me God and holydom, and by this Book. [*He kisses the Book.*]

The remainder were sworn in short form, to keep 'such oath as A.B. hath here sworn before you', whereupon the crier separated them into chief constables and constables, and commanded them to 'stand forth and hear your charge'. The charge was read by the presiding justice,[173] who after 1545 had to be an utter barrister.[174] And there, apart from precedents of instruments, the Suffolk formulary ends. A formulary from the time of Edward VI adds the oath taken by the informants who went before the grand jury:[175] 'The evidence and information which you shall give to this inquest against J.B. upon this bill shall be nothing but truth, and the whole truth, so nigh as God shall suffer you to have knowledge'. It also gives the proclam-ation of adjournment, which occurred at dinner-time, once the grand jury had embarked upon their task. The quarter sessions, not being a gaol delivery, had no power to deliver suspects by proclamation but could only proceed further if an indictment was found.[176] Nor could it arraign suspects on the same day that they were indicted.[177] When prisoners were arraigned, however, the trial procedure—which is omitted from the manuals—was no doubt the same as at the assizes.[178] The whole proceedings might last anything from a day to a week.[179]

[172] The Edwardian form in the Bodl. MS. is substantially similar, but has an added clause against false accusation: '... I shall nothing conceal from the said justices nor yet present for any affection, but the only truth and the whole truth say as nigh as I can'. Cf. a slightly earlier form (from BL MS. Harley 773) pr. in *Proceedings before Justices of the Peace in the 14th and 15th Centuries*, ed. Putnam, p. xcviii.

[173] Specimens may be found in BL MS. Harley 1777, fo. 84v (a fifteenth-century form similar to that pr. in *Boke of Justices*, sig. A5–C1); Fitz. J. P. 18–24 (38 articles). [174] 37 Hen. VIII, c. 1.

[175] Bodl. Lib. MS. è Mus. 57, fo. 87v (sp. mod.). This is arguably a charge rather than an oath.

[176] Littleton's reading (Inner Temple, 1493) 105 Selden Soc. 274; Marow, *Reading*, ed. Putnam, 404; Fitz. J. P. 13v. For delivery by proclamation at the assizes, see above, 258–9.

[177] Yorke 203, no. 301 (Serjeants' Inn, c.1535); Dalison's reports, BL MS. Harley 5141, fo. 11, *per* Hales J. (1553).

[178] For which see below, 516–20. For some procedural divergences between sessions and assizes, see Marow, *Reading*, ed. Putnam, 404–11. [179] Zell, 'Early Tudor Justices of the Peace', 138.

15

The Metropolis

THE principal courts outside Westminster Hall were located but a few miles away, in the city of London. London and Middlesex were in several respects excluded from the legal system which operated in other counties: Middlesex because it was the county in which the two benches normally sat, and London because of its ancient privileges. The city of London was a county in itself, with two sheriffs. There were also two under-sheriffs who, by the Tudor period, were actually judges; unlike under-sheriffs in ordinary counties, they were always lawyers of some standing and held office during good behaviour.[1] The normal work of an under-sheriff was carried out in London by the secondaries,[2] who were also usually members of the inns of court[3] and were assisted by clerks. On the other hand, the two under-sheriffs of Middlesex were commonly attorneys, and performed the usual duties of an under-sheriff.[4] The city courts were governed by immemorial customs which were not subject to outside review; in the event of dispute, a custom was tried by the mayor and aldermen and certified orally in the royal courts by the recorder.[5] These customs were justified in 1527 on the grounds

---

[1] Order of 1441, *Calendar of Letter-Book K*, 257. The first in our period was John Watno (d. 1484), a bencher of Gray's Inn: *Letter Book L*, 227; BL MS. Harley 2051, fo. 45v; Ramsay, 'Legal Profession', app. 8. Sir Thomas More held the office from 1510 to 1518. The under-sheriffs were sometimes called prothonotaries.

[2] B. R. Masters, 'The Secondary' (1968) 2 *Guildhall Miscellany* 425–33.

[3] e.g. Robert Elryngton (of the Middle Temple), who succeeded Owen Meredyth (of the Inner Temple) as secondary of the Bread Street Compter in 1506, apparently in exchange for the lucrative Common Pleas filazership for London: 2 *Guildhall Miscellany* 431; CP 40/975–976 (filazers). Their membership of the inns does not imply that they had followed the learning exercises there; they were not of the class which proceeded to the bench.

[4] They seem to have changed frequently: e.g. CP 40/876, m. 274 (John Elyot, Pas. 1481); CP 40/878, m. 23d (Thomas Staunton, Mich. 1481); CP 40/881, m. 253 (Robert Staunton, Trin. 1482); CP 40/882, m. 59; CP 40/883, m. 274 (John Stokker, Mich. 1482, Hil. 1483); CP 40/888, m. 250d (Thomas Luyt, 1484); CP 40/896, m. 178d (William Swan, 1486); CP 40/903, m. 85 (Edward Cheseman, before 1488); CP 40/909, m. 264 (Richard Stone, 1489); KB 27/1018, m. 38 (Richard Hawkys, 1491); CP 40/919, m. 299 (William Hungate, before 1492) and m. 238d (Edmund Wylly, 1492); CP 40/924, m. 140d (Roger Rydley, Pas. 1493); CP 40/925, m. 189 (Edmund Wylly, Trin. 1493); KB 27/948, Rex m. 8d (Edmund Wylly, 1498).

[5] *Bourgchier* v. *Colyns* (1482–6) Mich. 22 Edw. IV, fo. 30, pl. 11; CP 40/878, m. 404; Jenour's entries, fo. 270v; Mich. 2 Ric. III, fo. 2, pl. 7; KB 27/893, m. 80 (error); Pas. 1 Hen. VII, fo. 21, pl. 8; KB 27/897,

that Londoners needed speedy justice to meet the demands of commerce: 'London is the great fair of the realm'.[6]

Although nearly all the judicial records for our period have been lost,[7] indirect evidence points to a city jurisdiction of major importance, in terms of the number of suits, and of the sums of money involved, and of its possible influence on lawyers who practised in Westminster Hall.[8] The principal surviving sources of information are the Chancery *corpus cum causa* files (C244),[9] in which numerous London cases are found each year, and the files of Chancery petitions (C1) which often contain narrative accounts of proceedings in London. The returns to writs of *corpus cum causa* and *certiorari*, made either by the sheriffs or by the mayor and aldermen of London, reveal an extensive jurisdiction in debt. However, it was very rare for the tenor of the record to be certified in Chancery, and so the 'causa' was returned in general terms. In cases of debt, the return stated the sum in demand but not the basis of the claim. Most actions other than debt were described merely as 'trespass', without further details.[10] Since a surviving plaint of 1485 from the Sheriffs' Court reveals that 'trespass', in the understanding of the sheriffs, included actions on the case such as *assumpsit*,[11] it follows that the general returns are not very illuminating about the range of actions. More can sometimes be discovered if the bill in Chancery has survived.[12] As to the volume of litigation, although it is impossible to calculate with precision, it seems clear that the expansion of London business in the Common Pleas before the beginning of the Tudor period had not diminished the activity of the city courts. This steady continuity nevertheless probably meant that the city was receiving a diminishing share of a rapidly increasing number of suits.[13]

m. 30 (affirmed on a writ of error); *Ernley* v. *Garth* (1490) Port 96; Pas. 11 Hen. VII, fo. 21, pl. 8 (misdated). The method of trial and certification was itself a custom of London, which the central courts recognized to avoid circularity.

⁶ *Marmyon* v. *Baldwyn* (1527) 120 Selden Soc. 61 at 63, *per* Shelley J.

⁷ It is thought that they may have been destroyed in the fire of 1838 at the Royal Exchange.

⁸ The principal studies to date are P. Tucker, 'London's Courts of Law in the Fifteenth Century: the litigants' perspective', in *Communities and Courts in Britain 1150–1900*, ed. C. Brooks and M. Lobban (1997), 25–41; 'Relationships between London's Courts and the Westminster Courts in the Reign of Edward IV' in *Courts, Counties and the Capital in the later Middle Ages*, ed. D. E. S. Dunn (1996), 117–37.

⁹ These also include writs of *certiorari*.

¹⁰ Cf. *Onehand* v. *Wattes* (1488) C244/139/111 (plea of 'deceit' in the Mayor's Court, probably an action on the case).

¹¹ *Asshe* v. *Hayle* (1485) C244/139/100 (judgment for the plaintiff in the Sheriffs' Court; removed into the Mayor's Court, and from thence into Chancery in 1488).

¹² e.g. *Povy's Case* (1505/15) C1/348/39 (deceit for winning £10 with false dice); *Kygan* v. *Goodale* (1529/33) C1/649/27 (calling a lawyer a heretic); *Bradwey* v. *Starkey* (1529/33) C1/747/29 (defamation). These were all in the Sheriffs' Court.

¹³ See Tucker, 'London's Courts of Law in the Fifteenth Century', 27.

The city possessed the inconvenient privilege that the decisions of its courts could not be removed to the King's Bench by writ of error,[14] but could only be reviewed by ad hoc commissioners or delegates sitting at St Martin's-le-Grand.[15] Commissions to hear error from the city courts were occasionally issued in the sixteenth century to judges of the two benches, though there are but few examples enrolled on the patent rolls.[16] On the other hand, interference with London cases by *certiorari* or *corpus cum causa* from the central courts[17] became increasingly frequent during the early Tudor period. The procedure did not infringe the privilege because the London record was not removed but merely summarized in the return to the writ, and the object was to stay the proceedings pending in London rather than to reverse a judgment given there. In the case of the Chancery, the petitioner for a *corpus cum causa* had to show some cause for relief in conscience, and the suit would be remanded by *procedendo* if the cause was not made good.[18] In the case of the two benches, a *corpus cum causa* was issued on the footing that the applicant was engaged in litigation in the superior court and—according to its wording—had been arrested while coming to court.[19] If the London suit could be pursued in the superior court, it was necessary to do so by taking out an original writ, or by suing a bill of Middlesex, as if it were a fresh action.[20] But it did not always follow that the same suit could be pursued in the higher court, and so there might be a *procedendo* to the London court once the cause of privilege ceased or if the suit at Westminster was found to be collusive.[21] There was a contrast with writs of privilege for officers, which were intended to remove the cause permanently and would therefore only lie in the first place if the suit was of a kind which could be conducted in the higher court.[22] The explosion of London privilege cases

[14] Sir Robert Brooke, sometime recorder of London, noted with disapproval that in 1499 an indictment for forcible entry was removed from London by *certiorari*, contrary to the privilege: Brooke Abr., *London*, pl. 11, commenting on Pas. 14 Hen. VII, fo. 28, pl. 5.

[15] *Diversite de Courtz* (1533), sig. A3; FNB 23–4. The record was certified by the recorder of London: Trin. 20 Edw. IV, fo. 7, pl. 9, *per* Bryan CJ.

[16] e.g. *Archer v. Poyntz* (1523) *LP*, iii. 3586(16) (Broke and Fitzherbert JJ; debt in Mayor's Court); *Bulkeley v. Gylson* (1530) *LP*, iv. II. 6543(12) (Fitzherbert and Englefield JJ; action in Mayor's Court on a pledge for £10); *Staple v. Broun* (1557) *CPR 1555–7*, p. 311 (Broke CJ and Browne J.; debt in Mayor's Court for £500, and attachment); *Castell v. Mounde* (1558) *CPR 1557–8*, p. 250 (sim., debt for £100); *Panell v. Mercers Company* (1558) ibid. 453 (Saunders CJ and Dyer J.; assize of fresh force in Court of Husting).

[17] Including even the Exchequer: *Apprice v. Swyft* (1533) *LP*, vi. 1668 (petition to Cromwell as chancellor of the Exchequer).   [18] See e.g. Guy, *Public Career of More*, 68–9, 71–3, 77–9.

[19] This requirement was taken strictly in *Croftes' Case* (1486) Mich. 2 Hen. VII, fo. 2, pl. 6. An example from the end of Hen. VII's reign is *Re Sir Adrian Fortescue* (1508) CP 40/986, m. 111.

[20] *Anon.* (1544) Brooke Abr., *Priviledge*, pl. 48.

[21] The reported cases are not easy to interpret: see *Anon.* (1484) Mich. 2 Ric. III, fo. 16, pl. 43; *Anon.* (1486) Hil. 1 Hen. VII, fo. 12, pl. 20; *Pind v. Lumbard* (1486) Pas. 1 Hen. VII, fo. 22, pl. 12; *Anon.* (1494) Port 30, pl. 34; *Anon.* (1496) Port 36, pl. 36; *Anon.* (1498) Mich. 14 Hen. VII, fo. 6, pl. 15; *Anon.* (1505) Mich. 21 Hen. VII, fo. 39, pl. 48; *Anon.* (undated) Spelman 74, pl. 1–2. These are all King's Bench cases.

[22] *Anon.* (1534) Yorke 229, no. 380, *per* Fitzjames CJ (and affirmed by Fitzherbert JCP). Cf. Dyer 287a, §48.

in the Common Pleas in the 1550s hints that the court may have relaxed its surveillance of the procedure or even encouraged the business. The King's Bench also, by developing *assumpsit*, became at the same time attractive to city litigants, and may have drawn business away from the city courts.[23]

Contemporaries generally spoke of three courts in London: the Guildhall Court and the two sheriffs' compters. However, this distinction was based on the place of sitting rather than the underlying legal theory, which was more complex. The Guildhall was used for sittings of three principal courts, the Court of Hustings and the Sheriffs' Court (for cases adjourned from the sheriffs' compters), which sat in the hall, and the Mayor's Court, which sat in the chamber.[24] The shrieval jurisdiction was in theory unitary, although for convenience it was divided between the two sheriffs and exercised in different locations. Each sheriff had a 'compter', or counter, where proceedings were commenced;[25] but adjournment into the Guildhall did not involve a transfer of jurisdiction to a different body.

THE COURT OF HUSTINGS

The Court of Hustings had the jurisdiction of a county court. In later times it was called the Court of Husting, in the singular; but in strictness there were two Hustings,[26] one for pleas of land (in real and mixed actions) and the other for common pleas, the rolls being kept separately.[27] Like all county courts, an important part of its business was the proclamation of outlawries, which could take place in either Husting; but outlawry business was not entered on the Hustings plea rolls. It could also in theory hear error from the sheriffs' courts, by royal writ,[28] and after 1494 it could hear attaint in respect of any verdict given in the city courts,[29] though no early Tudor records in either category have been found. The court was held, at any rate notionally, before the mayor and aldermen; but by the mid-sixteenth century at the latest the judges seem in practice to have been the under-sheriffs.[30] Many of the warrants of attorney in the rolls were received

---

[23] See above, 158; below, 859. In 1554 the city itself brought *assumpsit* in the King's Bench against an executrix: *City of London* v. *Wylloughby* (1554) KB 27/1172, m. 187.

[24] An action by original bill of debt before the mayor and alderman *in magna camera* is set out in *Tomworthe* v. *Clyfton* (1555) CP 40/1164, m. 1310.

[25] For the compters see below, 284.

[26] On this ground, it was held to be erroneous to refer to the Court of Husting in the singular: *Grubham's Case* (1491) Hil. 6 Hen. VII, fo. 15, pl. 7; Mich. 11 Hen. VII, fo. 10, pl. 33, *per* Huse CJ. The statute 11 Hen. VII, c. 21, uses the plural even for the individual branches ('Hustings of Common Pleas').

[27] They are in the Corporation of London Record Office (CLRO). Usually each roll represents a separate case; the rolls were sewn together later, unnumbered and not always in order.

[28] *Diversite de Courtz* (1533), sig. A3; FNB 22v–23.   [29] 11 Hen. VII, c. 21.

[30] See Plowd. 90, 91v (Randle Cholmeley and John Southcote, 'deputies to the sheriff of London and judges in the cause', in an assize of fresh force in 1553; Southcote is said to be under-sheriff on fo. 93).

'per recordatorem', and it was the recorder who was responsible for producing the record, when required, before the central courts;[31] but there is no evidence as yet that he had judicial functions in the Hustings.

The jurisdiction of the Husting of Common Pleas overlapped with that of the Mayor's Court, but it seems by the time of Henry VII to have been confined to actions of *namia detenta*, the London equivalent of replevin, usually concerning rent of city land. These actions were commenced before one of the sheriffs and then adjourned into the Husting, either by the court itself or by a special imparlance with the assent of the plaintiff. The last surviving bundle of common pleas rolls contains a mere six such cases for the entire reign of Henry VII.[32]

The Husting for Pleas of Land continued to be used for occasional real actions, including writs of right.[33] Writs of right for land in the city were addressed to the mayor and aldermen, and were writs patent not removable by tolt.[34] After 1460 the Husting was chiefly used for conveying city land by means of collusive common recoveries in writs of right. It had therefore come to complement the court's older function of registering deeds and wills relating to land within the city, which were entered on a third series of rolls.[35] It was also used for assizes of fresh force in respect of land in the city.[36]

THE MAYOR'S COURT

The Mayor's Court was a court of record with an unlimited jurisdiction in personal actions at law and in equity,[37] but unfortunately its plea and memoranda rolls end in 1484 and they seem even by that date to have stopped recording suits by bill.[38]

In later times it was the recorder's court. For its later history and law see A. Pulling, *Laws and Customs of the City of London* (1843), 170–7. See also P. E. Jones, 'The City Courts of Law' (1943) 93 *Law Jnl* 285.

[31] *Osbarn (infant)* v. *Jakson* (1493) CP 40/923, m. 369; *Osbarn* v. *Dor…ys* (1494) CP 40/928, m. 369 (debt). For a dower case removed from the Hustings, but eventually remanded, see *Danyell* v. *Curtis* (1549) CP 40/1139, m. 458; CP 40/1141, m. 444.

[32] CLRO, Hustings Rolls, CP 169. The last known case is *Clothiers Company* v. *Abbot of Evesham* (1506) ibid., CP 169, mm. 7–8.

[33] e.g. *Osbarne* v. *Jakson* (1493) CP 40/923, m. 369 (removed into the Common Pleas by the recorder for the purpose of enabling a foreign voucher). [34] FNB 6 /.

[35] Wills of land had to be so registered where land was devised in mortmain, but it was not clear in other cases whether registration was essential to their validity: Brooke Abr., *London*, pl. 31.

[36] Two late examples were reported by Plowden: *Pollard* v. *Jekell* (1553) Plowd. 89v; *Panel* v. *Moore* (1553–6) Plowd. 91v.

[37] For its later history and jurisdiction see Pulling, *Laws and Customs of London*, 177–200. In later times, much of the business was brought by common informers for breach of city regulations.

[38] The last suit enrolled was in 1476. The only suits enrolled in the 1470s concerned either land in the city or the custom of foreign attachment: P. E. Jones, *Calendar of Plea and Memoranda Rolls 1458–1482* (1961), 86–7, 94–5, 104. There are only five files of bills surviving in CLRO before Eliz. I.

The activities of the court in the early Tudor period will therefore have to be reconstructed from the records of other courts, particularly the Chancery.[39]

Like the Hustings, the court was notionally held before the mayor and aldermen in the Chamber of the Guildhall, but it seems probable that the recorder was beginning to sit with them—or deputize for them—as the judge.[40] In the time of Henry VII, the common serjeant sometimes sat with the recorder, and in cases of difficulty the common-law judges might be directly consulted by these officers.[41] The recordership was certainly seen as a major office in the legal profession, and the holders frequently became serjeants at law and royal judges in due course. The court was served by four common attorneys (or 'clerks'), notionally clerks of the common clerk of the city, who served as chief clerk of the court.[42] The third clerk was responsible for enrolling deeds in the Court of Hustings, and the fourth was clerk of the Orphans' Court.[43] By the end of our period the attorneyships seem to have been treated as saleable offices. At any rate, John Norden thought it appropriate to bring a Chancery suit against Barnaby Blagge, of the Inner Temple, for failure to perform an agreement to sell such a post for £12 and surrender it to Norden's use.[44] The attorneys are mostly obscure characters, but some at least were—like Blagge— members of the inns of court and chancery. At some time during our period, the court came also to have its own exclusive Bar, the common pleaders or common counsel, who were benchers or senior barristers of the inns of court.[45] Their number was fixed, and by the 1540s the position was sometimes granted in reversion.[46] These counsel practised not only in the city courts, but also in sittings of the royal courts at the Guildhall.[47]

Proceedings were commenced by original bill, and defendants were summoned by a serjeant-at-mace without more ado. A surviving record from 1503, filed in

---

[39] See e.g. Guy, *Public Career of More*, 68–9, 75. Occasionally suits in the Guildhall Chamber were set out in actions at common law: e.g. *Dunnyng* v. *Bray* (1502) CP 40/961, m. 503 (maintenance of suit there); *Harpesfeld* v. *Earl of Wiltshire* (1518) CP 40/1020B, mm. 485, 488 (judgment pleaded in bar); *Aylmer* v. *Dykar*, recited in *Dykar* v. *Redder* (1522) KB 27/1042, m. 70 (debt for 340 marks).

[40] Jones, 'City Courts', 301–2, thought this had been so since the fourteenth century; but he did not cite his sources.   [41] *Ernley's Case* (1492) 105 Selden Soc. 259 (action of trespass).

[42] In 1535 Thomas Rushton of Lincoln's Inn, 'town clerk', was accused of helping a fellow member of the inn to obtain a favourable jury in an action on the case: *Harbart* v. *Andrewes* (1535) C1/824/51.

[43] B. R. Masters, 'The Town Clerk' (1969) 3 *Guildhall Miscellany* 55–74, at 59–60.

[44] *Norden* v. *Blagge* (temp. Audley C.) C1/863/36. Norden is named as an attorney in the Sheriffs' Court in 1550: *Foster* v. *Turke* (1550) E13/232, m. 1. In the 1550s there are examples of clerkships being held only for a few months, which strongly suggests dealing in them.

[45] The first record is in 1518, when Roger Cholmeley and William Martin were sworn: Tucker, 'London's Courts of Law in the Fifteenth Century', 32–5. Martin was a bencher of Gray's Inn; Cholmeley became a bencher of Lincoln's Inn in 1520 and a serjeant in 1531, remaining one of the common counsel in London until he became recorder in 1535.

[46] Tucker, 'London's Courts of Law in the Fifteenth Century', 33.

[47] e.g. *Broun* v. *Atherly* (1519) CP 40/1026, m. 101d (demurrer to the evidence; William Martin mentioned as *legis peritus de consilio* at the Guildhall).

Chancery, shows that the pleadings followed common-law forms very closely.[48] By immemorial custom, however, the Mayor's Court had a contract jurisdiction which differed in important respects from that of the central courts of law at the beginning of our period. It could entertain actions on promises to settle accounts stated without details of the individual transactions (the action of debt *sur concessit solvere*),[49] actions for breach of covenant without specialty,[50] and actions of debt against executors without specialty;[51] it enforced contracts made by married women traders as if they were single;[52] and it could relieve against penalties.[53] Wager of law in debt could be barred not only by a deed but by any holograph writing of the defendant which bore witness to the contract,[54] or by producing two citizens who swore to the truth of the contract.[55] London also had peculiar procedural advantages in the custom of foreign attachment, whereby a debt could be enforced not only against the principal debtor but also against third parties owing money to him,[56] and sequestration, whereby the household goods of an absent defaulting debtor could be seized by court order.[57] The King's Bench, in developing its commercial jurisdiction in the second quarter of the sixteenth century, was able to emulate the first three advantages but not the others. No doubt the London courts entertained other actions of a kind not encountered in Westminster Hall.[58]

THE SHERIFFS' COURTS

The only surviving records of the sheriffs' courts from the early Tudor period are a few rolls of actions from 1554. In the absence of records, it is not easy to

---

[48] *Walker v. Yorke* (1503) C244/153/49 (plaint of battery; defendant appears by attorney and pleads self-defence; plaintiff replies *de injuria*; verdict and judgment for the plaintiff).

[49] *The Lombard's Case* (1460) Pas. 38 Hen. VI, fo. 29, pl. 12; *De Furnariis v. Curteys* (*c.*1485) recited in C1/88/52 (cloth of gold and satin purchased for wardrobe of Edw. IV); *Pind v. Lumbard* (1486) Pas. 1 Hen. VII, fo. 22, pl. 12; FNB 161B; *Hawkens v. Jakson* (1527) CP 40/1053, m. 442 (brought for an informal penalty). For the earlier history see S. F. C. Milsom, 'Account Stated in the Action of Debt' (1966) 82 *LQR* 534–45.

[50] Pas. 22 Edw. IV, fo. 2, pl. 6, *per* Vavasour sjt; John Grene's reading, Inner Temple (*c.*1490/1) 105 Selden Soc. 206; *Cleymond v. Vyncent* (1521) Port 10, *per* More J.; FNB 145. Wager of law was used, but not against a writing: *Calendar of Letter-Book L*, ed. R. R. Sharpe (1912), 24 (ruled in 1463). For an alleged custom not to allow wager of law in debt for tabling, see Mich. 1 Edw. IV, fo. 5, pl. 14.

[51] Mich. 1 Edw. IV, fo. 6, pl. 14, *per* Danby CJ.

[52] Mich. 1 Edw. IV, fo. 6, pl. 14; Mich. 9 Edw. IV, fo. 35, pl. 11.   [53] See below, 823.

[54] Custom to that effect confessed in *Hawkens v. Jakson* (1525–7) CP 40/1053, m. 442.

[55] Mich. 2 Ric. III, fo. 16, pl. 43.

[56] Hil. 17 Edw. IV, fo. 7. pl. 3; *Bourgchier v. Colyns* (1482–6), above, 277–8 n. 5; Rast. Ent. 139 (142v); *Coke v. Barnys* (1526) CP 40/1049, m. 521 (plea sets out custom and proceedings in London); *Chune v. Thrower* (1544) KB 27/1133, m. 127 (demurrer to sim. plea); *Roberthon v. Norroy King of Arms* (1553) Dyer 83a; *Tomworthe v. Clyfton* (1555) CP 40/1164, m. 1310 (demurrer); *Harwood v. Lee* (1561) Dyer 196b. It was also the custom of some local courts: below, 309.

[57] *Anon.* (1495) Mich. 11 Hen. VII, fo. 1, pl. 4.

[58] e.g. an action to recover a share in a lottery (recited in C1/808/20).

distinguish the Mayor's Court from the Sheriffs' Court which also sat at the Guildhall,[59] and was usually presided over by one of the under-sheriffs.[60] It had the same common-law jurisdiction over all personal actions other than pleas of the Crown, including trespass, debt, covenant, account, defamation,[61] *assumpsit*,[62] and other actions on the case,[63] and it was by no means restricted to small claims.[64] No doubt much of the business was commercial.[65] Cases of difficulty could be removed before the Mayor's Court.[66] A surviving law report provides a glimpse inside the Sheriffs' Court in 1544. It was evidently by this time a learned court of common law, where technical questions of pleading in an action of detinue *sur trover* were argued by Robert Curson, bencher of Lincoln's Inn, one of the common counsel, before Guy Crafford, a fellow bencher, sitting as under-sheriff, apparently with the assistance of the recorder.[67]

The Sheriffs' Court sat in vacation as well as in term.[68] Suits were commenced by 'affirming' a plaint with a 'clerk-sitter' in one of the compters (or counters). Each sheriff had his own compter, which were both prisons[69] and offices, administered by the respective secondaries. One was in Bread Street,[70] and the other in the Poultry. It was not necessary, however, for the defendant to be in the custody of one of the compters for a suit to be commenced against

---

[59] For a session of the full Sheriffs' Court at the Guildhall in 1461, see *Calendar of Letter-Book L*, ed. Sharpe, 12.

[60] Guy, *Public Career of More*, 5–6. More referred to his judicial work as routine in a letter of c.1516: *Correspondence of Sir Thomas More*, ed. E. F. Rogers (1947), 78. Cf. *Gale v. Blakeman* (1557) KB 27/1182, m. 191, where the defendant pleads a suit commenced in the Poultry Compter and continued in the Guildhall before one of the sheriffs.

[61] e.g. *Kygan v. Goodale* (temp. More C.) C1/649/27 (clergyman said to have accused lawyer of heresy); *Gale v. Lowe* (1557) Chr. Yelverton's reports, fo. 248v (tr. 'An action on the case was brought this year in the Guildhall … for these words …').

[62] e.g. *Asshe v. Hayle* (1485) C244/139/100 (above, 278 n. 11).

[63] e.g. *Popham v. Rysley* (temp. Audley C.), recited in C1/880/97 (action by master for enticing and inveigling apprentice to play at dice and lose master's money, the winners being 'rufflers' who had absconded).

[64] e.g. *Lynam v. Prior of Wenlock* (1488) C244/139/55 (debt for 1,500 marks). The sheriffs had no equitable jurisdiction, and could not hear ejectment. For the later history and law, see Pulling, *Laws and Customs of London*, 200–3.

[65] Note e.g. *Vyvalde v. Norrey* (1536) C1/914/31 (action by a Frenchman against a Genoese merchant on a marine insurance contract with a 5% premium).

[66] Jones, 'The City Courts', 301; e.g. *Asshe v. Hayle* (1485) C244/139/100 (*assumpsit*); above, n. 62.

[67] *Anon.* (1544) LI MS. Misc. 189, ff. 249–250 (pr. 121 Selden Soc. 450–3), noted in the autograph of Randle Cholmeley, also of Lincoln's Inn. Cholmeley was under-sheriff in 1553: Plowd. 91.

[68] See C1/64/454, 672 (c.1480/3). P. Tucker drew attention to this.

[69] They were used, *inter alia*, for the temporary custody of accused felons: e.g. *R. v. A Plough* (1507) KB 27/983, Rex m. 18 (pleads that he took sanctuary while being moved from the Bread Street Compter to Newgate).

[70] The Bread Street Compter was used from the fifteenth century until 1555, when—because of misconduct by its keeper, who refused to quit—it moved to Wood Street: R. B. Pugh, *Imprisonment in Medieval England* (1968), 110; *Lisle Letters*, ed. Byrne, i. 613.

him.[71] The volume of business at the beginning of the Tudor period is evident from an order of common council in 1486 that each sheriff should have no clerks other than the secondary and his clerk, a clerk of the papers, and four other clerk-sitters.[72] The Sheriffs' Court had separate attorneys from those of the Mayor's Court.[73] It seems that some of the debt business might be managed by brokers.[74]

CRIMINAL JUSTICE

The counties of London and Middlesex were outside the assize system[75] and possessed their own self-contained system of criminal justice,[76] though—as with civil justice—most of the records have been lost. In London, the principal gaol deliveries were held at least five times a year for Newgate gaol,[77] in the 'Justice Hall' at the Old Bailey,[78] before commissioners who usually included the mayor, the recorder, and some or all of the common-law judges.[79] The jurisdiction extended to Middlesex as well as London cases, since Newgate held prisoners from both counties. The clerk of the Crown, or clerk of the arraigns, at these sessions was the common clerk of the city of London,[80] who also acted as clerk of the peace for London.

[71] e.g. *Platte* v. *Aylyfe* (1551–3) E13/234, mm. 3–5, 6d–7, 9; CP 40/1153, m. 101; Plowd. 35; Dyer 81b (defendant in Ludgate gaol sued in the Bread Street Compter on a bond for £200, and brought to answer before the sheriffs in the Guildhall). This was an action against one of the sheriffs for an escape from Ludgate. There are a number of similar cases in the Exchequer: e.g. *Foster* v. *Turke and Yorke* (1549) E13/232, m. 1 (£30); *Pyke* v. *Turke and Yorke* (1549) ibid., m. 4; E13/233, m. 11 (£300); *Thrower* v. *Aylyfe* (1551) E13/234, m. 11–13.

[72] *Calendar of Letter-Book L*, ed. Sharpe, 235. A week later this was amended to allow existing clerks to continue: ibid. 236.

[73] John Melsham (of Lincoln's Inn) was attorney there in 1525: CP 40/1053, m. 442. Three mentioned in the Exchequer plea rolls are Richard Staverton in 1535 (E13/214, m. 6), John Norden and Robert Maddy in 1550 (E13/232, m. 1). Norden later became an attorney in the Mayor's Court: but cf. above, 282 n. 44. The ambiguous title 'attorney of the Guildhall' occurs in 1494: *Black Books*, i. 101 (Roger Fitz).

[74] See *Huse* v. *De Grimaldis* (1506) KB 27/981, m. 99, where the defendant (an Italian described as a 'broker') justified maintenance of an action in the Guildhall as the other party's retained servant.

[75] Civil trials from the two benches with a London venue were held at St Martin's-le-Grand until 1518, and then at the Guildhall: *LP*, ii. II. 4233. Middlesex trials took place in banc. An assize for lands in Middlesex was likewise taken in banc: *Charleton* v. *Saunders* (1552) Dyer 78d.

[76] In Middlesex cases this was shared with the King's Bench, which could take over or stop proceedings in the sessions: Mich. 21 Hen. VII, fo. 29, pl. 2.

[77] It was ordered in 1475 that the sessions be held at least five times a year: *Calendar of Letter Book K*, 137.

[78] For this name see *CPR 1554–5*, p. 94 (1555).

[79] e.g. *CPR 1485–94*, p. 393 (1491); *CPR 1494–1509*, pp. 87 (1496), 247 (1501), 293 (1502), 437, 456 (1505); *LP*, i. 218(1) (1509); *LP*, iv. I. 787(29) (1524). For commissions of 1517 see William Porter's precedent book, C193/142, fo. 48.

[80] e.g. in KB 27/929, Rex m. 11 (1493), Nicholas Pakenham is the officer 'qui pro domino rege sequitur'. Pakenham, a member of Gray's Inn, was common clerk 1490–1510: 3 *Guildhall Miscellany* 72; C1/215/12. See also *R.* v. *Lincoln* (1517) Port 123 at 124 (William Paver, common clerk).

The Newgate sessions were of comparable importance to the assizes in the country, dealing predominantly with capital cases; but occasionally the Guildhall was used for a London state trial under a special commission of oyer and terminer.[81]

Since there were no justices of the peace in London, the equivalent police function was exercised by the mayor, recorder, and aldermen,[82] assisted by the parish beadles and constables. The principal officers held the city's own sessions of the peace at the Guildhall. Besides the normal common-law powers of arrest, city customs were said to permit arrest for offences against immorality such as adultery[83] or frequenting a bawdy house,[84] and the aldermen even claimed a power of arrest for insolence towards themselves.[85] The king's Council held the lord mayor directly responsible for misbehaviour in the city.[86]

In Middlesex there were commissions of the peace, as in other counties, but sessions were not required to be held quarterly and, because of the presence of the King's Bench in the county, they could not be held in term-time. The general sessions were generally kept twice a year—immediately after Michaelmas and Easter—at Westminster.[87] In term-time, the King's Bench could charge Middlesex grand juries to find indictments, and these survive in some quantity throughout our period.[88]

It is probable that many of the prisoners tried at the Old Bailey were arraigned upon indictments found previously at sessions of the peace. The Middlesex justices held intermediate 'sessions of inquiry', at which there was a grand jury on hand to review bills of indictment, but no trials. Some files of indictments preserved by the clerks of the peace for Middlesex have survived from 1550 onwards. Theft and homicide predominate, but there are also accusations of forcible entry, extortion, and lechery.[89] After 1552, the magistrates also had responsibility for licensing and controlling alehouses.[90] The corresponding

---

[81] e.g. R. v. Bagnall (1494) 102 Selden Soc. 32 n. 4; R. v. Lincoln (1517) ibid. 124; R. v. Dudley (1554) 109 Selden Soc. 10.

[82] For the position of the aldermen see Shakton v. Aylmer (1512) KB 27/1004, m. 34d (imprisonment justified by custom for aldermen to commit to gaol for opprobrious words; replication De injuria); Cumberford v. Aleyn (1520) CP 40/1029, m. 614 (imprisonment justified as aldermen and conservators of the peace, for refusing to keep the peace; demurrer).

[83] Gylys v. Walterkyn (1485) CP 40/893, m. 244; Hil. 1 Hen. VII, fo. 6, pl. 3 (custom pleaded in false imprisonment).

[84] Corby v. Alsoppe (1507) CP 40/981, m. 316 (custom pleaded in false imprisonment). The pillory was ordered as a punishment for immorality in 1489-90: Calendar of Letter Book K, 269, 276.

[85] Shakton v. Aylmer (1512) KB 27/1004, m. 34d (custom pleaded in false imprisonment).

[86] e.g. BL MS. Lansdowne 639, ff. 31v, 37 (lord mayor summoned to the Star Chamber for allowing unlawful games and dicing in London at night, 1510).

[87] Middlesex County Records, ed. J. C. Jeaffreson, i (1886), introd.

[88] The files of indictments are KB 9.

[89] R. v. Harryson (1550) Middlesex County Records, ed. Jeaffreson, i. 4 (extortion by bailiff of city of Westminster); R. v. Tredway (1551) ibid. 8 (lecherous behaviour: luxuriose vitam suam degit). See ibid. 3, 5, 16, 23, for examples of forcible entry. Jeaffreson's texts are only a selection, not a complete calendar.

[90] ibid. 10-11; 5 & 6 Edw. VI, c. 25.

London indictments, which were preserved by the common clerk of the city, have not survived before 1605.

MINOR COURTS

By one of the customs of London,[91] the guardianship of orphans of freemen belonged to the mayor and aldermen rather than the personal representatives of the parent, and a Court of Orphans was held before the city chamberlain in the inner chamber of the Guildhall to supervise the welfare and the administration of the estates of such orphans while they were under age.[92] London custom gave a freeman's children the right to one-third of his net estate;[93] this third part was looked after by the court, which settled the children's shares as between themselves and made them living allowances ('finding money') until they were given the capital. The business was handled separately from that of the Mayor's Court under the supervision of the common serjeant, who acted as counsel for the orphans, and by the fourth attorney of the Mayor's Court as clerk of the Court of Orphans.[94] There were about twenty cases a year until the 1550s, when a surge in the number of freemen coincided with a threefold increase in business.[95]

The city had a number of other jurisdictions, such as that of the conservancy of the River Thames.[96] A Court of Requests was established by act of the Common Council in 1518 for the recovery of debts not exceeding 40s., the aldermen and commoners sitting by rotation twice a week, apparently without legal assistance; but no records survive from this period.[97]

In addition to Newgate and the two compters, the city had a substantial gaol at Ludgate which was used for debtors as well as for criminal defendants. Debtors were given considerable freedom, and were allowed to leave the prison in company with a warder, if they paid for the latter's food and drink, so that they could better raise money to pay their debts.[98] However, in 1533, the weakness of this regime was revealed when such a prisoner escaped from his keeper and took

---

[91] See the custom as to orphans set out in the declaration in *Knap* v. *Prior of St Bartholomew's, Smithfield* (1511) KB 27/998, m. 8d.

[92] C. Carlton, *The Court of Orphans* (1974), on which this paragraph is based.

[93] Another third went to the widow, and the remaining third could be left by will. A child's share could be reduced to the extent of any advancement, and after 1551 by 'Judd's Law' (an act of Common Council) a child who misbehaved could be barred from his share.

[94] This name was in use by 1529: Carlton, *Court of Orphans*, 36.

[95] Carlton counted 603 cases between 1550 and 1559, compared with 200 between 1500 and 1509: *Court of Orphans*, 25.   [96] See 4 Hen. VII, c. 15.

[97] 93 *Law Jnl* 312. The later practice is described in Pulling, *Laws and Customs of London*, 203–7.

[98] See 109 Selden Soc., pp. lxxxii–lxxxiii; *LP*, vi. 1614 (alleges this cost 18d. or 20d. a day, 1533); *CPR* 1553–4, p. 73. It was alleged to be a custom of London, though in 1532 the Star Chamber disapproved of it: below, 383–4.

sanctuary at Westminster.[99] There were at that time nearly thirty minor debtors in Ludgate, and complaints were made of overcharging and other abuses.[100] The outcome of such complaints was the appointment of standing commissions to hear the complaints of the prisoners there, and to settle their debts according to equity and good conscience.[101]

A court was held at the Tower of London, nominally before the constable but in practice before the steward of the Tower liberty, for matters arising within the precincts of the liberty.[102] According to a decision of 1459, it was only a court baron and not a court of record; but it had an unlimited jurisdiction over personal actions arising within the verge, and a piepowder jurisdiction.[103] Occasional cases of removal show that the court was still in existence in the time of Henry VII, but it was not a court of much importance.[104] Another liberty having its own court was that of St Katharine's Hospital by the Tower; this was a court of record.[105]

The court of the Marshalsea of the King's Household, presided over by the steward and marshal of the household, continued to function in the early Tudor period, though none of its records appears to have survived.[106] It had a jurisdiction over criminal causes[107] and trespasses committed within the verge of the household, and contracts made within the verge or between members of the household.[108] Since it followed the king's person, it was not always in or near the metropolis.[109] Its continued existence may be discerned from occasional actions in the benches for suing in the Marshalsea in contract when neither party was of the household,[110] from justifications under the process of the

---

[99] *Lisle Letters*, ed. Byrne, i. 610–11, no. 73.

[100] *LP*, vi. 1614. Among the complaints was an allegation that the keeper would 'labor to fulfil his foul lust' with visiting wives. For a list of 28 debtors around this time, see *LP*, Add., i. 821.

[101] e.g. *LP*, xiv. I. 403(1) (1539); xvii. 1012(27) (1542); *CPR 1547–8*, p. 65 (1547); *CPR 1553–4*, pp. 73–4 (1553). See also Pugh, *Imprisonment in Medieval England*, 187–8.

[102] The Tower was not within the county of the city of London: see Pas. 4 Edw. IV, fo. 16, pl. 30.

[103] *Skargyll v. West* (1459), noted in *Calendar of Letter-Book L*, ed. Sharpe, 1–3; *Lawley v. Walwin* (1464) Mich. 4 Edw. IV, fo. 36, pl. 18.

[104] *Peverell v. Rothewell* (*c.*1490) C1/107/69 (trespass); *Mercer v. Campyon* (1507) CP 40/980, m. 396d; Rast. Ent. 504 (550v) (debt upon a *concessit solvere*, according to the alleged custom of the court).

[105] *Dykar v. Redder* (1522) KB 27/1042, m. 70 (debt on a bond for 50 marks; error; assigns *inter alia* that the liberties were in the king's hand by virtue of a *quo warranto*).

[106] It is the first court described in *Diversite de Courtz* (1533), sig. A2.

[107] See *Derby v. Lanton* (1502) KB 27/964, m. 79 (conspiracy to indict before steward and marshal; verdict for plaintiff but c.a.v.). Cf. 3 Hen. VII, c. 14, which created a special household court to try alleged conspiracies by household servants; it is not known whether it ever functioned.

[108] Articuli super Cartas, c. 3. For this purpose *assumpsit* was considered as contract rather than trespass: Brooke Abr., *Action sur Lestatute*, pl. 38; *Delandose v. Gose* (1553) KB 27/1168, m. 186 (error from the Marshalsea; undertaking at Southwark).

[109] e.g. *Hore v. West* (*c.*1485) C1/82/107 (marshalsea court at Winchester).

[110] e.g. Rast. Ent. 397 (432v–433); *Oldale v. Cheryngton* (1527) KB 27/1064, m. 32 (damages recovered).

court,[111] or from the removal of cases into the central courts.[112] In 1541 a detailed statute was passed to increase and regulate the powers of the court in dealing with murder and bloodshed in the king's palaces.[113] One of its more sanguinary provisions introduced amputation of the right hand as a mandatory penalty for maliciously drawing blood by striking, and detailed an appalling ceremony for carrying out the surgery. This very sentence was forthwith passed by the court, sitting at Greenwich, upon Sir Edmund Knyvet, for striking a servant of the earl of Surrey; but the sentence was never carried out.[114] Despite the extensive civil jurisdiction of the court, members of the household in our period made extensive use of the Requests, and this may have become a preferable forum in practice. The prince of Wales's court had its own marshalsea after 1492.[115]

[111] e.g. *Tyllysworth* v. *Rutter* (1514–15) KB 27/1013, m. 94 (justifies false imprisonment by attachment of the Marshalsea Court in a bill of trespass; demurrer; judgment for the plaintiff).

[112] e.g. in the second half of the 1480s, *Townton* v. *Chapman*, C1/76/106; *Ederiche* v. *Cole*, ibid. 112; *Garset* v. *Astley*, C1/79/7; *Stonor* v. *Dormer*, ibid. 17; *Borough* v. *Derant*, C1/80/13; *Gunnace* v. *Vernon*, C1/82/89; *Roweland* v. *Whiteheed*, ibid. 104; *Townley* v. *Wynprawe*, ibid. 105; *Leght* v. *Aylmer*, C1/83/43; *Wyot* v. *Danyell* (1488) C244/139/109 (*certiorari*). The record of *Barghus* v. *Denys* (1484), with jury panel attached, is in C244/136/91 (£26 damages awarded for trespass to goods). For *corpus cum causa* in the Common Pleas, cf. *Baker* v. *Regeway* (1555) CP 40/1164, m. 1379. Note also *Wykes* v. *Colysone* (*c.*1544/7) C1/1168/87 (suit in Chancery for suing in Marshalsea when not of the household).

[113] 33 Hen. VIII, c. 12. The statute did not extend to noblemen who struck their servants by way of chastisement.   [114] Below, 590.

[115] *CPR 1485–94*, p. 408 (Prince Arthur given power to appoint persons to hold pleas of the marshalsea before himself).

16

Local Courts

OF the myriad local jurisdictions which still operated in England in the early Tudor period it is impossible to provide minute detail, and we must be content with an outline of the general picture. Even to suppose that there might be a general picture to see is problematic, since the varieties in local custom, and in the wording of royal charters governing jurisdiction, seem on their face to render generalization impracticable. But what is most striking about the records of local courts in the period is the remarkable extent to which diverse jurisdictions had come to operate in much the same way in different parts of the country, in conformity with the norms represented by the central royal courts. The forms of action, the forms of pleading and demurrers,[1] and the prevalence of the jury, were almost as regular in the records of local courts as they are in the plea rolls of the two benches. This could be ascribed partly to direct control, since local courts were subject to the discipline of the King's Bench through writs of error, but it was probably more a consequence of increasing professionalization. By the sixteenth century local courts were usually presided over by recorders, stewards, or under-stewards trained in the inns of court;[2] and at least some of the attorneys and clerks of local courts had Westminster experience or had spent some time in the inns of chancery. It is to this professional influence that we may attribute such modern devices as actions on the case, ejectment, and common recoveries, all of which were copied in jurisdictions supposedly tied by immemorial local custom. Since the spreading influence of the legal profession had clearly been playing upon local courts before our period began, a full account of their evolution belongs more appropriately in the preceding volumes.

The complexities of local and private jurisdiction could not be better illustrated than by the case of the bishop of Durham.[3] In addition to his ecclesiastical courts,

---

[1] Even demurrers to the evidence: e.g. *Wyld v. Smyth* (1551) KB 27/1160, m. 79 (an example from the Guildhall Court of Worcester). In 1542, the court of the lordship of Halton, Cheshire, ordered that demurrers were to be 'according to common law': BL MS. Harley 2115, fo. 100.

[2] This is the general impression gained from a prosopographical study. Moreover, the readers on *quo warranto* asserted that a court was liable to be forfeited if the lord appointed a steward who was not learned in the law. But there were exceptions in practice: Brooke, *Pettyfoggers and Vipers*, 38–41.

[3] G. T. Lapsley, *The County Palatine of Durham* (1900), chs. 5–6; M. H. Dodds, 'The Bishop's Boroughs' (1915) 12 *Arch. Aeliana* (3rd ser.) 81 at 132–5; K. Emsley and C. M. Fraser, *The Courts of the*

he had regalian rights within the county palatine of Durham, which included full royal jurisdiction.[4] Indeed, Durham seemed so distinct from England for legal purposes that its inhabitants were not represented in Parliament and were exempt from parliamentary taxation.[5] The bishop was—in right of the palatinate—a temporal judge, and was able (for instance) to punish by *praemunire* those clergy who exceeded their spiritual jurisdiction.[6] The Durham Court of Pleas exercised virtually the same jurisdiction as the King's Bench and Common Pleas at Westminster, and also an Admiralty jurisdiction. The bishop's Chancery issued writs and commissions, in the bishop's name, and the temporal chancellor was beginning to assume an equitable jurisdiction. The bishop appointed the justices of the peace and of gaol delivery, who until 1535 were styled the bishop's justices rather than the king's. In 1535 the right to appoint judges was abrogated, though the bishop's temporal chancellor then became an *ex officio* justice of the peace.[7] As a feudal lord, the bishop also held halmote courts with unlimited jurisdiction in personal actions. Then again, in virtue of his palatine authority, the bishop held borough courts in Durham, Darlington, and Stockton, with a civil jurisdiction limited to 40s. Outside the county, the bishop owned the liberty of Allertonshire,[8] comprising over thirty vills in north Yorkshire, and here he held courts baron and halmote courts, again with civil jurisdiction under 40s., a forest court, a sheriff's tourn, and a borough court at Northallerton which had its own view of frankpledge, exempt from the tourn.[9] No doubt the bishop had a greater diversity of jurisdictions than any other English subject; but diversity and local peculiarities were characteristic of the country as a whole.

The jurisdictional morass could sometimes be exploited to unfair advantage, as when a party in one of the central courts pleaded a foreign plea which was triable only in a franchise 'where the king's writ runneth not'. In an attempt to prevent this abuse, the attorneys' oath of office included a promise to 'plead no foreign pleas nor sue any foreign suits unlawfully to hurt any man, but such as stand with the order of the law and your conscience'.[10] It was nevertheless alleged

County Palatine of Durham (1984); C. Kitching, 'The Durham Palatinate and the Courts of Westminster under the Tudors' in *The Last Principality*, ed. D. Marcombe (1987), 49–70; T. Thornton, 'Fifteenth-Century Durham' (2001) 11 *TRHS* (5th ser.) 83–100, at 84–9.

[4] Disputes concerning these rights might nevertheless be taken to the King's Bench at Westminster: e.g. *Re Earl of Westmoreland, decd* (1510) KB 27/996, Rex m. 15 (wardship).

[5] Thornton, 'Fifteenth-Century Durham', 89–94. Cf. *Hall's Chronicle*, 443, which says that Durham was brought to heel in 1489.   [6] Trin. 15 Hen. VII, fo. 9, pl. 8, *per* Fyneux CJ.

[7] 27 Hen. VIII, c. 24, s. 19; Lapsley, *Durham*, 196–8.

[8] See *Bishop of Durham* v. *Constable* (1512) CP 40/1001, m. 690 (case for infringing liberty of return of writs in Allertonshire; confessed).

[9] C. M. Newman, 'Local Court Administration within the Liberty of Allertonshire, 1470–1540' (1995) 22 *Archives* 13–24; 'Order and Community in the North: the liberty of Allertonshire in the later fifteenth century' in *The North of England in the Age of Richard III*, ed. A. J. Pollard (1996), 47–66.

[10] Oath of the 1550s, in 109 Selden Soc. 176.

in the time of Lord Audley C. that an attorney had advised his client to plead an improper foreign plea in person, contrary to his oath, so that he (the attorney) would not be liable to punishment.[11] A person living in a franchise might also be able to take advantage of local friendships to keep outsiders with good claims at bay.[12]

THE PALATINATES

The counties palatine were wholly outside the first-instance jurisdiction of the central courts of common law,[13] and had their own courts with full royal jurisdiction. Some thought Chester and Durham to be outside even the legislative jurisdiction of the English Parliament, on the grounds that the inhabitants were not represented there, though the matter was not formally tested.[14] No one doubted that the common-law jurisdiction remained almost fully independent. Unlike lesser franchises, palatinate jurisdiction excluded that of the central courts whether or not the parties themselves took exception or a formal claim was made.[15] If an issue of fact in a palatinate arose in litigation properly begun at Westminster, it could not be tried by the ordinary assize judges but had to be tried by special mandate.[16] On the other hand, the central courts could be invited to enforce palatine judgments by *scire facias*,[17] as would be necessary if the defendant moved out of the county. Cases were also removed into the Common Pleas in the case of a foreign voucher in a palatinate.[18] Although Fyneux CJ is reported as saying in 1505 that error did not lie from a county palatine to the King's Bench,[19]

---

[11] *Parker* v. *Selybank* (temp. Audley C.) C1/866/22. The attorney (Henry Mynne) was a busy Norfolk practitioner, and filazer of the King's Bench in the 1550s.

[12] e.g. *Haydon* v. *Toker* (temp. Audley C.) C1/812/48 (attorney unable to sue client by writ because he remains within the stannaries).

[13] Not, however, of the Chancery and Star Chamber, which increased their palatinate business under Wolsey: see T. Thornton, *Cheshire and the Tudor State, 1480–1560* (2000), 103–15.

[14] For such a claim in relation to Cheshire in the 1520s, see Thornton, *Cheshire and the Tudor State*, 120. However, several statutes from the 1530s onwards expressly applied to Cheshire, and parliamentary representation was granted in 1542: 34 Hen. VIII, c. 13; *HPHC 1509–58*, i. 43; Thornton, *Cheshire*, 125–37. (Durham did not send members to Westminster until 1672.)

[15] Anon. (1493) Mich. 9 Hen. VII, fo. 12, pl. 7; *Caldecote* v. *Daveson* (1522) Spelman 157; *Eston* v. *Fletcher* (1532) Spelman 124 at 126.

[16] *Anon.* (1496) Hil. 11 Hen. VII, fo. 16, pl. 13, *per* Vavasour J.; *Anon.* (1529) Spelman 219. An example is *Holcroft* v. *Standishe* (1558) CP 40/1174, m. 835 (debt on bond made in London; issue on fact in Lancs.; record remanded to justices itinerant at Lancaster).

[17] e.g. *Mascy* v. *Mascy* (1516) KB 27/1020, m. 97 (debt of £20 recovered before Conyngesby and Brian Palmes JJ. Ass. at Lancaster).

[18] Thomas Marow's reading (Inner Temple, 1497) Port 126; *Swetenham* v. *Warde* (1526) CP 40/1051, m. 311; Mich. 18 Hen. VIII, fo. 1, pl. 4; *Tochett* v. *Bunbury* (1534) CP 40/1080, m. 122; *Legh* v. *Moldesworth* (1535) CP 40/1086, m. 136; CP 40/1089, m. 431 (remitted because Moldesworth died). All these examples are from Chester. Cf. 34 & 35 Hen. VIII, c. 26.   [19] Mich. 21 Hen. VII, fo. 33, pl. 32.

but only to special commissioners, this was contrary to the usual practice at that time in relation to both Lancaster[20] and Chester.[21]

Lancaster was a county palatine vested in the king as duke of Lancaster, the duchy having been preserved by various acts of Parliament from merger in the Crown. The palatinate jurisdiction was, however, quite distinct from that of the duchy, which was nationwide and in some respects extraordinary.[22] The county palatine was a microcosm of the national system at Westminster but with jurisdiction confined to Lancashire.[23] It had its own Chancery,[24] which had common-law functions similar to those of the Chancery of England, issued original writs, and kept its own patent and close rolls. By 1485 there was an equitable jurisdiction, evidenced by the files of bills preserved from that time onwards (PL 6).[25] There is said to have been a Court of Exchequer, though its records have not survived; the administrative department was more or less dormant until 1501, when its revenue functions were revived.[26] The Court of Pleas combined the functions of a King's Bench and Common Pleas, and until 1501 its rolls contain personal and real actions, traverses to inquisitions, appeals of felony, and proceedings on indictment.[27] There were two sessions a year, usually but not necessarily at Lancaster,[28] presided over by a pair of judges who were normally members of the order of the coif but not necessarily the assize judges.[29] The court was served by a clerk of the common

---

[20] e.g. *Laurance* v. *Lomley* (1488–92) 1 Caryll 77; KB 27/909 m. 32; KB 27/923, m. 22d (judgment in darrein presentment reversed); *Lord la Warr* v. *Orell* (1491) KB 27/919, m. 36 (ravishment of ward); *Holcroft* v. *Holcroft* (1500) KB 27/955, m. 37; *Huetson* v. *Baynes* (1505) KB 27/977, m. 38; *Dale* v. *Pemberton* (1512) KB 27/1004, m. 33; *Totheill* v. *Southworth* (1516) KB 27/1021, m. 95. There are later examples: e.g. *Eccleston* v. *Parr* (1553) KB 27/1165, m. 84.

[21] e.g. *Savage* v. *Cotton* (1504) KB 27/970, m. 34; *Savage* v. *Venables* (1506) KB 27/978, m. 66; *Vernon* v. *Legh* (1506) KB 27/981, m. 92 (eyre of Chester before justices of Prince Arthur); *Legh* v. *Colyn* (1515) Dyer 321a; *Sutton* v. *Dudley* (1529) KB 27/1071, m. 68.   [22] For the duchy see above, 223.

[23] For the general background see R. Somerville, 'The Palatine Courts in Lancashire' in *Law-Making and Law-Makers in British History*, ed. A. Harding (1980), 54–63.

[24] The chancellor was in practice the same person as the chancellor of the duchy, though the offices were separate. Much of the judicial work was performed by a deputy or vice-chancellor (a title in use by 1482): see the list in Somerville, *Duchy of Lancaster*, 478–9. The vice-chancellor seems also to have acted as a master or cursitor responsible for issuing original writs: ibid. 477.

[25] The earliest so-called book of decrees and orders begins in 1524 (PL 11/1), but is really only an appearance book with occasional interlocutory decrees.

[26] Somerville, *Duchy of Lancaster*, 58–9, 272–3, 485 (list of barons).

[27] The roll for Lent 1500 (PL 15/91) is headed 'Placita apud Lancastriam coram Johanne Vavasour et Humfrido Conyngesby justiciariis domini regis de sessione Lancastrie tenta ibidem' (on 30 Mar. 1500). It is composed as follows: mm. 1–5, common pleas (including a traverse); 6–7, pleas of the crown: 8, assizes: 9, recognizances: 10, a presentment of burglary: 10d (and 1d), warrants of attorney and estreated fines: 11, common recoveries: 11d, appeals of death. After 1501, the clerk of the crown kept separate rolls.

[28] e.g. the session in the summer of 1485 was at Clitheroe (PL 15/61), while that in Lent 1520 was at Preston (papers in PL 21/2).

[29] See the list in Somerville, *Duchy of Lancaster*, 469–73. Unlike Chester and Durham, Lancaster was incorporated within the assize system, though it had a separate commission: J. S. Cockburn, *History of*

pleas (or prothonotary) responsible for civil actions and appeals of felony, and for issuing judicial writs on the plea side,[30] a king's serjeant or attorney,[31] a clerk of the crown,[32] a clerk of the peace,[33] and at least eight local attorneys.[34] The forms of procedure were almost exactly the same as those used in Westminster Hall, and a particular interest of the Lancaster archive is that it includes some paper pleadings from the time of Henry VIII (PL 21) which are almost certainly of the same character as the long lost 'papers' of the King's Bench.[35] The plea rolls (PL 15) and writ-files with jury panels (PL 20) survive more or less intact, together with the prothonotary's dockets (PL 16) and occasional remembrances and working notebooks,[36] thus providing a remarkably complete picture of a common-law court at work in the time of Henry VIII. Durham was similarly organized,[37] with a nascent equity jurisdiction in the bishop's Chancery, and there are plea rolls from the whole Tudor period (DURH 13). However, some of the attorneys in Durham were Common Pleas practitioners.

The county of Chester[38] (Cheshire) was a county palatine vested in the prince of Wales as earl of Chester, during those periods when there was a prince,[39] but otherwise continuing as a separate jurisdiction vested in the Crown.[40] Its courts were arranged quite differently from those at Lancaster. The County Court, which sat in Chester castle, was not an ordinary county court but a superior regalian jurisdiction. It had an unlimited civil and criminal jurisdiction within the county palatine, and also heard error from the Pentice Court of the city of Chester. It met

the English Assizes 1558–1714 (1972), 44–5. From 1485 to 1495 the judges were those of the Midland circuit (Fairfax and Vavasour JJ), and until 1538 the chief justice of Lancaster was usually the senior judge of that circuit; thereafter he was usually from the Northern circuit.

[30] The principal prothonotaries in our period were Brian Bradford, 1495–1514; Thomas Strey, 1515–31; and John Birkhened, 1531–c.1550. Their names appear on judicial writs in the writ files (PL 20) and in the dockets (PL 16).

[31] See Somerville, Duchy of Lancaster, 483. His name, rather than that of the clerk of the crown, appears in the rolls when an appeal is taken over in the king's name.   [32] ibid. 487.

[33] ibid. 489.

[34] Eight were noted in 1500 and 1547, but in Lent 1526 as many as eleven occur at one session: PL 15/140.   [35] 'Sessional Papers', PL 21/1–5; see below, 341.

[36] Thomas Strey's remembrance roll for Lent 1528 survives in PL 21/3. It is of the same character as the Common Pleas remembrances (CP 45). Strey's sewn paper notebooks (headed Billa Placitorum) for Summer 1529 and Lent 1531 are in the same box.   [37] See above, 291–2.

[38] B. E. Harris, 'The Palatinate 1301–1547' in A History of the County of Chester, ii, ed. B. E. Harris (VCH; 1979), 9–35; D. J. Clayton, The Administration of the County Palatine of Chester, 1442–85 (35 Chetham Soc., new ser.; 1990); Thornton, Cheshire and the Tudor State.

[39] Only twenty years in our period: 1483–4 (Prince Edward), 1489–1502 (Prince Arthur), 1504–9 (Prince Henry). There was no prince of Wales between the accession of Henry VIII and 1610.

[40] See Savage v. Cotton (1504) KB 27/970, m. 34 (question whether county vested in king or prince of Wales). In Legh v. Legh (1506) KB 27/977, m. 63, the privilege of the county palatine is laid in the prince. Cf. Caldecote v. Daveson (1522) Spelman 157, where it was argued that in between princes of Wales the jurisdiction was in suspense.

eight or nine times a year. Unlike ordinary county courts, the sheriff did not preside; there was a justice of Chester, who until 1504 was honorific—the earl of
Derby held the office from 1486 to 1504—and a deputy justice who actually
presided.[41] In 1504, Thomas Englefield, deputy to the earl of Derby, succeeded to
the office of justice (later called chief justice), and thereafter lawyers were always
appointed to the full office.[42] Civil actions were commenced by original writ
tested at Chester; but the law terms were not observed. Not only do plea rolls survive,[43] but files from as far back as the fourteenth century. In addition there was
an Exchequer of Chester, which also sat in the castle and doubled as a Chancery.
Here the chamberlain or his deputy held pleas according to the usage of the
English Exchequer, and also followed the course of the Chancery, with both a
Latin side, for revenue business,[44] and—from the beginning of our period—
a nascent court of equity with process by subpoena.[45] A further peculiarity of
Chester was that from time to time it appointed justices in eyre, the last-known
occurrence being in 1499–1500 when Serjeants Kebell and Mordaunt rode circuit
around Cheshire to hear pleas of *quo warranto*.[46] The prince of Wales (or, failing
a prince, the king) as earl of Chester had his own palatinate law officers,[47] and the
County Court had its own attorneys, many of whom also practised at Lancaster.
A considerable step was taken in 1535 to assimilate Chester to the rest of England
when Parliament enabled the king to appoint justices of the peace within the
county palatine. As a result of this the criminal work of the County Court was
considerably reduced, and it was enacted five years later that the latter need only

[41] The succession was: William Bulkeley (formerly king's serjeant in the county) 1441–50;
John Nedeham (likewise) 1451–80; John Fyneux (a bencher of Gray's Inn with no obvious Cheshire
connections) and Randle Billington 1480–1; John Hawarden (formerly king's serjeant in Lancs.)
1481–91.

[42] Englefield was succeeded by his son Sir Thomas (d. 1537); then Sir William Sulyard 1538–40; Sir
Nicholas Hare 1540–5; Sir Robert Townshend 1545–57; Sir John Pollard 1557; George Wood 1558. See
Williams, *History of the Great Sessions in Wales*, 29–31; Thornton, *Cheshire and the Tudor State*, 144–6.
Deputy justices were still appointed, and were in effect secondary justices. George Bromley and
Richard Snede, benchers of the Inner Temple, held the office for much of Henry VIII's reign.

[43] CHES 29. The contents of each bundle are divided into 'Placita Comitatus Cestrie' and 'Placita
Corone', with some gaol deliveries as well.

[44] For proceedings in the Exchequer of Chester on the death of a tenant in chief of Prince Arthur,
see 109 Selden Soc. 327–8. The chamberlain also kept the seal, and issued original writs.

[45] See T. Thornton, 'Local Equity Jurisdictions in the Territories of the English Crown: the
Palatinate of Chester, 1450–1540' in *Courts, Counties and the Capital in the Later Middle Ages*,
ed. D. E. S. Dunn (1996), 27–52; *Cheshire and the Tudor State*, 88–100.

[46] BL MS. Harley 2115, ff. 137v–171v; MS. Harley 2079, fo. 116 (copy of writ to earl of Derby); BL Add.
Roll 51531; BL MS. Add. 76947 (writ to Sir William Troutbeck); W. D. Selby, *Lancashire and Cheshire
Records*, i (7 Record Soc. Lancs. and Chesh.; 1882), 68; R. S. Brown, 'The Cheshire Writs of Quo
Warranto in 1499' (1934) 49 *EHR* 676–84; Thornton, *Cheshire and the Tudor State*, 185–6. See also
Vernon v. Legh (1506) KB 27/981, m. 92 (record removed by writ of error).

[47] 102 Selden Soc., p. xv.

meet twice a year instead of the customary eight or nine times,[48] thus bringing it into line with the Lancaster Court of Pleas. The legislation had to be modified the following year, so as to require the sheriff to keep an ordinary monthly county court for the proclamation of exigents and for suits under 40s.[49] Under the statute of 1543 which established the Great Sessions of Wales, the jurisdiction of the justice of Chester was extended to Flint and Montgomery.[50]

Only Durham, Lancaster, and Chester, were undoubted palatinates. Nevertheless, a statute of 1541 referred to Hexham and Ely as counties palatine 'within' the counties of Northumberland and Cambridge respectively.[51] These two were regalian liberties of considerable legal but small geographical extent, and not normally reckoned to be counties palatine. The archbishop of York exercised jurisdiction in Hexham through his steward or temporal chancellor, and appointed his own justices of assize. The bishop of Ely appointed a steward or judge (known by 1575 as the chief justice) of the Isle of Ely,[52] and his own assize judges;[53] it was a liberty 'where the king's writ runneth not'.[54] There was no separate sheriff in Ely, but only a franchise bailiff as in other liberties. Nor was there a county court, though the bishop claimed a jurisdiction in false judgment over the hundred court.[55] In fact, these liberties were not materially different from the soke of Peterborough, where the dean and chapter had a court of Common Pleas and appointed their own justices of gaol delivery.[56] By statute of 1535, the privilege of appointing assize judges was taken away, but the judges of both Hexham and Ely thereupon became *ex officio* justices of the peace.[57] Hexhamshire effectively came to an end in 1545, when the archbishop surrendered the liberty to the Crown by way of exchange, though it was not legally clear until 1572 whether it subsisted as a separate entity like Lancaster and Durham.[58] The duchy of

---

[48] 27 Hen. VIII, c. 5; 32 Hen. VIII, c. 43.   [49] 33 Hen. VIII, c. 13.

[50] 34 & 35 Hen. VIII, c. 26; above, 107. A new seal was ordained for judicial writs; the seal for originals remained in the custody of the chamberlain of Chester.

[51] 33 Hen. VIII, c. 10, s. 12. Note also Rast. Ent. 137 (138v), where Ely is mentioned (in a cross-reference) as a county palatine.

[52] In 1525 John Hynde was 'steward or bailiff of the liberty': *Lucas* v. *Bishop of Ely* (1525) cit. Dyer 156b. By 1547 he was described as '(tr.) the lord king's justice for pleas within the liberty of the bishop of Ely within the Isle of Ely': *Spencer* v. *Wheldale* (1547) CP 40/1134, m. 88/ (*recordari facias* to try foreign plea from Ely).

[53] VCH, *Cambridgeshire*, iv. 18, 22, 111, 181; *LP*, viii. 1088. It seems that by 1515 there was uncertainty over the assize judges, and the king and the bishop thereafter made simultaneous appointments of the same persons: J. Bentham, *The History and Antiquities of Ely* (1771), App. 27, p. 24; Cockburn, *History of English Assizes*, 33–4.   [54] *Parker* v. *Selybank* (temp. Audley C.) C1/866/22.

[55] Rast. Ent. 521 (570v), prints a writ of *recordari facias* issued by the bishop in 1480 to remove a case from the hundred court.   [56] VCH, *Northants.*, ii. 427.

[57] 27 Hen. VIII, c. 24, ss. 18, 20.

[58] It was settled by 14 Eliz. I, c. 13 that it was extinct. See also A. B. Hinds, *A History of Northumberland*, iii (1896).

Cornwall was not a county palatine, and did not have courts outside the common-law system apart from the stannaries.[59]

FORESTS

Forest jurisdiction belonged solely to the king, or to those with regalian authority, because when hunting or forestry rights were granted to private persons—in the form of park, chase, warren, or rights to timber—no court passed.[60] Incident to every forest, however, were a number of courts. The court of swanimote (or swainmote), held three times a year before a steward, was analogous to a court leet in that it could make presentments but could not give judgment.[61] It was principally concerned with offences against the vert and venison by taking timber or hunting without licence.[62] The principal court was the 'justice seat', this being the colloquial name for the sessions held by the justices of the forest. These justices, appointed by royal commission, had a criminal jurisdiction to try forest trespasses, and also a *quo warranto* jurisdiction to try claims to liberties within the forest, such as rights of chase and warren, or exemptions from the forest laws.[63] They were therefore sometimes regarded as akin to justices in eyre.[64] Where a presentment was transmitted to them from the swanimote, they had only to pass judgment, unless there was a demurrer in law or a plea of title, because the facts in such a presentment were not traversable. Indictments found before themselves, however, were tried by a jury of suitors.[65]

The officers of the forest—forester, verderers, regarders, and agisters—had the police function of keeping watch in the forest. In some forests, by prescription, the officers could punish minor offences summarily.[66] But their usual role was to prosecute, by presenting offences at the swanimote. Indeed, the oath of the deputy

---

[59] For the stannaries see below, 318–19.

[60] George Treherne's reading (Lincoln's Inn, 1520), fo. 5; BL MS. Stowe 414, fo. 47v. However, a forest could be leased by that name: e.g. BL Add. Ch. 34198 (1542; no mention of courts).

[61] Treherne's reading (1520), ff. 3v–4, 27v. There is an extended discussion of the swanimote (mostly on the technicalities of indictments) in Hesketh's reading (c.1506/08), ff. 42v–51v.

[62] See the New Forest rolls for 1487–94 printed in *A Calendar of New Forest Documents*, ed. D. J. Stagg (5 Hants Record Ser.; 1983); and R. H. Hilton, 'Swanimote Rolls of Feckenham Forest' (1 Worcs. Hist. Soc., new ser.; 1960), 37–52; Clayton, *Administration of the County Palatine of Chester*, 33–4. A surviving roll of the Windsor forest swanimote on 26 Sept. 1548 contains only presentments that all was well, or specifying timber which had been cut by warrant: C154/1/1.

[63] For some specimen presentments see the Savernake forest rolls for 1486–91 in H. C. Brentnall, 'Venison Trespasses in the Reign of Henry VII' (1949) 53 *Wilts. Archaeological and Natural History Magazine* 191–212. Note also *Abbot of Rufford's Case* (Mansfield in Sherwood, Notts., 1505) BL MS. Add. 36790, fo. 65.

[64] Treherne says of such a justice, 'he hath as much authority as a justice in eyre and more': reading in Lincoln's Inn (1520), fo. 7v. However, it does not seem that he could try felony or cases of contract.

[65] Treherne's reading (1520), ff. 8, 40.   [66] Hesketh's reading (c.1506/8), fo. 44v.

forester of Sherwood Forest closely resembled that of the grand jurors at assizes and sessions:[67]

I shall be loyal and true to the master forester of this forest, and to his lieutenant. I shall truly keep and walk the office of the forestership, and true watch make, both early and late, both for vert and venison; truly attach and true presentment make of all manner trespasses done in the said forest to my knowledge and in special within the keeping of my bailiwick; the king's counsel, my fellows', and mine own, truly keep, and no concealment make for no favour, mede nor dread, but well and truly behave me therein. So help me God and holydom.

The laws of the forest, which the justices applied in their sessions, differed in some details from the common law and were outlined in the thirteenth-century *Carta de Foresta*, but remained generally obscure until the sixteenth century. Two learned and popular readings on the charter, given early in the century, brought the subject into order and served as authoritative guides to forest law throughout the Tudor period.[68] It seems probable that these readings were prompted by a plan to revive the forest law for fiscal purposes, though how far such a plan may have proceeded has not been established.[69]

The justices were chiefly concerned with criminal business, the principal offences being assarts, purprestures, nuisances, wastes, and trespasses to the vert and venison.[70] Vert (or greenhue) meant the trees and underwood which provided cover for the beasts,[71] while venison meant the beasts of venery, such as the hart, roe, and deer, and also in theory wild hogs, bulls, and boars, though the last three categories were no longer to be found in England.[72] Hunting such wild animals was not criminal at common law,[73] but within a forest it was punishable under the forest law. The protection of that law extended to birds and beasts of warren—namely partridges, pheasants, hares, and rabbits—though these were not technically venison.[74] Forests were also home to 'vermins of chase', such as foxes and wolves, and 'petty vermin' such as squirrels and wild cats. Even these

---

[67] Documents relating to Sherwood forest, BL MS. Add. 36790, fo. 64v (sp. mod.).

[68] The first was given by Richard Hesketh in Gray's Inn (*c*.1506/8); the second by George Treherne in Lincoln's Inn (1520). Both were widely circulated in manuscript, but neither was printed.

[69] The *quo warranto* cases do not appear in the King's Bench rolls, presumably because they would have been heard by justices of the forest. A *quo warranto* enquiry in Ashdown Forest in 1519–20 was mentioned in evidence in *Earl de la Warr v. Miles* (1881) 17 Ch.D. 535 at 562.

[70] Treherne's reading (1520), ff. 29, 60–63v.

[71] The kinds of tree included might vary according to local custom. For instance, in Waltham Forest hawthorn, crabtree, and holm were the king's vert: Treherne's reading (1520), fo. 63. There is a discussion of the law relating to trees in Hesketh's reading (*c*.1506/8), fo. 25.

[72] Treherne's reading (1520), ff. 2v, 63v–64; BL MS. Stowe 414, ff. 46, 88. One version (BL MS. Stowe 414, fo. 88) speaks of wild 'bears', and says they were not extant at the time of the *Carta de Foresta*, but that there were still wild bulls and boars in Wales and in Chartley Park, belonging to Lord Ferrers.

[73] See below, 729–31. Cf. 1 Hen. VII, c. 7 (hunting in the night, or in disguise, made felony).

[74] Hesketh's reading (*c*.1506/8), fo. 76; Treherne's reading (1520), ff. 5, 65v; BL MS. Stowe 414, fo. 47. Treherne said (MS. Stowe 414, fo. 46, tr.) that rabbits were 'not at all belonging to the wood, for they

were not supposed to be taken without the king's licence, though there might in some places be a custom to do so, especially in the case of wolves, which were 'enemies to the common wealth'.[75] Treherne did not regard the taking of hares or vermin as properly being pleas of the forest.[76] But the forest jurisdiction was not narrowly confined, and could even extend its reach to those who wrongfully abstracted inanimate produce of the forest, such as minerals and honey.[77]

COUNTIES AND HUNDREDS

County courts were still functioning throughout England, and in accordance with Magna Carta were supposed to be held monthly before the sheriff.[78] They were essential for the purpose of proclaiming outlawries,[79] but they still exercised in addition a jurisdiction in personal actions under 40s.[80] The normal method of trial in personal actions was wager of law, and therefore actions could not be brought on deeds, even for debts under 40s.[81] Few records appear to have survived, though proceedings in county courts occasionally left their mark in the Common Pleas rolls in the form of justifications pleaded in trespass by reason of county court process,[82] or writs of false judgment.[83] Proceedings were not formally of record, unless removed into a central court and affirmed, and disputes about them in the central courts were therefore triable by jury.[84] Probably the day to day records were kept in minute-books. A paper indenture of 1537 between Sir Godfrey Foljambe, late sheriff of Nottinghamshire and Derbyshire, and Sir Nicholas Strelley, his successor, noted delivery of 'the county books of

have a mind of returning again, and therefore are not of such nature as the other beasts be; but yet they cannot be chased within the forest'.

[75] Treherne's reading (1520) BL MS. Stowe 414, fo. 46. Hesketh had added the fox to his list of beasts of warren.   [76] Treherne's reading (1520), ff. 2v, 63v–64.

[77] Treherne's reading (1520), ff. 24v, 54–55v.

[78] This was alleged in 1534 to be the law in all counties and cities except London, York, and Lincoln: *Lownde* v. *Orrell* (1534) KB 27/1090, m. 40; *Fuljambe* v. *Barley* (1534) KB 27/1091, m. 23; 94 Selden Soc. 282, 318. It was confirmed by 2 & 3 Edw. VI, c. 25.   [79] See below, 331–2.

[80] See the exposition of county courts, probably from Richard Littleton's reading (Inner Temple, 1493) in Port 119–20. For replevin in the county court, see Spelman 204. For abuses, see 11 Hen. VII, c. 15.

[81] Yorke 158, no. 182. Cf. the jurisdiction of courts baron, which Yorke treated as analogous: below, 316. Francis Mountford said 'the county court is only the king's court baron': Caryll (Jun.) 414, no. 114.

[82] *Clerk* v. *Bullock* (1494) CP 40/928, m. 363 (plaint of replevin in Suffolk county court at Ipswich); *Cole* v. *Faux* (1494) CP 40/929, m. 424 (plaint of trespass in Devon county court held at Exeter); *Jenney* v. *Eston* (1503) CP 40/962, m. 330 (withernam in Suffolk county court). Cf. *Bolyngeham* v. *Dyke* (1518) CP 40/1022, m. 547 (plea mentions custom of forest of Dean to sue in Gloucester county court in respect of iron-working).

[83] e.g. *Teyngcomb* v. *Hyll* (1523) CP 40/1041, m. 525 (replevin in county court of Devon; judgment reversed).

[84] *Purser* v. *Calney* (1492) 1 Caryll 104; CP 40/922, m. 308 (referring to *justicies*).

Nottingham and Derby, with divers plaints hanging in the same...also the processes of the said shire of Nottingham'.[85] There was a county clerk, who acted as clerk to the county court and was also responsible for closing the sheriff's account at the Exchequer.[86] The appointment of county clerk—unlike that of clerk of the peace[87]—belonged to the sheriff. In the time of Henry VIII a number of appointments were in fact made by the Crown, though they were held void later in the century.[88]

The hundreds were still of administrative importance, since the sheriff routinely delegated some of his functions to the bailiffs of hundreds, sometimes called bailiffs errant.[89] They were also in evidence as courts hearing personal actions,[90] and occasionally their records were removed into the Common Pleas by *recordari facias*.[91] But their functioning was not as uniform as that of the shires. Some were now in private hands, or belonged to boroughs, in which case they were usually called courts leet[92]—though some held that a leet was incident to every hundred.[93] In a court leet, the steward had the same judicial powers as the sheriff had in the hundred.[94] A hundred had a similar jurisdiction to the county,

[85] C146/7243 (sp. mod.). The 'processes' were proclamations of outlawry and exigents, and one *supplicavit*.

[86] See *Eggecombe* v. *Whyte* (1524) CP 40/1045, m. 647 (debt on bond to perform indenture granting the clerkship of the county of Devon to John Whyte and others in 1512; demurrer to plea of performance); *Calverley* v. *Beseley* (1558) CP 40/1176(1), m. 1136 (debt on bond to enter into and end the plaintiff's account; Beseley, described as clerk of the county and castle of York, was an attorney). In 1516 the office of sheriff's clerk of Devon was granted to five men: *Speke* v. *Flemyng* (1523) 119 Selden Soc. at 190.   [87] Above, 268.   [88] *Mitton's Case* (1584) 4 Co. Rep. 87.

[89] The duties of hundred bailiffs were set out in the conditions of bonds entered into with the sheriff: e.g. *Bedyngfeld* (*sheriff of Norf.*) v. *Golspyn* (1523) CP 40/1040, m. 442; *Hevenyngham* (*sheriff of Norf.*) v. *Fysshe* (1526) CP 40/1049, m. 332; *Heydon* (*sheriff of Norf.*) v. *Corbett* (1530) CP 40/1067, m. 761; *Blount* (*sheriff of Heref.*) v. *Perle* (1539) CP 40/1101, m. 642; *Blonte* (*sheriff of Heref.*) v. *Ap Richard* (1543) CP 40/1118, m. 421; *Songer* (*under-sheriff of Essex*) v. *Candeler* (1545) CP 40/1125, m. 303; *Souche* (*sheriff of Notts.*) v. *Walden* (1551) CP 40/1146, m. 125.

[90] e.g. *Flassheman* v. *Hele* (1528) CP 40/1058A, m. 628 (trespass justified by order of hundred court of Ermington, Devon, in an action of detinue; but judgment for plaintiff on demurrer).

[91] E.g. *Etton* v. *Aunger* (1522) CP 40/1034, m. 409 (reversal of judgment in trespass in hundred court of Tendring, Essex); *Frende* v. *Fortescue* (1551) CP 40/1146, m. 454 (next note); *Selfe* v. *Longe* (1551) CP 40/1147A, m. 753 (next note). Cf. *Lowth* v. *Wellys* (1520) KB 27/1037, m. 28 (writ of error from king's hundred of Colchester).

[92] Cf. *Corne* v. *Twygge* (1535) CP 40/1087, m. 303 (rescue; counts on seizure of cow by precept of the steward of the hundred of 'Sherewyll', Devon, belonging to John Chechester esq.); *Frende* v. *Fortescue* (1551) CP 40/1146, m. 454 (record of hundred court of Ermington, Devon, belonging to Francis Stonore; errors not assigned); *Selfe* v. *Longe* (1551) CP 40/1147A, m. 753 (reversal of judgment in hundred court of Potterne, Wilts., belonging to John Tregonwell). See also *Browne* v. *Scot* (1495) CP 40/933, m. 228 (avowry for distress for not attending private tourn at 'Hirstington', Hunts); Hil. 10 Hen. VII, fo. 15, pl. 12; Pas. 12 Hen. VII, ff. 15–18, pl. 1.

[93] It was argued on both sides in *Anon.* (1498) Pas. 12 Hen. VII, fo. 15, pl. 1.

[94] *Anon.* (1482) Mich. 22 Edw. IV, fo. 2, pl. 2, *per* Huse CJ. Cf. Hil. 3 Hen. VII, fo. 4, pl. 15, *per* Fairfax (a leet is the king's court though in the hands of a common person).

in personal actions, with an upper limit of 40s.[95] In addition, a leet could punish assaults, affrays, public nuisances,[96] regrating and forestalling,[97] and failures to perform public duties,[98] and could make bye-laws, which were enforceable by amercement,[99] though such laws could not bind 'strangers'.[100] The criminal jurisdiction over misdemeanours was highly summary in form, because presentments by the pledges were treated as 'gospel', which meant they were untraversable and did not require trial.[101] It was not even permissible to traverse the premise that the offence occurred within the precinct of the leet.[102]

The jurisdiction of hundreds and leets, and the difference between them, was discussed at some length in an avowry of 1493 for amercements of a leet where a hundred had been granted to an abbot.[103] It was said there that a hundred contained in itself a leet and a court baron, apparently meaning a view of frankpledge and a minor civil jurisdiction, though the same proposition was denied in the King's Bench two years later.[104] Despite repeated exposition in the readings, there was evidently great uncertainty about the history and nature of these institutions.

[95] This is mentioned in 34 & 35 Hen. VIII, c. 26, s. 28. The jurisdiction was not necessarily in decline: see Baker, 'Personal Actions in the High Court of Battle Abbey', 263 at 284 n. 100 (Mere, Wilts.).

[96] This was a very broad category. In 1498 the court leet of Dunwich fined a clergyman for associating illicitly with married women in the borough: BL Add. Ch. 40733. In a roll from Hastings (1528–9) we find a husband and wife charged as barrators and common scolds, and tradesmen charged with taking excessive profits: BL Add. Ch. 31621.

[97] Yorke 159, no. 184 (said to be a form of common nuisance).

[98] e.g. failing to repair ways and bridges (see Yorke 159, no. 184), failing to keep watch under the Statute of Winchester, and failing to attend the court itself. All these are found in BL Add. Ch. 31621 (Hastings, 1528–9).

[99] A prescription to make bye-laws, and enforce them, was pleaded in e.g. *Hale* v. *Huntley* (1557) CP 40/1170, m. 940 (Hempsted, Gloucs.). Cf. Spelman's reading (1519), 88.

[100] *Anon.* (1497) Hil. 11 Hen. VII, fo. 13, pl. 8; Mich. 21 Hen. VII, fo. 40, pl. 61 (same case); Brooke Abr., *Leete*, pl. 34. A leet might, however, be entitled to make village bye-laws extending beyond a particular manor: C. Oestmann, *Lordship and Community* (1994), 117–19.

[101] *William Dean's Case* (1484) Mich. 2 Ric. III, fo. 11, pl. 25; *Anon.* (1505) 2 Caryll 460; Spelman 160 ('every amercement in a leet is like a gospel'); reading in Gray's Inn (c.1525) BL MS. Harley 25239, fo. 56 (tr. 'note that a presentment in a leet is as true as the gospel'); *Anon.* (1536) Dyer 13, §64 ('a presentment of bloodshed in a leet...is taken for gospel'). Englefield J. said the reason was that the law did not favour personal property: *Marmyon* v. *Baldwyn* (1527) 120 Selden Soc. 61 at 64. St German said it was to avoid trouble: *Little Treatise*, ed. Guy, 117.

[102] *Burbury* v. *Tydnam* (1529) CP 40/1061, m. 693; pr. 121 Selden Soc. 311 (avowry for amercement), as reported in Wm Yelv. 311, no. 6 (tr. 'the law gives such high credence to the verdict of the pledges, that what they have presented is true, that no one shall traverse this presentment unless it touches the inheritance').

[103] *Tawndye* v. *Abbot of Winchcombe* (1493) 1 Caryll 151; Trin. 8 Hen. VII, ff. 1–5, pl. 1 (says Tewkesbury); Pas. 13 Hen. VII, ff. 19–20, pl. 2; CP 40/922, m. 412. See also Port 119–20.

[104] Pas. 12 Hen. VII, fo. 17, pl. 1, *per* Fyneux CJ. See also Brooke Abr., *Leete*, pl. 24 (a leet is not *incident* to a hundred but may be appurtenant).

Sheriffs still kept their tourns twice a year in the hundreds,[105] except when they had become leets in private hands.[106] The function was to record accusations and transmit them to the appropriate royal judges rather than dispose of them. Indictments could be received but not tried,[107] and even this limited authority was restricted to common-law offences.[108]

CITIES AND BOROUGHS

The possession of jurisdiction seems to have been an inseparable incident of any city or borough, even when the town was in the possession of a bishop,[109] religious house,[110] or other subject,[111] and municipal jurisdiction was in practice extensive in scope and regularly exercised. In the first place, a town very often had a criminal jurisdiction exclusive of the county around it. A few large cities were even counties in themselves, with their own sheriffs, county courts, and assizes; many other towns had their own commissions of the peace, in which the mayor and aldermen took the place of the landed gentry who dominated the country commissions. Many towns also possessed a leet jurisdiction—that is, a view of frankpledge and a hundred[112]—which enabled them to control unsocial

[105] The court had to be held at the times specified in Magna Carta, c. 35: *Anon.* (1491) Pas. 6 Hen. VII, fo. 2, pl. 4. It was held in 1532, however, that the provisions did not apply to a leet in private hands: Brooke Abr., *Leete*, pl. 23.

[106] See discussions in readings: Port 119–21 (probably Richard Littleton, Inner Temple, 1493); BL MS. Hargrave 87, ff. 372–78 (anonymous reading on Westminster II, c. 13). According to Francis Mountford (Inner Temple, 1527), 'the sheriff's tourn is the king's leet, and a leet is a common person's tourn': Caryll (Jun.) 414, no. 114.

[107] They were to be sent to the justices of the peace in accordance with 1 Edw. IV, c. 2.

[108] See Mich. 22 Edw. IV, fo. 22, pl. 2 (rape excluded); Mich. 1 Ric. III, fo. 1, pl. 1 (statutory misdemeanours excluded, e.g. uttering badly tanned leather); Hil. 3 Hen. VII, fo. 1, pl. 1, *per* Fairfax (referring to same case); *R.* v. *Wheler* (*c.*1480/90) Crown Office entries, fo. 10v (tourn may not enquire into rape); *R.* v. *Bregyn, R.* v. *Patte* (1491) KB 27/920, Rex m. 3d and m. 5 (sim.); *Anon.* (1491) Trin. 6 Hen. VII, fo. 4, pl. 4 (leet sim.); Richard Littleton's reading (Inner Temple, 1493) 105 Selden Soc. 278, pl. 109; *R.* v. *Rede* (1513) KB 27/1007, Rex m. 3 (steward of view may not take indictment for forcible entry). Note also *Anon.* (1487) Hil. 2 Hen. VII, fo. 10, pl. 6 (tourn cannot take indictment for trespass other than bloodshed). For the jury qualifications see 1 Ric. III, c. 4.

[109] e.g. the court in Salisbury Guildhall was held before the bailiff of the bishop of Salisbury's liberty of New Sarum: *Eliott* v. *Brodyate* (1523) CP 40/1038, m. 422; *Blathewit* v. *Lobbe* (1535) KB 27/1097, m. 31 (deputy bailiff); *Potter* v. *Stephyn* (1556) KB 27/1178, m. 182. The town court of Ripon was called the *curia militaris* of the archbishop of York: *Redeshawe* v. *Hardwyke* (1539) KB 27/1113, m. 61 (debt on an account stated); *Exilbe* v. *Chauner* (1558) KB 27/1187, m. 20 (debt on bond).

[110] e.g. the court at Bury St Edmunds, held before the abbot's steward: *Rokewode* v. *Kelyng* (1516) KB 27/1020, m. 92 (sim. records on mm. 89, 93).

[111] e.g. the town court of Burgavenny was held in the name of Lord Burgavenny: *Herberd* v. *Oldesworthe* (1554) KB 27/1169, m. 78 (debt on bond); cf. *Baker* v. *Watkyn* (1557) KB 27/1181, m. 34.

[112] The borough court at Monmouth was styled a 'hundred': *Dyer* v. *Gryff* (1552) KB 27/1161, m. 142.

behaviour and suppress public nuisances.[113] There seems to have been an increasing preoccupation with social control at the beginning of our period, exercised either through leets or through the municipal justices of the peace.[114] And all towns possessed their own civil jurisdictions, mostly without financial limits,[115] Even a small and impoverished town such as Maldon, in Essex, with under a thousand inhabitants, was incorporated in 1554 and granted a weekly court of record with unlimited jurisdiction over personal actions.[116] As in the central courts, the staple business in local courts was debt. However, the business of most of these courts is difficult to reconstruct in detail because their archives have not survived well from this period, and there are virtually no records even for large cities such as London, York, and Norwich. When records do survive, they are usually bare minutes of the proceedings.[117] The usual practice was for pleadings to be filed in paper, and very few of these files have been preserved.[118] Such information as we find in local archives is therefore, in general, less informative than the plea rolls of the central courts.

The nomenclature and procedure of municipal courts of civil jurisdiction varied from place to place. Some towns, such as Oxford, had constitutions modelled on that of London. Thus, Oxford had a court of husting for pleas of land, a bailiffs' court (corresponding to the sheriffs' court), and a mayor's court.[119] Other cities had a different multiplicity of courts, founded either on prescription or on the terms of their charters,[120] but often with a similar distinction between the jurisdiction of the corporation (exercised by the mayor) and that of the sheriffs,

[113] See F. J. C. Hearnshaw, *Leet Jurisdiction in England* (Southampton Record Soc.; 1908); F. A. Bailey (ed.), *A Selection from the Prescot Court Leet and other Records 1447–1600* (89 Record Soc. Lancs. and Ches.; 1937); C. Dyer, *Lords and Peasants in a Changing Society* (1980), 347 (bye-laws as to brewing, in unincorporated town).

[114] See M. K. McIntosh, *Autonomy and Community: the royal manor of Havering 1200–1500* (1986), 255–9; 'Social Change and Tudor Manorial Leets' in *Law and Social Change*, ed. Guy and Beale, 73–85; *Controlling Misbehaviour in England, 1370–1600* (1998); G. Rosser, *Medieval Westminster 1200–1500* (1989), 243–4; Newman, 'Local Court Administration within the Liberty of Allertonshire', 22–3; 'Order and Community', 63–5.

[115] A few were limited by their charters. Some were limited to £50 (e.g. St Albans, Tewkesbury) or £100 (e.g. Harwich, Leominster, Tiverton). Arundel and Plympton had a lowly 40s. limit: C. Muldrew, *The Economy of Obligation* (1998), 205, app. 2. Carlisle had the same limit, but contrived to ignore it from the 1550s onwards: H. Summerson, *Medieval Carlisle* (1993), ii. 531.

[116] R. Tittler, 'The Incorporation of Boroughs 1540–58' (1977) 62 *History* 24 at 38.

[117] Full records were made up when writs of error were brought; these records were entered in the King's Bench rolls (KB 27), which have been extensively used for the present account.

[118] See below, 310.

[119] J. Cooper and A. Crossley, 'Courts' in VCH, *Oxfordshire*, iv. 336 at 337–8. For example, *Gowght v. Busshell* (1539) KB 27/1113, m. 63 (error from mayor of Oxford).

[120] Many had courts of piepowder: below, 312. Some also had admiralty jurisdiction: see above, 210. At Ipswich, records of an occasional 'curia maritima' and court of piepowder are inserted among those of the regular borough courts: SfRO, C5/12/1 (examples of both kinds in 1488).

who perhaps in county towns represented a county court. York, for example, had a sheriffs' court (called Domesday) for personal actions,[121] and a superior court before the mayor and sheriffs to hear real and personal actions, bills of nuisance, and error from the sheriffs' court,[122] with wardmote courts to try minor misde- meanours.[123] Bristol had a mayor's court,[124] a sheriffs' court (known as the Tolzey Court),[125] and also a staple court.[126] Although the name Tolzey is peculiar to Bristol, it is echoed in East Anglian courts held in a town's Tolbooth or Tollhouse.[127] The mayor and sheriffs of Bristol were supposed to sit in the Counter every day to hear suits,[128] but the exact line between the jurisdiction of the mayor and that of the sheriffs alone was the subject of controversy.[129] Chester had a Crownmote, with criminal jurisdiction, a Portmanmote, which dealt with land transactions and breaches of the peace, and a Pentice Court, which heard personal actions.[130] Exeter had a court held before the mayor and four bailiffs in

[121] Two sheriffs' court books survive temp. Hen. VII (1497–8, 1499–1500): YCA, E25a, F1. See *Sheriffs' Court Books of the City of York 1471–1500*, tr. P. M. Stell (1999), 96–194. Specimen full records from the next century are *Wylde* v. *Prior of Newborough* (1515) KB 27/1017, m. 21; *Tubly* v. *Kelke* (1557) KB 27/1181, m. 60 (debt by physician for counsel and medicines; demurrer); *Tyllesley* v. *Bynkes* (1558) KB 27/1187, m. 28 (debt on bond).

[122] No records survive from this period. See 'De curia majoris civitatis Ebor. et custumis civitatis ejusdem in diversis casibus terminabilibus in eadem curia' (*c*.1471), printed in *York Memorandum Book*, pt ii, ed. M. Sellers (125 Surtees Soc.; 1915), 251–66; and VCH, *Yorks., The City of York* (1961), 75–7. An example of a writ of error to the mayor and sheriffs is *Spurriour* v. *Preston* (1531) KB 27/1081, m. 39 (action for defamation, with demurrer in English).

[123] See e.g. the fines from wardmote courts (1520–5) in the Chamberlains' Accounts, YCA, CC 2, ff. 18, 55, 137v–139, 142, 227.

[124] e.g. *Barrett* v. *Pottell* (1558) KB 27/1186, m. 92 (action of battery before mayor and aldermen).

[125] A stray Tolzey Court roll of 1517 is printed in 23 Selden Soc. 131. Some earlier examples are *Gylham* v. *Pardy* (1485) C244/136/16 (covenant); *Hylle* v. *Rysse* (1486) KB 27/899, m. 31 (debt on account stated); *Popley* v. *Archbishop of Canterbury* (1488) C244/139/46 (debt); *Sheryve* v. *Bishop of Annadown* (1490) KB 27/914, m. 31; *Arthure* v. *Duffeld* (1492) KB 27/925, m. 64.

[126] See *Smyth* v. *Weston* (1492) 1 Caryll 88; C1/175/45 (*certiorari*, but remitted to Bristol); KB 27/921, m. 32 (error from the mayor and constables of the staple of Bristol, following the law merchant).

[127] e.g. *Synger* v. *Barett* (1500–2) KB 27/956, m. 38; KB 27/963, m. 39 ('Le Tolhous' at Great Yarmouth); *Dey* v. *Kelyng, Rokewode* v. *Kelyng, Tassell* v. *Kelyng* (1516) KB 27/1020, mm. 89, 92, 93 ('Le Tollehouse' at Bury St Edmunds; dispute whether held before bailiffs or the bishop's steward); *Raye* v. *Swanne* (1556) KB 27/1178, m. 31 (Cambridge toll-booth); *Pegrem* v. *Atkyns* (1558) KB 27/1185, m. 96 (Cambridge toll-booth); *Joye* v. *Coke* (1558) KB 27/1188, m. 138 ('Le Tolhouse' at Southwold).

[128] See R. Ricart, *The Maire of Bristowe is Kalendar* (1479), ed. L. T. Smith (5 Camden Soc., 2nd ser.; 1872), 84.

[129] S. D. Cole, 'English Borough Courts' (1902) 18 *LQR* 376 at 380–4. In *Hayman* v. *Coxe* (1556) KB 27/1179, m. 197, the style of the Tolzey ('Tolsett.') court was before the sheriffs, but they were also stated to be acting as bailiffs of the mayor and commonalty. Cf. *Whetcombe* v. *Grene* (1558) KB 27/1188, m. 98 (sim., but sitting in Guildhall *secundum legem mercatoriam*, not mentioning the Tolzey).

[130] H. Lloyd, 'The Pentice and other ancient Law Courts in Chester' (1909) 16 *Jnl Chester Arch. Soc.* (new ser.), pt ii, 1–25; A. W. Kennett, *Archives and Records of the City of Chester* (1985), 23–31; Clayton, *The Administration of the County Palatine of Chester*, 31–2. A full account has been promised for VCH, *Chester*, v (forthcoming). See also Thornton, *Cheshire and the Tudor State*, 115–16.

the Guildhall,[131] which sometimes entertained real actions,[132] and a Provost Court held before the bailiffs alone;[133] and it claimed a custom for the mayor, bailiffs, and citizens to punish misdemeanours.[134] Norwich had a Guildhall Court, held before the sheriffs alone,[135] and a mayor's court which had a petty sessional jurisdiction.[136] Canterbury had a sheriffs' court, in essence a county court, a burghmoot, which heard real actions and assizes, a court of piepowder, sessions of the peace, and a view of frankpledge or lawday.[137] In some towns we find mention of a Foreign Court (*curia forinseca*), as at Colchester, Grimsby, Hull, Leominster, Lincoln, and Nottingham,[138] with jurisdiction beyond the confines of the borough.[139] And several towns, like Bristol, had a staple court for mercantile business within the purview of the staple.[140] In a case concerning the mayor of the staple of Chichester in 1527, it was pleaded that staple courts were held weekly in accordance with the law merchant (*lex mercatoria*) and the immemorial custom of England of the faculty of the wool staple, to hear actions of debt, covenant, and trespass, and that the mayor was elected as someone knowledgeable in mercantile law (*lex mercandizabilis*).[141]

Most boroughs, however, seem to have had only one court, held—or at least stated to be held—before the bailiffs (or sheriffs) alone,[142] or before the mayor

---

[131] e.g. *Straiche* v. *Crokhay* (1526) KB 27/1061, m. 65; *Hunte* v. *Cotton* (1554) KB 27/1172, m. 132.

[132] *Trevylyan* v. *Hyll* (1555) KB 27/1174, m. 162 (writ of right sued (tr.) 'in the form and nature of the lord king's writ of assize of novel disseisin at common law'; reversed).

[133] e.g. *Vyncent* v. *Kewe* (1500) C 1/246/54 ('Court of Provostry' belonging to the bailiffs and commonalty); *Bonyfant* v. *Hackewill* (1516) KB 27/1020, m. 26; *Webbe* v. *Colston* (1552) KB 27/1164, m. 128. Cf. Cole, 'English Borough Courts', 385, who equates the Provost Court with the mayor's court.

[134] *Filmore* v. *Hamlyn* (1528) CP 40/1058A, m. 528 (false imprisonment justified under the custom, but plea held bad on demurrer).

[135] Only one roll (for 1556) has survived: NfRO, NRC Case 8b/1. Examples of earlier cases are *Blomvyle* v. *Grigges* (1485) C244/136/126 (debt for £231); *Marskey* v. *Peterson* (1510) KB 27/997, m. 70 (trespass); *Berwyke* v. *Foster* (1552) KB 27/1161, m. 126 (*assumpsit*).   [136] NfRO, NRC Case 16a.

[137] E. Hasted, *History of the City of Canterbury* (1800), ii. 623 (referring to records around 1498), below, 307 (oath of recorder, c.1535).

[138] Pontefract, Yorks., had a *curia burgensium et for' apud praetorium* (see *Alford* v. *Barley* (1529) KB 27/1070, m. 29) which seems to refer to 'foreigners' rather than foreign causes.

[139] See Cole, 'English Borough Courts', 379. Colchester: *Breton* v. *Teryngton* (1516) KB 27/1021, m. 68 (*assumpsit*) and m. 86 (trespass). Kingston upon Hull: *Busshell* v. *Norman* (1534) KB 27/1092, m. 20 (debt); *Jacklyng* v. *Thornton* (1552) KB 27/1164, m. 115 (detinue). Nottingham: *Colles* v. *Byrde* (1550) KB 27/1153, m. 26 (debt on bond); *Howyde* v. *Garthe* (1553) KB 27/1165, m. 126 ('debt on the case'); *Travysse* v. *Leighe* (1553) KB 27/1166, m. 136 (debt); *Saunders* v. *Ascoughe* (1557) KB 27/1183, m. 88 (trespass justified by process of Foreign Court).

[140] See e.g. *Rasour* v. *Sybsey* (1500/01) C 1/245/9 (action in staple court of Boston, Lincs, on a bill payable to bearer according to the custom of merchants).

[141] *Bolley* v. *Stelle* (1527–30) CP 40/1055, m. 154 (demurrer to justification in false imprisonment).

[142] e.g. Bridgnorth, Dunwich, Ipswich, Lichfield, Ludlow, New Sarum (one bailiff), Shrewsbury, Southwold, Winchester, Worcester, and Great Yarmouth: records noted in KB 27. As to Worcester, cf. *Holder* v. *Harvey* (1557) KB 27/1181, m. 168 (suit before the two bailiffs, two aldermen and two

and bailiffs (or sheriffs).[143] Rather less frequently, a borough court was held before other combinations of officials and prominent citizens. For example, at Rochester the style of the borough court was 'before the mayor and other principal citizens',[144] while under its charter of 1488 Guildford held a court every three weeks before the mayor and 'two of the more discreet suitable men of the town'.[145] At Chichester a 'court for real and personal pleas' was held at the Guildhall before the mayor alone.[146] How far these laymen performed their judicial work unaided is far from clear. No doubt many cases were disposed of by arbitration or compromise, since only a small minority proceeded to trial, and the mayor or sheriffs may commonly have acted more like arbitrators than judges.[147] However, by early Tudor times there was in almost every city and borough a recorder or steward, learned in the law, who may have presided at some courts or at least attended to give legal assistance.[148] The oath of the recorder of Canterbury shows that he was expected to preside at the sessions, lawday, burghmoot, and court of piepowder, and at the common courts held twice a week.[149] Since he sat as representative of the corporation, and—in the absence of a specific provision in the charter—probably could not act as a delegate of the proper judges,[150] a recorder is seldom mentioned in the formal captions of

chamberlains of the city); *Tollye* v. *Blagdon* (1557) KB 27/1183, m. 24 (sim.); *Cycell* v. *Blagdon* (1557) KB 27/1184, m. 74 (sim.).

[143] e.g. Barnstaple, Bedford, Cambridge, Coventry, Dartmouth, Gloucester, Hull, Monmouth, Newcastle-upon-Tyne, Northampton, Nottingham, and Winchester: records noted in KB 27.

[144] *Burwell* v. *Lynke* (1553) KB 27/1167, m. 90.

[145] E. M. Dance, *Guildford Borough Records 1514–46* (24 Surrey Record Soc.; 1958), p. xxxi. The borough court at Totnes was held before the mayor and four burgesses: 94 Selden Soc. 302; *Cockesworthy* v. *Bullegh* (1552) KB 27/1163, m. 25; *Myller* v. *Swadell* (1552) KB 27/1164, m. 36. Kingston-on-Thames had a court before two bailiffs and five freemen: *Saunders* v. *Keyne* (1553) KB 27/1167, m. 157; cf. KB 27/893, m. 20 (two bailiffs only, 1484).

[146] *Wakford* v. *Unkle* (1539) KB 27/1113, m. 33; *Hardham* v. *Chatfeld* (1553) KB 27/1167, m. 87; *Tolpatt* v. *Grovet* (1557) KB 27/1182, m. 35. Likewise at Higham Ferrers: *Jenkyns* v. *Saunderson* (1558) KB 27/1187, m. 65 (writ to mayor and aldermen).

[147] See Ricart, *The Maire of Bristowe is Kalendar*, 85, where he says that the mayor and sheriffs at their daily sittings were 'to set parties in rest and ease by their advertisement, compromise or otherwise, unless then it so require that they must remit them to the law' (sp. mod.).

[148] In *Rokewode* v. *Kelyng* (1516) KB 27/1020, m. 92 (from Bury St Edmunds), the first error assigned is that although the style of the court was before the bailiffs (Sir Robert Drury and William Powle), Drury did not attend and the court was held before the steward.

[149] Precedent book of C. Levyns (*c.*1535) BL MS. Stowe 856, fo. 121. For courts of piepowder, see below, 312–14.

[150] In *Martyn* v. *Warren* (1543) KB 27/1128, m. 34, it was assigned as error in a record of the New Sarum Guildhall court that judgment had been given by a 'deputy' bailiff and no judge can appoint a deputy ('secundum legem et consuetudinem hujus regni... nullus judex sub se substituere potest aliquem inferiorem judicem sive deputatum'). The judgment was reversed, but this was not the only error assigned. Cf. *Blathewit* v. *Lobbe* (1535) KB 27/1097, m. 31 (court held before deputy bailiff of liberty of New Sarum).

courts.[151] But recorders must have had a general influence on the way municipal courts functioned. And they were not the only trained lawyers at hand. The town clerks, who were responsible for keeping the record and issuing process,[152] and might give legal advice in the absence of the recorder,[153] were commonly expected to be men of court; and there is evidence that Common Pleas attorneys practised in many borough courts.[154] In some towns there were professional local attorneys and common pleaders.[155]

For all these superficial local divergences, the procedure of municipal courts throughout England was on the whole remarkably uniform. Actions were commenced by plaint, or occasionally by bill, and process was by summons and distraint or attachment. When trial was required it was now nearly always by jury,[156] although wager of law had once been more usual[157] and seems to have been kept up in some towns, at any rate in those cases where it was still in use at Westminster.[158] In the city of York, for instance, we find wager of law with twelve hands, as well as occasional jury verdicts in both debt and trespass.[159]

[151] e.g. BL MS. Stowe 850, fo. 45 ('John Hales, learned in the law of this realm of England' present with the mayor and aldermen at Canterbury sessions, 1536). Cf. *Norman* v. *Owen* (1557) KB 27/1181, m. 163 (writ of error to bailiffs and freemen of Kingston upon Thames; caption mentions court before bailiffs and town steward; error assigned that steward not always present and the custom allowing him to be sometimes absent was not set out). See also *Bishop of Llandaff* v. *Button* (1557) KB 27/1182, m. 101 (debt before steward and bailiffs of Chepstow).

[152] The range of duties is indicated by the table of fees claimed by the town clerk of Canterbury in 1505: precedent book of C. Levyns, BL MS. Stowe 856, fo. 5.

[153] According to Ricart, *The Maire of Bristowe is Kalendar*, 85, the mayor and sheriffs of Bristol were advised by the recorder if present, but otherwise by the town clerk. The sheriffs' court of York was advised by the recorder for a fee: *Fairfax* v. *Neelson* (1497) CP 40/942, m. 210 (debt on retainer); A.K.R. Kiralfy, *The Action on the Case* (1951), 235.

[154] e.g. KB 27/997, m. 70 (John Corbet in Guildhall Court of Norwich, 1510); KB 27/1020, m. 26 (Richard Duke in Provost Court of Exeter, 1516); ibid., mm. 89, 92, 93 (John Holt, Thomas Lopham, and William Markaunt in Bury St Edmunds, 1516); KB 27/1092, m. 20 (Richard Brynkeley in Foreign Court of Kingston on Hull, 1534); ibid., m. 66 (Thomas Hyll in Guildhall Court of Worcester, 1534); KB 27/1160, m. 79, and 1161, m. 104 (Edward Darnell and Thomas Hill, Worcester, 1551); KB 27/1183, m. 24 (Edward Darnell, Worcester, 1557).

[155] e.g. Canterbury: precedent book of C. Levyns, BL MS. Stowe 856, fo. 10 (oath of attorney and counsellor of Canterbury, temp. Hen. VIII), and fo. 93v (oath of attorney and common pleader). Levyns was presumably himself such an attorney; he was admitted to Gray's Inn in 1526.

[156] Usually by twelve jurors, but there were customary variations: e.g. in Barnstaple trials could be made by four common councilmen: *Wychehalfe* v. *Walshe* (1557) KB 27/1182, m. 36.

[157] See C. Gross, 15 *Harvard Law Rev.* at 695–701.

[158] e.g. at Sudbury, where in 1508–9 law was waged—with two, three, or four hands—in eight debt actions as against two in which the issue was referred to a jury, though only two defendants successfully performed their law: Bodl. Lib. MS. Rawlinson B.425. In nearby Ipswich, a much larger town, law was rarely waged, though there is an instance (with seven hands) in 1488: SfRO, C5/12/1, Tues. after Trin. 3 Hen. VII. In the 1530s, a plaintiff complained in Chancery of a perjured wager of law in Taunton: *Mynshull* v. *Archer*, C1/850/44 (demurrer).

[159] Only three verdicts are recorded in the two Sheriffs' Court books: *Baynbrig* v. *Johnson* (1497) YCA, E25a, fo. 18v (6s. damages for trespass); *Wright* v. *Kyldale* (1498) ibid., fo. 29 (53s. 4d. damages for

The common-law forms of action were usually followed in the framing of plaints, except where local custom permitted variation. Several towns, including Bristol, Coventry, Gloucester, Ipswich, Ludlow, Much Wenlock, New Sarum, Nottingham, Shrewsbury, and Worcester, followed London in allowing debt upon a *concessit solvere*,[160] and it was also common to find the custom of suing without specialty in covenant or debt against personal representatives.[161] Bristol and Exeter used the London custom of foreign attachment.[162] In Norwich we find an example of *assumpsit* to indemnify a surety some twenty years before anything similar is found at Westminster.[163] And in Ipswich there was a custom of suing for 'the trespass of slander' before it was recognized as a cause of action by the central courts of common law at the beginning of the sixteenth century.[164] These few examples show that sometimes local practices could prefigure changes in the common law. Conversely, borough courts also reacted directly to changes at the centre. For instance, as actions on the case became established at common law, they were generally adopted in exactly the same forms in the borough courts,[165] and there were parallel trends in the popularity of certain causes of

trespass); *Hardsang* v. *Dogeson* (1500) F1, fo. 43v (debt of 40s.) The third case was delayed by a Chancery *certiorari*, and the writ of *procedatis* (complete with tag) is sewn into the book on fo. 33. In a fourth case, the defendant confessed when the jury appeared: *Kyrk* v. *Besewyk* (1499) ibid., fo. 29.

[160] e.g. *Alestre* v. *Alestre* (1490) C244/138/3 (Nottingham); *Tofte* v. *Clerke* (1519) KB 27/1033, m. 67 (Shrewsbury); *Blyke* v. *Barston* (1530) KB 27/1075, m. 26 (Coventry); *Sadler* v. *Richardes* (1533) KB 27/1088, m. 31 (Worcester); *Blathewit* v. *Lobbe* (1535) KB 27/1097, m. 31 (New Sarum); *Wytherby* v. *Percyvall* (1539) KB 27/1113, m. 25 (Ipswich); *Prince* v. *Cole* (1544) 15 JLH 219 n. 24 (Shrewsbury); *Travysse* v. *Leighe* (1553) KB 27/1166, m. 136 (Nottingham); *Phillippes* v. *Heynes* (1553) KB 27/1168, m. 150 (Ludlow); *Hobbolde* v. *Nesshe* (1555) KB 27/1177, m. 173 (liberty of Much Wenlock); *Doryngton* v. *Evans* (1556) KB 27/1179, m. 73 (Gloucester; alleged custom not to wage law in such cases); *Boraston* v. *Gryff* (1556) KB 27/1180, m. 132 (Ludlow); *Holder* v. *Harvy* (1557) KB 27/1181, m. 168 (Worcester); *Tollye* v. *Blagdon* (1557) KB 27/1183, m. 24 (Worcester); *Whetcombe* v. *Grene* (1558) KB 27/1188, m. 98 (Bristol). In the Sudbury minute book for 1508–9, six of the thirteen declarations in debt are upon *concessit solvere*: Bodl. Lib. MS. Rawlinson B.425. See further below, 815.   [161] See below, 814–15.

[162] Pulling, *Laws and Customs of London*, 187–92 (also Lancaster); Cole, 'English Borough Courts', 379–80. Bristol was said to have used London customs generally: see Ricart, *The Maire of Bristowe is Kalendar*, 93.   [163] *Fenby* v. *Baly* (1485) KB 27/896, m. 40; below, 855.

[164] *Lambe* v. *Gauge* (1487) SfRO, C5/12/1, Tues. after Mich. 3 Hen. VII ('de placito transgressionis scandali secundum consuetudinem ville Gippewici'; pleads 'Non scandalizavit').

[165] e.g. *Breton* v. *Teryngton* (1516) KB 27/1020, m. 68 (Colchester; *assumpsit*); *Knyght* v. *Farley* (1534) KB 271092, m. 66 (Worcester; slander); *Marler* v. *Wilmer* (1539) KB 27/1111, m. 64 (Coventry; *assumpsit*); *Gatacre* v. *Broke* (1542) KB 27/1122, m. 128 (Bridgnorth; slander); *Savage* v. *Morres* (1550) KB 27/1156, m. 48 (Coventry; trover); *Berwyke* v. *Foster* (1552) KB 27/1161, m. 126 (Norwich; *assumpsit*); *Howyde* v. *Garthe* (1553) KB 27/1165, m. 126 (Nottingham; 'debt on the case'); *Saunders* v. *Keyne* (1553) KB 27/1167, m. 157 (Kingston-on-Thames; unusual form of declaration for profits of joint trading); *Gune* v. *Seymore* (1554) KB 27/1172, m. 108 ('Downevet', i.e. Launceston; slander); *Modie* v. *Coxhed* (1556) KB 27/1180, m. 210 (Winchester; *assumpsit*); *Baker* v. *Watkyn* (1557) KB 27/1181, m. 34 (Abergavenny; *assumpsit*); *Wychehalfe* v. *Walshe* (1557) KB 27/1182, m. 36 (Barnstaple; *assumpsit*); *Langford* v. *Ap Howell* (1557) KB 27/1183, m. 188 (Ludlow; *assumpsit*); *Cycell* v. *Blagdon* (1557) KB 27/1184, m. 74 (Worcester; slander); *Hewyt* v. *Robartes* (1558) KB 27/1188, m. 86 (Hull; slander). See also Kiralfy, *Action on the Case*, 233.

action. There was thus a boom in defamation actions in the mid-sixteenth century, when such actions reached epidemic proportions at Westminster.[166] Such innovations as the replacement of debt by *assumpsit* were also followed, though with less good reason.[167]

Proceedings in error show that local courts of record were expected to follow the common-law forms of action unless a local custom was averred and acknowledged by the parties. For example, it was allegedly manifest error to omit *contra pacem* in trespass,[168] or to insert it in *assumpsit* for nonfeasance;[169] or to bring a plaint of 'trespass' where the declaration was in case;[170] or to bring a plaint of covenant[171] or account[172] to recover a debt; or to combine debt with elements of actions on the case;[173] or for a defendant in *assumpsit* to plead 'Did not lend'.[174] Errors such as these seldom occurred in the more professional world of the two benches at Westminster. Yet, underlying such proceedings in error, there is a clear assumption that borough courts followed the common law, as modified by local custom, rather than a distinct body of custom or law merchant.

The forms of pleading are less easy to trace in the borough records themselves, because of the tendency towards the end of the fifteenth century to file paper pleadings and only to keep a bare minute in the register-books.[175] The use of papers may well have followed the innovation at Westminster,[176] with the difference that in borough courts the parchment roll was often abandoned altogether and no full record routinely made up. The disappearance of these papers for most boroughs[177] usually means the loss of detail vital to the legal as well as the local

---

[166] Helmholz, 101 Selden Soc., p. lxiv; Champion, 'Litigation in the Boroughs', 208 and 219 n. 29.

[167] See e.g. Champion, 'Litigation in the Boroughs', 208 (Shrewsbury); Baker, 'Personal Actions in the High Court of Battle Abbey', *CLT*, 273–6.

[168] *Smyth* v. *Baker* (1551) KB 27/1160, m. 207 (Bridgnorth; trespass for depasturing *vi et armis*).

[169] *Modie* v. *Coxhed* (1556) KB 27/1180, m. 210 (Winchester; '(tr.) he alleges that the non-performance of the promise and undertaking aforesaid was against the peace of the king and queen, although nothing is alleged in the same count to have been done with force and arms or against the peace of the king and queen').   [170] *Spurriour* v. *Preston* (1531) KB 27/1081, m. 39 (York).

[171] *Welsshe* v. *Hoper* (1533) KB 27/1088, m. 26 (Hereford; pr. 94 Selden Soc. 324).

[172] *Parkes* v. *Dackhouse* (1556) KB 27/1179, m. 188 (Ludlow; '(tr.) the plaint contains a plea of account and the conclusion of the same plaint sounds in a plea of debt, which plaint containing such contrariety ought to be quashed'; no judgment).

[173] *Howyde* v. *Garthe* (1553) KB 27/1165, m. 126 (Nottingham; 'debt on the case' in an irregular form; reversed); *Tubly* v. *Kelke* (1557) KB 27/1181, m. 60 (York; demurrer in the sheriffs' court on the ground that debt and case confused).

[174] *Alen* v. *Edwardes* (1555) KB 27/1174, m. 170 (Shrewsbury Curia Parva; assigned as error).

[175] See e.g. HMC, *Fifth Report*, App., 489 (Rye); Champion, 'Litigation in the Boroughs', at 203–4 (Shrewsbury and Hereford); SfRO, C5/12/1; C5/14/1A (Ipswich); Bodl. Lib. MS. Rawlinson B.425 (Sudbury). See also Baker, 'Personal Actions in the High Court of Battle Abbey', *CLT*, 277–8, 282–3.

[176] See below, 337–9 (King's Bench), 341–2 (Lancaster).

[177] Some have survived, e.g. from Macclesfield and Shrewsbury.

historian. Nevertheless, a record was made up in full if a writ of error was brought, and the King's Bench rolls present a wide range of full borough records from various parts of the country. It is evident from these examples in the King's Bench rolls that the forms of pleading in municipal courts, like the forms of action themselves, also generally followed the common law. In some boroughs, indeed, this was an explicit requirement in the charter of incorporation, as at Guildford—where the court was to proceed 'according to the law and custom of the realm', using the same forms of action.[178] No doubt in practice it was largely a matter of available expertise. When appropriate expertise was not available, we do indeed find some outlandish and amateurish formulations. Even in such cases there was evidently an attempt to emulate the known forms of law, but there was a high risk of challenge by writ of error if the losing party obtained professional advice. A shortage of clerical expertise in some towns may explain the increasing though probably not very widespread tendency to record proceedings in English,[179] despite the view of the King's Bench that the statute of 1362 made Latin indispensably necessary in all courts.[180] Law French also intrudes here and there.[181]

There have been few detailed studies of levels of litigation in borough courts during the early Tudor period, but the research which has been done indicates that they followed the same pattern as in the central courts. That is to say, there was a decline or stagnation towards the 1520s and 1530s, followed by a marked increase from about the 1550s onwards.[182] It certainly cannot be shown that in this period there was a migration of litigants from urban jurisdictions towards Westminster Hall.

[178] Charter of 1488 printed in *Guildford Borough Records*, ed. Dance, p. xxxi.

[179] *Spurriour* v. *Preston* (1531) KB 27/1081, m. 39 (demurrer in English at York); *Prince* v. *Cole* (1544) 15 *JLH* 219 n. 24 (Shrewsbury); *Myller* v. *Swadell* (1552) KB 27/1164, m. 36 (English record from Totnes; error not assigned); *Burwell* v. *Lynke* (1553) KB 27/1167, m. 90 (sim., Rochester); *Tubly* v. *Kelke* (1557) KB 27/1181, m. 60 (demurrer in English at York; this not assigned as error). In *Stacy* v. *Standon* (1529) CP 40/1063, m. 616 (false judgment), there is a record in English of an action on the case in the manor court of Bere Ferrers, Devon.

[180] See the following reversals of borough judgments: *Heth* v. *Stokephorte* (1530) KB 27/1077, m. 28 (pr. 94 Selden Soc. 302 at 303–4: Totnes); *Busshell* v. *Norman* (1534) KB 27/1092, m. 20 (Hull; English record, but this not assigned as error); *Predyaux* v. *Warwyke* (1550) KB 27/1156, m. 28 (Dartmouth); *Cockesworthy* v. *Bullegh* (1552) KB 27/1163, m. 25 (Totnes).

[181] e.g. *Wykes* v. *Palyngton* (1506) C 244/156/71 (Winchester; demurrer in law French); *Alford* v. *Barley* (1529) KB 27/1070, m. 29 (Pontefract; plea in bar in law French); *Wakford* v. *Unkle* (1539) KB 27/1113, m. 33 (Chichester; demurrer in law French). Some of the paper pleadings at Shrewsbury are drafted in law French.

[182] See Bailey, *A Selection from the Prescot Court Leet*, 320–2; J. L. Bolton and M. M. Maslen, *Calendar of the Court Books of the Borough of Witney 1538–1610* (54 Oxfordshire Rec. Soc.; 1981–2); R. H. Britnell, *Growth and Decline in Colchester 1300–1525* (1986), 281 (recovery begins in 1520s); Champion, 'Litigation in the Boroughs', 205 (Shrewsbury; here there is no obvious intermediate decline); Muldrew, *Economy of Obligation*, 217, 230–1, 234.

COURTS OF PIEPOWDER

A court of piepowder was incident as a matter of common right to every fair,[183] whether or not it was mentioned in the charter granting the fair, and—although in theory it might have been possible to make a prescriptive claim for such a court independently of a fair[184]—the court which was incident to a fair could never be severed from it.[185] It was accepted in 1508 that a court of piepowder was also incident to every market.[186] This meant that in some towns a piepowder court was available to sit every day of the year,[187] though of course it would only have had to do so if there was business to be transacted. No doubt the most active courts were those functioning in market-towns, where they belonged to the borough or city, but there were many markets and fairs in private hands[188]—especially in the hands of religious houses[189]—and they were also supposed to have courts of piepowder. In theory, according to the readers on *Quo Warranto*, it was a ground of forfeiture of a fair if the proprietor did not keep a piepowder or refused to hold court for someone with a good cause of action.[190] The records of the Chancery and King's Bench contain evidence that courts of piepowder were indeed still active in the early Tudor period.

The principal feature of such courts was that process was continued from hour to hour. Thus, in an action of account in the Colchester Moot Hall in 1482 the plaintiff made his plaint at 7 a.m., the defendant was summoned by a serjeant-at-mace to attend the next court at 8 a.m., the same day; the serjeant returned *nihil*, and a precept was made to arrest the defendant and bring him before the next court at 9 a.m.; the defendant appeared at 9 a.m., and the plaintiff declared;

---

[183] 1 Ric. III, c. 6; *Tawndye* v. *Abbot of Winchcombe* (1493) Trin. 8 Hen. VII, fo. 4, pl. 1, *per* Vavasour J; Pas. 12 Hen. VII, fo. 16, pl. 1, *per* Yaxley sjt; ibid., fo. 17, *per* Fyneux CJ; Pas. 13 Hen. VII, fo. 19, pl. 2, *per* Vavasour J.; *Marmyon* v. *Baldwyn* (1527) 120 Selden Soc. 61 at 63, *per* Shelley J; *Anon.* (1527/28) Brooke *Abr.*, *Incidents*, pl. 34. Some writers use the word 'piepowders', but the Latin of the plea rolls was *curia pedis pulverizati* in the singular.   [184] Pas. 13 Edw. IV, fo. 8, pl. 2.

[185] *Anon.* (1527) Brooke *Abr.*, *Incidents*, pl. 34.

[186] *Whittell* v. *Besaunce* (1508) 2 Caryll 579; KB 27/988, m. 34 (piepowder court for the market of Banbury, Oxon., which was held weekly; no judgment entered); and cf. Pas. 12 Edw. IV, fo. 9, pl. 22, *per* Jenney sjt. The statute of 1483, however, refers only to fairs.

[187] The caption of the Hereford piepowder court stated that it was held '(tr.) by reason of the market had in the same city every day': *Webbe* v. *Croft* (1520) KB 27/1037, m. 76, *Bodman* v. *Carwardyn* (1555) KB 27/1174, m. 86; *Thomas* v. *Lorymare* (1556) KB 27/1178, m. 63. Cf. *Webster* v. *Halle* (1537) KB 27/1105, m. 29 (merely *ratione mercati*).

[188] e.g. the fair court of the duchess of York at Grantham: see the records of 1493–4 printed in 23 Selden Soc. 129.

[189] For piepowder courts belonging to priors, see 23 Selden Soc. 127 (Norwich, 1472); KB 27/917 m. 30 (St Bartholomew's, Smithfield, 1490); KB 27/1075 m. 22 (Royston, 1530).

[190] e.g. John Spelman's reading in Gray's Inn (1519) GI MS. 25, at ff. 284, 285v–286.

the defendant imparled until the next court at 3 p.m., when he pleaded, and the plaintiff demurred.[191] Steps which might have consumed a year or more in Westminster Hall were thus compressed into a single day. Even more remarkably, when issues of fact were triable by jury, a jury could be produced overnight.[192] This was no doubt the principal attraction of these tribunals, whose jurisdiction, though supposedly confined to personal actions upon matters arising within the market or fair,[193] was without financial limits.[194] However, proceedings were not as informal or as divergent from the common law as is sometimes claimed. Although it has been asserted that 'the procedure of the court of piepowder resembles the procedure of the international law merchant as it was administered in all European tribunals',[195] this was certainly not the case in our period. Speed apart, the courts used common-law forms of action—such as actions on the case[196]—with mesne process similar to that of borough courts; they used formal common-law pleadings which might, as in the Colchester case, result in a demurrer,[197] or even a demurrer to the evidence;[198] and they could, at any rate in some places, try cases by jury.[199] The record, when made the subject of proceedings in error, was drawn up with all the formalities of the common law. This was no doubt because parties might be represented by Common Pleas attorneys,[200] and it seems probable that legally trained stewards sometimes presided or assisted.

---

[191] Whitefoot v. Page (1489) KB 27/906, m. 39. The question of law (not decided on the writ of error) was whether account lay for the profits of a ship between co-owners.

[192] e.g. Webbe v. Croft (1520) KB 27/1037, m. 6 (issue joined in court held in Hereford at 9 a.m.; venire facias for 3 p.m.; habeas corpora for 9 a.m. the next day, when the trial took place). Cf. Straunge v. Walpole (1500) KB 27/957, m. 26 (issue joined at 9 a.m., jury appeared at 11 a.m.; but here the case had been adjourned for a week before the pleading to issue).

[193] Hall v. Wykes (1502) C 1/249/7 (complains of action in the Winchester piepowder court on a bond made at Salisbury); Webbe v. Croft (1520) KB 27/1037, m. 6 (assigned as error that action brought for negligence unconnected with market). Cf. Whitefoot v. Page (1487) KB 27/905, m. 64 (Colchester; account for moiety of profit of a ship); Straunge v. Walpole (1500) KB 27/957, m. 26 (bishop of Norwich's piepowder court at Bishop's Lynn; debt on lease of a manor in 'Southwotton'). For matters arising from a previous fair, see below, 314.

[194] A debt of £300 was claimed in the Southampton piepowder court in Isbury v. Portynary (1485) C244/136/120. In Webbe v. Croft (1520), above, £129. 6s. 0d. was recovered for negligence.

[195] C. Gross, 'The Court of Piepowder' (1906) 20 Qly Jnl Economics 231–49, at 237.

[196] e.g. Webbe v. Croft (1520), above (Hereford; assumpsit for negligence); Myddelton v. Foxley (1523) CP 40/1038, m. 452 (Leicester; assumpsit to exchange a horse); Ex parte Parker (1535) C 244/174/33 (Exeter; unspecified); Tolson v. Wylkyns (1552) KB 27/1161, m. 141 (Gloucester; negligence by a bailee); Pynder v. Hall (1556) KB 27/1178, m. 183; Dyer 133a (Sturbridge Fair, Cambridge; assumpsit to return goods bailed).

[197] Another example is Walter v. Veale (1558) KB 27/1187, m. 25 (Hereford; demurrer in replevin).

[198] Pender v. Beche (1506) KB 27/981, m. 63 (Canterbury).

[199] See above, n. 192; Webster v. Halle (1537) KB 27/1105, m. 29 (Hereford).

[200] e.g. Straunge v. Walpole (1500) KB 27/957, m. 26 (John Prent in Bishop's Lynn); Bonyfaunte v. Hackewill (1516) KB 27/1020, m. 26 (Richard Duke in Exeter).

Moreover, these were courts of record from which error lay to the King's Bench,[201] and the latter did not hesitate to reverse judgments on technical grounds.[202]

Considerable restrictions had been placed on courts of piepowder by legislation of 1477, perpetuated in the first year of Richard III.[203] Stewards had been entertaining actions in respect of matters outside their jurisdiction, and so an affidavit was required that the contract, trespass, or deed, was made or done in the time of the fair and within its bounds. The courts were not only restricted to matters arising within the ambit of the fair, but had no jurisdiction over contracts made in a previous fair.[204] On the other hand, successful plaintiffs could make use of the common law to enforce judgments in piepowder courts beyond the purview of the fair.[205]

MANORS

Although we find honorial courts still functioning[206]—usually in the king's name[207]—and some great lords had the privilege of holding court for all their tenants in one place,[208] most seignorial jurisdiction was exercised in the courts of individual manors. Manorial courts in theory comprised a court baron for freehold tenants, a court customary (or hallmote) for copyhold tenants, and sometimes a view of frankpledge or leet.[209] The minimum legal requirements for a manor were a prescriptive court baron and at least two suitors to attend it.[210]

---

[201] Mich. 6 Edw. IV, fo. 3, pl. 9, *per* Littleton J.; Hil. 7 Edw. IV, fo. 23, pl. 27, *per eundem*. This is borne out by the plea rolls.

[202] e.g. *Pender* v. *Beche* (1506) KB 27/981 m. 63 (Canterbury); *Taylor* v. *Ap Hye* (1523) KB 27/1047 m. 74 (Hereford); *Prudman* v. *Chamberleyn* (1530) KB 27/1075 m. 22 (Royston); *Spencer* v. *Parys* (1531) KB 27/1081, m. 73 (Winchester).

[203] 1 Ric. III, c. 6, perpetuating 17 Edw. IV, c. 2. See also Spelman 139.

[204] *Hall* v. *Pyndar* (1555) KB 27/1178, m. 183; Dyer 133a (Sturbridge Fair, Cambridge; counts on bailment at previous fair; judgment reversed).

[205] e.g. *Key* v. *Warner* (1517) CP 40/1017, m. 532 (debt on recovery in Rochester piepowder court); *Myddelton* v. *Foxley* (1523) CP 40/1038, m. 452 (debt on recovery in Leicester piepowder court). If the record was removed into the King's Bench, a *scire facias* could be used: e.g. *Rowlond* v. *Asshe* (1486–7) KB 27/899, m. 36; KB 27/905, m. 53.

[206] e.g. *Bocher* v. *Hamper* (1528) CP 40/1059, m. 552 (duke of Northumberland's court of the honour of Petworth); *Sherman* v. *Grey* (1540) CP 40/1105, m. 440 (Eye, Suffolk).

[207] e.g. *Harper* v. *Tankerd* (1536) CP 40/1088, m. 456 (Knaresborough, Yorks.); *Bykener* v. *Browne* (1537) CP 40/1093, m. 619 (Pleshey, Essex); *Randall* v. *Dere* (1557) KB 27/1181, m. 25 (writ of error to the constable of the honour and castle of Windsor). Knaresborough and Pleshey were both parcel of the duchy of Lancaster.

[208] e.g. the Rochester Palace Court: *Bishop of Rochester* v. *Stevynson* (1528) CP 40/1059, m. 703 (rescue; counts on right by patent to hold all manorial courts before his steward in his palace, with cognizance of all pleas, and a court of piepowder).

[209] This was in theory a hundredal jurisdiction in private hands: above, 301.

[210] Two were sufficient: *Browne* v. *Lyon* (temp. Hen. VIII) Brooke Abr., *Court baron*, pl. 17; *Anon.* (1531) ibid., pl. 22.

This meant that no new manor could be created. And a manor would be extinguished for ever if all the free tenancies except one escheated or were surrendered, for although new tenancies could still be created by means of gifts in tail, the court had to be continuous since time immemorial.[211] Whatever the theory, a manorial court was in practice controlled by the steward (*senescallus*)—or, where the stewardship was honorific, an under-steward—appointed by the lord. Stewards were usually legally trained, though there was a lower class of persons performing similar functions known as courtholders. The steward controlled proceedings by summoning the suitors,[212] swearing in the homage and delivering a charge,[213] and by keeping the rolls; and there exist a number of written guides for those performing these functions.[214] It was judicially stated in 1505 that the steward in such a court was merely a recorder of the pleas and not a judge.[215] Nevertheless, it seems that stewards acted in a manner which appeared to be judicial; and defamation actions by stewards reveal both that they were perceived as having considerable power to do wrong, and that they were themselves anxious to preserve their reputation for impartiality.[216] In one case of 1555, a steward was accused of having angrily refused to charge the homage to enquire into an alleged withdrawal of mill-suit, as requested by the bailiff, and of threatening to charge them to enquire into extortion, presumably hinting at misconduct by the bailiff. The plaintiff claimed that his reputation as a manorial steward to various lords was thereby injured.[217]

[211] *Anon.* (1541) Brooke Abr., *Comprise*, pl. 31; *Mannor*, pl. 5.

[212] Notice might be very short. A pleading of 1557 revealed that the steward of a court baron warned the suitors on 21 May to attend a court on 23 May: *Harryson* v. *Smyth* (1557–60) KB 27/1181, m. 90.

[213] See *Cooke* v. *Horne* (1556) CP 40/1168, m. 950d (custom for every customary tenant to owe suit and to be elected to the homage, and to make presentments upon the steward's articles of charge; defendant charged upon oath but refused to make a verdict, and was therefore removed from his tenancy). The plea alleges that the charge was: (i) whether all tenants owing suit were present, (ii) whether any tenants had died since the last court, (iii) whether any alienations or surrenders had occurred, 'and likewise the other common articles'. Note also *Felde* v. *Cade* (1531) CP 40/1071, m. 628 (case for slandering plaintiff as a villein; justifies by presentment of homage, which had been charged by the steward to produce a list of villeins).

[214] They were known as *Curia Baronis* or *Modus tenendi Curiam Baronis*: see CELMC, 161, 619. Two texts have precedents dated 1482. CUL MS. Ee.1.3, ff. 13–20, John Rylands Library, Manchester, MS. Eng. 288, ff. 1–24. The printed version of *Modus tenendi Curiam Baronis* was first printed *c*.1501. Note also *Modus observandi Curiam cum Leta* (c. 1525), versions of which also circulated in manuscript: see Derbs. Rec. Office MS. D2440; and Oslo/London, the Schøyen Collection, MS. 1641 (see 13 *JLH* 180, no. 337).

[215] *Ewnet* v. *Arderne* (1505) 2 Caryll 473. See also *Capell* v. *Church* (1485) Benl. 4 (royal manor court held before suitors, but process goes to bailiffs).

[216] e.g. *Songer* v. *Wever* (1553) KB 27/1167, m. 99 (steward of courts accused of polling and pilling). In *James* v. *Feld* (1549) CP 40/1140, m. 429, an attorney accused of deceit alleged it had cost him an annuity of 5 marks as steward of the earl of Warwick's manors in Shropshire.

[217] *Humfrey* v. *Lane* (1555) KB 27/1176, m. 122 (details from plea; the plaintiff alleged the words were (sp. mod.) 'You sit here as steward, but you will not hear indifferently; but rather you keep this court

The court baron had jurisdiction in pleas of land by little writ of right addressed to the lord, and a jurisdiction in personal actions. The latter was limited at common law to suits for less than 40s., and to suits in which wager of law was available— excluding, therefore, debt on a bond, debt for rent, and detinue for charters.[218] These limitations could be varied or dispensed with by custom or royal grant. Thus, we find a plaintiff recovering £40 damages in an action on the case for slander, by verdict of a jury, in a specially privileged manorial court in 1527.[219] Although procedure was in theory governed by manorial custom, it had been so far assimilated to the common law that in 1534 it was alleged—apparently with success—that a judgment in a manorial court was invalid if it did not appear what common-law form of action had been pursued in the plaint.[220] Jury trial was, moreover, said to be generally available by consent of the parties, though not otherwise.[221] Other aspects of common-law procedure not normally belonging to manorial courts, if used in a particular court for long enough, could be legally justified by the custom of the manor in question.[222]

The principal business of courts customary was to record the transfer of copyhold land, for which a surrender and admittance recorded in court was essential.[223] If custom so permitted, both the surrender and the admittance could be made out of court, before the steward, provided it was recorded at the next court; but it was said that an under-steward could only act in open court.[224] In practice it was not usual for courts customary and courts baron to be distinguished in the captions of court rolls, and the business was handled confusedly; indeed, the decline of the distinction may be associated in some manors with the disappearance of villein status or with the gradual enfranchisement of copyhold land.[225] By 1557 even a professional pleader will see no incongruity in alleging that a court baron was summoned to effect a transfer of customary land.[226]

to poll my lady's tenants than to minister justice according to your duty'). Richard Humfrey was steward of the manor of Kettering, Northants.

[218] Richard Littleton's reading (Inner Temple, 1493) Port 119; Yorke 158, no. 182; *Diversite de Courtz* (1533), sig. A7v–A8.

[219] *Legat v. Bulle* (1527–33) KB 27/1073, m. 70 (pr. 94 Selden Soc. 250); reported in Spelman 6 (error from Queen Katharine's manorial court of Havering-atte-Bower, Essex).

[220] *Vaughan v. Vaughan* (1534) CP 40/1080, m. 455 (false judgment from Wilton, Heref.; error assigned because 'non habetur aliquid mentio in qua natura sive forma brevis domini regis ad communem legem predictus Henricus queritur querelam suam'). Judgment was reversed, but this was not the only error assigned.

[221] 33 Hen. VIII, Brooke Abr., *Trialles*, pl. 143. Cf. Yorke 158, no. 182 (trial solely by wager of law).

[222] e.g. *Trewynnard v. Kempe* (1556) CP 40/1166, m. 836 (false imprisonment; pleads custom of king's manor of Bliston in Blisland, Cornwall, to arrest strangers to answer complaints of trespass by inhabitants).

[223] For the decline of other kinds of business see Whittle, *The Development of Agrarian Capitalism*, 46–63.   [224] *Anon.* (1548) Brooke Abr., *Court Baron*, pl. 22.

[225] Newman, 'Local Court Administration within the Liberty of Allertonshire', 17.

[226] *Harryson v. Smyth* (1557–60) KB 27/1181, m. 90 (demurrer, probably on another ground). Counsel in London had advised on a surrender and admittance, and a court was held for the purpose,

Also liable to confusion in practice were the court baron and the court leet, at any rate in manors which had leets.[227] It has been pointed out that the confusion was encouraged by some of the printed treatises and formularies related to court-holding, which made no sharp distinction between the two kinds of business.[228] A leet jurisdiction gave a manorial court the authority to exercise considerable social control,[229] for instance by clamping down on disorderly houses, gaming, and drunkenness,[230] or even adultery,[231] and by means of bye-laws.[232] But courts baron or customary could also make bye-laws, or ordinances (*ordinationes*), if they had always done so, and prescriptive claims found in the plea rolls of the 1550s show that the power was exercisable by majority vote of the tenants, even in the case of customary tenants.[233] Most manorial ordinances were agrarian in character,[234] but they could also regulate social behaviour, including the behaviour of residents and visitors who were not tenants and therefore not part of the voting assembly: for example, at Great Horwood in the time of Henry VIII substantial fixed penalties were laid down for gaming and keeping loose women 'for more than one night'.[235] In some places there were courts or assemblies of the

though the admittance did not occur. Cf. *Hoxwood* v. *Creswell* (1555) CP 40/1164, m. 941 (prescription to hold court baron for all free and customary tenants).

[227] Dyer, *Lords and Peasants*, 265–9.

[228] M. Griffiths, 'Kirtlington Manor Court 1500–1650' (1980) 45 *Oxoniensia* 260 at 264, 267.

[229] See above, 304; and also C. Harrison, 'Manor Courts and the Governance of Tudor England', in *Communities and Courts in Britain, 1150–1900*, ed. C. Brooks and M. Lobban (1997), 43–59.

[230] See e.g. Griffiths, 'Kirtlington Manor Court', 276–81. An instance is given (ibid. 280) of a punishment awarded at Kirtlington in 1525 for playing with 'painted playing cards'. Cf. BL MS. Harley 2115, fo. 89 (court of lordship of Halton, Ches., 1535; presentment for keeping bowls), and fo. 102 (view of frankpledge at Widnes, Lancs., 1542; presentment for playing at cards).

[231] A presentment for adultery made in the prior of Sheen's view of frankpledge at Greenwich resulted in a defamation suit: *Awldwyn* v. *Aleyn* (1527) KB 27/1064, m. 35.

[232] See e.g. Griffiths, 'Kirtlington Manor Court', 272–5.

[233] e.g. *Frankeleyn* v. *Chapman* (1552) KB 27/1162, m. 84; *Cokeman* v. *Brese*, ibid., m. 86; *Monye* v. *Brese*, ibid., m. 87 (bye-laws made by a court baron at Folsham, Norfolk; three demurrers); *Stokes* v. *Kykby* (1555) CP 40/1162, m. 549 (ordinances concerning the grazing of horses in the fields, made by the homage, with the consent of the majority of freeholders, in a court baron with view of frankpledge at Abbots Ripton, Hunts.); *Hoxwood* v. *Creswell* (1555) CP 40/1164, m. 941 (bye-laws made by common consent of the tenants, apparently meaning the homage, in the court baron at Upton Snodbsury, Worcs.); *Gerye* v. *Knyght* (1556) CP 40/1167, m. 551 (custom for tenants in the court baron at Osbaston, Leics., to make bye-laws by a majority, and order made by homage with consent of all the tenants); *Coke* v. *Symondes* (1557) CP 40/1170, m. 1173 (bye-law made by consent of the customary tenants in the court baron of Whitwell, Norfolk); and next note.

[234] See W. O. Ault, *Open-Field Husbandry and the Village Community: a study of agrarian by-laws in medieval England* (1965), 80–86, for the text of 37 examples (drawn from seven manors) between 1483 and 1555. Cf. Dyer, *Lords and Peasants*, 329–32, 335, 368–9 (noting an increase in bye-laws in Worcestershire after 1470).

[235] Court rolls of Great Horwood, Bucks., cited by Ault, *Open-Field Husbandry*, 82–3, nos. 178 (tr. 'It is ordered by concession of the lord and tenants that no tenant or inhabitant within the lordship should play at cards or dice—*carpinas*—except at Christmas, on pain of 20s. for every default', 1515),

inhabitants, rather than of the manorial tenants, and in these the power to make ordinances, though similarly founded on prescription, had no dependence on manorial jurisdiction except for purposes of record.[236]

OTHER FRANCHISES

Two other peculiar franchises need specific mention. The Cinque Ports had such extensive jurisdictional privileges that they were placed by Sir Robert Brooke under the same heading as the palatinates.[237] They were not actually palatinates and did not possess *jura regalia*, but were nevertheless deemed to be ancient demesne with exclusive jurisdiction in real and personal actions.[238] Each of the constituent towns had a court before the mayor and jurats, and there was a principal court at Shepway before the lord warden or vice-warden of the Cinque Ports, who also had an admiralty jurisdiction.[239] Their exclusiveness was maintained by prayers of cognizance and pleas to the jurisdiction; but in the last years of Henry VII the judges decided in the Duchy Chamber that the privilege of being sued only in the Cinque Ports could not prevent the king as duke of Lancaster from holding a court leet in one of the ports.[240] It remained uncertain whether judgments were liable to review in the central courts by error or false judgment,[241] though in 1540 it was held that *habeas corpus* would lie to the lord warden.[242]

The stannaries of Devon and Cornwall each had their own courts, held before the steward or chief steward, with jurisdiction in personal actions and matters relating to tin-mining in accordance with the laws and customs of the stannaries.[243] Their jurisdiction was not merely geographical, for it was limited to suits by or against tinners (*stannatores*), defined in 1524 as those who owned an interest in

---

183 (tr. 'It is ordered that no labourer, workman, or servant, should play at tables or cards on pain of 12*d*. . . .', 1521), 189 (tr. 'It is ordered that no one should harbour or comfort any woman or women of ill fame for more than one night, on pain of 6*s*. 8*d*. for each offence', 1534).

236 Ault, *Open-Field Husbandry*, 54 (referring to the first half of the sixteenth century).

237 Brooke Abr., *Cinke Ports et Countie Palantine*.

238 For pleas to the jurisdiction see *Hylles* v. *Worme* (1519) KB 27/1033, m. 56 (issue whether in Kent); *Grey* v. *Kyrkelond* (1528) KB 27/1069, m. 80 (sim.); *Eston* v. *Fletcher* (1532) Spelman 124; KB 27/1082, m. 68 (demurrer; pr. 94 Selden Soc. 326); *Couper* v. *Cumber* (1535) CP 40/1086, m. 647. Also in criminal cases: *R.* v. *Chauncy* (1506) KB 27/978, Rex m. 5d (riot; issue whether place in Pevensey). Cf. *Anon.* (1556) Benl. 47, pl. 82 (writ to constable of Dover).

239 As to the last see R. G. Marsden, 11 Selden Soc., pp. xxi–xxiv; 27 Hen. VIII, c. 4; 28 Hen. VIII, c. 15 (criminal jurisdiction).

240 *Cinque Ports* v. *Duchy of Lancaster* (1507–9) 2 Caryll 546, 549–51 (Pevensey). It was also confirmed that the Cinque Ports were ancient demesne.

241 *Anon.* (1571) Dyer 376a. Cf. Brooke Abr., *Cinke Ports*, pl. 25, which says that error did lie.

242 *Anon.* (1540) Spelman 186, pl. 5.

243 See *Bevyll* v. *Michell* (1512) CP 40/1001, m. 633 (stannary court of Blakemore; action of debt on a bond for delivery of tin; heard before Sir Henry Marney as chief steward); *Re Turnour* (1512)

tin-works or were employed in making things needed for working tin.[244] From the stewards' courts an appeal lay to the warden or vice-warden of the stannaries, and in Cornish cases from thence—in theory—to the prince of Wales's duchy council. Judgments were not liable to review by writs of error or false judgment, but were within the purview of the Star Chamber and Chancery.[245] When in 1508 the king pardoned a number of Cornish tinners for offences against some restrictive ordinances made in the name of the late Prince Arthur as duke of Cornwall, the patent provided that 'no statutes, acts, ordinances, provisions, restraints, or proclamations, shall hereafter be made within the aforesaid county of Cornwall to the prejudice of the same tinners' unless a convocation of tinners—later known as the Stannary Parliament—gave its prior consent.[246] This has been mistakenly supposed to have conferred a measure of legislative autonomy on the stannaries, or even a veto on parliamentary legislation.[247] But that could hardly have been imagined. The patent refers only to statutes 'made within the aforesaid county': in other words, to local regulations made for the stannaries by the king, or the duchy council, similar to those with which the pardon was concerned.

KB 29/144, m. 16 (trespass suit in same court mentioned in return to *habeas corpus*). In the 1530s a lawyer from Westminster might be retained for 40s. to appear in a case in a Cornish stannary court: C1/812/48 (George Haydon, an attorney, retained as counsel in the court at Stoke Climsland).

[244] G. R. Lewis, *The Stannaries: a study of the English tin miner* (1908), ch. 4, at 98; R. L. Pennington, *Stannary Law* (1973), 35–6. The statute 23 Hen. VIII, c. 8, uses the expression 'king's court of stannary'.

[245] Lewis, *The Stannaries*, 99–100; Pennington, *Stannary Law*, 30, 199; *Trewynarde* v. *Killegrew* (1562–5) Co. Inst. iv. 229–30.

[246] Patent roll, C66/605, mm. 29–31 (tr.); BL MS. Add. 6713, ff. 168–180.

[247] See e.g. Lewis, *The Stannaries*, 126; Pennington, *Stannary Law*, 20–1. The argument was advanced without success by the defendant in *Sec. State for Trade and Industry* v. *Trull* (Chancery Division, 1992), unreported.

Part IV

CIVIL PROCEDURE AND PLEADING

17

Commencing an Action[1]

NEARLY all actions in the Common Pleas, other than those brought against attorneys and officers, had to be commenced by original writ issued from the Chancery. Likewise, every such action in the King's Bench had to begin by original writ unless the cause of action arose in Middlesex or the defendant was a prisoner in the custody of the marshal. Since the original writs governed the whole course of proceedings at law, and varied according to the form of action, they had come to be regarded not only as 'the foundation of every suit'[2] but as the foundations of the law itself, on which the whole law depended.[3] A law student began his studies by learning the writs, and the first book placed in his hands in the inns of chancery was the *Natura Brevium*,[4] a version of which was printed in the 1490s 'at the instance of my masters of the company of Strand Inn'.[5] After 1534 students and practitioners alike could use the more detailed, and more up to date, guide by Sir Anthony Fitzherbert called the *New Natura Brevium*.[6] The formulae were not peculiar to the two benches, but were copied in the Exchequer and in many local courts.

The writs exerted their dominion not only over procedure but over the common-law mind. If there was no writ, there was no remedy. And the forms had been frozen in an earlier period. The cursitors of the Chancery who issued the writs had long been constrained to adhere to the old forms in the Register, and their bureaucratic discipline was reinforced by the refusal of the common-law courts to admit variations from tradition.[7] A writ which departed from the proper form was

---

[1] This section is largely confined to the common-law procedure of the two benches, the principal features of which were reproduced in many lesser courts of law. Accounts of Chancery procedure will be found in the preceding and succeeding volumes.

[2] *Diversite de Courtz* (1530 edn), sig. B8v (tr. 'Note that the writs are the principal and first things in our law... and the foundation of every suit'). Cf. *Articuli ad Narrationes Novas* (1533 edn), sig. A2v (tr. 'the writ, which is the foundation and original of all actions').　　　　　　　[3] FNB, pref. (1534).

[4] Simpson in 87 *LQR* at 103–4, 110. Cf. the preface of 'William Rastell to the gentyllmen studentes of the law' in *Natura Brevium* (1534 edn).

[5] Colophon in Pynson's edition: J. H. Beale, *A Bibliography of Early English Law Books* (1926), 119, no. T69 (sp. mod.).

[6] *La Novel Natura Brevium* (1534). The first edition is anonymous, but Fitzherbert's name appears in the preface to the 1537 edition and he was acknowledged as the author thereafter: Dyer 45a (1538); Gell's reports, I, 33 Hen. VIII, fo. 4v (1541); *Penyngton v. Hunte* (1544) Cholmeley 454 at 458.

[7] There was a problem if different registers, or Fitzherbert, disagreed: *Penyngton v. Hunte* (1544) Cholmeley 454 (*fuerunt* for *fuerint* in writ of assize); *Bishop of Carlisle v. Smith* (1556) Dyer 129a.

considered to be void and unamendable: for instance, if a trespass writ omitted the words 'vi et armis' or a writ of debt said 'praecipe quod solvat' instead of 'reddat'.[8] 'Notwithstanding that the writ passed the Chancery,' taught Spelman, 'if the writ is not good this court will abate it; for the course of the Register... is as a law positive, which no one may vary'.[9] The older writs contained phrases which were not even regarded as meaning anything at all; for instance, the 'praecipe quod reddat' formula was no longer regarded as giving the defendant or tenant an option to do right out of court instead of appearing.[10] And sometimes inappropriate language was ruled preferable to innovative modification, despite the statutory power to formulate writs *in consimili casu*. Thus, the writ for forging false deeds had to say 'deeds' even if only one deed was in dispute, and the writ for waste against a termor had to say 'who holds for a term of years' even if the term was for less than a year.[11] The wording was hallowed by usage, and to have permitted alteration would have thrown the study of the law into confusion.

It would nevertheless be very misleading to suppose that the forms of action were as rigid and static as these examples suggest. Nearly all the cases of abatement for want of form arose from technical mistakes and not from attempts to frame new remedies.[12] The invention of new writs had some statutory authority, under the terms of the *In consimili casu* clause of Westminster II, c. 24, and—whether or not this statute was taken to be the warrant for actions on the case[13]—it seems to have been possible throughout the period to obtain a writ on the case in almost any conceivable form. No objection seems ever to have been taken to a new action on grounds of form rather than substance; most of the cases on form are concerned with the long-established writs in the Register, which had reached its final stage of development by the mid-fifteenth century and was frozen in print in 1531.[14] The vulgate Register included a small selection of prototypical actions on the case, but the development of such actions in the Tudor period was completely unconstrained by any register. Only one formulary of special cases has so far been discovered, a collection of over two hundred recent but undated writs on the case made by Rowland Shakelady, a Chancery clerk in the second half of Henry VIII's reign; but there is no evidence that it was in general circulation as a supplemental register.[15] Since the possibility of experimentation through actions on the case is

---

8 *Hatley's Case* (1482) Mich. 22 Edw. IV, fo. 21, pl. 1; below, 325 n. 22.

9 John Spelman's reading in Gray's Inn (1514) Bodl. Lib. MS. Rawlinson C.705, fo. 95v. Cf. *Wimbish v. Lord Willoughby* (1552) Plowd. 73 at 77 (tr. 'the Register is the foundation of the law in these points').

10 Inner Temple moot (*c.*1485) Keil. 116v, pl. 57.   11 Examples from Port 142, pl. 3.

12 Fitzherbert himself once lost a writ for want of proper form: *Fitzherbert v. Welles* (1532) Spelman 15.

13 94 Selden Soc. *86*; below, 840.

14 The first printed edition, *Registrum Omnium Brevium* (1531), corresponds with mid-fifteenth century manuscript texts, though the king's name in the first writ was altered to Henry VIII. See below, 503.

15 BL MS. Harley 1856. Shakelady, admitted to Lincoln's Inn in 1527, was evidently a cursitor; his signature appears on original writs in CP 52.

the key to so many of the legal changes in the Tudor period, to regard the 'forms of action' as somehow inhibiting development of the common law would therefore be a distortion. The principal vehicle of change was virtually formless, and provided the law with a temporary escape from the formulary system.[16]

THE FORMULATION OF WRITS AND BILLS

This brings us to a basic question of some importance. Who was responsible for drawing new writs of trespass on the case? Were they devised in Chancery by the cursitors and masters, or were they drawn by the attorneys or counsel of the plaintiffs? The practice with respect to writs of settled form, such as debt and trespass, seems to have been as follows. The plaintiff's attorney made out a note of instruction called a 'titling',[17] and took this to the cursitor to inform him in making out the writ.[18] He would also show the cursitor the bond or other document on which the action was founded.[19] The cursitor, or his under-clerk, then put the matter into the proper legal form, engrossing the writ in Chancery hand on a strip of parchment which was signed with the cursitor's name at the bottom right-hand corner, and making a note in his 'book of titlings'.[20] The practice is reflected in the rule that the clerk was held responsible for mistakes in form and wording, whereas the client was responsible for mistakes in the factual content of the instructions. If the clerk was negligent in not following his factual instructions, he was summoned to the court where the writ had been returned and examined on oath; if the error was found to be his, he amended the writ sitting in court.[21] But this procedure was not allowed where the party was responsible for giving incorrect instructions, or where the clerk through ignorance failed to follow the correct form[22]—unless the errors were immaterial grammatical or orthographical slips,

---

[16] A new formulary system emerged as lawyers began to group actions on the case under headings such as *assumpsit*, *trover*, and so forth; but the systematization happened after our period.

[17] This term was apparently used for any note of instruction for an officer, e.g. the 'titling' of a warrant of attorney given to the clerk of the warrants: *Memorandum* (1512) CP 40 / 1001, m. 618d.

[18] Mich. 38 Hen. VI, fo. 4, pl. 10; *Anon.* (1535) Spelman 15, pl. 6. The same practice is stated in the Elizabethan practice books.   [19] Hil. 14 Hen. VII, fo. 13, pl. 1 (deed granting annuity).

[20] The books have not survived, but see *Memorandum* (1507) CP 40/980, m. 403d (sp. mod. 'which original one Richard Colyngbourne made . . . and the said [*client*] desired the said Colyngbourne that he should not put it in his book of titlings for because he would not have it seen'). Colyngbourne was a Chancery clerk.

[21] 8 Hen. VI, c. 12; Trin. 11 Edw. IV, fo. 2, pl. 3; Trin. 20 Edw. IV, fo. 7, pl. 9; *Anon.* (1499) Hil. 14 Hen. VII, fo. 13, pl. 1; *Anon.* (c.1516) Chaloner 279, no. 4; *Anon.* (1524) Spelman 14, pl. 1.

[22] *Hatley's Case* (1482) Mich. 22 Edw. IV, fo. 21, pl. 1; *Anon.* (1494) Hil. 9 Hen. VII, fo. 16, pl. 8, and fo. 19, pl. 13; Gray's Inn moot (1514) Bodl. Lib. MS. Rawlinson C.720, fo. 97, *per* Goring. See also the reporter's note to *Spynell v. Taillour* (1485) Mich. 2 Ric. III, fo. 12, pl. 30; 64 Selden Soc. 96; KB 27/895, m. 56.

in which case they were amendable.[23] Nor would the court permit the amendment of a substantial error of form, because that would be tantamount to making a new writ.[24] Such errors were nevertheless not fatal, because the plaintiff could sue out a better writ and start again.

This distinction between form and substance would have made sense in a situation where a clerk was writing out a standard form to a client's instructions. But when, as with actions on the case, the formal content of the writ was minimal, it would have been unworkable. Since the writ was in virtually the same form as the declaration, it seems more likely than not that the lawyer took a draft declaration to the cursitor as his instruction. There is no direct evidence for this, but it seems the best explanation for the diversity of forms; so far from there being any standardization, the 'special cases' in writs are virtually unclassifiable. Spelman reports a case in which he was consulted, as a serjeant, as to the validity of a writ of trespass; but he did not draw it himself, because he was able to find a precedent in the Register; and in any case it is not stated whether he was consulted before or after the writ was issued.[25] He also reports a case where a writ of slander was amended because of the clerk's mistaken verb-endings,[26] though this is not in itself inconsistent with the possibility that the writ had been drafted by counsel and that the clerk had made the error in transposing the matter into the form of a writ. Dyer provides some stronger evidence. He mentions in 1555 a defect in the date of an original writ attributable to the negligence of the attorney, and in 1573 refers to a writ being drawn by counsel.[27] It is therefore clear that by the 1570s, at the very latest, Chancery clerks were willing to issue writs drawn in their entirety by private practitioners; and it is likely that this was the position in our period as well.

Another argument in favour of this having occurred earlier may be drawn from King's Bench bills. Although they are in court-hand and unsigned, it is fairly clear that—like bills in Chancery—these were drawn by counsel. The bill was in the nature of a petition, and was therefore not a document emanating from a court official—unless, of course, a clerk of the court was asked to draw it up on behalf

---

[23] *Anon.* (1487) Hil. 2 Hen. VII, fo. 11, pl. 11, *per* Huse CJ; *Fitzherbert* v. *Welles* (1532) Spelman 15 (*idem* for *eidem*); *Wolley* v. *Leche* (1532) Spelman 111, 112 (*notificavit* for *notificaverunt*); *Dean and Chapter of Salisbury* v. *Martin* (1534) Spelman 118 (*revertere* for *reverti*); *Gell's reports*, 34 Hen. VIII, fo. 13 (*quas* for *que*); 36 Hen. VIII, fo. 23 (*fuerunt* for *fuerint*). Cf. *Anon.* (1494) Hil. 9 Hen. VII, fo. 16, pl. 8, *per* Vavasour J. (*hac breve* for *hoc breve* said to be unamendable).

[24] *Hatley's Case* (1482) Mich. 22 Edw. IV, fo. 21, pl. 1, *per* Catesby J.; *Anon.* (1483) Hil. 22 Edw. IV, fo. 48, pl. 14, *per* Jenney J.); *Anon.* (1494) 1 Caryll 229–30; *Colyns* v. *Arundell* (1519) KB 27/1030, m. 22 (*attachias per corpus* in trespass said to be '(tr.) against the form and course of the law of England'); *Wellys* v. *Wenne* (1532) Spelman 113. Cf. *Anon.* (1549) BL MS. Hargrave 4, fo. 102 (*procreatis* for *exeuntibus* in formedon: said to be amendable); *Vaughan* v. *Lord Burgh* (1550) ibid., fo. 114v; Moo. 5 (omission of *ostensurus* in trespass: amended). [25] *Hudson's Case* (1522) Spelman 32.

[26] *Wolley* v. *Leche* (1529–32) Spelman 111, 114 ('misprision de le clerke').

[27] *Molyneux* v. *Willock* (1573) 110 Selden Soc. 265.

of the party.[28] There was no register of bills, and no particular form was enjoined,[29] although the formal phrases used in common-law declarations were closely followed. The extant bills are of varying shapes and sizes, and in different hands, and are plainly the work of a multitude of practitioners. Only one surviving bill formulary has survived. It dates from the mid-fifteenth century and probably belonged to William Jenney (d. 1483), justice of the King's Bench. It is of interest as illustrating the variety of forms rather than official standardization.[30] However, an examination of actions on the case in the King's Bench rolls in the first half of the sixteenth century reveals no obvious differences in draftsmanship between writs and bills; experiments were constantly being made in both, and copied from one to the other. After 1548, bills were even filed in court under the heading 'Declarationes', which was an unhistorical but realistic description of their function.[31]

It seems unlikely, therefore, that the Chancery by this period exercised any real control over the development of actions on the case. The clerks there were not so unworldly as to deny themselves fees by refusing to oblige those who sought writs on the case instead of using bills, though the Common Pleas attorneys knew well enough that some novelties would not find favour with the judges there. The decision to proceed by bill rather than writ was probably not related to the novelty of the claim, except in so far as it affected the choice of forum, but rather to the procedural advantages of suing by bill.[32] Some plaintiffs even attempted to litigate without using writs or bills at all, or with a forged writ,[33] hoping they would not be caught out. The sheriff was not bound to ask for a sight of the original when executing process, and was therefore excusable.[34] But it was an abuse by the filazer or clerk to make out process without verifying his authority, and so the clerk in such a case was said to be liable to an action for damages[35] and any subsequent

---

[28] This seems to have been usual by the end of the sixteenth century, when the chief clerk charged by the sheet for drawing declarations: KB 15/41, fo. 43v.

[29] Hil. 19 Hen. VI, fo. 50, pl. 7, per Paston J. Thus it was said that bills lay for a wider range of trespasses vi et armis than were remediable by writ: Yorke 228, no. 378 (assault without battery).

[30] 'Modus formulandi billas in banco domini regis quando defendens est in custodia mariscalli', CUL MS. Add. 7912, ff. 294–302. The precedents are mostly from the 1440s to the 1460s, though a few date back to Hen. V. See C. A. F. Meekings, 'A King's Bench Bill Formulary' (1985) 6 JLH 86–104.

[31] KB 152. Meekings attributed the change of name to Richard Heywode, chief clerk from 1549.

[32] For these see above, 152–3.

[33] In Colbarne v. Smyth (1551) KB 27/1158, m. 147, an action was brought for slander in saying that the plaintiff had sued out a false writ which could not be found in the files, and the defendant pleaded a justification.

[34] Anon. (1492) Hil. 12 Hen. VII, fo. 14, pl. 1, per Rede sjt; More v. Halyngworth (1506) Pas. 21 Hen. VII, fo. 22, pl. 14, per More sjt; Courteney v. Chamond (1545) Dyer 60b–61a. See also Anon. (1546) Wm Yelv. 354 (rescue not permissible).

[35] Anon. (1488/9) BL MS. Harley 1691, fo. 67v; and cf. Anon. (1490) 1 Caryll 26 at 27; Anon. (1492/3) 1 Caryll 118; Whittell v. Besaunce (1508) 2 Caryll 579 at 580, per Brudenell CJ.

judgment was liable to reversal by writ of error.[36] However, when in 1505 a *capias* was issued in an action of trespass without any original being filed, the blame was laid on the plaintiff's attorney. It appeared upon enquiry by the court that the plaintiff's attorney had asked one of the clerks of the filazer for Worcestershire to make an entry in the rolls for Trinity term and to issue the *capias* as if an original had been filed that term, and the clerk had done so in reliance on this information. The attorney was an officer of the court and finable, but in fining the attorney rather than the filazer's clerk the court tacitly recognized that the mechanics for issuing mesne process had been substantially privatized.[37]

MESNE PROCESS

Having obtained his original writ from the Chancery,[38] the plaintiff was supposed to take the writ to the sheriff of the county in which the action was laid, together with his two pledges of prosecution, and, on the fourth day of the return,[39] the sheriff returned the writ to the court in which the action was commenced with the names of the pledges.[40] The court of return filed the original writ and then began to issue the appropriate judicial writs, under the seal of the court, to the same sheriff. So much is evident on the face of the files and rolls. But the common forms conceal what happened in reality. Although it was a material error if the sheriff failed to return the names of two pledges,[41] the names were in almost every case fictitious. Moreover, the party did not actually have to go to the county and seek out the sheriff, because all sheriffs were required to appoint attorneys of the court as deputies to receive writs on their behalf.[42] Every sheriff appointed another attorney as his under-sheriff, with the duty (amongst many others) of executing and returning writs.[43] Nor was there any need to trouble the judges sitting in Westminster Hall when obtaining or returning routine writs which

[36] *Halle* v. *Rolfe* (1505) KB 27/974, m. 35; *Standyshe* v. *Hennage* (1555) KB 27/1174, m. 161 (common recovery reversed on this ground), probably the case cited in Brooke Abr., *Judgement*, pl. 114.

[37] *Stokes* v. *Yardeley* (1505) CP 40/974, m. 112. John Middelmore, the attorney, was fined £5. One of his pledges was John Grosvenour, the filazer's clerk.

[38] The process was similar where the action was commenced by bill.

[39] *Anon.* (1529/30) Wm Yelv. 323, no. 23. This was the beginning of full term, the first four days being essoin-days: *Anon.* (1553) Dal. 10, pl. 8.

[40] Cf. *Anon.* (1527) Mich. 19 Hen. VIII, fo. 5, pl. 18; 121 Selden Soc. 435, no. 9 (dated 1534), where a sealed original writ was brought into court and delivered to the sheriff there; but this was evidently unusual.   [41] 94 Selden Soc. 89.

[42] Fitz. J.P. 27v–28. The statute 5 & 6 Edw. VI, c. 26, extending this requirement to Lancashire, recognizes that it was already the rule elsewhere. The deputy was not the same person as the under-sheriff, whose duty it was to return but not to receive writs.

[43] The full duties are set out in detail in C146/7236 (indenture of 29 Nov. 1511 between Sir Roger Lewkenor, sheriff of Sussex, and Thomas Polsted); PRO, Ancient Deed C7236 (sim.); *Dawtrey* v. *Bedon* (1529) CP 40/1062, m. 459 (bond to discharge office of under-sheriff of Sussex); *Nedeham* v. *Thornes*

purported to go to and from the court. A visit to Westminster was required when a writ needed a seal, since the seal could only be affixed while the court was sitting. All that happened otherwise was that pieces of parchment were moved from one office in the inns of court or chancery to another. So far as one can tell, a vast amount of parchment was handled in this way efficiently and scrupulously. In 1507 a judicial enquiry revealed that an attorney—who was also the under-sheriff—had tried to persuade a filazer, and the deputy custos brevium, to file a writ with the bundle of the previous term so that he could outlaw the defendant more quickly. Both officers refused. The attorney, who had subsequently misused his position as under-sheriff to expedite the return of the exigent, was fined £10 and removed from office.[44] In the 1550s an attorney of many years' standing thought to streamline the process by issuing his own judicial writs, in the name of the filazer, without purchasing an original. The filazer, on discovering several instances of this practice, made complaint to the court, and the attorney was expelled with much solemnity. The gravamen was not that he had harmed any of the litigants—his client had benefited from a saving of costs—but that he had deprived both the filazer and their majesties of their respective fees.[45]

A helpful glimpse of the routine procedure may be caught through an entry of a similar disciplinary enquiry in the Common Pleas rolls for Michaelmas term 1509. It had come to light that eleven judicial writs addressed to the sheriff of Lincolnshire in Trinity term had never been sealed, and the court conducted an investigation which was recorded by the chief prothonotary.[46] The writs had all been sued out by Thomas Palmer as attorney for the plaintiffs. Palmer gave evidence that he had sued the writs out of the office of Edward Warner, the filazer for Lincolnshire, and at 11 a.m. on the fourth day of the quindene—the last day of the return—he was walking towards Westminster from London to get the writs sealed when he met Warner in King Street. Warner asked the attorney where he was going, and he replied, 'To Westminster, to put in my writs', whereupon Warner replied, 'You have come too late because the court has adjourned for the day till tomorrow'. Palmer then explained that he had to go to Richmond to attend the King's Council in various matters, and he asked Warner—who was also the sheriff's deputy, and on better terms with the custos brevium than Warner was—if he

(1539) CP 40/1103, m. 523 (sim., Shropshire); *West* v. *Jakys* (1544) CP 40/1120, m. 321 (sim., Essex). It appears from the last case that a sheriff of two counties (e.g. Essex and Hertfordshire) might appoint a separate under-sheriff for each county; but such a sheriff usually only appointed one deputy to receive writs.

[44] *Memorandum* (1507) CP 40/980, m. 403d (presentment in English by a jury of attorneys and officers). The attorney was John Peycok, then under-sheriff of Berkshire. Perhaps this was the John Pecok who, as a scrivener, had been imprisoned in 1493 for forging a Common Pleas *supersedeas* and writ of privilege (tr.) 'to the grave obloquy of the good reputation of the court here': *Att.-Gen.* v. *Pecok* (1493) CP 40/926, m. 295d.

[45] *Re Selyard* (1558) CP 40/1176(1), m. 992d; below, 440. The writs mentioned dated back to 1553 and 1556.

[46] *Memorandum* (1509) CP 40/989, m. 505; 109 Selden Soc. 67 (noted by Dyer, 1561).

would receive and return the writs and deliver them in to the custos brevium for filing at the least possible cost. Warner had agreed to perform this favour and had taken the writs, but by negligence they were never sealed. Warner was then questioned. He confessed all that Palmer had said, adding that he had taken the writs back to his chamber in 'the New Temple'[47] and that later, forgetting that the writs were unsealed, he had given them in to the custos brevium together with the fee of 12*d*. for putting them in after the return-day. Warner took an oath that his conduct had been merely negligent and not deceitful. Both officers were committed to the Fleet, but the following day at the instance of sureties they were admitted to their fines. The record does not tell us what Palmer would have done if he had arrived at Westminster Hall in time, since everyone would have known that; but it does reveal some of the practice behind the routine 'optulit se quarto die' of the filazers' rolls. Evidently the expression was not literally true, because it was possible to conduct business after the fourth day on payment of a late-entry fee, though care had to be taken not to date the writ after the return.[48] It seems, moreover, that the filing of the writs by the court officers was done in their inns rather than at Westminster. This is borne out by a Star Chamber investigation of 1484, reported in the year books, when Thomas Danby—described as custos brevium, but actually the deputy—was accused of consenting to the erasure of filed writs in his chambers in Clifford's Inn.[49] The officers may also have made up their rolls in their offices in the inns.[50] Rather more remarkable is the revelation in 1509 that a judicial writ could quite properly be delivered to and returned by the same man who had issued it. It is therefore perhaps surprising that the seal was still kept at Westminster, and that it could only be used during court hours, especially since the keepers of the seals of the two benches exercised little or no control once they had received their fees.[51]

The entry of 1509 incidentally shows us that on the day in question—in the summer—the court had risen well before noon. According to Fortescue, the central courts did not sit in the afternoons.[52] And we should remember that they only sat on about ninety-nine working days in the year.[53] This left the judges and

[47] He was admitted to the Middle Temple on 5 Feb. 1509: *MTR*, i. 5.

[48] See *Marrow* v. *Drew* (1555) Dyer 129a.

[49] Mich. 2 Ric. III, fo. 10, pl. 22. This is not mentioned in the record: Crown Office entries, ff. 155v–157.

[50] See *Memorandum* (1512) CP 40/1001, m. 618d (titling of warrant of attorney given to a member of Lyon's Inn to take to the under-clerk of the clerk of the warrants 'at the Temple').

[51] *Att.-Gen.* v. *Pecok* (1493) CP 40/926, m. 295d (scrivener admits forging two Common Pleas writs, (tr.) 'but as to the sealing of the the writs and forging the seal . . . he says that he procured them to be sealed with the lord king's seal appointed for sealing writs before the king himself, then in the custody of James Starky, who was quite unaware of the aforesaid falsehood . . .'). The seals were merely touched on the wax.   [52] *De Laudibus*, ed. Chrimes, 128.

[53] Meekings, 'King's Bench Files', 111, reckoned the working days around 1558 to be: Michaelmas term 43, Hilary term 17, Easter term 22, and Trinity term 17. The days when the courts at Westminster

attorneys free the rest of the time for their other legal activities, and explains the importance of being able to continue the routine business of the courts after hours.

APPEARANCE, NON-APPEARANCE, AND DISCONTINUANCE

The principal sanction against a defendant who did not appear was imprisonment, either by writ of *capias ad respondendum* or—if he let things slip as far as outlawry—by *capias utlagatum*. From 1504, the same process was available in actions on the case as in trespass and debt, which meant that defendants were liable to arrest upon mesne process in the great majority of actions.[54] Sureties or bail might be given at the stage of the defendant's appearance, if he appeared in custody, so that he could be released from the Fleet or Marshalsea; such sureties were answerable for his further appearance and for payment of the debt if it was found to be due. Execution could be levied against the sureties if the principal judgment debtor defaulted.[55] It was therefore held in 1529 that they could maintain the principal's defence at their own charges for the sake of their indemnity.[56]

A high proportion of common-law entries, especially in the Common Pleas rolls, record the issue of writs of *capias* under the 'optulit se' formula. The majority of cases proceeded no further. In 1535, for instance, when an estimated 10,000 to 12,000 new suits were being commenced in the Common Pleas each year, only about 400 judgments were entered and fewer than 900 other cases were pleaded to issue without determination. In other words, around 90 per cent of the suits—perhaps 9,000 or 10,000 cases a year—were discontinued before issue was joined. Most of these ended before the defendant even appeared.

The number of writs which were ignored was even larger than this. The initial process could usually be ignored with impunity. The ancient process of essoining was confined to the real actions, and had long been taken over by fictional common essoiners.[57] In the commonest personal actions, there was no judgment in default of appearance and most judicial writs could safely be ignored, at any rate by those with means. Even if a defendant ignored them to the point of becoming

did not sit in term-time were Sundays, the Ascension, the Nativity of St John the Baptist, All Saints, and Candlemas: act of convocation (1536) pr. in E. Gibson, *Codex Iuris Ecclesiastici* (1713), i. 277. See also FNB 17 (no pleas on a Sunday). For a Saturday sitting see Plowd. 121v (1555).

[54] 19 Hen. VII, c. 9.

[55] e.g. *Rolfe v. Mantell* (1555) KB 27/1174, m. 61 (£302 recovered against surety for judgment debt).

[56] *Anon.* (1529) Port 61. The implication is that all sureties could maintain their principal's defence, the question here being whether sureties found after appearance could maintain an action already commenced.

[57] After 1506, Adam Doo (a cousin of John Doe) monopolized the business. Adam Pye, after working since the thirteenth century, retired in the time of Hen. VII, but returned in 1530 as the common

an outlaw, the outlawry could often be reversed on a technicality or, failing that, a pardon could be purchased for about 20s. to 30s.[58] Plaintiffs, on the other hand, were permitted no short-cuts. If they proceeded to outlaw the defendant after only two writs of *capias*, instead of the requisite three, as often happened, this was error.[59] Since fees were payable for each writ, the incentive to continue litigation was easily lost if the prospects of success were not good.

The sheriff presented another obstacle, even where there was no improper pressure upon him. Unable until 1542 to claim expenses[60]—as opposed to certain customary fees[61]—but liable both for excessive zeal and for negligence in allowing escapes of those they had arrested, sheriffs may sometimes have been tempted to avoid action. The sheriff executed process through his officers, principally the under-sheriff and the 'bailiffs errant' (*ballivi itinerantes*) appointed to execute process in particular hundreds.[62] Among the causes of delay at this stage were the many franchises of return of writs, where the sheriff could not use his own bailiffs but had to ask the officer of the franchise-owner to execute process; and a sheriff or bailiff who omitted this formality was liable to be sued for damages for infringing the franchise.[63]

A sheriff disposed to delay on his own account could not simply ignore the writ, because he could be fined for failing to return it. But he had at his disposal a gamut of fictitious returns which, according to contemporary commentators, were used to achieve delay or to avoid the expense and risk of carting bodies around. *Nihil* was the excuse for not distraining, *Non est inventus* for not arresting, and *Languidus detentus* for not bringing a body.[64] The return *Non est inventus* was

agent for opposing essoins: *Lists and Indexes Supplementary Series*, i. 77–8, 152–3. For the practice see *Waren* v. *Bele* (1516) 109 Selden Soc. 41; 120 Selden Soc. 2; *Anon.* (1529/30) Wm Yelv. 323, no. 23.

[58] Hastings, *Common Pleas*, 180, 253, calculated the cost as 23s. 3d. A late fifteenth-century note in LI MS. Hale 77, fo. 118v, gives the total charges as 32s. 2d. and details the tedious procedure involved. For an attempt to extort a good deal more under Henry VII, see Chrimes, *Henry VII*, 163 n. 1.

[59] 94 Selden Soc. 91 n. 1.

[60] 34 & 35 Hen. VIII, c. 16; 2 & 3 Edw. VI, c. 4. New fees, as opposed to expenses, could not be claimed until 1587 (29 Eliz. I, c. 4).

[61] There was a fee of 2s. for executing a *capias*: specimen charge for a tourn (1538) BL MS. Add. 48047, fo. 67; Fitz. J.P. 27. Fitzherbert said sheriffs also took 2s. for the return of a panel, but that this seemed to be extortion, since they should only have taken 4d. Cf. *Broun* v. *Carte* (1535) CP 40/1087, m. 159 (debt on 23 Hen. VI for taking unlawful fee of 5s. as bailiff of St Albans on arresting party in an action on the case).   [62] See above, 301.

[63] e.g. *Bishop of Exeter* v. *Bryt* (1510) KB 27/995, m. 18; *Bishop of Rochester* v. *Atterbery* (1512) KB 27/1004, m. 91; *Lord Dacre* v. *Venner* (1513) KB 27/1006, m. 11; *Prior of Dunstable* v. *Grigge* (1517) KB 27/1023, m. 62; *Queen Katherine* v. *Hartescong and others* (1523) CP 40/1041, mm. 540d, 620d, 681d; *Bishop of Lincoln* v. *Wymbusshe* (1523) ibid., m. 680; *Shrewsbury* (*bailiffs and burgesses*) v. *Vernon* (1526) CP 40/1051, m. 304.

[64] John Hales's reading in Gray's Inn (1514) Gray's Inn MS. 25, fo. 295; *Retourna Brevium* (*c.*1523), sig. a2–a3 (quoted at 94 Selden Soc. 91 n. 4).

very common indeed, and resulted in large numbers of writs of *alias capias* (a second writ to arrest the defendant), *pluries capias* (a third or subsequent writ), and *latitat* (a writ addressed to a different sheriff upon suggestion that the defendant was in another county). There was said to be no general procedure for challenging the veracity of the sheriff's return,[65] though in the unlikely event that the party could establish deceit it was possible to sue the sheriff in an action on the case for damages;[66] and if a sheriff returned *Languidus*, and the defendant then appeared in person, the sheriff would be amerced.[67] There are, nevertheless, precedents in both benches for a false return of *Languidus* to be challenged by informing the court that the party was in good health and the sheriff fraudulent; the sheriff would then be ordered to bring the body whether sick or well, 'because we will not have our subjects delayed in suing their actions or our court deceived'.[68]

The foremost reason for the discontinuance of suits, however, was neither the impudence of defendants nor the inertia of sheriffs but the straightforward fact that most lawsuits—in all ages—are settled or abandoned. The issue of a writ is as much an inducement to reach a compromise as it is a threat to pursue the law to its conclusion. Some suits, no doubt, were referred to arbitration,[69] though this is formally recorded as the outcome only in the Chancery and conciliar jurisdictions. The common-law records nevertheless contain many oblique references to arbitration, usually in actions of debt on bonds conditioned to abide by awards; but only very minute research would reveal how far these were preceded by actions at law.[70] The awards themselves usually refer merely to 'variances' between the parties, which does not necessarily imply a lawsuit. But a submission to arbitration could certainly occur at any stage in legal proceedings, and in a case of 1532 we even find an arbitration returned in a postea, where after the trial the parties had agreed—through the intercession of the jury-bailiff—to abide by the award

---

[65] *Note* (*c*.1530) Caryll (Jun.) 393, no. 55; *Anon.* (1531/2) Pollard 275, no. 69. A party could, however, confess and avoid a return: Yorke 190, no. 261.

[66] Caryll (Jun.) 393, no. 55, *per* Bradshaw; Hales's reading, n. 64 above. Most of the early Tudor precedents are inconclusive: *Corbet v. Marsham* (1512) KB 27/1005, m. 87d (*optulit se* against undersheriffs); *Lynde v. Corbett* (1538) CP 40/1096, m. 328 (*nihil dicit*); *Frigge v. Seyntlowe* (1538) CP 40/1098, m. 513 (imparlance); *Arnwey v. Seyntlowe* (1538) CP 40/1101, m. 614 (demurrer to *qui tam* action on the case); *Alleyn v. Basset* (1541) CP 40/1109, m. 615 (count only); *Fytz v. Jakes* (1541) CP 40/1111, m. 834 (case against under-sheriff of Middlesex; imparlance).   [67] *Staverton v. Logan* (1530) Port 71 at 72.

[68] Common Pleas entry in BL MS. Add. 37488, fo. 394v (tr.); *Wadham v. Legh* (1513) CP 40/1004, m. 152d. This was called a writ of *ducens tecum*.

[69] e.g. *Goddard's Case* (1539) Dyer 46a; *Dormer v. Clarke* (1555) Dyer 110a at 111a; *Bulkeley v. Thomas* (1555) Dyer 113b; *Anon.* (1558) Dyer 163a. For the use of arbitration in general see R. H. Britnell, *The Commercialisation of English Society 1000–1500* (1993), 214–15.

[70] An example is *Lord Beauchamp v. Croft* (1497–8) 1 Caryll 349; below, 797; BL Add. Ch. 73699 (arbitration bond, 7 May 1498). For two examples of arbitration pleaded since the last continuance, see *Prioress of Clerkenwell v. Bishop of London* (1513) CP 40/1004, m. 415 (demurrer); *Anon.* (1521) Spelman 17, pl. 2.

of four of the jurors.[71] A submission to arbitration effectively ousted the jurisdiction of the courts with respect to the substance of the dispute,[72] though there could still be litigation as to whether the arbitrators had made a valid award or whether the parties had performed it. Arbitrators were usually established lawyers, sometimes superior judges acting privately, and gave their decisions in writing.

It is reasonable to guess that the commonest single cause of discontinuance was a settlement between the parties themselves, or at least a resigned acceptance by the plaintiff that there was no point in continuing. Such an outcome is visible only in cases where the plaintiff was formally nonsuited.[73] A formal nonsuit could be entered on the plea rolls at any time before trial, or before judgment in the case of a demurrer,[74] or it could occur after a jury retired if the plaintiff decided after hearing the evidence not to risk the verdict; in the latter case, the plaintiff simply absented himself when the jury was called back, and a nonsuit was recorded.[75] A nonsuit of this kind could also be the outcome of a judicial ruling on the evidence.[76] Strictly speaking a nonsuit was not a discontinuance, and may have been less advantageous to the plaintiff than a simple abandonment.[77] Formal nonsuits nevertheless represented only a tiny proportion of the whole number of unconcluded actions. The prevalence of compromise is only apparent on the face of the record in local courts, where fines were payable 'for leave to accord' (*pro licencia concordandi*);[78] but the high proportion of such cases is an indication of what was probably happening in the central courts as well.

---

[71] *Yoman* v. *Thomas* (1532) CP 40/1075, m. 151d. One of the parties refused to accept the award, and so a verdict was taken. The court in banc took advisement, and no judgment was entered. Cf. *Browne* v. *Coke* (1531/2) C1/614/32 (unsuccessful attempt to settle at the assizes, followed by an arbitration).

[72] An award of 1521 (by Brudenell CJ and Conyngesby J.) contained a clause providing that any questions as to its terms were to be referred back to the arbitrators, whose determination was to be as effective as if contained in the award itself: JHB MS. 201 (sealed indenture of award).

[73] Cf. *Blomvyle* v. *Rawe* (1493) CP 40/924, m. 110 (defendant justifies battery in expelling the plaintiff who came intending to catch coneys; plaintiff's attorney, when called, says *Nihil dicit*, and judgment is entered for the defendant). This procedure is highly unusual.

[74] *Anon.* (1546) Brooke Abr., *Nonsuit*, pl. 67.   [75] 94 Selden Soc. *114*; below, 370.

[76] See *Holgyll* v. *Baynard* (1535) Mich. 27 Hen. VIII, fo. 29, pl. 19 (tr. 'Fitzherbert to Brown: now it appears . . . that this action brought in the way that you have is not maintainable'); CP 40/1086, m. 538 (formal nonsuit after evidence given).

[77] See *Moots*, 291, *per* Frowyk. It is unclear how a nonsuit could estop the plaintiff.

[78] Baker, 'Personal Actions in the High Court of Battle Abbey' (1992) repr. in *CLT*, 263 at 281–2; *Guildford Borough Records*, ed. Dance, p. xxxviii.

18

Pleading

THE evolution of pleading from an oral process conducted in open court to an exchange of papers has long been held responsible for profound changes in the common-law system.[1] Holdsworth thought the change occurred some time in the fifteenth and sixteenth centuries,[2] but the chronology has never been satisfactorily established. The difficulty arises from another kind of fiction in the records. The plea rolls always make the parties come into court and speak their pleadings, in words such as 'P complains that...' or 'D comes and says that...'. Such phrases may once have approximated to reality—even if they omit to mention the counsel who actually did the speaking—but the same language was retained even into the eighteenth and nineteenth centuries, when it is quite clear that no one came and said anything in court at the pleading stage, except in special cases such as common recoveries. In fact, we know that the oral discussion of pleadings at the bar had been forbidden by the middle of the seventeenth century at the very latest.[3] It is therefore clear that the change from oral to written pleadings occurred without leaving a mark on the face on the record.

ORAL AND PAPER PLEADING

Under the oral system, the pleadings were recited in law French by counsel, sometimes with an interval for imparlance, or a shorter period for consultation,[4] between the various stages of the pleading.[5] The pleadings were taken down in Latin translation by clerks—usually by the prothonotaries—on parchment membranes which were gathered in at the end of term and bound up to form the record.[6] Once this happened the rolls became sacrosanct, and it was felony to alter

---

[1] M. Hale, *History of the Common Law of England*, ed. C. M. Gray (1971), 111–12; J. Reeves, *History of English Law*, ii. 621–2; Holdsworth, *HEL*, iii. 640–56; Milsom, *HFCL*, 70–2.

[2] Holdsworth, *HEL*, iii. 641.   [3] 94 Selden Soc. 156.

[4] e.g. *Bishop of Norwich v. Skrene* (1482) Hil. 21 Edw. IV, fo. 75, pl. 7 (leave to consult client by next day); *Whitewood's Case* (1482) Trin. 22 Edw. IV, fo. 19, pl. 46 (leave to advise with client *sedente curia*).

[5] For the French forms, which obviously derive from those of an earlier period, see 94 Selden Soc. 92–4. The Latin entries on the plea rolls at this period only record imparlances between declaration and plea.   [6] See above, 138.

them except by way of addition. Entries were routinely extended with additions as process continued beyond issue, but the pleadings once entered of record could not be altered without the consent of both parties or an order of court. A party could 'relinquish the averment'—that is, retract a previous plea—in order to confess, a procedure which was not uncommon; and this was recorded as an addendum to the original entry. But it could not be done in order to plead a different plea, once term had ended.[7] Before the end of term, on the other hand, the record 'lay in the hearts of the justices'[8] and amendments were freely permissible;[9] there are occasional examples in the rolls of the parties repleading within the term.[10] Cancellations, erasures, or interlineations are commonly visible on the membranes, and no doubt many draft membranes were cancelled when more substantial revisions were made.[11] The clerks also sometimes left 'windows', or blank spaces for missing information such as names, but these were supposed to be filled in by the end of term.[12] Untimely alterations could be guarded against by a *recordatur*, which was an authenticated marginal note to the effect that certain words (marked with dots) were written without erasure or interlineation, or that certain necessary words had been omitted,[13] or that there was no continuance beyond a certain point.[14]

In the early Tudor period the French forms of pleading were still well known. The old oral forms were still used at moots in the inns of court, and it is probable that counsel continued to think about their pleas and to draft them in French rather than in the full-dress Latin of the record. Richard Morison, it will be recalled, had poured scorn on learned counsel who had to rely on clerks to turn their French drafts into Latin,[15] and some draft paper pleadings in French still

---

[7] *Anon.* (1492) 1 Caryll 81, 82. That was allowed only with the other side's consent: *Colepeper* v. *Lucas* (1535) Pas. 27 Hen. VIII, fo. 4, pl. 11; CP 40/1084, m. 511.

[8] Mich. 2 Ric. III, fo. 16, pl. 43, *per* Fairfax J.; *Warner* v. *Hudson* (1495) Hil. 10 Hen. VII, fo. 17, pl. 17, *per* Kebell sjt (misprinted as 'corps des justices').

[9] *Anon.* (1483) Trin. 1 Edw. V, fo. 3, pl. 5 (tr. 'And then, on another day, Brigges came and waived the demurrer and said...'); *Barret* v. *Lokington* (1484) Mich. 2 Ric. III, fo. 11, pl. 24; *Anon.* (1518) 2 Caryll 722. See also Dyer CJ's remarks in his charge of 1567: 94 Selden Soc. 95; 109 Selden Soc. 132 (different version).

[10] e.g. *Riche* v. *Sherewode* (1526) CP 40/1050, m. 609 (demurrer to bar; entry vacated), m. 619 (new entry with demurrer to replication).

[11] There is a stray draft King's Bench roll of the 1480s, from the chief clerk's office, in Bodl. Lib. MS. Talbot c. 104(6), containing three routine entries on the dorse, and on the recto a demurrer in *Norres* v. *Goldsmyth* (c.1486). The entry has been reused, apparently in drafting a similar entry between other parties. At the top the roll is marked: *Vacat iste rotulus*.

[12] Hil. 20 Hen. VI, fo. 18, pl. 9; Pas. 4 Edw. IV, fo. 14, pl. 23; *Anon.* (1489) Mich. 5 Hen. VII, fo. 1, pl. 2. Many windows still remain in the rolls.

[13] e.g. *R.* v. *Benson* (1527) CP 40/1056, m. 457 (demurrer; omission of word *inductus* recorded); Spelman 195 (judgment on that ground). In *Wynslowe* v. *Cleypole* (1489) CP 40/907, m. 327, there is a *recordatur* which goes so far as to state that the declaration is insufficient.

[14] Cf. Hastings, *Common Pleas*, 119–20, where the purpose seems to have been misunderstood.

[15] See above, 24–5.

survive from this period.[16] Whether the French oral forms were still used in open court in all actions is doubtful, though in Henry VIII's reign we hear complaints by litigants that their lawyers spoke at the bar in French when pleading,[17] and in 1552 it was alleged to be the law of the realm that all counts and pleas should be pleaded in French (*in lingua gallicana*) and enrolled in Latin.[18] There are other indications that French was still used for dilatory pleas.[19] However, the explicit mention of oral pleadings when new serjeants were created,[20] and when recoveries passed at the bar, suggests that they were becoming confined to ceremonial use. In 1596, Walmsley J. rebuked the serjeants drawing a recovery before him for not reciting the pleadings in their ancient form, and added that until Edward III all pleas were pleaded orally at the bar.[21] The implication of his remark, clearly, is that in most cases oral pleading had ceased long before his own time. But no light is thrown on the date of the general change by the survival of oral forms in special cases. Nor is much to be gained by putting a date on the introduction of draft written pleas, which had begun as far back as the thirteenth century.[22] The filing of papers is apparently alluded to in the Statute of Amendments 1429 as a regular practice,[23] and 'papers' are certainly mentioned in the year books of that time.[24] Yet it is clear that discussion in court of difficult or controverted pleas continued to be possible into the sixteenth century. The circulation of a written draft merely shifted the subject of discussion from the French words retained in the memory to the equivalent Latin words placed on paper. It was not the use of writing which made pleas unalterable, nor even the copying of paper pleadings on to parchment membranes, but only the incorporation of the membranes into the 'record' after the end of each term. What needs to be established, therefore, is when pleadings

[16] HEHL MS. HAM Box 70. They are double spaced and full of corrections. In HEHL MS. Temple (Legal Papers) Box 1, are some draft pleadings in Latin with corrections in French. The prothonotary's papers from the Court of Pleas at Lancaster (PL 21) contain numerous examples of draft pleadings in French, especially from the 1530s and 1540s.

[17] *Miscellaneous Writings and Letters of Thomas Cranmer*, ed. J. E. Cox (Parker Soc.; 1846), 170 ('I have heard suitors murmur at the bar, because their attornies have pleaded their cases in the French tongue, which they understood not', 1549). The reference to 'attornies' is puzzling, unless even common-form pleas were put forward in French. Cf. Denton, Bacon, and Cary, *Report*, 545, which says that moots were pleaded in French 'even as the serjeants do at the bar in the king's courts to the judges' (sp. mod.).

[18] *Cockesworthy* v. *Bullegh* (1552) KB 27/1163, m. 25 (record of Totnes borough court, with demurrer in English, reversed on this ground).

[19] The paper pleadings at Lancaster (PL 21) use third-person forms both in Latin or French, save that pleas in abatement or to the jurisdiction are always in the forms used orally ('Vous avez ci...').

[20] Baker, *Serjeants at Law*, 92.   [21] Were's reports, BL MS. Hargrave 7, fo. 41.

[22] See Sayles in 57 Selden Soc., pp. ci–cii.

[23] 8 Hen. VI, c. 12, s. 2. The statute refers to 'la scripture que en domoert en le tresorie', which Bryan CJ in 1495 took to refer to paper copies: Trin. 10 Hen. VII, fo. 25, pl. 2.

[24] *Haukeford* v. *Mason* (1428) Mich. 7 Hen. VI, fo. 15v, pl. 24 (tr. 'nothing but a paper'); *Anon.* (1429) Mich. 8 Hen. VI, fo. 7, pl. 16, *per* Martin J. (tr. 'Argue upon our record, for the paper is nothing but an aid to memory').

began to pass as a matter of course from paper to parchment record without any intervening discussion in banc.

The question may conveniently be approached backwards. Treatises on Common Pleas procedure around 1600 show that pleadings were by that date prepared entirely in chambers and then filed with the prothonotaries in the office.[25] In the King's Bench, the chief clerk was willing to draw as well as enter pleadings.[26] Exchange of pleadings did not yet take place literally, as in later times, because the office was the proper channel of communication; but clearly the pleading was completed when the papers were handed to the clerk. When issue was joined specially, the pleadings on both sides were put into a 'paper book'[27] and taken to a serjeant for signature; once counsel had settled them, the 'issue' could be engrossed on a roll. The exact relationship between the serjeant, the instructing attorney, and the clerks, is blurred in the early practice manuals. But it seems that the copy signed by counsel was the authoritative version which warranted the file copy, which in turn warranted the engrossment.[28] The serjeants thus continued to be fixed with the responsibility for pleading which had necessarily been theirs when issue had been joined orally, and the embodiment of the signature requirement in a formal order of the Common Pleas in 1573 indirectly acknowledged the disappearance of the older system.[29]

Such evidence as may be pieced together for the reigns of Henry VII and Henry VIII suggests that this was a period of transition between the old and new systems, both of which are found in operation concurrently. In 1490, a Norfolk attorney brought an action on the case in the King's Bench for negligently injuring his wife, and the defendant wished to plead specially that she had caused her own injury. The discussion turned to the cost of special pleading, and Fairfax J. remarked with a smile, 'Norfolk people are full of wiles and will not pay for anything of their own free will unless it is an absolute duty; and the paper is always at the plaintiff's cost; so will you, the defendants, pay for the paper?' The defendant's counsel agreed to do so, but in fact the general issue was entered.[30] The report plainly shows that the preparation of pleadings in a paper book was already common form in the King's Bench, but it also shows that this practice did not preclude discussion of the

---

[25] T. Powell, *The Attourneys Acadmy* (1623) is probably based on earlier guides. For some of the manuscript tracts see 94 Selden Soc. 96 n. 7; *CELMC*, 114, 128.

[26] Fees of the King's Bench (*c.*1590) KB 15/41, fo. 43v.

[27] For references to 'the book', meaning the paper pleadings, see Trin. 10 Hen. VII, fo. 28, pl. 19 (tr. 'Vavasour [J.] awarded that it be put out of the book'); *Anon.* (1518) 2 Caryll 722 ('He prayed that this might be struck out of the book'); *Anon.* (1527/8) Wm Yelv. 318, pl. 13 ('troubled with a tedious book'); *Guldeford* v. *Frankwell* (1529) ibid. 318 at 319 ('put out of the book'); *Anon.* (1544) below, 339 n. 36; *Anon.* (1550) Brooke Abr., *Action sur le Case*, pl. 112 (tr. 'struck out of the book').

[28] See *Ramsey* v. *Bird* (1591) Cro. Eliz. 258; and also 8 Co. Rep. 61.

[29] *Praxis Utriusque Banci* (1674), Common Pleas, '44' (*recte* 60).

[30] *Frankessh* v. *Bokenham* (1490) 1 Caryll 27 at 29.

pleadings in banc, that pleas could still be put forward at the bar—apparently without papers—and that the paper pleadings were not necessarily those entered on the roll. The King's Bench procedure may have been different from that of the Common Pleas, since there was an officer in the former called the clerk of the papers whose function was apparently to control the exchange of paper pleadings—and probably to prepare the 'paper books'—before engrossment on the roll.[31] A bill of costs from 1471 indicates that counsel (two serjeants and an apprentice) were retained to 'see the paper' and settle the issue, a clerk (John Nethersole) was paid 2s. 6d. for 'making of the paper' and another 2s. 6d. for a copy, and the chief clerk was paid 5s. to enter the pleadings.[32] Nethersole, evidently clerk of the papers in function if not in name,[33] appears here simply as a copyist. But no doubt the clerk of the papers actively assisted with the formulation of pleadings. The first certainly known holder of the office, Robert Maycote (d. 1533), left a number of books of entries, including a compilation of his own making which reveals a keen interest in unusual pleas and recent innovations.[34] The very existence of such an officer testifies to the establishment of a regular practice of drawing pleas on paper. The Common Pleas did not have a comparable office, and by 1596 it was the prothonotaries' clerks who prepared the paper books there—six copies, four for the judges and two for the serjeants.[35] The use of paper books reminds us that papers served two objects. They were not merely instructions for the prothonotary, but were used to provide judges and counsel with a written text for reference—and advance preparation—when a motion was made in court.[36] This latter function must have been practically essential when complex pleas of title might contain many thousands of words.[37]

In the Common Pleas it was the prothonotaries who bore the primary responsibility for overseeing the pleading process, though in exercising this role they were considered to be acting for the parties rather than on behalf of the court.[38]

---

[31] 94 Selden Soc. 99, 364.   [32] *Paston Letters*, ed. J. Gairdner, v (1904 edn), 120–1, no. 788.

[33] The clerk of the papers in 1532 received a fee equal to half the chief clerk's fee: *Ayer v. Stonard* (1543) KB 27/1126, m. 113 (costs included 40d. for entering the plea, and 20d. to Maycote).

[34] Library of Congress (MSS Div.) MS. Phillipps 9071. For Maycote see *CITR*, i. 461; Spelman 209; 94 Selden Soc. 364.

[35] Recital in an action of 1596 (brought for fees) in R. Aston, *Book of Entries* (1673), 215–16.

[36] See Pas. 7 Hen. VII, fo. 13, pl. 3, *per* Wode sjt (tr. 'my copy is not so'); *Anon.* (1544) Gell's reports, I, Pas. 36 Hen. VIII, fo. 51v, *per* Baldwin CJ (tr. 'Bring us books of the case and we will give a day for it to be argued').

[37] The longest pleadings noticed in this period are about 100 ft long: *Garneys v. Spencer* (1514) CP 40/1008, m. 788 (20 mm., with different pleas as to different parcels of land, culminating in a demurrer to the second replication to the third plea in bar); cf. *Garneys v. Lucy*, ibid., m. 789 (9 mm., demurrer to a single replication).

[38] See *Anon.* (1495) Mich. 11 Hen. VII, fo. 1, pl. 2, *per* Fairfax J. (tr. 'This was adjudged in the Common Bench, that someone gave a clerk a paper to enter his plea, and he entered other matter, and

A Chancery petitioner around 1490 informs us that a prothonotary might be retained to prepare the 'writings' for a common recovery, evidently as the principal counsel and draftsman and not merely as a copyist.[39] When, in 1521, the executors of John Muscote sued several attorneys for fees due to the estate, they declared that it was the customary office of the prothonotaries 'to enter and enrol the declarations and pleas, and other enrolments of whatever kind, of plaintiffs and defendants, pleaded here in court by their attorneys'.[40] According to the declaration, the defendant attorneys had on 9 October 1498, in the parish of St Dunstan in the West, requested the deceased to enrol and enter various declarations and pleas.[41] The place referred to was presumably Muscote's office in the Middle Temple, though the retainer appears to have been treated as a general retainer to enter pleadings from time to time rather than a specific transaction. Nevertheless, the implication is that usually the pleading was entered on the instructions of the attorney.

The role of the serjeants is less easy to trace. We have noted that it was probably no longer necessary for a serjeant to recite every plea in court, though it remained possible for serjeants to plead at the bar by handing in a paper to the prothonotary in open court.[42] In other cases, the serjeant might amend a plea orally at the bar after argument, and then it was apparently the prothonotary's responsibility to circulate paper copies before making the entry.[43] It may also have been possible for counsel to deal directly with the prothonotaries out of court, as when counsel was told, after argument, to 'make the papers'.[44] In a King's Bench

yet this could not be amended; for the law says that the plea is always the saying of the party himself and not of the prothonotary'). The case cited may be *Holybrond* v. *Pyryton* (1456) 94 Selden Soc. *98* n. 2. But Bryan CJ thought the 1429 statute had given some formal authority to the paper version: Trin. 10 Hen. VII, fo. 25, pl. 2.

[39] *Viscount Lisle* v. *Conyngesby* (*c*.1486/93) C1/100/62.

[40] From the declaration (tr.) in *Osberne* v. *Fitz* (1522) CP 40/1036, m. 409d (action for fees).

[41] *Osbern* v. *Oreng* (1521) CP 40/1033, m. 138; *Osbern* v. *Fitz* (1522) CP 40/1036, m. 409d (Latin quoted in 94 Selden Soc. *98* n. 5); *Osbern* v. *Treheyron* (1522) CP 40/1036, m. 475. The date is the same in all three. Muscote became second prothonotary earlier in 1498.

[42] Above, 339 n. 38; *Anon.* (1481) Pas. 21 Edw. IV, fo. 6, pl. 18 (tr. 'Copley, clerk: your paper is false...'); *Anon.* (1482) Hil. 21 Edw. IV, fo. 76, pl. 9 (tr. 'Pigot... delivered to Vavasour in the court a paper of his demurrer'); *Eriche's Case* (?1490) Pas. 11 Hen. VII, fo. 22, pl. 10, *per* Bryan CJ (tr. 'Take his paper from him and be advised against the morrow...'); Jenour's entries, fo. 260 (paper delivered by Serjeant Frowyk to Mordaunt, the chief prothonotary). See also Spelman 199 (claim to franchise put in at the Lynn eyre of 1522).

[43] *Anon.* (1515) 2 Caryll 661 (tr. 'Therefore More, perceiving the opinion of the court, pleaded that way, although it was [already] entered in the roll the same term, as Conyngesby the prothonotary said, which was remaining in his office; but because neither Serjeant More nor the defendant's attorney ever had a copy of the paper after the replication made by the plaintiff, the officer was blamed and More was told by the court to plead afresh...').

[44] Cf. Pas. 10 Hen. VII, fo. 19, pl. 5, *per* Bryan CJ (tr. 'Make the papers of the matter'); Trin. 10 Hen. VII, fo. 26, pl. 5 (tr. 'the other [serjeant] said, "Make the papers"').

case of 1534, an attorney was sued for pleading a plea without authority and successfully defended himself on the grounds that the plea had been pleaded by
Serjeant Willoughby through John Talbot, of counsel, in the name of the attorney.
It is not easy to understand how a serjeant could plead through junior counsel
except on the footing that this is an oblique reference to signature of the draft; but
it is left unclear whether Talbot recited the plea orally or merely handed in the
paper.[45] No doubt paper pleadings required the approval of counsel, as in a suit of
1518 for which a surviving bill of costs shows that two serjeants were paid 'to look
over the paper'.[46] Sometimes filazers were also involved in the pleading process,
since declarations and simple pleas could be enrolled by them. In a year-book case
of 1506, John Jenour—the future prothonotary—is said to have been 'of counsel' in
drawing a declaration, which he then defended in court by reference to precedents.[47]

   No papers remain among the archives of either bench for the Tudor period.
However, there survives among the records of the Court of Pleas for the
county palatine of Lancaster a collection of papers from the beginning of
Henry VIII's reign which are almost certainly of exactly the same character as the
documents which would have been filed with the clerk of the papers of the
King's Bench at the same period.[48] The collection consists of bundles of paper
rotulets, some of which are still strung on files made for particular sessions. The
drafts are double-spaced, with interlined corrections. Some are draft entries
evidently made by or for the prothonotary, written in full for copying directly
on to the plea rolls; they include draft posteas, judgments, recognizances, and
other matter, besides pleadings. Others contain drafts in short form,[49] occasionally
in law French,[50] and there are sometimes successive drafts. The use of French, and
the memoranda which John Birkhened wrote on the papers when he was
prothonotary in the 1540s, indicate that at least some of the drafts emanated from
counsel, or were drawn in consultation with counsel.[51] Similar paper pleadings

---

[45] *Constable* v. *Frobussher* (1534) KB 27/1092, m. 70.

[46] *Roche* v. *Fawke* (1517–19) E101/518/4, Hil. 9 Hen. VIII ('pro feodo consilii supradicti [6s. 8d.], pro
factura papiri placiti [3s. 4d.], pro feodo consilii supradicti ad supervidendum papirum [6s. 8d.], pro
intratione placiti [6s.], pro copia ejusdem placiti [2s. 4d.]'). This may mean that counsel first advised
on the pleading, and then had another fee for settling the paper. Cf. above, 339 (1471).

[47] Trin. 21 Hen. VII, fo. 28, pl. 8 (tr. 'junor, one of the prothonotaries, who was of counsel with the
matter, said that he would not change the count because he had sufficient precedents of it'). Jenour,
who 'Junor' must be, was not then a prothonotary but was filazer for Devon and Dorset 1503–13.

[48] 'Sessional Papers', PL 21/1–5. The earliest date noted was 1 [Hen. VIII]. There are draft pleadings
of exactly the same appearance in HEHL MS. HAM Box 70; MS. Temple (Legal Papers) Box 1.

[49] e.g. 'Ad vi et armis non culpabilis et ad residuum actio non quia...' (plea in bar), 'Defendens bene
advocat captionem...' (avowry), 'Precludi non quia...' (replication).

[50] The frequency of pleadings in French seems to increase towards the end of Henry VIII's reign.
The forms are the same as the Latin: e.g. the *actio non* formula is 'L'action ne doit il quar...'.

[51] e.g. the following notes all occur in the bundle for Lent 1541 (in PL 21/5) (tr. from French): 'Query
what Mr Hassall intends by his paper'; 'Remember that Mr Hassall restored a paper according to this

from the 1540s were preserved by the prothonotaries of the Great Sessions in Wales, whose practice was modelled on that of Westminster Hall.[52]

From 1524 onwards there is direct evidence concerning the mechanics of pleading at Westminster in the surviving remembrance rolls of the Common Pleas.[53] These contain memoranda of the 'rules'[54] whereby each stage in a case was controlled by the court and the prothonotaries. They are extremely hieroglyphic, and not always easy to interpret, but they take us behind the plea rolls and reveal a tight bureaucratic control over the system. The practice may be illustrated by a particular example, the reported case of *Bolde* v. *Molyneux*, in which a demurrer was entered in the plea roll for Easter term 1535.[55] The progress of the case may be traced through the following entries in Jenour's remembrances for that term:[56]

London. [The sheriff is] again [ordered to] take William Molyneux of Sefton in Lancashire, knight, to answer in the octave of Hilary [20 Jan. 1535] unto Richard Bolde of Bold in Lancashire, esquire, for £90 upon a bond made at London in the parish of St Sepulchre, in the ward of Farringdon Without. [Attorneys:] William Chalfount for the plaintiff, Lawe for the defendant. To answer on the Monday [26 April 1535] after the feast of St George. <Unless he answers by the Saturday [1 May 1535] after one month of Easter, let judgment

plea, and then he relinquished this plea and pleaded a new plea ... as appears among the new papers drawn; and I have written this plea for my own fancy, and it is invalid for various reasons'; 'Afterwards, in Lent 31 [Hen. VIII], the answer was made, and at St Bartholomew 32 [Hen. VIII] the replication was restored *ut arguitur*'; 'Remember that in my book of remembrances it is specified how Christopher and Richard have restored a plea, to which the said Wrightyngton demurred—ask the plaintiff's counsel whether the demurrer should be entered'; 'Remember that in Lent 31 [Hen. VIII] the said Hoskyn and Jane Sherard pleaded the condition performed, as appears in my book of remembrance, and therefore I believe that this plea ought to be a rejoinder—so speak with H[umphrey] Hurleton, who made this plea, for the plaintiff has demurred upon this plea'.

[52] See G. Parry, *A Guide to the Records of the Great Sessions in Wales* (1995), pp. xcvi–xcviii, 54 (Denbighshire, 1548), 235 (Radnorshire, 1542?), 264 (Glamorganshire, 1548–9), 316 (Carmarthenshire, 1543, 1547), 361 (Cardiganshire, 1546).

[53] CP 45. The first (CP 45/1) is that of John Jenour, second prothonotary, for Pas. 1524. The earliest prothonotary's remembrance roll from Lancaster seems to be from Lent 1528 (in PL 21/3). Nothing similar survives from the King's Bench, where some rules were noted or endorsed on the bills in the files: e.g. *Conyngesby* v. *Machell* (1512) in KB 147/2/4/3 (bill marked 'Intretur paupirum super ista billa'); the endorsements are usually of days to appear.

[54] This term is rarely found in the reports, but it was already in use: e.g. *Anon.* (1481) Mich. 21 Edw. IV, fo. 53, pl. 18; *Anon.* (1520) 120 Selden Soc. 44, pl. 28; cf. *Throckmerton* v. *Tracy* (1555) Plowd. 145 at 149v–150 (rulings on exceptions to pleading).

[55] CP 40/1085(1), m. 331 (demurrer to replication, Pas. 1535; judgment for defendant, Pas. 1537); reported in Dyer 14b; Benl. 13.

[56] CP 45/8, mm. 3, 10 (tr. and freely extended). The original is heavily abbreviated: m. 3, 'London. § Pl. ca. Will'm Molyneux de Sefton in com. Lancastr. militem ... r. oct. Hillarii Ric'o Bolde de Bolde in com. Lancastrie armig. lxxxx li. quil't per oblig. f. apud London. in parochia S'c'i Sepulchri in Warda de Faryngdon extra. W. Chalf. q. Lawe def. <r. Lune p^t f'm Georgii. [*margin*]> <n^i r. Sabbati p^t m. Pas. intr. jud'm et da^a xiij ^{s} iiij d.> [*interlined over entry*]'; m. 10, '... n^i def. r. Mercurii p^t f'm Georgii intr. jud'm et da^a xiij ^{s} iiij d. H'et ulterius diem Lune p^t f'm Ph'i et Jac. ex obl. s.'

be entered and damages of 13*s*. 4*d*.> [57] ... Unless the defendant answers by Wednesday [28 April 1535] after the feast of St George let judgment be entered and damages of 13*s*. 4*d*. He has a further day until Monday [3 May 1535] after the feast of Philip and James on his own offering.

The entry on the roll this term contains a demurrer to the replication, suggesting that all the pleadings were put in together, as was the practice in later times; and that might explain why there is no entry in the remembrance concerning the replication or the demurrer. Certainly the completed pleadings were always engrossed together, on what was called the issue roll. But the remembrances show that each pleading could be brought into the office separately. There are rules in other cases to plead, reply, rejoin, or amend. Rules may be 'peremptory', or on pain of judgment by default (as in Molyneux's case), or in the case of a plaintiff on pain of a nonsuit; but the threats are not always as final as they sound since further indulgence is often shown. Sometimes the pleading is to be done when the court is sitting (*sedente curia*), or rising (*in levatione curie*), or after it has risen (*post levationem curie*), but usually there is no such qualification. Paper drafts are sometimes mentioned in rules to 'bring in the paper',[58] presumably meaning that it must be brought into the office, while other memoranda refer to counts in paper.[59] When a demurrer is noted, the name of the serjeant is usually given, and occasionally a named serjeant is given a day to amend a plea or a demurrer will be entered.[60] Despite all the detail, however, the rolls leave us in a state of bewilderment about the nature of the routine being recorded. We are not told whether the rules themselves were made in the office or in open court. And when a rule is silent as to the manner of pleading, we cannot tell whether it is to be done in the office or in court. The explicit references to papers are very few; but this can hardly mean that papers were seldom used. The evidence is, in truth, consistent with both the earlier and later practice. This could be simply because the wording of the routine memoranda had failed to reflect a change, but it could also indicate that the system enabled pleading to be conducted either way.

---

[57] Interlined over entry, but seemingly out of sequence.

[58] e.g. *Capel* v. *Pigott* (1535) CP 45/8, m. 19 (quare impedit; tr. 'unless the defendant brings in the paper (*inf. papir.*) on Monday by the time the court rises (*in lev. cur.*), let a writ be made out to the bishop'). The plea roll shows that the pleadings were entered the same term, though subsequently the defendant pleaded a release puis darrein continuance: CP 40/1086, m. 537. The case is reported in Pas. 27 Hen. VIII, fo. 11, pl. 28. [59] e.g. CP 45/8, m. 2 ('quer. narr. in papiro').

[60] e.g. *Abbot of Westminster* v. *Stephynson et al.* (*executors of Leman*) (1536) CP 45/8, m. 29 ('M[agis-ter] Mervyn h[ab]et diem Lune p[os]t f[estu]m Pur[ificationis] ad emend[endum] pl[acitu]m ex[ecu-torum] Leman ad [sectam] Abb[at]is Westm[onasterii] vel intret[u]r mora[tio] in lege'). A demurrer was entered the following term: CP 40/1089, m. 524 (judgment for plaintiff, Hil. 1537). Serjeant Mervyn was for the defendant: Dyer 26b, 28a.

The survival of tentative pleading is, nevertheless, beyond doubt and will be discussed later.[61]

FORMS AND FORMALISM

The science of pleading was rooted in the fourteenth century, and had been hardened by the learning exercises of the inns of court into a highly formalized and esoteric discipline quite unintelligible to the outsider.[62] Some of the technicalities were occasioned by the difficulty of applying the logic so as to produce a proper issue for trial, such as the rules about when the replication *de injuria* was appropriate,[63] the distinction between single and double pleas,[64] and how far double pleading could be avoided by the use of the 'protestation' (*protestando* clause).[65] On the other hand, there were many instances of entrenched formalism in daily practice which had little substance to them, such as the rigmarole of new assignment,[66] and the requirement of ficititious 'colour',[67] when pleading title in trespass *quare clausum fregit*. Equally formalistic were the rules about the correct use of the *absque hoc* and the averment. Briefly, an *absque hoc* clause was required at the end of a special traverse, and an averment—*Et hoc paratus est verificare*—at the end of an issuable affirmative statement of fact.[68] A negative plea which resulted in an issue triable by jury was supposed to conclude to the country— 'And thereof he puts himself upon the country', or, if pleaded by a plaintiff, 'And

---

[61] Below, 386–9.   [62] For the basic principles see 94 Selden Soc. *143–9*.

[63] There is a detailed discussion in *Anon.* (1493) 1 Caryll 193–5 (misdated in Mich. 16 Hen. VII, fo. 2, pl. 7); Port 99; apparently overruling *Tylly* v. *Michell* (1486) Mich. 2 Hen. VII, fo. 3, pl. 12; CP 40/898, m. 496. There was an intermediate discussion at Brudenell's reading (Inner Temple, 1491): *Moots*, 228–9. See also *Fyssher* v. *Burnham* (1489) Mich. 5 Hen. VII, fo. 6, pl. 12; KB 27/913, m. 37d; *Markewyke* v. *Sherman* (1501) KB 27/961, m. 61 (demurrer); *More* v. *Halyngworth* (1506) Pas. 21 Hen. VII, fo. 22, pl. 21; CP 40/977, m. 459; *Anon.* (1526) Yorke 209, no. 318, *per* Fitzherbert J.

[64] 94 Selden Soc. *149–50*. In *The Serjeants' Case* (1531) Wm Yelv. 293 at 297, Serjeant Cholmeley said double pleas were disallowed in order to avoid 'the inveigling and incumbrance of the court'. Cf. *Ryshton* v. *Cripce* (*c.*1531) Wm Yelv. 290 at 291 ('le court serra envegle').

[65] Matter in a protestation would avail the party if the verdict passed in his favour: Anthony Browne's reading (Middle Temple, 1555) BL MS. Hargrave 199, fo. 10v; 94 Selden Soc. *149–50*. Protestations are common; usually one is taken, but in *Myllys* v. *Rogers* (1539) KB 27/1113, m. 34d, there are six prefaced to the plea *Non assumpsit*. A *protestando* without a substantive plea was held bad in *Grenefeld* v. *Conquest* (1528) CP 40/1059, m. 556.

[66] Below, 721 n. 19. The procedure could also be used in other general actions: e.g. *Broughton* v. *Thorneton* (1511) KB 27/998, m. 30d (maintenance).

[67] *Gilford* v. *Godyng* (1493) KB 27/927, m. 21 (lack of colour assigned as error in forcible entry); Yorke 211–13, nos. 326–9; Pollard 250, no. 11; *Guldeford* v. *Frankwell* (1529) Wm Yelv. 318, no. 14; *Doctor and Student*, ed. Plucknett and Barton, 297–8; Brooke Abr., *Colour*, pl. 64. Cf. Mich. 11 Hen. VII, fo. 2, pl. 7, *per* Mordaunt sjt (tr. 'it is but a thing of form').

[68] A negative could not be averred because it could not be tried: *Moots*, 175.

he prays that this be inquired into by the country'.[69] An averment was not supposed to conclude to the country.[70]

The forms for which precedents existed were collected in precedent books known as books of entries, the word 'entry' distinguishing the Latin form as entered on the roll from the oral French form as found in the *Novae Narrationes*. The book of entries emerged as a genre around the time of Henry VI,[71] though most of the great collections current in the early Tudor period began with precedents from the time of Edward IV. Many of the earlier entries in these books are from the rotulets of William Copley, chief prothonotary from 1468 to 1490, suggesting that he or one of his clerks may have been the original source. One such volume, now in the British Library, seems to have belonged to Copley's successor, William Mordaunt (d. 1518).[72] We know that Mordaunt had a book of entries, of which he thought so highly that he attempted to entail it by will,[73] and which was cited by Sir James Dyer in 1558.[74] Another similar book belonged to Mordaunt's successor Edward Stubbe (d. 1533), and this has additions from the time of Henry VII and Henry VIII, many of them from Mordaunt's rolls.[75] Stubbe's book came into the hands of William Rastell, whose niece married Stubbe's son, and was heavily used by him in compiling the valuable alphabetically arranged *Colleccion of Entrees* which was first printed in 1566.[76] A third collection, likewise beginning with cases from Copley, is the book of entries compiled by John Jenour (d. 1542), second prothonotary, which was often cited after his death by Dyer[77]—his former

---

[69] *Ryshton* v. *Cripce* (*c*.1531/2) Wm Yelv. 290 at 291; *Anon.* (1534) Trin. 26 Hen. VIII, fo. 3, pl. 12, *per* Hales A.-G.; Anthony Browne's reading (Middle Temple, 1555) BL MS. Hargrave 199, fo. 9v.

[70] *Anon.* (1511) BL MS. Add. 35936, fo. 67v, *per* Rede CJ; *Jobbeson* v. *Stile* (1517) KB 27/1024, m. 64 (undetermined demurrer); *Ryshton* v. *Cripce* (*c*.1531/2) Wm Yelv. 290 at 291. Cf. *Moile's Case* (1486) Mich. 2 Hen. VII, fo. 4, pl. 15.

[71] An early example is CUL MS. Ee.1.3, compiled by Simon Elryngton, filazer of the Common Pleas 1442–75, with entries mostly from the 1430s and 1440s.

[72] BL MS. Add. 37488. See fo. 175v ('vide in remembranciis meis Mich. 19 Hen. VII'); Mordaunt was prothonotary in 1493. Mordaunt is mentioned by name on ff. 354v, 434v, and there are other cases from his rolls; but there is also a dated entry of 1510 from the rolls of Muscote, second prothonotary. There are later additions down to 1561, with material from the rolls of the first and second prothonotaries.

[73] PCC 8 Ayloffe; *Testamenta Vetusta*, ed. N. H. Nicolas (1826), ii. 554.

[74] Dyer 174b. It was in the possession of Sir Anthony Browne JCP (d. 1567), who directed by his will that it be returned to his kinsman Robert Mordaunt: PCC 20 Stonarde; PROB 11/49, fo. 50v.

[75] BL MS. Add. 24078. There is a reference to the serjeants' call of 1521, from the remembrances (fo. 35), to the patent of Ernle CJ (fo. 239), and to the oath of Mordaunt's successor (fo. 261v), all of which point to Stubbe.

[76] Most of the later entries can be identified as coming from Mordaunt's rolls.

[77] *Anon.* (1544) Gell's reports, I, Pas. 36 Hen. VIII, fo. 54; Dyer 172a (1558); Dyer 189b (1560); 109 Selden Soc. 54 (1560). This was also in the hands of Browne J. (above, n. 74), who described it as 'the president booke of my olde master John Jenour, myche of it his owne hande': PROB 11/49, fo. 50v. Jenour apparently cites it himself in Pas. 27 Hen. VIII, fo. 1, pl. 2. He probably had other books of entries as well: see 109 Selden Soc. 41 n. 2.

pupil—and had some influence on the anonymous *Intrationum Liber* of 1546.[78] A fourth example, with cases from the time of Henry VII and Henry VIII, interspersed with a few reports of the cases in French, may also have been the work of a prothonotary or prothonotary's clerk.[79] Similar compilations were made in the King's Bench. The most important was that made by John Lucas (d. 1525), filazer and secondary of the court, with entries from the reigns of Edward IV and Henry VII; this also came into the hands of Rastell and accounts for most of the King's Bench precedents in his *Colleccion*.[80] Notice has already been taken of the slightly later collection made by Robert Maycote (d. 1533), clerk of the papers,[81] and there were others for use on the Crown side.[82] What is striking about these collections is their dependence on recent material. There is very little before the time of Edward IV,[83] and the compilers seem more interested in the latest inventions than the earliest precedents. Thus, despite the longevity of the common-law system, and the seeming timelessness of the forms of action and the formalities of written entries, there may well have been a sense that the forms of pleading were only just settling down.

In reality the number of cases won or lost on points of form in pleading was small. Unless a party risked all the merits of his case by demurring, the usual consequence of a plea being held bad was that the party withdrew the plea and pleaded again. If the parties overlooked a flaw in the pleading at the appropriate time and proceeded to issue and verdict, the flaw was often 'cured'.[84] If it was not curable but constituted a 'jeofail', or a material misjoinder of issue,[85] the consequence was not that one of the parties lost but that the parties would be ordered to replead from the stage immediately before the error.[86] In such cases the record formally noted that the court considered the first plea insufficient in law and ordered a repleader.[87] A jeofail could be pointed out to the court at any stage

---

[78] Library of Congress (MSS Div.) MS. Phillipps 26752, which is in a fair hand and may be a copy.

[79] BL MS. Harley 1715; 109 Selden Soc. 41 n. 2; 120 Selden Soc. 1–7.

[80] Library of Congress (MSS Div.) MS. Phillipps 11910; 94 Selden Soc. 364–5.

[81] ibid., MS. Phillipps 9071; above, 339.

[82] KB 15/42 is a Crown Office book of entries, *c.*1500; BL MS. Add. 25168 is a later copy with some additions.

[83] Even the learned Dyer seems to have regarded 1400 as a line beyond which research in the records was seldom attempted: 109 Selden Soc., p. xxix.   [84] 94 Selden Soc. 151 n. 7.

[85] Jeofail is defined as a misjoinder of issue in *Anon.* (1532) Pollard 265, no. 45. Cf. Anthony Browne's reading (Middle Temple, 1555) BL MS. Hargrave 199, fo. 5v, where a distinction is drawn between a misjoined issue (tr. 'when the issue is found for him although the law is against him') and a jeofail ('when the issue is upon a point which is not the effect of the plea, or issue is joined upon a matter which is not a bar and is immaterial').

[86] Hil. 5 Hen. VII, fo. 13, pl. 4; Mich. 7 Hen. VII, fo. 3, pl. 3; Pas. 13 Hen. VII, fo. 18, pl. 1, *per* Bryan CJ.

[87] e.g. *Pope* v. *Fox* (1488) KB 27/909, m. 38; *Marsshe* v. *Archer* (1492) KB 27/924, m. 36; 1 Caryll 111; *Wyat* v. *Atkynson* (1510) CP 40/990, m. 518; *Pett* v. *Moyle* (1520) KB 27/1037, m. 67; *Goderd* v. *Dervy* (1535) CP 40/1086, m. 668; Mich. 27 Hen. VIII, fo. 26, pl. 8; *Wullacombe* v. *Arundell* (1536) CP 40/1089, m. 517; *Coppyng* v. *Coppyng* (1555) CP 40/1161, m. 622.

before judgment—not only before trial, which seems to have been the usual case, or when the jury appeared[88]—but even by motion in arrest of judgment after verdict, which in such a case was tantamount to a motion for a new trial upon new pleadings and if successful had the effect of annulling the verdict.[89] In a case of 1515, Anthony Fitzherbert as plaintiff in the King's Bench attempted to cure a jeofail by making a new averment of fact after verdict, but this unusual procedure resulted only in further adjournments for advisement.[90] A repleader could also be ordered after a demurrer, if a jeofail arose from pleadings prior to that which was the subject of the demurrer.[91]

The procedure was straightforward enough where the pleadings resulted in an issue which was incapable of trial, but in practice the line between errors of substance and curable errors had been drawn distinctly in favour of the former, to the encouragement of purely technical objections. There was apparently a proposal, emanating from John Rastell, to reform the law of jeofails in the 1530s; and a second bill to effect a reform during the time of Cromwell foundered in the Lords in 1539 for lack of time.[92] In 1540, however, a Statute of Jeofails was finally passed, despite near defeat after an attempt to add a clause in the Commons.[93] According to the preamble, the mischief was the overturning of verdicts as a result of 'subtle and negligent pleadings'. It was therefore enacted that after verdict the judges should proceed to judgment notwithstanding any 'mispleading, lack of colour, insufficient pleading, or jeofail, or any miscontinuance or discontinuance, or misconveying of process, misjoining of the issue, lack of warrant of attorney[94] ... or any other default or negligence of any of the parties', and that such judgments

---

[88] *Anon.* (1543) Brooke Abr., *Repleder*, pl. 54.

[89] *Anon.* (1532) Pollard 265, no. 45 (described as a plea in arrest of judgment). Examples are *Culpeper v. Clerk* (1488) CP 40/906, m. 421; *Rawe v. Lanchyne* (1518) CP 40/1022, m. 454; *Dey v. Marche* (1535) CP 40/1085 (2), m. 311. See also below, 395.

[90] *Fitzherbert v. Welles* (1515) KB 27/1017, m. 67 (court takes advisement after verdict, the flaw being indicated by a *recordatur* that there was no averment in the replication that a cestuy que use was living; in Trin. 1517 the plaintiff makes the averment, *in manutentione placiti sui*, and the case is continued for advisement to Trin. 1518). The dispute was also taken to the Chancery: C1/590/56; KB 27/1020, m. 83d (suit on 42 Edw. III, c. 3).

[91] *Lord North v. Buttes* (1555) CP 40/1164, m. 459; Dyer 139b, 140b (repleader of avowry ordered after demurrer to replication). Cf. *Browning v. Beston* (1555) Plowd. 131, 138.

[92] Rastell's proposal was for the reformation of pleading: SP 1/85, fo. 100. (G. R. Elton, *Reform and Renewal* (1986), 139, suggested it was about a change from French to English, but that seems highly unlikely.) For the 1539 bill, see *HLJ*, i. 112b, 114a; Elton, *Reform and Renewal*, 152.

[93] 32 Hen. VIII, c. 30; *HLJ*, i. 138a, 139a, 140b; Elton, *Reform and Renewal*, 154. It was renewed by 33 Hen. VIII, c. 17; 37 Hen. VIII, c. 23; and perpetuated by 2 & 3 Edw. VI, c. 32.

[94] For the prevalence of such cases, and of errors by discontinuance, see 94 Selden Soc. 122. For the distinction between miscontinuance (which was not usually fatal) and discontinuance, see *Lord Willoughby de Broke v. Lord Latimer* (1497) Port 26; *Lomnor v. Byrde* (1532) Spelman 112, 113; *Welsshe v. Hoper* (1534) Spelman 120; 94 Selden Soc. 123. For the effect of the statute, see *Drope's Case* (1563) 109 Selden Soc. 87.

should not be reversed for error. The result was that the last opportunity for objecting to a jeofail or other formal defect of this kind was by motion at nisi prius in arrest of the verdict.[95] The statute had no effect on the availability of repleader before verdict, which continued to be ordered on seemingly very technical grounds.[96] It could be said, therefore, that the statute did nothing to remove the requirements of good form, but merely regulated the time within which formal objections could be made.[97] And the courts soon decided that the wording was not broad enough to cover defects in the original writ, the declaration (if it disclosed no cause of action), the verdict, or the judgment.[98] Indeed, since the statute referred to the default or negligence of the parties, it even became the general learning that it had no application to errors which were attributable to the court and its officers.[99]

The greatest difficulties arose not from failures to observe forms, in which the student had been steeped since his first entry into the law, and which were in any case primarily for the discipline of the prothonotaries and entering clerks, but from the devising of new forms for situations where there was no precedent. In such cases the parties were more or less free, using the framework of established idioms and the appropriate openings and conclusions, to state the effect of their matter in the best words they could find. In the first term that he sat on the bench, Fitzherbert J., one of the most erudite experts on pleading and the older year books, pronounced that 'the law is only that the truth of every matter should be set out and declared in a good sentence'; and therefore a plea which made good sense ought not to be rejected on formalistic grounds.[100] True it is that this provoked a rather strong reaction from Broke J., who replied that formality was 'the chiefest thing in our law' and that 'form must be kept and used, or else everything will be in confusion and orderless'. It is also to be contrasted with a remark made twelve years later by Fitzherbert J., when he grew angry with a serjeant for using a novel form of pleading which had not been seen until the last two years, threatening that 'if anyone will demur upon such pleas I will give judgment against

---

[95] *Collett* v. *Crusshe* (1541) CP 40/1108, m. 401 (motion at Essex assises; verdict taken *de bene esse*, advisement).

[96] e.g. *Lord Scrope* v. *Nevell* (1542) CP 40/1115, m. 553; *Berde* v. *Heddon* (1542) CP 40/1115, m. 790; *Bosse* v. *Waters* (1549) CP 40/1142, m. 732; *Sear* v. *Sear* (1553) KB 27/1168, m. 85. Anthony Browne said in his reading on the statute (Middle Temple, 1555) that exceptions to pleading were '[as] much allowed before verdict taken as they were before [the statute]': BL MS. Hargrave 199, fo. 2.

[97] Anthony Browne's reading on the statute (1555) BL MS. Hargrave 199, ff. 2, 18, 20v.

[98] *Anon.* (1553) BL MS. Harley 1691, fo. 91 (King's Bench decision reported in the Common Pleas); *Clifford* v. *Wariner* (1554) Dyer 96b at 97a; Benl. 37; 1 And. 26, pl. 60; Plowd. 209. Dyer adds a query.

[99] Anthony Browne's reading on the statute (1555) BL MS. Hargrave 199, fo. 16. Cf. *Courtney* v. *Wychehalfe* (1555) CP 40/1164, m. 914, 915b (repleader ordered after verdict because replication bad in law); Dalison's reports, BL MS. Harley 5141, fo. 26v.

[100] *Speke* v. *Flemyng* (1522) Pas. 14 Hen. VIII, fo. 26, pl. 7 (119 Selden Soc. 180–1).

them, so that such corrupt pleas shall be utterly abolished in time to come'.[101]
Fitzherbert was, however, given to shows of impatience, and his impatience in this
case was consistent with his policy of requiring 'good sentence' and stopping
undesirable trends. It is more worthy of note that a Common Pleas judge, who
had lectured on pleading in Gray's Inn, compiled a great abridgment of year-book
cases, and probably knew more about the technicalities of pleading than any of his
contemporaries, felt able to reduce the science to its one basic purpose and to
regard the forms as ancillary to its attainment.[102]

FICTIONS

Fictions had long been deeply rooted in the common-law system and they were
still in daily use, as may be seen from the many examples in this volume.[103] Yet it
is of the essence of a fiction that it should be invisible on the face of the record,
and in consequence it is difficult to assess how far fictions were used in pleading
as a matter of routine. The language of fiction is not frequently encountered in
informal sources either; but we read now and again of matters which have to be
pleaded even though they are not issuable, and that amounts to the same thing.[104]
Some fictions we know to have been not only common but compulsory, as in
the requirement of 'colour', whereas others we know to have been assailed as
mischievous and improper. The clearest example of the latter is the feigned
'foreign plea', which the courts did their best to eradicate.[105] Fictions were good
if they promoted justice, bad if they frustrated it. But generalized analysis is
impossible. Each fiction had its own story; yet none can be confidently traced back
to its origins.

[101] Trin. 26 Hen. VIII, fo. 5, pl. 26 (tr.).

[102] Cf. *Bulkeley* v. *Thomas* (1554) Plowd. 118 at 128, *per* Brooke CJ (tr. 'our law does not necessarily
require a thing to be alleged by one sole precise order of words'). The court there held that an affirmative averment could be made in a *licet* clause.

[103] The most notorious are the bill of Middlesex (above, 151) and geographical fictions to extend
jurisdiction (above, 213), the claiming of clergy by laymen to avoid the death penalty (below, 532), the
bastardization of villeins to achieve liberty (below, 605), and the common recovery to bar entails
(below, 694). For fictions in writs see 105 Selden Soc. 80; Mich. 7 Hen. VII, fo. 2, pl. 2; Port 142; *Burgh*
v. *Potkyn* (1522) 120 Selden Soc. 82 at 83; *Eland's Case* (1528/9) Spelman 31.

[104] e.g. Yorke 221, nos. 357–8.

[105] e.g. Pas. 21 Edw. IV, fo. 22, pl. 3 (attorney examined on oath); and see the later oath of an attorney
not to plead foreign pleas, below, 438–9.

19

Trial by Jury

B Y the Tudor period nearly all issues of fact in the common-law courts were tried by a jury of twelve men.[1] Battle could on rare occasions still be proffered, as a tactical manoeuvre, in appeals of felony[2] and writs of right,[3] but it was virtually obsolete and almost certainly no combat was fought in Tudor times.[4] Spiritual matters, such as bastardy or profession, were tried by certificate from the bishop.[5] But the principal exception to jury trial was wager of law, which was still commonly available in actions of debt and detinue. It will be more appropriate to discuss it in the context of debt.[6]

JURY TRIAL

In most cases, when the pleadings resulted in an issue of fact, the parties put themselves upon the country and the sheriff was ordered to summon twelve lawful men, who were not related to the parties, to determine it. The entry of the precept for a *venire facias* was a matter of course. The trial, however, was very far from being a matter of course, and was perhaps the weakest link in the common-law system.[7] The year books often refer to the 'peril' or 'ambiguity' of the unpredictable 'lay gents' who constituted the jury, and it has been observed that the logic of medieval pleading was directed against the possible misleading of jurors.[8] Yet the lay character of the jury occasioned other and greater perils than those which arose from their ignorance of law. The jurors were selected by the sheriff to

---

[1] For juries of women see below, 552.

[2] e.g. *Smyth* v. *Ruston* (1499) KB 27/950, m. 61 (followed by nonsuit); Rast. Ent. 50v; *Reade* v. *Schuyther* (1552) KB 27/1164, m. 139 (demurrer to wager of battle), reported in Dyer 120a. For ways of ousting battle see *Anon.* (1482) Trin. 22 Edw. IV, fo. 19, pl. 46; Brooke Abr., *Battail*, pl. 7; 94 Selden Soc. 116 n. 6. For the approver's oath, and justices' proclamation, in English see *Bernard* v. *Halley* (1448 or 1458) Crown Office entries, ff. 119v–121 (37 Hen. VI); BL MS. Add. 25168, fo. 292v (27 Hen. VI).

[3] e.g. Rast. Ent. 103v (undated writ of right of advowson), 323 (343v), 324 (344v) (writs of right in seignorial courts, 1490 and 1503); *Milborne* v. *Baskervile* (1512) CP 40/998, m. 348 (sim.). See also *Lowe* v. *Paramore* (1571) 109 Selden Soc. 212; Dyer 301a.

[4] There is an undated precedent of a battle being fought in an appeal in Rast. Ent. 42v.

[5] For certification of bastardy see below, 605. For profession see below, 609.   [6] Below, 835–7.

[7] For unsuccessful reform proposals see Elton, *Reform and Renewal*, 148, 152, 153.

[8] Milsom, *Historical Foundations*, 42, 83; *SHCL*, 185–8.

try the issue between particular parties. If, therefore, one of the parties held influence with the sheriff, it was no difficult task to procure a favourable panel or to stave off trial altogether. Men of standing in a county who were involved or likely to be involved in litigation would go to considerable lengths to ensure that the right sheriff was pricked at the annual election.[9] Favour was not necessarily on the side of the mighty: in one case an earl successfully challenged an array which he claimed had been made on the nomination of his alleged villein.[10] And it is not always easy to identify corrupt motives. Parties rarely asked openly for improper favour. They sought an impartial ('indifferent') jury; and urging jurors to give a verdict according to conscience was not unlawful or a ground of challenge.[11] But the implication of such requests is that the sheriff or under-sheriff chose jurors in a way which could very easily be seen to favour one side or the other. Bribery to that end was certainly a source of complaint.[12]

The defects of jury trial led some to reflect that trial by judge alone might be at least as effective. Sir Thomas More, indeed, wrote: 'I never saw the day yet but that I durst as well trust the truth of one judge as of two juries'.[13] The general public, he added, would rather submit their affairs to a judge than a jury, 'except haply some such as trust more in the favour of the country than in the truth of their cause'.[14] It will be recalled from More's conversation with Roper[15] that the judges declined to undertake such a task because they would not meddle with questions of fact; and favour, bribery, and maintenance infected all issues of fact. They knew that if they took such questions upon them, they themselves would be subjected to pressures that they would sooner avoid. Even More did not maintain that trial by judge alone would have been better than jury trial, merely that it would be at least as reliable.[16] But it was not a realistic possibility. The judges were not, and had no wish to be, chancellors. Instead, they made use of the pre-existing formal safeguards against abuse.[17] These, as we shall see, were in theory rigorous but in practice rigid and somewhat artificial. One form of safeguard looked to the quality of the jurors and the other to the actual or potential bias of sheriffs.

[9] e.g. *Plumpton Letters*, ed. J. Kirby (8 Camden Soc. 5th Ser.; 1996), 138, no. 146 (George Emerson, an attorney, to Sir Robert Plumpton, 1500); *LP*, vi. 1337 (Sir William Parr to Cromwell, 1533). For the choice of sheriffs favourable to the Crown, cf. *LP*, v. 1517–18. For maintenance see above, 69.

[10] *Earl of Suffolk v. Revet* (1499) KB 27/951, m. 66.   [11] Dyer 48a (1540).

[12] e.g. Richard Bishop, attorney of the Common Pleas, was accused of taking 10s. when under-sheriff of Herts. to make up a favourable panel: *Baron v. Bishop* (1504–5) CP 40/970, m. 506; CP 40/972, m. 418.

[13] *The Apologye of Syr Thomas More*, ed. A. L. Taft (1930), 150; More, *The Debellacyon of Salem and Bizance* (1533), sig. G7v, repr. in *Complete Works of More*, x. 131, line 32.

[14] *Debellacyon of Salem and Bizance*, sig. H3v; repr. in *Complete Works of More*, x. 135, line 18.

[15] See above, 47.

[16] *Debellacyon of Salem and Bizance*, sig. H4, repr. in *Complete Works of More*, x. 135, line 25.

[17] The punishment of perjury belonged to the Star Chamber: above, 198.

QUALIFICATIONS OF THE JURORS

According to official thinking, the likelihood of corruption varied in inverse proportion to wealth, and so the root cause of perjury was considered to be the impanelling of men who were insufficient in substance to withstand temptation. The solution was found in a property qualification, a rough test of social commitment which was to survive in England until 1972. Some reformers in the fifteenth century thought of strengthening the safeguard by raising the qualification. One suggestion was that jurors should be armigerous gentlemen having an annual income at least equivalent to the subject-matter of the case to be tried.[18] But the higher the qualification the more difficult it was to find jurors to serve, and even the existing 40s. qualification made it difficult for sheriffs in some parts of the country to find enough men to impanel. The solution to one problem was thus the occasion of another, and it was especially acute in cities where land ownership was necessarily restricted. In practice, therefore, there was a tendency to extend the qualifications sideways rather than upwards, by recognizing that personal and equitable substance might be equivalent to real property.

In 1513 it was enacted that jurors summoned to sit at nisi prius in London should no longer be required to possess land worth 40s. a year if they had goods to the value of 100 marks.[19] The judges also relaxed the operation of the general rule by allowing all feoffees to uses of land worth 40s. a year to be sworn on juries, and also—by 'discretion' but not of right—the cestuy que use.[20] But sheriffs continued to return unqualified men, and in 1543 Parliament rendered them liable to fine by requiring that the 40s. qualification be mentioned in the *venire facias*.[21] Lack of qualification was still a good ground of challenge.[22]

The other general qualification for juries was that, if freehold was in issue, at least four members should be inhabitants or owners of freehold in the hundred where the land in issue lay.[23] Jurors could therefore be challenged for 'nothing within the hundred'.[24] Once four jurors had been sworn, however, no further

---

[18] Westminster Abbey Muniments no. 12235 (quoted in 94 Selden Soc. *107* n. 2).

[19] 4 Hen. VIII, c. 3, explained (and perhaps impliedly perpetuated) by 5 Hen. VIII, c. 5. There was already a similar qualification in the city's own courts for suits over 40 marks: 11 Hen. VII, c. 21.

[20] Litt. s. 464; *Lady Hastings v. Hungerford* (1492) 1 Caryll 102 at 104, *per* Wode sjt; *Dod v. Chyttynden* (1502) 2 Caryll 395 at 396, 407; *Thornedon v. Bewregard* (1507) 2 Caryll 559; Yorke 126, no. 101, *per* Fitzherbert J.   [21] 35 Hen. VIII, c. 6.

[22] *Anon.* (1523) Spelman 35, pl. 2; *Anon.* (1541) Benl. 28, pl. 42.

[23] Either residence or freehold was sufficient, but not leasehold: *Anon.* (1534) Spelman 37, pl. 10. The value was immaterial: Yorke 123, no. 92. It was sufficient even to be a trustee: ibid. 126, no. 101.

[24] e.g. *Norris's Case* (1498) Mich. 14 Hen. VII, fo. 2, pl. 6; *Anon.* (1501, 1510, 1515) Rast. Ent. 116v (118), 117v (118v), 250v (267v); *Calthorp v. Yelverton* (1520) CP 40/1030, m. 331; *Morgan v. Mogrygge* (1526) CP 40/1050, m. 453; *More v. Higham* (1529) Spelman 36, pl. 5; *Anon.* (1547) Dyer 61b; *Anon.* (1555) 110 Selden Soc. 404. Numerous cases on this subject are put in Edmund Dudley's reading (Gray's Inn, 1496) CUL

challenge could be taken on this ground, and any jurors previously stood by for this cause might be brought back and sworn.[25] The rule had to be relaxed where the lord of the hundred was a party, in which case jurors were summoned from adjacent hundreds;[26] and likewise where there were insufficient qualified persons within the hundred.[27] Since it was no longer supposed that jurors were likely to make much use of personal knowledge, the rule itself was seen as an anachronism and given little favour. It was held sufficient if the juror lived in the hundred and had land elsewhere in the county.[28] And in 1529 and 1557 it was decided by the judges, reversing earlier precedents, that where an action was brought for land in different hundreds there did not have to be hundredors from each of them.[29]

There was in general no attempt to adjust the composition of the jury to match the social position of the parties, though it was held in 1555—reviving a practice long dormant—that where a peer was party to a civil cause the jury had to contain some knights.[30] This was a privilege belonging to the peer, who alone could challenge the jury for want of knights.[31] The only other class of society to enjoy a comparable privilege were aliens, who were entitled to ask for a jury half composed of aliens.[32] However, there was no general principle that a jury should consist of either party's social peers. An esquire could not object to being tried by common merchants or anyone else who met the property qualification.[33] In fact, the only other established form of special jury qualified by status was the jury of twelve matrons used in criminal cases to determine whether a woman felon was pregnant.[34] But a special

MS. Hh.3.10, ff. 73–74; Thomas Williams's reading (Inner Temple, 1558) pr. as *The Excellency and Praeheminence of the Common Law asserted* (1680), 121–34.

[25] *Anon.* (1524) Yorke 125, no. 96; *Anon.* (1529) Spelman 35, pl. 4; 94 Selden Soc. *108*. See also Yorke 128, no. 108.

[26] e.g. Rast. Ent. 252 (269); *Abbot of Tavistock v. Whytefeld* (1531) CP 40/1069, m. 306d; *Nunny v. Abbot of St Albans* (1534) CP 40/1083, m. 150; *Assheley v. Frye* (1535) CP 40/1085(2), m. 322d; *Anon.* (1537) 121 Selden Soc. 437, no. 16.

[27] *Wryght v. Oxenbrygge* (1485) KB 27/895, m. 61 (London action; sim. plea of nothing within the ward; triers say there are no others in the ward; sheriff to include *tales* from adjacent ward).

[28] Dudley's reading (1496), fo. 73v; Yorke 127, no. 105.

[29] *Heigham v. Colt* (1529) 120 Selden Soc. 76 at 77; *Manwood v. Allen* (1557) Benl. 47, pl. 85; Brooke Abr., *Challenge*, pl. 216 (tr. 'by the Exchequer and both benches in the time of Edward VI and Trin. 4 Mar. I').

[30] *Newdegate v. Earl of Derby* (1555) Dyer 107b; Plowd. 117; Gell's reports, I, Mich. 2 & 3 Phil. & Mar., fo. 6v; Rast. Ent. (1670 edn), fo. 116; *Countess of Oxford v. Earl of Oxford* (1558) BL MS. Hargrave 4, fo. 137v; MS. Harley 1624, fo. 78v. It was doubtful whether this extended to bishops, since they were not themselves knights: *R. v. Bishop of Rochester* (1535) Brooke Abr., *Enquest*, pl. 100.

[31] *Lord Windsor v. Ferrers* (1557) 110 Selden Soc. 410. See also 109 Selden Soc., p. lviii.

[32] See below, 612. The form of *venire facias* (with a clause 'quorum una medietas sit de indigenis et altera medietas sit de alienigenis...') is printed in Rast. Ent. 157 (159). Such a jury could be claimed at the stage of the *distringas juratores*, even if it was overlooked at the *venire facias*: *Anon.* (1505) Mich. 21 Hen. VII, fo. 32, pl. 23. If such a jury was ordered, a verdict given by a jury otherwise constituted was void: *Bradschawe v. Savage* (1490) CP 40/914, m. 260 (*venire de novo* awarded).

[33] *R. v. Thomas* (1554) Dyer 99b.   [34] Below, 552.

jury of greater substance than normal could be ordered in appropriate cases, apparently at the court's discretion.[35] Age was no disqualification, since the 1285 provision that men over 70 should not be put in juries was held to be solely for the benefit of the aged, whose remedy was to sue the sheriff.[36]

IMPANELLING AND CHALLENGING THE ARRAY

Besides these rules concerning the composition of juries, the common law provided safeguards against the partiality of sheriffs both at the time of issuing the process to summon the jurors and by way of challenge at the trial.[37] If the sheriff was himself a party, or was related to one of the parties, then either at the time of entering the issue—if the other party consented[38]—or upon a successful challenge to the array the court was often asked to award a *venire facias* to the coroners,[39] or (where there was more than one sheriff) to the other sheriff alone.[40] If some of the coroners were also involved in the litigation or connected with the parties, which was quite common since they were often lawyers, then the *venire facias* went to the remaining coroners only,[41] or to the coroners generally with a proviso that those involved should not intermeddle.[42] If neither the sheriff nor the coroners were competent to execute the writ, the parties had to ask the court to nominate two electors ('elisors' or 'esliers') from among 'certain persons here standing around' to perform the duty by their consent. The court usually appointed two of its senior clerical officers,[43] commonly two of the prothonotaries,[44] but it was not

[35] In *Thurland* v. *Godley* (1518) CP 40/1022, m. 529, a 100s. qualification was inserted in the *venire facias* to try a trespass case before justices of oyer and terminer.

[36] *Anon.* (*c.*1545/50) Wm Yelv. 357, no. 93.

[37] There is a detailed discussion of this subject in Dudley's reading (1496), ff. 70v–74, glossing *legales homines*; William Staunford's reading (Gray's Inn, 1545) BL MS. Hargrave 92, ff. 91–94; Thomas Williams's reading (1558), 164–70. See also 94 Selden Soc. 108 n. 1.

[38] *Wimbish* v. *Lord Willoughby* (1552) Plowd. 73 at 74v. This was to avoid delay. If the other party did not admit the allegation, the writ went to the sheriff and the point had to be taken by challenge.

[39] e.g. 94 Selden Soc. 104–5. Subsequent process went to the coroners even if the sheriff changed: *Anon.* (1490–1) 1 Caryll 38–9, pl. 40.

[40] e.g. *Grewe* v. *Reve* (1528) CP 40/1058A, m. 414d (plaintiff a sheriff of Norwich).

[41] e.g. *Vyall* v. *Norris* (1497) KB 27/942, m. 34 (sheriff married defendant's niece, one of coroners of counsel with plaintiff, another coroner a party); *Abbot of St Augustine's, Canterbury* v. *Goldwyn* (1523) CP 40/1038, m. 130 (sheriff and two coroners were plaintiff's tenants); *Earl of Northumberland* v. *Wedall* (1523) ibid., m. 449; CP 40/1039, m. 103 (sheriff a son-in-law of the plaintiff, and one of the coroners his counsel). There were often a good number of coroners in a county: e.g. CP 40/1038, m. 130 (five in Kent, 1523); CP 40/1039, m. 103 (eight in Yorks., 1523); CP 40/1079, m. 439 (likewise, 1533).

[42] Dudley's reading (1496), fo. 72; *Fuljambe* v. *Leche* (1526) Mich. 19 Hen. VIII, fo. 2, pl. 9.

[43] e.g. *Fenkyll* v. *Fenkyll* (1504–7) KB 27/970, m. 65; KB 27/984, m. 73 (chief clerk and clerk of the crown); *Corke* v. *Selman* (1515) CP 40/1012, m. 443 (first prothonotary and a filazer).

[44] e.g. the first and second: *Cheyne* v. *Cheyne* (1508) CP 40/983, m. 147; *Bassett* v. *Long* (1529) CP 40/1061, m. 633; *Bradley* v. *Wovaston* (1529) CP 40/1063, m. 134; *Bagshawe* v. *Browne* (1531) CP 40/1069,

constrained to do so and might appoint men of quality from the county concerned.[45] The sheriff was not allowed to circumvent this procedure by saying, in response to challenge, that the choice of jurors had actually been delegated to a deputy[46]—as was no doubt often the truth. On the other hand, bias in the sheriff's delegate was a ground for issuing a *venire de novo* to the coroners.[47] Where bias was discovered in an under-sheriff after a challenge, the *venire de novo* might contain a proviso that the under-sheriff should not intermeddle in its execution.[48]

Since a challenge could be made to the array if the sheriff executed a *venire facias* notwithstanding his relationship to one of the parties,[49] it was quite common for a party to point out his own relationship to the sheriff to ensure that the case was not delayed by a challenge when the jury appeared. The array could not be quashed on the ground that some of the *jurors* were related to a party, or biased, because it was necessary to show that the sheriff, under-sheriff, coroners, or electors, had been partial in making the selection; but an unbalanced selection might be evidence of favour in the sheriff.[50]

The rules guarding against bias by reason of family relationship were extensive in scope. Consanguinity between the sheriff and a party was always recognized. Affinity was recognized if it existed at the time of making the panel;[51] but if it was traced through the party's wife it was necessary to show that she had some potential interest in the suit, which was usually achieved by showing that she had issue by the party.[52] Spiritual affinity was also recognized, as where the sheriff was godfather to one of the parties.[53] Somewhat remarkably, affinity with a corporation was also a ground of challenge, as in a case of 1529 where the Priory of St John was plaintiff and the sheriff had married the great-great-granddaughter of

m. 344; *Grenehall* v. *Cocke* (1535) CP 40/1087, m. 326d. Or the second and third: *Archbishop of Canterbury* v. *Newman* (1531) CP 40/1069, m. 319.

[45] e.g. *Ive* v. *Hudson* (1532) CP 40/1073, m. 109 (two esquires); *Cumberland* v. *Berdesey* (1555) KB 27/1175, m. 176d (sim.). Dudley said the parties could nominate 'esliers', if they agreed: reading (1496), fo. 72.   [46] *Bellewe* v. *Baron* (1546) KB 27/1138, m. 34 (so held on demurrer).

[47] e.g. *Roos* v. *Hurleston* (1524) CP 40/1042, m. 157d (array challenged for favour shown by hundredor of St Albans, who gave the panel to the sheriff; *venire de novo* to coroners).

[48] e.g. *Brograve* v. *Botery* (1510) CP 40/993, m. 645; *Pyerpont* v. *Abbot of Missenden* (1515) CP 40 / 1010, m. 527; *Littleton* v. *Hunkleton* (1552) Dyer 78a (citing a record of 1474); *Dermer* v. *Rotherham* (1555) CP 40/1162, m. 749. Cf. *Kyppyng* v. *Olyver* (1527) CP 40/1056, m. 511d (one of coroners not to intermeddle because he is defendant's attorney).

[49] This included real parties standing behind nominees or trustees: *Smyth* v. *Stanley* (1518) CP 40/1021B, m. 606 (*venire facias* to coroners because plaintiffs sue to use of Conyngesby J., whose wife was a cousin of the sheriff's wife).   [50] *Norris's Case* (1498) Mich. 14 Hen. VII, fo. 1, pl. 5.

[51] *Anon.* (1500) Trin. 15 Hen. VII, fo. 9, pl. 9; *Marshall* v. *Eure* (1537) Dyer 37b; CP 40/1090, m. 402; *Lyttleton* v. *Huccleton* (1553) Dyer 91b.

[52] 94 Selden Soc. 105; *Anon.* (1503/9) Port 130, pl. 86; *Essex* v. *Feteplace* (1518) CP 40/1026, m. 847 (challenge upheld on demurrer).

[53] e.g. *Hynde* v. *Thressher* (1555) KB 27/1174, m. 110 (*venire facias* to coroners).

the preceptor of Beverley's great-great-great-grandfather.[54] The number of degrees to which a relationship could be traced was apparently unlimited, and Richard Littleton held that for this purpose the law took notice even of a relationship outside the prohibited degrees of marriage so long as it was capable of supporting an inheritance.[55] This is confirmed by an Irish statute of 1541, which abolished challenges beyond the fifth degree of consanguinity or affinity in relation to both sheriffs and jurors; it had allegedly become almost impossible to find juries in Ireland who were not related in some way to the parties.[56] In England, challenges rarely set out relationships beyond the third degree.[57] The rules were applied with an artificial rigidity which sometimes lost sight of their purpose; for instance, in replevin the relationship that counted was the relationship with the avowant rather than with the freeholder in whose name he avowed.[58]

The practice in a relationship case was for the party making the challenge to submit a written pedigree; and several such pedigrees, on paper, survive in the prothonotaries' papers from Lancaster[59] and the Great Sessions in Wales.[60] It was not necessary to prove the pedigree precisely as alleged, however, so long as the relationship was established.[61] Bias in the sheriff must have been more difficult to establish than a family relationship. The usual approach was to establish some circumstance from which it might be inferred: for instance, by showing that the sheriff was the party's counsel[62] or

---

[54] *Prior of St John's of Jerusalem* v. *Baynbrige* (1529) CP 40/1061, m. 424. Beverley was another house belonging to the Order of St John. For consanguinity with members of a corporation see the note in Port 130, pl. 87.

[55] Richard Littleton's reading (Inner Temple, 1493) CUL MS. Hh.3.6, fo. 8v. See also *Dean and Chapter of Lincoln* v. *Prat* (1481) Mich. 21 Edw. IV, fo. 63, pl. 33 (kinship even in ninth degree sufficient).

[56] 33 Hen. VIII (Ir.), c. 4. According to the preamble, all Irishmen were related in the ninth degree.

[57] For exceptions see *Strangways* v. *Graunger* (1523) CP 40/1039, m. 158d (sheriff is great-great-grandson of plaintiff's great-great-grandfather on the grandmother's side); *Ratclyffe* v. *Sayvell* (1530) CP 40/1065, m. 131 (sheriff is great-great-great-grandson of the great-grandmother of the plaintiff's wife); *Danby* v. *Girlyngton* (1532) CP 40/1075, m. 352d (coroner is great-great-great-grandson of plaintiff's great-great-grandfather). Cf. the 1525 case from Lancaster, below, n. 59.

[58] *Anon.* (1531) Spelman 37, pl. 9; *Lyster* v. *Maude* (1532) CP 40/1075, m. 506 (sheriff's great-great-grandfather was great-great-grandfather of plaintiff's lessor, in whose right defendants distrained; challenge held bad on demurrer).

[59] e.g. in PL 21/2 there is a pedigree of Robert Standissh (four degrees), Robert Orell (six degrees) and Ralph Orell (five degrees), submitted for the purpose of excluding the coroners as well as the sheriff in a case of 1525; the court here appointed two attorneys as electors.

[60] G. Jones, *A Guide to the Records of the Great Sessions in Wales* (1995), pp. xcix–c. The corresponding 'papers' of the King's Bench and Common Pleas have been lost.

[61] *Yeo* v. *Mychell* (1526) CP 40/1049, m. 129 (triers find that sheriff is plaintiff's kinsman, but not exactly in the manner alleged; *venire de novo* awarded).

[62] e.g. *Lane* v. *Muschamp* (1518) CP 40/1020B, m. 343; *Goldney* v. *Flemmyng* (1520) CP 40/1030, m. 451; *Abbot of St Augustine's, Bristol* v. *Bradston* (1529) CP 40/1060, m. 528; *Prior of Bodmin* v. *Gille* (1537) CP 40/1093, m. 131. Cf. *Abbot of Hyda* v. *Clerke* (1520) CP 40/1030, m. 453d (sheriff of plaintiff's fee and counsel but because he is a man of high discretion and good conscience the defendant waives any

attorney,[63] his steward,[64] his tenant,[65] or of his livery,[66] or that there had been a previous dispute between the party and the sheriff. A nice point, discussed in the Inner Temple in 1493, arose where the sheriff had previously been a juror between the parties in the same dispute.[67] It is obvious from the involvement of the Star Chamber in accusations of bias by sheriffs that these principles were not always in practice wholly effective.[68] They could also be manipulated to delay proceedings, as in the case where—so it was alleged—one prominent Suffolk knight had brought a collusive action against another and left it undetermined for several years, so that if ever he was sued while the defendant was sheriff he could challenge the array.[69]

A challenge was treated as a miniature lawsuit within a lawsuit. It was supposed to be made in French in the form 'Vous aves cy...', entered of record in Latin, and returned with the postea. Often the opposing party would confess the facts. If he did not, the parties pleaded to an issue of fact, which was put to triers (triatores) drawn from the panel, who were charged and sworn.[70] In the case of a challenge to the array, this logic might seem somewhat defective, since the triers were necessarily themselves under challenge; but in fact triers did sometimes quash arrays.[71] Whether the judges were able to exert an independent influence on the triers is beyond our knowledge, though obviously the system was far from perfect; Spelman could not contain his astonishment when an array was affirmed in a case where the sheriff was the uncle of the wife of the avowant's lessor in replevin.[72]

objection); Anon., Rast. Ent. 117 (118), pl. 8. Likewise in the case of coroners: Avon v. Jace (1494) CP 40/929, m. 321 (array quashed); Arundell v. Rawe (1495) CP 40/934, m. 128; Veer v. Stafford (1516) CP 40/1014, m. 502; Earl of Northumberland's Case (1523) CP 40/1039, m. 103; Gascoigne v. Prior of Bolton (1532) CP 40/1075, m. 511 (John Swynhowe).

[63] This was more likely to occur in the case of a coroner: e.g. Cheyne v. Cheyne (1508) CP 40/983, m. 147; Gascoigne v. Prior of Bolton (1532) CP 40/1075, m. 511 (John Lambert); Earl of Cumberland v. Burton (1533) CP 40/1079, m. 439 (John Swynhowe).

[64] e.g. Bishop of Exeter v. Ackelond (1518) CP 40/1020B, m. 321; CP 40/1079, mm. 343d, 439; Prior of Maxstoke v. Est (1530) CP 40/1067, m. 718.

[65] e.g. Re Trussell, Earl of Arundel v. Regem (1500) Trin. 15 Hen. VII, fo. 9, pl. 11; KB 27/957, Rex m. 5; Anon. (1528) Caryll (Jun.) 390, no. 49 (Exeter assizes); Abbot of St Augustine's, Canterbury v. Edyell (1529) KB 27/1071, m. 26; Earl of Cumberland v. Burton (1533) CP 40/1079, m. 439 (John Lambert, coroner).

[66] Anon. (1490) 1 Caryll 38–9, pl. 40. Dudley said there was no challenge if the sheriff was of the fee or clothing of both parties: reading (1496) at fo. 72.

[67] Richard Littleton's reading (1493) 105 Selden Soc. 276.

[68] See Guy, The Cardinal's Court, 32–3.

[69] This was alleged by the Crown in R. v. Jenney (1508) 2 Caryll 573. The triers found the covin as alleged, but the reporter doubted the result.

[70] Cf. Dermer v. Rotherham (1555) CP 40/1162, m. 749, where a challenge to the array for bias by the under-sheriff was '(tr.) found true by examination of the aforesaid undersheriff'.

[71] e.g. Barton v. Bryce (1526) CP 40/1049, m. 335 (array quashed for favour shown by earl of Cumberland as sheriff).

[72] Anon. (1531) Spelman 37, pl. 9. It was the lessor's title which was in issue.

The usual number of triers was two,[73] though the court could appoint more at its discretion.[74] If two or more jurors had already been sworn before the challenge in question, they acted as the triers.[75] And if one juror only had been sworn in, he might be asked to choose someone indifferent as the other trier.[76] Otherwise, in the case of a challenge to the array, the court nominated the triers, for instance by choosing the third and ninth names in the panel.[77] Serjeant Hynde commended the trick ('policy') of challenging two or three, and then allowing a friend to be sworn in so that he would be one of the triers.[78] The triers were not subject to challenge.[79] The evidence to inform them was usually provided by judicial exam-ination of the person challenged,[80] though it was said that there could be no examination unless the triers requested it.[81]

Favour might also take the form of delay, where the sheriff did not produce a jury at all. The party then had to seek further process, the *habeas corpora juratorum*, the *distringas juratores*, and sometimes an *alias* and *pluries distringas*, each requir-ing a fee for the writ, a fee for a warrant to the sheriff, and a fee to the sheriff's bailiff for warning the jury.[82] Here the common law could not ultimately help, and the rolls often record the continuance of such process for a year and more without success. However, if the plaintiff tried to stave off trial by not suing the *venire facias*, it was open to the defendant to sue a *venire facias cum proviso*.[83] In 1543 Parliament introduced legislation to prevent delays because of the practical difficulties in assembling juries. Sheriffs were to be finable if they did not return at least six hundredors in every panel. And if there were insufficient jurors, before or after challenges, at the *habeas corpora* or *distringas juratores*, either party could pray a *tales de circumstantibus*: that is, to have the number made up from persons

[73] Yorke 128, no. 106. This was also true in criminal cases: e.g. *Anon.* (1529) Port 56.

[74] In *Duke of Buckingham* v. *Lucas* (1514) KB 27/1010, m. 38, three triers were charged (at Henhow assizes) and retired to the 'house' (*domus*) used for jurors, about 20 yards from the bar.

[75] *Norris's Case* (1498) Mich. 14 Hen. VII, fo. 1, pl. 5. Cf. *Kyppyng* v. *Olyver* (1527) CP 40/1056, m. 511d (five sworn before challenge to the array at bar; they try it and quash the panel).

[76] *Hoggeson* v. *Abbot of St Albans* (1490) 1 Caryll 49; *Anon.* (1537) Dyer 25a; 121 Selden Soc. 437, no. 15.

[77] *Anon.* (1506) Trin. 21 Hen. VII, fo. 29, pl. 10.   [78] Yorke 128, no. 107.

[79] *Anon.* (1510/11) 120 Selden Soc. 9, no. 3.

[80] *Anon.* (1506) Trin. 21 Hen. VII, fo. 29, pl. 10; *Helghum* v. *Colt* (1529) 120 Selden Soc. 76. Cf. Yorke 124, no. 94 (Exeter assizes, 1522/36), which says that the jurors were not examined in the case of a principal challenge.   [81] *Anon.* (1503) Port 130, no. 85, *per* Frowyk CJ.

[82] Bill of costs (1518) E101/518/4. The *venire* cost 2*s.*, with 7*d.* for the seal; the *habeas corpora* and *distringas juratores* cost 13*d.* each, with 8*d.* for a warrant to the sheriff; the *distringas* and two writs of *alias distringas* were accompanied by fees of 40*d.* each time to the sheriff's bailiff for warning the jury.

[83] *Ogard* v. *Knyvet* (*c.*1545/50) Wm Yelv. 343. In *Ive* v. *Drury* (1494) CP 40/929, m. 410, it appeared that the sheriff had returned both the plaintiff's *venire* and the defendant's *venire facias cum proviso*; upon enquiry, it appeared that the defendant's writ was sued first, and so the plaintiff's was taken off the file and the panel endorsed upon it was deleted.

who happened to be present at the assizes.[84] This seems, from the posteas entered in the plea rolls, to have been common. The judges assembled in Serjeants' Inn ruled in 1557 that this procedure extended to the case where there were insufficient hundredors.[85]

CHALLENGES TO THE POLLS

Individual jurors could be challenged for favour or kinship, as well as for lack of qualification. Favour, or bias, could be demonstrated in many ways. It was rare to rely on a direct admission or prior statement of bias towards one party,[86] and again recourse was had to facts which raised inferences: for instance, that the juror was a lessee of one of the parties,[87] or his steward,[88] or had his badge,[89] or had received past favours from a party,[90] or that a party had stood godfather to the juror's child,[91] or that party and juror were fellows of the same inn of court,[92] or that a juror was a member (or related to a member) of a corporation which was party to the suit,[93] or—conversely—that the party had committed some past wrong against the juror.[94] Less clear was the case of a juror who had already tried

---

[84]　35 Hen. VIII, c. 6, s. 3, continued by 37 Hen. VIII, c. 22, and perpetuated by 2 & 3 Edw. VI, c. 32. Thomas Williams read on this statute (Inner Temple, 1558) and put numerous cases concerning *tales*: *The Excellence and Praeheminence of the Common Law asserted* (1680), 137–61. See also *Anon.* (1547/50) Wm Yelv. 341, no. 61.　　　　　　　　[85]　Ruling of the assize judges (1557) 110 Selden Soc. 412, 413.

[86]　e.g. where a juror said he would find for the party whether the matter was true or false: *Trafford's Case* (1506) Mich. 21 Hen. VII, fo. 32, pl. 21. Cf. Staunford's reading (1545), fo. 91 (bias towards the king has same effect in a criminal case).

[87]　Dudley's reading (1496), fo. 71; *Hoggeson v. Abbot of St Albans* (1490) 1 Caryll 49 at 50; *Anon.* (1491) ibid. 55, pl. 55; *Anon.* (1495) Pas. 10 Hen. VII, fo. 20, pl. 10; *Bishop of Chester's Case* (1506) Mich. 21 Hen. VII, fo. 37, pl. 46 (principal challenge); *Heigham v. Colt* (1529) Spelman 36, pl. 7; 120 Selden Soc. 76.

[88]　Dudley's reading (1496), fo. 71 (receiver or rent-gatherer); *Norris's Case* (1498) Mich. 14 Hen. VII, fo. 2, pl. 6; *Anon.* (1535) Benl. 15, pl. 17; Moore 3, pl. 7 (steward of avowant's manor); *Heigham v. Colt* (1529) 120 Selden Soc. 76 (rent-gatherer).

[89]　Dudley's reading (1496), fo. 71. For retaining by badges see above, 69–71.

[90]　*Anon.* (1529) Spelman 36, pl. 6; Wm Yelv. 315, no. 10 (treating jurors to dinner before trial).

[91]　*Dean and Chapter of Lincoln v. Prat* (1481) Mich. 21 Edw. IV, fo. 63, pl. 33, per Nele J.; *Abbot of Stratford v. Pykeryng* (1494) Mich. 10 Hen. VII, fo. 7, pl. 13; 105 Selden Soc. 277; CP 40/930, m. 323; Old Benl. 23, pl. 37; Williams's reading (1558), 165. But not vice versa: Dudley's reading (1496), fo. 71.

[92]　*Geinsford v. Gilford* (1504) Mich. 20 Hen. VII, fo. 3, pl. 10 (common membership of Gray's Inn). Cf., however, Dudley's reading (1496), fo. 71 (no challenge because (tr.) 'the juror and the party are sworn brethren, or bedfellows, or served together for twenty years with a great lord, or for familiarity').

[93]　*Dean and Chapter of Lincoln v. Prat* (1481) Mich. 21 Edw. IV, fo. 11, pl. 3; Hil. 21 Edw. IV, fo. 20, pl. 29; Pas. 21 Edw. IV, fo. 31, pl. 28; Mich. 21 Edw. IV, fo. 63, pl. 33; Williams's reading (1558), 166 (e.g. kinsman to the mayor, or any member of the commonalty, of a town, or kinsman to an abbot or monk of a religious house).

[94]　Dudley's reading (1496), fo. 71. This is a rare instance of bias against a party; the main concern was favour.

a similar case between the same parties,[95] or had given evidence in a related case,[96] or acted as an arbitrator between them,[97] since it did not follow that prior knowledge of relevant facts was evidence of bias; but the law on this question was not settled in our period. In trying a challenge for favour, no regard was to be had to the effect which taking the oath might have on the potential juror, since it was his impartiality before being sworn which was in issue.[98] The triers were not limited to finding the facts alleged in the challenge, since it was open to them to find a juror 'indifferent' (impartial) despite the establishment of the facts shown against him.[99]

EVIDENCE

A jury in theory needed no formal evidence to support their verdict,[100] since they might use their own knowledge acquired before the trial. It was on this footing that the common law did not require any particular number of witnesses to prove a fact.[101] Nevertheless, the jury had long ceased to be and were no longer regarded even in theory as being a body of witnesses. As Sir Thomas More pointed out, the jurors were judges of fact and in most cases weighed the evidence produced before them in court and based their decision upon it:[102]

I never took the twelve men for witnesses in my life; for why should I call them witnesses whose verdict the judge taketh for a sure sentence concerning the fact, without any examination of the circumstances whereby they know or be led to believe their verdict to

[95] *Anon.* (1491) 1 Caryll 55, pl. 55; *Anon.* (1503) Port 130, no. 85; *Tomson v. Robynson* (1539) CP 40/1101, m. 446d (demurrer to challenge; verdict taken *de bene esse*, but no judgment); *Anon.* (1556) BL MS. Add. 24845, fo. 31v (tr. 'In trespass for breaking a close it was awarded a good challenge that one of the jurors was previously one of the indictors of the defendant for the same trespass'); Williams's reading (1558), 167 (a principal challenge).

[96] Dudley's reading (1496), fo. 71 (good challenge in the case of positive evidence, but not if negative).

[97] *Anon.* (*c.*1511) 120 Selden Soc. 21, pl. 13 (not a peremptory challenge, if no award made). Dudley's reading (1496), fo. 71, says it is a challenge if he was nominated by one party, but not if his appointment was mutually agreed.   [98] Yorke 124, no. 95.

[99] *Hoggeson v. Abbot of St Albans* (1490) 1 Caryll 49, 50 (juror admits kinship but found indifferent); *Geinsford v. Gilford* (1505) above, n. 92; *Bishop of Chester's Case* (1506) Mich. 21 Hen. VII, fo. 37, pl. 46 (party held land of juror, but juror found indifferent). Cf. *Anon.* (1542) Gell's reports, I, Hil. 33 Hen. VIII, fo. 9v (juror found indifferent but then admitted kinship, not withdrawn but stood by).

[100] *Lucas v. Cesse* (1499) Trin. 14 Hen. VII, fo. 29, pl. 4, *per* Vavasour J.; *Reniger v. Fogassa* (1550) Plowd. 1 at 12, *per* Brooke. Cf. Hales, *Oration*, fo. 37 (quoted in 94 Selden Soc. *109*).

[101] See Wm Yelv. 333, no. 43, *per* Bromley J. Ass. ('It is requisite that there be two witnesses in those cases where a judgment is to proceed upon their depositions and declarations. But in cases where no judgment is to proceed thereon, but it is only to inform a jury or inquest according to his knowledge, there it is not requisite to have more than one witness'); *Reniger v. Fogossa* (1550) 1 Plowd at 8v, *per* Atkins, and 12, *per* Brooke (sim.). For the statutory two-witness rule introduced in 1552 for treason trials, see below, 518.

[102] More, *The Debellacyon of Salem and Bizance* (1533), sig. K5; repr. in *Complete Works of More*, x. 149 (sp. mod.).

be true? And also wherefore should I mean to call them witnesses, whom I see desire witnesses at the bar to inform them in the matter, as witnesses inform a judge?

The reality is well illustrated by a case of 1555 on Dyer's circuit, where the evidence of five or six witnesses in a criminal case was deemed to be 'weak and slender', and the trial was postponed to enable more information to be gathered.[103] Even when a particular juror did claim to have relevant personal knowledge, the other jurors were supposed to give more weight to the evidence of any witnesses sworn in court than to such informally shared information.[104] Indeed, in 1558 Thomas Williams went so far as to state that jurors were not allowed to proceed 'barely upon their own knowledge, but the parties shall be heard by their counsel and witnesses shall be sworn to give in evidence what they can for the proof or disproof of the matter in issue'.[105] Nevertheless, it was still acceptable for trial jurors to take account of their own local knowledge, in particular their knowledge of the witnesses and their character.[106]

Since the law reporters did not usually notice ordinary trials, there is little information about either the law of evidence or the ways in which facts were usually proved.[107] The usual course was for the plaintiff to begin, though this was not invariable;[108] in replevin, for instance, it was for the avowant to begin by making good the title in his avowry.[109] According to Dyer, it was the defendant's place to begin where the issue was a negative requiring affirmative evidence from the defendant. For instance, if the issue was 'Fully administered', it was for the defendant to show what he had done with the goods of the deceased; but Dyer thought even this case doubtful, because the plea ended with a negative 'nothing in his hands'.[110] Dyer's contemporary, Anthony Browne, stated the rule in 1555 to be that the party making the first affirmative was to begin, but that a 'causative negative'

---

[103] *R.* v. *Gunn* (1555) 110 Selden Soc. 406.

[104] *Anon.* (1557) 110 Selden Soc. 410; and see *Reniger* v. *Fogassa* (1550) 1 Plowd at 8v, *per* Atkins. Cf. STAC 4/10/35, where six jurors claimed that 'their own knowledge was as good to them and better' than evidence given in court.   [105] Williams's reading (1558), 18.

[106] Hales, *Oration*, fo. 37; T. A. Green, *Verdict according to Conscience* (1985), 142 n. 154 (two cases where jurors accused of perjury defended themselves on the basis that they had personal knowledge).

[107] There is a brief exposition by Richard Hesketh of Gray's Inn in Trinity Coll. Cambridge MS. R.15.7, ff. 98v–99 ('Nota bon erudytionz per Heskett'). But there are only two main points: (i) an affirmative must be strictly proved by 'matter apparent', or direct factual evidence, whereas a negative may be maintained by matter in law; (ii) justifications may not be given in evidence on the general issue.

[108] This appears from demurrers to the evidence: see below, 398. In *Aynesworth* v. *Pilkington* (1493), the defendant complained that he was required to begin, contrary to the usual order, because of favouritism: *Pilkington Narrative*, 33.

[109] *Aysshley* v. *Boxley* (1551) CP 40/1148, m. 612 (avowry for damage feasant; plaintiff alleges lease and traverses defendant's seisin in demesne; evidence concerning a chantry granted by Edward VI).

[110] *Dean and Chapter of Exeter* v. *Trewynnard* (1551–3) Dyer 80a; CP 40/1148, m. 601 (issue *Plene administravit*; defendant shows how he used the goods to pay debtors on bonds; plaintiff prays oyer of

could be treated for this purpose as an affirmative.[111] There is no mention, in these discussions, of burdens of proof; but the burden presumably fell on the party who began.

Most legal discussion of evidence in the early Tudor period concerns relevance and conformity with the issue. The courts would exclude not only evidence which was factually irrelevant but also evidence which was 'contrariant' to the issue, such as evidence of a justification when the general issue had been pleaded.[112] It was also possible for legal argument to occur 'upon the evidence', and such argument might be reported if the trial was in banc or in London.[113] But there seem to have been no exclusionary rules to prevent unsafe testimony reaching the jury. Hearsay evidence was admissible,[114] and the courts may not have been very rigorous even in enforcing the rules on relevance and consistency. Indeed, it was said at the beginning of the sixteenth century that some learned men thought it good practice to plead the general issue, so as to avoid giving prior notice of the facts on which they relied, and then 'give various dark matters in evidence so that the other party does not know what he will do, and by this means blind the jury and everyone else'.[115]

Evidence might be written or oral, though no doubt written evidence was regarded as better, and in demurrers to the evidence we encounter only written testimony. Documents proffered as matters of record—for instance, under the issue *Nul tiel record*—had to be exemplified under the great seal; but if they were merely shown as evidence of the facts recorded they were exemplified under the seal of the court which made them.[116] Written evidence was not confined to records and charters, but might include letters, bills, or merchants' books.[117]

bonds and demurs). Dyer said it was unusual in this case for the defendant to begin. See also *Peeres* v. *Bishop* (1554) Dyer 112a.

[111] Reading on jeofails (Middle Temple, 1555) BL MS. Hargrave 199, fo. 10. His example of a causative negative was special *Non est factum*; so it probably meant a negative conclusion resting on an affirmative 'cause' (such as misrepresentation).

[112] Trinity Coll. Cambridge MS. R.15.7, fo. 99, *per* Hesketh; *Browne* v. *Elmer* (1520) Trin. 12 Hen. VIII, fo. 1, pl. 1 (119 Selden Soc. 2); *Anon.* (1527) Pas. 19 Hen. VIII, fo. 6, pl 2; *Anon.* (1533) Brooke Abr., *General Issue*, pl. 82. It was occasionally complained in Chancery that an attorney had entered the general issue and thereby precluded the defendant from justifying.

[113] e.g. *Anon.* (1535) Trin. 27 Hen. VIII, fo. 20, pl. 10; *Anon.* (1536) Dyer 18a (tr. 'It was moved upon evidence by Knightley...'); Dyer 18b (tr. 'At another time this question arose upon evidence to a jury by Knightley...').

[114] In *Rolfe* v. *Hampden* (1542) Dyer 53b; CP 40/1112, m. 416; there were three witnesses to prove a will, two of them by hearsay; the evidence was admitted, but the jury rejected it. For hearsay in criminal trials see below, 518.   [115] Trinity Coll. Cambridge MS. R.15.7, fo. 99, *per* Hesketh (tr.).

[116] *Anon.* (1530) Brooke Abr., *Record*, pl. 65. The commonest instances in the Tudor period are common recoveries (below, 695) exemplified under the seal of the Common Pleas in dark green wax. In 1498 the judges refused to allow a recovery to be put in evidence without exemplification: *Pilkington Narrative*, 42.

[117] See below, nn. 123-5. For wills see *Bill* v. *Bill* (1538) CP 40/1097, m. 558; *Bisshop* v. *Somer* (1544) CP 40/1121, m. 104.

Depositions of living witnesses were probably widely used in criminal cases,[118] and it seems that they could be used in civil cases provided they were under seal.[119] In one unusual case, we even find a litigant asking Sir Thomas Cromwell to provide eye-witness evidence for him in the form of a letter to the judges.[120] If a witness appeared to be near death, his evidence could be perpetuated in written form by the Chancery,[121] and it must be assumed that depositions *in perpetuam rei memoriam* were admissible as evidence in the common-law courts.

Some difficulty must have been occasioned in practice by the rule which prevented the parties themselves from giving sworn evidence.[122] However, we learn from demurrers to the evidence that it was permissible to produce documents emanating from the parties,[123] and these did not have to be formal. Therefore a parol contract could be proved by means of a letter written by the defendant,[124] or a merchant's books.[125] Moreover, it seems from the same source that informal statements by the parties or their counsel might be treated as evidence—as in a case of 1504 where the defendant executors 'stated in evidence that no other goods or chattels belonging to the said testator came into their hands at the time when the writ was obtained or ever thereafter'.[126] Such a negative could hardly have been proved by witnesses.

MISCONDUCT OF THE JURY

The rolls sometimes record enquiries into alleged misconduct by jurors, but these are not a useful source of information about trial procedure because the only

---

[118] *Hall's Chronicle*, 623–4; Langbein, *Prosecuting Crime in the Renaissance*, 27–8.

[119] *Gynys* v. *Hille* (1518) CP 40/1021B, m. 335 (English deposition in the Marches set out in demurrer to evidence); *Broke* v. *Gardener* (1541–6) CP 40/1108, m. 354; below, 368; *Reniger* v. *Fogassa* (1550) Plowd. 1, at fo. 2 (depositions used but deponents called); *Sydenham* v. *Viscount Howard* (1569) 109 Selden Soc. 164. The unconventional English record from Calais in *Bereworth* v. *Wollar* (1551) KB 27/1158, m. 171, actually sets out the depositions in an action of debt. In *Core* v. *Whalley* (1535) CP 40/1087, m. 147 (demurrer to evidence), a notarially authenticated inventory was shown to jurors on the issue *Plene administravit*.

[120] *Viscount Lisle* v. *Debenham* (1535) CP 40/1085(1), m. 338; *Lisle Letters*, ed. Byrne, ii. 459, no. 368 (*scandalum magnatum* for words spoken in Cromwell's presence). [121] See above, 185.

[122] *Diversite de Courtz* (1530), sig. C3v, says that a party may not be sworn ('il mesme ne serra resceu a jurer'), which might be taken to mean that he could give unsworn evidence, as in criminal cases (below, 519).

[123] e.g. *Dunton* v. *Bird* (1516) KB 27/1019, m. 72d (sealed bill of sale given in evidence before Fyneux CJ at St Martin-le-Grand; plaintiff demurs to defendant's evidence showing his counterpart of the bill); *Baynard* v. *Maltby* (1525) KB 27/1054, m. 23d (pr. in 94 Selden Soc. 264 at 265; receipt); *Core* v. *Whalley* (1535) CP 40/1087, m. 147 (notarized inventory).

[124] e.g. *Buller* v. *Arundell* (1532) CP40/1073, m. 117d. See also *Russell* v. *Wareyn* (1516) CP 40/1015, m. 443 (unsealed acknowledgment of debt).

[125] e.g. *Buller* v. *Arundell* (1532) CP40/1073, m. 117d; *Tuthyll* v. *Cogan* (1540) CP 40/1104, m. 355; *Sapcotes* v. *Strangeways* (1561) 110 Selden Soc. 430. They were also used in local courts: e.g. *Dalton* v. *Pays* (1527) C47/24/16/11–14 (Staple Court of Calais).

[126] *Langtone* v. *Dyne* (1504) CP 40/969, m. 331; 2 Caryll 440 at 444.

forms of misconduct noticed were those which involved breaches of the terms of their custody after retirement from the bar. The jury bailiff was charged and sworn that he should not, without leave of the court, allow the jurors 'any bread, drink, meat, fire, or light, nor suffer the same jurors to speak to any person or persons', and that he should not speak to them himself save to enquire whether they were agreed upon their verdict.[127] The jurors themselves may have been given a similar oath.[128] If the jurors were alleged to have misbehaved, this could be investigated on oath at the request of one of the parties and the facts enrolled with the postea.[129] In case of doubt, the verdict would be taken *de bene esse* and a motion made in banc 'in arrest of verdict'—that is, in effect, what was later called a motion for a new trial.[130]

There are many recorded cases of eating and drinking by jurors, suggesting that in practice it was a common occurrence. It was indeed openly permitted with the consent of the court or of the parties.[131] But the prohibition on eating or drinking without permission was strictly enforced, on the grounds that if the jurors were given such comforts they might never agree, especially since it might enable a few dissentients to hold out against the rest.[132] The jurors and their bailiff were therefore liable to a fine for eating and drinking without permission, even if they claimed to have taken food and drink on account of the 'weakness and infirmity of their bodies and not by fraud or collusion'.[133] Ale is the beverage always

---

[127] Rast. Ent. 251 (268v); Hales, *Oration*, fo. 37; 26 Hen. VIII, c. 4 (for jurors in Wales, but embodying the common law). Cf. similar form in *Long Quinto*, fo. 61v. In an assize there were sworn keepers nominated by each party: *Lord Stafford v. Seymour* (1466–1503) CP 40/963, m. 389.

[128] *Norris's Case* (1498) Mich. 14 Hen. VII, fo. 2, pl. 5, is ambiguous (tr. 'Rede ordered the jurors to go to their house, and assigned them the place under the custody of the marshals, until the next day, and caused them to be sworn that they would not eat or drink all that day and night except at their own expenses, and would not allow them to speak with anyone until the morrow').

[129] Without a recorded 'exception' the verdict would be final: *Clerkson's Case* (*c.*1530) Yorke 126, no. 102.

[130] For 'arrest of verdict' see *Lucas v. Cesse* (1500) Hil. 15 Hen. VII, fo. 1, pl. 2; *Wodmancye v. Gyrton* (1515) Dyer 37b, §45; CP 40/1009, m. 356. When formally entered it was in the form, 'Unde predictus A non intendit quod curia hic ad captionem alicujus veredicti de juratoribus predictis super premissis procedere debet': *Re Trussell, Earl of Arundel v. Regem* (1500) KB 27/957, Rex m. 5 (verdict taken notwithstanding objection).

[131] *Norris's Case* (1498) Mich. 14 Hen. VII, fo. 1, pl. 5; *Geinsford v. Gilford* (1504) Mich. 20 Hen. VII, fo. 3, pl. 10; *Lord Zouch v. Zouch* (1533) Spelman 221, pl. 1; *Fulmerston v. Hussey* (1547) CP 40/1133, m. 403 (jurors given leave to drink *in facie curiae* in the Guildhall, Thetford, but no drink could be obtained there and so they ate and drank at their own costs after retirement; verdict taken and no punishment); St German, *Doctor and Student*, ed. Plucknett and Barton, 293.

[132] *Lucas v. Cesse* (1500) Hil. 15 Hen. VII, ff. 1–2, pl. 2, per Kebell sjt; 64 Selden Soc. 183; *Littilbury v. Pennington* (1504) Mich. 20 Hen. VII, fo. 3, pl. 8, per Brudenell sjt and Frowyk CJ.

[133] *Shukburgh v. Agard* (1497) CP 40/939, m. 305. In *Duke of Buckingham v. Lucas* (1512) CP 40/1001, m. 659, a juror said he had taken a drink of ale because of thirst and illness ('propter nimiam sitim et egritudinem quas tunc patiebatur'). A sick juror might ask the court's permission to take sustenance: see *Lord Zouch v. Zouch* (1533) Spelman 221, pl. 1 (where the parties consented but the other jurors were against it).

mentioned, though the 'bread' and 'meat' of the oath were not interpreted exclusively: it was forbidden also to eat fish, fruit, or even sweets.[134] The effect of such misconduct on the validity of a verdict was controversial in the late fifteenth century, and in the 1490s the prevailing view—the view of Bryan CJ—was that the verdict should always be quashed and a *ventre de novo* awarded.[135] Spelman records that in 1536 Fitzjames CJ and Fitzherbert J. were still adherents of this doctrine, because of the precedents.[136] However, there were earlier precedents in favour of accepting the verdict,[137] and this contrary view prevailed in two King's Bench decisions of 1499 and 1500.[138] After 1500 it was the general practice in both benches to treat eating and drinking merely as a finable offence rather than an error which could affect the verdict,[139] unless it was suspected that the provisions emanated from one of the parties,[140] and the verdict passed for the culpable party.[141]

The same principles governed the separation of the jurors before giving their verdict. They were the subject of a well-known Exchequer Chamber case of 1499,[142] where the jurors at Amesbury in a case concerning the earl of Kent, after

---

[134] *Anon.* (1474) cit. Dyer 78a (box of sugar-candy); *Re Trussell, Earl of Arundel* v. *Regem* (1500) KB 27/957, Rex m. 5; Rast. Ent. 251 (268) (comfits, dredge, sugar-candy, raisins, prunes, and dates, which the jurors had brought in their purses); *Snawsell qui tam etc.* v. *Malory* (1521) CP 40/1032A, m. 101d; Rast. Ent. 252 (268v) (a pear); *Wilson* v. *Creswell* (1523) CP 40/1040, m. 115d (bread and fish).

[135] *Lother* v. *Lancaster* (1494) CP 40/930, m. 444 (verdict taken, but no judgment after advisement); *Rogers* v. *Cotton* (1494) KB 27/932, m. 63; *Anon.* (1498) Mich. 14 Hen. VII, fo. 1, pl. 3; *Lucas* v. *Cesse* (1499) Trin. 14 Hen. VII, fo. 30, pl. 4, *per* Hody CB and Bryan CJ; *Littilbury* v. *Penington* (1504) Mich. 20 Hen. VII, fo. 3, pl. 8.

[136] *Anon.* (1536) Spelman 223, pl. 5 ('the verdict is not good where they eat before they are agreed; and it was so adjudged several times, as they said'). To the same effect is the undated note in Yorke 126, no. 102 (tr. 'Note that if the jury drink after their charge it is error, if the aggrieved party will put in his exception . . . And this was Clerkson's case, of Gray's Inn'); but there may have been suspicion of treating in this case.

[137] e.g. *Prior of Canterbury* v. *Pencrove* (1421), cited by Dyer CJ in 110 Selden Soc. 428 (1560); *Tanfeld* v. *Loche* (1485) CP 40/893, m. 157.

[138] *Lucas* v. *Cesse* (1499) Trin. 14 Hen. VII, ff. 30–31, pl. 4, *per* Tremaile J. and Fyneux CJ (as to eating and drinking after agreement); *Re Trussell, Earl of Arundel* v. *Regem* (1500) KB 27/957, Rex m. 5 (judgment given); Rast. Ent. 251 (268).

[139] *Anon.* (1509/21) Spelman 222, pl. 5 (before or after agreement); *Palmer* v. *Morton* (1510) KB 27/997, m. 69 (before agreement; here each juror took a draught of ale from a pot before the verdict was discussed); *Duke of Buckingham* v. *Lucas* (1512) CP 40/1001, m. 659 (drinking from a pot of ale before deliberation); *Barnabe* v. *Parker* (1514) CP 40/1106, m. 333 (after agreement); *Wodmancye* v. *Gyrton* (1515) CP 40/1009, m. 356, cited in Dyer 37b (after agreement); *Wilson* v. *Creswell* (1523) CP 40/1040, m. 115d; *Trolove* v. *Sheref* (1531–4) CP 40/1070, m. 308 (before agreement; court takes advisement after verdict; no judgment); *Anon.* (1536) Spelman 222, pl. 4; *Pulter* v. *Taylour* (1539) CP 40/1101, m. 432 (after agreement); *Skewes* v. *Trewynnard* (1540) CP 40/1104, m. 406; Dyer 55b (before agreement); *Anon.* (1554) Dal. 16, pl. 2; *Paul Securis's Case* (c.1558) 110 Selden Soc. 431. The cases of 1514 and 1515 were both challenged by writ of error; the 1540 case was affirmed on a writ of error.

[140] As in *Gadbury* v. *Andrewes* (1500) KB 27/957, m. 34 (where the jury remained to be taken).

[141] *Anon.* (1554) Dal. 16, pl. 2.

[142] *Lucas* v. *Cesse* (1499) Trin. 14 Hen. VII, fo. 29, pl. 4 (speeches of judges); Hil. 15 Hen. VII, fo. 1, pl. 2 (argument of Kebell sjt, presumably misdated); 64 Selden Soc. 183 (sim. text, but dated 13 Hen. VII,

being sworn, went off without leave of the court because of a thunderstorm. Although the report does not explain why this was a reason for leaving, the implication is that the assize judges were sitting in the open air or in booths and that the proceedings necessarily halted until the rain stopped.[143] Whatever the reason, it was alleged that before their return some of them had come into contact with one of the earl's supporters, who gave them a drink and told them that the earl's 'matter' was better than his opponent's. Of course this was the very problem which the sequestration of the jury was designed to prevent, though in the event the verdict went against the earl. The judges were divided. Most—including Fyneux CJ— thought the verdict should stand; the storm was arguably a sufficient excuse to leave the court, and should not in itself render the verdict void; the attempt to influence the jury might have been an objection if the verdict had gone that way, but it had not; and in any case the objection should have been taken and recorded when the jury returned and not after verdict. However, Hody CB and Bryan CJ took the view that such misconduct rendered the verdict void without reference to the possibility of corruption. The matter was left unresolved, though in a case of 1523 where the jurors were allowed to go home to bed—a sin requiring a mulct for jurors and bailiffs alike—the verdict was nevertheless accepted.[144]

There are only a few cases concerning the third branch of the oath, that which forbade communication with the jury after retirement. It was a rigid rule that no one, not even the judges, could have any private dealings with the jury once they had retired from the bar. If the jurors wished to ask questions,[145] or were to be offered fresh evidence,[146] they had to return to court so that the proceedings could take place in public. Not only speaking to other people, but receiving documents passed to them privately, were offences capable of rendering a verdict null and void.[147] However, the effect of improper communications depended on the circumstances. In 1466 the jurors in an assize had put factual questions to the keepers, had been given a penner (*calamarium*) and ink, and had then been given a draft special verdict in a bill written in English; but the formal verdict was upheld many years later on the strength of evidence that the jurors had followed their

---

from BL MS. Hargrave 105); Spelman 223 (recollected by Conyngesby J.), CP 40/940, m. 393. See also D. Seipp, 'Jurors, Evidences and the Tempest of 1499' in *The Jury in the History of the Common Law*, ed. J. W. Cairns and G. McLeod (2002), 75–92.

[143] According to Fyneux CJ, it would have been in vain for anyone to remain until the rain had stopped. On the other hand, Bryan CJ remarked that rain was a feeble reason for leaving.

[144] *Wilson* v. *Creswell* (1523) CP 40/1040, m. 115d.

[145] *Pynde* v. *Tendale* (1492) 1 Caryll 120–1; KB 27/924, m. 29; *R.* v. *Lord Dacre* (1534) Spelman 54–5.

[146] *Anon.* (1534) Trin. 26 Hen. VIII, fo. 5, pl. 24; *R.* v. *Sherwin* (1555) 110 Selden Soc. 407.

[147] e.g. *Maunde* v. *Staunton* (1525) KB 27/1056, m. 31 (assize adjourned to Serjeants' Inn; verdict quashed); *Anon.* (1555/6) Brooke Abr., *Jurors*, pl. 8 (scroll taken from plaintiff which was not delivered in open court; verdict for plaintiff quashed).

consciences rather than the bill.[148] Even in a case where the defendant offered the jury £200 for their verdict the only outcome was a fine.[149] In a case of 1507, the jurors at Oxford assizes sent one of their number under escort to follow one of the judges and the associate—whom they saw passing down the street—to ask permission to eat and drink, and while he was on this errand the others were said to have spoken with two strangers who entered the room 'by subtlety' while the door was being guarded by the other keeper; fines were imposed, but the verdict was accepted.[150] And in 1541 a jury at Hertford assizes, while locked in a house, received a paper containing an unsealed deposition of the evidence given in court, a form of assistance which had been refused on application in open court because the paper was unsealed; nevertheless, after five years of debate, the verdict was allowed to stand.[151] Likewise in 1555, when a copy of court roll was given to the jurors by a person unknown, after they had retired, without being read in court or delivered to the jurors by the justices,[152] the verdict was recorded.[153]

An obvious solution to the problem of misguided juries would have been to give the judges greater power to overturn verdicts, for instance after examining the jurors individually as to their reasons and motives.[154] Hales recommended this course, even though he acknowledged that it would prolong the circuits considerably:[155]

me thinketh that a little pain and diligence would occur and stop all these and such like mischiefs in trials if judges in their judgments upon the verdict given would examine every of the jurors ('jurates') secretly by himself of the circumstances of the matter and of the causes that moved his conscience so to give it. For commonly in every jury there be two or three doers and ringleaders, and the rest be consenters. Although the justices did thus consume ten or twelve days in the circuits, where now they bestow one or two, were this loss of time? Were this pain?

The judges, as we have seen, were not keen on such enquiries, though in criminal cases they sometimes intervened to prevent an unjust acquittal.[156] In any case, the availability in civil cases of the action of attaint, however awkward it was in

---

[148] Lord Stafford v. Seymour (Wilts. assizes, 1466), recorded in (1503) CP 40/963, m. 389.

[149] Tanfeld v. Loche (1485) CP 40/893, m. 157.

[150] Pakyngton v. Newers (1507) CP 40/982, m. 524.

[151] Broke v. Gardener (1541–6) CP 40/1108, m. 354. The jurors, and the bailiff, were fined 6s. 8d. each.

[152] These words (tr. 'never read by the court to the jurors aforesaid before the aforesaid justices nor ever delivered to the jurors aforesaid by the court') suggest that the court could allow the jurors to take documents with them when they retired.

[153] Bayspole v. Gryse (1555) CP 40/1162, m. 538. The jurors were fined 6s. 8d. each. The verdict passed against the defendant, who raised the objection; but no judgment is entered.

[154] Cf. 3 Hen. VIII, c. 12, which authorized judges to alter jury panels in criminal cases at their discretion. [155] Hales, Oration, fo. 38v (sp. mod.).

[156] e.g. Shelley v. Penyngton (1492) KB 27/925, m. 87d; 1 Caryll 98 (distringas juratores stayed because of pressure on the jurors by the appellee's adherents).

practice, was thought to tie the judges' hands. An alternative form of judicial control was exercised through the Star Chamber, in those cases where attaint was
unavailable, but it came after the event and operated by way of punishment rather
than by overturning the verdict.[157]

VERDICTS

When the jurors had heard the evidence, they received their charge from the court.
Very little is known about the nature of the directions they were given, and it is not
even certain whether judges routinely summed up the evidence. All we can say with
confidence is that a summing up was not unknown in the time of Henry VIII, and
that directions might be given both on the issue to be decided and on the damages
and costs to be assessed.[158] Among the prothonotary's papers for the Court of Pleas
at Lancaster there survive a few written instructions, in English, for the recognitors
in assizes of novel disseisin; these contain quite detailed instructions as to their
duties of enquiry, but no summing up.[159] Plowden's report of a trial in 1553 hints
that the judges only gave directions on the law if requested to do so by counsel:[160]

Portman [J.] recited the evidence to the jury and said, 'Jurors, the counsel of each party has
prayed us, the judges, to tell you what the law is in this point—whether the lord may seize
heriot-service or not; and we have discussed it together and are agreed, and take the law to
be that the lord may seize heriot-service perfectly well. Therefore take the law to be so, by
the ruling of the court.

After the charge, the parties withdrew and the jurors proceeded to consider
their verdict. It seems that very often, perhaps even as a matter of course, they
retired to a 'house' near the court for this purpose.[161] Sometimes this was a private house,[162] though in 1512 we hear of a 'house' (domus) barely twenty feet from
the bar at Henhow assizes, which was customarily used by jurors,[163] and in a case

---

[157] See below, 373.   [158] 94 Selden Soc. 112, 295.

[159] e.g. in Cauncefeld v. Thorneton (1520) PL 21/2, concerning the earl of Derby (sp. mod. 'The first
issue is if William Thorneton and John Olyver disseised Thomas Cauncefeld of two messuages . . . or
not. If ye find they did it not, say no more. If they did it, then ye shall find whether it was with force
or not, and then if it were done after the eighth year of King Henry the VI . . .').

[160] Woodland v. Mantell (1553) Plowd. 94 at 96v (tr.). This was in the King's Bench. For a detailed
direction on the law in a homicide case at the assizes see R. v. Salisbury (1553) ibid. 101.

[161] e.g. Pynde v. Tendale (1492) 1 Caryll 120; Lucas v. Cesse (1500) 64 Selden Soc. 183 n. 1; Lord Zouch v.
Zouch (1533) Spelman 221, pl. 1; Broke v. Gardener (1541) CP 40/1108, m. 354 (house in Hertford).

[162] Shukburgh v. Agard (1497) CP 40/939, m. 305 (house of John James in Warwick); Skewys v.
Trewynnard (1540) CP 40/1104, m. 406 (house of Thomas Comer in Launceston); Fulmerston v. Hussey
(1547) CP 40/1133, m. 403 (house of Robert Crane in Thetford).

[163] Duke of Buckingham v. Lucas (1512) CP 40/1001, m. 659 ('quandam domum vix viginti pedibus a
barra illa distantem ad hujusmodi juratores juratos includendos et custodiendos consuetam'). Perhaps
this was an open-air session.

of 1523 a jury was sent back to a corner of the court to discuss an award of damages.[164] When they had agreed upon their verdict, the jurors were supposed to return to the bar so that the parties could be formally called to hear the verdict. It was at this moment that the plaintiff could absent himself so that a formal nonsuit could be recorded.[165]

If the jury reached agreement after the court had risen for the day, it was permissible—in civil cases only[166]—for them to give an informal 'privy verdict' so that the restrictions on their comfort could be relaxed.[167] They then gave in their formal verdict the next day, in the usual manner, apparently after the privy verdict had been read over to them.[168] It was, however, the formal verdict which was recorded, and therefore the jury were able to change their minds overnight.[169] It followed that if the jury failed to appear in the morning, the privy verdict was not returned as a formal verdict, though the circumstances might be mentioned in the postea.[170] It is difficult to trace the history of the privy verdict, since the procedure is rarely mentioned in the plea rolls and then only indirectly.[171] The practice of reading out the privy verdict, even if the parties were not informed of the result prior to the formal announcement in open court, enabled the plaintiff to elect to be nonsuited at that stage if the verdict was against him;[172] and so it seems highly probable that the privy verdict developed in connection with the formal nonsuit procedure.[173]

[164] *Wilson* v. *Creswell* (1523) CP 40/1040, m. 115d ('juratores predicti iterum adinvicem in angulo curie transierunt'). [165] See above, 334.

[166] See Spelman 222, pl. 4; 223, pl. 6; *Note* (1530) Port 71. In *R.* v. *Rice ap Griffith* (1531) Spelman 48, the judges remained on the bench for two hours, apparently doing nothing, awaiting the return of the jury; but in that case, being commissioners *pro hac vice*, they had no power of adjournment.

[167] *Long Quinto*, fo. 61v; *Note* (1505) 2 Caryll 456, pl. 318 (single judge sent to receive it). In *Saunders* v. *Freeman* (1561) CP 40/1189, m. 1321, Dyer CJ allowed the jurors to eat and drink if they wished, 'as was the custom'.

[168] This is implicit in *Cosyn* v. *Serlys* (1534) Spelman 222, pl. 3, where the privy verdict was not read out in view of a doubt whether it was proper to take one at all.

[169] *Cosyn* v. *Serlys* (1534) Spelman 222, pl. 3 (appeal of robbery); *Anon.* (1536) Spelman 222, pl. 4 (adjourned assize); *Saunders* v. *Freman* (1561–2) CP 40/1189, m. 1321 (*quid juris clamat*; judgment after advisement); 110 Selden Soc. 430; Plowd. 210; Moo. 33; Dyer 209a; Chr. Yelverton's reports, fo. 251.

[170] *Grubbe* v. *Doddes* (1554) CP 40/1157, m. 318 (Ware summer assizes; tr. 'the same jurors returned before the same justices in the justices' room to give a secret verdict therein, and were adjourned by the same justices to appear before them in the court aforesaid at 6 a.m.').

[171] Examples are *Lord Thame* v. *Porter* (1523) CP 40/1038, m. 421 (triers of challenge could not agree before the sessions were adjourned, but later came before the justices 'et secrete veredictum suum in hac parte reddiderunt et dixerunt' that the juror was indifferent); *Saunders* v. *Freeman* (1561) CP 40/1189, m. 1321 ('secrete dixerunt super sacramentum suum quod…'). In *Fane* v. *Style* (1510) CP 40/992, m. 425, the circumstances of a privy verdict are recorded in detail.

[172] This is explicitly stated in *Rolfe* v. *Hampden* (1542) Dyer 53b ('the jury gave a privy verdict…by means of which the plaintiff was nonsuited'); *Gardiner* v. *Lovell* (1569) 109 Selden Soc. 164 ('the plaintiffs, after a privy verdict, were nonsuited').

[173] The two are discussed together in *Note* (1505) 2 Caryll 456.

Once a formal verdict had been given at the bar it could not be changed.[174] Even if the jurors had evidently miscalculated the damages, the court could not direct them to amend their verdict.[175] A Chancery litigant in the 1530s alleged that a jury at nisi prius had given a verdict contrary to their conscience, and that when they went back to the judges and asked to amend it, the judges could not and would not accept the alteration. The facts were denied by the defendant, but the underlying assumption that a verdict was absolutely final seems not to have been in dispute.[176]

A note of the verdict was indorsed on the nisi prius roll (or postea), which was a transcript of the record containing the issue—if necessary written on two or more membranes sewn together—attached to the writ of *venire facias* or other writ summoning the jury. The indorsement was usually in simple form: 'The jurors say for the plaintiff and assess damages at *n* shillings, and *p* shillings for costs'.[177] The postea was then returned to the court, with the jury panel attached, so that the record of the trial and verdict could be made up in proper form ('Postea die et loco infracontentis...'). The original posteas are still preserved in the files of both benches.

ATTAINT

Unless it could be quashed, the verdict of the jury established the facts beyond further dispute, because the judges could not reject or interfere with findings of fact. We have already noted ways in which the court could quash a verdict before giving judgment, on grounds of irregular conduct, in which case a *venire de novo* normally issued to summon a new jury. After judgment was given, it was still open to the losing party to bring an action of attaint against the first jury and the successful party, for the purposes of quashing the verdict and reversing the judgment on grounds of perjury. In conformity with the principle that decisions of fact were for jurors, the issue in attaint—the false oath of the first jury—was tried by a grand jury of twenty-four. This was not an appeal, and the procedure did not allow the plaintiff to reopen the facts with fresh evidence. Although the defendant in the attaint might bring new witnesses to support the verdict, the plaintiff was not allowed to introduce any factual evidence that was not given to the trial jury,[178] and

---

[174] Except in a capital case: *R.* v. *Archer* (1539/53) cit. at Plowd. 211.

[175] *Capell* v. *Scott* (1494) 1 Caryll 216, printed as Pas. 16 Hen. VII, fo. 6, pl. 4. But the court could perhaps press the plaintiff to remit the excess: below, 382.

[176] *Foster* v. *Pydman* (temp. Audley C.) C1/797/3–5.

[177] Files in CP 52. The form is: 'Jur[atores] dic[unt] pro quer[ente] et assid[ent] da[mpn]a ad... et pro misis ad...'. For rules indorsed on the postea see below, 393.

[178] *Tusser* v. *Walgrave* (1529) Port 69; KB 27/1073, m. 27 (verdict against petty jury but no judgment); Yorke 217, no. 344; *Rolfe* v. *Hampden* (1542) Dyer 53b; *Anon.* (1553) BL MS. Add. 24845, fo. 17; *Heydon* v. *Ibgrave* (1556) Dyer 129b; KB 27/1176, m. 150; *Anon.* (1558) BL MS. Hargrave 4, fo. 140v; MS. Harley 1624, fo. 55v.

the charge of the grand jury was to decide in its conscience whether it would have decided the case the same way.[179]

Hales and Fitzherbert regarded attaint as one of the great safeguards of the common law,[180] but it was less than effective in practice. For one thing, it was expensive, and in about 1522 a party sought relief in Chancery on the ground that he had no other remedy 'but by attaint, which is so chargeable that your said orator is not able to sue the same attaint'.[181] It was extremely difficult to make a grand jury appear.[182] An even greater problem, perhaps, was that the penalties for the petty jury were so harsh that grand juries were most unwilling to convict them.[183] In fact, only one precedent has been found in our period when the full and dread common-law judgment was pronounced: that the petty jurors be excluded from being witnesses again, and barred from their free law (the right to wage law), that their goods and chattels be forfeit to the Crown, that their lands and tenements be seized into the king's hands, wasted, and spoiled, that their wives and children should be taken away, and that they should suffer indefinite imprisonment. Mercifully, the jurors who received this sentence were able to purchase pardons.[184]

In an attempt to render attaint more workable, Parliament in 1496 simplified the procedure and reduced the penalties to a fixed monetary forfeiture, a fine, damages and costs, and loss of credence.[185] The statute lapsed but was revived in 1531.[186] There does not seem to have been any noticeable increase in the number of attaints commenced, in consequence of this legislation, but there were certainly a few more judgments,[187] and the statute may have provided the judges with a useful threat against troublesome juries.[188] There is evidence that Audley C., by the late 1530s, thought the reform had gone too far in the wrong direction; but the legislation remained in place.[189]

---

[179] *Rolfe* v. *Hampden* (1542) Dyer 53b–54a, *per* Shelley J.

[180] Hales, *Oration*, fo. 38; *Marmyon* v. *Baldwyn* (1527) BL MS. Hargrave 388, fo. 234v, *per* Fitzherbert J. (quoted at 94 Selden Soc. *118*).   [181] *Rychardson* v. *Wyberd* (*c.*1522) C1/561/58.

[182] Examples of attaints which were discontinued when the grand jury failed to appear are KB 27/985, m. 97; KB 27/995, m. 27; KB 27/1000, m. 36; KB 27/1034, m. 42; KB 27/1037, m. 75; KB 27/1052, m. 60. There are many others.

[183] Hales, *Oration*, fo. 38v. Cf. T. Smith, *De Republica Anglorum* (1583), 90.

[184] *Guldeford* v. *Gaynesford* (1504–5) KB 27/975, m. 24 (judgment in attaint); KB 27/979, m. 65 (second judgment in attaint); Maycote, *Entries*, fo. 28v; 2 Caryll 517; Mich. 20 Hen. VII, fo. 3, pl. 10; *CPR 1494–1509*, pp. 468–9.

[185] The same Parliament extended attaint to the city of London: 11 Hen. VII, c. 21.

[186] 11 Hen. VII, c. 24; continued by 12 Hen. VII, c. 2; 1 Hen. VIII, c. 11 (lapsed); 23 Hen. VIII, c. 3.

[187] *Conyngesby* v. *Edmundes* (1532) CP 40/1074, m. 442; *Gaynesforde* v. *Gressham* (1543) CP 40/1116, m. 414 (damages reduced); *Raye* v. *Swanne* (1556) KB 27/1178, m. 31 (successful attaint of jury for verdict in the mayor's court of Cambridge).

[188] For an example of the statute being used as a threat in 1498, see *Pilkington Narrative*, 43.

[189] Elton, *Reform and Renewal*, 153. The 1531 act was continued by 33 Hen. VIII, c. 17; 37 Hen. VIII, c. 23; revived and perpetuated by 13 Eliz. I, c. 25.

Attaint was not available in cases where the king was party, such as criminal prosecutions and *qui tam* actions or informations.[190] In these cases the only recourse was to the extraordinary justice of the Council. The Star Chamber took upon itself to punish jurors for perjury, a power which the trial judges themselves could not exercise.[191] Perjury, in this context as in others, almost certainly implied a deliberate disregard for the jurors' oath, typically as a result of corruption, rather than merely disregarding a judge's directions.[192] Punishment of jurors by the Star Chamber was well established in criminal cases in the time of Henry VII,[193] and was mentioned in a statute of 1534.[194] A good number of criminal juries were brought before the Star Chamber in the early Tudor period, but the proceedings were always to punish the offending jurors; their verdict of acquittal could not be reversed by any court. The most celebrated acquittal in our period was that of Sir Nicholas Throgmorton, who was discharged after a state trial for treason in Westminster Hall, to the jubilation of the populace. The jurors were promptly punished for their supposed perversity, but Throckmorton remained a free man.[195]

There was some thought of extending the jurisdiction to civil cases, in order to provide an effective alternative to attaint. As early as 1508 there is an example of a jury being brought before the Council for a verdict given between private parties, though the suit was dismissed because the complainant showed no clear evidence of perjury.[196] In 1539, two civil juries were committed to the Fleet prison for perjury,[197] and there were one or two further examples in the 1540s. However, in 1551 the Star Chamber dismissed such an action on the ground that the proper and only mode of challenging a civil verdict was by writ of attaint,[198] and this decision seems to have been observed thereafter.[199]

---

[190] *Tay* v. *Toft* (1505) Mich. 20 Hen. VII, fo. 5, pl. 16. The only recourse in such cases was to the Star Chamber: e.g. *Cheseman's Case* (1546) HEHL MS. EL 2652, fo. 17v (Exchequer information); *Quarles's Case* (1557) ibid. (information for forestalling).

[191] *Note* (1554/5) Dalison's reports, BL MS. Harley 5141, fo. 27; Dal. 18, pl. 10.

[192] Some evidence from the 1550s is set out in Green, *Verdict according to Conscience*, 141–2.

[193] There are examples from 1498 in 75 Selden Soc. 69, 74. Another instance occurred in 1507, when Fyneux CJ ordered a Kent jury to appear in Council, and the JPs were summoned to bring the evidence: DL 5/2, ff. 103v, 104v.

[194] 26 Hen. VIII, c. 5 (referring only to the acquittal of felons).

[195] *R.* v. *Throgmorton* or *Throckmorton* (1554) 1 St. Tr. 869, Dyer 90b, Dal. 13; KB 8/29; KB 29/197, m. 33; *Att.-Gen.* v. *Lucar* (1554) 1 St. Tr. 901; 109 Selden Soc., p. lxxxix n. 39, and p. 12.

[196] *Higham* v. *Higham* (1508) DL 5/4, ff. 119v, 132v (writ of entry *dum non fuit compos mentis*).

[197] *Skidmore* v. *Dawbery* (1539) HEHL MS. EL 2657 (detinue, but concerning the customs); *Ayson* v. *Mason* (1539) HEHL MS. EL 2768, fo. 23v (debt).

[198] *Hyndemershe's Case* (1551) HEHL MS. EL 2652, fo. 17v.

[199] *Lowe* v. *Sumpter* (1556) 109 Selden Soc. 15, pl. 28 (held on demurrer, 'they are not compellable to answer, because it was the particular and private suit of the party'); *Anon.* (1557) BL MS. Hargrave 216, fo. 147 (sp. mod. 'in civil causes the party grieved with a false verdict is driven to his attaint against the jury, for this court will not meddle in such cases'); *Shelgar's Case* (1560) Hudson, *Star Chamber*, 76. In the first case, the plaintiff did bring an attaint: *Lowe* v. *Sumpter* (1556) KB 27/1180, m. 60 (process only).

20

Damages and Costs

As part of their verdict, if they found wholly or partly for the plaintiff, the jury in most actions were required to assess the damages occasioned by the defendant's wrong and also the costs laid out by him in prosecuting his suit. The costs were regarded as part of the damages, and the plaintiff could ask for the damages and costs to be awarded jointly if he so wished.[1] Whether or not the award was composite, the total sum was limited to the sum laid in the 'Et dampnum habet...' clause of the declaration, and it was therefore advisable for a plaintiff to overestimate the possible future costs when laying his damages.[2] In practice composite awards were unusual, and nearly all verdicts found the costs separately. In actions such as trespass or waste where a number of different wrongs were complained of, the plaintiff could ask for the damages themselves to be 'severed'—that is, specified separately in the verdict. This had obvious advantages if part of the claim was upset for any reason.[3] For the same reason, the damages could be severed against joint defendants.[4] But it was not necessary for damages to be severed in such cases,[5] and in fact it was uncommon.

The assessment of damages was seen as an exercise in establishing facts rather than applying law. The plaintiff did not have to explain in his declaration how he arrived at the sum laid as damages, and so it was purely a matter of evidence off the record. Even if it became necessary to assess damages where the parties had not pleaded to an issue triable by jury, as in the case of a demurrer adjudged for

---

[1] *Anon.* (1496) Port 21, 56. It was the plaintiff's election, not the defendant's: *Nelinger's Case* (1479) Hil. 18 Edw. IV, fo. 23, pl. 4.

[2] *Bigott* v. *Rydley* (1497) 1 Caryll 338; KB 27/941, m. 25 (counts for £40; jury awards £40 damages and £10 costs; verdict said to be void as to £10); *Durel* v. *Ylues* (1498) Hil. 13 Hen. VII, fo. 16, pl. 17 (counts for 20 marks; jury awards 22 marks damages and costs; judgment for 20 marks); *Brograve* v. *Sprever* (1501) KB 27/961, m. 39 (counts for £10; verdict for £7 damages and £8 costs; judgment for £10); *Barley* v. *Hunwicke* (1563) 109 Selden Soc. 86. See also Rast. Ent. 172 (173v) (plaintiff waives excess).

[3] Note at Grene's reading (Inner Temple, c.1490) *Moots*, 213; *Anon.* (1523/4) Port 79. Cf. the difficulty caused by unsevered verdicts in *Sheffield* v. *Percy* (1490) Pas. 11 Hen. VII, fo. 19, pl. 4 (misdated); CP 40/915, m. 95; KB 27/921, m. 29 (affirmed); *Radclyff* v. *Penyngton* (1491) 1 Caryll 61; KB 27/917, m. 56; *Anon.* (1494) 2 Caryll 262; Trin. 9 Hen. VII, fo. 3, pl. 4.

[4] Pas. 6 Hen. VII, fo. 1, pl. 2; *Anon.* (1560) 109 Selden Soc. 34 (separate damages but joint costs).

[5] See *Sutton* v. *Forster* (1483) Mich. 22 Edw. IV, fo. 29, pl. 10; Trin. 1 Edw. V, fo. 5, pl. 11; Mich. 1 Ric. III, 64 Selden Soc. 56, pl. 20; CP 40/882, m. 349 (damages of £58).

the plaintiff or a judgment by default, the assessment was made by a jury summoned for the purpose by a writ of inquiry.[6] The jury upon a writ of inquiry appeared before the sheriff in the county, and the sheriff returned the award to the court. There was no opportunity for the court to direct such a jury; and if no direction was needed in that case, it may be presumed that none was needed at trials.[7] It follows from the absence of pleadings or reported directions that—despite the large number of recorded awards of damages—there was virtually no law relating to their assessment in the early modern period. The principal exception to this was the case of debt, where the wrong consisted solely in withholding a known sum of money. Here the court was able to assess the damages itself, in the absence of a verdict, and commonly did so.[8] The usual practice in the case of judgments by default was for the court to assess a conventional sum, such as 6s. 8d., without severing the costs.[9] But the court would not assess damages in debt or detinue for fungibles, where a writ of inquiry was needed because of possible changes in value.[10] Yet the court was, in those cases, willing to give guidance as to the effect of inflation,[11] and in this context we find a reference to a judicial direction at assizes in 1558.[12]

REFORMS IN THE LAW OF COSTS

The law relating to costs underwent significant changes in the early Tudor period. There was no principle of common law that a court could award costs, but it had been established by the Statute of Gloucester 1278 that wherever damages were recovered the jury could award costs as part of the damages, and this was the invariable practice thereafter.[13] Costs were also recoverable by statute in certain real actions. But in forms of action where damages were not recoverable in 1278, such as *quare impedit* and waste,[14] or writs of error, no costs could be awarded by

---

[6] e.g. Spelman 108 (default), 255 (demurrer). Cf. *Moots*, 315, where Brudenell hints at the possibility that judges could assess the damages upon a demurrer. This is denied in *Anon.* (1535) Pas. 27 Hen. VIII, fo. 2, pl. 8.

[7] For an example of a general charge as to damages see *Strete* v. *Yardley* (1528) Wm Yelv. 313, no. 8 (trial at bar).   [8] An example in print is *Ernley* v. *Garth* (1491) CP 40/913, m. 411; Port 96 at 99.

[9] In the Common Pleas in the year 1535, 6s. 8d. was awarded in 27 out of 56 cases of judgment by default. The lowest sum given was 3s. 4d., and the largest £6. 13s. 4d.

[10] *Anon.* (1495) Mich. 11 Hen. VII, fo. 5, pl. 20.

[11] *Anon.* (1524) Spelman 87, pl. 11 (in debt, the jury may have regard to an increase in value between the contract and the delivery date; query as to a decrease); *Anon.* (1558) 109 Selden Soc. 419, pl. 57 (in detinue, the jury may have regard to a decrease in value).

[12] *Anon.* (1558) 109 Selden Soc. 419, pl. 57.

[13] The king, however, could never recover damages or costs: Yorke 123, no. 90; Caryll (Jun.) 386, no. 36, *per* Englefield J.

[14] *Doreward* v. *Ingow* (1451) Trin. 27 Hen. VI, fo. 10, pl. 7; *Anon.* (1497) 1 Caryll 349; *Anon.* (undated), Spelman 82, pl. 6; *Anon.* (*c.*1514/16) Lincoln's Inn MS. Misc. 486, §7a (tr. 'adjudged at York within the

virtue of the statute. This was true even of statutes which provided for penal actions of debt, because the cause of action was statutory and not common-law debt.[15] Nor were costs recoverable if proceedings to recover damages did not in fact end in an award of damages, as where the suit was discontinued, or the plaintiff was nonsuited,[16] or the defendant won the verdict. And there was no provision for a successful defendant to be awarded any costs in an action at law, though they were available in Chancery[17] and Star Chamber.[18]

The first reform came in a statute of 1487,[19] which entitled successful defendants in writs of error to recover their costs in the event of a judgment to affirm the court below or of a discontinuance or nonsuit. The purpose was to discourage vexatious litigants from delaying execution by means of unfounded writs of error, and to this end the statute also gave the defendant damages 'for his delay and wrongful vexation'.[20] This was a model for further legislation, since it acknowledged the justice of awarding costs to a successful defendant, or to a defendant who had been vexed by an action which was not pursued to its end.

The next reform was suggested by the back-to-front nature of replevin, in which the defendant (or avowant) was in effect the claimant. This was another obvious case in which a defendant ought to be allowed costs, and it was enacted in 1515 that successful defendants in replevin should have 'their damages and costs that they have sustained, as the plaintiff should have done' if he had won.[21] A particular reason for this reform, touched upon in the preamble, was the increasing difficulty in making avowries. Unlike the 1531 statute, to be considered presently, but following the precedent of 1487, the replevin legislation allowed the court to award damages for the vexation and delay as well as costs. Two undesirable gaps in the 1515 legislation soon emerged, as a result of careless or unduly cautious drafting. In the first place, it only applied where the avowry or acknowledgment

last two years'); *Anon.* (1530) Hil. 22 Hen. VIII, Brooke Abr., *Costes*, pl. 25, *per* Spelman J. Cf. Mich. 5 Edw. IV, fo. 7, pl. 13 (waste).

[15] *Anon.* (1543/4) Brooke Abr., *Costes*, pl. 32; *Damages*, pl. 200.

[16] *Prestall* v. *Champion* (1500/30) Spelman 82, pl. 5.

[17] See *Fitzherbert* v. *Welles* (1529/32) C1/634/7 (Fitzherbert, having borne the costs of three defendants in another suit, seeks a contribution). The authority was probably the statute 17 Ric. II, c. 6.

[18] e.g. *Bromwich's Case* (1510) BL MS. Lansdowne 639, fo. 33; *Debyn* v. *Duelly* (1512) ibid., fo. 43; *Chichester* v. *Billon* (1517) ibid., fo. 57v. It remained a wider jurisdiction than the later statutory provisions: e.g. *Brereton* v. *Bolton* (1557) BL MS. Harley 2143, fo. 5v (costs of counsel awarded where plaintiff failed to attend hearing).

[19] 3 Hen. VII, c. 10, confirmed by 19 Hen. VII, c. 20 (because the former act had 'not been as yet duly put in execution'). The statute had the effect of giving damages and costs in error upon *quare impedit*, though no costs were recoverable at first instance: *Wadham* v. *Rogers* (1529) 120 Selden Soc. 78; *Henslow* v. *Keble* (1552) Dyer 77a.

[20] For precedents of the form of entry, see *Hussey* v. *Huse* (1523) Spelman 300; KB 27/1047, m. 30; *Southwull* v. *Huddelston* (1524) Port 90, 95; *Logat* v. *Bulle* (1529) Spelman 253; KB 27/1073, m. 70; *Lomnor* v. *Byrde* (1532) Spelman 115, 310; KB 27/1071, m. 70.   [21] 7 Hen. VIII, c. 4, s. 2.

was for 'rent, custom, or service'. Second, a verdict had to be found for the defendant, or the plaintiff 'otherwise barred';[22] it did not, therefore, apply in the case
of a nonsuit.[23] The principal gaps were supplied by a statute of 1529,[24] which
extended the remedy to the case of a successful avowry for damage feasant, and
allowed costs in the case of a nonsuit in replevin. The damages and costs were
assessed by jury, where the nonsuit occurred after the jury were charged,[25] and in
practice the court sometimes added an increment for costs as well.[26] The remedy
was still not quite comprehensive, because the statutes did not extend to a count
upon *uncore detient*.[27]

The preparation of the 1529 legislation doubtless suggested the more radical
reform which came in 1531, to the great potential benefit of defendants generally.[28]
Now it was enacted that, from Lady Day 1531, if any plaintiff in forcible entry
(upon the statute of 5 Richard II), covenant, debt on a bond or contract,[29] detinue,
account, action on the case, or action on a statute, was nonsuited after the appearance of the defendant, or if a verdict passed against him, the defendant should
'have judgment to recover his costs'. If the plaintiff was a pauper, he was to be
punished instead—though no example of this has been found in the rolls.[30]

---

[22] e.g. by demurrer: *George* v. *Sedler* (1522) Spelman 81; CP 40/1036, m. 469. Or upon nonsuit in
second deliverance, because this was a 'bar': *Gylby* v. *Saunders* (1524–5) Spelman 81; Brooke Abr.,
Retorne de avers, pl. 37; *Seconde deliveraunce*, pl. 15; CP 40/1035, m. 543; *Anon.* (1527) Spelman 81; Pas.
19 Hen. VIII, fo. 8, pl. 11; Trin. 19 Hen. VIII, fo. 11, pl. 7; *Abell* v. *Heron* (1528) CP 40/1059, m. 506; *Partridge* v.
Straunge (1553) Plowd. 77 at fo. 82.

[23] *Adurley* v. *Kendall* (1529) KB 27/1071, m. 31 (jury assess damages and costs after nonsuit in
replevin, but court gives judgment for defendant without damages or costs). This case may have
prompted the statute.

[24] 21 Hen. VIII, c. 19, s. 2; *Anon.* (1556) Dyer 141b, §46.

[25] e.g. *Longysford* v. *Speccolt* (1533) CP 40/1079, m. 326 (40s. damages, £8 costs); *Welsshe* v. *Dewentre*
(1533) ibid., m. 451d (40d. damages, £6 costs, but 40s. remitted); *Cowarne* v. *Acton* (1535) CP 40/1085(2),
m. 303 (nonsuit at assizes; damages and costs for the defendant assessed by the jury, with increment at
the justices' discretion); *Leeke* v. *Baxster* (1535) CP 40/1086, m. 454 (nonsuit at assizes; 3s. 4d. damages
and 3s. 4d. costs awarded to the defendant, with increment of £6. 6s. 8d.; writ of error received, 1541).

[26] e.g. *John* v. *Horsmonden* (1532) CP 40/1075, m. 502 (12d. damages, 40s. costs, 59s. increment); *Hyll*
v. *Roger* (1533) CP 40/1078, m. 420 (26s. 8d. damages, 13s. 4d. costs, 26s. 8d. increment); *Wolston* v. *Miles*
(1533) CP 40/1079, m. 452 (2d. damages, 20s. costs, 20s. increment). The court charged the jury to assess
the damages 'both by reason of the foregoing and for the outlay and costs' (tr.).

[27] *Robyns* v. *Beston* (1531) Spelman 82.

[28] 23 Hen. VIII, c. 15. The Harleian text of James Hales's important reading on this statute (Gray's
Inn, 1532) does not deal with costs as such, but with the forms of action in which a defendant's costs
were now permitted. However, some of the reader's cases in BL MS. Hargrave 253 do touch on the law
of costs.

[29] It was made clear by 24 Hen. VIII, c. 8, that this was not to extend to actions of debt brought by
informers to the king's use. But it was decided that it applied to debt for rent, because a lease was a
'contract': *Rokyngham* v. *Ketell* (1542) CP 40/1112, m. 112; *Anon.* (1554/5) Brooke Abr., *Costes*, pl. 23.

[30] Paupers were excused from paying the court fees if they sued *in forma pauperis*, though recorded
examples are surprisingly rare: e.g. *Rede* v. *Appowell* (1539) KB 27/1113, m. 29d.

A glaring and presumably deliberate omission in the statute was the action of trespass,[31] and it seems probable that this omission was designed to protect the fictitious bill of Middlesex procedure from attracting costs. The wording also circumscribed the award of costs in actions of debt, since it referred only to bonds made to the plaintiff or contracts made with the plaintiff; this excluded debt on a record, or for arrears of an account, and also actions of debt by executors or administrators.[32] Moreover, since the statute spoke of actions brought by a person or persons, it was held not to sanction the award of costs against a plaintiff corporation.[33]

The statute was put into effect at once. In 1532, two defendants in an action on the case for slander recovered 20s. costs jointly, upon the statute, after a nonsuit at the assizes, though not before the court had taken advisement.[34] In 1533, the defendant in an action of debt to recover costs awarded under the 1531 Act pleaded that he had already commenced error to reverse the judgment, but the court held that the action nevertheless lay. Indeed, Fitzherbert J. took the rather pedantic view that the costs would be recoverable by the terms of the statute even if the judgment was reversed.[35] After a few years, however, awards seem to have become relatively scarce and mostly confined to cases where there was a formal nonsuit— in which case there was probably an agreement as to costs.[36] There are very few enrolled judgments for defendants in any case, and it may be that the threat of a judgment for costs simply became another factor in prompting informal settlements out of court.

THE CONTROL AND MITIGATION OF AWARDS

The general principle that the judges knew nothing of the facts of a case usually prevented them from interfering directly with the jury's award of damages or costs. But in reality there were a number of ways in which excessively high or low awards could be modified.

[31] This is pointed out in Yorke 110, no. 61.

[32] Yorke 109, no. 61; *Allen* v. *Allein* (1537) Benl. 19; Hales's reading in Gray's Inn (1532) BL MS. Hargrave 253, fo. 11.   [33] Hales's reading (1532) BL MS. Hargrave 253, ff. 11, 11v.

[34] *Alyn* v. *Tregean* (1532–3) CP 40/1075, m. 501. This did not deter the plaintiff from bringing a second action in 1533: CP 40/1079, m. 455 (issue).

[35] *Playfote* v. *Cokkys and Argall* (1532) CP 40/1074, m. 316 (defendants awarded costs); *Cokkys and Argall* v. *Playfote* (1533–7) CP 40/1079, m. 515 (demurrer in debt on the judgment, which had not been reversed); KB 27/1089, m. 38 (error; no judgment); Dyer 32a.

[36] e.g. *Humfrey* v. *Cook* (1532–3) CP 40/1074, m. 313 (debt on a contract; defendant prays costs; no judgment); *Holgyll* v. *Baynard* (1535) CP 40/1086, m. 538 (covenant; defendant recovers 33s. 4d.); *Maynard* v. *Dyce* (1542) KB 27/1125, m. 110 (*assumpsit*; defendant recovers 40s.). Cf. *Petyt* v. *Lacye* (1539) KB 27/1113, m. 37 (recovers £4 after verdict for defendant in action on the case); *Chaunsy* v. *Tyson* (1541) KB 27/1121, m. 135 (trover; plaintiff defaults at trial; defendant recovers 40s.).

Where inadequate damages were awarded, the plaintiff's remedy was to abstain from praying judgment and to commence a fresh action, because he was not allowed an attaint.[37] However, the court could increase the damages in cases of personal injury where the injury could be inspected by the judges themselves.[38] This was well established in appeals of mayhem, and it was established in the 1550s that it could be done in actions of battery as well.[39] Sometimes the court would give reasons for the increase, such as the seriousness of losing a hand.[40] Although the rationale for overriding the jury in such cases was that the court could form a judgment by its own inspection, the court was not confined to eye-witness evidence but could take account of consequential loss and of medical evidence.[41]

The court had a much larger discretion to increase costs,[42] and this was done in the majority of cases when entering judgment. The form of entry was that the plaintiff should recover the damages and costs assessed by the jury 'and also n shillings adjudged by the court here to the plaintiff, at his request, for his outlay and costs aforesaid, by way of increment'.[43] Sometimes the jurors assessed the costs at a conventional sum, such as 20s., and the real taxation was left for the court in banc. For the purposes of taxation the plaintiff probably had to submit a written statement of the items of expenditure; several such bills of costs survive among the papers of the Court of Pleas at Lancaster.[44] The advantage of postponing the taxation was that the

[37] Anon. (undated) Spelman 22.

[38] e.g. Mynes v. Causton (1487) KB 27/903, m. 14d (award of 20s. for loss of two fingers increased by £5. 13s. 4d., tr. 'inasmuch as the mayhem appeared to the lord king's court here').

[39] Trypcony v. Chynnowith (1554) KB 27/1169, m. 84; Dyer 105a (jury award of £40 for cutting off hand increased to £100); Goffeton v. Puttrell (1555) CP 40/1164, m. 314 (jury award of £6 for battery doubled because a blow on the head had lost the plaintiff a great part of his memory and several bones of his brain-pan). Cf. More v. Fowler (1532) Yorke 197, no. 280, which says the principle does not extend to trespass 'for the trespass does not appear to them'; but the distinction seems to turn on the visibility of the injury rather than the form of action.

[40] e.g. Custe v. Tempest (1508) KB 27/986, m. 31 (damages increased from £22. 13s. 4d. to £44, for loss of use of right leg and left hand, because the maiming seemed to the court to be serious and quite horrible); Rast. Ent. 46; Betson v. Crips (1518) KB 27/1026, m. 69 (damages increased from £4 to £10. 13s. 4d. for loss of the index and middle fingers); Baryngton v. Baker (1532) 93 Selden Soc. 82; More v. Fowler (1532) Yorke 197, no. 280; Lye v. Shelton (1541) KB 27/1121, m. 127 (damages of £23. 6s. 8d. doubled because plaintiff had lost four fingers of left hand and thereby the use of his hand); Trypcony v. Chynnowith (1554) KB 27/1169, m. 84; Dyer 105a (£40 damages increased to £100 because they were too low, in that it appeared by inspection that he had lost the use of his right hand and right arm, and was seriously injured in his body). Cf. the brain damage found in Goffeton v. Puttrell (1555), last note.

[41] Anon. (1533) Spelman 82, pl. 5 (steward of courts maimed in both hands so that he lost his living); perhaps the same as Baryngton v. Baker, last note; More v. Fowler (1532) KB 27/1085, m. 74 (damages increased from £46. 13s. 4d. to £86. 13s. 4d. after consulting seven surgeons); Yorke 197, no. 280.

[42] Anon. (1535) Pas. 27 Hen. VIII, fo. 2, pl. 8. This had been common in the fifteenth century: 94 Selden Soc. 115 n. 1.

[43] Cf. the simpler form in Pennyng v. Blakborn (1488) KB 27/906, m. 30d (tr. 'and thereupon, at the petition of the aforesaid P, the court here increased his damages for his outlay and costs...').

[44] The earliest noticed was from 1534 (in PL 21/3). There was a standard counsel's fee of 3s. 4d., and attorneys received 20d. a term. The bills do not name the counsel, attorneys, and officials.

court in banc could take account of costs incurred between the verdict and judgment, and of incidental expenses such as the costs of defending successfully a Chancery suit brought by the opponent to delay the principal action.[45] The sums awarded were not usually large. In Hilary term 1535, the average costs awarded by juries in the Common Pleas were 30s.; eight awards were increased to 40s. or more, but the largest award (66s. 8d.) was reduced by the court to 30s.[46] However, although usually adjustments were modest, there are cases of very substantial increases which raise at least a suspicion that the court could have used this procedure as a pretext for increasing the damages.[47]

The court was more frequently faced with awards of damages which were alleged to be excessive. Here they had no general power of mitigation,[48] because the aggrieved defendant had the remedy of an attaint against the jury.[49] An attaint to reduce the damages, though very rare, was still a practicable possibility. In 1529, for example, an attaint jury found that the petty jury in a trespass action had found damages of £40 when they should have been no more than £5; but the King's Bench took advisement, and no judgment was entered.[50] In 1543, however, judgment was given in the Common Pleas against a petty jury for assessing damages at £8, which was 4 marks too high.[51] More frequent and more effective than the cumbrous and draconian attaint was the procedure for adjustment in court before judgment was entered. The records frequently record that the plaintiff, having recovered damages, freely ('gratis') remitted part or all of them. The word 'freely' may represent some kind of truth, though sometimes it looks as though the plaintiff's benevolence may have been the result of a settlement under which the defendant agreed to confess the action if the plaintiff would waive damages.[52]

---

[45] Anon. (1482) Hil. 21 Edw. IV, fo. 78, pl. 20; Brooke Abr., Costes, pl. 22. As to successive actions in the same court, cf. Moots, 100; Port 161, no. 61.

[46] From an analysis of CP 40/1084. Four were increased to 40s. (from 8d., 2s., 20s., and 26s. 8d.); one to 45s. (from 5s.); one to 53s. 4d. (from 40s.); one to 60s. (from 20s.); and one to £6. 13s. 4d. (from 13s. 4d.).

[47] e.g. Vyllers v. Mylner (1536) CP 40/1091, m. 549 (20d. damages for trespass, with 3s. 4d. costs; court awards 66s. 8d. increment); Kendall v. Copston (1537) CP 40/1092, m. 128 (1d. damages and debt of £10, with 12s. costs; court awards 30s. increment); Salter v. Holte (1543) KB 27/1126, m. 60 (20d. damages for false imprisonment, with 5s. costs; court awards £10 increment).

[48] Anon. (1535) Pas. 27 Hen. VIII, fo. 2, pl. 8; Bonham v. Lord Stourton (1554) Dyer 105a; CP 40/1158, m. 609 (300 marks awarded for defamation, judgment for plaintiff, with an increment for costs); Anon. (1558) BL MS. Harley 1624, fo. 80; MS. Hargrave 4, fo. 139.

[49] An unsuccessful example, where the plaintiff lost because he had released part of the damages, is Anon. (1488) Mich. 14 Hen. VII, fo. 5, pl. 11 (King's Bench).

[50] Tusser v. Walgrave (1529) Port 69; KB 27/1073, m. 27. See also Spelman 22 (undated note).

[51] Gaynesforde v. Gressham (1543) CP 40/1116, m. 414. The jurors were adjudged to forfeit £5 each, half to the king.

[52] e.g. Earl of Cumberland v. Crakanthorp (1532) CP 40/1073, m. 323, 328 (confession at the assizes); Hungerford v. Temmys (1535) CP 40/1084, m. 301 (writ of inquiry not returned; court awards £40 damages at prayer of plaintiff, who then remits the whole); Abbot of Bermondsey v. Warham (1535) CP 40/1085(2), m. 143 (remits all damages on non potest dedicere in annuity); Lord Scrope v. Nevell (1542)

It was also common for plaintiffs in debt on a bond to waive part of the debt when obtaining judgment by default,[53] which suggests some kind of collusion.[54] An agreed settlement seems a strong inference in those cases where the defendant withdrew a demurrer and suffered a judgment by *non potest dedicere*.[55] In other cases we sometimes see very substantial sums being waived, apparently in return for a confession.[56] Here we may guess at the exertion of some pressure to abate a penalty, rather than a dispute as to the facts or the law.

A less frequently used formula explicitly refers to pressure from the court: 'it appears to the same justices that the aforesaid P will mitigate his damages... reasonably releasing somewhat before judgment is given therein, and so he is told to do so; and the same P freely remits... and prays judgment for the residue'.[57] This may have been proper only in the case of damages found upon writs of inquiry, where it was allowed on the footing that the defendant could not bring an attaint.[58] But instances may be found of its use after verdict,[59] especially in cases

---

CP 40/1115, m. 553 (remits all damages on *non potest dedicere* after repleader in *quare impedit*, and defendant in return releases all errors); *Poyner* v. *Chorleton* (1556) Dyer 135a ('at length the plaintiff relinquished his damages and had judgment'). See also *Pilkington Narrative*, 43 (damages awarded by a partial jury abated by half).

[53] An earlier example than those below is *Covert* v. *Kyrton* (1502) CP 40/961, m. 156 (defendant does not deny debt of £40 but plaintiff remits 40 marks).

[54] The following nine examples were noted in 1535: CP 40/1084, m. 133d (remits £4 of £6. 13s. 4d. upon confession), m. 134 (remits all damages of 10s. when debt of £34. 6s. 8d. recovered upon confession; writ of error received, 1539), m. 141d (remits £4. 13s. 4d. of debt of £20 upon bond for payment of £8. 13s. 4d.); CP 40/1085(1), m. 132d (remits £15 of debt of £20 recovered by verdict upon default); CP 40/1086, m. 108 (remits £22. 6s. 8d. of £48 recovered upon *non est informatus*), m. 302 (after judgment on *non potest dedicere*, remits £12 of £30 upon bond for payment of £12; writ of error received, 1537), m. 331 (remits £3. 6s. 8d. of £13. 6s. 8d. recovered by verdict); CP 40/1087, m. 308 (after judgment on *non potest dedicere*, remits £26. 13s. 4d. of £66. 13s. 4d.), m. 424 (after judgment upon *non potest dedicere*, remits £15 of £40 upon a bond to perform an award to pay £21).

[55] e.g. *Vaughan* v. *Caldecot* (1543) CP 40/1116, m. 305 (remits £40. 6s. 8d. of 100 marks); *Hawes* v. *Copwoode* (1543) CP 40/1117, m. 422 (remits £14 of £30); *Redman* v. *Denham* (1554) KB 27/1171, m. 169 (remits £45. 13s. 4d. of £66. 13s. 4d.).

[56] e.g. *Thomas* v. *Walsche* (1538) CP 40/1097, m. 323d (remits £80 of £100 upon *non est informatus*); *Altham* v. *Rope* (1552) KB 27/1164, m. 122 (remits £200 of £433. 6s. 8d. upon *non potest dedicere*). Cf. *Beryton* v. *Chapleyn* (1524) CP 40/1044, m. 114d (remits 26s. 8d. of 40s. upon *nihil dicit*; both parties were attorneys).

[57] e.g. *Apsley* v. *Bishop of Chichester* (1512) CP 40/1000, m. 320 ('Super quo videtur justiciariis hic quod predictus P mitigabit dampna sua predicta, aliquid inde rationabiliter defalcando sive relaxando priusquam judicium inde reddant, per quod dictum est ei per curiam quod sic faciat etc. Et idem P gratis hic relaxat prefato episcopo...'); *Romney* v. *Yonge* (1516) CP 40/1014, m. 483 (sim., but 'gratis remittit').

[58] *Anon.* (1542) Brooke Abr., *Damages*, pl. 144. Examples are: *Romney* v. *Young* (1516), last note; *Branstell* v. *Tygo* (1530) CP 40/1065, m. 154; *Warde* v. *Arderne* (1534) CP 40/1080, m. 142 (remits £2 of £10 damages and £4 costs).

[59] *Gardyner* v. *Baldwyn* (1535) CP 40/1085(2), m. 392 (remits 20s. of 40s. damages in trespass, but court awards 33s. 4d. increment of costs).

where costs were to be reduced.[60] In an entry of 1540, where the costs were reduced, it is explicitly stated that the costs were 'assessed excessively and too high' by a stated amount, and the excess was deducted by the court before judgment was given. Since there was no mention here of a release by the plaintiff, the court—or at least the prothonotary making the entry—clearly believed there was a jurisdiction to reduce excessive awards of costs whether or not the plaintiff consented.[61]

EXECUTION

The chief sanction used in enforcing judgments was imprisonment by means of a *capias ad satisfaciendum*. Although it might be thought that debtors would have stood a better chance of finding money if they were at large, the philosophy behind the widespread use of imprisonment was that most defendants would have friends and potential sureties who would rally to their aid if their liberty was threatened. An unfriended indigent debtor was not worth suing unless he had property which could be seized, since imprisonment only produced ready money if the defendant had friends who would lend it to him or stand surety for him,[62] whereupon he could be released to raise it.[63] Nevertheless, it was argued in the 1530s that 'forasmuch as a great part of every man's substance for the most part lieth in debts' a man would sooner pay his own debts if he was free to pursue his own debtors. This was said to be the basis of a supposed custom of the city of London that prisoners in execution for debt in Ludgate prison were allowed to go abroad with a keeper, though the Star Chamber in 1532 denied the lawfulness of the custom.[64] Although it seems to have remained a general practice in London,[65]

---

[60] e.g. *Abbot of Bindon v. Marten* (1532) CP 40/1075, m. 323 ('super quo...' formula, as in *Apsley v. Bishop of Chichester*, above, but inserting 'pro misis et custagiis suis' after 'dampna sua'); *Armyn v. Pratt* (1536) CP 40/1088, m. 38d; *Robynson v. Johnson* (1536) CP 40/1088, m. 152; *Burwell v. Whychecote* (1546) CP 40/1125, m. 522d; *Light v. Milles* (1555) CP 40/1163, m. 624. Likewise a defendant's costs: *Welsshe v. Dewentre* (1533) CP 40/1079, m. 451d (nonsuit in second deliverance; inquest awards defendants 40d. damages and £6 costs; 40s. of costs waived); *Keble v. Pragnell* (1555) CP 40/1163, m. 329 (nonsuit in replevin; inquest awards 40d. damages and 30s. costs; 23s. 4d. of costs waived).

[61] *Cooke v. Legh* (1540) CP 40/1106, m. 313 ('Super quo videtur justiciariis hic quod misi et custagia predicta per juratores predictos excessive et nimis alte per sex solidos et octo denarios sunt assessa. Ideo, sex solidis et octo denariis illis de predictis quinque marcis deductis et defalcatis per justiciarios hic, consideratum est...' that the plaintiff recover the residue). Cf. *Custe v. Tempest* (1508) CP 40/986, m. 31; Rast. Ent. 172v (174), pl. 12 (£20 reduced to £10).

[62] See e.g. *Holygrave v. Knyghtysbrygge* (1535) KB 27/1094, m. 30d (printed in 94 Selden Soc. 256); Mich. 27 Hen. VIII, fo. 24, pl. 3; Spelman 7.

[63] On the Tudor philosophy of imprisonment for debt see 109 Selden Soc., pp. lxxxii–lxxxiii.

[64] *Holand v. Catanys* (temp. Audley) C1/824/2; Bassett, 'The Fleet Prison', at 397; 109 Selden Soc., p. lxxxii. See also above, 287.

[65] A commission of 1553 to examine the complaints of the prisoners in Ludgate expressly authorized the sheriffs to allow them to go abroad with keepers to collect their debts: *CPR 1553–4*, p. 73.

it could only benefit the principal creditor, because the release was at the gaoler's risk; if a prisoner escaped or was allowed his freedom the debt transferred to the official responsible for the gaol,[66] and so the official was well advised to seek some surety himself before allowing his charges any liberty.[67] The problem may have been particularly acute in London, because of the large number of debtors in execution, and there was a spate of actions against the sheriffs of London around 1550.[68]

Many creditors required sureties to be found before lending money, and if bonds were taken the surety—or multiple sureties—might well be sued in debt rather than, or as well as, the principal debtor. Where more than one defendant was in consequence adjudged to pay the same debt, the judgment would be followed by a note that there should only be a single execution (*unica executio*),[69] though this could be levied against any or all of the judgment debtors. The development of *assumpsit* for money in the early sixteenth century enabled sureties to be pursued for debts even where no bonds were taken.[70]

---

[66] Port 115; *Bevyll* v. *Michell* (1512) CP 40/1001, m. 633 (debt against bailiff of stannary court for releasing debtor); *Eliott* v. *Brodyate* (1523) CP 40/1038, m. 422 (debt against mayor of Salisbury); 5 Edw. VI, Brooke Abr., *Escape*, pl. 45; *Langracke* v. *Calverley* (1556) CP 40/1168, m. 1270 (debt against sheriff of Yorks.); *Thurland's Case* (1558) Dyer 162b.

[67] e.g. *Fytzwyllyam* v. *Adams* (1558) KB 27/1186, m. 158 (under-marshal of Marshalsea recovers £320. 6s. 8d. against prisoner whose custody was relaxed so that the under-marshal became liable for his debt).

[68] e.g. *Mynours* v. *Turke* (1549) Dyer 66a; E12/1, fo. 21v; *Foster* v. *Turke* (1550) E13/232, m. 1; *Pyke* v. *Turke*, ibid., m. 4; E13/233, m. 11; *Langrave* v. *Calverley* (1551) E13/233, m. 15 (demurrer to plea that prisoner satisfied plaintiff); *Platt* v. *Aylyfe* (1551) E13/234, mm. 3–5, 6d–7, 9 (error in Council Chamber); Plowd. 35; Dyer 81b; CP 40/1153, m. 101 (attaint); *Thrower* v. *Aylyfe* (1551) E13/234, mm. 11–13. Cf. *Clarke* v. *Woodroffe* (1555–7) CP 40/1168, m. 357 (case against sheriffs of London for allowing debtor to become a sanctuaryman; recovers £100 damages).

[69] For an example in print see Rast. Ent. 172 (173v), pl. 9.

[70] See *Grafton* v. *Bold* (1520) KB 27/1037, m. 88d (judgment against surety); *Cleymond* v. *Vyncent* (1520–1) Mich. 12 Hen. VIII, fo. 11, pl. 3 (119 Selden Soc. 46); Port 10; *Squyer* v. *Barkeley* (1532–3) Spelman 7; below, 856.

21

Legal Discussion in Court

Iᴛ has already been suggested that one of the biggest changes in English law during the early Tudor period was a transformation in procedure and methodology rather than any specific innovation in theory or doctrine.[1] The essence of this transformation was that the jury was no longer seen as the final arbiter of fact and law combined, with lawyers making their chief contribution in defining the issue to submit to the laymen and—in the last resort—in presenting the facts to them. Trial of the facts was now coming to be seen as a preliminary step in the process whereby the court reached a reasoned decision. There were advantages in enabling the court to make its determination on the law after the facts were found, since it enabled the final decision to be given with legal reasons. A party who thought he had a good case on the law as well as on the facts thus gained an opportunity to pursue both sides of his case to a conclusion.[2] And, in a world imbued with the humanist spirit, reasoned decisions were doubtless more satisfying than the inscrutable verdicts of laymen.[3] The procedural changes which resulted from this sharper division of authority meant that legal principle was increasingly discussed in banc in relation to facts established by verdict rather than hypothetical facts which it was proposed to try later, and the consequence was that the judgment of the court in banc after such discussion not only settled the lawsuit in hand but also determined a point of law authoritatively for the future. All the various means of achieving this transformation existed before our period, in embryonic form, and the continuity of forms in the records has all but hidden the largest changes from our sight. Nevertheless, it is possible to show that the transformation took place between the reign of Henry VII and that of Elizabeth I. Before coming to the changes, however, we should first consider the fate of the older regime in which legal principle was secreted in the interstices of pleading.

---

[1] See above, ch. 1.

[2] A judgment on the law could not be obtained under the old system without waiving the possibility of a trial of the facts: below, 392.

[3] For evidence of a similar shift on the Continent see above, 9–12, 52. Note also the contemporary comments on judge and jury, above, 352.

TENTATIVE PLEADING

The change was once thought to have resulted from the disappearance of tentative oral pleading and its replacement by written pleadings settled in chambers; but we have already observed that the use of written drafts preceded the end of oral pleading by a considerable length of time. The introduction of paper pleadings was intended to facilitate rather than to preclude the oral discussion of pleadings in court.[4] And it is clear from the last year books, and the reports of the 1540s and 1550s, that argument as to the form of the pleadings could still occur in court before the pleadings were finally settled and entered of record, although it had become far less common than in the fifteenth century. Such argument was presumably based on the 'paper book', and would have arisen upon what in later language was a motion to show cause against a pleading rule. The motion could be made by either party.[5] When it took the form of an objection to a plea already pleaded, it was in effect a 'tentative' demurrer whereby the law could be tested without a formal commitment to the outcome. On occasion the court would put an end to the tentative stage of pleading by requiring a firm joinder in demurrer,[6] but even then there were ways of discovering the law without risking everything—for instance, by demurring (where possible) with respect to a small part and pleading to an issue of fact for the rest.[7] Perhaps the more common way of raising a question of pleading was the tentative plea, where the party wishing to plead in effect sought the court's advice after making an unsworn or hypothetical statement of the facts upon which he proposed to rely.[8] Moving 'questions' was certainly part of a barrister's practice in the early Tudor period.[9] A fragmentary bill in Chancery, referring to a Common Pleas suit which is reported both in the year books and by Spelman, hints that there may have been more discussion of the facts at this stage than theory would seem to permit. The question was the form

[4] For the mechanics of pleading see above, ch. 18.   [5] See 94 Selden Soc. 153–4.

[6] e.g. *Anon.* (1558) BL MS. Hargrave 4, fo. 131v, where Brooke CJ and Dyer J. disagreed, and Dyer J. said to Serjeant Bendlowes: (tr.) 'Well, you have my lord with you, so demur'.

[7] e.g. *Brome* v. *Hyotte* (1488) 1 Caryll 15, *per* Kebell sjt; *Savell* v. *Stansfeld* (1489) CP 40/910, m. 113 (demurrer to plea as to one twentieth part, issue as to rest); *Trussell* v. *Maydeford* (1493) 1 Caryll 156 at 159, *per* Kebell sjt (tr. 'Kebell, on account of the opinion of the two justices, did not dare demur but pleaded only as to one cartload of clay, and said he would risk so much to ascertain the law').

[8] See e.g. Mich. 14 Hen. VIII, fo. 4, pl. 3 (119 Selden Soc. 104: 'now the defendant comes and shows that...and he asks whether he may plead this'); Mich. 26 Hen. VIII, fo. 7, pl. 3 (repeated as Mich. 27 Hen. VIII, fo. 11, pl. 26: 'Mountagu asked this question...'); *Dawney* v. *Lepton* (1535) Hil. 26 Hen. VIII, fo. 9, pl. 2; Pas. 27 Hen. VIII, fo. 5, pl. 15 (tr. 'Mountagu: I am to make an avowry, and my case is thus...'); ibid., fo. 7, pl. 21; Trin. 27 Hen. VIII, fo. 22, pl. 16; Mich. 27 Hen. VIII, fo. 23, pl. 1 (tr. 'Denshill: I am to make a counterplea to this voucher and I pray your advice...'); *Anon.* (1537) Dyer 31b (tr. 'Mountagu asked the advice of the court in the joinder of an issue...').

[9] There are three examples in William Staunford's fee-book (BL MS. Add. 71134): 'Of one for putting of a case' (1542), 'For a question demanded' (1552), and 'For a question moved at the bar' (1552).

of plea available to a 'layman' who claimed that some of the conditions of a bond had been misread to him but that he had performed the rest. It was the case in which Fitzherbert J. had made his remarks about the fundamental object of pleading.[10] According to the complainant in Chancery, the Common Pleas had been regaled at the pleading stage with statements that the defendant had been seen reading a service-book and must therefore have been literate.[11] If this was an accurate recollection, it would seem that detailed evidence could still be discussed before pleas were framed, perhaps because counsel were allowed considerable latitude in outlining their facts off the record before the issue was settled.[12] In the event the plaintiff in this case demurred formally to the plea, and after six adjournments for advisement he discontinued the action and commenced a second, in which the parties pleaded to an issue of fact.[13]

The reports suggest that oral discussion of draft or tentative pleadings continued longer in the Common Pleas than in the King's Bench, and this could well be explained by the complexities of real-property litigation which were prominent in the former. However, the first rule-book from the plea side of the Exchequer, dating from the 1550s, shows the procedure in action more clearly than the Common Pleas remembrances: a plaintiff is given a day to show why the defendant's plea is not sufficient in law or else to reply, and if he makes out his case the defendant is given a day to make his plea perfect and sufficient in law or else a demurrer will be entered.[14] This strongly suggests oral argument preceding the formal demurrer, though we must turn to the law reports for confirmation that this practice survived.

Spelman's reports afford at least six instances from the 1520s where it can be shown, by collation with the record, that tentative pleas were withdrawn after discussion in court and never entered in their draft form.[15] St German in the same period states that the judges were accustomed, out of favour and not of right, to assist parties and their counsel in framing pleas.[16] Instances of assistance in open court can still be found in the reports of the 1550s,[17] and it may safely be

---

[10] See above, 348.

[11] *Flemyng* v. *Speke* (*c.*1521) C1/506/11–13 (pr. in 94 Selden Soc. 288–90); *Speke* v. *Flemyng* (1521–3) Pas. 14 Hen. VIII, fo. 25, pl. 7 (119 Selden Soc. 180); Spelman 84–6; CP 40/1032B, m. 306 (pr. in 119 Selden Soc. 189; demurrer). The record printed in 94 Selden Soc. 284 is of a second action.

[12] Note also *King's College, Cambridge* v. *Hekker* (1520) Pas. 14 Hen. VIII, fo. 31, pl. 8 (misdated), *ad finem* (119 Selden Soc. 76), where the court seems to have considered facts off the record even after demurrer.

[13] (1523) CP 40/1038, m. 439d (imparlance); CP 40/1039, m. 539 (issue; pr. in 94 Selden Soc. 284–8). No verdict is recorded. See further below, 830–1.   [14] Above, 168; and cf. 343.

[15] 94 Selden Soc. 100 n. 4.   [16] *Doctor and Student*, ed. Plucknett and Barton, 285.

[17] E.g., *Anon.* (1550) BL MS. Hargrave 4, fo. 111v (Serjeant Coke asks for, and is given, advice on making an avowry); *Anon.* (1558) BL MS. Hargrave 4, fo. 135; MS. Harley 1624, fo. 76 (tr. 'Rastall came to the bar and said that he was of counsel in an ejecment . . . now he moved how he should plead . . .', and was answered).

concluded that tentative pleading remained possible throughout our period. St German's point, indeed, was that the judges could not in conscience allow a party to run any risk by mispleading when he had sought their advice on the 'rules and formalities' of the law. Typical of the questions put to the court would be whether a traverse was called for, and if so what should be traversed.[18] But these kinds of question as to form were no longer the dominant agenda of the courts in banc. They were inappropriate for actions on the case, since the legal problems to which they gave rise were founded on the original bills and writs, and these could not be put forward tentatively. Even in the Common Pleas, the judges were unwilling to give counsel if they themselves lacked unanimity. Presumably they did not wish to prejudice any decision they might be asked to make on demurrer.[19] 'We will not make your pleas,' said Bryan CJ to Serjeant Kebell in a case where the judges were evenly divided.[20] 'Plead at your peril,' came the warning when the court wished to avoid a ruling.[21]

Not only were the judges becoming reluctant to advise parties on the law at the pre-trial stage, but reports of extempore pleading discussions were coming to be regarded as jurisprudentially inferior to final decisions upon points of law after verdict. To Plowden, educated in the 1530s, the distinction was fundamental, and his refusal to report inconclusive discussions marks his *Commentaries* as strikingly different from anything which had gone before:[22]

...other reports be made most of the sudden speech of the judges upon motion of cases of the serjeants and counsellors at the bar; but all the cases here be matter in law tried upon demurrers, or be special verdicts containing matters in law, of which the judges had copies, studied them, and in most of them argued, and after great deliberation have given judgment—and so, as I think, there is most firmness and surety of law in this report.

In the previous generation, too, one finds year-book cases explained away as having been 'argued but not adjudged', as if that indicated that a point was still unsettled.[23]

---

[18] 94 Selden Soc. 154.

[19] This was the explanation given for the change once it had occurred: 94 Selden Soc. 156 n. 2.

[20] Trin. 11 Hen. VII, fo. 29, pl. 15.

[21] ibid.; *Sherborne's Case* (1522) Spelman 18, pl. 3; *Anon.* (1529/30) Keil. 203, pl. 1, *per* Brudenell CJ; St German, *Doctor and Student*, ed. Plucknett and Barton, 285.

[22] *Les Comentaries* (1571), prologue, sig. B (sp. mod.).

[23] *Anon.* (1488) Mich. 4 Hen. VII, fo. 17, pl. 5 (tr. 'not adjudged, though well argued'); *Anon.* (1498) Trin. 13 Hen. VII, fo. 28, pl. 6, *per* Jay sjt (tr. 'well debated but not adjudged'); *Sherborne's Case* (1522) Spelman 18, 85 (case of 1468); *Anon.* (1527/8) Spelman 135, pl. 2 (case of 1489); *Anon.* (1529) Spelman 30 (case of 1481), pl. 7; *Anon.* (1544) Gell's reports, I, Trin. 36 Hen. VIII, fo. 40, *per* Saunders sjt (tr. 'there is a more recent book than this which is not adjudged'); ibid., fo. 41, *per* Foster (tr. 'by your patience, the book of assize is not ruled'). Cf. *Woodland* v. *Mantell* (1553) Plowd. 92 at 96, *per* Bromley sjt (tr. 'this distinction which you put is moved obiter—*per le voy*—in the years of Hen. VII, but there is no principal case there adjudged upon it'); *Case of the Duchy of Lancaster* (1559) 109 Selden Soc. 31 ('not ruled but only a holding by the serjeants').

And it was not unknown for the rolls to be searched to find whether a case had been adjudged upon advisement, that is, after a continuance 'because the court wishes to be advised' (*curia advisari vult*).[24] For Bryan CJ there was all the difference between a point which had been merely 'agreed' or even 'held' and a point which had been 'adjudged'.[25] A decision is more authoritative than a mere opinion or interlocutory ruling; and a decision after advisement is especially authoritative. And it seems that the courts were increasingly expected to provide authoritative judgments, to serve as case-law. The status of judicial advice on pleading motions fell into the same category as judicial dicta at readings, at the dinner table, or on the return-journey from Westminster Hall.[26] These were all evidence of the *communis opinio* which passed for law in the absence of better authority.[27] But opinion had always to give way to judicial determinations,[28] and the latter were on the increase as a result of the procedural developments to which we are about to turn. Only in formal decisions, as Plowden saw things, could one find 'most firmness and surety of law'.

FORMAL DEMURRERS

A decision on the pleadings could still, as in the past, result from a formal demurrer entered on the record, and in fact a substantial proportion of the principal cases in the reports of the sixteenth century arose upon demurrers which were formally entered of record. They seem often to have had a different function from the generality of tentative oral demurrers, in that the pleading questions raised by the latter were often matters of form and practical convenience, whereas formal demurrers were more often concerned with matters of substance.[29] As questions of law came increasingly to be framed in advance of argument at the bar, by means of a written demurrer, the practice of framing or perfecting pleadings orally remained appropriate for purely practical questions where there was no intention of staking the whole case on a technicality. The first half of the sixteenth century might therefore be regarded as a transitional period between the old world of

[24] e.g. Trin. 13 Hen. VII, fo. 25, pl. 1. Cf. *Dodge* v. *Bedingfield* (1565) 109 Selden Soc. 115, 116–18. For recourse to the rolls see further below, 486.

[25] *Anon.* (1496) Trin. 11 Hen. VII, fo. 24, pl. 2 (tr. 'Vavasour [J.]: We have all in effect agreed before this time... Bryan [CJ]: That has been held, as you say, within two years before ourselves; but it was not adjudged, and perhaps never will be...').

[26] For opinions rendered on the way to and from the Hall see Hil. 6 Hen. VII, fo. 15, pl. 8; Pas. 10 Hen. VII, fo. 23, pl. 27; Mich. 20 Hen. VII, fo. 9, pl. 18; *Anon.* (1526) 120 Selden Soc. 58, pl. 44; *Anon.* (1535) Mich. 27 Hen. VIII, fo. 26, pl. 5; cf. *Anon.* (1553) Dyer 92b (tr. 'by the report of the bishop of Ely returning from Westminster Hall').   [27] See further below, 467.

[28] See *Anon.* (1490) 1 Caryll 38, pl. 39, *per* Huse CJ (tr. 'I do not see how that can be right, although if the precedents are that way we will respect them').

[29] For examples in Spelman see 94 Selden Soc. 156.

tentative pleading and the newer ways of raising legal questions. Not only did demurrers increase in frequency during this period, but so—at least for a time— did the chances of their leading to a decision.[30] It was even possible for the judges to indicate in a clear case that argument was unnecessary: indeed, a leading case of 1549–50 was very nearly disposed of without any argument at all.[31]

In the late fifteenth century, there were normally around four to six demurrers a year, of which perhaps one or two at most were decided.[32] By the first decade of Henry VIII's reign the courts seem to have become more decisive. For example, of a large crop of eighteen demurrers joined in the one year 1514, only eight were left undecided. In the ten years from 1514 to 1523 there were on average a dozen demurrers a year, of which as many as 40 per cent resulted in judgment.[33] The frequency of demurrers thereafter remained more or less constant until the 1550s, though in the second quarter of the century the proportion of judgments fell slightly, to about one-third of the total.[34] By 1555 the chances of a plaintiff obtaining judgment on demurrer seem once more to have improved, rising by that year to 45 per cent.[35] These figures probably under-represent the number of decisions, since the very small proportion of judgments entered for the defendant hints that judgments may not regularly have been entered up unless needed by plaintiffs for the purpose of suing out execution.[36]

The high point of the demurrer is particularly marked in the printed year books for 1520–3 (12–14 Henry VIII), which have a distinctive character and are clearly by a different hand from the rest of the Henrician year books.[37] Of the twenty-two

---

[30] The figures in the following paragraph are based on notes taken over a long period and should not be regarded as exact. The samples seem nevertheless large enough to support generalizations. The dates given are the years when the demurrers were entered rather than when they were decided, which could be several years later.

[31] *Anon.*, identifiable as *Colthirst* v. *Bejushin* (1549) BL MS. Hargrave 4, fo. 104v (tr. 'Hales J. If it be the pleasure of my companions to have this argued I will not be against it, but I think the case is clear... Mountagu [CJ]. I think my brother Hales has well said... and Hynde [J.] affirmed this. But in the end the court gave a day to the serjeants for the matter to be argued.'). For the subsequent proceedings see below, 704.

[32] Full figures are not available, but this impression is confirmed by a close analysis of the Common Pleas rolls for the two calendar years 1494 and 1495 (omitting Trin. 1495, which was unfit for production). Nine demurrers were noted, of which only two were decided (one each year).

[33] Of 123 demurrers noted in these years, 47 were decided for the plaintiff and 4 for the defendant. There seems to have been a dip in the numbers in 1517–19, which may be attributable to the decline and end of Rede's chief justiceship and the shortness of Ernley's.

[34] Of 243 demurrers noted between 1532 and 1553, inclusive—an average of 11 a year—75 were decided for the plaintiff and 7 for the defendant. The proportion of judgments was thus 33%. This was much the same as the fourteenth-century rate: 100 Selden Soc., p. xxvii.

[35] As many as 24 demurrers were counted in CP 40/1161–4. In 11 cases judgment was entered for the plaintiff; no judgments were entered for the defendant.

[36] Note also *Wiseman's Case* (1557) Chr. Yelverton's reports, fo. 241v (tr. 'Wiseman said to me in Westminster Hall that the judgment was not entered because the demandant prayed it *instanter*').

[37] *Year Books 12–14 Henry VIII*, ed. J. H. Baker (119 Selden Soc.; 2002).

cases reported in these books which have been identified in the plea rolls, as many as sixteen went to judgment, seven of them upon demurrer; four more arose from undetermined demurrers, and two were pleaded to issue without any verdict being recorded. In other words, half the identifiable cases resulted from formal demurrers, and the greater part of them were decided demurrers. There could not be a greater contrast with the year books of the fifteenth century. Our anonymous reporter was setting a pattern for the future. Like Plowden, he wanted reasoned judgments rather than inconclusive tussles over the joinder of issue. A similar trend, though less marked, may be observed in the reports of Spelman (1500–40)[38] and Dyer (1532–81).[39] In a relatively unusual case of a demurrer on a clear point of substance, where the judgment was affirmed on a writ of error, Spelman could make the equally unusual claim that the law had now been made clear.[40]

The demurrer did not usually, however, work such clear results and in fact it did not settle as much law as might have been expected. For one thing, neither the joinder in demurrer nor the entry of judgment explicitly identified the point of the demurrer. A pleading was objected to in its entirety, and either upheld or condemned in general terms.[41] In many cases the point of law may be deduced by intelligent guesswork, but in many it cannot. By far the commonest use of the demurrer was in actions of debt upon a bond, where the defendant had pleaded performance of the condition, and in these cases the effect was usually to refer to the court a very nice point of construction.[42] Such cases, though dominant in the rolls, were very rarely reported because they did not raise any point of general application. And there are a good many other enrolled demurrers where the point cannot easily be guessed at without the benefit of a report. A second shortcoming of the demurrer was that, when there was any division of judicial opinion on a point of principle, the court was unwilling to give judgment.[43] Most of the demurrer cases in Spelman's reports stood undecided; at least, no decision is reported or

[38] 94 Selden Soc. 156.

[39] Dyer did not always state how questions of law arose, but in the old edition (1585/6) demurrers are mentioned in over 50 cases between 1535 and 1558, three times more than any other specified procedure.

[40] See King's College, Cambridge v. Hekker (1521) Spelman 193, 194 (whether corporation may present its head to a benefice); CP 40/102/, m. 539 (pl. lii 119 Selden Soc. 76); KB 27/1039, m. 21 (pr. in 94 Selden Soc. 352). This is also in Pas. 13 Hen. VIII, fo. 12, pl. 2 (119 Selden Soc. 76; Common Pleas); Mich. 14 Hen. VIII, fo. 2, pl. 2 (119 Selden Soc. 98; King's Bench).

[41] A special demurrer was possible, but rarely used: e.g. Axstell v. Normanvyll (1495) CP 40/932, m. 266 (demurrer to plea in abatement for misnomer, on grounds of estoppel); Mordaunt v. Mountegue (1513) CP 40/1004, m. 414d (demurrer to plea in abatement of writ, because too late after view); Estland v. Prior of Leeds (1516) CP 40/1015, m. 531 (justification on behalf of keepers of Rochester Bridge; demurrer because no foundation shown for corporation); Skelton v. Haneball (1517) CP 40/1017, m. 349 (demurrer to declaration on a deed, because words interlined in deed).   [42] See below, 824–5.

[43] A majority in the Exchequer Chamber may have carried more weight: thus in Sutton v. Forster (1483) Mich. 1 Ric. III, 3, pl. 2, Bryan CJ reluctantly agreed to give judgment according to the majority view, with which he disagreed.

recorded. A leading case was as often the outcome of an indecision as a decision. For example, two notable cases in the 1530s—which had the distinction of being noted by at least three different reporters—resulted from an even or almost even division of opinion which left the respective points undetermined.[44] Divided opinions on the bench were no more decisive than majority verdicts. Indeed, it might be said that a demurrer on a controversial point of law, if left undecided, served only to confirm that the law was uncertain.[45] Equal uncertainty could result if the King's Bench as a court of error failed to pronounce on a Common Pleas judgment which had been given upon demurrer. Perhaps the worst instance of judicial delay in the reign of Henry VIII was the notorious case of *Millys* v. *Guldeforde*, which turned on the straightforward question whether a bond was rendered void by indorsing a condition upon it after execution. The Common Pleas held in 1510, upon demurrer, that it was not; but the case depended in the King's Bench for twenty-five years without a decision ever being made.[46] The fault was probably that of the parties, for the year book says the case was not argued; but the failure to decide the case for such a long time was considered 'a bad example for the students'.[47] This leading indecision was noticed by at least five different reporters.

From the parties' point of view, indecision and procrastination by the judges— not to mention the inability to record any reasons for decisions—were not as objectionable as they seem to the legal historian searching for explanations. The same characteristics beset all common-law procedures,[48] and not merely the demurrer. Fighting a demurrer to the end was often a mark either of immoderate confidence or of desperation. By intimating to both parties that their position was precarious, and that a compromise might be preferable to a clear ruling, the judges gave the parties a salutary opportunity to settle their differences. But the demurrer did have the severe shortcoming that, if judgment was given, it was peremptory. A party who demurred was taken to confess the truth of the

[44] *Ryshton* v. *Cripce* (1530–1) Spelman 16, 93; Yorke 193, no. 267; Pollard 247–8, nos. 5–6; Dyer 4; Wm Yelv. 290, no. 1; KB 27/1076, m. 33 (94 Selden Soc. 290); *Pope* v. *See* (1533–4) Spelman 215; Dyer 31b, §219; Port 22; KB 27/1089, m. 33 (94 Selden Soc. 357).

[45] See *Anon.* (1536) Dyer 7a (tr. 'and so query, because Marvin and Browne demurred in judgment'); *Anon.* (1537) Dyer 33b (tr. 'And Mountagu said they were on the point of demurring in law upon the case, so query').

[46] The case was not unique: cf. *Culpepyr* v. *Haryngton* (1488–1508) KB 27/908, m. 64 (demurrer to title pleaded in trespass; continued for 80 terms without judgment); *Marmyon* v. *Baldwyn* (1527–41) 120 Selden Soc. 61, 71 (continued for 48 terms without judgment).

[47] *Millys* v. *Guldeforde* (1507–35) CP 40/986, m. 617; KB 27/1005, m. 26 (94 Selden Soc. 344); Spelman 167; 2 Caryll 616, 625; Chaloner 281, no. 8; Yorke 205, no. 307; Hil. 26 Hen. VIII, fo. 10, pl. 4 (tr. 'Englefield said that the continuation of the aforesaid plea, without being reversed, for all the aforesaid time *est in malum exemplum studentium*'); Dyer's reports, 110 Selden Soc. 384.

[48] But not necessarily in less formal jurisdictions. The Court of Wards could make decrees on points of law with reasons: e.g. *Re Townsend* (1554) Plowd. 115.

assertions in the pleading to which he objected, and if the law was decided against him he had no chance to present his case on the facts.[49] It was this practical, tactical problem, rather than the indecisiveness of the courts, which prompted litigants to seek ways of raising legal questions after trial. There was no sense in staking a case on demurrer, and thereby waiving trial, if the same point of law could be held in reserve until the party had tried his fortunes before the jury.

MOTIONS IN ARREST OF JUDGMENT

The simplest way of achieving discussion after trial was by motion in arrest of judgment. Where the plaintiff won the verdict, the defendant could move the court in banc to withhold judgment from the plaintiff on some legal ground arising on the face of the record. It seems likely that, in the absence of such a motion, judgment would be entered in the office during term-time without any motion to the court in banc. Of course, it was necessary for the defendant to be given notice of an intention to enter judgment,[50] and this was achieved by means of a rule. The filed Common Pleas posteas, where verdicts were given for the plaintiff,[51] are usually marked at the foot with a rule for judgment to be entered 'unless the defendant alleges something in arrest of judgment (*in retardationem judicii*)' by a specified date,[52] and similar rules may be found in the remembrance rolls.[53] The rule would also specify any increment of costs to be included in the judgment. In the case of a verdict for the defendant, there would be a rule to show cause why judgment should not be entered for the defendant;[54] but this procedure was

[49] A repleader was only possible if both parties were formally at fault, so that a jeofail occurred: above, 346–7.

[50] In *Graynfeld* v. *Atmere* (1536) C1/803/18–21, a Common Pleas attorney was accused of improperly suing out a writ of nisi prius without due warning and entering judgment before the quindene of Michaelmas, 'the like whereof hath been seldom seen or put in ure' (sp. mod.). The attorney answered that he had given notice of the nisi prius to the petitioner's attorney, and that judgment was entered after the quindene by consideration of the judges 'after the due order of the law'.

[51] Most of them were, probably because successful defendants did not always press for judgment. Twenty-four posteas were examined in the file for Mich. 1535; of these, 16 contained verdicts for the plaintiff, 4 recorded failures to convene the jury, 2 recorded nonsuits, and 2 recorded confessions by *non potest dedicere, there were no verdicts for the defendant.*

[52] Files in CP 52. The wording is: 'N[isi] def[endens] aliquid allegav[er]it in retard[ationem] judicii ... intr[etur] jud[iciu]m ... et *n* s[olidos] de incr[emento] p[ro] misis'.

[53] e.g. *Prior of St John's* v. *Baker* (1535) in Jenour's remembrance, CP 45/8, m. 10 ('Nisi Baker allegaverit in retardationem judicii Lune ante festum Ascensionis adversus priorem Johannis intretur judicium...'); *Holte* v. *Audeley* (1556) in Rokewoode's remembrance, CP 45/18, m. 15d ('Nisi tenens aliquid allegaverit in retardationem judicii Sabbati ante levationem curie intretur judicium').

[54] There is a clear example in the Exchequer remembrance book: *Tytley* v. *Port* (1555) E12/1, fo. 70v ('Et super hoc juratores reddierunt veredictum coram justiciariis ad assisas cum defendente, super quo idem defendens petit judicium. Dies datus est querenti usque diem Mercurii xiii diem Novembris ad ostendendum quare judicium non intretur cum defendente').

uncommon, chiefly because verdicts for defendants were infrequently filed, but
also in part because the opportunities for the plaintiff to obtain judgment
notwithstanding an adverse verdict were far fewer than in the converse case. What
remains unclear is whether the prothonotary was able to make these rules himself,
out of court, or whether they had to be sanctioned by a judge sitting in court or
in chambers. Certainly judges were beginning to deal with routine business in
their chambers in one of the Serjeants' Inns before the end of our period, though
very little is known of its scope.[55] But it makes little difference to our general
understanding of the procedure. The rule for judgment operated more or less
automatically once the verdict was returned, unless the losing party had anything
to move to the court in banc to stay the giving of judgment.

Since a verdict for the plaintiff had the effect of confirming all the plaintiff's
factual allegations, the procedure could be used only where there was some legal
defect on the face of the record—including, for this purpose, the postea—which
prevented the plaintiff from winning even though his factual case was established
beyond dispute. And so long as the plaintiff used a well-known form of action,
after winning a verdict he needed to fear only technical objections. The motion in
arrest was familiar in the fifteenth century,[56] and is marked in the reports by the
opening phrase 'You ought not to go to judgment...' ('Al jugement ne deves
aler...').[57] In the fifteenth-century cases it often signalled an objection to a jeofail
or defective verdict. But it came into its own, as a means of raising substantive
points of law, with the development of actions on the case. Here there were no
truly settled forms, and the original writ or bill set out with some particularity the
variable facts on which the plaintiff relied. Therefore there was ample room for
legal argument after trial as to whether the facts which had been proved were

---

[55] Note *Ayra* v. *Goodale* (1541) CP 40/1109, m. 118 (defendant, committed upon a *capias pro fine*,
appears before Baldwin CJ 'in camera sua in hospicio de Sergyantes Inne in Fletestrete', where the
plaintiff confesses satisfaction of the debt and Baldwin CJ sets the fine). Writs of *habeas corpus* were
sometimes returnable in a judge's house or in Serjeants' Inn (109 Selden Soc., p. lxxxi) and the plea
rolls frequently refer to deeds being produced for enrolment before a single judge in Serjeants' Inn: 94
Selden Soc. 136 n. 6. The references to chambers in Dyer (see 109 Selden Soc., p. xlvi n. 3) are to non-
routine judicial discussions, though Dyer 140b may indicate a rule made in chambers after consulting
the judges.

[56] In *Combe* v. *Elryngton* (1493) 1 Caryll 145 at 146, Bryan CJ refers to an argument in arrest of
judgment in 1464 (tr. 'I tell you that I was retained of counsel in that case, and the matter was well
argued in arrest of judgment...'). Note also *Rednesh's Case* (1486) Pas. 1 Hen. VII, fo. 19, pl. 4 ('duae
exceptiones captae ad retardandum judicium...').

[57] e.g. *Anon.* (1480) Trin. 20 Edw. IV, fo. 4, pl. 2; *Anon.* (1481) Pas. 21 Edw. IV, fo. 22, pl. 5, 6; *Anon.*
(1481) Pas. 21 Edw. IV, fo. 29, pl. 24; *Anon.* (1482) Hil. 21 Edw. IV, fo. 83, pl. 37; *Hatley's Case* (1482) Mich.
22 Edw. IV, fo. 21, pl. 1; *Sutton* v. *Forster* (1482) ibid., fo. 29, pl. 10; Trin. 1 Edw. V, fo. 5, pl. 11; Mich. 1 Ric.
III, fo. 1, pl. 2; 64 Selden Soc. 56; *Prior of St Mary Overy* v. *Walton* (1493) 1 Caryll 195; *Capell* v. *Scott*
(1494) 1 Caryll 216 at 217 (tr. 'You ought not to get to judgment... Bryan [CJ]: That matter is of no avail
in arrest of judgment...'); Mich. 14 Hen. VIII, fo. 10, pl. 6.

sufficient to found a cause of action. The post-trial motion in such cases gave the defendant the same scope for argument as a demurrer to the declaration,[58] but without obliging him to admit the truth of the plaintiff's factual case. Demurrers to the declaration in actions on the case are still occasionally found in the sixteenth century,[59] and one is reported by Spelman,[60] but their rarity is not surprising; parties would not wish to risk all on the law unless they lacked a good case on the facts.

Motions in arrest were being used to challenge the sufficiency of the declaration by the beginning of our period,[61] and they became increasingly frequent with the rise of *assumpsit* and defamation actions in the sixteenth century.[62] Unfortunately, their history cannot be traced with any precision because they were off the record: motions were not mentioned in the plea rolls. It may fairly be assumed when the record mentions a continuance for advisement after verdict that there has been such a motion,[63] but it can be demonstrated by comparing reports and plea rolls that where a motion in arrest was followed by judgment the same term the record gives nothing away.[64] Moreover, a comparison of different reports shows that reporters did not always trouble to mention the procedure when it was used.[65] While denying us the facts and figures, this circumstance in itself demonstrates how well established the motion in arrest of judgment had become by the middle of Henry VIII's reign.

The post-trial motion known in later times as the motion for a new trial was a particular species of the motion in arrest of judgment,[66] sometimes called a motion in arrest of verdict.[67] But it was still limited to cases where the verdict was

---

[58] For an example of a demurrer to the declaration, in account, see *Say* v. *Dokket* (1495) Mich. 10 Hen. VII, fo. 6, pl. 12; Trin. 10 Hen. VII, fo. 30, pl. 28; Port 1; CP 40/930, m. 410 (102 Selden Soc. 2).

[59] Six examples have been noted in the Common Pleas between 1509 and 1553, all of them undecided: *Hayden* v. *Raggelond* (1510) CP 40/992, m. 451 (negligence); *Wryght* v. *Grove* (1533) CP 40/1079, m. 641 (defamation); *Howse* v. *Bert* (1540) CP 40/1104, m. 319 (*assumpsit*); *Gatacre* v. *Broke* (1542) CP 40/1112, m. 429 (defamation); *Bayly* v. *Davye* (1550) CP 40/1144A, m. 425 (*assumpsit*); *Barne* v. *Johnson* (1553) CP 40/1155(2), m. 608 (*assumpsit*).

[60] *Squyer* v. *Barkeley* (1532) Spelman 7; KB 27/1085, m. 32d (*assumpsit*; pr. in 94 Selden Soc. 253). Other King's Bench examples are *Lyon* v. *Wakefeld* (1544) KB 27/1133, m. 73 (conversion by bailee); *Symond* v. *Thomas* (1550) KB 27/1154, m. 128d (*assumpsit*); *Norwood* v. *Read* (1557) Plowd. 180b; KB 27/1182, m. 188 (*assumpsit*).

[61] See e.g. *Sarger's Case* (King's Bench, 1481) Pas. 21 Edw. IV, fo. 22, pl. 6; B. & M. 513; *Johnson* v. *Baker* (Common Pleas, 1493) 1 Caryll 135; CP 40/914, m. 104; B. & M. 399 at 400.

[62] For explicit examples, see Spelman 2, 3, 4, 7.   [63] As in *Johnson* v. *Baker* (1493), above, n. 61.

[64] e.g. *Cleymond* v. *Vyncent* (1520-1) Mich. 12 Hen. VIII, fo. 11, pl. 3 (119 Selden Soc. 46); Port 10; KB 27/1037, m. 40 (pr. in 102 Selden Soc. 10); *Pykeryng* v. *Thurgoode* (1532) Spelman 4; KB 27/1083, m. 65 (pr. in 94 Selden Soc. 247).

[65] e.g. *Burgh* v. *Potkyn* (1522) Spelman 136; Mich. 14 Hen. VIII, fo. 10, pl. 6 (119 Selden Soc. 125); 120 Selden Soc. 82, no. 4; CP 40/1036, m. 319; 94 Selden Soc. *158, 183–4*. In *Pecke* v. *Redman* (1555) Dyer 113a; KB 27/1172, m. 106; Dyer refers to a verdict being 'traversed', probably meaning a motion in arrest of judgment; but there is no postea on the roll.

[66] See St German, *Doctor and Student*, ed. Plucknett and Barton, 293 (sp. mod. 'if they [the jurors] do the contrary it may be laid in arrest of the judgment...').   [67] See above, 348, 365.

rendered unsafe by reason of the jurors' misconduct,[68] or was void as the result of a jeofail[69] or technical error.[70] It was not a means of examining in banc questions which arose upon the evidence given at the trial. There was, for a time, a belief that such an examination could be achieved by asking the trial judge to seal a bill of exceptions. The bill of exceptions was sanctioned by the Statute of Westminster II, c. 31, which was not intended to apply to rulings on circuit.[71] Yet in the one known example from Henry VII's reign it was used to review a ruling by the assize judges at York on a challenge to the array. This was a sufficiently unusual precedent to find its way into two manuscript books of entries.[72] But in 1535 the King's Bench put paid to any hope of developing this irregular procedure as a method of raising questions in banc. In *Jordan's Case* (1535),[73] the plaintiff in *assumpsit* proved at the trial a promise made to his wife, which she had later told him about, and claimed that this supported his averment of a promise to himself. Luke J., sitting at nisi prius at the Guildhall, evidently agreed and a verdict was taken for the plaintiff. The defendant, however, persuaded the judge to seal a bill setting out the evidence so that he could argue the point in banc. When the matter was moved in banc, Spelman J. objected that the statute of 1285 only provided that a bill of exceptions could be made the subject of a writ of error, and that the court in banc could therefore take no notice of it. Fitzjames CJ responded that, although this was true in strictness of law, it would cause hardship in the case of the King's Bench because a writ of error could only be brought in Parliament; therefore by 'good discretion' the court in banc should examine the exception before giving judgment. In all likelihood, it was Spelman's view that prevailed. He makes no mention of the bill of exceptions, or the point which it raised, in his own report of the case, and there is no mention of the bill in the record. Had the procedure been extended in the way Fitzjames CJ suggested, it would have anticipated by well over a century one of the later functions of the motion for a new trial. But this did not happen. Since it could not be used as a means of raising questions of

---

[68] See above, 364–8.

[69] See above, 346–8. This is referred to as 'matter in arrest of judgment' in *Anon.* (1506) Trin. 21 Hen. VII, fo. 26, pl. 3, *ad finem*. The motion 'in arrest of judgment' in *Bourgchier* v. *Cheseman* (1504) Mich. 20 Hen. VII, fo. 4, pl. 13, seems to turn on an alleged jeofail.

[70] e.g. *Milles* v. *Archbishop of Canterbury* (1528) Spelman 173 ('counsel alleged this matter in arrest of judgment', in this case to bar the plaintiff); *Drope's Case* (1563) 109 Selden Soc. 87 ('moved in arrest of judgment after verdict' and *habeas corpora de novo* issued).

[71] In 1481, Bryan CJ sitting alone in banc offered to seal a bill of exceptions with his own signet: Mich. 21 Edw. IV, fo. 53, pl. 18. Cf. *Dean and Chapter of Lincoln* v. *Prat* (1481–2) Mich. 21 Edw. IV, fo. 11, pl. 3; fo. 63, pl. 33; Hil. 21 Edw. IV, fo. 20, pl. 29; Pas. 21 Edw. IV, fo. 31, pl. 28 (challenge to a juror in an assize of novel disseisin).

[72] *Bubwyth* v. *Plumpton* (1503) KB 27/967, m. 62; copied in Jenour's entries, fo. 287; Maycote's entries, fo. 154v. See also 94 Selden Soc. 117 n. 5.

[73] Mich. 27 Hen. VIII, fo. 24, pl. 3, identifiable as *Holygrave* v. *Knyghtysbrygge* (1535) Spelman 7; KB 27/1094, m. 30d (pr. 94 Selden Soc. 256). The bill of exceptions is mentioned only in the year book.

law in banc, the bill of exceptions would not be much used at all.[74] The proper way of reserving a point arising from the evidence at the trial was by demurring to the evidence.

DEMURRERS TO THE EVIDENCE

The demurrer to the evidence became established during the fifteenth century,[75] and remained in regular use throughout our period and beyond. It accounts for at least thirteen reported cases in the first half of the sixteenth century,[76] while over fifty examples have been noted in the plea rolls of both benches during the same period. The effect of a demurrer to the evidence was to admit the truth of the evidence proffered by the other side, to prevent any further evidence being given,[77] and to discharge the jury from giving a verdict, so that the court in banc could be asked to determine whether the evidence so admitted was sufficient to support the position of the party who proffered it. The method of achieving this was to summarize the evidence, with the joinder in demurrer, and return it with the postea; the jury, before being discharged, would be asked to assess the damages and costs which should be recovered in the event of the demurrer being decided in favour of the plaintiff, so as to obviate the expense of a writ of inquiry. The evidence was not entered on the record in the way that a Chancery examiner wrote depositions. Although documents shown to the jury could be set out verbatim,[78] whether or not they were under seal,[79] oral evidence was summarized in Latin in the same style as pleadings, without any mention of individual witnesses and their statements.[80] Only rarely are the particular facts given from which conclusions are to be inferred.[81]

[74] It could still be used to support a writ of error: e.g. *Markham's Case* (1567) 110 Selden Soc. 443 (challenge overruled at Nottingham assizes). The 'bill of exception' mentioned in *Holwey* v. *Hale* (1529/32) C1/642/16, was different in kind; it was a petition signed by counsel asking the judges of the Common Pleas to set aside a fraudulent confession by a vouchee (which they did).

[75] The procedure was mentioned (but not used) in *Prior of Tickford* v. *Prior of Tickhill* (1456) Pas. 34 Hen. VI, fo. 36, pl. 7; *Babington* v. *Venour* (1465) *Long Quinto* 58, at fo. 60. The earliest example we have so far noted in the plea rolls is *Stanter* v. *Touke* (1493) CP 40/925, m. 136. See also *Dale* v. *Broune* (1496) Port 18; KB 27/939, m. 62 (pr. 102 Selden Soc. 19; Rast. Ent. 146 (148), pl. 12).

[76] 94 Selden Soc. 111 n. 6. To the ten cases there should be added *Abbot of Buckfast* v. *Horswyll* (1505) 2 Caryll 485; CP 40/974, m. 448; *Core* v. *Whalley* (1535) Dyer 32; CP 40/1087, m. 147; *Reniger* v. *Fogassa* (1550) Plowd. 5 (in the Exchequer).

[77] *Browne* v. *Elmer* (1520) Trin. 12 Hen. VIII, fo. 1, pl. 1 (119 Selden Soc. 2), *per* Broke J. The demurrer is entered in CP 40/1023, m. 124d.

[78] In *Master of Welshgate Hospital, Shrewsbury* v. *Owen* (1524) CP 40/1043, m. 303, the transcripts of the relevant deeds occupy two membranes. [79] Above, 363–4.

[80] An exception is *Grynys* v. *Hille* (1518–20) CP 40/1021B, m. 335 (Hereford assizes), where the defendant's counsel prayed that a particular witness be examined and his evidence was entered in Latin; the plaintiff's counsel put in a deposition (in English) from the Council in the Marches.

[81] e.g. *Boylston* v. *Hunt* (1537–9) CP 40/1095, m. 537 (issue whether arbitrators made award; evidence that arbitrators sent messenger to defendant's home and offered the sealed award to a servant, but the servant said she had orders not to receive it; judgment for plaintiff; writ of error brought, 1541).

Most demurrers to the evidence give the names of the 'counsel learned in the law of the land' who 'showed' the evidence to the jury. These were almost invariably serjeants at law or benchers of the inns of court,[82] only one being named on each side.[83] The mention of counsel 'showing' the evidence suggests that the demurrer may not have been to evidence in the sense of sworn testimony given by witnesses, but to the opening statement of counsel in which he stated what he intended to prove.[84] Indeed, in a case of 1548 we find counsel praying oyer of an indenture 'shown' by the other side, indicating that it had not been read out.[85] This conclusion may also explain why the party joining in demurrer sometimes offered to 'verify' or 'aver' (*verificare*) the evidence, which makes little sense if it had already been given on oath. Probably most demurrers to the evidence were mutually agreed upon by opposing counsel, in the same way as the later special case stated.[86] However, it seems from a remark of Dyer that a demurrer might on occasion be pressed on the parties by the trial judge himself, in the course of a trial, where a difficult point of law was being clouded by doubtful testimony already given.[87]

The procedure was not in such constant use that the precedents are wholly consistent. Usually the plaintiff began, and in most cases the demurrer was to the plaintiff's evidence alone. Where a cause of action was severable, it was possible to demur to some of the plaintiff's evidence and accept a verdict for the plaintiff on the rest.[88] In the celebrated case of *Orwell v. Mortoft* (1505),[89] the plaintiff's evidence added nothing to the declaration and the only effect of the demurrer seems to have been to occasion a motion in arrest of judgment; but this stands alone. In some other cases the defendant proffered his own evidence in answer to the plaintiff's and then either he or the plaintiff demurred, in which case the evidence on both sides was set down.[90] Less commonly, the defendant's evidence was

---

[82] See above, 259 n. 36.

[83] The only exception noted is *Broun v. Atherly* (1519) CP 40/1025, m. 101d (evidence at the Guildhall submitted by three counsel—*legis periti de consilio*—Shelley, Pakyngton, and Martyn).

[84] Note also *Russell v. Wareyn* (1516) CP 40/1015, m. 443 (plaintiff gives in evidence—*in evidenciis*—that the defendant borrowed money from him, and to prove it—*ad illud probandum*—produces a memorandum acknowledging the debt).

[85] *Harry v. Willyng* (1547-8) CP 40/1134, m. 723d (Exeter assizes).

[86] See *Anon.* (1549) Wm Yelv. 346, no. 72 (tr. 'The case, which arose upon the evidence, was this...and as it appeared upon the case, *as it was agreed upon...*'). The words in italics are in English in the original report.

[87] *Stokes v. Somersall* (1558) 110 Selden Soc. 418 ('because the evidence was doubtful, and it was doubtful whether the entail was determined...the court moved the parties...to discharge the jury and demur', though one of the parties declined).

[88] *Brereton v. Egge* (1522) CP 40/1035, m. 301 (judgment for plaintiff on demurrer, verdict for plaintiff as to residue). Cf. *Philipp qui tam etc. v. Percyvall* (1501-2) KB 27/959, m. 69 (demurrer to the evidence on one of two issues); *Tofft v. Tay* (1502-4) KB 27/963, m. 38 (sim.).

[89] Mich. 20 Hen. VII, fo. 8, pl. 18; 2 Caryll 465, 493; CP 40/972, m. 123 (B. & M. 406); below, 853-5.

[90] e.g. *Stanter v. Touke* (1493) CP 40/925, m. 136; *Dale v. Broune* (1496) Port 18; KB 27/939, m. 62 (102 Selden Soc. 19; Rast. Ent. 146, pl. 12); *Anon.* (1514) Dyer 2a; *Southwall v. Huddelston* (1523-4) Hil. 14 Hen. VIII, fo. 17, pl. 6 (119 Selden Soc. 150); Spelman 136; Port 90; CP 40/1030, m. 731 (pr. 102 Selden Soc. 90

given first and the plaintiff demurred.[91] For instance, in an action on the case for fire, in which the general issue was joined, the defendant produced an indenture of lease to prove that he was the termor in possession, and the plaintiff demurred because he was tenant by the curtesy and unable to bring an action of waste.[92] In a few cases the evidence proceeded as far as a rebuttal by the plaintiff of the defendant's evidence, so that three stages in the submission of evidence were enrolled.[93]

The chances of a demurrer to the evidence resulting in judgment were about the same as in the case of a demurrer to pleading. About one-third produced a decision in the first half of the sixteenth century, with perhaps a slightly higher rate of decisiveness in the first half of Henry VIII's reign. The object was similar to an ordinary demurrer, in that it dispensed with a verdict and transferred the burden of decision to the court in banc; and sometimes the kind of question raised was the kind of question which could have been raised by a special plea. But, generally speaking, demurrers to the evidence enabled more detailed questions to be raised than could be generated by pleading. From this point of view, their principal drawback was the need to frame *ex parte* versions of the facts, which had to be accepted or rejected as a whole,[94] rather than a mutually agreed statement of the facts which required approval by a jury before legal argument occurred. The latter could be achieved by means of a special verdict, but it was

at 93); *Milles* v. *Archbishop of Canterbury* (1528) Spelman 173; CP 40/1059, m. 734 (pr. 94 Selden Soc. 346 at 349); *Core* v. *Whalley* (1535–6) Dyer 32a; CP 40/1087, m. 147; *Bill* v. *Bill* (1536–8) CP 40/1097, m. 558; *Harry* v. *Willyng* (1547–8) CP 40/1134, m. 723d (plaintiff prays oyer and then demurs); *Meynell* v. *Gervesse* (1548) CP 40/1138, m. 331; *Scullard* v. *Tarrant* (1550–1) CP 40/1044A, m. 160; *Coucheman* v. *Paynell* (1551) KB 27/1160, m. 64d; *Person* v. *Andrewe* (1552) KB 27/1162, m. 40d; *Warren* v. *Lee* (1555–9) KB 27/1174, m. 115; Dyer 126b; *Rychardson* v. *Hewer* (1558–9) KB 27/1185, m. 22.

[91] e.g. *Philipp qui tam etc.* v. *Percyvall* (1501–2) KB 27/959, m. 69 (forcible entry; issue on seisin to uses; defendant shows will and charter of feoffment; judgment for plaintiff); *Tofft* v. *Tay* (1502–4) KB 27/963, m. 38 (debt on 23 Hen. VI, c. 9, for extortion; defendant admits taking money but shows custom for under-sheriff to take gaol fee from prisoner on acquittal); *Dean and Chapter of Exeter* v. *Trewynnard* (1551–3) Dyer 80a; CP 40/1148, m. 601; *Aysshley* v. *Boxley* (1551) CP 40/1148, m. 612; *Peeres* v. *Bishop* (1554) Dyer 112a (*non est factum*); *Marten* v. *Hardy* (1555) CP 40/1161, m. 603; Dyer 122b (replevin); *Sachet* v. *Norden* (1556) CP 40/1166, m. 839 (trespass; issue on title pleaded by defendant).

[92] *Gravener* v. *Squyer* (1522) CP 40/1037, m. 452d.

[93] e.g. *Scydmore qui tam etc.* v. *Parkgate* (1522) KB 27/1042, m. 23 (forcible entry); *West* v. *Mede* (1553) CP 40/1155, m. 671 (plaintiff and defendant show evidence; then the plaintiff '(tr.) maintaining his prior evidences... for further proof thereof further shows in evidence to the jurors aforesaid...'); *Granado* v. *Dyer* (1554) Dyer 123a; KB 27/1169, m. 84d (trespass to grain; plaintiff shows grant of impropriated rectory; defendant shows earlier grant by prior of Plympton; plaintiff shows surrender of priory); *Whytney* v. *Gough* (1556) Dyer 140b; CP 40/1166, m. 140.

[94] This might cause a problem if the evidence conflicted: *Reniger* v. *Fogassa* (1550) Plowd. 1 at 8. In *Fyncheley* v. *Creswall* (1512) CP 40/1001, m. 604, a demurrer to the plaintiff's evidence unusually resulted in a *venire de novo* and a verdict for the plaintiff.

only towards the end of our period that special verdicts began to creep into regular use as a vehicle for reserving points of law.

SPECIAL VERDICTS

Although special verdicts had been more freely allowable in earlier times, and the old precedents were to be of use in justifying the Tudor revival, by the end of the fifteenth century the orthodox learning espoused by Bryan CJ was that they were only allowed in trespass and the assize,[95] and that was because the writ, count, and plaint in those kinds of action were factually uninformative ('general').[96] Even then they were allowed only upon the general issue.[97] It was arguable that actions on the statutes of forcible entry could be brought within the same reasoning, since they operated in a similar way to trespass,[98] though in practice demurrers to the evidence rather than special verdicts were used in actions for forcible entry as well.[99] The logic certainly could not extend to a *praecipe* action.[100] In a dower case of 1538, where the demandant's serjeant wanted to demur to the evidence, and the tenant's serjeant wanted the jury to find a special verdict, the judges would not allow the latter course.[101]

The distinction between the two procedures may not always have been very clear even to contemporaries,[102] though the advantage of the special verdict was probably thought to be that it eliminated factual disputes and presented a legal question in clear form to the court in banc.[103] Whatever the relative merits of the alternatives, however, it was the policy of the courts until about the 1540s to give preference to the demurrer and to confine verdicts 'at large' to the cases allowed

[95] Examples of special verdicts in novel disseisin are *Newdygate* v. *Punchyn* (1531) CP 40/1068, m. 303d; *Villers* v. *Beamonte* (1556) CP 40/1166, m. 516; Dyer 146a. In *Trafford* v. *Assheton* (1506–7) KB 27/978, m. 36; 2 Caryll 556–7, judgment was given on a special verdict in attaint upon an assize of novel disseisin.   [96] *Anon.* (1494) Trin. 9 Hen. VII, fo. 3, pl. 4; 2 Caryll 262.

[97] *Anon.* (1493) Mich. 9 Hen. VII, fo. 13, pl. 8, *per* Fairfax J. (*pace* Tremaile J.); *Anon.* (1500) Fitz. Abr., *Verdit*, pl. 44. Tremaile's contrary opinion was commended by Brooke Abr., *Verdite*, pl. 83; but by Brooke's time the general opinion had changed.

[98] *Anon.* (1490) Mich. 6 Hen. VII, fo. 12, pl. 12, *per* Bryan CJ.

[99] e.g. *Philipp qui tam etc.* v. *Percyvall* (1501) KB 27/959, m. 69; *Rooper* v. *Oxenden* (1520) 120 Selden Soc. 29; KB 27/1035, m. 81 (judgment for plaintiff); *Scydmore* v. *Parkgate* (1522) KB 27/1042, m. 23. Cf. *Bele* v. *Benet* (1526) 120 Selden Soc. 58, where Fitzherbert J. ordered a special verdict but the jury insisted on giving a general verdict.

[100] *Anon.* (1531) Brooke Abr., *Verdite*, pl. 85 (refused in *quibus*).

[101] *Anon.* (1538) Dyer 41a. Cf. *R.* v. *Muschamp* (1542) Dyer 53a, where the Court of Exchequer (upon an information) apparently directed a special verdict because the king's counsel refused to join in a demurrer to the evidence.

[102] *Toft* v. *Cromer* (1505) is reported in Mich. 20 Hen. VII, fo. 12, pl. 22, as arising from a verdict, and in Hil. 21 Hen. VII, fo. 16, pl. 28, as a demurrer to the evidence.

[103] There is some slight evidence that this could also be achieved by means of an agreed case, or case stated: *Anon.* (1549) Wm Yelv. 346, no. 72 (quoted above, 398 n. 86).

by Bryan CJ.[104] Special verdicts were, in fact, very uncommon in either bench between the 1450s and the 1550s. Why the policy changed in the middle of the sixteenth century is not recorded, though it is possible to trace the steps whereby special verdicts became generally available. The reform seems to have been promoted primarily by the Common Pleas judges.

The first restriction to be abandoned was that concerning the forms of action in which special verdicts were allowed. To allow them in actions on the case would have flown in the face of the Bryan theory, since writs tailored to meet special cases were the very reverse of 'general'; on the other hand, the trespass rationale might reasonably be extended to other 'general' personal actions. That was the teaching in Gray's Inn in the 1530s: a special verdict might be allowed in debt or detinue, upon the general issue, but not in an action on the case.[105] Yet by the middle of the century special verdicts were allowable even in case, and in 1552 the practice was justified by the equity of the statute of Westminster II, c. 30—which in terms applied only to the petty assizes[106]—and by the earlier precedents concerning personal actions. In 1545 the Common Pleas were presented with a conundrum where a defendant in debt had pleaded *Non est factum*, but then the alleged deed—which had been in existence when the plea was pleaded—had been eaten by mice while in the custody of the court. The solution was to direct the jury to find these facts specially so that the matter could be decided by the court.[107] By 1558 it seems that special verdicts were allowable in all or most other kinds of action,[108] including real actions such as entry in the *quibus*.[109]

The other restriction—that special verdicts could only be given on the general issue—was not finally removed in our period, though it was sometimes ignored. In 1540, 1553, and 1554 we find judges directing special verdicts in trespass where

[104] Note *Banister* v. *Benjamin* (1540) Dyer 47b, where there was a difference of opinion and the court asked the serjeants to demur and discharge the jury, but they declined; the jury was therefore given the option of finding a special verdict. This was in trespass, but upon the issue of disseisin.

[105] Notes from a reading, perhaps that of James Hales (1532) BL MS. Hargrave 253, fo. 15v.

[106] *Anon.* (1540/1) Brooke Abr., *Verdite*, pl. 90 (partial verdict in *assumpsit*); *Arundell* v. *Carye* (1549) KB 27/1149, m. 75 (special verdict in trover); *Brugis* v. *Warneford* (1552–3) Dyer 75a; Dalison's reports, BL MS. Harley 5141, fo. 12; Dal. 9 (partial verdict in defamation). In the last case, a partial verdict is treated by the reporter as a species of special verdict.   [107] *Nichols* v. *Haywood* (1545) Dyer 59a.

[108] e.g. *Panel* v. *Moor* (1553) Plowd. 91, 92 (decision in Guildhall); *Warcop* v. *Musgrave* (1555) Dyer 111b (debt); *Anon.* (1555) Dyer 124a (debt); *Newman* v. *Punter* (1556) Benl. 47 (appeal of murder); *Anon.* (1558) BL MS. Hargrave 4, fo. 148 (attaint); *Stokes* v. *Porter* (1558–9) Dyer 166b; 1 And. 11; CP 40/1176(1), m. 422; Benl. 72 (debt); *Wylloughby* v. *Dawbeney* (1558–9) CP 40/1176(1), m. 957 (replevin); *Barham* v. *Hayman* (1561) Dyer 173a; Moo. 24; Chr. Yelverton's reports, BL MS. Hargrave 388, fo. 251v (replevin; allowed only after 'long debate, argument, and consideration had by the justices'). For the general principle see *Dowman* v. *Vavasour* (1586) 9 Co. Rep. 7, 11–14.

[109] e.g. *Drew* v. *Marrow* (1558) Dyer 158a (special verdict in *quibus* discussed without adverse comment); sub nom. *Marwood* v. *Drew*, 1 And. 37; Benl. 37; *Bowyer* v. *Warren* (1558) CP 40/11/5, m. 154 (judgment for plaintiff upon special verdict in *quibus*). (Both from Devon.) Cf. Brooke Abr., *Verdite*, pl. 85, where amazement is expressed at the 1531 decision rejecting a special verdict in *quibus*.

issue had been joined upon a title,[110] but in the 1550s a halt was called to any further sliding away from the old position. In 1553 and 1555 the Common Pleas held that a special verdict was only acceptable on the general issue.[111] That appears to have remained the orthodox position until the middle of Elizabeth I's reign,[112] save that a special verdict was said to be allowable on a special issue if it 'tended to the point of the issue',[113] and it was permitted on common-form traverses such as 'His freehold' or 'Never executor'.[114] In 1559, Serjeants Weston and Harpur as assize judges at Dorchester accepted a special verdict upon a title pleaded specially in replevin, but no judgment was entered.[115]

The principal practical difficulty with the special verdict was the need to settle a text before the jury was discharged, though it seems that this could be done in the form of an English draft which would be translated into proper form later.[116] The draft would have to be the work of counsel, and because the procedure was unusual the forms differ. For example, in a trespass case of 1500 the jury set out the facts of an informal lease for life, and said that if the law willed that nothing passed by the words set out then they found further facts; the verdict ends without a conclusion or a submission to the court.[117] It was more usual, however, to end with a prayer for the judges to decide the doubt. Dyer mentions a trespass case of 1551 in which, just before he took the coif, he drew the special verdict in a Common Pleas action tried at Winchester assizes.[118] The verdict may be found enrolled on a separate membrane from the issue, which had been entered the previous term. The formula he used was: 'The jurors say upon their oath that... and upon the foregoing the same jurors pray the advice and discretion of the justices aforesaid whether the [defendant] should... by the law of the land be adjudged guilty of the aforesaid trespass, or not'. The jurors then assessed the damages in case the verdict should be adjudged for the plaintiff. This form of verdict, embodying a question for the court, was used

---

[110] *Banister* v. *Benjamin* (1540) Dyer 47a (Shelley J. in banc); *Belgrave* v. *Bennett* (1549–53) CP 40/1142, m. 606 (Marvin J. at Leicester assizes, 1553); *Mount* v. *Hodgkin* (1554) Benl. 38 at 39; Dyer 116a (no mention of verdict).

[111] *Anon.* (1553) Benl. 37; 1 And. 37; *Trevylyan* v. *Parkyn* (1552–5) Dyer 114a; CP 40/1150, m. 804; *Jones* v. *Weaver* (1555) Dyer 117b at 118a.

[112] It was a particular interest of Edmund Anderson, who reopened it in *The Serjeants' Case, Parker* v. *Francis* (1577) 1 And. 58. The extension was settled in the time of Anderson CJ: *Gewrt* v. *Sydenham* (1584) 1 And. 118 at 119; *London* v. *James* (1584) 1 And. 128; *Lewen* v. *Mody* (1586) 3 Leo. 135 at 136.

[113] *Panel* v. *Moore* (1555) Plowd. 91 at 92 (in Guildhall).

[114] *Myldon* v. *Harrawood* (1556–7) KB 27/1178, m. 155 ('His freehold' in trespass); *Stokes* v. *Porter* (1558–9) Dyer 166b; CP 40/1176(1), m. 422 ('Never executor' in debt).

[115] *Wylloughby* v. *Dawbeney* (1558–9) CP 40/1176(1), m. 957.

[116] An English draft used in *Lord Stafford* v. *Seymour* (1466) is copied in (1503) CP 40/963, m. 389. It was recorded verbatim because of an allegation of misconduct in handing it *ex parte* to the recognitors in an assize.   [117] *Fyncham* v. *Fabyan* (1500) CP 40/951, m. 115 (judgment for plaintiff).

[118] *Kydwelly* v. *Brande* (1551) Dyer 68a; Plowd. 69v; CP 40/1146, m. 355. Dyer's *'treya'* (drew) was mistranslated by Vaillant as 'tried', which makes no sense.

in other cases at this period, sometimes posing a more specific question at the end.[119] In a case of 1553 we even find it recorded that the jurors answered a specific question put to them by the assize judge and prayed discretion.[120] These specific questions, however, related to special issues, and were therefore ruled out of order for the time being by the decision not to allow special verdicts again in such cases. The special conclusions gave way in any case to the more general conclusion which merely prayed the court's discretion whether judgment should be given for the plaintiff or the defendant,[121] or found for one party or the other contingently upon the court's advice.[122] The judges in banc would be given copies of the special verdict, on paper, and in the Hampshire case where Dyer drew the verdict we learn that they resolved the case among themselves without even hearing counsel.[123]

There is a slight increase in the number of special verdicts in the King's Bench after the mid-1550s, but only upon the general issue in trespass,[124] and even in the 1550s they were less common than demurrers to the evidence. A fruitful new procedure had been re-established for raising legal questions, though the fruit was borne later.

WRITS OF ERROR

If a party could find an error in 'the record, the process, or the rendering of judgment' against him, he could bring a writ of error with the object of having the judgment

[119] e.g. *Trevelyan v. Parkin* (1552–5) Dyer 114a; CP 40/1150, m. 804 (tr. 'the jurors pray the discretion of the justices whether the aforesaid tenements with the appurtenances, being thus demisable for sixty years... should be adjudged by the law of the land to be customary land of the aforesaid manor...'); *Josse v. Joysse* (1556–7) KB 27/1178, m. 29 (tr. 'and they pray the discretion and advice of the aforesaid justices whether the aforesaid W. J. be guilty of the aforesaid trespass by the law of the land, or not'); *Myldon v. Harrawood* (1556–7) KB 27/1178, m. 155 (jurors set out terms of will and pray the advice and discretion of the justices whether the land was the defendant's freehold); *Whytstones v. Nethewey*, ibid., m. 186 (pray discretion and advice whether the defendant be guilty).

[120] *Belgrave v. Bennett* (1549–53) CP 40/1142, m. 606 (tr. 'hereupon the jurors were asked by the justices here whether the within-mentioned three messuages are parcel of the manor... and they say that they are agreed among themselves and are in accord to state the truth of the foregoing in the following form... and they pray the advice and discretion of the aforesaid justices therein').

[121] Cf. the very general forms in *Villers v. Beamonte* (1556) CP 40/1166, m. 516 (tr. 'and they pray the discretion of the justices etc.'); *Brett v. Terre* (1558) KB 27/1186, m. 107 (tr. 'And thereupon the jurors pray the advice of the court, and the jurors assess the damages...').

[122] e.g. *Robynson v. Goddyng* (1557) KB 27/1183, m. 126d (tr. 'upon the whole matter aforesaid the jurors pray the advice of the court, and if it seems to the court that... then the jurors say that [the defendant] is guilty of the trespass'); *Bowyer v. Warren* (1558) CP 40/1175, m. 154 (tr. 'if upon the whole matter aforesaid it seems to the justices that the aforesaid re-entry... was a disseisin... then the aforesaid jurors say upon their oath that [the defendant] disseised [the plaintiff]', and assess damages, but if it seems no disseisin then they find that the defendant did not disseise the plaintiff).

[123] *Kydwelly v. Brande* (1551) Plowd. 69v at 70.

[124] e.g. *Ellys v. Rokesbye* (1555) KB 27/1175, m. 32; *Josse v. Joysse* (1556–7) KB 27/1178, m. 29; *Whytstones v. Nethewey* (1556–7) ibid., m. 186; *Robynson v. Goddyng* (1557–9) KB 27/1183, m. 126d; *Brett v. Terre* (1558–9) KB 27/1186, m. 107.

reversed. The writ was usually addressed to the justices in whose record the error was supposed, commanding them to send the record and process for inspection to the court of error. From minor local courts, such as manorial courts, writs of false judgment lay to the Common Pleas.[125] From local courts of record, such as borough courts, and also from Calais,[126] Ireland,[127] the palatinates,[128] and (after 1543) the Great Sessions of Wales,[129] error lay to the King's Bench. Error also lay to the King's Bench from the Exchequer[130] and the Common Pleas, and the latter constituted the largest single category. Where the writ was brought to reverse a judgment or an outlawry it was addressed to the chief justice; but where it was brought to reverse a final concord—there being no judgment on the plea roll—it was addressed to the custos brevium.[131] Errors in process in the King's Bench— including outlawry[132]—could be corrected by the King's Bench itself on a writ of error *coram nobis*, on the theory that these were not the errors of the court but of its officers. But errors, whether of fact or of law, in a judgment of the King's Bench could be corrected only by Parliament.[133] This remedy was not available unless Parliament was in session; it was extremely expensive; and it was exceptionally rare.[134] The records of the House of Lords mention only five cases between 1514 and 1589, and none of them reached the law reports.[135] The only reported examples in our period occurred in the mid-1480s.[136]

[125] See the discussion in Henry White's reading (Inner Temple, 1531) BL MS. Hargrave 87(2), ff. 237–239v. White pointed out that false judgment could not be used for courts of record held by patent—such as Chester, Oxford, Cambridge, and Exeter—or courts of piepowder. This is borne out by the rolls.

[126] See above, 294–5.   [127] See above, 112.   [128] See above, 109.

[129] 34 & 35 Hen. VIII, c. 26. An example is *Baynton* v. *Bishop of St Asaph* (1555) KB 27/1175, m. 116 (error from Flint in *quare impedit*). The jurisdiction was limited to real or mixed actions. Error in personal actions lay to the Council in Wales and the Marches.   [130] See above, 170.

[131] e.g. *Coryton* v. *Calwodley* (1520) KB 27/1035, m. 68. Such cases become common in the 1550s: e.g. *Seyntyll* v. *Smart* (1554) KB 27/1171, m. 174; *Bayly* v. *Cooke* (1555) KB 27/1175, m. 173; *Tompkyns* v. *Lyster* (1555) KB 27/1176, m. 295; *Salter* v. *Style* (1556) KB 27/1177, m. 171; *Colepepyr* v. *West* (1556) KB 27/1178, m. 124; *Toftes* v. *West*, ibid., m. 173; *Paramoure* v. *Cheveine*, ibid., m. 194 (reversed); *Eyer* v. *Rye* (1557) KB 27/1182, m. 93 (reversed); *Chamber* v. *Terrye* (1557) KB 27/1184, m. 171; *Brokett* v. *Fyshe* (1558) KB 27/1186, mm. 79, 90, 168 (affirmed). The *certiorari* for the original writ of covenant went to the chirographer.

[132] e.g. *Oxenbrigge* v. *Horne* (1489) KB 27/966, m. 57 (reversed). Such cases are quite common.

[133] *Saxcy* v. *Hudson* (1555) KB 27/1173, m. 163 (error *coram nobis*; adjudged that error lay only to Parliament). See also *Jordan's Case* (1535) Mich. 27 Hen. VIII, fo. 25, pl. 3, *per* Fitzjames CJ; *Diversite de Courtz*, sig. A3; FNB 211.

[134] Yorke 202, no. 297 ('quod raro accidit'). An example is *Stourton* v. *Benger* (1485) Mich. 2 Ric. III, fo. 1, pl. 1; fo. 20, pl. 49; 64 Selden Soc. 66; KB 27/894, m. 27 (error to reverse judgment in a writ of error). Note also the form of writ (for removal 'in presens parliamentum nostrum') in Rast. Ent. 284 (302), identifiable as *Pynde* v. *Flouredewe* (1486), below.

[135] E. R. Foster, *The House of Lords 1603–49* (1983), 179.

[136] *Stourton* v. *Benger* (1485), above, n. 134; *Pynde* v. *Flouredewe* (1486) Pas. 1 Hen. VII, fo. 19, pl. 5; 64 Selden Soc. 109, pl. 33; KB 27/885, m. 32 (judgment at first instance); Rast. Ent. 284 (302) (writ of error).

The court of first instance, on receiving a writ of error, had to send the record as directed, within one term, and in default process would issue against the justices, though this was seldom found necessary. In Common Pleas cases, a note of the writ of error was made on the rotulet containing the judgment, and it is noticeable that many cases so marked cannot be traced in the King's Bench rolls. It may be supposed that they were subject to the same vagaries as other forms of litigation and could be settled before the defendant's appearance. When the record arrived in the King's Bench, the plaintiff in error assigned the matters which he intended to argue as errors, and prayed a writ of *scire facias ad audiendum errores* to warn the opposing party to attend and hear them alleged. There is a detailed description of the proceedings in an error case of 1499. The points alleged as errors were first written on paper and then on parchment by Serjeant Brudenell's clerk, and the chief clerk of the King's Bench was paid 5s. to enter them; counsel were retained to appear at the bar three times, first to 'demand' the defendant in error, then to join issue upon the errors, and finally to argue the point of law, which in this case occupied the court from 8.30 until 11 a.m.[137]

It was only when the *scire facias* was issued that the opposing party became defendant to the writ of error, since the latter was not addressed to him, and it was normally only at this stage that the suit was entered of record in the King's Bench.[138] If the record was removed and no errors were assigned, the defendant could pray a *scire facias ad ostendendum errores* to compel his adversary to show why he should not have execution of the original judgment.[139] If the writ of error was discontinued, or if it abated for any reason, the plaintiff might with leave obtain a new writ of error *coram nobis* to revive or recontinue the proceedings.[140] The record, once removed, remained in the King's Bench. If, therefore, the judgment was not reversed, the plaintiff in the original action could elect either to proceed to execution in the court of first instance[141] or—and this whether or not the King's Bench had original jurisdiction in the matter—to sue execution in the latter.[142] A writ of error therefore incidentally provided a convenient device for

[137] *Pilkington Narrative*, 52–3.

[138] FNB 20G, 22F; *Scoles* v. *Hogon* (1506) Spelman 121, 122. The rolls, however, sometimes contain records transmitted with no errors assigned.

[139] *Scoles* v. *Hogon* (1506) Spelman 121 at 122; *Anon.* (1531) Spelman 109–10; Yorke 208, no. 314.

[140] FNB 20G; *Wolley* v. *Leche* (1532) Spelman 91, 115; *Brough* v. *Copledyke* (1529) KB 27/1073, m. 61 (writ abated by death of a party); *Rawlyns* v. *Raynolds* (1552) KB 27/1164, m. 85 (writ abated by death of a party); *Rythe* v. *Fuller* (1552) KB 27/1164, m. 162 (writ abated by marriage of a party; second writ, purchased in 1558, abated by death of a party; third writ purchased in 1564).

[141] e.g. *Prior of St Mary Overy* v. *Culpeper* (1524) Spelman 109; CP 40/1043, m. 561; *Anon.* (1529) Port 62; *Cokkys* v. *Playfote* (1537) Dyer 32a; CP 40/1079, m. 455.

[142] Hil. 14 Hen. VII, fo. 14, pl. 3, *per* Fyneux CJ; anon. reading on Magna Carta, CUL MS. Ee.5.22, fo. 31v; *Hogekynson* v. *Leche* (1534) Spelman 118; KB 27/1093, m. 63d (writ of entry).

having the same judgment entered on the records of two different courts, for greater security.[143]

The plaintiff in error was allowed to assign an error in fact, such as the minority or death of one of the parties, or the party's absence on royal service at the time of his outlawry, or the technical incompetence of the judge, provided he did so before the *scire facias ad audiendum errores*.[144] In this case, the other party could traverse the fact assigned and have the issue tried by jury,[145] or he could demur.[146] An error could alternatively be assigned in some essential part of the Common Pleas proceedings which did not appear on the plea roll, such as the lack of a warrant of attorney or original writ. In this case, a *certiorari* had to be sent to the custos brevium of the Common Pleas before the *scire facias ad audiendum errores*.[147] A third alternative was to assign error 'in diminution of the record', by showing that the record as certified was incomplete.[148] In addition, or alternatively— and far more commonly—the plaintiff could assign errors in law apparent on the face of the record. Since the King's Bench had a general duty to correct any manifest errors which it found in the record, and since the usual plea for the defendant was the general No error (*In nullo est erratum*), which put the whole record in issue, manifest errors could be assigned at any stage in the proceedings. Special replies by the defendant in error were possible, but unusual.[149]

Proceedings in error were an important part of the work of the King's Bench, accounting for about twenty to thirty cases a year in Henry VIII's reign. Spelman took a particular interest in them, as a judge of the King's Bench, and reported no fewer than forty examples. Yet very few of those cases turned on what we should regard as substantive points of law. Certainly it was possible to raise pure questions of law upon a writ of error, or fundamental questions about the forms of action; but by far the greatest number of error cases were concerned with minute procedural technicalities. This is especially true of the large category of suits to reverse outlawries, in which the most trifling slips were sniffed out to justify reversal.

---

[143] This is pointed out in BL MS. Harley 1691, fo. 62; Yorke 202, no. 297.

[144] *Anon.* (1493/1500) Port 102, pl. 31; *Scoles* v. *Hogon* (1506) Spelman 121; Yorke 193, no. 269, *per* Spelman.

[145] 94 Selden Soc. *120–1*. Because it led to an issue of fact, only one error in fact could be assigned: Yorke 206, no. 310; Caryll (Jun.) 377, no. 18.

[146] e.g. *Anderson* v. *Warde* (1554) KB 27/1172, m. 133; Dyer 104a (infancy alleged as a ground for reversing a recovery by default in *dum fuit infra aetatem*; evidence of witnesses enrolled; demurrer; judgment reversed). Cf. *Juysse* v. *Dormer* (1556) KB 27/1178, m. 178 (infancy alleged and found; advisement).

[147] *Anon.* (1492) 1 Caryll 134, pl. 125; *Palmer* v. *Loveys* (1533) Pollard 258. As to what should be done if the certificate was overtaken by events, see *Wolley* v. *Leche* (1532) Spelman 111–12, 114–15; *Botiller* v. *Garlonde* (1532) Spelman 116. See also 94 Selden Soc. *122*.

[148] e.g. *Culpepur* v. *Harryngton* (1487) KB 27/905, m. 70 (omission of formal words by misprision of clerk corrected); *Anon.* (before 1500) Port 102.

[149] e.g. *Hussey* v. *Huse* (1523) KB 27/1047, m. 30 (94 Selden Soc. 298); *Hogekynson* v. *Leche* (1534) KB 27/1090, m. 20 (94 Selden Soc. 322).

Thus, in 1515 an outlawry was reversed because one of the hustings was recorded as having been held on the Monday after the feast of Mary the Virgin, without specifying which feast.[150] Another fortunate defendant was restored to inlawry because he had been described as 'of Norwich', which was considered somehow ambiguous.[151] Yet the court of error was not compelled to reverse judgments for any error, however trivial, since it had authority by a statute of 1429 to amend such errors as were attributable to the 'misprision' (mistake) of the clerk.[152] The Statute of Jeofails 1540 gave further protection against purely formal hazards.[153] But the court evidently had a wide discretion as to what was material and unamendable, and probably treated outlawries to more meticulous scrutiny than judgments on the merits.

As with all the other procedures, judgments in error did not always make clear the point that had been decided. Although the records are more informative than most, in that the plaintiff was required to show his reasons when assigning errors, entries of the judgments were not adorned with explanations. If a judgment was affirmed, it may safely be taken that all the errors assigned were rejected. But if a judgment was reversed, it was expressed to be 'for the aforesaid errors and others appearing in the record', which leaves the reasoning wholly uncertain. Since only one material error was needed to justify reversal, the words of form obviously ought not to be read as meaning that all the assigned errors were in truth accepted by the court. Yet there is no sure way of telling, unless there is a report, what really persuaded the court to reverse judgment. Spelman adverted to a practice of 'crossing' errors if they were rejected by the court, which meant marking a + in the left-hand margin of the roll against each error which failed. If this had been a consistent practice it would have been very helpful, but a study of the rolls reveals that crosses were seldom used at all, and that—even when they were—judgments were sometimes affirmed without all the errors being crossed.[154]

---

[150] *Hylley* v. *Rede* (1515) KB 27/1016, m. 38.

[151] It might denote the city or the county of the city: *Rede* v. *Drury* (1519) KB 27/1033, m. 25.

[152] 94 Selden Soc. 122–3.   [153] See above, 347–8.   [154] 94 Selden Soc. 122.

Part V

THE LEGAL PROFESSION AND
ITS LEARNING

22

The Judiciary

COLLEGIALITY OF THE JUDGES

T HE legal profession was headed by the senior members of the order of the coif, the judges of the two benches, with the lord chief justice of England as their head.[1] They acknowledged each other as brethren,[2] and were formed in the same professional mould. All former readers in the inns of court, they were also— with only two exceptions in our period[3]—all former practising serjeants at law. As serjeants, they were no longer members of the inns of court, though most of them were members of the two serjeants' inns.[4] They nevertheless retained a connection with their former societies by attending the readings there during the two learn- ing vacations; and they also enjoyed a collegiality of their own, centred for formal purposes on Westminster Hall and the Exchequer Chamber. If legal doubts arose while the judges were sitting at Westminster, it was a regular practice—if some- thing of a last resort[5]—for the opinion of the other bench to be sought without a formal meeting in the Exchequer Chamber. In 1531, we read of the King's Bench sending the puisne judge across to the Common Pleas, escorted by the marshal, and with a clerk carrying the record, to learn their views.[6] It is possible that the judges travelled to and from the hall in each other's company. At any rate, in 1481 the judges of the King's Bench collectively asked the opinion of those of the Common Pleas while returning from Westminster.[7]

---

[1] The lord chancellor was, in a sense, the senior figure in the legal system; but until 1529 he was not a member of the same profession as the judges.

[2] The practice of calling each other 'brother' was established before our period, and was by the 1480s adopted by the serjeants as well: Baker, *Serjeants at Law*, 21. But serjeants did not so address the judges: below, 423.   [3] In 1519 and 1545: below, 426.

[4] For judges who kept town houses of their own, see 94 Selden Soc. *135* n. 6, *136* n. 1. This did not in itself preclude membership of one of the serjeants' inns.

[5] See Trin. 11 Hen. VII, fo. 24, pl. 2, *per* Vavasour J. (tr. 'Vavasour [J.]: If you like, I will go into the King's Bench to know their opinions, and if they say the same as you then in God's name let it be so adjudged. Bryan [CJ]: Do not do that until we have discussed it further').

[6] *Lewys* v. *Cam* (1531) Spelman 124. Likewise the Common Pleas would send its puisne judge with a question to the King's Bench: *Anon.* (1543) Gell's reports, I, Pas. 34 Hen. VIII, fo. 12. Cf. *Bellengeham's Case* (1537) Dyer 34a (where the King's Bench sent Baker, A.-G., to ask the Common Pleas judges a question).

[7] Pas. 21 Edw. IV, fo. 30, pl. 24 ('veniendo de Westm.'). For opinions expressed by individual judges on the way to and from the Hall, see above, 389 n. 26.

But the principal informal means of consultation must have been the two serjeants' inns. By 1500 these were located in Chancery Lane (south of the Rolls) and in Fleet Street (between the Temple and the Whitefriars),[8] though in the 1480s and early 1490s Scrope's Inn (near St Andrew's church in Holborn) seems to have been used as a serjeants' inn instead of the Chancery Lane house.[9] Whenever lawyers eat together they talk law, and once the judges and serjeants began to keep commons together it was inevitable that their inns should become centres of legal discussion. The two serjeants' inns never rivalled the inns of court by developing formal learning exercises, but by the early Tudor period they were beginning to be used as an alternative to the Exchequer Chamber for adjourned assizes[10] and assemblies of the judges.[11] These were public transactions, attended by counsel not of the coif, and the choice of a venue in one of the serjeants' inns rather than Westminster Hall reflected professional convenience in the arrangement of judicial assemblies rather than spontaneous debate between members of the same order. However, it is from the same period that we first learn something of the informal intellectual life of these inns.

The year books contain only one explicit mention of an informal discussion among members of one of the serjeants' inns: in 1486, Huse CJ is reported to have put certain questions to Sulyard and Townshend JJ 'at his inn after dinner', probably referring to the Fleet Street inn.[12] But Spelman's reports show that, under Henry VIII, discussions frequently took place in Serjeants' Inn, Chancery Lane. The group of participants regularly mentioned by Spelman were evidently the judicial members of that inn,[13] and this preference shown by a reporter for opinions expressed in his own inn may indicate that these societies had a deeper influence on common-law traditions than is apparent on the surface. A more simple explanation for Spelman's bias could be that in his time the other King's Bench judges happened all to belong to the same society, whereas the Fleet Street

---

[8] The first reference to this inn by name is in 1516: PCC 25 Holder (will of Guy Palmes). But serjeants had been there in the 1430s, and were probably there in the 1480s: see below, n. 12. In 1521 its usages could be described as 'old': Baker, *Serjeants at Law*, 279.

[9] In 1640 Dugdale noted a reference to the inn in the bishop of Ely's accounts for 1484 (now lost) as 'now called the Serjeants' Place': *Origines Juridiciales*, 333 (tr.). In 1494 it was conveyed to Lord Scrope's feoffees, and by 1499 was 'lately called Serjeants' Inn': *CIPM Hen. VII*, ii. 138, no. 214. During this period the Chancery Lane inn was let to Sir Thomas Grey; but in 1496 the bishop of Ely granted a new lease to the judges and serjeants. See E. Williams, *Early Holborn and the Legal Quarter of London* (1927), i. 293–314.   [10] Above, 260.

[11] e.g. Pas. 19 Hen. VIII, fo. 6, pl. 5; Trin. 19 Hen. VIII, fo. 12, pl. 10.

[12] Hil. 1 Hen. VII, fo. 10, pl. 12. Sulyard referred in his will to (tr.) 'my inn next to the Carmelite friars', which must be the Fleet Street inn: PCC 21 Milles. Townshend desired burial in the Whitefriars, which carries the same implication: PCC 2 Vox.

[13] 94 Selden Soc. 136–7. Fitzherbert J. recorded deeds in this inn: CP 40/1078, Hord m. 1 (1533); 1079, m. 632d (1533); (1537), 1093, Hord m. 13 (1537). So did Luke J.: CP 40/1088, Hord m. 1 (1536); KB 27/1102, m. 37 (1537); KB 27/128, m. 20 (1543).

inn was dominated by the Common Pleas. On the other hand, Serjeant Yorke, who as a practising serjeant must have been more concerned with the Common Pleas, shows the same predilection in his reports for the opinions of Spelman's group of judges; and this can only be a result of his membership of their inn.[14] It is no surprise that Spelman and Yorke should have reported with a Gray's Inn focus, but their preference for Chancery Lane over Fleet Street demonstrates the importance of informal interchanges of opinion in developing a judicial consensus on points of principle.

JUDICIAL INDEPENDENCE

The judges were thus exposed to collegial learning, and the interchange of opinion, at four distinct levels: in occasional assemblies of all the judges in the Exchequer Chamber, in their own courts in banc, at readings in the inns of court, and at table in the serjeants' inns. They were also, in this period, still active members of the legislature, and individual judges might be sent from the House of Lords to negotiate the wording of a bill with the Commons.[15] However, in asssessing the role of the judiciary in the development of the common law, we must confront the question whether the only influences upon their minds were intellectual. For, with respect both to their legal pronouncements and to the exercise of their discretion in granting motions, the judges were open to the same kinds of pressure as the jurors were in making their decisions of fact. At the beginning of our period, powerful men certainly regarded the judges as amenable to undue influence, and it was necessary for Henry VII to remind his councillors not to 'conceive against any judge or officer indignation or displeasance for doing of his office in form of law'.[16] The judges officially resisted improper pressure, and the year books tell us that Huse CJ had occasion to rebuke Sir Thomas Brandon in open court for seeking favour on account of royal service.[17] Yet pressures must have been ever present. Assize judges were treated to meals and presents, though usually by corporations rather than private litigants.[18] Sir Thomas More and Sir John Fitzjames were each

[14] 94 Selden Soc. 137. Serjeant Caryll was a member of the Fleet Street inn, and in one place reported an opinion entertained by 'Pollard [J.] and all the members of our house': *Poynes' Case* (c.1514/15) 2 Caryll 655 at 657.

[15] e.g. *HLJ*, i. 5b (Brudenell and Conyngesby JJ sent to Commons with bill concerning assize judges (tr.) 'to treat concerning the reform of the same bill, and when it should begin to have force', 1510).

[16] Condon, 'An Anachronism with Intent?', 247, art. 16 (sp. mod.). Cf. Edmund Dudley's remarks to the same effect in *The Tree of Commonwealth* [1509], ed. D. M. Brodie (1948), 35.

[17] *Wingfield's Case* (1481) Mich. 21 Edw. IV, fo. 71, pl. 55. Note also the case of Lord Cobham and Fitzherbert J., above, 69.

[18] E. W. Ives, 'The Reputation of the Common Lawyer in English Society 1450–1550' (1960) 7 *Univ. Birmingham Historical Jnl* 130–61, at 148–50. The city of York commonly presented the judges with 16d.

praised for refusing all gifts,[19] which carries the implication that many judges were less scrupulous. It now seems almost incredible that a solicitor could advise his client that 'if ye send the said lord Norwich [CJCP] a firkin of sturgeon, it will not be lost';[20] though we have to remember that some kind of moral distinction was then made between a bribe and an unconditional gift. It is also rather shocking to find a judge begging for 'good lordship' from a peer with whose financial business he was officially concerned.[21] Yet if bribery had been prevalent, the wealthy would always have won their lawsuits. Litigants were no doubt more concerned to ensure an impartial judge than to buy an unfair favour, and if the judges were at fault in not making clear that their impartiality did not rest on tokens of respect, that is not the same thing as corruption. It is significant that no serious allegations of corruption were made by contemporaries,[22] and that a study of disbursements in litigants' accounts does not reveal evidence of corruption.[23] If we may credit Sir Thomas More, who was not a judge of the coif, judges were in fact more independent than juries.[24]

The least resistible form of pressure was that applied by the Crown, whose servants the judges were.[25] No judges were removed from office by Henry VII or Henry VIII,[26] and this has been taken to indicate that their compliance could invariably be counted upon.[27] On the other hand, the removal of judges was so uncommon before Stuart times that it may not have been in practice a serious weapon of coercion. Perhaps more telling is the fact that judges were appointed on the nomination of royal advisers such as Cromwell,[28] who continued to hold the purse-strings, sometimes tightly, after they were in office.[29] The difficulty is to establish the effects of pressure, and the extent (if any) to which it may be said to have influenced the law itself.

worth of wine and bread: e.g. YCA, CC 3, sub dat. 1535, p. 129; CC 4, fo. 90v ('presents to the king's justices of assize', comprising two gallons of Gascon wine, 1542–3).

[19] Roper, *Lyfe of Moore*, ed. Hitchcock, 61–4; D. Lloyd, *State-Worthies* (1670), 114–18 (Fitzjames: source not stated).

[20] Letter from George Rolle to Lady Lisle (1534) SP 3/13, fo. 74; *Lisle Letters*, ed. Byrne, ii. 223, no. 239. Cf. Ives, *Common Lawyers*, 309.

[21] *Lisle Letters*, ed. Byrne, i. 503–4, no. 27; ii. 159, no. 196 (Lyster CB to Viscount Lisle).

[22] For some vague complaints see Ives, 'Reputation of the Common Lawyer in English Society', 139; *Common Lawyers*, 308.

[23] Ives, *Common Lawyers*, 311–12.

[24] *The Debellation of Salem and Bizance*, ed. J. Guy and others (1987), 131, 134–5.

[25] Edmund Dudley acknowledged this to be a serious threat to judicial impartiality: *The Tree of Commonwealth* [1509], ed. Brodie, 34.

[26] Mary I refused to reappoint Cholmeley CJKB and Mountagu CJCP in 1553, for their part in witnessing Edward VI's will, and the following year (for reasons now obscure) dismissed Morgan CJCP.

[27] K. Pickthorn, *Early Tudor Government: Henry VII* (1934), 53; Ives, *Common Lawyers*, 233.

[28] For the appointment of Luke J. see *LP*, vi. 1370, 1371, 1381; vii. 263.

[29] The salaries were two years in arrear in 1534: *LP*, vii. 848 (and cf. nos. 50, 108).

Most of the comment on this issue has centred upon the highly untypical state trials of Sir Thomas More and Queen Anne, trials which have brought a good deal of obloquy on the judges who participated. Professor Amos went so far as to comment that 'men who could prostitute their learning, talents, and stations in committing murders, by legal sophistry, to please a king, would not hold the scales of justice even between party and party'.[30] This grave charge is as difficult to disprove as it is to maintain. We now know that the judges were commonly consulted before indictments for treason were preferred, and that as a result of their advice many accused persons were released without trial.[31] This being so, one would not expect the judges as a rule to countenance purely legal objections by those who had been brought to trial on their advice, at least when they were the very objections which they had already considered privately. The trial of the facts was, of course, for the jury and not the judges. No doubt judges could exert influence on a jury, but the forms of charge and oath made it plain that the ultimate responsibility for a conviction rested upon the jurors' consciences. The judges' task was to see that the procedural rules were observed, and they evidently performed that limited role with propriety.[32]

In the surviving correspondence between assize judges and Secretary Cromwell, we encounter an obsequiousness, even a hint of subservience, which a modern English reader might find offensive to the ideal of judicial independence. But here again we must distinguish between executive cooperation and interference with the course of a trial. Justices of assize represented the views of the government to the country, and they were not above advising the government on what we should regard as political matters, in the light of their local knowledge gained on circuit.[33] Even in proceedings at law they had some discretion to help the prosecution: for instance, by putting off a trial so that further evidence could be collected, or by binding over a suspect to appear at the next assizes in the expectation that better evidence would become available. This would not have been regarded as improper, but as a necessary flexibility if difficult prosecutions were to succeed at all. There was no independent public prosecutor, and it is doubtful whether the Crown was represented by counsel even in major capital cases on circuit. In treason and other cases of public importance, the king's Council were usually the moving force as prosecutors; and in view of the political delicacy which such cases involved it was advisable for the judge to be directly acquainted with the

---

[30] A. Amos. *Observations on the Statutes of the Reformation Parliament* (1859), 137. Cf. Lord Campbell, *Lives of the Chief Justices of England* (1849), i. 68.

[31] Elton, *Policy and Police*, 274–5, 301 ff. Prosecution decisions were commonly taken in Council, with the judges present: Condon, 'Ruling Elites in the Reign of Henry VII', 109 at 129–30. An early example is *Earl of Warwick's Case* (1499) 75 Selden Soc. 32. See also above, 202–3 (Privy Council, 1540).

[32] 94 Selden Soc. 138. See further above, 68.   [33] See above, 261.

background—not so that he might do anything unlawful or unfair to secure a conviction, but so that he might know whether to press on with or simply drop cases which turned out to present problems. There is at least no hint in Cromwell's correspondence that the judges were under pressure to bend or lay aside the law to suit the government. A judge no doubt regarded himself as a Crown servant, and perhaps believed (rightly or wrongly) that through Cromwell he was receiving the king's personal instructions. Nevertheless, he was not afraid to reprieve a convicted traitor if he felt legal scruples. Like all servants, he could only carry out lawful commands; and the king, like other masters, was legally powerless to command something that was wrong.

One of Henry VIII's judges, Sir John Spelman, has left first-hand accounts of a number of state trials which he attended. They read more like news items than law reports, suggesting that the judges felt no reservations about the Crown evidence, or did not regard it as their business to question it. By and large, the cases did not involve difficult legal questions; and, when they did, the judges were assembled to discuss them in advance of the arraignment, so that an agreed ruling could be given in public if the point was taken.[34] The practice of extrajudicial consultation had been questioned in 1486, when Humphrey Stafford's plea of sanctuary was referred to the judges in the Exchequer Chamber, though the case has no direct bearing on pre-trial conferences, because there was no trial. The puisne justices began to discuss Stafford's case in the presence of the lord chancellor, but protested that it was not 'good order' to state their opinions before the matter had been brought before them judicially. Shortly afterwards, Huse CJ went to the king in person and asked him not to seek their opinions, 'for they thought it would come into the King's Bench judicially, and then they would do what by right they ought to do'.[35] This the king conceded, with a complaint about the delay, and the judges of both benches then assembled in the King's Bench, where Stafford was arraigned upon his earlier attainder and offered to plead sanctuary.[36] Huse CJ's objection cannot have been to the consideration in advance of points of law and procedure which might arise at a trial, because there was no prospect of a trial: it was presumably expected from the outset that the Crown would demur to the plea. There were a number of unusual problems in the case, including a potential

[34] R. v. Lord Dacre of the North (1534) Spelman 54; 121 Selden Soc. 415–16. See also R. v. Lincoln (1517) Port 123 n. 5 (conference at Fyneux CJ's house); HEHL MS. EL 2654, fo. 23v (conference in the Star Chamber, in the king's presence); R. v. Charterhouse Priors, and R. v. Sir Thomas More (1535), conference noted in LP, viii. 606, 892. For examples later in the century see 109 Selden Soc., p. lxii.

[35] R. v. Stafford (1486) Trin. 1 Hen. VII, fo. 25, pl. 1, at fo. 26 (tr.). For this case, see also Ives, Common Lawyers, 245–6; below, 546. Ives refers to a 'trial', but the record and the report show that there was a demurrer.

[36] Cf. the Latin report in 64 Selden Soc. 118 (tr. 'all the justices of both benches, sitting in the King's Bench, were unanimously of one opinion . . .').

conflict between the Church and the common law, and the judges may have been subjected to undue pressure from the king's Council. But the principal difficulty was that the judges could not begin a sensible discussion of such a complex matter without seeing how Stafford would frame his plea. For that purpose he was allowed counsel, causing a delay which further annoyed the king, and the matter was then argued upon a formal demurrer. After much discussion, the judges decided in favour of the Crown. Their resistance to committing themselves in advance was probably less to do with political sensitivity than with sheer practicality, including the desire not to give the convicted traitor Stafford any guidance on how he might frame a plea which would meet all possible objections. The development of the pre-trial conference was not, therefore, incompatible with the position taken by Huse CJ in 1486.

There is no reason to suppose that in pre-trial discussions the judges blindly favoured the Crown. In 1534, they laid down the important principle that the court could not communicate with the jury, or peers triers, in the absence of the accused.[37] And the following year, in More's case, they apparently agreed that a refusal to answer questions was not an overt act of treason.[38] There are instances of judges reprieving 'political' convicts because of doubts about the validity or technical propriety of their indictments.[39] In major cases, however, the indictments were drawn with great care and consideration, so that the defence had to be made upon the evidence rather than upon legal technicalities. And if a judge such as Spelman treated the evidence with a spirit of credulity, when jotting it down in a private notebook, we ought not too hastily to condemn jurors who found verdicts of guilty against prisoners charged with treason.[40] Even packed juries sometimes acquitted,[41] and without a detailed study of jury panels no one is in a position to say how far juries were packed with men of known bias. In the case of More's trial, in which the conduct of the prosecution left much to be desired by the standards of today, it is not clear that the evidence was perjured. It would have been easy enough to hire rogues to put words into More's mouth, whereas every attempt was made to trap him into a genuine treasonable statement. The uneasiness which posterity has felt about More's conviction stems largely from the obnoxious character of a statute which virtually forced a man to condemn himself on a matter of conscience; but that was the work of Parliament, not the judges. Although the judges were invited to declare the statute invalid, in deciding that Parliament was sovereign they were hardly 'prostituting their

[37] R. v. Lord Dacre of the North (1534) Spelman 54–5.

[38] Derrett, 'The Trial of Sir Thomas More', 449 at 459, 462. It is not quite clear whether this was a ruling, or a concession by prosecuting counsel.

[39] See Elton, Policy and Police, 299–300, 303, 305.

[40] For the contemporary credibility of the evidence against Queen Anne see R. M. Warnicke, The Rise and Fall of Anne Boleyn (1989), 228.   [41] ibid. 314–17.

learning'. The only contemporary standard by which the fairness of a prosecution could be measured was that of the ecclesiastical courts, which was admitedly not a high standard; but it is evident that the procedures of the secular law in this intolerant age were decidedly more favourable to the accused than those which More (when in power) had thought appropriate for the eradication of those whose consciences were at odds with his own.[42] In this and in other state trials of the period the judges were certainly involved in a sanguinary process, but they seem on balance to have conducted the proceedings in accordance with contemporary standards of fairness. The earl of Northumberland grudgingly admitted this after a trial in 1531, when, despite pressure from the Crown, the judges remained (in his words) 'nevertheless very indifferent'.[43]

The clearest example of pressure being applied successfully on the judges by the Crown comes from the sphere of feudal revenue, and again our most revealing source is Spelman.[44] The celebrated case of Lord Dacre of the South (1535), which will be discussed in Chapter 35, was of the greatest concern to the Crown in enabling the restoration of feudalism for fiscal purposes and preparing the way for the execution of uses.[45] It arose from a traverse in Chancery to an inquisition *post mortem*, and the Chancery judges (Audley, the chancellor, and Cromwell as master of the rolls) referred it to all the judges of England in the Exchequer Chamber. After hearing counsel in the presence of a year-book reporter, the judges reconvened in private. On the first show of hands, the judges (including Audley and Cromwell, who were of course for the king) seemed evenly divided. However, Audley counted Port J. on the wrong side and thereby reckoned a majority of one in favour of the king. Spelman does not say whether the miscounting was deliberate, but at any rate Audley did not ask Port to raise his voice and Port did not see fit to correct the result. The judges were then convoked before the king himself, who promised his 'good thanks' if they—presumably meaning all of them—would decide the case in his favour. Now, deciding the case in the king's favour required overturning the orthodox learning of the time, learning which had been accepted by Parliament in 1490. What manner of inducement or threat underlay the words 'good thanks' one can only guess; but the 'minority' (including Spelman) did subsequently give way, ostensibly out of deference to the wisdom of the 'majority'. At least two of the judges, and perhaps Port as well, had the good fortune or the tact to absent themselves when the final vote was taken. And so the king managed to obtain the opinion of his judges, *nemine contradicente,*

---

[42] See e.g. *The Debellation of Salem and Bizance*, ed. J. Guy and others (1987), 104, where More argued that if common-law standards of openness were extended to heresy proceedings, 'the streets were well likely to swarm full of heretics' (sp. mod.).　　　　　　　　　[43] SP 1/66, fo. 295.

[44] For some less clear examples, see 94 Selden Soc. *140* n. 3.

[45] *Re Lord Dacre of the South* (1535) Spelman 228–30; B. & M. 105–11; above, 66; below, 669.

overturning the common law as previously understood—and stunning the House of Commons. It may reasonably be assumed that the Crown brought similar pressure in other cases. It is well known that Sir James Hales was imprisoned on Queen Mary's orders in 1553 for charging a grand jury to the effect that the statutes concerning religious conformity stood unrepealed, and was placed under so much pressure to change his religious views that he took his own life.[46] However, although his position was one of legal and constitutional propriety, his was an individual and rather hopeless stand against a new regime. We know that heavy pressure could sometimes be withstood.[47] For example, when Queen Mary sent a token to the judges in 1557 to decide a case against Sir Nicholas Throgmorton, they refused to comply, 'inasmuch as the law was against the queen'.[48] Whatever occasional lapses may have occurred, independence was unquestionably hailed throughout the period as a virtue and as an attainable ideal: the story of Gascoigne CJ, Prince Henry, and King Henry IV, was a popular lesson even with Henry VIII's chief justices.[49]

If we turn to ordinary criminal cases, there is so little information available to us that we cannot safely make any assumptions about the standard of justice applied in them. We should not be surprised to see favour playing a part in securing the discharge of the guilty. The most obvious example is the reprieve of a convicted felon so that he could obtain a pardon, a practice which was not confined to cases where the conviction was thought unsafe, or where there were mitigating circumstances, but might be extended as a favour to persons of rank or connection.[50] A letter from Cromwell,[51] or some other person known to the trial judge, would doubtless have been effective. This is not a criticism of the judges, since the grant of a pardon was an executive act of clemency, and no judge would authorize execution knowing that a pardon was available. But it is possible that the judges used an analogous discretion themselves, when exercising their jurisdiction to quash indictments for minor flaws. Spelman reports a case where an

---

[46] New DNB; R. Wingfield, Vita Mariae Reginae, ed. D. McCulloch (29 Camden Soc., 4th ser.; 1984), 242–3, 292. The death was held to be a felonious suicide and gave rise to three reported cases: Bishop of Chichester v. Webb (1554) Dyer 107b; Hales v. Petyt (No. 1) (1558–60) Dyer's reports, 109 Selden Soc. 46; Hales v. Petyt (No. 2) (1561–2) ibid. 72; Plowd. 253.

[47] e.g. The Princess's Case (1536), noted in LP, xi. 7, 236.

[48] Throgmorton's Case (1557) Chr. Yelverton's reports, fo. 247 at 248v (tr. 'Mr Gerrarde, now the queen's attorney, who was of counsel with Mr Throgmorton but did not argue, recently told me in his chamber that Queen Mary sent her ring and token to the justices to give judgment in the case for her, but they would not, inasmuch as the law was against the queen'). This was a scire facias to repeal a grant of Brigstock Park.

[49] Baker, Serjeants at Law, 285–6, 300 (speeches to new serjeants); T. Elyot, The Boke named the Governour (1531), ff. 122–123.

[50] Elyot, The Governour, fo. 128v, mentioned a tendency to allow gentlemen to escape punishment; he may have been referring to jury verdicts, but more likely to pardons.

[51] e.g. LP, vi. 872 (pr. in R. B. Merriman, Life and Letters of Cromwell (1902), 359, no. 49); LP, vii. 1252.

indictment was quashed because of a minor uncertainty, and we know from other sources that the fortunate defendant was an usher of the duke of Richmond's bed-chamber and that the duke had asked Cromwell to intercede for him.[52] Spelman reports only the point of law, which was decided in a manner consistent with the traditional insistence on precision in indictments. But are we to assume that Cromwell wrote or spoke to the judges, and that his intervention swayed the out-come? Would an unfriended defendant have received a different judgment? The answer is not known. However, even if we assume from this example that favour may have influenced the quashing of indictments, it is not certain that contem-porary morality would have been more affronted by this than by the failure to prosecute crime in the first place. Was it any injustice for the unfavoured criminal to suffer death, when he had been duly convicted? If one convict was shown grace and another left to his fate, that was unfortunate for the latter, but had any wrong been done him? Favour could not convict the innocent, for no judge could sub-stitute a conviction for an acquittal, and if favour occasionally helped the guilty it betokened a flexible standard of mercy rather than corruption. It was from such a discretion that sentencing policies would eventually emerge, to mitigate the fixed death penalty; but we should not expect in our period to see a sharp distinction in the categories of mercy between a ground of mitigation and a favour.

---

[52] R. v. Delarever (1534) Spelman 52, 100; KB 27/1092, Rex m. 5 (pr. 94 Selden Soc. 283–4); LP, vii. 762 (pr. 94 Selden Soc. 284). For an interesting sidelight on Delarever, see Elton, Policy and Police, 315.

23

The Bar

SERJEANTS AT LAW

THE most clearly identifiable and best-documented branch of the English legal profession was the order or fraternity of serjeants at law, who provided the Bar of the Court of Common Pleas, the principal common-law court throughout the period.[1] There were usually fewer than ten in practice, and indeed for two memorable months in 1559 the number dwindled to one, William Bendlowes, who was proud to claim that he had been 'solus serviens ad legem in Anglia'.[2] Every ten years or so, when numbers had fallen through death or promotion, there would be a group call of eight to ten new serjeants,[3] chosen from the double readers in the inns of court.

By 1495 the procedure for creating a serjeant was for the king to sign a warrant for the issue of a writ of subpoena under the great seal, stating that the recipient had been chosen on the advice of the 'Council', and commanding him to prepare to take the degree at an appointed day.[4] The performance of this command required much elaborate ritual, and up to a year's notice might be given.[5] The central feature of the creation was the ceremony in the Common Pleas when the graduands were heard to recite a count for the first time at the bar, in a feigned real action brought between two real-life patrons.[6] There was also a magnificent feast, which the king himself sometimes attended.[7] Only eighty-nine serjeants were created in our period, forming a distinct elite. As an exclusive order of dignity, they were invested at their creation with the distinctive parti-coloured robes

---

[1] For general information see Baker, *Serjeants at Law*.

[2] Inscription formerly in Serjeants' Inn, Fleet Street: see Baker, *Serjeants at Law*, 111.

[3] The largest call was in 1531, when 11 were created.

[4] Baker, *Serjeants at Law*, 30. Until 1495 the writs were enrolled on the close rolls. They were not enrolled on the patent rolls until 1552.

[5] The serjeants created in June 1540 had been chosen as early as July 1539: *Lisle Letters*, ed. Byrne, v. 584–5.

[6] For the patrons at the 1555 call of serjeants see Baker, *Serjeants at Law*, 434. Each serjeant at a group call used a different form of action.

[7] Henry VII attended the feasts of 1495 and 1503, and Henry VIII those of 1521 and 1531: Baker, *Serjeants at Law*, 100, 165, 168, 279. These were all kept at Ely House except for the 1503 feast, which was in Lambeth Palace.

and cowled hoods of murrey (mulberry colour) on one side and deep blue or black on the other,[8] with white linen coifs tied over their heads. They were also required, on taking the coif, to leave their inns of court. In the fifteenth century, some of them kept private town-houses, though by 1558 most had become members of one of the two serjeants' inns (in Chancery Lane and Fleet Street respectively).[9] They were nevertheless expected to maintain close relations with their former inns, giving general advice, and attending the readings.

Since the degree of serjeant came into existence through controlling the pleaders in the Common Bench, serjeants enjoyed the monopoly in that court of oral pleading,[10] and probably (by extension) the settling of written pleadings and demurrers. By the sixteenth century they in practice undertook most of the advocacy in banc as well.[11] As a consequence of this monopoly they were supposed to keep the Common Pleas bar—that is, to make it their principal place of practice[12]—in return for which they were entitled to be excused from knighthood.[13] Yet they were not debarred from appearing in other central courts, and the law reports show that they regularly did so; their signatures are also found on bills in Chancery, showing that they settled pleadings in the newer courts as well. Towards the middle of the sixteenth century the special relationship with the Common Pleas, and the special nature of the degree itself, were weakened by a few serjeants who chose not to practise at Westminster at all. Robert Mennell (d. 1563), created in 1547, seems to have lived in the far north of England and no one remembered him when Bendlowes was reckoned as the sole serjeant in 1559. He had been general attorney to the earl of Northumberland, though the stringent terms of his retainer had been relaxable if he became a serjeant.[14] He served as attorney-general, steward, and chancellor, to the bishop of Durham, and as clerk of the peace in Durham, after becoming a serjeant,[15] but his name does not appear in reports of Common Pleas cases. Doubtless he had an informal dispensation from the duties of a serjeant. That was the proper course. In 1550, John

---

[8] These were worn at the creation, and for some time thereafter; each half of the robes was a different colour, adjoining at the front and back. By 1500 serjeants also wore violet robes on certain occasions, perhaps when appearing in banc, and scarlet robes for best: Baker, *Serjeants at Law*, 73–8.

[9] For the serjeants' inns see above, 412.

[10] i.e. in the technical sense of framing pleadings orally.

[11] See Baker, *Serjeants at Law*, 42–3. It seems, however, that apprentices also stood at the bar: see Trin. 1 Edw. V, fo. 4, pl. 6 (tr. 'it was said by various apprentices present there at the bar...').

[12] Baker, *Serjeants at Law*, 44–5.

[13] *Re John Brooke* (1514) E159/293, m. 9d; Baker, *Serjeants at Law*, 44, 52. From the 1530s onwards, however, there are several examples of serjeants being knighted: below, 597.

[14] *Mennell v. Earl of Northumberland* (1533–6) CP 40/1077, m. 610; CP 40/1090, m. 501; Baker, *Serjeants at Law*, 44 n. 5.

[15] Baker, *Serjeants at Law*, 44 n. 5; 199 Surtees Soc. 344; *Valor Ecclesiasticus* v. 300.

Pollard obtained a formal patent of discharge from the degree of serjeant, and of 'all attendance and service' due as a serjeant, and from wearing the coif and the 'vestures and habits' of a serjeant, in order to become a member of the Council in the Marches.[16] A similar patent was granted to Ralph Rokeby when he joined the Council of the North in 1555.[17] The patents show how strictly the duties of serjeants were still regarded; and yet no serjeant before Mennell seems to have put himself in the position of needing one.

Another privilege of the order was that only serjeants could be appointed as judges of the Common Pleas and King's Bench. Of the eighty-nine serjeants created in our period, no less than fifty-four received such an appointment; and another (Audley) became lord chancellor, the first serjeant to attain this office since the reign of Edward III.[18] Serjeants were also commonly appointed as chief baron of the Exchequer,[19] though the junior barons were not of the coif and therefore did not share in the circuit duties of the other judges.[20] The judicial element in the order of the coif was thus stronger than the practising element,[21] and the brotherhood between judges and serjeants enhanced the prestige of the order still further.[22] Nevertheless, the serjeants did not address the judges in court as 'brother'. Arguments in the year books were generally prefaced with 'Sir' in the singular, which may mean 'my lord'[23]—*sire* being the vocative of *seignior*—but seems to have been used for counsel also, unless they were deemed to be addressed through the chief justice. By the 1550s serjeants were beginning to address the judges in banc plurally, as 'my lords', a practice first noted in Plowden.[24]

Almost half the serjeants at some stage in their careers served the Crown as king's serjeants,[25] an office to which they were appointed by patent with a

---

[16] Patent roll, C66/828, m. 13; pr. (sp. mod.) in Baker, *Serjeants at Law*, 65–6; noted in Plowd. 89v.

[17] Dugdale, *Origines Juridiciales*, 139–40.   [18] *Memorandum* (1532) Spelman 38.

[19] Five of the nine appointed between 1483 and 1558 were serjeants. The last non-serjeant was Clement Heigham (Mar. to Nov. 1558): Baker, *Serjeants at Law*, 170.

[20] Above, 159–60. This changed after 1579, when Serjeant Shute was appointed a junior baron.

[21] Moreover, some serjeants who did not receive permanent appointments served as commissioners of assize.

[22] Note Pas. 14 Hen, VII, fo. 21, pl. 2, *per* Bryan CJ (tr. 'the contrary is agreed by all my fellows, as well upon the bench as at the bar').

[23] A new serjeant on making his count addressed the CJCP (as 'my lord'), rather than the whole court, and it may be supposed this reflected the general practice with oral pleadings.

[24] *Colthirst* v. *Bejushin* (1550) Plowd. 21 at 23, *per* Pollard sjt ('Vous mes seigniors...'); *Wimbish* v. *Tailbois* (1550) ibid. 42, *per* Coke sjt; *Partridge* v. *Straunge* (1553) ibid. 78v, *per* Morgan sjt. The courtesy title 'lord' (*seignior*) had previously been reserved for the chief justices—none of whom were peers.

[25] For lists see J. Sainty, *List of English Law Officers, King's Counsel and Holders of Patents of Precedence*, 7 Selden Soc. Supp. Ser.; 1987, 12–15; 94 Selden Soc. 386–90.

small salary of £20 and some minor perquisites.[26] There were between two and four king's serjeants at any one time, and they were the pre-eminent leaders of the Bar. The appointment amounted to a general retainer on behalf of the Crown without otherwise restricting private practice. In collaboration with the attorney-general they were responsible for prosecuting important criminal cases,[27] especially in state trials,[28] they were summoned to attend the House of Lords as assistants,[29] and they also represented the Crown in civil cases. They were not allowed to appear or advise against the Crown,[30] and in 1540 Serjeant Browne was punished for devising a revenue-avoidance scheme.[31] On the other hand, the prohibition was relaxed where the king had only a formal interest in a civil suit, as in trespass against the king's peace. Thus, it was held in 1558 that the king's serjeants might be of counsel with the petty jury in an attaint, though if the verdict passed against them they could then change sides and pray judgment for the king.[32]

Notwithstanding their privileges, the serjeants in the Tudor period no longer benefited from them as fully as they had in earlier times. Indeed, the new serjeants called in 1540 obtained the king's permission to curtail the length of the feast on the grounds that 'the gain of the law was not as it had anciently been'.[33] This seems on the face of it to be an allusion to the general decline in litigation in the previous generation, though recovery should have been noticeable by 1540.[34] But one of the growing threats to the order of the coif was the rise of central courts other than the Common Pleas, courts where their monopoly of audience did not obtain. The number of serjeants was not increased sufficiently to man all the central courts when the boom occurred, and so other senior members of the Bar inevitably began to share the work. The greater ultimate threat to the serjeants, posed by the rank of king's counsel, had not yet emerged. But its origins lie in the growing authority and professional standing during the Tudor period of the law officers who were not of the coif.

[26] They received £1. 6s. 11d. in lieu of robes, and also 'rewards', defined temp. Eliz. I as ink, paper, and a document bag: Baker, *Serjeants at Law*, 59.

[27] The 'king's serjeant' (in the singular) was named with the attorney-general in the proclamation for evidence at assizes and sessions: above, 259.   [28] Sta. P.C. 152.

[29] Curiously, this did not disqualify them from election to the Commons. Dyer, for example, was MP and Speaker in 1553 while he was queen's serjeant.

[30] *Elyot v. Tofte* (1513) KB 27/1006, m. 62; below, 786.

[31] Below, 681 n. 191 Browne had also been temporarily removed from office in 1532 for advising felons to sell their goods to avoid forfeiture: Spelman 183 (misdated).

[32] *Memorandum* (1558) BL MS. Harley 1624, fo. 55v. Cf. *Anon.* (1556) BL MS. Hargrave 388, fo. 296v (tr. 'Dyer, who put the case, held the contrary, and yet was the queen's serjeant').

[33] R. Owen, *History of the Common Law*, BL MS. Harley 1572, fo. 246. The effect seems to have been to concentrate on a single grand day, at which the entertainment was far from parsimonious: Baker, *Serjeants at Law*, 100.   [34] Above, 121–2, 142–3.

THE LAW OFFICERS

The principal law officers of the Crown were the king's serjeants, and the king's attorney-general and solicitor-general.[35] Of almost equal importance and rank in the first half of the Tudor period were the king's law officers in the duchy of Lancaster and in the new revenue courts.[36] There were corresponding officers in the palatinates, though they had far less business.[37] The nomenclature of 'attorney' and 'solicitor' disguised the fact that these were necessarily men of legal eminence, mostly benchers of their inns of court. Indeed, all but two of the attorneys-general were double readers, and therefore possessed the same qualification as was generally required for the coif. They were in reality by this period learned counsel to the Crown, the normal functions of attorneyship being carried out by under-clerks or separate officers.[38]

The attorney-general became in the Tudor period a major government official, and service in the office was already a qualification for appointment to preside over one of the central courts, usually the Exchequer,[39] though promotion was not a right.[40] No holder of the office in the Tudor period accepted a puisne judgeship. The lesser office of king's solicitor had been established in 1461, and the title solicitor-general was first used in a patent of 1485, though it did not become standard until 1536.[41] Both offices carried a salary of £10 in the fifteenth century, but by the end of Mary I's reign that of the solicitor-general had doubled, while that of the attorney-general had increased to over £80, four times that of a queen's serjeant.[42] This growing differential shows not only the relative importance of the two offices, but also the growing status of the attorneyship. The solicitor-general was usually considerably junior to the attorney-general on appointment, sometimes not even being a reader in court, though the appointment was almost always a stepping-stone towards higher office. Of the fourteen holders of the office in our period, five were promoted to attorney-general, two were appointed directly to

---

[35] For lists see Sainty, *Law Officers*, 44–5, 60–1; 94 Selden Soc. 390–2.

[36] For a list of attorneys-general of the duchy see Somerville, *The Duchy of Lancaster*, 406–9. For the law officers in the revenue courts, see above, 227, 230.

[37] For a list of king's serjeants in the county palatine of Lancaster see Somerville, *Duchy of Lancaster*, 483–4. For those in Chester see 102 Selden Soc., p. xv n. 31, below, 434.

[38] For the clerk to the attorney-general, and the clerk of the king's process, see 94 Selden Soc. 385; above, 127. In the duchy, the Crown had (in addition to the A.-G.) a separate attorney in each of the four courts at Westminster: Somerville, *Duchy of Lancaster*, 456–9.

[39] Hody CB (1486), Ernle CJ (1519), Fitzjames CB (1522), Lyster CB (1529), Hales MR (1536), and Bradshaw CB (1552), were all formerly A.-G. The only previous examples were Babington CB (1419), Nottingham CB (1479), and Huse CJ (1481), of whom only Babington was appointed directly from A.-G. The office of CB was probably favoured because it did not require the coif.

[40] In 1539 it was thought that Sir John Baker A.-G. would become CJKB (*Lisle Letters*, ed. Byrne, v. 377), but Mountagu, K.Sjt, was appointed. [41] Sainty, *Law Officers*, 59.

[42] Sainty, *Law Officers*, 41–2, 59.

judicial office,[43] one (Port) became a serjeant, one (Rich) became chancellor of
the Augmentations and later lord chancellor, and one died in office; only three
disappeared from royal service.

Despite the growing fortunes of these officers, no one could yet have foreseen
that the king's counsel would eclipse the serjeants, a development which would
not begin until after the invention of the rank of king's counsel extraordinary
enabled the number of king's counsel to be increased. The degree of serjeant was
still the higher rank, and its acceptance automatically terminated appointment
as a law officer.[44] Nevertheless, a major Crown appointment was as highly valued
as the coif, and became a *de facto* qualification for the bench as a result of the practice of bestowing the coif *pro forma*. This device was used twice in our period.[45]
In 1519, John Ernle of Gray's Inn, then attorney-general, was chosen in preference to
all the serjeants to be chief justice of the Common Pleas, and was created serjeant
a few days before his judicial patent was sealed.[46] This was the first instance of a
single call to the degree of serjeant since the fourteenth century. The precedent
was followed in different circumstances in 1546, when Lyster CB, a former solicitor-
general, was translated to the King's Bench.[47]

RIGHTS OF AUDIENCE

When the year books mention counsel other than serjeants, their usual description
is the vague 'apprentice', which no longer denoted a student but had come to mean
those lawyers who had rights of audience at Westminster.[48] There is, however, no
definition of the qualifications of an apprentice in the year-book period. Most of
the names appearing in the reports are those of benchers rather than utter barristers,
who do not appear under that title before the 1540s.[49] The only clues to the legal
definition of those entitled to practise as counsel are in pleas in bar of actions of
maintenance. Throughout our period these are framed in terms of being 'learned
in the law' and a member of an inn of court or chancery, without referring to any
specific degree.[50] Likewise when counsel brought actions for defamation, relying

[43] Dymmok B. in 1497, Cordell MR in 1557.
[44] The Exchequer treated Ernle A.-G. and Fitzjames A.-G. as having vacated their offices on the day
they became serjeants in 1519 and 1521: E356/25, mm. 38, 40d. Likewise Port S.-G. vacated the solicitor-
ship on creation as a serjeant in 1521: 94 Selden Soc. 392.
[45] Note also that William Conyngesby was appointed JKB within a week of his creation at the general
call of 1540, but died before he could sit.   [46] Baker, *Serjeants at Law*, 167; E101/210/1.
[47] Baker, *Serjeants at Law*, 169; E101/4/4/14, fo. 19.
[48] The title is less common in the middle of the sixteenth century, but see *Anon.* (1556) Chr.
Yelverton's reports, fo. 41v (tr. 'held clearly by all the apprentices at the Chancery bar', i.e. present in
court). Yelverton also used the newer term 'counsellor': ibid., fo. 41 (tr. 'not denied by any counsellor
on the other side').   [49] Below, 428 n. 56.
[50] *LPCL*, 109–10.

on their professional status as 'learned in the law', it is simple membership of an inn rather than a degree which is pleaded.[51] The obvious explanation is that there were no specific rules about rights to practise as counsel. However, the custom that only benchers were usually heard in the superior courts is confirmed by a list of 'the pleaders or apprentices of the king's courts' drawn up in 1518 for Cardinal Wolsey.[52] There were thirty-seven apprentices 'supposed now to be present at this term', and twelve 'supposed now to be absent', giving a total Bar of about fifty, besides the serjeants. All but five of the men listed as apprentices were readers in court. Three of the five had recently been elected benchers of the Inner Temple without reading; another read in 1519, and his name seems to have been added to the original list. Only one name (Edmund Knightley) is difficult to account for, though we may guess that he was another bencher elected prior to reading.[53] The list demonstrates that in 1518 the practising Bar at Westminster, the 'apprentices of the king's courts', were simply the benchers of the inns of court. Barristers and others were not included. A further piece of evidence is provided by bills in Chancery, which in the first half of our period are mostly signed by serjeants and benchers.[54]

Election to a readership normally came about ten years after call to the bar,[55] and an utter barrister who did not procure appointment to an office had to spend those years soliciting causes, devilling for a bencher, practising in lesser courts, or undertaking non-contentious work, including draftsmanship, manorial court-keeping, and stewardship. When the volume of litigation increased after the 1530s, there must have been pressure for these practising barristers to take on some of the work of apprentices at Westminster; and indeed we begin to notice counsel

[51] e.g. *Rowley* v. *Roberdys* (1538) KB 27/1109, m. 68d (fellow of Gray's Inn, learned in law, accused of theft; recovers £20 damages); *Vaus* v. *Serle* (1540) KB 27/1116, m. 110 (fellow of Middle Temple: cf. mis-dated citation from a book of entries in *LPCL*, 134 n. 44); *Pyle* v. *Ascue* (1541) CP 40/1108, m. 632 (fellow of Middle Temple); *Sayntpole* v. *Norton* (1545) KB 27/1136, m. 153 (elaborate declaration as fellow of Lincoln's Inn, where he 'bestowed no little diligence in hearing the laws of the realm': *LPCL*, 41 n. 12); *Tusser* v. *Rede* (1553) KB 27/1167, m. 179 (fellow of the Middle Temple); *Manwood* v. *Worland* (1557) KB 27/1183, m. 190 (fellow of the Inner Temple). See also *LPCL*, 111, 124.

[52] C82/474/36 (sp. mod.); discussed in *LPCL*, 90. The date must be before 26 Jan. 1519, when Ernle became A.-G., though a name seems to have been added in 1519.

[53] He was adm. Middle Temple 1505 but did not read until Lent 1523, by which time he was A.-G. of the duchy (app. 11 Nov. 1522): Somerville, *Duchy of Lancaster*, 407. He acted as counsel in the Requests in 1520: REQ 1/104, fo. 51v. He became a serjeant in 1531, after a second reading in 1528.

[54] For Wolsey's period (when counsel begin regularly to sign bills and pleadings) see Guy, *The Cardinal's Court*, 112–13; *St German on Chancery and Statute*, 65–6. Before then, the names of counsel and six clerks are often marked at the top left-hand corner of answers (though not of bills or other pleadings). Of eleven legible counsel's signatures in C1/238–9 (1500–1), six were of serjeants and five of benchers.

[55] J. H. Baker, 'The English Legal Profession, 1450–1550' in *Lawyers in Early Modern Europe and America*, ed. W. Prest (1981); repr. in *LPCL*, 91–2. Fewer than half of all barristers, however, proceeded to read.

described in the reports as 'utter barristers'.[56] It is from the 1530s also that call to the utter bar begins to be officially recognized as a qualification for public office.[57] This no doubt explains why attempts began to be made, in the 1540s, to clarify rights of audience. The method chosen was not legislation but the use of the royal prerogative.

In 1546 a proclamation was issued restricting rights of audience in the superior courts at Westminster—including the new revenue courts—to readers and such others as should be 'thereunto admitted and appointed' by the lord chancellor and two chief justices, acting on the advice of two of the benchers and ancients from each inn of court; at the assizes, the admission of counsel was to be at the discretion of the justices of assize.[58] The proclamation was issued on the advice of the lord chancellor (Wriothesley) and all the justices of both benches, and was appointed to take effect in Michaelmas term. The proposed procedure for augmenting the Bar with non-readers was clearly new, and this provides further confirmation that, prior to 1546, the regular Bar of the central courts was thought to consist of readers and not utter barristers. The purpose was to permit expansion, but subject to official control. There is no evidence, however, that the new procedure was ever put into effect. The king died before the Hilary term 1547, Wriothesley was dismissed from the lord chancellorship in May, and in November a different policy was announced by a second proclamation, perhaps attributable to the new chancellor, Lord Rich.[59] The element of discretionary control was removed, and a qualification by continuance introduced in its place:

Whereas always heretofore the utter barristers and other students of the four houses of court for the time being have been from time to time admitted and allowed to be pleaders and setters forth of the causes and suits of the king's highness's subjects in all and every of his courts, the Court of Common Pleas at Westminster only excepted, his most royal majesty therefore minding the due execution and ministration of justice, and the expedition of his said subjects' causes in this behalf, is pleased and contented that all and every such person and persons, now being or that hereafter shall be student, utter barrister, or utter barristers, in any of the said houses of court, and being fellow in any of the said houses by the space

---

[56] e.g. *Anon.* (1544) Gell's reports, I, Mich. 36 Hen. VIII, fo. 25v ('Forster, utter barester'); *Penyngton* v. *Hunte* (1544) Cholmeley 454 ('William Rastell, un dez utterbarresters de Lyncolnes Inne'). There is a much earlier example in Pas. 4 Hen. VII, fo. 7, pl. 4 ('les barresters'; reads 'lez barrestez' in 1531 edn, fo. 6v). There are also a few examples without the title: e.g. John Talbot, a barrister of ten years' standing, argued in the Exchequer Chamber in *Marmyon* v. *Baldwyn* (1527) 120 Selden Soc. 61 at 62.

[57] See 23 Hen. VIII, c. 5, s. 7, where it is made a qualification for commissioners of sewers to be 'learned in the law of the realm', that is, 'utter barrister in one of the four principal inns of court'. The previous statute referred only to 'justice of *quorum* learned': 6 Hen. VIII, c. 10.

[58] BL MS. Harley 442, fo. 176; pr. (sp. mod.) in *Tudor Royal Proclamations*, i. 371, no. 270 (dated 28 June 1546). For its enforcement against laymen see *LPCL*, 83 n. 25 (1546–7).

[59] MS. in Society of Antiquaries Library (sp. mod.), pr. in *Tudor Royal Proclamations*, i. 408, no. 294 (dated 28 Nov. 1547).

of eight years, shall and may from henceforth lawfully plead and be counsellors and pleaders at or in any court of record within this his realm of England and the marches of the same, the said Court of Common Pleas at Westminster only excepted; any proclamation, order, and decree heretofore had or made to the contrary in any wise notwithstanding.

The eight-year rule would have excluded most students below the bar, but would have given 60 per cent of barristers rights of audience within two or three years of call.[60] It is noteworthy that it was still not thought appropriate to define rights of audience generally by reference to call to the bar. It was a matter of standing since admission. For the central courts, however, the proclamation added a further provision:

And furthermore his highness straitly chargeth and commandeth that no manner of person or persons being no serjeant at law, reader, or utter barrister of any of the said four houses of court, nor any utter barrister not being a fellow of any of the said four houses of court by the space aforesaid, shall presume or enterprise to plead or be a pleader in any of his highness's said courts at Westminster, upon pain of imprisonment and further to make fine at his majesty's will and pleasure.

At Westminster, therefore, but only at Westminster, call to the bar was to be an indispensable minimum qualification. On the face of it, the recital in the proclamation seems to contain a very liberal interpretation of previous custom, in the light of which this second clause would seem to introduce a new restriction on rights of audience in the central courts to utter barristers, to the exclusion of 'other students'. However, this may be a piece of legerdemain. We have seen that, in the central courts, utter barristers had only recently been treated as 'pleaders and setters forth of the causes'. And there is no known example of a student below the bar appearing in Westminster Hall. But the recital does not refer exclusively to the superior courts at Westminster, and the body of the proclamation makes it clear that (unlike its precursor of 1546) it referred to local as well as central courts; and in local courts, even in the city of London, there may have been no conventions as to rights of audience.[61] Moreover, it is consistent with the old pleading tradition of associating the status of 'learned in the law' with continuance in an inn rather than with graduation.

Comparing the two proclamations, it may be deduced that there had been instant opposition to any attempt by the lord chancellor to impose a discretionary control on rights of audience—especially since the lord chancellor at the time was Wriothesley[62]—and that the intention of widening the class of practitioners in the

[60] Of 84 barristers called by Lincoln's Inn between 1518 and 1550, 33% had five years' standing, 27% had six years, 21% had seven years, and only 19% were of longer standing.

[61] We find Randle Cholmeley arguing in the sheriffs' court, London, within a year of call: *Anon.* (*c.*1544) Cholmeley 452.

[62] For the clash between Wriothesley and the common lawyers see above, 179.

central courts was achieved instead by building upon the vagueness of existing law and usage. There was no rule of law against utter barristers assisting clients in litigation, and no obvious reason for distinguishing as a matter of law between different forms of practice in contentious causes. Therefore the usage could be restated in such a way that it permitted (or confirmed the right of) utter barristers of sufficient standing to appear in the central courts, and of inns of court members below the bar to appear in local courts. We do not know whether the proclamation had any immediate impact, because there is no formal record of the names of counsel appearing in banc, and the continuing concentration of reporters on the speeches of serjeants and benchers might have resulted from silently editing out the lesser voices. Likewise, the virtual monopoly of serjeants and benchers in demurrers to the evidence at the assizes, until the end of our period,[63] may reflect the obvious need to retain counsel of standing in cases of legal difficulty. Nevertheless, there is reason to think that in the second half of the sixteenth century the Bar at Westminster was more fully opened up to utter barristers, and it is more likely than not that this relaxation was greatly assisted by the 1547 proclamation.

PROFESSIONAL ETHICS

This is the period in which principles of professional conduct—above and beyond the basic requirement of honesty—began to be formulated for the Bar. Our principal evidence is provided by three exhortatory speeches delivered by chief justices to new serjeants at law in the reign of Henry VIII,[64] from which it appears that serjeants were expected to observe high standards of conduct: to assist the poor and oppressed without reward;[65] to give counsel to anyone who should seek it;[66] to dissuade clients from pursuing unjust causes, and to advise them to abandon causes if it appeared they were in the wrong; to deal with business expeditiously and not prolong it for gain; to keep their clients' business secret; to avoid corruption by money or favour, not merely in deceiving their clients but also, for instance, in pretending to be 'blind'—that is, unable to assist in a worthy cause; 'to stick with

[63] The only form of entry in which counsel are named: above, 259 n. 36, 398.

[64] Baker, *Serjeants at Law*, 280–302. Note also Sir Nicholas Bacon LK's speech to the new serjeants sworn in Chancery in 1559: ibid. 302–4.

[65] See further above, 97, 194, 203, 207 n. 126. Cf. *Anon.* (1561) Chr. Yelverton's reports, fo. 251 (tr. 'At Bedford assizes in the same year I was assigned of counsel with a poor woman defendant by my lord Catlyn', in an action of trespass).

[66] See Baker, *Serjeants at Law*, 292 (sp. mod. 'ye shall refuse to take no man under the protection of your good counsel'). This seems to refer to what is now called the cab-rank principle. Sir Nicholas Bacon LK added the rider that they should not take on more work than they could advisedly consider: ibid. 303.

hand, foot, and nail' to the truth, never pretending that a wrong is right; and to do nothing contrary to good conscience. It is unlikely that these were new ideas; but we have no earlier guidance for comparison. No doubt the judges were always trying to raise the standards. Sir Nicholas Bacon even suggested in 1559 that it was improper to 'offer jeofail or error', that is, to take technical points after a hearing; but that was something of a cry in the wilderness.

RETAINERS

The ways in which counsel earned their fees in the early Tudor period are understood in a general way,[67] but patterns of professional income are impossible to reconstruct in detail as a result of the loss of individual fee books.[68] Some lawyers, typically at the outset of their careers, derived their living principally from the patronage of a single great man whose employment they entered as in-house counsel. Thus, Serjeant Kebell began his career as adviser to the Hastings family, and Chief Justice Lyster began as receiver to Lord Darcy.[69] They gained wider recognition by acting as feoffees to uses, probably an unpaid position but invaluable in securing the notice of potential clients.[70] As they made their way, they might also act in such diverse capacities as court-keeping, moneylending,[71] and arbitration.[72] Probably most professional income arose from small fees for individual pieces of work, whether in court or in conference or on paper: 'even with prominent counsel, little and often was the rule'.[73]

In an important case several counsel might be retained to appear in court on each side. The year books usually report multiple arguments, though it is difficult to know whether all the serjeants were retained *ex parte* or were simply joining in the debate. It was obviously safer for a party to retain as many as possible than to leave them free to express their own opinions.[74] Likewise in private consultation there was safety in numbers. Since an important matter might be laid before as many as eight counsel,[75] there were frequent opportunities for the established lawyer to give impromptu opinions. William Staunford's fee book shows that when he began to practise in 1539 his income was made up principally of

---

[67] See Ives, *Common Lawyers in pre-Reformation England*, 93–146.

[68] Only one survives from our period. William Staunford's fee book for the period 1538–55 is now BL MS. Add. 71134, ff. 38–70. [69] Ives, *Common Lawyers in pre-Reformation England*, 94–100.

[70] Ives, *Common Lawyers in pre-Reformation England*, 94–5, 101–2, 104–11, 119.

[71] Ives, *Common Lawyers in pre-Reformation England*, 120–1.

[72] ibid. 126–30. See also above, 333. [73] ibid. 306.

[74] An explicit example is Trin. 5 Hen. VII, fo. 36, pl. 3 (tr. '... and others to the contrary, namely all the serjeants retained against him').

[75] e.g. John Husee reported to Lady Lisle in 1538 that eight named counsel had been consulted concerning a family settlement which had become insecure: *Lisle Letters*, ed. Byrne, v. 146.

hundreds of small fees of 3s. 4d., increasing later in his career to 5s., 6s. 8d., or even 10s.,[76] though the highest fees were paid for drawing lengthy documents, going out specially on circuit, or acting as an arbitrator.[77] Opinions seem still to have been sought and given orally, and we have not yet encountered before the mid-sixteenth century a written counsel's opinion of the kind found in the Elizabethan period.[78] At the beginning of the century, counsel could still be sought out directly in Westminster Hall, or (in the afternoon) in the 'parvise' or concourse of St Paul's,[79] or in Temple Church.[80] New serjeants at law were even assigned their own pillars in St Paul's where they could attend in the afternoons for the convenience of clients and potential clients.[81] Conferences might also be arranged in taverns, such as the Cardinal's Hat.[82] By the end of our period, however, counsel seem for the most part to have retreated into chambers.[83] Serjeants and leaders of the Bar, at any rate, were too busy to stand around in public places waiting for business. When the assignment of pillars to new serjeants ceased in 1567 it had presumably for some time been a meaningless ceremony.

As a barrister achieved reputation or influence,[84] he would expect to receive permanent retainers from the religious houses, civic corporations, and principal landowners in his part of the country, often in the form of a written contract granting an annuity 'for counsel given and to be given' (pro consilio impenso et impendendo), or for more specific services such as those of stewardship, or the recordership of a borough.[85] A monastery might have half a dozen lawyers on its

---

[76] 'My gains of the law since I began to practise (sp. mod.)', BL MS. Add. 71134, ff. 38–70. His total fees in 1539–40 were £36. 1s. 2d., and in 1540–1 they rose to £51. 19s. 4d. In Easter term 1553, just after becoming a serjeant, he listed 146 fees averaging 7s. 7d. each (total £52. 19s. 4d.). Even as a serjeant, 10s. fees were exceptional.

[77] e.g. (in 1547) 10s. for drawing marriage covenants for Sir John Rogers, 10s. for an arbitration, 10s. for drawing an indenture, and 40s. for drawing a 'great indenture'. In 1552 he was paid 40s. 'to ride to Hertford assizes'.

[78] For an early instance (1561/2), written in the first person in English, see Chr. Yelverton's reports, fo. 253 (with endnote, tr. '...This was Mr Caryll's opinion written thus with his own hand verbatim in Foster and Morgan's case against Staple of Gray's Inn, which was never drawn into suit because the parties agreed...').

[79] For an example (1501) see Ives, Common Lawyers in pre-Reformation England, 299; Baker, Serjeants at Law, 103. In the 1520s David Broke was arrested while returning from St Paul's to the Inner Temple: 94 Selden Soc. 78 n. 2.

[80] In 1540 it was said that 'all the term times [the church] hath in it no more quietness than the parvise of Paul's by reason of the confluence and concourse of such as are suitors in the law': Dugdale, Origines Juridiciales, 195.   [81] Baker, Serjeants at Law, 101–4.

[82] Baker, The Law's Two Bodies, 69.

[83] Note the remarks of Harrison (1587) quoted in LPCL, 102. But cf. the reference to Temple Church in 1540, above, n. 80. For notes of a conference in Serjeants' Inn in 1535 see CLT, 376.

[84] Thus Lord Lisle's attorney recommended retaining Richard Pollard at a fee of £10 per annum because he was in good favour with Cromwell: Lisle Letters, ed. Byrne, iv. 41, no. 841.

[85] Ives, Common Lawyers in pre-Reformation England, 132–40, 286–93.

payroll.[86] The sums of money granted by way of annuity were usually only a pound or two,[87] but even a modest number of such retainers would produce a steady income of £10 or more a year, and a senior practitioner could receive several times that sum. A good cross-section has come to light of the annuities granted in the time of Henry VII to Thomas Lucas (d. 1531) of the Inner Temple, as a result of lawsuits brought by him and his administrators. He had begun his career in the service of Jasper Tudor (d. 1495), duke of Bedford;[88] and while solicitor-general (1497–1509) to Henry VII he was retained with annuities by Lady Fitzwalter (1498),[89] Sir William Berkeley (d. 1501),[90] King's College, Cambridge (1501),[91] the priory of Huntingdon (1502),[92] the bishop of Ely (1502–5),[93] Sir William Willoughby (1503), Sir Richard Wentworth (1504), Sir George Tailboys (1506), Sir William Gascoigne, and Sir Robert Peyton (d. 1518).[94] These ten alone brought him over £18 a year,[95] much more than the 40s. he received as the king's solicitor, and—given that only the unpaid annuities were put in suit—they were presumably only a fraction of all those he had. A list of the annual retaining fees received in 1524 by Richard Snede (d. 1537), another bencher of the Inner Temple, provides a more complete picture from the next generation. The total came to £84. 16s. 8d., of which £48. 10s. came from private clients—four abbeys (Chester,

[86] *The Last Days of Peterborough Monastery*, ed. W. T. Mellows (12 Northants. Record Soc.; 1947), p. xlviii (Peterborough in 1504–5 had seven counsel and an attorney).

[87] Richard Snede in 1524 (below) received retainers ranging from 6s. 8d. (one) to £6. 13s. 4d. (one, from the earl of Derby), the commonest sums being 20s. (nineteen) and 13s. 4d. (eighteen).

[88] Window formerly in St Mary's, Bury St Edmunds: J. Weever, *Ancient Funeral Monuments* (1767 edn), 510 ('servant and secretary, and one of the counsell to Jasper, duke of Bedford, and earl of Pembroke').

[89] *Grenefeld and Lucas (administrators of Lucas)* v. *Fitzwater* (1533) CP 40/1078, m. 332 (annuity of 40s. granted 20 Jan. 1498).

[90] *Lucas* v. *(Anne) Berkeley* (1515) CP 40/1011, m. 90 (arrears of annuity of 26s. 8d.; no declaration).

[91] *Grenefeld and Lucas (administrators of Lucas)* v. *King's College, Cambridge* (1533) CP 40/1078, m. 504d (annuity of 20s. granted *pro consilio*, 28 Dec. 1501).

[92] *Lucas* v. *Prior of Huntingdon* (1514–16) CP 40/1007, m. 358; CP 40/1016, m. 444; No. 2 (1526–8) CP 40/1051, m. 422; CP 40/1059, m. 119; *Grenefeld and Lucas (administrators of Lucas)* v. *Prior of Huntingdon* (1533–4) CP 40/1078, m. 522; CP 40/1083, m. 521 (app. steward of manors and lands, with annuity of 40s., a Apr. 1502).

[93] CUL, Ely Diocesan Records, G2/3, ff. 150v (pension of 8 marks granted *pro consilio*, 20 Jan. 1502), 163v (grant of stewardship, *pro consilio*, 23 Aug. 1504); *Lucas* v. *Bishop of Ely* (1526) CP 40/1050, m. 629; Dyer 157a (app. steward of all courts and manors outside the isle of Ely, with annuity of 40s., 21 Aug. 1505).

[94] *Grenefeld and Lucas (administrators of Lucas)* v. *Willoughby* (1543) CP 40/1078, m. 543 (annuity of 40s. granted 22 Nov. 1503); *Grenefeld and Lucas (administrators of Lucas)* v. *Wentworth* (1541) CP 40/1108, m. 332 (annuity of 26s. 8d. granted 12 Dec. 1504); *Lucas* v. *Taylboys* (1516) CP 40/1013, m. 200 (annuity of 40s. granted 31 Jan. 1506); *Lucas* v. *Gascoigne* (1515) CP 40/1011, m. 90 (arrears of annuity of 20s.; no declaration); *Grenefeld and Lucas (administrators of Lucas)* v. *Peyton* (1535) CP 40/1084, m. 92d (debt of £22. 10s.; no declaration).

[95] Cf. the estimate of over £40 a year from Richard Empson's retainers in the same period: Ives, *Common Lawyers in pre-Reformation England*, 292.

Furness, Vale Royal, and Whalley), two peers, sixteen knights, seventeen esquires, two clerks, two ladies, and eight others—and the remainder from his offices as justice of North Wales, recorder of Chester, serjeant and attorney in the county palatine of Chester, attorney of the prince of Wales and king's attorney in North Wales.[96] He would in addition have earned the usual ad hoc fees for specific work done. A really eminent practitioner might have earned more. Sir Thomas More was alleged to have earned £400 a year while in practice, but that included his income as under-sheriff of London.[97] An indication of the more typical fee income of a younger barrister is provided by John Rastell's recollection that he had earned 40 marks a year pleading at the bar in the early 1500s.[98] All in all, then, a bencher in the early sixteenth century might hope to earn at least £100 a year from the law, and a barrister less, though a serjeant or law officer might expect two or three times as much.[99] In the next generation, William Staunford earned £51. 19s. 4d. in his second year of practice at the Bar in 1539, at the age of about 30,[100] including over £12 gained at the summer assizes. In his third year, his fees totalled £127. 16s. 7d., a level which he did not exceed from private fees until he became a serjeant twelve years later, though much of his intermediate income doubtless came from government work.[101] His first year as a serjeant (1552–3) brought him £315. 1s. in fees.[102]

Retainers, especially from religious houses, might include benefits in kind as well as money. The old tradition of an annual livery robe, and accommodation when visiting, was kept up into the early sixteenth century. Lucas, for instance, was entitled to an esquire's robe, and lodging at Ely House, by virtue of his retainer by the bishop of Ely in 1502.[103] John Pulleyn of Lincoln's Inn had a livery and a room as solicitor to Fountains' Abbey in 1503.[104] Waltham Abbey provided its steward in 1504 with a robe of the gentlemen's suit, and a furnished bedchamber in the abbey, with board, lodging, and stabling for three horses, besides his annuity of 40s.[105]

[96] 'Feoda Ricardi Sneyde in festo Pasche 16 H. 8', BL MS. Harley 2079, fo. 116 (seventeenth-century copy 'ex libro antiquo Ricardi Sneyd de Bradwall armigeri').

[97] Roper, *Lyfe of Moore*, ed. Hitchcock, 8–9.

[98] Letter to Thomas Cromwell (*c.*1535), pr. in *Original Letters illustrative of English History*, ed. H. Ellis (3rd ser., 1846), ii. 308–12 at 310. Rastell was called to the bar before 1502.

[99] Ives, *Common Lawyers in pre-Reformation England*, 321–5.

[100] He himself stated that he 'began to practise' in Lent 1538 (BL MS. Add. 71134, fo. 38), but this was over ten years after admission and eight years after call to the bar.

[101] He mentions that his fee book did not show income as attorney of the Court of Surveyors (1542–6). Between 1544 and 1547 there is a gap while he was in the service of Lord Wriothesley, and his fee income from private practice seems not to have recovered until he took the coif in 1552.

[102] BL MS. Add. 71134, ff. 38–70. The 1552–3 fees included 75s. for 17 common recoveries and 8 fines (each charged at 3s.).   [103] CUL, Ely Diocesan Records, G2/3, fo. 150v.

[104] C. Pullein, *The Pulleyns of Yorkshire* (1915), 145–55.

[105] *Broun v. Sapurton* (1522) CP 40/1037, m. 627; Spelman 32; *Browne v. Abbot of Waltham and Wroth* (1523–4) CP 40/1041, m. 687; same parties (1524–5) CP 40/1043, m. 525 (three actions of detinue for the

Even ad hoc retainers and conferences required the sustenance of counsel with food and drink.[106] Many of these forms of legal remuneration ceased in our period. Livery robes for lawyers—though permitted under Henry VII's legislation against liveries[107]—disappeared, and the rights of board and lodging were mostly swept away by the dissolution and sale of the monasteries. Nevertheless, occasional payments in kind were still offered and accepted by members of the Bar in the mid-sixteenth century.[108]

deed of appointment, Serjeant Browne claiming to have bought the office from Robert Sapurton; each ends with a demurrer). It is not known whether Sapurton was a member of an inn, though other members of the family belonged to Furnival's Inn.

[106] Ives, *Common Lawyers in pre-Reformation England*, 304–5.

[107] The statute 19 Hen. VII, c. 14, exempts household servants and officers, and men 'learned in the one law or the other' (evidently in this context meaning common lawyers or canonists).

[108] e.g. the ell of taffeta and cypress chest alleged to have been given to Roger Manwood in part payment for drawing up a conveyance: *Manwood* v. *Worland* (1557) KB 27/1183, m. 190.

24

Attorneys and Clerks

THE largest branch of the legal profession consisted of those who practised attorneyship or clerkship. The attorneys and law clerks constituted an inferior group of general practitioners, lowly men for the most part, who managed litigation and the mundane affairs of their clients, helping them to find counsel when the nature of their business required it. Yet they were not rigidly separate from barristers, because their career structure was unrelated to the degree structure of the inns of court. There was nothing impossible or improper about a barrister practising as an attorney or solicitor, or acting as clerk of a court. Indeed, it was quite common for young lawyers to begin their training in this branch of the profession while following the learning exercises of the inns of court. For instance, William Eyre (d. 1507), who was a Norfolk attorney in the 1480s, became treasurer of the Inner Temple, practised as counsel, and was described on his brass as 'learned in the law' (*legis peritus*).[1] Walter Roudon (d. 1513) was admitted to Lincoln's Inn in 1485 while practising as an attorney and holding office as clerk of the parcels in the Exchequer, though he seems to have given up these occupations on or before call to the bar.[2] From the next reign, it will be enough to mention that Dyer CJ began his professional training in the early 1530s as a prothonotary's clerk,[3] while Serjeant Bendlowes started in practice as an attorney at the end of the 1530s.[4] Nevertheless, a lawyer intending to practise as a pleader or advocate, and to gain advancement in the profession, would leave off attorneyship at an early stage. We do not find attorneys as benchers of the inns of court,[5] and the great majority of them seem to have been senior members of the inns of chancery. They

---

[1] Noted in CP 40 as an attorney in 1480, 1485; JP Norfolk 1494–150?, *CITR*, i. 1; C1/240/3 (counsel in Chancery, 1500/1); REQ 1/3, fo. 120v (counsel in Requests, 1504); brass at Great Cressingham, Norfolk.

[2] *LI Adm. Reg.*, 23 (Rudon); Wegwood and Holt, 720 (Roden); clerk of the parcels 1480–91 (information kindly supplied by Sir John Sainty); last noted in CP 40 as an attorney in 1486; *BBLI*, i. 102 (barrister by 1494), 139 (associate of the bench, 1505).

[3] 109 Selden Soc., p. xxii; below, 452.

[4] His name appears as an attorney in several cases in 1539–42, in one case for Matthew Parker, clerk, the future archbishop (CP 40/1106, m. 407), and in another for Lady Lisle (CP 40/1112, m. 404).

[5] However, a senior clerical official such as a prothonotary would sometimes become a bencher or an associate bencher by virtue of that office.

nevertheless claimed, in the formal language of pleadings, to be 'learned in the law of the land',[6] and to give 'counsel'.[7]

ATTORNEYS

In principle, every court had its own attorneys, but it was generally understood that the attorneys of the Common Pleas were the leaders of this branch of the profession, and by the end of our period they claimed the informal title 'attorney at the common law' or 'attorney at law'.[8] They could practise also in the King's Bench, and in local courts, and some even ventured into the ecclesiastical and admiralty courts,[9] though the Exchequer and Chancery—and (from the 1520s) the Council—had separate cadres of attorneys.[10] No admission rolls survive, but the names of all practising attorneys are found in the warrants enrolled at the end of the termly bundles of plea rolls.[11] The Common Pleas attorneys in the 1480s numbered well over 100, and the number rose to around 200 by the 1550s.[12] The specialist attorneys of the other courts at Westminster probably did not number more than about twenty in addition.

Attorneys were officers of the courts, and their branch of the profession was therefore controlled primarily by the judges of the Common Pleas, who were supposed to examine candidates before swearing them into office. The earliest surviving form of the attorney's oath dates from the mid-1550s, since in two surviving versions it mentions the king and queen:[13]

You shall do no falsehood nor consent to any to be done in this court; and if you know of any to be done you shall give knowledge thereof to my lord chief justice and other my masters his

---

6 Baker, 'English Legal Profession, 1450–1550', 87.

7 e.g. *Denne* v. *Furbysshour* (1494–9) CP 40/928, m. 367 (retainer in 1486 'ad essendum de consilio ... tanquam ejus attornatus'); *Sparry* v. *Hubaud* (1537) CP 40/1095, m. 448 (defamation of 'attornatus et consiliarius'); *Ayer* v. *Bussey* (1542) CP 40/1114, m. 653 (debt on retainer of attorney 'ad essendum de consilio'); *Gray* v. *Irby* (1548) CP 40/1137, m. 425 (sim.).

8 *Sparry* v. *Hubaud* (1537) CP 40/1095, m. 448 (defamation of 'attornatus ad communem legem'); *Lee* v. *Forman* (1551) CP 40/1146, m. 445 (annuity granted to 'attornatus ad legem' in 1545); CP 40/1193, m. 1025 (Richard Clyff, sp. mod. 'one of the attorneys at the common law', 1561).

9 Reynold Beesley LLB is mentioned as judge of the admiralty at Chester in 1544 (BL Add. Ch. 50247) and as counsel in a York ecclesiastical case in 1558 (*Wyllson* v. *Tompson* (1558) CP 40/1174, m. 1029; above, 236). He is also found in the warrants in CP 40 (between 1546 and 1555) as an attorney in Yorks., and he was recorder of Scarborough and clerk of the county and of the castle of York: CP 40/1176(1), m. 1136; HPHC 1509–58, i. 425. No other example is known of an attorney with a law degree, and so it may be more appropriate to regard him as an unusual civil lawyer who happened to become admitted as an attorney.   10 See above, 161, 183, 200.

11 CP 40 (for the Common Pleas). The original warrants are filed in the *Brevia* series. The Common Pleas dockets (IND 1/1–) contain reckonings of attorneys' dues to the officers, and may provide a convenient guide to their engagements. The King's Bench warrants are enrolled in KB 27, and filed in KB 150, though only a few files survive from the early Tudor period.   12 Above, 136.

13 109 Selden Soc. 176–7 (Dyer's version temp. Eliz. I, collated with two versions temp. Phil. & Mar.). For a slightly earlier form used by the attorneys of the borough court of Canterbury, see the precedent book of C. Levyns (c.1535), BL MS. Stowe 856, fo. 10 (and cf. fo. 93v).

brethren, that it may be reformed. You shall delay no man for lucre or for malice. You shall increase no fees, but be content with the fees accustomed. You shall plead no foreign pleas nor sue any foreign suits unlawfully to hurt any man, but such as shall stand with the order of the law and your conscience. You shall seal all such process as you shall sue out of this court with the seal thereof or see the [king's and] queen's majesty or my lord chief justice satisfied for the same. Also, you shall not wittingly sue or procure any false suit, nor give aid or counsel to the same, on pain to be expelled from this court for ever. And further use your self in the office of an attorney within this court according to your learning and discretion. So help you God etc.

It must be older than this example, however, because in the time of Lord Audley C. an attorney was accused of pleading a foreign plea 'not regarding his oath that he took in the Common Pleas when he was sworn attorney that he should plead no foreign pleas'.[14] A similar oath was taken by the court officers, who are mentioned as being sworn in the fifteenth century; they were to use every effort to hinder falsehoods and reveal them to the court.[15]

For a serious offence, proved by evidence upon oath in a formal investigation, an attorney might be formally 'forejudged' from the court.[16] By the early sixteenth century it was the custom for an attorney so evicted by judgment to be physically thrown over the bar into the outside world. This humiliating ceremony is only indirectly alluded to in the records,[17] but it was familiar enough to be known by the colloquialism 'turning up one's heels'.[18] Indeed, John Perkins of the Inner

[14] Parker v. Selybank (temp. Audley C.) C1/866/22. In 1529, an attorney referred to himself as 'attornatus de eodem Banco juratus': Elford v. Lankesforde (1528) CP 40/1059, m. 631. Note also Re E. U. (1515) Rast. Ent. 96 (fine for presuming to act as an attorney when not sworn in court).

[15] Such an oath was mentioned by a filazer in 1558 as a reason for informing against an attorney: Re Selyard (1558) CP 40/1176(1), m. 992d ('pro eo quod ipse ex vinculo juramenti in ejus officio philizarii et attornati hic facti ad falsitates si quas in curia hic perpetrandas intellexerit ad posse suum impediendas meliori modo quo sciverit eaque celeritate qua convenit curie hic revelare et notificare astringitur').

[16] e.g. R. Moyle, Judicial Writs, 49 (Rowland Brugge forejudged, 1497; incorrect roll citation); Memorandum (1507) CP 40/980, m. 403d (John Pecock fined £10 and forejudged for backdating a writ; detailed presentment in English by a jury of attorneys); Memorandum (1533) JHB MS. 55 (book of entries), fo. 88v (Edward Borden forejudged for failing to appear to a bill of privilege; incorrect roll citation); Ashborne v. Sheffeild (1557/8) BL MS. Harley 1124, fo. 70 at 71v; MS. Hargrave 4, fo. 127v (attorney forejudged for failing to appear to a bill); Memorandum (1558) CP 40/1176(1), m. 992d (John Selyard forejudged for forging writs of capias without an original).

[17] In actions of slander: e.g. Anon. (1525) BL MS. Lansdowne 1076, fo. 146 ('pickt over the barre'); Hale v. Thorneton (1531) CP 40/1068, m. 404 ('thou art a false harlot and a crafty, and a poller, and for that thou were cast over the bar in Westminster Hall'); Danby v. Thwyng (1532) KB 27/1083, m. 32 (sp. mod. 'thou wast attainted and casten over the bar at London'; declares as attorney of Common Pleas); next note. (All quotations here in mod. sp.)

[18] Biryton v. Abbot of Reading (1535) CP 40/1085(2), m. 500 ('For falsehood Thomas Biryton's heels were turned up in Westminster Hall'); Hogekynson v. Lyndhop (1540) CP 40/1104, m. 365 ('Thou art a false harlot and pointed thy heels upward at Westminster'); Nasshe v. Chaunce (1546) CP 40/1129, m. 124 ('Master Nasshe you be a false man . . . which in case it were known your heels would be turned up in Westminster Hall'); Woodward v. Nicolles (1555) KB 27/1175, m. 199 ('Daniel Woodward is a false harlot, his heels were turned upward in Westminster Hall').

Temple, author of the *Profitable Book*, complained in 1537 of a rumour that his 'heels was turned upward' twenty years earlier.[19] For a lesser offence a fine or sentence of imprisonment might be imposed.[20] In 1528 an attorney complained of having been expelled and taken out of the roll of attorneys on account of a bill sent to the chief justice alleging extortion, though he was restored after examination by the court,[21] which shows that there was some kind of suspension pending a full hearing. In serious cases an investigation might be made by a grand jury of attorneys.[22] The court evidently took its disciplinary jurisdiction very seriously, and in grave cases could impose penalties *in terrorem*. In 1558 the court summoned all the officers and attorneys to hear the sentence imposed on an elderly attorney of forty years' standing, 'to the terror of other offenders', making the offender take the following oath:[23]

This hear ye justices that I, John Selyard, late one of the attorneys of this court, having my name by you for divers misdemeanours by me committed in the exercise of my said office justly drawn out of the attorneys' roll,[24] and my self therefor forejudged this court and put from all exercise of the same office, shall not from henceforth directly or indirectly as attorney pursue or defend or otherwise intromit in any action, suit, or cause, in this court here, or in any of the king's and queen's majesties' courts at Westminster. So help me God and all saints, and by the contents of this Book.

COURT OFFICIALS

The four superior courts of law at Westminster had between them over fifty senior legal officials, and if each of them had on average one or two under-clerks there must have been well over one hundred men earning their living from the clerical side of those courts alone. They belonged for the most part with the attorneys' branch of the profession, and were commonly members of the inns of chancery rather than of court, at least until they reached the highest offices. Indeed, a career might begin in an office even before admission to an inn of chancery. John Lucas (d. 1525), who rose to be secondary of the King's Bench, noted that he had gone to his 'master' in the King's Bench (probably John Rooper) on 6 November 1492, but had not been admitted to New Inn until

[19] SP 1/115, fo. 110v; Elton, *Star Chamber Stories*, 21.
[20] e.g. *Memorandum* (1521) CP 40/1033, m. 110d (Robert Smalbroke fined 6s. 8d. for 'pursuing certain process erroneously' against a party, to whom he had made amends, 1521). Cf. *Vernon* v. *Butler* (1536) CP 40/1090, m. 427 (attorney committed to Fleet after being found guilty of misconduct upon demurrer in a bill of complaint).
[21] *Elford* v. *Lankesforde* (1528–9) CP 40/1059, m. 631 (pleading in debt on a bond to keep the peace; attorney plaintiff recovers 40s. damages). [22] See above, 136.
[23] *Memorandum* (1558) CP 40/1076(1), m. 992d. John Selyard had practised in Kent since at least 1519, and died within a year of the judgment. [24] No such roll of attorneys has been found.

1 August 1501; after serving five years as a filazer, he was specially admitted to Lincoln's Inn in 1508, at the instance of Rooper, who was then reader of the inn.[25] Most of those who began such a career were at the lowest economic level of the legal profession, but since the usual way of filling vacancies was by promotion within a department, men of ability like Lucas could reasonably hope for advancement. Very few officials received a salary, and their income was derived from fees which they were entitled to charge for each item of business transacted. Approved scales of fees show that, even in the two benches, these were not set at more than a few pence or shillings; but the volume of business in the major courts was such that the total receipts could amount to a respectable or even a large income. Many officers augmented their official income by practising as attorneys in the central courts, and those who did so were among the busiest attorneys. Some acquired other positions. Several acted as clerks of the peace and clerks of assize, while Edward Cheseman (d. 1510), filazer of the King's Bench for twenty-five years, even managed to become cofferer of the household to Henry VII.[26] The fact that Robert Maycote (d. 1533), the first known clerk of the papers in the King's Bench, left a collection of books on surgery to his son Richard (an attorney) may be evidence that his Kent practice took in surgical patients as well.[27]

Those fortunate enough to ascend to the higher clerkships prospered noticeably.[28] The way in which the Roper family fortunes were founded on the chief clerkship of the King's Bench is well known.[29] The first founder of those fortunes, John Roper or Rooper (d. 1525), possessed more movable wealth than any other lawyer in the land, and his son married the lord chancellor's daughter. Both he and his predecessor, Reynold Sonde (d. 1491), were armigerous. His colleagues on the Crown side, Henry Harman (d. 1502) and William Fermour (d. 1552), also bore arms. The like status was attained by the chief officers in the other courts: for instance, William Porter (d. 1521), clerk of the Crown in Chancery; Robert Blagge, who was probably granted arms while he was king's remembrancer of the Exchequer, and his secondary, John Copwode, who also received a grant of arms in Henry VIII's reign; and John Raymond, who obtained arms when he was prothonotary of the Common Pleas.[30] Even some of the filazers and lesser clerks achieved armigerous status: Thomas Jakes (d. 1514), clerk of Hell and clerk of the warrants in the Common Pleas, and Oliver Southworth (d. 1537), filazer of the King's Bench, each directed that their arms should be placed on their tombs.

---

[25] 94 Selden Soc. 365. Another King's Bench filazer spent 28 years in Clement's Inn before being admitted to the Inner Temple in 1522: ibid. 128 n. 2.

[26] He described himself as an esquire, became a JP, and was of some substance: PCC 33 Bennett (will); C1/302/82 (inventory); HPHC 1509–58, i. 631; inscription on brass at Chipping Barnet, Herts.

[27] PCC 8 Hogen. For the Maycotes, see 94 Selden Soc. 364.

[28] For what follows see Baker, 'The English Legal Profession, 1450–1550', 83–4.   [29] Above, 148–9.

[30] Miscellaneous Grants (77 Harleian Soc.; 1926), 178.

At the other end of the spectrum, however, there were clerks who barely earned the style of a gentleman.[31]

SOLICITORS AND OTHERS

Besides the two or three hundred Westminster attorneys and court officials, whose identities may be ascertained with reasonable precision, there were an indeterminate number of lesser 'practitioners' who cannot safely be treated as professional lawyers until more is known about them. Attorneys in local courts were usually not Westminster attorneys,[32] and it is possible that most of them were not lawyers at all, in the sense of being members of the inns of court or chancery. Into the same category fall 'courtholders', whose very designation probably indicates that they were not qualified as learned in the law and were perceived as not quite belonging to the ranks of gentlemen. A few of them, nevertheless, may have gained admission to the inns and thereby to a semblance of gentle status.[33] Scriveners, or professional writers, drew contracts and conveyances of a straightforward character, and might act in minor administrative capacities such as that of courtholder;[34] but writing legal documents was not in itself a legal role and we should not consider these men as being necessarily lawyers.[35] Some scriveners also practised as attorneys,[36] but of 140 scriveners admitted by the London company during our period only nine were or became attorneys of the Common Pleas,[37] though a few more were members of inns. In the absence of professional control, the categories were imprecise; and in 1557 we find an action for defamation brought by a common court-keeper who was also a common conveyancer.[38] Notaries were in much the same position on the fringes of legal practice; they

[31] e.g. Thomas Thomson, cursitor of the Chancery, pardoned in 1559 as gentleman, *alias* yeoman: *CPR 1558–60*, p. 238. Cf. below, 450   [32] Some were: above, 308 n. 154, 313 n. 200.

[33] Thomas Sneth, pardoned in 1509 as yeoman, *alias* gentleman, *alias* courtholder, *alias* attorney of the Common Pleas, may be the one adm. Lincoln's Inn 1512: *LP*, i. 438(4), at p. 269; *LI Adm. Reg.*, i. 36. Cf. Richard Doune, pardoned in 1509 as yeoman, *alias* courtholder: *LP*, i. 438(1), at pp. 210–11.

[34] e.g. Thomas Trendill, pardoned in 1509 as yeoman, *alias* scrivener, *alias* courtholder: *LP*, i. 438(2), at p. 232.

[35] See Ramsay, 'Scriveners and Notaries as Intermediaries in Later Medieval England', 118–31.

[36] e.g. John Pyne of Gray's Inn, attorney and clerk of the essoins (1525–31), was admitted scrivener in 1527: *Scriveners' Company Common Paper 1357–1628*, ed. F. W. Steer (London Record Soc. 4; 1968), 25; CP 40/1059, m. 130; CP 40/1072, m. 482; warrants in CP 40. William Pyerson or Pyreson was a scrivener and attorney of the Common Pleas in the 1550s: *Scriveners' Company Common Paper*, 26 (adm. 1543); CP 40/1144A, m. 591d (1550); *CPR 1558–60*, p. 190 (1559); J. Stow, *Survay of London* (1598), 205 (inscription in St Mary-le-Bow, London). See also Ramsay, 'Scriveners and Notaries', 131 n. 58 (1483).

[37] Ralph Tilghman, Ralph Caldewell, William Blakwell, John Mountague, John Pyne, Geoffrey Caldwall, William Charnocke, William Pyerson, and Humphrey Broke. These were not all necessarily in practice as scriveners and attorneys simultaneously.

[38] *Hunt* v. *Gylberd* (1557) CP 40/1170, m. 1138 (declares as 'communis custos curiarum et communis scriptor cartarum, indenturarum, et aliorum scriptorum et munimentorum') .

had no official place in the secular legal system, but they had employment in ecclesiastical and mercantile affairs and their status was recognized by law.[39] Many of them were also scriveners,[40] and some may have practised as attorneys.[41] Auditors, or accountants, were another professional class on the fringes of the law; they might or might not have legal knowledge, but a good many of them were members of the inns of court and chancery.[42]

It is too early, in the period under survey, to regard solicitors as constituting a distinct profession. The word was already in use, and generally indicated the solicit-ing of causes in a court where the solicitor was not himself an officer or attorney.[43] Most references to solicitors in the plea rolls are thus to Common Pleas attorneys retained to solicit business (*ad negocia solicitanda*) in the King's Bench, Chancery, and other courts.[44] The payment of fees to counsel, even by someone himself learned in the law, was *ipso facto* an act of soliciting.[45] The position of 'solicitor' might therefore be merely transitory. It was not a recognized legal office or rank, and an attorney would not have regarded soliciting as a job description. Probably the only kind of solicitor who would use the description for general purposes was the in-house lawyer, who did not practise as a common attorney but as a servant retained by a noble landowner or religious house to look after its legal affairs. In that capacity he would be required not only to solicit causes, by retaining attorneys and counsel where needed, but to draft entries, keep manorial courts, audit accounts, and to act as bailiff, receiver, household steward, clerk of the kitchen, clerk of works, comptroller, and paymaster: in other words, to serve as a general man of business.[46] A solicitor was likely to have 'had the speculative' in one of the inns of court or chancery,[47] like Guthlac Overton (d. 1537) of Lincoln's Inn, who was a solicitor and a practising auditor and gave private instruction in 'the faculty of auditorship'.[48] Likewise John Bowyer or Boyer served Henry Grey, duke of

---

[39] See above, 236. Cf. CP 40/1127, m. 566d (Edmund Scotte of Newcastle-upon-Tyne, 'notarius publicus in lege', 1546).   [40] Ramsay, 'Scriveners and Notaries', 124–5.

[41] There was a monumental inscription in St Botolph Aldersgate to John Milsam (d. 1567), described as a notary and attorney of the Guildhall: J. Stow, *Survey of London*, ed. J. Strype (1720), i. III. 113.

[42] See Baker, 'English Legal Profession, 1450–1550', 92–3.

[43] An example just before our period is in C1/32/60 (Robert Pert, solicitor to Winchcomb abbey, Glos., temp. Edw. IV).

[44] e.g. *Samuell* v. *Talany* (1490) CP 40/913, m. 429 (retainer as 'attornatus et solicitarius' in courts at Westminster); *Denne* v. *Furbysshour* (1494–9) CP 40/928, m. 367 (retainer as 'attornatus . . . ac solicitator'); *Grote* v. *Steyk* (1496) CP 40/935, m. 379 (retainer 'ad negocia . . . solicitanda' as 'attornatus et solicitarius'); *Symon* v. *Hatche* (c.1530) C1/674/19 (defendant an attorney, and 'solyster' of a Chancery suit). Cf. 94 Selden Soc. 385 n. 3; *LPCL*, 150.   [45] Pas. 5 Hen. VII, fo. 19, pl. 1, at fo. 20, *per* Kebell sjt.

[46] These duties were all performed by John Fairechild, of Gray's Inn, as solicitor in the service of the duchess of Norfolk around 1520: Ives, 'The Common Lawyers in pre-Reformation England' (1968) 18 *TRHS* (7th ser.) 145 at 152.   [47] As Fairechild claimed: ibid.

[48] *Overton* v. *Sharpe* (temp. Wolsey C.) C1/551/49 (retained for six years as defendant's 'solicitor in all his causes and business in the law and otherwise'); 94 Selden Soc. 263 n. 2.

Suffolk, in various characters from about 1546 until the duke's execution in 1554, first as clerk of his kitchen, then as his solicitor, and latterly as his secretary; but, although he was admitted to the Inner Temple in 1556, he is not known as a legal practitioner.[49] Solicitors were not necessarily lawyers at all. We may instance the case of Edmund Lentall, who was retained in 1533 by the parson of Morley, Devon, to take 'some labour and pains in soliciting and labouring his causes and matters', for which he was given an annuity of 13s. 4d. for life, and yet claimed in subsequent litigation that he was not learned in the law.[50] Nevertheless, without a legal qualification or a master-servant relationship, a solicitor who assisted in litigation committed the offence of maintenance.[51] Enforcement of this principle would almost extinguish 'common' solicitors in the time of Elizabeth I; but the common solicitor is a species not yet encountered.

[49] CSPD 1553–8, p. 344, no. 781 (deposition of 14 June 1558).   [50] C1/840/26 (replication).
[51] LPCL, 112–13.

25

The Education of Lawyers

THE procedural revolution outlined in Part IV, above, does not in itself explain how law was transmitted from one generation to another, or how new legal ideas were introduced and reconciled with the old. Contemporary sources suggest that, although the opinions of judges usually carried more weight than the opinions of individual serjeants or apprentices, the functions of expounding and developing the princples of the common law were not appropriated exclusively to the courts. Maitland's remark that law schools make tough law[1] rested on an assumption that law schools are capable, in some sense, of making law. And indeed the early-modern common law was to some extent the creature of the inns of court, which with the inns of chancery constituted the third university of England.[2]

Law can be 'made' not only by acts of legislation and judgment, but by shaping the thoughts of the profession which produces the legislators and judges. And the common learning[3] of the profession was generated and nurtured in the halls of the inns rather than in the hall of Westminster Palace, where it was given practical effect. The common opinion of the serjeants at dinner, or of the benchers at a moot, or of the readers in their lectures—especially an opinion which had often been repeated without challenge over the years[4]—was good evidence of the state of legal doctrine, and might arguably be more cogent evidence than the unprepared speeches and sudden remarks of the judges in banc. We could hardly assert today that whatever passes for law in the law schools *is* the law; but it was closer to the truth when the inns of court were at their zenith as residential colleges of law. It was a law school in which the lecturers of one generation would provide the judges of the next.[5] The reports and notebooks of the early Tudor period, such as those of Port and Spelman,[6] mingle dicta from learning exercises with dicta from the courts so freely that it is not always easy to disentangle the one kind from the

---

[1] Above, 12.

[2] Although the expression 'third university' is not found in this period, we find Parliament referring in 1498 to the study of law at Oxford, Cambridge, *London*, 'or any other university': *CPR 1494–1509*, p. 128, para. 3.   [3] For this expression see below, 467.

[4] Litt. s. 481 implies as much: (tr. 'to prove that … I have often heard the reading on the statute of Westminster II which begins *In casu quo vir…*').

[5] Only a reader could become a serjeant, and only a serjeant could become a judge.

[6] Below, 470.

other. Doubtless there was no need to do so. No less weight attached to what Sir John Fyneux stated as law if he said it in Gray's Inn rather than the King's Bench.[7] As reasoned judicial decisions became increasingly available as sources of law, the inns would lose their lawmaking role; but that had not obviously happened by 1550. The inns of court and chancery at the accession of Elizabeth I were both academies of law for intending practitioners and finishing schools for gentlemen with no intention of living by the law. But equally important was their creative role in facilitating the transmission, discussion, and refinement of legal doctrine and procedural learning.

In this role they were greatly admired by contemporaries as models of academical discipline. Sir Thomas Elyot, himself a product of the Middle Temple, considered the exercises to be perfect if unconscious revivals of classical rhetoric,[8] while Sir Thomas Smith, in his inaugural lecture in the Cambridge faculty of Civil law, lavished praise on the methods of argument in the other law school.[9] Indeed, in the later 1530s, prompted by humanist thinking such as Elyot's, there was a project to found a new secular royal academy for selected mature students, modelled closely on the inns of court but with 'all good sciences and knowledges' on the curriculum, for the purpose of improving the education of the upper classes. It is thought to have foundered only because of the sudden downfall of Thomas Cromwell in 1540.[10]

Our legal university was a body of considerable size, not much smaller than Cambridge, with four main colleges containing over one hundred resident members each,[11] and nine lesser colleges containing on average about sixty: in total, a resident membership of around a thousand.[12] Perhaps as many as one-third of the gentry of England passed through them, something which can by no means be confidently asserted of the universities in this period. The majority of its members were probably pursuing their first academic course, though some had come from the other kind of university, and that is where our account should begin.

---

[7] See e.g. Trin. 15 Hen. VII, fo. 11, pl. 21 (tr. 'In Thatcher's reading this case was stated to be law—*dit pur ley*—by Fyneux CJ'); Spelman 140 ('Note that the Lord Fyneux CJKB said in Gray's Inn for law...'). His most important dictum in Gray's Inn was his observation in 1499 about *assumpsit* for nonfeasance: below, 844, 847.

[8] *The Boke named the Governour* (1531), fo. 56; new edn by S. E. Lehmberg (1962), 53–4.

[9] Cited in Maitland, *English Law and the Renaissance*, 89–90.

[10] R. M. Fisher, 'Thomas Cromwell, Humanism and Educational Reform, 1530–1540' (1977) 50 *BIHR* 151–63.

[11] Even in a learning vacation there might be 80 members of Lincoln's Inn in residence: *Lisle Letters*, ed. Byrne, iv. 86, no. 862.

[12] Baker, 'The English Legal Profession, 1450–1550', in *LPCL*, 75 at 94. The total admissions 1450–1550 were probably more than 10,000: ibid. 95.

COMMON LAWYERS AND THE UNIVERSITIES

It is difficult to ascertain how much preparation or general education a typical law student would have received between grammar school and going up to London, since university membership records in this period are so defective. There are allusions to university attendance by common lawyers before our period, and we may deduce from the occasional testamentary exhibition for a student to read at university before proceeding to an inn[13] that it may have been a more common course than the meagre records suggest. One of Henry VII's judges attended the Wykehamist foundations at Winchester and New College, Oxford, before going to the Middle Temple around 1480;[14] Sir Thomas More went to Canterbury College, Oxford, before New Inn and Lincoln's Inn;[15] and two of his near contemporaries began their studies at the twin royal foundations of Eton and King's College, Cambridge.[16] We know of one Henrician judge who even took a Bachelor of Arts degree at Oxford.[17] Nevertheless, graduation was rare for common lawyers even in later periods, and since most exhibitions for legal study do not provide for a preliminary spell at university it may still have been the exception rather than the rule. Thomas Elyot complained in 1531 that lawyers lost the opportunity to acquire an essential liberal education because they were set to the study of law as young as 14 or 15,[18] and there is certainly little school learning discernible in the year books. When Bryan CJ showed off his academical expertise in 1496 by discussing universal and particular negatives, referring to 'the figure' and citing a sophister's verse, his brother Townshend J.'s admission that he was 'not a good sophister' was doubtless intended to draw a sympathetic smile from those in court rather than dismay at his ignorance.[19]

There is no reason to suppose that the common lawyers as a class were enemies of learning. Two chief justices (Huse and Rede) endowed lectureships at

[13] e.g. Serjeant Constable in 1501 provided for Marmaduke Constable to spend three years at Cambridge (from the age of 15) and then three in an inn of chancery: 53 Surtees Soc. 195. In 1504, Thomas Markenfield provided for his son Ninian to spend two years at Oxford followed by three in an inn of court: *Testamenta Eboracensia*, iv. 125; *CIPM Hen. VII*, ii. 108, no. 163. In 1529, John Williamson provided for his son to attend Oxford from age 15 to 20, and then to spend four years in an inn of court: PCY, ix. 462; *Testamenta Eboracensia*, v. 279. And in 1542, John Hawarden provided for his son Adam (aged 17) to spend one year at university, two in an inn of chancery, and at least one in an inn of court: BL Add. Ch. 53039 (marriage settlement). None of these four children is mentioned in the university records.

[14] John Kingsmill (d. 1509), fellow of New College 1476–9, serjeant at law 1495, JKB 1503.

[15] 94 Selden Soc. 126 n. 6.

[16] William Conyngesby (d. 1540) of the Inner Temple and Edward Halle (d. 1547) of Gray's Inn: 94 Selden Soc. 126 n. 4.

[17] Edmund Molyneux (d. 1552), reader of Gray's Inn 1532, JCP 1550: 94 Selden Soc. 126 n. 7.

[18] *The Boke named the Governour* (1531), fo. 53v; new edn by S. E. Lehmberg (1962), 51.

[19] Trin. 11 Hen. VII, fo. 23, pl. 1. Two years earlier, Bryan CJ had been in favour of consulting masters of grammar on a question of Latin: Hil. 9 Hen. VII, fo. 16, pl. 8.

Cambridge, some benchers of the Inner Temple helped to found a college at Oxford,[20] and others practising in our period would found schools.[21] It may even be possible to discern in the legal sources of the early sixteenth century a greater awareness of the value of a liberal education. Academic learning—especially in philology—is particularly noticeable in the reports of James Dyer[22] and Edmund Plowden,[23] educated in the 1520s, while a Henrician chief justice (probably Sir Edward Mountagu) could address the new serjeants created in 1540 with a speech containing references to Boethius, 'the excellent clerk Cicero', Faber, Florus, 'Justinus the excellent historiographer', Livy, Sallust, Valerius Maximus, and 'Ulpian the great civilian'.[24] There is perhaps a note of pride in Sir Edward Saunders's remark in 1555 that 'we do not despise sciences other than our own, but allow and commend them as things worthy of commendation'.[25]

Nevertheless, the prevalence of classical allusions was really little more than a show of fashionable rhetoric.[26] Even if we suppose that in the early sixteenth century a university education was becoming more normal for inns of court men, it is difficult to argue that this had a major impact on the discipline of the common law. The universities themselves were hardly beacons of enlightenment, and it is significant enough that the college founded at Oxford by benchers of the Inner Temple was intended to entrench a distinctly medieval philosophy of education in the face of the new learning.[27] Few common lawyers seem to have resided long enough to graduate in Arts, let alone in Law— which was a postgraduate study for those bent on a different career—and those few who did become engrossed in scholastic disciplines are unlikely to have found the transition to London congenial. One recalls the example of the translator Richard Taverner, who proceeded to Strand Inn and the Inner Temple, his head full of philosophy and divinity, in the middle of Henry VIII's reign, and provided some amusement for his contemporaries by rendering bits of English law into Greek;[28] remembered as a minor man of letters, he never became a

---

[20] Brasenose College, co-founded by Richard Sutton: 94 Selden Soc. 126–7. The arms in the old college hall included those of four of Sutton's fellow benchers (Brudenell, Grevill, Port, and Pygot) and a clerk of the Crown (William Fermour): 102 Selden Soc., p. xvi.

[21] Highgate School was founded by Cholmley CJ: HPHC 1558–1603, i. 605. Brentwood School was founded by Sir Anthony Browne J.: HPHC 1509–58, i. 518. Repton School was founded by John Port of the Inner Temple, law reporter and son of Port J.: 102 Selden Soc., p. xxiii.

[22] 109 Selden Soc., pp. xxi–xxii.   [23] See above, 16 n. 52.

[24] Baker, Serjeants at Law, 294–302.

[25] Bulkeley v. Thomas (1554) Plowd. 118 at 124v (tr.). The context was a grammatical dispute.

[26] Cf. above, 16.

[27] I. S. Leadam, 'The Early Years of the College', in Brasenose College Quatercentenary Monographs (1909), ii. IX. 24, 44.

[28] J. K. McConica, English Humanists and Reformation Politics (1965), 117–18. Taverner may have been responsible for a nutshell guide to land law in English: above, 27 n. 115.

serious man of law and perhaps found the law's intricacies too prosaic for a Master of Arts.[29]

ACCESS TO LEGAL EDUCATION

An intending law student would join an inn of chancery at around the age of 18, with the hope of progressing to an inn of court around the age of 20 and pursuing several years' further study before call to the bar.[30] This was not free from expense, and without long-term maintenance there was little hope of completing the course. Maintenance was presumably normally paid by fathers, though—unlike colleges at the universities—the inns made their contractual arrangements directly with their members and no parent–tutor agreements have been found. Some entrants obtained the means of support through a fortunate legacy, or a family settlement,[31] others (such as young heirs) by way of mortgage or something similar.[32] The cost was probably greater than university. Fortescue, a generation before our period, had said that only the sons of gentry could afford the inns of court, because an allowance of at least £13. 6s. 8d. a year would be needed.[33] Some had more than that. Serjeant Constable provided in his will (1501) for his son to have £25 a year for three years at an inn of chancery,[34] and Mr Baron Rouclyff in 1494 left his nephew Guy Palmes (later a serjeant) £20 a year to study in the Middle Temple.[35] On the other hand, Serjeant Caryll (d. 1523) left his son John only £10 to study in the Inner Temple, saying that he knew it would suffice 'if he live and use himself well and honestly and wisely like a learner and student'; the son went on to become attorney of the duchy and a bencher of the inn.[36] Caryll's estimate seems to have been widely accepted,[37] but some had to make do with still less. Anthony Fitzherbert's mother left him but 5 marks a year to keep him at

---

[29] A similar example is provided by John Dethick, who had spent twelve years at Oxford and Cologne universities by the time he was admitted to Clement's Inn in the 1530s to learn some law; he was at various times a Latin tutor, Portuguese translator to Audley LK, clerk in Chancery under Southwell MR, clerk of the market at Boulogne, and steward of Lord Grey: deposition of 1556 in *CSPD 1553–58*, p. 213, no. 442.   [30] Baker, 'English Legal Profession, 1450–1550', 96.

[31] e.g. the marriage settlement which provided for the 'finding in court' of Eustace Hill (c.1504/15): C1/325/10.

[32] In 1484, Gerard Stukeley, an heir apparent aged 23, contracted with a London merchant to find him with necessaries 'at court for his learning in the law' for seven years or more, by assigning him his share in a lease: *Calendar of Ancient Deeds*, vi. 410, no. C6972 (8 Aug. 1484). He was born in 1461/2: *CIPM Hen. VII*, i. 412. Although his father was a member of Lincoln's Inn, he joined Gray's Inn, which sued him for dues in 1494: CP 40/927, m. 28. He died in 1506: C142/30/64.

[33] *De Laudibus Legum Anglie*, ed. Chrimes, 118.   [34] PCC 15 Blamyr; 53 Surtees Soc. 195.

[35] *Testamenta Eboracensia* iv. 105 (1494).   [36] PCC 10 Bodfelde (sp. mod.).

[37] Baker, 'English Legal Profession, 1450–1550', 96. A later example is PCC 3 Wrastley (John Maynard leaves his son £10 a year to study law, 1556).

Gray's Inn in the 1490s, though he may have had other sources of income.[38] And Richard Wye, a bencher of the Inner Temple, had been sent to the inn with only 6 marks a year under his father's will of 1504.[39] Although even such modest requirements would have put the inns beyond the reach of the majority of the population, legal education was by no means exclusive to the nobility and gentry. The title of gentleman was bestowed on all entrants to the inns, thereby confusing social origins for the historian; and yet it is known that yeomen could in fact gain admission. Thus Thomas Underhill, yeoman, went from his inn of chancery to Lincoln's Inn on becoming clerk of the juries in 1474; and either he or his son became armigerous.[40] Luke Langland, formerly of Clifford's Inn, yeoman, was admitted to the Inner Temple in 1510 as a servant of the new earl of Wiltshire.[41] Many names in the records suggest an obscure background, and some indeed found that they could not manage. One Leonard Perpoint was expelled from the Inner Temple in 1547 because 'he lacketh exhibition and is not able to pay his dues'; but he was a member of Furnival's Inn when he died in 1566.[42] Such drastic action as expulsion was probably unusual. Many men were outlawed, or at least put in exigent, for non-payment of their dues, but there are reasons for doubting the effectiveness of such proceedings. The inns appear rather to have shown considerable forbearance with respect to the debts of members, and although no evidence has come to light of any endowed exhibitions or hardship funds, communal charity could sometimes assist a member in adversity. An explicit instance occurs in 1482, when William Lancaster, a member of Lincoln's Inn of six years' standing, was pardoned various debts on account of poverty.[43] The proportion of poor students making careers in the law is difficult to estimate, but it has been shown that of the fifty-three serjeants at law created between 1463 and 1510 only half came from a social background of any consequence, and that all the serjeants called in 1486 were of obscure origin.[44] The highest places in the common law were therefore comparatively open: open, at any rate, to the very able who either had a small exhibition or could support themselves through seven or eight years of education. At the lower levels of the profession, it was often an attorney who first lifted a family into the landed gentry.

[38] R. H. C. Fitzherbert, 'The Will of Elizabeth Fitzherbert' (1898) 20 *Jnl Derbs. Archaeological and Natural Hist. Soc.* 38. Adam Hawarden was likewise promised 5 marks a year, once he was of age, in the 1540s: marriage settlement, BL Add. Ch. 53039. Cf. the will of Thomas Godsalve (1545), Norwich Consistory Court, Reg. Mingayes 275 (10 marks a year for a student already at Gray's Inn).

[39] PCC 21 Holgrave.

[40] C67/48/24 (described as gentleman *alias* yeoman in pardon, 1471); *BBLI*, i. 75; arms on brass at Great Thurlow, Suffolk (1508).   [41] *CITR*, i. 21; *CPR 1494–1509*, p. 343.

[42] *CITR*, i. 146; PCC 29 Crymes.   [43] *BBLI*, i. 75.

[44] Ives, *Common Lawyers of pre-Reformation England*, 30–2.

PUPILLAGE

There is no evidence in the early Tudor period for the existence of pupillage, in the sense of a formal relationship for learning purposes between an established member of the Bar and a pupil. However, something like it was achieved by the practice of sharing chambers in the inns of court with seniors, who were often relatives or family acquaintances.[45] When Viscountess Lisle's son (John Basset) went to Lincoln's Inn in 1535, considerable efforts were made to find him a suitable chamber-fellow to act as his 'creancer',[46] and the barrister who accepted this role undertook to give him instruction.[47] In addition, two benchers—William Sulyard and John Densill, who acted as the viscount's counsel—kept a friendly eye on him. For good measure, he was also taken under the wing of another bencher, John Danaster, as a 'special friend' with whom Basset and his chamber-fellow stayed in the 'holidays'—until, that is, his mother was informed that Danaster kept house with a mistress and her illegitimate children.[48] Master Sulyard regarded Basset as his 'pupil', and wrote reports on his progress.[49] These arrangements are known to us through the happy survival of the Lisle letters; but there are no hints of such supervision in the records of the inns, and it is a matter for conjecture whether Basset's experience was typical. On the face of it, admittances to chambers were primarily residential arrangements. As yet there was no such thing as a 'set' of chambers, with a professional goodwill of its own.

A form of pupillage which was fully established and highly esteemed was a clerkship with an officer of one of the courts at Westminster, this being the best way of learning the practice of litigation and the finer points of special pleading. It may be considered the lineal ancestor of pupillage with a special pleader, which arose after the art of pleading had itself shifted from the court offices to private chambers. In the early Tudor period, the prothonotaries of the Common Pleas were both the leaders of the clerical establishment and the principal experts in special pleading, and they enjoyed considerable professional and social prestige.[50] Their learning in forms and precedents was oracular, and they were consulted by

---

[45] e.g. in 1486 Humphrey Starkey (of the Inner Temple) required his son to be placed under the 'oversight, guiding, and rule' of Thomas Marow of the same inn: PCC 25 Logge. For two other examples see Ives, *Common Lawyers of pre-Reformation England*, 58.

[46] *Lisle Letters*, iv. 14, no. 825 ('a discreeter creancer cannot be found for him in all that Inn than Mr Lane, who shall be in chamber with him'). Thomas Lane, who became a bencher the following year, did not in the event take on this role.

[47] Augustine Skerne to Lady Lisle, *Lisle Letters*, iv. 33–5.

[48] A minute insight into the life of a well-born inns of court student is provided by the correspondence concerning Basset in *Lisle Letters*, ed. Byrne, iv. 1–94. For Danaster as Basset's 'special friend' see ibid. 27. For 'holidays' see ibid. 30, 51; and ii. 396.   [49] *Lisle Letters*, ed. Byrne, iv. 64, 154.

[50] See above, 129.

the court with due respect for their expertise. They formed libraries, and compiled books of entries,[51] which alone would have educated a young man fortunate enough to be given access to them. Such a clerkship was essential for appointment to a clerical office,[52] and invaluable for an intending practitioner, whether an attorney or a member of the Bar. It might be undertaken before or after admission to an inn. In 1496, a London alderman provided for his son to be placed under the 'rule and governance' of one of the prothonotaries, or at one of the inns of court, as if these were alternatives.[53] And we know from his own memorandum that John Lucas spent eight or nine years training as an under-clerk in the King's Bench office before he entered New Inn in 1501.[54] But in 1515 we find a Norfolk testator providing for his son to spend two years in an inn of chancery, and then in a 'prenatoris file' with Mordaunt or Mountford; William Mordaunt was chief prothonotary of the Common Pleas, seated in north Essex, while Francis Mountford was filazer of that court for Norfolk and perhaps known to the family.[55] When John Jenour, second prothonotary, died in 1542, his former pupil Robert Catlyn listed among his former clerks the names of no less than four future chief justices (himself, Brooke,[56] Anthony Browne,[57] and Dyer[58]) and two future puisnes (Corbet and Frevile)—all fellow members of the Middle Temple, where Jenour probably kept his office.[59] The training left an indelible mark on the legal mind, and even the handwriting, of Sir James Dyer,[60] and it would be instructive to know how many other judges and leaders of the Bar underwent the same kind of formation.[61] Probably it was common; and those who could not secure a place with a prothonotary might work under an attorney.

At the very end of our period, we find an example of a pupillage of this kind which seems to be associated with chambers in an inn of chancery. Henry Attemer, a Norfolk attorney and a member of Clifford's Inn, agreed with a father to retain his son as a writing clerk or servant 'in arte et facultate scribendi', whereby he taught him at his own cost for two and a half years; but the student, according to Attemer, stole from two of his chamber-fellows in the same inn and had to be dismissed.[62]

---

[51] See below, 345–6.　　　[52] See above, 133 (untrained nominee rejected by the judges).

[53] Will of Hugh Brice, PCC 2 Horne.　　　[54] Above, 440.

[55] NfRO, Norwich Consistory Court, Register Spurlinge, fo. 94 (will of Nicholas Beaupré). An Edward Beaupré was admitted to Lincoln's Inn in 1523 and called in 1529.

[56] Anthony Browne (next note) received from Brooke 'a greate written booke of presidentes', which seems to betoken a shared interest in pleading: PROB 11/49, fo. 150v.

[57] Browne referred to him as 'my olde master John Jenour': above, 345 n. 77.

[58] For Dyer's use of Jenour's book of entries, see above, 345.

[59] MS. Phillipps 24108 (now in the Ess collection, HLS), memorandum by Catlyn on verso of title page; 94 Selden Soc. 130. Jenour was treasurer of the Middle Temple 1517–20.

[60] 109 Selden Soc., pp. xxii–xxiii.　　　[61] For a conjecture about Serjeant Bendlowes see below, 483.

[62] *Attemer* v. *Lachelos* (1551) CP 40/1146, m. 402d (claiming damages from the father for loss of future services). The defendant was a Norfolk husbandman, and the retainer was alleged to have been made at Norwich in 1545.

This shows that the attorney not only took residents into his chambers, but that at least one of them was admitted for the purpose of learning the craft of draftsmanship.

THE INNS OF CHANCERY

The study of the common law usually began with at least eighteen months in one of the inns of chancery.[63] There were nine at the beginning of our period[64]—a tenth inn or lodging house of uncertain status,[65] called the Long Entry in Holborn, having perhaps disappeared.[66] In 1549 one of the nine, Strand Inn, was demolished by the duke of Somerset in order to build Somerset House, and the society thereupon dissolved, leaving only eight.[67] By 1540, all the inns of chancery had become linked to parent inns of court,[68] whereas at the beginning of our period external control seems rather to have rested with the lord chancellor, sometimes with the assistance of the Council.[69] It is far from clear when the affiliations with inns of court developed, but our earliest evidence is from 1496, when Lincoln's Inn provided an entertainment for Furnival's Inn;[70] and already by 1502

[63] For the length of time spent in these inns, see 94 Selden Soc. 127–8.

[64] Barnard's, Clement's, Clifford's, Davy's (or Thavie's), Furnival's, Lyon's, New, Staple, and Strand Inns.

[65] Fortescue had said there were ten inns of chancery: *De Laudibus*, ed. Chrimes, 116 ('decem... et quandoque vero plura'). John Norden identified the tenth as 'an ancient church next the Steelyard', which had belonged to the Templars, known as the White Hall: *Speculum Britanniae* (1593), i, Middlesex, 33. This has not been verified. The Outer Temple was sometimes mentioned as a nominal addition, but there is no evidence of a distinct society there either.

[66] In 1476 the 'pensionarius hospicii vocati Le Longentre' sued four gentlemen for dues: CP 40/859, m. 439. (One of the four was sued the following year by Thavie's Inn, and so it is possible that the two were connected.) Cf. G. Pursloe, *Wardens' Accounts of the Founders' Company* (1964), 26 ('Item paid at the Long Entre for drinkyng iiij d. ob.', in connection with an Exchequer suit, 1507). It was probably the old Tamworth's Inn (named after a Chancery clerk who died in 1374): Williams, *Early Holborn*, i. 149, 157.

[67] J. Stow, *Survey of London* [1598], ed. C. L. Kingsford (1908), i. 77; *CITR*, i. 178. The last principal, Richard Sherard, tried to recover outstanding dues from 147 members: CP 40/1134, m. 841 (debt against three knights and 144 gentlemen, 1548); CP 40/1135, m. 494a–b (exigent); CP 40/1138–9 (58 separate declarations, 1548–9); CP 40/1143, m. 251d (debt against six, 1550); CP 40/1144A, mm. 296d, 568 (exigent).

[68] Denton, Bacon, and Cary, *Report*, 545 (as to readers). In 1561, it was said to be an immemorial custom that Clement's, Clifford's, and Lyon's Inns were 'united and annexed' to the Inner Temple: *CITR*, i. 215.

[69] As to the chancellor see *Furnival's Inn v. Leycrofte* (c.1487) C1/93/66 (petitioner says 'the rule and governance of all court' belongs to chancellor); *Early Records of Furnival's Inn*, ed. D. S. Bland (1957), 39 (election dispute referred to chancellor, 1503); *Copwode v. Sherarde* (c.1528) C1/401/9 (petitioner says inns of chancery under rule of chancellor). For investigations in Council see e.g. 16 Selden Soc., pp. cix–cx.

[70] Williams (*Early Holborn*, §482) speculated that from this date Lincoln's Inn had a head-lease of Furnival's Inn from the earl of Shrewsbury; but this is no more than a guess. Lincoln's Inn bought the freehold in 1547: *BBLI*, i. 286.

there seems to have been some duty on the former to support readings in the latter.[71] On the other hand, an order made by the lord chancellor and judges in 1529, under which the Inner Temple appointed readers for Clement's Inn and Lyon's Inn,[72] suggests that there may have been some uncertainty before then. By the 1530s, however, internal problems in an inn of chancery were being referred to its guardian inn of court rather than the lord chancellor.[73] And it became increasingly common during this time for members of the inns of court to be admitted from their satellites, though it was far from being the rule.[74]

No contemporary administrative records survive for any of the inns of chancery in the Tudor period,[75] and our information about their working and membership is therefore fragmentary. Their constitutions were not written down, but were probably broadly similar in all the societies. For Clement's Inn, Clifford's Inn, and New Inn we possess statutes from this period; but these were not constitutions, in the sense of coherent frameworks of government, so much as compilations of regulations probably made at different times. Even their date is a matter of some doubt. The Clifford's Inn statutes survive in the form of an illuminated vellum triptych of 1528, headed by the royal arms, which formerly hung in the hall there in an oak case with folding doors, and was transferred to the Inner Temple in 1903 when the society was dissolved.[76] These were transcribed from something earlier, and refer in the defaced heading to the time when Laurence Holland was principal in the time of Henry VII.[77] One of the statutes refers to a decision made by the council of the Inn in the time of King Edward IV,[78] and the bulk may be older than that. The Clement's Inn statutes survive in a copy made in 1635,[79] and are very similar in character. One of the individual statutes is said to be dated

---

[71] *BBLI*, i. 111, 125, 235 (clear association with readings in 1533). The first comparable reference to Thavie's Inn is in 1534: ibid. 238 (election of new reader discussed).

[72] *CITR*, i. 95 (*bis*). There may have been some connection in 1521: ibid. 65; *Pension Book of Clement's Inn*, ed. C. Carr (78 Selden Soc.; 1960), pp. xxiii–xxiv. On the other hand, the Inner Temple had in 1523 persuaded someone to serve as principal of Thavie's Inn, which did not become one of its satellites: *CITR*, i. 81; 78 Selden Soc., p. xxiv.   [73] *BBLI*, i. 225, 245.

[74] 78 Selden Soc., p. xxiv.

[75] Some extracts from the lost records of Furnival's Inn survive in a seventeenth-century transcript: *Early Records of Furnival's Inn*, ed. D. S. Bland (1957).

[76] IT MS. Misc. 189; seventeenth-century transcript in IT Archives, CLI/4/1; S. Ireland, *The Inns of Court* (1800), 76–8; C. M. Hay-Edwards, *A History of Clifford's Inn* (1912), 59–66 (extracts from a transcript). Ireland (p. 78) provides a woodcut showing its general appearance.

[77] Holland is mentioned as principal in 1504 and 1508: CP 40/970, m. 171; CP 40/984, m. 27d. He was no longer principal in 1511.

[78] Clifford's Inn statutes, no. 20. The words after 'Edward' have been treated with a chemical agent and are no longer legible. Carr read them as indicating Edward III (78 Selden Soc., p. liii), but an old transcript says Edward IV (Hay-Edwards, *History of Clifford's Inn*, 59–60).

[79] PRO, PRO 30/26/74/4; tr. only in *Pension Book of Clement's Inn*, ed. Carr, 218–26. An inaccurate transcript was privately printed, with parallel translation, as *The Book of Constitutions and Orders of the Honble. Society of Clement's Inn* (1880).

1479,[80] but the very circumstance that a date is mentioned in the text may mean that it was not coeval with the rest. These documents both appear, then, to be consolidated collections of rules and orders, perhaps issued with the authority of the lord chancellor, and put together around the beginning of the Tudor period. The New Inn constitutions seem, from their contents, to have been coeval with the other two.[81] In 1662 they were kept chained in hall, and were so old that they could be described as 'made tyme out of mynde';[82] but they survive today only in a translation made in 1668 and contain no internal dates. Staple Inn had statutes in Dugdale's time which were thought to date from the time of Henry V, but these had been lost by the end of the eighteenth century. A new edition of the inn's orders, made in 1624, incorporated material from the old statutes but without indicating what was old and what was new.[83] Nothing is known of the statutes of the other inns, though doubtless they all possessed them at one time.

All the inns of chancery except Lyon's Inn were presided over by a principal. Lyon's Inn, like the inns of court, had a treasurer instead.[84] Clement's Inn at the very beginning of our period was governed by two joint principals,[85] though from 1502 at the latest it had single principals like the other inns.[86] The office was elective,[87] but the tenure varied. Staple Inn was ruled at the beginning of the Tudor period by Martin Ferrers (d. 1503), who was principal for at least thirty years but is not known as a lawyer,[88] while Barnard's Inn had another long-term principal in Richard Massy, probably the Lancashire practitioner.[89] However, the

[80] Clement's Inn constitutions, no. 47; It reads 'le xix anne de nostre senior le roy', which the 1880 translation renders as '19 of our late King Edward IV', though the evidence for this reading is not stated.

[81] 'Constitutiones Novi Hospicii', MT archives, MT 12/MIS17; and an eighteenth-century copy, inscribed on the cover, 'New Inn Constitutions Translated from the French in the Year 1668', MT 12/CON1.

[82] MT 12/MIS16 ('fixed with a chayne in the common hall of this house, and made tyme out of mynde').   [83] JHB MS. 198.

[84] The first known mention of this office is in 1486: CP 40/897, m. 298 (Thomas Gower, 'thesaurarius de Lyons Inne').

[85] Those whose names are known from the plea rolls are: William Babthorp and Henry Tedyngworth (1476), Robert Fulwode and Henry Tedyngworth (1477), Robert Fulwode and William Bret (1481–2), John Baff and Nicholas Hughson (1484–5), Nicholas Hughson and John Pole (1487–8).

[86] Clifford's Inn had joint principals before our period: William Elys (sole principal 1471–2) and Thomas Roche (1474–8), Thomas Danby and Thomas Roche (1481–2), then Thomas Roche alone (1486). No similar instances are known in the other inns.

[87] New Inn constitutions, which imposed a fine of 40s. on those who refused office after election by 'the company' (unless they had held it before). In Furnival's Inn also the election was by the company or fellowship, which presumably meant the whole society: *Principal of Furnival's Inn* v. *Pottyer* (1499) CP 40/949, m. 484 (referring to election 'per cometivam ejusdem hospicii'). A dispute concerning the next election there (c.1505/6) reached the chancellor: C1/364/2–3.

[88] Ferrers brings numerous actions, probably as principal, from 1474: CP 40/849, m. 434.

[89] C. W. Brooks, *The Admissions Registers of Barnard's Inn* (1995), 16 (1488); 75 Selden Soc. 28 (1494); DL 5/2, fo. 28 (1502). Massy first sues members for dues in 1484 (CP 40/888, m. 320), though he is not named as principal in the record. A Richard Massy was an attorney in Chester in 1465 (CHES 37/6/4) and serjeant of the county palatine of Lancaster in 1473 and 1485 (*DKR*, xxxi. 169).

tenure of office was usually brief. The typical principal was not a senior member of the profession, but a young member waiting for admission to an inn of court;[90] and it seems that service as a principal was a recognized way of earning admission on favourable terms, since many were so admitted on ending their term of office. There were a few other officers, such as the pensioner and the steward, and special officers for Christmas. The senior members of each society were known as ancients, and they seem to have enjoyed a status similar to benchers in the inns of court; they were probably for the most part attorneys who remained in residence in the inns of chancery. It is not clear whether the principal's council who governed Clifford's Inn,[91] or the 'great council' of New Inn,[92] were the whole body of ancients or smaller governing bodies.

The bulk of the members, to judge from the names in the many actions brought by the principals to recover outstanding dues, were gentlemen (or even knights[93]) not destined for the practice of the law, including what the statutes of Clifford's Inn call 'noble pensioners'. In this they imitated the inns of court. They also followed the festivities of the court, so that in Clifford's Inn at Christmas 1482

daily the company exceeded in largesse of diet, their tables being replenished with store of venison and costly viands, change of wines, selected songs, choice music, majestical masques, stately stage-play, bountiful banquettings, dicing, dancing, and many other rare invented court-like pastimes, with like rarity of oratory speeches whereby was unfolded the brave wits and ingenious capacity of sundry persons resorting hither...[94]

For the professional student, however, the main purpose of the inns of chancery was to provide a studious environment in which he could become acquainted with Littleton and the wording of writs, and master the forms and rudiments of pleading.[95] For this purpose, there was a collegiate structure and a rigorous

[90] A documented example is discussed in 'The Legal Education of Richard Empson' (1984) 57 BIHR, 98–9.

[91] e.g. Clifford's Inn statutes, no. 12 ('il est ordeignez et establies per le principall et son councell que...'); no. 37 provides that any question as to the construction of the statutes should be referred to the principal 'and those who are of his council' ('et ceux de son counsell'); no. 47 ('accord est per le principall et tout le councell de le dit hostell'). In Lincoln's Inn the 'council' were, and still are, the benchers.

[92] New Inn constitutions, which also indicate that the council met in a 'parliament chamber', as in the Temple.

[93] In 1484 the Christmas steward of Clifford's Inn was a knight: MT, 'Brerewood' MS., fo. 57.

[94] MT, 'Brerewood' MS., fo. 57 (sp. mod.), citing lost stewards' books. In 1487 there were also 'mummeryes... martial stratagems, heroicall inventions in matters of honour and armes, and other wyttye devises there acted and contrived': ibid., fo. 57v. Lords and ladies attended in 1488: ibid. For the Christmas banquet in Furnival's Inn in 1518, see J. H. Baker, *Readers and Readings in the Inns of Court and Chancery* (13 Selden Soc. Suppl. Ser.; 2001), 438.

[95] See SP 1/82, fo. 140, where John Amadas (writing to Thomas Cromwell) says of a law student, '(sp. mod.) he hath been this two years at Lyon's Inn, and there hath his principles of the common law of England, as Littleton's *Tenures* and *Natura Brevium* etc.... and he shall to the Temple to his book

educational regime enforced by pecuniary mulcts. It is nowhere stated that graduation in such a course was essential for admission to an inn of court, or for practice as an attorney, and yet some such normal expectation must have been the underlying sanction for submission to the regime.

Although we have only a few statutes for guidance, a reference in the Clifford's Inn statutes to education 'according to the custom of the court',[96] and the known circumstance that vacation exercises in each inn of chancery were attended by members of other inns,[97] both demonstrate that the course of study was substantially common to all the societies. The statutes, however, provide only fleeting glimpses of the system and show that there were variations in points of detail. All the members ('companions') of Clement's Inn under twelve years' standing, other than attorneys and clerks attending offices, were obliged to attend moots and readings on pain of fine; they were divided, as in the inns of court, into utter and inner barristers, the principal having the power to 'call to the bar' those who were competent to moot; acceptance of call was compulsory, on pain of fine. There was a lesser exercise, called a 'report', which is not described. Everyone who mooted or reported was 'to do so perfectly, without a book', on pain of fine. On working days every member under two years' standing was to 'hear the reading' of a writ from the *Natura Brevium* by the principal, and at dinner a case in law was to be put by the youngest of the first mess at each table; a fine of 4*d.* was payable for defaults in these daily exercises.[98] The Clifford's Inn statutes are more concerned with social misbehaviour, but they refer in passing to the same four exercises of writ-reading, lecture, moot, and report, and they also mention a 'declaration of the court baron'—presumably a course on *Curia Baronis*, the written guide to procedure in manorial courts.[99] They direct that a student should begin after half a year's residence to 'bear all manner of learnings which belong to an inner barrister', without waiting to be asked, and that after a year and a day from his admission he was bound—again without call—to perform the learnings of an utter barrister.[100] The short time-scale shows the elementary nature of the course, and confirms that the normal minimum period of residence was eighteen months or two years.[101]

and to continue his learning'. Cf. *MTR*, i. 5 (Thomas Empson adm. Middle Temple, but to remain in New Inn until he becomes proficient in study, 1503).

[96] Clifford's Inn statutes, no. 9 ('tout ceux que entrent en le avantdit hostiell a cause de laprise solonc le custume del courte').   [97] 94 Selden Soc. *133*.

[98] Clement's Inn constitutions, nos. 10–15.

[99] Clifford's Inn statutes, nos. 8 ('declaration de le aptur. ou courte baron'), 40 (tr. *LPCL*, 18). The meaning of 'aptur.' is obscure, and it may be a clerical mistake.

[100] Clifford's Inn statutes, no. 46. (Cf. no. 12, which requires every member of at least one year's standing 'to bear all learnings of this Inn for his proper course'.) Inner and utter barristers are also mentioned in Clement's Inn constitutions, no. 13.

[101] Robert Catlyn spent only 18 months in Clement's Inn in 1529–31 before joining the Middle Temple: 94 Selden Soc. *127–8* n. 1.

These degrees had no significance outside the inns of chancery, and may already have been obsolescent in our period; but their existence proves that the title 'barrister' refers to the 'bar' of an inn, for mooting purposes, and has nothing to do with the bar of the courts. The New Inn constitutions are less helpful than the other two in educational matters, but they refer to three principal kinds of exercise, namely moots, 'the statutes', and 'the writ'.[102] Each of these exercises involved all the 'fellows', in the order of their chambers; but the last occurred only in the Lent and autumn vacations. As in the other two inns, both utter and inner barristers took part in the moots. There was also a 'reading of the writ every day in the term', indicating that there were two different exercises concerning writs.

The form of mooting in chancery is revealed by two separate series of pleadings, in French, using the names of members of Lyon's Inn, one from around 1490 and the other from around 1502–6.[103] These moots were elementary pleading exercises. Participants learned the basic forms of writs and pleadings by drawing them up for comparatively simple fact situations taken from moot-books—collections of set problems—using each other's names as parties; and, since the statutes would have them perform 'without book', it must be supposed that at the exercise they recited them from memory. A few points of law in each case would be argued upon the pleadings, in medieval fashion. In the learning vacations, the exercises were performed to a high standard, and were attended by members of other inns, including formal representatives of the inns of court.[104] Double was the penalty for any student who let an exercise slip when the society was thus on public display.[105] The exercises were sufficiently serious for Edmund Dudley to refer in Gray's Inn on more than one occasion to opinions he had heard there.[106] There may even have been a tendency in the early sixteenth century to make the vacation-moot cases too showy, because the judges directed in 1557 that they should not contain 'above two points argumentable'.[107]

The writ-readings were probably mere recitals of the formulae, by rote, or at most lessons read from the *Natura Brevium*, rather than full lectures. The *Natura*

[102] New Inn constitutions, which refer in different places to 'the course of the moot', 'the course of the statutes', and 'the course of the writ'. The 'course' here refers to the order in which students performed the exercise, according to the location of their chambers.

[103] John Rylands Lib., Manchester, MS. Eng. 288, ff. 171–174 (*c.*1490); Lambeth Palace Lib. MS. 270, ff. 8–13 (*c.*1502/6); identified in *Moots*, pp. liii–liv.

[104] *Moots*, pp. lii, clx–clxxxiii (specimen). Each inn of court sent one barrister and one student as 'assistants' to the reader in chancery: Dugdale, *Origines Juridiciales*, 195 (1540).

[105] Clement's Inn constitutions, no. 40, tr. *LPCL*, 18 (40*d.* for loss of a moot, as opposed to 20*d.* for a moot in term-time, and only 6*d.* for a writ or report).

[106] Bodl. Lib. MS. Rawlinson C.705, ff. 66v (tr. 'by Dudley, and so he said Eleson had held at Strand Inn once upon a time'), 74 ('. . . and he said that he had learned this case at Davy's Inn in a moot from Baker, bencher of the Inner Temple, who was well learned in the law').

[107] *CITR*, i. 192; *BBLI*, i. 320; *MTR*, i. 112.

Brevium was certainly one of the standard textbooks for the inns of chancery. An edition was printed in the 1490s 'at the instaunce of my maistres of the company of Stronde Inne',[108] and the Harvard Law School possesses a copiously annotated copy of the 1537 edition which belonged successively to Thomas Rolleston and Anthony Gell, principals of Clement's Inn.

It is through Anthony Gell that our first identifiable readings in an inn of chancery have been preserved. They are from Clement's Inn in 1543–4, the year before Gell became principal. The main course reported is that of Richard Blackwall, a barrister of the Inner Temple, who lectured on Magna Carta. The course began in Trinity term, with lectures on chapters 2 and 3, and resumed in Hilary term—Michaelmas term having been adjourned because of plague—with chapters 5 to 10, followed by eleven more chapters in the Lent vacation. The preceding course is not complete, but the text in Hilary term 1543 was the first chapter of Westminster I, on 'the peace of the realm', and in the Lent vacation the reader digressed over numerous other statutes concerning justices of the peace; in Easter term, however, there was a complete change of subject and of statute.[109] Thus it is evident that, as in later times, the custom was for readings in chancery to begin in the summer and continue through the year, both in term and in the principal vacations. Although the reader could work his way through a statute, chapter by chapter, he does not seem to have been obliged to do so. The only other identifiable reading from our period is Plowden's in New Inn (1550), which was on the statute *De Donis*.[110] Since these readings used the same texts as readings in court, it is quite possible that some of our anonymous earlier readings on statutes are from inns of chancery rather than inns of court.[111] It was said in a later period to be an 'ancient custom' that readings in the inns of chancery could be given on a section of Littleton instead of a statute,[112] and this would account for the Elizabethan readings on copyholds, but no pre-Elizabethan evidence one way or the other has yet been found.

THE INNS OF COURT

From his inn of chancery, the fortunate law student would gain admission to clerks' commons in one of the four inns of court, there to continue his studies for two or more years before he became a full member, a 'master' or 'fellow' (*socius*).[113]

---

[108] Colophon in Beale, *Bibliography*, 119, no. T69.

[109] CUL MS. Add. 8871; *CELMC*, 641–2. The MS. belonged to Anthony Gell, who was principal in 1545–7: HMC, *Ninth Report*, ii. 385.

[110] BL MS. Hargrave 89, ff. 38–47. This began in the Easter term.

[111] For a reading on Marlborough delivered in term-time, and so presumably in an inn of chancery, see 23 *JLH* 63.   [112] *BBLI*, ii. 265 (1626).

[113] 94 Selden Soc. 129.

These fellows comprised not only the benchers but also the utter barristers. Indeed, the pristine constitution of the inns of court was apparently independent of the degree system which grew up during the fifteenth century.[114] Each was self-governing, in the sense that the whole society or fellowship made orders for its regulation, and once a year elected three or four governors to act as an executive governing body for the next twelve months.[115] The assembly of the society was known as a parliament in the two Temple societies,[116] as a general council in Lincoln's Inn, and as pension in Gray's Inn.[117] Already three of the inns had a treasurer, who was one of the governors or was associated with them. But the office did not necessarily have the primacy of later times; it was sometimes held by a relatively junior fellow, and might be renewed for several successive years.[118] In the course of the early Tudor period, the government of the inns gradually passed from the fellowship at large, and their elected governors, to the masters of the bench: that is, those fellows who had graduated as benchers. In Lincoln's Inn, orders were made at the very beginning of our period by the governors and benchers.[119] On the other hand, an account of the inns of court around 1540 says that the parliament or pension was still a general assembly of the benchers and utter barristers, and this seems to reflect the practice in the Middle Temple.[120] Although governors were still elected by some of the inns at the end of our period,[121] they were abandoned soon afterwards.[122]

Gray's Inn had a markedly different constitution from the other three societies at the start of the sixteenth century.[123] It apparently did not have governors, and

[114] For what follows see also A. W. B. Simpson, 'The Early Constitution of the Inns of Court' (1970) 28 *CLJ* 241–56 (repr. *Legal Theory and Legal History*, 17–32).

[115] Lincoln's Inn had four governors after 1427. The Inner Temple had three by 1484: CP 40/888, m. 218d (three described as the treasurer and governors); cf. CP 40/898, m. 97d (four so described in 1486); CP 40/914, m. 319d (four governors, not mentioning the treasurer, in 1490). Middle Temple had three governors and a treasurer in 1498: CP 40/946, m. 543.

[116] The term is in use when the Middle Temple records begin in 1501, and those of the Inner Temple in 1505.

[117] The term is found in 1529: Dugdale, *Origines Juridiciales*, 108a. It was also used in some of the inns of chancery.

[118] Lincoln's Inn introduced the office in 1455: *BBLI*, i. 21. Middle Temple had a treasurer by 1479: CP 40/870, m. 440 (William Poulet). Inner Temple had one by 1484: CP 40/888, m. 218d (Thomas Welles).   [119] *BBLI*, i. 89 (1489), 116 (1494).

[120] Simpson, 'Early Constitution of the Inns of Court', 31. As late as 1551, utter barristers were amerced 3s. 4d. for not attending a parliament: *MTR*, i. 80.

[121] They are not mentioned in *MTR*, though the Middle Temple had three governors (besides the treasurer) in 1498: above, n. 115.

[122] In 1566 in the Inner Temple, 1574 in Lincoln's Inn: Simpson, 'Early Constitution of the Inns of Court', 25, 30.

[123] A. W. B. Simpson, 'The Early Constitution of Gray's Inn' (1975) 34 *CLJ* 131–50 (repr. in *Legal Theory and Legal History*, 33–52); J. H. Baker, 'The Old Constitution of Gray's Inn' (1977) 81 *Graya* 15–19 (repr. *LPCL*, 39–43).

it did not have a treasurer until 1530,[124] after which it sometimes had two joint treasurers.[125] The society was divided into two parts, the 'grand company' (*magna societas*), comprising the readers and ancients, and the 'company of masters and clerks', comprising the students and other gentlemen. Gray's Inn used the term 'readers' for constitutional purposes, in preference to 'benchers'; it was possible for lesser members to sit on the bench at moots, but only those who had read were governing benchers. The position was not in that respect greatly different from that in the other inns, save that elsewhere benchers (or associates of the bench) were occasionally—albeit rarely—elected before they had read.[126] The ancients were utter barristers of several years' standing who had been elected into the grand company, and they had duties in relation to readings and moots. It seems likely that this *magna societas* corresponded to the democratic fellowship of masters which once ruled in the other inns,[127] before the introduction of the degree system, and that it retained its coherence longest in Gray's Inn because of the special status of the ancients. Nevertheless, by the middle of the sixteenth century, the government of the inn was falling to the readers alone, and by 1585 this had been established long enough to seem 'immemorial'.[128] By the reign of Elizabeth I, therefore, the organizational differences between the inns of court were very slight, and the inns had begun to harmonize their arrangements by making joint regulations.[129]

Whatever his status had been in the inns of chancery, the student 'in court' started the exercises of learning as a beginner. Until he was qualified to argue in moots, his status was again that of an inner barrister.[130] In due time, by following a course to be sketched below, he would aspire to become an utter barrister and then a bencher. This, at any rate, was the course of graduation for the professional student. As in the lesser inns, however, the great majority of members were young

---

[124] Lost pension book, cited by Dugdale, *Origines Juridiciales*, 115a (William Walsyngham 'primus thesaurarius' elected Mich. 22 Hen. VIII). The finances were controlled prior to this by the steward and the pensioner, offices which also existed in the other inns.

[125] Dugdale, *Origines Juridiciales*, 152b (Edmund Grey and Robert Urmyston app. 1540), 182b; CP 40/1138, m. 609 (Sir Walter Hendley and William Staunford, 1548); CP 40/1168, m. 16 (Nicholas Bacon and Gilbert Gerrard, 1556). Bacon had served alone from 1552 to 1556: *Origines Juridiciales*, 201b, 216b.

[126] e.g. in the Inner Temple, Edward Tame (1507), John Baker and Richard Wye (1517): *CITR*, i. 7, 39.

[127] Including the inns of chancery, where the government continued to reside in the 'ancients'.

[128] *Treasurers of Gray's Inn* v. *Gargrave* (1585) CP 40/1447, m. 2428d (tr. *LPCL*, 42: 'the readers for the time being of the same house are accustomed, and have been accustomed since time immemorial, to hold common councils commonly called pensions within the same house, and in the same pensions to make and appoint decrees, laws, and ordinances for the good rule and government of the said ancients, masters, and clerks...').

[129] 'Orders made and agreed upon to be observed and kept in all the four houses of court' (1557) *BBLI*, i. 320–1; *MTR*, i. 111–12; *CITR*, i. 192–3; Dugdale, *Origines Juridiciales*, 310-11. These do not mention any external authority, though similar orders were made in 1559 by the judges.

[130] In the Middle Temple, inner barristers are referred to as 'no utter barristers': 105 Selden Soc., p. lix.

noblemen and gentlemen finishing their general upbringing in the metropolis but not needing any acquaintance with the forms of pleading. More than half the members of Lincoln's Inn make no appearance in the records beyond their admission, and it seems probable that no more than a third of the resident membership of the inns were following the law.[131] For the majority of members, the wider advantages offered by these communities, so conveniently located between the city of London and the palace of Westminster, were doubtless more important than the rudiments of a legal education. It was here, rather than among the scholarly clergy of Oxford and Cambridge, that the future statesmen, members of Parliament, sheriffs, magistrates, and administrators of the secular commonwealth were brought together in their formative years. Here they joined in work and play, learned the names which would matter to them, dined and prayed together, displayed their wealth or their talent—whichever was more conspicuous—talked of law and much else, drank, diced, and misbehaved. If English society possessed any common characteristics, a community of attitudes and aspirations, it was the inns of court and chancery as much as any other central institutions which helped to foster it.

It could be maintained that the inns contributed more to the general cultural life of the nation—more historians, translators, and poets—than both universities.[132] The music, the 'disguising',[133] and the courtly ceremony associated with the Christmas vacation, provided the renaissance gentleman with polite accomplishments and laid the foundations of an English musical and dramatic tradition. Let it be said also that the inns had a rougher side. The atmosphere of the Christmas festivities, which were compulsory for the young clerks commoners and their elected mock officers, was at times like that of a rumbustious children's party, while at others it recalled the social ritual of an age long gone by: a curious mixture of officially tolerated horseplay and carefully preserved medieval tradition. The young man elected as lord of misrule sometimes over-indulged his dramatic licence, and in 1519 Lincoln's Inn felt obliged to abolish the custom of electing a mock traitor (Jack Straw); five years later, a lord of misrule elsewhere actually killed someone. Quite apart from Christmas, student behaviour was often rude and sometimes violent. On several occasions in Henry VII's reign the inns were in trouble before the Council for rioting,[134] sometimes resulting in death; gaming and loose living were rife; and in 1506 even a future chief justice was fined for frequenting a brothel. The misbehaviour may have been worse than that of the

[131] See 'English Legal Profession, 1450-1550', 93-6.

[132] For what follows see 94 Selden Soc. 130-1.

[133] 94 Selden Soc. 130 n. 9. See also *Lisle Letters*, ed. Byrne, ii. 20, no. 108 ('The inns of court hath kept revel this Christmas with such disguisings and pastimes as hath not been seen', 1533/4).

[134] In addition to the three instances in 94 Selden Soc. 131 n. 4, see C244/153/137, 149 (1503); 75 Selden Soc. 36-7; C244/154/21 (1504).

students in the universities, who were younger and *in statu pupillari*, and perhaps the traditional scholarly virtues were less valued by men of the world. Yet the frequency of disorderly incidents over the period as a whole compares favourably with modern universities, and for the realities of serious student life we should look rather at the students' notebooks than at the disciplinary records which fate has so unkindly preserved.

LEARNING EXERCISES IN THE INNS OF COURT[135]

The system of exercises in the inns of court was similar in form to that in the inns of chancery, but more advanced.[136] Its origins lie in an earlier period, and it was already by 1483 a well-established routine. However, it is in the early Tudor period that the first detailed descriptions are found,[137] and we may also detect certain changes in the way the routine operated. In addition to the degrees of inner and utter barrister, as found in the inferior inns, there was the degree of reader or bencher. The length of training considerably exceeded that in the preparatory schools, since 5 or 6 years were required before call to the utter bar, and a further 10 to 12 years before the call to read.[138] Between his calls to the bar and bench, the utter barrister would be expected to deliver a reading in an inn of chancery.

The readings were not given in term-time, as they were in the inns of chancery, but in the two 'grand' vacations during Lent and the early autumn (August). Unless the sequence was broken because of plague, or a call of serjeants, or a default, the Lent reading was normally a 'double' reading—that is, the second course of lectures expected of a bencher some five to ten years after his first reading. These readings, especially in Lent, were the chief events in the educational cycle, and were regularly attended by those judges and serjeants who were former benchers of the inn. They were always given on statutory texts, and at the beginning of our period it may still have been the custom to proceed through the *statuta vetera* from Magna Carta until the reign of Edward I, each reader starting where his predecessor left off. That course is still discernible in the Inner Temple readings from the early 1490s, and seems to have been returned to at the beginning of Henry VIII's reign, though between 1494 and 1508 there was no

---

[135] For private study, as evidenced by the ownership and exchange of books, see below, 491–3.

[136] For what follows, see 94 Selden Soc. 132–5; *Moots*, pp. xlv–lxxv; *Spelman's Reading on Quo Warranto*, 113 Selden Soc. (1997), introd.; *Readers and Readings*, 227–34.

[137] The most important is the report prepared for Henry VIII in 1539, pr. E. Waterhous, *Fortescutus Illustratus* (1663), 543–6; repr. by D. S. Bland, 10 *JSPTL* 178–94. (For the circumstances of composition, see R. M. Fisher, 14 *JSPTL* 108–9.) Cf. related account of the Middle Temple in BL Cotton MS. Vitellius C.IX, ff. 319–323v; pr. by Fisher, 14 *JSPTL* 111–17.

[138] Baker, 'English Legal Profession, 1450–1550', 91; 105 Selden Soc., p. lix.

coherent sequence at all.[139] The old cycle may first have been broken by readers anxious to impress the Crown by glossing a text of concern to the government. Prominent in this movement were the serjeants-elect of 1495, at least two of whom (Constable and Frowyk) chose *Prerogativa Regis*,[140] though precedents had been set in the 1480s by Edmund Dudley's first reading in Gray's Inn, on the Statute of *Quo Warranto*,[141] and by Gregory Adgore's first reading in the Inner Temple, on the 1484 statute of uses:[142] choices which show that, even before 1490, the traditional sequence was not rigidly insisted upon for readers in course. Other readers followed suit, introducing for instance the *Carta de Foresta*,[143] which had not previously been included within the old cycle, or—like Adgore—selecting a recent statute. Once readers had a free choice, they were able to introduce an element of practical usefulness into a course which was still necessarily random in its coverage. After 1530, it was not at all unusual to expound the statutes of Henry VIII, including those concerned with technical matters.[144] As this shift occurred, the statutes between Edward I and Richard III were almost completely ignored.[145]

The readings consisted of exposition followed by disputation. The reader read a clause of his statute each day, commented upon it, and then explained its operation with the aid of a spectrum of illustrative cases 'put as law'.[146] The fifteenth-century tradition, emulating that of the universities, was to gloss each phrase in the statute seriatim, and this method was still followed by some readers in the earlier Tudor period; but the new form of reading introduced by Dudley and his contemporaries laid more emphasis on the analytical treatment of a topic, ranging if need be far away from the wording of the set text. Both the old and the new traditions recognized the importance of interactive exercises, and the most intellectually testing part of the reading was the disputation of the readers' 'cases'.

[139] 102 Selden Soc., pp. xxxiv–xxxviii.

[140] These are the subject of detailed studies by McGlynn, 'The King and the Law'(1997); *The Royal Prerogative and the Learning of the Inns of Court* (forthcoming in 2003). Part of Constable's reading (omitting the later chapters) was printed in 1949 by Professor S. E. Thorne.

[141] 113 Selden Soc., p. xvi n. 35. *Quo Warranto* was, of course, an Edwardian statute; but it does not seem to have been included in the course of readings earlier in the fifteenth century.

[142] For this, and the other nominate readings referred to, see the bibliography, below, 888–92.

[143] This was chosen by Richard Hesketh (Gray's Inn, c.1506/8) and George Treherne (Lincoln's Inn, 1520), in each case for a first reading.

[144] The first example noted is Walter Hendley's reading (Gray's Inn, 1530) on 21 Hen. VIII, c. 3 (abridgment of plaints).

[145] Very few exceptions have been noted. BL MS. Lansdowne 1138, ff. 116–118v, contains brief fifteenth-century readings on the statutes of Lincoln (9 Edw. II) and York (12 Edw. II), the latter 'secundum Pygot'. Staundford read in 1545 on 34 Edw. III, c. 12 (forfeiture for treason). And in Sir Richard Morgan's MS., Univ. Illinois at Urbana-Champaign MS. 27, ff. 63–67, there is an anonymous reading on 9 Ric. II, c. 3 (errors).

[146] See Spelman 219, referring to Fitzherbert's reading (Gray's Inn, 1510).

Each day a few of the cases put by the reader were challenged for argument by the barristers, benchers, serjeants, and judges who were present.[147] The process is fully described in 1540:[148]

[The reader], openly in the hall before all the company, shall read from one such act or statute as shall please him to ground his whole reading on for all that vacation; and that done doth declare such inconveniences and mischiefs as were unprovided for, and now by the same statute be [remedied], and then reciteth certain doubts and questions which he hath devised that may grow upon the said statute, and declareth his judgment therein; that done, one of the younger utter barristers rehearseth one question propounded by the reader, and doth by way of argument labour to prove the reader's opinion to be against the law; and after him the rest of the utter barristers and readers one after another in their ancienties do declare their opinions and judgments in the same; and then the reader who did put the case endeavoureth himself to confute objections laid against him, and to confirm his own opinion; after whom the judges and serjeants, if any be present, declare their opinions; and after they have done the youngest utter barrister again rehearseth another case, which is ordered as the other was. Thus the reading ends for that day: and this manner of reading and disputations continues daily two hours, or thereabouts...And besides this daily, in some houses, after dinner, one at the reader's board before they rise propoundeth another of his cases to him, put the same day at his reading, which case is debated by them in like form as the cases are used to be argued at his reading; and like order is observed at every mess at the other tables; and the same manner always observed at supper, when they have no moots.

The reports of readings contain both kind of exercise, not always in conjunction.[149] Readers' cases in isolation have little or no apparent coherence, since the points challenged did not necessarily have a very direct relationship with the main topic of the lectures. We may find a debate on *specificatio*, or on whether stealing one's own goods can be felony, in a reading on *quo warranto*;[150] a discussion of *assumpsit* in a reading on coheirs;[151] or a discussion of hunting in a reading on the abduction of nuns.[152] Reporters were most interested in the views of the reader, the leading benchers, and the visiting judges and serjeants,[153] and rarely mentioned the barristers who started the discussion.[154] However, as in the

---

[147] See 113 Selden Soc., pp. xii–xvi.   [148] Waterhous, *Fortescutus Illustratus*, 544–5.

[149] Three susbtantial series of readers' cases from the Inner Temple *c.*1485–99 are in print: Keil. 102v–137 (1480s); 105 Selden Soc. 68–301 (mixed with moots). The cases from Spelman's reading (Gray's Inn, 1519) are printed in *Spelman's Reading on Quo Warranto*, 113 Selden Soc. 143–72.

[150] *Spelman's Reading on Quo Warranto*, 113 Selden Soc., pp. xiv–xv, 160, 165.

[151] Peter Dillon's reading (Gray's Inn, 1516) 94 Selden Soc. 272.

[152] Spelman 17 (Gray's Inn, 1512). It arose because of a case put concerning a licence to hunt granted to an abbess by way of accord for taking a nun.

[153] These speakers might sometimes relate cases from their own experience: 105 Selden Soc., pp. lxxi–lxxii; 113 Selden Soc., pp. xvi, 154, 170.

[154] Cf. BL MS. Add. 35939, fo. 216 (*c.*1530), where the utter barristers of the Middle Temple said after a moot, at the cupboard, that all the benchers were wrong in ruling a case to be clear.

year books, they seem to have been more concerned with the debate itself than with any result, and they did not aim to find a clear solution of the problems. Discussion might well continue after the formal exercise was over.[155]

These disputations in the course of readings have sometimes been confused with moots, but they were an entirely different exercise. Moots were primarily pleading exercises, founded upon sets of facts provided to the students for the purpose, like examination questions. The problems were mostly taken from moot-books of some antiquity, in which some of them are given mnemonic names such as Jacob and Esau, The Rod (Le virge), The Rose between Thorns (Rosa inter spinas), The Sparrowhawk (Lesperver), The Little Rose (Parva rosa), and Cat in the Pan. Unlike moots in the inns of chancery, those in the inns of court were extremely complex. The object was not to thrash out a contested point of law in a single sitting, but to practise the art of pleading, and incidentally of oral argument, in an exercise which could be divided up into manageable instalments. The first task would be to draw a writ in Latin, and then suitably elaborate pleadings in law French bringing out all the questions in the case, recited orally and with argued exceptions at each stage. A prolonged 'casus notabilis' in the Inner Temple in the 1490s proceeded as far as a demurrer to a surrebutter.[156] The exercise could occupy many days, or even a whole vacation.[157] Nevertheless, there may sometimes have been pressure to rush things. In the early years of Henry VIII, the students in Gray's Inn complained that a problem was 'an unreasonable case to be mooted at one time, for there are twenty-eight points in it if it be well scanned'.[158] As with readings, discussion of moots could continue after the formal exercise, for we find a member of Gray's Inn noting what he heard Nevill and Tingleden saying in the Fields about a moot-case, and a Middle Templar jotting down what Mawdley said in his room.[159] Other less formal exercises are first encountered in our period, such as library and chapel moots,[160] clerks' commons cases,[161] and discussions 'at the cupboard'.[162]

Law school, for the serious student, was no soft option. But the daily commitment to learning was not supposed to end with call to the bar or bench: the

---

[155] 94 Selden Soc. 132; 113 Selden Soc., pp. xiv, 147. See also BL MS. Add. 35939, fo. 281v (Gray's Inn, c.1500, tr. 'Dudley said, when he came into the buttery, that the better opinion is...').

[156] 105 Selden Soc. 1, 179–92.

[157] The case called Le virge (the rod) occupied the whole of the autumn vacation 1529 in the Inner Temple: 105 Selden Soc. clxxxiii. The case is printed ibid. 30–1. Another case, called Isaac and Jacob, occupied the autumn vacation 1533: ibid. 18.

[158] Bodl. Lib. MS. Rawlinson C.705, fo. 20v; HLS MS. 125, no. 82; tr. LPCL, 21.

[159] 94 Selden Soc. 132. See also 113 Selden Soc. 147–8 ('After the reading, Spelman said...[and] Goring asked Fyneux [CJ]...').

[160] Library moots are mentioned in Gray's Inn in 1514, and in the Inner Temple by the 1550s. Chapel moots are mentioned in the Middle Temple in 1539, and in Lincoln's Inn in 1553.

[161] First mentioned in the Inner Temple in the 1530s or 1540s: BL MS. Harley 1691, fo. 162; 105 Selden Soc., p. lxxiv n. 396.   [162] 105 Selden Soc., p. lxxiv.

student remained an 'apprentice of the law' until he took the coif,[163] and even then was expected by custom to participate in the readings in his old inn. The benchers had their own continuing educational routine, besides the readings at which they assisted, since cases could be moved at 'the board' or 'the board's end' (the high table in hall).[164] Benchers sometimes moved their own real cases for discussion. Sir James Dyer recalled in 1558 that, when he was a bencher, Sewster had asked a question concerning his own ward; moreover, Dyer treated the answer as authoritative.[165]

COMMON LEARNING

The arguments reported at readings and moots, in the early Tudor period, closely resemble in style those found in the later year books.[166] The range of reference is much the same; the few citations are to the year books, and (more rarely) to text-books such as Littleton and the *Natura Brevium*, or even *Bracton*. Although the readings were on statutory texts, it did not require much ingenuity to introduce expositions of parts of the common law by using particular words as triggers.[167] It was quite common to discuss recent cases, not only those reported in the year books but cases remembered from the assizes and other courts. How far the learn-ing exercises themselves were used as authorities is more difficult to judge, since there is only an occasional reference in the texts to an old reading, or what some-one had said at a moot.[168] A holding of the whole house was obviously of special significance,[169] as was a 'common distinction' made at moots.[170] It is in the same

[163] Plowden used the description on the title-page of *Les Comentaries* (1571), when he was a double reader aged 53 and perhaps the most eminent common lawyer of the day. For the equation of apprent-ice and bencher see above, 427.

[164] Caryll (Jun.) 402, no. 78, and 409, no. 101; Gell's reports, II, fo. 40 ('un bordesend case'); BL MS. Hargrave 253, ff. 56, 81v; 105 Selden Soc., p. lxxiv. These are perhaps the cases known later as bench-table cases.   [165] *Anon.* (1558) BL MS. Harley 1624, fo. 64.

[166] For what follows see 105 Selden Soc., pp. lxxi–lxxiii.

[167] Note the remark of Richard Hesketh, introducing a common-law subject into his reading on the *Carta de Foresta* (Gray's Inn, *c.*1506/8), fo. 44v (tr. 'Now for the full explanation of this word *distress*, I will declare and treat somewhat for learning and remembrance of the nature of distress...'). Later in the reading (ff. 70v–72), glossing the phrase *liber homo* in the charter, he introduced a discussion of the common law of villeinage.

[168] 94 Selden Soc. *133*; 105 Selden Soc., p. lxxii n. 374.

[169] e.g. HLS MS. 47, fo. 113 (tr. 'Note that it was held by all the barristers and readers in Gray's Inn...'); HLS MS. 125, no. 100 (tr. 'Broke said that Adgore of the Temple said that the opinion of the Templars was clearly so...').

[170] e.g. *Dyve* v. *Maningham* (1550) Plowd. 60v at 62v (tr. 'there has been a common distinction held by those who moot in court and chancery...'); *Anon.* (1559) Gell's reports, II, fo. 65v, *per* Browne J. (tr. 'it has been a distinction taken at moots'), and fo. 66, margin ('mote point'). Cf. 1 Caryll 27 for an apparent contrast between a distinction and a 'learning'.

vein that we also hear of 'common learning' (*common erudition*) without further qualification.[171]

This last expression sometimes—especially when used with the indefinite article[172]—meant much the same as a maxim,[173] ground,[174] rule,[175] or principle,[176] all of which denoted well known propositions which—unless challenged or qualified[177]—required no proof.[178] 'There are two principal things upon which arguments may be made,' said Serjeant Morgan, 'namely maxims and reason, the mother of all laws; but the maxims are the foundations of the law and are the conclusions of reason, and therefore they ought not to be impugned but always admitted'.[179] If a proposition could be disproved, it could not be a maxim or

---

[171] For use of this phrase in the year books see 94 Selden Soc. *161* n. 1; and Hil. 4 Hen. VII, fo. 1, pl. 1, *per* Fyneux sjt; Trin. 4 Hen. VII, fo. 9, pl. 2, *per* Bryan CJ; next note. It continued in use throughout the period: see e.g. *Gawen* v. *Hussee* (1537) Dyer 38a at 40a; *Mynours* v. *Turke* (1549) Dyer 66a at 66b (tr. in 1794 edn as 'common doctrine'); *Wimbish* v. *Tailbois* (1550) Plowd. 38v at 56 ('est tenus en nostre learning'); *Fulmerston* v. *Steward* (1554) Plowd. 102 at 103v; 113 Selden Soc., p. xxi n. 73.

[172] e.g. Trin. 9 Hen. VII, fo. 4, pl. 4, *per* Bryan CJ ('un common erudition'); *Moyle* v. *Abbot of Battle* (1494) 1 Caryll 266, from Trin. 16 Hen. VII, fo. 16, pl. 17 ('un commen lerning'); *Speke* v. *Flemyng* (1522) Pas. 14 Hen. VIII, fo. 25, pl. 7, at fo. 28 (119 Selden Soc. 185), *per* Pollard J. ('un comon erudition'); *Wimbish* v. *Tailbois* (1550) Plowd. 38v at 57v, *per* Mountagu CJ ('nous avomus un erudition en nostre ley'); *Dean and Chapter of Bristol* v. *Clerke* (1553) Dyer 83a at 84a ('un erudition'); *Throgmorton's Case* (1557) Chr. Yelverton's reports, fo. 247, *per* Prideaux sjt ('jeo apprise ceo pur un erudition').

[173] See 94 Selden Soc. *161* n. 3; *Colthirst* v. *Bejushin* (1550) Plowd. 21 at 27v.

[174] See 94 Selden Soc. *161* n. 2; *Moots*, 67, 119, 124, 144, 322, 323; Port 149, no. 29. Cf. Keil. 124; *Moots*, 94 ('le commen grounds'); Trin. 6 Hen. VII, fo. 5, pl. 5; *Lord Broke* v. *Lord Latimer* (1497) Mich. 12 Hen. VII, fo. 11, pl. 7, at fo. 13, *per* Danvers J. ('il est un ground in le ley'); Mich. 14 Hen. VII, fo. 12, pl. 21, *per* Bryan CJ ('contrary a vostre ground'); Port 149, no. 29; Yorke 103, no. 44, and 221, no. 356 ('Nota pur un grounde...'); Caryll (Jun.) 379, no. 21 ('comen grownde'); *Anon.* (1549) Wm Yelv. 349, no. 74, *per* Mountagu CJ ('ceo fuit son grounde'); *Partridge* v. *Straunge* (1553) Plowd. 77v at 83 ('les groundes del ley'), and 85v ('un grounde en le ley'); *Bulkeley* v. *Thomas* (1554) Plowd. 118 at 121v (sim.); *Throckmerton* v. *Tracy* (1556) Plowd. 145 at 160v ('Staunford J. prist trois groundes...'). Littleton was a fruitful source of 'grounds': 94 Selden Soc. *161* n. 7.

[175] The word 'rule' is found in *Anon.* (1549) Wm Yelv. 349, no. 74 ('prist pur un ruele'); *Reniger* v. *Fogassa* (1550) Plowd. 1 at 17 ('les rules del commen ley'); *Colthirst* v. *Bejushin* (1550) ibid. at 33v ('general rule').

[176] *Moots*, 124 ('un principle del ley'); Mich. 8 Hen. VII, fo. 8, pl. 4 ('le common principle de remitter'); *Scrope* v. *Hyk* (1511) 2 Caryll 618 ('un principal en le ley'); *Reniger* v. *Fogassa* (1550) Plowd. 1 at 10v ('un principal ou foundation'), and 15 ('jeo entend ceo come un principle'), and 17 ('un principle en le common ley'); *Colthirst* v. *Bejushin* (1550) ibid. 28v ('un principall en le ley') and 33v ('principles en nostre ley'); *Norwood* v. *Rede* (1557) ibid. 182v ('principles del ley'); *Wiseman's Case* (1557) Chr. Yelverton's reports, fo. 241v.

[177] e.g. *Anon.* (1550) BL MS. Hargrave 4, fo. 106v, *per* Mountagu CJ (tr. 'to prove this, there is a common case against the ground of my brother Hales...').

[178] St German, *Doctor and Student*, ed. Plucknett and Barton, 57, 59; *Colthirst* v. *Bejushin* (1550) Plowd. 21 at 33v, *per* Mountagu CJ (tr. 'these are observed as principles in our law, and therefore I have shown them briefly without multiplying cases upon them, because they do not need much proof inasmuch as they are so well known').

[179] *Colthirst* v. *Bejushin* (1550) Plowd. 21 at at 27v.

ground.[180] Self-proving propositions could certainly emerge from experience of argument in the courts, or from the 'common opinion' of the profession.[181] But the word *erudition* more particularly connoted academical doctrine: it was the settled learning of the inns of court, referred to in the 1490s as the 'old learning of court',[182] or the 'common learning in moots'.[183] Common learning, by its nature, did not require chapter and verse to support it. It was what the whole system of exercises was implicitly calculated to transmit, to test, and to teach.[184]

The principal focus of the readings and moots, not surprisingly, was the law of real property and the procedure of the real actions. This learning was, for the most part, very conservative. Until the readers began to lecture on recent statutes, there was a reluctance to discuss innovations such as uses or common recoveries; and there was an equal unwillingness to abandon familiar anachronisms, such as the finer points of the law of villeinage, or real actions which were seldom used in practice. There was hardly any discussion—so far as we can discover—of trespass, or the law of contract.[185] Fictions were tacitly off the syllabus. But the main object was not to provide the student with the latest case-law or with vocational guidance. What was being taught was a method, a cast of mind, rather than mere rules. Some of the questions were clearly designed to stretch the mind rather than to establish principles which might be of practical utility: for instance, whether a woman justice of the peace could commit her own husband to gaol,[186] or how a person could be a villein every other day of his life.[187] These were conundrums thrown up by teaching rather than practice. The cases in the moot-books also betoken a love of the improbable; they are full of expectant heirs becoming monks and then inconveniently returning to life when claimed by deserted fiancées. The emphasis on the 'deraignment' of monks is out of all proportion to any practical repercussions of this rare procedure, but entirely justified in terms of its trouble-some theoretical consequences; and the same could be said of villeinage, which seems to occupy a disproportionate share of time if judged merely in terms of

---

[180] Mich. 20 Hen. VII, fo. 8, pl. 17, *per* Fyneux CJ (tr. 'there is in our law no general maxim or ground for the showing of deeds but that such maxim may be disproved').

[181] For this phrase see *Pollard* v. *Jekell* (1553) Plowd. 89v at 90v (tr. 'the common opinion among the learned in the law has always been that...'); *Woodland* v. *Mantell* (1553) Plowd. 94 at 96 (tr. 'the common opinion among men learned in the law').

[182] *Hulcote* v. *Ingleton* (1493) 1 Caryll 138 at 139 (also in B. & M. 57 at 58), *per* Kebell sjt.

[183] 105 Selden Soc. 272 (Inner Temple, 1492).

[184] For this and what follows, see J. H. Baker, 'The Inns of Court and Legal Doctrine' in *Lawyers and Laymen*, ed. T. M. Charles-Edwards *et al.* (1986), 274–86, repr. *CLT*, 37–51; 102 Selden Soc., pp. xxxii–xxxiii; 113 Selden Soc., pp. xvi–xxi; *The Law's Two Bodies* (2001), ch. 3.

[185] The only full treatment of actions on the case was in James Hales's reading on costs (Gray's Inn, 1532) B. & M. 345–51. Only one moot on *assumpsit* has been found (Gray's Inn, 1516): B. & M. 401–2.

[186] Bodl. Lib. MS. Rawlinson C.705, fo. 127 (Gray's Inn, 1520s).

[187] HLS MS. 47, fo. 59 (Gray's Inn, 1520s). For other examples see Baker, 'The Inns of Court and Legal Doctrine', 277–8, 280.

practical usefulness. In any case, the participants were less concerned to discover any right answer than to know whether a point was 'good and arguable' or 'mootable',[188] a true 'moot point'.[189] There could be an instructive exercise even when it led nowhere in law. In one case where the benchers eventually held a case not sufficient to raise 'a doubt in law', the reporter nevertheless noted with satisfaction that good learning had arisen from it.[190] Common learning was not necessary stable.[191] Moreover, not everything that was said in disputation—even by the great—was law, for the reason that the procedure was not designed, any more than that of the courts of law was designed, to produce oracular pronouncements. The object was to produce good pleadings. Then again, a mooter could not choose his side, any more than a serjeant at law could choose his client. And, whereas real judges must follow their trained consciences, the benchers had no such judicial responsibilities and might, in order to provoke thought or controversy, argue against their own minds for the sake of argument.[192] Occasionally we hear that the benchers were not sufficiently stimulated by the argument to perceive any doubts worth arguing at all.[193] In so far as the law was 'made' in these exercises, it was by consensus rather than by authoritative rule.

Yet we can hardly doubt that law was, in a very real sense, made here. The young students of the Inner Temple in Port's day hung eagerly on the words of Serjeant Kebell or Serjeant Frowyk when they graced the inn with their presence, just as those of Gray's Inn in Spelman's day revered the remarks which fell from Fyneux CJ. Lecture notes were copied and passed round and studied as evidence of the law, and dicta from readings and moots were inserted into notebooks and collections of reports, such as Port's and Spelman's, as if they had the same authority as judicial remarks in court.[194] Even when the readers passed over the latest developments in silence, and concentrated on the property law of the fourteenth century, they were making law in the sense that they were arranging, consolidating, analysing, and explaining, unwritten principles which could only be glimpsed fleetingly and tangentially in the year books. A reading was not intended as a practical guide to current law, let alone an original account of a discrete legal topic, so much as a reiteration of inherited learning, an introduction to legal

[188] See Trinity Coll. Cambridge MS. R.15.7, fo. 65 ('quere bene quar est motable').

[189] This expression is found by 1514: below, n. 193. Cf. HLS MS. 125, no. 39 (Middle Temple, 1530s); above, 467 n. 170 (1559). [190] 105 Selden Soc. 174, no. 60 (and cf. note at p. lxxiii n. 386).

[191] See J. H. Baker, *The Law's Two Bodies* (2001), 68–9. For two areas where 'common learning' reversed direction twice within fifty years, see below, 576, 637–8.

[192] For a possible example, see the contrary arguments by Hendley on the question of a lease for years granted to uses: below, 634 n. 12.

[193] Bodl. Lib. MS. Rawlinson C.705, fo. 43 (tr. 'Thomas Nevill said, "We are all agreed that it is a clear case…", and thus they rose; but Hendley believed the reason was because it was getting late and they were not disposed to argue, for it is an old moot point', 1514). See also above, 465, n. 154.

[194] Above, 445–6; 94 Selden Soc. *134*; 102 Selden Soc., pp. xxxi–xxxiii.

method, and an occasion for formal disputation.[195] Yet by constant repetition of the 'common cases'[196] and testing of opinion, the system established a tradition as to what was received learning and what was dubious[197]—something which could not be so effectively achieved in the courts, where questions arose extempore in the throes of litigation. In any case, the debates reported in the year books, so often obscured by procedural considerations which are not easily visible, presupposed a grasp of the underlying principles; and it was in the inns, rather than in Westminster Hall, that those principles were expounded and refined as a coherent body of law. That was the sense in which these law schools made tough law.

In the field of criminal law, a larger claim may be made for the role of the inns of court in refining legal doctrine. Very few criminal cases were decided in Westminster Hall, and, after the cessation of eyres and circuit reporting in the fourteenth century, only a relatively small number of criminal cases trickled into the year books. Yet questions must have been arising constantly on circuit, or at Newgate, which could not be resolved by recourse to *Bracton* or *Britton*, and the inns provided an obvious forum for their discussion. Although readers could not lecture on the common law as such, there were several provisions in the *statuta vetera* which provided the pretext for explaining such terms as 'felony', 'misadventure', or 'clergy', under the guise of statutory interpretation. The dozens of extant readings on the law of felony, between about 1450 and 1550, show that nearly all the law found in the sixteenth-century textbooks had been current for the best part of a century; and the expositions went much further in detail than either the reports or the textbooks of the Tudor period.[198]

Criminal law was perhaps an exception. Nevertheless, the increased range of statutory texts in the early Tudor period enabled the new exposition of other aspects of public law, and we find new treatments of older topics such as the forest law, franchises, or the law relating to the king's feudal revenue.[199] In lecturing on revenue legislation, readers were not introducing new ideas directly, but exploring the interpretation of controversial new measures. They sometimes asked questions ahead of the courts, and it would be surprising if the courts were

[195] For a reader's range of sources, and the extent of repetition over the generations, even when dealing with seemingly new subjects, see *Spelman's Reading on Quo Warranto*, 113 Selden Soc. (1997), pp. xvi–xxi.

[196] See Dudley's reading (Gray's Inn, 1496) CUL MS. Hh.3.10, at fo. 62v (tr. 'Fairfax to the contrary... and he put the common cases upon his ground').

[197] Nevertheless, there could be divergences between the teaching of different inns, or even within the same inn: Baker, 'The Inns of Court and Legal Doctrine', 282.   [198] Below, 528–9.

[199] See above, 120 (*quo warranto*), 299 (forest law); below, 662 (prerogative rights), 666 (uses), 683 (wills). Cf. the readings on *Prerogativa Regis*, for which see M. McGlynn, 'Teaching the Law in a Time of Change: the Royal Prerogative and the Statute of Uses' in *Learning the Law: Teaching and the Transmission of English Law, 1150–1900*, ed. J. A. Bush and A. Wijffels (1999), 211–25; *The Royal Prerogative and the Learning of the Inns of Court* (forthcoming in 2003).

uninfluenced by their suggested answers. Were it otherwise, it would have been unnecessary for Lord Chancellor Audley to warn the readers publicly in the Star Chamber, on behalf of Henry VIII, 'truly and justly to interpret and expound his laws and statutes in the readings and moots'.[200] The warning was delivered in 1540, when the government's immediate concern was that loopholes were being found in the Statute of Uses. Within months the Crown acted more directly by promoting the Statute of Wills.[201] The feared evasions had been found in private conference as well as in the lecture room, but the incident affords evidence of a kind of lawmaking by professional opinion, in the formation of which the inns played a vital part.

[200] Lost Star Chamber register, 23 Feb. 1540, pr. in 94 Selden Soc. 351.   [201] See below, 681.

26

Case-Law

IT has been customary to regard the reign of Henry VIII as the period in which the moribund year books finally passed away, leaving a gap later filled by the nominate or 'private' reports. This change has generally been interpreted as a shift from one kind of reporting to another, from a medieval to a newer style. And the interpretation used to be coloured by the belief, occasioned by Plowden's troublesome allusion to the four paid reporters of 'ancient time',[1] that the year books had been the work of Crown officials. The change could then be seen as a movement from state control to private enterprise. Even Maitland, who finally laid the official-reporter theory to rest,[2] subscribed to the old view that something significant happened to law reporting in 1535 when the year books ceased to flow, and went so far as to suggest that this was another ominous indication of a state of crisis in the life of the embattled common law.[3] The dearth of surviving printed reports from the first half of the sixteenth century led Plucknett and others to conclude that law reporting barely survived the fifteenth century, and that the profession must somehow have lost the need for access to recent case-law in written form.[4] Such a remarkable conclusion cries out for explanation. Was the profession truly so myopic or backward-looking that it regarded recent cases, in which new ideas were tested, as experiments or aberrations which were not worth paper and ink? Was Maitland right, after all, to hint that the common law itself was in serious straits?

THE LAST YEAR BOOKS

It has already been suggested that Maitland was on the wrong track in this respect, and that the common law was entering one of its more creative phases.[5] If law reporting had dwindled to a virtual standstill during this burst of intellectual activity it would certainly be startling. But there is no such incongruity to explain,

---

[1] Plowd., preface, sig. ii.   [2] *Year Books of Edward II* (1903) 17 Selden Soc., pp. xi–xiii.
[3] *English Law and the Renaissance*, 21–2; above, 7. Cf. Pollard, *Wolsey*, 68 n. 1.
[4] T. F. T. Plucknett, *Early English Legal Literature* (1958), 111; L. W. Abbott, *Law Reporting in England 1485–1585* (1973), 13 (but cf. 35–6, 60–1). The notion that official reporting ceased at the end of Henry VII's reign may be traced to 3 Co. Rep., preface, sig. Cii, Diii.   [5] See above, ch. 1.

because the supposed changes which caught the notice of Maitland and Plucknett are an illusion. The accepted teaching was true only in the narrow bibliographical sense that the last reports to be printed in year-book form relate to the year 1535. But printed reports at that date were the exception. Despite enormous losses of paper manuscript texts, it is possible to show that reporting continued as steadily in Henry VIII's reign as in the previous century, both during the unprinted years before 1535 and in the black hole which followed. Indeed, as we shall see, more individual reporters can be identified in this period than in any previous reign.[6]

Perhaps many writers have been misled by the name 'year books'[7] into supposing that it represents a genre of legal literature clearly distinct from the later reports. Yet the year books, stretching over 250 years, were themselves hardly a uniform series. They had evolved a good deal between 1300 and 1500, and naturally reflected changes in the kinds of argument taking place in banc at Westminster. The chief common feature of the fifteenth- and sixteenth-century books which we call year books is that printers happened to arrange and publish them, anonymously, in a continuous series. Yet it is now becoming clear that the superficial uniformity and continuity of the later year books was not the result of some regular organization of a reporting system, but rather of the desire of the law printers of a subsequent generation to create from existing materials the appearance of a 'complete set' of reports which the profession would feel obliged to purchase. In creating that appearance, they jumbled the texts into whatever confusion gave them the most saleable character. In fact there were at least two independent reporters at work by 1450,[8] and we know the names of three major reporters who overlapped in the second half of the century: Roger Townshend (d. 1493), justice of the Common Pleas, John Caryll (d. 1523), prothonotary of that court and later a serjeant, and John Port (d. 1540) of the Inner Temple, later a judge.[9] All three began reporting as students or young barristers and continued throughout their careers. There is no obvious connection between them, and no evidence that they acted in concert.[10] Port and Caryll were near contemporaries in the same inn,

---

[6] There may have been as many hands at work on the reports of Edw. II, but we cannot identify them.

[7] This expression was not yet in use, though Tottell referred to 'books of years' in 1556: below, 499. In 1531 Serjeant Densill referred to 'auncient yerez': *The Serjeants' Case* (1531) Wm Yelv. 294 at 300. And in 1553 Serjeant Bromley referred to 'the years of Henry VII': *Woodland* v. *Mantell* (1553) Plowd. 92 at 96 (tr.). The traditional title was 'terms' rather than years. Cf. St German's reference to 'years of terms': *Little Treatise*, ed. Guy, 107.   [8] 94 Selden Soc. 165.

[9] 94 Selden Soc. 165 (where two other possible reporters are mentioned); *The Notebook of Sir John Port*, ed. Baker (102 Selden Soc.; 1986). There are also anonymous reports, not part of these series or of the year books as printed: e.g. Free Library of Philadelphia, MS. LC 14.35 (Hen. VII to 1498).

[10] Only one case occurs in the same words in both Port and Caryll: *Anon.* (1493) 1 Caryll 193; slightly abridged in Port 99, pl. 28; see 102 Selden Soc., p. xxxii n. 60. It is also in the printed year book Mich. 16 Hen. VII, fo. 2, pl. 7, taken directly from Caryll.

the Inner Temple, and so it seems unlikely that Plowden's four reporters can be explained on the basis that each of the inns had one recognized reporter.[11] The pattern which emerges from these identifications, and which is followed in the early sixteenth century by reporters such as John Spelman, James Dyer, and Edmund Plowden, is that those who wrote reports were men of the highest standing in the profession who carried on the activity throughout their professional careers. They were not professional reporters, and in the case of Port the notes were so private that no one else saw them until the 1970s. Some of the reporters, on the other hand, made their notes available to others for transcription or comment. We know from Plowden's own words that that was how he worked, and, although his published reports do represent a new departure in terms of quality and selectivity, he was probably continuing professional tradition in the way he kept his autograph notes. His four officials still need explaining, but perhaps not too precisely, since he was referring to a legend rather than personal knowledge. He might have heard of a committee of barristers used by the early law printers to prepare works for publication;[12] though not reporters themselves, editors were responsible for producing a readable text and were not above adding the kind of comment for which Plowden, and later Coke, were famous.[13]

Some degree of cooperation between the reporters and their professional fellows in the inns is evident from the contents of the books themselves.[14] Some reporters relied a good deal on hearsay,[15] and were sometimes unable to complete a report because of absence,[16] or an inability to hear what was said.[17] One reporter in 1491 even referred, in two separate places, to the opinion in Gray's Inn concerning the cases in question.[18] There is some evidence that the judges also took an interest in the accuracy of what was circulating. Fitzherbert J., on more

[11] This was Lambert's suggestion: *Les Year Books de Langue Française* (1928), 140–6. See also G. J. Turner, 26 Selden Soc., p. xxiv; 42 Selden Soc., p. xli; A. W. B. Simpson, 87 *LQR* 94.

[12] Below, 500.

[13] The most notable example is Redman's *Annus quadragesimus Edwardi tercii* (1534), e.g. at fo. xiii [*recte* xvi]; but this was apparently the work of a single editor. This volume even shows signs of textual criticism: ibid., and fo. xlviii^v.   [14] Simpson, 87 *LQR* at 113–14; Ives, 89 *LQR* at 82–4.

[15] e.g. Hil. 5 Hen. VII, fo. 12, pl. 4 (tr. 'well argued, as it was said, but I was not there (*sed non interfui*)'); Pas. 8 Hen. VII, fo. 12, pl. 5 (tr. 'as I have heard from the others, *sed non interfui*'); Trin. 15 Hen. VII, fo. 9, pl. 9 (tr. 'nevertheless the serjeants... told me that...'); Mich. 20 Hen. VII, fo. 9, pl. 18 (tr. 'coming from Westminster, I heard my lord Fyneux say that...').

[16] e.g. Trin. 13 Hen. VII, fo. 26, pl. 5 (tr. 'at which arguments I was not present').

[17] e.g. Pas. 8 Hen. VII, fo. 11, pl. 2 (tr. 'Query well, for although that is what he said I did not hear the reason'); Hil. 21 Hen. VII, fo. 6, pl. 2 (tr. 'Fisher and Vavasour JJ were of the same opinion, but I know not how to report them for they spoke so low that I could not hear them'); Mich. 21 Hen. VII, fo. 37, pl. 45 (tr. 'but I could not hear them'); 121 Selden Soc. 297 (1531).

[18] Pas. 6 Hen. VII, fo. 1, pl. 5 (tr. 'Query, for in Gray's Inn everyone thought that...'); Trin. 6 Hen. VII, fo. 6, pl. 5 (tr. 'I think so; and so held several in Gray's Inn...'). Cf. Mich. 5 Hen. VII, fo. 10, pl. 22 (tr. 'And see Fairfax the younger of Gray's Inn, who thought that...'); Spelman 40, pl. 1 (tr. 'Query, for many of Gray's Inn wondered at this opinion').

than one occasion in the 1530s, ordered the correction of year books which he considered wrong, either because they were misreported[19] or because the decision was mistaken and ought to be expunged.[20] A remarkable instance of judicial involvement in the reporting process at the beginning of our period occurs in a note by John Caryll of the Inner Temple.[21] Caryll, during the first few years of his legal studies, had noted (on a blank leaf between some older year books) an Exchequer Chamber session in 1488 at which Thomas Fitzwilliam, reader of the Inner Temple and recorder of London, put a series of questions concerning criminal law to the assembled judges. Caryll's note is particularly interesting because it has an interlineation inserted three years later:[22]

And afterwards, in Michaelmas term in the seventh year of the same king [1491], because various books of report of this matter varied, Blount, at the request of a certain doubter, asked of Bryan [CJ] the said doubts. And Bryan affirmed everything as above, according to the new interlining: which note. But Vavasour [J.] was of opinion that... according the interlining of Hilary term in the seventh year of the same king [1492].

The interlineations here referred to are in Caryll's hand. The first, in Michaelmas term 1491, refers to 'the report of Frowyk... which Bryan and Vavasour affirmed as law the same term and year'; and the second, in Hilary term 1492, includes a comment attributed to 'Snede and Tame, fellows of the Inner Inn'. We have here a rare example of a draft report in year-book form—though not the vulgate text of the same case in print—in the course of revision. It shows that several reports of the 1488 assembly were in circulation soon after the event, and that they varied. This in itself is hardly consistent with an official report. As it is, two quite different texts have survived—the other is in the vulgate year book of 3 *Henry VII*[23]—and we can only speculate how many others have been consigned to oblivion. What is even more interesting is that the doubts were resolved by direct recourse to some of the judges concerned. The doubt here arose in the Inner Temple, where Caryll, Frowyk, Snede, Tame—and (we must guess) Blount—were fellows, and Blount as one of their number was sent to Bryan CJ and Vavasour J. for clarification. It seems unlikely that the question was put to them judicially in the Common Pleas, since the question concerned criminal law. It was rather a matter of personal contacts: Vavasour was a former member of the inn, and Blount may have been

---

[19] Brooke Abr., *Executours*, pl. 23 (case of 34 Hen. VI said to be misreported because contrary to the record, and so Fitzherbert J. in 1531 ordered the book to be amended). See also 109 Selden Soc., p. xxix.

[20] Trin. 27 Hen. VIII, fo. 23, pl. 21 (tr. 'put that case out of your books, for it is not law'); for the context, see below, 870.

[21] BL MS. Harley 5158, fo. 188. For the date and authorship, see 94 Selden Soc. *166–7*.

[22] Tr. from the French text pr. in 94 Selden Soc. *167*.

[23] Hil. 3 Hen. VII, ff. 1–2, pl. 3–5; Mich. 3 Hen. VII, fo. 12, pl. 5, 8; Fitz. Abr., *Corone*, pl. 51, 56–58. The manuscript version is dated Pas. 3 Hen. VII. See below, 526–7.

Bryan's step-father.[24] We see something similar occurring the following year, when Thomas Pygot of the Inner Temple related to the reporter an opinion of Bryan and Huse CJJ.[25]

How such raw texts came to take the shape of the printed year books, and what proportion of the manuscript reports was destroyed, are questions which will never be fully answered. But a good deal may be worked out from internal evidence alone. The textual confusion appears to be at its worst in the reign of Henry VII, for which virtually no manuscripts survive.[26] An example of demonstrable textual confusion is the year *15 Henry VII* (not printed until 1555), which combines cases from three or more collections: one of 18 Henry VII,[27] another of about 16 Henry VII,[28] and the third from 21–3 Edward IV,[29] with at least one case from 2 Ric. III.[30] Another is *21 Henry VII*, which contains cases from 11–19 and 22 Henry VII.[31] The year *16 Henry VII* is also spurious, and contains cases from the 1490s. The chaos is not merely chronological. Clearly the work of many hands has been combined. Some of the earliest reports of Henry VII are in Latin, and can in many cases be matched by reports from a different author in French.[32] Likewise, some of the wrongly dated reports in *16 Henry VII* occur in a different form, evidently by a different hand, in *9–10 Henry VII*. The former appear to be the work of John Caryll, and they belong with a series from 8–9 Henry VII printed in *13 Henry VII*.[33] One of the sections interpolated in *21 Henry VII*, at the very end of the reign, is a series of eighteen cases apparently extracted from Fitzherbert's *Graunde Abridgement* to fill up blank pages at the end of the printed volume; these are mostly datable to Trinity term 14 Henry VII (1499).[34] Another series of twenty cases, mostly from

---

[24] 94 Selden Soc. 167.

[25] Pas. 8 Hen. VII, fo. 13, pl. 5. Pygot also occurs as a relator of a case in Spelman 217, pl. 8.

[26] The only substantial text is BL MS. Hargrave 105, which is close to the print. Selden had a manuscript of 21 Hen. VII: J. H. Baker, *English Legal Manuscripts*, ii (1978), 18. Sir Anthony Browne JCP (d. 1567) bequeathed 'an olde booke written of yeres of Kyng Richarde the thirde and of other covered with bordes': PCC 20 Stonarde; PROB 11/49, fo. 150v.

[27] Mich. 15 Hen. VII, fo. 13, pl. 1, is (tr.) 'the first case that Thomas Frowyk argued after he was made chief justice', which places it in Mich. 18 Hen. VII. [28] These are in Fitz. Abr.: below.

[29] In pl. 7–13 the speakers include Brigges and Choke (both d. 1483), Sulyard, Catesby J. (1481–5), and Tremayle sjt (1478–88).

[30] Mich. 15 Hen. VII, fo. 14, pl. 6, appears to be the same as Mich. 2 Ric. III, fo. 7, pl. 14.

[31] It mentions Marowe and Adgore sjts (d. 1504, 1505), Palmes 'un des novel serjeants' (created Nov. 1503), and Rede CJ (appointed Mich. 1506). Some interpolations from Fitz. Abr. are dated 11–19 Hen. VII: below.

[32] Most of 2 Ric. III, ff. 1–13, and some of 1–3 Hen. VII is in Latin; a late specimen is Pas. 21 Hen. VII, ff. 20–21, pl. 1–4. See M. Hemmant, 64 Selden Soc. at pp. xlii–xliii, lviii.

[33] The Caryll texts appear to be Pas. 13 Hen. VII, ff. 18–24, pl. 1–9; Trin. 13 Hen. VII, ff. 24–28, pl. 1–7; Mich. 16 Hen. VII, ff. 9–17, pl. 1–20. These are now printed, with a translation, in 115 Selden Soc.

[34] Mich. 21 Hen. VII, ff. 39–41, pl. 49–67. The latest case is pl. 53, a case at Warwick assizes which Frowyk CJ explained to the reporter in the Common Pleas in 19 Hen. VII.

16 Henry VII (1500–1), which are found in the printed *15 Henry VII*,[35] are also in Fitzherbert (with slight differences). Both series are of Gray's Inn provenance, with a case from Thatcher's reading and no less than eleven references to Fyneux CJ. They were either the work of Fitzherbert himself or gathered by him as a young barrister of the inn. The dearth of year-book manuscripts from this period is such that it may never be possible to separate decisively the constituent elements of the printed *Henry VII*. But at least we can no longer believe the later year books to have been a regular, organized series.

The printed year books of Henry VIII are less suspect, if only because there are fewer of them to have become confused. The printers never attempted to fill out a more complete series for this reign, probably because they concentrated at first on older texts and by Tottell's time—when a full edition of *Henry VIII* might have been chronologically appropriate—the addition of new year-book material to the canon had virtually ceased. For the first eleven years of the reign there are no printed reports. The *12–14 Henry VIII* section with which the vulgate edition begins has a distinct bibliographical history from the rest, and until 1591 was printed separately.[36] No manuscripts are known. There are only thirty-four cases, but the quality of the reporting is superior to that of any other Tudor law reporter before Plowden.[37] The author selected cases in which points of law were raised by demurrer or motion in arrest of judgment, and generally gave the speeches at length. Most of the cases may be traced in the plea rolls, which confirm the reports as being very accurate. Given that the cases were printed more promptly than any others had been, within ten years of decision, and that—although the press-editing left much to be desired[38]—they were self-evidently of superior quality, it is surprising that the precedent did not create a professional demand. As we shall see, the gap was filled for the time being by private notes. But the law printers missed a golden opportunity.

Only four further years of the reign were printed (18–19 and 26–27 Henry VIII), and those not until William Middleton undertook an edition in about 1545–6. These texts had circulated before they were printed,[39] though no complete manuscript has survived. The fullest manuscript text known is that copied by or for Anthony Gell, principal of Clement's Inn in the 1540s and later a bencher of the Inner Temple;[40] this is particularly interesting in that it continues with reports from the early 1540s, in the same style and perhaps by the same hand. The author is evidently not the person who wrote *12–14 Henry VIII*, for the style is that of the

---

[35] Trin. 15 Hen. VII, ff. 8–11, pl. 2–21. The last case ('en lectura Thetcher') has not been found in Fitz. Abr.

[36] There is now a new edition in 119 Selden Soc. (2002). [37] See above, 390–1.

[38] One case lacks its ending, one is reported twice (verbatim), and some of the dates are demonstrably wrong: 119 Selden Soc., p. xviii. [39] See 94 Selden Soc. *169*.

[40] Library of Congress (Law Div.) MS. 15. The reports jump from 27 to 33 Hen. VIII, but resume in a very similar style.

older year books, in which extempore motions predominate. In the last portion of the printed text, from 1535, Fitzherbert J. is extremely prominent. He was, of course, a great judge whose opinions merited attention; but the fact that the reporter knew what he said privately to another judge, and discussed cases with him personally, suggests that the reporter was either a member of Serjeants' Inn, Chancery Lane, or of Gray's Inn.[41]

THE UNPRINTED REPORTS

Since it was a mere bibliographical accident that some reports were printed in year-book form and others were not, any substantial distinction between the year books and other reports of the Tudor period is misplaced. Moreover, the decision as to which reports to include in the year-book canon was not taken at the time of reporting, but at the end of our period or even later. The last year books from Henry VII's reign were not printed until 1555, and so the law printers might have been expected to fill in the missing years of Henry VII and Henry VIII during the reign of Elizabeth. It was Richard Tottell, law printer from 1553 to 1593, who decided not to extend the year-book series any further.[42] His decision necessarily affected the sources available to posterity, but can have no direct bearing on the history of reporting in our period. What is more interesting to us is what we learn from surviving manuscripts about the state of law reporting in general during the early Tudor period. And the salient fact is that there are, besides the year books, twelve substantial series of law reports for Henry VIII's reign still surviving, and several more under Edward VI and Mary I, most of them the work of identified individuals. Far from there having been an alarming decline in the production of law reports during this half-century, it is the first period in which we can distinguish the work of a multitude of individuals whose careers are known to us.

As might be expected, there are great differences between the work of different authors. But these are not differences between year-book reporters and 'private' reporters; there are similar stylistic contrasts within the printed year books. The principal reporters so far identified for Henry VIII's reign are: two John Carylls (father and son), John Port, and Anthony Gell of the Inner Temple; John Spelman, William Yelverton, and Roger Yorke of Gray's Inn; Richard Pollard, Robert Brooke, and James Dyer of the Middle Temple, and William Bendlowes of Lincoln's Inn. The twelfth series circulated under the title *En temps Henry VIII* and has so far defied affiliation; but there are internal clues indicating a Lincoln's Inn author.

---

[41] 94 Selden Soc. 170.

[42] He omitted not only the residue of Hen. VII and Hen. VIII but also Edw. II, 1–16 Edw. III and the whole of Ric. II. For Tottell see further below, 497–9.

Dyer and Serjeant Caryll effectively followed the year-book tradition of chronological reporting. Caryll's reports began soon after his admission to the Inner Temple in the early 1480s, perhaps with the Exchequer Chamber case of 1488 mentioned above. His reports from 1497 to 1519 were printed in 1602 from a manuscript of Robert Keilwey, while substantial fragments of the earlier portion from 1489 to 1496 survive in at least four manuscripts and in some of the vulgate year books.[43] The anonymous *En temps Henry VIII* continues in a similar form from 1509 to 1535.[44] Dyer's notebooks—the contents of which can be reconstructed with some precision[45]—began with a few extracts from the year books and other early reports of Henry VIII, presumably copied from manuscript sources in the 1530s,[46] and continued with his own reports running from 1532, around the time of his admission to the Middle Temple,[47] until 1581, shortly before his death as chief justice of the Common Pleas. They were not intended for publication, but over half the contents were printed in 1585/6 and the remainder enjoyed a limited circulation in manuscript. It is a mere coincidence that these three collections continue almost in series, because they overlapped with the work of our other reporters. But the circumstance is significant, since these three men alone represent a continuous tradition of law reporting from almost the beginning of Henry VII's reign until the middle of Elizabeth I's. By the end of our period there were other reporters in the same tradition, most notably William Dalison in the time of Edward VI and Mary I.[48]

The work of our other reporters represented new methods of arrangement. While the style of each individual report was not markedly different from that of the year books, the schemes of arrangement indicated some revised thinking about the most convenient method for preserving case-law. We might be tempted to associate them with humanist concepts of order and form; yet the authors and contents of these series are so far removed from humanist jurisprudence in the accepted sense of the word that we should rather believe that they were carrying on, or building upon, older traditions.

No less than five of our reporters—Port, Spelman, Yorke, Pollard, and Brooke—arranged their cases by subject rather than adding them to a chronological register. This method may have been widespread at the time. The only extant

[43] 94 Selden Soc. *171*; above, 476. They have now been printed as *The Reports of John Caryll* (115–16 Selden Soc.; 2000).

[44] There are three known texts, all somewhat corrupt: BL MS. Hargrave 3, ff. 140–156v; MS. Hargrave 388, ff. 273–295v; MS. Lansdowne 1072, ff. 35–48; pr. 120 Selden Soc. 8–80.

[45] J. H. Baker, introd. to *Reports from the lost Notebooks of Sir James Dyer*, i (109 Selden Soc.; 1993), pp. xxxv–xlvi.   [46] The year books were not printed until 1545–6: above, 478.

[47] See 109 Selden Soc., p. xxiii.

[48] BL MS. Harley 5141 (1552–8). Note also the reports of Anthony Gell (*c.*1541–62), Richard Harpur (*c.*1546–76), and Christopher Yelverton (*c.*1556–75): 109 Selden Soc., pp. xiii, xiv, xv. Plowden began reporting by 1550, though his work is known only from the printed edition of 1571 (with suppl., 1578).

autograph example (Sir John Port's notebook) was completely unknown before it
turned up at auction in 1979; and four more commonplace books or abridgments
compiled by Henry VIII's judges, but now lost, are known from casual references.[49]
Yorke's reports, which come down to us in four manuscript copies, were arranged
for the most part under non-alphabetical titles in a notebook which also contained
a good deal of Gray's Inn material.[50] The other reports were alphabetical, and in
at least some cases—Port and Brooke, and perhaps Spelman[51]—they were added
into abridgments of year books, a practice anticipated in a more limited way by
Fitzherbert's reports from 1499–1501 which we have already noticed,[52] and by an
anonymous reporter of the 1490s.[53] Since abridgments constitute a genre which
itself dates from the 1460s,[54] we may suppose that the idea of bringing them up
to date occurred to the profession within a generation or two of its invention. If
the abridgment was becoming the first recourse in legal research, it might have
seemed sensible to omit the intermediate chronological format. Our reporters
were not mere abridgers, but alphabetical reporters intent on making their work
easier to search. Their intention was laudable, but with hindsight we can easily
see why the new technique did not prevail. The loose-leaf filing system had not
been invented, and a bound volume would eventually be filled; but it would be
filled at varying rates, since it was difficult to predict at the outset which titles
would prove hungry for material and which would not. Port was obliged for this
reason to continue some of his titles in other parts of his volume, and to cram
minute writing into spaces inadequate to receive it, while many expectant pages
stood blank.[55] Moreover, although the alphabetical notebook provided a useful
vade-mecum for the compiler's own use, it could not easily be transcribed in a
way which subsequent generations could supplement. We find Christopher
Yelverton, at the beginning of Elizabeth I's reign, undertaking the labour of recast-
ing Spelman in chronological form—adding in the contents of Pollard for good
measure—and others went to the trouble of distilling chronological reports from
the printed abridgments.[56] A second disadvantage of the alphabetical system was
that the task of fitting reports into pre-existing alphabetical volumes led to undue
compression of the texts, and also to repetition when the same case fitted under
multiple headings. By the 1540s it was perceived that abridged reports could not

[49] 94 Selden Soc. 172. The judges were Sir Richard Elyot, Sir Thomas Englefield, Sir Richard Lyster,
and Sir Edward Mountagu: all, as it happens, from the Middle Temple. Port was an Inner Templar.
[50] 93 Selden Soc., p. xxvii; 94 Selden Soc. 172.
[51] Spelman's book certainly had year-book cases in it, though his titles do not correspond exactly
with any of the printed abridgments: 94 Selden Soc. 173–4.   [52] Above, 477.
[53] Free Library of Philadelphia, MS. LC 14.35. There are also a few cases temp. Hen. VII (down to 1505)
added into Sir John More's abridgment, BL Royal MS. 17 E. VI. More became a serjeant at law in 1503.
[54] Below, 501.   [55] 102 Selden Soc., pp. xxvi, xxviii–xxix.
[56] 93 Selden Soc., pp. xiv–xxvi; 94 Selden Soc. 174.

properly be combined with full reports, and so the chronological format was
allowed the final victory. But the short-lived popularity of the alphabetical method
may go some way to explain the dearth of printed reports. Brooke's reports
reached the press by association with his larger venture, the *Graunde Abridgement*
which gave ready access to the year books as well.[57] Spelman's new reports were
much more voluminous—they contain more cases than all the printed year books
of Henry VIII, albeit in shorter form—and, as Yelverton found, were more difficult
to rearrange in 'year book' form. If most lawyers of the time were experimenting
with similar schemes for their own private use, there would have been more
textual chaos than the law printers could manage, and little which—even with
their disregard for true dates—they could pass off as year books.

Whereas the alphabetical reports resulted from adding cases into abridgments
of year books, another related category consisted of cases inserted into volumes of
inns of court exercises or precedents of pleading. This is not to be regarded as a
distinct tendency in reporting, since several reporters of the period (including
Spelman, Pollard, and Yorke) mixed inns of court material in varying proportions
with cases from Westminster Hall.[58] Port's notebook, indeed, contains more Inner
Temple material than cases from the courts, because most of it was written while
he was a student.[59] Serjeant Caryll apparently kept his Inner Temple material separate from the reports; at least, his reports circulated separately. But his son John
Caryll (d. 1566) reported fewer Westminster cases (from the 1530s), which he
inserted into what is essentially a notebook of Inner Temple discussions.[60] There
are similar notebooks from Gray's Inn: one probably written by William
Yelverton, admitted around 1515 and later a bencher, another which belonged to
William Coke, admitted in 1528 and later a judge, and a third bearing the name of
William Porter, whose career is obscure.[61] Cases are less likely to be mixed with
texts of readings, as opposed to notes from readers' cases and discussions, but in
some cases reports may be found inserted on blank leaves in collections of readings: for example, Chaloner's reports of King's Bench cases added into a volume
of Gray's Inn readings around 1520,[62] and the reports from 1544 written by Randle
Cholmeley of Lincoln's Inn.[63]

[57] The new cases in Brooke (*c.*1515–58) were distilled and printed chronologically as *Ascuns Novell Cases* (Bro. N.C.) in 1578.   [58] Above, 445–6, 470.

[59] 102 Selden Soc., pp. xxxi–xxxxiii.

[60] BL MS. Harley 1691, ff. 98–133, which is surrounded by other Inner Temple material possibly compiled by Caryll. There is an edn in 121 Selden Soc. 366–416.

[61] BL MS. Hargrave 253 (Yelverton); HLS MS. 47 ('Porter', arranged alphabetically); BL MS. Harley 5103 (Coke). Yelverton's notebook is the only one to contain a substantial proportion of cases from Westminster Hall. Coke's notebook contains only one (the new serjeants' case of 1531), which is also in Yelverton; 121 Selden Soc. 294.   [62] GI MS. 25; 121 Selden Soc. 278–88.

[63] LI MS. Hale 189, ff. 249–256 (pr. 121 Selden Soc. 450–68). In Dyer 310, §79, a case of 1558 reported by Cholmeley is cited posthumously; but no continuous series by him has yet been found.

Reports are also found in books of entries, where they serve the useful purpose of illuminating the Latin forms of pleading by reference to discussion in court. There is an example in the British Library of a book of entries containing six reports in law French, from the period 1509–26, and a few other notes in French.[64] But the best-known example of this genre is the widely disseminated collection by William Bendlowes. Bendlowes's earliest cases consist merely of transcripts from plea rolls, some from the fifteenth century; but from about 1534, when he was admitted to Lincoln's Inn, he annotated them in French.[65] He occasionally acted as an attorney in the mid-1530s, and it seems highly likely that he studied as a clerk to one of the prothonotaries, perhaps Nicholas Rokewode of Lincoln's Inn.[66] Serjeant Caryll had been a prothonotary, but had not thought to link the Latin texts of pleadings with his reports of what occurred in court. Serjeant Bendlowes, and his anonymous precursor of 1509–26, had perceived the value of such a link but did not develop it to advance the quality of reporting. Their 'reports' were simply brief notes appended to the pleadings. Many of the cases in Bendlowes's entries were reported more fully by Dyer, and when the two sources are laid side by side the cases are much easier to understand. It was left to Plowden to perfect the idea. Instead of producing an annotated book of entries, Plowden would print the entries of pleadings as preliminaries and the entries of judgments as postscripts to each of his very full reports.

Most of the reports in our period are still from the Common Pleas, though the growing importance of the King's Bench naturally brings that court into greater prominence. There are a considerable number of King's Bench cases even in the year books of Henry VII, and of course when Spelman and Port sat in that court they reported it almost to the exclusion of the Common Pleas; Port indeed left off his alphabetical system to produce a series of King's Bench reports for 1529–34.[67] Spelman and Yorke were the first reporters to record private discussions between the judges at table in Serjeants' Inn, a practice continued by Dalison and Dyer in the middle of the century. There are as yet no separate collections of cases in the Chancery, Star Chamber, Wards, or Exchequer, though occasional cases from all these courts may be found. However, a new departure at the end of our period provides us with a continuous series of notes of civil and criminal cases on circuit. Dyer began to keep his circuit notebook when he was first appointed an

---

[64] BL MS. Harley 1715, which gives references to several of the rolls; reports pr. 120 Selden Soc. 1–4. One of the reports (1514) is also pr. in 109 Selden Soc. 150.

[65] The principal edition is *Les Reports de Gulielme Benloe Serjeant del Ley Des divers Pleadings et Cases* (1689). Note p. 14 (tr. 'the author of this book heard and was present at the said argument and judgment', 1535). For other reports possibly by Bendlowes, and recurring in some other printed volumes, see 94 Selden Soc. 176.

[66] Cf. above, 452, for the Middle Temple pupils of Mr Prothonotary Jenour.

[67] Port 56–76.

assize judge in 1554 and he continued it until his last circuit in 1581.[68] It is the only full collection of circuit cases between the *Liber Assisarum* and the seventeenth century.[69]

THE CIRCULATION OF REPORTS

Although there was no decline in law reporting in the early Tudor period, there does seem to have been a change in the general patterns of circulation.[70] No doubt reporting was always a mixture of private initiative and communal sharing; but, so far as we can tell, the year books from Edward III to Henry VI circulated widely in the profession as standard texts and were still being transcribed at the start of the printing era.[71] We do not know how much time usually elapsed between reporting and circulation, but it is assumed to have been fairly short, since the standard unit of dissemination was the single year rather than a longer-range collection. Caryll's note of the 1488 case, with the 1491–2 interlineations, confirms that contemporary reports were shared and collated even at that date. This is not to say that 'private' reports did not exist as well. The Henry VI years printed by Machlinia seem to have been such; at any rate, they are different from the manuscripts which survive for those years and which, before the age of printing, represented the vulgate text. And the *Long Quinto* did not come to light until Powell printed it in 1552, presumably from a unique manuscript; it is quite different from the vulgate year 5 *Edward IV*. Nevertheless, by the end of the fifteenth century the uncirculated manuscript seems to have become more common, and this accounts for the textual chaos in the printed years of Henry VII. To the extent that Caryll and Spelman circulated in the sixteenth century, they did so as posthumous compilations covering a professional lifetime, rather than as annual instalments of recent material. Port's notebook, the only one to survive, did not circulate at all.

The explanation for this change is uncertain. It might be argued that the advent of printing rapidly led to over-reliance on the press, so that the practice of multiplying manuscript reports by hand was simply given up. This cannot be a complete explanation, because the law printers rarely tackled reports which were anywhere near contemporary and seem to have aimed rather at giving the

---

[68] 109 Selden Soc., pp. xcii–xcvi; printed in 110 Selden Soc. 400–65. The autograph notebook has not survived, but there is a transcript in IT MS. Petyt 511/13.

[69] A few scattered circuit cases are to be found in Spelman, Yelverton, and Yorke; and see 121 Selden Soc. 469–70 (three cases on the Midland circuit, 1544–5).

[70] For the circulation of law manuscripts generally see below, 491–3.

[71] See A. W. B. Simpson, 'The Circulation of Year Books in the Fifteenth Century' (1957) 73 *LQR* 492–505.

profession texts which were hard to come by, to fill gaps in the retrospective series. Moreover, the copying of manuscripts by scriveners remained a viable trade until the Civil War, and Bendlowes (for example) was widely published in manuscript before it was printed in 1689. Nor does the function of reporting seem to have changed hands. Like the year-book reporter Townshend, most of our early Tudor reporters began as young members of the inns of court and continued to note cases throughout their careers; the majority of them became judges or serjeants at law. What seems, therefore, to have happened is that it became an accepted part of legal education, at least for the most serious students, to make their own notes. Their notebooks, as we have seen, would contain reports of both inns of court exercises and cases in the central courts, in varying proportions. They would be tailored to individual needs, and would reflect individual careers. Caryll's reports concentrate on the Common Pleas once he becomes a prothonotary in 1493, but contain some important public-law cases after he becomes a king's serjeant in 1514. Spelman's interest shifts from the Common Pleas to the King's Bench when he becomes a judge there and likewise the principal subject-matter shifts from pleading to criminal law and writs of error; unlike Caryll and Port, he made a practice of noting memorable events—such as the death of Henry VII, the coronation of Anne Boleyn, a creation of serjeants, the appointment of judges and chancellors, and even the discovery of an enormous fish in the Thames.[72] Dyer noted still more material of this kind, though some of it was edited out of the printed version of 1585/6, and he also included the results of historical research in the plea rolls.

Here, then, is the distinction between the year books and their immediate successors. It lies not in the content, or the class of author, but in the circumstance of publication. Year books, as currently understood, were published in manuscript for more or less immediate circulation, whereas the notebooks of our known early Tudor reporters did not, for the most part, become public or available for copying until after the writers' deaths. How many of the latter we have lost is a matter for conjecture; but it is a fair guess that there were once many more well-thumbed notebooks like Port's, written on paper, in atrocious hieroglyphs, with no title-pages or headlines to explain to the uninitiated what they contained. Some may have fallen to pieces from constant use. The old year books, written in regular scribal hands, were far less likely to be thrown away than these personal notes, which, however precious to legal historians in later ages, must have struck the average executor as highly ephemeral. Indeed, but for the foresight of a handful of copyists in the time of Elizabeth I, and a few happy chances in the preservation of libraries, the entire corpus would have been lost for ever.

[72] 94 Selden Soc. 177.

THE FORCE OF PRECEDENT

Another difference between the typical fifteenth-century year book and the typical law report of the mid-sixteenth century is that emphasis has shifted from tentative pleading, and other procedural questions arising before trial, to post-trial motions in banc, demurrers, and special verdicts. The judges have been acquiring an enhanced role as authorities, since their final judgments in such cases represent legal decisions which settle the law. The apparent transformation in reporting has nothing to do with the cessation of the year-book format as such, but reflects the changes taking place in legal procedure and in the law-making role of the courts.[73] These changes were under way before the year books ended. Indeed, one of the last year-book reporters—the anonymous author of *12–14 Henry VIII*—perceived them and reacted to them more positively than any of the named reporters before Plowden.

Before these changes have occurred, the year books seem very indecisive. Discussions often end abruptly with no resolution. The final judgment is irrelevant to what is being reported, and since it is given in a subsequent term it is usually ignored. At the start of our period, therefore, the common law was not perceived of as case-law in the modern sense, as a body of judicial decisions. It was better characterized as accepted teaching, or rather learning: the *common erudition* which we have already encountered.[74] This learning was found not only in the opinions occurring in the year books themselves, and in a few works of authority such as Littleton, but in the oral traditions of the inns of court and chancery, and in the plea rolls.

The primary sense of the word 'precedent' was a judgment of record, and recourse was had to the plea rolls when a point was unfamiliar or an earlier report unclear.[75] Yet the rolls were not a friendly guide to legal doctrine. No doubt they were relatively inaccessible to practitioners.[76] Most cases did not result in judgment, and most judgments were mere formalities following the verdict of the jury. The record did not show whether there had been a motion in arrest of judgment, or—in the absence of a formal adjournment for advisement or repleader—whether any legal difficulty had been considered by the court at all. When an issue of law was raised by demurrer or writ of error, judgments were not as common as indecisions, and such judgments as there were came without enrolled reasons. It

---

[73] See above, ch. 21. Cf., in similar vein, D. J. Ibbetson, 'Case Law and Judicial Precedents in Medieval and Early-Modern England' in *Auctoritates: xenia R. C. van Caenegem oblata*, ed. S. Dauchy, J. Monballyu, and A. Wijffels (1997), 55–68.   [74] See above, 467.

[75] Above, 389; 94 Selden Soc. *161*; 109 Selden Soc., p. xxix.

[76] See above, 139. Cf. *Anon.* (1558) BL MS. Hargrave 4, fo. 150, *per* Prideaux sjt (tr. 'such an action was brought and well debated within these three years... and I have seen the roll myself and judgment was entered').

is not surprising, therefore, if we fail to encounter any clear notion that a particular precedent might have binding force. Judges might 'reprove' earlier cases which they considered erroneous.[77] An old decision might be dismissed as out of date, a new one as an aberration.[78] Obiter dicta and submissions, and interlocutory rulings on procedure, were to be distinguished from final judgments on the law, which were relatively uncommon.[79] Reports were prima-facie evidence of common learning, but not the law itself. Indeed, the evidence of the later year books is that precedents were still used in a rather vague way when arguing in court.[80] There was no law library in Westminster Hall, apart from some odd volumes in the offices;[81] neither the judges nor counsel had desks or lecterns in court; and there was no tradition of producing books in court, even when cases were cited. We find vague references to 'the books' or 'our books' (*nos livers*), and sometimes a vague offer to produce a book if pressed ('I could show you a book...'),[82] but not the reading of specific texts in the course of argument.[83] A citation might be countered by a bald assertion that there were 'other books to the contrary', when it is evident that no one had the books before them; argument might therefore degenerate into a memory contest, or a threat to bring books if driven to do so.[84] This no doubt explains why so many citations appear to be wrong—though we must remember that the reporters also were relying on memory.[85] Even when a mistaken summary of a case was corrected from the bench, the authority seems to have been superior memory rather than a text in hand.[86] Sometimes, without

[77] See Sir Nicholas Throckmorton's remark about Spelman J. in 1 St. Tr. 892. Cf. Fitzherbert J.' s comment in 1535 on a 1520 decision which (though resulting from the success of his own advocacy) he thought wrong: above, 476 n. 20; below, 870. [78] 94 Selden Soc. 162. See also above, 28.

[79] Above, ch. 21.

[80] The tradition of citing cases had begun in the thirteenth century. See further P. H. Winfield, *Chief Sources of English Legal History* (1925), 152; T. E. Lewis, 'The History of Judicial Precedent III' (1931) 47 *LQR* 411–27 at 423; J. P. Dawson, *Oracles of the Law* (1968), 50–65; J. H. Baker, 'English Law as Case-Law' (1989), repr. in *CLT*, 158–64. [81] See above, 140–1, 151.

[82] A late example is *Anon.* (1550) BL MS. Hargrave 4, fo. 107, *per* Hales J. ('jeo poy monstre un liver...').

[83] Cf. the Inner Temple custom, noted in 1656, of not allowing specific citations by barristers arguing moots: 105 Selden Soc., p. cxcii. Benchers, however, were allowed to cite cases by year; so this may have been thought more fitting for judges than counsel.

[84] 94 Selden Soc. 162; *CLT*, 158 9; Ives, 89 *LQR* at 69 70. A reporter thought it worth remark, when in 1482 Fairfax J. quoted a statute, that he did so from a book in his hand: Pas. 22 Edw. IV, fo. 11, pl. 30.

[85] For a specific example see *Anon.* (1556) Chr. Yelverton's reports, fo. 241v (tr. 'Brooke CJ vouched the book in 47 [Edw. III], naming it to be in 43 [Edw. III] ...'). Most citations consisted simply of the regnal year, or term, since pagination varied from manuscript to manuscript.

[86] See e.g. *Sutton* v. *Forster* (1483) Mich. 1 Ric. III, fo. 2, pl. 2 (Huse CJ corrects Donington's recollection of a Hen. VI case); *Anon.* (1493) Hil. 8 Hen. VII, fo. 10, pl. 2 (tr. 'Huse [CJ]: that case [in 11 Hen. IV] was otherwise; and he rose and went away...'); *Anon.* (1493) Mich. 9 Hen. VII, fo. 6, pl. 1 (tr. 'Vavasour [J.] said, first, that his book is contrary, and he said he had seen several times in his book ...'); *Conyngesby and Mallom* v. *Regem* (1509) 2 Caryll 595 at 600 (Rede CJ corrects Boteler J.' s recollection of a Hen. IV case).

doubt, books were brought and perused, and different texts compared.[87] But there is very little in the way of critical discussion of reported opinions. It was not merely practical inconvenience which discouraged citation. There was a professional tradition that the law should be stated in a way which appealed to the right reasoning of a legally trained audience or readership; a proposition was therefore backed up not by strings of citations but by examples which showed its correctness, preferably familiar examples.[88] There is implicit in all the arguments a reverence, not for the single ruling decision,[89] but for the current of authority or the most reasonable opinion: that, presumably, is what 'common erudition' was.

Starkey was more or less correct when he wrote in the 1530s:

The judgments of years [year books] be infinite and full of much controversy, and beside that, of small authority. The judges are not bounden, as I understand, to follow them as a rule, but after their own liberty they have authority to judge according as they are instructed by the serjeants, and as the circumstance of the cause doth them move.

But he was probably exaggerating when he concluded that 'this maketh judgments and process of our law to be without end and infinite', and that 'the subtlety of one serjeant shall evert and destroy all the judgments of many wise men before time received'.[90] That he should characterize law reports as containing 'the judgments of many wise men' is an interesting reflection on the changes under way by the 1530s, and perhaps expresses what the ideal law report was coming to be; but it is not the way most lawyers would have seen the year books. We have seen why an individual case was of 'small authority'. Common erudition, on the other hand, was almost sacrosanct.

Citation of cases from memory must often have been superficial or inaccurate, and at the beginning of our period only a few of those who heard an earlier case mentioned in court would have had convenient access to a manuscript text of it. It is hardly surprising that the citation of particular cases was regarded as less important than the propositions derived from them. Nevertheless, in the early Tudor period fashions were changing. We have already linked this with a growing judicial positivism;[91] but we may fairly suppose that the change was greatly

---

[87] 94 Selden Soc. 163 nn. 1–2. In 1553 Bromley J., sitting at Shrewsbury assizes, ordered a *Liber Assisarum* to be fetched from his home (which was in Wroxeter): Plowd. 98v.

[88] Cf. the 'common cases' mentioned in an educational context: above, 471.

[89] Except, perhaps, for an Exchequer Chamber decision by all the judges. In *Anon.* (1557) Chr. Yelverton's reports, fo. 242, Brooke CJ refused to allow counsel to argue against a recent decision of that kind.

[90] T. Starkey, *Dialogue between Pole and Lupset*, ed. T. F. Mayer (1989), 128 (sp. mod.). In the 1878 edn, S. J. Herrtage rendered 'everte' (i.e. overturn) as 'enerte'. Cf., to the same effect, Morison, *A Perswasion to the Kyng that the Law of his Realme shulde be in Latin* [c.1536], fo. 8v.

[91] Above, 48–52.

facilitated by the printing of the year books.[92] The availability of a common text encouraged the specific citations which seem to be increasingly expected, while research into case-law with a view to citation was greatly eased by the publication of Statham's abridgment in about 1490 and Serjeant Fitzherbert's *Graunde Abridgement* in 1514–17.[93] In Spelman's reports alone, there are over sixty explicit citations of cases by year, ranging in date from 1312 to 1505, and all but two of the cases are identifiable in the printed year books.[94] Several of the citations in Spelman seem to be from Fitzherbert rather than from the books at large. Port certainly made constant use of Statham.[95] Fitzherbert was also, in his *Novel Natura Brevium* (1534), the first legal writer to make a practice of discussing earlier cases, some of which are cited from 'les abridgements' (meaning his own book). By the 1550s—unless we are deceived by the variable quality of the law reports—we seem to have reached a different and more familiar world. The speeches reported by Plowden are full of specific citations to printed year books, which are offered as 'proof' of legal propositions, and are discussed critically by counsel and judges. In the same decade, Sir William Staunford—while serving as a judge—wrote an important textbook on criminal law chiefly by the technique of digesting the printed authorities found under the title *Corone* in Fitzherbert.[96] There could hardly be a greater contrast with Littleton, written less than a century earlier, in which hardly any cases are mentioned at all.[97] Authority is now sought in reported cases as a matter of routine, and no legal proposition can safely be advanced without chapter and verse—or rather year and folio—to support it. The common law has apparently become case-law, in the modern understanding of that term.

[92] See E. G. Henderson, 'Legal Literature and the Impact of Printing on the English Legal Profession' (1975) 68 *Law Lib. Jnl* 288–93, at 293.   [93] For the abridgments see below, 501.

[94] 94 Selden Soc. *162* n. 4.

[95] 102 Selden Soc., p. xxxi. Port also cited numerous manuscript year books, probably from his own library: ibid., pp. xxix–xxxi. But these were mostly notes for his own use, not citations in court.

[96] Staunford, *Les Plees del Coron* (1557); below, 502.

[97] The same dearth of citations is found in St German, Rastell, and Perkins.

27

Law Books and Publishing

LAW LIBRARIES

THERE were no common-law libraries comparable with those of the universities or large monasteries. The inns of court had nascent libraries around 1500, but few books in them, not all legal. For instance, of the six chained books which Edmund Pykeryng (d. 1488) left in his will to the library of Gray's Inn, only one—a statute-book of Edward III—was connected with law.[1] The same inn formerly possessed a fifteenth-century register of writs inscribed 'Iste liber pertinet societati de Greysynn',[2] and still owns a number of medieval books of monastic prove-nance, doubtless acquired after the Dissolution. The earliest gifts to have survived to the present in Lincoln's Inn are the five or more volumes from the Cholmeley bequest of 1563. Nevertheless, Lincoln's Inn had had a library as early as 1475, and rebuilt it in 1505–9. In 1519, Sir John Boteler, justice of the Common Pleas, bequeathed to it his own law library—'all my books of law which I have in my house in Silver Street and Serjeants' Inn in Chancery Lane'[3]—and by 1550 it had a number of volumes of medieval reports and a *Bracton*.[4] But security was weak, and the contents were simply lost. Likewise all the books in the 'symple lybrary' of the Middle Temple went missing before 1540.[5] None of the pre-1550 books in the Inner Temple, which had a library by 1506,[6] survived to the nineteenth century.

Law libraries were mostly personal, and books changed hands frequently, usu-ally within the walls of each inn of court, but sometimes by bequest. For instance, law books might be left to children or close relatives who had embarked on the law. When Serjeant Rudhale (d. 1530) bequeathed the contents of his Serjeants' Inn chamber to his younger son Charles, he provided that his elder son John (a member of the Inner Temple and an attorney) should 'have such books there as he will choose for the furtherance of his learning, leaving to the said Charles books convenient for his age and learning'.[7] Borrowed books might also be

---

[1] PCC 32 Milles ('libraria de Grays Inne').
[2] Now BL MS. Add. 34901 (inscription no longer present).   [3] PCC 22 Ayloffe (tr. from Latin).
[4] Baker, *English Legal Manuscripts*, ii. 1; 94 Selden Soc. *131*.
[5] 94 Selden Soc. *132* n. 3.   [6] *CITR*, i. 6. For a bequest to the library in 1514 see below, 493.
[7] PCC 26 Jankyn (sp. mod.).

restored to their rightful owners by will.[8] Unfortunately for us, the testators rarely listed the titles.

Changes of ownership, and even loans,[9] were often carefully recorded on the flyleaves of the books themselves.[10] Legal manuscripts of the fifteenth and early sixteenth centuries frequently end with an 'Explicit... quod John Style' (or whatever the name might be). There has been some controversy as to whether these names after the *quod* were the names of scribes, as Ker supposed, or of owners.[11] No doubt frequently they were the same, since law students learned by copying. In fact, the names seem nearly always to belong to lawyers or law students, and the explicits were clearly treated as ownership inscriptions, substitutions of names being made by subsequent owners. We even find an early printed year book with a blank space provided in such an explicit for the owner's name to be inserted. Other inscriptions are in the common form 'Iste liber pertinet...', sometimes witnessed by fellows of the owner's inn. There was a good deal of exchanging and borrowing, or even giving.[12]

Although few detailed lists of law libraries exist from our period,[13] a good idea of their typical contents can be reconstructed from several different kinds of source. We may take by way of illustration three members of the Inner Temple and a serjeant at law. For two of them we have probate inventories. William Catesby (d. 1485), bencher of the Inner Temple and chancellor of the Exchequer, had eight (unspecified) law books, a psalter, a book of chronicles, and a book *De Natura Legis Naturae* (doubtless Fortescue).[14] This may be compared with the rather larger library of William Cutler or Cutlerd (d. 1506), serjeant at law, formerly of Lincoln's Inn.[15]

---

[8] John Watnow (d. 1484) of Gray's Inn left to Huse CJ (formerly a fellow bencher) three or four quires of parchment 'the which I understond been parcellis of bokes which I suppose I had of hym': PCC 6 Milles.

[9] C. Moreton, *The Townshends and their World: gentry, law, and land in Norfolk c.1450–1551* (1992), 27 (loans in 1490s by Roger Townshend JCP). For an example of lending, probably for copying, see *ELMUSA*, i. 17, no. 43.

[10] For what follows see J. H. Baker, 'The Books of the Common Law' in *The Book in Britain: Volume III, 1400–1557*, ed. L. Hellinga and J. B. Trapp (1999), 411–32.

[11] See Simpson, 'The Circulation of Year Books in the Fifteenth Century', 492 at 501; with the further note (referring to Ker) in 87 *LQR* 108. For statute-books in which *quod* apparently denotes the scribe, see Baker, 'The Books of the Common Law', 422 n. 83.

[12] For records of gifts, see e.g. *ELMUSA*, i. 18 ('Heydon ex dono Butery anno xvii° H. viii. vii die Julii', both members of Lincoln's Inn), 30 ('Iste liber constat Willelmo Good de Furnyvals Ynne etc. muneris D. H.'), 32 ('Johannes Whittyngton est hujus libri possessor ex dono Thome Troute de Bodmyn in com. Cornubie', Troute being an attorney of the Common Pleas).

[13] See R. J. Schoeck, 'The Libraries of Common Lawyers in the Renaissance' (1962) 6 *Manuscripta* 155–67; E. W. Ives, 'A Lawyer's Library in 1500' (1969) 85 *LQR* 104–16; and the present writer's forthcoming contribution to *The History of Libraries in Britain*.   [14] PRO, E154/2/4.

[15] PRO, PROB 2/472. Though not described as a serjeant, the identification of the deceased as the serjeant is confirmed by his having left a scarlet gown with a hood and a ray gown with a hood; he was also in debt to 'the sargeantes of the comen lawe' (presumably one of the serjeants' inns).

Besides a manuscript *De Dictis Philosophorum,* he owned twenty-seven law books (seven of them printed), including three volumes of statutes, an abridgment of statutes, nine volumes of year books from Edward III to Edward IV and a *Liber Assisarum,* two abridgments of cases (one the printed Statham), a book of entries, and two books of 'raportes'—evidently meaning readings in the inns of court rather than reports of cases.[16] These books were at the time of his death mostly kept in his study at Boston, Lincolnshire, though six printed law books (not described) were found in the chapel. They seem, nevertheless, to have been his working law library.

The more impressive library of Sir Thomas Frowyk (d. 1505) can be glimpsed through surviving manuscripts. His three volumes of year books of Edward I, Edward II, and Edward III are all in the British Library,[17] as is his illuminated volume of *Statuta Nova* which had previously belonged to another judge, William Calow (d. 1487).[18] Calow mentions in his will a 'book of new statutes', perhaps this one, together with a book of assizes, a *Bracton,* and 'two books of abridgments, one of mine own labour and th'other of Lincoln's Inn labour'.[19] We know that Frowyk also owned a 'great book of entries', because Lady Frowyk's second husband Thomas Jakes (d. 1514) left to the Inner Temple 'my fair book of the new statutes written and limned and my great book of entries, which were my singular good Lord Frowyk's'.[20] These were all precious treasures; Frowyk would certainly have owned other less valuable books.

In the case of Sir John Port (d. 1540), his library may be conjecturally reconstructed from the citations in his autograph notebook. It included year books of Edward I, Edward II, and Edward III, the *Liber Assisarum,* year books from Henry IV to Edward IV, a *Natura Brevium,* Littleton, Statham's abridgment, and some readings.[21] It is possible that some of these were borrowed, though the numerous scattered references suggest constant access.

Readings and recent reports are seldom mentioned in wills and inventories, doubtless because their commercial value was minimal, though Port's notebook shows that manuscript readings were consulted and cited. Law libraries were evidently small by later standards, and even a judge might own no more than a selection of year books which had chanced to come his way. Access to legal literature can hardly have been constricted by the size of individual libraries, and must have depended on borrowing, copying, and remembering. This began to change in the early Tudor period with the advent of law publishing.

---

[16] The second reference is to 'raporttes of statutes'.

[17] BL MS. Add. 37657 (Edw. I), Add. 37659 (Edw. III); MS. Hargrave 210 (Edw. II).

[18] BL Cotton MS. Nero C.1 (with Calow arms).   [19] PCC 7 Milles (dated 1483) (sp. mod.).

[20] PCC 2 Holder (sp. mod.). This suggests that Jakes had only one such statute-book, and it may therefore be the Cotton MS. There is no record of either book having been in the Inner Temple library.

[21] 102 Selden Soc., pp. xxix–xxxi.

THE LAW BOOK TRADE AND THE PRESS

The books of the common law, even in the second half of our period, were primarily handwritten. Many of them would have been written or copied out by the lawyer himself or his clerk, or a junior member of his inn. Apart from the well-known series of *Statuta Nova*, mentioned below,[22] we do not find illuminated law books in our period; nor is there any known evidence from this period of a bookselling trade in law manuscripts. The vast majority of law books were written on paper, without decoration, and many of them have an amateurish appearance. Although it is conceivable that some of them were bought 'new', many were produced by borrowing and copying. Even books in print (such as Littleton) were sometimes copied by hand in the later fifteenth century.[23]

There was nevertheless, by the sixteenth century, a bookselling trade in law, dominated by the law printers.[24] It had begun in 1481 or thereabouts with the immigrants John Lettou and William de Machlinia, who had acquired some of Caxton's type. Together they printed Littleton's *Tenures* and the year books of 33, 35, and 36 Henry VI; Machlinia working alone added 34 and 37 Henry VI.[25] These years were apparently chosen not because they were well-known texts, but because the printers had come by some unique reports which were quite different from the manuscript versions of those years already in circulation. Machlinia's largest undertaking was the first printing of the *Statuta Nova* in the time of Richard III.[26]

The trade of law printing passed in the 1480s to Richard Pynson (d. 1530), a Norman by birth, who may have acquired Machlinia's goodwill and stock; some of Machlinia's waste has been found in his earliest bindings. As his first ventures, he had Littleton and Statham printed in Rouen, but thereafter he seems to have used London presses. In around 1500 he moved from St Clement's parish to The George in Fleet Street, near St Dunstan's church and opposite the Temple. He had a lease for forty-seven years of this or another house in Fleet Street from the dean and chapter of Westminster, and in 1520 he had some dealings with John Rastell

---

[22] Below, 505.

[23] In 1484, William Esyngwold (town clerk of Nottingham) claimed 22s. 6d. from John Mapurley [of Staple Inn] for writing out (in Nottingham) a book of *New Tenures* containing 61 leaves at the rate of 4d. a folio and 2s. 2d. for materials: *Records of the Borough of Nottingham*, ii. 340–1. CUL MS. Mm.5.2 contains a copy of Littleton apparently written out by Christopher Hanyngton (d. 1490), a Chancery clerk; an inscription now gone recorded that the book was bought in St Paul's churchyard in 1480 (see F. Hargrave in the 1832 edn of Coke on Littleton, p. xxv). Littleton was printed *c*.1481.

[24] The oeuvre of the law printers to 1600 was surveyed by Beale, *A Bibliography of Early English Law Books* (1926), with supplement by R. B. Anderson (1943), both reprinted in 1966. The subject has been placed on a new footing by K. F. Pantzer in the 2nd edn of *STC*.

[25] They are now very rare. The only complete set appears to be in CUL.

[26] K. Pantzer, 'Printing the English Statutes 1484–1640: some historical implications' in *Books and Society in History*, ed. K. E. Carpenter (1983), 74–5.

concerning its renewal by Pynson's daughter-in-law.[27] He printed numerous year books, beginning before 1500 with a continuation of the Machlinia series into 1–9 Edward IV. The first two years of Edward IV have explicits 'secundum Townsend', the only identified year books in print.[28] All the year books were issued singly, for a few pence each,[29] to be made up into volumes by the purchaser. Pynson has been credited with a total legal output of at least 139 editions, including ninety-two year books.[30] In 1506 or 1507, he succeeded William Faques as king's printer, and thereafter used the title *regius impressor* on his books. Although this office apparently carried a modest stipend, it conferred no privilege in relation to law books generally and from around 1513 Pynson had competition, especially from John Rastell and Robert Redman.

John Rastell (d. 1536), a barrister of the Middle Temple, made an impressive contribution. He continued the printing of the year books, and printed the first edition of the *Liber Assisarum* in 1514, the first English translations of the *Old Tenures* (1523?) and of Littleton's *New Tenures* (1525), and the first part of *Doctor and Student* (1528).[31] His *Exposiciones Terminorum* (1523?) was not only the first law dictionary but also served—by means of parallel texts—to introduce students to law French; it was to enjoy a long life under its later title *Les Termes de la Ley*. However, Rastell's principal achievement in the history of printing was his publication of Serjeant Fitzherbert's three-volume *Graunde Abridgement* (1514–17), the production of which is thought to have consumed a quarter of a million large sheets of paper.[32] It was so far superior to Statham that the latter was never reprinted.

An inventory of John Rastell's stock in 1538, two years after his death, reveals that he left 700 copies of his *Expositiones* (480 in English, 220 in French only), 430 Littletons in English, 124 *Old Tenures*, 100 'Talis' (*Novae Narrationes*, new tales), twelve acts of 21 Henry VIII (printed by Rastell, who served in this parliament), and eight abridgments of statutes in English. The *Narrationes* and the statutes were small pamphlets valued at 1*d.* each, the abridgments somewhat larger and priced 4*d.* each; but the rest were not individually valued.[33] There is no mention

[27] *Rastell* v. *Pynson* (1529) KB 27/1072, m. 60. Jane, the widow of Pynson's son Richard (an attorney), had married John Heywode, a relative of Rastell's.

[28] Beale, *Bibliography*, 78–9, nos. R225, R233. For Roger Townshend see above, 474.

[29] Rastell's colophons indicate a rate of 2*d.* per five sheets. Cf. the valuation of Kebell's pre-1500 printed year books: Ives, *Common Lawyers in pre-Reformation England*, 445.

[30] Beale, *Bibliography*, 188–90.

[31] He was very keen to promote English as a language suitable for expressing even technical information: Baker, 'Rastell and the Terms of the Law'. See also Reed, *Early English Drama*; A. J. Geritz and A. L. Laine, *John Rastell* (1983).

[32] H. J. Graham, 'The Rastells and the Printed English Law Book of the Renaissance' (1954) 47 *Law Library Jnl* 6–25, at 17. See also H. J. Graham and J. W. Heckel, 'The Book that "Made" the Common Law' (1958) 51 *Law Library Jnl* 100–16; F. L. Boersma, *An Introduction to Fitzherbert's Abridgement* (1981).

[33] PROB 2/692; pr. in R. J. Roberts, 'John Rastell's Inventory of 1538' (1979) 1 *The Library* (6th ser.) 34–42. The valuation may be on the low side, since in 1554 Rastell's abridgment of statutes cost 2*s.* 8*d.*: 13 *British Library Jnl* 46 (1989).

of Fitzherbert or the year books, which may have sold out, and the legal portions of this remaining stock were mostly student books. John had given up printing in 1530, though since 1529 his son William Rastell had become a printer in his own right and had probably taken over some of his father's stock. William's principal contribution as a law printer was the first edition of the *Registrum Omnium Brevium* in 1531; this is not mentioned in the 1538 inventory either. He also produced in 1534 an omnibus handbook combining the *Natura Brevium*, the old and new tenures, the book for justices, *Novae Narrationes*, *Returna Brevium*, and *Carta Feodi*. However, William did not continue long in the business. Firmly opposed to the Reformation, he ceased printing in 1534, was called to the Bar in 1539, and after a few years in practice fled to Louvain.[34]

Robert Redman (d. 1540) also provided stiff competition for Pynson in the 1520s, acquiring Pynson's old premises in St Clement Danes—and, in what looks suspiciously like passing-off—using Pynson's sign of The George. Pynson attacked Redman as incompetent, calling him 'Rudeman', and Redman retaliated. Editorial work on the year books suggests that Redman was in fact the better.[35] His new edition of 40 Edward III in 1534 even shows unusual signs of thorough editing, with copious notes and cross-references throughout by an anonymous editor ('my frende'); there is an English preface criticizing Pynson and calling for the profession to support Redman's enterprise. Redman also introduced a best-seller in the form of Perkins's *Profitable Book* (1528).[36] Eventually he purchased Pynson's business, and may have taken over some of Rastell's type. The office of king's printer, however, went to Thomas Berthelet (d. 1555), who exercised it for the rest of Henry VIII's reign. The king's printer had monopolized the production of statutes since Pynson's time; Berthelet also printed a few year books, but after 1532 the king's printers did not concern themselves at all with reports or with the more advanced law books.

The George passed after Redman's death to William Middleton (d. 1547), who reprinted several law books. Middleton's widow married William Powell, who succeeded to the business and is best known as the first printer of the *Long Quinto*, a unique long year book of 5 Edward IV similar in style to the long reports of late Henry VI printed by Machlinia. Powell continued in business until 1567, but stopped printing law books in 1553. A lawsuit against Powell in 1553 lists the contents of a London house, including the entire stock of a bookseller.[37] Plomer

---

[34] He returned under Mary, became a serjeant in 1555, and published his alphabetical *Collection of all the Statutes* in 1557. He was appointed a judge by Mary I in October 1558, and reappointed by Elizabeth I a month later, but he resigned in 1562 and went into exile again. He died in Louvain in 1565. For his *Colleccion of Entrees* (1566) see above, 345–6.   [35] 119 Selden Soc., p. xix.

[36] Below, 502.

[37] CP 40/1156, m. 525. This was discovered by H. R. Plomer: 'An Inventory of Wynkyn de Worde's House "The Sun in Fleet Street" in 1553' (1915) 6 *The Library* (3rd ser.), 228–34.

suggested that the house might be identified as The Sun, where de Worde's successor Whitchurch ceased printing in 1553; the stock certainly included many non-law books. But there may instead be some connection with Powell's financial difficulties and the loss of his law business. Law is more strongly represented than might be expected of a general bookshop. There are over 1,500 year-book pamphlets, on average fifty copies of each year.[38] Some had dwindled to three or four copies, but there were over 100 copies of some years of Edward IV and 170 copies of 7 Edward III. Some of the titles are known today only in editions by Redman, Berthelet, or Rastell. There were also 100 copies of *Britton* (printed by Redman in 1540), 100 of *Diversite de Courtz*, fifty *Old Tenures*, fifty *Natura Brevium* in French (and forty of the English translation), and fifty Littletons (only sixteen of the English translation, which had obviously sold well). These figures, like those of the 1538 inventory, suggest original print-runs well into three figures for books which now survive only in a handful of copies. Such numbers are confirmed by evidence that Pynson's abridgment of statutes (1499) ran to 409 copies.[39]

The underlying cause of the Powell litigation does not appear from the record, but 1553 was a critical year in the history of law printing. Berthelet was dismissed as king's printer, for religious and political reasons, and Powell ceased publishing common-law books, probably for financial reasons, leaving Richard Tottell as the sole law printer. The printing of common-law books thereupon became virtually a *de facto* monopoly. The reason was largely economic. Law printing was a specialized craft, requiring a familiarity with abbreviated French and some Latin, and it could not easily be carried on as a sideline. The bulk of the work lay, not in printing new texts for immediate sale, but in maintaining permanent stocks of the traditional books of the law.[40] Lawyers collected, and probably bought, their year books in miscellaneous bundles of single-year pamphlets; it is not uncommon to find volumes made up of a few Pynsons, a few Redmans, and perhaps the odd Berthelet or Middleton.[41] If a bookseller had a good stock of Pynson remainders, he would not have needed to order more copies of the same year from Redman. The printer therefore came to make his living by continuous reprinting of years already in circulation. This was the state of the business to which Tottell succeeded in 1553, and he did not greatly change it in nearly forty years of law printing.

Tottell had been an apprentice of Middleton, worked briefly for Elizabeth Middleton (later Mrs Powell), and around 1553 took over the printing house and

[38] Details of the law books are taken from the original record.
[39] H. R. Plomer, 'Two Lawsuits of Richard Pynson' (1909) 10 *The Library* (2nd ser.) 115 at 131.
[40] For the economic factors see H. J. Byrom, 'Richard Tottell: his life and work' (1927) 8 *The Library* (4th ser.) 195–232, at 210.
[41] There are good examples of such composite volumes in BL, LI, and Norwich Public Library.

shop of Henry Smyth (d. 1550) near the Temple, which he called The Hand and Star in allusion to the well-known watermark. He must at the same time have acquired the law side of the Powell business. It is difficult not to think that there is some connection here with the lawsuit of 1553, but the precise way in which Tottell established his monopoly remains a mystery. It is possible that the judges had intervened to rescue law printing from disarray by securing the advancement of a prominent youngster; at any rate, it was said in 1582 that Tottell 'at suit of the judges hath the common law books', which seems to import that the judges were somehow involved in the formal grant of monopoly.[42] Certainly Tottell managed at this time to obtain new privileges by patent. Previous law printers had obtained limited grants of copyright in respect of particular titles, such as that given to Rastell in 1531 for seven years in respect of the *Registrum Omnium Brevium*.[43] Following various precedents from other fields in the 1540s, Tottell was granted a patent in 1553 which gave him and his assigns the privilege of printing all common-law books for the next seven years, excepting those in which anyone else had a specific privilege—meaning those already in print *cum privilegio regali ad imprimendum solum*—and provided the books were licensed by a judge, two serjeants at law, or three apprentices of the law.[44] Tottell does not seem in practice to have been under any restraint in reprinting law books first printed by others, doubtless because there was no competitor left in business. He did, however, have to negotiate with William Rastell over Rastell's own compilations.[45] The patent did not in terms grant a monopoly, but provided that if anyone printed a book which Tottell had printed first it would be forfeited; in other words, it was a grant of limited future copyright in all the books he chose to print, obviating the need for specific licences. A more extensive patent followed in 1555, which omitted the licensing requirement and also made Tottell the sole printer of common-law books; and in 1559 this privilege was renewed for life.[46] These last two patents turned Tottell into a monopolist, prohibiting all other printers and booksellers from printing common-law books on pain of fine. For the next two and a half centuries, law printing would remain a monopoly, preserved despite protracted and bitter litigation with the disgruntled Stationers.

Tottell's possession of the patent for sole printing of common-law books was to give him the undoubted supremacy in law publishing for forty years. He claimed to have put the trade on a new footing. As early as 1556, he invited his readers to cast their minds back a few years to the pre-Tottell era, when the books of law were

---

[42] Burghley papers, BL MS. Lansdowne 48, fo. 186 (sp. mod.). Cf. Byrom, 'Richard Tottell', 220.

[43] According to the colophon: Beale, *Bibliography*, p. 148, no. T310.

[44] Pat. 7 Edw. VI, pt 3, m. 29; *CPR Edw. VI*, v. 47 (12 Apr. 1553).   [45] Graham, 'The Rastells', 15.

[46] Pat. 2 & 3 Phil. & Mar., pt 1, m. 28; *CPR 1555–7*, p. 18 (5 May 1555); Pat. 1 Eliz. I, pt 4, m. 23; *CPR 1558–60*, p. 62 (12 Jan. 1559).

imperfect, 'the most part marvellously mangled, and no small part nowhere to be gotten', so that the scarcity had raised the prices. He boasted that:[47]

there be enough...that...can truly witness...sithence I took in hand to serve your uses, that imperfections have been supplied, the price so eased as the scarceness no more hindereth but that ye have them as cheap (notwithstanding the common dearth of the times) as when they were most plentiful, the print much pleasanter to the eye in the books of years than any that ye have been yet served with, paper and margin as good and as fair as the best, but much better and fairer than the most, no small number by me set forth newly in print that before were scant to be found in writing, I need not my self to report it.

This self-assessment is not, of course, to be taken as an objective evaluation. When the printing monopolies came under attack in the 1570s and 1580s, Tottell would be accused of abusing the monopoly to raise prices, 'to the hindrance of a great number of poor students'.[48] And although he undertook some new titles of importance in our period, such as Staunford's *Les Plees del Coron* (1557), much of Tottell's legal work consisted in repeatedly reprinting the haphazardly established canon of year books. His principal achievement in year-book printing was to collect most of the existing individual year books into composite volumes, beginning with *Henry IV* in 1553, and ending with *Henry VIII* in 1591. With Tottell, therefore, the issuing of individual years—apart from the *Long Quinto*—ended. This policy of consolidation must have brought to his attention the glaring gaps in the series, and it is a principal criticism of his stewardship that, with the exceptions mentioned above, he generally chose not to fill them.[49]

THE LAW PRINTERS AND THE LEGAL PROFESSION

The law printers must obviously have kept closely in touch with the needs of the profession they supplied. Their premises were conveniently situated close to the inns of court. Pynson's shop The George, which was the principal outlet for common-law books throughout the reigns of Henry VIII and Edward VI, was on the corner of Chancery Lane, close to Clifford's Inn and Serjeants' Inn, facing the Temple. Tottell's shop, The Hand and Star, was just across the street, next to the Middle Temple gateway; it has been identified as No. 7, Fleet Street, immediately east of the gatehouse. Law books were probably also available in St Paul's church-yard: the colophon to one impression of Rastell's *Registrum Omnium Brevium*

---

[47] *Magna Charta cum Statutis quae Antiquae Vocantur* (dated 12 June 1556), preface, sig. *ii (sp. mod.).

[48] 'The griefes of the printers...susteined by reson of priviledges granted to privatt persons', BL MS. Lansdowne 48 (Burghley Papers), fo. 180 (sp. mod.).

[49] His collected edition of Hen. VII (1555) nevertheless included a number of reports after the year 8 Hen. VII which had never before been printed. Many of these additions are misdated, and some can be shown to be the work of John Caryll (d. 1523): above, 477.

(1531) says that it was to be sold in Rastell's own house, or in Paul's churchyard, or in Redman's house at Temple Bar.[50] But no evidence has yet been discovered of sale in Westminster Hall.

How far the printers worked on commission for members of the profession must be a matter of conjecture, though the fact that Pynson printed a *Natura Brevium* in the 1490s at the instance of Strand Inn[51] suggests that orders for student books might sometimes have been placed by the inns. Some professional involvement in bookselling might also be inferred from the fact that an attorney in 1492 complained of the loss from his house (in 1485) of sixty copies of Littleton and two bales of paper; but his stock also included sixty copies of *The Fox*— presumably Caxton's—and it is possible that he was dealing in books, or taking them as surety for a loan, rather than selling.[52]

The work of editing law books for these printers is largely concealed from our sight, since it was rare for editors to be mentioned by name on title-pages or in explicits. Yet it is certain that members of the inns of court were employed as editors, and most of those known to us were members of the Middle Temple. Plomer's discovery of a dispute with Pynson and three Middle Temple editors, concerning the printed abridgment of statutes, showed that Christopher St German was one of them,[53] and it seems possible that editing was St German's principal occupation in the missing years between his quitting chambers and his becoming a successful writer in the late 1520s. Another member of the inn heavily involved in editing was William Owen (admitted 1514). He was given public credit for *Le Bregement de Toutes les Estatutes... par Guillaume Owen du Medile Temple* (1521), and he is said to have acted as Fitzherbert's amanuensis in copying out the *Graunde Abridgement*.[54] Legend had it that Owen was Fitzherbert's chamber-fellow. If that is true, he may have migrated to the Middle Temple from Gray's Inn; but his son described him as a 'fellow student and neere cozen' to Sir Thomas Elyot, who was admitted to the Middle Temple in 1510. According to Dyer CJ, a former bencher of that inn, Owen was also an editor of the old *Natura Brevium*.[55]

---

[50] Beale, *Bibliography*, 148, no. T309b. For a purchase in Paul's churchyard see above, 494 n. 23.

[51] Above, 459. Strand Inn was one of the inns of chancery, where students went to learn by rote the writs in the *Natura Brevium*.

[52] *Parsons v. Johnson* (1492) CP 40/919, m. 134d ('sexaginta libros de novis tenuris et sexaginta libros vocatos Le Fox'; pleads Not guilty). Hugh Parsons was an attorney of the Common Pleas.

[53] Plomer, 'Two Lawsuits', 130–1. A related piece of evidence, unknown to Plomer, is *Boweryng and Seyntgerman v. Pynson* (1506) CP 40/978, m. 617 (action of debt for £40).

[54] G. Owen, *The Description of Pembrokeshire* [1603], ed. H. Owen (1892), i. 237.

[55] See his remarks in *Brett v. Rigden* (1568) CUL MS. Gg.2.5, fo. 98; Bodl. Lib. MS. Rawlinson C.112, pp. 370 (tr. 'he utterly denied the case in *Natura Brevium* which one Owen of the Middle Temple has put in [as an] addition') and 371–2 (tr. 'he also denied the case put by Owen of the Middle Temple in the additions of *Natura Brevium*'). Pynson's edition (Beale, *Bibliography*, 120, no. T.82) was said to have been edited by a learned lawyer ('emendata castigataque a viro in legum multum solerti studio'). Redman's (ibid., no. T.87) claimed to be 'cum additionibus novis'.

LAW BOOKS IN MANUSCRIPT AND PRINT

First and foremost among the contents of a learned lawyer's library were the year books and other law reports. Not that anyone had a complete set—the very concept is meaningless in an age of manuscript texts—but a judge, serjeant, or apprentice needed access to a full range of case-law. In order to know what information was to be found in this ever-growing chronological series, lawyers used 'abridgments': that is, digests of case-law under alphabetical titles.[56] These are not found until the time of Henry VI, but become quite common in the 1460s.[57] A typical abridgment of that period was printed at Rouen in about 1490, without title; it has been known since the 1490s as *Statham*, after a bencher of Lincoln's Inn who is supposed to have compiled it in the 1460s.[58] Two much larger ('graunde') abridgments were compiled in the early Tudor period. The first, by Anthony Fitzherbert, was prepared for the press by the compiler—perhaps beginning the work in the reign of Henry VII—and printed in 1514–17.[59] The other, by Sir Robert Brooke (d. 1558), was apparently a private exercise and did not appear in print till 1573. These rapidly became the first recourse of a lawyer embarking on a particular piece of research into case-law. Until well after our period, however, lawyers continued to make their own alphabetical commonplaces of material in the year books.[60]

A medieval Civil lawyer looking at the common law would have been struck by the virtual absence of treatises or monographs. The most erudite of the common lawyers owned or knew about the Latin treatises called *Glanvill* and *Bracton*, but those ancient books were of little practical use and copies had ceased to be made long before they were first printed: *Glanvill* in about 1555, *Bracton* in 1569.[61] No one would attempt another comprehensive survey of the common law until long after our period. The only current legal treatise of any significance in the fifteenth century was Littleton—Sir Thomas Littleton's *New Tenures* (*c*.1460)—first printed in 1481, the year of the author's death. It soon superseded the much shorter *Old Tenures* (*c*.1380), manuscripts of which ceased to be produced in the fifteenth century, though the older work was given a brief extension of life by the printing press. Littleton had achieved a biblical authority in the profession,[62] and was an

---

[56] See also P. Winfield, 'Abridgments of the Year Books' (1923) 37 *Harvard Law Rev.* 214–44.

[57] 94 Selden Soc. *172–3*; *CELMC*, pp. xl–xli, 418; Baker, 'The Books of the Common Law', 418.

[58] The book has no title, but it was cited in the 1490s as 'abbr[igemen]tes Staham': BL MS. Add. 14030, fo. 11. Port (a student in the 1490s) cited it as 'S'.

[59] Fitz. Abr. contained 13,845 entries. For its importance see Boersma, *An Introduction to Fitzherbert's Abridgement*. See also below, 502–3.   [60] For original reports in this form see above, 480–2.

[61] Above, 23–4.

[62] See *Wimbish* v. *Tailbois* (1550) Plowd. 38v at 58, *per* Mountagu CJ (tr. 'the first edition of Littleton's book, in which the recent additions are omitted, is the true and most sure register of the fundamentals and principles of our law'); 94 Selden Soc. *161* n. 7.

enormous success in the history of printing. There were more than sixty editions in the sixteenth century alone. But it was very much a student primer. It stated the axioms of land law, with few doubts and few citations. A lawsuit of 1534 between two Berkshire attorneys, concerning the possession of a mattress, some bedding, 'et unum librum vocatum Lytylton tenures',[63] tellingly reveals the pride of place which this little book enjoyed among the most basic requirements for a law student or attorney going to London.

Almost as successful in the sixteenth century was *Doctor and Student* (1528–30), written by Christopher St German (d. 1540). This was not a law book in the usual sense, though its elementary discussions of selected legal topics made it useful for the student. It was probably not aimed at lawyers at all, but was part of St German's intellectual campaign—supported by the government—to justify the separation of canon law in England from papal authority by showing that the common law had a parallel and equal relationship with conscience and divine law.[64] A third popular work was John Perkins's *Profitable Book* (1528).[65] This was a kind of supplement to Littleton, dealing chiefly with points of conveyancing which were not to be found in the *Tenures*, and it therefore lacked the coherence or elegance of Littleton's great work. It nevertheless had a thoughtful jurispru-dential preface, was clearly written, and was considered authoritative. Like Littleton, Perkins did not think it needful to provide legal citations. His was the last generation of authors to present common learning in that form,[66] without referring to specific authorities.

The abridgments, though intellectually inferior to treatises, contributed to the evolution of legal literature by making it easier for readers in the inns of court and writers of treatises to find and expound the relevant case-law. William Staunford, reader of Gray's Inn, recognized this in 1548 when he expressed the hope that the availability of Fitzherbert would facilitate the compilation of treatises on the subject-matter of the various titles:[67]

I would wish that amongst such plenty of learned men as be at this day something were devised to help the students of their long journey... Which thing might well come to pass, after my poor mind, if such titles as be in the great abridgment of Justice Fitzherbert were

---

[63] *John Knyght* (of the Middle Temple) v. *Edmund Grey* (of Gray's Inn) (1534) CP 40 /1083, m. 798.

[64] J. H. Baker, introduction to *Doctor and Student* (reprint of 1787 edn, 1988); above, 42.

[65] First published as *Perutilis Tractatus Magistri Johannis Parkins Interioris Templi Socii* (1528), though the text is French. BL MS. Hargrave 244 seems to be more or less coeval. After three further editions in French, an English translation appeared in 1555 as *A Verie Profitable Booke treating of the Lawes of this Realme*. The English versions are divided into 11 chapters and 845 numbered sections.

[66] Similarly St German and Rastell did not provide citations for common-law propositions. There are very few citations of authority in Fitzherbert's *Natura Brevium* (1538).

[67] An *Exposition of the Kinges Prerogative, collected out of the great Abridgement of Justice Fitzherbert* (1567), sig. A4 (preface dated 1548, addressed to Nicholas Bacon, A.-G. of the Wards; sp. mod.).

by the judges or some other learned men laboured and studied, that is to say, every title by itself by special divisions digested, or ordered and disposed, in such sort that all the judicial acts and cases in the same might be brought and appear under certain principles, rules, and grounds, of the said laws... which now as things scattered abroad and out of order be hidden within the... title.

Staunford himself led the way with his *Exposition of the King's Prerogative* (1548), not printed until 1567, and his *Plees del Coron*, printed the year before his death in 1557. No one else in this period, however, followed the same method. The nearest approach to orderly exposition of other branches of the law was to be found in the readings, which were not printed.[68] In truth, the content of Staunford's two printed books did not differ greatly in kind from that of manuscript readings on the prerogative and the criminal law; the chief difference lay in the citation of authorities, now rendered uniform by the existence of a great printed abridgment, and the omission of propositions which could not be matched with a printed authority.

Formularies were also needed in substantial quantity. The body of available forms of action had ceased to grow before 1400 and most lawyers made do with old manuscripts containing precedents of writs, the most recent being the most valuable: a Chancery clerk in the 1460s might pay as much as 41s. for one.[69] In the legal mind there was one notional 'register of writs'. In practice, the contents of the old manuscript books differed somewhat, and they had varying encrustations of notes and *regulae* emanating from the teaching of masters and clerks in Chancery up to the time of Edward IV. It seems that no further changes were made in our period, and once the *Registrum Omnium Brevium* was printed (in 1531) the fiction of a single common register at last became reality. There was no need for a continuing manuscript tradition, as there was with law reports, since there was nothing to update;[70] the only new writs were actions on the case, and the newer varieties of these were soon to be found in the books of entries. A commentary on the register was provided by the *Natura Brevium*, containing the most important writs with French commentary. The medieval (or *Vieux*) *Natura Brevium* was superseded in 1534 by Sir Anthony Fitzherbert's *Novel Natura Brevium*, which survived as the primer on the writ system until the nineteenth century.

Precedents of conveyancing and pleading were made by lawyers for their own use, the former sometimes by lowly practitioners, the latter chiefly by prothonotaries and clerks. Substantial books of entries were printed in 1510 (*Intrationum*

---

68 Above, 463–6. For a select bibliography of manuscript readings see below, 888–92.

69 *ELMUSA*, i. 33 ('Explicit registrum novum precium istius libri xli s. quod constat Baldewino Hyde clerico uni clericorum cancellarie domini regis Edwardi quarti'). Hyde was admitted to Lincoln's Inn in 1466.

70 A solitary exception is Rowland Shakelady's unpublished collection of writs on the case: above, 324.

Excellentissimus Liber), 1546 (*Intrationum Liber*, a different anonymous compilation), and 1566 (William Rastell's *Colleccion of Entrees*), and these are matched by
some large manuscript compilations.[71] By contrast, the printed precedents of conveyancing from our period were archaic and slight in content. The *Carta Feodi
Simplicis*, first printed around 1505, was probably of fourteenth-century origin.
A New Boke of Presidentes (1543), with a preface by Thomas Phaer, was also—despite
the promising title—decidedly out of date.

Guides to the law and practice of inferior courts were less advanced than those
relating to the courts in Westminster Hall, and at the lowest level practice was
learned without the aid of books at all. But some local courts followed country-
wide usages, and there was a growing practical literature by the end of the fifteenth century. The oldest genre was that of manuals of procedure in manorial
courts, originally known as *La Court Baron* or *Curia Baronum*, which may have
been a textbook in the inns of chancery.[72] A late redaction of this kind of manual,
which has an ancestry stretching back to the thirteenth century, was printed by
Pynson around 1501 under the title *Modus Tenendi Curiam Baronis*.[73] It was
reprinted many times, and was joined by the *Modus Tenendi unum Hundredum*
(1521?), the *Modus Observandi Curiam cum Leta* (1525?),[74] the *Diversite de Courtz*
(1526), and *The Office of Sheryffes* (1538?).

Justices of the peace were rather better served, since the active justices were inns of
court lawyers and questions arising at quarter sessions could be discussed centrally.[75]
The first coherent treatment of the authority of county magistrates is found in
lecture-form, most notably in Thomas Marow's widely circulated reading of
1503 in the Inner Temple.[76] But there were also fifteenth-century collections of
precedents for clerks of the peace, including indictments, warrants, and other
instruments. One of these, from Suffolk in the 1490s, enjoyed a circulation in
manuscript; it included 'La forme doffice dun clerk de peas', a practical guide to
sessions procedure of a type not represented in print until the 1660s.[77] In 1505 or
thereabouts Richard Pynson printed a simplified version of one of these collections as *The Boke of Justices of Peas*. In 1538, a much larger and far superior work,
The New Boke of Justices of the Peas by Sir Anthony Fitzherbert, was printed by
Robert Redman. This was a translation, with some variations, of *Loffice et
Auctoryte des Justyces de Peas*, printed earlier the same year.[78] These two 'books
of justices' are hailed as the first printed treatises on English criminal law, and

---

[71] See above, 345–6.   [72] See above, 457.   [73] See above, 315.   [74] See above, 315 n. 214.
[75] See below, 528–9. For the law relating to JPs see above, 265.
[76] The only printed edition is by Putnam, *Early Treatises on the Practice of Justices of the Peace*,
286–414. There is no translation.   [77] Above, 274.
[78] For the differences between the two versions, see the introduction by P. R. Glazebrook to the 1972
reprint by Professional Books Ltd of the *Newe Boke*. Fitzherbert died in May 1538.

Fitzherbert's 'new' book remained in use (in revised editions) until it was over-taken by Dalton and Coke in the seventeenth century. Nevertheless, their treatment of substantive criminal law was less thorough than that found in the manuscript readings and in Staunford's *Plees del Coron* (1557).[79]

STATUTE BOOKS[80]

Statutes have a somewhat different bibliographical history from law books produced within the closed world of the inns of court and chancery. Here there are more signs of an organized manuscript trade in the fifteenth century, especially in the series of illuminated books of *Statuta Nova*—the acts of Parliament from 1 Edward III to the middle or second half of the fifteenth century. A beautifully executed group from the third quarter of the century is particularly notable.[81] The volumes frequently have coats of arms painted in on the first page, apparently for the original purchaser,[82] and many of these arms can now be identified as belonging to prominent lawyers,[83] painted around the time they became benchers of their inns.[84] Serjeant Kebell's 'great boke of lawe wreten in velom and covered with blak velvet', with latten clasps, valued at ten marks, was probably of the same type.[85] But these were hardly working copies—Kebell's, if we have correctly identified it, was kept at his country home rather than in chambers. They may be considered rather as status symbols, and were doubtless marketed as such.

The printing press here displaced manuscript production entirely in the 1480s.[86] No manuscript statute-books were made after 1500. The printed texts were readily available, were much more reliable, and there was no scope for

---

[79] See above, 502–3.   [80] For legislation as a source of law, see above, 34–9, 76–82.

[81] K. L. Scott, 'Additions to the Oeuvre of the English Border Artist: the *Nova statuta*' in *The Mirrour of the Worlde* (1980), 45–60, 66–8. Few of the arms had then been identified.

[82] LI MS. Hale 183 has the escutcheons left blank for this purpose.

[83] BL Cotton MS. Nero C.1 (arms of William Calow, JCP, d. 1487); LI MS. Hale 71 (arms of Gregory Adgore, serjeant at law, d. 1504); Yale Law School MS. G. St.11.1 (arms of Richard Elyot, JCP, d. 1522: *ELMUSA*, i. 73–4); Philadelphia Free Library MS. LC 14 9.5 (paternal arms of Robert and Thomas Molyneux, both of Gray's Inn: *ELMUSA*, i. 59–60); BL MS. Lansdowne 522 (arms—painted in reverse—of Elryngton of Hackney: probably for John Elryngton, officer of the Common Pleas; above, 127, 137); Bodl. Lib. MS. Hatton 10 (arms of Thomas Pygot, serjeant at law, d. 1520); Dyson Perrins sale, Sotheby, 9 Dec. 1958, lot 21 (arms of Sir Thomas Fitzwilliam, d. 1497).

[84] Adgore, Kebell, Pygot, and Fitzwilliam were benchers of the Inner Temple in the 1480s and 1490s; Calow and Elyot were benchers of the Middle Temple; Molyneux of Gray's Inn. Five of them became serjeants.

[85] Cf. Ives, *Common Lawyers*, 445, where *Bracton* is suggested; but the book apparently began with c. 1 of a French statute.

[86] For the printing history see G. R. Elton, 'The Sessional Printing of Statutes, 1484–1547' in *Wealth and Power in Tudor England*, ed. E. W. Ives (1978), 68–86; Pantzer, 'Printing the English Statutes, 1484–1640', 69–114.

private versions (as in the case of the other sources). Moreover, they were in English. Machlinia printed the statutes of Richard III in French, but thereafter—according to Rastell, at Henry VII's personal suggestion—English was used.[87] Of course, there were those who still revered the old manuscript texts, and we learn of two members of Clement's Inn who in around 1508 exchanged a new printed collection of statutes for a fourteenth-century manuscript.[88] However, as far as current production was concerned, all statutes would now be printed.

If statutes are an exception to the general characterization of law books offered above, it is as well to remember that statutes circulated widely outside the legal profession, especially once they were promulgated in the vernacular, and that, even if a common lawyer of our period would have regarded them as only a subsidiary source of law, they were texts which no lawyer could afford to be without. It is noteworthy that the books left by Mr Justice Townshend (d. 1493) included eleven volumes of statutes (some old, some more recent, and two printed) but only four or five year books.[89]

IMPACT OF THE PRINTING PRESS ON THE LAW

The introduction of printed law books certainly had an impact on the law, though it was not wholly beneficial. The most positive consequence of printing, no doubt, was the introduction of a single authoritative and carefully printed text of the current statutes. This, however, was offset by a more literal approach to the interpretation of legislation which now left little room for textual manipulation.[90] In the context of case-law, it made possible specific folio-citations to reported cases, a practice which became commonplace during the sixteenth century, and thereby perhaps increased reliance on individual reported precedents.[91] It is a matter of taste whether the addiction to citations, which has beset the English lawyer ever since, represents an improvement in legal technique; but at least the profession now had common access to what was being cited. The most negative effects of the existence of law printing, and more particularly of Tottell's monopoly, were that it served over time—more or less unconsciously—to reduce the canon of known or

[87] Above, 26. For the retrospective translation of the older statutes by George Ferrers (d. 1579) see H. J. Graham, ' "Our Tong Maternall Marvellously Amendyd and Augmentyd": the first Englishing and printing of the medieval statutes at large, 1530-8' (1965) 13 *UCLA Law Rev.* 58–98.

[88] MS. sold at Sotheby's, 10 Dec. 1996 (lot 54), at fo. 12v ('Liber Johannis Lambart senioris...de Clementis In London. sibi perquisitus de Roberto Hilton...in escambio pro alio libro statutorum impresso'). Hilton was also a member of Clement's Inn: CP 40/1050, m. 622.

[89] C. E. Moreton, 'The "Library" of a Late-Fifteenth Century Lawyer' (1991) 13 *The Library* (6th ser.) 338–46.   [90] 109 Selden Soc., pp. lix–lxi; above, 77.

[91] Above, 488–9.

citable authorities, and to discourage recourse to manuscripts which might have corrected errors in the vulgate text.[92]

The profession soon forgot how year-book printing had begun. From the beginning in the 1480s, and throughout our period, reports were usually printed in pamphlets containing one year each. No doubt these printed pamphlets were originally intended merely to supplement those available in manuscript; indeed, in some early books we find the printed and manuscript years bound up together. But the printers had started by choosing rare texts from previous generations rather than current material, because there was a greater demand for such rarities than for currently circulating material. The closest they ever came to printing recent cases was the unusual edition of 12–14 Henry VIII, printed about ten years after the event, though even this seems not to have been prepared for the press by the reporter.[93] This publishing policy had the odd consequence that texts which were originally rare or unique became the vulgate reports, while the reports which had been the standard text in manuscript were never printed and passed out of use. Here the tyranny of the printing press had a harmful effect on legal literature, and has even damaged modern historical scholarship. We should not be too hard on the printers themselves, who presumably relied on professional advice both in selecting texts for publication and in editing and proof-reading them. Moreover, the profession seems generally to have acquiesced in the prevailing balance between print and manuscript. Recent material may have been difficult to obtain, if reporters preferred to keep their notes to themselves, though Tottell did eventually make some attempt to fill the post-1535 gap with the important volumes by Plowden (1571) and Dyer (1585/6), the contents of which stretched back to the 1530s. Nevertheless, an arbitrary and partly accidental printed canon of legal literature placed unintended limitations on the range of legal source-material. The most drastic narrowing of the canon resulted from the complete omission of readings. It was no doubt commendable to encourage students to attend lectures themselves, or at least copy texts by hand. But the failure to print readings helped to exclude doctrinal literature completely from the later common-law mind. For better or worse, the common law of the future was to be case-law, and printed case-law at that.

[92] See also above, 29–30, 499.
[93] *Year Books of Henry VIII: 12–14 Henry VIII*, ed. J. H. Baker (119 Selden Soc.; 2002).

Part VI

CRIMINAL LAW AND PROCEDURE

28

Criminal Procedure

A CHIEF justice addressing new serjeants at law in the reign of Henry VIII said they would be consulted in 'two sorts or kinds of causes' represented by the two sides of their parti-coloured robes: blue for the *causae pecuniariae*, the civil cases, and murrey for the *causae sanguinis*. The implication was that 'matters of blood' were of equal importance with pecuniary business, though in reality serjeants were more likely to be engaged in the former as judges than as counsel. The title *Corone* in Fitzherbert's abridgment is sufficiently lengthy to demonstrate that concern with criminal law was of long standing, though the case-law had declined since the demise of the general eyre in the 1330s. But the law reports, and also the readings in the inns of court, suggest that interest was growing during the early Tudor period. Since the punishment for murder and felony was death, miscarriages of justice were regarded with particular horror.[1] And justice ought to be mediated by reason.

Some contemporaries, it is true, regarded the severity of the English legal system as inherently barbarous.[2] Starkey complained that thieves who stole 'for necessity' were 'hanged without mercy or pity'.[3] Yet it is difficult to believe that the system worked routinely in that way, and such glimpses as we can achieve through the law reports suggest otherwise.[4] The better view was that the necessity of hunger was a defence to larceny,[5] though the matter was rarely of serious importance because taking a small item of food would only be petty larceny and therefore not capital. Moreover, poaching wild animals was not a felony at common law,[6] and Parliament was only just beginning to create exceptions.[7] Hanging a man for any kind of theft seems harsh to modern eyes, and it was the main complaint of those contemporaries who attacked the law for severity.[8] They understated, however, the extent to which

---

[1] See *R. v. Anon.* (1538) Spelman 60, pl. 40. [2] 94 Selden Soc. 299 n. 5.

[3] Starkey, *Dialogue*, ed. Mayer, 80 (sp. mod.). Cf. T. More, *Utopia* [1516], sig. b4, c3.

[4] See e.g. *R. v. Barbour* (1490) 1 Caryll 22 (tr. 'because the value of the goods was but twelve pence, Fairfax J. had pity on him', and found a technical excuse for discharging him). [5] Below, 566.

[6] Below, 568.

[7] e.g. 11 Hen. VII, c. 17 (taking pheasants and partridges); 14 & 15 Hen. VIII, c. 10 (tracking hares in snow); 25 Hen. VIII, c. 11 (wildfowling). For 32 Hen. VIII, c. 11, see below, 569.

[8] e.g. Starkey had no objection to the death penalty for robbery or homicide: *Dialogue*, ed. Mayer, 80, 131. When the hangman of London was himself hanged for robbery in 1538, a crowd of 2,000 came to watch: *Hall's Chronicle*, 826.

benefit of clergy, pardons, sanctuary, abjuration, and the jury system itself, saved lesser felons from the gallows. The *peine forte et dure* for those who refused trial was certainly barbarous, and judges strove to see that it was not lightly imposed.[9] Yet the absence of a law of pre-trial investigative torture,[10] which was routine in northern Europe, the insistence on due process, and the double safeguards of the grand and petty juries, ensured that—as Fortescue had put it[11]—the common law was free from that cruelty and inhumanity which disfigured continental legal systems. The worst severities in early Tudor England were those introduced by Henry VIII and Parliament,[12] who were firm believers in the value of fearsome deterrents. The sanguinary legislation of Henry VIII shocked lawyers of the time,[13] and yet it was a Henrician legislature which took the admiralty criminal jurisdiction from the civilians, thereby ending the last possibility of lawful torture in England.[14]

A harsh penal system punishes heavily and indiscriminately, making no allowance for human weaknesses or the variety of circumstances. The ordinary criminal law of the early Tudor period was not of that kind. If anything, in the absence of a power of discretionary sentencing,[15] it tended to permit the indiscriminate discharge of the guilty. Given the immutable premise that felony attracted the death penalty, it was equally axiomatic that 'life is greatly favoured and preferred in law',[16] and a Henrician judge could direct a jury, 'If you be in doubt, lean rather to life than to death'.[17]

APPEALS OF FELONY

Persons suspected of murder and felony could be arraigned either upon an appeal, brought by an individual appellor, or upon an indictment found by a grand jury or—in the case of homicide—by a coroner's jury.[18] Since appeals of

[9] See e.g. *Marsshe* v. *Archer* (1492) 1 Caryll 111 at 112, *per* Fairfax J. (likening it to suicide); *R.* v. *Anon.* (1506) 2 Caryll 469, pl. 330, *per* Frowyk CJ.

[10] Torture was sometimes used *de facto* in matters of state: Elton, *Policy and Police*, 145 n. 4, 165, 384; *Lisle Letters*, ed. Byrne, ii. 88, no. 150 (investigation into escape from the Tower, 1534); Bernard, 'The Tyranny of Henry VIII', 113–29, at 129 n. 64. But it had no legal sanction.

[11] *De Laudibus Legum Anglie* [*c.*1470], ed. S. B. Chrimes (1942), 64–5.

[12] e.g. 22 Hen. VIII, c. 9 (boiling to death); 33 Hen. VIII, c. 12 (striking off the hand).

[13] See the reference to 'Draco's laws', below, 587.

[14] 27 Hen. VIII, c. 4, which mentions torture in the preamble. It is probable, however, that convictions were easier to obtain from a jury: above, 212.

[15] We see, however, the antecedents of transportation in the occasional commutation of the death sentence to galley service: e.g. *APC*, ii. 556 (1548); and see *CLT*, 334.

[16] Porter's notebook, HLS MS. 47, fo. 39 (tr.), from a moot in Gray's Inn (*c.*1520).

[17] *R.* v. *Benger* (1540) noted in Elton, *Policy and Police*, 319–20, *per* Browne J. (He did, however, offer his own view that there was no doubt.)

[18] For a possible exception see 3 Hen. VII, c. 14 (conspiracy by member of king's household).

treason were practically defunct, treason cases could only be prosecuted upon an indictment found by a grand jury.[19]

The appeal procedure differed from that used for Crown prosecutions in that proceedings were entered on the plea side of the King's Bench,[20] counsel were allowed,[21] and trial was at nisi prius, as in civil cases. It had long been overtaken numerically by trial upon indictment; but appeals were still in regular use at the beginning of the Tudor period,[22] and there were twenty-eight pending in the King's Bench in 1500.[23] They were still fairly common in the 1550s, when Staunford's treatise on Crown law devoted almost twice as much space to them as to indictments,[24] though their frequency had more than halved since 1500.[25] Most appeals throughout the period were for murder[26] or robbery, but there were also appeals of mayhem and (very rarely) of rape. Until 1529 the appeal of robbery had the advantage that it enabled the owner of stolen goods to obtain restitution.[27] The appeal of mayhem was brought for damages, which could be augmented by the court on its own sight of the wound.[28] Appeals of death—the largest category—were usually brought by widows, ostensibly for revenge, but they hardly ever resulted in verdict or judgment. Evidently their prime purpose, in most cases,[29] was not to secure a conviction but to obtain a settlement in return for compensation.[30] If there was no widow, the appeal could be brought by the victim's heir.[31]

[19] Persons accused of treason were sometimes attainted by act of Parliament without trial; but this was an act of sovereign power rather than of judicature.

[20] i.e. they were not Crown Office business. They could also be commenced at a gaol delivery, or before the sheriff and coroners: 3 Hen. VII, c. 1.

[21] In *Sir Henry Owen's Case* (1516) 2 Caryll 662, the defendant was offered counsel but declined.

[22] Some 398 appeals were entered in the King's Bench rolls between 1485 and 1495: C. Whittick, 'The Role of the Criminal Appeal in the Fifteenth Century' in *Law and Social Change in British History*, ed. J. A. Guy and H. G. Beale (1984), 55–72, at 55.

[23] IND 1/1327, mm. 6d–8d (eighteen for death, seven for robbery, three for mayhem).

[24] Staunford, *Les Plees del Coron*, ff. 58v–83v (then indictments, ff. 83v–98). The more summary *Diversite de Courtz* (1533), sig. Bii–Bvi, devotes ten pages to appeals.

[25] In 1550 there were only four appeals pending in the King's Bench, but in 1551 there were thirteen (ten of them for death): IND 1/1337, mm. 13–22.

[26] When murder by poisoning was made treason by statute, it was held that an appeal did not lie: *Saccomb v. Saccomb* (1541) Dyer 50a; KB 27/1121, m. 117 (nonsuit after demurrer).

[27] In 1529 the remedy was extended to prosecutions on indictment: 21 Hen. VIII, c. 11. Prior to the statute, the goods would have been forfeited to the Crown in case of conviction on indictment.

[28] See above, 380.

[29] Cf. *Salmon v. Mando* (1532) Spelman 155, where the purpose was to obtain a speedier conviction. In *Ley v. Froston* (1534) Spelman 56 the defendant was found guilty in self-defence.

[30] Whittick, 'The Role of the Criminal Appeal', 63. Dyer says that *Abyngton v. Oldcastell* (1553) Dyer 88b; KB 27/1167, m. 88; was settled when the appellor remarried pending the appeal.

[31] This sometimes raised points of law: *Anon.* (1494) 1 Caryll 265; Mich. 9 Hen. VII, fo. 5, pl. 1 (heir dies after commencement); *Bell v. Crakenthorpe* (1551–3) KB 27/1158, m. 160; Dyer 69a; BL MS. Hargrave 4, fo. 120 (appeal by brother; pleads an elder brother living; reply that he has died; nonsuit after demurrer); *Jorden v. Jakes* (1554) KB 27/1169, m. 96 (appeal by son; pleads an elder son living; demurrer). A husband had no appeal for his wife's death: Mountford's reading, CUL MS. Ee.5.19, fo. 115.

In later periods, the principal use of the appeal was to initiate a prosecution where a grand jury would not approve an indictment; but in the early Tudor period it was common for an appeal to be accompanied by a parallel prosecution on indictment. This had the advantage to the prosecutor that it ousted battle, and also served to demonstrate that the appeal was not malicious. The appeal took priority, and the judges decided in 1482 that arraignment on an indictment for homicide should in all cases be delayed for a year and a day 'so that the party's suit may be saved'.[32] This rule was reversed by statute in 1487, on the grounds that 'the party is oftentimes slow, and also agreed with, and by the end of the year all is forgotten, which is another occasion of murder'.[33] Nevertheless, if an appeal had been commenced it was still given priority,[34] and in practice arraignment 'at the king's suit' often followed the formal discontinuance of an appeal by nonsuit.[35] In such cases the defendant was arraigned at the king's suit upon the declaration in the appeal rather than upon the indictment.[36] The statute of 1487 may have diminished the bargaining power of the widow or heir,[37] though an acquittal on indictment did not free the defendant from the possibility of conviction upon a subsequent appeal.[38] The principal deterrent to potential appellors was no doubt the risk of having to pay heavy damages on acquittal if the appeal was found to have been malicious.[39]

PUBLIC PROSECUTION

In the minority of cases prosecuted by appeal, the source of prosecutorial energy was obviously the appellor. In other cases the record indicates an accusation by grand jurors, 'who make presentment for our lord the king', or by the verdict of a coroner's inquest;[40] but this was form rather than reality. It is very unlikely that the presenting jury any longer made much, if any, use of its own knowledge, since its

---

[32] Mich. 22 Edw. IV, Fitz. Abr., *Corone*, pl. 44 (tr.).   [33] 3 Hen. VII, c. 1.

[34] An appeal could be commenced when the defendant was arraigned upon indictment: *Owen* v. *Feld* (1508) 2 Caryll 585.

[35] It also followed a demurrer decided in favour of the appellee: *Anon.* (1556) Chr. Yelverton's reports, fo. 240v.   [36] Port 42; Spelman 63, 64.

[37] See also D. R. Ernst, 'The Moribund Appeal of Death: compensating survivors and controlling jurors in early modern England' (1984) 28 *AJLH* 164–88, esp. at 175.

[38] This was noted in *Lownde* v. *Orrell* (1534) Spelman 51 as the only form of double jeopardy permitted by the law. See also *Ley* v. *Froston* (1534) ibid. 56; *Anon.* (1537) ibid. 60, pl. 39.

[39] See *Fissher* v. *Ketford* (1496) KB 27/941, m. 30 (20 marks for false appeal of murder); *Rede* v. *Rochforth and Swynborne* (1555–7) Dyer 120a, 131b; Dalison's reports, BL MS. Harley 5141, ff. 43v–44; KB 27/1164, m. 159; KB 27/1182, m. 120 (£120 damages recovered against an abettor of the appeal).

[40] For coroners' inquests see R. F. Hunnisett, *Calendar of Nottinghamshire Coroners' Inquests 1485–1558* (25 Thoroton Soc. Record Series; 1969); *Sussex Coroners' Inquests 1485–1558* (74 Sussex Record Soc.; 1985). For the grand jury see above, 258, 275. For the form of indictments see below, 523–4.

function was to approve or reject bills of indictment laid before them, in the light of the supporting evidence.[41] Someone else had to coordinate the prosecution, either independently or on behalf of a victim or complainant. In cases of treason and other matters of public importance, the king's Council oversaw investigations, which it might delegate to an individual judge or justice of the peace.[42] Moreover, the king's chief minister—at any rate Thomas Cromwell, whose correspondence alone survives in any quantity—kept in close touch with the assize judges and county magistrates concerning the arrangements for important trials.[43] However, there was no way in which the central authorities could supervise all the criminal prosecutions throughout the country. Bills of indictment might, like appeals, emanate from individual complainants with some legal or clerical assistance.[44] But a general oversight of capital cases was becoming the responsibility of the justices of the peace, assisted by town and parish constables. We have already noticed that the investigatory role of the justices seems to have been a novelty in the later fifteenth century,[45] and that the police powers of individual justices were largely limited to matters within their personal knowledge. In the first half of the sixteenth century the pre-trial functions of the magistrates were regularized into a routine,[46] and it became prudent practice for them to take down statements of witnesses in the form of depositions, to prompt their memory at the trial. Though it is impossible to discover how widespread this practice was, for want of records, it was evidently used in ordinary cases—as well as state prosecutions[47]—in the time of Henry VIII.[48] The legislation of the 1480s which enabled bail to be granted by justices out of court[49] led to complaints of laxity and eventually to a statute of 1555 which linked bail with the taking of depositions.[50] The statute confirmed that bail should not be granted by a single justice, or two

[41] See J. Bellamy, *The Criminal Trial in Later Medieval England* (1998), 23–6; above, 258.

[42] Above, 202; 102 Selden Soc., p. xviii n. 57.

[43] 102 Selden Soc., pp. xviii, liii–lvi; Zell, 'Early Tudor Justices of the Peace at Work', at 133–4.

[44] In an action for slander by a parish constable, one of the allegations complained of was that he had conveyed away a woman who was robbed so that she could not put in a 'bill' against the suspect: *Nycolle* v. *Kyllowe* (1558) CP 40/1174, m. 715.   [45] Above, 270.

[46] Langbein, *Prosecuting Crime in the Renaissance*, part 1. Langbein compares the legislation of 1555 with the German provisions of the Constitutio Criminalis Carolina (1532) and concludes that the English development was independent.

[47] Depositions were used in *R.* v. *Duke of Buckingham* (1521) reported in *Hall's Chronicle*, 623; *R.* v. *Rice ap Griffith* (1531) Spelman 47 at 48. The Privy Council considered a 'book' of evidence compiled against Lord Leonard Grey in 1540: above, 203 n. 95.

[48] e.g. Langbein, *Prosecuting Crime*, 91, 98–103 (Norwich, 1519: murder), and 87 (Leicester, 1532–4: seditious words).

[49] 1 Ric. III, c. 3, gave power to a single justice, but this was altered to two by 3 Hen. VII, c. 3. See Yorke 112, no. 69.

[50] 1 & 2 Phil. & Mar., c. 13. The session began in 1554 but the statute was not passed until January 1555, after extensive discussion in the Commons: Langbein, *Prosecuting Crime*, 57–9; Loach, *Parliament and the Crown in the Reign of Mary Tudor*, 125–6.

acting at different times, but only by two acting together, and then not before they (or one of them) had taken 'the examination of the prisoner, and information of them that bring him,[51] of the fact and circumstances thereof'; and it further required that so much as was material to prove the crime was to be put in writing and certified to the next gaol delivery.[52] The informants could be bound over to attend the trial, and for this reason their recognizances were likewise to be certified to the gaol delivery. By a statute passed later in 1555, similar depositions and recognizances were to be taken where a prisoner was committed for trial without bail.[53] These statutes were in formal terms the foundation of the preliminary hearing before magistrates, but they codified and made routine a procedure which had already begun informally.

TRIAL ON INDICTMENT

Most trials for murder and felony were initiated by indictment and were held at assizes and quarter sessions or—in London—at Newgate.[54] As with civil trials, information about the courtroom proceedings is very sparse, and for criminal cases in the country there is a dearth of formal records as well. What little we know of Tudor criminal trials is mostly derived from reports of state trials for treason, which were obviously untypical, the prosecution evidence being presented by the law officers of the Crown with a view to public consumption, and the journalistic reports were often slanted and unreliable. In most criminal cases there were no counsel on either side, no reporters, and seemingly little interest on the part of the legal profession.

The procedure at an ordinary criminal trial is outlined towards the end of our period in a brief clerical manual with the title 'The Manner of Entering the Gaol Delivery' (*Modus intrandi Deliberationem Gaole*), which dates from around 1550.[55] There is no reason to suppose that any of it was new, and most of it remained the same long afterwards; but, given the paucity of earlier evidence, it is worth noting the details which come into view at this time.[56] The accused persons who had been indicted by the grand jury were brought to the bar, bareheaded,[57] and

---

[51] Langbein suggests that this would normally be the constable, accompanied by complainants or witnesses: *Prosecuting Crime*, 11-12.

[52] This could be taken to mean that evidence helpful to the defence was to be omitted: Holdsworth, *HEL*, iv. 529. [53] 2 & 3 Phil. & Mar., c. 10.

[54] For the principal courts of criminal jurisdiction see above, 257, 263, 266, 285.

[55] Bodl. Lib. MS. è Mus. 57, ff. 88–89 (quoted here in sp. mod.). It gives a specimen commission in the name of King Edward VI. [56] For jury trial in general see also above, ch. 19.

[57] Mountagu CJ once ordered a prisoner at Norwich assizes to remove his hat, because by the law of the land he was to come to trial bareheaded, ungirt, and barefooted: Wm Yelv. 357, no. 94.

arraigned in the following manner:

'John Dale, hold up thy hand. Thou art indicted by the name of... for that thou...' (and so rehearse the indictment[58]). 'What sayest thou to this felony, guilty or not guilty?' If he say 'Not guilty': 'How wilt thou be tried?' If he put himself upon the country:[59] 'Po. se.'[60]

The prisoner was at this time entitled to have any irons or shackles removed, since he was to be free from any appearance of duress at his trial.[61] The clerk then turned to the panel of jurors in waiting and asked them to answer their names as they were called. The prisoner was also warned, 'Take heed to thy challenge, for this inquest shall pass upon thee'. At common law the defendant was at this point entitled to make up to thirty-five challenges without cause,[62] though the number was reduced in 1530 to twenty.[63] The Crown could challenge jurors, but apparently only for lack of qualification.[64] Each unchallenged juror was individually sworn:

You shall truly enquire and true <presentment and>[65] deliverance make betwixt our sovereign lord the king and John Dale, prisoner at the bar, of all such things, points and articles touching him whereof he is indicted <and nothing conceal>. So help you God, etc.

When all twelve had been sworn, the prisoner was again asked to hold up his hand (for identification), and the 'inquest of deliverance',[66] or trial jury, was charged:[67]

Sirs, the prisoner at the bar before this was indicted... (as is contained in the indictment), upon which [felony][68] he hath been arraigned and hath pleaded Not guilty, and hath put him upon the country, which be you. Your charge therefore is to enquire if he be guilty of this felony or not guilty. If ye find him guilty, ye shall enquire what goods and chattels, lands, or tenements, he had at the time of this felony done or at any time since. And if ye

---

[58] i.e. summarizing it in English.

[59] The proper response was, 'By God and the country': R. v. Throckmorton (1554) 1 St. Tr. 871.

[60] This abbreviation for *ponit se* was what the clerk wrote upon the indictment, and presumably he said it out loud.   [61] Sta. P.C. 78.

[62] This was decided in 1488: *Note* (1488) 1 Caryll 6; Hil. 3 Hen. VII, fo. 2, pl. 5; Mich. 3 Hen. VII, fo. 12, pl. 5; and see Mich. 14 Hen. VII, fo. 7, pl. 16 (same number in an appeal). A prisoner had been hanged in 1467 for challenging 37 jurors: Bodl. Lib. MS. Rawlinson C.703, fo. 22 (Maidstone assizes, Laken J.). Spelman said he could challenge 36, being three full panels. Yorke 127, no. 104.

[63] 22 Hen. VIII, c. 14; 32 Hen. VIII, c. 3; 33 Hen. VIII, c. 23; 1 & 2 Ph. & Mar., c. 10 (35 restored for treason trials); and see *Newman v. Punter* (1555) Moo. 12 (same number in an appeal). The defendant could not challenge for favour but only for insufficiency: Yorke 123, no. 90; 125, no. 97.

[64] Yorke 123, no. 90.

[65] So reads the Bodleian manuscript, but these words (and the 'nothing conceal') seem to have strayed in from the grand jury oath. For the classic oath, ending 'and a true verdict give according to your evidence', see *LPCL*, 285.

[66] Dyer uses this expression in 1555: 110 Selden Soc. 406, 407.

[67] In R. v. Throckmorton (1554) 1 St. Tr. 869 at 897, this charge was given to the jury at the end of the trial.

[68] Reads 'felonies, treasons, and heresies'.

find him not guilty, ye shall enquire whether he withdrew himself, and of his goods and chattels.

A proclamation was then made for anyone to come forward and give information against the prisoner, for 'the prisoner standeth upon his deliverance'.[69]

The evidence for the Crown was then presented. It was not yet settled that evidence should necessarily be *viva voce*, and so depositions could be read to the jury,[70] though it does seem to have been an accepted principle that testimony ought normally to be given in person in the presence of the accused.[71] A single witness was sufficient, even in cases of treason.[72] However, a few months after the duke of Somerset's trial in 1552, when his request for the witnesses against him to be brought face to face was refused,[73] Parliament enacted that in trials for treason and misprision of treason no one should be convicted unless two 'accusers' were brought in his presence to 'avow and maintain that that they have to say against the said party to prove him guilty'.[74] Since 'accusers' was not a term of art, and the statute did not speak of witnesses or evidence, the judges were thrown into some doubt as to what it meant. Serjeant Dyer and Saunders J. treated accusers as synonymous with witnesses, as in an earlier statute of 1547,[75] but Brooke CJ said it was agreed to be a term of the Civil law and meant something different from both witnesses and counsel.[76] In 1554 the judges emasculated the provision by holding that a hearsay witness who merely repeated what an accuser had told him could be the second 'accuser'.[77] This incidentally confirms that there was as yet no objection to hearsay evidence.[78] Another limitation was that the statute itself permitted the depositions of deceased accusers to count, and in treason cases there might be

[69] Cf. *R.* v. *Throckmorton* (1554) 1 St. Tr. 869 at 871, which is in virtually identical words.

[70] e.g. *R.* v. *Duke of Buckingham* (1521) reported in *Hall's Chronicle*, 623 (119 Selden Soc. 58); *R.* v. *Rice ap Griffith* (1531) Spelman 47, 48; *R.* v. *Benger* (1540) noted in Elton, *Policy and Police*, 319–20; *R.* v. *Duke of Somerset* (1551) 1 St. Tr. 515 at 520; *R.* v. *Throckmorton* (1554) 1 St. Tr. 869 at 873, 883; *Note* (1556) 109 Selden Soc. 16–19; and see *R.* v. *Hall* (1571) 110 Selden Soc. 242.

[71] *R.* v. *Benger* (1540) noted in Elton, *Policy and Police*, 319–20 (objection to unsworn written evidence); *R.* v. *Sherwin* (1555) 110 Selden Soc. 407 ('new evidence came; and the jury was caused to return to court in the prisoner's presence, so that he might hear it'). The statute of 1552 (below) provided that the accusers were to give evidence in the presence of the accused, though only 'if they be then living'.

[72] *R.* v. *Fisher* (1535) 1 St. Tr. 395 at 401. A fortnight later, More was condemned on the evidence of a single witness.

[73] *R.* v. *Duke of Somerset* (1 Dec. 1551) 1 St. Tr. 515 at 520. He was tried on the depositions alone.

[74] 5 & 6 Edw. VI, c. 11. It was not a wholly new idea: see L. M. Hill, 'The Two-Witness Rule in High Treason Trials: some comments on the emergence of procedural law' (1968) 12 *AJLH* 95–111.

[75] 1 Edw. VI, c. 12. This required an accusation by 'two sufficient and lawful witnesses', but said nothing about their having to be present at the trial.

[76] This was discussed by the assembled judges in 1556: Dyer's notebook, 109 Selden Soc. 16–17; Saunders' reports, ibid. 19; Brooke Abr., *Corone*, pl. 219 (tr. 109 Selden Soc. 18). Cf. Sta. P.C. 163v–164v.

[77] *R.* v. *Thomas* (1554) Dyer 99b, §68.

[78] In an action of conspiracy, a defendant could plead in justification that he had given evidence to the grand jury as to what someone else told him: *Anon.* (1528/9) Wm Yelv. 317, no. 12; *Walker* v. *Collyns*

incriminating confessions from men who had already been executed for their part in the same treason.[79] The legislation was partly repealed under Mary I.[80]

To return to the manual. As the individual prosecution witnesses came forward they were given their oath:[81]

The evidence of information that you shall give to this inquest against John Dale, prisoner at the bar, shall be truth and nothing but the truth, and the whole contents thereof. So help ye God etc.

The manual does not record what happened next, since it was not a matter of formal concern to the clerk, and does not even tell us whether the prisoner could call witnesses. Although defence witnesses were not unknown, by the middle of the sixteenth century there seems to have been a prevailing notion—perhaps influenced by the Civil law—that witnesses ought not to give evidence to contradict clear evidence for the Crown. This rule was applied in Sir Nicholas Throgmorton's case, although it was reported that the queen had personally instructed Morgan CJ that 'whatsoever could be brought in favour of the subject should be admitted to be heard'.[82] Four years later Dalison J. sought to justify to the queen his refusal to allow witnesses to prove an alibi in a robbery case at Lincoln assizes, arguing that it was a matter of judicial discretion.[83] The question was not settled until later in the century, and even then defence witnesses were unsworn.[84] On the other hand, the defendant was expected to give his version of events, and in that way could proffer what was in effect unsworn testimony.[85] He might even be interrogated as to the facts.[86] The conduct of the defence was probably a mixture of personal statement and confrontation with the witnesses, in the manner described in the 1560s by Sir Thomas Smith.[87] When the evidence had been given, the judge would summarize it for the jury and guide them as to the law.[88] Trials were over quickly, and each jury was usually charged to try several

and *Melley* v. *Stafford* (1534) CP 40/1081, mm. 444, 449; Pollard 252, no. 14; Yorke 216, no. 340. See also above, 363 (as to civil cases).

[79] e.g. *R.* v. *Throckmorton* (1554) 1 St. Tr. 869 at 883.

[80] 1 Mar. I, sess. 2, c. 2; revived by 1 Eliz. I, c. 1. The repeal was not comprehensive: see Dyer's comments in 109 Selden Soc. 16, 17.

[81] Cf. *R.* v. *Throckmorton* (1554) 1 St. Tr. 869 at 878 (witness sworn 'to say nothing but the truth').

[82] *R.* v. *Throckmorton* (1554) 1 St. Tr. 869 at 885, 88/=8.

[83] *R.* v. *Thymblebie* (1558) SP 11/13/47, cited by J. G. Bellamy, *Criminal Law and Society in Late Medieval and Tudor England* (1984), 48, 53; *Criminal Trial*, 108; C. Knighton (ed.), *State Papers of Mary I: domestic series, 1553–8* (1998), 350–1, no. 802.

[84] Holdsworth, *HEL*, v. 192–3; Baker, *LPCL*, 288. Dalison J. (previous note) said that when defence witnesses were allowed it was 'always without oath'.

[85] See e.g. *R.* v. *Armysby* (1533) Spelman 50; *R.* v. *Smith* (1555) 110 Selden Soc. 404.

[86] In *R.* v. *Throckmorton* (1554) 1 St. Tr. 869 at 873, the defendant was in effect examined by the law officers throughout the trial.

[87] *De Republica Anglorum*, ed. M. Dewar, 113–14. This was first printed in 1583, but written in the mid-1560s.   [88] See *R.* v. *Throckmorton* (1554) 1 St. Tr. 869 at 897.

cases at one sitting.[89] Yet the jurors might retire to consider their verdicts, and Dyer noted cases where a jury came back to hear additional evidence[90] or sought an adjournment so that better evidence could be obtained.[91]

Trial by peers

If a nobleman[92] was indicted for a capital offence he was tried before the lord high steward and his peers. The procedure was best known in cases of treason, though it was settled in 1541 that it was also to be used in case of felony,[93] and in 1556 that it extended to misprision of treason as well.[94] It was not available, however, in an appeal of felony.[95] Nor was it available to sons of peers who had courtesy titles only.[96]

Little is known of the procedure at such trials before the sixteenth century,[97] but it was fully described in two reports of the duke of Buckingham's trial in 1521.[98] It was not a trial in the House of Lords, there being no Parliament then in session. The duke of Norfolk was appointed lord high steward by letters patent of commission, solely to preside over the trial, and he sent out precepts summoning about twenty peers to attend. A scaffold or stage was erected in Westminster Hall for the peers, with rails and counter-rails for the judges (who attended to give legal advice), and the lord steward sat beneath a cloth of

[89] At the end of our period, it was common to charge each jury with four or five trials, each of which can rarely have exceeded thirty minutes: J. S. Cockburn, *Calendar of Assize Records: Introduction* (1985), 64, 110–11. Treason trials took longer, since the evidence was led by counsel, and four hours was considered quite speedy: *R. v. Knell* (1538) cited in Elton, *Policy and Police*, 295.

[90] *R. v. Sherwin* (1555) 110 Selden Soc. 407.

[91] *R. v. Gunn* (1555) ibid. 406; above, 362. The application was granted, but it was doubted whether the same jury could continue in being until the evidence was obtained.

[92] The position of bishops was unclear. Bishop Fisher was tried for treason before commissioners of oyer and terminer, but had by then been deprived of his bishopric: *R. v. Fisher* (1535) Spelman 57–8; Brooke Abr., *Trialles*, pl. 142; Pike, *House of Lords*, 220–1. Thomas Cranmer made no claim to be tried by peers in 1553: Pike, *House of Lords*, 221.

[93] *R. v. Lord Dacre of the South* (1541) 109 Selden Soc. 2; Brooke Abr., *Jurours*, pl. 48; *Trialles*, pl. 142.

[94] *Anon.* (1556) Dalison's reports, BL MS. Harley 5141, fo. 38; misreported by Whiddon in 110 Selden Soc. 250–1; Sta. P.C. 153D.

[95] *Radford v. Earl of Devon* (1456) 109 Selden Soc., p. lvii n. 93; Pas. 10 Edw. IV, fo. 6, pl. 17, *per* Littleton J.; Sta. P.C. 152A.

[96] *R. v. Lord Leonard Grey* (1541) 109 Selden Soc. 2; 1 St. Tr. 439; *R. v. Earl of Surrey* (1547) Brooke Abr., *Treason*, pl. 2; 1 St. Tr. 460. Wives of peers, on the other hand, were triable 'in the same manner as peers' by virtue of 20 Hen. VI, c. 9.

[97] The principal earlier authority was *R. v. Earl of H[untingdon]* (1400, but dated 1399) Mich. 1 Hen. IV, fo. 1, pl. 1 (plea of guilty). The report was first printed in 1553 and L. W. Vernon Harcourt considered it a forgery: *His Grace the Steward and Trial of Peers* (1907), 416–29, 444–60. Cf. Pike, *House of Lords*, 209–13.

[98] Pas. 13 Hen. VIII, fo. 11, pl. 1 (119 Selden Soc. 56); *Hall's Chronicle*, 623.

estate. The prisoner was brought in by the constable of the Tower of London, with the Tower axe borne in front of him. After the commission and indictment were read by the clerk of the Crown,[99] the prisoner pleaded Not guilty and was asked how he would be tried, to which the response was, 'By God and my peers'. The peers were not technically a jury, since they were not sworn; and they did not have to be unanimous. When the evidence had been given, and the defendant had put his side of the case, they retired for deliberation; and on their return they were asked individually for their votes, beginning with the most junior.[100] In case of conviction, sentence of death and dismemberment was passed by the lord steward, at which chilling moment the blade of the axe was turned towards the convict before he was taken back by barge to the Tower. We learn from Spelman a few years later that, as soon as judgment was given, the usage was for the lord steward to break his wand of office to signify the dissolution of the court.[101] Most of these procedures would remain in use for the next four centuries.

Before Lord Dacre of the North was tried by his peers in 1534, the judges assembled to discuss the procedure so that they could avoid any disagreement in public.[102] They decided that a peer could not refuse to be tried by his peers and put himself on the country instead,[103] that a majority decision was acceptable provided there were at least twelve in the majority, and that peers who had served on the commission of oyer and terminer to receive the indictment were not disqualified from sitting as triers. At the trial itself, they held that the defendant could not challenge any of the peers, since they were not jurors: a harsh rule that led to apparent injustice in later cases.[104] In the event the peers had great difficulty reaching agreement, thinking the principal witnesses to have been tainted by malice. They asked to hear a new witness, which the lord steward would not allow, and there was some discussion as to whether the proceedings could be adjourned and, if so, whether the triers should be held in ward like a jury. Eventually they returned and, one by one, declared the defendant to be not guilty. Observers noted that the decision was received by the common people in Westminster Hall with joyous shouting and clapping.

---

[99] His record of such proceedings was kept in the King's Bench *baga de secretis* (KB 8).

[100] According to the year book—though Hall says the opposite.

[101] *R. v. Marquess of Exeter* (1538) Spelman 61 at 62.

[102] *R. v. Lord Dacre of the North* (1534) 1 St. Tr. 407–8; Spelman 54; Caryll (Jun.) 415–16 (report also attributed to Thomas Gawdy); KB 8/6.

[103] This decision was apparently reversed in *R. v. Grey* (1555) BL MS. Add. 24845, fo. 34v; 109 Selden Soc., p. lviii. In 1554, the marquess of Dorset was tried by jury, and it was said he could waive his privilege, but it was not clear whether the peerage had descended to him: *R. v. Marquess of Dorset* (1554) Dalison's reports, BL MS. Harley 5141, ff. 22v–23; Dal. 16, pl. 1.

[104] *R. v. Duke of Somerset* (1551) 1 St. Tr. 515 at 521; *R. v. Duke of Northumberland* (1553) ibid. 766.

SUMMARY PROCEDURE

Trial by jury was *de rigueur* in cases of life and death, and whenever an accusation was made by indictment, but not for all misdemeanours. Misdemeanours were indeed commonly tried on indictment at the quarter sessions, but other procedures were available. A succession of statutes from the time of Richard II onwards had empowered justices of the peace to try offenders against various regulatory measures by 'examination', which meant that they—or sometimes just one or two of them, acting out of sessions—determined guilt without a jury.[105] Moreover, between 1494 and 1509 justices of the peace and assize judges alike were empowered by statute to try any non-capital statutory offence upon information, without indictment, though the statute was silent as to the mode of trial. Because of abuse by means of 'sinister and crafty feigned and forged informations', the experiment was not continued under Henry VIII.[106] It was, wrote Coke a century later, 'A good caveat to parliaments to leave all causes to be measured by the golden and straight metwand of the law, and not to the uncertain and crooked cord of discretion'.[107] Summary procedure was nevertheless normal in Star Chamber, where prosecutions were commenced by the law officers without indictment or bill of information and tried without a jury.[108]

A different kind of summary procedure presumably lies behind a kind of formal plea-bargain sometimes recorded in misdemeanour cases.[109] The defendant would sometimes plead Not guilty but, 'in order to spare the outlay, labour, and expenses with respect to trying an issue by the country in that behalf, [pray] to be admitted to a fine with the lord king'.[110] Nothing is known of the kind of negotiation which must have underlain such an outcome.

[105] Langbein, *Prosecuting Crime in the Renaissance*, 66–75; Bellamy, *Criminal Law and Society*, 8–32.

[106] 11 Hen. VII, c. 3, repealed by 1 Hen. VIII, c. 6. Coke attributed the 1494 measure to Empson and Dudley, and said it was to 'the utter subversion of the common law': Co. Inst. iv. 39–41.

[107] Co. Inst. iv. 41.

[108] There is little information from this period: above, 199. For the early Elizabethan period see 109 Selden Soc., pp. lxxxviii–lxxxix.

[109] Cockburn, *Calendar of Assize Records*, 68–9. For examples from quarter sessions see *Calendar of Caernarvonshire Quarter Sessions Records 1541–58*, ed. W. O. Williams (1956), 229, 235, 236 (1552–3).

[110] e.g. *R. v. Hawtry* (1498) KB 27/948, Rex m. 3d: 'dicit quod ipse in nullo est inde culpabilis, et de hoc ponit se super patriam etc., sed ut parcatur misis, laboribus, et expensis circa exitum patrie in hac parte triandum petit se ad finem cum domino rege occasione predicta admitti. Et admittitur, prout patet per rotulos finium istius termini.' The rolls of fines record the fines as being 'for a certain trespass whereof he has put himself in the lord king's grace' (tr.). For a similar procedure in Exchequer informations see above, 162.

29

The Development of Criminal Law[1]

THE absence of special pleading from most criminal cases[2] prevented the development of substantive legal principles by oral interchange between counsel and judges at the pleading stage, as in civil cases; but it would be misleading to deduce from this that criminal jurisprudence was lightly regarded, or incapable of development, in the dark days before Staunford and Coke put so much of it into print.

The formal means of raising questions of substantive criminal law were certainly limited. The only factually informative part of the record was the indictment, which summarized the accusation. The indictment could occasion discussion either at the trial[3] or in the King's Bench, which could inspect a record removed by *certiorari* and quash it for insufficiency. When cases were removed into the King's Bench, the Rex rolls specified the prisoner's 'exception', as Spelman called it, and its outcome, with the result that they contain explicit records of the disposal of points of law. This makes criminal records of this kind potentially more informative than the common plea rolls; but in reality the scope for raising points of substance was heavily restricted by the formality of indictments. Since the defendant did not plead facts in detail, new questions of law could only arise from new forms of indictment, and yet the vast majority of indictments followed set formulae. Most exceptions were therefore to points of form. Indictments had already settled into certain forms, in which certainty as well as formality were requisite;[4] and the King's Bench seems to have been very pernickety about the correct use of additions, the particulars of places and dates,[5] essential terms of art such

---

[1] See further 'The Refinement of English Criminal Jurisprudence 1500–1848' in *Crime and Criminal Justice in Europe and Canada*, ed. L. A. Knafla (1981), 17–42; repr. *LPCL*, 303–24.

[2] There were exceptions, e.g. the plea of self-defence: *R.* v. *Jenyn* (1499) KB 27/953, Rex m. 7 (indictment); *Hyde* v. *Assheton* (1538) Spelman 60 (appeal). [3] Below, 525 n. 19.

[4] Hil. 3 Hen. VII, fo. 1, pl. 1, *per* Fairfax J. (tr. 'Every indictment is the king's declaration, which must be certain to every common intent'); *R.* v. *Delarever* (1534) Spelman 52, pl. 23 ('Every indictment must contain more certainty than an original writ').

[5] Not their factual truth, which the court could not know, but their formal correctness. Thus it was insufficient to allege an offence on the feast of St Thomas, without saying which of the feasts of St Thomas: Pas. 3 Hen. VII, fo. 5, pl. 2; Brooke Abr., *Inditements*, pl. 47.

as *felonice* and *vi et armis*,[6] good Latin, and other matters of form.[7] Indeed, Spelman reports a case in which an alleged murderer was saved by the mistake of a single letter in his indictment.[8] Since the formal particulars did not all have to be proved true, the concern was very much with form rather than substance. On the other hand, evident technical errors seem sometimes to have passed unchallenged. This selective attachment to formality may perhaps be explained by supposing that technical errors could be used as pretexts for quashing indictments on more substantial grounds which are invisible on the face of the record. There is a reported instance of this being done in 1490, when Fairfax J. searched out a very technical error because he had taken pity on a burglar charged with taking twelve pennyworth of wool.[9]

Occasionally the removal procedure could be used to raise points of substance: for example, whether importing forged ducats was treason,[10] whether the year-and-day limitation in murder applied to poisoning,[11] whether the stones of a wall could be the subject of larceny,[12] or whether a clandestine burial could be felonious.[13] Records even of such cases are nevertheless less informative than reports, for—as with writs of error in civil cases[14]—the court could consider errors which were not assigned, and therefore we cannot tell with certainty from the record what was the true ground of the decision to quash.[15]

Another limitation of the procedure from the point of view of jurisprudence is that an exception was normally entered on the record only if it was successful. We are therefore deprived of an important part of the picture. According to later doctrine, demurrers were as peremptory in criminal cases as in civil; but a case

---

[6] The allegation of force and arms was arguably indispensable until the statute 37 Hen. VIII, c. 8: *R. v. Anon.* (1535) Yorke 97, no. 29 (which says *contra pacem* implies it); but cf., as to an accessory, *R. v. Salysbery* (1538) Spelman 104. As the statute indicated, it was usually embellished with the staves, knives, bows, and arrows, found in trespass actions; but it could be more verisimilitudinous: e.g. *R. v. Pygeon* (1508) KB 27/987, Rex m. 16 ('vi et armis, videlicet baculis et aliis instrumentis vocatis *handpekys* et *garfangihokes*').

[7] See 94 Selden Soc. *301*; 'Refinement of English Criminal Jurisprudence', *LPCL*, 306–8. For the requirements see Richard Hesketh's reading on forest law (Gray's Inn, *c*.1506/8), ff. 47–49; Sta. P.C. 95–6; G. de C. Parmiter, 'Tudor Indictments, Illustrated by the Indictment of Sir Thomas More' (1961) 6 *Recusant Hist.* 140–56.

[8] *R. v. Rogers* (1531/3) Spelman 52; KB 27/1081, Rex m. 1d (*quidam* for *quidem*); 'Refinement of English Criminal Jurisprudence', *LPCL*, 307.

[9] *R. v. Barbour* (1490) 1 Caryll 22. For later examples see 'Refinement of English Criminal Jurisprudence', *LPCL*, 308.

[10] *R. v. Anon.* (1539) Spelman 62, pl. 45.

[11] *R. v. Pyteous* (1532) Spelman 48, 97; KB 27/1079, Rex m. 9.

[12] *R. v. Gardiner* (1533) Spelman 99; KB 27/1087, Rex m. 1d (pr. 94 Selden Soc. 295).

[13] *R. v. Ames* (1518) KB 27/1028, Rex m. 6Bd.   [14] Above, 407.

[15] e.g. *R. v. Ap Rhys* (1533) Spelman 98; KB 27/1085, Rex m. 12 (pr. 94 Selden Soc. 293); *R. v. Delarever* (1534) Spelman 52, 100; KB 27/1092, Rex m. 5d (pr. 94 Selden Soc. 283).

reported by Dyer in 1540 shows that exceptions or demurrers to indictments were not so treated in practice.[16] If the exception was disallowed, the prisoner was in practice allowed to waive his demurrer and plead over, *in favorem vitae.* Criminal pleading could therefore be, in a sense, tentative.[17] The rolls are full of pleas of Not guilty to removed indictments, and only in the rare cases where a report can be found may it emerge that the roll has omitted to mention the exception which occasioned the removal.[18] Maybe there could be other invisible reasons for removing indictments. At any rate, the evidence provided by recorded exceptions is one-sided, and may be assumed to be deficient in respect of decisions to uphold indictments.

QUESTIONS ARISING AT THE TRIAL

Questions of law could arise at the trial, either upon the indictment[19] or upon the evidence,[20] or they could be anticipated before trial upon the charge to the grand jury;[21] but the rulings of the court only became sources of law to the extent that they were reported orally or in writing so that they could be absorbed by the profession as 'experience'.[22] They were not formally recorded, since the records of criminal proceedings were if anything more opaque than those on the civil side, though they might sometimes have been noted informally in the clerk's minutes. A surviving fragment of the Newgate gaol delivery minute-book for 1541–3, now in Aberystwyth,[23] does indeed minute a legal difficulty arising 'upon the evidence to the jury';[24] but this is a rare survival, and we cannot know how far legal questions and answers were preserved locally in this way. Some lawyers, such as

[16] *R.* v. *Gwyer* (1537/40) Dyer 46; KB 27/1109, Rex m. 10.

[17] Cf. *R.* v. *Olyffe* (1532) Spelman 49, where the court ordered a plea to be recorded so that it could not be amended, because the prisoner was of bad reputation: the implication is that this was an unusual course.

[18] For examples see 94 Selden Soc. 302 n. 3.

[19] e.g. *R.* v. *Anon.* (1520/1) Spelman 45, pl 5; *R.* v. *Lupton* (1536) ibid. 103 (presentment); *R.* v. *Anon.* (1553) BL MS. Hargrave 388, fo. 240 (tr. *LPCL,* 321); *R.* v. *Anon.* (1554) Dyer's circuit notebook, 110 Selden Soc. 402.

[20] e.g. *R.* v. *Armysby* (1533) Spelman 50 (trial at bar); *Snore's Case,* Spelman 67 (appeal in banc); *R.* v. *Anon.* (1554) Dyer's circuit notebook, 110 Selden Soc. 409, pl. 31.

[21] e.g. *R.* v. *Newbolt* (1512) 2 Caryll 613 at 614, *per* Fyneux CJ.

[22] This was the term for informal precedent of this kind: see Yorke 89, 97; Spelman 44, pl. 2 ('common experience', 1533); Gell's reports, II, fo. 170v (1562).

[23] National Library of Wales, Chirk Castle MS. A.17. This was discovered in the 1970s by C. H. C. Whittick. The first 63 leaves are missing.

[24] *R.* v. *Penley* (1542) ibid., fo. 82v; 94 Selden Soc. 301 n. 1. The question was whether someone could steal goods in his own possession or keeping: below, 567–8.

Spelman and Dyer,[25] took written notes of circuit rulings; but such notes had a very limited circulation, and they influenced the general development of criminal law chiefly to the extent that the reporters themselves made subsequent use of them. The first example in print seems to have been Plowden's report of some cases at Shrewsbury sessions in July 1553, published in 1571.[26] Perhaps Plowden had made a practice of noting such cases regularly; but it is significant that he did not think them generally worth printing.[27]

Criminal law may have developed in the first instance as a corpus of 'experience', although practice could still differ from one circuit to another,[28] or even (we may suppose) from one town to another, and if the law was to develop in a coherent and uniform manner it was necessary to find ways of centralizing discussion. Proceedings in error were inappropriate for this purpose. Error had the same limitations as *certiorari* before judgment: the record omitted the evidence, any judicial guidance to the jury, and most of the facts necessary for the making of legal distinctions. The verdict itself was final, even if perjured.[29] Recourse was therefore had to informal devices.

RESERVED CASES

It was natural that judges meeting with points of difficulty on circuit, or at the sessions, should consult their brethren. Their first recourse, no doubt, would have been to legally trained justices of the peace on the spot. But the judges might also be expected to raise questions with their fellows in one of the serjeants' inns, or the inns of court, when they came together in the following term. There was no tradition of preserving the outcome of such ephemeral discussions, and it is impossible to trace exactly the transition from purely informal conversation to a more regular procedure for 'reserving' crown cases. The principal hallmark of a 'reserved' case is a respite of the defendant, so that his fate depended on the advice sought. But it is this procedural link which is difficult to establish in the early cases. A more obvious indication is that a reserved case was usually discussed by all the judges, whereas an informal discussion only involved members of the trial judge's own inn.

The first clear example of formal reservation occurred in 1488,[30] when Sir Thomas Fitzwilliam, recorder of London, reprieved several prisoners at Newgate

---

[25] Dyer's circuit notebook (1554–81) is the first known example of its kind: see 109 Selden Soc., pp. xcii–xcvi. A stray example of a query by Fitzherbert J. at Stafford assizes is to be found in Brooke Abr., *Corone*, pl. 85.   [26] Plowd. 97–101v; below, 576–7.

[27] A notorious exception was his report (pr. 1578) of *R. v. Saunders and Archer* (1573) Plowd. 473–6 (Warwick assizes). His autograph notes have not been traced.

[28] For an example, see 'Refinement of English Criminal Jurisprudence', *LPCL*, 321–3 (fluctuating opinions between 1553 and 1588 as to stealing lead from a church roof).   [29] Above, 371–3.

[30] For earlier Exchequer Chamber cases, which might have arisen from such a procedure, see 64 Selden Soc. 125 (*c.*1470/80); Trin. 20 Edw. IV, fo. 5, pl. 3 (question put by Bryan CJ to Billyng CJ, 1480);

so that legal difficulties in their cases could be considered by all the judges in the Exchequer Chamber.[31] The occasion was sufficiently unusual to attract the notice of at least two reporters,[32] and one of the cases was still being discussed four years later, when Bryan CJ was asked to clarify what had been decided.[33] In 1491 and 1504 we find a similar procedure used to dispose of questions arising prior to arraignment.[34] Only two clear instances of reservation have been encountered in the following reign.[35] In 1520 Conyngesby J. reprieved a convict at Coventry assizes until the advice of all the justices of England could be taken on a question of sanctuary.[36] And in 1532 a priest was executed for clipping or counterfeiting coin 'by advice of all the justices', the advice in this case being given after conviction.[37] Spelman reports other discussions of points of criminal law argued in Serjeants' Inn, some of which may have been reserved cases, though they could equally have been informal conversations at table.[38]

In the reign of Mary I the reservation procedure seems to have become routine, and was sometimes furthered by the use of special verdicts instead of general convictions which might have to be set aside by pardon.[39] Certainly the procedure was more often noticed in mid-century, in the reports of Plowden,[40] Dalison,[41] and Dyer.[42] Both reporters also noted a special assembly in 1557 when ten

Trin. 22 Edw. IV, 64 Selden Soc. 55, pl. 19 (1482); ibid. 125, pl. 35 (1485/6). In Mich. 3 Hen. VII, fo. 12, pl. 8, Huse CJ referred to a ruling on criminal law in the Exchequer Chamber temp. Edw. IV.

[31] According to Mich. 3 Hen. VII, fo. 12, pl. 10, one of the cases arose before Fairfax J. Cf. 3 Hen. VII, 64 Selden Soc. 134, pl. 41 (case before Fairfax J. at Newgate and later in Exchequer Chamber). These were probably part of the same reference.

[32] Hil. 3 Hen. VII, ff. 1–2, pl. 3–5, and (perhaps a different report) Mich. 3 Hen. VII, fo. 12, pl. 4–6, 8–10; 1 Caryll 6–8, pl. 10A–C. The versions in Spelman 44, pl. 2, and Fitz. Abr., *Corone*, are derived from the year book.   [33] 1 Caryll 7 (1491–2); 94 Selden Soc. *166–7*; above, 476.

[34] *R*. v. *Preston* (1491) Spelman 44; KB 27/921, Rex m. 2d; copied in Crown Office entries, fo. 34v; *R*. v. *Aprice* (1504) 2 Caryll 426 (reserved by Frowyk CJ from Shaftesbury assizes). Another example may be *R*. v. *Cressede* (1505) 2 Caryll 462 (Exchequer Chamber).

[35] The procedure seems also to be mentioned in *Anon*. (1530/1) Caryll (Jun.) 381, no. 23, *per* Hare. Cf. *Anon*. (1526) Mich. 18 Hen. VIII, fo. 2, pl. 11, where Wolsey C. moved the justices whether stealing tame peacocks was felony; it is not clear how the case arose.

[36] *R*. v. *Spencer* (1520) 2 Caryll 707–8.   [37] *R*. v. *Anon*. (1532) Spelman 49, pl. 15; Yorke 90, no. 5.

[38] Spelman 44 (pl. 2), 45 (pl. 7), 65 6 (pl. 55 8), 69 (pl 68), 72 (pl, 71, 73), 105 (pl. 28), 140–1 (pl. 1–2), 207 (*Riottz*, pl. 1). For civil cases discussed 'at table' see above, 412–13.

[39] Cockburn dates the use of special verdicts for this purpose to the mid-sixteenth century, though they were rare: *Calendar of Assize Records: Introduction* (1985), 112. However, there are no surviving assize records for most of the period.

[40] *R*. v. *Salisbury* (1553) Plowd. 100 at 101v (tr. 'although the court held it clear . . . nevertheless they thought it good, and the court agreed, to reprieve the prisoner until the opinions of the other sages of the law were known').

[41] Criminal cases before all the justices are reported by Dalison in BL MS. Harley 5141, ff. 17, 17v–18v, 19, 20, 21v–22, 23v, 27–28 (1554); ff. 30, 30v–31 (1555); and often thereafter.

[42] e.g. 110 Selden Soc. 402, pl. 7 (1554), and 404, pl. 12 (1555); 109 Selden Soc. 13, pl. 23 (1555); Dyer 128a, §57, and 128b, §60–1 (1556).

questions of criminal procedure from different circuits were moved at Serjeants' Inn, Fleet Street, before the assize judges—presumably including the serjeants in commission as well as the judges of the two benches;[43] but these are not stated to have been reserved cases, and the idea of holding regular sessions of all the assize judges to deal with circuit difficulties seems not to have caught on. Crown cases reserved were to play an important part in the development of the criminal law in later periods; but, unless our sources are very misleading, they were probably not the means whereby the principal outlines of Tudor criminal law were settled.

ROLE OF THE INNS OF COURT

It was once thought that the principal sources of doctrine in the criminal law of the Tudor period were the treatises by Fitzherbert (1538) and Staunford (1557).[44] In fact, those books only mark a transition from aural to visual learning of the criminal law. The authors were not inventing the law which they expounded, but setting down what was for the most part already common learning.[45] Dozens of extant readings on the law of felony, delivered between about 1450 and 1550, show that nearly all the law in the textbooks—and more besides—had been current for the best part of a century.[46] In the absence of centralized judicial procedures, the inns of court provided a natural forum for the exploration of criminal law. The benchers were mostly justices of the peace themselves, and the students would have found questions of criminal law an interesting diversion from the intricacies of property law. Of course, readers could not lecture on the common law as such, but there were several provisions in the old statutes which provided the pretext for doing so under the guise of statutory interpretation. They did not have to restrict themselves to the point of the statute. For instance, in lecturing on homicide, the readers discussed such novel questions as whether it was felony to cause the abortion of a foetus, to frighten someone to death, to refuse to open one's door to a man fleeing from a murderous assault, to make a suit of armour so negligently that its wearer was killed through a defect of design, to hire out a dangerous horse which threw the hirer to his death, to kill from afar with a machine, such as a mantrap, or trained animal; whether the concept of misadventure extended to shooting and other sporting accidents; whether automatism and drunkenness

[43] 110 Selden Soc. 411–12 ('amongst the justices for all circuits'); Dalison's reports, BL MS. Harley 5141, ff. 39, 31v–32v (pr. 110 Selden Soc. 412–14).

[44] A. Fitzherbert, *The Newe Boke of Justices of the Peas* (1538); W. Staunford, *Les Plees del Coron* (1557).

[45] This became evident on the publication of Thomas Marow's reading on the peace (Inner Temple, 1503) by B. Putnam in 1924.

[46] See 94 Selden Soc. 299–346; 'The Refinement of English Criminal Jurisprudence', *LPCL*, 313–15; 'The Inns of Court and Legal Doctrine', repr. *CLT*, 37–51, at 44–5. For a provisional bibliography of readings on criminal law, c.1450–1550, see 94 Selden Soc. 347–50.

were defences; and many other questions which are not hinted at in the statutory texts and did not reach the printed reports or treatises till much later.[47] Disputed cases at readings could range even wider from the text: for instance, whether it was possible to steal one's own goods feloniously was debated at Spelman's reading on *Quo Warranto*.[48]

Some of the classroom examples were suggested by real but unreported cases.[49] Others were from *Bracton*, which continued to possess some influence on the criminal law for want of later authority. It was by way of *Bracton* that an Inner Temple reader of Henry VIII's time commented on a case of misadventure first debated by Mela, Proculus, and Ulpian in the ancient world.[50] Besides real cases and textbook cases, the readers now and then invented a mind-stretching remote contingency—such as that of the blind Italian who prayed benefit of clergy,[51] or the alleged *bigamus* who prayed clergy in an appeal of felony brought by a bishop and his archbishop.[52] Even if some of these cases never occurred in practice, the readers' attempts to analyse and rationalize doctrine must have had considerable effect on real Crown proceedings. It is not too great an exaggeration to say that the criminal law of the early Tudor period was reduced to a coherent and sophisticated science—and in that sense made—by the inns of court.

[47] 94 Selden Soc. *304-16*; 'The Inns of Court and Legal Doctrine', repr. in *CLT*, 45; above, 471.

[48] 113 Selden Soc., pp. xiv, 160-1 (cf. pp. 103, 131, for the lecture on which the point arose).

[49] e.g. the abortion case: 94 Selden Soc. *306*. For the citation of real cases, see also *Moots*, 271, no. 95 (Newgate, perhaps a report); 274, no. 100 (King's Bench case of 1492); 280, no. 110 (recent case at Newgate); Bodl. Lib. MS. Rawlinson C. 705, fo. 75v, *per* Dudley (1496; case at Southwark gaol delivery); BL MS. Hargrave 87, fo. 140v (temp. Edw. IV and Hen. VII).

[50] Francis Mountford's reading (1527), above, 23 n. 92.

[51] Case put at Thomas Kebell's reading: Baker, *The Law's Two Bodies*, 132.

[52] Another Inner Temple case, perhaps from Richard Littleton's reading (1493): Port 127 at 128.

30
Privileges and Immunities

THE working of the criminal law in the early Tudor period was dominated by the two great ecclesiastical privileges of clergy and sanctuary. Introduced to protect ordained clergy and sanctified places from sacriligious interference by secular authority, both privileges had come to provide extensive protection to lay as well as clerical felons. By the end of Henry VIII's reign, however, sanctuary had been all but abolished, while statutory modifications of clergy were turning it into a vehicle for the adjustment of punishment to fit the crime. By a 'noble alchemy' the legislature was beginning to extract 'rich medicines out of poisonous ingredients'.[1]

BENEFIT OF CLERGY

As a result of the conflict between Becket and King Henry II, it had been established since the twelfth century that the lay courts were incompetent to proceed with the trial or sentence for felony of someone who proved himself a clerk in orders. If a prisoner was claimed by the ordinary[2] as a member of the clergy—and such claims were now invariably made after trial—the secular judge had to deliver him to the ecclesiastical authority to undergo canonical purgation. Yet the notion that clergy should be privileged in this way was not calculated to appeal to the laity. Priests were by no means above felonious activities, and it was arguable that, if any distinction was to be made, an educated man of the cloth who transgressed the law deserved greater punishment than a layman.[3] The Church, however, had St Thomas on her side. He had become a national saint, and the occasion of his canonization was not forgotten by temporal lawyers.[4] The doctrine of immunity was therefore accepted, while the practice was dramatically modified by judicial and parliamentary legislation.

At some point—as yet undetermined by historians—between the mid-fourteenth and the mid-fifteenth centuries, benefit of clergy had become secularized.[5] No

---

[1] Bl. Comm. iv. 371.

[2] Usually the bishop, though in Westminster Hall it was the abbot of Westminster. The claim was actually made by a deputy, who was himself colloquially called the ordinary.

[3] This was argued by Starkey, *Dialogue*, ed. Mayer, 92–3.

[4] Caryll's reading (Inner Temple, 1510) CUL MS. Ee.3.46, fo. 50; above, 21, 237.

[5] See Baker, 94 Selden Soc. 327–32; *CLT*, 177–85; *The Law's Two Bodies*, 39, 127–33.

longer did the judges do their utmost to ensure that only genuine clergy were allowed the privilege; on the contrary, it had become widely available to laymen.[6] The canonical requirement of tonsure and clerical habit had been abandoned,[7] and—unless there was written proof of ordination[8]—the only test of clergy was the ability to read a biblical passage (in Latin). It was now the judges who made the real decision. The ordinary's deputy still had to make the claim; but the judges could fine him if he claimed as a clerk someone who patently could not read, or if he refused someone who could. Until the time of Henry VII there was arguably a distinction between a general and a special refusal by the ordinary. If the ordinary refused generally, without assigning any cause, it was said that his decision was unreviewable because he might have taken into account spiritual factors— such as bigamy or heresy—which were outside the knowledge of the lay judges.[9] If, however, he gave as a reason something within the judges' cognizance, such as the failure to read, or the lack of a tonsure, the judges could review the decision by virtue of their own direct knowledge. This distinction was abandoned around 1490, when a member of the Middle Temple was convicted at Newgate and the ordinary's deputy refused him generally, but the court fined the ordinary—who was alleged to have been bribed—and coerced him to accept the prisoner as a clerk. This was said to be an exercise of judicial discretion *in favorem vitae*.[10] Against this approach it was said that, if the ordinary had no discretion, there was little point in his attendance. Yet in practice there seem to have been few conflicts between judges and ordinaries, who now colluded in allowing clergy to literate laymen. The reading test was administered by handing to the prisoner a book, which was usually a psalter,[11] and requiring him to read an assigned verse. The chosen passage was known as the neck-verse,[12] but there is no evidence that it was as yet always the same text. Kebell said the justices chose the passage,[13] and could by discretion assign whatever book they pleased so long as it was legible. A blind defendant was given an oral test, and a dumb defendant a written test. In these

---

[6] This was acknowledged by Parliament in 1489: 4 Hen. VII, c. 13; *The Law's Two Bodies*, 132–3.

[7] Kebell mentioned an (undated) decision by all the judges to this effect: reading in the Inner Temple (*c.*1470/5) BL MS. Hargrave 87, fo. 304v (tr. *The Law's Two Bodies*, 132).

[8] A priest with a certificate of ordination was not required to read: C. St German, *Division betwene the Spirytualtie and Temporaltie* (1532), fo. 32v.   [9] Pas. 21 Edw. IV, fo. 21, pl. 1.

[10] Richard Littleton's reading (Inner Temple, 1493) BL MS. Hargrave 87, ff. 110v–111, *per* Frowyk (tr. *Moots*, 280); *Diversite de Courtz* (1533), sig. B5 (change attributed to Huse CJ).

[11] In *Ferrant* v. *Phelippe* (1536) CP 40/1091, m. 344, the defendant pleaded a conviction at Exeter assizes and that the prisoner prayed clergy and the judge told the ordinary to proffer him a psalter, from which he read.

[12] *Applyard* v. *Fowler* (1527) KB 27/1063, m. 38 ('... but thou cannyst thy neke vers tho shouldyst be hanged').

[13] So also BL MS. Harley 4990, fo. 159v (1530s), which says the ordinary produces the book but the court appoints the verse.

cases, the record stated that the defendant 'read as a clerk', which was fictitious; but, as Kebell said, 'the acts of speaking and writing Latin presuppose that they know how to read, and are nobler and worthier than mere reading'.[14]

The case of the blind man raised another difficulty: a blind man could not be made a priest. One reader succumbed to the fallacy of supposing that, for this reason, he could not claim clergy at all.[15] But the objection was misconceived, because he could have become blind since ordination, in which case he would not have lost his clerical status. The same was true of maimed or limbless persons, excommunicates, and outlaws. Most readers in court also allowed that bastards and villeins could have clergy, even though their disability began at birth, either because they could have taken orders by dispensation or because full priests' orders were unnecessary to claim clergy.[16] Richard Littleton went so far as to hold that clergy could be allowed to Jews.[17] The line was drawn, however, at convicted heretics, infidels, and women.

The most bizarre of the exclusions was canonical bigamy. By virtue of obscure medieval theology, founded on a passage in Leviticus, a man was disqualified from ordination if he had either married a widow or had lawfully married two wives in succession. Yet there was no similar objection, apparently, to a man who had a multitude of mistresses, or who was a bigamist in the modern sense—so that only one of his 'marriages' was valid.[18] The objection was to two lawful marriages by either the husband or the wife. This strange learning had been incorporated into English law by a statute of 1276,[19] which operated to bar any real or presumed dispensation,[20] with the result that a man's life often depended on the details of his matrimonial history.[21] Indeed, men were regularly sentenced to death because they had married widows.[22] That would have been absurd enough even when

[14] Kebell's reading (c.1470/5) BL MS. Hargrave 87, fo. 304 (tr. The Law's Two Bodies, 132). Note the problems with foreigners, discussed by Littleton and Mountford: 94 Selden Soc. 330. Brooke said that Greeks were entitled to read from books in Greek characters: Brooke Abr., Clergie, pl. 20.

[15] CUL MS. Ee.2.26, fo. 92. He also excluded the maimed, for the same reason.

[16] 94 Selden Soc. 331; Brooke Abr., Clergie, pl. 21–22. Cf. BL MS. Harley 4990, fo. 159 (1530s), which says a villein or bastard may have clergy, because they may be ordained by dispensation, but not a blind or maimed person.

[17] Cf. Brooke Abr., Clergie, pl. 20 (probably from a Middle Temple reading), where Jews and Moslems are excluded from clergy together with heretics.

[18] The second point is expressly stated in a fifteenth-century reading on De bigamis, BL MS. Lansdowne 466, fo. 169v. The reverse is stated in BL MS. Harley 4990, fo. 159v (1530s), but the practice bears out the earlier statement.   [19] 4 Edw. I, De Bigamis, c. 5. See Port 127–8.

[20] A fifteenth-century reader said that a papal dispensation for a bigamus was not noticed in 'our law', presumably because it would be contrary to the statute: BL MS. Lansdowne 466, fo. 169v.

[21] Counterpleas of bigamy are often found in the rolls. The question of fact was referred to the bishop for later certification rather than disposed of by the deputy present in court. For a certificate of Non est bigamus see R. v. Ap Howell (1499) KB 27/950, Rex m. 2d.

[22] e.g. R. v. Annott (1516) KB 27/1019, Rex m. 9; R. v. Jenyns (1539) KB 27/1111, Rex m. 12; R. v. Brewe (1539) KB 27/1113, Rex m. 5. In R. v. Carter (1541) KB 27/1121, Rex m. 10d, a pardon was obtained.

clergy was only claimed by priests, but it caused mischief on a larger scale now that the privilege was more widely available. The full extent of its absurdity is illustrated by a case of 1527. A prisoner claimed clergy and read as a clerk, and the king's attorney counterpleaded that he had married a widow; the bishop certified a marriage de facto, but said that the prisoner had been precontracted at Calais to another woman, by whom he had issue, so that the marriage with the widow was void. The prisoner was therefore allowed to be a notional clergyman, precisely because he was a bigamist in today's language and had lived in sin. Had he lived chastely, and married the widow lawfully in the eyes of the Church, he would have been hanged.[23] Edward Hall related another case in which a dutiful wife, to save her husband from the gallows, waived her reputation and swore that her previous partnerships were not marriages.[24] This intolerable law was finally abrogated in 1547,[25] and was not revived by the restoration of papal authority in 1553.[26]

Perhaps because it rarely mattered, but perhaps also because the canon law was unclear,[27] the courts did not authoritatively settle which orders were sufficient to attract the privilege. Opinion favoured deacons and subdeacons as well as priests,[28] and it seems probable that minor orders had also been allowed: in fact, a papal bull of 1516 noted that men in England were receiving minor orders to cover their criminal activities, and abolished minor orders except for those with benefices.[29] It was clear, however, that the common law only allowed the privilege for murder,[30] felony, and (probably) petty treason.[31] It was not allowed for high treason,[32] and in 1532 a priest was executed for clipping coin—though 'several of the spirituality grumbled at this'.[33] Nor was clergy available for the non-capital

---

[23] R. v. Bagnall (1527) KB 27/1065, Rex m. 9; and likewise R. v. Bromeham (1530) Caryll (Jun.) 379, no. 10A. Cf. R. v. Riche (1512) KB 27/1047, Rex m. 8 (denies that widow is his wife).

[24] R. v. Calaway (1543) Hall's Chronicle, 859; below, 577.   [25] 1 Edw. VI, c. 12, s. 6.

[26] R. v. Anon. (1557) 109 Selden Soc. 21, pl. 36; 110 Selden Soc. 411; Dalison's reports, BL MS. Harley 5141, fo. 39 (tr. 110 Selden Soc. 412). The contrary view was held by Staunford (Sta. P.C. 134v), but this was a decision by all the judges.

[27] R. H. Helmholz, The Ius Commune in England (2001), 208–10.

[28] See R. v. Dolfyn (1500) 3 DKR, app. ii, 219–20 (alleged bigamus says he was ordained as a sub-deacon, and was a friar preacher, before he married the widow); R. v. Boswell (1513) KB 27/1008, Rex m. 12 (pr. 102 Selden Soc. 39) (claims clergy as subdeacon and deacon, having previously been benet and acolyte; then pleads sanctuary). The matter was touched on in Dr Standish's Case (1515) 2 Caryll 683 at 686, 687, 688. The clergy statute of 1531 (23 Hen. VIII, c. 1) recognized that subdeacons and deacons were entitled to the privilege.   [29] Bellamy, Criminal Law and Society, 138.

[30] R. v. Anon. (1507) 2 Caryll 556, pl. 399.

[31] R. v. Sherman (1498) KB 27/948, Rex m. 2; R. v. Smith (1555) 110 Selden Soc. 404; R. v. Parker (1560) ibid. 428. The matter was uncertain: 94 Selden Soc. 333.

[32] 94 Selden Soc. 333 n. 3; anon. reading (1530s) BL MS. Harley 4990, fo. 159v. Numerous actual clergy—including Bishop Fisher—were put to death in the 1530s for denying the supremacy.

[33] R. v. Anon. (1532) Yorke 90, no. 5; Spelman 49, pl. 15. Little did they foresee what was coming.

offences of petty larceny[34] or misdemeanour. Even a real clergyman could be sentenced to a corporal punishment for misdemeanour.[35]

The extension of clergy to literate laymen may have given the judges some control over the fixed death penalty, since their discretion in administering the reading test could sometimes be influenced by policy factors.[36] However, it did not bring the law closer to a state of perfection. As late as the seventeenth century, some would defend the protection of the literate 'in favour of learning in general, and in reverence of mankind, and man's blood (which in persons of use is not to be shed lightly)';[37] and yet the protection was almost as arbitrary as the punishment it relieved. The felon who was literate, or who could manage to appear so, had little to fear from detection and prosecution save the loss of his goods,[38] and those might be restored to him after canonical purgation. Bishops were supposed to punish criminous clerks by imprisonment, but it seems that in practice their officials were so negligent or corrupt that many 'manifest thieves and murderers' escaped scot-free both before and after purgation.[39] This led to what may be regarded as the third element of secularization. By 1500 the judges classified the ordinary's custody as temporal, and claimed to be able to fine the ordinary if a 'clerk' was imprisoned too harshly or too leniently, or was bailed or released or allowed to escape before purging himself.[40] Escape by the clerk was felony,[41] which after 1531 was unclergiable.[42] Only the king could pardon the imprisonment by the ordinary, and in that case release could be obtained by *habeas corpus*.[43] Unless the trial and judgment in the ecclesiastical court took its due course, the royal courts therefore possessed some notional control. Yet it seems from the complaints of readers in court, and the dearth of reported or recorded cases in point, that no rigorous surveillance was exercised. In return for these slight risks of disability, or of brief loss of liberty, the literate felon earned the decided advantage that conviction in the temporal court wiped out all previous felonies and outlawries, even for debt:[44] a great mischief, lamented a fifteenth-century reader, whereby many men were often defrauded.[45] What better way for a rogue to escape

---

[34] Kebell's reading (*c*.1470/5); anon. reading (1530s) BL MS. Harley 4990, fo. 159v.

[35] *Stephenson's Case* (1545) 110 Selden Soc. 339 (priest set on pillory by order of Star Chamber, 'his clergy not regarded').   [36] This is made explicit in *R. v. Brasier* (1531) Spelman 46.

[37] *Searle* v. *Williams* (1620) Hob. 288.

[38] This was a disadvantage of the privilege in comparison with a pardon: *Wyse's Case* (1530) Caryll (Jun.) 378, no. 20.   [39] 23 Hen. VIII, c. 1, preamble.

[40] Trin. 15 Hen. VII, fo. 9. pl. 8, *per* Fyneux CJ; Hil. 16 Hen. VII, Fitz. Abr., *Imprisonment*, pl. 28; Fitz. J.P. 64v. See, e.g., *R. v. Bishop of Exeter* (1508) KB 27/987, Rex m. 18 (indictment for escape of clerks convict); *R. v. Abbot of St Albans* (1520) 120 Selden Soc. 56 (ordinary chargeable even if there was no indictment).   [41] *R. v. Anon.* (*c*.1523) Spelman 66, pl. 57.

[42] 23 Hen. VIII, c. 11.   [43] *R. v. Smyth* (1534) Spelman 52, 169.

[44] Spelman 41–2, pl. 6; Spelman 65, pl. 55; Yorke 90, no. 7.

[45] Reading in Gray's Inn (*c*.1474) CUL MS. Ee.5.22, fo. 117v.

creditors than to learn to read and then get convicted of felony? However, the common-law judges—having changed their minds once so as to facilitate the claiming of clergy—were unwilling to retreat to a middle position. They could hardly put the law back a century and confine the privilege to the real clergy alone; and yet—despite their discretionary control of the reading test—they did not feel able to do more than tinker with the fiction. Reform was needed, to enable benefit of clergy to operate more discriminatingly and to prevent its flagrant abuse by habitual criminals. But it had to be effected by legislation.

STATUTORY RESTRICTIONS ON CLERGY

The first reform was a statute of 1489 which provided that a layman could only enjoy the privilege of clergy once,[46] a measure attributed by a contemporary to Henry VII in person.[47] To ensure against evasion, murderers and manslayers were to be marked in the brawn of the left thumb with the letter M, thieves and other felons with a T. Clerks who were actually in orders could escape branding by producing the letters of their ordination; but that was the only permissible method of proof.[48] For those who were branded, the mark was not itself a matter of record, but a warning to the officers to search out the record of the previous conviction.[49] The procedure in such cases was for the Crown to counterplead *auterfoits convict* to a prayer of clergy, and if need be for the matter to be tried on a plea of *Nul tiel record*,[50] or on the factual issue of identity.[51] To facilitate the necessary record-keeping, the assize judges were required after 1518 to maintain lists of those to whom clergy was granted.[52]

The next step was to place further limitations on the offences for which clergy was available. This device may at first have been suggested by softening the boundaries of treason.[53] When John Spynell and others were attainted by

[46] 4 Hen. VII, c. 11.

[47] P. Vergil, *Anglica Historia*, ed. Hay, 116–17, 130. It had, however, been proposed as early as 1449: *RP*, v. 151 (below).

[48] Spelman 46, pl. 10–11; Yorke 90, no. 4, and 92, no. 13; *R. v. Rogers* (1532) KB 27/1084, Rex m. 13. In *R. v. Davy* (1536) KB 27/1100, Rex m. 7, a chaplain obtained adjournments for three years to produce his letters but was eventually ordered to be branded.　　　　　　　　　　　　　[49] Yorke 91, no. 11.

[50] 94 Selden Soc. 332.

[51] e.g. *R. v. Chylde* (1493) Crown Office entries, ff. 161v–163v (jury finds he is same person); *R. v. Richevell* (1494) ibid., ff. 163v–166 (sim.); *R. v. Anon.* (c.1516) Chaloner 278–9, no. 2 (issue as to whether defendant is the priest named in the letters); *R. v. Ludman* (1541) KB 27/1121, Rex m. 10d (jury find he is same person); *R. v. Anon.* (1545) 121 Selden Soc. 469, no. 2 (sim.). The mark in the hand is mentioned in the 1541 record but was evidently not conclusive.

[52] Cockburn, *Calendar of Assize Records: Introduction*, 118–19. A Home Circuit list from 1509 to 1520 is preserved in KB 9/477, mm. 35–36d. The practice continued until the mid-seventeenth century.

[53] It had been proposed as early as 1449 and 1455 that second offences of felony, after clergy had once been allowed, should be deemed high treason: *RP*, v. 151, 333–4.

Parliament in 1487 of felony, for plotting against the great officers of the realm, the act provided that they should not have benefit of clergy.[54] And when in 1491 it was made a statutory felony for a soldier to desert, the benefit of clergy was again removed, because 'his offence stretcheth to the hurt and jeopardy of the king our sovereign lord, all the nobles of the realm, and of all the common weal thereof'.[55] In each case the new offence was felony, not constructive treason, and yet the policy of denying clergy seems likely to have been associated with the canonical exception of treason. Three years later, but only in Ireland, clergy was removed from murder by the expedient of declaring it to be treason.[56] Then, in 1496— provoked by a recent incident in Essex—the English Parliament declared that murder by way of petty treason was not clergiable,[57] thereby clearing up a genuine doubt as to the law. Henry VIII was later to turn murder by poisoning into high treason.[58] Such changes were achieved without bringing the Crown into direct conflict with the Church, since the exception of treason was acknowledged by the canonists. But it was a disingenuous technique, and this was not to be the general line of development in England.

A more direct method of limitation was adopted in 1512, when Parliament passed a temporary statute to remove the benefit of clergy from murder of malice aforethought and from robbery in a church, highway,[59] or dwelling-house.[60] Nothing is known of the statute's origin, save that it seems to have been the end-result of a failed bill of 1510 to remove clergy from robbers and burglars.[61] According to Serjeant Caryll, the statute operated 'to the great increase and advancement of the public weal of the whole realm, and to the great discomfort and fear of all common murderers and thieves'.[62] Like the 1489 statute, it was not to apply where the offenders had actually been ordained, and that ought to have prevented any collision with the Church. But in that respect it did not succeed. Even allowing for the fact that our principal report of the ensuing dispute comes from the pen of one of the king's serjeants, the attitude of the prelates in defending

---

[54] *RP*, vi. 402. There was no felony here at common law: below, 590.

[55] 7 Hen. VII, c. 1; continued in the next reign by 3 Hen. VIII, c. 5; renewed and enlarged by 2 & 3 Edw. VI, c. 2.   [56] 10 Hen. VII (Ir.), c. 21. This referred to murder 'of malice prepensed'.

[57] 12 Hen. VII, c. 7. The statute was passed, according to its preamble, because of the recent murder of Richard Tracy, gentleman, at Brentwood, Essex, by his servant James Grame, 'to the right perilous ensample of other evil disposed'. Grame was attainted by the statute itself.

[58] 22 Hen. VIII, c. 9; below, 539.

[59] As to whether this extended to a footpath (*via pedestris*) see *R. v. Anon.* (1546) BL MS. Hargrave 4, fo. 98v (judges at Newgate divided).   [60] 4 Hen. VIII, c. 2.

[61] For the 1510 bill see *HLJ*, i. 7a (tr. 'A bill against plundering thieves [*latrones spoliantes*] not to be allowed the privilege of clergy unless their orders can be proved, delivered to Master Elyot [king's serjeant], read for the first time'; 'A bill concerning plunderers by night, read the third time, delivered to Porter [clerk of the Crown] to be written afresh and expedited').

[62] *Dr Standish's Case* (1515) 2 Caryll 683–4.

the fictitious form of the privilege—the privilege of real clergy being unchallenged at this time—seems to have been theologically vacuous, legally inept, politically bone-headed, and on any view irrational.[63] The matter came to a head after Dr Richard Kidderminster, preaching a convocation sermon at Paul's Cross following the indictment of an ecclesiastical judge for murdering Richard Hunne,[64] and fortified by a papal decree of 1514,[65] declared the statute of 1512 to have been against the law of God and that its makers had incurred the censures of the Church. Whatever the preacher meant by 'makers', this was an attack upon the king himself. Upon complaint by the Commons—led by their speaker, Sir Robert Sheffield, formerly recorder of London[66]—the king appointed various doctors of law to argue the point before his judges and temporal counsel at the Blackfriars. The doctor supporting the preacher relied on an ignorant scriptural error and failed to substantiate his case, but the matter was left undetermined. The affair exploded later in the year when Henry Standish, a doctor of divinity, was cited to appear before Convocation on trumped-up charges of heresy. His real offence was to have argued the legal case against Kidderminster. The citation for heresy was reported to the king as an attack on royal jurisdiction, and the matter was again referred to the judges at the Blackfriars. After discussion, the judges agreed that all those who had participated in the process against Dr Standish—and they included Archbishop Warham—were guilty of *praemunire*. At a later session, in Baynard's Castle, the two archbishops knelt before the king and prayed a reference to the pope, inasmuch as the statute of 1512 was contrary to the law of God and that 'various holy fathers' (an allusion to Becket) had in former times suffered martyrdom in the dispute. Fyneux CJ responded that, since the Church had no authority to try murder or felony, there was little point handing convicts over. This the bishops could not answer. The king warned, ominously, that the kings of England had no superior but God and that he would see his temporal jurisdiction maintained. Standish was discharged, and in 1518 was rewarded with the bishopric of St Asaph. The stand taken by the bishops had considerably weakened their authority, and had probably disposed many members of Parliament to look favourably on the king's notion of the royal supremacy nearly twenty years before the great divorce.

Despite this moral victory, the king and Parliament did not reassert the supremacy for the time being, and the statute of 1512 was allowed to expire.[67]

[63] *Dr Standish's Case* (1515) 2 Caryll 684–92.

[64] Above, 241; Ogle, *The Tragedy of the Lollards Tower*, 141–3.

[65] Bellamy, *Criminal Law and Society*, 133–4.

[66] See *History of Parliament 1509–58*, iii. 305. The dispute with Wolsey cost Sheffield his freedom and probably his life: above, 93.

[67] A bill for its renewal passed the Commons in 1515, but the parliament was dissolved before it could complete its passage in the Lords: *HLJ*, i. 31–3, 54.

The Church did little to reform matters, save that Wolsey procured a papal bull in 1528 to facilitate the degrading of clerks who committed atrocious offences.[68] Early in 1531, however, the matter was resurrected after a number of servants and paupers at Lambeth Palace became violently ill and one died. It was discovered that Richard Roose, the bishop of Rochester's cook, had put some poisoned powder in a pail of yeast used to make porridge. The case attracted the interest of the king, who attended the House of Lords in person to speak at length on the subject.[69] Roose was attainted by Parliament without trial, the chief object being to authorize the barbarous new punishment of boiling to death: a striking example of the king's viciousness when alarmed. The bill as first introduced treated the offence as 'voluntary murder'; but in the statute as passed it was elevated into high treason.[70] This alteration—harking back, doubtless unconsciously, to the Irish precedent—was presumably designed to prevent any possible claim to benefit of clergy without incurring clerical opposition. But it stirred a renewed interest in that subject. Later in the year, Parliament restored the 1512 provision and again removed clergy from murder of malice aforethought, highway robbery, robbery in a church or dwelling-house, and now also (an innovation) arson.[71] Over the next five years Parliament added piecemeal to the list of non-clergiable offences,[72] thereby imposing or reintroducing a mandatory death penalty for buggery, piracy, embezzlement by a servant to the value of 40s., and all felonies within the Admiralty jurisdiction.[73] Clergy was also removed from convicts who escaped by breaking out of the ordinary's prison, which was accounted a new felony.[74] An attempt was made to evade these statutes by claiming clergy on arraignment, without pleading or putting oneself upon the country, so that the defendant would not have become 'convicted by verdict' as the wording of the legislation required. This escape-route was closed by a further statute in 1534.[75] Later additions to the list of non-clergiable felonies in this period were contradicting the

---

[68] Bellamy, *Criminal Law and Society*, 139–40. This perhaps referred chiefly to treason, which was not clergiable.   [69] See Lehmberg, *The Reformation Parliament*, 125.

[70] 22 Hen. VIII, c. 9; repealed by 1 Edw. VI, c. 12; and see Stacy, 'Richard Roose and the Use of Parliamentary Attainder in the Reign of Henry VIII', 1–15. The bill is E175/6/12; printed in K. Kesselring, 'A Draft of the 1531 "Acte for Poysoning"' (2001) 116 *EHR* 894–9. Roose was duly executed by boiling: *Hall's Chronicle*, 780–1. There is some evidence that he only intended a jest, thinking the powder would act as a laxative.   [71] 23 Hen. VIII, c. 1.

[72] Cf. also *Tudor Royal Proclamations*, i. 263, no. 179 (clergy withdrawn from those killing officers of justice while resisting arrest or slaying with 'sudden foins', 1538; the word 'murder' is used, but the situations were usually treated as chance-medley).

[73] 25 Hen. VIII, c. 6; 27 Hen. VIII, cc. 4 and 17; 28 Hen. VIII, c. 15. Note also the short-lived statute of 1539 making incontinency by priests a capital felony: 31 Hen. VIII, c. 14; repealed by 32 Hen. VIII, c. 10. The clergy legislation was perpetuated by 28 Hen. VIII, cc. 1, 2, 6; 32 Hen. VIII, c. 3.   [74] 23 Hen. VIII, c. 11; above, 535 n. 42.

[75] 25 Hen. VIII, c. 3. See *HLJ*, i. 78, 79.

articles of faith (1540),[76] sorcery (1542),[77] horse-stealing (1545),[78] assembling to destroy enclosures (1549),[79] robbery in a booth or tent in a fair or market (1552),[80] and remaining in the country as a gypsy (1554).[81] In some of these instances clergy was restored in 1547.[82]

The two statutes of 1531 preserved the privilege of clergy for genuine clerks in orders—including deacons and subdeacons—albeit with 'liberty' for the ordinary (if he saw cause) to 'disgrade' his clerk, in accordance with canon law, so that he could be sentenced to death by the King's Bench.[83] No such saving was contained in the statutes concerning buggery and piracy, and when the earlier legislation came to be continued in 1536 it was enacted that clerks in holy orders should thereafter suffer the same 'pains and dangers' as other persons not in orders.[84] Benefit of clergy had finally become, and was for nearly three centuries to remain, a lay privilege governed entirely by the secular law of the land. The logical next step would have been to remove the reading test; but for the time being this was done only for peers. From 1547 a lord of Parliament was entitled to claim clergy even if he could not read.[85] Another statute of 1547 seems to have been designed to reduce the enormous discrepancy in the severity of punishments for those who could and could not read; but the means adopted—the turning of clerks convict into 'slaves'—was so unpalatable that it was repealed two years later.[86]

Despite the restrictions, the incidence of benefit of clergy seems to have increased markedly between the mid-fifteenth and the mid-sixteenth centuries.[87] Clearly it was becoming easier to claim, and yet—for whatever reason—it was still beyond the reach of at least half of those convicted of felony.

SANCTUARY AND ABJURATION[88]

The second great privilege of the Church which seriously interfered with the administration of criminal justice was that of sanctuary, which was a consequence

[76] 31 Hen. VIII, c. 14.

[77] 33 Hen. VIII, c. 8. This was the precursor of the witchcraft acts: 109 Selden Soc., pp. lxix–lxxii; below, 594.

[78] 37 Hen. VIII, c. 8 ('horse'); 1 Edw. VI, c. 12 ('horses, geldings, or mares'); 2 & 3 Edw. VI, c. 33 (explained that 1547 act extends to single animal).

[79] 3 & 4 Edw. VI, c. 5; below, 652. [80] 5 & 6 Edw. VI, c. 9.

[81] 1 & 2 Phil. & Mar., c. 4 ('outlandish people calling themselves Egyptians').

[82] 1 Edw. VI, c. 12. The exact operation of the act caused difficulties: e.g. in relation to piracy.

[83] 23 Hen. VIII, c. 1 (to find two substantial sureties for their good bearing or suffer life imprisonment); 23 Hen. VIII, c. 11. This effectively restored the terms of the Provisions of Clarendon 1164.

[84] 28 Hen. VIII, c. 1; perpetuated by 32 Hen. VIII, c. 3.

[85] 1 Edw. VI, c. 12. The statute also enabled peers to claim clergy in all cases other than treason and murder, and exempted them from branding.

[86] 1 Edw. VI, c. 3; repealed by 3 & 4 Edw. VI, c. 16. For other aspects of the slavery statute, see above, 99.

[87] Bellamy, Criminal Trial, 136. There are, however, virtually no gaol delivery records between 1460 and 1550. [88] For what follows see 94 Selden Soc. 334–9.

of the peace or 'grith'[89] which inhered in sanctified places. Unlike clergy, the privilege of sanctuary attached at common law to the place and not the person,[90] and was therefore available to any person who was bodily within its bounds, including women, excommunicates, bigamists, and probably heretics.[91] It was available for all offences, arguably even treason,[92] though this last case was modified by papal and royal legislation.[93] It could even, in some places, provide an escape from civil debts.[94] The common law fully acknowledged the privilege, so that if someone was improperly brought out he could pray sanctuary and the courts would restore him. That was the main distinction between ecclesiastical sanctuaries and secular liberties, such as the palatinates, with which they have sometimes been confused. If a plea of sanctuary was counterpleaded by the Crown, the issue of fact was tried by a jury of the county where the sanctuary was alleged.[95] One reader argued that this precluded a man from pleading sanctuary in a church outside England, such as Wales.[96]

Every church and churchyard in England was a common sanctuary in which criminals might seek refuge from the criminal law, subject to certain limitations. The privilege was said to attach not only to ancient parochial churches but also to newly founded chapels and hospitals.[97] The protection extended to the whole of the sanctified area of church and cemetery,[98] including the steeple, and it was held sufficient to place any part of the body within the sanctuary or merely to grasp the door-ring. In special sanctuaries the area of protection might be wider, and was sometimes marked by crosses. Protection did not extend, however, to the profane

[89] The English word was still used. It was called 'church gree' in *Re Bowmer* (1511) KB 29/143, m. 17.

[90] The canon law did not follow the logic so clearly and admitted a number of rather disparate exceptions which were confused in theory and largely ignored in English practice: Helmholz, *The Ius Commune in England*, 34–7, 42–55. For an attempt in 1516 to introduce the canon law exceptions see below, 548.

[91] The canon law excluded non-Christians and heretics: Helmholz, *The Ius Commune in England*, 50.

[92] See e.g. *R. v. Stafford* (1486), below, 546.

[93] See the bulls of Innocent VIII and Julius II (Rymer, *Foedera*, xii. 541; xiii. 104; *Calendar of Papal Letters*, xviii. 151–2, no. 116), the first of which was enrolled in the central courts at the instance of Fitzjames A.-G. in 1520: KB 27/1037, Rex m. 25; CP 40/1030, m. 1; Helmholz, *The Ius Commune in England*, 48; 26 Hen. VIII, c. 13.

[94] 3 Hen. VII, c. 4 (deeds of gift made to support debtors fleeing to sanctuary); below, 547.

[95] e.g. *R. v. Sawyer* (1499) KB 27/953, Rex m. 4 (jury finds he was taken from St Mary Overy, Southwark; judgment to be restored); *Thornedon v. Bewregard* (1507) 2 Caryll 559; *Owen's Case* (1516) ibid. 662; *R. v. Torre* (1530) KB 27/1075, Rex m. 3 (prisoner in Newgate pleads he was taken from sanctuary in Somerton church, Somerset; Crown says he was arrested wandering in highway at Somerton; issue to be tried at Somerset assizes); *Gawen v. Calverley* (1534) Spelman 53. For the venue see 4 Hen. VIII, c. 2.

[96] Richard Snede's reading (Inner Temple, 1511) CUL MS. Ee.3.46, fo. 60v. Cf., however, trials of *quare impedit* for churches in Wales: above, 103.

[97] Kebell's reading (c.1470/5), ff. 305v–306. According to Richard Littleton, it did not attach to a private chapel.

[98] Yorke 90, nos. 4 and 6, refers to sanctuary being taken in a cemetery as if this was the usual practice.

parts of a monastery, such as the gardens and fields, the barns and sheep-houses, or parts which had been made profane by keeping common shops or bawdy houses there.[99] A fugitive was permitted to leave sanctuary temporarily without forfeiting its protection for necessary purposes, such as to follow the call of nature or to escape fire or flood.[100] If required to give evidence in court in another case, he might attend in the custody of a keeper and then be led back.[101]

The privilege of common sanctuary lasted for only forty days at common law. At the end of that period, it was still illegal to take the fugitive out, and it was contrary to the canon law for the church authorities to eject him.[102] But anyone who fed the fugitive, or took his goods to him, after the expiration of the forty days, was regarded as an accessory after the fact; and so a felon could be starved into surrender. There was also a notion, said to be of canonical origin, that the felon might be 'immured' after the forty days—apparently meaning that he could be closely confined—but the common-law authorities denied this. At any rate, the felon in a common church, whose time was running out, had four alternative strategies open to him besides suing for a pardon.[103] He could escape and flee to another church, where he could have another forty days' protection; he could escape and commit another felony and return to the same church, in which case he also had another forty days; he could take refuge in one of the special sanctuaries, which had no time-limit imposed on their protection; or he could pray a coroner to come and record his abjuration of the realm.

Abjuration was much discussed by the readers, but it had changed little in essence since the fourteenth century. Though closely associated with sanctuary, it was not an ecclesiastical concept. At the felon's request, a coroner came to the church,[104] accompanied by the neighbours he was supposed to summon as witnesses; the felon confessed his offence, and the confession was recorded in writing; the coroner then assigned him a port, to which he was sworn to proceed for embarkation, promising never to return to England without the king's licence. His possessions were forfeited, except for essential clothing, and he was given a wooden cross to serve as a passport.[105] The felon was supposed to proceed from vill to vill, escorted by the constables of each place, and at the port he was to do

---

99 Hil. 9 Hen. VII, fo. 20, pl. 15; *Pauncefote* v. *Savage* (1519-20) 2 Caryll 704 at 707, 711-12; *Spencer's Case* (1520) cited ibid. 707-8. See also the readings cited in 94 Selden Soc. 335 n. 13.

100 On this see also BL MS. Harley 4990, fo. 154v.

101 Spelman 48, pl. 12, referring to James ap Hywel (Powel).

102 The forty-day rule was not acknowledged by the canon law: Helmholz, *The* Ius Commune *in England*, 61, 70.

103 For the manner of obtaining pardons in criminal cases see Bellamy, *Criminal Trial*, 140-4.

104 In theory a felon could abjure elsewhere, even in court, though not after the evidence against him had been given: Mich. 2 Hen. VII, fo. 3, pl. 8.

105 e.g. Spelman 53, pl. 24 (precedent of 1461, copied in 1534). A plea of abjuration in *R.* v. *Jenyns* (1537) KB 27/1104, Rex m. 8, refers to a passport.

his utmost to obtain a passage overseas—if need be, going down to the sea each day to call out for a ship.[106] How effective the system was in reality is difficult to gauge. But if the abjured felon was ever caught in any place other than the assigned route and destination, he could be arraigned upon the abjuration—which was tantamount to a conviction upon his recorded confession of guilt—and sentenced to death. The rules were applied generously, so that the felon was excused if he accepted a ride instead of walking, or genuinely lost his way, or deviated temporarily from the route in order to follow the call of nature or seek food. But the judges did not take kindly to those who sought to abuse the privilege by prevaricating before the coroner or escaping afterwards. Before the coroner, the felon had to give precise details of the felony which he was confessing, so that a proper record could be made;[107] and this created a serious dilemma for someone who had dealt a possibly mortal blow to a victim who had not yet died, since it was impossible to confess a felony which had not yet occurred.[108] Then again, the excuses for deviation from the route did not justify failing to return to it.[109] In 1491 a felon who had tried for fourteen days to find a ship pleaded that he had been compelled by hunger to return inland with the intention of abjuring again; but the court held that he should have stayed in the port and begged alms there.[110] Equally short shrift was given the same term to a felon who pleaded that he had been imprisoned en route, but failed to say that he had returned once he was freed.[111] And in 1532 a felon who had actually boarded a ship found no sympathy when he pleaded that it had been driven back to shore by gales and the Flemish mariners had declined to take him any further; he should have stayed near the sea until he could find another ship.[112]

Abjuration was allowed at any time, even—so the judges held in 1529[113]—after conviction, sentence, and escape. But it differed in scope from sanctuary in that it was only available for murder and felony, and could not be used in cases of treason, misdemeanour, or debt. Moreover, it could not be allowed twice, because the

---

[106] Rastell, *Exposiciones Terminorum* [*c.*1523], sig. A4, says he must wade up to his knees every day.

[107] *Marsshe v. Archer* (1492) 1 Caryll 111; *Moots*, 274; KB 27/924, m. 36 (noted 115 Selden Soc. 112); *Justice v. Ap Morgan* (1510) KB 27/996, m. 103 (appellant says accused would not confess a specific felony; issue joined as to whether a coroner came at all).

[108] *R. v. Anon.* (*c.*1525/35) Spelman 66–7; Yorke 90, no. 6.

[109] See the cases in 94 Selden Soc. 337–8.

[110] *R. v. Preston* (1491) Spelman 44; KB 27/921, Rex m. 2d; copied in Crown Office entries, fo. 34v.

[111] *R. v. Whatman* (1491) Mich. 7 Hen. VII, fo. 7, pl. 11; Fitz. Abr., *Corone*, pl. 65; KB 27/921, Rex m. 6; copied in Crown Office entries, fo. 35.

[112] *R. v. Danby* (1532) Spelman 49; KB 9/519, m. 147 (filed abjuration); KB 27/1084, Rex m. 7 (abstract tr. 94 Selden Soc. 278). Cf., to the like effect, *R. v. Olyffe* (1532–3) Spelman 49, pl. 14 and 16; KB 9/519, m. 119 (filed abjuration); KB 27/1083, Rex m. 4d (tr. 94 Selden Soc. 277).

[113] *R. v. Anon.* (1528/9) Spelman 46, pl. 8 ('un graund case'); Caryll (Jun.) 394, no. 60; cf. 22 Hen. VIII, Brooke Abr., *Corone*, pl. 110. The decision was noted incorrectly in 94 Selden Soc. 339.

attainder on the first abjuration could be put into execution if the person was arrested in England. But the abjured felon who was caught at large could plead benefit of clergy,[114] or mistaken identity.[115] To prevent abuse in this regard, it was enacted in 1529 that a felon who abjured was to be branded on the brawn of the right thumb with the letter A immediately upon confession.[116] This mark operated in the same way as the M or T ordained for clerks convict, not as a conclusive record in itself.

In 1531 the nature of abjuration was drastically altered by statute. The government were worried that able-bodied Englishmen, skilled in archery, were abjuring the realm and enlisting in foreign armies. These criminals would be better kept as potential recruits for the English army, or at least kept out of the field. It was therefore enacted that felons who abjured were not to quit the realm but to give up their liberty; instead of a port, they would be assigned to a designated English sanctuary, there to remain for life.[117] Parliament did not say what was to happen if and when these sanctuaries became full,[118] nor did it consider too carefully why certain parts of the country should bear the brunt of a somewhat outmoded privilege. The new policy could only exacerbate the evils attending special sanctuaries, and tied the future of abjuration to their fate.

SPECIAL OR PRIVATE SANCTUARIES[119]

The trouble caused by the abuse of abjuration was as nothing compared with that caused by the communities of malefactors who congregated in the great special or 'private' sanctuaries which gave protection for life. Often in the centre of important towns and cities—such as London,[120] Beverley,[121] and Durham[122]—they provided the professional criminal with an ideal base for his forays into the outside world. Polydore Vergil complained that 'our Christian world today, and especially England, is full of sanctuaries; which admit not only those in fear of

[114] *R. v. Preston* (1491) Spelman 44; *R. v. Wolmer* (1500) KB 27/956, Rex m. 2 (copied in Lucas's entries, fo. 153; Rast. Ent. 1v); *R. v. Anon.* (1518) 2 Caryll 695; *R. v. Cheslett* (1530) KB 27/1075, Rex m. 2; *R. v. Olyffe* (1532–3) Spelman 49; *R. v. Smyth* (1534) ibid. 169. Kebell said in his reading (*c.*1470/75) that the law had once been otherwise, but opinion had changed.   [115] Spelman 63, pl. 48.

[116] 21 Hen. VIII, c. 2.   [117] 22 Hen. VIII, c. 14.

[118] In *R. v. Harrys* (1533) KB 27/1086, Rex m. 4, the defendant pleaded that he was branded with an A and assigned to Beaulieu, but the abbot would not let him in.

[119] For what follows see 94 Selden Soc. 339–46.

[120] The principal sanctuaries in or near the metropolis were St Martin's-le-Grand, London; St John's Priory, Clerkenwell; and St Peter's, Westminster (i.e. the abbey).

[121] Beverley received over 250 felons between 1506 and 1539: *Sanctuarium Dunelmense et Sanctuarium Beverlacense*, ed. J. Raine (5 Surtees Soc., 1837), pp. xxvi–xxvi.

[122] Durham received over 300 felons between 1464 and 1524: ibid.

attack, but also all manner of criminals, even traitors'.[123] A Venetian visitor to England in Henry VII's reign could scarcely believe that so many villains were permitted to organize crime under the eye of the Church.[124] Starkey put into the mouth of Cardinal Pole the rhetorical question whether it were 'well' for a man who had committed murder or robbery, or deliberately deceived his creditors, to take all his goods into sanctuary and live there quietly and unmolested: 'This thing', he said, 'is a plain occasion of all mischief and misery, and causeth much murder in our country and nation; for who will be afraid to kill his enemy if he may be saved by the privilege of sanctuary?'[125] And in his *History of King Richard III*, written in about 1513, even Thomas More—not known for tempering his view of ecclesiastical privilege to suit secular concerns—provided a strong case against the unreformed sanctuaries. The remarks were attributed to the duke of Buckingham (in 1483), but have been credibly supposed to represent More's own views at the time of writing. The burden of the speech was that sanctuary was a wise and God-sent institution which man had notoriously abused, but which could still be reformed without breaking the spirit of the privilege. It might in unsettled times have given justifiable protection to political offenders, but the shelter it now gave to thieves was indefensible, since the king's pardon provided all that mercy required. Sanctuaries had become 'a rabble of thieves, murderers, and malicious heinous traitors'. Men ran to them with other men's money and goods, and spent them there, 'and bid their creditors go whistle them'. Thieves brought in stolen goods and lived on the proceeds, devised new robberies, and crept out at night to commit them, sure of a safe refuge afterwards: as if the places gave them not merely protection for past misdeeds but a licence to repeat them. That could not have been God's intention.[126]

Some claims to privilege were extraordinarily wide and of very dubious authenticity. This was particularly true of the privileges claimed for the order of St John of Jerusalem. It was thought that one could obtain sanctuary merely by touching a knight of St John.[127] In Salisbury they claimed the right to rescue felons from the gallows by sending the 'St John's cart' with a banner for the felon to touch.[128] Sanctuary was also alleged to attach to some non-religious properties of the Hospitallers.[129] Another foundation of St John's, at Beverley, claimed a peace or

---

[123] P. Vergil, *De Inventoribus Rerum* (1528), fo. 55 (tr.).

[124] *Venetian Relation*, 34–5.   [125] Starkey, *Dialogue*, ed. Mayer, 94 (sp. mod.).

[126] T. More, *The History of King Richard III*, ed. R. S. Sylvester (1963), 27–33, 115–19 (sp. mod.).

[127] See two pleas to this effect in *R. v. Pulham* (1507) KB 27/984, Rex m. 4 (verdict taken); *R. v. Toker* (1507) ibid., m. 12 (demurrer). The pleas were ineffective, apparently for failure to plead over to the felony.   [128] Hil. 1 Hen. VII, fo. 6, pl. 2; Fitz. Abr., *Corone*, pl. 48.

[129] e.g. Temple Fee in Bristol, an ancient house which passed to the Hospitallers when the Templars were dissolved: *R. v. Johnson* (1516–22) KB 27/1020, Rex m. 21; KB 29/148, m. 22d; *R. v. White* (1516–22) KB 27/1020, Rex m. 22 (both pleas met with undetermined demurrer). Cf. *Rollesley v. Toft* (1495) KB 27/936, m. 60 (Templar house at Winkburn, Notts.).

sanctuary extending one league from the church door, the boundaries of which were marked by finely carved stone crosses. Most special sanctuaries, even if more limited in space, were unlimited in time, and so there was no need for inmates to abjure. The criminals were, instead, received by the church as residents, enrolled in its register of sanctuarymen, and given an oath of fealty to the superior of the house. Sometimes they were required to perform household chores and assist at services, but it is far from clear that the church attempted to supervise their lives or reform them. Their oath forbade them to carry weapons or to go out and commit felony in hope of returning; but the only sanction was imprisonment at the abbot's discretion, and enforcement seems to have been lax. They seem, in short, to have had the benefits of monastic life without the burdens of its rule. It was not easy to pursue civil actions against them. Moreover, since they had not abjured, they suffered neither the disabilities of an attainted felon nor the forfeiture of a clerk convict. In some places the sanctuarymen even carried on trades, and one Westminster inmate (John Milles) was plaintiff in a series of celebrated Common Pleas cases.

Since the Church proved unwilling or unable to reform these scandalous abuses, and Parliament had in 1482 rejected a bill to that end,[130] the most effective limitations on sanctuary in its last phase before the break with Rome were those introduced by the common-law judges. The attack seems to have begun in the time of Henry VII.[131] In the first year of the reign, the abbot of Westminster sought confirmation of the privileges of his house—including the sanctuary— and was advised by the lords in Parliament and the judges not to bring the matter to open argument but rather to ensure that the privileges were not abused.[132] Soon afterwards the case of the alleged traitor Humphrey Stafford fell to be argued by the judges. Stafford, arraigned in the King's Bench, pleaded that he had taken refuge in the Benedictine house at Culham, near Abingdon, and prayed to be restored. The abbot was summoned by *scire facias* and produced a charter[133] of King Coenwulf of Mercia granting various privileges, with a confirmation from King Edgar, reinforced by usage from time immemorial and several papal bulls. Eventually the matter was decided on a point of construction, but the judges held *obiter* that only the king could grant sanctuary for treason, and that neither by

---

[130] C40/40, no. 10 (bill marked, 'Le roy savisera'). The bill did not propose that sanctuary be directly violated. Reciting the evils of sanctuarymen committing felonies, it was proposed that governors of sanctuaries should be made liable to a fine if a felon was not handed over after proclamations made at the door for his appearance.

[131] See I. D. Thornley, 'The Destruction of Sanctuary', in *Tudor Studies Presented to A. F. Pollard*, ed. R. W. Seton-Watson (1924), 182–207, especially at 197–200.

[132] Hil. 1 Hen. VII, fo. 10, pl. 11. The treatise on the abuse of the Westminster sanctuary, now at Longleat House (MS. 38), may date from this period: Thornley, 'Destruction of Sanctuary', n. 67, 74; Helmholz, *The* Ius Commune *in England*, 71.

[133] Now known to have been forged, at a much earlier period.

prescription nor by papal bull could the terms of the royal grant be exceeded. Some of the judges went further and declared that the king could no longer grant such privileges, so that a grant before time of memory was necessary; and they also required proof that the sanctuary had been allowed by justices in eyre.[134] Some powerful weapons for further contest were thus provided. No one could plead sanctuary by special grant unless the governor of the sanctuary could produce the relevant records for scrutiny;[135] claims would not be favoured, and the requisite supporting evidence now comprised a royal grant before 1189, a papal confirmation, usage since 1189, and allowance in eyre. Pope Innocent VIII lent his support to the campaign by issuing a bull in 1487 which authorized the archbishop of Canterbury to investigate abuses and to modify or limit sanctuaries which operated against the public good.[136] Further means of attack were found later in the reign. For instance, Richard Littleton, in his Inner Temple reading of 1493, argued that it was legally impossible to create a sanctuary for debt,[137] trespass, or treason, so that any grant or usage to that effect was void. And in 1504 Pope Julius II confirmed that traitors could be removed from sanctuary, as could murderers and highway robbers (*insidiatores viarum*) who left sanctuary in order to commit new crimes and then return.[138]

The judicial assault on sanctuaries was headed by the two influential chief justices Huse CJ (1481–95) and Fyneux CJ (1495–1525). Huse CJ's hostility was clearly voiced in a case of 1495, reported by both Caryll and Port.[139] He likened a sanctuary to a 'den of thieves' (*spelunca latronum*),[140] and said that if the king could grant such places of protection it would—*vis à vis* an appellor—be a breach of his royal obligation to do justice. Prescription, he said, was immaterial, since such a privilege could only be validly granted by act of Parliament.[141] The case appears to have been left undecided, but sent a clear signal to the profession. At around the same time, though seemingly not in the same case, Huse CJ 'and all the

---

[134] *R. v. Stafford* (1486) Trin. 1 Hen. VII, fo. 25, pl. 1; KB 27/900, Rex m. 8; Crown Office entries, ff. 151–155v; 64 Selden Soc. 115; cited in Port 32, *per* Huse CJ (1495); 2 Caryll 709, *per* Fyneux CJ (1519); Yorke 191, no. 263. Discussed in Thornley, 'Destruction of Sanctuary', 198–208; Hemmant, 64 Selden Soc., pp. xlii–xlv.

[135] See also *R. v. Bagnall* (1494) 102 Selden Soc. 32 n. 4; record in Crown Office entries, ff. /3 75; (title to sanctuary of St Martin-le-Grand challenged by demurrer; dean summoned to show his title).

[136] *Calendar of Papal Letters*, xiv. 35 (bull of 6 Aug. 1487, exemplified 1493; with letter to the archbishop in support, 18 Mar. 1490); copy in BL MS. Add. 25168, fo. 565.

[137] A debtor who fled to sanctuary in fraud of his creditors could be outlawed: *Ayloffe* v. *Jakes* (1491) KB 27/921, m. 31. His goods were also liable to execution: 2 Ric. II, stat. 2, c. 3.

[138] *Calendar of Papal Letters*, xviii. 151–2, no. 116; above, 541.

[139] *Rollesley* v. *Toft* (1495–8) 1 Caryll 285; Port 31; KB 27/936, m. 60 (pr. Rast. Ent. 533 (584); tr. 102 Selden Soc. 33).   [140] The allusion is biblical: see Helmholz, *The* Ius Commune *in England*, 30.

[141] But it could arguably be justified by local custom: anonymous reading (Gray's Inn, c.1515) 113 Selden Soc. 12, no. 7. Cf. ibid. 4, no. 3 (does not lie in prescription).

justices' held that the privilege of St John's priory could not extend to its fields.[142]
The campaign continued in the time of Fyneux CJ. In 1506 it was decided by the
judges that a plea of sanctuary had also to answer the felony, and if it did not
it would be rejected on that ground alone.[143] And a major case arose in 1513,
when Hugh Boswell pleaded sanctuary in the Cluniac priory of St Andrew,
Northampton, relying on prescription and also on bulls of Innocent IV and
Benedict XII granted to the Cluniac order in general under the sanction of 'horrible curses'. By the advice of all the justices of England he was sentenced to death,
because his plea did not show a royal grant and allowance in eyre. It was impossible to prescribe to be outside the law; and a papal grant by itself was not enough.
The prior of St Andrew's chose not to lay any evidence before the court, or to
claim any sanctuary, and so it appears that he had made a decision not to press a
possible claim; but it is improbable that he had any better evidence than that
recited by Boswell.[144] It was around this time that More's passage on sanctuary
was written, though it was not published for another thirty years.

The matter came to a head after a bloody incident in 1516 when John
Pauncefote, a Gloucestershire justice of the peace embroiled in local feuds,[145] was
shot dead and mutilated on his way to the spring quarter sessions at Cirencester.
The murderers, together with a number of thieves, caused a public outcry by taking sanctuary. When the matter was discussed in the Star Chamber, some of the
legally qualified bishops argued that sanctuary was not available under the canon
law to manifest thieves and waylayers of highways (*publici latrones et insidiatores
viarum*),[146] but Wolsey C. seems to have had doubts and asked for more time. The
point of canon law had already occurred to the law officers earlier in 1516, when
the attorney-general set up a counterplea of 'communes et publici latrones et
insidiatores viarum' and a writ was sent to the bishop of London to certify the law
of the Church.[147] Yet in neither case did the bishops take this opportunity to
cooperate by restricting abuses of sanctuary in accordance with the law of the
Church and the bulls obtained in the previous reign. Under Wolsey's leadership—
and in the context of the simultaneous furore over Richard Hunne and benefit of

[142] *Anon.* (1494) Hil. 9 Hen. VII, fo. 20, pl. 15.

[143] *R. v. Anon.* (1506) 2 Caryll 469, pl. 330 (judgment of *peine forte et dure*); *R. v. Cowley* (1518) ibid.
693; and see *R. v. Elys* (1516) KB 27/1018, Rex m. 7 (plea held bad on demurrer; judgment of *peine forte
et dure*); *R. v. Wenwryght* (1508) KB 27/986, Rex m. 6d (tr. 'as to the felony he says nothing but refuses
the royal laws'; later changes plea to Not guilty). The rule did not apply if sanctuary was pleaded in
another county: *R. v. Bradbury* (1507) ibid. 553; *R. v. Anon.* (1516) ibid. 662, pl. 482.

[144] *R. v. Boswell* (1513) Port 31; 2 Caryll 708–9; KB 27/1008, Rex m. 12 (tr. 102 Selden Soc. 38);
KB 29/145, m. 14d.

[145] In 1514–15 he was himself in prison for security of the peace: KB 29/146, m. 46 (*habeas corpus*).

[146] For this canonical exception see Helmholz, *The* Ius Commune *in England*, 34, 42–8; letter of
Julius II (1504) *Cal. Papal Letters*, xviii. 151–2, no. 116.

[147] *R. v. Dodde* (1516–17) KB 27/1018, Rex m. 11 (writ not returned).

clergy[148]—they chose instead to take an absolute stand against any change to the status quo. The immediate result of the Star Chamber discussion is unknown, but the case came before the King's Bench when Pauncefote's widow commenced an appeal of murder against various defendants who included Sir John Savage, sheriff of Worcestershire, and his namesake Sir John Savage the younger.[149] The latter pleaded that he had taken sanctuary in a house in St John's Street, Middlesex, belonging to the priory of St John, but had been forcibly removed and taken to the Tower. In a lengthy plea he made out the priory's title to the sanctuary by prescription, papal bull, royal confirmation, allowance in eyre, and allowance in recent times by justices of assize and at Newgate. The appellor demurred. The principal question of law was whether the general privileges of the priory extended to profane houses outside the 'ambit' of the priory proper—meaning the church, cloister, dorter, and cemetery. Fyneux CJ indicated that they did not, since they had already been held not to extend to the fields.[150] He also indicated that he thought it was impossible to prescribe for a sanctuary beyond forty days, since that was 'so much in derogation of justice and against the common weal of the realm'.[151] A third objection was that sanctuary could not be created by prescription or papal bull, and therefore the royal confirmation and the judicial allowance were of something void in its inception. According to Serjeant Caryll's account, Savage was minded to waive the plea and put himself on the king's grace, a course which Fyneux CJ commended. Nevertheless, the record shows that the case continued until 1520 and that discussion ranged more widely. The matter was returned to in Council, where Wolsey debated it with the two chief justices in the inner Star Chamber; and on 10–11 November 1519 it was argued in the king's presence, with the assistance of the assembled judges and a number of canonists. The wide claims made by St John's and Westminster Abbey were on the agenda,[152] and their supposed sanctuary for debt was questioned. The king observed that he did not suppose that those who created sanctuaries ever intended them to serve for wilful murder and theft committed outside the sanctuary in the hope of returning, and warned: 'I will have this reformed which has been encroached by abuse, and brought back to the true intention of the makers'.

---

[148] Above, 537–8.

[149] *Pauncefote* v. *Savage* (1516–20) 2 Caryll 704; Port 34; Yorke 191, no. 263; KB 27/1020, m. 60 (noted in 116 Selden Soc. 714). For the local context see E. W. Ives, 'Crime, Sanctuary, and Royal Authority under Henry VIII: the exemplary sufferings of the Savage family' in *On the Laws and Customs of England*, ed. M. S. Arnold *et al.* (1981), 296–320; Guy, *The Cardinal's Court*, 33.

[150] i.e. in Hil. 9 Hen. VII, fo. 20, pl. 15. Note also *R.* v. *Spencer* (1520) 2 Caryll 707 (interpolated), in which the justices held that the sanctuary of the Greyfriars in Coventry did not extend to an orchard within its walls.

[151] 2 Caryll 708. Cf. Port 41, no. 40, which says that privileges could be 'enlarged' in respect of consecrated ground.   [152] See also Port 41, no. 39.

Although no final judgment was given, and Savage was indeed pardoned, the reform of sanctuary had now been promised. As with benefit of clergy, the legislative solution had to wait for some fifteen to twenty years. In the meantime, however, pleas of sanctuary were nearly always contested by the Crown and—using the substantial armoury of weapons now assembled for the attack—regularly rejected by the courts.[153] The Chancery was prepared to issue writs for the removal of those who reoffended while in sanctuary.[154] And Wolsey took note of the king's command to instigate reform by commissioning individual judges to investigate particular sanctuaries.[155] The Star Chamber played some part in this surveillance.[156] There were also threats of enquiry by *quo warranto*,[157] a procedure used twice against Beaulieu,[158] and in 1526 the Council in the Marches was ordered to investigate all sanctuaries within its purview by that means.[159]

When Parliament met again in 1529, a more sweeping solution could be contemplated. The Reformation Parliament began, as we have seen, by introducing branding and inland abjuration.[160] In 1534 it reduced the scope of the privilege itself by abolishing sanctuary for high treason,[161] though—by way of contrast with the policy on benefit of clergy—this approach was not carried much further.[162] The following year a different kind of reform was initiated with a statute for controlling sanctuarymen. They were to lose their privilege if caught at large without the prescribed ten-inch badges, or carrying weapons other than table-knives, or if caught out at night on three occasions, or if they disobeyed the governor of the place.[163] That control was still preferred to eradication indicates the weight of opposition from the Church, and the position taken by conservatives like More who held that sanctuaries were not in themselves evil but needed reform. Even the king was not unwilling to support ecclesiastical privileges which derived from the Crown.[164] Nevertheless, Cromwell's private notes show that he had

---

[153] 94 Selden Soc. 344–5.   [154] *Anon.* (1521) Port 42, no. 41.   [155] 94 Selden Soc. 345 n. 3.

[156] See *R.* v. *Symondson* (1529–31) KB 27/1071, Rex m. 14, where the defendant said he was collared and shackled in Ilchester priory because the prior was bound over to keep him until the Council were consulted.

[157] See H. Garrett-Goodyear, 'The Tudor Revival of Q*uo Warranto*' in *On the Laws and Customs of England*, ed. Arnold *et al.*, 231–95, at 246–8. There are, however, very few examples in the records; and the topic is not mentioned in Spelman's reading on *quo warranto* (1519).

[158] *Att.-Gen.* v. *Abbot of Beaulieu* (1520) ibid. 275, no. 14, citing KB 9/480, m. 53 (file); KB 29/151, mm. 35, 37d (controlment roll); *Att.-Gen.* v. *Abbot of Beaulieu* (1531–3) KB 9/518, m. 8; KB 27/1087, Rex m. 5. See also *Att.-Gen.* v. *Bradstone* (1530) KB 27/1074, Rex m. 2.

[159] BL MS. Harley 6068, ff. 30v-31.   [160] Above, 544.   [161] 26 Hen. VIII, c. 13.

[162] Sanctuary was taken away for embezzlement by 27 Hen. VIII, c. 11; and for stealing the king's goods by 33 Hen. VIII, c. 12. In 1538 the king decreed by proclamation that those killing officers of justice in the execution of their duty, or killing in the course of a sudden affray, should not have clergy or sanctuary: *Tudor Royal Proclamations*, i. 263, no. 179. In 1547 it was taken away after conviction of a non-clergiable felony: 1 Edw. VI, c. 12; *Note* (1557) 110 Selden Soc. 411, no. 8.   [163] 27 Hen. VIII, c. 19.

[164] Elton, *Reform and Renewal*, 137.

nurtured a more radical solution for some years, as part of his policy of destroying sectional privilege.[165] He may have forced the issue in a case of 1539, when he ordered a wanted murderer to be taken out of the Westminster sanctuary, and then arranged for a suitably reliable commission of gaol delivery—including himself and Rich—to overrule the man's not obviously bad plea.[166] He may have drawn encouragement from the fact that François I had, that same year, struck down the privilege in France with papal approval. The dissolution of monastic sanctuaries, such as Glastonbury and Beaulieu, may also have attracted renewed attention to the subject. Whatever prompted it, the Cromwellian solution was finally achieved by statute in 1540.[167] The preamble explained how wilful offenders had saved their lives by means of 'licentious privileges', and thereby avoided the 'just and condign punishment of his grace's laws, both contrary to the expressed word of God and the common tranquility of this his grace's realm and the public wealth and surety of the same'. The privilege was therefore completely abolished in cases of murder, rape, burglary, robbery, and arson, leaving it in place principally for simple larceny (which was clergiable); all special sanctuaries not expressly named were abolished;[168] and, with limited exceptions, all sanctuaries were limited to the common forty-day period. Though sanctuary was to linger on into the next century, it was effectively stifled by this act of 1540, read in conjunction with the previous legislation of Henry VIII's reign. Abjuration, not being itself an ecclesiastical privilege, was preserved for the time being; but, since it depended (after the 1530 statute) on the provision of English sanctuaries, it disappeared with them. The legislation did not affect the Westminster sanctuary for debt, which was finally declared unlawful by the Star Chamber in 1569.[169] The last vestiges of ecclesiastical sanctuary would be eradicated in 1624.[170]

PREGNANCY

A very different kind of privilege was available to women, who could take sanctuary and abjure[171] but were unable by reason of their sex to have benefit of clergy. A female convict could instead allege pregnancy, in which case she was sentenced to death at once but execution was deferred until after the birth.[172] It is not known whether—as in later times—execution was in practice suspended indefinitely, though it was said that the privilege would not avail if the woman became pregnant

---

[165] 94 Selden Soc. 345 n. 8.

[166] R. v. Maynwaryng (1539) KB 27/1112, Rex m. 9. Other cases of pleas of sanctuary being held bad for no obvious reason are R. v. Smyth (1534) Spelman 52, 169; R. v. Brewe (1539) KB 27/1113, Rex m. 5.

[167] 32 Hen. VIII, c. 12 (sp. mod.).

[168] Manchester was added to the list of sanctuary towns, though this proved controversial. Chester was later replaced with Stafford: Tudor Royal Proclamations, i. 311, no. 212 (1542).

[169] Ex parte Hampton and Whitacres (1569) 109 Selden Soc. 121, 173-4.   [170] 21 Jac. I, c. 28.

[171] Yorke 91, no. 8.   [172] Yorke 92, no. 12.

a second time.[173] The plea of pregnancy was quite common, and was sometimes expressed to be 'for the reverence of God and the Blessed Mary the Virgin',[174] or with the explanation 'lest the issue in her belly should suffer death for the fault of its mother'.[175] It was usually challenged by suspicious clerks of the Crown, in which case a jury of married women (*legales mulieres matrones*) was summoned to inspect the body of the accused and decide whether she was indeed pregnant. The number of women impanelled for this purpose seems to have varied between twelve and twenty-four.[176] In later times the verdict of pregnancy became virtually fictitious, but there is no clear evidence that this was already so. It was, at any rate, not the invariable outcome.[177]

[173] *Anon.* (1536/7) Brooke Abr., *Corone*, pl. 97.

[174] e.g. *R. v. Gybson* (1516) KB 27/1019, Rex m. 8. Sometimes the phrase is simply 'ob reverenciam Dei': e.g. Maycote's entries, fo. 31; *R. v. Mathewe* (1506) KB 27/981, Rex m. 4; *R. v. Kewell* (1508) KB 27/986, Rex m. 9; *R. v. Franke* (1512) KB 27/1047, Rex m. 8.

[175] Maycote's entries, fo. 31; *R. v. Mathewe* (1506) KB 27/981, Rex m. 4.

[176] See e.g. *R. v. Mathewe* (1506) KB 27/981, Rex m. 4 (twenty-four); *R. v. Multon* (1508) KB 27/989, Rex m. 16 (twelve); *R. v. Franke* (1512) KB 27/1047, Rex m. 8 (twelve); *R. v. Smith* (1555) 110 Selden Soc. 404 (twenty).

[177] See *R. v. Gybson* (1516) KB 27/1019, Rex m. 8 (woman convicted of petty treason found not pregnant; sentenced to death by burning).

31

The Law Relating to Felonies[1]

OFFENCES AGAINST THE PERSON

HOMICIDE was the only common-law felony arising from violation of the person, though rape had also been made a felony by thirteenth-century legislation. The appeal of mayhem was still in use, and the count used the word 'feloniously';[2] but wounding or maiming was not an indictable felony[3] and a successful appeal did not lead to capital punishment. Appeals apart, the most material distinction in relation to assaults was whether or not they resulted in death. If they did not, the law did not distinguish offences according to the gravity of the attack, though that would affect the punishment. Maiming and simple battery alike were indictable misdemeanours,[4] and indictments may even be found for assaults by words alone.[5]

Homicide[6]

The unlawful killing of another person was a capital felony, and—if the readings are a safe guide—the division of felonious homicide into murder and manslaughter was a distinction of secondary importance and not necessarily exhaustive.[7] Moreover, although the common declaration in appeals of death

---

[1] Misdemeanours were almost unlimited in scope (see above, 272–3, 317) and received much less discussion in the learned authorities. The law was probably still fairly crude. St German did not think ignorance of fact or law was a defence in proceedings upon a penal statute: *Little Treatise*, ed. Guy, 118. In some cases parties were still punished without trial: above, 302; *Anon.* (c.1550) Wm Yelv. 353, no. 81 (party fined upon the indictment, without trial, unless he wished to traverse).

[2] Yorke 113, no. 72 (c.1535), *per* Fitzjames CJ ('the appeal says *felonice*, although it is only a trespass; but that is the form').

[3] Except for the cutting out of tongues and eyes, which was made felony by 3 Hen. IV, c. 5. Cutting off ears was recognized as a finable misdemeanour by 37 Hen. VIII, c. 6.

[4] There are two indictments for maiming (1532–3) in NfRO, C/S3/1, mm. 22, 48 f.

[5] e.g. several from 1533 in NfRO, C/S3/1, mm. 63a and 63f (assault, affray, and imposing such threats and contumelious words that his life was despaired of), 72e (trespass to land and assault so that he dared not go about his business), 72h (riotous assault and affray so that life despaired of), 73d (assault, affray, and threats, so that he dared not exercise office of sheriff). For 'waylaying' with intent to assault, see W. Hudson, *Court of Star Chamber*, ed. F. Hargrave (1792 edn), ii. 88.

[6] For a more detailed study see 94 Selden Soc. *303–16*.

[7] The term 'felony' included murder: *Anon.* (1507) 2 Caryll 556, pl. 399. The converse was less clear, and an indictment for murder had to say 'feloniously' as well as 'murdered': Spelman 105, pl. 28.

spoke of murder by lying in wait and assault aforethought, these were formal allegations and probably did not exclude the kind of non-malicious killing later characterized as manslaughter.[8] The doctrinal treatment of homicide therefore tended to treat the subject as a unity. Although the discussion of misadventure, in readings on Marlborough, might seem to later legal minds to have more to do with manslaughter than murder, to the contemporary mind manslaughter was chiefly about sudden fighting.

The distinction between murder and other forms of homicide was nevertheless of practical importance, because pardons of 'felony' did not extend to murder by malice aforethought,[9] and statutory general pardons often excluded wilful murder.[10] It became even more important as a result of the statutes of 1512 and 1531 which took away benefit of clergy for murder by malice aforethought.[11] Whether malice aforethought differed from the *mens rea* required for all felonious homicide, and if so how, does not seem to have been resolved in this period.[12] The requirement of *mens rea* meant that felonious homicide could not be committed by an insane person, or a child who was not old enough to distinguish between right and wrong, or someone asleep. Voluntary drunkenness, however, did not excuse: 'he who killeth a man drunk, sober shall be hanged'.[13] To malice we shall return presently.

All felonies included 'force and arms against the king's peace', and therefore homicide caused by inaction or passive negligence was not felonious, except in the special case of deliberately neglecting an infant or helpless dependant.[14] Nor were bare words regarded as forcible acts, and so it was said that frightening someone to death with words could not be felonious.[15] It was, however, possible to commit felony through the agency of an animal, or an inanimate object such as a trap, or an innocent agent, without a direct act of violence by the killer.[16] A growing concern in Henry VIII's reign was the use of poison.[17]

---

[8] It is stated in Yorke 95, no. 22, that in appeals after 1512 the judges took to asking juries whether the killing was of malice aforethought or not. For uncertainty as to the meaning of the words of form see *Jackson v. Stratforth* (1539) Spelman 62–3.   [9] 13 Ric. II, stat. 2, c. 1.

[10] 94 Selden Soc. 305 n. 5.

[11] 4 Hen. VIII, c. 2; 23 Hen. VIII, c. 1; above, 537, 539. An earlier precedent was 12 Hen. VII, c. 7, which took away clergy for petty treason, where someone 'purpensedly' murdered his lord or master.

[12] 94 Selden Soc. 304, 309. For the requirements of 'discretion' and 'memory' see also *Anon.* (1530) 121 Selden Soc. 417 at 420.

[13] 94 Selden Soc. 309; *Reniger v. Fogassa* (1550) 1 Plowd. 1 at 19, *per* Pollard sjt.

[14] 94 Selden Soc. 307; *R. v. Page* (1559) 110 Selden Soc. 422. However, where a child of 6 died of cold through her parents' neglect, when left out all night in November to guard sheep, this was treated as a natural death: *Sussex Inquests*, 57, no. 204 (1555). Cf. leaving a wife out in the cold: *R. v. Gelder* (1558) *Notts. Inquests*, 156, no. 324 (not clear whether natural death or misadventure).

[15] Mountford's reading (Inner Temple, 1527) BL MS. Hargrave 87, fo. 177 (e.g. a menace, or telling someone he had the common sickness).   [16] 94 Selden Soc. 307–8.

[17] Not that it was new: see *Jurdan v. Jurdan and Phisician* (1488) KB 27/909, m. 97; Rast. Ent. 51v (appeal of death against a widow and a physician for poisoning wine with ratsbane); *Wynslowe v. Cleypole* (1489) Mich. 5 Hen. VII, fo. 4, pl. 10; CP 40/910, m. 340 (arrest on suspicion of poisoning).

There was no legal difficulty in holding it to be homicide if a poisoner created a situation in which the deceased unwittingly took the poison himself,[18] but there was a difficulty if the poison had a long-term effect. Some judges were willing in that case to relax the rule that death must occur within a year and a day,[19] though the matter was not settled. The poison scare did nevertheless result in the nastiest of Henry VIII's penal innovations.[20]

A general question which was not fully resolved concerned the killing of an unborn foetus. The readers differed as to whether this was felonious homicide or only a misdemeanour;[21] but precedents of indictments show that in practice abortion was sometimes treated as murder.[22]

Murder

Although the original meaning of murder had been a killing by stealth, and some definitions still included 'lying in wait' as a necessary element, the essence of murder by the end of the fifteenth century was a killing by malice aforethought or 'malice prepense' (*malicia praecogitata*), meaning premeditation.[23] What exactly had to be premeditated was not precisely defined.[24] Sometimes an intent to kill was expressly laid in the indictment,[25] but it was not necessary.[26] If a victim died unexpectedly from an unlawful beating it was felonious homicide, and so it seems that an intention to hurt was sufficient for murder.[27] From this notion there developed the broader doctrine that any unexpected death occasioned in the course of an unlawful enterprise was murder.[28] The doctrine seems to have been laid down by Fyneux CJ in 1512, in a case where there was an intent to beat, and it was held that

[18] R. v. *Dores* (1533) KB 9/523, m. 99 (poisoned soup taken to deceased by small boy).

[19] R. v. *Bradshaw and Pyteous* (1532) Spelman 48, 97; *Anon.* (after 1530) ibid. 71, pl. 70.

[20] 94 Selden Soc. 308–9; 22 Hen. VIII, c. 9 (above, 539).   [21] 94 Selden Soc. 306.

[22] c.g. R. v. *Wynspere* (1504) KB 27/974, Rex m. 4; *Notts. Inquests*, 8–9, no. 10 (suicide of mother and homicide of child in womb); *Boke of Justyces of Peas* (1515 edn), sig. F3 (murder of mother and of child in womb); R. v. *Wodelake* (1530) KB 9/513, m. 23 (rape of mother, and murder of unborn child); R. v. *Taillour* (1532) NfRO, C/S3/1, mm. 45c, 53 (rape of mother, and murder of two children *habentes vitas* in her womb).

[23] See the definitions in 94 Selden Soc. 309 n. 5. Cf. Scottish parallels from the same period: W. D. H. Sellar, 'Forethocht Felony, Malice Aforethought and the Classification of Homicide' in *Legal History in the Making*, ed. W. M. Gordon and T. D. Fergus (1991), 43–59.

[24] It was not even necessary to lay premeditation in the indictment, since it was implied in the word 'murdered': R. v. *Buckler* (1552) Dyer 69a.

[25] e.g. R. v. *Meurig ap Rhys* (1532) KB 27/1085, Rex m. 12 (tr. 94 Selden Soc. 293 at 294). The accessories in this case, however, were indicted for abetting the principal with intention to beat ('ea intentione ad verberandum') the deceased.

[26] It was not even necessary to say 'of malice aforethought', because this was implied in 'feloniously murdered': R. v. *Anon.* (1526) 120 Selden Soc. 57, no. 41; R. v. *Anon.* (1554) Dalison's reports, BL MS. Harley 5141, fo. 17v.

[27] This was expressly decided in R. v. *Anon.* (1558) Dalison's reports, BL MS. Harley 5141, fo. 41.

[28] For this doctrine see J. Kaye in 83 *LQR* at 579–87.

the person who struck the fatal blow was guilty of murder and all those who accompanied him with that intention were accessories.[29] By 1558, the doctrine was said to apply to any unlawful act, such as an unlawful entry on land, though it may have been a necessary assumption in such cases that there was an intention to counter resistance.[30] However, it was still of uncertain scope and received considerable discussion in the 1550s. There was now doubt as to whether an accessory who commanded a man to beat another, but had no intention to kill, was guilty of murder or only manslaughter if death resulted.[31] The unlawful-enterprise doctrine was thought inapplicable where the death was not directly connected with the wrongful act;[32] it was not clear that it extended to a defensive killing while resisting the forces of law;[33] and it was not clear that it operated where a stranger was killed.[34] The last point divided judicial opinion in 1558 in a *cause célèbre* involving two Glamorganshire knights.[35] Sir George Herbert went with a riotous party of forty or more to Sir Rhys Mansell's house 'with the purpose of having an affray and fight with the said Sir Rhys and his son, but with no intention of killing anyone'. While Mansell's sister was trying to restore peace, she was struck and killed by a rock or stone thrown over a wall by one of Herbert's servants. The question referred to all the judges in Serjeants' Inn was whether this was murder in Herbert and his retinue or only manslaughter. The judges were equally divided:[36]

Saunders CJ, Whiddon and Browne JJ, Heigham CB, and Dalison [Q.Sjt], were agreed that this was wilful murder, because it commenced upon an unlawful act to be done to a man's

---

[29] *R. v. Newbolt* (1512) 2 Caryll 613 at 614. The intention was critical. Merely being in company with a murderer, if the intention was unknown, did not inculpate: *R. v. Benett* (1518) *Notts. Inquests*, 34, no. 57.

[30] *Anon.* (1558) Dalison's reports, BL MS. Harley 5141, fo. 41v, *per* Brooke CJ (tr. 'an unlawful thing, such as beating someone, or disseising someone, or ousting him from his house'); *R. v. Wright* (1562) Gell's reports, 110 Selden Soc. 435, *per* Dyer CJ ('a wrongful act', such as entering to distrain for rent where no rent is in arrears).

[31] Cf. *Anon.* (1552) Dalison's reports, BL MS. Harley 5141, fo. 1 (murder); with *Anon.* (Star Chamber, 1553) BL MS. Add. 24845, fo. 19 (manslaughter). The doubt is also found in Sta. P.C. 21.

[32] e.g. *R. v. Potter* (1555–6) *Sussex Inquests*, 54, no. 190 (poacher who accidentally shot a fellow trespasser indicted for manslaughter). Cf. Mountford's reading (1527) BL MS. Hargrave 87, fo. 177v (deceased killed jumping out of window, or tripping on a weapon, while trying to escape).

[33] *Anon.* (1558) 110 Selden Soc. 417, pl. 52. Cf. the proclamation of 1538 which declared that those who murdered officers in the course of resisting arrest should suffer death without benefit of clergy: *Tudor Royal Proclamations*, i. 262, no. 179. But this said 'slay and murder', which seems not to extend to manslaughter.

[34] *Anon.* (1558) Dalison's reports, BL MS. Harley 5141, fo. 41v, *per* Brooke CJ, probably referring to the following case.

[35] *R. v. Herbert* (1558) Dalison's reports, BL MS. Harley 5141, ff. 40–41; Dyer 128b, §60. (Dalison refers to Mansell as Mansfield, and it is so cited in Moo. 87, pl. 217.) For the feud between the Mansells and the Herberts, including this incident (which arose from a vice-admiralty prize dispute), see *HPHC 1509–58*, ii. 338, 565, and the references there. Herbert, a member of Lincoln's Inn and former sheriff, was seemingly a JP at the time. He was restored to the bench in 1561.

[36] Dalison's report.

person, in which act they had malice to do something against the law, and in this malice the death of the woman occurred... Serjeant Browne and Catlyn, the queen's attorney, and Griffith, Sol.-Gen., were of the same opinion. Brooke CJ, Staunford, Dyer, and Morgan JJ, and Prideaux, Q.Sjt, were to the contrary: that it was not murder but manslaughter. For murder is a slaying of someone by malice aforethought (*occisio hominis ex mulicia praecogitata*), and towards this woman they had no malice;[37] but they said that if Mansell or any of his servants in his company had been thus dead this would certainly have been murder, whereas this woman did not come in aid of Mansell or Herbert but was a peacemaker between them, to whom both parties bore good will...

According to Dalison, the matter was adjourned for further enquiry as to whether the woman was 'in part taking with Mansell' or came as a stranger or a friend to both sides. It was thus agreed that the implied malice towards Mansell and his party was sufficient for murder, though the killing was merely negligent, and the principal question was whether this implied malice could be transferred to a third party. The notion of transferred malice was well established where there was an actual intent to kill, so that it was felony if A, intending to kill B, actually killed C.[38] Although most of the sources speak of felony rather than murder in this situation, at least two other authorities regarded transferred malice as sufficient for the purposes of murder.[39] This was another doctrine which proved useful in dealing with the consequences of poison, which could easily be taken by the wrong person.[40]

If a servant murdered his or her master, or a wife her husband, or a monk his superior, this was petty treason and attracted a more severe death penalty—in the case of a woman, death by burning.[41] It was the first form of homicide to be removed from the ambit of benefit of clergy.[42] Yet, as Robert Brooke pointed out in his 1551 reading, the difference between petty treason and murder could turn on fine points of marriage law. Moreover, if a man hired a woman to be his concubine for 40s. a year, and she killed him, it was not petty treason because she was neither his wife nor a lawful servant.[43] Other anomalies emerged at Serjeants' Inn

[37] Cf. Dyer's report: 'no malice was intended against the woman, and murder cannot be extended beyond what was intended'.

[38] 94 Selden Soc. 310; Note (c.1487) 1 Caryll 5, pl. 8; Littleton's reading (1493) *Moots*, 274; Port 107; R. v. *Salisbury and others* (1553) Plowd. 100.

[39] Note (after 1498) Port 86, pl. 21 ('murder by reason of the malice'); R. v. *Salisbury* (1553) Plowd. 100. The case cited by Port was actually a case of mayhem, not murder: Hil. 13 Hen. VII, fo. 14, pl. 5.

[40] Littleton's reading (1493) *Moots*, 274; differently reported in CUL MS. Hh.3.6, fo. 3v; R. v. *Dores* (1533) KB 9/523, m. 99; R. v. *Herbert* (1558) BL MS. Harley 5141, at fo. 40v; cf. R. v. *Saunders and Archer* (1573) Plowd. 473.

[41] Mich. 1 Ric. III, fo. 4, pl. 5. This was deemed to be a result of the Treason Act, since at common law it was only murder: Trin. 6 Hen. VII, fo. 5, pl. 4.   [42] 12 Hen. VII, c. 7; above, 537.

[43] *The Reading of M. Robert Brook upon Magna Charta* (1641), 14.

in the 1550s. A son did not commit petty treason by killing his parent, unless he performed services for his keep and could be deemed to be a constructive servant.[44] Since it was not clear that there could be accessories to petty treason, it was arguably possible for the person who killed the husband or master to be guilty of simple murder but for the procurer to be guilty of petty treason as a constructive principal.[45]

Manslaughter

The commonest category of felonious homicide falling short of murder was called killing by 'chance-medley', which meant a sudden fighting. Because of the suddenness of the encounter which led to the death,[46] the ill will of the killer—though felonious—could not be described as malice aforethought.[47] By the 1480s, at the latest, the English word manslaughter had also come into use. Although the word exactly translates the French *homicide*, it was from the first used more narrowly to denote killing by chance-medley,[48] or by sudden chance (*ex subito casu*),[49] and this usage was adopted by Fitzherbert.[50]

However, there were other forms of felonious killing which then or later were classified as manslaughter to distinguish them from murder. The terminology is obscure, not because such cases were rare but because there was no need to use a term of art in the indictment. The appropriate words alleging manslaughter were simply 'feloniously slew' (*felonice interfecit*), and the readers spoke merely of 'felony'. One of the additional categories of felonious homicide was killing by provocation, which had the same suddenness as chance-medley but did not necessarily involve mutual fighting. Many early examples of provocation by words could probably be

---

[44] *R. v. Anon.* (1554) Dalison's reports, BL MS. Harley 5141, ff. 18, 21v; Dal. 14 (son-in-law).

[45] This was a vexed question: Dalison's reports, ff. 19, 21v (1554), and fo. 41v (1558); Dal. 16, pl. 11; *R. v. Smith and Robinson* (1555) Dyer's notebook, 110 Selden Soc. 404; *R. v. Anon.* (1556) Dyer 128a, §57; Dal. 16; *Browne's Case* (1574) Dyer 332, §25. Cf. Marow's reading (1503), ed. Putnam, 380 (says the servant is accessory to simple felony).

[46] If the fight was by prearrangement, a resulting death would be murder: Dalison's reports, BL MS. Harley 5141, fo. 41 (1558). But this was not so of a sporting contest: below, 559–60.

[47] 94 Selden Soc. 304–5.

[48] See the form of charge in the fifteenth-century justices' manual in BL MS. Harley 1777, fo. 87 (sp. mod. 'Manslaughter is where a man or more by chance-medley fall at affray so that the one of them slayeth the other, that is but felony in itself'); Trinity Coll. Oxford MS. 30, fo. 84v ('Manslaughter is where two men or more by chance-medley meet together and fall at variance...'); *Boke of a Justyce of Peas* (1505?), sig. Av (sim. to last). Cf. Yorke 183, no. 243, *per* Elyot J. ('if a man kills someone by chance medley, without malice aforethought, this is not properly murder but manslaughter').

[49] *R. v. Pulter* (1531) KB 27/1079, Rex m. 4 (scholar of Christ's College, indicted for murder, pleads that the killing was '*homicidium vocatum* manslaughter *ex subito casu*'). Cf. 22 Hen. VIII, c. 14 ('manslaughter by chance-medley').

[50] Fitz. J.P. 19v (1538; sp. mod. 'and so appeareth the diversity between murder and manslaughter, of which the one cometh by malice prepensed and the other but by chance').

classified as chance-medley;[51] but the courts had begun to recognize other cases, such as the verbal insult,[52] or the adulterer found *in flagrante delicto*.[53] The other case was killing by gross or 'vehement' negligence.[54] This was not felonious if the death was caused indirectly, as where a fatal accident resulted from reliance on defective goods or building work, or from riding a hired horse known to be dangerous.[55] But negligence could result in direct harm, as in the classroom case of a man throwing a stone, or firing an arrow, over a house. Here a distinction had to be made between felonious negligence, which was manslaughter, and misfortune,[56] or misadventure,[57] which was not a complete defence but entitled the person responsible to a pardon.[58] The distinction turned chiefly on whether the conduct leading to the death was lawful or permissible,[59] which was a matter of public policy and general usage. There was probably never much difficulty in the case of the person who killed another accidentally in the course of his occupation or profession.[60] The test-case, which occasioned frequent discussion, was killing in the course of play or exercise.

Consent was only a limited defence in such circumstances, because one could not lawfully consent to unusual violence, and if someone asked another to kill him his request was no defence.[61] For the same reason, it was unlawful to take an unreasonable risk: as where the deceased invited someone to shoot at him to test his armour, and the armour failed the test.[62] On the other hand, death resulting from a friendly wrestling contest,[63] or even play with staves or swords, was

---

[51] e.g. *R. v. Wulf* (1540–1) *Sussex Inquests*, 31, no. 115.

[52] See *R. v. Eldred* (1560) 110 Selden Soc. 424 (doubted whether murder or manslaughter). A similar case (an insult at the table) is *R. v. Barcolf* (1540) KB 27/1116, Rex m. 1, where the indictment was for manslaughter but the trial jury found it self-defence.

[53] *R. v. Parker* (1520/1?) Spelman 72 ('all the justices held this to be felony'). According to Spelman, the indictment was cited by Fitzherbert J., who became a judge in 1523. In 1671 it was cited as 12 Hen. VIII: John Rylands Lib., MS. Eng. 288, p. 18.

[54] Francis Mountford required 'vehement negligence' for felonious homicide: reading (1527) BL MS. Hargrave 87, fo. 177.

[55] 94 Selden Soc. 307. Cf. William Staunford's reading (Gray's Inn, 1545) BL MS. Hargrave 92, fo. 99v (tr. 'if someone has an ox which is accustomed to misbehave, and the owner does not put it in a safe place but allows it to go at large, so that it kills someone, the owner in this case shall forfeit his land and his goods').

[56] The Statute of Marlborough, c. 25, provided that a killing 'per infortunium' was not murder.

[57] The Statute of Gloucester, c. 9, provided that a pardon was available as of course for a killing by misadventure. Elyot J. treated an archery or stone-throwing accident as misadventure: Yorke 183, 110. 244.

[58] See *Moots*, 74, pl. 27.   [59] Pas. 11 Hen. VII, fo. 23, pl. 14, *per* Fyneux CJ ('sufferable').

[60] e.g. dropping things at work. Serjeant Pollard pointed out that there was biblical authority for this defence: *Reniger v. Fogassa* (1550) Plowd. 1 at 19 (head of axe falling off). For medical treatments causing death see *R. v. Busshey* (1533) KB 9/525, m. 155 (foreign physician treating fever with *aqua vitae* and hot brickstones); *R. v. Smythe* (1548) *Sussex Inquests*, 40–1, no. 141 (surgeon treating syphilis with a bath; eventually presented as a natural death).

[61] Pas. 11 Hen. VII, fo. 23, *per* Fyneux CJ; Inner Temple moot, Keil. 136, pl. 120, *per* Kebell sjt.

[62] Francis Mountford's reading (1527) BL MS. Hargrave 87, fo. 177.

[63] Case from a reading on Gloucester, c. 9, in *Moots*, 74, pl. 27; *R. v. Bunting* (1549) *Notts. Inquests*, 133, no. 278.

regarded as misadventure, because 'such martial acts are good to be used for the defence of the realm'.[64] Archery practice fell on the same side of the line, provided it was carried out at the butts,[65] because archery was officially encouraged for the defence of the realm and indeed regularly enjoined by statutes and proclamations. Fatal shooting accidents were quite common, and were commonly presented as misadventure—or even as deaths caused by the arrow, or by the deceased's own conduct, rather than by the archer.[66] However, rougher ideas of sport and chivalry were waning and there seems in the early Tudor period to have been a reaction against violent sports. An anonymous fifteenth-century reader held that 'if a man plays with another with a sword or a knife, and by chance against his will so treats the other that he dies, in this case it is felony and not self-defence'.[67] In 1496, Fyneux CJ and others declared jousting and sword-play to be illegal without royal licence,[68] and it became a presentable nuisance to keep a sword-playing house.[69] A killing in the course of an unlicensed joust was felonious.[70] After 1504 it was prohibited to use a crossbow without royal licence.[71] Francis Mountford, reading in 1527, was perhaps the last to defend the use of weapons such as dagger and poleaxe in sport, though he denied a defence if injury resulted from malice or violence.[72] At some time in Henry VIII's reign, the judges reached the different conclusion that even the king's licence could not justify death from jousting.[73] The decision may have reflected a change in court opinion after the king's own serious jousting accident in 1536, for in 1533 the judges seem to have been willing enough to attend the queen's coronation jousts had they been invited.[74]

If a stricter attitude was to be taken towards martial exercises, it would have been inconsistent to tolerate socially useless activities such as throwing stones over houses. Fyneux CJ had considered it misfortune if death resulted from such an accident,[75]

[64] Inner Temple moot, Keil. 136, pl. 120, *per* Kebell sjt. For the other cases, see 94 Selden Soc. 313.

[65] This is usually mentioned in the discussions, and was held essential by William Wadham (reading in Lincoln's Inn, 1505) Taussig MS., fo. 193.

[66] 94 Selden Soc. 312. To the cases cited there may be added *R. v. Esterffeld* (1508) *Sussex Inquests*, 8, pl. 31; *R. v. Egglesfeld* (1512) KB 27/1003, Rex m. 1; *R. v. Marche* (1515) *Sussex Inquests*, 10, pl. 41.

[67] BL MS. Lansdowne 1138, fo. 43.   [68] Pas. 11 Hen. VII, fo. 23, pl. 14.

[69] *R. v. Smyth* (1531) KB 9/975, m. 35.

[70] See Littleton's reading (1493) CUL MS. Hh.3.6, ff. 3v (not felony with the king's licence), 5v (appeal lies for death in jousting or tourneying, because unlawful).

[71] 19 Hen. VII, c. 4. Hand-guns were added by 25 Hen. VIII, c. 17. The original reason for the legislation was the decay in long-bow proficiency, but by 1541 the concern was with crime: 33 Hen. VIII, c. 6. Note also Brooke Abr., *Charter de pardon*, pl. 76 (firing an 'albaster', i.e. arblast or crossbow, may be sanctioned by the king, because only *malum prohibitum*).

[72] Reading (Inner Temple, 1527) BL MS. Hargrave 87, fo. 177.

[73] Brooke Abr., *Corone*, pl. 228. Cf. *Proclamation*, pl. 13, where he states the older view.

[74] Spelman 68 at 70.

[75] Pas. 11 Hen. VII, fo. 23, pl. 14; and see *Moots*, 74. Serjeant Kebell took the same view even of shooting over a house: Keil. 136, pl. 120. For a contrary fifteenth-century view see the reading on Marlborough, c. 24, in CUL MS. Ee.5.22, ff. 101–102; Lib. Congress, Law MS. 139, p. 134 (where it is said

but a newer common-weal argument was propounded by a reader in the first half of the sixteenth century:[76]

Misadventure or misfortune (*infortune*) is where someone does a lawful act, such as [the work] of a carpenter or tiler, or shooting at the butts, and in doing such things— without any malice, by misfortune, and against his will—he kills another, this is misfortune and not felony or manslaughter (*homicide*) . . . But if someone does an unlawful act, which he is not compelled to do by any need or for any common profit—for example, where a man throws a stone over a house, or such like—and there by chance (*casuelté*) kills another, this is manslaughter and felony and he shall lose his life. The law is the same concerning play with sword and buckler, if one man kills another. And so there is a distinction: where the act is lawful and for the common good at the outset, and where not except in special cases.

This became the orthodox position by the middle of the century. A man who threw stones in play, for his own pleasure, could not be shown the same leniency as the tiler who dropped a tile in the course of his lawful labour.[77] Someone who practised medicine without proper training might find himself in the same position.[78] There seems thus to have been a tightening of the law of homicide to accommodate a more careful respect for human life. Although it was a heavy-handed form of social control, since manslaughter was a capital felony, the offence was always clergiable.

Excusable homicide

Killing in self-defence had the same consequences as misadventure.[79] Self-defence did not justify homicide, so as to remove all liability, but it entitled the person concerned to a pardon.[80] By Tudor times, the Bractonian doctrine of inevitable necessity was interpreted as requiring a retreat prior to the use of defensive force.[81] A presentment for killing in self-defence therefore almost invariably set out a retreat to a wall, ditch, or similar obstacle, or a falling down, before the defensive action was taken. One fifteenth-century reader, however, was in favour

that *necligencia neminem excusat*, negligence excuses no-one), and, apparently to the same effect, Port 86, pl. 21.

[76] BL MS. Harley 1210, fo. 145 (tr.).   [77] Brooke Abr., *Corone*, pl. 228.

[78] William Staunford's reading (Gray's Inn, 1545) BL MS. Hargrave 92, fo. 99v (tr. 'someone who is no surgeon or physician takes upon himself the craft of surgery, and undertakes to cure someone who is wounded, who dies at his hands: this is felony in the said surgeon').

[79] For this paragraph see 94 Selden Soc. 315–16.

[80] Statute of Gloucester, c. 9; Statute of Northampton 1328, c. 2. Fyneux CJ tried to soften the law, but was overruled: *R. v. Aprice* (1504) 2 Caryll 426. In 1532 it was enacted that self-defence against a highway robbery merited a full acquittal: 24 Hen. VIII, c. 5; applied in *R. v. Molde* (1534) *Notts. Inquests*, 71–2, no. 138.   [81] 94 Selden Soc. 315; *R. v. Slingesbie* (1488) 1 Caryll 5 at 6.

of allowing instant reaction in circumstances where retreat would have been dangerous.[82]

Self-defence was not the only form of excuse known to the common law. It was also excusable to kill in defence of one's master,[83] one's relations,[84] and (according to Francis Mountford) judges on the bench, priests saying mass, the king, and the heir to the throne. A man could kill to defend his wife from rape, but not to stop an act of adultery.[85] It was not permissible to kill in defence of goods, though some thought it might be permissible to kill a robber in the attempt. In practice this was a question of intention, since it was lawful to use force in defence of chattels. On the other hand, if a death occurred in the proper defence of a dwelling-house it was regarded as excusable;[86] but this may have been a particular application of self-defence, because when a man was in his own home he had no further retreat.[87] 'A man's home,' said Fyneux CJ in 1499, 'is to him as his castle and defence.'[88] Duress might be considered another case of self-defence. If a man's life was threatened, this might excuse his actions.[89] On the other hand, coercion of a wife by her husband would not excuse homicide.[90]

Sexual offences

Rape was said by Fitzherbert to be 'the most great offence next unto murder',[91] and yet it was little discussed by the readers,[92] perhaps because the definition was considered straightforward. *Rapere* (to ravish) was itself an ambiguous word, since it denoted primarily a seizure or abduction,[93] and therefore *rapuit* had to be accompanied in an indictment or appeal with the word 'feloniously' (*felonice*)[94] and the phrase 'carnally knew' (*carnaliter cognovit*). In fact the 'rape' or ravishment

---

[82] CUL MS. Ii.5.43, fo. 66.

[83] Trin. 14 Hen. VII, Fitz. Abr., *Trespas*, pl. 246, pr. as Mich. 21 Hen. VII, fo. 39, pl. 50, *per* Tremayle J.; Port 107, pl. 41, *per* Richard Littleton.   [84] Marow's reading (Inner Temple, 1503), ed. Putnam, 334.

[85] *R.* v. *Parker* (1520/1?) Spelman 72. For the date see above, 559 n. 53.

[86] Cf. *R.* v. *Harcourt* (1563) in Fitz. J.P., ed. R. Crompton (1617 edn), fo. 24v; 83 *LQR* 587 (shooting in defence of house, against someone with pretended title, treated as manslaughter).

[87] *R.* v. *Slingesbie* (1488) 1 Caryll 5; readings cited in 94 Selden Soc. *316* n. 1.

[88] Trin. 14 Hen. VII, Fitz. Abr., *Trespas*, pl. 246. Cf. the 'safehold and defence' passage, below, 573.

[89] 94 Selden Soc. *316* n. 3; *Moots*, 274. Mountford went further than Littleton, recognizing duress by a gaoler as providing a defence.   [90] Marow's reading (1503), ed. Putnam, 377.

[91] Fitz. J.P. 19v.

[92] It was made a felony in 1285 by the Statute of Westminster II, c. 34, but readers glossed the chapter very briefly. It was necessary for an indictment of rape to say 'against the form of the statute': *R.* v. *Anon.* (1554) 110 Selden Soc. 402, pl. 7.

[93] e.g. 'common ravisher of fish' in *Smyth* v. *Somerfeld* (1540) CP 40/1104, m. 191.

[94] Mich. 20. Hen. VII, fo. 7, pl. 17, *per* Brudenell sjt; Marow's reading (Inner Temple, 1503), ed. Putnam, 393; *Anon.* (c.1523) Spelman 65, pl. 56; 105, pl. 28; *Anon.* (1547) cited in Brooke's reading (pr. 1641), fo. 17.

was an irrelevance, or fiction,[95] because the essence of the felony lay in having carnal knowledge of a woman against her will.[96] It was no defence that the woman assented afterwards.[97] There was, however, said to be a defence if the woman conceived a child, on the evidential grounds that —as was then widely believed— this could not occur without her consent.[98] To this it was objected by a bishop that the body might consent but not the mind; the judges' retort was that their authority extended only to the body.[99] Evidence in rape cases might be given not only by the complainant but by women who had conducted an examination.[100]

Despite the views of the thirteenth-century authors, buggery did not become a felony at common law and is seldom met with in the records. Indeed, by Tudor times it was not certain that it was a common-law offence at all, unless by some abstruse logic it could be deemed to be a form of constructive treason.[101] In 1534, however, it was by statute made a non-clergiable felony,[102] perhaps at the personal behest of the king.[103] The statutory offence included bestiality, for which a woman could be convicted.[104] The records do not suggest a widespread concern with such offences, and the legislature seems to have been less concerned with sexual immorality as such than with black magic and the dangers of tampering with nature.[105]

---

[95] Cf. the statutory offences of abduction, which did not encompass sexual misbehaviour: below, 620–1.

[96] The statute says 'where she has not assented', but the usual wording in indictments was 'against her will' (contra voluntatem suam). The textbook definitions also say 'against her will': Boke of Justyces of Peas (1505?), sig. Avi; J. Rastell, Exposiciones Terminorum [c.1523], sig. E1, and (1527), fo. 60 ('inconter son agreement demesne'); Fitz. J.P. 19v. Cf. Mountford's reading (1527) CUL MS. Ee.5.19, fo. 114 (defined as taking a woman with violence and having carnal copulation with her).

[97] 6 Ric. II, stat. 1, c. 6 (assent to ravishment not to bar an appeal); manual for justices (fifteenth century) BL MS. Harley 1777, fo. 87 (sp. mod. 'though afterward she assenteth thereto, yet it is felony'); Boke for Justyces of Peas (1505?), sig. Avi (sim.); Fitz. J.P. 19v.

[98] Lady Butler's Case (1436) RP, iv. 497, cited in Babington v. Venour (1465) in Long Quinto, fo. 61v; Moots, 275; Sta. P.C. 24. We are grateful to Elise Histed for identifying the 1436 case.

[99] Moots, 275, where the remark is attributed to the counsel of George Nevill, archbishop of York (1465–76), but the context is unclear.

[100] R. v. Anon. (1558) 110 Selden Soc. 417, pl. 54, at 418 (clergyman convicted of raping girl of 10: cf ibid, 426, pl. 84).

[101] See Elton, The Tudor Constitution, 60 n. 140 (temp Edw. IV); Bellamy, Tudor Law of Treason 42–3. It was, however, punishable in the ecclesiastical courts.

[102] 25 Hen. VIII, c. 6; perpetuated by 32 Hen. VIII, c. 3; modified by 2 & 3 Edw. VI, c. 29; repealed by 1 Mar. I, sess. 1, c. 1; revived and perpetuated by 5 Eliz. I, c. 17 (after an attempted revival in 1559: 109 Selden Soc., p. lxix). Lord Hungerford was executed for this offence in 1540: Bellamy, Tudor Law of Treason, 43. However, in 1541 the headmaster of Eton received only imprisonment for sodomy with some of his pupils.

[103] This is conjecture: Elton, Reform and Renewal, 136–7, 148.

[104] Co. Inst. iii. 59 (since the statute says 'any person'). Coke informs us that 'somewhat before the making of this act [of 1534], a great lady had committed buggery with a baboon, and conceived by it'.

[105] For the background see R. M. Warnicke, 'Sexual Heresy at the Court of Henry VIII' (1987) 30 Historical Jnl 247–68; revised in The Rise and Fall of Anne Boleyn, ch. 8.

OFFENCES AGAINST PROPERTY[106]

Larceny

The other felony which received full treatment by the readers was theft, or larceny. The offence was often simply called 'felony', and the key words in the indictment were 'feloniously stole' (*felonice furatus fuit*). Petty larceny was distinguished only by the value of the thing stolen, while robbery (which always included larceny) and burglary (which did not) are best treated as separate felonies. As with homicide, the readers were content to discuss 'felony' without reference to a comprehensive definition. What few attempts there were at generalization seem all to have been based on *Bracton*.[107] Piecing together the contemporary discussions, the elements of felonious theft seem to have been well established as a taking and carrying away of a chattel of value from the possession of someone with better title, without that person's consent, intending permanently to deprive him of the possession.

Only a chattel could be the subject of theft, and so one could not be convicted of felony for stealing growing trees or crops, unless they were left to lie after severance and removed on a later occasion.[108] On the same principle, one could not steal fruit or nuts from trees,[109] or nesting birds, or minerals from the ground,[110] or muniments concerning land and their boxes. Fixtures, such as lead on a roof, were likewise outside the ambit of larceny.[111] In 1533 a man was indicted for stealing stones from the turrets of the town-walls of Oxford, and was discharged on the ground that the stones were part of the freehold.[112] Even a movable chattel could not be stolen feloniously unless it was a thing of substantial value in the eyes of the law. This principle was developed to mitigate the rigour of the law, and to ensure that no one lost his life for taking a 'thing of pleasure' only, even if its market value exceeded 12*d*.[113] But this humane policy was difficult to apply. In the fifteenth century, the classic examples of things which could not be

---

[106] For a more detailed study see 94 Selden Soc. *316–26*.

[107] See the attempts at definition cited in 94 Selden Soc. *316* n. 6. Mountford in his reading (1527) expressly quoted *Bracton*: CUL MS. Ee.5.19, fo. 113. Cf. Caryll (Jun.) 409, no. 102.

[108] For this paragraph see 94 Selden Soc. *317–18*. For the distinctions between realty and personalty, and fixtures, see also below, 733–8.

[109] Richard Littleton unaccountably maintained that fruit could be stolen, unlike the tree bearing the fruit; but perhaps he meant fruit which had been severed: reading (1493) CUL MS. Hh.3.6, fo. 2 (marked 'quere').   [110] Including silver, which belonged of right to the Crown.

[111] Anonymous reading (1530s) BL MS. Harley 4990, fo. 155; *R.* v. *Anon.* (1553) Chr. Yelverton's reports, fo. 240 (tr. *LPCL*, 321). Mountford said it was felony if churchwardens stole bells or gravestones, but not if they stole chalices; but he was making the point that the former were not in their custody and overlooking that they were fixtures: reading (1527) CUL MS. Ee.5.19, fo. 113.

[112] *R.* v. *Gardiner* (1533) Spelman 99; KB 27/1087, Rex m. 1d (pr. 94 Selden Soc. 295).

[113] *Fyloll* v. *Assheleygh* (1520) Trin. 12 Hen. VIII, fo. 3, pl. 3 (119 Selden Soc. 15), *per* Roo sjt.

stolen were game birds, hawks, and hounds; and a judge in 1520 concluded on the same principle that musical instruments could not be the subject of larceny.[114] It was also said that 'if someone steals relics, provided they are not enclosed in silver, it is not felony, because one cannot know the value'[115]—a rather different concept of pricelessness. The distinction between things of pleasure and things of profit was a favourite topic of jurisprudential reflection in early Tudor times;[116] but the generous attitude towards the theft of luxuries did not take a permanent hold. Some began to distinguish the bird-stealing cases as if they had been based on *animus revertendi*, so that a hawk could be stolen from a mew or perch. Then, in 1526, the matter was referred to all the judges by Wolsey C. The context has not come to light, but the question was whether peacocks could be stolen. After weighing many examples, the judges decided that, since peacocks were edible and 'commonly of the same nature as hens, capons, geese, or ducks', they could be taken feloniously.[117] This left open the question whether it was felony to steal animals which, though domesticated or reduced into possession, were kept purely for pleasure. That point arose a few years later when a courtier was indicted for stealing a tame hart. He was discharged on a technicality, but the court apparently refused to accept the substantive argument that a hart could not be the subject of larceny.[118] By the 1530s, Fitzherbert could write that peacocks, doves, and tame deer, were all larcenable.[119] But the shift of opinion was not universal, because Hales J. as late as 1553 delivered himself of the rather surprising pronouncement that diamonds could not be stolen.[120] That was testing the old doctrine to destruction. It was not heard of again.

There was normally no difficulty over the nature of the *actus reus* in theft, the taking and asportation.[121] The taking could be effected in person or through an innocent agent or animal, as where a man trained a dog to carry off pieces of plate.[122] But felony did have to be distinguished from attempted felony, and what

---

[114] *Fyloll* v. *Assheleygh* (1520) Trin. 12 Hen. VIII, fo. 4, pl. 3 (119 Selden Soc. 16), *per* Pollard J. (harps, lutes, and bows).

[115] Reading on the Statute of Winchester, CUL MS. Ee.5.22, fo. 364 (tr.). Likewise BL MS. Hargrave 87, fo. 397.   [116] See above, 33–4

[117] Mich. 18 Hen. VIII, fo. 2, pl. 11; Gell's reports, I, 18 Hen. VIII, fo. 2. Cf. Mountford's reading (1527) CUL MS. Ee.5.19, fo. 113v (swans and tame deer larcenable, because profitable as well as things of pleasure).

[118] *R.* v. *Delarever* (1534) Spelman 52, 100; KB 27/1092, Rex m. 5d (94 Selden Soc. 283). This was Mountford's view: last note. Cf. contrary views cited in 94 Selden Soc. *318* n. 4 and n. 9.

[119] Fitz. J.P. 20v.

[120] Dalison's reports, BL MS. Harley 5141, fo. 12 (tr. 'even though they are esteemed in price with all men, stealing them was not felony at common law'). Hales J. distinguished stones from fish and pigeons, which were 'profitable'.   [121] For this paragraph see 94 Selden Soc. *316–17*.

[122] Mountford's example (1527) CUL MS. Ee.5.19, fo. 113.

was required for the full offence was not merely a loss of control by the owner of goods but an assumption of control by the thief. If a cutpurse succeeded in severing a purse from its owner's girdle, and it fell to the ground, this was not a completed felony. Neither was it felony to chase another man's horse without catching it, or to mark another's sheep with one's own mark without separating it from the flock. In these cases there was no taking of possession. It was more difficult to draw the line where the miscreant began to remove goods from a house but did not get them out of the door. It seems that, if he was a guest or servant with lawful access to the chattels, he was not guilty of felony unless he hid them or moved them to a place whither he had no implied authority to move them.[123] It was not felony to obtain goods by a trick,[124] but it was if the owner handed them over under threat of violence.

The *mens rea* required for theft was an intention permanently to deprive the person entitled to possession of that possession.[125] It was therefore not felony if goods were taken for a temporary purpose only, as where a horse was taken for a single journey, or a weapon was seized for self-defence on a sudden occasion. It was also necessary that the taking should be—in the terminology of *Bracton*—'fraudulent'. Francis Mountford put the case of someone who took away his kinsman's goods because he considered him a spendthrift, and kept them to his use: this was a trespass, but not felony.[126] Mistake of law may have been a defence, as where a servant kept his master's goods after his employment was over as a 'lien' for his wages. Mistake of fact was certainly a defence, as where a man took a horse similar to his own under the belief that it was his own, or marked someone else's beast with his mark through carelessness. If goods were taken under colour of right, as for a distress, this was not felony unless the property was afterwards feloniously converted to the use of the taker, in which case the trespass *ab initio* principle converted it into felony *ex post facto*. The usual defences of lunacy, insanity, and want of discretion on account of infancy, were available in relation to theft as well as homicide. Necessity was considered a good defence,[127] and at least two readers took the view that it excused someone who took food because he or his family were starving.

Possession problems in larceny

The principal legal difficulties in the law of larceny related to the concept of theft as a physical violation of possession rather than as an interference with property

---

[123] *R.* v. *Anon.* (1554) Dalison's reports, BL MS. Harley 5141, fo. 27v. Likewise if he took possession of a domestic beast in a field but did not remove it from the field: ibid. (cited Co. Inst. iii. 109).

[124] The gap was not filled until 30 Geo. II, c. 24. But the trickster could be indicted for misdemeanour as a common cheat.   [125] For this paragraph see 94 Selden Soc. 323.

[126] Mountford's reading (1527) CUL MS. Ee.5.19, fo. 113v.

[127] Cf., in a different context, *Reniger* v. *Fogassa* (1550) Plowd. 1 at 18v, *per* Pollard sjt (tr. 'all laws give place to necessity, for it is a common proverb that necessity knows no law (*necessitas non habet legem*), and therefore necessity shall be a good excuse in our law and in all other laws').

in its more abstract sense.[128] The narrowness of this concept excluded from its scope numerous other forms of dishonesty. Indeed, this has been regarded as 'the great defect in the common law of larceny', because a string of statutes was needed over the centuries to plug the gaps.[129] Yet it was an inevitable consequence of treating 'force and arms' and asportation as necessary elements which had to be laid in the indictment and proved. He who was already in possession could not take it with force. Fraudulent conversion by a bailee was only a civil wrong at common law, remediable by an action on the case.[130] Therefore if a carrier stole the goods entrusted to him it was not felony. This rule had embarrassed the judges, and in the famous *Carrier's Case* of 1473 the doctrine of 'breaking bulk' had been invented—apparently by Choke J.—to circumvent it. By the last decade of the fifteenth century the judges, seizing upon a dictum of Nedeham J. in the 1473 case, had narrowed the rule still further so that the bailee was only exempt from the law of theft if he had an interest or possession distinct from that of the owner. For this purpose, a servant having the keeping or use of his master's goods did not acquire a separate possession, but the goods were deemed to remain in the possession of the master. In 1487 the judges had taken the older view that the servant's relationship with his master's goods was akin to that of a bailee, so that he could not be held to take them with force;[131] but the readers thereafter consistently maintained that, on the contrary, the servant could be found guilty of stealing the goods in his care.[132] The examples given were the butler who stole plate or napery, the shepherd who stole sheep, and the stable-man who stole horses or their accoutrements. Where, however, the servant was given the possession of a thing to carry to someone else—for instance, where he was sent with a bag or casket of mail to London—he was then in the same position as any other carrier and as a bailee could not take the thing feloniously: it was no longer considered in his master's possession. This position was not free from difficulty, and in 1529 it was declared by Parliament to be felony for a servant to abscond with or 'imbezil' goods worth 40s. delivered to him by his master to keep to his master's use.[133] According to the preamble, it 'was doubtful at the common law, whether it were felony or not'. But the statute did not extend to fraudulent conversion by a receiver.[134] It was debatable whether a shop-assistant who properly sold his master's goods but pocketed the money, or a servant who stole goods purchased with his master's money, were guilty of felony. When the question arose upon evidence given to the jury, in a

---

[128] For what follows see 94 Selden Soc. 319–22. For the cases in this paragraph see also Staunford's reading (Gray's Inn, 1545) BL MS. Hargrave 92, fo. 100.   [129] Plucknett, *CHCL* (5th edn), 449.

[130] Below, 802.   [131] Mich. 3 Hen. VII, fo. 12, pl. 9.

[132] The newer view is also found in Hil. 21 Hen. VII, fo. 14, pl. 21, *per* Cutler sjt; *Anon.* (c.1538) Wm Yelv. 356, no. 92, *per* Shelley J. ('this was felony at common law').   [133] 21 Hen. VIII, c. 7.

[134] *Anon.* (1533) Dyer 5, §2, *per* Englefield J.

case at the Old Bailey in 1542, the court considered the matter for a year before holding, for reasons not stated, that the appropriation of the proceeds was felony.[135]

A case reported by Spelman in 1533 illustrates the practical difficulties faced by the judges in this area. It appeared in evidence that a servant had been sent with a pannier of poultry from London to Aylesbury, and that his master had put a bag into the pannier—the contents of which were unknown to the servant—to be delivered in Aylesbury. The servant was later arrested at Grantham in Lincolnshire and found in possession of £5. 11s. 3d. He said he had 'found' some of the money in the pannier, out of the bag, and decided to keep it. Now, it was clear that he could not at common law have stolen the poultry or the bag, because they were in his possession, and since he had not taken the money out of the bag he had not broken bulk. The judges felt unable to reach a decision, which they avoided by discharging the jury on a point of venue. Eventually the poultryman was indicted on the statute of 1529.[136]

The newer theory of possession, which distinguished it from a bare custody, was extended in the early Tudor period from servants to independent contractors. When someone left cloth with a tailor, or his horse with a blacksmith, or grain with a miller, he did not part with the possession in law;[137] and therefore the tailor, the blacksmith, or the miller, could be found guilty of stealing the property deposited with them.[138] Similarly, an innkeeper was not a bailee of his guest's goods, and so if he stole them it was felony. Conversely, the guest did not have an independent possession of the plate and linen made available to him in the inn, and if he took them it was also felony. It was even said that an office-holder did not have full possession of his implements of office, so that a civic sword-bearer could steal the city sword, a city serjeant his mace, and a parish priest the chalice or vestments belonging to the parish. The distinction between possession and custody did not, however, affect third parties. If a third party stole goods from someone having only the custody, this was nevertheless felony.[139]

Wild animals could not be stolen, because while at large—even in a park or warren—they were not considered to be in the possession of the landowner.[140] Hunting and poaching were therefore not capital offences at common law. The ways in which a landowner might achieve a sufficient possession for the purposes

---

[135] *R. v. Penley* (1542–3) above, 525.

[136] *R. v. Armysby* (1533) Spelman 50; KB 27/1087, Rex m. 2 (pr. 94 Selden Soc. 280); second indictment, KB 27/1088, Rex m. 1d (pr. ibid.).

[137] On the other hand, if a third party stole them, the property could be laid in the tradesman: *R. v. Anon.* (1505) 2 Caryll 472, pl. 334.

[138] *Fyloll v. Assheleygh* (1520) Trin. 12 Hen. VIII, fo. 4, pl. 3 (119 Selden Soc. 16), *per* Pollard J.; Mountford's reading (1527) CUL MS. Ee.5.19, fo. 113.

[139] *Everard v. Chirch* (1484) Mich. 2 Ric. III, fo. 22, pl. 53 (appeal of robbery at Newgate).

[140] For this paragraph see 94 Selden Soc. 322.

of the law of theft occasioned much debate, especially concerning fish. Obviously fish which had been caught and placed in a receptacle such as a cistern or a pike-monger's trunk could be stolen;[141] and equally obviously fish in an open river or lake could not, except in the case of the fisherman who had fish in his net but had not yet landed them. As to intermediate cases, the better opinion seems to have been that it was felony to take fish from a stew or small pond.[142] Nevertheless, because of the doubt, Parliament in 1539 declared it felony to fish in any pond, stew, or moat.[143] Having pigeons in a pigeon-house did not give the landowner the same kind of possession, because the birds came and went as they pleased and could not be taken at the will of the owner.[144] Domesticated animals, on the other hand, could be stolen even though the owner did not confine them. Thus, clipping sheep and taking their wool in the open field was felony.[145] Some deer were regarded as tame for this purpose, and it was not necessary for them to be collared or belled to prove it;[146] but deer in a park were considered wild and not larcenable at common law. Swans, on the other hand, were not rendered domestic by mark-ing their beaks, and so even marked swans could not be stolen feloniously from a river. A hawk or falcon trained to return after the kill could be the subject of theft, even while it was at large, because it had *animus revertendi*; and its prey could also be stolen, for it vested in the owner of the bird or of the *locus in quo*. The common-law position concerning the poaching of game was modified in piecemeal fashion by Tudor legislation. In 1495 it was made a misdemeanour to take pheasants or par-tridges, or the eggs of hawks or swans, on another person's land.[147] And in 1540 it was made a felony to take the eggs of hawks or falcons, or to steal deer from a park or warren either at night or when disguised with visors or painted faces.[148]

A wife could not be guilty of stealing her husband's goods, because in law hus-band and wife were one person. This had the odd consequence that if she took his goods and gave them to an accomplice, the latter was not guilty of felony by receiving, because he was not a principal and could not be an accessory if the wife was not a principal. It was otherwise if he accompanied the wife when the goods

---

[141] Trin. 18 Edw. IV, fo. 8, pl. 7; John Goring's reading (Gray's Inn, c.1510/13) Spelman 64.

[142] A precedent of an indictment for stealing pikes in a pond is *R. v. Thomlyn and Colson* (1529) KB 27/1073, Rex m. 10.

[143] 31 Hen. VIII, c. 2. The preamble stated that the owners of ponds, stews, and moats, had stocked them with fish 'as well for the pleasure of their friends as for their own commodity and profit'.

[144] Trin. 18 Edw. IV, fo. 8, pl. 7.

[145] *R. v. Anon.* (1554) Dalison's reports, BL MS. Harley 5141, fo. 27v; abr. (under a later date) in Dal. 21.

[146] *R. v. Delarever* (1534) Spelman 100 at 101. Cf. George Treherne's reading (Lincoln's Inn, 1520) BL MS. Stowe 414, fo. 71v (felony to kill a hart which had a little leather collar).

[147] 11 Hen. VII, c. 17.

[148] 32 Hen. VIII, c. 11. These felonies had first been introduced in 1539 in the case of the king's falcons and hawks and the king's parks: 31 Hen. VIII, c. 12. The statutes were repealed in 1547 but temporarily revived by 3 & 4 Edw. VI, c. 17; 7 Edw. VI, c. 11.

were taken, because then he was a principal. The law was said to be the same of goods taken by a monk from his monastery.[149]

An even odder consequence of the nature of felony, as a violation of possession rather than title, was that in certain circumstances a bailor could steal his own goods.[150] Lawyers were naturally uneasy about this notion, but the only difficulty was the intent. In the case of a passive bailment to rebail, the bailor who seized his goods back could be said to take them with force; but he was only guilty of felony if he did so fraudulently, intending to sue the bailee for their loss.[151] Where the bailee had an interest, however, the matter was clearer. A bailor could steal his own goods from a pledgee,[152] or a distrainor, or a bailee who had changed the nature of the goods by specification; though in such cases evidence of stealth may have been necessary to prove that the taking was fraudulent.

Petty larceny

For stealing to amount to grand (capital) larceny, the goods had not only to be of some value but also to be of a greater value than 12d.[153] Stealing goods below that value was petty larceny or 'bribery', which carried forfeiture[154] and some other punishment—such as fine or pillory—at the discretion of the court.[155] There was some doubt, voiced by Fitzherbert J. at Stafford assizes,[156] whether stealing exactly 12d., or goods of that value, was petty or grand larceny. Marow, Fitzherbert, Spelman, and Rastell, all wrote that it was grand larceny; but it was the contrary view, espoused by Staunford, which became law. The rule, whichever it was, made it necessary to specify the value of stolen goods in the indictment, and if the value was omitted the prisoner was entitled to be discharged.[157] But if someone was indicted for the theft of several articles, which were collectively valued in the indictment at more than 12d., and the jury found him guilty of stealing only some of the articles, the court would presume *in favorem vitae* that the stolen items were worth less than 12d. If, on the other hand, several men were indicted

---

[149] Spelman 65, pl. 54; *Snore's Case* (c.1523/33) Spelman 67.

[150] For this paragraph see 94 Selden Soc. 321–2.

[151] Pas. 13 Edw. IV, fo. 10, pl. 5, *per* Nedeham J.; Hil. 5 Hen. VII, fo. 18, pl. 11; Marow's reading (1503), ed. Putnam, 376; anon. reading, MS. Hargrave 87, fo. 397. Cf. Brooke's reading of 1551 (pr. 1642), 14 ('. . . it is not felony, for the property is in himself; but it is adjudged contrary').

[152] See Spelman's reading (1519) 113 Selden Soc. 160.

[153] For what follows see 94 Selden Soc. 318–19.

[154] Trin. 27 Hen. VIII, fo. 22, pl. 17, *per* Fitzherbert J.; Dyer's notebook, 110 Selden Soc. 416, pl. 46 (1557), and p. 436, pl. 113 (1562).

[155] *Anon.* (1550) Wm Yelv. 352, no. 81, *per* Saunders sjt (pillory or stocks 'or otherwise, at the discretion of the justices').

[156] Brooke Abr., *Corone*, pl. 85. Cf. Fitz. Abr., *Corone*, pl. 178 (same point raised in 1349).

[157] *R. v. Hardwyk* (1532) Spelman 98; KB 27/1085, Rex m. 6 (pr. 94 Selden Soc. 293).

for stealing 12$\frac{1}{2}$d., there was no objection to finding them all guilty of capital felony. Some were even prepared to hold that the separate theft of items totalling 12d. was capital felony.[158]

Since the jury was free to set its own value on stolen goods, it could facilitate a punishment less than death by reducing a charge of grand larceny to petty larceny.[159]

Robbery

Robbery was larceny accompanied by personal violence or threats of violence, and it was capital even if the goods stolen were worth less than 12d.[160] A fifteenth-century manual for justices of the peace defined it rather cumbrously:[161]

Robbery is where as a man lieth in the king's highways to market town and from market town, in woods, ditches, or in any other secret places, where people cometh for by and robbeth them, albeit that he taketh away but the value of one penny or less it is felony, for the malapertness of the deed and the jeopardy that a man is in of his life; for when it is taken from his person it causeth the offence to be the greater than when it had been theftily stolen.

Yet it is clear from the readings that the archaic requirement of an ambush was no longer current. Rastell required only a taking from the person—or in the presence—of the owner. Serjeant Kebell required a taking from the person with menaces, while Marow and Yorke required also that the victim be put in fear. Francis Mountford went further and required actual violence.[162] The element of fear or violence distinguished the activity of the cutpurse, who it seems was guilty only of simple larceny if he stole by dexterity rather than violence.[163]

A statute of 1531 removed benefit of clergy from robbery in a dwelling-house, 'the owner or dweller in the same house, his wife, his children, or servants, then being within and put in fear and dread by the same', and for robbery in or near a highway.[164] Since the statute also spoke of 'robbing of any churches', there was a case for saying that 'robbery' was not here used in a technical sense; but no contemporary ruling on the point has been found.

---

[158] Littleton's reading (1493) CUL MS. Hh.3.6, fo. 2v; Mountford's reading (1527) CUL. MS. Ee.5.19, fo. 113v. Mountford held that this was so even if the thief had already been in the pillory for one of the thefts. [159] R. v. Anon. (1554) Dalison's reports, BL MS. Harley 5141, fo. 17.

[160] Brooke argued that it was robbery even if the goods stolen were of the kind which were not larcenable at all, such as a greyhound: reading of 1551 (pr. 1641), 10.

[161] BL MS. Harley 1777, fo. 87v (sp. mod.); variant in Trinity Coll. Oxford MS. 30, fo. 84v (temp. Edw. IV); pr. with variations in Boke of Justyces of Peas (c.1505), sig. Avi (pr. from 1515 edn in 94 Selden Soc. 324).

[162] Mountford's reading (1527) CUL MS. Ee.5.19, fo. 113v. He said that, without force, petty stealing was only 'petit brybery'. [163] Marow's reading (1503), ed. Putnam, 377.

[164] 23 Hen. VIII, c. 1. For its amendment in 1547 see below, 573.

Burglary[165]

Burglary was the felonious invasion of a house, and did not necessarily include theft or any other felony.[166] It was still the subject of varying definitions. Fitzherbert and Mountford both followed the *Liber Assisarum* in defining it, archaically, as the felonious breaking of a house, church, or town-walls, in time of peace. This omitted any mental element, though Mountford distinguished cases where breaking into a house was not felony: to extinguish a fire, to arrest a felon, to separate fighters, or to retake goods.[167] There was much diversity of opinion as to the requisite state of mind, which was not always inserted in indictments.[168] An intent to commit a non-felonious trespass would not suffice.[169] Marow distinguished the case where some other felony was actually committed from the case where it was the intent alone which made the breaking felonious. If another felony was actually committed in the house, any felony would suffice to make it burglary, whereas if no other felony was committed then only an intent to murder was sufficient. Other writers, however, thought a mere intent to steal or rob,[170] or perhaps to rape,[171] would be enough. Fitzherbert brought all these views together, and stated the settled common-law position that an intention to commit any felony would suffice.[172]

The *actus reus* was also differently defined by different writers. There was not yet much debate about the entry, perhaps because an entry was not always regarded as essential.[173] It was necessary to break into a dwelling-house, rather than a mere close,[174] and this requirement was occasionally discussed. Spelman held that it was possible to commit burglary in one's own house, if part of it was in separate possession, as where an innkeeper broke into his guest's locked room intending to commit a felony.[175] And it was held in 1548 to be burglary to break into a stable adjoining a dwelling-house with intent to commit a felony.[176] Some thought it necessary that there should be persons in the house at the time of the breaking in,

---

[165] For what follows see 94 Selden Soc. 325–6.   [166] *R.* v. *Slingesbie* (1488) 1 Caryll 5.

[167] Mountford's reading (1527) CUL MS. Ee.5.19, fo. 113v.

[168] In *R.* v. *Lawys* (1501) KB 27/961, Rex m. 14, an indictment for burglary was quashed because it did not lay an intention to rob or despoil.

[169] Reading on Magna Carta (fifteenth century) Lib. Congress Law MS. 139, p. 29 (intent to beat insufficient).

[170] Rastell, *Exposiciones Terminorum* [c.1523], sig. B2, mentions only an intention to steal.

[171] Rape was disputable only because it was not a felony at common law: Marow's reading (1503), ed. Putnam, 378; Fitz. J.P., ed. Crompton (1617 edn), 32.   [172] Fitz. J.P. 20.

[173] Yorke 183, no. 242, expressly says it was not. But other authorities require an entry (e.g. Rastell, *Exposiciones Terminorum*, sig. B2), and it seems to have been settled as necessary by the 1550s: *R.* v. *Anon.* (1554) Dyer 99, §58, *per* Bromley CJ; Dyer's notebook, 110 Selden Soc. 411 (1557); Dalison's reports, BL MS. Harley 5141, fo. 39v (tr. 110 Selden Soc. 412; pr. Dal. 22, pl. 2); Sta. P.C. 30.

[174] *Anon.* (c.1542/50) Wm Yelv. 353, no. 83 (Norfolk assizes).

[175] Spelman's reading (1519) 113 Selden Soc. 161, case 21.

[176] *R.* v. *Anon.* (1548) Brooke Abr., *Corone*, pl. 179.

and this is also mentioned in the statutes of 1512 and 1531 which removed clergy from the offence of housebreaking with robbery.[177] Mountford said it was not felony to break into a tavern or alehouse for meat, but he did not say whether this was because it was not a dwelling-house (as an inn was) or because the intention was not felonious. The law had always given special protection to dwelling-houses, and protection was especially needed at night when the inhabitants were off their guard; for 'the law would that every man's house against malefactors should be a safehold and defence for him'.[178] Darkness also afforded a ready means of escape in a world without street-lighting, and the expert burglar was already characterized by his dark nocturnal clothing.[179] All the readers and writers except Fitzherbert and Mountford held that burglary could only be committed at night, and Fitzherbert was criticized by Brooke and Staunford for omitting this element, though it may have been an innovation.[180] For this purpose, night began at sunset and ended at sunrise.[181]

Thus, although no single source in this period gives a definition of burglary which represents the settled state of law, it appears from the sources as a whole that the offence was generally coming to be seen as the breaking into a dwelling-house—or church[182]—by night with intent to commit any felony. Housebreaking in the daytime was not a felony,[183] though a statute of 1547 removed benefit of clergy from the offence of 'breaking of any house by day or by night, any person being then in the same house...and...thereby put in fear and dread'.[184] This replaced the 1531 provision as to 'robbery' in a dwelling-house, but suffered from an analogous defect: there was no felony for which clergy might be available in the case of housebreaking by day, unless it was accompanied by robbery or larceny.

Arson

Arson was another common-law felony protecting the dwelling-house, in this case from malicious burning. Unlike burglary, it could be committed by day as well as

---

[177] Yorke 183, no. 242; 4 Hen. VIII, c. 2; 23 Hen. VIII, c. 1; and see 5 & 6 Edw. VI, c. 9; above, 571.

[178] Charge for a leet (1538) BL MS. Add. 48047, fo. 65. Cf. Fyneux CJ's remark about it being his 'castle and defence', above, 562.

[179] *Lane v. Grove* (1533) CP 40/1077, m. 603 (burglar's black coat and hood mentioned in defamation action).

[180] Bellamy suggests that *noctanter* had originally been inserted in burglary indictments merely for aggravation and did not become essential until the Tudor period: *Criminal Trial*, 76, 83–4.

[181] *Anon.* (1505) 2 Caryll 483 at 484, *per* Frowyk CJ. This was a matter of evidence. Indictments merely said 'by night' (*noctanter*), sometimes specifying the time: see *R. v. Barbour* (1490) ibid. 22. Cf. *R. v. Paterson* (1532) NfRO, C/S3/1, m. 5c (house burglariously broken at 8 p.m. in January, not saying *noctanter*).

[182] Marow's reading (1503), ed. Putnam, 378. Examples are: *R. v. Fuller* (1539) NfRO, C/S3/2 (indictment at Norwich sessions for burglariously breaking a chapel and feloniously taking property of the parishioners in the custody of the churchwardens); *R. v. Anon.* (1554) Dyer 99, §58.

[183] Marow's reading (1503), ed. Putnam, 378.   [184] 1 Edw. VI, c. 12.

by night.[185] In 1496 the judges extended the scope of the protection to a barn adjoining a house,[186] presumably if it contained grain,[187] and in 1557 the assembled judges agreed that it extended also to a stable, ox-house, or sheep-house, which was part of and adjoining a dwelling-house.[188] In 1531 benefit of clergy was removed from the offence of wilfully burning a dwelling-house or a barn which contained grain.[189] Since the statute did not say that such a barn had to adjoin a dwelling-house, the assembly of 1557 was asked whether it had impliedly enlarged the common-law offence.[190] Dyer thought it had,[191] as did Coke,[192] but it would have been more natural to interpret the statute as merely removing clergy from the common-law offence in specific cases. A clearer example of a statute creating a new felony is provided by that of 1545, which explicitly made it felony to burn the timber frame of a house while it was being built.[193]

ACCESSORIES

Felons were either principals or accessories, and accessories could be before the fact or after.[194] Although accessories received the same judgment as principals, it was practically important to distinguish between the two categories of felon for at least four reasons. First and foremost, an accessory could not be convicted without a principal, and so an alleged accessory was entitled to be discharged if the principal was acquitted or pardoned,[195] or died,[196] or was attainted of another felony before judgment.[197] For this reason, it was the usual practice to arraign the

[185] Manual for justices (fifteenth century) BL MS. Harley 1777, fo. 87v; pr. with variations in *Boke of Justyces of Peas* (1505?), sig. Avi (sp. mod., 'If there be any man that burneth his neighbour's house maliciously by day or by night it is felony'). [186] Mich. 11 Hen. VII, fo. 1, pl. 3; Spelman 73, pl. 76.
[187] See Mountford's reading (1527) CUL MS. Ee.5.19, fo. 113v (arson may be of houses or grain).
[188] Dyer's notebook, 110 Selden Soc. 411; Dalison's reports, BL MS. Harley 5141, fo. 31v (tr. 110 Selden Soc. 413). [189] 23 Hen. VIII, c. 1.
[190] See the discussion of 1557 variously reported in 110 Selden Soc. 411, 413.
[191] 110 Selden Soc. 411 (reports the decision of 1557 in that sense), 441 (question in 1566 whether wilfully burning a windmill containing grain was arson). Dalison reported the 1557 decision more guardedly.
[192] Co. Inst. iii. 67.
[193] 37 Hen. VIII, c. 6 (said to be 'a new damnable kind of vice'); repealed by 1 Edw. VI, c. 12.
[194] Littleton's reading (1493) CUL MS. Hh.3.6, fo. 3v; *R.* v. *Bracier* (1530/1) Pollard 247, no. 3. Cf. Marow's reading (1503), ed. Putnam, 380, where there are said to be three kinds of accessory (adding accessory at the time of the felony). Marow was followed by Mountford (1527): CUL MS. Ee.5.19, fo. 114v.
[195] Mich. 3 Hen. VII, fo. 12, pl. 10; Pas. 3 Hen. VII, Crown Office entries, fo. 50; *R.* v. *Crips* (1508) KB 27/986, Rex m. 11d; *R.* v. *Symson* (1512) KB 27/1003, Rex m. 4. Spelman 44, 51, 67; *R.* v. *Whalley* (1553) Dyer 88a, §105.
[196] Littleton's reading (1493) CUL MS. Hh.3.6, fo. 4; Mich. 21 Hen. VII, fo. 31, pl. 15; *R.* v. *Mayne* (c.1480/90) Crown Office entries, fo. 51; *R.* v. *Kent* (1508) KB 27/988, Rex m. 20d; *R.* v. *Mason* (1518) KB 27/1026, Rex m. 9; *R.* v. *Holdesworth* (1538) Spelman 120; *R.* v. *Thorpe* (1539) ibid. 62. This made it impossible to be an accessory to suicide: *R.* v. *Wynspere* (1504) KB 27/974, Rex m. 4; *Notts. Inquests*, 8–9, no. 10.
[197] *Anon.* (1492/3) 1 Caryll 119–20, pl. 117. Attainder of felony was a form of civil death and wiped out all other felonies: *Moots*, 230; Yorke 90, no. 7; Dyer 214b, §48.

principal first.[198] It was widely thought that an accessory was not entitled to a discharge where the principal was allowed benefit of clergy after conviction;[199] but some held the true distinction to be that the accessory went free if the principal claimed clergy before judgment—which was the usual case—whereas he did not if clergy was claimed upon confession or after judgment.[200] The second reason for distinguishing principal and accessory was that—until 1555[201]—it was doubtful whether an accessory could be indicted if the principal felony was committed in a different county.[202] The third was that a coroner's jury could not indict someone for being an accessory after the fact to homicide.[203] And the fourth was that the felony of an accessory was a separate felony, so that it was possible for someone acquitted of being an accessory to be indicted and convicted as principal in respect of the same felony.[204] It was also arguable that the statutory removal of clergy from a felony did not, without express words, extend to accessories.[205]

An accessory before the fact was someone who counselled, abetted, commanded, moved, procured, or 'steered' a felon to commit a felony.[206] A person who actually did the deed was a principal.[207] But there was a difficult intermediate territory. Suppose someone procured or abetted a felony, or was in company with the principal and shared his unlawful purpose, and was present when the felonious act was committed, but did not perform the act himself. In 1488 it was

---

[198] *Anon.* (1488) 1 Caryll 8, pl. 10C, *per* Huse CJ ('amazing law to charge the same inquest with the principal and accessory at the same time'); Hil. 3 Hen. VII, fo. 1, pl. 3; Mich. 3 Hen. VII, fo. 12, pl. 10; Spelman 44, pl. 2; *Moots*, 72–3. Cf. *Anon.* (1530) Pollard 246, no. 2, *per* Fitzjames CJ (jury sworn upon both, but verdict taken first with respect to the principal).

[199] *R.* v. *Anon.* (1488) Hil. 3 Hen. VII, fo. 1, pl. 3 (where a contrary decision is also mentioned); Mich. 3 Hen. VII, fo. 12, pl. 10; 1 Caryll 8, pl. 10C; *Anon.* (1492) *Moots*, 271 (contrary decision remembered); *Anon.* (1533) Spelman 44, pl. 2. Cf. *Diversite de Courtz* (1533), sig. B ('quere quid sit lex?'); *Anon.* (1549/50) Brooke Abr., *Corone*, pl. 184; Sta. P.C. 48 (notes divergence of opinion).

[200] Littleton's reading (1527) CUL MS. Hh.3.6, fo. 4; *R.* v. *Anon.* (1557) 110 Selden Soc. 409, pl. 32; 411, pl. 38(2); 412 (decision of the assembled judges). This view is inconsistent with the cases of 1488 and 1533 (previous note), where clergy was claimed before judgment.

[201] 2 & 3 Edw. VI, c. 24, which enabled an indictment to be taken in the county where the accessory committed the act.

[202] *Anon.* (1515) Chaloner 288, no. 15; *Gawen* v. *Hussey* (1534) Spelman 53. Cf. *R.* v. *Cressede* (1505) 2 Caryll 462; Port's opinion (1516) in 102 Selden Soc., p. xlv.

[203] *R.* v. *Mulgan* (1492) KB 27/924, Rex m. 1d; *R.* v. *Cobyn* (1501) KB 27/961, Rex m. 2d; *R.* v. *Cressede* (1505) 2 Caryll 462; *Anon.* (undated) Spelman 65, pl. 53; *R.* v. *Jones* (1517) KB 27/1025, Rex m. 1.

[204] *R.* v. *Knightley* (1549/50) Brooke Abr., *Corone*, pl. 185. And vice versa: Littleton's reading (1493) CUL MS. Hh.3.6, fo. 2. Cf. also *R.* v. *Bales and Middleton* (1555) 110 Selden Soc. 407.

[205] The law was changed by 4 & 5 Phil. & Mar., c. 4, following an ad hoc enactment relating to a particular accessory the previous year (2 & 3 Phil. & Mar., c. 17).

[206] The manual for justices (temp. Edw. IV) in Trinity Coll. Oxford MS. 30, fo. 84v, uses all these verbs but the first two, which are found in Fitz. J.P. 21 (sp. mod. 'then is he that procured, abetted, or counselled the [felony] to be done, accessory to the felony'). Various combinations of verbs were used in indictments.

[207] He need not necessarily be present, e.g. where he laid poison or a trap: Littleton's reading (1493) CUL MS. Hh.3.6, fo. 3v.

decided by all the judges of England that someone present at a murder, moving another to kill, was himself a principal.[208] But when the point was discussed at Richard Littleton's reading in 1493, it emerged that opinions differed. The old opinion—apparently favoured by the reader—was that all those present were principals, because by their presence they both emboldened the actor and discouraged resistance; but the 'new opinion'—which had become the 'common learning nowadays'—was that they were accessories unless they actually set hands on the deceased.[209] This new learning, seemingly confined to murder, was adopted by Marow,[210] and Fyneux CJ,[211] and may have been current until the 1530s;[212] but it proved unstable. John Rastell took the contrary view in the 1520s,[213] and in 1534 it was again held by all the judges that someone present aiding and abetting a murder was a principal.[214] There the law settled.[215] In the two related cases of Lord Dacre of the South and John Mauntell, in 1541, it is even said to have been decided that all those who came in a single company to perform an unlawful act, where death resulted, were principals.[216] That was a strong case of actual malice, in that—according to the indictment—the defendants and their adherents had taken an oath to kill anyone who should oppose them. The case nevertheless considerably extended the application of the newer doctrine, since Lord Dacre is said to have been a quarter of a mile from the deceased when the blow was struck.[217]

The status of the secondary kind of principal was considered in some detail in 1553, at Shrewsbury assizes. Bromley CJ there suggested that the rule requiring the discharge of an accessory if the principal could not be convicted ought, by parity of reasoning, to extend to principals in murder who did not deliver the mortal blow but were alleged to have abetted those who did. Such abettors

[208] Mich. 4 Hen. VII, fo. 18, pl. 10. See also *Wingfield's Case* (1481) Mich. 21 Edw. IV, fo. 70, pl. 55, at fo. 71, and the older authorities collected in Sta. P.C. 40.

[209] *Moots*, 273–4; different version in CUL MS. Hh.3.6, fo. 3v, where the reader states the old rule with approval, adding '(tr.) But the new opinion is contrary, so query'.

[210] Marow's reading (1503), ed. Putnam, 381.

[211] *R. v. Anon.* (1499) Trin. 14 Hen. VII, fo. 31, pl. 7 (indictment quashed in King's Bench); *R. v. Newbolt* (1512) 2 Caryll 613 at 614 (direction to jury).

[212] See e.g. Mountford's reading (1527) CUL MS. Ee.5.19, ff. 114v–115 (rule in murder only); *Diversite de Courtz* (1533), sig. B (states both views); *R. v. Salysbery* (1538) Spelman 104; *Jackson v. Stratforth* (1539) ibid. 62 (unclear).   [213] J. Rastell, *Exposiciones Terminorum* [*c.*1523], sig. A4, and (1527 edn), fo. 4.

[214] *R. v. Anon.* (1534) Spelman 100, pl. 16. It was held that even if the indictment said 'ut accessorius', those words were surplusage. Cf. the Serjeants' Inn case of this period in Yorke 89, no. 3, to the same effect.

[215] So says Sta. P.C. 40G, noting that the law had formerly varied.

[216] *R. v. Lord Dacre of the South* (tried by peers) and *R. v. Mauntell* (1541) Brooke Abr., *Corone*, pl. 171 (misdated 34 Hen. VIII); *Hall's Chronicle*, 842; KB 8/12 (calendared in 3 *DKR*, app. ii, 259–60); KB 9/550, m. 71 (calendared in *Sussex Inquests*, 33–4); cited in Dalison's reports, BL MS. Harley 5141, fo. 41 (1557); Moo. 86, pl. 216 (1568); discussed in *Sussex Archaeological Collections*, iv. 176–8; xix. 170–9; *Sussex County Magazine*, v. 32–48, 89–99. Both defendants were executed for the murder.

[217] The fact, however, was off the record, since the indictment alleged (fictitiously) that he was present and delivered a mortal blow.

were now distinguished, in Bromley CJ's analysis, as principals 'in the second degree', or principals 'in law' (but not in fact), since formerly—as he pointed out—they had been regarded as accessories. However, Sir Robert Townshend (the other assize judge), Plowden, and the other justices present, held that those who were present were principals to all intents and purposes, and could be arraigned without the principal in the first degree, 'for the presence of the others is a terror to the one who is assaulted, and a reason that he durst not defend himself', and so they were equal offenders.[218] At the same session it was held that it was possible to be found an accessory to manslaughter where the principal was guilty of murder, if the accessory did not share in the malice aforethought of the principal.[219]

The offence of an accessory after the fact was defined in the reign of Edward IV as 'aiding, supporting, maintaining, or retaining' a felon, knowing him to have committed the felony.[220] The usual cases were 'receiving' or harbouring a felon and receiving stolen goods. A buyer or bailee of stolen goods was a receiver, though not—it was said—a mere donee.[221] Receiving stolen goods made the receiver an accessory even if they had been stolen in another county, because the theft continued in every county where they were taken;[222] and in a *cause célèbre* of 1543 a London goldsmith was convicted as an accessory to the theft of some silver from New College, Oxford.[223] But this was not true where the felon himself was received and harboured in a different county, and a statute was passed in 1548/9 to make this felony.[224] Some thought that endeavouring to secure the acquittal of someone known to be guilty, or taking him goods in sanctuary, was a sufficient act of support to amount to felony; but this position was disputed.[225] Certainly it was not felony to give food or alms to a felon in custody.[226] Rescuing a felon in the course

---

[218] *R. v. Griffith ap David* (1553) Plowd. 97–100 (tr.). Bromley CJ sent home for his copy of some year books, which bore out his view; but Plowden said the law had changed.

[219] *R. v. Salisbury* (1553) Plowd. 100–1; though it ought perhaps to have been a case of transferred malice (see 83 LQR 585–7). The defendant, Sir John Salusbury MP, JP, obtained a pardon and by 1559 was custos rotulorum for Denbighshire: *HPHC 1509–58*, iii. 264.

[220] Manual for justices (temp. Edw. IV) Trinity Coll. Oxford MS. 30, fo. 84v.

[221] Port 83, no. 13 (undated note); 110 Selden Soc. 402, pl. 8 (note dated 1554). Cf. Marow's reading (1503), ed. Putnam, 381 (buyer of stolen goods not a receiver).

[222] *R. v. Thorpe* (1539) Spelman 62; *R. v. Anon.* (1542) Brooke Abr., *Corone*, pl. 170. Cf. 2 & 3 Edw. VI, c. 24, preamble.

[223] *R. v. Calaway* (1543) *Hall's Chronicle*, 859. Hall attributed the prosecution to the malice of Dr London, warden of the college, because Calaway was of the 'new learning'. Calaway was convicted on slender evidence, and upon a false assertion that the principal had been convicted; but he had his clergy (above, 534). London was convicted of perjury and died in prison.

[224] Sta. P.C. 41v; 2 & 3 Edw. VI, c. 24. Likewise accessories before the fact: *Gawen v. Calverley* (1534) Spelman 53; Dyer 38; KB 27/1094, m. 40.

[225] Spelman 68, pl. 65 (undated note); 94 Selden Soc. 336. As to speaking kind words and seeking an acquittal, cf. Sta. P.C. 41v (citing Fitz. Abr., *Corone*, pl. 195).

[226] Littleton's reading (1493) CUL MS. Hh.3.6, fo. 3v; Mountford's reading (1527) MS. Ee.5.19, fo. 115.

of arrest was an independent felony and was not treated as making the rescuer an accessory to the original felony.[227] Releasing a suspect arrested for felony was also an independent felony, regardless of whether the suspect was subsequently indicted.[228] Concealing a felony was not in itself a felony,[229] though if a person agreed with the felon to conceal his misdeed and not to give evidence against him—whether or not this was for money—it might amount to supporting the felon and thereby make the concealer an accessory.[230] Merely approving of a felony after it was committed, even if it was for the benefit of the person concerned, did not make him a felon.[231] It was impossible to be an accessory after the fact until the principal felony was complete, and so receiving a man who had fatally wounded someone did not make the receiver an accessory to homicide unless his support continued after the victim died.[232]

An inchoate attempt to procure or commit a felony was not a felony. Where, therefore, a labourer was indicted for feloniously breaking Yarmouth gaol, unlocking the fetters on a woman prisoner, and counselling her to escape, he was discharged by the King's Bench for want of any direct assertion that she did in fact escape.[233] A few years later a cutpurse who was indicted for slipping his hand into the purse of a lawyer at the King's Bench bar, with the intention of stealing money, was discharged by the court.[234] An attempt was nevertheless said by Marow to be a punishable misdemeanour.[235] In burglary, as we have seen, it was not necessary for the intruder's felonious intention to be fulfilled, because the offence of burglary was complete when a house was broken at night with the intention of committing another felony.

There could be no accessories to treason,[236] or to a misdemeanour.[237] All plotters and abettors in such cases were therefore treated as principals.[238] Where

---

[227] Hil. 1 Hen. VII, fo. 6, pl. 2; 64 Selden Soc. 125; R. v. Grene (1537) Spelman 59–60. Cf. Mountford's reading (1527) CUL MS. Ee.5.19, fo. 115, where it is said that procuring the escape of a felon amounts to accessory after the fact.   [228] R. v. Anon. (1554) Dyer 99a, §60.

[229] Dalison's reports, BL MS. Harley 5141, fo. 3v (1552). Concealing treason, however, was misprision of treason.

[230] ibid.; Moo. 8, pl. 29 (Hales J. at Serjeants' Inn said it was felony, but others disagreed). Cf. the common practice of compounding an appeal: above, 513.   [231] Port 149, no. 30 (undated note).

[232] Dalison's reports, BL MS. Harley 5141, fo. 44 (1557/8).

[233] R. v. Osbern (1506) 2 Caryll 535; KB 27/980, Rex m. 5 (pr. 116 Selden Soc. 536).

[234] R. v. Petite (1510) KB 29/142, m. 27 (the lawyer was Edward Hales, bencher of the Inner Temple). The controlment roll gives no reason for the discharge ('exoneretur per curiam etc. eo quod etc.'). See also above, 566.   [235] Marow's reading (1503), ed. Putnam, 377 (cutpurse).

[236] R. v. Cokker (1488) Trin. 3 Hen. VII, fo. 10, pl. 2; 64 Selden Soc. 134; R. v. Mannok (1501) KB 27/961, Rex m. 14 (both cases of counterfeiting coin); Littleton's reading (1493) CUL MS. Hh.3.6, fo. 3v. This rule extended to petty treason: above, 558; Rastell, Exposiciones Terminorum [c.1523], sig. A4; Sta. P.C. 40C.

[237] Littleton's reading (1493) CUL MS. Hh.3.6, fo. 3v; Mountford's reading (1527) MS. Ee.5.19, fo. 114v.

[238] Cf. undated note in Port 123, no. 72, which says receiving or comforting a traitor is not treason.

a felony was created by statute, it was usually taken to be implied that accessories should also be guilty of felony. This was the case with rape,[239] though there was room for doubt as to whether it was true of all statutory felonies.[240]

[239] Dalison's reports, BL MS. Harley 5141, fo. 10v (1553), garbled in Dal. 11, pl. 12, cited in Co. Inst. iii. 59 as 3 & 4 Phil. & Mar.

[240] See R. v. Whalley (1553) Dyer 88a, §105 (multiplication, contrary to 5 Hen. IV, c. 4); Sta. P.C. 44 (accessories before the fact).

32

Treason and Offences against Public Order

HIGH TREASON[1]

TREASON is the point where law and politics meet, and the history of Tudor England seems to have treason trials and bloody executions on almost every page. Considering its importance, however, the subject is not well served by purely legal sources. The reports and textbooks suggest that judges and lawyers were chiefly concerned with forms and procedures, leaving the larger questions to juries. But here, as elsewhere in the law, there was often a gap between form and reality, a gap bridged by artificial constructions and fictions. This makes the true legal history of treason—as opposed to a bare catalogue of the statutes which extended its scope—remarkably elusive. Although many of the state trials of the early Tudor period are well known to posterity, the details are largely wanting; and the law reports provide little enlightenment about either the substantive law or the thinking of lawyers concerned in prosecutions and trials.

The law of treason at the end of the fifteenth century was governed by the Treason Act of 1351, the principal forms of high treason being compassing or imagining the death of the king, levying war against the king in his realm, and adhering to the king's enemies.[2] Already, however, the scope of the law had been increased by broad interpretation so as to accommodate what would later be called 'constructive treason'.[3] In particular, various forms of words spoken against the king, or magical prophecies as to his life expectancy, had been held to be a constructive compassing of the king's death, on the grounds that his life might

---

[1] Two major studies are Elton, *Policy and Police*; Bellamy, *The Tudor Law of Treason*. The principal records (from the *Baga de Secretis*, KB 8) are calendared in the appendices to *Reports of the Deputy Keeper of Public Records*, vols 3–4 (cited as 3, 4 *DKR*).

[2] 25 Edw. III, stat. 5, c. 2. Cf. 3 Hen. VII, c. 14, which *inter alia* treated compassing the king's death by a household servant as merely felony. For petty treason, which was an aggravated species of murder, see above, 557–8.

[3] For the process of enlargement see J. Bellamy, *The Law of Treason in England in the Later Middle Ages* (1970).

be shortened by the grief they caused him.[4] That notion reappeared in the indictment of Queen Anne Boleyn,[5] though in general the more imaginative forms of constructive treason were not pursued in the sixteenth century.[6] On the other hand, many early Tudor indictments for treason laid stress on plotting to depose the king, or to deprive him of his regal power, for instance by taking over the government,[7] as if this were a distinct species of treason, though there is no mention of it in the 1351 act. It was probably assumed to be a constructive compassing of the king's death, or a levying of war,[8] and was sometimes reinforced by overt acts of treason falling under the words of the 1351 act; but indictments did not always make the categories clear, and juries were unlikely to concern themselves with fastidious distinctions.

It is unfortunate that we have no law report of the trials of Edmund Dudley and Sir Richard Empson in 1509. Contemporaries probably hailed their execution as a fitting end to two unscrupulous lawyer-politicians who had enriched Henry VII at the expense of his people,[9] but in calmer retrospect their condemnation seems to have ushered in a new regime of harshness. Spelman thought they had been arrested for their rapacious activities under Henry VII,[10] and Dudley's petition from the Tower after his conviction shows that he too thought that was the reality.[11] They were indeed indicted for various deceits, extortions, and offences against Magna Carta;[12] but these indictments were not pursued. Their trials were for treason against the new king. The legal difficulty in prosecuting them for treason was that what had been done in Henry VII's time had been in his name

[4] See also I. D. Thornley, 'Treason by Words in the Fifteenth Century (1917) 32 *EHR* 556–61. Coke said a man had been hanged in 5 Hen. VII for libelling the king: *Bagnall's Case* (*c.*1490) cited in J. Hawarde, *Cases in Camera Stellata*, ed. W. P. Baildon (1894), 345, 372.

[5] i.e. the allegation that the queen promised to marry one of her lovers if the king died, and that she would never love the king in her heart, which on becoming known to the king caused him such grief that he suffered bodily: *R. v. Queen Anne* (1536) 3 *DKR*, app. ii, 243–5.

[6] e.g. using magic to prognosticate the king's death, which was treated as treason in *R. v. Burdett* (1477) 3 *DKR*, app. ii, 213; CUL MS. Ee.3.1, ff. 23–25, was not regarded as treason a hundred years later: see 25 Eliz. I, c. 2; Co. Inst. iii. 6. See further below, 593–4.

[7] Note e.g. the attainder of Thomas Stafford (1557) for proclaiming the queen not to be rightful queen and naming himself protector and governor of the realm: *Tudor Royal Proclamations*, ii. 75, no. 433.

[8] e.g. *R. v. Boltesby* (1498) KB 27/948, Rex m. 4 (treasonable assembly and levying war '(tr.) with the intention of resisting, annulling, and hindering the royal power and authority in administering law and justice, and in executing the statutes for the peace of the realm, in subversion of the king's realm and in annulment of the aforesaid laws and statutes'; pardoned).

[9] See *Hall's Chronicle*, 505–6, 515. For their activities as 'promoters', see above, 63, 222; 2 Caryll 605 ('haughty and cruel approvers'); Spelman 175, pl. 5 (tr. 'promoters who took no heed of the common weal').   [10] Spelman 175, pl. 5.

[11] Harrison, 'The Petition of Edmund Dudley', 82–99. See also Dudley, *The Tree of Commonwealth*, ed. Brodie.

[12] KB 29/140, m. 22 (indictments found at the Guildhall, London, before the duke of Buckingham and others). They were not tried on these indictments (each entry is marked 'mortuus').

and for his benefit.[13] Resort was therefore had to an extraordinary and self-evidently fictitious device. The charge against Dudley was conspiring with unnamed persons to depose and destroy the new king should he and his council refuse to be ruled and governed, against his will, by Dudley and his adherents, and in pursuance of this conspiracy writing to various knights and esquires to assemble in London in warlike array. Empson was indicted and tried independently, by different grand and petty juries, and there was no express suggestion of a conspiracy with Dudley. His charge was similar in essence to Dudley's but differently worded: perceiving the illness of Henry VII, he had intended after the king's death to govern the new king against his will, and—if he could not do so—to destroy the king by force and violence; and in pursuance of this intention he summoned various Northamptonshire gentlemen to gather under arms immediately after the accession.[14] They were both convicted in the summer of 1509, and an unsuccessful attempt was made to attaint them in the Parliament of 1510; but it was over a year before (in response to popular clamour) they were executed.[15] There was no suggestion in 1509 of any other contender for the throne, and the allegation of an intention to 'destroy' the new king can hardly have been credible. The charges therefore appear to have been purely about the wrongful exercise of political power, and the convictions legally unjustifiable.[16] Historians have attributed the prosecutions to Henry VIII's personal intervention, and to his ruthlessness. Indeed, they have been described as 'the first item in that long series of judicial murders for which the reign of Henry VIII was to become unique in English history'.[17] Contemporary legal opinions of the proceedings are not preserved,[18] but misgivings at the time may have caused a reaction. For the remainder of the period the law officers, and the judges, were careful to ensure that treason charges fell within the law, and if the law needed to be extended it was done by legislation rather than legal fiction. The charge of plotting to rule the king against his will, and to deprive him of his power, resurfaced in the indictments of the Lincolnshire rebels in 1537; but then there were clear acts of levying war, with thousands of

[13] Dudley's son, John, duke of Northumberland, said that his 'poor father' had 'suffered death for doing his master's commandment': C. S. Knighton in *Law and Government under the Tudors*, ed. C. Cross et al. (1988), 174 (sp. mod.)

[14] R v. *Dudley* and R. v. *Empson* (1509) KB 8/4; 3 *DKR*, app. ii, 226–7 (calendar of record). The Empson record was copied in Catlyn CJ's precedent book, Alnwick Castle MS. 475, fo. 44v. It was also recited in *Glover* v. *Empson* (1514) CP 40/1046, m. 553.

[15] *Hall's Chronicle*, 515. The form of writ for their execution was copied in William Porter's precedent book, C193/9, fo. 142.

[16] See Holdsworth, *HEL*, iv. 27; Chrimes, *Henry VII*, 316–17; Williams, *The Tudor Regime*, 383; Elton, *England under the Tudors*, 71; Bellamy, *Tudor Law of Treason*, 21–2. Cf. Brodie, 'Edmund Dudley' 133 at 151–2, who thought there might have been some colour of truth.   [17] Chrimes, *Henry VII*, 317.

[18] However, both common-law attainders were soon reversed: 3 Hen. VIII, c. 19 (Dudley); 4 Hen. VIII, c. 15 (Empson).

supporters in warlike array.[19] Where there was nothing that could be described as an overt act of war, as in the case of Thomas Cromwell in 1540, or Protector Somerset in 1549–51,[20] charges of political overbearing were pursued extra-judicially by an act of attainder rather than by judicial proceedings.

To find a formal scrupulousness in treason cases is not to conclude that those who lost their lives after trial at the king's behest were fairly convicted on the merits. But their deaths were not judicial murders in the formal sense. The forms of law were observed; evidence was given of facts falling within the scope of treason as defined by law; and jurors were put on oath to find the truth. Juries usually complied with the prosecution. But whether the evidence was cogent, or the verdicts reliable, were issues from which the judges felt able to remain aloof. Sir John Spelman made private notes of the evidence given in some of the state trials which he attended as a judge, but treated it more as newsworthy information than as material to be weighed and questioned.[21]

During the first twenty years of Henry VIII's reign there seem to have been few developments in the law of treason, apart from two instances in which the judges were prepared to treat serious forms of public protest as a constructive levying of war. In 1516 it is said to have been resolved by all the judges 'that an insurrection against the Statute of Labourers, for the enhancing of salaries and wages, was a levying of war against the king, because it was generally against the king's law, and the offenders took upon them the reformation thereof, which subjects by gathering of power ought not to do'.[22] The 'insurrection' apparently involved some interference with the quarter sessions, to prevent the enforcement of the statute.[23] There are, however, two recorded cases that same year where the assembly of armed crowds at the time of assizes and quarter sessions, in order to intimidate jurors and influence proceedings, was treated merely as riot.[24] Then, in 1517, after the Evil May Day insurrection in London, Fyneux CJ advised that a general rising to destroy foreign immigrants and their houses was high treason. It was, he said, 'a thing practised against the regal honour of our sovereign lord the king', as in the case of the Kentish labourers, though for

---

[19] e.g. *R. v. Mackerell* (1537) 3 *DKR*, app. ii, 245–7. Lord Darcy was even accused, *inter alia*, of plotting to compel the king to hold a parliament: *R. v. Lord Darcy* (1537) ibid. 247–9.

[20] His indictment for treason in 1551 owed a good deal to the precedents of 1509: *R. v. Duke of Somerset* (1551) KB 8/19; 3 *DKR*, app. ii, 228–30. He was acquitted of treason, but convicted of (and executed for) felony. Note also the similar charges against Lord Seymour (1549) 1 St. Tr. 483; *APC*, ii. 248.

[21] See above, 417.

[22] Co. Inst. iii. 10. The only citation in the margin is 'Ter. Mich. 8 H. 8'. It is probably the Kentish case noted in Port 123, no. 73 and n. 3 (undated).

[23] Port 123, no. 73 (mentions an intention to compel the justices not to enforce the statute).

[24] The instigators were men of rank: *R. v. Darcy* (1516) KB 27/1021, Rex m. 2d (riotous assembly of 200 armed malefactors by Sir George Darcy during the York assizes; pleads Not guilty but accepts a fine to spare trouble); *R. v. Floure*, ibid., m. 13 (riotous assembly by command of Sir Richard Sacheverell to influence jurors at Leicestershire quarter sessions; pleads Not guilty).

good measure—the evidence of premeditation being flimsy—the offenders were also held to have committed statutory treason by breaking a treaty of amity.[25] The real blame seems to have lain with two monks who had preached inflammatory sermons against foreigners, and in the event only four (out of over 400) prisoners were executed. These precedents do not seem to have started a trend. Riot was generally treated as such;[26] but in these two cases there was evidently serious alarm that the mob might impede the working of government. Preventing justices from holding their quarter sessions would again be treated as levying war in 1548.[27]

The royal divorce and the break with Rome prompted a severe extension of treason law in the 1530s, but the changes were wrought by Parliament rather than the judges. Indeed, the judges had declined to cooperate in 1533 when Elizabeth Barton, the 'Nun of Kent', was charged with slandering the king's second marriage and prognosticating the king's natural death if he persisted with it.[28] The judges were not prepared to follow the fifteenth-century precedents and hold this to be a constructive compassing of the king's death. Barton was therefore not prosecuted at law, but attainted by statute,[29] and shortly afterwards new treason legislation was passed.[30]

The First Succession Act 1534 declared it treason to do anything to the peril of the king's person, or to 'give occasion' whereby the king 'might be disturbed or interrupted of the Crown', or to act or write anything to the 'prejudice, slander, disturbance, and derogation' of the king's marriage to Anne Boleyn.[31] Of course, the statute required rapid alteration in 1536 when that marriage came to a bloody end.[32] It then became treason to slander the marriage with Queen Jane, or to affirm the marriage with Anne Boleyn to have been good.[33]

The original Succession Bill had proposed to go further and make words alone treason, but on the advice of counsel this was omitted and a separate clause was inserted making it misprision of treason to commit the like offences 'by words, without writing or any exterior deed or act'.[34] Such caution was abandoned in the

---

[25] R. v. *Lincoln and others* (1517) Port 123–4 (at Guildhall); 2 Caryll 607; HEHL MS. EL 2654, ff. 23v–24 (discussion in Star Chamber); Vergil, *Anglica Historia*, ed. Hay, 242–7; *Hall's Chronicle*, 588–91; R. Holinshed, *Chronicles* (1808 edn), iii. 622; R. Grafton, *Chronicle* (1568), 1023. Truce-breaking was made treason by the statute 2 Hen. V, stat. 1, c. 6.   [26] Below, 590–2.

[27] R. v. *Geffrey* (1548) 3 DKR, app. ii, 217–19. The other overt act alleged here was proclaiming that they would have no new laws until the king reached the age of 24.

[28] *LP*, vi. 1445. Chapuys thought they would give way; but no trial occurred.

[29] 25 Hen. VIII, c. 12.

[30] Some reform of the treason law had been under consideration since 1530, though the underlying purpose of the original measure is unclear: Elton, *Policy and Police*, 265–74.

[31] 25 Hen. VIII, c. 22. This was the statute on which Robert Feron, the Carthusian monk, was indicted for wishing the king the same fate as King John or Richard III: R. v. *Feron* (1535) 3 DKR, app. ii, 237; CUL MS. Ee.3.1, ff. 116–118v.

[32] 28 Hen. VIII, c. 7; replaced by 35 Hen. VIII, c. 1.

[33] Those who drew the bill had themselves technically committed treason under the 1534 act, and so the 1536 act included a retrospective pardon.   [34] Elton, *Policy and Police*, 276.

Treason Act passed six months later,[35] which may have been the brainchild of Thomas Cromwell—doubtless under orders from the king himself—with legal assistance from Audley C. This statute made it high treason, *inter alia*,[36]

if any person or persons... do maliciously wish, will, or desire, by words or writing, or by craft imagine, invent, practise, or attempt any bodily harm to be done or committed to the king's most royal person, the queen's, or their heirs' apparent, or to deprive them or any of them of their dignity, title, or name of their royal estates, or slanderously and maliciously publish and pronounce, by express writing or words, that the king our sovereign lord should be heretic, schismatic, tyrant, infidel, or usurper of the Crown...

Treason by words alone was not new:[37] indeed, Fyneux CJ had confirmed in 1521 that words could constitute the overt act proving a treasonable intention.[38] But now the mere private expression of opinion could be treason.[39] The Commons are said to have insisted on the qualifying adverb 'maliciously',[40] but it proved a worthless safeguard in practice. Within seven months Prior Houghton of the Charterhouse, Bishop Fisher, and Sir Thomas More, were convicted under this statute for denying the king's title of supreme head of the Church in England.[41] Moreover, the expression of opinion did not have to be public: in the case of More, the chief complaint was of evasive answers under interrogation rather than spontaneous open denial. The same statute led to the execution of Cardinal Pole's adherents in 1538, on the footing that Pole had denied the king's supremacy by accepting his red hat from the pope, and that the defendants had expressed their approval of his conduct.[42] In 1539 Sir Nicholas Carew was indicted, convicted, and beheaded, merely for having correspondence with the marquess of Exeter—lately attainted of treason—about 'change in the world', and saying, 'I marvel greatly that the indictment against the

[35] 26 Hen. VIII, c. 13. This was passed in November 1534. Note also 28 Hen. VIII, c. 10 (treason to refuse oath of supremacy); 35 Hen. VIII, c. 3 (treason to imagine to deprive the king of any titles, styles, names, degrees, royal estate, or regal power, annexed to the Crown).

[36] The new treasons also included (from the 1530 bill) rebelliously withholding from the king any of his castles, fortresses, ships, ordnances, artillery, or other munitions of war. This was very close to levying war. The statute also deprived traitors of sanctuary: above, 550.

[37] Examples of treason resting largely on spoken words were *R. v. Cowley* (1518) 2 Caryll 693–5 (saying the king was dead, and that if Wolsey were killed they would have a merry world); *R. v. Duke of Buckingham* (1521) Port 124–5; Pas. 13 Hen. VIII, fo. 1, pl. 1 (119 Selden Soc. 56); KB 8/5, mm. 1–15; Crown Office precedents, ff. 258*bis*–259*bis*; 110 Selden Soc. 234–5.

[38] *R. v. Duke of Buckingham* (1521) Port 124–5, *per* Fyneux CJ (charging grand jury); Pas. 13 Hen. VIII, fo. 11, pl. 1 (119 Selden Soc. 57), *per* Fyneux CJ (at trial).   [39] Or a heraldic error: below, n. 50.

[40] Elton, *Policy and Police*, 283.

[41] *R. v. Houghton and others* (1535) 3 *DKR*, app. ii, 238–9; Spelman 57; *R. v. Fisher* (1535) ibid.; *R. v. More* (1535) 3 *DKR*, app. ii, 240–1; Spelman 58; Derrett, 'The Trial of Sir Thomas More', 449–77. The records of all three are copied in CUL MS. Ee.3.1, ff. 118v–123v (*c.*1540).

[42] *R. v. Sir Geoffrey Pole* (1538) 3 *DKR*, app. ii, 251–2; *R. v. Nevyle* (1538) ibid. 252–3 (also for saying 'The king is a beast and worse than a beast'); *R. v. Lord Montague* (1538) ibid. 255–7; Spelman 61.

lord marquess was so secretly handled, and for what purpose, for the like was never seen'.[43] By another statute, of 1541, evidently the personal invention of an obsessed king, even silence could be treason—if someone failed to disclose to the king or his Council the sexual incontinence of a woman about to marry him.[44]

This series of statutes has been condemned, with justice, as the most repressive body of penal legislation ever passed in England. That was also the contemporary reaction, for we are told that the law officers in 1553 inveighed in Parliament against the 'cruel and bloody laws of King Henry the eighth . . . Draco's laws, which were written in blood'.[45] In 1547 Protector Somerset had them all repealed by the new king, as having been 'very strait, sore, extreme, and terrible'.[46] There could no longer be treason by words or thoughts alone, at any rate for the time being. The very first statute of Mary's reign confirmed the repeal, because 'not only the ignorant and rude unlearned people, but also learned and expert people minding honesty, are often and many times trapped and snared, yea many times for words only without other act or deed done'.[47] But it remained the case that words could sometimes constitute an overt act of treason, as where someone confided traitorous plans to another[48]—indeed, the year-book report of the duke of Buckingham's trial, with Fyneux CJ's ruling to that effect, was widely disseminated in print.[49] And constructive treasons were by no means laid to rest. In 1547 the earl of Surrey was charged with high treason for using a variant of some royal arms, thereby slandering the king's title to the throne;[50] and in 1555 William Constable was indicted for high treason in affirming Edward VI to be still alive.[51] In any case, Mary lost no time in reintroducing her father's brand of statutory treason by words, for those who said—or merely held the opinion—that the king of Spain ought not to have the style of king, or that she ought not to be queen.[52] It was at

---

[43] R. v. Carew (1539) KB 8/11/3; 3 DKR, app. ii, 258–9. The marquess had been tried by his peers: R. v. Marquess of Exeter (1538) KB 8/11/2; Spelman 61.

[44] 33 Hen. VIII, c. 21. The act attainted Queen Katharine Howard of treason for sexual misbehaviour.

[45] Quoted in R. v. Throckmorton (1554) 1 St. Tr. 869 at 896.

[46] 1 Edw VI, c. 12. This abrogated all treasons created by statute since 1351.

[47] 1 Mar. I, sess. 1, c. 1.

[48] R. v. Anon. (1555) Dalison's reports, BL MS. Harley 5141, ff. 27v–28; Dal. 14, pl. 5. This was also Staunford's opinion: Sta. P.C. 2v. Cf. R. v. Throgmorton (1554) Dyer 98b; R. v. Croft (1554) Sta. P.C. 19v; Dal. 14; where it was held that conspiring to levy war was not treason without an overt act by at least one conspirator, which suggests that conspiring was not itself an overt act.

[49] Above, n. 38.

[50] R. v. Earl of Surrey (1547) KB 8/14; Crown Office precedents, ff. 257v–258v; 3 DKR, app. ii, 267 (using the arms of Edward the Confessor with a label of three points argent, on a shield in his father's house, to the slander of the king's title to the crown, contrary to 28 Hen. VIII, c. 7); Brooke Abr., Treason, pl. 2; P. R. Moore, 'The Heraldic Charge against the Earl of Surrey 1546–7' (2001) 116 EHR 557–83.

[51] R. v. Constable (1555) indictment copied in Catlyn CJ's precedent book, Alnwick Castle MS. 475, fo. 44v.   [52] 1 & 2 Phil. & Mar., c. 10.

the same time made treason to pray for the queen's death unless she turned from idolatry.[53]

A third form of high treason mentioned in the 1351 statute was violating the king's companion, or his eldest unmarried daughter, or the companion of his eldest son and heir. In the case of Queen Anne Boleyn, this offence was held to be committed where the 'violation' was by the queen's consent, and in such case the queen was guilty as well as the violators.[54] The case may also have established that the king's 'companion' for this purpose included a *de facto* queen, so that the validity of the marriage was immaterial, although the king seems not to have asserted the nullity of the marriage until after the event. The unprecedented conviction of a queen for treason raised the appalling prospect of her being burned at the stake; but the lord steward, with some dissent from the judges, passed sentence that she be burned or beheaded at the king's pleasure,[55] and she was in fact beheaded with a sharp sword by an expert executioner brought from Calais.[56]

The list of treasons in the 1351 statute also included counterfeiting the king's great or privy seal, or his money,[57] or importing and uttering false money imitating the coin of the realm.[58] This was extended by legislation to counterfeiting or importing foreign coin current in the realm,[59] or counterfeiting the privy signet or sign manual.[60] Clipping, washing, and filing coin was treason until the general repeal of statutory treasons by Edward VI.[61] In 1540 it was held to be treason for a Chancery official to counterfeit patents by misusing the matrix of the true seal.[62] On the other hand, it was held in 1545 not to be treason to take a good seal off an old patent and affix it to a new;[63] but the decision was reversed in 1556.[64] Although

---

[53] 1 & 2 Phil. & Mar., c. 9.

[54] *R. v. Queen Anne* (1536) Spelman 70; KB 8/8; E. W. Ives, *Anne Boleyn* (1986), ch. 17. The indictments also supposed a constructive compassing of the king's death, and a constructive slandering of the king's issue by Queen Anne contrary to the statute.

[55] ibid. Spelman says, 'Note that the justices grumbled (*murmurront*) at this judgment' for want of a precedent. The warrant for execution was in the disjunctive: copy by Sir Robert Catlyn, Alnwick Castle MS. 475, fo. 175v.   [56] Spelman 59, pl. 37; Holinshed, *Chronicles*, iii (1587), fo. 940.

[57] This offence was said to be complete by the counterfeiting alone, even if the coin was not uttered: Mich. 1 Ric. III, fo. 1, pl. 1; Mich. 6 Hen. VII, fo. 13, pl. 13.

[58] See *R. v. Creyghton* (1536) Spelman 103; KB 27/1101, Rex m. 13.

[59] 4 Hen. VII, c. 18; repealed by 1 Edw. VI, c. 12; revived by 1 Mar. I, sess. 2, c. 6 (counterfeiting); and 1 & 2 Phil. & Mar., c. 11 (importing). Importing counterfeit foreign coin was not treason before 1554: *R. v. Anon.* (1539) Spelman 62, pl. 45 (French ducats). For counterfeiting Irish money see Trin. 3 Hen. VII, fo. 10, pl. 3.

[60] 27 Hen. VIII, c. 2; repealed by 1 Edw. VI, c. 12; revived by 1 Mar. I, sess. 2, c. 6. Examples of prosecutions for forging the sign manual: *R. v. Conysby* (1538) noted in Elton, *Policy and Police*, 307–8; *R. v. Hackney* (1554) 4 *DKR*, app. ii, 238–9 (granting himself an annuity purportedly warranted by 'Mary the Quene').   [61] 3 Hen. V, st. 2, c. 6; 1 Edw. VI, c. 12.

[62] *R. v. Egerton* (1540) noted in *Hall's Chroncicle*, 841. For the context see below, 615.

[63] *R. v. Anon.* (1545) Brooke Abr., *Treason*, pl. 3.

[64] *R. v. Anon.* (1556) Dalison's reports, BL MS. Harley 5141, fo. 30v; Sta. P.C. 3 (tr. 'and so it has been adjudged in my time'). This decision followed the year-book case Trin. 2 Hen. IV, fo. 25, pl. 25.

the Chancery official of 1540 suffered dismemberment, the better view was that this should not form part of the sentence for such treasons as did not touch the king's person.[65]

MISPRISION OF TREASON

There were no accessories in high treason.[66] Those who participated actively in a traitorous plot were principals, though the same language of aiding, counselling, and abetting, was used in indictments;[67] other forms of implication in treason might constitute the lesser offence of misprision. The prime meaning of misprision was concealment of treason,[68] though it was said to include also a traitorous intent which was not accompanied by any overt act.[69] In 1556 all the justices declared that 'misprision of treason is where high treason is revealed or declared to another person, and that person to whom it is so revealed or declared does not declare it to some of the Council or to some of the justices but keeps it secret'.[70] The punishment was perpetual imprisonment and forfeiture of goods, chattels, and the profits of land during the offender's life.[71] There were a few other species of misprision at common law, such as uttering counterfeit money made by others,[72] or receiving and aiding a counterfeiter after the fact.[73] In addition, a number of statutory forms of misprision were created under Henry VIII[74] and Edward VI.[75] The statute of 1553 which repealed statutory treasons also provided that no offence should be deemed to be treason or misprision of treason 'but only such as be declared and expressed to be treason, petty treason, or misprision of treason' in the statute of 1351.[76] In fact no misprisions were declared in the statute of 1351;

---

[65] Port 82, no. 11, per Grantham; R. v. Anon. (1554) Dalison's reports, BL MS. Harley 5141, fo. 20, per Portman J. [66] Above, 578. The position in petty treason was unclear: above, 558.

[67] e.g. R. v. Kebyll (1498) KB 27/948, Rex m. 6 (judgment to be hanged, drawn, and quartered for adhering to, counselling, comforting, abetting, and aiding Perkin Warbeck).

[68] This was confirmed by 2 & 3 Phil. & Mar., c. 10, s. 8. See specimen charge (1538) BL MS. Add. 48047, fo. 63 (sp. mod. 'misprision of treason . . . is where any person [knowing] that another intended to offend . . . the same did keep secret and not disclose and utter before the act done'). An example is John Hayes's attainder (1492) RP, vi. 455.

[69] Anon. (c.1497) 120 Selden Soc. 43, no. 26, per Townshend J. But an overt act by one conspirator was enough to make all of them principals: R. v. Throgmorton (1554) Dyer 98b; R. v. Croft (1554) Sta. P.C. 19v; Dal. 14.

[70] R. v. Anon. (1556) Dalison's reports, BL MS. Harley 5141, fo. 37v; and Dyer's note in 109 Selden Soc. 17 (1556). There is a similar definition in Sta. P.C. 37v.

[71] Brooke Abr., Treason, pl. 19 (1552) and 25 (1554/5). [72] Trin. 3 Hen. VII, fo. 10, pl. 3, ad fin.

[73] R. v. Coniers (1570) Dyer 296a, §21.

[74] e.g. 28 Hen. VIII, c. 7; above, 585. There were also a few parliamentary attainders for misprision, e.g. that of John Fisher in 1535: 26 Hen. VIII, c. 22; Spelman 58.

[75] 5 & 6 Edw. VI, c. 11, which revived in the inferior guise of misprision some of the Henrician treasons by words, e.g. slandering the king as a heretic or usurper. [76] 1 Mar. I, sess. 1, c. 1.

but the judges held that common-law misprision remained in being, the explicit intention of the 1553 statute being only to repeal statutory misprisions.[77]

Staunford also classified as misprision the offence of drawing a weapon or committing an assault in the presence of the king's justices, which carried the further penalty of having the offending hand struck off.[78] This offence was enlarged by statute in 1541 to include any malicious striking in any palace or house where the king was personally residing, if blood was drawn[79]—another sanguinary measure which bears the stamp of the king's personal influence, the immediate target being Sir Edmund Knyvet.[80] The statute required executions of amputation under the statute to be attended by various servants of the royal household, doubtless to serve them a dire warning, and they were all assigned suitably awesome duties: the serjeant of the woodyard was to provide a block, the master cook to bring a knife, the serjeant surgeon to sear the stump, and so on. As a small concession to humanity, the offender was to be allowed a pot of wine, though not until after the event. Perhaps this piece of terror was meant to be purely psychological. Knyvet was pardoned at the last moment and the elaborate ceremony never took place. The new offence was one of those swept away in 1553. But the common-law offence and its gruesome penalty, remarkably, have never been abolished.[81]

RIOT AND UNLAWFUL ASSEMBLY

The King's Bench rolls contain numerous indictments for unlawful assembly, in its various forms, whether arising from public discontent or—as was more usual—from attempts to resolve property disputes by force.[82] Although, as we have seen, there was sometimes a very thin line between an unlawful assembly and constructive levying of war, the lesser offence was not felony at common law but merely a trespass, or misdemeanour. In 1487 John Spynell and others were attainted by Parliament for felony committed by assembling and planning 'commotions, rumours, and insurrections,' and to slay, murder, and destroy divers of the king's great officers and members of the Council. Doubtless the device of an act of attainder was here resorted to because no treason or felony had been committed at common law.[83]

---

[77] R. v. Anon. (1556) Dalison's reports, BL MS. Harley 5141, ff. 37v–38.

[78] Sta. P.C. 38; and also mentioned in Marmyon v. Baldwyn (1527) 120 Selden Soc 61 at 63, per Shelley J. The penalty was still sometimes imposed: R. v. Anon. (1556) Dal. 23, pl. 6; R. v. Burchet (1573) Co. Inst. iii. 140; R. v. Jones (1575) KB 27/1252, Reg. m. 6. See also Dyer 188b, §10 (case of 1461 noted in 1560).

[79] 33 Hen. VIII, c. 12; above, 289.

[80] R. v. Knyvet (1541) Brooke Abr., Paine et Penance, pl. 16; 1 St. Tr. 443; HPHC 1509-58, ii. 483. It was another example of legislation intended to apply retrospectively: cf. above, 66. Knyvet was also sentenced to lose his inheritance, a penalty not mentioned in the statute.

[81] See Baker, 100 LQR 544–7.   [82] As to which see below, 722–3.   [83] RP, vi. 402.

The subject of unlawful assemblies received some doctrinal discussion because it was of special importance to justices of the peace. Since the statutory provisions governing the prosecution of rioters referred to the offences of riot, 'rout of people', and unlawful assembly,[84] lawyers came to regard these as three distinct offences, although the distinction between them was far from clear and did not bring any practical consequences. The essence of riot was clearly agreed to be the effecting of an unlawful purpose, whereas unlawful assembly was a complete offence even if nothing was done beyond the assembling.[85] Rout seems to have lain somewhere between the two. Although the French word *rout* suggests a mob or large crowd, Fitzherbert seemingly held rout and unlawful assembly to be the same thing. Marow held a rout to be a 'great assembly' without a leader to carry out a common unlawful purpose, whereas an unlawful assembly was a meeting to carry out the unlawful purpose of its leader.[86] The Middle Temple readers seem to have taken the same line, that a rout was committed where a multitude of people assembled for their own unlawful purposes but did nothing.[87] A generation later, however, Dyer CJ held it to be purely a question of numbers, so that at least thirty persons were needed to constitute a rout.[88] In practice it was usual to combine the elements indiscrimately in indictments, which used phrases such as 'riotously, in manner of rout, unlawfully assembled, and in warlike array' (*riotose, route, illicite congregati,*[89] *et modo guerrino arraiati*). Some definitions consequently included the warlike or forcible array as necessary elements,[90] but Marow and others held arms and armour to be immaterial.[91]

All three offences included an unlawful assembly of people, and what made an assembly unlawful was an unlawful purpose. An assembly—according to Marow—was a gathering of two or more people,[92] though later authorities held

---

[84] 13 Hen. IV, c. 7; 2 Hen. V, c. 8; 11 Hen. VII, c. 7 (continued by 12 Hen. VII, c. 2); 19 Hen. VII, c. 13. Cf. *Tudor Royal Proclamations*, i. 245, no. 168 ('routs, riots, and unlawful assemblies', 1536).

[85] Marow's reading (Inner Temple, 1503), ed. Putnam, 339; Port 122; William Saunders's reading (Middle Temple, 1533) Pollard 273, no. 64; Fitz J.P. (1538), fo. 64v; Brooke Abr., *Riots*, pl. 5.

[86] Marow's reading (Inner Temple, 1503), ed. Putnam, 339; Port 122. The leadership point is more clearly made in Port's version.

[87] Saunders (1525) held that 'Rout is where a community assemble to commit a wrong...in all their names': Pollard 273, no. 64. Cf. Brooke Abr., *Riots*, pl. 5, probably abridging Marow.

[88] *R. v. Hunt* (1559) Gell's reports, II, fo. 69v; tr. 110 Selden Soc. 421.

[89] Or 'gathered and assembled in unlawful conventicles' (*in conventiculis illicitis aggregati et assimilati*).

[90] *Boke of a Justyce of Peas* (1505?), sig. Bii ('them that accompany them selfe in forcyble aray ayenst the kynges peas puttynge the kynges people in fere'); charge for a tourn (1538) BL MS. Add. 48047, fo. 68 (sim.). Arms could perhaps turn a lawful assembly into a riot: *Anon.* (1570) Chr. Yelverton's reports, BL MS. Hargrave 322, fo. 70v; tr. 110 Selden Soc. 451.

[91] Marow's reading (1503), Port 122. It was lawful to wear armour on sporting occasions: Hil. 3 Hen. VII, fo. 1, pl. 1, *per* Kebell sjt.

[92] Marow's reading (1503), ed. Putnam, 339; Port 122. William Saunders held that only 'two or more' were needed for a riot: reading (1533) Pollard 273, no. 64.

the minimum number to be three.[93] Similar conduct by one or two might constitute an affray.[94] The requisite unlawfulness had to involve a breach of the peace, so that merely assembling to play an unlawful game, such as closh or dice, was not an unlawful assembly.[95] Nor was it *ipso facto* an unlawful assembly if two or three people committed a private tort in concert.[96] It was lawful to assemble friends and servants to defend one's person or one's home,[97] and perhaps when going on a journey,[98] but not when doing something wrong or if numbers were excessive.[99] However, an assembly lawful in its inception might become unlawful if it turned violent or exceeded its lawful purpose.[100]

The riot act passed in 1549, following Kett's rebellion, made it high treason if twelve or more assembled to attempt to kill or imprison any of the king's Council, or to alter any laws, and continued together for an hour after being commanded to depart by a justice of the peace, mayor, or sheriff. If the purpose of an assembly of twelve or more was to destroy a park, pond, conduit, or dove-house, or to have a common way in enclosed ground, or to pull down houses, barns, or mills, or to burn any stack of corn, or to abate the rents of any lands or the prices of any victual, the offence of remaining an hour after proclamation was made felony without clergy.[101] This statute was replaced by another in 1553, which reduced the new offence to felony and restricted it to assemblies 'to change any laws made for religion'.[102] The measure expired in 1603 but was the model for other enactments making it felony to defy proclamations to depart—the procedure popularly known in later times as 'reading the riot act'.[103]

---

[93] Brooke Abr., *Riots*, pl. 5, emended Marow to this effect.

[94] Charge for a tourn (1538) BL MS. Add. 48047, fo. 68 (two). For an affray by one person see *R. v. Anon.* (1497) 1 Caryll 347–8.

[95] Marow's reading, ed. Putnam, 340–1. The indictment for riot in *R. v. Sprewce* (1499) KB 27/952, Rex m. 6d, laid that it was 'as well in disturbance of the peace and the common law as in disturbance and affray of the lord king's lieges living there' (tr.).

[96] Marow's reading, ed. Putnam, 341 (if a number of people tortiously take a piece of timber it is not riot unless the number is excessive).

[97] *Anon.* (1499) Trin. 14 Hen. VII, Fitz. Abr., *Trespas*, pl. 246 (pr. as Mich. 21 Hen. VII, fo. 39, pl. 50); Marow's reading, ed. Putnam, 339–40; Port 122; *Anon.* (1556) Chr. Yelverton's reports, fo. 241 (identifiable as *Dalaber* v. *Lyster*, below, n. 99).

[98] So says Marow, but in the case of 1499 it was said that if someone feared attack in the open his proper course was to seek surety of the peace rather than to raise a protective force.

[99] See e.g. *R. v. Penson* (1498) KB 27/948, Rex m. 11 (indictment for unlawful assembly in obstructing a parochial procession in Bristol); *Dalaber* v. *Lyster* (1557) Dyer 141b (Star Chamber; forcible re-entry).

[100] Marow's reading, ed. Putnam, 340. It was questioned in *Anon.* (1531) Spelman 207, whether it was riot if a man sent twelve servants to distrain for rent and they took too many beasts.

[101] 3 & 4 Edw. VI, c. 5; renewed by 7 Edw. VI, c. 11.

[102] 1 Mar. I, sess. 2, c. 12; renewed by 1 Eliz. I, c. 16; expired 1603.

[103] Cf. *Tudor Royal Proclamations*, i. 245, no. 168 (proclamation of 1536 threatening martial law against persons unlawfully assembled who refused to return to their houses).

WITCHCRAFT AND MAGIC

The practice of magic was a feature of everyday life both at the beginning and at the end of our period. Professional necromancers, soothsayers, and charmers could be consulted in criminal investigations, witches could be hired to get rid of enemies, and even a deceased queen could be accused in Parliament of having engaged in sorcery.[104] Until the 1530s, however, the misuse of magical power seems to have been almost exclusively a matter for the ecclesiastical courts,[105] which could in extreme cases treat black magic as heresy but were tolerant of white magic.[106] Exceptions were only made if the magic was used for felonious purposes.[107] Secular legal concern with magic grew more extensive after the break with Rome, in part because it came to be associated with disaffected popish priests. The concern was not merely that it could be a vehicle for fraud. Fortune-telling, as practised by beggars and gypsies, was a different kind of criminal offence.[108] The more serious concern was that magic really could work—after all, priests could turn wine into blood—and might be misused to undermine the government and its religious settlement. The first major problem was prophesying. Prophecies also had an ambiguous character. On the one hand, they provided a coded language for otherwise dangerous comments on the desired fate of king or government. On the other, and especially when revealed by priests and monks, they might be seen as real predictions nurtured by religious mysticism and possessed of a self-fulfilling validity. In 1535 someone was committed to the Tower for prophesying death and war, not merely (it seems) to keep him quiet but also that he might be detained until it emerged whether he was right.[109] It is therefore not wholly surprising that, with some judicial misgivings,[110] it came to be accepted that treason by imagining the king's death could be committed—or at least

---

[104] *RP*, vi. 240-2 (above, 58); *Bishop of St David's* v. *Mayor and Sheriffs of Bristol* (1500) C1/267/41 (above, 236); *Coke* v. *Balynger* (1505) 75 Selden Soc., pp. clii, 151-9; Wunderli, *London Church Courts and Society*, 127; *CSPD 1553-8*, p. 46, no. 98.

[105] 'Certen Considerations why the Spirituell Jurisdiction wold be abrogatt and repelled or at the leest reformed' (c.1534) BL Cotton MS. Cleopatra F.II, fo. 243v, says (sp. mod.) 'we know not that the king's court hath meddled with sorcery, prophesying (*divinatio*), augury, idolatry, or blasphemy.

[106] Wunderli, *London Church Courts and Society*, 126-7.

[107] Note the case of Robert Wythe, accused in 1530 of using *ars magica vocata* 'wychecraft' to kill a sick man. He was committed to gaol by a JP, brought before the Norwich sessions and Thetford assizes, and made to appear before the Council in the White Hall, though it seems he was not charged or tried: the story emerges in *Wythe* v. *Alens* (1541) KB 27/1121, m. 115 (action against clergyman for defamation). Multiplication (turning base metal into gold) was made felony by a statute of Hen. IV: see *R* v. *Eden* (1553) Dyer 88a. [108] Above, 98; below, 615.

[109] *Lisle Letters*, ed. Byrne, ii. 493, no. 396.

[110] It was the principal difficulty for the judges in Elizabeth Barton's case (1533): above, 585. But it had been recognized in 1477: above, 582 n. 6.

evidenced by—the use of prophecies.[111] In 1542 Parliament carried the matter further by creating the new capital offence of making prophecies based on coats of arms or the letters of a person's name. Here the emphasis seems to have been on fraud or sedition rather than effective black magic.[112] But the same Parliament also turned its attention to improper applications of working magic, and made it capital felony—that is, without benefit of clergy—to use witchcraft, enchantment, or sorcery, to discover treasure, to destroy a person or his property, to provoke anyone to unlawful love,[113] 'or for any other unlawful intent or purpose'.[114] It will be noted that the offence consisted not merely in pretending or purporting to use magic, but in actually using it for an unlawful purpose. However, the statute only remained in force for five years, being swept away in 1547 by the general repeal of recent criminal legislation, and it was not resurrected until 1563.[115] This did not prevent the arrest of alleged sorcerers for activities which were potentially seditious or treasonable,[116] or just deceitful.[117] Nevertheless, the history of witchcraft prosecutions under the secular law belongs principally to the period after 1558.

[111] J. K. Van Patten, 'Magic, Prophecy and the Law of Treason in Reformation England' (1983) 27 AJLH 1–32; S. L. Jansen, Political Protest and Prophecy under Henry VIII (1991). Notorious examples are R. v. Duke of Buckingham (1521) Pas. 13 Hen. VIII, fo. 11, pl. 1 (119 Selden Soc. 56); R. v. Rhys ap Griffith (1531) Spelman 47.

[112] 33 Hen. VIII, c. 14. Cf. 3 & 4 Edw. VI, c. 15 (reintroduced as lesser offence, with punishment of imprisonment and forfeiture).

[113] Parliament may here have been primarily concerned with unnatural sexual acts, as a result of Lord Hungerford's case (1540): cf. above, 563 n. 102.

[114] 33 Hen. VIII, c. 8. For a view on its possible origin see Bellamy, Criminal Law and Society in late Medieval and Tudor England, 143–4.

[115] 1 Edw. VI, c. 12; 5 Eliz. I, c. 16. For the resurrection of legal concerns shortly after 1558 see 109 Selden Soc., pp. lxix–lxxi.

[116] See CSPD 1547–53, p. 67, no. 131 (Robert Alen in prison for 'calking' figures and prophesying, 1548); CSPD 1553–8, p. 98, no. 189; APC 1554–6, p. 143 (John Dee and others arrested and examined for calculating nativities of king and queen, 1555). For similar cases in the early 1540s see above, 202 n. 93.

[117] e.g. APC 1554–6, p. 362 (soothsayer deceiving people).

Part VII

PERSONS

33

Status and Legal Personality

WITH the limited exception of the peerage,[1] status for legal purposes was not generally related to social rank or precedence. For instance, a trial jury did not have to be composed of a party's social peers or equals.[2] Conversely—again with the exception of peers—social rank was not determined by law. Peerages devolved in accordance with the law of inheritance, but other ranks were not hereditary; and it was said that, if a knight's son took to husbandry, his correct legal description was 'husbandman', while a husbandman's son who 'used the office of a gentleman, such as an officer or clerk in the king's court' could be described as a gentleman.[3] Edmund Dudley held that if a corody was granted to a lord or knight, his 'reasonable sustenance' was more than that of a yeoman, and yet if the grantee became poor his entitlement would diminish accordingly: it was therefore dependent on *de facto* standing rather than legal rank.[4] Social mobility of this kind was not a figment of the legal imagination.[5] Self-made men such as lawyers and merchants were prominent investors in land, and the careers of Cromwell, Audley, and Rich showed that a humble beginning in law could lead ultimately to the peerage; physicians, too, were becoming a respectable landed class.[6] Knighthoods were conferred according to means rather than class, and were sometimes conferred on professional men such as practising lawyers and doctors.[7] Moreover, even in the case of the peerage, there was no noble caste in England.

---

[1] For the legal consequences of peerage status see above, 84.

[2] *R. v. Thomas* (1554) Dyer 99b, §67; above, 354.

[3] *Anon.* (1520) 120 Selden Soc. 41, *per* More J. As to whether a knight's daughter could be described as a spinster, see *Allington (recte Ahyngton)* v. *Oldcastell* (1553) Dyer 88a; KB 27/1167, m. 88. Cf. the effect of marriage on a woman's status: below, 618–19.

[4] Dudley's reading (Gray's Inn, 1496) CUL MS. Hh.3.10, at fo. 63.

[5] For social rising through the legal profession see above, 449–50.

[6] For the incorporation of the College of Physicians see below, 622. For professional regulation see above, 163 n. 37, 164 n. 49.

[7] This was not necessarily a welcome privilege, since knighthoods were expensive. Serjeants at law claimed to be exempt: above, 422. It was unheard of for practising serjeants to be knighted before the 1530s. The first examples were Thomas Willoughby and John Baldwin, knighted as king's serjeants in 1534 and 1536: Spelman 39, 208.

A peer's son—though entitled to social rank—was in law a commoner[8] and did not enjoy the privileges of the peerage.[9]

According to King Henry VII, 'all manner of men, as well the poor as the rich' were 'all one in due ministration of justice'.[10] Magna Carta and the statutes of due process guaranteed that no one should be harmed in person or property save in accordance with the law of the land (*lex terrae*). The 'no free man' (*nullus liber homo*) of Magna Carta had been enlarged in the later statutes to include everyone; and by the 1530s lawyers were prepared to interpret the phrase *liber homo* itself as including a villein, on the ground that a villein was free with respect to everyone other than his lord.[11] In consequence, 'every subject of this realm . . . may sue to the king, and against any subject, be he bond or free, woman or infant, religious, out-lawed, excommunicated, or otherwise, without any exception'.[12] Liberty and access to justice were not, however, synonymous with equality or uniformity of treatment for all purposes, and the *lex terrae* still recognized various forms of limited legal inequality or disability,[13] two of which came to an end in the sixteenth century.

VILLEINAGE DE SANK

Although many manorial tenants still held in 'villeinage'—the term used by Littleton—that species of tenure was now almost universally known by the more respectable name of copyhold.[14] But, whatever its name, tenure in villeinage did not make the tenant a villein, even if the services were of a lowly kind.[15] Villeinage as a status, the condition of bondage, could only be acquired by legitimate descent in the male line from time immemorial, or (in theory) by confession in a court of record or captivity in war.[16] Villeins were no longer a large proportion of the population by 1500, but villeinage was still of practical importance,[17] and it was often discussed in readings and moots. It was widely believed that bondage had originated at the Norman conquest, with the sparing of lives by the conqueror.

---

[8] He could be elected to the House of Commons: *HCJ*, i. 27 (1550).

[9] As to trial by peers see above, 520.   [10] *Tudor Royal Proclamations*, i. 19, no. 17 (1489).

[11] Anon. reading, BL MS. Harley 4990, fo. 161.

[12] *Anderson v. Warde* (1554) Dyer 104a at 104b; KB 27/1172, m. 133. Cf. *Wimbish v. Tailbois* (1550) Plowd. 38v at 55v, *per* Mountagu CJ (tr. 'every person may equally have the benefit of the law').

[13] e.g. infancy, which is not discussed here because the principles do not seem to have changed mat-erially. More esoteric was the alleged disability of a 'pagan': see *Fyloll v. Assheleygh* (1520) Trin. 12 Hen. VIII, fo. 4, pl. 3 (119 Selden Soc. 15), *per* Broke J.   [14] See below, 644-50.

[15] For the following see 'Villeinage' in 94 Selden Soc. *187-92*; and, for a broader historical survey, Baker, 'Personal Liberty under the Common Law of England 1200–1600' (1995), *CLT*, 325-34.

[16] Richard Hesketh, following *Bracton*, held that a captive in a just war against a foreign prince was a villein both by the law of arms and 'by the common law called *jus gentium*, which is derived immediately from the law of nature': reading in Gray's Inn (*c*.1506/8) BL MS. Lansdowne 1145, fo. 71. But contem-porary prisoners of war were more akin to slaves: see 'Personal Liberty under the Common Law', 334.

[17] I. S. Leadam, 'The Last Days of Bondage in England' (1893) 9 *LQR* 348-65; F. G. Davenport, 'The Decay of Villeinage in East Anglia' (1900) 14 *TRHS* (2nd ser.) 125-41; A. Savine, 'Bondmen under the

Four centuries and more later it was an anachronism, rationally indefensible but too well established to question. St German's Student thought it had been

admitted so long in the laws of this realm, and of divers other laws also, and hath been affirmed by bishops, abbots, priors, and many other men both spiritual and temporal which have taken advantage by the said law... that I think it not good now to make a doubt nor to put it in argument whether it stand with conscience or not.[18]

Arguably, however, it was 'the greatest inconvenience that is now suffered by the law', because it could so easily be abused: if a lord wrongfully seized a man as his villein, took away his property, and detained him, the man had little prospect of initiating or financing a suit to assert his liberty.[19] The very idea of villeinage had become socially unacceptable with changes in labour conditions since the Black Death and improvements in the general standards of living, and in many parts of the country—especially in the north—it had actually disappeared. There was no obvious social difference between the villein and his free neighbour, and some alleged villeins had entered the professions.[20] Yet we learn from defamation actions that reputed villeins could still be subjected to the unkindest taunts,[21] and that the mere suspicion of villeinage could harm a man's marriage prospects.[22] The stigma of bondage was therefore painful. The condition was also potentially ruinous, since a lord was entitled to seize the villein's real and personal property, whenever he wished, and to imprison and beat (though not maim) him.[23] With notable exceptions—which were not tolerated without challenge in the courts[24]—lords in

Tudors' (1902) 17 TRHS (2nd ser.) 235–89; Kerridge, *Agrarian Problems in the Sixteenth Century*, 90–1; Dyer, *Lords and Peasants in a Changing Society*, 269–75; P. D. A. Harvey, *The Peasant Land Market in Medieval England* (1984), 334–5; D. MacCulloch, 'Bondmen under the Tudors' in *Law and Government under the Tudors*, ed. C. Cross et al. (1988), 91–109; Whittle, *The Development of Agrarian Capitalism*, 37–46.

18 St German, *Doctor and Student*, ed. Plucknett and Barton, 213–14 (sp. mod.).

19 J. Fitzherbert, *The Boke of Surveyeng* (c.1526), fo. 24v.

20 e.g. *Hunston v. Bishop of Ely* (1484) Mich. 2 Ric. III, fo. 13, pl. 35; KB 27/893, m. 91; *Gelget v. Wymbyll* (1514) CP 40/1008, m. 306d. Thomas Hunston of Gray's Inn was JP and MP; Edmund Gelgelt of the Inner Temple was an attorney and filazer of the Common Pleas.

21 e.g. *Wythe v. Norgate* (1526) CP 40/1050, m. 418d ('W. is a bond churl and an whoreson churl and all his nation'; recovers 40s.); *Bordyop v. Danby* (1528) KB 27/1067, m. 30d ('Thou art a churl and thy puddings in thy belly be not thine own'); *Pygryme v. Butland* (1537) CP 40/1092, m. 329 ('a bound churl's chicken born and that I will prove'); *Brande v. Vaughan* (1540) CP 40/1107, m. 454 ('Thou art a false, subtle, crafty, and villein churl and so is all the blood and kindred that thou camest of', spoken of a grocer); *Forde v. Lewes* (1554) CP 40/1159, m. 333 ('Thou and thy brother are stark villeins'); *Harvye v. Gybbon* (1558) KB 27/1184, m. 97 ('Thou art a bond churl and all the ancestors that thou camest of...'). All sp. mod.

22 *Bateley v. Bexwell* (1535) CP 40/1087, m. 485d (op. se).

23 Note, however, *Howard v. Caundyssh* (1505–13) CP 40/974, m. 403, where an imprisonment was justified because the plaintiff was a villein and refused to be 'justiced' by the lord. The case was continued for eight years, upon a demurrer, until the plaintiff was nonsuited.

24 e.g. *Allington v. Childhuse* (1481) Hil. 21 Edw. IV, fo. 81, pl. 31 (ship and tackle seized); *Revet v. Earl of Suffolk* (1499) KB 27/951, m. 66 (tenements and a large stock of cattle and furniture seized; £120 damages recovered); *Salle v. Paston* (1498) KB 27/949, m. 95 (gold, silver, and jewels seized). In 1540

fact rarely availed themselves of these outmoded rights. The indignity may therefore have been in most cases more burdensome than the legal disability. That, however, also benefited lords. If they scrupled to confiscate their villeins' substance, they could yet with a semblance of decency bargain for a share of it as the price of manumission. A lord prepared to accept a capital loss could thus turn charity to profit by selling liberty.

As St German indicated, the Church—and particularly the religious houses[25]—had generally failed to take a stand against the institution of villeinage. But the common law was not similarly indifferent. It was an old maxim that the law favoured liberty,[26] and the general view of lawyers was probably that expressed in a Gray's Inn moot in the 1520s: 'villeinage is an odious thing in law and not to be favoured, for it is merely contrary to liberty, and liberty is one of the things which the law most favours… and so if by any lawful means one can be released from the bondage of villeinage, [the opportunity] shall be grasped'.[27] Accordingly, more attention was devoted in readings to methods of gaining liberty than to ways of exploiting the rights of lords.[28]

Even during the state of bondage, the villein's person was protected against the lord by the criminal law:

the villein is the king's subject as well as his lord, and if the lord slays him it is murder in him and he shall be hanged; and if the lord maims the villein, he shall not have an appeal of mayhem—for he would only recover damages, and the lord could take them back—but the lord shall be indicted for it at the king's suit, because his maiming is a weakening of the realm.[29]

Moreover, the villein was fully competent to own property real and personal, and to sue and be sued at common law. A grant of property to a villein did not vest the property in the lord in the way that a grant to a wife enured to the benefit of the husband;[30] for the lord only acquired title by seizure, and before seizure the villein's title was good and transmissible. There was no need, however, for the lord to lay his hands on every item of property. He could seize one item in the name of all, though such a seizure did not extend to after-acquired property.[31]

the earl of Bath was alleged to have seized goods worth £400 from two supposed bondmen: 12 Selden Soc. 49.

[25] Their qualms about the freeing of bondmen arose in part from the principle of canon law which forbade them to alienate permanently or waste real property.

[26] 'Personal Liberty under the Common Law', *CLT*, at 326.   [27] HLS MS. 47, ff. 59–60v, 114 (tr.).

[28] The fullest expositions were in glosses on the phrase *liber homo* in Magna Carta (e.g. Richard Snede's reading, Inner Temple, 1511) or the *Carta de Foresta* (e.g. Richard Hesketh's reading, Gray's Inn, c.1506/8).

[29] John Petit's reading (Gray's Inn, 1518) BL MS. Harley 5103, fo.19 (tr.), *per* Broke sjt.

[30] There was no analogy with husband and wife, because 'the lord and villein are two distinct persons': BL MS. Harley 5103, fo.19 (tr.), *per* Broke sjt, refuting the reader's assertion that a villein could not disseise his lord.

[31] St German, *Doctor and Student*, ed. Plucknett and Barton, 272; but cf. Litt. s. 177.

Enfranchisement could occur by reason of estoppel, or of privilege, or by means of a written instrument of manumission, which operated as a conveyance or release of liberty from the lord, or by a collusive action. If the lord did something inconsistent with villein status, such as making a bond in favour of the villein, or making a feoffment or lease to him, or bringing an action against him, or defend-ing an action brought by him without pleading villeinage, the villein was freed by reason of the estoppel.[32] But transactions which were consistent with villeinage did not have this effect: as where the lord gave the villein clothes or pocket-money,[33] or lent him a horse, or (perhaps) where he employed him as a bailiff or steward.[34] There were a number of doubtful cases, such as the moot-case of the feoffment made to lord and villein jointly,[35] or the villein who purchased a manor to which his own lord was regardant;[36] and another disputable area was the effect of a grant or gift by the villein to the lord.[37]

Villeins were undoubtedly useful to law schools. But this learning was largely academic, and much of it derived ultimately from *Bracton*. Equally academic was the learning on privilege by reason of place, profession, or dignity.[38] A personal immunity of a temporary or local nature attached to a villein in sanctuary or prison, or who escaped to ancient demesne, or who dwelt in certain cities (including London) for a year and a day.[39] It was an immunity rather than a privilege, because it did not protect the villein's property from seizure, or remove his legal disability; he remained a villein.[40] A villein who entered religion was held to acquire a personal immunity not limited to the cloister, because on profession he became the man of God and obedient only to his religious superior.[41] But the more practical question whether the same immunity followed ordination as a secular priest seems—despite

[32] See 94 Selden Soc. *188–9*. Such matters of estoppel had to be specially pleaded: *Anon.* (1533/4) Brooke Abr., *General Issue*, pl. 82.

[33] Hil. 11 Hen. VII, fo. 13, pl. 6 (misdated), *per* Huse CJ; and cf. *Moots*, 145.

[34] HLS MS. 47, fo. 60 (Gray's Inn). Edmund Dudley said employment worked an enfranchisement if wages were paid: reading in Gray's Inn (1496), fo. 70v.

[35] *Moots*, 33, no. 94 (case called 'Cat in the pan'); HLS MS. 47, fo. 260 (Gray's Inn); Spelman 225, lines 2–3 (Gray's Inn); HLS MS. 125, fo. 19 (Middle Temple).

[36] Moot in Middle Temple (1549) HLS MS. 12, no. 123. Hesketh held that if a lord confessed himself villein to his own villein, the villein would be free for ever: Hesketh's reading, fo. 72. See also *Moots*, 136, no. 22.   [37] *Moots*, 144, no. 31 (Inner Temple).

[38] See 'Personal Liberty under the Common Law', *CLT*, 329–30. No reported or recorded cases have been found which depended on this learning.

[39] e.g. *Anon.* (1521) Moo. 2, pl. 4 (custom of London). Hesketh said it was necessary to be sworn as a freeman: Hesketh's reading, fo. 71v.

[40] *Anon.* (c.1530) Caryll (Jun.) 386, no. 37 (referring to ancient demesne, ordination, and knight-hood); *Courteney and Tomyewe* (*executors of Skewes*) v. *Chamond* (1545) Dyer 59b at 60b (ancient demesne).

[41] That is the explanation in BL MS. Add. 35939, fo. 367v (Gray's Inn, c.1525/30). See also Litt. s. 202; reading on Magna Carta, HLS MS. 13, fo. 7; HLS MS. 47, fo. 59v; Caryll (Jun.) 386, no. 37; St German, *Doctor and Student*, ed. Plucknett and Barton, 273.

the statement in *Bracton*—to have been unsettled,[42] Edmund Dudley holding that an ordained villein could still be compelled to perform 'such suitable and condign services as belonged to a priest'.[43] A female villein who married a free man took on her husband's condition, because her subjection to her husband took priority over that to her lord,[44] though some thought that the lord could bring an action on the case against the husband for marrying his villein and thereby causing him loss.[45]

Explicit manumission, by charter, seems to have been uncommon. One reason for this is that problems arose if the manumission was made by a lord with an estate of limited duration. It was said that a manumission for one hour was a manumission for ever, in favour of liberty.[46] One could not grant freedom for a limited estate. However, if a tenant of the lordship in tail, for life, or for years, manumitted a villein, the state of bondage would return when the manumitter died or the lease ended;[47] and if the villein had had issue in the meantime, it was arguable that the issue, though free at birth, would revert to bondage when the reversion fell in.[48] The worst case—perhaps only imaginable in a law school—was that of the person who became a villein every other day of his life.[49] It may have been for such reasons that less direct methods of freeing bondmen came into general use.

Suits for liberty, and the end of villeinage

The proper remedy for a man wrongly seized as a villein was the action *de homine replegiando*, which was analogous to replevin in that the plaintiff's goods and also his liberty were returned to him on his giving surety to pursue the claim.[50] The action was only available if the villein was under physical restraint at the time, and this restriction may explain why it had more or less gone out of use by

[42] Hesketh's reading (c.1506/8), fo. 71v (priest enfranchised by his orders); cf. Gray's Inn moot (c.1525/30) BL MS. Add. 35939, fo. 367v (tr. 'a priest may be a villein well enough'). Cf. BL MS. Harley 5103, fo. 65 (inn of chancery, 1530s), where it is argued that a villein who becomes the king's chaplain is only privileged while in the king's presence; but the reader says he is enfranchised.

[43] Moot in Gray's Inn (before 1509) BL MS. Harley 5103, ff. 34v–35v; HLS 125, no. 167 (tr.); also masquerading as an Inner Temple moot in *Moots*, 158, no. 42.

[44] ibid., *per* Fairfax. Hesketh said it was by reason of the sacrament of espousals: Hesketh's reading, fo. 71v. But the converse did not hold: i.e. a free woman did not become unfree by marrying a villein.

[45] *Sherley v. Stammer* (1498) KB 27/948, m. 11; *Duke of Buckingham v. Sherman* (1508) CP 40/985, m. 57d; cf. *Abbot of Peterborough v. Roper* (1510) KB 27/996, m. 54 (trespass *vi et armis*, with *per quod servicium amisit* clause). St German's Student held that the lord could sue a religious superior in trespass for receiving his villein as a monk: *Doctor and Student*, ed. Plucknett and Barton, 273.

[46] *Courteney and Tomyewe (executors of Skewes) v. Chamond* (1545) Dyer 60b, §23.

[47] BL MS. Harley 5103, ff. 34v–35, *per* Erneley; Richard Broke's reading (Gray's Inn, c.1504/9) Spelman 224. Likewise as to manumission by the tenant in tail: *Anon.* (1473) Mich. 13 Edw. IV, fo. 2, pl. 4.

[48] Richard Broke's reading (Gray's Inn, c.1504/9) Spelman 224.

[49] HLS MS. 47, fo. 59 (Gray's Inn). This was said to occur if there was such a partition of the seignory between two coparceners, one of whom manumitted a villein. But it would be more usual for one of the coparceners to take the villein, as in Mich. 13 Edw. IV, fo. 2, pl. 4.   [50] FNB 67–8.

1500.[51] The action *de libertate probanda* was ineffective and almost completely defunct.[52] By the end of the fifteenth century, therefore, trespass had become the usual option.

For a past seizure of person or goods it had been possible for two hundred years to bring a general action of trespass *vi et armis*, in which the personal status could be tried by jury on a plea of villeinage;[53] and juries were invariably inclined towards liberty.[54] It had also become possible to bring a special action of trespass[55] for lying in wait to seize the plaintiff as a villein, in which case it was necessary to show threatenings but not an actual seizure and imprisonment.[56] This likewise regularly achieved a verdict that the plaintiff was free,[57] sometimes with substantial damages.[58] The form of action might be perceived as resting on a kind of aggravated defamation,[59] but its true function was to supplant *de homine replegiando*.

[51] Some late examples are *Newman* v. *Berney* (1494) KB 27/932, m. 66; *Revet* v. *Earl of Suffolk* (1499) KB 27/951, m. 66; *Palmer* v. *Dengayn* (1520) KB 27/1037, m. 65; *Pope* v. *Fortescue* (1533) CP 40/1079, m. 623 (20s. damages and £5 costs).

[52] FNB 77C said it was ineffective as a result of the statute 25 Edw. III, stat. 5, c. 18. There is an example in 1494: *Salle* v. *Paston* (1494–5) KB 27/933, m. 40d; KB 27/934, m. 26; KB 27/936, m. 93; Rast. Ent. 373v (401v); but the plaintiff gave up and later brought trespass. Cf. Rastell, *Exposiciones Terminorum* (1527 edn), fo. 74v.

[53] Pleading difficulties were encountered in *Howard* v. *Caundyssh* (1505–13) CP 40/974, m. 403 (pleads villeinage and Not guilty as to trespass; demurrer; plea eventually held bad); *Broke* v. *Garneys* (1510–18) CP 40/993, m. 517 (pleads villeinage and justifies seizure of animals; advisement after verdict).

[54] e.g. in *Mascall* v. *Cottesmore* (1491) 1 Caryll 59; CP 40/918, m. 117 (trespass to oxen, cows, and chickens); *Harberd* v. *Assheley* (1491) ibid., m. 337 (20s. damages); *Thomson* v. *Lee* (1498) KB 27/949, m. 33 (below); *Blake* v. *Venters* (1500) ibid., m. 24d (£26 damages); *Vyncent* v. *Drury* (1501) CP 40/955, m. 301 (19 alleged villeins found free); *Symmys* v. *Duke of Buckingham* (1501) CP 40/958, m. 436 (£14 damages); *Newcum* v. *Gybthorp* (1502) KB 27/965, m. 79; *Broke* v. *Garneys* (1510–18) CP 40/993, m. 517 (last note); *Seman* v. *Belyngford* (1535) CP 40/1087, m. 286d (8 marks damages; writ of error noted).

[55] It was *vi et armis*, but in *Hunston* v. *Bishop of Ely* (1484), next note, it is called an action on the case ('un especial brefe sur son case').

[56] See *Haukyns* v. *Broune* (1476–83) Trin. 17 Edw. IV, fo. 3, pl. 2 (tr. in B. & M. 629); KB 27/862, m. 30; *Hunston* v. *Bishop of Ely* (1484) Mich. 2 Ric. III, fo. 13, pl. 35; KB 27/893, m. 91 (above, 95 n. 63; after efforts to stop the action by using protections and a *non procedendo rege inconsulto*, Hunston was nonsuited). For earlier examples see 94 Selden Soc. *190* n. 4.

[57] e.g. *Baude* v. *Kendale* (1489) KB 27/913, m. 32 (£10 damages); *Trypp* v. *Artur* (1495) KB 27/935, m. 30 (20s. damages); *Wyggeston* v. *Knolles* (1500) KB 27/957, mm. 21, 21d (two actions: £50 damages and £40 costs but remits £20); *Steyde* v. *Kyme* (1503) CP 40/962, m. 514 (£65 damages and £20 costs but remits £10); *Palmer* v. *Morton* (1510) KB 27/997, m. 69 (£10 damages); *Hast* v. *Mylys* (1519) KB 27/1031, m. 28d (£6. 13s. 4d. damages); *Newman* v. *Harward* (1519) ibid., m. 36d (£15 damages); *Hawkyns* v. *Pagnam* (1525) KB 27/1054, m. 67 (pleads that he only discussed the matter with the plaintiff; found guilty with £6 damages); *Gybbe* v. *Poynes* (1537) CP 40/1095, m. 616 (issue only).

[58] e.g. *Fox* v. *Wykam* (1495) CP 40/932, m. 338 (£120); *Sheperd* v. *Worthe* (1501) KB 27/960, mm. 52, 52d (£100 damages in each of two actions, but one award remitted); *Smyth* v. *Prior of St Neots* (1509) CP 40/989, m. 419 (£340).

[59] See below, 782. In *Hale* v. *Cade* (1532) CP 40/1073, m. 509, the damages in such an action were said to be for defamation ('occasione scandali diffamationis').

The reality was recognized in the remarkable decision of 1498 that, since the nature of the action was to try liberty, and the plaintiff would be at an unfair disadvantage if he were not at liberty while pursuing the action, the plaintiff could replevy his goods and person just as he could in *de homine replegiando*.[60] From about 1511 it was possible to bring actions on the case for slandering someone as a villein, and since it was no longer necessary to allege force this extended the remedy to cases where the plaintiff was alleged to be someone else's villein,[61] or—more usually—just that he was a bondman or churl, or a 'bond churl'. Some of these actions were tried on the general issue, Not guilty, and the object was merely to obtain damages. But in others the defendant justified, so that the issue of villeinage went to the jury.[62]

Damages in the defamation actions were usually modest, but verdicts on the issue of liberty had more than monetary value. It is true that both the general and special forms of trespass were personal actions for a wrong done or threatened to the plaintiff or his property, not actions *in rem* to vindicate his free status. Yet in 1500 it was apparently held that a verdict on the issue of villeinage, even if the lord was not a party to it, would settle the status for ever;[63] and that would have made it theoretically possible to bring a collusive action to bar the lord. The awarding of damages suggests that most actions were genuine and contested; but it is known that actions were sometimes arranged with the lord's consent to resolve a dispute as to status,[64] or to effect a

---

[60] *Thomson* v. *Lee* (1497–8) 1 Caryll 369; Port 6–7; Free Lib. Philadelphia MS. LC 14.35, fo. 181v; KB 27/949, m. 33 (pr. 102 Selden Soc. 7); followed in *Newcum* v. *Gybthorp* (1501) KB 27/961, m. 35d; *Anon.* (1501) Rast. Ent. 608v (680v) (Common Pleas case); *Anon.* (1517) Yorke 219, no. 349.

[61] e.g. *Gelget* v. *Wymbyll* (1514) CP 40/1008, m. 306d; *Annot* v. *Gryffyn* (1520) CP 40/1030, m. 647; *Wolley* v. *Leche* (1529–32) Spelman 111; KB 27/1973, m. 63; *Pygryme* v. *Butland* (1537) CP 40/1092, m. 329 (sp. mod. 'bound churl to the abbot of Waltham'); *Godfrey* v. *Ryall* (1538) KB 27/1107, m. 7d (sp. mod. 'John Godfrey is Master Everard's bond man, which I will prove, for his father was carried to Mr Everard's house at his horse-tail').

[62] e.g. *Boller* v. *Serjaunt* (1520) CP 40/1028, m. 623; *Annot* v. *Gryffyn* (1520) CP 40/1030, m. 647; *Reymond* v. *Lord Fitzwater* (1521) Spelman 2; KB 27/1040, m. 40 (pr. 94 Selden Soc. 239); *Wolley* v. *Leche* (1529–32) Spelman 111; KB 27/1973, m. 63; *Nychol* v. *Cake* (1536) CP 40/1090, m. 405d; *Hurst* v. *Godman* (1540) CP 40/1105, m. 444. The cases cited in 94 Selden Soc. *191* n. 3, are mostly *vi et armis* actions. In *Nychol* v. *Cake* (1536) CP 40/1090, m. 405d, the plaintiff was the king's villein and the manor to which he belonged was in dispute.

[63] *Salle* v. *Paston* (1498–1500) Mich. 14 Hen. VII, fo. 5, pl. 12; KB 27/949, m. 95 (plea of villeinage; plaintiff alleges verdict in former action; defendant rejoins that other party in that action was not seised; judgment for defendant, on demurrer). See also Mich. 13 Edw. IV, fo. 2, pl. 4; fo. 4, pl. 11.

[64] *Lord Fitzwater* v. *Swalder* (1524) CP 40/1042, m. 433 (condition of bond that John Raymond should cause himself to be tried free after the course of the common law, or yield himself to Lord Fitzwater as his bondman, in such manner as the lord's counsel should devise; pleads that he brought false imprisonment in 1521, and villeinage was pleaded, but the parties went to arbitration and the action was stayed pending the award, which had not been rendered). This can hardly refer to *John Reymond* v. *Lord Fitzwater* (1521) KB 27/1040, m. 40 (pr. 94 Selden Soc. 239) Spelman 2 (damages recovered for slander). Cf. *William Raymond* v. *Lord Fitzwater* (1523) CP 40/1038, m. 528 (false imprisonment in 1521; recovers damages); verdict challenged by attaint in *Lord Fitzwater* v. *Raymond* (1525) CP 40/1044, m. 270.

manumission.[65] Fitzherbert acknowledged such possibilities when he wrote that, although the action was personal, the lord's heir could bring attaint to prevent an estoppel arising from the verdict.[66]

An even more effective method of establishing freedom was to obtain a certificate of bastardy, since a bastard could not inherit unfree status. This was a common form of proceeding by the later fifteenth century, and by the second quarter of the sixteenth century it had become more frequent than recourse to the jury in a trespass action.[67] Its advantage was that the bishop's certificate estopped everyone, without any risk of reversal by attaint, since it was presumed to be a final determination of the fact.[68] Such a certificate could be obtained in any law suit in which bastardy came in issue. The plea of bastardy could be a direct response to a plea of villeinage, as where trespass was brought against the lord, who pleaded that the plaintiff was his villein, and the plaintiff replied that he was a bastard.[69] The action was usually *quare clausum fregit*, but the action for lying in wait to seize the plaintiff as a villein was sometimes used for this purpose.[70] Alternatively, bastardy could be pleaded by the lord in response to a hereditary property claim by an alleged villein. Examples of two kinds of device are to be found in the rolls for Michaelmas 1488. One was an action of trespass by the lord in which the defendant pleaded descent from an ancestor who was seised, and the lord replied that he was a bastard;[71] the other was a writ of entry in the *quibus* against the lord, in which the defendant pleaded bastardy.[72] The latter was to become the commonest of all the procedures in the sixteenth century,[73] though it was necessarily confined to the Common Pleas.[74] To perfect the process, in all these cases, three proclamations had to be made in Chancery before the writ was sent to the bishop, in accordance with a statutory provision of 1430 designed to prevent collusion.[75]

[65] This seems to be the import of *Nicholls* v. *Heydon* (1516) CP 40/1016, m. 418, where the defendant confessed the plaintiff's liberty, and an exemplification of the record was made for the plaintiff.

[66] FNB 108B. Cf. Mich. 13 Edw. IV, fo. 2, pl. 4, at fo. 3, *per* Choke J.

[67] There is a valuable discussion in MacCulloch, 'Bondmen under the Tudors', 101–6.

[68] *Waller* v. *Debenham* (1493) 1 Caryll 125 at 127, *per* Kebell sjt; Richard Broke's reading (Gray's Inn, c.1504/9) Spelman 225; St German, *Doctor and Student*, ed. Plucknett and Barton, 187–8.

[69] 94 Selden Soc. *191* n. 5; *Hast* v. *Lord Bergavenny* (1524) CP 40/1044, m. 625 (three plaintiffs recover 40s.). This was common even in the 1550s: e.g. *Dawes and others* (18 *plaintiffs*) v. *Shelton* (1557) CP 40/1170, m. 603; *Heyluk and others* (13 *plaintiffs*) v. *Shelton*, ibid., m. 716 (but no certificate here).

[70] e.g. *Cullyour* v. *Lord Fitzwater* (1508) CP 40/983, m. 330; C263/1/2, no. 58

[71] *Tounesend* v. *Spynk* (1488) CP 40/906, m. 148. The plaintiff was Townshend J.

[72] *Galt* v. *Jenney* (1488) CP 40/906, m. 314.

[73] Early examples are Jenour's entries, Lib. Congress (MSS Div.) MS. Phillipps 26752, fo. 54; BL MS. Add. 37488, ff. 284v–285; *Intrationum Liber* (1546), fo. 35; *Smyth* v. *Seymour* (1488) CP 40/906, m. 336; *Jowell* v. *Spenser* (1491) *CPR 1485–94*, p. 3.

[74] Writs of entry could not be brought in the King's Bench. However, even in trespass cases the certification procedure does not seem to have been used in the King's Bench.

[75] 9 Hen. VI, c. 11. Some files of writs for proclamations (from the CJCP to the LC, endorsed with the dates of the proclamations) survive: C263/1/1–3. For the form of a writ sent to Frowyk CJ, certifying such a proclamation, see Bodl. Lib. MS. Rawlinson C.339, fo. 43v.

Since there is no mention of villeinage in the commonest of these cases—entry in the *quibus* with a plea of bastardy—the true purpose of the actions is a matter of inference. But, as in the overt villeinage cases, they are all actions for very small pieces of land, usually an acre or a rood, brought by plaintiffs or groups of plaintiffs—often bearing rustic surnames—against defendants who are usually peers, knights, or esquires.[76] In nearly every case, the bastardy is duly certified. Sometimes an action is brought by multiple members of the same family, who are all found to be bastards. Sometimes there is a group of actions by different villagers against the same lord, and again they are all bastardized. Such records smell of collusion, and evidence has been found of a villein paying his lord £20 to cooperate in such proceedings.[77] Ecclesiastical judges do not seem to have investigated illegitimacy too closely if it was uncontested; and in any case, since the proceedings were fictitious, the villein might as well allege his birth in a diocese known to be helpfully credulous, such as Norwich.[78] This, then, was the villein's equivalent of the common recovery: a collusive fictitious lawsuit, recorded on the rolls of the Common Pleas, with proclamations and episcopal certificate, all of which together barred the lord and his heirs and thereby conveyed an absolute title to liberty without mentioning it. The analogy with recoveries may explain the doubt which Dyer reported in 1557. A tenant for life of a manor had agreed to plead bastardy in a writ of entry in the *quibus*, in order to effect a manumission, and the court wondered whether the bishop's certificate would bar the remainderman or reversioner.[79] No answer is given, but the earlier authorities do not qualify the power of a certificate with proclamations to estop everyone, and almost certainly one of the attractions of the procedure had been that it would bar reversioners.[80]

[76] e.g. from a four-year sample: *Whele v. Stowe* (1523) CP 40/1040, m. 340; CP 40/1041, m. 690 (acre in Horsham, Norfolk); *Kyng v. Earl of Oxford*, ibid., m. 356 (rood in Knapton, Norfolk); *Hyde v. Fenys*, ibid., m. 608 (two acres in Burnham, Somerset); *Randolfe v. Reygate* (1523) CP 40/1041, m. 330 (acre in Reading, Berks.); *Tuk v. Gonnour* (1523) CP 40/1043, m. 124 (rood in Salthouse, Norfolk); *Rust v. Skypwyth* (1523) ibid., m. 327 (acre in Ingoldmells, Lincs.); *Lulham v. Lord La Warr* (1524) CP 40/1045, m. 160 (seven acres in Ripe, Sussex); *Bowde v. St Leger* (1525) CP 40/1048A, m. 104 (acre in Hankford, Devon); *Lulham v. Lord La Warr* (1525) ibid., mm. 142, 157 (ten acres in Ripe); *Cobbe v. Tyrrell* (1525) ibid., mm. 338, 338d, 527 (acres in Gislingham, Norfolk); *Tolwyn v. Duke of Norfolk* (1526) CP 40/1049, m. 340 (rood in Suffield, Norfolk); *Howard v. Duke of Norfolk* (1526) CP 40/1050, m. 147, 147d (acres in Little Framingham, Norfolk); *Wyrgar v. Lord Abergavenny*, ibid., mm. 160, 160d (acres in Rottingdean, Sussex); *Wheteholme v. Copuldyche*, ibid., m. 326 (rood in Freeston, Lincs.); *Selme v. Lord Burgavenny* (1526) CP 40/1051, mm. 142, 142d (acres in Rodmell, Sussex); *Happe v. Lord Burgavenny*, ibid., m. 143 (sim.); *Brakpole v. Lord Burgavenny*, ibid., mm. 148, 148d (acres in 'Pecham'); *Ade v. Lord Burgavenny*. ibid., mm. 149, 149d (acres in Rodmell).

[77] *Whele v. Stowe* (1523), last note, mentioned in the duke of Suffolk's accounts for 1523–4: MacCulloch, 'Bondmen under the Tudors', 104. See also *Symonds v. Nicolls* (1557), below.

[78] MacCulloch, 'Bondmen under the Tudors', 103–4. A surviving writ to the bishop of Norwich, and his certificate, in *Nerd v. Berkeley* (1503), are in BL Add. Ch. 54536–54537.

[79] *Symonds v. Nicolls* (1557) Dyer's reports, 109 Selden Soc. 19.

[80] MacCulloch, 'Bondmen under the Tudors', 105–6.

The procedure was still in regular use in the 1550s, chiefly for manumissions by peers,[81] and continued until the 1570s.[82]

Formal abolition of villeinage could only have been achieved by act of Parliament, but that step was never taken in the sixteenth century—or at any time since. Although Henry VII abolished it in parts of Wales by the use of his prerogative,[83] Parliament in 1504 legislated in the contrary direction, to protect lords from feoffments to the use of their villeins by giving them powers of seizure.[84] In 1536 there was a chance that the institution would be swept away when, in the wake of legislation about the poor and enclosures,[85] a bill was presented for a general manumission; but it was rejected on its third reading in the Lords.[86] The bill's rejection is indicative both of the potential economic value of villeins, and of the more conservative social attitudes prevalent among the peerage. Manumission, to a conservative view, was tantamount to wasting the inheritance.[87] It was nevertheless, as we have seen, profitable and—unlike other forms of waste—it could be indulged in with impunity by a tenant for life or in tail. Since establishing a claim to villeins was becoming in reality impossible,[88] and there was also a risk of completely losing the capital asset through legislation, lords proceeded to manumit all their villeins who owned enough to pay for the privilege. Thus did villeinage, for all practical purposes, come to an end in England.

RELIGIOUS PERSONS

Another legal status, or disability, which disappeared during the Tudor period was that of the professed religious—monks, friars, and nuns.[89] The common law

---

[81] Of 28 successful actions noted in the 1550s, all but 2 were against peers: Lord Burgavenny (13), duke of Norfolk (7), duke of Suffolk (3), earl of Arundel (1), earl of Rutland (1), and Lord Morley (1). Lord Burgavenny had freed 14 villeins, using the same means, in the mid-1520s: CP 40/1044, m. 625; CP 40/1050, mm. 160, 160d; CP 40/1051, mm. 142–143, 148–149d; CP 40/1057, mm. 136, 325. The duke of Norfolk had freed 6: CP 40/1049, m. 340; CP 40/1050, m. 147, 147d; CP 40/1053, mm. 127, 129, 446.

[82] MacCulloch, 'Bondmen under the Tudors', 107. There is an entry temp. Dyer CJ in Bodl. MS. Rawl. A.413, fo. 36v.

[83] Smith, 'Crown and Community: the principality of North Wales in the reign of Henry Tudor', at ɪɪɪ ɪꞈɐ.

[84] 19 Hen. VII, c. 15; Broke's reading on Magna Carta (Gray's Inn, c.1504/9), Spelman 224. It was arguable that the measure extended, by the equity, to chattels: St German, *Doctor and Student*, ed. Plucknett and Barton, 272.   [85] Above, 98–9.

[86] *HLJ*, i. 94a, 99a.

[87] See *LP*, xiii. 1263 (Earl of Arundel to Cromwell, 1536); MacCulloch, 'Bondmen under the Tudors', 106. In *Anon.* (1488) 1 Caryll 10, manumission is said to be a diminution of the manor.

[88] Not only because of the leanings of juries (above), but after 1540 through the working of the Limitation Act (32 Hen. VIII, c. 2): see *Butler v. Crouch* (1567) Dyer 266b.

[89] No cases have been found concerning nuns in this period. Edward Hall distinguished the nun from the anchoress, the sister in a hospital, and the avowess who 'takes the mantle and ring': reading

followed the canon law as to the effect of profession. Upon taking the habit and professing obedience,[90] the monk left the secular world, lost his surname,[91] gave up his worldly property, and became dead in law (*civiliter mortuus*). If he held land in fee, it descended to his heir as upon natural death,[92] while his personal property was distributed by his executors or administrators. In consequence he could not be sued in a real action or in an action for damages, though his executors would be liable on a bond made before profession.[93] Religious disability could not be avoided by means of uses, because a feoffment to the use of a monk—as of any other dead person—was void.[94] On the other hand, civil death was not absolute.[95] Although the monk could not enter into a secular contract, he could make a contract as agent for his religious superior.[96] According to Edmund Dudley, a monk could even contract a valid marriage, because profession was not a sacrament.[97] Then again, profession did not disable a monk from doing wrong. Although he could not be sued for damages for a tort, his superior could be sued vicariously, and he himself would undergo any punishment which the law imposed on a tortfeasor.[98] And the superior could sue for a tort committed against his monk.[99] A monk was also liable to prosecution and capital punishment for murder and felony, and—unless he was an ordained priest, which most were not—he could not claim benefit of clergy by virtue of his religious status.[100] Security of the peace could be demanded against a monk, though recognizances would be taken only from sureties and not from the monk himself.[101] When acting in other capacities,

in Gray's Inn (1541) BL MS. Hargrave 92, fo. 57. (For the mantle and ring, symbolizing a vow of chastity, see also Spelman 224.)

[90] This was the moment when the change occurred, not when entering a religious house: Hall's reading (Gray's Inn, 1541), fo. 57. The minimum age was 12: ibid.

[91] *Chamber* v. *Salley* (1491) 1 Caryll 65 at 66. The monk's correct description for legal purposes was as co-monk (*comonachus*) of his abbot: ibid.; *Abbot of Westminster's Case* (1490) Mich. 6 Hen. VII, fo. 7, pl. 2; *Lewys* v. *Cam* (1531) Spelman 11, 124.

[92] According to a reader on Magna Carta in the 1530s (BL MS. Harley 4990, fo. 165), the monk's heir paid relief, but his wife was not entitled to dower and the descent did not toll an entry.

[93] See Mich. 4 Edw. IV, fo. 24, pl. 2, at fo. 25.

[94] There was a resulting use in the feoffor: *Townsend's Case* (1555) Plowd. 111 at 114.

[95] Some further distinctions between civil and natural death are explored in a reading from the 1530s: BL MS. Harley 4990, fo. 165.

[96] *Anon.* (1490) 1 Caryll 25, pl. 32; which is identifiable as *Spark* v. *Abbot of Ramsey* (1489) CP 40/907, m. 101d. Note also *Moots*, 293 (sale in market overt by a monk).

[97] Reading in Gray's Inn (1496) BL MS. Harley 5103, fo. 55v; Bodl. Lib. MS. Rawlinson C.705, fo. 81 (speaking of monks who were not priests). An earlier marriage, however, would avoid the profession: below, 609.

[98] Mich. 4 Edw. IV, fo. 24, pl. 2 (action lies against superior and monk for tort before profession); *Moots*, 140–1 (action for abducting a nun, which carried statutory imprisonment).

[99] *Anon.* (1505) 2 Caryll 376, pl. 342, *per* Frowyk CJ; *Prior of Ely* v. *Thorpe* (1537) CP 40/1092, m. 348 (action for slandering monk).

[100] R. v. *Boswell* (1513) Port 37; KB 27/1008, Rex m. 12 (Carmelite friar with orders of benet and acolyte).   [101] 36 Hen. VI, fo. 23, pl. 17.

such as an executor, a monk could enter into transactions and bring actions as if he were living. The principal case was that of the abbot or prior, who as head of a corporation could sue and be sued despite his profession.[102]

The complexities of profession made it a common topic of discussion at readings and moots, and it was not wholly academic learning. There were almost 10,000 religious in England. Most of them stayed out of the central courts, but pleas of profession are encountered from time to time in the plea rolls. The form was to set out the place of profession and under whose obedience the monk was.[103] Profession was usually triable by certificate of the bishop of the place where it was alleged to have occurred,[104] though this was not the case with the order of St John of Jerusalem since it was outside episcopal jurisdiction.[105]

Profession was reversible and dispensable. It could be reversed either for some disqualification which affected its validity (which made it void *ab initio*) or by degradation. The process of reversal was called 'deraignment',[106] and the principal cause mentioned in the common-law sources was a precontract of marriage.[107] Since even fictitious death was an irreversible process, a deraigned monk was treated as if he had never been dead, so that any inheritance was revived.[108] Civil death could, however, be suspended for temporal purposes. A dispensation from regular obedience could be granted by papal bull to a monk who became a bishop or parson, enabling him to sue in respect of his office or freehold.[109] It was also arguable that any dispensation to hold a benefice worked an implied dispensation from obedience.[110] In a case of 1523, which is reported in the year books, it was

---

[102] See further below, 623–4.

[103] e.g. *Prior of Alvecote* v. *Grene* (1522) CP 40/1037, m. 403 (under prior of Malvern); *Trevelyan* v. *Verney* (1523) Hil. 14 Hen. VIII, fo. 16, pl. 4 (119 Selden Soc. 145); CP 40/1035, m. 642 (friar under obedience of prior of Benedictine house in Exeter); *Paten* v. *Edolff* (1526) CP 40/1051, m. 318 (Austin canon under obedience of prior of Combwell). See also Rast. Ent. 444 (482v) for two undated pleas, one by a Carmelite friar and the other by a friar preacher.

[104] Cf. Trin. 9 Hen. VII, fo. 2, pl. 3, *per* Huse CJ, as to when it might be triable by the country.

[105] Port, 128 (dictum in the Inner Temple); e.g. *Prior of St John's and Pecke* v. *Newnam* (1494) CP 40/929, m. 401 (defendant pleads that Pecke, preceptor of Baddesley, was 'miles professus in ordine militie hospitalis Sancti Johannis Jerusalem in Anglia' and under the obedience of the prior). Hall held that a profession overseas was recognized in England, but did not say how it would be tried: reading (1541), fo. 57.

[106] However, the statute of 1539 (below) also uses the term deraignment for the release of monks from a valid profession.

[107] If the man had married *in facie ecclesiae* or consummated the marriage before profession, the profession was void: James Hales's reading in Gray's Inn (1532) BL MS. Hargrave 253, fo. 11; Hall's reading (1541), fo. 57.

[108] Hall's reading (1541), fo. 57. Deraignment (where profession was a nullity *ab initio*) was different from degradation: *Moots*, 135.

[109] ibid. In *Abbot of St Mary Graces* v. *Palmer* (1518) KB 27/1028, m. 71, an unsuccessful attempt was made to challenge the purchase of such a bull as contrary to the statute of *praemunire*.

[110] See *Paten* v. *Edolff* (1526) CP 40/1051, m. 318 (debt on a bond; pleads testator was professed; plaintiff replies that testator was granted a dispensation by bull of Pope Julius II to accept a benefice with cure of souls, and so he was discharged from his profession).

apparently held that the mere act of inducting or collating a monk into a benefice had the like effect and rendered him capable of being sued, even though it was the act of the ordinary rather than of the pope.[111]

The peculiar legal status of monks could not survive the dissolution of the monasteries.[112] When the lesser monasteries were dissolved in 1536, provision was made for the monks either to be transferred to larger houses, where they could continue to live 'religiously', or to be given 'their capacities, if they will, to live honestly and virtuously abroad, and some convenient charity disposed to them for their living'.[113] By 'capacities' was evidently meant a general dispensation from religion, which would have to be sued out from the master of the faculties,[114] though the precise effect of such dispensations must have been fraught with doubt. As the greater monasteries were dissolved, and the option of transfer became impracticable, it was thought necessary to plan a general resurrection of monks to legal life. A government bill of 1539 for this purpose, which was introduced into the Lords by the solicitor-general, was replaced in the Commons with a more restrictive measure designed to give better protection to property interests.[115] All religious persons, men and women, were by reason of the dissolution of their houses 'put at their liberties from the danger, servitude, and condition of their religion and profession', with liberty to purchase unto them and their heirs, and to sue and be sued for matters arising since their discharge from religion, but with the important proviso that they should not succeed to property as heirs by reason of any title accrued before the departure from religion.[116] The legislation did not abolish profession—which may have been thought beyond the competence of Parliament—and it was still necessary under canon law for the displaced religious to obtain dispensations, though because of administrative confusion only about a third did so.[117] When the order of St John of Jerusalem was dissolved in 1540, the former knights of Rhodes and other brethren, though not members of religious houses, were given a similar release from obedience and granted legal capacity.[118] A third statute, in 1541, extended the same liberties to religious persons belonging to houses which were not suppressed but reincorporated.[119] A possible

---

[111] *Trevelyan* v. *Verney* (1523) Hil. 14 Hen. VIII, fo. 16, pl. 4 (119 Selden Soc. 145); CP 40/1035, m. 642 (plea of profession was held bad). It had been argued that only the pope could dispense. That question was not finally settled, because there was an estoppel. See, however, Hil. 44 Edw. III, fo. 4, pl. 17.

[112] For the dissolution see below, ch. 37.   [113] 27 Hen. VIII, c. 28.

[114] The power of dispensation was transferred from the pope by the statute 25 Hen. VIII, c. 21.

[115] Elton, *Reform and Renewal*, 151.

[116] 31 Hen. VIII, c. 6; explained by 33 Hen. VIII, c. 29, and 5 & 6 Edw. VI, c. 13.

[117] F. D. Logan, *Runaway Religious in Medieval England c.1240–1540* (1996), 167–77. According to Logan, 3,781 dispensations were issued.

[118] 32 Hen. VIII, c. 24. However, it was questioned in *Cave* v. *Handysshe* (1557–8) CP 40/1170, m. 525 (undetermined demurrer) whether a former knight could bring an assize of novel disseisin.

[119] 33 Hen. VIII, c. 29.

casus omissus was that of the apostate who was *de facto* outside the cloister at the time of the legislation.[120] But the combined effect of these statutes was to put a complete end to monastic status. According to Edward Hall, the last monastic habit seen in England was taken from a prisoner who had been in Newgate between the dissolution and his arraignment in 1540.[121]

One effect of the legislation was that it enabled former religious persons to marry, provided they were not priests and that they had not taken or confirmed their vows after the age of 21.[122] It was also intended that a former monk should be able to inherit land from an ancestor dying after the heir's discharge from religion, though the wording of the statute caused difficulty and judicial disagreement when it was considered by the Common Pleas in 1544,[123] and the position had to be clarified by another statute in 1552.[124]

ALIENS

There were an increasing number of aliens living in England in the early Tudor period, rising in London alone from over two thousand in 1485 to four or five thousand in the 1550s,[125] and so their legal position was a matter of some practical significance.[126] Aliens were understood to be persons born outside the realm—or outside the 'allegiance'—to parents likewise born outside the realm. If a born Englishman had a child while lawfully abroad, or an alien had a child while living in England, the child was not an alien.[127] Aliens were not deemed to be 'free men' for the purposes of Magna Carta,[128] and could not be sworn on grand juries,[129] but were entitled to the protection of the criminal law while in the country, even if they came without a passport,[130] and could bring and defend personal

---

[120] See *Gardiner v. Lovell* (1569) Dyer's reports, 109 Selden Soc. 163.   [121] *Hall's Chronicle*, 840.

[122] 31 Hen. VIII, c. 6, second proviso; considered in *Gardiner v. Lovell* (1569) Dyer's reports, 109 Selden Soc. 163–4 (inheritance dispute between daughter of former friar and daughter of friar's younger brother). Cf. Dudley's unorthodox opinion that this had been possible anyway: above, 608.

[123] *Chalfount v. Chalfount* (1544) Gell's reports, I, Mich. 36 Hen. VIII, ff. 26–30v; CP 40/1124, m. 144 (action by second son against first-born former monk, their father having died after the statute of 1539; undetermined demurrer).   [124] 5 & 6 Edw. VI, c. 6.

[125] For estimates of numbers see A. Pettegree, *Foreign Protestant Communities in Sixteenth-Century London* (1986), 16–17, 83.

[126] For the background to what follows see K. Kim, *Aliens in Medieval Law* (2000).

[127] J. Rastell, *Exposiciones Terminorum* [c.1523], sig. B1, and (1527 edn), fo. 16v; anonymous reading (1530s) BL MS. Harley 4990, fo. 161v; *Anon.* (1544) Brooke Abr., *Denizen*, pl. 9, 19. The first proposition was embodied in the statute of Edw. III *De Natis ultra Mare*, which Huse CJ considered a confirmation of the common law: Mich. 1 Ric. III, fo. 4, pl. 7. As to children born in Calais see *Tudor Royal Proclamations*, i. 93, no. 64 (1512).   [128] Anon. reading (1530s) BL MS. Harley 4990, fo. 161v.

[129] William Wadham's reading (Lincoln's Inn, 1505) Taussig MS., fo. 199.

[130] 94 Selden Soc. 306. However, the readers held that an alien was not entitled to demand surety of the peace: Marow's reading (Inner Temple, 1503), ed. Putnam, 324; Harlakenden's reading (Gray's Inn, 1525) Taussig MS., fo. 65v.

actions.[131] Some prominent aliens, indeed—notably the Genoese merchants Antonio Bonvisi, Raphael Maruffo, and Antonio Vivaldi[132]—are frequently encountered as litigants in the plea rolls. However, aliens could not bring real actions,[133] and could not own a freehold estate in land. A real action by an alien could therefore be answered by a plea of 'alien born' (alien né), which was triable by jury if he replied that he was born in a particular place in England.[134] In 1540 Parliament went so far as to forbid aliens to take leases of shops and dwelling-houses,[135] though in practice they had to find homes and the king promptly suspended the statute;[136] there are frequent references in the statute-book to alien housekeepers.

The London merchants tended to congregate in distinct communities, some of which—notably the Hanseatic community in the Steelyard[137]—lived under a measure of self-government.[138] It was no doubt their social distinctness as well as language difficulties which had led to the introduction of the jury de medietate linguae—'of half tongue'[139]—for the trial of cases in which aliens were parties.[140] The procedure was very common in the early Tudor period. Although the statute which introduced it spoke merely of a jury half-alien ('moitee des aliens'), suggesting that prejudice against foreigners rather than language was the chief concern, the expression 'half tongue' implied that linguistic differences were also important. The divergent philosophies were reflected in divergent practice, in that

---

[131] Frowyk's reading (Inner Temple, 1492) in *Moots*, 268–9; undated note, Yorke 211, no. 325; *Anon.* (1546) Brooke Abr., *Denizen*, pl. 10; *Nonabilitie*, pl. 62. Cf. *Anon.* (1531) Pollard 246, no. 1, which says (following Litt. s. 198) that they could not sue in tort either, but had a remedy in Council. Aliens could act as personal representatives: *Anon.* (1557/8) BL MS. Hargrave 4, fo. 130, *per* Dyer CJ.

[132] Amongst other activities, Maruffo and Vivaldi ran a thriving business obtaining and bringing papal bulls from Rome. Vivaldi was also involved in marine insurance: C1/914/31 (action in London on a contract made by Vivaldi's London agent in 1536). It is said that alien merchants controlled more than half the London export trade: Pettegree, *Foreign Protestant Communities*, 10.

[133] *Anon.* (1531) Pollard 246, no. 1; *Anon.* (1546) Brooke Abr., *Denizen*, pl. 10; *Nonabilitie*, pl. 62.

[134] Mich. 1 Ric. III, fo. 4, pl. 7, *per* Huse CJ; Hil. 7 Hen. VII, fo. 8, pl. 1, *per idem*. Cf. *Re Laurence* (1514) KB 27/1010, Rex m. 9 (inquisition traversed).

[135] The terms of the statute imply that such leases were formerly valid: 32 Hen. VIII, c. 16. But cf. Brooke Abr., *Denizen*, pl. 22 (tr. 'It was said in 5 Mar. in Parliament that if an alien born obtains a lease for years the king shall have it, for he may not have land in this realm for any estate').

[136] *Tudor Royal Proclamations*, i. 291, no. 195.

[137] They feature in a customs case in the Exchequer Chamber case in 1491: Hil. 6 Hen. VII, fo. 15, pl. 9; 64 Selden Soc. 158.

[138] Note a reference to a judgment of the council of the nation of Venetians in London: *Orio v. Trono* (c.1490) C1/104/16.

[139] This was a contemporary expression: see 11 Hen. VII, c. 21 ('wherein the trial and inquest was by half-tongue'); C49/42, no. 2 ('byll for juries of halfe tonge', 11 Hen. VII). Cf. 22 Hen. VIII, c. 10 ('medietatem linguae'). But the expression is not used in the plea rolls.

[140] 28 Edw. III, c. 13; 8 Hen. VI, c. 29. See M. Constable, *The Law of the Other: the half-alien jury and changing perceptions of citizenship, law and knowledge* (1994), which does not take account of plea-roll evidence.

sometimes the *venire facias* required a jury composed half of aliens—following the wording of the statute—whereas in other cases half the jurors were to be from the same country, or even the same region, as the party. It is impossible to discern any clear rules governing these variations. Indeed, in three cases involving the same Italian merchant three different forms of *venire facias* are found: one for a jury half from Lucca, one for a jury half Italian, and one for a jury half alien.[141] The choice, according to the wording of the record, was that of the alien who prayed the half tongue. In practice it seems to have been most common for an Italian party to ask for a jury half Italian, usually specifying the state,[142] while Germans and French tended to leave the region or even the nationality unspecified.[143] This may reflect the larger number of Italians in London. It is perhaps also possible to discern a trend towards the general half-alien jury from the mid-1520s, even at the prayer of Italians,[144] and in the 1550s it was judicially confirmed to be sufficient in law.[145] Obviously it must have been more difficult for the sheriffs to find six aliens from any particular country, though when they did so it must have been disconcerting to the other party to see six members of a close community on the jury. Even so, we find mention of juries half Genoese, half Florentine, and half Venetian, which not only appeared in court but proceeded to find against the Italian defendants.[146] An alien could waive the privilege, and it

---

[141] *De Gigliis* v. *Brograve* (1501) CP 40/958, m. 143d (half Italian); *same* v. *Amyvale* (1505) CP 40/971, m. 146d (half alien); *same* v. *Harsnap* (1506) CP 40/977, m. 454 (half from Lucca).

[142] e.g. *Lomeline* v. *Sparke* (1491) CP 40/924, m. 141 (Genoese); *De Gigliis* v. *Brograve* (1501) CP 40/958, m. 143d (Genoese); *Albert* v. *Goodwyn* (1503) CP 40/963, m. 471; Rast. Ent. 157 (159) (Florentine); *Corne* v. *Lomelyn* (1505) KB 27/974, m. 63d (Genoese); *Spinula* v. *Brograve* (1506) CP 40/975, mm. 342d, 353; *Waren* v. *Maruffo* (1512) CP 40/999, m. 530; *Boeris* v. *Hopwood* (1512) CP 40/1001, m. 652 (Genoese); *Bank* v. *Hatchet* (1515) CP 40/1010, m. 443 (Florentine); *Wythers* v. *Bonvixi* (1515) CP 40/1012, m. 436; *Baptiste* v. *Bulkeley* (1525) CP 40/1048A, m. 607 (born under the obedience of the Emperor Charles as duke of Genoa); *Rawlyns* v. *Maruffo* (1525) ibid., m. 614; *Slee* v. *Maruffo* (1528) CP 40/1059, m. 331 (Genoese); *Calvacant* v. *More* (1553) KB 27/1165, m. 113 (plaintiff prayed a half-Italian jury but there is no mention of this in the precept for the *venire facias*); *Ewarcy* v. *Cabot* (1555) CP 40/1162, m. 908.

[143] e.g. *Segrave* v. *Vaughan* (1491) CP 40/918, m. 355d (defendant from Cleves); *Coron* v. *Hethcote* (1524) CP 40/1045, m. 550d (German plaintiffs); *Ecclesfeld* v. *Bonhoffe* (1533) KB 27/1088, m. 65d (defendant from Cleves); *Fouler* v. *Wedy* (1534) KB 27/1092, m. 69d (defendant from Cologne); *Fressher* v. *Deacon* (1535) KB 27/1097, m. 39 (defendant from Brittany); *Cokerell* v. *Tolowrge* (1538) KB 27/1109, m. 61 (defendant from France). Cf. *Welforde* v. *Scotte* (1491) CP 40/918, m. 311 (jury half from 'Coleynland', presumably Cologne); *Parsons* v. *Johnson* (1492) CP 40/919, m. 134d (jury half German); *Reniger* v. *Fogassa* (1550) Plowd. 1 at fo. 2 (jury half Portuguese).

[144] e.g. *Cavalcant* v. *Gate* (1524) CP 40/1044, m. 458; *Ughuccioni* v. *Poynes* (1526) CP 40/1050, m. 344; *De Vivaldis* v. *Boughton* (1529) CP 40/1063, m. 549d; *Lomelyng* v. *Staunton* (1534) CP 40/1081, m. 515 (all Genoese plaintiffs); *Moreany* v. *Basyng* (1551) KB 27/1157, m. 40 (Venetian plaintiff).

[145] Brooke Abr., *Denizen*, pl. 4; Sta. P.C. 159.

[146] *Bradschawe* v. *Savage* (1490) CP 40/914, m. 260 (half from Genoa); *Husey* v. *Berty* (1506) KB 27/981, m. 30d (half from Florence); *Huse* v. *Baptyste* (1506) ibid., m. 99 (half from Venice). See also *Ecclesfeld* v. *Bonhoffe* (1533) KB 27/1088, m. 65d (verdict by general half-alien jury against German

was not error if an ordinary jury found against an alien who failed to claim it;[147] but in a case of 1531 the failure of counsel to claim a jury *de medietate linguae* in the Sheriffs' Court, London, was made the subject of a bill in Chancery.[148]

The foreign merchants who appear in these lawsuits probably accounted for only about 10 per cent of the aliens in Tudor London. Most of the remainder were immigrant tradesmen. Alien immigrants caused problems of a different character.[149] There was no common-law check on immigration,[150] and many foreign craftsmen were encouraged to settle in England to promote new trades and industries;[151] but the presence of immigrant craftsmen was often blamed for perceived economic and social problems. It was alleged that aliens not only took work from the English but tended to employ their own countrymen, thereby impoverishing the natives. This grievance was mentioned in the first parliament of Richard III, which addressed the problem by forbidding aliens to provide lodging for other aliens, except from their own countries; to buy, sell, or make woollen cloth; to 'occupy handicraft' other than as servants to English subjects; to sell by retail; or to employ alien household servants, other than their own children.[152] There were also some particular provisions concerning Italians which were repealed soon afterwards.[153] Despite these restrictions, hostility to aliens continued to grow as their numbers soared, and reached its zenith in the Evil May Day riots of 1517, when a massacre was only narrowly averted.[154] In response to the causes of this unrest, the Star Chamber and Parliament confirmed the restrictive measures of 1484 and also prohibited aliens from taking alien apprentices or more than two alien lodgers.[155] The legislation was regularly enforced by informers in the Exchequer,[156] and sometimes in other courts.[157] Indeed, its over-zealous

defendant). Examples of half-alien juries finding in favour of aliens are: *Boeris* v. *Hopwood* (1512) CP 40/1001, m. 652; *Ughuccioni* v. *Poynes* (1526) CP 40/1050, m. 344; *Moreany* v. *Basyng* (1551) KB 27/1157, m. 40.

[147] Dyer 28a, §180; *R.* v. *Sherleys* (1557) Dyer 144b; Dal. 22.

[148] *Femyngus* v. *Rolf* (1531) C1/634/19.

[149] See, generally, Pettegree, *Foreign Protestant Communities in Sixteenth-Century London* (1986).

[150] Specific legislation was therefore required to prohibit 'Egyptians' (gypsies) from entering or remaining in the realm: below, 615.

[151] e.g. the law printers John Lettou, William Machlinia, and Richard Pynson: above, 494. Two alien 'bookprinters' (John Hareford and Philip Skapullys) are mentioned in an information of 1540: E159/319, Trin., m. 28, 36.   [152] 1 Ric. III, c. 9.

[153] 1 Hen. VII, c. 10.

[154] Above, 584. For a riot committed by London apprentices and servants against the Easterlings, or Steelyard merchants, in 1494 see *Hall's Chronicle*, 468.

[155] 14 & 15 Hen. VIII, c. 2, perpetuated and enlarged by 21 Hen. VIII, c. 16; 32 Hen. VIII, c. 16. The 1523 statute confirmed a Star Chamber decree of 1521 to the like effect.

[156] e.g. a substantial crop of informations in 1540 (on the 1523 statute), mostly against shoemakers, by the notorious common informer George Whelplay: E159/319. For Whelplay see Elton, *Star Chamber Stories*, ch. 3.

[157] e.g. *Pole* v. *Sanyas* (1511) CP 40/994, m. 537 (information on 1484 statute against a goldsmith).

enforcement against certain trades which depended on immigrant labour soon led Parliament to introduce exemptions.[158] Aliens were still seen as a problem in 1554, when by royal proclamation all aliens other than merchants and ambassadors' servants were ordered to leave the realm.[159]

A different kind of problem was presented by gypsies—the 'outlandish people calling themselves Egyptians'—who had no proper trade but made a living by deceiving people with fortune-telling and by theft, and who also lived in irregular ('abominable') circumstances. They were perceived as part of the problem of the idle poor,[160] but since they were also foreigners they could be dealt with by expulsion.[161] By statute of 1531, all gypsies were required to leave the realm or suffer imprisonment and forfeiture of goods.[162] The measure was not very successful, and attempts were still being made to enforce it in the 1540s.[163] In 1554 it was made a capital offence for a gypsy to remain in the country, and a £40 fine was introduced for those who smuggled gypsy immigrants into England or tried to obtain passports for them.[164]

A common defence to informations for statutory offences by aliens was a patent of denizenation, by means of which an alien could be converted into a subject through the exercise of the royal prerogative. Several thousand such patents were issued in the first half of the sixteenth century, particularly after the statute of 1540;[165] and, indeed, a Chancery official was executed for treason in 1540 for trying to profit from the rush by sealing counterfeit patents.[166] The letters patent conferred upon the grantee all the liberties, franchises, and privileges which liege subjects used and enjoyed, including leave to acquire real property. The effect was to make the alien a subject for most purposes, so that—for instance—he could plead a general pardon available only to 'subjects'.[167] The king could not, however, alter the law of nationality, and so it was held that denizenation of a father did not enable his children previously born outside England to inherit, since they were

---

[158] 22 Hen. VIII, c. 13 (bakers, brewers, surgeons, and scriveners).

[159] *Tudor Royal Proclamations*, ii. 32, no. 404.   [160] For the poor law of 1531 see above, 98.

[161] There was a precedent of a kind in the proclamation of 1503, following a treaty with the Emperor Maximilian, requiring Turks (as traitors to the emperor) to leave the realm on pain of instant death: *Tudor Royal Proclamations*, i. 58–9, no. 52.   [162] 22 Hen. VIII, c. 10.

[163] See e.g. *APC 1542–7*, pp. 88 (order for vagabonds called Egyptians to leave the country, 1543), 128, 320 (1546).

[164] 1 & 2 Phil. & Mar., c. 4. A decision of 1562 explaining this statute was reported in Dyer's notebook but can no longer be found: Dyer 96a, §42.

[165] Of over 900 patents granted up to 1540, about 400 were issued in the immediate wake of the statute. Another 3,000 were granted in 1544, following a proclamation. See Pettegree, *Foreign Protestant Communities*, 15.

[166] Ralph Egerton, servant to Lord Audley C., was hanged, drawn, and quartered: *Hall's Chronicle*, 841; BL MS. Add. 25168, fo. 554v.

[167] *R. v. Lomelyn* (1518) KB 27/1026, Rex m. 2 (Italian pleads general pardon of 1515 for all subjects, and that by virtue of his patent he was a subject; pardon allowed).

still aliens. The father's first son born in England would inherit his English land.[168] It was also found necessary to limit the tax advantages of denizenated aliens, since their exemption from customs duty was open to abuse.[169]

Friendly aliens who were not denizenated were nevertheless subject to the law,[170] and could even be convicted of treason by virtue of the local allegiance which they owed on coming into the realm.[171] Enemy aliens, on the other hand, did not owe allegiance if they entered the country to levy war against the king, and could not therefore be convicted of treason. That is why Perkin Warbeck, who conspired to depose Henry VII by pretending to be the rightful heir to the throne, and came to England to effect that purpose, was tried under martial law rather than upon indictment.[172] The decision was later criticized by Serjeant Catlyn, on the ground that Warbeck, in claiming to be a king's son, entered England as an Englishman rather than as an alien;[173] but, since Warbeck's claim was false, it could not alter the fact that he was an alien. During hostilities, it was said to be lawful to kill an enemy alien, though according to Marow the burden of proof was on the killer, so that if an unidentified alien was killed it would be treated as murder.[174] Marow was presumably not here referring to the battlefield, but rather to isolated private attacks. Enemy aliens could also in theory be taken prisoner,[175] and sold into bondage.[176] Although the category of enemy aliens included

[168] Frowyk's reading (Inner Temple, 1495) in *Moots*, 297; St German, *Doctor and Student*, ed. Plucknett and Barton, 49; *Anon.* (1544) Brooke Abr., *Denizen*, pl. 9, 19. Frowyk also held that an elder son born in England before the father became a denizen (being an English subject) could inherit, but the other benchers denied this.

[169] 1 Hen. VII, c. 2 (reciting that some aliens made denizens allowed other aliens to import in their own names to avoid customs); renewed by 11 Hen. VII, c. 4; 21 Hen. VIII, c. 16; 22 Hen. VIII, c. 8. For other remaining disabilities, see Pettegree, *Foreign Protestant Communities*, 15–16.

[170] *Note* (1558) BL MS. Hargrave 4, fo. 136 (tr. 'Note that it was said by Prideaux, serjeant, that all strangers coming to any realms . . . are bound to the laws of the realm within which they are, and vouched 13 Edw. IV', i.e. *The Carrier's Case*). It had nevertheless been thought necessary to enact (in prospective terms) in 1540 that all aliens should be subject to the laws and statutes of the realm: 32 Hen. VIII, c. 16.

[171] *R. v. Sherleys* (1557) Dyer 144a (Frenchman triable at law for treason, since no state of war with France); sub nom. *Sheres*, Catlyn's precedent book, Alnwick Castle MS. 475, at fo. 178v (tr. '. . . at which judgment I was present, being one of the same queen's serjeants'); sub nom. *Sheires*, Dalison's reports, BL MS. Harley 5141, fo. 38v (which says an alien would be triable by martial law—*la ley martiall*—if he came in as an enemy in battle array in time of war); Dal. 22, pl. 5; Brooke Abr., *Treason*, pl. 32.

[172] *Perkin Warbeck's Case* (1499) Port 125; 1 Caryll 383; James Hobart's report, 109 Selden Soc. 206 (also copied in Catlyn's MS., ff. 178, 236*bis*); lost Star Chamber register, 75 Selden Soc. 32; commission in *CPR 1494–1509*, pp. 115, 118; above, 216–17.

[173] Catlyn's precedent book, Alnwick Castle MS. 475, fo. 178. Since it was presumably more advantageous to be treated as an Englishman, estoppel was irrelevant.

[174] Marow's reading (1503), ed. Putnam, 379.

[175] *Whele v. Reynold* (1483) KB 27/885, m. 34d; Hil. 22 Edw. IV, fo. 45, pl. 9 (where the alleged Scot was a King's Bench filazer); *Moots*, 269. The liability of Scots to arrest and imprisonment is mentioned in several defamation actions (below, 786) and in *Anon.* (1544/5) Brooke Abr., *Propertie*, pl. 38 (prisoners bought by king after capture of Boulogne).

[176] 'Personal Liberty under the Common Law', 334; above, 598 n. 16.

Scotsmen,[177] in practice the Scots were not treated as outlaws, and even during hostilities they were given time to leave peacefully;[178] but they were not permitted to use the courts.[179]

WOMEN

There were no significant changes in the legal position of women in the early Tudor period. For most purposes other than inheritance, and the operation of the death penalty,[180] unmarried women were in the same legal position as men.[181] They could and did use the courts of law and equity, albeit to a far lesser extent than men, but perhaps with increasing confidence in the Tudor period.[182] They could and did own property, real and personal, though the rules of inheritance— in the absence of contrary provision—favoured men in the same degree of consanguinity. Lawyers accepted in principle that land could be settled in tail upon female heirs only,[183] but in a patriarchal society this would have been absurd and no real instance has been found. Family settlements were designed to ensure that land passed in the male line, suitable provision being made for the marriage of daughters who were not heiresses.[184] Nevertheless, apart from the automatic rules of inheritance, which applied only to land held in fee, there was no presumption against female succession: a remainder limited to 'issue' or 'children' passed to daughters as well as sons.[185] And Dyer J. held that a statute which restrained 'the lawful liberty of women at the common law' with respect to alienating their own inheritances ought to be narrowly construed, since women were not represented in Parliament.[186]

---

[177] See n. 175, above; below, 786 (falsely calling someone a Scot). However, around the time of the battle of Blackheath, a Scotsman is said to have been tried before Townshend J. in Southwark and executed for treason: *Anon.* (*c.*1497) 120 Selden Soc. 43, no. 26.

[178] 7 Hen. VII, c. 7. Cf. *Anon.* (1544/5) Brooke Abr., *Propertie*, pl. 38 (as to a Frenchman who enters England as a friendly alien and then war is declared).   [179] See 110 Selden Soc. 257.

[180] See above, 551 (respite for pregnancy), 557, 588 (burning for treason).

[181] The canonists no doubt expressed a generally accepted principle in the maxim that the word 'man' in law included a woman: *Reformatio Legum Ecclesiasticarum* (1551), ed. G. Bray in *Tudor Church Reform*, 743, maxim no. 76. Cf. *Anon.* (1551) BL MS. Hargrave 4, fo. 115v, *per* Whiddon sjt (tr. 'women are *gentes as well as men*, referring to the Statute of Winchester, and distinguishing *homines*); but note the *homo laica*, below, 830 n. 84.

[182] Sampling suggests that in the earlier part of the period about 5% of common-law litigants and 15% of litigants in Chancery were women: E. Hawkes, 'Women's Knowledge of Common Law and Equity Courts in Late-Medieval England' in *Medieval Women and the Law*, ed. N. J. Menuge (2000), 145 at 148, 151. Other samples suggest a considerably increased proportion by 1560: T. Stretton, *Women Waging Law in Elizabethan England* (1998), 38–42.

[183] i.e. tail female: *Moots*, p. lxix; Litt. s. 22; *CLT*, 40.   [184] See further below, 687.

[185] *Anon.* (1549) Wm Yelv. 347, no. 73.

[186] *Villers* v. *Beamont* (1557) Dyer 146a at 148b; CP 40/1166, m. 516 (concerning 11 Hen. VII, c. 20). He was, however, dissenting. Cf. Hales J.'s comments on the same statute in *Wimbish* v. *Tailbois* (1550) below, n. 190.

With the exception of the queen,[187] women did not in practice hold high public office, unless it descended to them in fee, in which case it was performed by deputy.[188] It was accepted in theory that a woman could be a justice of the peace,[189] 'even though'—in the ungenerous opinion of Edmund Dudley—'she has not so perfect a discretion as a man'.[190] No actual instance has been found, though at a Gray's Inn exercise around 1500 a lady justice is said to have been named.[191] Women regularly served on juries to try pregnancy,[192] though it was said that no woman could be sworn on a grand jury.[193] The fullest discussion of the matter occurred around 1530 when a lady pleaded a writ of protection issued by reason of royal service, in company with her husband, in victualling Berwick. Norwich CJ held that 'a woman is just as able in the law to do various things in law as a man, especially for the common weal, as here', while Shelley J. thought 'a woman by her providence and policy may get victuals as well as a man, and perhaps better than some men'.[194] In any case, since the king had selected her for the appointment, it was not for the court to question her suitability. Moreover, according to Englefield J., 'a woman shall have as much advantage as a man, and shall be helped by the law as much as a man shall be'. Fitzherbert J. alone dissented, on the grounds that it was unsuitable for a woman to bear arms, and that this unsuitability somehow extended to supporting men at arms.[195] Whatever legal conclusions may have been reached in later times—when women started to seek public positions—it seems from these discussions that the exclusion of women from formal public service in the early Tudor period was a matter of convention rather than of legal dogma.

Most legal questions concerning women arose in relation to married women and the relationship between husband and wife. Many such questions were litigated, and discussed in the inns, but the main principles of coverture—and the various exceptions to the doctrine that husband and wife were as one person in law[196]—were

---

[187] And female monarchy raised doubts in some minds: above, 61–2.

[188] *Duke of Buckingham's Case* (1514) 2 Caryll 645 at 646 (constableship of England). Note also the settlement of the wardenship of the Fleet for life upon Elizabeth Venour, who performed by deputy: above, 128.

[189] Marow's reading (Inner Temple, 1503), ed. Putnam, 310, 318; Port 113; Walter Hendley's reading (Gray's Inn, 1530) BL MS. Harley 5103, fo. 24, *per* Molyneux; MS. Add. 35939, fo. 352v; Bodl. Lib. MS. Rawlinson C.705, fo. 127; next note. See also P. Hogrefe, Tudor Women: commoners and queens (1975), 27–36.

[190] BL MS. Add. 35939, fo. 12v (in Gray's Inn). Cf. *Wimbish* v. *Tailbois* (1550) Plowd. 38v at 50v, *per* Hales J. (tr. 'the makers of the statute considered the frailty and inconstancy of women, who will easily be led astray by soft words', adding that they have 'so little discretion').

[191] ibid., *per* Fairfax (tr. 'and he named a lady who was a justice of peace'). In the same case it was stated that the countess of Warwick (d. 1449) had been a hereditary sheriff.   [192] Above, 552.

[193] Wadham's reading (Lincoln's Inn, 1505) Taussig MS., fo. 198v.

[194] For a woman surgeon in 1554 see below, 820. Women did not practise as lawyers until the twentieth century.

[195] *Re Lady E. S.* (*c.*1530/5) Wm Yelv. 292, no. 2 (anon.); identified from Spelman 189, pl. 2.

[196] For explicit exceptions see Hendley's reading (Gray's Inn, 1530) BL MS. Harley 5103, fo. 24, *per* Molyneux (tr. 'even though husband and wife are but one person etc., yet in some respects they are

already well settled. A woman took her husband's surname on marriage,[197] and also his status,[198] even if it was inferior to hers.[199] Thus the widow of an earl who married a gentleman lost her 'name of honour'.[200] In the case of Lady Powys in 1552, a herald gave evidence that in the law of arms a peer's widow retained her dignity (and former name of dignity) on marriage to a commoner; but this was held not to be the law of England.[201] If a title was retained on remarriage, it was purely a matter of courtesy. The decision was, however, questioned in 1557 in the case of Frances, dowager duchess of Suffolk, who married her groom, Adrian Stokes.[202] A similar question arose if a peer's daughter married a commoner. When Frances Plantagenet, daughter of Viscount Lisle, married Mr John Basset in 1538, her mother was concerned about the loss of status and obtained an opinion from the heralds that she did not lose her 'degree' on marriage; but this opinion seems to have been thought unreliable.[203] A title gained by marriage was lost by divorce; and so even Queen Katherine of Aragon became, after the divorce, the princess dowager.[204]

The degree of autonomy which women possessed in fact is a matter more of social than of legal history. The law acknowledged that a married woman was subject to her husband's will,[205] and so she was given protection against forced conveyances of her inheritance by fine or collusive lawsuit. She could also be given a separate estate in land during the marriage by means of a feoffment to her use.[206] And she could demand some personal protection against a violent husband.[207]

distinct persons in law'); *Anon.* (1535) Mich. 27 Hen. VIII, fo. 27, pl. 12; *Abbot of Bury* v. *Bokenham* (1536) Dyer 7b at 8b, *per* Knightley sjt (tr. 'although husband and wife are in some respects as one and the same person in law, yet in this respect, namely to become the purchaser of a use, she is as a stranger').

[197] *Chamber* v. *Bulcombe* (1491) 1 Caryll 65 at 66. She reverted to her former name if the marriage was annulled, and changed her name again if the divorce was revoked: *Moots*, 180.

[198] *Allington* (recte *Abyngton*) v. *Oldcastell* (1553) Dyer 88a; KB 27/1167, m. 88 (gentleman).

[199] Except in the case of a villein.

[200] This did not apply to a peeress in her own right: anon. reading, BL MS. Harley 4990, fo. 163v (1530s).

[201] *Howard and Lady Powys* v. *Duke of Suffolk* (1552) Dyer 79, *per* Mountagu CJ and Hales J.; cited in BL MS. Add. 24845, fo. 18; MS. Harley 5141, fo. 7v; MS. Harley 1624, fo. 59, *per* Dyer (mentions herald); Owen 82; J. Ferne, *Blazon of Gentrie* (1586), 62–4. Anne, widow of Lord Powys, had married Ranulph Howard, esquire, and it was held that she could no longer use the name Lady Powys for legal purposes.

[202] *Stokes and Duchess of Suffolk* v. *Bishop of London* (1557) BL MS. Harley 1624, fo. 59; MS. Harley 5142, fo. 11; MS. Add. 25001, fo. 22v; MS. Add. 35940, fo. 40v. Another dowager duchess of Suffolk, Katharine Willoughby, likewise married a commoner (Richard Bertie); they were parties in a famous case of 1560: below, 686 n. 236.

[203] *Lisle Letters*, ed. Byrne, iv. 74–5, no. 856; 148, no. 884; 151, no. 887 (where the countess of Rutland thought the contrary).

[204] *Tudor Royal Proclamations*, i. 209, no. 140. The title of princess dowager derived from her marriage with Prince Arthur. She was generally called the Lady Katherine: e.g. *HLJ*, i. 67.

[205] See Hendley's reading (Gray's Inn, 1530) BL MS. Harley 5103, fo. 24, *per* Hales A.-G. (tr. 'during the coverture the wife lacks free will, for she is *sub potestate viri* and amenable to his pleasure').

[206] Below, 685.

[207] Harlakenden's reading (Gray's Inn, 1525) Taussig MS., fo. 65v, says she may demand surety of the peace against her husband. Nevertheless, the law allowed the husband some powers of

Marriage nevertheless brought about a drastic alteration of status. Entry into matrimony was supposed to be dependent on free will, but marriages were commonly arranged—especially in landed families—when the parties were very young,[208] and there was considerable pressure, on young men as well as women, to do a guardian's bidding. There was even a legal sanction behind such pressure, in the form of an action for the value of the marriage against wards of either sex who refused suitable marriages when tendered.[209] Yet there were limits. A statute passed in 1487 recited that heiresses apparent and other women of substance were 'oftentimes taken by misdoers, contrary to their will, and after married to such misdoers, or to others by their assent'. It therefore enacted that 'taking' a woman against her will, whether maid, widow, or wife, was to be felony.[210] The immediate occasion for the measure was probably the abduction of Jane Sacheverell (née Statham) by Henry Willoughby.[211] It was limited in scope, in that it did not apply to guardians 'claiming' wards, or to lords 'claiming' bondwomen, and it was probably passed as much in the interests of guardians and lords as of women. It was also, perhaps, too severe to be easily enforced.

Caryll noted two notorious examples of abduction in the reign of Henry VII, both of which gave rise to protracted litigation. In the first, Alice Shelley, the 15-year-old daughter of Sir Thomas Shelley, was abducted by Adam Penyngton, a gentleman of the king's household,[212] and forced to go through a marriage ceremony. According to counsel, the 'horribleness of the deed' was well known. Alice was advised to bring an appeal of felony upon the statute, and this was allowed to proceed even though the statute did not mention an appeal. Then the defendant pleaded in abatement that she was his wife, which she denied. That was an issue of fact triable by jury; but, after the jurors had reached a decision, the appellant allowed herself to be nonsuited and the prosecution was taken over by the attorney-general. No outcome is recorded.[213] Equally inconclusive, it seems,

chastisement: *Fyloll* v. *Assheleygh* (1520) Trin. 12 Hen. VIII, fo. 4, pl. 3 (119 Selden Soc. 15), *per* Broke J. (who says this is because she cannot sue him).

[208] Below, 690.

[209] FNB 147D. The action was usually brought against male wards: e.g. *Wyll* v. *Nott* (1526) CP 40/1052, m. 402 (denies tender of marriage while under 21); *Colepeper* v. *Lucas* (1534–5) CP 40/1083, m. 619d; Pas. 27 Hen. VIII, fo. 3, pl. 11; *Foljambe* v. *Leke* (1535) CP 40/1084, m. 509; *Pygot* v. *Nevile* (1542) CP 40/1112, m. 328 (£120 damages recovered); *Folyambe* v. *Leeke* (1548) CP 40/1135, m. 629.

[210] 3 Hen. VIII, c. 2 (sp. mod.); E. W. Ives, ' "Ayenst taking awaye of Women": the inception and operation of the abduction act of 1487' in *Wealth and Power in Tudor England*, ed. Ives *et al.* (1978), 21–44.

[211] A. Cameron, 'Complaint and Reform in Henry VII's Reign: the origins of the statute of 3 Hen. VII, c. 2?' (1978) 51 *BIHR* 83–9. There was a forced marriage, and a divorce. For other prominent abductions see B. J. Harris, 'Aristocratic Women in Early Modern England' in *States, Sovereigns and Society in Early Modern England*, ed. C. Carlton *et al.* (1995), 3–24, at 18 n. 30.

[212] He is so described in 1507: CP 40/982, m. 487. He was also of Furnival's Inn. He lived until 1526: C142/45/6; PCC 21 Porch.

[213] *Shelley* v. *Penyngton* (1492) 1 Caryll 98; KB 27/925, m. 87d (pr. 115 Selden Soc. 100–1).

were Alice's action for false imprisonment, her father's actions for abduction, and Penyngton's action against the father for falsely imprisoning his wife.[214] The second case concerned Serjeant Kebell's widow Margaret, who at the age of 24 was forcibly carried off by Roger Vernon and forced into a wedding ceremony.[215] Margaret brought an action of trespass and then an appeal of rape; and, when Vernon pleaded that she was his wife, she replied that the marriage was void for duress. The Common Pleas held that duress was a good plea to avoid a marriage, but once again the actions seem not to have led to a final judgment.[216] Vernon's own action for abducting Margaret, as his wife, raised the interesting question whether a friend could justify taking a wife away and providing her with transport, so that she could attend to her divorce proceedings. The judges of the King's Bench thought such intervention proper, on grounds of necessity, but there were qualms about the details and no judgment was entered.[217] The absence of judgments in all these cases may indicate the ineffectiveness of the law in securing the capital punishment of abductors,[218] but is otherwise typical of litigation in general. Margaret Kebell certainly gained her freedom in practice, together with her substantial jointure.[219]

In 1557 the judges placed a restrictive construction upon the 1487 act by requiring it to be laid in the indictment that the woman was abducted with the intention either of marrying her against her will or of deflowering her, since these were mentioned in the preamble.[220] It was also said to be unclear whether the offence was committed if no marriage or copulation in fact occurred.[221] Further legislation was enacted at the end of the period to punish those who 'took' unmarried girls under the age of 16 away from their fathers or testamentary guardians, having obtained the girl's consent by means of 'flattery, trifling gifts, and fair promises'. This offence, which was not capital, could be committed without using force and seems to have been created to combat a different kind of abuse. According to the preamble, lewd persons were trading in heiresses and luring them into marriages with unsuitable partners.[222] As in 1487, Parliament was more concerned with property interests and parental control than with the autonomy of the ward.

[214] 115 Selden Soc. 98, headnote.   [215] Like Jane Sacheverell's case, it arose in Derbyshire.

[216] *Kebell* v. *Vernon* (1504) 2 Caryll 424 (trespass); (1506) Mich. 21 Hen. VII, fo. 31, pl. 13, and fo. 34, pl. 35 (appeal of rape). For related Star Chamber proceedings see 16 Selden Soc., pp. cx–cxiv.

[217] *Vernon* v. *Gell* (1504–6) KB 27/972, m. 85 (undetermined demurrer); Mich. 20 Hen. VII, fo. 2, pl. 4; Hil. 21 Hen. VII, fo. 13, pl. 17.

[218] Note also *R.* v. *Sturges* (1539) Spelman 104; KB 27/1111, Rex m. 14 (indictment on statute of 1487). The defendant was discharged because of an ambiguity; but it was held that the statutory offence did not require that the victim be forced into marriage.

[219] Ives, *Common Lawyers in pre-Reformation England*, 392–3.

[220] *Anon.* (1557) BL MS. Harley 5141, ff. 34v–35; Dal. 22, pl. 3.

[221] *Tichborne* v. *Eyre* (1558) 109 Selden Soc. 22 (disagreement in Star Chamber). The case concerned an heiress who refused marriage before and after the abduction.

[222] 4 & 5 Phil. & Mar., c. 8. The new offence was not a felony, but was punishable by imprisonment.

CORPORATIONS

In 1483 there were many bodies and fellowships in England owning land or privileges, though the nature of corporate personality was still being worked out by lawyers.[223] In the absence of earlier theory, most of the old kinds of corporation—religious houses, deans and chapters, colleges, cities, boroughs, guilds, and corporations sole—had never received explicit grants of corporate status and it had to be supposed, when theory came to matter, that they had acquired it by the common law,[224] by or under custom,[225] by prescription,[226] or by implied grant—as where privileges were granted by letters patent to a society or to a fluctuating body, such as the members of a community or the inhabitants of a place.[227] So uncertain was the law at this time that the existence of a corporation could be left to a jury without pleading how it was alleged to have been established.[228]

It was only around the middle of the fifteenth century that new corporations, such as colleges and craft guilds, began to be given perpetual corporate status explicitly by royal grant.[229] During the early Tudor period several new species of corporation were created by royal charter, in each case principally to facilitate a grant or lease of land to a professional or skilled body: for example, the College of Physicians (1518),[230] the Fraternity of St George or Guild of Artillery

---

[223] For the late emergence of corporate theory see also S. Reynolds, 'The History of the Idea of Incorporation or Legal Personality' in *Ideas and Solidarities* (1995), pt VI, 1–20.

[224] e.g. churchwardens were said to be common-law corporations, though not for the purpose of acquiring land: *Baker* v. *Johnson* (1497) 1 Caryll 361; Trin. 12 Hen. VII, fo. 27, pl. 7, at fo. 29, *per* Fyneux CJ; KB 27/945, m. 34d (undetermined demurrer); *Anon.* (1525) Yorke 232, no. 393. The chattels of the parish were not vested in the churchwardens either, but were in their custody: below, 625.

[225] e.g. it was alleged to be a custom of the city of London to found colleges, chapels, and chantries: *Cetito* v. *Duke of Suffolk* (1526–33) CP 40/1052, m. 844 (concerning the chaplains of Corpus Christi next St Lawrence, Candlewick Street). Cf. the London guilds: Trin. 12 Hen. VII, fo. 27, pl. 7, *per* Frowyk sjt. A liberty of making corporations could only be claimed by custom, not by grant or prescription: Hil. 2 Hen. VII, fo. 13, pl. 16, *per* Kebell sjt; Spelman's reading (Gray's Inn, 1519), 123; but (as to a grant) cf. Mich. 20 Hen. VII, fo. 6, pl. 17, at fo. 7, *per* Rede J.

[226] *Prior of Huntingdon* v. *Men of Huntingdon* (1487) Trin. 2 Hen. VII, fo. 17, pl. 1; *Mayor of Oxford's Case* (1498) Hil. 13 Hen. VII, fo. 14, pl. 6, *per* Kebell sjt. See also Mich. 12 Edw. IV, fo. 17, pl. 21 (prescription for priory to sue and be sued without superior house). Cf. *Stele* v. *Newton* (1527–30) Mich. 18 Hen. VIII, fo. 1, pl. 5; CP 40/1054, m. 254 (inhabitants of Derby may not prescribe for common unless they prescribe to be incorporated).

[227] Trin. 7 Edw. IV, fo. 14, pl. 7; reading on Magna Carta, c. 9, BL MS. Harley 1336, fo. 128 (pr. 113 Selden Soc. 3); Spelman's reading (Gray's Inn, 1519), 89; *Note* (1554) Dyer 100a, §70. Cf. the arguments against an implied indirect incorporation in Hil. 2 Hen. VII, fo. 13, pl. 16.

[228] *Brotherhood or Guild of the Nine Orders of Angels* v. *Pokelyngton* (1482) Mich. 22 Edw. IV, fo. 34, pl. 13; CP 40/882, m. 121.

[229] J. H. Baker, 'The Inns of Court and Chancery as Voluntary Associations' (1983) 11–12 *Quaderni Fiorentini*, pt i, 9–38; repr. *LPCL*, 45–74, at 47–9.   [230] 14 & 15 Hen. VIII, c. 5.

(1537),[231] and the Six Clerks' Company (1539),[232] all based in London. By the end of our period the incorporation of trading enterprises, in order to confer monopolies and powers of control, was also just beginning. In 1555 the Merchants Adventurers of England for the Discovery of Lands Unknown, otherwise known as the Muscovy Company or Russia Company, were incorporated by letters patent which granted that no one other than the company's members or licensees should visit the mainlands of Russia or lands further north.[233] On the other hand, there were countervailing advantages for an association in remaining unincorporated, in that its constitution could remain flexible. The inns of court, for instance, could surely have obtained incorporation if they had desired it; but they did not.[234] Some trading companies likewise were still being formed as unincorporated associations.[235]

This was the period in which the distinctions between bodies politic and natural persons, and between corporations and their individual heads and members, began to receive full examination by the courts. The common law was in the process of refining a doctrine of corporate personality, though different kinds of corporation attracted different legal rules and there were few generalized principles. Indeed, according to Serjeant Broke—speaking in Gray's Inn hall in 1519— it would have been such a large task to define the qualities of a corporation that it would have taken an entire vacation.[236] Most of the earlier case-law concerned monasteries, which required special treatment in law because all the members were legally dead.[237] The legal powers of a religious house were reckoned to repose in the head, who alone was deemed to be alive for the purpose of exercising them. The head could make contracts, give oral instructions,[238] and sue or be sued, without naming the convent.[239] This circumstance made it largely unnecessary to

---

[231] E159/319, recorda, Pas. 32 Hen. VIII, m. 2; *The Royal Charter of Incorporation granted to the Honourable Artillery Company*, ed. G. A. Raikes (1889). The patent was belatedly enrolled on the patent rolls in 1829. Within months of the charter the guild took a 99-year lease of an exercise garden, and it later came to be known as the Company of the Artillery Garden. It is now called the Honourable Artillery Company.   [232] Above, 185.

[233] *CPR 1554–5*, pp. 55–9.

[234] The inns of court are still not incorporated. For the legal consequences see Baker, 'The Inns of Court and Chancery as Voluntary Associations', *LPCL*, 45–74.

[235] e.g. the Company of Adventurers to the New Found Lands, granted privileges and powers by a patent of 1506; being unincorporated, they did not survive. The patent contained an unusual limitation to the patentees, their heirs, attorneys, agents, or deputies: *CPR 1494–1509*, p. 320. The only Henrician charter in *Select Charters of Trading Companies 1530–1707*, ed. C. T. Carr (28 Selden Soc.; 1913), 1–3, granted privileges to the Andalusia Merchants (1530) without explicitly incorporating them.

[236] Spelman's reading (Gray's Inn, 1519) 113 Selden Soc. 154. Fyneux CJ made a start in *King's College, Cambridge v. Hekker* (1522) Mich. 14 Hen. VIII, at fo. 3 (119 Selden Soc. 101: 'we must examine what a corporation is, and what kinds of corporations there are…').   [237] Above, 608.

[238] See *Note* (1492) 1 Caryll 93, pl. 104; Hil. 7 Hen. VII, fo. 9, pl. 2; cf. *Anon.* (1493) 1 Caryll 192, pl. 148.

[239] *Hoper v. Abbot of St Albans* (1490) Pas. 5 Hen. VII, fo. 24, pl. 7, at fo. 26, *per* Bryan CJ.

invest such corporations with an artificial legal personality, other than for the purposes of succession, since the legal entity was identifiable with the human person of the abbot or prior.[240] There was no great difference for most purposes between such a body and a corporation sole,[241] though it was often remarked that it was different from a secular corporation aggregate in which the head and members had dual capacities and could not act as a body without written authority approved by them in common.[242] The chief remaining legal doubt with respect to monasteries was whether an abbot could wage law in debt on a contract made in the time of a predecessor. Since the essence of such an indebtedness was that the merchandise had come to the use of the house, it was arguable that this was as much within the knowledge of the successor as of the predecessor.[243] Yet Bryan CJ was against allowing wager of law, apparently regarding privity as a matter of human rather than corporate personality,[244] and he was also against allowing an abbot to wage law in respect of a contract made through one of his own monks.[245] Although his view was unorthodox by the end of the fifteenth century,[246] it seems to have prevailed in the next generation.[247] Bryan CJ also took the view that an abbot could be sued on a bond made as abbot even after his translation to another house.[248] His opinions may perhaps be understood as conservative in terms of acknowledging corporate personality, though they seem rather to be predicated upon the special circumstance that in monasteries only the head was legally alive. At any rate, corporate theory was to be more significant in the context of lay communities.

[240] Cf. *Case of Dean and Canons of Westminster*, Spelman 154 (corporation cannot do homage).

[241] For the differences between a parson and an abbot see the discussion at Spelman's reading (1519) 113 Selden Soc. 153–5.

[242] *Dean and Chapter of St Paul's* v. *Gloss* (1483) Trin. 1 Edw. V, fo. 4, pl. 10, at fo. 5, *per* Bryan CJ; *Case of Dean and Chapter of St Paul's* (1488/9) Pas. 4 Hen. VII, fo. 6, pl. 2; Mich. 4 Hen. VII, fo. 17, pl. 7; *Note* (1492) 1 Caryll 93, pl. 104; Hil. 7 Hen. VII, fo. 9, pl. 2, *per* Oxenbridge sjt ('corps politique aggregate' distinguished from abbot and convent, who are dead in law); Trin., 7 Hen. VII, fo. 16, pl. 3; Hil. 10 Hen. VII, fo. 16, pl. 15; *Case of the Master and Wardens of Rouncival* (1496) Trin. 11 Hen. VII, fo. 27, pl. 12; *Case of Dean and Chapter of St Paul's* (1497) Trin. 12 Hen. VII, fo. 25, pl. 6; *Anon.* (1498) Hil. 13 Hen. VII, fo. 17, pl. 21.

[243] See *Wivel* v. *Abbot of Durford* (1443) Hil. 21 Hen. VI, fo. 23, pl. 3 (point left undecided); *Cowplond* v. *Abbot of Wymondham* (1515) 2 Caryll 679, *per* More sjt.

[244] See *Anon.* (1486) Pas. 1 Hen. VII, fo. 25, pl. 18; *Tabor* v. *Prior of Dunstable* (1497–8) Mich. 13 Hen. VII, fo. 3, pl. 2; CP 40/942, m. 301d (undetermined demurrer).

[245] *Spark* v. *Abbot of Ramsey* (1490) CP 40/907, m. 101d; 1 Caryll 25, pl. 32 (pr. anon.).

[246] In *Tabor* v. *Prior of Dunstable* (1497–8), above, the other judges were in favour of wager of law. The point was undecided in *Skelbroke* v. *Abbot of Westminster* (1498–1502) CP 40/943, m. 261d (demurrer to wager of law); *Carnebull* v. *Prior of Lenton* (1512) CP 40/1000, m. 410 (sim.).

[247] *Cowplond* v. *Abbot of Wymondham* (1515) 2 Caryll 679 (by all the the judges); Pollard 264, no. 41; CP 40/1010, m. 404 (judgment for plaintiff); *Anon.* (1534) 121 Selden Soc. 433, no. 7 (citing the case of 1515); Spelman 95, pl. 5, and 160, pl. 2 (citing the case of 1443, above).

[248] *Hoper* v. *Abbot of St Albans* (*Prior of Bath's Case*) (1488–90) Mich. 3 Hen. VII, fo. 11, pl. 2; Pas. 5 Hen. VII, fo. 24, pl. 7; Pas. 9 Hen. VII, fo. 23, pl. 4; CP 40/910, m. 599d. Note also the question whether an abbot could be punished for a nuisance (by omission) commenced in time of his predecessor: Mich. 5 Hen. VII, fo. 3, pl. 9.

It was already recognized in the later fifteenth century that incorporation was needed if an otherwise ill-defined group of people was to take a valid grant of property, other than (perhaps) chattels.[249] Neither the Church nor an individual parish church was a corporation capable of owning property,[250] though the unincorporated body of parishioners was said to be capable of owning chattels.[251] A gift or grant to a fluctuating body, such as the inhabitants from time to time of a particular parish,[252] or to a voluntary society—such as the 'company' of the Inner Temple[253]—could not be given legal effect without incorporating them.[254] Yet such groups could be recognized for some purposes. Property could be held in trust for them.[255] Both kinds of body were able to sue and be sued in Chancery and Star Chamber, though their recognition by such courts should perhaps be seen as anticipating the class-action rather than as recognizing an equitable or quasi-corporation.[256] Inhabitants of hundreds were liable to pay compensation for robberies, under the Statute of Winchester, and could in consequence be sued as a group;[257] but, here again, recognition of the group for this purpose does not seem to have given it any corporate characteristics. A succession of customary office-holders, such as the sheriffs of a county, or the chief justices and officers of the Common Pleas, were allowed to claim privileges by prescription, as if they were a corporation sole, even though they were not.[258] On the other hand, it was

[249] The only case-law concerns parishioners (below). But the inns of court, for instance, owned chattels such as plate and books.

[250] R. v. Watlyngton (1499) KB 27/953, Rex m. 10 (goods cannot belong to 'parish church').

[251] They were described in indictments and pleadings as 'the goods of the parishioners' (boni parochianorum): Mich. 7 Edw. IV, fo. 14, pl. 1; R. v. Boswell (1513) Port 37 at 39; Anon. (1530/1) Caryll (Jun.) 381, no. 23; R. v. Fuller (1539) above, 573 n. 182. But they were in the custody of the churchwardens, in whose name actions for them were brought.

[252] Baker v. Johnson (1497) Trin. 12 Hen. VII, fo. 27, pl. 7, at fo. 29; Mich. 13 Hen. VII, fo. 9, pl. 5; KB 27/945, m. 34d (undetermined demurrer). According to Tremayle J., '(tr.) it is only a body gathered together, which implies no manner of certainty'.

[253] This example was put at an Inner Temple moot in 1491: Moots, 229. The word 'company' does not here have its later connotation but means the same as fellowship.

[254] For incorporation of societies by charter in order to take a grant of land see above, 622. For incorporation of parishioners by statute for the same purpose see Reynolds, 'History of the Idea of Incorporation', 14 (example of 1540). For implied incorporation where a grant was made by royal letters patent see above, 622 n. 227.

[255] This was disputed in Baker v. Johnson (1497) above, n. 252. But it was common practice de facto.

[256] See Holdsworth, HEL, iv. 439 (suit by parishioners to enforce a guild charity temp. More C.); S. C. Yeazell, From Medieval Group Litigation to the Modern Class Action (1987), 127–9.

[257] e.g. Coveney v. Bromfeld and other Inhabitants of Denton (1521) CP 40/1032A, m. 508; Webbe v. Inhabitants of Hundred of Amesbury (1554) CP 40/1158, m. 422. Similar actions could be brought against the community of the forest of Dean by virtue of the statute 8 Hen. VI, c. 27: Inhabitants of Tewkesbury v. Communities of the Forest of Dean (1514) CP 40/1007, m. 510; Garett v. Communities of the Forest of Dean (1521) CP 40/1034, m. 571.

[258] Anon. (1497) Pas. 12 Hen. VII, fo. 15, pl. 1, at fo. 18, per Fyneux CJ; Note (1502) 2 Caryll 410, pl. 268; Toft's Case (1506) Hil. 21 Hen. VII, fo. 17, pl. 28; Spelman's reading (Gray's Inn, 1519), 86 at n. 3.

not possible for an indefinite body, such as the inhabitants of a place, to prescribe for rights of common.[259] The correct course was to lay the prescription in the municipal corporation, if there was one, as being for their benefit.[260] But the corporation could not itself take advantage of a custom for the inhabitants to take common, because, in the words of Serjeant Kebell in 1489, the corporate body unlike its individual members—is a 'dead person in law' and cannot do anything by itself.[261] Here, then, was an explicit recognition of the distinction between a corporation, which was a legal abstraction, and the living members by whom it was constituted at a particular moment. Yet it was only beginning to matter at a rather technical level. Even for the learned members of the inns of court, we may imagine, the societies to which they and their contemporaries belonged were readily understood without reference to corporation theory.

The first major reported discussion of corporate personality occurred in 1481–3 in a case concerning a civic corporation. The abbot of St Benet Hulme sued the corporation of Norwich in debt upon a bond.[262] The defendants pleaded that the bond was void for duress, since the mayor at the time of execution was imprisoned in the Fleet at the suit of the abbot's predecessor. The plaintiff demurred on the ground that the mayor as a person was only an individual member of the corporation, and that the corporation itself had not been imprisoned. A civic corporation was a body of natural persons which could only act through human will, by the consent of the majority; and so perhaps, as Choke J. suggested, it would have been a defence if a majority of the members had been imprisoned, 'because in the majority their body resides'. However, as Serjeant Pygot argued, a corporation is a different entity from the people who belong to it. The reason why no *capias* lay against a corporation was that it could not be imprisoned. It had no substance at all. It was merely a name, a concept which could not be seen or suffer physical injury. Choke J. agreed, adding that 'although a body politic is made of natural men, yet this body can only be created by the king, and when it is created it is a dead person in law'. Catesby J. also agreed, observing that 'It is not like a natural

---

[259] Spelman's reading (1519), 87, 123; Mich. 18 Hen. VIII, fo. 1, pl. 5, *per* Fitzherbert J. (but queried by reporter); tentatively identifiable as *Stele* v. *Newton* (1527–30) CP 40/1054, m. 524 (prescription for inhabitants of Derby to have common appurtenant to the vill; demurrer; nonsuit); also reported in Yorke 232, no. 392. Cf. *The Case of the Borough of Dunster* (1525) Yorke 232, no. 393, where Broke J. and others said an unincorporated township could prescribe for common if they also prescribed to take by grant.

[260] *Boteler* v. *Bristow* (1475) Trin. 15 Edw. IV, fo. 29, pl. 7.

[261] *Case of the City of York* (1489) 1 Caryll 20, pl. 28; Trin. 4 Hen. VII, fo. 13, pl. 11.

[262] *Abbot of St Benet Hulme* v. *Mayor etc. of Norwich* (1481–3) Mich. 21 Edw. IV, fo. 12, pl. 4, and fo. 67, pl. 53; Pas. 21 Edw. IV, fo. 27, pl. 22; CP 40/876, m. 308 (undetermined demurrer); discussed in H. Lubasz, 'The Corporate Borough in the Common Law of the late Year-Book Period' (1964) 80 *LQR* 228–43. There is a contemporary account in English in the Norwich *Liber Albus*, ff. 72–73, abstracted in *Records of the City of Norwich*, ed. W. Hudson (1906), i. 353–4. The year book seems to include two independent reports.

body, for one cannot touch my hand without doing a wrong to my person, whereas if I do wrong to the mayor, the corporation is none the worse'. On the other hand, Bryan CJ inclined to the view that subjecting the mayor to duress did affect the validity of the deed, because it undermined his consent; and so the case was left undecided. Again, perhaps, we see Bryan CJ more inclined than his brethren to treat a corporate body as no different from a group of individuals.[263] The terms of the discussion nevertheless show that by the 1480s a corporation was generally perceived as an artificial body distinct in law from its members.[264]

The second major case was argued in 1521 and concerned the master of a hospital.[265] The defendant cleric in *quare impedit* pleaded a previous presentation to the church in question by the master of the hospital of St Giles in Norwich, which was a corporation, and that he himself was presented by the same hospital on the present vacancy. The plaintiffs replied that each of the two presentations was of the current master of the hospital, and demurred on the grounds that a corporation could not present its own head to a benefice. Serjeant Fitzherbert, for the defendant, argued that the head of a corporation was an individual distinct from the corporate body and so the presentation was effective. The court was at first evenly divided, but later gave judgment for the plaintiffs, and the judgment was affirmed the following year by the King's Bench.[266] The rejection of Fitzherbert's argument revealed a further obstacle to treating a corporation as completely separate from its members. But the decision, like Bryan CJ's opinion in the mayor of Norwich's case, was predicated on the special position of the head. While a presentation of one of the brethren of the hospital would have been valid, the head was inseparable from the body.

---

[263] Cf. Trin. 14 Hen. VII, fo. 32, pl. 8, where Bryan CJ (dissenting) held that a condition to be performed by a named abbot could not be performed by his successor; the other judges held that the abbot was named only in right of the house.

[264] Note also Mich. 2 Ric. III, fo. 7, pl. 13 (question by chief baron as to whether an acquittance by a mayor binds the corporation).

[265] *King's College, Cambridge* v. *Hekker* (1521–2) Pas. 13 Hen. VIII, fo. 12, pl. 2 (119 Selden Soc. 68); report duplicated in Pas. 14 Hen. VIII, fo. 29, pl. 8; CP 40/1027, m. 539 (pr. 119 Selden Soc. 76).

[266] Mich. 14 Hen. VIII, fo. 2, pl. 2 (119 Selden Soc. 98); Spelman 193; KB 27/1039, m. 21 (pr. 119 Selden Soc. 102).

Part VIII

THE LAW OF PROPERTY

34
Agrarian Changes and Security of Tenure

At the end of the fifteenth century the law of real property, as set down in Littleton's *Tenures*,[1] seems still to have been predicated on a feudal world in which little had happened since the reign of Edward I. The daily exercises of the inns of court, which introduced generations of lawyers to the minutiae of property law, were rooted in the same world and initiated students into the intricate learning of the ancient real actions and assizes. Sound legal education has to look back to the past; but in this instance, without question, the real world was becoming very different. The most onerous feudal incidents had largely disappeared as a result of uses—a phenomenon barely mentioned by Littleton or the pre-Tudor readers in the inns of court. They were about to be revived, however, for fiscal purposes; and the side-effects of the legislation would soon transform the land law beyond Littleton's imagination. Family settlements depended on the fee tail, expounded in the second chapter of the *Tenures* and the many readings on *De Donis*. But entails could now be barred by fines and recoveries, and counsel were experimenting with new forms of perpetuity. Even the contingent remainder, firmly rejected by Littleton, was beginning to gain acceptance. The real actions were now rarities, and before the end of the sixteenth century would be virtually defunct, taking with them to the grave half the law of England. Patterns of landholding were changing across the country, first because of developments in agrarian management, such as the enclosure movement, and second (from the 1530s) as a consequence of the dissolution of the monasteries and the redistribution of vast quantities of monastic land to laymen. Monastic grants greatly swelled the number of tenants in chief by knight-service, to the benefit of the king's revenue. But since 1290 the creation of new mesne tenures in fee simple had been impossible. A new form of quasi-tenure had in consequence become prevalent, in the form of the husbandry lease for years; and lessees now needed protection as tenants rather than as mere investors. Copyholders also now needed protection, as owners of property which differed from freehold only by reason of historical accident. For all these reasons, the law of real property underwent more fundamental changes in sixty years than in the previous two hundred. Littleton

---

[1] First printed in 1481, but probably written around 1460: above, 501.

would retain its biblical authority throughout the sixteenth century, and beyond; but it was now an old testament which students read as background to the new law which will be the principal focus of this Part.

By the middle of the fifteenth century, at the latest, most of the manorial demesne land throughout the country, which had increased in proportion as a result both of *Quia Emptores* and of the Black Death, had become leased for years to farmers.[2] A lease enabled the lord of a manor to create a tenancy, in return for services (usually rent), without breaking up the manor.[3] As a result of this change, the term of years had largely lost its ancient association with moneylending and had typically become the grant of a beneficial interest to be worked by the farmer, or at least sold on to someone who would work it for his own profit. Indeed the word 'farm', which had once primarily meant rent, by the sixteenth century normally denoted a messuage (the farmhouse), the demesne, and lands let out for years.[4]

The advantage of the term of years over copyhold, from the landlord's point of view, was that it enabled fixed customary provisions to be replaced by flexible agreements, while for tenants it gave security for a fixed term, free from the casual fines that might be due on the unpredictable death of a lord or tenant. A lease was also a good investment for a gentleman or city merchant,[5] who could sub-let parcels to the farmers on the land. This was doubtless why leases began in the early Tudor period to be granted for longer terms, such as twenty-one or even ninety-nine years, leases conceded in some cases by landlords more interested in substantial cash premiums than long-term revenue.[6] In some parts of the country the rise of leasehold may have led to the partial extinguishment of copyhold;[7] for it was coming to be accepted that a lease made to a copyholder by indenture or patent (rather than by copy) would be treated as a lease of the freehold, which

---

[2] For the chronology see e.g. Dyer, *Lords and Peasants in a Changing Society*, 209–17, 292–3; Harvey, *The Peasant Land Market in Medieval England*, 181–2, 228–9, 311–13, 333–4. See also F. R. H. Du Boulay, 'Who were Farming the English Demesnes at the End of the Middle Ages?' (1965) 47 *Economic Hist. Rev.* (2nd ser.) 443–55.

[3] A grant in fee would sever the land from the manor, as a result of *Quia Emptores*. But a lease might reproduce many of the features of feudal tenure, including even something like knight-service: e.g. BL Add. Ch. 50908 (lease for 61 years with covenant by the lessee to find an able man to serve in time of war, 1498); Add. Ch. 43332 (sim., 1538); both examples are from Cheshire.   [4] See Plowd. 195.

[5] There was similar investment in copyhold, so that in some manors many of the copyholders were non-resident.

[6] Kerridge, *Agrarian Problems*, 47–8; R. B. Smith, *Land and Politics in the England of Henry VIII: the West Riding of Yorkshire 1530–46* (1970), 81–3; Dyer, *Lords and Peasants*, 209–17; Oestmann, *Lordship and Community*, 59–62; cf. J. M. W. Bean, *The Estates of the Percy Family 1416–1537* (1958), 51–68 (no clear evidence of use of long leases to exact larger fines), 146–7 (long leases granted through profligacy of sixth earl of Northumberland). Kerridge and Oestmann say that leases became shorter again after 1540.

[7] Kerridge, *Agrarian Problems*, 53–4; Smith, *Land and Politics in the England of Henry VIII*, 81–3; Whittle, *The Development of Agrarian Capitalism*, 64–84.

would enfranchise the copyhold for ever.[8] On the other hand, a lease of the demesnes did not necessarily affect the manorial copyholds.[9] At any rate, it was common for both manorial tenants and investors to hold some of their land by copy and some by common-law lease, the distinction being from their point of view more or less fortuitous. This did not lead to legal assimilation, since there were differences in the incidents attaching to the different forms of tenure, and therefore in their capital and rental value; but it perhaps led to both forms of tenure being regarded as broadly similar in kind, and in need of similar legal protection.

Long before our period both forms of tenancy had for different reasons been excluded from the common-law concept of freehold, with the consequence that they were unprotected by the old real actions; but the transformation brought about by social changes had already led the law to extend some limited protection. Within our period the process was completed. Both leasehold and copyhold achieved more or less complete protection *in specie*, against the lord as well as strangers,[10] and thereby came to be accommodated within the common-law structure of real property. Security of tenure was not solely a matter of law, since much depended on local custom and on the practice of surveyors in renewing leases and setting fines; the Chancery also played a major part in improving the position of the copyholder. But it can hardly be doubted that the changes in the common law during the early Tudor period represented a major shift towards the recognition of non-freehold tenants as landowners with a real interest in their property.

TENANTS FOR YEARS

The lessee for years, according to Serjeant Kebell in 1492, had nothing but a chattel, 'and a chattel is not favoured in law like a freehold'.[11] A term was not hereditary, but like a movable chattel passed to personal representatives on death, and could be devised by will at common law. It was arguably not even 'land', and

[8] See *Compton* v. *Brent* (1537) Dyer 30b; *Trevilian* v. *Parkins* (1555) CP 40/1150, m. 804; Dyer 114a; but cf. Gell's reports, I, Pas. 1 & 2 Phil. & Mar., fo. 12 (probably same case, but reported contra). The point was thought unsettled until slightly later: *Hide* v. *Newport* (1575) cit. 2 Co. Rep. 17a, 4 Co. Rep. 31b, Moo. 185, Cro. Eliz. 8; *Frenche's Case* (1576) 4 Co. Rep. 31a; *Anon.* (1584) Moo. 185; *Smith* v. *Lane* (1585–8) 1 And. 191; 2 Co. Rep. 16b; 1 Leon. 170. A lease for years could be granted by copy if the custom warranted it.

[9] W. G. Hoskins, *The Age of Plunder* (1976), 63.

[10] And eventually against the king: 2 & 3 Edw. VI, c. 8 (where both are mentioned together).

[11] *Rede* v. *Capel* (1492) Pas. 7 Hen. VII, fo. 10, pl. 2, at fo. 11 (tr.). Cf. *Moots*, 75, pl. 29; *Anon.* (1492) 1 Caryll 123 at 124, *per* Townshend J. ('a tenant for years has but a chattel'); Dudley's reading (1496), fo. 82 (tr. 'it is only a chattel').

some held that it could not support a use in fee.[12] On the other hand, it was not a mere chattel but a 'chattel real'.[13] Already by the later fifteenth century leasehold was regarded as a form of quasi-feudal tenure, at any rate if rent was reserved:[14] the lessee was a 'tenant' who 'held' the land of a 'lord', and owed him fealty.[15] The lessee's interest was such that he could arguably disseise the lessor by making a feoffment;[16] and his consent was necessary to enable the lessor to deliver seisin to a grantee.[17] These propositions hint at something akin to seisin in the termor.[18] It was not, however, usual to speak of the tenant for years as seised,[19] except (after 1535) by operation of the Statute of Uses,[20] but rather as 'possessed' (*possessionatus*). Livery of seisin could not be made to him.[21] And, not being seised of freehold, the tenant was unable to use any of the real actions for recovery of his term.[22] Nor could he vouch his lessor to warranty, though if ousted he could sue the lessor in a separate action of covenant.[23]

The action of *quare ejecit* had been designed to provide a remedy for the tenant against eviction by a grantee from the lessor, in which case there was no privity to

[12] It was held for a time that a lease for years was not included in 'lands, tenements, or hereditaments' for the purposes of 1 Ric. III, c. 1: Gregory Adgore's reading (Inner Temple, c.1489) CUL Hh.3.10, ff. 27v–28; Gray's Inn moot (c.1520) BL MS. Harley 5103, fo. 85, *per* Walter Hendley. Hendley deduced from this that a term could not be subject to a use. When Spelman said the same in 1519 (tr. 'the term is but a chattel and shall not be charged with a use'), Hendley said it was otherwise if there was a remainder to the same use: ibid., fo. 82v.

[13] *Earl of Arundel v. Brent* (1505) Mich. 20 Hen. VII, fo. 4, pl. 11.

[14] There was a view that lordship and fealty depended on the reservation of rent: see *Anon.* (1490) Hil. 5 Hen. VII, fo. 10, pl. 2, at fo. 11, *per* Fairfax J. (queried by the reporter); Spelman 26 (copy of year book); *Ryshton v. Cripce* (1531) Spelman 93 at 94, *per* Spelman J.

[15] Litt. s. 132; *Anon.* (c.1516) Chaloner 280, no. 6, *per* Brudenell J., citing 5 Hen. VII (last note); *Ryshton v. Cripce* (c.1531/2) Wm Yelv. 290.

[16] Edmund Dudley's reading (Gray's Inn, 1496) Bodl. Lib. MS. Rawlinson C.705, fo. 68v (tr. 'Note by Dudley, reader, that if I lease lands for a term of years, the lessee may make a feoffment against the will of the lessor...'); CUL MS. Hh.3.10, fo. 82.

[17] *Anon.* (1537) Dyer 33a (Shelley J. dissenting). The lessee's consent in such a case was arguably a surrender of the term: *Anon.* (1506) Hil. 21 Hen. VII, fo. 7, pl. 6, *per* Frowyk CJ; *Anon.* (1537) Dyer 33a, *per* Baldwin CJ (Fitzherbert J. dissenting, citing a case of 5 Hen. VII).

[18] Cf. A. W. B. Simpson, *A History of the Land Law* (2nd edn, 1986), 247–8.

[19] Cf. the Clifford's Inn moot case in BL MS. Harley 5103, fo. 47: (tr.) 'A lease is made for a term of years, by indenture, upon condition that if the lessee should have issue during the term he should have the land to him and his heirs, and livery of seisin is made to the lessee for term of years...'. But in this case it was very unclear where the fee resided before the condition was fulfilled: see the discussion in Clifford's Inn, ibid., fo. 36.

[20] If a freeholder bargained and sold a term he was seised to the use of the purchaser for years, and by operation of the statute (27 Hen. VIII, c. 10) the purchaser was 'seised' of like estate (i.e. for years).

[21] Yorke 98, no. 32.

[22] Dudley held that an assize would lie on a grant of an *office* for 100 years, but that was because it would end on the grantee's death and was therefore a grant for life: reading in Gray's Inn (1496) CUL MS. Hh.3.10, at fo. 68.

[23] *Earl of Arundel v. Brent* (1505) Mich. 20 Hen. VII, fo. 4, pl. 11; Yorke 233, no. 396 ('for it is but a chattel real').

support an action of covenant, and it gave recovery of the term as well as damages. Yet in our period it was rare.[24] Although it had the advantage that it enabled the lessee to recover possession of the land, it had at least four drawbacks: process was by summons rather than *capias*, and there was no outlawry; it was necessary to show that the lessor had re-entered in order to make the grant to the defendant; it was not available to an assignee of the lease; and it did not lie after the end of the term.[25]

The action of ejectment (*de ejectione firmae*) was not quite so rare, though it was not in widespread use before the 1550s. Whatever its origins, it now overlapped with the other remedies, because it could be brought not only against a stranger but against the lessor himself,[26] or against a grantee from the lessor.[27] Although in form it was a species of trespass *vi et armis*, and therefore on one view ought to have been regarded as a personal action for damages only,[28] it seems to have been widely accepted by the beginning of our period that judgment could be given to recover the outstanding term against the lessor.[29] However, the point was not fully settled, and this may explain occasional recourse to Chancery or the Star Chamber for relief.[30] The uncertainty is usually taken, on the strength of a passage in Fitzherbert's *Natura Brevium*,[31] to have been ended by a decision of the Common Pleas in 1499; but it seems probable that the court was concerned in that case with the narrower and newer question of whether judgment could be given to recover the term against a mere stranger.[32] Fitzherbert said the judgment was affirmed in the King's Bench. The proceedings in error have not been traced,

[24] Examples are *Dorker* v. *Hardyng* (1496) KB 27/940, m. 63 (action against head lessor; judgment to recover damages only); *Baker* v. *Conyngesby* (1555) CP 40/1164, m. 921 (judgment to recover term and damages).

[25] FNB 197U, 198D; *Pynchemore* v. *Brewyn* (1481) Mich. 21 Edw. IV, fo. 10, pl. 1, *per* Bryan CJ; *Note* (*c.*1495) Port 127, pl. 80.

[26] e.g. *Williams* v. *Barnard* (1498) KB 27/949, m. 78 (action by executrix of lessee; issue).

[27] FNB 198A, C.

[28] Pas. 6 Ric. II, Fitz. Abr., *Ejectione Firme*, pl. 2, *per* Belknap CJ; *Note* (*c.*1495) Port 127; *Old Natura Brevium* (*c.*1516 edn), fo. 49 (tr. B. & M. 179).

[29] *Pynchemore* v. *Brewyn* (1481) CP 40/876, m. 315; Mich. 21 Edw. IV, fo. 10, pl. 1; Pas. 21 Edw. IV, fo. 30, pl. 25; tr. *SBEL*, 110; Brooke Abr., *Quare Ejecit*, 2; *Case of J. B.* (King's Bench, 1481) Mich. 21 Edw. IV, fo. 11, pl. 2, *per* Huse CJ; *Trussell* v. *Maydeford* (1493) 1 Caryll 156 at 157, *per* Kebell and Wode sjts. For earlier precedents and dicta to the same effect see Plucknett, *CHCL* (5th edn), 373 n. 5, 574; Simpson, *A History of the Land Law*, 144 n. 3; Arnold, 100 Selden Soc., p. lxxiii n. 560.

[30] For the latter, see Guy, *The Cardinal's Court*, 58.

[31] FNB 220H, citing a precedent of 14 Hen. VII which is identifiable as *Gernes* v. *Smyth* (1499) CP 40/948, m. 303; Lucas's entries, fo. 107; pr. Rast. Ent. 244 (252v). Another precedent came within a year: *Deyster* v. *Godyer* (1500) CP 40/953, m. 116; pr. Rast. Ent. 243 (251v).

[32] That is how the point is stated in FNB 220H, having been left in a state of uncertainty by the reports of *Pynchemore* v. *Brewyn* (1481), above. Cf. also *Anon.* (1530) Pollard 256, no. 24 (tr. 'Note that it was held by the whole court that the lessee for term of years may recover his term by writ *de ejectione firmae* against a stranger ... Note also that this writ is only a writ of trespass in its nature; and the writ shall be *vi et armis*').

though the judgment roll notes a writ of error dated 11 Oct. 1499 and there is no reason to doubt Fitzherbert's contemporary observation—which permits us to regard this as yet another of the legal developments sanctioned by Fyneux CJ. The new law is noticed by John Rastell as well as Fitzherbert.[33] On two or three occasions in the reign of Henry VIII the availability of specific relief was confirmed by the judges, though the action was still sufficiently unusual for the decisions to be remarked on by reporters.[34] During the same period, opinion seems also to have turned in favour of giving termors protection under the 1429 statute of forcible entry, so that they could obtain restitution through the justices of the peace.[35]

Despite the obvious advantages of ejectment in giving specific recovery, it seems from the plea rolls that the usual actions for trying leasehold title until the middle of the sixteenth century continued to be trespass *quare clausum fregit* and replevin.[36] In trespass the plaintiff was frequently driven by the defendant's pleading to set out a leasehold interest, so that the issue became one of leasehold title.[37] It was decided in 1490 that the action could be used even against the lessor himself.[38] Ejectment does not finally explode into wide use until the 1550s, when its ascendancy is marked in both benches at the same time. A high proportion of the actions in the first wave were to recover rectories,[39] which could only be made the

---

[33] *Exposiciones Terminorum* [*c*.1523], sig. F4v; (1527 edn), fo. 86.

[34] *Soole v. Edgare* (1524–5) CP 40/1044, m. 505, as reported in Yorke 226, no. 373, and FNB 220I; *Anon.* (1530) Pollard 256, no. 24 (quoted above); cf. *Anon.* (?1545) JHB MS. 55, fo. 148 (entry dated Pas. 37 Hen. VIII, roll 428, an incorrect reference). The 1525 case is probably the one intended in *Anon.* (1572) BL MS. Hargrave 374, fo. 125v (tr. 'Dyer said that the opinion that the plaintiff should recover his term in ejectment had its first beginning in 17 Hen. VII [*sic*], but he said that the same opinion was never grounded upon law. Bendlowes: Yorke in 27 Hen. VIII moved this matter to the court here, and the opinion then was that the plaintiff should recover his term in this action...').

[35] William Saunders's reading (Middle Temple, 1525 or 1533) Pollard 263, no. 39. Cf. Hil. 1 Hen. VII, fo. 12, pl. 21; FNB 248E.

[36] In replevin the defendant initiated proceedings, and so the majority of cases where a lease is pleaded in the replication may be considered as actions against lessees. However, actions by lessees are sometimes found: e.g. *Bysshop v. Frankelyn* (1535) CP 40/1087, m. 432 (avows as lessee; jury finds sub-lease from defendant to plaintiff; judgment for plaintiff); *Whytney v. Mylle* (1535) ibid., m. 437 (acknowledges as bailiff of lessee of manor; issue on earlier lease by same lessor).

[37] e.g. nine such cases were counted in the Common Pleas rolls for 1535.

[38] *Anon.* (1490) Hil. 5 Hen. VII, fo. 10, pl. 2; and see *Anon.* (1558) Gell's reports, II, fo. 39r–v. Cf. *Anon.* (1547) BL MS. Hargrave 4, fo. 99v (tr. 'Note that it was held by all the justices that the lessee shall not have a writ of trespass *quare vi et armis* against his lessor'); abr. Dal. 3, pl. 9.

[39] e.g. *Anon.* (1554) Gell's reports, I, Mich. 1 & 2 Phil. & Mar., fo. 7 (lease of tithes); *Elryngton v. Reymond* (1555) KB 27/1175, m. 201d; *Cottesford v. Waynman* (1555) KB 27/1176, m. 85; *Cornwell v. Warberton* (1555) ibid., m. 94; *Harley v. Vaughan* (1555) ibid., m. 228; *Ibgrave v. Lee* (1555) Dyer 116b (lease of tithes); *Adee v. Nayler* (1556) KB 27/1178, m. 113; *Belassis v. Pepper* (1557) KB 27/1182, m. 66; *Blynkynsopp v. Dawston* (1557) KB 27/1183, m. 22 (lease of tithes); *Bushe v. Collyns* (1558) KB 27/1188, m. 66. The availability of ejectment for a rectory was discussed in *Anon.* (1494) 1 Caryll 219, pl. 164, and settled by *Case of St Dunstan in West* (1500) Trin. 15 Hen. VII, fo. 8, pl. 1; Pas. 16 Hen. VII, fo. 7, pl. 6; Pas. 21 Hen. VII, fo. 21, pl. 11 (misdated); confirmed in *Anon.* (1558) BL MS. Hargrave 4, fo. 124, *per* Dyer J. (where it was also held that ejectment would lie for mill-tolls).

subject of ordinary trespass actions indirectly.[40] A good number were also brought on leases of manors,[41] monastic leases,[42] or leases of former monastic lands.[43] The rise of ejectment may therefore have some connection with the title disputes arising from the confusion of leaseholds granted prior to the dissolution of the monasteries and in the rapid succession of land transfers afterwards— commercial dealings which may have generated a tougher attitude towards investments in real property and their protection. Its wider use, as a means of trying freehold and copyhold title, may already have suggested itself to the legal mind by the 1550s; but its exploitation lay in the future.[44]

Thus the lessee was confirmed in the full protection of his term against the lessor, grantees deriving title from the lessor, and mere strangers without title. For eviction by strangers with good title paramount to the lessor, there could obviously be no remedy,[45] save an action of covenant against the lessor.[46] But there were three intermediate situations which gave rise to difficulties. The first concerned the title of the lessor's lord in the event of his becoming guardian: that is, where the lessor died leaving an infant heir to the reversion. It had been settled law since earlier times, indeed 'common learning', that the guardian could oust the termor during the wardship.[47] Doubts about this harsh position were stirred in 1490,[48] and in

[40] e.g. by suing for trespass to grain set aside as tithes.

[41] e.g. *Carter* v. *Goddard* (1551) KB 27/1160, m. 119; *Warde* v. *Warde* (1552) KB 27/1164, m. 27; *Plankney* v. *Cowper* (1553) KB 27/1170, m. 113 (judgment for plaintiff); *Ludlowe* v. *Kente* (1553) CP 40/1153, m. 819d; *Halden* v. *Trappes* (1553) CP 40/1154, m. 518 (judgment for defendant); *Daunce* v. *Lord Pagett* (1553) CP 40/1155, m. 621 (demurrer to plea); *Pawlyn* v. *Heyward* (1555) KB 27/1175, m. 104; *Elryngton* v. *Reymond* (1555) KB 27/1175, m. 201d; *Grotewyche* v. *Willoughbye* (1555) KB 27/1176, m. 37; *Pleydell* v. *Wellys* (1557) KB 27/1184, m. 126; *Colthirst* v. *Crowche* (1558) KB 27/1186, m. 82.

[42] e.g. *Berdge* v. *Broke* (1549-50) CP 40/1142, m. 639 (demurrer to plea setting out attainder of abbot of Woburn and dissolution of abbey); *Newdigate's Case* (1551) Dyer 68b; *Gardyner* v. *Coldyche* (1552) KB 27/1163, m. 33; *Moone* v. *Clyfforde and Waryner* (1552-3) KB 27/1166, m. 159; CP 40/1151, m. 541; sub nom. *Clifford* v. *Warrener* (1553) Dyer 89a, 96b; *Capstock* v. *Turnor* (1554) KB 27/1172, m. 202; *Pawlyn* v. *Heyward* (1555) KB 27/1175, m. 104; *Blynkynsopp* v. *Dawston* (1557) KB 27/1183, m. 22; *Rede* v. *Style* (1557) ibid., m. 123; *Pleydell* v. *Wellys* (1557) KB 27/1184, m. 126; *Johnson* v. *Grene* (1557) ibid., m. 129; *Bushe* v. *Collyns* (1558) KB 27/1188, m. 66.

[43] This is not usually mentioned in the record. Occasionally the plaintiff counted on a lease sanctioned by the Court of Augmentations: *Luce* v. *Smyth* (1554) KB 27/1169, m. 86; *Barley* v. *Punter* (1555) KB 27/1175, m. 155.   [44] See also below, 724.

[45] *Ferrour* v. *Rodley* (1522) Mich. 14 Hen. VIII, fo. 4, pl. 4 (119 Selden Soc. 105); *Anon.* (1532/3) Brooke Abr., *Leases*, pl. 19.

[46] This remedy required a deed, and was beset with difficult distinctions: Port 151, no. 36.

[47] In our period see *Delariver's Case* (1490) Trin. 5 Hen. VII, fo. 36, pl. 3, *per* Kebell sjt; *Rede* v. *Capel* (1492) Pas. 7 Hen. VII, fo. 10, pl. 2, at fo. 12, *per* Huse CJ; *R.* v. *Bishop of Chester* (1499) Pas. 14 Hen. VII, fo. 21, pl. 4, at fo. 22, *per* Heigham sjt; *Anon.* (1500) Pas. 15 Hen. VII, fo. 6, pl. 2, at fo. 7, *per* Kebell sjt; S. E. Thorne, introd. to *Prerogativa Regis: tertia lectura Roberti Constable* (1949), 20 n. 47. For this as the old 'common learning' see Spelman 142; but the readers were not unanimous (inf. M. McGlynn).

[48] *Delariver's Case* (1490) Trin. 5 Hen. VII, fo. 36, pl. 3, at fo. 37, *per* Townshend J.; cf. inconclusive discussion soon afterwards in the Inner Temple, *Moots*, 143-4, pl. 30.

about 1514 it was held by Fyneux CJ and his brethren in the King's Bench that the lord could not have the land while the term was running.[49] Spelman informs us that after Fyneux's death (in 1525) the decision was rejected by Fitzherbert J. (of the Common Pleas) and others.[50] Before the end of the reign, however, opinion had swung back in favour of the termor.[51] Part of the problem underlying this debate was to identify an appropriate remedy; but by 1534 even Fitzherbert J. was willing to allow the lessee to bring *quare ejecit* in the case where the reversion escheated to the lord, and to treat the allegation of a 'sale' in the writ as a non-traversable fiction.[52] Logic had led to uncomfortable results, and the willingness of even conservative judges to discard the old learning is fair proof of the increased status of the tenant for years.

The second difficulty concerned the effect on the lessee of a common recovery suffered by the lessor. Since a recovery depended on a supposed title paramount, it was not obvious how the termor could be helped. The action of *quare ejecit* provided a remedy against a purchaser from the lessor, but it was difficult to treat a recovery as tantamount to a sale, even fictionally.[53] The lessee could intervene pending the action, in which case execution of the recovery would be stayed by judgment until the expiry of the term;[54] but usually he would not have an opportunity to do so.[55] If his lease was in writing under seal, he could falsify the recovery by bringing covenant, and the view was expressed in 1492 that the termor under an informal lease should have the same remedy by means of ejectment.[56] But the more generous view did not prevail, and by the sixteenth century it was accepted that a collusive recovery would extinguish a term of years, saving to the termor his last crop.[57] Here the solution was found in Parliament, which in 1529

---

[49] *Anon.* (1513/14) Spelman 142 (dated 5 Hen. VIII), 144 (dated '15' Hen. VIII), 176; *Anon.* (*c.*1516) Chaloner 280, no. 6; B. & M. 183.   [50] Spelman 142; and see FNB 142B–C.

[51] *Anon.* (1544) Brooke Abr., *Leases*, pl. 58 (tr. B. & M. 185).

[52] FNB 198F, where he says that this seems reasonable, though the point is doubted. Cf. FNB 142C, where he says it seems reasonable that the lord should have the land because of his older title.

[53] FNB 198E was in favour, saying the words of sale were 'forsque del forme'.

[54] Statute of Gloucester, c. 11; *Moots*, 75, 101. Examples: *Earl of Shropshire* v. *Lord Grey of Wilton* (1505) CP 40/971, m. 352 (c.a.v. after receipt); *Osmond* v. *Gervys* (1512) CP 40/999, m. 437; *Wentworth* v. *Amyas* (1529) CP 40/1060, m. 158; *Anon.* (1529/30) Wm Yelv. 319, no. 15; *Symondys* v. *Petytt* (1535) CP 40/1086, m. 550; Pas. 27 Hen. VIII, fo. 7, pl. 20. In the similar case of *Ferrour* v. *Rodley* (1522) CP 40/1037, m. 439; Mich. 14 Hen. VIII, fo. 8, pl. 4 (119 Selden Soc. 105), Pollard J. was in favour of receiving the termor, while Fitzherbert J. was not.

[55] He had to act before the vouchee defaulted: *Anon.* (1529/30) Wm Yelv. 319 at 320, *per* Brudenell CJ.

[56] *Rede* v. *Capel* (1492) Pas. 7 Hen. VII, fo. 10, pl. 2. Perhaps he meant *quare ejecit*: FNB 198E. Note also Hil. 1 Hen. VII, fo. 9, pl. 7, *per* Bryan CJ.

[57] *Anon.* (1507) 2 Caryll 561, pl. 403; FNB 198E; Perk., sig. Oi. See also the Inner Temple discussion of the 1480s in *Moots*, 75 ('it would have been inconvenient for a person who had only a term, which is a mere chattel, to avoid a recovery which is real'). However a proposal to reform the law in 1511 was rejected on advice, probably from Fyneux CJ, that there was already a remedy at common law: *HLJ*, i. 15.

legislated to enable the termor to falsify a recovery in the same way as a free-holder.[58] Parliament further legislated in 1540 to protect those taking short leases from tenants in tail, or from other particular tenants, against eviction by those in reversion after the death of the lessors.[59] The statute was imperfectly drawn and occasioned much dispute over the effect of leases by tenants in tail.[60]

The third problem was that lessees had no protection against eviction by the king, where the king came into possession of the freehold by virtue of an inquisi-tion which made no mention of the lease, because 'their interest is but a chattel in the law ... and no estate of freehold'. This was remedied in 1548.[61]

It was generally accepted in our period that a lease for years was freely alienable, following much the same principles as applied to freehold. Little is known about the extent of sub-letting in practice, since it occurred off the manorial record,[62] but it is thought to have increased in the Tudor period as a result of the growing prac-tice of purchasing substantial leases as investments.[63] On the other hand, it was common for a landlord who wished to preserve a quasi-feudal control over his ten-antry to forbid sub-letting or assignment of smaller holdings without his leave,[64] and it was sometimes the practice to require the tenant to reside on the premises.[65] The lessor could not impose a general condition against alienation,[66] though he could restrain assignment to anyone other than the person or persons named in the covenant or condition, and either by covenant or condition could forbid assignment without his own leave.[67] Sometimes we meet with a covenant not to assign to anyone above the rank of yeoman or gentleman, which was presumably

[58] 21 Hen. VIII, c. 15. According to Fitzherbert's interpretation, this could be achieved by using *quare ejecit* or ejectment: FNB 198E, 220I. Thomas Moyle read on the statute in Gray's Inn (1533) BL MS. Hargrave 92, fo. 41.

[59] 32 Hen. VIII, c. 28. This only applied to leases for not more than 21 years, or three lives, and to land which had commonly been in lease for 20 years before the lease in question.

[60] *Earl of Bridgewater's Case* (1541) Dyer 48b; *Anon.* (1547) BL MS. Hargrave 4, fo. 99; Brooke Abr., *Acceptance*, pl. 19; *Baker* v. *Austen* (1555) Gell's reports, I, Pas. 1 & 2 Phil. & Mar., fo. 12; *Anon.* (1558) BL MS. Hargrave 4, fo. 134v; *Anon.* (1558) ibid., fo. 147v. The statute was the subject of readings by John Gosnold (Gray's Inn, 1542) BL MS. Hargrave 92, ff. 63–85; and William Symonds (Inner Temple, 1549) CUL MS. Ll. 3. 12, ff. 1–15v.

[61] 2 & 3 Edw. VI, c. 8, s. 1. This limb was the subject of readings by Reynold Corbet (Middle Temple, 1552) and John Ramsey (Gray's Inn, 1556).

[62] Note the remarks of Oestmann, *Lordship and Community,* 77–8; J. Whittle and M. Yates, 'Pays réel ou pays légal?' (2000) 48 *Agricultural History Rev.* 1–26, at 18–19.

[63] Kerridge, *Agrarian Problems,* 48–9; Dyer, *Lords and Peasants,* 214–16, 313–14; A. C. Jones in *The Peasant Land Market,* ed. Harvey, 242–3.

[64] Note also BL Add. Ch. 40283 (lessee of manor covenants not to sub-demise without licence, 1488).

[65] Du Boulay, 'Who were Farming the English Demesnes?', at 447–8. An example in the reports is *Chickeley's Case* (1553) Dyer 79a (lease of a parsonage by Clare Hall).

[66] Cf. John Gosnold's reading (Gray's Inn, 1542) BL MS. Hargrave 92, at fo. 75, where he says that a general condition is good.

[67] *Anon.* (1492) 1 Caryll 123, pl. 122, *per* Vavasour J.; *Parry* v. *Herbert* (1539) Dyer 45b; *Anon.* (1549) Dyer 66a, 79a; *Anon.* (1557) Dyer 152a (covenant not to assign except to A or B); *Anon.* (1558) BL MS.

an attempt to keep out major speculators.[68] It was not wholly clear whether restraints on assignment, if expressed as covenants,[69] passed with the land.[70] The obligation to pay rent certainly passed on assignment of the lease, so that the lessor could recover rent against the assignee by writ of debt, notwithstanding the want of privity;[71] and a grantee or devisee of the reversion likewise could bring debt on the lease.[72] However, the lessee could not by his own unilateral act cause the rent to be apportioned, and therefore if he assigned only part of the subject-matter of the lease he remained liable for the whole rent.[73] Covenants which ran with the land, such as a covenant to repair houses, could also be enforced against assignees.[74]

Although a lease could thus be assigned *inter vivos* or devised, it was in contemplation of law only a chattel, and therefore (according to the medieval learning) was not capable of assignment by way of settlement, which would result in a temporal division into present and future estates.[75] Towards the end of our period, however, we find a growing acceptance of the notion that a term of years could be settled by the lessee's will, a notion fortified by the broad language of the

Hargrave 4, fo. 128v (covenant not to assign except to his own wife or children); *Note* (1559) Gell's reports, II, fo. 76 (condition not to assign except to A). The law was the same with respect to leases for life: Brudenell's reading (Inner Temple, 1500) Port 177–8, no. 103.

[68] e.g. PRO Ancient Deeds C7162 (limitation to assigns not passing a yeoman's estate, 1496), C2404 (limitation to assigns below the rank of esquire, *c.*1530).

[69] For the principle that covenants in a lease passed with the land, see *Thirkill* v. *Gore* (1529) Spelman 75. A covenant to repair bound an assignee even without mention of assigns, because 'the covenant goes with the land': Yorke 201, no. 294 (tr.; so held in the Common Pleas).

[70] *Anon.* (1535/6) Caryll (Jun.) 397, no. 65; 413, no. 110 (question of construction); *Anon.* (1536) Dyer 13b; *Anon.* (1539) Dyer 45a (principle of construction only, that restraint on named lessee does not bind others); *Anon.* (1549) Dyer 66a; *Anon.* (1557) Dyer 152a (judges divided; but not clear whether a covenant or a condition); *Anon.* (1558) BL MS. Hargrave 4, ff. 125, 128v (executors bound). The difference between a condition and a covenant is fully discussed in *Docwra's Case* (1535) Trin. 27 Hen. VIII, fo. 14, pl. 6; Mich. 27 Hen. VIII, fo. 28, pl. 16; *Anon.* (1558) BL MS. Hargrave 4, fo. 128v; Gell's reports, II, ff. 41–42.

[71] *Ernley* v. *Garth* (1491) 1 Caryll 65; *Moots*, 261, pl. 78; Port 96, no. 27; *Anon.* (1498) Mich. 14 Hen. VII, fo. 4, pl. 9, *per* Bryan CJ; *Note* (*c.*1520/30) Yorke 231, no. 389. Cf. *Grove* v. *Bromwiche* (1558–9) CP 40/1176(1), m. 782 (debt against assignee of assignee of under-lease; demurrer to declaration).

[72] *Ernley* v. *Garth* (1490) CP 40/913, m. 411 (judgment for plaintiff); Pas. 5 Hen. VII, fo. 18, pl. 12; Port 96 at 97. Cf. *Ernley* v. *Garth* (no. 2) (1491–1500) CP 40/918, m. 335 (undetermined demurrer); 1 Caryll 65; last note. The plaintiff, John Ernley of Gray's Inn, was later CJCP. Cf. also Yorke 231, no. 389, where it is said that the grantee of the reversion may distrain for the rent but not bring debt.

[73] *Ryshton* v. *Cripce* (1531) KB 27/1076, m. 33; Spelman 16, 93, 290; Yorke 193, no. 267; Pollard 247–8, nos. 5–6; Dyer 4; Wm Yelv. 290, no. 1. There was no unanimity on this question.

[74] *Thirkill* v. *Gore* (1529) Spelman 75; *Anon.* (1533/4) Brooke Abr., *Covenant*, pl. 32; (1534/5) Caryll (Jun.) 413, no. 109. In Yorke 201, no. 294 (undated), it is said that this is so even if 'assigns' are not mentioned in the covenant.

[75] Moreover, Walter Hendley argued in Gray's Inn (*c.*1530) that a lease for years could not be granted to the use of someone in fee, because a lease was not 'real': BL MS. Harley 5103, fo. 85. A change of view may be discerned in *Anon.* (1559) Gell's reports, II, fo. 100 (tr. B. & M. 186–7), *per* Browne CJ and Weston J. (good remainder but destructible by particular tenant).

Statute of Wills.[76] In 1541, for instance, the prothonotary John Jenour devised the lease of a house to his wife for life, remainder to his son.[77] By 1550 a majority of judges allowed that a lease could be entailed, or settled with life estates and remainders, by means of a last will.[78] Yet a settlement of a term by devise did not have the same legal effect as a common-law setlement of the freehold, because the prevailing opinion until 1578 was that the first devisee took the whole of the outstanding term, and could therefore destroy the executory devise if he aliened in his lifetime.[79] It was held in Chancery by two successive lord chancellors that there was no equitable relief for the devisee in remainder if his expectation was thus destroyed.[80]

The principal restriction on a lessee's exercise of the attributes of ownership was that he was not permitted to waste the inheritance, since that belonged to the reversioner.[81] The relationship between lord and tenant was in this respect unaffected by the changes in the nature of leasehold, since the temporal limitation on the tenant's estate necessarily presupposed that the reversion should be preserved intact. Thus, although the tenant had an interest in the trees on his land during the term—so that the lessor could not fell them (without a reservation in the lease)—he was nevertheless unable to take them, unless they were felled by the lessor or by the wind.[82] The tenant was not even permitted to improve the tenement, for instance by carrying out internal alterations to a house in order to enlarge the rooms,[83] or by knocking down a ruined house,[84] without the lessor's consent. Likewise he could not alter irreversibly the course of husbandry, whether

[76] The older view had been challenged even before the statute, on the premise that wills should take effect according to the intention of the testator, but this was open to the objection that testators had no power to change the law: *Anon.* (1536) Dyer 7a. The later view was that a remainder could only be created in a term by devise and not by assignment *inter vivos*: *Anon.* (1568) Dyer 277a. But that point was left open in *Anon.* (1559) Gell's reports, II, fo. 100 (tr. B. & M. 186 at 187), *per* Browne J.

[77] PROB 11/29, fo. 81. The remainder was conditional upon the son, Robert, continuing his learning in the Temple.

[78] *Anon.* (1541) Brooke Abr., *Chattelles*, pl. 23 (tr. B. & M. 185); *Anon.* (1548) Brooke Abr., *Devise*, pl. 13 (tr. B. & M. 185–6); *Anon.* (1550) BL MS. Hargrave 4, fo. 116v (tr. B. & M. 186); *Anon.* (1553) Dalison's reports, BL MS. Harley 5141, fo. 6v. Cf. *Lord North* v. *Butts* (1557) CP 40/1164, m. 459; Dyer 139b at 140b ('a remainder of a term is not good').

[79] *Anon.* (1541) Brooke Abr., *Chattelles*, pl. 23 (tr. B. & M. 185); *Anon.* (1552) Dyer 74; *Anon.* (1559) Gell's reports, II, fo. 100 (tr. B. & M. 186–7); *Foster* v. *Foster* (1572) B. & M. 185. The opinion was reversed by *Weltden* v. *Elkington* (1578) B. & M. 188.

[80] B. & M. 185 (Wriothesley C.) and 186 n. 18 (Lord Rich C.).

[81] There are discussions of the law of waste in the readings by William Wadham (Lincoln's Inn, 1505) Taussig MS., fo. 200; and George Browne (Gray's Inn, 1547) BL MS. Hargrave 92, fo. 116v.

[82] Below, 735.

[83] *Abbot of Stratford Langthorne* v. *Pykeryng* (1494–7) CP 40/930, m. 323 (discontinued Pas. 1497); Mich. 10 Hen. VII, fo. 2, pl. 3, and fo. 5, pl. 7; 1 Caryll 375 (dated Trin. 1498).

[84] *Anon.* (1558) BL MS. Hargrave 4, fo. 144v; MS. Harley 1624, fo. 58. It was otherwise if he rebuilt, though if he built on a different site he needed the lessor's consent: *Trussell* v. *Maydeford* (1493) 1 Caryll 156 at 158, *per* Danvers J.

or not the result was an improvement. Converting a wood into arable was waste, and so was anything which damaged the soil in some permanent way, as by digging up or killing off thorns;[85] but uprooting slips of trees in arable land,[86] or ploughing up a meadow, or damaging crops, was not, because these had only a temporary effect.[87] Even draining fishponds and selling all the fish, without restocking, or replacing carp with roach, was held in 1558 not to be actionable waste.[88] In case of doubt, the lessor could insert conditions or covenants in the lease to prevent alterations in the course of husbandry or cutting wood, or even to require improvements.[89] A covenant to repair could also modify or clarify the operation of the law of waste by preventing the tenant from relying on an act of God,[90] or by limiting the scope of the repairs for which the tenant was to be responsible—for instance, to the outer covering of a house rather than its main timbers.[91]

A licence to occupy land for a fixed term might amount to a lease, provided that it gave exclusive occupation to the licensee; but a term of years was distinguished from a mere licence to use land or to take profits from it, without exclusive occupation, which at best was a covenant and might in some cases be revocable.[92]

[85] Yorke 208, no. 315, *per* Hesketh; cf. Thomas Gawdy's reading (Inner Temple, 1554) Cardiff Public Lib. MS. 3.38, fo. 36 (tr. 'an action lies for digging the land leased so that the soil is impaired; but it does not lie for ploughing the land, unless in the parts which are not apt to bear grain according to the custom of the country; if the lessee permits the land to lie fresh, or to be overgrown with thistles and bushes, it is waste').

[86] *Anon.* (1530) Yorke 209, no. 317 (as to 'slippes' which were not timber). If, however, the land was leased as 'wood', then it was waste to cut any little trees or slips: ibid., *per* Fitzherbert J.

[87] *Abbot of Stratford Langthorne* v. *Pykeryng* (1494) Mich. 10 Hen. VII, fo. 2, pl. 3 (tr. 'destruction of all the saffron heads of a saffron garden is not waste, nor is ploughing up a meadow, all of which is but bad husbandry, because they are things which may be done and undone by yearly manual labour'); *Malyverer* v. *Spynke* (1537) Dyer 35b (converting wood into arable is waste, but rooting up bushes, thorns, and furze is good husbandry and justifiable for fuel); CP 40/1089, m. 345 (demurrer but no judgment). For lopping and topping trees see *Samwell* v. *Johnson* (1547–8) Dyer 65a; CP 40/1134, m. 719 (pleads he lopped ash and elm in seasonable time to repair hedges; judgment for plaintifff on demurrer); *Anon.* (1553) Dyer 92a.

[88] *Anon.* (1558) BL MS. Hargrave 4, fo. 149–v, *per* Brooke CJ and Dyer J. However, it was a breach of an express condition not to spoil, waste, or destroy the fishponds.

[89] ibid. (as to a condition). For examples of covenants see Du Boulay, 'Who were Farming the English Demesnes?', at 447.

[90] *Colthirst* v. *Bejushin* (1550) Plowd. 21 at 29, *per* Saunders sjt. According to Browne J., however, it was waste if the lessee failed to repair storm damage: *Anon.* (1557/8) BL MS. Hargrave 4, fo. 133.

[91] e.g. BL Add. Ch. 39337 (1536): landlord to repair timbers, the tenant providing food and accommodation for his workmen; tenant to repair covering ('in tylyng, thakyng, splentyng, [and] cleyng'). Cf. covenants as to 'hornhigh': 119 Selden Soc. 51 (exception of 'thatche et hornehigh', 1520), 51 n. 1 (liability for 'hornehye', 1529); BL Add. Ch. 38695 ('walling, hornehy, heyging, and other closing', 1531).

[92] Pas. 10 Edw. IV, fo. 4, pl. 7, contd at fo. 5, pl. 11; Mich. 5 Hen. VII, fo. 1, pl. 1; *Note* (*c.*1520) Spelman 161, *per* Broke sjt; Thomas Moyle's reading (Gray's Inn, 1533) BL MS. Hargrave 92, fo. 41v (a licence to put in beasts for one year is not a lease; but a licence to occupy for one year 'a le meliour profit que il poet' is a lease).

A covenant to grant a lease was not itself a lease.[93] On the other hand, an informal agreement for a lease might amount to a lease even if the intended deed was never executed.[94]

TENANTS AT WILL

The security given to the leaseholder could not be extended to the tenant at will, for in his case the freeholder had parted with the possession only on the understanding that he could have it back on giving reasonable notice of his will and pleasure. The lessor could therefore re-enter at will; but an actual re-entry was required, not merely a determination of his will.[95] When the estate was determined by the lessor, the tenant was permitted time to remove his belongings, and to take his last crop (emblements), because he could not have known in advance when the end would come.[96] While in possession he could maintain trespass against strangers, and by 1524 it could even be argued that he was entitled to take timber for estovers.[97] But he obviously had no legal protection against eviction by his lessor, because the lessor was entitled to evict him at will.

It was extremely common for tenants to occupy land under running tenancies,[98] or under other informal arrangements with no agreed term, such as holding over after a formal lease. The courts were urged to interpret such arrangements if possible as leases from year to year rather than as tenancies at will, since this was more to the advantage of both parties,[99] though the position was not always clear. In 1505 a tenancy at will from year to year was held to be a tenancy at will, because it could hardly be a lease for years if the years were not specified.[100] However, this may have been a result of careless pleading, since the more usual course was to plead a lease for one year and thereafter from year to year at the will of the lessor,[101] or at the will of both parties.[102] In 1511, in a case pleaded in the latter form, it was argued that such an arrangement amounted to a succession of yearly terms, each requiring notice in the preceding year to determine it.[103] The point

---

[93] *Anon.* (1537/8) Brooke Abr., *Lease*, pl. 49. Cf. *Anon.* (1545) ibid., pl. 60 ('covenants and grants').

[94] *Anon.* (1550) BL MS. Hargrave 4, fo. 111v; Dal. 7, pl. 2 (abr. Moo. 8).

[95] Before re-entry, therefore, he could not sue the tenant for holding over: *Scrope* v. *Hyk* (1511) 2 Caryll 618; Spelman 135 at 136, pl. 1.   [96] 94 Selden Soc. 183.

[97] *Abbot of Bury St Edmunds* v. *Tyes* (1524) CP 40/1044, m. 537d (trespass to trees; pleads that plaintiff's tenant at will commanded him to cut two ash trees as ploughbote; demurrer). The tenant at will was not liable for waste: Yorke 208, no. 316.

[98] See Pollard J. in *Burgh* v. *Potkyn* (1522) Mich. 14 Hen. VIII, fo. 10, pl. 6 (119 Selden Soc. 132).

[99] A tenant at will was entitled to emblements, which could be very detrimental to the lord.

[100] *Anon.* (1505) 2 Caryll 457; Mich. 21 Hen. VII, fo. 38, pl. 47.

[101] e.g. *Burton* v. *Harding* (1507–8) CP 40/980, m. 434 (imparlance).

[102] e.g. *Essex* v. *Freer* (1507) CP 40/981, m. 150 (action confessed).

[103] *Scrope* v. *Hyk* (1511) CP 40/995, m. 429; 2 Caryll 621.

was made the subject of a leading case in the Common Pleas in 1522. It had arisen as a technical question, namely whether a lease for one year, and then from year to year at the will of both parties, would support an action of waste in a wood 'which he holds for a term of years' (*quem tenet ad terminum annorum*). The tenancy had in fact been running for thirty years, but, as Fitzherbert J. observed, the mere effluxion of time could not turn a lease at will into a term of years. There was no doubt that there was a lease for the first year, but if that was the only term of years the writ should have said 'held' (*tenuit*). Pollard J. expressed a worry at the 'inconvenience' which would be caused if such a tenancy were not held to be a good lease for years, and thought it sufficient if the end of the term was ascertainable before it came. Brudenell CJ agreed, but the other two judges, Broke and Fitzherbert JJ, took the older view that beyond the first year there was only a tenancy at will.[104] And so the question was left unsettled. The form of pleading was nevertheless very common, and suggests that periodic tenancies of this kind were in practice widely used.[105]

Besides tenants under running yearly tenancies, the most important kinds of tenant at will were the beneficiary under a use,[106] and the copyholder.[107] Both acquired legal protection at much the same period, though in different circumstances and for different reasons.[108]

MANORIAL TENANTS BY COPY OF COURT ROLL

Customary tenure was still extremely widespread. Though taking various forms, and known by different local names,[109] most varieties were now classified by lawyers under the general description of tenancy by copy of court roll.[110] It did

[104] *Burgh* v. *Potkyn* (1522) CP 40/1036, m. 319; Mich. 14 Hen. VIII, fo. 10, pl. 6 (119 Selden Soc. 125); Spelman 136, pl. 3; 120 Selden Soc. 82.

[105] Six examples were noted in the Common Pleas rolls for 1535 alone. Three were mentioned in declarations in debt for rent: *Bay* v. *Rolf* (1535) CP 40/1085(1), m. 105; *Lamberde* v. *Walkotte* (1535) CP 40/1086, m. 559d; *Stokton* v. *Isodde* (1535) CP 40/1087, m. 116. The other three were mentioned in pleadings as to title: *Bukland* v. *Sharp* (1535) CP 40/1085(2), m. 156 (replevin for damage feasant; plaintiff sets out lease from third party in reply to avowry); *Egerton* v. *Dex* (1535) CP 40/1086, m. 644 (pleaded in trespass); *Beaumount* v. *Thakwro* (1535) CP 40/1087, m. 333 (pleaded in trespass).

[106] More strictly, he was a tenant at sufferance, or even a trespasser: Hil. 15 Hen. VII, fo. 2, pl. 4; Trin. 15 Hen. VII, fo. 12, pl. 23; *Dod* v. *Chyttynden* (1502) 2 Caryll 395 at 396. See further below, ch. 35.

[107] He held 'at the will of the lord according to the custom of the manor': next section.

[108] Note, however, Serjeant Knightley's suggestion that the copyholder had a use (albeit not a trust): *The Serjeants' Case* (1531) Wm Yelv. 294 at 299.

[109] Kerridge, *Agrarian Problems*, 35–41; Harvey, 'Forms of Tenure' in *The Peasant Land Market*, 328–38, especially at 329–34. Cf. Litt. s. 80 (tr. 'in various lordships and in various manors there are many and various customs in such cases'). Tenancy by the virge was still common.

[110] The word 'copyhold' is rarely found in legal texts before the end of the period, doubtless because it is not French: but see e.g. 1 Ric. III, c. 4 (where it occurs also in the French version: *SR*, ii. 479); Yorke 156 (heading); 2 & 3 Edw. VI, c. 8 (also 'customary hold'); 1 Mar. I, sess. 2, c. 12, s. 7 ('copy or customary holds');

not greatly matter whether the customary tenant actually possessed a copy of the court roll or not,[111] since his tenancy was governed by the same customs whether or not he had a copy as evidence.[112] According to the common law as enshrined in Littleton, the tenant by copy held 'at the will of the lord according to the custom of the manor'. Such a tenant could not alien his land directly, but only by surrendering it to the lord on trust to admit the grantee;[113] and that is why the grantee's title was dependent on the admission as recorded on the court roll. Moreover, according to Littleton, such a tenant could not sue or be sued for his tenement by the king's writ, but had to seek his remedy in the lord's court.[114] Littleton added that the lord would not break a reasonable custom in such a case; and it seems in reality to have become uncommon by 1500 for copyholds to be seized into the lord's hands as forfeited.[115] If the lord did behave unreasonably, it is clear that protection was routinely available in Chancery by the end of the fifteenth century,[116] though some lawyers denied its correctness.[117] And by 1484 Parliament was prepared to recognize copyhold as a sufficient landowning qualification for jury service in the tourn.[118] Yet the precise status of a copyholder at common law was still unsettled, and had perhaps remained so because copyholders as a class were still mostly smallholders with no taste for expensive litigation against their local superiors.[119]

Anon. (1553) BL MS. Add. 24845, ff. 20v ('copihold'), 21 ('copieholder'). It is more often found in English bills: e.g. C. M. Gray, Copyhold, Equity, and the Common Law (1963), 185, 188, 194.

[111] Customary tenure 'without copy' (sine copia) was still quite common in the time of Henry VIII: Hoskins, The Age of Plunder, 61. Note also Alman v. Saunder (1530) CP 40/1067, m. 702 (customary tenancy transferred by entry in 'covent boke' of abbot of Buckfast).

[112] See [J. Fitzherbert], The Boke of Surveyeng and Improumentes (1523), ff. 25v–26. Littleton's definition of tenant by copy of court roll (Litt. s. 73) does not mention possession of a copy as being of the essence but only as explaining the name.

[113] This was a 'trust' recognized by the common law, to the extent that the lord could not validly admit someone to a larger estate than that specified by the surrenderor: Constable's Case (1555) Co. Litt. 59b. The rule applied also to uses, so that a use could not be raised by the bargain and sale of a copyhold without a surrender: Anon. (1551) BL MS. Hargrave 4, fo. 118. Likewise, a fictitious recovery of copyhold land in the manorial court, to effect a resettlement, had to be followed by a surrender: Anon. (1547) Dal. 2, pl. 4.

[114] Litt. ss. 73–7; tr. in Kerridge, Agrarian Problems, 138–40; B. & M. 200–1. See also Yorke 156, no. 176.

[115] Dyer, Lords and Peasants, 294–5. However, forfeiture for waste or non-repair was not unknown in the sixteenth century: e.g. BL Add. Ch. 45559 (copyhold forfeited for felling ash trees and failing to repair, 1555).

[116] See Gray, Copyhold, Equity, and the Common Law, 23–51. Cases are also found in the Requests and Star Chamber: ibid. 51–3. The availability of a remedy in Chancery was accepted by 1454: B. & M. 200.

[117] In The Serjeants' Case (1531) Wm Yelv. 294 at 299, Serjeant Knightley said that a subpoena would not lie against the lord because there was no trust or confidence, the tenant having consented to take his tenancy at the will of the lord. [118] 1 Ric. III, c. 4; Port 121.

[119] This thesis is advanced by Harvey, The Peasant Land Market, 328–9. See also Hoskins, The Age of Plunder, 60–5. However, investment in copyholds by city merchants and gentlemen was not unknown: Jones in The Peasant Land Market, ed. Harvey, 234–5.

It was said that the copyholder had a kind of seisin, a word regularly used in pleading copyhold estates;[120] and he could pray aid of his lord if sued in the royal courts.[121] But the copyholder was not seised of a free tenement, and was even regarded by some as having no more than a chattel.[122] On the other hand, copyholds were in practice increasingly treated as family estates extending beyond a particular tenant's lifetime, secured by the expedient of a surrender and admittance to the use of a family settlement or will.[123] Copyhold customs in some parts of the country permitted more or less automatic inheritance and free alienation, like freehold,[124] perhaps even the right to fell timber.[125] Yet copyhold interests were not governed by the common-law rules of real property. They were in theory dependent upon the customs of each individual manor, and these, however homogeneous they might have become, were not formally known to the judges but had to be ascertained from the manorial court rolls.[126] The extent to which the common law may have begun to control the lord and to protect the tenant, before the time of Coke, has in consequence been a matter of considerable controversy.[127] Tawney was so bewildered by the problem that he took refuge in equivocation: 'one must reconcile a good deal of insecurity with a good deal of protection'.[128] More recently it has been asserted that the copyholder was protected against his lord at common law, by means of the action of trespass, at

[120] *Tropnell* v. *Kyllyk* (1505) CP 40/974, m. 445; 2 Caryll 489, 492–3 (plea that copyholder was 'seised and possessed according to the custom of the manor'); *Brooke* v. *Payntour* (1526) CP 40/1050, m. 415 ('(tr.) seised as of fee at the will of the lord according to the custom of the manor'); Gray's Inn moot (1530s) MS. Rawlinson C.705, fo. 126 (tr. 'A man may be seised of lands held by copy of court roll to the use of another'); *Warreyn* v. *Whyker* (1552–3) CP 40/1154, m. 738 ('(tr.) seised as of freehold for life according to the custom of the manor').

[121] *Anon.* (1500) Trin. 15 Hen. VII, fo. 10, pl. 13; *Anon.* (1535) Mich. 27 Hen. VIII, fo. 28, pl. 15 (both cases where aid was prayed of the king).

[122] See *Anon.* (1558) BL MS. Hargrave 4, fo. 132v (remainder for life in copyhold destroyed by forfeiture of prior life estate, (tr.) 'inasmuch as it is only a chattel and *de minimis non curat lex*'). Cf. 2 & 3 Edw. VI, c. 8, which distinguishes the termor as having a chattel and the copyholder as having 'a customary hold and no estate of freehold'.

[123] e.g. L. R. Poos and L. Bonfield, *Select Cases in Manorial Courts 1250-1550* (114 Selden Soc.; 1998), pp. cxiv, 38–40 (a sophisticated copyhold settlement of 1483). Examples of admittances to the use of a will: BL Add. Ch. 48483 (1487), 41492B (1538); Poos and Bonfield, *Select Cases*, pp. cxl–cxli (deathbed transfers, 1484, 1497). Copyhold entails were not fully accepted, because there could not be an immemorial custom to follow a statute of 1285: *Anon.* (1545/8) Wm Yelv. 342, no. 62. Nor could a copyhold estate be barred by common recovery in the central courts: below, 695.

[124] Poos and Bonfield, *Select Cases*, pp. xcix–cxii. For an apparent difference between a sample of Norfolk manors (where copyholds were inheritable and freely alienable) and a sample from Berkshire (where copyholds were held for life or lives) see Whittle and Yates, '*Pays réel* or *pays légal*?', at 8, 12. The authors recognize, however, that the distinction may relate more to the way records were kept than to the reality.   [125] *Anon.* (1550) BL MS. Hargrave 4, fo. 109v; Dal. 8, pl. 8.

[126] This is explicitly stated in *Anon.* (1558) BL MS. Hargrave 4, ff. 126v–127, *per* Brooke CJ (as to a question of inheritance, tr. 'You must search the court rolls...and not ask anything of us about it').

[127] For older views see 94 Selden Soc. 184 n. 5.

[128] R. H. Tawney, *The Agrarian Problem in the Sixteenth Century* (1912), 292.

least since the end of the fifteenth century, and that his security of tenure 'was not agitated in the courts in the sixteenth and seventeenth centuries for the simple reason that the question had been settled long before'.[129] The assertion rested on two dicta in the year books of Edward IV, both admittedly explicit,[130] yet 'as obiter as dicta could be'.[131] The dicta should be regarded as signs of a change in thinking about copyhold rather than a change in legal practice, for the manuscript evidence suggests that common-law protection was not fully established until just after our period.

There is no known reported case before the second half of the sixteenth century in which a copyholder successfully maintained trespass against his lord. It was, however, considered possible by the beginning of the century for the tenant to plead a copyhold estate by way of defence to an action of trespass brought by the lord, so long as it was supported by a custom general to the whole manor and not particular to his estate.[132] This had first been judicially approved in 1491, on the footing that the tenant by copy was not merely a tenant at will but a tenant at will according to the custom of the manor.[133] An immemorial custom had the force of law, and a manorial custom had as much force as any other—though customs might just as well favour the lord, and in some cases a lord who had ousted his tenant replied to a plea of copyhold by pleading a custom of forfeiture.[134] The plea rolls show that legal difficulties often arose when tenants tried to frame pleas of copyhold, but the demurrers are difficult to interpret and probably do not represent a substantive doubt.[135] If the copyholder could in theory plead against the

[129] Kerridge, *Agrarian Problems*, 74. This passage provoked a storm of criticism from legal historians: see M. J. Prichard, [1971] *CLJ* 158–60; D. E. C. Yale, 86 *LQR* 404–6; J. L. Barton, 86 *LQR* 618–19.

[130] *Anon.* (1467) Mich. 7 Edw. IV, fo. 19, pl. 16, *per* Danby CJ; tr. in B. & M. 201; *Anon.* (1482) Hil. 21 Edw. IV, fo. 80, pl. 27, *per* Bryan CJ. These cases are cited in Litt. s. 77; but the citations are an interpolation in the 1530 edn.   [131] F. W. Maitland, 7 *LQR* 175.

[132] Litt. s. 82 (tr. 'the custom of the manor in some cases may help him bar his lord in an action of trespass'); *Earl of Devon* v. *Cole* (1503) CP 40/963, m. 355 (lord replies that he had re-entered; issue on the re-entry); *Prioress of Amesbury* v. *Bryne* (1505) CP 40/973, m. 550 (lady replies *de injuria*); *Tropnell* v. *Kyllyk* (1505–7) 2 Caryll 489; CP 40/974, m. 445 (demurrer but no judgment); *Anon.* (1506) 2 Caryll 490, pl. 351B; *Prior of Nostell* v. *Wrayth* (1507) CP 40/978, m. 418 (lord pleads surrender). These were all trespass cases.

[133] *Anon.* (1491) 1 Caryll 51, pl. 49. For an issue of fact joined by a manorial lord on the footing that the copyholder defendant was never seised, see *Abbot of Ramsey* v. *Skecher* (1530) CP 40/1067(a), m. 94.

[134] *Arundell* v. *Squyer* (1506) CP 40/975, m. 355 (lord alleges custom to oust non-residents); *Long* v. *Long* (1524) CP 40/1045, m. 411 (lord alleges custom to oust widow who remarries); *Chapell* v. *Nichols* (1525) CP 40/1047, m. 306 (custom of forfeiture for waste pleaded in rejoinder); *Danvers* v. *Henne* (1531) CP 40/1071, m. 796 (lord alleges custom to oust non-residents).

[135] e.g. *Tropnell* v. *Kyllyk* (1505–7) CP 40/974, m. 445 (above); *Saye* v. *Penreth* (1516) CP 40/1016, m. 517d (pleads demise by plaintiff according to custom of manor; judgment for plaintiff on demurrer); *Gilberd* v. *Toker* (1520) CP 40/1030, m. 444 (pleads demise by plaintiff's steward according to custom of manor; plaintiff replies that he gave the steward contrary instructions; demurrer); *Scullard* v. *Tarrant* (1550–1) CP 40/1144A, m. 160 (demurrer to evidence, in trespass by the lord's freehold grantee, showing that the lord had granted a copyhold to the defendant). Similar difficulties arose in

lord, *a fortiori* rival copyhold tenants of the same lord could litigate in trespass at common law.[136]

It was another matter to allow an action against the lord, in view of the position as stated in Littleton that such suits were outside the jurisdiction of the common-law courts. Although the fifteenth-century dicta already mentioned supported such an action, and apparently Fitzherbert J. added the weight of his support in 1529,[137] its availability was not established during the first half of the sixteenth century. Copyholders seeking redress in Chancery around 1500 are found complaining of the lack of a remedy against the lord at common law.[138] This might have been dismissed as mere form if examples of such actions could be found in the plea rolls; but they can not. There are indeed instances in the 1520s of actions by a copyholder against a servant of the lord, who relied on the lord's freehold, where issue was joined without demur.[139] These may indicate a further step towards protection of the copyholder, since in 1506 the defendant's demurrer in a similar case had effectively stopped the action.[140] But actions of trespass against the lord himself there are not; and in 1526 an attempt to bring an action on the case against the lord, in the nature of mort d'ancestor, for refusing to admit the plaintiff as heir according to the custom, likewise came to grief with an undetermined demurrer.[141]

At about the same time, John Rastell reiterated the Littletonian doctrine that if the lord ousted the tenant by copy of court roll the latter had no remedy but to sue to the lord by petition.[142] A few years later, in 1531, the question was made the subject of the serjeants' case,[143] and was fully argued by the eleven new serjeants.

replevin: *Alygh* v. *Sherfold* (1542) CP 40/1113, m. 427 (copyhold pleaded against lord's bailiff; demurrer); *Morefewe* v. *Blomefeld* (1546–7) CP 40/1130, m. 718 (sim.); cf. *Hopkyns* v. *Guyer* (1551) CP 40/1148, m. 857 (verdict for plaintiff in similar case).

[136] e.g. *Berkeley* v. *Wood* (1535) CP 40/1085(2), m. 153 (conflicting admissions to copyholds; judgment for plaintiff after verdict); *Shirclyff* v. *Bromeley* (1535) ibid., m. 441 (likewise, in replevin); *Gue* v. *Milward* (1543) CP 40/1117, m. 337 (conflicting admissions; issue on custom for widows to hold over). Cf. earlier difficulties in *Whytton* v. *Broune* (1515) CP 40/1009, m. 595 (undetermined demurrer to plea); *Smoker* v. *Tommes* (1511) CP 40/995, m. 410 (plea of copyhold title, and that plaintiff came in by later title; held bad on demurrer); *Burton* v. *Burton* (1525) CP 40/1047, m. 339 (copyhold pleaded against lord's lessee; judgment for plaintiff on demurrer).

[137] *Anon.* (1529) Pollard 274–5, no. 68; B. & M. 202. The reporter added a 'query'.

[138] Gray, *Copyhold, Equity, and the Common Law*, 58; E. B. Fryde, *Peasants and Landlords in Later Medieval England* (1996), 240–1. Gray (at pp. 59, 198–9) detects a possible change in the time of Henry VIII.

[139] *Grace* v. *Gryffyth* (1523) CP 40/1041, m. 502d (issue on copyhold tenure); *Chapell* v. *Nichols* (1525) CP 40/1047, m. 306 (issue on licence to commit waste).

[140] *Bastard* v. *Johnson* (1506–9) CP 40/978, m. 599 (no judgment). Cf. *Wetheryge* v. *Lake* (1551) CP 40/1147A, m. 643 (demurrer to replication setting out copyhold title against lord's freehold grantee).

[141] *Gatacre* v. *Dean and Chapter of Lichfield* (1526) CP 40/1049, m. 631.

[142] *Exposiciones Terminorum Legum Anglorum* (c.1525), fo. 100v.

[143] It was the custom after a call of serjeants to appoint a difficult case to be argued by all the new serjeants, to display their learning.

Six serjeants argued that the lord could not oust his tenant, because it would be contrary to his own grant. The tenant had an inheritance according to the custom, and the custom was binding on the lord, so that the tenant had a right of entry and a right to the profits even though he did not have the freehold. Upon a conveyance by surrender and admittance, according to Cholmley and Audley, the lord was 'merely an instrument' to pass the estate. However, they were less clear as to the evicted tenant's remedy, and only two of the serjeants (Baldwin and Audley) went so far as to hold that trespass lay against the lord for taking the profits.[144] The opposing serjeants argued that the custom only operated within the manor, that there could not be two fee simples in the same land, and that the tenant had accepted the tenancy on the terms that he could be evicted at the absolute will of the lord. No judgment is reported on the point.[145] That it was made the main point for the serjeants' case shows that it was still considered to be controversial and unsettled. About ten years later an elementary introduction to the law reported that men of 'learning and prudency' were to be found on both sides of the question, which was still *sub judice*.[146] This may possibly refer to a dispute in the king's Council around that time. No report of that case has been found, but it is referred to in a revealing passage in Gell's reports in 1544:[147]

Note that it was said by Shelley J. that the lord by copy of court roll can put out his tenant at will, and the tenant at will shall have no remedy against him: for he cannot have any action against him. And if all the books are looked at, including Littleton, Bracton, and the *Natura Brevium*, and other old records, and they are well noted and construed, I doubt not that the better opinion is that the lord may oust him. I have seen tenants sue in such cases for a remedy, and they could have none. If it were to be proved by reason it would be hard to prove that the tenants should have any remedy.

Browne J. to the contrary. In the present king's time this matter was appointed to be argued, but on account of the mischief which would have ensued if it had been adjudged as your opinion is, a command was sent by the king's Council that it should not be argued.

Baldwin CJ confirmed this, and was against Shelley in it. But query what the law is.

It seems from this passage that the better opinion in the 1540s continued to deny an action for the copyholder, and that the Council had been worried that the reassertion of what was undoubted law might put wrong ideas into the heads of manorial lords. The Council had taken the remarkable step of stopping the argument rather than overturning the old law; and therefore legal opinion in the 1550s

[144] The question was not in issue, since the point arose upon an avowry for damage feasant.

[145] *The Serjeants' Case* (1531) Wm Yelv. 294, no. 3. Only four serjeants were reported in favour of the lord (identified as Lord Bray), but that is because Mountagu spoke so softly that he was inaudible; the arguments were strictly pro and con in order of seniority.

[146] [?R. Taverner], *Institutions of the Lawes of England* (c.1540), sig. A7; pr. 94 Selden Soc. 186.

[147] Gell's reports, I, fo. 22v (tr. B. & M. 202). Cf. also the fuller passage by Shelley J. to the same effect, at fo. 51v (tr. 94 Selden Soc. 186).

continued to treat the matter as doubtful.[148] At much the same time, however, Parliament gave the copyholder protection against eviction by the Crown acting under an inquisition which omitted to mention the copyhold estate.[149] A general remedy had to await the flowering of ejectment, which enabled an action to be founded on the possession enjoyed by a copyholder's lessee.[150]

ENCLOSURES

The law could react to social changes by developing new remedies, but it proved virtually powerless to control general changes in the course of husbandry which were perceived by intellectuals as damaging to the common weal. The enclosure movement had begun before our period and would continue long after. Enclosure was the appropriation of a piece of manorial waste or common land, by planting hedges, so that it could be exploited more effectively as a separate entity. Whether or not it was an 'approvement' sanctioned by medieval legislation,[151] enclosure was often done by consent and might be seen as 'a sensible and reasonable plan of agrarian improvement'.[152] The value of the land was greatly improved by enclosure, and the displaced commoners could be given their own farms by way of compensation. On the other hand, when it involved the conversion of arable land into pasture, the practice led to unemployment, depopulation, and a decay of agriculture, and for those reasons it was often regarded with suspicion or even warm opposition.[153] Conversion to pasture was a strong temptation, where practicable, since sheep provided a better return than crops and were therefore good investments for merchants and even lawyers:[154] for instance, in 1490 Mr Justice Townshend owned 12,000 of them in Norfolk.[155] The interests of investors led to 'engrossing', that is, the multiplication of farms in the same hands, which further increased the same evils. There was also a good deal of illegal enclosure, as appears from consequent legal proceedings. Such proceedings could take a number of forms. Commoners were entitled to break down the offending hedges themselves,[156]

---

[148] e.g. *Anon.* (1550) BL MS. Hargrave 4, fo. 109v (concerning the validity of a custom for the copyholder to fell timber), where Mountagu CJ suggested a legislative solution. According to Gray, *Copyhold, Equity, and the Common Law*, 61-4, the first clear statement in favour of the copyholder's action is found in 1564.   [149] 2 & 3 Edw. VI, c. 8, which helped lessees in the same way: above, 639.

[150] Gray, *Copyhold, Equity, and the Common Law*, 65-6 (dating it to the 1570s and 1580s).

[151] Merton, c. 4; Westminster II, c. 46. There could be no approvement where the common was without stint: Yorke 226, no. 370.

[152] J. Thirsk, 'Enclosing and Engrossing' in *Agrarian History of England and Wales* iv. *1500-1640*, ed. J. Thirsk (1967), ch. 4, at 201; repr. in *Agricultural Change: Policy and Practice* (1990), ch. 2. References below are to the former.   [153] See e.g. Starkey, *Dialogue*, ed. Mayer, 113-14.

[154] Merchants were specifically mentioned in a bill of 1515: Thirsk, 'Enclosing and Engrossing', 215.

[155] Moreton, *The Townshends and their World*, 164.

[156] Yorke 226, no. 370. Some justifications by commoners: *Prior of Worcester* v. *Hyll* (1494) 1 Caryll 239 (breaking hedges); *Prior of St Katharine outside Lincoln* v. *26 husbandmen of Skeldingthorp* (1503)

or they could bring an action on the case,[157] or initiate an indictment.[158] Copyholders were driven to seek redress in Chancery or Star Chamber. Occasionally there might even be disputes between neighbouring lords.[159]

At the beginning of the 1484 parliament, the lord chancellor mentioned enclosures and depopulation as evils to be tackled,[160] but no legislative measures were passed until the following reign. After a preliminary measure limited to the Isle of Wight, a general statute was passed in 1489.[161] The preamble recited the prejudice to the common weal caused by pulling down houses and towns and converting tilled land to pasture, but the statute dealt only with the first problem. Anyone who owned a farm with at least twenty acres of land lying in tillage or husbandry was to maintain the houses and buildings necessary to support the tillage and husbandry, upon pain that the lord would be entitled to half the profits of the land until the building or repairs were carried out. This was to attack the effect rather than the cause, and it does not seem to have been very successful. The evils of engrossing farms and converting tillage to pasture were addressed by a proclamation of 1514, followed by a temporary statute of 1515, made perpetual in 1516.[162] Although the statute may have been prompted by new fears about a dearth of grain, it recited the same two evils as in 1489 and this time dealt with the second one. Enclosed lands which had been commonly used in tillage were to be restored to tillage, according to the usage of the region, under the like penalty as in the 1489 act. The statute was not to extend to parks and enclosed marshes. The following year Wolsey C. decided on more active measures. General commissions of enquiry were appointed—a new Domesday—and in 1518 their detailed findings were returned before the judges in the Exchequer Chamber.[163] The judges pointed out that the Chancery procedure could only be used in respect of land held immediately of the king, because in other cases the enforcement was by statute given to the lord. The proceedings then hit a further difficulty, in that most offences were within the general statutory pardon of 1515, and so the king could only recover profits since the pardon.[164] But Wolsey C., without statutory sanction, made a

CP 40/962, m. 401 (breaking hedges); *Hastynges v. Turvyle and 24 husbandmen of Normanton Turvyle* (1503) ibid., m. 535 (trespass to trees and shoots); *Nowers v. Cobbe* (1503) ibid., m. 549 (trespass to trees).

[157] e.g. *Wulward v. Ingleby* (1537) KB 27/1105, m. 88 (issue on the prescription for pasture).

[158] See e.g. *R. v. Bartylmewe* (1506) KB 27/979, Rex m. 3 (defendant discharged because indictment did not state whether the common was used by the free tenants of the manor or the tenants at will).

[159] e.g. as to neighbouring rights of common: *Anon.* (1518) Yorke 225, no. 369.

[160] Thirsk, 'Enclosures and Engrossing', 214.

[161] 4 Hen. VII, c. 19. The Isle of Wight was singled out in the earlier statute (4 Hen. VII, c. 16) for defence reasons: Hoskins, *The Age of Plunder*, 66.

[162] 6 Hen. VIII, c. 5; 7 Hen. VIII, c. 1; Heinze, *Proclamations of the Tudor Kings*, 94–8; *Tudor Royal Proclamations*, i. 122–3, no. 75. Commentators have assumed the proclamation antedates the first statute.

[163] I. S. Leadam, *The Domesday of Inclosures 1517–18* (1897); 2 Caryll 721. See also Pollard, *Wolsey*, 85–7.

[164] *Case of Enclosures* (Mich. 1518) 2 Caryll 723. Wolsey C.'s decree was made on 12 July 1518.

general decree in Chancery that those who pleaded the pardon should nevertheless restore converted land to tillage, on pain of a £100 fine. It does not seem to have been effective, because a proclamation of 1526, referring to Wolsey's 'industry and diligence' in the matter, admitted that 'very little reformation thereof as yet is had or made'.[165] As Holdsworth pointed out, the root of the problem was that the governing classes were themselves the principal delinquents.[166]

In 1534 the campaign was renewed with a statute limiting the number of sheep which any one farmer was permitted to own to 2,400 and forbidding the occupation of more than two farms, or the holding of farms by non-residents.[167] Cromwell boasted to the king that this was the most beneficial measure since the time of King Brut, though it had been somewhat diluted in the Commons[168]— probably after reference to the judges[169]—and it fell far short of Cromwell's overall scheme for redressing the decay of husbandry.[170] The only further reform effected by Cromwell came in 1536, when the problem detected by the judges in 1518 was removed by allowing the king to enforce the statutes if the mesne lord failed to act.[171] A further onslaught on enclosures at the beginning of Edward VI's reign led to the appointment of a new commission in 1548, a new tax on sheep, and a supporting proclamation in 1549.[172] But this time there was something of a retreat when it was perceived that the measures had given encouragement to rioters and rebels, purporting to use their common-law rights to abate enclosures, and it became necessary to threaten dire legal consequences for those who 'presumed to pluck his highness's sword out of his hand' by pulling down enclosures without judicial sanction.[173] A new statute for restoring land to tillage, with more elaborate savings, followed in 1552,[174] and another commission in 1555. Proceedings arising from these various statutes may be traced in the records of the Court of Exchequer,[175] the other central courts, and even manorial courts; but the net effect on enclosures seems to have been very limited.

[165] *Tudor Royal Proclamations*, i. 155, no. 110. This heralded another Chancery campaign, which ended with Wolsey's fall in 1529: ibid. 163–4, nos. 113–14; and pp. 174–5, no. 119; 186, no. 123.

[166] Holdsworth, *HEL*, v. 366.

[167] 25 Hen. VIII, c. 13. The limit was two thousand, counting 120 to the hundred, excluding lambs.

[168] Elton, *Reform and Renewal*, 90–1, 101–6; Lehmberg, *Reformation Parliament*, 188–9. A number of provisos were added in the Commons—the chief of which exempted tenants in fee, in dower, or in curtesy, keeping sheep upon their demesnes—and it was a Commons amendment which led to the thousands being reckoned by the 'long hundred' (six score).

[169] Elton, *Reform and Renewal*, 103–4. For a paper listing objections to the bill, see *LP*, vii. 58.

[170] See Elton, *Reform and Renewal*, 100–1.

[171] 27 Hen. VIII, c. 22. This, however, only applied to certain counties (mostly in the Midlands).

[172] Jordan, *Edward VI*, 410–16, 419–23, 428–32, 436–7; *Tudor Royal Proclamations*, i. 427–9, no. 309; 451–3, no. 327.

[173] *Tudor Royal Proclamations*, i. 461–4, nos. 333–4; 474–6, nos. 340–1. For the riots see J. Loach, *Edward VI* (1999), 59–69. The common law had permitted self-help: above, 650 n. 156.

[174] 5 & 6 Edw. VI, c. 5. Cf. 3 & 4 Edw. VI, c. 3 (improvement of commons and wastes).

[175] The 1533 and 1552 statutes were enforceable by common informers.

35

Uses, Wills, and Fiscal Feudalism

ANOTHER prolonged discussion, culminating in a more fundamental and far-reaching reform, concerned another class of tenant altogether, the tenant by knight-service. Here the debate concerned a different aspect of feudal tenure, the valuable 'incidents' which belonged to the lord on the descent of such a tenancy to an heir. The lord was entitled to wardship and marriage if the heir was under the age of 21,[1] and relief when the heir assumed his inheritance. The king as lord was entitled in addition to primer seisin and livery, without respect to the age of the heir, and priority over other lords in claiming wardship (prerogative wardship).[2] These profits were casual; but for a lord with numerous tenants in chivalry, such as the king, they fell in frequently enough to form a substantial part of their revenue. Their incidence, however, was becoming drastically reduced as a result of the growing practice of granting lands to trustees, or feoffees to uses. Since lands vested in multiple feoffees never descended to heirs,[3] the incidents of descent could never attach. The consequent loss of revenue, especially to the king, who was always lord and never tenant, occasioned a prolonged counter-attack on the use. Seen from above, the feoffment to uses might well be regarded as a scheme for avoiding feudal revenue. But the story was complicated by the fact that uses were not designed solely, or even primarily, for the avoidance of tenurial incidents. One of their main objects was to give landowners the power to devise or charge their lands by will,[4] without relinquishing any of their powers of ownership while living. Uses also gave them greater flexibility in making family settlements unencumbered by dower,[5]

---

[1] i.e. in the case of a male heir. A female heir was in ward only if she was under 14 at the time of the descent, though (if she was) the lord retained his rights of wardship until she was 16: Westminster I, c. 22; Litt. s. 103.

[2] There is a full discussion of the king's prerogative incidents in Constable's reading (Lincoln's Inn, 1495), pr. in *Prerogativa Regis: tertia lectura Roberti Constable*, ed. S. E. Thorne (1949).

[3] The feoffees were joint tenants, so that on the death of any feoffee his share went to the others by the *jus accrescendi*. The incidents would only attach if, by oversight, there was a single surviving feoffee who died; and then it was, inappropriately, the feoffee's infant heir (not the beneficiary's) who would be in ward. The heir of the last feoffee was bound by the use: *Tey* v. *Pawne* (1507) KB 27/983, m. 62 (replication).

[4] This was always implied, since a feoffment to the use of A and his heirs was in law the same thing as a feoffment to perform A's will: *Anon.* (1549) Wm Yelv. 346, no. 72.

[5] A widow could still claim dower in respect of lands of which the husband made a post-nuptial feoffment to uses, but not of lands which were in use at the time of marriage or came to him in use: cf. Bean, *The Decline of English Feudalism*, 136-7.

often to the bride's advantage, and with features (such as discretionary powers) unknown to the common law.[6] And they were convenient in other contexts, for instance in creating new forms of mortgage.[7] These unobjectionable aims would have been frustrated by the simple prohibition of uses, which would have restored strict primogeniture and dower. The prevalence of uses therefore provoked a conflict of interests which could not be reduced to a simple question of revenue evasion. And it was no small problem. According to Serjeant Frowyk, by 1489 'the greater part of the land of England was in feoffments upon trust'.[8]

USES AND THE COMMON LAW

Before the beginning of our period uses had not been part of the law of the land. The feoffment to uses,[9] or 'feoffment of trust',[10] was a familiar situation, if not yet a legal institution.[11] It was certainly a legal device, in the sense that it was frequently recommended by conveyancing counsel, in order to achieve clear legal consequences, such as the power to devise. Lawyers were therefore well acquainted with trusts and commonly served as feoffees. Nevertheless uses operated outside the law, inasmuch as the common law treated the feoffees as having an absolute title and the beneficiary—assuming he was not himself one of the feoffees[12]—as having no legal status.[13] The trust which was reposed in the feoffees bound them by ties of

---

[6] For powers of appointment see below, 678.   [7] Below, 706.

[8] Mich. 15 Hen. VII, fo. 13, pl. 1 (misdated but identifiable as *Dod* v. *Chyttynden*, 1502), *per* Frowyk sjt, referring to the date of the statute 4 Hen. VII, c. 17.

[9] In conveyances the phrase 'use and behoof' was already in common use, as representing the Latin doublet *opus et usum*: e.g. CP 40/916, m. 135 ('youse and behoff', 1487); BL Add. Roll 51523 ('thuse and behove', 1508); BL Add. Ch. 53062 ('use and behove', 1531); BL Add. Ch. 56692 ('use and behouf', 1540); *Lyte* v. *Peny* (1541) Dyer 49a; CP 40/1099, m. 340d; BL Add. Ch. 48798 ('uses and behoffe[s]', 1547). Cf. T. Madox, *Formulare Anglicanum* (1702), 438 ('behove, profet, and use', 1487).

[10] A common expression throughout our period: e.g. Mich. 21 Edw. IV, fo. 38, pl. 1 ('enfeffa... de trust'); Pas. 22 Edw. IV, fo. 6, pl. 18 ('feoffement de trust'); Adgore's reading (c.1489), fo. 24 ('feffez de trust'); Madox, *Formulare*, 413 ('feoffement of trust' in a deed of 1508); Bodl. Lib. MS. Rawlinson C.705, fo. 46v ('feffe de trust', 1513); KB 27/1021, m. 38 (deed enrolled by feoffees in trust, 1516); John Petit's reading (1518) BL MS. Harley 5013, fo. 18 ('per cest feffement de confidence est implie un confidence et trust inter le feffour et feffe'); Knightley's reading (1523) CUL MS. Hh.3.9, fo. 91v ('feffe de trust'); Yorke 126, no. 101; 139, no. 134; 147, no. 158; 148, no. 160; 150, no. 167; 152, no. 170 ('feoffees del trust', c.1520/30); BL Add. Ch. 53062 ('feoffez of truste', 1531); St German, *Doctor and Student*, ed. Plucknett and Barton, 222–3.

[11] Cf. Plucknett, *CHCL* (5th edn), 579, writing of the previous century.

[12] Sometimes he was: e.g. Madox, *Formulare Anglicanum*, 213 (1499; the endorsement states that seisin was delivered to that feoffee only).

[13] If in occupation, he was merely a trespasser or (at best) a tenant at sufferance: *Anon.* (1464) Pas. 4 Edw. IV, fo. 8, pl. 9; *Anon.* (1500) Hil. 15 Hen. VII, fo. 2, pl. 4 (tenant at sufferance); Trin. 15 Hen. VII, fo. 12, pl. 23 (trespasser); *Dod* v. *Chyttynden* (1502) 2 Caryll 395, pl. 258.

conscience and of professional fidelity but was not recognized as a legally enforceable obligation. Littleton, presumably for this reason, had barely mentioned uses at
all.[14] And conservative orthodoxy deemed them extra-legal even at the time of the
statute of 1536. 'The use is nothing in law', said Fitzherbert J., 'but is a trust, which
trust might be broken . . . for the common law never favours the use, for a use is not
a right, nor is any action given in law to recover it if someone is deforced of it . . .'.[15]
Yet the requirements of good conscience had long since brought them to the notice
of the Court of Chancery, where they were well known and were coming to be
governed by consistent principles.[16] Uses had also been recognized by the judges
for the purpose of qualifying the beneficiary to serve on juries.[17] During our
period, the use was transformed into a fully-fledged legal institution, chiefly as a
result of legislation which compelled the judges to notice its existence and determine its characteristics.[18]

   The initial legal transformation was brought about by the very first legislative
measure of Richard III.[19] According to the preamble, the statute was passed to end
the 'great uncertainty' which was increasing among purchasers, devisees, and
lessees of land with respect to their title. The problem, evidently, was that title
depended on seisin, and yet a great many landowners who were visibly in possession and in receipt of the rents and profits—and, we may suppose, in possession of
the title-deeds[20]—were beneficiaries under uses and therefore did not in law have
seisin. To this end, it enacted that every grant of land or other hereditament,[21] by
a person of full capacity, should be 'good and effectual' against both the grantor's
heirs and those holding to his use.[22] Although the object was the protection of the

---

[14] Trusts are mentioned in Litt. ss. 462–4 (feoffments 'sur confidence').

[15] *Abbot of Bury* v. *Bokenham* (1536–7) Dyer 7b at 12a. Cf. his earlier opinion that uses were at common law: below, 659. See also *Anon.* (1533/4) Caryll (Jun.) 372, no. 10, *per* Willoughby sjt ('a use . . . is
not a thing in possession and is not regarded in our law').

[16] The rules concerning the creation and transfer of express and implied trusts were expounded in
Gregory Adgore's reading on uses (Inner Temple, *c.*1489) CUL MS. Hh.3.10, ff. 19–28 and other manuscripts (references below are to the CUL MS.); extracts pr. B. & M. 102–3, 482–3. The main principle,
however, was that uses were flexible: below, 658, 678.

[17] Litt. s. 464; Mich. 15 Hen. VII, fo. 13, pl. 1 (misdated report of *Dod* v. *Chyttynden*), *per* Frowyk sjt.
Cf. *Dod* v. *Chyttynden* (1502) 2 Caryll 395, 396, where it is said that this '(tr.) began by sufferance, for
the benefit of the king'; and Yorke 126, no. 101, *per* Fitzherbert J. (not in strictness of law but 'at the
discretion of the justices').

[18] For a useful survey of the process whereby the profits of feudalism were revived by the Crown see
Bean, *Decline of English Feudalism*, 235–305.

[19] 1 Ric. III, c. 1; B. & M. 101. A few years later (*c.*1489) the statute was the subject of the reading
by Adgore noted above. Note also 1 Hen. VII, c. 1 (formedon against pernor of profits); Caryll (Jun.)
388, no. 43.   [20] Trin. 6 Hen. VII, fo. 3, pl. 2.

[21] e.g. a rent (Pas. 4 Hen. VII, fo. 8, pl. 9); or an annuity (*Athowe* v. *Waller* (1504) CP 40/969, m. 309).

[22] The statute did not refer to 'feoffees', and so it applied to recoveries to uses and to implied uses.
If the use was sold, the purchaser of the use acquired the power of disposal given by the 1484 act:
Adgore's reading (*c.*1489), fo. 19.

person acquiring title from the beneficiary, and not the advantage of the latter,[23] the effect was to give the latter a power to dispose of the freehold estate which was held to his use.[24] The beneficiary could even change his own feoffees simply by entering and making a new feoffment to his own use.[25] The statute was a remarkable piece of legal conjuring, since it enabled the legal estate to be transferred by someone who did not have it. Such an innovation inevitably begat new difficulties.

Although the statute gave the cestuy que use[26] the power to deliver seisin of the freehold, he was still not himself seised, and therefore it was held that he could not distrain except in the name of his feoffees.[27] Nor did he necessarily have possession to support an action of trespass or forcible entry.[28] Such a novel division of ownership gave rise to particular problems concerning leases.[29] The act specifically validated a lease by cestuy que use, but it was not clear whether he could reserve a rent to himself, since the reversion remained in the feoffees.[30] The prevailing view was that a rent could be reserved to the beneficiary, but only by deed.[31] The proper remedy for the beneficiary was an action of debt,[32] since he could not distrain, though it may also have been possible to reserve a right of re-entry.[33] On the other hand, it was for the feoffees to bring an action of waste against a lessee, since waste

[23] *Anon.* (1489) Mich. 5 Hen. VII, fo. 5, pl. 11; *Anon.* (1500) Hil. 15 Hen. VII, fo. 2, pl. 4; Trin. 15 Hen. VII, fo. 12, pl. 23. See also Milsom, *HFCL*, 215.

[24] For grants by particular tenants and remaindermen in use see *Anon.* (1488) Mich. 4 Hen. VII, fo. 18, pl. 9.   [25] *Castelen* v. *Morleyn* (1503) CP 40/963, m. 348.

[26] This shortest form is contemporary, but Adgore spoke of both 'cestui a que use est' and 'cestui que ad use': reading (*c.*1489), ff. 25, 27v. See also Trin. 13 Hen. VII, fo. 26, pl. 5, at fo. 27 ('cestuy a qui use le feoffement fuit fait' and 'cestuy que use'). It is clear from the longer phrases that 'use' is here a noun and not a verb.

[27] *Dokker* v. *Slyngesby* (1488) KB 27/909, m. 37 (discontinued demurrer); *Dod* v. *Chyttynden* (1502) CP 40/960, m. 437 (judgment on demurrer); 2 Caryll 391, 395, 407; Hil. 15 Hen. VII, fo. 2, pl. 4; Trin. 15 Hen. VII, fo. 12, pl. 23; Mich. 15 Hen. VII, fo. 13, pl. 1; sim. Rast. Ent. 508v (554v), pl. 3 (wrong KB roll-reference). Cf. *Atwode* v. *Elice* (1498) CP 40/946, m. 113; Rast. Ent. 570 (629v) (pleads distraint by cestuy que use as servant of feoffee).   [28] Adgore's reading (*c.*1489), fo. 25v.

[29] As to whether seisin passed on a lease pur auter vie by cestuy que use for life, see *Mordaunt* v. *Byrde* (1523) CP 40/1040, m. 435 (undetermined demurrer).

[30] Cf. the problem of the mortgage. Edmund Knightley thought cestuy que use could as a general rule enter for breach of a condition imposed by him (cf. Mich. 5 Hen. VII, fo. 6, pl. 11, per Bryan CJ), but not upon a feoffment in mortgage: reading (1523) CUL MS. Hh.3.9, fo. 92.

[31] *Moots*, 132–3 (moot point in Inner Temple, mid-1480s); *Anon.* (1489) Mich. 5 Hen. VII, fo. 5, pl. 11, per Bryan CJ; *Warre's Case* (1493) Hil. 8 Hen. VII, fo. 9, pl. 1, per Keble sjt ('peradventure' rent can be reserved with a deed, but not without), also in Trin. 13 Hen. VII, fo. 26, pl. 5; Adgore's reading (*c.*1490), fo. 25v (tr. '. . . and yet the reversion is not in him except by operation of law'); *Anon.* (1535) Trin. 27 Hen. VIII, fo. 13, pl. 1 (cestuy que use may devise rent reserved on a lease by deed, though the rent is part of the reversion); Yorke 141, no. 139 (deed necessary); Perk. s. 691.

[32] *Anon.* (1493) Hil. 8 Hen. VII, fo. 9, pl. 1, per Keble sjt; *Anon.* (1506) Trin. 21 Hen. VII, fo. 25, pl. 2; Yorke 141, no. 139 (where there was a deed).

[33] As to distress see *Anon.* (1535) Trin. 27 Hen. VIII, at fo. 14, per Shelley J.; Perk. s. 692. As to re-entry for non-payment see *George* v. *Sedler* (1522) CP 40/1036, m. 469; Spelman 81, 227; (no. 2, 1527) CP 40/1054, m. 530 (right of re-entry reserved by feoffees carrying out will of cestuy que use); *Bygge* v.

was an injury to their reversion.[34] If an action was brought against a tenant having a lease from cestuy que use, it was not clear that he could pray aid of the feoffees as reversioners.[35] What is more, since the use was in suspense during the lease, the beneficiary could not enter and make a grant of the reversion until the lease ended.[36] Another odd consequence of the division of ownership was that, although cestuy que use of an advowson could grant the next presentation to someone else,[37] it was not possible for him to make a presentation himself.[38]

One of the effects of the 1484 act was that it gave the beneficiary what was tantamount to a legal power to devise the land. Strictly speaking, it was not the freehold but the use which was devised, as before the act; but since the devisee now acquired the power to alienate the freehold, by the equity of the statute,[39] this was a distinction which only a lawyer would have understood.[40] Furthermore, the beneficiary could by will empower his representatives to sell timber or grant leases.[41]

The orthodox view that the beneficiary had no more to do with the land than a mere stranger obviously did not sit very well with these legislative changes. No doubt the statute was contrary to the common law;[42] but it was becoming somewhat pedantic to disentangle the common law from the statutory position. Indeed, when the 'greatest stranger' doctrine was propounded by Serjeant Frowyk in 1502, he was driven to concede that the beneficiary now had the power to fell timber as well as make leases.[43] A cestuy que use who could alienate, lease, or

Hyett (1524–5) CP 40/1045, m. 513 (right of re-entry reserved for beneficiary; undetermined demurrer); above, n. 30.

[34] Adgore's reading (*c.*1489), fo. 25v; *Moyle's Case* (1493) Hil. 8 Hen. VII, fo. 9, pl. 1; *Anon.* (1534) Trin. 26 Hen. VIII, fo. 6, pl. 31.

[35] *Moyle's Case* (1493) Hil. 8 Hen. VII, fo. 8, pl. 1; 1 Caryll 177 (plaintiff in replevin pleads lease from cestuy que use and prays aid of feoffees; aid granted); *Bradbury* v. *Lyle* (1531) CP 40/1070, m. 103 (sim.; judgment for defendant upon demurrer).

[36] Gray's Inn moot (1519) BL MS. Harley 5103, fo. 82v; HLS 125, no. 104; Rawlinson C.705, fo. 10, *per* Spelman; *Note* (*c.*1530) Yorke 139, n. 136 (lease for life); *Anon.* (1533/4) 25 Hen. VIII, Brooke Abr., *Uses*, pl. 45.   [37] *Litton* v. *Harvy* (1502) CP 40/960, m. 102.

[38] *Sandys* v. *Bray* (1511) 2 Caryll 610; Spelman 234; 120 Selden Soc. 4, 24; *Brudenell* v. *Abbot of St Werburgh's, Chester* (1516) CP 40/1014, m. 445; 120 Selden Soc. 4. The point was left undecided in *Lady Hastings* v. *Hungerford* (1492) Trin. 10 Hen. VII, fo. 29, pl. 24; Hil. 13 Hen. VII, fo. 18, pl. 24; 1 Caryll 75, 81, 102.

[39] *Anon.* (1494) Pas. 9 Hen. VII, fo. 26, pl. 13; *Anon.* (1506) Hil. 21 Hen. VII, fo. 19, pl. 30, *per* Tremayle J.; *Anon.* (*c.*1522/6) Yorke 144, no. 149; *Anon.* (1527) Trin. 19 Hen. VIII, fo. 10, pl. 4, *per* Shelley and Englefield JJ; Perk. s. 544; *Putbury* v. *Trevilian* (1556) Dyer 142b at 143a.

[40] Cf. *Abbot of St Mary Graces* v. *Duplage* (1495) CP 40/932, m. 349; 102 Selden Soc. 48 at 51 (lease by the devisee of a use).   [41] *Anon.* (1499) Hil. 14 Hen. VII, fo. 14, pl. 4, at fo. 15.

[42] *Lady Hastings* v. *Hungerford* (1492) Trin. 10 Hen. VII, fo. 29, pl. 24, *per* Vavasour J.

[43] *Dod* v. *Chyttynden* (1502) 2 Caryll 395 at 396, *per* Frowyk sjt (tr. 'by the course of the common law he has no more to do with the land than the greatest stranger in the world... And it was touched upon that cestuy que use may take trees, just as well as he may make a lease... by the equity of the new

devise the land, fell timber, and exercise other powers of ownership over the free-hold, could hardly be anything but the owner. And even before 1500 lawyers were referring to him as the 'owner',[44] an English word not normally used for the ten-ant in fee. Moreover, the statute necessarily familiarized common-law pleaders and judges with titles traced through uses,[45] thereby compelling the courts of law to take notice of the manner of devolution of a use. For instance, pleadings in the time of Henry VII make the right in use ('jus usus' or 'jus in usu') of an intestate cestuy que use descend automatically to the heir at law,[46] or (in the case of land subject to local custom) to the customary heir.[47] The use was therefore no longer merely an interest in conscience, nor even a mere power, but a form of property or ownership governed by legal rules noticed by the courts of common law.[48]

In deciding what those rules were, the courts might have interpreted the 1484 statute as requiring them to receive the doctrines that had been developed by the fifteenth-century Chancery; but there is no evidence that they overtly did so, or indeed that the Chancery had developed many clear doctrines prior to 1484.[49] Certainly some of the relevant principles had already been recognized in Chancery, such as those which governed the descent of uses on intestacy; but these

statute (query): which Frowyk conceded'); cf. *Brent* v. *Bere* (1502) CP 40/960, m. 400 (defendant in trespass pleads grant of trees by cestuy que use). The right to trees was agreed in *Lady Hastings* v. *Hungerford* (1492), previous note (and 1 Caryll 102 at 104), though it was denied that cestuy que use could license someone else to take trees: Adgore's reading (*c*.1489), fo. 25v.

[44] Pas. 4 Hen. VII, fo. 8, pl. 9, *per* Wode sjt. Adgore repeatedly used this word in his reading (*c*.1489), ff. 22v, 23, 24r-v, 25r-v, 26.

[45] See 94 Selden Soc. *196* n. 2. Earlier examples are *Rous* v. *Pope* (1490) KB 27/916, m. 73 (use traced through devise and sale by executors; demurrer relinquished); *Abbot of St Mary Graces* v. *Duplage* (1495) CP 40/932, m. 349; 102 Selden Soc. 51 (pleads a lease for years by the devisee of a use); *Stubbe* v. *Fletcher* (1499–1502) CP 40/949, m. 415; Rast. Ent. 606v (676) (pleads sale of trees by executors as directed by will); *Wagge* v. *Choune* (1501) CP 40/958, m. 360 (pleads feoffment by cestuy que use); *Brograve* v. *Sprever* (1501) KB 27/961, m. 39 (sim.); *Boteler* v. *Lee* (1502) CP 40/962, m. 134 (sim.); *Blechynden* v. *Filpot* (1503) CP 40/964, m. 372, 370A (pleads feoffment to use of will, and terms of will); *Spysour* v. *Grubbe* (1504) CP 40/969, m. 428 (pleads will by cestuy que use in 1457 directing the feoffees to sell the land, and that they sold to G., who made a feoffment to his own use); *Randall* v. *Eston* (1510) CP 40/993, m. 541 (bargain and sale by cestuy que use pleaded in replication); *Merbury* v. *Mordaunt* (1512–13) CP 40/998, m. 437 (avowry traces use from testator to executors, and thence to the plaintiff; demurrer).

[46] e.g. *Dod* v. *Chyttynden* (1502) CP 40/960, m. 437 ('jus usus'); *Glover* v. *Lucas* (1502) CP 40/962, m. 444 (sim.); *Frebody* v. *Baker* (1506) CP 40/978, m. 454 ('jus in usu'); and see *Sandys* v. *Bray* (1510) CP 40/993, m. 541 (pr. 116 Selden Soc. 611). For the descent of 'usus' see also *Atwode* v. *Elice* (1498) CP 40/946, m. 113; Rast. Ent. 570 (629v); *Athowe* v. *Waller* (1504) CP 40/969, m. 309; *Carter* v. *Grene* (1506) CP 40/974, m. 594; *Anon.* (1506) Mich. 21 Hen. VII, fo. 33, pl. 28; *Morton* v. *Chippenham* (1507) KB 27/983, m. 66.

[47] *Parcyvall* v. *Phylippe* (1502–4) CP 40/962, m. 570 (defendant pleads that a use of gavelkind land descended to two brothers, one of whom enfeoffed the other).

[48] Even Thomas Audley, a strong critic of the development of the use, defined it as a kind of prop-erty or ownership: reading on uses (Inner Temple, 1526) BL MS. Hargrave 87, fo. 438 (tr. B. & M. 104); abstracted as 'Diffinitio usus' in Catlyn's precedent book, Alnwick Castle MS. 475, fo. 186v.

[49] See J. L. Barton, 81 *LQR* at 574–6; Simpson, *Rise of Assumpsit*, 327–9; Milsom, *HFCL*, 216.

were no doubt perceived as rules of law noticed by the Chancery rather than the converse. On the other hand, the requisites for a use binding at law were necessarily qualified by the terms of the statute. Thus, although in conscience feoffees were bound by a charitable use, for instance a use in favour of a parish,[50] such a use was not valid at law because neither the parishioners nor the churchwardens were a corporation capable of owning real property or of making grants and leases under the statute of 1484.[51] There was therefore a possibility of conflict between equity and law, such as that which beset executory interests in a later period.

Be that as it may, when the time came for the common-law courts to state the principles governing uses, they proceeded on the basis that uses were a form of property recognized by the common law. The precise relationship between uses and the law was soon to be of critical importance in relation to royal revenue;[52] but the first reported debate (in 1522) is of interest for being apparently innocent of revenue implications.[53] The facts of the 1522 case, as confessed by demurrer, were that feoffees to uses had granted a rent to the defendant,[54] who had notice of the use; they had then enfeoffed a third party of the land, and cestuy que use had released all his right to this third party. The question was whether the rent had thereby been extinguished. For the release to be effective, under the 1484 act, the rent must have been held to the use of the releasor, and the problem was that the rent had had no existence in the hands of the feoffees. It was argued for the plaintiff that the defendant, having notice, took the rent subject to the use, since the rent followed the nature of the land. Serjeant Shelley, for the defendant, countered this with the fifteenth-century argument that the feoffees had the land at common law and (subject to the 1484 act) could bind cestuy que use. But this view was going out of fashion, and the judges rejected it. Fitzherbert J. responded that

Uses are at common law and not by reason of the statute of Richard III.[55] A use is nothing other than a trust and confidence which the feoffor puts in the person of his feoffee,[56] according to his estate. And that was at common law ... [and] the way in which a use shall be changed is governed by the common law, and it shall be taken and determined in accordance with reason. Every use follows the feoffees' estate.

[50] See 23 Hen. VIII, c. 10. Such uses were in practice frequently constituted by last will

[51] *Baker* v. *Johnson* (1497) KB 27/945, m. 34d; Trin. 12 Hen. VII, fo. 27, pl. 7; Mich. 13 Hen. VII, fo. 9, pl. 5; 1 Caryll 361. The case turned on the validity of a lease by churchwardens under such a use, and so the ratio decidendi might be confined to the operation of the 1484 statute; but the judges made much broader statements to the effect that the use was void in law.   [52] See below, 661.

[53] *Gervys* v. *Cooke* (1522) Mich. 14 Hen. VIII, fo. 4, pl. 5 (119 Selden Soc. 108; quotations from 114, 115, 116); Spelman 227; CP 40/1035, m. 510 (pr. 119 Selden Soc. 123). Cf. *Parker* v. *Pateshall* (1520) 120 Selden Soc. 42, *per* Fyneux CJ ('uses were at common law').

[54] Actually to the defendant's wife, when she was married to the feoffor (who was not the cestuy que use).   [55] Cf. his statement of 1536, quoted above, 655.

[56] Cf. *Anon.* (1549) Wm Yelv. 347, no. 72.

Broke J. agreed:

As has been said, uses are at common law, and by common reason, and shall be taken and qualified accordingly. Sir, even as the feoffor puts his confidence and trust, so shall be his use. And the use is in the feoffor, in conscience, even though the feoffee has the land by the common law ... Every intermeddling with the land must be at the feoffor's desire, for if the feoffee does otherwise he is chargeable in conscience ... [And yet] it is not conscience which makes uses but common reason, which is common law; and common law is indifferent to all laws both spiritual and temporal.

Pollard J. agreed, but judgment was never entered because Brudenell CJ had doubts. It is not wholly clear from the report why the judges felt it necessary to assert that uses were at common law, or why Broke J. chose to insulate them from the canon law; but the majority view is clear enough: uses were not simply a matter of conscience, seen as distinct from the law, but were now fully noticed by the law.

The following year the Common Pleas had to consider the possibility of a common-law remedy for cestuy que use. An action had been brought against feoffees to use, and one of them refused to plead as his feoffor directed. We learn from a subsequent Chancery suit that the feoffor had suffered a recovery, and the action seems to have been an attempt to falsify it. The court rebuked the feoffees' attorney, who was placed in an uncomfortable dilemma, but admitted that they could do no more than exert moral pressure because they could not take judicial notice of a use which had not been pleaded.[57] They did suggest, however, that an action on the case would lie against the feoffees.[58] That was legally thinkable,[59] but—apart from isolated experiments in a later period[60]—it was not to be.[61] As Fitzherbert J. said in the case of 1522, it was logically consistent for the law to determine the rules for the transfer and devolution of uses while denying a remedy against the feoffees. The copyholder, it may be recalled, was currently in an analogous plight.

---

[57] Cf. *Anon.* (1467) Hil. 7 Edw. IV, fo. 29, pl. 15, where the judges held that the feoffee was bound to plead as directed by cestuy que use; but they did not indicate the remedy. See also Trin. 27 Hen. VIII, fo. 20, pl. 7, where the judges accorded cestuy que use the privilege of a litigant; the problem of judicial notice was circumvented by taking evidence as to the use.

[58] *Gresley* v. *Saunders and Sprott* (1522) Pas. 14 Hen. VIII, fo. 24, pl. 2 (119 Selden Soc. 170); Spelman 22; Brooke Abr., *Feffements al uses*, pl. 48; CP 40/1037, m. 413; CP 40/1038, m. 112d. Actions were also brought in the King's Bench (KB 27/1043, m. 78) and Chancery (C1/513/35, 36). Similar issues were raised in *Holwey* v. *Hale* (1529/32) C1/642/16; *Browne* v. *Coke* (1531/2) C1/614/32.

[59] See also *The Serjeants' Case* (1531) Wm Yelv. 294 at 299, *per* Cholmley sjt ('by the common law, if the feoffees execute some other estate than [cestuy que use] wishes them to have, an action upon his case lies against them, because he put his confidence and trust in them to do it, and the action on the case lies for the deceit').

[60] e.g. *Megod's Case* (1586) B. & M. 497, identified by N. G. Jones as *Meggott* v. *Broughton and Davy* (1586) KB 27/1298, m. 342; KB 27/1299, m. 57; 4 Leon. 60, 225.

[61] See 94 Selden Soc. *197-8*. See also Fitzherbert J.'s dictum of 1536 quoted above, 655.

LEGISLATIVE REMEDIES

Although the Statute of Marlborough 1267 had addressed the loss of incidents resulting from devices which prevented a descent of the fee, it was too narrowly drawn to catch feoffments to uses.[62] One possible exception was the use which indirectly carried land to the heir, either by requiring the feoffees to convey to the heir at full age or by requiring them to perform the feoffor's will, where the will in the event required them to re-enfeoff the heir. Such uses might be treated as collusive feoffments within the equity of the statute.[63] If, however, a feoffment was made to the use of the feoffor's last will, and then he simply failed to make a will, so that the use devolved on the heir by operation of law, this was not considered to fall within the statute.[64] Closing this loophole seems to have been the sole purpose of the statute of 1490,[65] which was not so much a radical innovation preparing the way for the great statute of 1536 as a supplement to Marlborough, which is recited in the preamble. The measure may have been prompted by negotiations over the estates of the earl of Northumberland, who died in 1489 leaving most of his land in use.[66] But it was not new thinking. It was closely modelled on a short-lived statute of 1483, possibly penned by Empson, which had applied only to the duchy of Lancaster.[67] The 1490 version provided that if feoffees were seised of land held by knight-service 'to the use of any other person or persons and of his heirs only',[68] and cestuy que use died leaving an infant heir, 'no will by him declared or made in his life touching the premises', then the lord should have a writ of right of ward for the body and land of the heir just as if the cestuy que use had died seised. It also provided that if the heir was of full age the lord should have relief.

The statute of 1490 was limited in several respects. It only touched wardship and relief due from tenants in chivalry and did not affect relief and heriot in respect of socage tenure, though these were the subject of a further supplemental

[62] Statute of Marlborough 1267, c. 6. See 94 Selden Soc. *193*.

[63] So held John Baldwin (Gray's Inn reading, *c*.1454) CUL MS. Hh.2.6., at fo. 67v (tr. 94 Selden Soc. *193*); and Thomas Audley (Inner Temple reading, 1526) CUL MS. Ee.5.19, at fo. 5v. (For fourteenth-century case-law on the point, see Bean, *Decline of Feudalism*, 183, 203–4.) For other difficulties with c. 6, see John Grene's reading (Inner Temple, 1499) Port 169–73.

[64] Baldwin's reading (last note). A passive use in fee simple was found to be collusive in 1487: *CIPM Hen. VII*, i. 143, no. 339.

[65] 4 Hen. VII, c. 17. The legal date was 1489, since the Parliament began in Jan. 1489, but the statute applied to persons dying after Easter 1490 and was probably passed in the 1490 session: Bean, *Decline of Feudalism*, 242. It is more convenient to assign it to 1490. A contemporary copy in the Paston Letters, BL MS. Add. 27446, fo. 7, has the commencement date miscopied as 'mcccclxxx'.

[66] Bean, *Decline of Feudalism*, 245–7.

[67] C49/40, no. 3; *RP*, vi. 207b (Jan. 1483; not printed as a statute); W. Hardy, *Charters of the Duchy of Lancaster* (1845), 337–40. Empson was at this time A.-G. of the duchy. The measure was repealed by Richard III in Jan. 1484 (*RP*, vi. 261b).   [68] i.e. in fee simple, not in tail.

provision in 1504.[69] Nor did it affect the king's right of primer seisin, since that was not mentioned.[70] Even with respect to wardship, it was debatable whether it operated to give the king prerogative wardship, since he had that as king and not as lord.[71] It did not apply to settlements, where the heir in use had a fee tail rather than a fee simple; and an heir in use in remainder was not subjected to wardship during the particular estate.[72] More importantly, it applied only on intestacy. There was as yet no thought of impeding the power to devise, the main object of most uses, and since the majority of beneficiaries probably left wills the statute may not have been intended to make a major impact on seignorial revenue. Yet the statute, like that of 1484, had a more subtle intellectual impact. It familiarized lawyers with the idea that cestuy que use could be treated for certain purposes as if he were seised,[73] a fiction that was to be carried to the furthest extent by the statute of 1536. And then there was a critical chink, to be ripped open in the case which led to the latter statute. Although the 'no will by him declared' clause suggested that the mere existence of a will 'touching the premises' would be enough to exclude the operation of the statute, legal opinion was inclined to give this an extensive equitable construction. Obviously the statute could not be evaded merely by making a will leaving the land to the heir,[74] and it was arguable that a will of land did not in any case affect the lord's right to wardship of the body.[75] More significantly, however, it was held—held, at any rate, by readers favouring the prerogative—that where a will did not dispose of the entire inheritance in fee simple, the statute could come into operation once the will was performed.[76] It is not certain whether this principle bore fruit in practice, in view of the difficulty of

[69] 19 Hen. VII, c. 15, s. 2. The statute also made the land of cestuy que use liable to execution for a judgment debt.

[70] Constable's reading (1495) on *Prerogativa Regis*, ed. Thorne, 53–4; Thomas Frowyk's reading (1495) ibid. 54 n. 135; reading in the Inner Temple (perhaps by John Port, 1507) BL MS. Hargrave 87, fo. 171 (pr. ibid.); notes by Serjeant Caryll (1514) 2 Caryll 531, pl. 373B; (1516) ibid. 669, pl. 486; John Spelman's reading (Gray's Inn, 1521) Gray's Inn MS. 25, fo. 305v.

[71] *Re Stonor* (1497) KB 27/938, Rex m. 4; Trin. 12 Hen. VII, fo. 19, pl. 1; Mich. 13 Hen. VII, fo. 11, pl. 12; tr. in 64 Selden Soc. 161; 1 Caryll 363, pl. 226; 2 Caryll 530, pl. 373A; Robert Constable's reading (Lincoln's Inn, 1495) on *Prerogativa Regis*, ed. Thorne, 20 n. 48; Gray's Inn reading (before 1514) Spelman 176, pl. 6. By 1514, the king seems to have won in practice: see 2 Caryll 531, pl. 373B. Priority between other lords was likewise governed by the common law: *Earl of Rutland* v. *Constable* (1529) Spelman 143.

[72] *Abbot of Bury* v. *Bokenham* (1536–7) CP 40/1088, m. 420; Dyer 7b; Benl. 16; 1 And. 2.

[73] This led to some curious puzzles: e.g. Spelman 146.

[74] Yorke 143, no. 147 (tr. '...and the reason why he shall be in ward is because such a will is void, because if he had not made such a will the son would have had the land anyway').

[75] Constable's reading (1495) on *Prerogativa Regis*, ed. Thorne, 36; *Abbot of Bury* v. *Bokenham* (1536–7) Dyer 7b at 10b, *per* Willoughby sjt. See also n. 78, below.

[76] Constable's reading (1495) on *Prerogativa Regis*, ed. Thorne, 20–1; reading in the Inner Temple (perhaps by John Port, 1507) BL MS. Hargrave 87, fo. 174v (pr. in *Prerogativa Regis*, ed. Thorne, 21 n. 49); Spelman's reading (1521) GI MS. 25, fo. 303 (pr. ibid.). This was expressly provided for in the 1483 statute: *RP*, vi. 207b.

superintending wills,[77] and in any case it did not obviously bear upon the common arrangement of a devise to the heir in tail.[78] But the creeping exceptions prepared the way for the major debate of 1535.[79]

The appointment of a master of the wards in 1503, and the development of his new revenue department,[80] confirm the implication arising from the law reports and readings that the enforcement of revenue from tenants by knight-service was seen as a matter of major importance by Henry VII and his advisers. Nevertheless, the gaps in the legislation of 1490 were left unplugged for forty years. On the face of it the Crown already had a means of protecting its interests, because a feoffment to uses by a tenant in chief required a licence to alienate.[81] However, the Crown was prevented by statute from requiring the tenant to compound for the loss of wardship, and a licence could not be unreasonably withheld.[82] The best the Crown could achieve by means of licences was a stipulation that the licensee retain a portion of land held in chief, so as to preserve wardship of the body and prerogative wardship with respect to other lands.[83] The lack of further legislative proposals until the 1520s may seem puzzling with hindsight, but is perhaps explained simply by the social importance and complete general acceptance of wills of land. An attempt to restore the lost feudal revenue by abolishing uses would have threatened the existence of wills and would therefore have been broadly unacceptable.[84]

A compromise solution had been essayed in the 1483 statute for the duchy. Although the statute contained a proviso that it should not affect wills, this was subject to a saving to the king of 'such reasonable portion of the same lands...as shall be sufficient for the finding of such heirs during their nonage'. The statute stood in force for less than a year, and there is no evidence that the saving was ever put into effect. It would have required some kind of decision as to what proportion of a tenant's lands should reasonably be left to descend to his heir, and an

---

[77] Bean, *Decline of Feudalism*, 253–4.

[78] See Yorke 143, no. 147, *per* Hesketh and Spelman (tr. 'if he makes his will that the feoffees should make an estate tail to the son...the body shall be in ward (for the fee simple) and not the land').

[79] *Re Lord Dacre* (1535) below, 669.

[80] See above, 229. For the tightening of central control over inquisitions *post mortem* see D. Luckett, 'Henry VII and the South-Western Escheators' in *The Reign of Henry VII: proceedings of the 1993 Harlaxton symposium*, ed. B. Thompson (1995), 54–64.

[81] See J. A. Guy, 40 *CLJ* at 161. Fines could be imposed on tenants in chief for making feoffments to uses: e.g. *CCR 1485–1500*, p. 205, no. 700 (1494); ibid. 281, no. 949 (1497). That licences were essential is indicated by 14 Edw. IV, c. 1, and 7 Hen. VII, c. 2/3 (exempting tenants in chief from obtaining licences when going on war service).

[82] 1 Edw. III, stat. 2, c. 12. Constable held that the reasonable fine was one-third of the annual value of the land: reading (1495) on *Prerogativa Regis*, ed. Thorne, 155–6. Spelman held that it was one half: Yorke 176, no. 224. The fine for alienating without licence was a whole year's profits: ibid.; *Anon.* (1529) Pollard 269, no. 54.   [83] Bean, *Decline of Feudalism*, 198–200, 207–9.

[84] See further ibid. 255–6.

even more difficult decision about how to pare down testamentary provisions which purported to leave an unreasonable proportion elsewhere. When Richard III repealed the statute he gave as the reason 'the great hurt and thraldom of his subjects'; but at least some of its shortcomings must have been related to the difficulty of administering the principle of the 'reasonable portion'. The saving clause was not repeated in the 1490 statute, and the problem was shelved for forty years.

A renewed campaign to revive the lost feudal revenues was begun in 1526, perhaps prompted by heavy recent public expenditure.[85] In that year the Crown began to take penal recognizances from tenants in chief wishing to make feoffments, to ensure that the Crown did not suffer financial loss,[86] and the Star Chamber ordered suits to be brought in respect of unlicensed alienations which affected wardships.[87] Likewise, when a common recovery was suffered, the attorney-general—or sometimes the assize judges—began to extract recognizances that the recovery would not be prejudicial to the king in respect of wardship, primer seisin, or other profits.[88] Further evidence of the new policy is a document containing the heads of a proposed piece of legislation agreed between the king and the peers in 1529–30.[89] The first draft clause proposed to give the king prerogative wardship of lands in use, where there was no will, thereby supplying the apparent omission in the 1490 act. The bulk of the agreement, however, would have resuscitated in a different and general form the failed experiment of Edward IV. In respect of land held by knight-service in use, where a will or jointure had been made, and the heir was under age at the time of the ancestor's death, the king was to have wardship of one-third of all the land. Where the heir was of full age at the ancestor's death, the king was to have primer seisin and the heir to have livery in return for half a year's profits of the land. Mesne lords were to have the same wardship rights as the king, namely one-third of lands held by knight-service, save where they were ousted by the prerogative. This definition of the reasonable portion destined for the Crown, or the lord, was doubtless an attempt to dispel the uncertainty which may have doomed the earlier measure.

---

[85] Bean associates the campaign with the appointment of William Paulet as joint master of the wards in 1526: *Decline of Feudalism*, 237. Elton did not think Cromwell was involved until the 1530s: *Reform and Renewal*, 143. For Audley's possible involvement see below, 666.

[86] J. Guy, *Christopher St German on Chancery and Statute* (1985), 78, citing unsorted fragments of Supplementary Close Rolls.

[87] Order of 30 June 1526, cited ibid. 79. The lawyers present were Fyneux and Brudenell CJJ, Sir Thomas More (as chancellor of the duchy), and Sir Thomas Nevill (bencher of Gray's Inn).

[88] By the end of the 1520s these are enrolled in CP 40 on the attorney-general's rolls.

[89] BL Cotton MS. Titus B.IV, ff. 114–118 (*LP*, vi. 6044, at p. 2694). For the date, see Bean, *Decline of Feudalism*, 265–7. The text is printed in Holdsworth, *HEL*, iv. 574–7 (dated 1529). For comment, see Plucknett, 'Some Proposed Legislation of Henry VIII', 121–4; Holdsworth, *HEL*, iv. 449–61; E. W. Ives. 'The Genesis of the Statute of Uses' (1967) 82 EHR 673 at 677–80; Bean, *Decline of Feudalism*, 258–70; S. E. Lehmberg, *The Reformation Parliament 1529–36* (1970), 95–6.

It has been suggested that the peers were persuaded to agree to these proposals by an exemption conceded to the peerage from the proposed legislation of 1529 which would have annulled all entails and turned them into fee simple.[90] Whether or not this is correct,[91] there was clearly no corresponding benefit to offer the commons, apart from a two-edged provision that uses should be invalid unless registered in the Common Pleas. In the House of Commons, therefore, the scheme foundered in 1532. According to the Imperial ambassador Chapuys, the proposals were 'the occasion of strange words against the king and Council' in February of that year.[92] The chronicler Edward Hall, who was a member of the lower house at the time, and a barrister of Gray's Inn, says that the king originally proposed to take half of a tenant's lands in ward, so that only half could be left by will, and that this caused much grief among 'ignorant persons' in the House of Commons—and anger directed against the king's learned counsel. According to Hall, those with better foresight were willing to settle for a scheme allowing ward-ship of a quarter or even a third, which the king would have accepted. But in the event no compromise was reached, and the proposals were rejected outright. Henry VIII reacted with an angry threat. 'I assure you,' he warned, 'if you will not take some reasonable end now when it is offered, I will search out the extremity of the law, and then will I not offer you so much again.'[93]

Doubtless the majority were untroubled by this warning, secure in the knowledge that the law was on their side. Uses had been recognized by the Court of Chancery for over a century, and wills had in consequence become accepted as commonplace. The validity of a will of land held in use had indeed been acknowledged by Parliament in the 'no will by him declared' clause in the statute of 1490. But, as Hall noted, wiser men foresaw that this was not necessarily an impregnable position. Such a threat from such a king might well be made good. And so it turned out, as Henry VIII and his ministers set about to undermine the commons by getting the common law changed.[94] In this bold endeavour the way had already been prepared by the lawyers themselves.

THE ASSAULT ON USES

The debate which began in the mid-1520s provided an opportunity for lawyers desirous of serving the Crown, and in the period when the political solution seemed beyond reach it was left to them to save the king's cause by altering the

---

[90] Holdsworth, *HEL*, iv. 450–1; Bean, *Decline of Feudalism*, 259–61. The provision is in cl. 1 of the bill (SP 1/56, fo. 36), pr. Holdsworth, *HEL*, iv. 572.

[91] Ives, 'Genesis of the Statute of Uses', 680, argues against a connection between the bill (which was abandoned) and the agreement with the peers. This view is followed by Lehmberg, *Reformation Parliament*, 94–5.   [92] Letter to the Emperor, *LP*, v. 805.

[93] *Hall's Chronicle*, 785.   [94] For the constitutional significance of this event see above, 66.

intellectual assumptions of the profession. Thus it happened that, just as the reception of the use into the common law was gaining momentum in the early sixteenth century, it received a powerful rebuff from Thomas Audley in 1526 as autumn reader of the Inner Temple.[95] Audley selected as his text the 1490 statute of uses, and it may be supposed that he seized the occasion to mark his recent entry into the Crown's service—in Empson's old office as attorney-general of the duchy[96]—and his commitment to the new campaign to improve feudal revenue. His reading began with a lecture on tenure in chivalry and its incidents, followed by an exposition of the fifteenth-century learning on collusion and the sixth chapter of Marlborough. Then came the more radical doctrine, which was to shake the very foundation of uses. He claimed that uses had been 'imagined and compassed' since the Statute of Marlborough in order to defraud lords of their wardships, contrary to the learning of the common law, which held repugnant any condition upon a feoffment that the feoffor should take the profits. Warming to his theme, Audley expatiated on the problems of uncertainty caused by making title to land rest on conscience rather than legal rules; and it is as well to remember that the audience would not have failed to detect the latent allusion to Wolsey C.:[97]

Although these wills were at first contrived for a good purpose, namely for power to make wills of land in this realm, whereas inheritances in old times were ruled and governed by the common law (which for the most part consists of ordinary and certain rules): nevertheless to a great extent they have been pursued by collusion for the evil purpose of destroying the good laws of the realm, which now by reason of these trusts and confidences are turned into a law called 'conscience', which is always uncertain and depends for the greater part on the whim (*arbitrement*) of the judge in conscience. And by reason of this no man can know his title to land with any certainty; for now land passes by words and bare proofs in the Chancery, whereas by the common law it could only pass by solemn livery on the land or something equivalent, or by matter of record or in writing. Also, the trial of title to land in this realm was never by proofs but by verdict, whereas now it is contrary.

This passage could be taken as a manifesto for the campaign to follow, though no one could yet know that in ten years Audley himself would be the 'judge in conscience' and in a position to practise his preaching. The survival of three old copies of the reading may indicate that it circulated more widely than most. The key passage was certainly remembered in the Inner Temple in the 1530s, when

---

[95] The three extant texts are virtually identical: BL MS. Hargrave 87, ff. 427–457; CUL MS. Ee.5.19, ff. 1–17v; Univ. Illinois at Urbana-Champaign MS. 27, ff. 69–95v.

[96] Somerville, *Duchy of Lancaster*, 407. He was also a member of Princess Mary's Council in the Marches: above, 104 n. 31. He joined Wolsey's household in 1527.

[97] From the text in B. & M. 104 (and cf. 94 Selden Soc. *198*), including the suggested emendation to remove an obscurity in the texts.

Master Hare told how:[98] 'A use was invented in the beginning with the intention of making a fraud at common law, namely to make a declaration of a will and so to defraud the right heir and oust the wife of her dower or oust tenancy by the curtesy... And he said that Audley was of this opinion in his reading; and so he held the law.' The same passage was also known to Robert Catlyn, who copied it out in the 1550s.[99]

Another exponent of Audley's teaching was the anonymous 'serjeant at the laws of England' who in about 1530 wrote the intemperate *Replication* to St German's *Doctor and Student*.[100] St German had made the Student explain to the Doctor that uses were founded on a 'secondary conclusion of the law of reason', and that, although a reservation of profits on a feoffment was void in law, the arrangement was binding in conscience. He had also listed some of the deceitful objects for which uses had been employed in the past, and shown how these had been remedied by statute. The principal reasons for uses, according to the Student, were to enable wills to be made of land and to facilitate marriage settlements.[101] The implication was that these were proper objects. But, for the serjeant, St German had been too uncritical by far:[102]

I say that [uses] began of an untrue and crafty invention to put the king and his subjects from that [which] they ought to have of right by the good, true common law of the realm... And though some of these inconveniences be holpen by divers statutes, as ye have said, yet there resteth many and great inconveniences, more than I can rehearse at this time, that be not yet remedied. And in especial one, and that is this: by such uses the good common law of this realm, to the which the king's subjects be inherit, is subverted and made as void. For if he claim and prove his title by deed of feoffment, the other party will say that he was but a feoffee of trust... What a falseness is this, to speak and do one thing, and think another thing clean contrary to the same. Every man may perceive, in my mind, that of this can come no goodness, but craft and falsehood. And so me seemeth that these uses began by an untrue and a crafty invention, and is continued by an untruth and for a deceit.

After more invective of the same kind, and an argument that uses were even against the law of God, since they were against truth, the serjeant's peroration was an equally close paraphrase of Audley's reading:[103]

...all the law that now is used is to determine which is conscience and which is no conscience; and so the common law of the realm is nowadays by you that be students turned all into conscience, and so ye make my lord chancellor judge in every matter, and bring the laws

---

[98] Inner Temple moot (*c.*1533) Caryll (Jun.) 374–5, no. 13. Hare curiously omitted to mention the loss of feudal incidents.   [99] 'Diffinitio usus', Alnwick Castle MS. 475, fo. 186v.

[100] For this text, and speculations about its authorship, see above, 43–4.

[101] St German, *Doctor and Student*, ed. Plucknett and Barton, 222–5.

[102] *Replication of a Serjeant*, ed. Guy, 103–4 (sp. mod.).   [103] ibid. 105 (sp. mod.).

of the realm into such an uncertainty that no man can be sure of any lands, be it inheritance or purchase, but every man's title shall be by this means brought into the Chancery...

This might have been Audley speaking, though Audley did not himself take the coif until November 1531. At any rate, it represented a view which Audley was prominent in promoting at a critical moment in the history of the use. St German's rejoinder was that, if uses were permitted by law, it could not be deceitful to take advantage of them; and, of course, until that moment they had been permitted by law—not merely in the sense that they were enforced by the Chancery, but also in that they were not contrary to the common law. That being so, it could not be unconscionable to take lawful steps to avoid the incidents of tenure, or dower. One may properly avoid, but not fraudulently evade, the legal rules which apply to particular forms of settlement. On the other hand, St German declined to debate for the time being 'whether it were good to break all uses', merely observing that if a remedy was needed it was not because of deceit but because of the uncertainty and trouble which they occasioned.[104] Even St German, therefore, accepted that there was some kind of case to be made against uses.

That general case was formulated shortly afterwards in a tract entitled (in an endorsement) 'Damna usuum'.[105] This was a random catalogue of the 'mischiefs, wrongs, and inconveniences' which flowed from uses. Among the forty-three complaints, the evasion of feudal incidents appears only as the thirty-ninth item, and the financial harm to the Crown is noticeably under-stressed. This does not prove that it was of unofficial origin; for, if the commons were to be won over, it was necessary to make the case independently of revenue considerations. A recurrent theme, as in Audley's reading and the *Replication*, was the uncertainty resulting from the substitution of conscience for legal title. 'The opinions of the justices do change daily,' it claimed, 'upon the sureties for lands in use'; it was doubtful whether cestuy que use in tail could bar the issue;[106] a claimant to land did not know whom to sue; uses still encouraged forms of mortmain; and there were numerous doubts arising from the statute of 1484. Moreover, the common law was being subverted by 'double law'.[107] The proposed remedy is hidden away in the middle:[108] 'If the uses, which [are] but the shadow of the thing and not the thing indeed, were clean put out of the law, men that had right should hereafter rather come to their remedies.' This tract was not a specific proposal for legislation, but shows both careful preparation of a damning indictment of the use, on a variety of counts, and also serious contemplation of a drastic remedy.

[104] *Little Treatise concerning Writs of Subpoena*, ed. Guy, 113–15. He particularly mentioned the trouble caused by uses in tail: ibid. 114.

[105] SP 1/101, fo. 282; pr. Holdsworth, *HEL*, iv. 577–80 (sp. mod. in quotations here). It is also endorsed 'Inconveniences for sufferance of uses'.   [106] See below, 695–6.

[107] See *HEL*, iv. 579–80, nos. 32 ('uses make double law'), 36 ('uses subvert the laws and customs of this realm'). Double here means deceitful.   [108] *HEL*, iv. 578, no. 15.

Another extra-parliamentary approach was to attack individual wills. Audley devoted the later part of his reading to defects in wills, the point being—as he held—that, when a will was invalid, the testator could be treated as having died with 'no will by him declared' for the purposes of the 1490 statute.[109] This had already occurred to the legal advisers of the Crown before 1526. In 1516 a traverse to an inquisition raised the issue (amongst others) whether a feoffment to the use of a last will had been made to defraud the king of his wardship and marriage; but the traverse had failed.[110] It is said that in *The Earl of Derby's Case* (1522), the Crown actually succeeded in obtaining wardship despite the existence of a will; the grounds are unclear, though it seems that much of the land had been devised to the testator's heir.[111] However, in *Re Longford* (1523), in which Fitzherbert J. was personally involved as a feoffee, it was accepted that if a feoffment was made to the use of a last will it could not be condemned as a collusive feoffment to deprive the king of wardship.[112] Consistently with this view, wills devising uses were regularly pleaded in the common-law courts down to 1535,[113] without objection to their validity.[114] This orthodox position had now to be shaken, and the attack was launched just after the rejection of the king's legislative proposals in 1532.[115]

The first peer to die after the king's defeat in Parliament was Thomas Fiennes, seventh Baron Dacre (Lord Dacre of the South), who died in 1533 leaving an heir aged 18. His was to be the leading case. Much of his land was vested in feoffees to uses, and by his will he had charged various legacies on some parcels and had settled others. One of the provisions in the will which struck blatantly against the

[109] CUL MS. Ee.5.19, ff. 11v–13.

[110] *Re Sir Christopher Wroughton, Hungerford v. Regem* (1516) KB 27/1021, Rex m. 8 (inquisition finds feoffment was fraudulent; Hungerford says it was made to the use of Wroughton's last will, which he sets out, and traverses the fraud and collusion; att.-gen. joins issue). The controlment roll shows that Hungerford was nonsuited and judgment given for the Crown: KB 29/148, m. 55; but cf. different proceedings in KB 27/1021, Rex m. 11.

[111] 2 Caryll 731, pl. 524. Thomas Stanley, first earl of Derby, died in 1504. For his will see PCC 19 Holgrave; *Testamenta Vetusta*, ed. N. H. Nicolas (1826), ii. 460.

[112] *Re Ralph Longford* (or *Langforth*) (1513–26) Spelman 212 (pleadings drawn on this assumption); C142/79/173 (inquisition); KB 27/1047, Rex m. 3 (traverse); E159/304, Hil. 17 Hen. VIII, mm. 23–25 (ousterlemain); S. M. Wright, *The Derbyshire Gentry in the Fifteenth Century* (1983), 41, 162 nn. 94–7, 242. See also Port 136, no. 102.

[113] Late examples are *Basse's Case* (Hil. 1535) CP 40/1084, m. 442 (issue on terms of will); *Capell v. Pygot* (Trin. 1535) CP 40/1086, m. 537 (sim.); reported in Pas. 27 Hen. VIII, fo. 11, pl. 28; *Tylden v. Lylle* (Mich. 1535) CP 40/1087, m. 601 (devise of use confessed by pleading; judgment for plaintiff after verdict). Note also *Roberts v. Sadler* (1527) CP 40/1054, m. 530 (issue concerning Lady Frowyk's will).

[114] Three such cases in 1525–7 produced demurrers, but not on the ground that wills were collusive: *Bele v. Benet* (1527) CP 40/1054, m. 316 (judgment); probably Spelman 228, pl. 3; *Archbishop of Canterbury v. Wyatt* (1524–5) CP 40/1044, m. 419, and *Archbishop of Canterbury v. Morley* (1527) CP 40/1054, m. 615 (demurrers concerning will of Robert Morley; no judgments).

[115] Cf. a case of 1534 in which Cromwell became involved in the selection of an inquisition *post mortem* to prevent the king's rights being 'cloaked': *LP*, vii. 383; Holdsworth, *HEL*, iv. 454 n. 4.

king's rights was that which directed the feoffees to convey the residue of the lands to the heir when he reached the age of 24, and to maintain him out of the profits in the meantime. Inquisitions were held in January 1534, apparently at Cromwell's instance,[116] and duly found that Lord Dacre's will was made by fraud and collusion between him and Thomas Polsted,[117] with other legal advisers, to defraud the king of the wardship of the body and lands of the heir. The feoffees demurred to the office, and so the matter came judicially before the Court of Chancery.[118] Given that the lord chancellor was now Audley, and that Cromwell conveniently became master of the rolls in October 1534, the court must have been strongly inclined to decide the case against the feoffees; but a judgment by Audley and Cromwell would hardly have carried conviction without the approval of the common-law judges. And so the case was adjourned into the Exchequer Chamber for argument before the assembled judiciary, an argument which is fully reported in the year book for Easter term 1535.[119]

Since the fact of collusion and fraud had been found by the inquisition, counsel for the feoffees had to base their submissions on the law. Their first contention was that a man on point of death had to be presumed not to have acted fraudulently; but this was matched by the argument that jurors must be presumed not to have perjured themselves. The next contention was that uses were a well-established legal institution. Indeed, it was argued, consistently with the year-book case of 1522, that uses were at common law:[120]

... for a use is nothing but a trust which the feoffees put in the feoffee upon the feoffment; and if we were to say that there was no use at common law, it would follow that there was no trust at common law, which cannot be: for trust or confidence is a thing which is very necessary between man and man, and at least no law prohibits or restrains a man from putting his confidence in another... Moreover, it has been held for many years that a use was at common law, by the common opinion of the whole realm; and so it seems to me that it is no longer to be disputed.

Serjeant Mountagu added that, even if this had originally been a mistake, 'it would be a great mischief to change the law now, for so many inheritances in the realm today depend on uses that there would be great confusion if this were done'.[121]

[116] Cromwell's remembrances, *LP*, vi. 1382; Bean, *Decline of Feudalism*, 276–7.

[117] Probably the well-established attorney practising in Sussex since the 1490s, who died in 1529. His son, the barrister Thomas Polsted (A.-G. of the Wards 1540–1), was a protégé of Cromwell: *HPHC 1509–58*, iii. 126–8.

[118] *Re Lord Dacre of the South* (1533–5) C142/80/24–5 (inquisition); C43/2/32 (traverse); Pas. 27 Hen. VIII, fo. 7, pl. 22 (arguments in the Exchequer Chamber), part tr. B. & M. 105–10; Spelman 228 (judicial conferences); Bean, *Decline of Feudalism*, 275–83.

[119] Pas. 27 Hen. VIII, fo. 7, pl. 22. The year book does not state the outcome, and misled Holdsworth, who—mistakenly assuming that Serjeant Mountagu was already CJKB—thought the feoffees had won: *HEL*, iv. 447–8.　　　[120] Pas. 27 Hen. VIII, fo. 7, pl. 22, at fo. 9, *per* Yorke sjt.

[121] ibid., at fo. 10.

Richard Pollard, on behalf of the Crown, argued that uses could not have existed at common law, for two reasons: first, it was repugnant to make a feoffment to someone else and yet still retain the property; and, second, a feoffment before 1290 would have created a tenure, and the tenure would have been a consideration for the feoffee to hold to his own use, and so uses could not be immemorial. These were not very good general arguments, because they were directed solely at the resulting use. The first argument would not reach a feoffment to the use of a third party, and the second would not reach an express use of any kind. A rather stronger argument was that a use such as that in the present case should be treated as falling within the equity of the Statute of Marlborough. The final argument was, however, something of a bombshell. Admit that uses were at common law, then they should follow the common law—and in that case they could not be testamentary, because land could not be left by will at common law. There the year book leaves the matter.

The significance of the case emerges from Spelman's report of the secret judicial meetings with Cromwell and the king.[122] According to Spelman, there was an even division among the judges at the first assembly in the Exchequer Chamber. The traditionalists, including himself, favoured the view that the beneficial interest in a use could be disposed of by will. The will was no more, they said, than a direction to the feoffees and did not itself alter their title: 'by his will he gives nothing of the land but only his use'. It was not therefore a disposition of the land and did not fall within the common-law rule. However, three judges (Lyster CB, Baldwin CJ, and Luke J.) sided with Audley and Cromwell in holding that a will of the use was void, because it was 'against the nature of land' to pass by will, and absurd that the testator should be able to devise someone else's property. The deadlock was broken when Port J.—who 'spoke so low' that he was misunderstood—was counted on the wrong side, making a majority of six to four in favour of the king. Pressure was then exerted on the judges by the king in person to make their decision unanimous, and they later 'conformed'.[123] Although the 'nature of land' argument seems somewhat at odds with the clear legal acceptance of local customs to devise land, the decision was not necessarily a complete perversion of law; it had a certain logic once it was accepted that uses followed the rules of common law. But the conclusion that uses of land were incapable of being left by will was hardly foreseeable, and was perhaps the most disconcerting piece of judicial legislation in English legal history. There was no longer any need to find fraud by means of special inquisitions:[124] since all wills were invalid, the 1490 statute would apply

[122] Spelman 228–30; B. & M. 110–11.

[123] By this stage the king did have a majority, because another of the 'traditionalists' was absent on grounds of illness. See also above, 418.

[124] Bean's statement to the contrary (*Decline of English Feudalism*, 284) seems to rest on a misapprehension that the finding of fraud was necessary to the final decision.

automatically on every death. Strict primogeniture was back with a vengeance, and not even limited to lands held by knight-service, since the incidents of tenure were immaterial to a decision founded on the 'nature of land'. Worst of all, as a judicial declaration of the existing law the decision was necessarily retrospective. It did not merely deprive landowners of their power of testation for the future, but unleashed the devastating legal conclusion that no will made in the past could have been valid. Any landowner whose title was traced through a will, however far back in the past, now faced eviction by the heir at law of the testator. The 'great confusion' which Serjeant Mountagu had predicted was now reality.

THE STATUTE OF USES 1536

The decision in *Lord Dacre's Case* stunned the legal profession, and its landed clientele, by unsettling most landed titles in the country. The lawyer members of Parliament might well regret that they had declined the king's offer of 1532 and paid so little heed to his warning. Legislation was now the only way of resolving the intolerable state of confusion, and a settlement would have to be reached with the king on his own terms. The commons, who in 1532 had refused to be cowed by the forceful personality of 'an extremely strong-willed king',[125] were now reduced into submission by the alarming legal logic of 1535. The king had, of course, already gained by the decision of the judges more than he had formerly offered to accept. But he had yet more to gain from legislation, in that uses still deprived him of prerogative rights such as primer seisin. These matters were already on Cromwell's mind, for in the autumn of 1534 he had on his agenda 'that some reasonable ways may be devised for [the king's] wards and primer seisin'.[126] The original intention may have been some extension of the 1490 statute,[127] but the victory of 1535 suggested a more radical approach. A new session of Parliament began in February 1536, and a bill for dealing with uses was read and passed before it ended in April. Cromwell was doubtless the moving force.[128]

The statute would not only put the king's entitlement to feudal incidents on a statutory footing, ending any possible doubts about the decision in Chancery,[129]

[125] F. W. Maitland, *Equity* (1936), 34. Maitland's point was that the preamble could not be taken at face value.

[126] BL Cotton MS. Titus B.I, fo. 159v (*LP*, ix. 725) (sp. mod.). For the date see Ives, 'Genesis of the Statutes of Uses', 692.

[127] See the draft bill pr. Holdsworth, *HEL*, iv. 580–1, which also deals with a number of other points. For the three successive drafts see SP 1/101, ff. 252–291; *LP*, x. 246; Lehmberg, *Reformation Parliament*, 236–7.

[128] See *LP*, ix. 725(ii); Elton, *Reform and Renewal*, 143 (where the context is misunderstood). Lehmberg says the final draft of the statute bears some stylistic improvements in Cromwell's hand. See also the earlier notes in *LP*, iv. 6043(3); v. 394; vi. 120(1).

[129] In *Tylden v. Lylle* (Mich. 1535) CP 40/1087, m. 601, after the decision in *Lord Dacre's Case*, a devise of a use was pleaded by the defendant and confessed by the replication.

but would restore his prerogative rights to their full extent at common law. His subjects, in return, would be protected from the retrospective effects of the decision in *Lord Dacre's Case*. The only explicit evidence of this compromise is section nine, but its sense is clear once the context is understood.[130] Because 'great ambiguities and doubts may arise of the validity and invalidity of wills heretofore made' of land, 'to the great trouble of the king's subjects', it was provided by section nine that all wills of persons dying before 3 May 1536:

shall be taken and accepted good and effectual in the law after such fashion, manner and form as they were commonly taken and used at any time within forty years next afore the making of this act, anything contained in this act or in the preamble thereof or any opinion of the common law to the contrary thereof notwithstanding...

The only 'opinion of the common law' which contradicted the previous common understanding was the decision of the judges in *Lord Dacre's Case*; and the section was in effect a declaration that it should not have retrospective effect. It was this protective assurance, rather than some supposed deal with the legal profession to overlook its abuses and augment its business,[131] which persuaded Parliament to restore the king to all the revenue which the common law gave him. The full victory was to be short-lived,[132] but even after the king's partial retreat in 1540 the newly revived feudal revenue was sufficiently substantial to justify the creation of a new department of state to handle it.[133]

The technical means of achieving the result was prepared with considerable skill. It was not sufficient to codify the decision of the judges—by declaring that uses could not validly be devised by will—because that would not have restored the king to his full rights. Nor did the statute merely abolish uses, because at best that would have left existing feoffees (mostly lawyers) with an unfettered discretion to deal with the freehold as they saw fit. In order to bring about the desired object it was necessary to transfer the seisin of all land held to uses from the feoffees to the beneficiaries, so that the latter would die seised, their wills would be invalid, their heirs would inherit, and feudal incidents would attach at common law. Yet it would have been impracticable to require all the feoffees in the country to make conveyances to their beneficiaries. So resort was had to the statutory magic which had been released in smaller quantities in 1484 and 1490. Any beneficiary under a use would be deemed thenceforth to be seised, not merely for the specific purposes mentioned in those statutes, but for all purposes. In other words, the seisin would be

---

¹³⁰ 27 Hen. VIII, c. 10 (sp. mod.); B. & M. 112.

¹³¹ Holdsworth, *HEL*, iv. 450–61; Plucknett, *CHCL* (5th edn), 583–7. Neither was aware of Spelman's report.

¹³² For the Statute of Wills 1540, which reverted to the one-third principle, see below, 679.

¹³³ For the Court of Wards and Liveries (1540) see above, 229. The feudal revenue was further augmented by the conversion of monastic land to knight-service, but this was effective chiefly because of the Statute of Uses.

made actually to pass to him: not by the physical delivery which at common law was requisite for the conveyance of a freehold in possession, but instantaneously by operation of law. This was accomplished by providing that whenever anyone was— or should in the future be—seised to the use of any other person or persons,[134] the latter should 'stand and be seised, deemed, and adjudged in lawful seisin, estate, and possession ... of and in such like estates as they had or shall have in use'.[135] The feoffees became 'only an instrument to cause the thing to pass'.[136]

LEGAL CONSEQUENCES OF THE STATUTE

Serjeant Mountagu (later Mountagu CJ) was wont to refer to the 1536 Act as 'the statute for extinguishing uses',[137] alluding to the technical sense of extinguishment rather than to outright extinction or abolition,[138] and Robert Catlyn (later Catlyn CJ) likewise referred to it in 1547 as 'the statute which extinguishes uses'.[139] Within twenty years, however, pleaders were calling it 'the statute for transferring (or transmuting) uses into possession',[140] while Chancery draftsmen around the end of our period adopted the reverse form, 'the statute for transferring (or uniting) possessions to uses':[141] a formula favoured by Mountagu as chief justice in 1550.[142] Both expressions describe more exactly the essence of the operation known to later generations as 'executing the use'.[143] Although the purpose of transmuting

---

[134] Including corporations.   [135] Statute of Uses 1536, s. 1; B. & M. 113.

[136] *Anon.* (1550) Wm Yelv. 351, no. 79, at 352, *per* Mountagu CJ.

[137] Dyer 23, §148 (1536); Dyer 32, §3 (1537). Cf. *Anon.* (*c.*1540/8) Wm Yelv. 358, no. 96, *per* Shelley J. ('by the vesting and execution of the possession where the use was, the use is gone and confounded').

[138] The first reader on the statute, John Boys of Gray's Inn (1536), was said to have been in 'trouble' for interpreting the statute as an abolition of uses for the future: *The Learned Reading of Francis Bacon on the Statute of Uses* (1642), 34; Baker, *Readers and Readings*, 36.

[139] Reading in the Middle Temple (1547) BL MS Lansdowne 1133, fo. 4 ('lestatute anno 27 H. 8. que extinct uses').

[140] e.g. *Baker* v. *Conyngesby* (1555) CP 40/1164, m. 921 ('statutum de usibus in possessionem transfer-endis'); *Padyham* v. *Gerves* (1555) ibid., m. 937 ('statutum de usibus in possessionem transmutandis'); *Chamberleyn* v. *Darry* (1556) CP 40/1168, m. 1460; *Lady Mountjoy* v. *Cokysworthye* (1556) CP 40/1169, m. 743. Cf. *Anon.* (*c.*1540/8) Wm Yelv. 358, no. 96, *per* Shelley J. ('in the place where the use was there shall be the possession').

[141] N. G. Jones, 'Trusts in England after the Statute of Uses: a view from the 16th century', in *Itinera Fiduciae*, ed. R. Helmholz and R. Zimmermann (19 CSC; 1998), 173–205, at 191 n. 115 (citing cases from 1566 to 1584).

[142] *Anon.* (1550) Wm Yelv. 351, no. 79, *per* Mountagu CJ ('by the operation of the statute the feoffee's possession was *hoc instante* transposed and conveyed to the use'). Cf. *Re Townsend* (1554) Plowd. 111 at 112 (tr. 'the statute gives the feoffees' possession to cestuy que use according to the estate, quality, and form of the use').

[143] Contemporaries preferred to speak of executing the possession: *Anon.* (1542) 121 Selden Soc. 448, no. 26, *per* Portman sjt ('the statute of 27 [Hen. VIII] which executes possession to the use'); *Wimbish* v. *Tailbois* (1550) Plowd. 38v at 46v, *per* Whiddon sjt (tr. 'when the statute of 27 Hen. VIII executes the possession...').

uses into possession was to restore feudal revenue, the device brought with it a great many tangential consequences and new conveyancing possibilities, not all of which were foreseen by the draftsman.

First, the statute did away with wills for the time being. Although section nine expressly validated the wills of testators dying before 1536, the effect of executing the use was that beneficiaries under existing and future uses would die seised at common law, so that their wills—even if made before 1536—could no longer take effect. This position, as we shall see, lasted for only five years. But it remained the case that wills of persons dying after 3 May 1536, if made at any time before 20 July 1540, were invalid, except in the case of a testator who survived until the latter date and then ratified and approved such a will.[144]

Second, the statute put an end to resulting uses. That was indeed necessary to its purpose, since most uses created before 1536 had been tacit resulting uses arising from feoffments made without a consideration moving from the feoffees.[145] If a conveyance was made without consideration after 1536, however, the livery of seisin had no effect: the feoffees became seised to the use of the feoffor, the use was instantaneously executed by the statute, and so the seisin rebounded on the feoffor.[146] The only practical consequence of this was to make conveyancers more careful to recite a consideration and to express a use in favour of the feoffees.[147]

The statute also executed implied uses, and this raised an awkward problem. Execution of the implied use which arose in favour of the purchaser on a bargain and sale of land would have removed the distinction between the contract to sell land and the conveyance. This would have thrown conveyancing practice into confusion, since an interval was necessary to make enquiries, to take counsel as to the best form of conveyance, for legal advisers to draw the instrument transferring title, and in appropriate cases to arrange for a common recovery or final concord to clear the title.[148] The problem seems to have been spotted at a rather late stage, and a separate bill was rushed through Parliament to deal with it.[149] The solution

---

[144] The ratification was effective as a new will: *Putbury* v. *Trevilian* (1557) Dyer 142b at 143b (testator made will in 1531 and died in 1545).

[145] The resulting use was accepted Chancery doctrine by the beginning of our period. Some lawyers nevertheless thought it repugnant to the express words of grant: see John Hynde's reading (Gray's Inn, 1518) HLS MS. 125, case no. 170, *per* Broke sjt and Fyneux CJ; *Anon.* (1542) 121 Selden Soc. 448, no. 26, *per* Baldwin CJ (referring to the position before 1536); pr. Baker, *The Law's Two Bodies*, 104, 107.

[146] Cf. Catlyn's reading (Middle Temple, 1547) BL MS. Lansdowne 1133, fo. 4 (tr. 'if he makes a feoffment to his use, the possession reverts [*reverse*] immediately in him').

[147] It was held sufficient before the statute to limit the use expressly to the feoffee: *Anon.* (1535) Benl. 16.

[148] The written contract of sale commonly contained, besides the covenant to make an estate (i.e. convey the title), a covenant to make such further assurance as counsel should advise: e.g. the precedent of 1499 in Madox, *Formulare Anglicanum*, 287–8.

[149] For the haste see Elton, *Reform and Renewal*, 146–7 (where the purpose is misunderstood). The draftsman may have been Robert Urmeston, clerk of the House of Commons, and a barrister of Gray's Inn.

was to provide that a bargain and sale of land should not operate to pass an estate of inheritance or freehold 'except the same bargain and sale be made by writing indented, sealed and enrolled in one of the king's courts of record at Westminster' or in the county where the lands were situated.[150] The 'bargain and sale enrolled' thus became a new way of passing freehold title, without livery of seisin, on condition of public registration.[151] The device had no connection with the schemes for compulsory registration of deeds which were currently under consideration but came to nothing.[152] It did not even become the usual method of conveyance, though there was a marked increase in the number of deeds enrolled in the central courts after 1536.[153] Moreover, enrolling the contract evidently did not in practice preclude a second stage in the conveyancing process, because these enrolled deeds commonly contained covenants by the vendor to make a good estate by deed, fine, feoffment, recovery, release, or otherwise, and sometimes also to make such further assurances from time to time[154] as counsel learned should devise, and to hand over muniments of title. A covenant to make a good estate was not fulfilled by the enrolment alone.[155]

Another kind of contract fell outside the enrolment legislation. If a landowner covenanted upon good consideration to stand seised to certain uses—provided it was not an executory covenant to be performed in the future[156]—he was thereby immediately seised to those uses,[157] and so they would be executed by the Statute of Uses; and yet there was no bargain and sale within the provisions of the

[150] Statute of Enrolments 1536, 27 Hen. VIII, c. 16; B. & M. 115. See J. M. Kaye, 'A Note on the Statute of Enrolments 1536' (1988) 104 LQR 617–34. For the first draft see Lehmberg, *Reformation Parliament*, 238.

[151] For the manner of pleading title through the statute see *Omer v. Lord Cromwell* (1539) CP 40/1102, m. 357 (defendant in replevin pleads bargain and sale enrolled in Chancery according to the form of the statute, as a result of which he entered and was seised).

[152] As to these see Elton, *Reform and Renewal*, 144–6; Lehmberg, *Reformation Parliament*, 238. For the proposed registration of uses see above, 665.

[153] e.g. in Mich. 1538 the clerk of the enrolments in the Common Pleas had over 30 membranes of enrolled deeds, mostly bargains and sales: CP 40/1099, sub nom. Hord.

[154] It was important to use a phrase such as 'whenever and as often as he shall be requested', or else the covenant would be executed by the first conveyance made: Caryll (Jun.) 376, no. 15 (note, c.1530).

[155] *Anon.* (1552) Benl. 36; 3 Leon. 1, pl. 2. Cf. *Anon.* (c.1538) Wm Yelv. 355, no. 90 (enrolment void unless both parties present, but in that case each party can require enrolment under the original covenants).

[156] Hil. 21 Hen. VII, fo. 18, pl. 30; *Anon.* (1530) Yorke 146, no. 154; *Anon.* (1532/3) Pollard 276, no. 72; *Lord Burgh's Case* (1543) Dyer 54; *Bainton v. Reginam* (1553) Dyer 96; *Constable's Case* (1554) Dyer 101b; *Lady Wingfield v. Littleton* (1557) Dyer 162. Cf. *Anon.* (1550) BL MS. Hargrave 4, fo. 110 (effect of covenant to make a feoffment to uses, where covenantor dies before performance).

[157] *Drax's Case* (c.1501/6) 2 Caryll 501; *Note* (c.1520/30) Yorke 135, no. 124; *Anon.* (c.1525/35) Caryll (Jun.) 401, no. 74 (conditional covenant changes use when condition performed); *Lord Burgh's Case* (1543) Dyer 55a. Cf. *Anon.* (1502) 2 Caryll 395, where Frowyk sjt argued that a covenant could not make a use. As to whether a past or continuing consideration would suffice, see *Anon.* (1544) Brooke Abr., *Feffements al Uses*, pl. 54.

Statute of Enrolments. This conclusion was confirmed by all the judges 'upon great deliberation' in 1542.[158] The device was very common in marriage agreements.[159]

A different difficulty which was foreseen in 1536 was the effect of the Statute of Uses on dower and jointures. Estates in use did not carry dower,[160] and in practice dower had to a considerable extent been replaced by jointure.[161] But if the husband-beneficiary was now to die seised, his widow would be entitled to dower at common law, and if provision had been made for a jointure she would be entitled to that as well. The Statute of Uses therefore provided that a widow who had a jointure or separate use could not also claim dower, save that in the case of a jointure given after marriage the woman could—after her husband's death— refuse the jointure and demand her dower at common law.[162] Her common-law right to dower operated as a kind of insurance for the jointure, since, if evicted from any of the jointure lands, she could claim dower up to the value of the lands which she had lost. Although the statute gave rise to a number of conundrums,[163] the general principle was that a jointure could be pleaded in bar to a writ of dower.[164]

The draftsman seemingly did not give so much thought to the effect of the legislation on future and contingent interests in use. Since he was principally concentrating on feudal incidents, the estates foremost in his mind were estates of inheritance: that is, the passive resulting use in fee simple and the use in fee (often fee tail) created by will or marriage settlement.[165] It has been suggested that most other testamentary provisions were essentially 'ministerial'.[166] But uses were also the basis of marriage settlements and testamentary settlements with remainders; and some settlors had begun to experiment with devices unknown to the common

---

[158] *Mantell's Case* (1542) Brooke Abr., *Feffements al Uses*, pl. 16, ad finem; BL MS. Harley 1691, fo. 91v, *per* Broke CJ (cited, 1554); followed in *Anon.* (Serjeants' Inn, 1553) Dalison's reports, BL MS. Harley 5141, fo. 15; *Anon.* (1556) Brooke Abr., *Feffements al Uses*, pl. 59. [159] See further below, 688.

[160] It was, however, doubtful whether a jointure in use 'in satisfaction of all dower' could operate as legal recompense: *Anon.* (1533/4) Caryll (Jun.) 371, no. 10, at 372, *per* Fitzherbert J.

[161] See below, 689.

[162] This reproduced the previous law: *Anon.* (1533/4) Caryll (Jun.) 371, no. 10.

[163] In *The Duchess of Somerset's Case* (1554) Dyer 97b, a jointure in tail was held to bar dower, though not within the words of the statute. See also *Anon.* (1551) BL MS. Hargrave 4, fo. 117v, where Hales J. agreed with counsel that the wording of the statute was obscure. Legal ingenuity would in due course uncover situations in which a widow might claim both jointure and dower, or neither: John Brograve's reading on jointures (Gray's Inn, 1576), pr. in *Three Learned Readings* (1648), at 83–6.

[164] e.g. *Hanmer* v. *Hanmer* (1546) CP 40/1129, m. 456 (life estate 'in name of all dower and jointure' pleaded in bar; demurrer); *Elryngton* v. *Rowe* (1556) CP 40/1165, m. 425 (jointure of copyhold, granted by surrender and admittance, pleaded in bar; demurrer).

[165] Sometimes the feoffees would be directed to make a conveyance, but often the entail was left in use. John Norwode in 1493 directed his feoffees that if their numbers fell to three or four they were to take more in, and never to make an estate to the heirs: *CIPM Hen. VII*, i. 518, no. 1169.

[166] See Milsom, *HFCL*, 226–7.

law, such as powers of appointment,[167] shifting uses,[168] springing uses,[169] and perpetuities.[170] The statute drew no distinctions, but stated in general terms that persons having uses in fee simple, fee tail, for life, for years, 'or otherwise', or in reverter or remainder, should be seised 'of and in such like estates as they had or shall have in use'. It thus appeared to be the clear intention to turn any kind of settlement in use into a legal settlement.[171] The inevitable question which was to vex future generations, namely whether this gave legal form to varieties of settlement not permitted under the rules of the common law, does not seem to have been ventilated and may not have been foreseen. It was a perfectly reasonable failure of foresight, since the doctrine which supported the decision in *Lord Dacre's Case*—that uses should follow the common law—would, if applied to future estates, have prevented the later difficulties from arising. Well might the draftsman have assumed that to be the legal position. Spelman had held in 1519—anticipating Coke's successful argument in *Shelley's Case* (1581)—that settlements in use followed the same rules as settlements of the legal estate ('the land'), so that a feoffment to the use of A for life, remainder to A and his heirs, or to A's heirs, gave A an immediate fee simple which extinguished the life estate in use.[172] If that had indeed become the common learning after 1535, much confusion might have been avoided. On the other hand, it was agreed in 1540—following the Chancery practice before 1536—that limitations of uses were to be construed according to the intention rather than the strict rules of law.[173] And the

[167] Baker, *IELH* (4th edn), 289. Examples of powers in settlements: *CIPM Hen. VII*, i. 439, no. 1025 (1482; life tenant given power of sale if heir disobeyed will); iii. 92, no. 172 (1501; similar); BL Add. Ch. 59344 (1501; lands to be divided at discretion of feoffees, or of others chosen by them); *CIPM Hen. VII*, ii. 397, no. 628 (1503; power for settlor to nominate ultimate remainderman in fee simple); Dyer 136, §17 (1505; power to appoint remainders on failure of issue); *CCR 1500–9*, no. 509 (1505; power for tenant in tail to assign jointure to future wife). The common law recognized powers given to executors (who were often given a power of sale) and powers of attorney (e.g. to deliver to seisin). Some members of Gray's Inn around 1510 even held good a remainder to such person as the tenant for life would assign: Trinity Coll. Cambridge MS. R.15.7, fo. 89.

[168] e.g. *CCR 1485–1500*, pp. 357–60 (1499; to use of settlor in tail until son marries); Madox, *Formulare Anglicanum*, 413 (1513; fee to shift when first feoffee has received £24. 10s.).

[169] Executors were often directed to raise money from the land for a fixed term, in order to carry out bequests, before they transferred the fee. See also *CIPM Hen. VII*, ii. 1, no. 1 (1496; to use of wife for life, remainder for 21 years after testator's death, if wife dies within that term, for benefit of younger children, then to convey to eldest son in tail male).   [170] Below, 699.

[171] The execution of uses in tail was pleaded in *Robertys* v. *Lynke* (1538) CP 40/1099, m. 644; *Smalham* v. *Hawke* (1539) CP 40/1101, m. 519 (plaintiff replies that it was barred by recovery, and jury so finds); *Reyner* v. *Rayner* (1548) CP 40/1137, m. 452 (plaintiff replies that feoffees had notice of prior use); *Garneys* v. *Browne* (1548) Brooke Abr., *Formedon*, pl. 49. For uses in tail see further below, 695–6.

[172] Moot in Gray's Inn (1519) BL MS. Harley 5103, fo. 82v; HLS MS. 125, no. 104; Bodl. Lib. MS. Rawl. C.705, fo. 10. Note also *Bele* v. *Benet* (1527) below, 680 (sim. settlement in will). The same conclusion seems to have been made by the escheators in *CIPM Hen. VII*, i. 380, no. 888; ii. 355, no. 562 (will of Elizabeth Russell, 1481).

[173] *Anon.* (1540) Brooke Abr., *Conscience*, pl. 25, *per* Lord Audley C. (the words 'for ever' may create a fee simple in use, without the words 'his heirs'). Cf. (before the statute) *Anon.* (1532) Benl. 11 (devise 'to A. to do his will therewith' creates a fee simple).

courts of law seemed inclined to go further. Soon after the statute we find mention of springing uses[174] and shifting uses,[175] which, though not recognized by the common law, were turned by the statute into legal estates.[176] The same appears to have been true of powers of appointment, which are still found after 1535.[177] Doubtless no one at first saw the full significance of applying the statutory magic to them. The conflicting logics were to wreak their revenge in later ages.

THE STATUTE OF WILLS 1540

The king's victory of 1536 was absolute but not permanent. In fact it stood for only five years. In 1540, the king 'of his most blessed disposition and liberality' restored the power to devise land and retreated to the one-third scheme which he had proposed in 1530.[178] This volte-face—or defeat[179]—has generally been understood as a response to popular disquiet about the reintroduction of compulsory and unqualified primogeniture, and an attempt to appease the landed gentry.[180] The duke of Norfolk had pronounced the Statute of Uses the worst statute ever made,[181] and it was among the grievances listed by the Pilgrims of Grace in 1536. Robert Aske, a barrister of Gray's Inn and one of the ringleaders, had urged that landowners should be allowed to leave part of their lands by will, so that they could pay their debts and provide for their children's marriages, or else lawyers would exploit loopholes in the legislation—loopholes which, as he warned ominously, had already become apparent.[182] The king loftily told the protesters that the statute did not concern them, as 'base commons',[183] and Aske was soon afterwards executed for treason. Yet the preamble to the Statute of Wills expressed

---

[174] Anon. (1538/9) Brooke Abr., Feffements al Uses, pl. 50 (tr. B. & M. 120); Anon. (1554) Dyer 99b, §64; 110 Selden Soc. 400, pl. 2. There is here no mention of the statute.

[175] Anon. (1546) Brooke Abr., Assuraunces, pl. 1; Anon. (1552) Brooke Abr., Feffements al Uses, pl. 30 (tr. B. & M. 134). In both cases, the use was held to be executed by the statute.

[176] The Chancery took the same view, in cases on the legal title in the 1540s and 1550s: see Henderson, 'Legal Rights to Land in the Early Chancery', 97 at 110–17. See also below, 706.

[177] e.g. The Pudsay Deeds, ed. R. P. Littledale (56 Yorks. Arch. Soc. Rec. Ser.; 1916), 269, no. 290 (1542; power reserved for settlor, as tenant for life, to give lands to younger sons). See also below, 680.

[178] Statute of Wills 1540, 32 Hen. VIII, c. 1; B. & M. 115. Cromwell was executed in 1540, but the bill may originally have been his: Elton, Reform and Renewal, 143–4. Cf. below, n. 197.

[179] Bean, Decline of English Feudalism, 301, called it 'a compromise which marked a real and substantial defeat'.

[180] See T. E. Scrutton, Land in Fetters (1886), 94; Holdsworth, HEL, iv. 465; Plucknett, CHCL (5th edn), 587; Simpson, History of the Land Law, 191.

[181] M. H. Dodds and R. Dodds, The Pilgrimage of Grace (1915), i. 266. Lord de la Warr said it was 'a very sore act', and he 'grudged much at it': LP, xiii. II. 822.

[182] M. Bateson, 'Aske's Examination' (1890) 5 EHR 550–73, at 563; LP, xii. I. 406; D. S. Berkowitz, Humanist Scholarship and Public Order (1984), 228–9, 232–3.

[183] Dodds and Dodds, Pilgrimage of Grace, i. 137. Cf. LP, xi. 780, where he retorted that 'the rude commons of one shire' ought not to dispute a piece of law reform approved by Parliament.

the king's desire to make the very concession which Aske had sought. What could have brought about such a major political retreat? The principal grievances of the pilgrims were religious, and there were no concessions on that front. It therefore seems unlikely that the government were unduly perturbed by popular unrest. Much more likely it was Aske's juristic warning. Lawyers were already beginning to contemplate devices which threatened the entire working of the Statute of Uses. Aske, after his arrest, was interrogated closely as to what he had in mind, and it seems that it involved making a settlement on the landowner for life with remainders, in the manner of the later strict settlement.[184] If the heir apparent or other intended beneficiary took by remainder, rather than by descent, the feudal incidents would be lost.[185] If Aske was thinking of vested remainders, such a settlement would still not have given the landowner the flexibility of a will which could be revised at any time before death. But he had hinted that there were 'more ways than before', implying that the statutory magic could be turned to new ends. Something very like a power to devise could be created by drawing a feoffment to the use of the settlor for life, with remainders[186] to such persons as he should by will appoint. Such devices had been contemplated before the statute,[187] and were discussed at Walter Hendley's reading of 1530.[188] If the statute were now to operate on such remainders when the power was executed—and it was difficult to see why it should not—the persons designated by will would obtain seisin without taking by devise or inheritance, and the feudal incidents would again be lost.

By 1539 Cromwell was sufficiently worried to ask the king to seek the advice of the judges.[189] He had also come to learn of settlements which turned the landowner into a lessee for a long term of years, with remainder to his eldest son,

---

[184] Such an arrangement was already common in respect of jointure land, settled on the husband and wife for lives with remainder to the heir, but this was not necessarily a true remainder (see above, 678 n. 172).

[185] Bateson, 'Aske's Examination', 565; *LP*, xii. I. 901. For the relevant interrogatory, see *LP*, xii. I. 945. Aske doubtless assumed that a remainder to an heir in the singular, or by name, was not a limitation but the designation of a person intended to take by purchase.

[186] The word 'remainder' itself was seldom applied to uses, the usual formula being 'to the use of A for life, and after his death to the use of ...'.

[187] Cf. *Bele* v. *Benet* (1527) CP 40/1054, m. 316; as reported in Spelman 228, pl. 3 ('to the use and intent to perform his last will as follows, namely, to his own use for term of his life, and he willed that after his death the tenement should remain to B. his son...'); Trin. 19 Hen. VIII, fo. 11, pl. 5, and fo. 13, pl. 11; 120 Selden Soc. 58; Wm Yelv. 365, no. 105. However, the record shows that the 'will' was expressed in the deed of feoffment itself (tr. 'to the use, intention and performance of the last will of the same John Benet ... namely, to the use of the aforesaid John Benet for term of his life, and after his decease he willed by the same charter that' the feoffees should stand seised to the use of the defendant in tail, with remainder over). A majority of judges held that the defendant—the testator's son—took by purchase and not by descent.

[188] Reading in Gray's Inn (1530) BL MS. Harley 5103, ff. 24–25; part tr. in *The Law's Two Bodies*, 142–3. It was argued that the remainder was too uncertain, but the reader held it good.   [189] *LP*, xv. 439.

so that he could devise the estate in possession by will.[190] Leases for years, being chattels, were devisable at common law and unaffected by the statute. It was a scheme of that kind which sent four lawyers to the Tower in February 1540.[191] Their imprisonment was avowedly a punishment for advising the late Sir John Shelton to settle his lands in lease, so that he could make a will,[192] conduct which was regarded as a breach of their 'oaths and duties' as royal officials;[193] but presumably the government also hoped that the secret might be suppressed until legislation could be prepared.[194] The readers of the inns of court were at the same time summoned to the Star Chamber for a lecture by Lord Chancellor Audley on the evils of tax avoidance by 'subtle practices or invention of crafty wits', and a warning not to propagate learning which might deprive the king and other lords of their feudal incidents.[195] The Statute of Wills was passed the following July.[196] It was evidently the fear of lawyers' skills, rather than any alarm at popular wails of protest, which necessitated the dramatic revision of policy.[197]

Parliament could hardly abolish remainders as well as wills, and the best legislative strategy was to reintroduce the power to devise but with statutory restrictions safeguarding a proportion of the feudal revenue. The scheme in principle was the same as that proposed in 1530, though since the Statute of Uses was left in force it operated in a slightly different way. The statute enabled every landowner to devise hereditaments 'at his free will and pleasure', thereby introducing for the first time a general power to devise the legal estate in land.[198] In the

---

[190] *LP*, xv. 1028 (a young lawyer assures Cromwell that he has not 'devised any estates to bring a term of years to the owner of the inheritance with a remainder over to declare a will'). It is ambiguous whether the power to declare the will related to the term or the remainder. Holdsworth (*HEL*, iv. 465) assumed it was the term; but cf. Bean, *Decline of English Feudalism*, 297. The similarity to Shelton's arrangement suggests that Holdsworth was right.

[191] Lost register of the Star Chamber, 23 Feb. 1540, pr. 94 Selden Soc. 351-2; *Hall's Chronicle*, 837; repr. from Hall, *Henry VIII*, ii. 303 in Bean, *Decline of English Feudalism*, 296; C. Wriothesley, *A Chronicle of England*, ed. W. D. Hamilton (1877), ii. 116. Cf. Spelman 183, which (contrary to what is stated there and in 94 Selden Soc. 203) relates to Serjeant Browne's earlier dismissal in 1532.

[192] The nature of Shelton's settlements is set out in the statute 33 Hen. VIII, c. 26, which annulled them; Bean, *Decline of English Feudalism*, 296-7. Shelton had died on 21 Dec. 1539, and Hall referred to a fraudulent will; the will is filed in PCC (PROB 10/8).

[193] The decree recited that Humphrey Browne was a king's serjeant, Sir Nicholas Hare a privy councillor, and William Conyngesby attorney of the duchy. The fourth prisoner (one Grey) was doubtless Edmund de Grey, barrister of Gray's Inn, steward of the sheriffs' court, Norwich.

[194] The prisoners were released in March, but only on giving heavy sureties.

[195] 94 Selden Soc. 351; above, 472.   [196] *HLJ*, i. 154-7.

[197] Cf. Bean, *Decline of English Feudalism*, 297-301, who argues convincingly against the statute being a response to the Pilgrimage of Grace, and against any connection with the statute erecting the Court of Wards, but suggests some unspecified connection with Cromwell's fall in June 1540.

[198] It had always been allowed by local custom, such as the customs obtaining in most cities. The statute did not validate other wills (i.e. those made between 1536 and 1540) retrospectively: *Putbury* v. *Trevilian* (1555) Dyer 142.

case of socage land, the power was unrestricted, save that if the land was held in chief the king was to retain his right to primer seisin, relief, and livery, and was to be entitled to a fine for the alienation made by the will. In the case of land held by knight-service, only two-thirds of it could be devised by will, reserving to the lord all the feudal incidents in respect of the one-third left to descend; and the king was to have a fine for alienation of the two-thirds if the land was held in chief. Moreover, and this was some *quid pro quo* for the king, the one-third principle applied not only to devises but to all land of which the deceased had been at any time seised for an estate of inheritance. This was achieved somewhat obliquely, by expressing the power to devise as exercisable not only by last will but also by 'any act or acts lawfully executed in his life'.[199] The result struck at least one legal commentator as 'very strange, for the law—which is like unto reason and equity—wills that everyone may do with his land as he pleases'.[200]

The general principle was clear enough, but the subject-matter was complex and the wording raised so many legal questions that another statute had to be passed two years later to explain it.[201] The seemingly comprehensive statutory power to devise land was not intended to enable wills to be made by tenants in tail, or by those who lacked testamentary capacity.[202] If a tenant by knight-service overlooked the statute and devised all his land, this would be good as to two-thirds and a division would have to be made by commissioners.[203] A conveyance by way of lease for life or years, with remainders, if made by covin to defraud the king or other lords of their feudal incidents, was to be ineffective for that purpose: the limitations were not rendered void,[204] but the lord was entitled to claim the incidents (and the king his prerogative rights) if the fraud was found by inquisition *post mortem*. This last section put beyond further doubt the fate of the two kinds of settlement which had provoked the hurried enactment of the 1540 statute in the first place.

Despite these clarifications, the Statute of Wills, like its elder sister of 1536, created many problems for posterity, not least through the generality of the words

---

[199] On this provision see *Anon.* (1549) Brooke Abr., *Testament*, pl. 24. Its interpretation was later narrowed by the courts: J. L. Barton, 82 *LQR* at 222–3.

[200] *Lady Long's Case* (*c*.1546/50) Wm Yelv. 344, no. 68.

[201] 34 & 35 Hen. VIII, c. 5; B. & M. 118–20. For problems of interpretation see M. C. Mirow, 'Readings on Wills in the Inns of Court, 1552–1631' (Cambridge Ph.D. diss., 1993); P. Vines, 'Land and Royal Revenue: the Statute for the Explanation of the Statute of Wills, 1542–1543' (1997) 3 *Australian Jnl of Legal History* 113–30.

[202] For incapacity see M. C. Mirow, 'Monks and Married Women' (1997) 65 *RDH* 19–39.

[203] This provision was held to apply to wills made since 1540: *Hyde* v. *Umpton* (1556) Dyer 150b; Brooke Abr., *Testament et Volunt*, pl. 26.

[204] This was confirmed by *Anon.* (1547) Brooke Abr., *Testament et Volunt*, pl. 24. Cf. *Lady Long's Case* (*c*.1546/50) Wm Yelv. 344.

'at his will and pleasure', which would enable executory devises outside the rules of the common law.[205] It appears from Dyer's reading on wills, delivered in the Middle Temple in 1552, that these possibilities were already coming into view.[206] Another basic question still causing trouble in 1550 concerned a devise to the heir. Should the heir sue livery for the two-thirds devised to him as well as for the third which descended to him? According to the earl of Wiltshire, lord treasurer, it had been the standard practice since the statute to require him to sue livery for the devised portion; but the master and attorney of the Court of Wards—Keilwey and Bacon—held that the king was not entitled to livery if there was no descent.[207]

TRUSTS AFTER THE STATUTE OF USES

The extent to which the Statute of Uses reduced the jurisdiction of the Chancery over equitable interests in land has not yet been established in quantitative terms;[208] but it is clear that the wording of the statute did not turn all uses into legal estates. The statute applied where feoffees were seised to the use of someone else for an estate which could be executed. It obviously could not apply to feoffees who had duties to perform beyond passively holding an estate for another. It could not conceivably 'execute' purposes, such as charitable objects,[209] or indeed any kind of active trust: for instance, where the profits were to be collected to pay debts,[210] or even where the feoffees were directed to collect them and pay them over directly to the beneficiary.[211] Not only did the freehold in such cases remain in the feoffees, so that they could carry out the trusts,[212] but the trusts themselves

---

[205] This was not meant as innovation, since the pre-1536 law was that wills should be given effect according to the testator's intention: *Anon.* (1527) Wm Yelv. 361 at 362, 363; *Fortescue v. Stonor* (1532) Spelman 225–6, 230–1.

[206] See *Three Learned Readings* (1648), 5 (term of years devised to a man and his heirs, passes to the heir), 7 (springing devise). See also *Warren v. Lee* (1555–9) KB 27/1174, m. 115; Dyer 51 (the words 'free will and pleasure' permit a devise upon condition).

[207] *Anon.* (1550) BL MS. Hargrave 4, ff. 105v–106.

[208] The question is complicated by the fact that, before and after the statute, the Chancery was often concerned with legal title: see above, 189.

[209] See Gray's Inn reading (c.1536) BL MS. Hargrave 253, fo. 5v, *per* Fitzherbert J. A charitable use, created by will, is pleaded (without mention of the statute) in *Cawston v. Mounford* (1538) CP 40/1097, m. 506.

[210] *Smalham v. Hawke* (1539) CP 40/1101, m. 519 (feoffees to use of will; testator wills that executors should take profits for seven years to pay debts and legacies; feoffees enter after the Statute of Uses claiming the profits to this use: it is notable that the statute is pleaded, even though it did not execute any use).

[211] Gray's Inn reading (c.1536) BL MS. Hargrave 253, fo. 5v, *per* Fitzherbert J. (feoffees directed by will to find younger son at Oxford, which they cannot do without taking the profits); *Anon.* (1544) Brooke Abr., *Feffements al Uses*, pl. 52.

[212] *Anon.* (1557/8) BL MS. Hargrave 4, fo. 129 (feoffment in trust that if the feoffor did not pay £20 by a certain day the feoffees would sell the land and use the proceeds to pay the money).

remained alive in conscience in order that the Chancery could compel the feoffees to carry them out.[213]

Since the statute spoke only of persons who were 'seised' to the use of others, it did not on a natural interpretation apply to possessions which did not technically amount to seisin, such as copyholds and leases for years. This was not necessarily a *casus omissus*, because at the time of the statute it was doubted whether a copyhold[214] or a term[215] could be impressed with a use. Doubts about terms of years lingered into the second half of the century.[216] Nevertheless, it seems that by the end of our period the Chancery was prepared to enforce trusts both of copyholds[217] and of terms,[218] on the footing that they were not executed by the statute. In the lease for years, then, the conveyancer had—at any rate by the 1550s—found a means whereby an unexecuted trust could be deliberately created.[219] The same result could be achieved by giving the feoffees active duties, and indeed most trusts found in the mid-sixteenth century were 'active'.

It was once thought that the deliberate creation of equitable interests could not have been tolerated by the Chancery between 1535 and the abolition of feudal incidents in 1645.[220] The revenue considerations were, however, irrelevant after the Statute of Wills.[221] And there were various good reasons for wishing to create equitable trusts.[222] One was to prevent the disappearance of the married woman's

[213] For a list of bills in Chancery for the enforcement of charities between the 1530s and the 1550s, see G. H. Jones, *History of the Law of Charity 1532-1827* (1969), 184-9. The disputes mostly arose from wills, the commonest object being a chantry.

[214] *Brooke v. Payntour* (1526) CP 40/1050, m. 415 (undetermined demurrer); moot in Gray's Inn (1530s) Bodl. Lib. MS. Rawlinson C.705, fo. 126 (tr. 'Of lands held by copy of court roll one may not be seised to the use of another...').

[215] Moots in Gray's Inn (*c.*1520) BL MS. Harley 5103, fo. 82, *per* Spelman, and fo. 85, *per* Hendley. The reason given in both cases is that a use is real, whereas a lease is but a chattel; but there are contrary arguments (and see Spelman at fo. 33). Trusts of chattels personal were common in practice: see e.g. R. H. Helmholz, 'Trusts in the English Ecclesiastical Courts 1300-1640', in *Itinera Fiduciae*, ed. Helmholz and Zimmermann (1998) 153 at 160-5.

[216] Simpson, *History of the Land Law*, 194; Jones, 'Trusts in England after the Statute of Uses', 178-9, 180-1. Cf. *Anon.* (1556) Brooke Abr., *Feffements al Uses*, pl. 60 (tr. 'A gift of land for years or of a lease for years to a use is good...').

[217] See *Byllyngesley v. Barons* (1548/9) C78/5/24 (decree in favour of beneficiary); cited in Jones, 'Trusts in England after the Statute of Uses', 180 (and see 184).

[218] For cases in 1558-9, see Jones, 'Trusts in England after the Statute of Uses', 184 n. 73, and 185 n. 77. There are less clear cases in the later 1540s: ibid. 181 n. 57.

[219] An example is BL Wolley Ch. XII. 119 (1553), a lease of a manor for 90 years in trust for the lessor.

[220] See Holdsworth, *HEL*, iv. 471-3.

[221] See N. G. Jones, 'The Influence of Revenue Considerations upon the Remedial Practice of Chancery in Trust Cases, 1536-1660', in *Communities and Courts in Britain, 1150–1900*, ed. C. Brooks and M. Lobban (1997), 99-113.

[222] In later terminology, the word 'trust' was used to distinguish an interest which was not executed by the statute and therefore subsisted in equity, whereas a 'use' was executed by the statute. This verbal distinction was not clearly in place in our period.

separate use. It had been common before the statute for lands to be conveyed to feoffees for the use of a married woman, usually under the provisions of her marriage agreement, so that she could receive the profits independently of her husband;[223] but the statute put an end to this device by executing the use on which it depended and turning it into a form of jointure.[224] By the 1550s, the same result could be achieved by making a lease for years to the use of the married woman; such an arrangement made in 1553 for Lady Bourchier was enforced in Chancery in 1561.[225] A lease in trust might also be employed to protect an estate from a spendthrift.[226]

In later times, equitable interests were created by means of a 'use upon a use', that is, a conveyance to A to the use of B to the use of (or in trust for) C. The effectiveness of this strange device depended upon the failure of the Statute of Uses to execute the second use; but the law on this point was not settled until the very end of our period. The validity of a use upon a use had been considered before the statute, usually in the context of an express use which conflicted with an implied or resulting use.[227] Although the second use had sometimes been ruled repugnant,[228] St German's student treated the matter as one of interpretation rather than of law, on the basis that implied and resulting uses themselves rested on rebuttable presumptions of intention.[229] The matter came to a head twenty years after the statute in *Jane Tyrrel's Case* (1557).[230] Jane Tyrrel, a widow, had in 1550 bargained and sold land for money to her son George, by indenture enrolled according to the Statute of Enrolments, to the use of herself for life and then to George in tail. The question arose in the Court of Wards, which may be considered for this purpose a court of common law, whether the uses of the settlement were not void in that they were reserved upon the implied use raised in favour of

[223] See *Anon.* (1467) Trin. 7 Edw. IV, fo. 14, pl. 8; B. & M. 98; *Moots*, 298 (Inner Temple, 1496); John Petit's reading (Gray's Inn, 1518) BL MS. Harley 5103, fo. 18. There are some examples in *CCR 1485–1500*, pp. 83 (no. 304), 88 (no. 322), 225–6 (no. 770), 269 (no. 915), and 343 (no. 1157).

[224] The statute expressly mentions a feoffment 'to the use of the wife' as a species of jointure. The conveyancing practice continued: e.g. BL Add. Ch. 39244 (feoffment 'ad solum opus et usum' of feoffor's wife for life, and then to the feoffor and his heirs for ever, 1560).

[225] *Anne, Lady Bourchier* v. *Walgrave* (1561), discussed in Jones, 'Trusts in England after the Statute of Uses', 186–9.

[226] For an example of 1558 see Jones, 'Trusts in England after the Statute of Uses', 184 n. 73. For a possible earlier example (c.1536/9) see *LP*, xv. 1028, para. 1.

[227] Cf. *CIPM Hen. VII*, i. 453, no. 1055 (feoffment to the use of A and his heirs to the use of A's last will): this looks like a use upon a use, but 'and his heirs' were words of limitation, merely indicating that A could devise the fee simple and that if A made no will the use would be to his heirs. The usual form was 'to the use of A and his heirs to perform A's last will'.

[228] e.g. uses implied from the consideration in a bargain and sale: *Anon.* (1532) Brooke Abr., *Feffements al Uses*, pl. 40; *Anon.* (1544) ibid., pl. 54.

[229] *St German's Doctor and Student*, ed. Plucknett and Barton, 220–1.

[230] *Jane Tyrrel's Case* (1557) Dyer 155a; 1 And. 37; Benl. 61. See N. G. Jones, 'Tyrrel's Case (1557) and the Use upon a Use' (1993) 14 *JLH* 75–93.

George by reason of the consideration in the bargain. There seems little doubt that Mrs Tyrrel's legal advisers had intended the settlement to be executed by the Statute of Uses,[231] and the escheators took the view that it had been.[232] Whether they had all been careless in overlooking the implied use,[233] or had simply taken a wrong view as to the effect of the Statute of Enrolments,[234] is a matter of controversy. However, after taking the advice of the Common Pleas judges and Saunders CJ, the Court of Wards held that the second use was void, both because it was repugnant to the first and—which is not quite the same thing—because 'a use cannot be engendered of a use'. The first reason might have rested merely on interpretation, but the second was evidently a rule of law. It may not have been as wide a rule of law as later generations made it, because it was limited to bargains enrolled under the Statute of Enrolments.[235] The enrolled bargain could only transfer the freehold if there was an implied use executed by the Statute of Uses, and once that use was acknowledged there was no room for interpretation: the second could not override it. If, on the other hand, the enrolled bargain did not transfer the freehold, then there was no seisin to support the second use. Understood as a general rule, that a use upon a use was not good in law and therefore not executed by the statute, it opened up the possibility that the second use might be enforced by the Chancery on grounds of conscience. That possibility was presumably in the minds of counsel advising the duchess of Suffolk and a number of other protestants fleeing religious persecution under Queen Mary. To safeguard their lands from forfeiture, the departing landowners granted them away to nominees ostensibly upon valuable consideration but subject to secret trusts to reconvey.[236] But there is no evidence that the Chancery pronounced on the enforceability of the second use in equity until the return of the duchess to England after the accession of Elizabeth I.

[231] Cf. *Milborn* v. *Ferrers* (1555) Dyer 114b, where there is an express use upon an express use, but no decision. For this case see Jones, 'Tyrrel's Case', 78.

[232] Jones, 'Tyrrel's Case', 92 n. 14 (citing inquisitions *post mortem* in Bucks. and Oxon.).

[233] This was the older view: Plucknett, *CHCL* (5th edn), 600; Simpson, *History of the Land Law*, 202.

[234] The statute may have been seen as making the bargain and sale equivalent to a feoffment, the implied use being somehow spent upon enrolment. See Jones, 'Tyrrel's Case'.

[235] Note Dyer CJ's opinion that it might not apply to the use implied upon a render in a final concord: *Anon.* (1563) Moo. K.B. 45, pl. 138; B. & M. 123.

[236] The best-known case was that of Katharine Bertie, dowager duchess of Suffolk, in which the Chancery made an important general pronouncement in 1560: Baker, 'The Use upon a Use in Equity, 1558–1625' (1977) 93 *LQR* 33–8; *Bartie* v. *Herenden* (1560) B. & M. 121. But there were several similar cases: Jones, 'Trusts in England after the Statute of Uses', 185.

36

Family Settlements

ONE of the principal occupations of learned counsel in the early-modern period, as in many others, was to provide advice to landed families on estate planning and the conveyancing operations associated with it. These were the most important everyday transactions requiring legal assistance, and the degree of expertise required in dealing with large estates was very considerable. In the absence of contemporary guides to the subject, recovering that expertise is not easy.[1] In broad terms, the typical landowner's strategy would have been dynastic: that is, to leave as substantial an estate as possible to descend in the senior male line. But he would also wish to make adequate provision for his wife, by means of a life estate in jointure; for his younger sons, if possible by grants of land; and for his daughters, usually by means of marriage portions in cash. Decisions had to be made upon the marriage of the landowner or his children, and when he was approaching death. At marriage it was usual for the bride's father to provide a portion in money, though sometimes in land as well, and for the groom's father to settle land on the couple in tail. When making a will, the testator might wish to make the payment of his debts and legacies the first charge, to make further provision for his wife, and to provide for any sons and daughters who had not been advanced in his lifetime, leaving the residue to pass in the main line of descent. In practice, there were many complicating factors which might necessitate departure from such simple schemes. Some of the settlor's land might be affected by earlier entails and wills, and by the claims of earlier wives and children by other unions;[2] and some of it might be burdened with earlier debts. Life's uncertainties were also to be brought into account. No settlor could know, when one of his children married, how many more children he might have, nor indeed how many more wives. Nor could he know, at the time when his heir apparent married, whether

---

[1] No one has yet written a history of conveyancing. The best account of estate-planning in the period is J. P. Cooper, 'Patterns of Inheritance and Settlement by Great Landowners from the Fifteenth to the Eighteenth Centuries' in *Family and Inheritance*, ed. J. Goody, J. Thirsk, and E. P. Thompson (1978), 192–327. See also the helpful study by Wright, *Derbyshire Gentry*, ch. 3.

[2] For an agreement of 1488 to resettle land on a married man whose five children were illegitimate, see *CCR 1485–1500*, pp. 75–6, no. 281. For the generous treatment of illegitimate children, see also Wright, *Derbyshire Gentry*, 49.

that child would in fact survive to inherit.[3] Not all marriages produce sons, and in settling the patrimony decisions might have to be made whether daughters and their sons should be preferred before male collaterals. The terms of family settlements and resettlements were therefore a cause for anxious reflection, for detailed discussions with counsel, and, in the case of marriage settlements, for negotiation between the respective parents. Settlements were not confined to the nobility or even the gentry.[4] But the larger the estate, the more complex were the possible solutions, since different parcels of land could be (and often were) settled on different terms.

MARRIAGE TREATIES[5]

Upon a marriage between landed families, a detailed contract or 'treaty' would be drawn up by counsel after negotiation. It was frequently in English, whereas the ensuing deeds would most often be in Latin. A surviving paper draft for a marriage contract of 1536, with corrections, is signed by the bride's father but provides that the articles and agreements are to be 'reducyd in due forme' later,[6] showing that the process of agreement might require several stages. The agreement was usually concluded between the intending spouses' parents or nearest relatives, though a groom who was of age would make it on his own behalf.[7] In its 'due form' it was framed as a series of covenants, engrossed on parchment in indentures under seal; and it was common for the parties to execute performance bonds, so that the agreement could be enforced more effectively by an action of debt.[8] The treaty would usually be concluded before the marriage took place, but post-nuptial settlements are occasionally encountered.[9]

[3] Some men did not even know at death whether they would have issue at all. For a will making provision in case the testator's wife was pregnant and had a child (which she did nine months later) see *CIPM Hen. VII*, ii. 368, no. 578 (1502).

[4] For marriage agreements by yeomen see e.g. BL Add. Ch. 52487 and 52490 (1545). Cf. BL Add. Ch. 50251 (groom a merchant, 1551).

[5] The following attempt to describe the usual elements in marriage agreements is based on an examination of about fifty such agreements during the period. See also S. J. Payling, 'The Politics of Family: late medieval marriage contracts' in *The McFarlane Legacy*, ed. R. H. Britnell and A. J. Pollard (1995), 21–47, especially at 34–8.

[6] BL Add. Ch. 53041 (signed by David Myddelton, whose daughter Anne Seyton was to marry Sir William Norres). Cf. BL Add. Ch. 51523 (draft marriage contract in a paper roll, with draft conveyances and bonds also, 1508).

[7] e.g. *CCR 1485–1500*, p. 82, no. 302 (1488); *CIPM Hen. VII*, iii. 339, no. 568 (1499); iii. 105, no. 190 (1502); iii. 185, no. 301 (1507); BL Add. Ch. 50241 (1536).

[8] This was the usual remedy for breach of a marriage agreement: e.g. *Duke of Buckingham* v. *Darrell* (1514–21) CP 40/1008, m. 450; *Sapcotys* v. *Fitzwaren* (1515) CP 40/1009, m. 520 (penalty of £1,000); *Wastnes* v. *Thurland* (1520) CP 40/1026, m. 839; Trin. 12 Hen. VIII, fo. 5, pl. 4 (119 Selden Soc. 21); *Wulverston* v. *Bendysshe* (1535) CP 40/1085(1), m. 304; *Earl of Bath* v. *Chechester* (1537) CP 40/1095, m. 607; *Harper* v. *Makand* (1540) CP 40/1107, m. 337; *Gower* v. *Delarever* (1545) CP 40/1124, m. 454.

[9] e.g. BL Add. Ch. 72173 (1526), 46060 (1535).

The core of any marriage agreement was a covenant by the groom's father, perhaps in return for a sum of money paid or payable by the bride's father, to transfer lands of an agreed value to trustees for the bride's jointure. The jointure most commonly took the form of joint life estates to the bride and groom, though in about one instance in three it was a joint estate tail, the effect for the wife being the same. A separate life estate for the wife was also called a jointure.[10] The land so settled upon the bride was often said to be in 'recompense'[11] and 'satisfaction'[12] of both jointure and dower,[13] or 'in the name of' jointure and dower;[14] and it might be provided for good measure that she would lose the jointure if she claimed dower.[15] However, a jointure was sometimes made supplementary to dower.[16] The learning on these matters became critical and complex as a result of the jointure provisions of the Statute of Uses.[17] As a further precaution for the beneficiaries, the father of an heir apparent usually covenanted that he would not encumber the land, except as agreed,[18] and that he would not alienate it but leave it to descend.[19] A younger son would normally expect a life estate, or an annuity, rather than an inheritance.[20] The father sometimes reserved to himself a life estate in at least some of the land settled.

There would be covenants that the children would marry, and it was prudent to make these conditional on their consent.[21] There were usually default provisions in case the marriage failed to take place or came to an end before consummation,[22]

[10] BL Add. Ch. 72173 (1526; post-nuptial); Add. Ch. 53062 (1531); 27 Hen. VIII, c. 10 (above, 677).

[11] BL Add. Ch. 51186 (1512; 'in full recompence of all hyr joyntor and dower'); *Anon.* (1533/4) Caryll (Jun.) 371, no. 10 (sim.; but questioned whether a jointure in use could be a legal recompense for dower of other land).

[12] e.g. BL Add. Ch. 53039 (1542); cf. Port 136 ('in plenam contentationem totius dotis et juncture sue').

[13] Cf. *CCR 1485–1509*, p. 278, no. 945 (1496), where the settlement is to the use of bride and groom for life, and (as to one-third) after the husband's death to the use of the widow for her dower.

[14] BL Add. Ch. 50241 (1536; 'in name and for her holl dower and jointure'); *Hanmer* v. *Hanmer* (1546) CP 40/1129, m. 456 ('nomine totius dotis ac juncture sue'). Cf. *Standish Deeds*, 131, no. 321 (1487; in name of dower); BL Add. Ch. 53062 (1531; in name of jointure).

[15] e.g. BL Wolley Ch. V. 18 (1505); BL Add. Ch. 53062 (1531).

[16] See e.g. BL Wolley Ch. VII. 48 (1490) (wills that wife should have both); will of William Whorwood A.-G. (1545) cited in *Whorwood* v. *Lisle* (1546) Dyer 61b.

[17] See above, 677; and also J. Drobac, 'The "Perfect" Jointure: its formulation after the Statute of Uses' [1988] *Cambrian Law Rev.* 26–44.

[18] The usual exception is jointure or dower for the settlor's own wife or successive wives.

[19] See the discussion of such clauses in Hil. 21 Hen. VII, fo. 18, pl. 30; Yorke 135, no. 124; 146, no. 154 (1530); Pollard 276, no. 72 (1532/3); *Constable's Case* (1554) Dyer 101b. For a bond by a groom's father to permit lands to descend see *Hasylden* v. *Nycoll* (1533) CP 40/1078, m. 407 (demurrer to plea).

[20] For younger sons see Wright, *Derbyshire Gentry*, 47–50; Cooper, 'Patterns of Inheritance', 220–1, 315–18.

[21] *Wastnes* v. *Thurland* (1520) Trin. 12 Hen. VIII, fo. 5, pl. 4 (119 Selden Soc. 21) arose from a refusal by the son where there was no mention of consent. Consent was required by the canon law, but the guardian could sue the ward for damages for refusing a marriage: e.g. *Pygot* v. *Nevile* (1541) CP 40/1110, m. 339.   [22] Or in case of divorce: BL Add. Ch. 52795 (1500).

or was obstructed by the guardian in chivalry.[23] Such provisions commonly included an agreement for the intended bride or groom to marry another available child of the other parent,[24] not always named,[25] 'if the ecclesiastical laws should permit'.[26] Such terms clearly indicate marriages arranged on behalf of the children,[27] and before they had reached the age of puberty.[28] If the children were under age, they would remain in ward, and the agreement often provided for the revenues of the settled land to be taken by one of the parents until the groom reached a certain age—usually 20.[29] There might be more specific provisions for the maintenance of the infant spouses, such as an exhibition to study at university and the inns of court.[30] Some agreements also dealt with the cost of the wedding.[31]

The next stage after the treaty would be for specific lands to be selected and conveyed to feoffees to uses in accordance with the covenants for jointure. This may be called the marriage settlement[32] proper. There might then be a third stage, if the agreement required the settlor or the feoffees to perfect the title by arranging for common recoveries or final concords, or licences to alienate.

[23] See CIPM Hen. VII, iii. 120, no. 198 (William Basset's settlement, c.1500/6).

[24] For an example of such a covenant in 1468 see BL Add. Ch. 73901. For cross-covenants of this kind see CCR 1485–1500, p. 358, no. 1201 (1499); The Pudsay Deeds, ed. R. P. Littledale (56 Yorks. Arch. Soc. Record Ser.; 1916), 269, no. 290 (1542); BL Add. Ch. 53039 (1542).

[25] It was usually the next in seniority. In a settlement of 1499 between Lord Latimer and Lord Willoughby de Broke, there is a further covenant that if all the former's daughters die before carnal knowledge had, the latter's son shall wed such maiden of the house of Nevill as shall be most meet and convenient of age: CCR 1485–1500, p. 358, no. 1201.

[26] As to whether this phrase extended to a marriage within the prohibited degrees, which required a dispensation, see Wastnes v. Thurland (1520) Trin. 12 Hen. VIII, fo. 5, pl. 4 (119 Selden Soc. 21); CP 40/1026, m. 839 (undetermined demurrer). For a covenant by the bride's mother to obtain a dispensation see BL Add. Ch. 52795 (1500).

[27] Some agreements left it to the bride's father to select the daughter to be married: CIPM Hen. VII, iii. 61, no. 113 (1486); Standish Deeds, 85, no. 143 (1490).

[28] In Gyfford v. Prust (1544–7) CP 40/1123, m. 318, the intended bride was under 5 at the time of the agreement. Marriages occurred at much later ages among the lower classes: R. Houlbrooke, 'The Making of Marriage in mid-Tudor England' (1985) 10 Jnl Family History 339–52.

[29] e.g. CIPM Hen. VII, ii. 61, no. 86 (before 1498); CCR 1485–1500, p. 358, no. 1201 (1499); CIPM Hen. VII, ii. 363, no. 573 (1500); Moreton, The Townshends and their World, 221.

[30] See e.g. PCC 3 Maynwaryng; PROB 11/20, fo. 12v (before 1520; John Erneley had found Master Culpeper's son at an inn of chancery under the terms of marriage agreement); BL Add. Ch. 53039 (1542; groom's father to find him at university, and at an inn of chancery and inn of court, until 21, with an exhibition of 5 marks while he diligently applies himself). Wright, Derbyshire Gentry, 47, 164 n. 142, cites two further examples.

[31] e.g. Madox, Formulare Anglicanum, 112 (1507; bride's father to pay); BL Add. Ch. 51186 (1512; parents to share costs, and each to clothe own child with suitable 'apparel'); CP 40/1085(1), m. 304 (1519; groom to pay for wedding clothes and supper); BL Add. Ch. 40761 (1524; bride's father to pay for the bride's apparel 'and to bear the charge of the dinner at the day of marriage', sp. mod.).

[32] The expression was not commonly used until the Elizabethan period (e.g. 3 Leon. 27, 'settlement of marriage', 1573), but the writer has a deed of 1554 which recites 'the setling of the sayd messuage' as a consideration (JHB MS. 114).

Occasionally the settlor or the feoffees might be required to convey a legal title to the bride and groom,[33] perhaps at a later date;[34] though after the Statute of Uses this would happen automatically through execution of the uses.

OTHER FORMS OF SETTLEMENT

Some settlements were still made in the traditional manner, by means of legal gifts in tail,[35] or even (albeit rarely) in frank-marriage.[36] When the donor was a real donor, as distinguished from a trustee under a marriage settlement, the gift was still very often made to a son and his wife, suggesting that the object was either to give effect to a marriage agreement or to make further provision after marriage. Settlements were also widely effected by means of uses, the commonest categories being family settlements and dispositions by will. A charter of feoffment did not properly mention uses, but a bill or schedule declaring the uses or 'intents' of the feoffment might be annexed to it.[37] Such a declaration of uses could not be changed afterwards.[38] Similarly, the uses of a common recovery might be declared in indentures made with the recoverors.[39]

Wills of land before 1540 were not dispositive instruments, but directions—or declarations of intent—to feoffees,[40] and they did not require probate by the ecclesiastical authorities.[41] In practice, a last will of land often was proved, together with the testament disposing of money and chattels, and sometimes the two were combined in a single document. But a will could be expressed in indentures declaring the uses upon which the feoffees held the title, and directing the feoffees to stand seised to those uses.[42] Such a will took effect *inter vivos*,[43] and

[33] e.g. *CCR 1485–1500*, pp. 277–8, no. 945 (1496).

[34] e.g. *CIPM Hen. VII*, ii. 396, no. 628 (1503; to make estate in tail when groom is 21).

[35] e.g. Madox, *Formulare Anglicanum*, 411, 414. For entails in use see above, 668, 677–8; below, 695–6.

[36] A gift of 1529 'in liberum maritagium' is mentioned in *Webb v. Potter* (1581) 110 Selden Soc. 396.

[37] e.g. BL Add. Ch. 43620 (1503); *CIPM Hen. VII*, iii. 165, no. 262 (1503); BL Add. Ch. 49199A–B (1521); *Standish Deeds*, 141, no. 393 (1522). The uses might alternatively be declared in indentures: e.g. *CIPM Hen. VII*, iii. 204, no. 342 (1494).

[38] *Anon.* (*c.*1521/30) Spelman 232, pl. 8, ad fin.; *Anon.* (1538) Brooke Abr., *Feffements al Uses*, pl. 47.

[39] For settlements so established, with remainders, see e.g. BL Add. Ch. 43606 (1492); *CIPM Hen. VII*, iii. 175, no. 277 (1506); Madox, *Formulare Anglicanum*, 113 (1538). For an indenture which the recoveror enrolled in court a term after the recovery, expressing the uses of a marriage agreement, see CP 40/1075, Hord m. 1 (1532). An example of an agreement to lead the uses by way of jointure is BL Add. Ch. 33271 (1557). [40] See above, 671.

[41] See above, 243.

[42] e.g. *CIPM Hen. VII*, ii. 355, no. 562 (shortly before death, 1481); ii. 262, no. 423 (week before death, 1501); iii. 207, no. 344 (seven weeks before death, 1505; last will annexed to charter in a schedule); Madox, *Formulare Anglicanum*, 413 (1508); *Bele v. Benet* (1527) CP 40/1054, m. 316 (tr. above, 680 n. 187); *Lord Burgh's Case* (1543) Dyer 55a.

[43] The person making such a will sometimes limited a use to himself for life: e.g. BL Wolley Ch. VII. 48 (1490); *CIPM Hen. VII*, ii. 566, no. 888 (1493). The first of these is said to be the party's will '(sp. mod.) at this time, without I declare my will in writing hereafter . . . otherwise, under my seal'.

some thought it was unalterable if made upon the livery of seisin;[44] that, however, would have been inconsistent with the rule that a will could always be changed,[45] and it was held by the judges in the 1520s that this rule applied even if the will was declared upon the livery of seisin by deed,[46] unless the intent was expressed solely as a use without reference to a will.[47] It was therefore a matter of construction whether a declaration of the intent of a feoffment was a changeable will or a binding declaration of the uses. The Statute of Wills 1540 altered the nature of wills of land by giving them the force of a conveyance,[48] but this still did not bring them within the cognizance of the ecclesiastical courts,[49] and it was still not necessary to appoint executors since the devolution of title was automatic.[50]

PRIMOGENITURE AND ENTAILS

Although the evidence of settlements and wills shows that the heads of landed families were concerned to furnish suitable support for their wives, younger sons, and daughters, it is equally clear that they were at pains to do so in a way which left a substantial patrimony to descend to the heirs in the male line.[51] They also preferred, if possible, to provide for their wider family out of acquired wealth rather than by alienating any of the patrimony which they had themselves inherited. Primogeniture was still the basis of landed society, though much legal and political debate in this period was directed to its appropriateness. Indeed, the extent of a landowner's reach into the future was one of the more difficult legal questions of the Tudor period.

Freedom to trade in land was more in accord with the spirit of the times than the policy of *De Donis*, which St German's Student thought had been 'made of a singularity and presumption of many that were at the said Parliament for exalting and magnifying of their own blood'.[52] Entails subjected parents to the cradle, by taking away a man's authority over his eldest son: the heir apparent, confident in his inheritance, had no incentive to self-sufficiency and industry. Moreover, it was not merely a kindness but a moral duty to make provision for one's younger

---

[44] The point was left undetermined in *The Duke of Buckingham's Case* (1505) Mich. 20 Hen. VII, fo. 10, pl. 20. [45] *Fortescue* v. *Stonor* (1532) Spelman 225–6, 230–1.

[46] *Foljambe* v. *Barley* (1522) Spelman 228; *Anon.* (Serjeants' Inn, 1521/30) ibid. 231–2; *Anon.* (1527) ibid. 228, pl. 3; Trin. 19 Hen. VIII, fo. 11, pl. 5; *Anon.* (1538) Brooke Abr., *Feffements al Uses*, pl. 47. See also *Moots*, 89–90, *per* Baker (Inner Temple, 1480s).

[47] *Anon.* (Serjeants' Inn, 1521/30) Spelman 232; *Anon.* (1527) ibid. 228; Trin. 19 Hen. VIII, fo. 11, pl. 5; Wm Yelv. 365, no. 105: which is probably *Bele* v. *Benet* (1527) CP 40/1054, m. 316. Cf. Perk. s. 480, where the exception is stated more widely. [48] Above, 681.

[49] *Rolfe* v. *Hampden* (1542) Dyer 53b; *Thymolby* v. *Gray* (1557) Dyer 152b, §8.

[50] *Anon.* (1545) Brooke Abr., *Testament et Volunt*, pl. 20.

[51] See Wright, *Derbyshire Gentry*, ch. 3.

[52] *Doctor and Student*, ed. Plucknett and Barton, 159 (sp. mod.).

children. The humanist attack on entails was therefore inevitable.[53] And the reformist position almost became law. The ill-fated bill of 1529, which we have already noticed, would have converted all fee tail into fee simple with an exemption for the peerage.[54] Although that would not have ended primogeniture, it would have made it easier to distribute landed wealth by gift *inter vivos* or by will. But the commons were as imbued with the dynastic spirit as the peers, and the project foundered.

Whatever misgivings there may have been about entails and primogeniture, they did not find support in legislative programmes during this period: rather the contrary. The spirit of primogeniture was at work in 1539, when lands from dissolved monasteries in Kent were distributed to lawyers and members of Parliament, who passed a disgavelling statute to prevent partition under the custom of Kent.[55] The disgavelling of Welsh land in 1542 brought primogeniture to parts of Wales, to the further detriment of younger sons.[56] A statute passed in the same year barred feigned recoveries where the king had given land in tail to a subject. In such a case, the king's reversion was protected against barring by the common law;[57] but Henry VIII thought the issue in tail should share in the protection, for by giving land in tail the king willed that the heirs of the body should continue the estate and 'have in special memory and daily remembrance the profit that they have and take by the service of their ancestors done to the kings of this realm, and thereby be the better encouraged to do the like service to their sovereign lord'. In such cases, therefore, the feigned recovery was to be of no effect, so that a species of unbarrable entail was created.[58] It was also made clear in 1542 that the Statute of Wills did not apply to entails, so that tenants in tail could not bar the entail by will.[59]

The same spirit is encountered in private affairs.[60] Serjeant Yaxley excepted entailed lands from his will, in 1505, because he did not want them on his conscience.[61] John Spelman's first recorded retainer, in 1508, was to advise on the resuscitation of a barred entail, because the tenant in tail (a priest) had 'remorse in his conscience' at having suffered a common recovery. The reason for his remorse was that he had opened the way for female heirs, and the prospect of the land descending to his sister drove him to put things back as they were.[62] William

---

[53] See e.g. Starkey, *Dialogue*, ed. Mayer, 74–6, 129, 130. Starkey acknowledged that primogeniture was appropriate for the nobility, but for gentlemen he preferred the equal distribution of the Civil law.

[54] Holdsworth, *HEL*, iv. 450–1; Bean, *Decline of Feudalism*, 259–61; above, 665.

[55] 31 Hen. VIII, c. 3. The 34 beneficiaries included Lord Cromwell, Willoughby J., Serjeant Cholmeley, the attorney-general (John Baker), William Rooper, and four benchers of Gray's Inn (Hales MR, Thomas Moyle, Thomas Harlakenden, and James Hales). [56] 34 & 35 Hen. VIII, c. 26, s. 91.

[57] *Anon.* (1537) Dyer 32a; *Anon.* (1541) Brooke Abr., *Recoverie in Value*, pl. 31; *Discontinuance*, pl. 32.

[58] 34 & 35 Hen. VIII, c. 20. [59] 34 & 35 Hen. VIII, c. 5.

[60] See also Cooper, 'Patterns of Inheritance', 201.

[61] *CIPM Hen. VII*, ii. 306, no. 496; PCC 39 Holgrave. [62] Spelman 21–2; 94 Selden Soc. 270.

Fitzwilliam referred in his will of 1516 to an entail established by his 'dear ancestor' of the same name, and placed on record that God had so blessed his family with worship and ancestry 'that I think such as go about to prejudice the same cannot avoid his plague and indignation; and therefore I have given nothing away at all . . .'.[63] These are isolated examples; but it is probably an accurate generalization to assert that the barrability of entails did not usually work against the dynastic instinct. Families were proud to hold their land under ancient entails.[64] When an entail was barred—and it was a common occurrence—the usual purpose was probably not to alienate land from the family, but to effect a resettlement.[65]

COMMON RECOVERIES

By the beginning of our period, it was established that entails could be barred by common recovery,[66] provided the tenant in tail was of full age.[67] Recoveries were already in regular use, and in the first half of the sixteenth century over 200 were enrolled by the Common Pleas every year.[68] They were at first effected by a writ of right *quia dominus remisit curiam*,[69] the procedure hallowed by *Taltarum's Case*,[70] but after 1489 it was almost invariable to use a writ of entry sur disseisin in the *post*.[71] The reason for the change is obscure. It may simply have been to save costs;[72] but it also allowed lands in different manors or lordships to be included

---

[63] *Testamenta Vetusta*, ed. Nicolas (1826), i. 545–6.

[64] e.g. *CIPM Hen. VII*, iii. 368, no. 640 (gift of 1313 still effective in 1487). The dates of gifts were not recited in actions of formedon, but esplees were often laid in the fourteenth century. In *Cleyton* v. *Robynson* (1535) CP 40/1084, m. 408, formedon was brought upon a fine of 19 Edw. II.

[65] Simpson, *Land Law*, 126, 132.

[66] For the origins, which may be traced to the time of Henry VI, see J. Biancalana, *The Fee Tail and the Common Recovery in Medieval England 1176–1502* (2001), ch. 5.

[67] As to this see *Pudsey* v. *Stanley* (1532) Spelman 113; 94 Selden Soc. 312–13 (final concord). The practice of allowing infants to suffer recoveries, subject to special safeguards, is said to have begun *c.*1531: see the precedents cited at Hob. 197.

[68] 252 were counted in 1535, 211 in 1540. Professor Biancalana counted 240 in 1502. They could also be used in local courts. For greater security they could be removed from local courts into the Common Pleas for a foreign voucher of the common vouchee: e.g. CP 40/874, m. 562 (duchy); CP 40/879, m. 421 (queen's court of honour of Mandeville); cf. CP 40/1062, m. 640 (recovery by writ of right sued in the nature of entry in the *post* in the queen's court of Cookham, Berks.). Fitzherbert J. recommended a writ of error to affirm a recovery in a local court: Yorke 202, no. 297.

[69] e.g. *Wylkynson* v. *Hopton* (1488) CP 40/906, m. 326 (vouches Earl Rivers, who vouches the common vouchee, who puts himself on the grand assize and defaults).

[70] i.e. *Hunt* v. *Smyth* (1472) CP 40/844, m. 631; Mich. 12 Edw. IV, fo. 14, pl. 16, and fo. 19, pl. 25; Mich. 13 Edw. IV, fo. 1, pl. 1 (pleading a recovery in 1464). The defaulting vouchee in 1464 was Robert Kyng, who acted as common vouchee into the 1480s: 94 Selden Soc. 204. (There was a Westminster scrivener of this name in 1492: CP 40/919, m. 302.) Many of the vouchees before then had been practising lawyers.

[71] M. M. Condon, 'From Caitiff and Villain to Pater Patriae' in *Profit, Piety and the Professions in Later Medieval England*, ed. M. Hicks (1990), 137 at 148.

[72] The details are elusive. Biancalana, *The Fee Tail*, 277, suggests that writs of entry were more expensive but avoided the cost of obtaining a waiver of court from the lord. In 1529 it was proposed to

in the same recovery.[73] At first the writ named a real person as disseisor, but there can have been no legal advantage in so doing. From the mid-1490s the names begin to look unreal, and in the sixteenth century the imaginary Hugh Hunt began to monopolize the role of fictitious common disseisor.[74] Very occasionally a formedon was used.[75] The cost of a straightforward recovery was approximately 30s., with 4s. or 5s. in addition for a sealed exemplification.[76] Exemplifications of recoveries were becoming common muniments of title and many have survived. They were written in court-hand under the name of the prothonotary responsible for the entry on the roll, and sealed with the Common Pleas seal in dark green wax, pendent on a tag; occasionally the initial letter was decorated with elaborate penwork.

The recovery was not effective to bar copyhold entails, even assuming such estates were legally feasible at all,[77] or entails in use, which were in any case not obviously affected by De Donis.[78] Although some held that cestuy que use in tail could bar the entail by virtue of the first statute of 1484,[79] a larger body of opinion held that such a discontinuance was only effective during the life of cestuy que use, and that the feoffees could falsify to the use of the issue.[80] Final concords by

legislate that writs of right could be used as 'surety' for certain purposes, paying the same fine as entry in the post: LP, vi. 6044, at p. 2694, cl. 16.

[73] Biancalana, The Fee Tail, 278–80.

[74] The names were still quite variable in Henry VIII's reign, though names beginning in H were preferred. In 1533, for instance, the disseisors included Hugh Hunt, his relatives Henry Hunt and Humphrey Hunt, and his friends Humphrey Hert, Humphrey Coke and Humphrey Thorpe: CP 40/1077, passim. For the 1490s see Biancalana, The Fee Tail, 284.

[75] e.g. Colepeper v. Eldryngton (1490–91) CP 40/913, m. 351 (demurrer); Cary v. Gilbert (1494) 1 Caryll 273; Mich. 10 Hen. VII, fo. 1, pl. 1; CP 40/930, m. 346 (action confessed by collusion); Strelley v. Ayscough (1542) CP 40/1112, m. 324 (with common vouchee). In Viscount Lisle v. Earl of Nottingham (c.1485/93) C1/100/62, counsel advised a collusive writ of right followed by a collusive formedon against the recoverors.

[76] Bodl. MS. Rawl. C.246, fo. 108v (notes by John Palmer of the Inner Temple, c.1500/10: costs of 34s. 8d. including exemplification); Bodl. Lib. MS. Lat. misc. c. 66, fo. 279v (notes by Humphrey Newton, sim. date: 29s. without exemplification); BL Add. Roll 41529 (39s., and 6s. 8d. 'reward to Master Baldwyn', 1512).

[77] There could be no voucher to warranty or execution in value: Note (c.1530) Caryll (Jun.) 393, no. 57. See also above, 646 n. 123.

[78] Some thought they were a conditional fee simple, as in Bracton's day. Trin. 19 Hen. VII, fo. 13, pl. 11; Anon. (1532/3) Pollard 276, no. 73; Anon. (1538) Brooke Abr., Feffements al Uses, pl. 56. See also Anon. (c.1535/6) Wm Yelv. 326, no. 28.

[79] 1 Ric. III, c. 1; Trin. 27 Hen. VIII, fo. 20, pl. 9, per Fitzherbert J.; Anon. (1537) Brooke Abr., Feffements al Uses, pl. 56; Recoverie in Value, pl. 29; Yorke 144, no. 150 (recovery); 165, no. 200 (fine). A feoffment by cestuy que use in tail is pleaded in Cade v. Dawe (1532) CP 40/1074, m. 317.

[80] Constable's reading on De Donis (Lincoln's Inn, 1489) 71 Selden Soc. 184; Mich. 4 Hen. VII, fo. 18, pl. 9; Anon. (1507/21) Spelman 231, pl. 7 (feoffment); Gresley's Case (1522) Brooke Abr., Feffements al Uses, pl. 48 (as to which see 94 Selden Soc. 197 n. 2); Anon. (1527) Trin. 19 Hen. VII, fo. 13, pl. 11; Brooke Abr., Feffements al Uses, pl. 2 (feoffment or recovery); Anon. (1533) Spelman 226–7 (feoffment); Anon.

cestuy que use in tail, though effective to bind the issue, were thought by some not to bar the remaindermen or reversioner.[81] These uncertainties were complained of by opponents of the use,[82] and must have made the use in tail more effective than a legal entail by deterring purchasers from buying an unsafe title.[83] Uses thus gave protection to remaindermen and reversioners until 1536,[84] when the position was altered by the operation of the Statute of Uses. In 1538 it was reported to Lady Lisle that the execution of a settlement by the statute had the inescapable consequence that the reversioner, her son John Basset, could be barred—or at any rate seriously disadvantaged[85]—if the tenant in tail, Lord Daubeney, suffered a recovery. Her numerous counsel were of the unanimous opinion that Basset was entitled in law, yet 'all these can find no means ne ways by the law to debar or let any recovery to pass against the Lord Daubeney... and all by the Statute of Uses lately enacted'. Attempts to persuade Cromwell and the Council to stop the recovery by injunction ultimately failed,[86] a committee having reported—after four hours of debate—that 'the Lord Daubeney may put away the land quite from Mr Basset, by reason of the new statute that was last made'.[87] The only relevance of the statute was that it had turned the estates into legal estates, and thereby subjected them to the power of a recovery. And that was evidently a major side-effect, unsettling settlements which had been secure when made.

In the early sixteenth century, recoveries became more sophisticated as increasing use was made of double and multiple vouchers.[88] In the case of a double voucher

(1538/9) Brooke Abr., *Feffements al Uses*, pl. 56 (second case; recovery); *Entre Congeable*, pl. 123; *Fauxefier de Recoverie*, pl. 49; *Fines Levies*, pl. 109.

[81] Yorke 145, no. 151; but cf. p. 140, no. 137 (fine levied by feoffees); 146, no. 155 (fine levied by cestuy que use for life, remainder in tail); 148, no. 160 (feoffment or lease for life, followed by fine).

[82] Above, 668.

[83] The problem was later eased by judicial acceptance of the practice of vouching the cestuy que use in a recovery against the feoffees: *Anon.* (temp. Edw. VI) Brooke Abr., *Feffements al Uses*, pl. 56, *ad finem*; below, 697.

[84] See also *Tendring's Case* (1533) Benl. 12 (recovery against cestuy que use for life does not bar remainder in tail).

[85] The fullest report said that if Lord Daubeney discontinued the tail it would 'drive Mr Basset hereafter, after the decease of the Lord Daubeney, to sue a formedon for the recovery of his right; which were a shrewd matter to do if he should be entangled with any great personage': *Lisle Letters*, ed. Byrne, v. 146. Basset was still under age.

[86] *Lisle Letters*, ed. Byrne, v. 146, 149, 167–8, 176–7, 183, and *passim*. The solution was to attempt to purchase the particular estate in possession; negotiations were still continuing in 1540. The settlement had been made in 1500, and the feud with Lord Daubeney (later earl of Bridgewater) dragged on into the 1550s: *Earl of Bridgewater's Case* (1541) Dyer 48b; *Basset's Case* (1556–7) Dyer 133a, 136a; Chr. Yelverton's reports, fo. 242v; Dal. 22, pl. 4 (petition of right by the heir).

[87] ibid. 187–8. The committee comprised Lord Hertford, Lord Beauchamp, and eight lawyers.

[88] Biancalana, *The Fee Tail*, 299–312. For a quintuple voucher, see *Taylboys* v. *Forster* (1555) CP 40/1163, m. 619, where the tenant vouched Sir Ambrose and Lady Elizabeth Dudley, sister and heir of George Tailboys; she vouched Lord Willoughby of Parham; he vouched Sir Edward Dymmok; he vouched William Tailboys, clerk; and he vouched Henry Selybarn, the common vouchee.

the tenant in tail caused the collusive writ of entry to be brought against a collusive feoffee, who vouched him, a device which was effective to bar 'all the interests and tails' of the tenant in tail, and his heirs, in case he was in possession under a different title.[89] In other cases the vouchee was the heir apparent,[90] in order to bar the reversion,[91] or the vendor, where the recovery was suffered by a purchaser,[92] or the cestuy que use, where the recovery was suffered by feoffees to uses.[93] The double voucher may explain the growing practice, from the 1530s, of entering on the roll a note of execution of judgment—obviously fictitious—against the common vouchee.[94] Unless that judgment was executed, there was a risk that the issue in tail might at some time in the future seek compensation against a real landed vouchee or his heirs.

The recovery was not completely watertight. Where there was a tenant for life, and a remainder in tail, the usual form of recovery was held in the 1530s not to be safe, because the recompense did not go to the remainderman.[95] This view was confirmed by statute in 1540.[96] If he could be persuaded to consent, the solution was to pray aid of the remainderman, who then vouched the common vouchee.[97] Another shortcoming of the recovery was that it would not bar dower.[98]

---

[89] See the explanation in Brooke Abr., *Taile*, pl. 32 (1531/2); examples in Robert Catlyn's reading (Middle Temple, 1547) BL MS. Lansdowne 1133, fo. 12v.

[90] This is made explicit in *Dormer and Goodwyn* v. *Earl of Huntingdon* (1537) CP 40/1095, m. 107 (vouches Francis, Lord Hastings, his son and heir apparent); *R.* v. *Colepeper* (1538) CP 40/1097, m. 605 (vouches Thomas Colepeper, his son and heir). For a more complex example see *Nevill* v. *Danvers* (1543) BL Add. Ch. 38882–3 (land earlier recovered against J to use of W; W, now seised, covenants to suffer recovery to use of himself in tail, remainder to S, the right heir of J; the recovery is against W, who vouches S, who vouches the common vouchee).

[91] See the discussion in *Anon.* (1557) MS. Hargrave 4, ff. 125v–126v; Benl. 58, pl. 97.

[92] An indenture of 1554 enrolled in KB 27/1172, m. 61, sets out an agreement to this effect. Richard Heywode bought land from Charles Yarburgh; he covenants with his nominees, William Rooper and William Rastell, to allow them to bring a writ of entry, in which he will vouch Yarburgh, who will vouch the common vouchee 'accordyng to the manner and forme of the common recoveryes'; and this will be to Heywode's use in fee simple.

[93] The effectiveness of such a voucher seems not to have been settled until the 1550s: Brooke Abr., *Feffements al Uses*, pl. 56. But it had been in use since the previous century.

[94] Biancalana, *The Fee Tail*, 292–9.

[95] *Lord Zouche* v. *Stowell* (Chancery, after 1535) Brooke Abr., *Recoverie in Value*, pl. 28, by all the judges; ibid., pl. 30. Cf., to the contrary, *Sir William Danvers' Case* (1488) 1 Caryll 13; *Anon.* (1535) Brooke Abr., *Recoverie in Value*, pl. 28, per Mountagu CJ and others.

[96] 32 Hen. VIII, c. 31.

[97] See Brooke Abr., *Recoverie in Value*, pl. 27 (1531) and pl. 30 (1538). Examples: *Throgmerton* v. *Smyth* (1535) CP 40/1084, m. 341; *Perott* v. *Bray* (1539) CP 40/1100, m. 543; *Powlet* v. *Lady Mountjoy* (1539) CP 40/1101, m. 454; *Rodney* v. *Harecourt* (1540) CP 40/1105, m. 148; *Lewson* v. *Kyrton* (1548) CP 40/1136, m. 355. For earlier examples see Biancalana, *The Fee Tail*, 288–90.

[98] *Fowler* v. *Lyndesell* (1529) Yorke 200, no. 292; Wm Yelv. 322, no. 20; CP 40/1059, m. 828, 830 (judgment on demurrer). The widow falsified the recovery by bringing a writ of dower against the recoveror.

FINES WITH PROCLAMATIONS

As a result of a statute passed in 1484, entails could also be barred by final concord. It may have been an earlier doubt as to the effect of recoveries on remaindermen and reversioners which led to the statutory provision that a final concord with proclamations should bar 'as well privies as strangers'.[99] The avowed object of the statute was to ensure that fines should be 'of the greatest strength to avoid strifes and debates', and it expressly enabled them to be used for barring entails.[100] It used the word 'conclude', indicating that the proclamations worked a kind of estoppel. But the logic of estoppel could only bind strangers to the fine if they had a reasonable opportunity to intervene. The effect was therefore a precarious compromise, preserving the rights of remaindermen and reversioners claiming under gifts in tail, so long as they pursued their claims within five years of their right descending, remaining, or coming to them—which might be far into the future. There was a similar saving for those who were unable to make a claim by reason of incapacity, absence, or imprisonment. The statute was re-enacted in 1490.[101]

Doubts arose in the sixteenth century about the effect of the statute on the issue of a tenant in tail who levied a fine, and this was the subject of a major debate in the Exchequer Chamber in 1527.[102] Three judges thought the issue were not immediately barred, but could make their claim within five years of inheriting, because of the express saving of rights which descended by force of any estate tail. But a strong majority—including Fitzjames and Brudenell CJJ and Fitzherbert J.—adopted a purposive interpretation, stressing the intention of the statute to make a 'final end', and held that the issue of the person who levied the fine, though they were not parties to the fine, were 'privies' and therefore barred.[103] The saving as to descended rights applied only to issue claiming through a different ancestor, as where the fine was not levied by the tenant in tail.[104] All the judges agreed that

---

[99] 1 Ric. III, c. 7. For the contemporary procedure in levying a fine see Robert Catlyn's reading (Middle Temple, 1547) BL MS. Lansdowne 1133, ff. 1v–2v.

[100] Since *De Donis* (1285), fines had been ineffective to bar the issue or reversioners: B. & M. 50; Yorke 165, no. 200.

[101] 4 Hen. VII, c. 24. The legal date was 1489, since the session began in January of that year, but the operative date was Easter 1490 and the statute was probably passed in the 1490 session: cf. the statute concerning uses (above, 661). The statute was the subject of the famous reading by John Densell in Lincoln's Inn (1530).

[102] *Anon.* (1527) Pas. 19 Hen. VIII, fo. 6, pl. 5; Dyer 3a–b (same text); Brooke Abr., *Fine*, pl. 1; *Taile*, pl. 2.

[103] The justices in Serjeants' Inn, Chancery Lane, were of the same opinion this year: Yorke 151, no. 169.1(B). Hare's report, 120 Selden Soc. 87, no. 2, says it was 'held clearly by the justices' that a fine with proclamations immediately barred the tenant in tail who levied the fine, all feoffees claiming to his use, his issue, and all his blood who were privy to the fine. The date is given as 2° Hen. VIII, which is perhaps a slip for 20 Hen. VIII. The effect of fines on entails in use is also discussed in Trin. 27 Hen. VIII, fo. 20, pl. 9; *Anon.* (1538) Brooke Abr., *Fines Levies*, pl. 108; and see 32 Hen. VIII, c. 36 (below).

[104] In this case the tenant in tail and his immediate issue each had five years to make claim, after which the more remote issue were bound: *Anon.* (1540) Brooke Abr., *Fines Levies*, pl. 109.

if a remainderman in tail failed to make his claim within the five years, his issue
were barred for ever.[105]

The 'diversity of interpretations' led to an attempt at statutory clarification in
1540.[106] In accordance with the majority opinion in 1527, it was declared that a fine
by tenant in tail should be an immediate bar to him and to his heirs in tail, and to
anyone claiming the land to the use of him or the heirs of his body. This did not
apply where the reversion or a remainder was in the king, or where the 'posses-
sioners and owners' were restrained from alienation by act of Parliament. The
statute had no effect on remainders and reversions upon estates tail, which were
still to be barred only if the person entitled failed to make claim for five years after
they fell in.

PERPETUITY CLAUSES

Although widespread advantage was taken of these means of barring the entail, it
does not follow that settlors were unanimously in favour of allowing later generations a free hand in dealing with the inheritance. From the beginning of our
period, and indeed in earlier periods, there had been experiments with various
devices designed to reinforce the entail. There were essentially two ways of going
about this. One was to try to keep the inheritance in the future, so that there
would be a succession of life estates for as many generations as the law would permit, with remainders in fee thereafter. The other was to impose upon the fee tail
a condition against alienation, so that a tenant in tail who attempted to bar the
entail would forfeit his estate. There was no legal difficulty about creating an entail
with a condition against alienation, so long as it was enforceable by the heir of the
donor.[107] In 1493, after much debate, it seemed the better opinion that such a
condition was enforceable even if there was a remainder in fee simple following
the entail, because the entire future estate depended upon the same condition.[108]
A similar condition could probably be annexed to an entail in use.[109] This was not
an ideal remedy, because the heir of the donor might well be the very person who
was trying to bar the entail; even if he was not, allowing him to re-enter would

---

[105] This is difficult to reconcile with the decision of 1540 reported by Broke (last note).

[106] 32 Hen. VIII, c. 36. This was a government measure, in which Cromwell had taken an interest:
LP, xv. 615; Elton, Reform and Renewal, 155. It was the subject of the reading by Robert Catlyn (Middle
Temple, 1547). The prothonotaries feared it would lead to a decline in common recoveries: LP, xvi. 690.

[107] Hil. 8 Hen. VII, fo. 10, pl. 3; Hulcote v. Ingleton (1493) next note (agreed by all the JJ); Anon. (1529)
Pollard 251, no. 13.

[108] Hulcote v. Ingleton (1493) 1 Caryll 138–44; Port 87; Mich. 10 Hen. VII, fo. 11, pl. 28; Mich. 11 Hen.
VII, fo. 6, pl. 25; CP 40/924, m. 156 (pr. 102 Selden Soc. 87–9; undetermined demurrer). This arose from
a settlement of 1360.

[109] Serjeant Rudhale annexed such a condition to the entail created by his will in 1516, and it was
held seventy years later to have survived execution by the Statute of Uses: PCC 26 Jankyn; Rudhale v.
Miller (1586) 1 Leo. 298; Sav. 76; Moo. K.B. 212.

destroy the purpose of the settlement. What the common law could not permit, however, was a condition operating to carry the estate by way of remainder to the person next entitled under the settlement.[110] That, according to a reader of Gray's Inn in 1530, would be contrary to 'the common ground in our law that no right of entry may be reserved except to the donor, grantor, or lessor'.[111] Nor did the common law allow an endless succession of life estates. It was permissible to limit remainders to living sons and grandsons, but it was not permissible to limit them to unborn heirs—a form of contingent remainder—unless they happened to be born before the first estate came to an end.[112]

To these difficulties, uses seemed to offer a possible solution. Although there was a view that uses followed the rules of common law,[113] this did not always prevail in practice. An ambitious perpetuity clause may be found in the will of Sir Richard Haddon, alderman of London, in 1516.[114] He directed his feoffees to stand seised to the use of his wife for life, then to his son William for life, and then to the next heir of William's body for life, and then to the heir of that heir, for life, and so on successively to every heir of the body for life only. He then added the condition that if any of the said heirs, during their lives, would suffer any recovery or do anything whereby their heirs might be disinherited, 'the use of that heire soo doyng shalbe voyde and of noon effect', and the feoffees would stand seised to the use of the next heir apparent as if the offending heir were naturally dead. The devise thus deliberately broke the two rules of common law mentioned above. It did not become the subject of litigation until 1576, and even then the court was evenly divided.[115] But the counsel who advised Sir Richard were not alone in believing that such schemes would be effective. In 1517, John Fitzherbert made a devise in tail with a similar perpetuity clause providing that upon any attempt to alienate or mortgage the estate the use was to pass to the next heir male, whether lineal or collateral.[116] Since the chief executor and next heir was John's brother Anthony, it is difficult to think that the great lawyer was not involved in its drafting, though the clause would have restricted his own

---

[110] Litt. ss. 720–3 (tr. B. & M. 67–8), referring to *Rikhill's Case* (*c.*1395); and cf. Hil. 21 Hen. VI, fo. 33v, pl. 21 (tr. B. & M. 68–9), referring to *Thirning's Case* (*c.*1400); *Anon.* (1506) Hil. 21 Hen. VII, fo. 11, pl. 12.

[111] Walter Hendley's reading in Gray's Inn (1530) BL MS. Harley 5103, fo. 24v, referring to 'Riclez Case' (i.e. Rikhill's). [112] For debate on this point see below, 701.

[113] Above, 678.

[114] PCC 29 Holder; PROB 11/18, ff. 226v–228v. Haddon was commemorated by a brass in St Olave, Hart Street.

[115] *Manning* v. *Andrewes* (1576) 1 Leo. 256 (testator misspelt as 'Hart'); BL MS. Harley 2036, ff. 57–73 (will misdated to 1536); sub nom. *Haddon's Case*, CUL MS. Ll.3.8, fo. 263 (tr. B. & M. 134–5).

[116] Will in Lichfield Record Office: see J. C. Cox, 'Norbury Manor House and the Fitzherberts' (1885) 7 *Jnl Derbs. Arch. and Nat. Hist. Soc.* at 231, cit. Cooper, 'Patterns of Inheritance', 204 n. 1; Wright, *Derbyshire Gentry*, 36–7.

freedom.[117] Fitzjames CJ seems to have shared Fitzherbert's faith in shifting conditions. In 1537 he settled manors on his wife for life, remainder to his son, remainder to the son's sons (all by name), on condition that if the wife alienated a different manor her estate in these manors would be void and of no force in law, and the manors would immediately remain to the next remainderman.[118] This settlement was enrolled in the King's Bench, and was known to Dyer CJ, who treated it with respect thirty years later.[119] According to Brooke, it was held judicially in 1546 that a remainder to the use of X and his heirs until he decided to alienate, and then to the use of B and his heirs, was good and executed by the Statute of Uses.[120] Opinions would change over the next sixty years. It seems, however, that in the first half of the sixteenth century legal opinion generally favoured perpetuity clauses effected by means of uses. Indeed, they may have become common in the 1550s.[121]

CONTINGENT REMAINDERS

According to Littleton, whose treatise was first printed in 1481, a valid remainder had to be vested in the person to whom it was limited at the time when livery of seisin was made to the tenant of the preceding estate.[122] That view completely ruled out contingent remainders, such as a remainder to the heir of a living person. However, the profession had already come to accept the validity of a remainder to the heirs of a living person, where that person died before the particular tenant. In that case the uncertainty was removed before the first estate came to an end, so that there was no danger of the remainder being in abeyance.[123] And it was not uncommon in a marriage settlement to add a remainder to the husband's heirs after a separate estate in the wife for life.[124]

---

[117] When John died in 1531, the terms of the will occasioned a riotous altercation at the funeral and a Star Chamber suit: F. Boersma, *Sir Antony Fitzherbert and La Graunde Abridgement* (1978), i. 24.

[118] KB 27/1102, m. 36; pr. 110 Selden Soc. 237-8.

[119] *Newis v. Larke* (*Scholastica's Case*) (1571) Plowd. 414; Dyer's reports, 110 Selden Soc. 237. Dyer CJ's explanation is that the clause must have been treated as a limitation rather than a condition.

[120] Brooke Abr., Assurances, pl. 1.

[121] See Cooper, 'Patterns of Inheritance', 207 (Sir Thomas Pope, 1554); Plowd. 405 (Henry Clerke, 1556: the subject of *Scholastica's Case*). The classic perpetuity clause used by Sir Walter Mildmay in 1588 (B. & M. 158, 163) was of the same type. [122] Litt. s. 721 (tr. B. & M. 67).

[123] *Faryngton v. Darell* (1431) B. & M. 70 at 72, *per* Martin J.; *Anon.* (1454) Statham, *Done*, pl. 6; Fitz. Abr., *Feffements*, pl. 99, *per totam curiam*. This was said in Gray's Inn to have been 'always held as a principle in the law, and it was so held by all the justices in Hilary term 8 Hen. VII [1493]': Trinity Coll. Cambridge MS. R.15.7, fo. 89 (tr.). The case cited is doubtless *Hulcote v. Ingleton* (1493), above, 699.

[124] c.g. *CCR 1485–1500*, pp. 22–3, no. 83 (1486); BL Add. Ch. 52795 (1500); *Hussey's Case* (1545) Brooke Abr., *Discent*, pl. 1; *Done*, pl. 61; *Nosme*, pl. 1, 40.

At a Gray's Inn reading in 1518, Serjeant Broke held that a remainder to the heirs of a living third party was void, as was a remainder to the abbot of Westminster if there was a vacancy at the time of the limitation. On the other hand, a remainder to a person's heir apparent, or eldest son, or to the person who first came to the reading, was good, because the person was immediately ascertainable.[125] Broke's point does not seem to have been the same as Littleton's, but related to the ascertainability of the remainderman. Twelve years later, at another reading in the same inn, Littleton was completely rejected on this point. The reader (Walter Hendley), the attorney-general (Christopher Hales), and the common serjeant of London (William Walsingham), all agreed that a remainder to the heirs of a living person was good if the latter died before the particular tenant.[126] Hales referred to this as a 'contingent' remainder, and recognized the problem of locating the fee before the contingency was determined. The fee could not be in abeyance, or in 'the consideration of the law'; but Hales's solution was to hold that the fee was 'preserved in the person of the lessor until the remainder becomes certain'.[127] This was the view of the courts around the same period.[128] It was also held that a second remainder could take effect on failure of a prior remainder to an heir.[129]

This one situation, though already called a contingent remainder, was not yet a legal category.[130] Whether any other kind of contingent remainder might be acceptable in law was settled by a decision by the Common Pleas in *Colthirst v. Bejushin* (1550).[131] However, in his judgment in that case, Mountagu CJ recalled another case in which he had been concerned fifteen years earlier:[132]

When I was at the bar, I was of counsel with Mr Melton in the following case: a fine was levied... whereby the conusee granted and rendered the tenements to the conusor in tail, upon condition that the conusor and his heirs of his body should bear the conusee's standard when he went into battle, and if the conusor or his heirs failed in doing this the land was to remain to a stranger. And I moved the case to the court then, and there was great amazement (*graund marvel*) that the fine had been received upon condition. But Mr [Justice] Fitzherbert held the remainder good, and they did not wonder at that or hold it any great question but that it might commence upon condition.

[125] Case at John Petit's reading (1518) BL MS. Harley 5103, fo. 21v.

[126] Hendley said Littleton was wrong to draw a conclusion about contingent remainders from *Rikhill's Case*, where the principal point was the shifting condition.

[127] Case at Hendley's reading (1530) BL MS. Harley 5103, ff. 24–25. If the remainder was to the heirs of two living people, there was a divergence of opinion whether it vested in the heir of the first to die, or (as Hendley thought) in both: ibid., fo. 30v.

[128] *Anon.* (1538/9) Hare's reports, 84, no. 3 (Common Pleas); *Hussey's Case* (1545) Brooke Abr., *Done*, pl. 61, *per* Hare MR.

[129] *Anon.* (c.1535/45) Wm Yelv. 355, no. 88, *per* Baldwin CJ (upholding a remainder after a failed remainder to an heir male).   [130] Cf. Milsom, *HFCL*, 196 ('a well-known anomaly').

[131] *Colthirst* v. *Bejushin* (1550) Plowd. 21; below, 704.

[132] Plowd. 34v (translated from the French).

The case may be found reported anonymously in the year books for 1535.[133] The report says that Serjeant Mountagu put the case before the Court of Common Pleas and asked whether the remainder was good. Fitzherbert J. said he had never seen a fine levied with a condition, but that it was good and that the remainder took effect from the moment of livery. Serjeant Mountagu questioned this last proposition, on the ground that the remainder could not take effect before the condition was broken; but Fitzherbert J. replied that, if that were so, it could never take effect at all, concluding that 'the case is good to be advised [upon].' Both reports conceal the context of the case, which appears from the record.[134] It was a *scire facias* brought by Sir John Melton against Henry Percy, sixth earl of Northumberland, to enforce a final concord levied in 1384. The effect of the fine was to grant and render the castle and honour of Cockermouth in tail to Henry Percy, then earl of Northumberland, and his wife Maud (née Lucy)—heiress of Cockermouth—with remainder to the heirs male of Maud's body, remainder to the earl's eldest son Henry in tail male, and with various remainders over, the last being to Maud's right heirs. The remainder to Henry, and the three remainders following, were conditional upon their bearing the arms of Percy quartered with Lucy on all banners, penons, and coats of arms which they displayed; so that, if any of them failed, his estate—and, it seems, any further Percy remainders—should become void and the premises should 'remain' to the right heirs of Maud. The original purpose of the clause was to preserve the memory of the Lucy family. It was unusual, not only in the armorial context,[135] but also in providing for the condition to be enforced by a remainderman rather than the heir of the donor. Since it was drawn before the Rikhill experiment was declared a failure,[136] it may not in 1384 have been so obviously offensive to basic principles. Unfortunately we do not have a full analysis of it as interpreted by the lawyers of 1535, though it had an obvious affinity with the perpetuity clauses discussed above.[137]

Melton made claim to the contingent remainder as the right heir of Maud, on the ground that on 6 May 1531, in St George's Chapel, Windsor, the present earl had displayed his banner without the quartered arms of Lucy as required by the condition. The date refers to the earl's installation as a knight of the Garter, and it seems likely that Melton had been told about the banner by Lord Darcy KG, whose

---

[133] Mich. 27 Hen. VIII, fo. 24, pl. 2; Gell's reports, I, ff. 41v–42 (same text). For a full discussion see J. H. Baker, 'Sir John Melton's Case (1535): Cockermouth Castle and the three silver luces' (1996) 55 *CLJ* 249–64; repr. in *CLT*, 365–82.

[134] *Melton v. Earl of Northumberland* (1535–6) CP 40/1087, m. 138 (imparlance, Mich. 1535); CP 40/1089, m. 438 (stayed).

[135] It has been well known to heraldic historians, and may have been unique. It anticipated by more than three centuries the classical 'name and arms' clause (see Squibb, 69 *LQR* 220); but cf. the name and arms clause of c.1390 in PRO, Ancient Deed A11372 (Ralph Basset).

[136] Above, 700 n. 110.   [137] Above, 700–1.

son Sir George had married Melton's heiress presumptive. However preposterous, Melton's claim seemed sufficiently cogent to worry not only Percy but also Cromwell and the king—to whom Cockermouth had been mortgaged between 1531 and 1535.[138] Under some obscure bargain with the king, Percy immediately resettled Cockermouth with remainder to the king in fee simple, with the result that Melton's suit could be stayed *rege inconsulto*; and this high-handed arrange-ment was embodied in an act of Parliament in Hilary term 1536.[139] Melton peti-tioned the king without success for a hearing by the king's counsel, but he failed to win support at court and his suit collapsed.

It is not surprising that *Melton's Case* was reported in such an elliptical manner. It nevertheless affords an interesting illustration of the power of abstract theory, and perhaps even of judicial independence, in the face of practical politics. It would obviously have suited the men of influence in the case—King Henry VIII, Thomas Cromwell, and the earl of Northumberland—if the judges had displayed a little more wonderment when the case was moved in 1535. It would have suited them even better for instant purposes if the Melton 'remainder' could have been firmly stamped upon by a judgment on demurrer. But Fitzherbert J.—who had himself been one of Percy's advisers—thought differently; and the attorney-general did not dare risk a demurrer. It was a general policy that ancient conveyances by way of final concord should if possible be upheld.[140] And it may be that the king himself was not in his heart averse to strict entails, and arms clauses, in noble families. The true authority of the case rested on the extreme lengths to which it was felt necessary to go to frustrate Melton's inconvenient claim. For those in the know, such as Mountagu, that gave the incident in the Common Pleas a special force which most readers of the year book could not have perceived. According to Mountagu, it was the tolerant reception of the contingent remainder in 1535, without expressions of amazement from the bench, that helped to settle the old doubt. In that rather limited sense, though not formally decided, the case of 1535 represented some kind of turning-point.

The 1550 case was more decisive, and became much better known after the publication of Plowden's report of it in 1571.[141] The Grange in Barton, near Bath, had been settled in 1529 on Henry Bewshin and his wife for lives, remainder to their son for William for life, and, if he should die before his parents, remainder

---

[138] See Bean, *Estates of the Percy Family*, 148, 151.

[139] 27 Hen. VIII, c. 47. The statute extended to all the earl's castles, honours, and lands, without listing them.

[140] That was Brooke CJ's view of the case: Brooke Abr., *Fines Levies*, pl. 5. He was a young barrister of the Middle Temple in 1535.

[141] *Colthirst* v. *Bejushin* (1550–1) CP 40/1141, m. 441; Plowd. 21 (extracted in B. & M. 78); briefly reported in BL MS. Hargrave 4, ff. 104v, 112. The defendant, Peter Bewshin or Bewchin, is 'Beiushin' in the plea roll. The plaintiff was an auditor of the Augmentations who purchased Bath Abbey.

to their son Peter for life. William did die before his parents, and the question raised by demurrer was whether Peter's remainder was valid. There was disagreement as to whether the 'if he should die' clause was a condition or a limitation. If it was a condition, it fell foul of the rule that no one could enter for breach of a condition other than the donor and his heirs.[142] But the remainder was on any view contingent, because if William had survived his parents it would never have fallen in. On the other hand, the contingency here was determined before the life estates came to an end, and so there was an analogy with a remainder to the heirs of a living person who died before the rermainder fell in. The court gave judgment upholding the remainder; indeed, their first reaction was that there was no point worth arguing.[143] It is difficult to extract a general principle from the judges' opinions,[144] other than that there was no fundamental objection to a contingent remainder provided that it did not cut short the particular estate. The whereabouts of the fee was, however, still a puzzle. Hales J. repeated his cousin Christopher Hales's doctrine that the fee continued in the settlor until the contingency was resolved; but Mountagu CJ, following Fitzherbert J.'s opinion in *Melton's Case*, held that the fee passed out of the settlor immediately, 'upon a possibility to be performed afterwards', and was therefore 'in abeyance' until the remainder vested.

MORTGAGES AND RECOGNIZANCES

The classic mortgage at the beginning of the Tudor period was the feoffment on condition of repayment, as described by Littleton.[145] The mortgagor granted the fee simple to the mortgagee—Littleton called him the tenant in mortgage—upon condition that he might re-enter if he paid the debt on time. That is how John Rastell defined a mortgage in the 1520s, taking his law straight from Littleton.[146] If the mortgagor died before the day of payment, his heir was allowed to redeem; but if there was no day of payment, the mortgagee could keep the land.[147] The main disadvantage of this form of mortgage was that, if the mortgagee died before receiving payment, the land descended to his heir and was subject to dower and feudal incidents, whereas the debt which it secured devolved on his representatives

---

[142] This was still troubling the courts a few years later: *Anon.* (1556) Chr. Yelverton's reports, fo. 241.

[143] BL MS. Hargrave 4, fo. 104v (Mich. 1549); above, 390 n. 31.

[144] There was the further complication that each remainder was qualified by the words 'if he will reside in the Grange'. These were held to be limitations, or at least conditions subsequent, so that they did not prevent the second remainder from vesting; but the points are not easily distinguished in the arguments and may have become confused in the excerpts in B. & M.

[145] Litt. ss. 332–44.

[146] *Exposiciones Terminorum* (1527 edn), fo. 27v; and likewise Yorke 106, no. 51.

[147] Litt. s. 337; Rastell, loc. cit.; *Martin Docwra's Case* (1535) Trin. 27 Hen. VIII, fo. 14, pl. 6, at fo. 19, *per* Audley C.; Yorke 106, no. 51.

as personal property.[148] It may also have been difficult for the mortgagor to regain seisin,[149] for instance if the condition was not in writing.[150] For these reasons, common-law mortgages in this form—to judge from the paucity of surviving deeds[151]—were becoming less common, and were giving way to mortgages by way of use. Land would be conveyed to feoffees on the terms that if the feoffor paid the debt as agreed they would stand seised to his use,[152] or would allow him to re-enter,[153] whereas if he did not pay they would stand seised to the use of the lender, either outright,[154] or on payment of an agreed price for the land,[155] or until the loan was repaid out of the issues and profits.[156] The feoffees were usually third parties, though the mortgagee might be one of their number. Occasionally the mortgagee received sole seisin of the land to his own use, on terms that he would be seised to the use of the mortgagor once the debt was paid.[157] In this case it was advisable to convey the land to the mortgagee by bargain and sale to prevent an immediate resulting use in favour of the mortgagor.[158] Sometimes the use might provide for the lender to receive the profits in the interim until the loan was paid off,[159] sometimes for the mortgagor to receive the profits.[160] The variability of the formulae shows the advantage of uses in giving effect to the wishes of the parties in a flexible manner. Mortgages by way of use were said to be executed by the Statute of Uses 1536, so that the mortgagee became seised; but the seisin would shift to the mortgagor on payment.[161] The principal drawback was that the mortgagee might alienate the land, before redemption, to a bona fide purchaser for value. An attempt to prevent this, by providing that any sale by the mortgagee should be

---

[148] Unless it was expressed to be payable to the mortgagee 'and his heirs'.

[149] See *Mayhowe* v. *Glynn* (*c.*1500) C1/267/48, where a mortgagor sought relief in Chancery on the grounds that he could not recover the land, though he had paid the debt; but the mortgagee apparently claimed—the answer is almost illegible—that he had been sold the land. This may therefore have been a conditional sale of the kind noted in n. 151, below (1555).

[150] Trin. 9 Edw. IV, fo. 25, pl. 34. Serjeant Pygot said the Chancery would here give relief.

[151] Two examples in the BL are Add. Ch. 56989 (1479) and 56789 (1558). A hybrid form was the bargain and sale with condition of re-entry on repayment of the £10 purchase price at any one time within ten years: BL Add. Ch. 40830 (1555): until completion, the mortgagor himself was seised to the use of the mortgagee.   [152] e.g. BL Add. Ch. 33212 (1512).

[153] e.g. BL Add. Ch. 72130 (Lady Stafford's feoffment, 1473).

[154] e.g. *Capell's Case* (1494) Port 13, 14 (mortgage made in 1480s); BL Add. Ch. 48798 (1547; mortgage to king).   [155] e.g. *CIPM Hen. VII*, ii. 446, no. 688 (1498); BL Add. Ch. 33212 (1512).

[156] *CIPM Hen. VII*, ii. 420, no. 669 (1501); iii. 228–9, no. 366 (1505).

[157] e.g. BL Add. Ch. 41201 (1536). The feoffment is here made in the words 'hath set to pledge'. Cf. *CIPM Hen. VII*, iii. 178, no. 283 (1505; mortgagee recovers land against mortgagor to use of mortgagor if he pays 220 marks by instalments as agreed).

[158] e.g. *Powtrell's Case* (*c.*1549/50) Wm Yelv. 339 (and below).

[159] e.g. *CIPM Hen. VII*, i. 280, no. 679 (before 1490).

[160] e.g. BL Add. Ch. 48798 (1547). In BL Add. Ch. 41201 (1536) the mortgagee is to occupy the land until payment, and in case of non-payment is to receive a penalty as well.

[161] *Anon.* (1552) Brooke Abr., *Feffements al Uses*, pl. 30 (tr. B. & M. 134).

to the use of the mortgagor, was defeated in 1547 on the grounds that such a provision could only sound in covenant and could not affect the innocent purchaser.[162]

Merchants could charge debts on land by having recognizances—statutes merchant and statutes staple—enrolled in mercantile courts under the provisions of medieval legislation. The title to the land was not conveyed, as in the case of a mortgage, and it remained in the debtor's possession; but if the debt was unpaid the land could be delivered in execution to the creditor, to be retained until the money was raised from the income.[163] The convenience of this form of security, especially of statutes staple, was such that it came to be coveted by non-merchants; and since the officials of the relevant courts were not over-anxious to reduce their potential income by enquiring too closely into the context of recognizances brought for enrolment, the legal requirements concerning the mercantile character of the parties and their contracts seem to have become fictitious.[164] A statute of 1532 put an end to this by imposing a heavy penalty—recoverable by common informers—on officials who thereafter recorded non-mercantile recognizances. The occasion for this measure may have been the arrest of the earl of Northumberland's servant upon a statute staple while Parliament was sitting, a possible breach of privilege on which the Council sought the advice of the judges.[165] Parliament nevertheless acknowledged the popular demand for such securities by introducing at the same time a new form of recognizance 'in the nature of a statute staple'.[166] These recognizances were to be available to 'every of the king's subjects', but only, in reality, in the metropolis, because they had to be registered before the chief justices of the two benches or the mayor of the staple of Westminster and the recorder of London.[167]

---

[162] Powtrell's Case (c.1549/50) Wm Yelv. 339, per Hales J.

[163] See Duplege v. Debenham (1484) Mich. 2 Ric. III, fo. 7, pl. 14; 64 Selden Soc. 75; Mich. 15 Hen. VII, fo. 14, pl. 6 (misdated); Rede v. Capell (1492) Pas. 7 Hen. VII, fo. 12, pl. 1; Capell v. Scott (1493) 1 Caryll 165, 216; Stanter v. Touke (1493) CP 40/925, m. 136d (demurrer to evidence concerning a statute staple); Robert Brudenell's reading on De Mercatoribus (Inner Temple, 1500) 102 Selden Soc. 176–80. For the effect of dower on the creditor's interest, see Anon. (1530) BL MS. Harley 1691, fo. 102.

[164] See Dutton v. Manley (1544) Cholmeley 462, in which there is a long technical debate about the validity of a statute merchant enrolled in Chester (cf. Dyer 34b, §27), but no objection was taken to the fact that the parties were obviously not merchants.

[165] Spelman 184 (the judges ruled it was not a breach of privilege, Trin. 1532). The statute was passed in the session which ended on 28 March 1532.

[166] 23 Hen. VIII, c. 6. See also 32 Hen. VIII, c. 5, for 'continuing debts upon execution' where the land was the subject of a recovery. The 1540 statute gave rise to difficulties of interpretation and was the subject of many readings, the earliest known being that of Thomas Stanley (Gray's Inn, 1550) BL MS. Hargrave 199, ff. 22–62.

[167] Even statutes merchant were geographically limited: see Anon. (1537) Dyer 35a, §27 (authority of mayor of Chester denied).

37

Dissolution of the Monasteries[1]

THE dissolution of religious houses, and the redistribution of their lands to laymen, was the biggest upheaval in landholding in England since the Norman conquest. Somewhere between a fifth and a quarter of all the land in the country was probably affected. However, the process of dissolution, and the administration of land transfers, did not themselves raise many fundamental legal questions. Although the scheme was linked politically with the first wave of Reformation, and with Henry's newly assumed supreme headship of the Church, it was not legally dependent upon freedom from papal authority. Edward III had set a precedent for seizing religious houses and their temporal possessions when he confiscated houses belonging to alien priories on grounds of war;[2] and it had been held that when these priories were resumed and seized by Henry V, by authority of an act of Parliament,[3] the corporations were thereby dissolved.[4] Monasteries had also been dissolved by kings—albeit with papal licence—in order to endow new institutions, such as colleges at Oxford and Cambridge. In that context, it had been held by all the judges of England at the beginning of the century that when a religious house came into the king's hands and was granted over to another corporation, the first corporation was dissolved.[5] Cardinal Wolsey had arranged the suppression of a number of monasteries, chiefly in order to found

---

[1] For detailed accounts of the whole exercise see D. Knowles, *The Religious Orders in England, III: the Tudor Age* (1959); Youings, *The Dissolution of the Monasteries*. See also Elton, *Reform and Reformation*, 230–49; Dickens, *English Reformation*, 167–91.

[2] See *Prior of Castleacre v. Dean of Westminster* (1503) 2 Caryll 411; Hil. 21 Hen. VII, fo. 1, pl. 1 (misdated); *Prior of Sheen v. Prior of Little Malvern* (1514) 2 Caryll 650; *Parkhurst v. Prior of Lewes* (1514) CP 40/1008, m. 759; (No. 2, c.1530) Spelman 15; *Dean of Windsor v. Bishop of Hereford* (1526) Spelman 198.

[3] *RP*, iv. 13 (not in *SR*).

[4] *Prior of Castleacre v. Dean of Westminster* (1503), as reported in Hil. 21 Hen. VII, fo. 1, pl. 1, at fo. 4, *per* Frowyk CJ. See also *Abbess of Barking v. Dean of Barking Chapel* (1489) CP 40/906, m. 305; Pas. 4 Hen. VII, fo. 6, pl. 3 (defendant pleads dissolution of religious corporation by Parliament).

[5] *Anon.* (1506) Hil. 21 Hen. VII, fo. 1, pl. 1, at fo. 5, *per* Frowyk CJ (said to be 'ore tard', i.e. recent). This may refer to the abbey of Creyke, Norfolk, which was suppressed (with papal licence) in 1505 to support the foundation of Christ's College, Cambridge. For other precedents see R. Burn, *Ecclesiastical Law* (1763), ii. 62–3; Knowles, *Religious Orders*, iii. 157–8.

his college at Oxford, which was itself dissolved following his conviction by *praemunire*.[6] But in 1532—still before the break with Rome—a precedent was set for a new kind of dissolution when the priory of Christchurch, Aldgate, was dissolved by deed of surrender to the Crown, as founder, without papal sanction.[7] The priory had been in financial difficulties, and the surrender seems to have been voluntary. But the surrendered property was not devoted to pious uses: indeed, much of it was purchased by Sir Thomas Audley, the new lord keeper.[8] This was a convenient legal precedent for the general dissolution of the later 1530s. In 1534 an act of Parliament was passed to put beyond doubt what had been done, apparently at Audley's behest. Reciting the surrender by deed, the statute declared the 'actual and real possession' of the priory's real property to be in the king and his heirs, without the need to find an office, and that the king might grant the property by letters patent, saving the rights of others.[9] This, in short-form, was the model for the various dissolution statutes to come.

The general dissolution was justified on grounds of misconduct and abuse, as uncovered by visitations held under authority of the king's supreme headship,[10] and was in many cases achieved by means of a pressured surrender. Although these mechanisms were already in existence, the chief novelty of Henry VIII's scheme—besides its scale—lay in the notion that the confiscated properties could be applied to secular or non-charitable purposes, following the Christchurch example. The general scheme was very much Thomas Cromwell's, though he was assisted in the legal aspects of the business by Audley as lord keeper and Sir Richard Rich as chancellor of the Augmentations. Already in 1535, before he became the king's vicar-general and vice-gerent of the spirituals,[11] Cromwell had superintended a general visitation of the monasteries by royal commission. The adverse findings of the visitors were a necessary prerequisite to drastic action. Whether they were wholly justified by the evidence is another matter.

Cromwell may have had a general dissolution in mind from the beginning, but decided on a gradualist approach and began in 1536 with a statute concerning the

---

[6] Above, 246. For the suppression of monasteries by Wolsey see Knowles, *Religious Orders*, iii. 159–64.

[7] Calwich, Staffordshire, was also suppressed without papal sanction in 1532: Knowles, *Religious Orders*, iii. 200 n. 7.

[8] Audley was K.Sjt at the time of the deed of surrender but became LK a few months later. He did later leave some of his lands to endow Magdalene College, Cambridge.

[9] 25 Hen. VIII, c. 33. See E. J. Davis, 'The Beginning of the Reformation: Christchurch, Aldgate, 1532' (1925) 8 *TRHS* (4th ser.) 127–50.

[10] Similar visitations had occurred, with papal sanction, in the time of Archbishop Moreton and Cardinal Wolsey. The king's duty to visit monasteries was mentioned in the Act of Supremacy 1535 (26 Hen. VIII, c. 1).

[11] He received these appointments in July 1536, a few months after the dissolution of the lesser houses (in March).

smaller houses.[12] Whether or not they were wholly independent and impartial, his visitors produced such telling evidence of shameful misconduct that the statute seems to have passed with little or no opposition in Parliament, even from the mitred abbots—who perhaps hoped that the sacrifice of the lesser monasteries would save their own. Reciting the 'manifest sin, vicious, carnal, and abominable living' which was daily used in the smaller houses, the wasting of monastic revenues, and the failure of successive visitations to impose any effective reform, the statute gave the king and his heirs all religious houses which did not have lands of an annual value exceeding £200.[13] This effected a statutory conveyance to the king of the corporations, their sites, lands, tithes, jurisdictions, and other appurtenances, in fee simple, subject to any prior rights of others, such as lessees, provided they had not been acquired within the previous year.[14] Annexing the monasteries to the Crown worked an automatic suppression or dissolution of the corporations, in accordance with the earlier case-law.[15] With respect to the lands and all the other property rights, the statute provided—following the Christchurch precedent—that the king should have 'the actual and real possession' of them,[16] and full power to dispose of them by letters patent, without the need for an inquisition. The king was also given the ornaments, jewels, goods, chattels, and debts, of the houses concerned. As compensation, the heads of each dissolved house were to receive 'such yearly pensions and benefices as for their degrees and qualities shall be reasonable and convenient', and their convents were either to be supported by charity for life or transferred to one of the greater monasteries. In order to cope with the vast new administrative business created by the management of so much property and revenue, a separate statute of the same year established the Court of Augmentations.[17]

The second statute of dissolution followed in 1539 and dealt with the larger religious houses.[18] It did not directly transfer to the Crown any undissolved

---

[12] Lehmberg, *Reformation Parliament*, 223–9. On the other hand, the preamble to the 1536 statute speaks favourably of the greater houses where 'religion is right well kept and maintained'.

[13] 27 Hen. VIII, c. 28.

[14] According to the statute, various fraudulent grants and leases had been made by heads of houses foreseeing dissolution. All such dispositions, even if effected by common recovery, were declared void.

[15] This is assumed in the statute itself. In *Martyndale v. Adamson* (1548–50) CP 40/1136, m. 317d, it was relied on by the defendant in an action of debt for the price of bread; he pleaded he was the late prior of Coxford, Norfolk, and the bread was bought to the use of the house, and that in 1536 the monastery came into the king's hands as not having lands worth £200; there is an undetermined demurrer.

[16] The 1539 statute (below) used the expression 'very, actual, and real seisin and possession'. But this fiction did not extend as far as turning rights of entry into seisin: *Anon.* (1541/2) Brooke Abr., *Chose in Action*, pl. 14.   [17] Above, 227.

[18] 31 Hen. VIII, c. 13. This started in the House of Lords, but the bill was rewritten in the Commons: Elton, *Reform and Renewal*, 151.

monasteries, but followed the different policy of supporting their piecemeal surrender or forfeiture.[19] That process had already begun,[20] and the legislation applied to houses which had already been surrendered since February 1536 as well as to those which should be surrendered in the future. Although the statute recited that the surrenders were 'free and voluntary...without constraint, coaction, or compulsion', the facts were often rather different; but this was not open to challenge. There had been some legal qualms about the legal effect of the deeds of surrender,[21] and the main purpose of the 1539 legislation was to confirm the king's title in and seisin of all surrendered monasteries, saving the rights of third parties—with various complex exclusions. The practical object was no doubt to give assurance to patentees taking grants of monastic lands from the Crown.[22] This time leases made within a year of the statute were protected only if the lands had been usually let to farm before then, and on the same terms. The statute transferred to the king the right to enforce covenants and conditions in leases made by religious houses to the same extent as the heads of house could have done before dissolution; and in 1540 it was necessary to pass a supplementary statute extending this fictional privity to the king's grantees,[23] though even then the scope of the provision remained unclear.[24] Another clarificatory statute of 1540 'revived' all franchises and temporal jurisdictions belonging to monasteries, and provided that, after coming into the king's possession, they should be under the survey of the Court of Augmentations and exercised by stewards and bailiffs as before, without interference from sheriffs.[25] The legislation was needed because the monasteries came to the king as king and not as lord,[26] and therefore the franchises should have been extinguished in the king's hands and lost any attributes claimed by prescription.

A third dissolution statute, in 1540, dealt with the priory of St John of Jerusalem in England, which had vast possessions throughout the country. In this case the statute itself expressly dissolved the priory, on grounds of traitorous adherence to Rome; but there were similar provisions to those in the earlier legislation vesting

---

[19] The friars were suppressed at the same time, without recourse to legislation: Knowles, *Religious Orders*, iii. 360–6. Friars were unincorporated and therefore did not own real property.

[20] Some houses had been deemed to be forfeited as a result of the attainder of their heads for treason, though there seems to have been little legal justification for this conclusion.

[21] Knowles, *Religious Orders*, iii. 350–1. Audley C. seems to have thought a fine and recovery the proper way, but that sometimes a deed would be more expedient: *LP*, xii. II. 153.

[22] Youings, *Dissolution of the Monasteries*, 83–4.

[23] 32 Hen. VIII, c. 34. This was the subject of a reading by George Browne (Gray's Inn, 1547) BL MS. Hargrave 92, ff. 108–118v.

[24] See *Hill* v. *Grange* (1556) CP 40/1165, m. 412; Plowd. 164 at 173–178v; reported on other points in Dyer 130b; *Anon.* (1558) BL MS. Hargrave 4, fo. 137v.   [25] 32 Hen. VIII, c. 20.

[26] *Gilbert's Case* (1538) Dyer 44a, 44b, §32, citing *R.* v. *Darcy* (1332) Trin. 6 Edw. III, fo. 31, pl. 15. Cf. *Anon.* (1505) 2 Caryll 477, where the King's Bench held that a liberty was not extinguished in the king's hands.

seisin of its real property in the king and his heirs, saving the rights of third parties.[27] The final statute in the series, passed in 1545, gave to the Crown the lands of those colleges,[28] free chapels, chantries, and hospitals, which had been dissolved or extinguished by reason of the misapplication of their endowments, with powers for commissioners to seize others on the like grounds.[29] The dissolution of the chantries was completed in 1547.[30] Another pair of statutes, in 1539 and 1542, dealt with the legal status of the 9,000 or so displaced religious:[31] from the time of their deraignment—or discharge from religious obedience—they were brought back to life again for legal purposes,[32] and most of them were given reasonable pensions.[33]

The dissolution gave the king not only a source of revenue but an enormous source of patronage wherewith the goodwill of the nobility and gentry, and their easier reconciliation to the new settlement of religion, could be secured. It inevitably created an enormous market in land for investors and middlemen.[34] Many of the patentees were attorneys,[35] probably acting on behalf of others. By 1546 over half the lands had been sold or given away by the Crown, and by 1558 over three-quarters: perhaps one-sixth of all the land in the realm. Monastic lands were not only plentiful but normally blessed with clear titles and other legal advantages,[36] though when they were granted out as tenancies in chief to be held

[27] 32 Hen. VIII, c. 24. The savings here were unqualified.

[28] See J. J. Scarisbrick, 'Henry VIII and the Dissolution of the Secular Colleges' in *Law and Government under the Tudors*, ed. C. Cross et al. (1988), 51–66. For the meaning of 'college' see also below, 716 n. 54.

[29] 37 Hen. VIII, c. 4. As with the greater monasteries, the dissolution before 1547 was achieved by means of 'voluntary' surrenders: Scarisbrick, 'Dissolution of the Colleges', 58. See, generally, A. Kreider, *English Chantries: the road to dissolution* (1979), 165–85; Dickens, *English Reformation*, 230–42. Grants of land to ecclesiastical uses, including obits and chantries, had been forbidden since 1532 on the grounds that it was tantamount to mortmain: 23 Hen. VIII, c. 10. [30] See further below, 715.

[31] See Logan, *Runaway Religious in Medieval England c. 1240–1540*, 167–77.

[32] 31 Hen. VIII, c. 6. This had been hastily redrawn (Elton, *Reform and Renewal*, 151), which may explain the further legislation in 33 Hen. VIII, c. 29. See also the explanation in 5 & 6 Edw. VI, c. 13. For the effects of this legislation see above, 610–11.

[33] Youings, *Dissolution of the Monasteries*, 16. An example of a grant of a pension is BL Add. Ch. 42608 (£6 a year granted to a former monk of Pershore—dissolved in 1540—until he should be promoted to a benefice of like value).

[34] See Knowles, *Monastic Orders*, III. 393–401; J. Youings, 'The Monasteries' in J. Thirsk (ed.), *Agrarian History of England and Wales*, iv. 332–55; *Dissolution of the Monasteries*, 117–31; Dickens, *English Reformation*, 181–91.

[35] More so than previous writers have been aware. Of the nine prominent purchasers mentioned by Youings (Thirsk (ed.), *Agrarian History*, iv. 350), five (Andrews, Bellow, Dyon, Rolle, and Heydon) were attorneys of the Common Pleas, and another (Chamberlain) an attorney of the Exchequer. Two more were members of inns (Broxholme of the Inner Temple, Brokylsbye of Clement's Inn) but not necessarily lawyers. Only one (Temple) is not known in a legal context.

[36] Usually the freehold title was clear and there could be no claims to dower. Many abbey lands were exempt from the payment of tithes, and the statute of 1539 confirmed that tithes were not revived when the land came into lay hands.

by knight-service—as the original legislation required—they became subject to wardship, primer seisin, and other feudal incidents.[37] Since it was found that these feudal burdens made some of the smaller parcels of land unsaleable, the law was amended in the 1540s to enable tenements worth less than 40s. a year to be granted by other forms of tenure.[38] As a result, many lesser properties were granted out in free and common socage to be held of the manor of East Greenwich, or some other royal manor, so that they would not be held *in capite*.[39]

The many successive transfers of title and changes of lordship which followed the distribution of property by the Court of Augmentations were a major source of the complaints voiced by the Pilgrims of Grace as early as 1536,[40] and would cause confusion and strife for generations.[41] However, the only really troublesome practical questions of law generated directly by the legislation—judging from the law reports, and from undetermined demurrers in the plea rolls—were those arising upon the construction of the various exceptions and provisos concerning monastic leases.[42]

No real attempt was made under Queen Mary to undo the work of Henry VIII and Edward VI in regard to monasteries and chantries, though Cardinal Pole made known his wish to restore monasticism in some form and the many owners of former monastic land must initially have been worried.[43] Upon the repeal of Henry VIII's reformation legislation in 1554, the Lords and Commons supplicated the queen to intercede with Pole for some resolution of the uncertainty, so that purchasers of monastic land might 'without scruple of conscience enjoy them without impeachment or trouble by pretence of any general council, canons, or ecclesiastical laws, and clear from all dangers of the censures of the Church'. The pope granted a general dispensation, though the cardinal—doubtless correctly—declined to accept that such an act of mercy could cure bad titles.[44] It was therefore left to Parliament to make it clear that the previous legislation relating

[37] It was, however, not wholly clear that the monasteries were given to the king 'in right of his Crown': *Dean and Chapter of Bristol* v. *Clerke* (1553) Dyer 83a at 86a.

[38] 35 Hen. VIII, c. 14; explained by 37 Hen. VIII, c. 20; and see 1 Edw. VI, c. 4.

[39] See J. Hurstfield, 'The Greenwich Tenures of the Reign of Edward VI' (1949) 65 *LQR* 76–81.

[40] Thirsk, 'Enclosing and Engrossing' in *Agrarian History*, ed. Thirsk, 219.

[41] For early examples of disputes over titles deriving from the Court of Augmentations, see *Willughby* v. *Welstede* (1542) CP 40/1112, m. 508; *Ireland* v. *Poyner* (1548) CP 40/1138, m. 393; *Wade* v. *Smyth* (1550) CP 40/1143, m. 511; *Pexall* v. *Long* (1551) CP 40/1147A, m. 726.

[42] *Berdge* v. *Broke* (1549) CP 40/1142, m. 639 (demurrer); *Hosteler* v. *Gybbes* (1551) CP 40/1147A, m. 623 (issue whether land usually leased); *Eppes* v. *Dabbes* (1552) KB 27/1163, m. 20 (demurrer); Dyer 73a; *Abbot of Kingswood's Case* (1552) Dyer 77b; *Abbot of Keynsham's Case* (1553) Dyer 80b; *Fulmerston* v. *Steward* (1553–61) KB 27/1162, m. 162 (demurrer); Dyer 102b; Plowd. 102; *Granado* v. *Dyer* (1555) KB 27/1169, m. 84d (demurrer); Dyer 123a.

[43] For Pole's plans see T. F. Mayer, *Cardinal Pole* (2000), 283–9. A few new houses were created, but the queen continued to sell off the lands of monasteries already dissolved.

[44] Guy, *Tudor England*, 234–6.

to monastic land remained in force, that titles derived therefrom remained fully effective, and that any attempt to molest an owner of monastic land in the ecclesiastical courts would incur the penalty of *praemunire*.[45]

IMPROPRIATION OF TITHES

A novel consequence of transferring monastic tithes to the king, with an unrestricted power to grant them over, was that the freehold property in tithes came for the first time into the hands of laymen.[46] This process was called lay appropriation,[47] or impropriation.[48] The whole tithes of a parish could be transferred to a patentee by a grant of the parsonage or rectory to which they belonged. Benefices thus transferred to laymen were later called lay rectories, though the expression is not found in this period. Portions of tithes in the parish of another rector, which could be claimed by monasteries if received from time immemorial, were also mentioned in the statute and could therefore be impropriated.[49] It was necessary to pass another statute in 1540 to clarify the position of lay impropriators, who were not given any remedy to protect their property by the earlier legislation. As a result of the 1540 statute, they were enabled to sue in the ecclesiastical courts for non-payment of tithes, to bring actions in the temporal courts if dispossessed of their parsonages,[50] and to levy fines of parsonages.[51] Thus the impropriated benefice, or lay rectory, became a new form of real property, assimilated for most legal purposes to land.

CHANTRIES AND CHARITIES

The dissolution of the chantries, which began piecemeal in the mid-1540s,[52] turned into a general exercise in 1547. Henry VIII had not been theologically

[45] 1 & 2 Phil. & Mar., c. 8, ss. 13–16.

[46] It was said in 1503 that the king could not be a parson even by act of Parliament: *Prior of Castleacre* v. *Dean of Westminster* (1503) Hil. 21 Hen. VII (misdated), fo. 4, pl. 1; CP 40/964, m. 416 (noted in 116 Selden Soc. 413). Vavasour J. said in that case (tr.), 'I know several lords who have parsonages in their own use', giving details of their names and places; but Frowyk CJ asserted that this had been done with papal permission. It had been common before 1536 for parsonages to be leased.

[47] Before 1536, parsonages and tithes could only be appropriated to corporations.

[48] Appropriation and impropriation are interchangeable words in this period, though in later usage impropriation became the usual term for appropriation by laymen. The distinction may originate in *Crimes* v. *Smith* (1588) 12 Co. Rep. 4.

[49] See e.g. *Dean and Chapter of Bristol* v. *Clerke* (1553) Dyer 83a.

[50] Ejectment was already available, and remained in common use: above, 636–7.

[51] 32 Hen. VIII, c. 7. This was the subject of a reading by William Coke (Gray's Inn, 1546) BL MS. Hargrave 92, ff. 104–107v. The statute 1 & 2 Phil. & Mar., c. 8, ss. 17, 26, confirmed this legislation as unaffected by the repeal of the king's supremacy.

[52] Above, 713. For an attempt at anticipatory evasion see *Hall* v. *Spencer* (1557) CP 40/1170, m. 1009 (Richard Blackwall alleged to have acquired chantry lands in Wirkworth church, Derbs., by collusive recovery in April 1545; issue on collusion). Blackwall was a barrister of the Inner Temple.

opposed to the concepts of purgatory and intercession, and indeed provided for masses in his own will. But Edward VI and his ministers—adopting the Lutheran position that they had no biblical or theological foundation[53]—immediately rejected the doctrines as superstitious and no longer defensible. The whole basis of chantries being thus officially removed, it was necessary to bring them all to an orderly end. But it was a more difficult exercise than the dissolution of religious houses, because chantries had commonly been created in conjunction with other charities which deserved to be maintained. The statute of 1547 followed the precedent of 1536 by deeming 'all manner of colleges,[54] free chapels, and chantries', and their lands and possessions, to be in the king's seisin and possession, without the need for an inquisition, saving the rights of lessees and other third parties.[55] The Crown was also given the jewels, plate, ornaments, and other chattels, belonging to chantries.[56] The act went on to transfer to the Crown all fraternities, brotherhoods, and guilds, other than craft guilds, together with their lands. But a new distinction had to be drawn between superstitious and other objects. Lands which had been given wholly for the maintenance of an anniversary or obit, or for a light or lamp in a church or chapel, were to be enjoyed by the Crown for ever; but where only part of the revenues of land had been given for such purposes, the Crown was to receive such sums of money only as were payable for those purposes, with power to distrain. Commissioners were to be appointed to investigate all chantries in order to protect proper charitable objects, and to examine the account-books of all craft guilds to discover what revenues were devoted to chantry purposes and what lands should therefore be assigned to the king. Most of this work was in the event done by Sir Walter Mildmay and Robert Keilwey.[57] Perhaps by oversight, the statute did not make any provision with respect to future transfers of land to superstitious uses, and it did not therefore prevent the endowment of new chantries under Mary I.[58]

[53] The issue had been in public controversy since the 1520s, and common lawyers had played a prominent part: Simon Fish of Gray's Inn wrote the tract of 1529 which prompted defences of purgatory by Sir Thomas More and John Rastell.

[54] By express saving, the statute did not apply to colleges in the universities, St George's chapel, Windsor, or the colleges of Winchester and Eton. See also *R. v. Lord Dacre of the North* (1553) Dyer 81a (Greystoke College held not to have been a college for the purpose of the act).

[55] 1 Edw. VI, c. 14; discussed in Kreider, *English Chantries*, 186–208. There is some evidence that the draftsman was John Hales (d. 1572): BL MS. Hargrave 4, fo. 299v; Kreider, *English Chantries*, 262.

[56] For legal disputes about personalty from chantries see *Walkelyn v. Lendall* (1550) CP 40/1144A, m. 539 (vessels; demurrer); *Nethersole v. Cartwryght* (1551) KB 27/1157, m. 118 (bells, vestments, plate, altar cloths, and a bible; demurrer). The first case arose from a wider dispute concerning chantry property at Chelsfield, Kent: *Walkelyn v. Lendall* (1552) CP 40/1150, m. 617 (demurrer); *Lendall v. Walkeleyn* (1552) CP 40/1154, m. 721 (general issue).

[57] Kreider, *English Chantries*, 13, 47.

[58] See Jones, *The History of the Law of Charity*, 13–15.

The distinction which the legislation drew between superstitious uses and 'good and godly' uses was the foundation of the secular law of charities.[59] However, charity was not yet a legal term of art or a distinct legal concept—indeed, the word is not used in the 1547 act[60]—and the only forms of charity which the statute required to be preserved were the maintenance of preachers and schoolmasters, the payment of benefits to poor people, and the maintenance of piers, jetties, and sea-walls.[61] The education of youth 'in virtue and godliness' was specifically mentioned in the preamble, and one of the principal and long-lasting achievements of the chantry commissioners was the re-foundation of a considerable number of chantry schools as King Edward VI grammar schools.[62] These were established as corporations, created by letters patent, the supporting lands and the management being vested in local governors.[63] The commissioners also sought to ensure that any deficiencies in parish clergy consequent upon the dissolution of the monasteries were made good by the support of vicars and curates.

[59] G. H. Jones, 'The Reformation and the Law of Charity', ibid. 10–15.

[60] The 1545 act, however, referred to 'charitable deeds'.

[61] A draft chantries bill of 1545 had wider provisions, dealing with the relief of poverty, the maintenance of religion and liberal sciences, and the repair of highways and bridges: *LP*, xx. II. 852; Kreider, *English Chantries*, 178.

[62] The foundation of Berkhamstead School (see 2 & 3 Edw. VI, c. 59) is pleaded in *Davers* v. *Reve* (1551) CP 40/1146, m. 351 (trespass against master and usher, who plead the foundation and incorporation by the king and pray that the judges should not proceed *rege inconsulto*).

[63] e.g. King Edward VI Grammar School Chelmsford—which derived from Sir John Mountney's chantry (1375) in Chelmsford church—was established by letters patent of 24 March 1551 as a corporation of four governors endowed with land, having power to appoint a master and usher and to make statutes, and with licence to acquire further land in mortmain: *CPR*, iv. 116; original patent in Essex Record Office; J. H. Johnson, *Chelmsford Grammar School* (1946).

38

Litigation over Real Property

THE fifteenth and sixteenth centuries saw a revolution not only in the substance of the land law but also in the law and practice of real actions, though contemporaries did not remark on it until it was largely over. It is difficult to pin down the details because appearances can be deceptive. For instance, the learning on assizes was evidently considered very important in the early sixteenth century: there are 472 entries under that title in Fitzherbert's *Abridgement*, and notable readings were still delivered in the inns of court on assize-related topics.[1] Yet cases of novel disseisin are scattered very thinly in the plea rolls and law reports. Although their low visibility is itself misleading, since they only found their way to Westminster if adjourned from the country,[2] it is evident from the Chancery records that the number of writs of assize issued each year never reached double figures.[3] Novel disseisin still had the advantage that it enabled land to be specifically recovered, and it was the only appropriate action to recover a freehold office.[4] Formedon was used regularly to enforce gifts in tail, since there was often no alternative,[5] though sometimes it seems to have been collusive.[6] Dower and partition were also in regular use, since there was no other judicial means of achieving the supervised division of property which they sought. The various writs of entry are encountered from time to time in the rolls, and several are to be found in the law reports, though—apart from the fictional writs of entry

---

[1] e.g. Edmund Dudley on Westminster II, c. 25 (Gray's Inn, 1496), and Walter Hendley on 21 Hen. VIII, c. 3, concerning abridgment of plaints (Gray's Inn, 1530). [2] Above, 263.

[3] D. W. Sutherland, *The Assize of Novel Disseisin* (1973), 179–80 (eight in 1499–1500, six in 1525–6, four in 1534–5, three or four in 1550).

[4] e.g. *Croftes* v. *Beauchamp* (1486) Trin. 1 Hen. VII, fo. 28, pl. 6 (forestership); *Croftes* v. *Hemperden* (1487) KB 27/901, m. 30; Mich. 2 Hen. VII, fo. 7, pl. 23; Hil. 2 Hen. VII, fo. 11, pl. 12; Spelman 13 (parkership of Woodstock); *Savage* v. *Bishop of London* (1507) CP 40/982, m. 601 (parkership of Harringay); *Dyne* v. *Leverey* (1514) CP 40/1005B, m. 422 (forestership); *Rudhale* v. *Salwey* (1519–20) CP 40/1026, m. 560 (clerkship of peace in Glos.); Dyer 7b, pl. 10 (1536), *per* Mountagu sjt (filazership); *Vaus* v. *Jefferne* (1555) CP 40/1162, m. 955; Dyer 114b; above, 133 (filazership).

[5] When, in 1539, an attorney reported to his client that a formedon would be necessary, he noted that it was 'much dilatory': *Lisle Letters*, ed. Byrne, v. 408, no. 1359.

[6] e.g. all three examples in CP 40/1084 (Hil. 1535) end in a judgment upon confession (*non potest dedicere*). Note also *Carewe* v. *Courteney* (1539) CP 40/1102, m. 357 (*non potest dedicere*, but judgment not given until 1542). See also above, 695 n. 75.

in the *post* used for common recoveries—they are hardly more numerous than novel disseisin. Writs of right were even less common,[7] and usually attracted the attention of law reporters.[8]

The whole gamut of real actions was therefore still within range for the more learned practitioner, and their intricacies remained central to the curriculum of the inns of court. However, what is most striking about the patterns of actual lit-igation as revealed by the plea rolls is that the vast majority of actions involving title to land, or other questions of real property law, were now personal actions: forcible entry, replevin,[9] and—first and foremost—trespass. An analysis of the 149 cases in the plea rolls of the Common Pleas for 1535 in which the issue was essen-tially one of real property,[10] excluding common recoveries and debt for rent, shows that more than half (78 cases) were trespass *quare clausum fregit* and over one-fifth (32 cases) were replevin, while no other category of action occurs more than five times.[11] It is likely that some of the many other trespass actions in which the defendant pleaded Not guilty were also concerned with title. Other possible remedies were detinue of title deeds, or a bill in Chancery for discovery of title deeds;[12] and account for the profits of land.[13] But trespass was the principal medium for disputing property rights throughout our period,[14] and had indeed been gaining ground since the fourteenth century.[15]

The reason behind this marked preference for personal actions is not explicitly spelt out in the sources, but it must have been the greater simplicity of procedure—for instance, speedier and more effective mesne process, simpler pleading, and the unavailability of dilatory measures such as essoins, vouchers to

---

[7] They were used for common recoveries until 1489: above, 694.

[8] e.g. *Anon.* (1497) Mich. 12 Hen. VII, fo. 10, pl. 6; *Lord Fitzwaryn* v. *Swayne* (1535) Trin. 27 Hen. VIII, fo. 14, pl. 2; CP 40/1087, m. 517 (right of advowson); *Abbot of Bury* v. *Bokenham* (1536) Dyer 7b; CP 40/1088, m. 420 (right of ward; demurrer to count); *Marvin* v. *York* (1538) Dyer 104b (judgment by default); *Lord Windsor* v. *St John* (1553–5) Dyer 79b, 98a, 103b (ends with appearance of four knights 'girt with swords above their garments'); Benl. 42; CP 40/1150, m. 543; CP 40/1163, m. 756.

[9] Professor Biancalana has pointed out to the writer that these seem to have fallen off after about 1555.

[10] CP 40/1084–1087. Only cases in which the defendant appeared were counted.

[11] The other categories are: formedon (5), quare impedit (5), actions on the case (5), debt on a bond (4), entry in the *quibus* (4), forcible entry (2), entry in the *post* (1), entry *in consimili casu* (1), account against a receiver (guardian in socage) (1), covenant (1), dower (1), forfeiture of marriage (1), forgery of a will (1), and right of advowson (1). The absence of forcible entry is remarkable.

[12] See above, 189. Such a suit was not, however, a 'claim' to land for the purposes of the Statute of Limitations: *Anon.* (*c.*1545/9) Wm Yelv. 345, no. 70.

[13] Sutherland, *Assize of Novel Disseisin*, 176. Account would not, however, lie against a disseisor or anyone else who took profits in his own right: see *Anon.* (1554) Brooke Abr., *Accompt*, pl. 65, 89; below, 877 n. 21.

[14] Cf. Sutherland, *Assize of Novel Disseisin*, 179, who counted forty trespass cases 'turning on freehold rights' in Mich. 1499 alone, in the rolls of both benches. The figure was even higher in 1439.

[15] According to Sutherland (p. 173), 'trespass to lands became a major partner with the assize during the last decades of the fourteenth century'.

warranty, aid-prayers, receipts, and parol demurrers.[16] The plaintiff was also freed from the need to name the tenant or tenants of the freehold; he could bring the action against a servant or lessee of the freeholder; and he did not have to be a freeholder himself. Personal actions were formally less advantageous, in that seisin of the land could not be recovered, and in practice the damages awarded were seldom substantial. But it may be that a plaintiff's principal object was not to obtain a remedy so much as to win the verdict of a jury. A verdict in favour of someone out of possession would justify an entry without the need for a writ to the sheriff;[17] and, if a question of title was specially pleaded, it would be settled by the jury's finding, since the verdict would work an estoppel in any future proceedings.[18] Yet the pleadings in trespass actions were hardly designed as a means of recording the plaintiff's title for posterity. For one thing, the property in dispute was not defined at all (beyond naming the vill), unless the plaintiff was driven to make a new assignment;[19] and, if he did that, the defendant usually simply pleaded Not guilty.[20] For another, the defendant would often plead generally that the land was his own freehold or the freehold of his master, without setting out the title.[21]

It is difficult to see how a general verdict in trespass, upon such pleadings, would furnish either party with any useful kind of recorded title, or how an adversary could be restrained from reopening the same question in a second or subsequent action.[22] In one case in our sample from 1535 we find the plaintiff giving up once the evidence was shown to the jury,[23] and it may be that in some cases the object of the litigation was no more than to obtain discovery and test the opponent's case. We know from demurrers to the evidence that all kinds of documentary evidence

[16] *Anon.* (1482) Hil. 21 Edw. IV, fo. 82, pl. 36; Pas. 22 Edw. IV, fo. 4, pl. 14. See generally Sutherland, 'Trespass takes Over' in *The Assize of Novel Disseisin*, 169–203.

[17] Sutherland, *Assize of Novel Disseisin*, 173.

[18] See *Anon.* (1492) 1 Caryll 78, pl. 86 (verdict as to disseisin, in an action of forcible entry, estops party in trespass).

[19] The plaintiff in trespass was not allowed to specify the land in his declaration but merely alleged the breaking of a 'close' in a certain vill. If the defendant pleaded his freehold in particular land, the plaintiff could 'new assign' the trespass elsewhere and the pleading began again: e.g. *Anon.* (1522) Mich. 14 Hen. VIII, fo. 4, pl. 3 (119 Selden Soc. 104); *Anon.* (1535) Pas. 27 Hen. VIII, fo. 7, pl. 21, *per* Baldwin CJ (tr. 'by the new assignment the bar is out of doors', meaning that the defendant could plead generally); *Saunders* v. *Lord Burgh* (1558) Dyer 161b. Sometimes a new assignment would even define the property with abuttals: *Saunders* v. *Lord Burgh* (1558) Dyer 161b. See also *Anon.* (*c.*1516) Chaloner 279, no. 5.

[20] Fourteen examples were noted in 1535. Note also *Beamount* v. *Wood* (1535) CP 40/1087, m. 326 (justifies as servant of freeholder, doubtless a fiction; plaintiff new assigns; defendant pleads own freehold).　　　　[21] Eight examples were noted in 1535, besides that in the following note.

[22] This must be the explanation of *Anon.* (1491) 1 Caryll 55, pl. 55 (juror challenged because he had found for the plaintiff on the same title in a previous action: here it seems to be assumed that there was no estoppel).

[23] *Purde* v. *Holgyll* (1535) CP 40/1086, m. 437 (nonsuit after evidence given to jury).

could be shown to the jury on the general issue in trespass,[24] as could parol evidence—for instance of a sale by cestuy que use,[25] a livery of seisin without a letter of attorney,[26] or a partition.[27] But this evidence was not usually placed on the record; and the occasional demurrer—which achieved that result[28]—required the other party to admit its authenticity for the sake of legal argument. Uncovering and testing the evidence seems therefore to have been in itself a principal end of trespass litigation. In those cases where a verdict was obtained, the conclusion of the jury was presumably taken as a sufficient indication of local opinion to settle the matter for most current purposes.

Only in the event of a prolonged feud would repeated actions be brought, perhaps proceeding in due course to the assizes and real actions. Some notes in law French on the progress of a lawsuit between Reynold Andrewe and Thomas Wyse, for land in Hampshire, provide a simple illustration. An action of forcible entry had been brought around 1484 but discontinued by the death of Richard III; Andrewe had then brought novel disseisin, in which the assize gave a verdict which Andrewe claimed was false; and so finally, in 1490, the plaintiff brought a writ of entry in the *post*, which was pending when the notes were written.[29] But there was probably no such thing as a textbook lawsuit. A real feud would drag on for years, even decades, with entries and intrusions and expulsions, suits in Chancery and Star Chamber besides those in the courts of law, perhaps a prosecution at the sessions for forcible entry, and sometimes recourse to arbitration as the only sensible way of achieving a final settlement.[30]

Self-help remained a serious temptation—whether it was viewed as an alternative to litigation, or as a preliminary—and the prevalence of actions of forcible entry at the beginning of the Tudor period doubtless reflects the continued use of real force in property disputes.[31] A particularly serious case arose in 1532 during the long-standing legal feud between the Fortescues and

[24] e.g. *Brynys* v. *Hille* (1518) CP 40/1021B, m. 335 (deposition in Council of Marches); *Hyllyng* v. *Courties* (1521) CP 40/1032B, m. 130d (lease of 1481 and sub-lease of 1518); *Bill* v. *Bill* (1538) CP 40/1097, m. 558 (will, set out in English); *Bisshop* v. *Somer* (1544) CP 40/1121, m. 104 (sim.); *Gale* v. *Furman* (1549) CP 40/1142, m. 675 (copy of court roll); *Scolland* v. *Tarrant* (1550) CP 40/1144A, m. 160 (sim.).

[25] *Harley* v. *Potter* (1536) CP 40/1088, m. 157d.   [26] *Meynell* v. *Gervesse* (1548) CP 40/1138, m. 331.

[27] *Bill* v. *Bill* (1538) CP 40/1097, m. 558.

[28] Of the eight cases in the previous four notes only two (*Hyllyng* v. *Courties* and *Gale* v. *Furman*) resulted in judgment for the plaintiff. But the demurrer itself could be taken as a formal confession of the evidence.   [29] Bodl. Lib. MS. Lyell 35, ff. 28v–32.

[30] See e.g. the lengthy struggles described in R. Virgoe, 'Inheritance and Litigation in the Fifteenth Century: the Buckenham disputes' (1994) 15 *JLH* 23–40 (and the references to an earlier period on p. 39 n. 1); J. Kirby (ed.), *The Plumpton Letters and Papers* (8 Camden Soc., 5th series; 1996), 10–18.

[31] The actions were sometimes founded on the statute of 1381 (5 Ric. II, stat. 1, c. 7), sometimes on that of 1429 (8 Hen. VI, c. 9). The 1429 remedy was only available to freeholders: *Anon.* (1491) 1 Caryll 74, pl. 80. However, Saunders held in his reading (Middle Temple, 1525) that a lessee could obtain restitution from the justices under the 1429 statute: Pollard 263, no. 39.

the Stonors over lands in Oxfordshire. After Sir Walter Stonor had re-entered the manor of Stonor with a force of some thirty men, Sir Adrian Fortescue returned with a posse of eighty men, one of whom was killed with a bolt from a crossbow. The case attracted the king's personal concern, and the eventual solution was an arbitration award embodied in an act of Parliament.[32] There is no doubt that other examples of violence occurred,[33] and forcible entries were statutory misdemeanours which could be prosecuted at the quarter sessions,[34] where restitution could be ordered.[35] The crime was committed whether or not the person who entered with force had good title.[36] But restitution was not available in the civil action for forcible entry,[37] the primary use of which was to try title, and the judges sought to further that purpose by treating the force as more a matter of form than of substance.[38] We cannot therefore be sure whether all allegations of force were genuine.

It may be that the technical problems encountered in forcible entry account for its decline,[39] and for the choice of a simple action of trespass *quare clausum fregit* whenever possible. They were not theoretically interchangeable actions. The essence of forcible entry, like novel disseisin, was a complaint of dispossession; whereas trespass *quare clausum fregit* complained of an entry on land still in the plaintiff's possession.[40] A reversioner out of possession could not complain of a trespass committed before he had re-entered.[41] On the other hand, it seems to have been necessary only that the plaintiff should have been in possession at the time of the trespass, and so a disseisee could maintain trespass against the disseisor without alleging a re-entry.[42] It was indeed quite common in trespass

[32] *Fortescue* v. *Stonor* (1533) Spelman 106 (and references in headnote); 28 Hen. VIII, c. 36.

[33] Gunn, *Early Tudor Government*, 102–3. For the preceding period see S. J. Payling, 'Murder, Motive and Punishment in Fifteenth-Century England: two gentry case-studies' (1998) 113 *EHR* 1–17, and the citations there.   [34] See above, 273.

[35] The restitution did not bar an assize: see FNB 248–9; *Anon.* (1553) MS. Add. 24845, ff. 18v–19, *per* Hales J. (Portman J. *contra*).   [36] *Fortescue* v. *Stonor* (1533) Spelman 106 at 107.

[37] *Paschall* v. *Tendring* (1554) Benl. 37. Cf. Hil. 10 Hen. VII, fo. 14, pl. 7, where Vavasour sjt argued that a successful plaintiff could obtain restitution, perhaps meaning that the justices would give effect to the civil judgment.

[38] *Rednesh's Case* (1486) Pas. 1 Hen. VII, fo. 19, pl. 4; *Forster* v. *Frowike* (1487) Pas. 2 Hen. VII, fo. 16, pl. 2; *Anon.* (1500) Mich. 15 Hen. VII, fo. 17, pl. 12. FNB 249D refers to 'the usage today' (1534) that, although a defendant who pleads in bar must deny the entry with force, this is not traversable by the plaintiff, who must answer the bar.

[39] Besides the question of force, it was necessary in forcible entry to plead a specific title: *Hoppyng* v. *Benet* (1502) 2 Caryll 406 (noting this as a distinction from trespass); *Anon.* (1532/3) Brooke Abr., *Action sur Statute*, pl. 15. For another difference see *Anon.* (1505) 2 Caryll 481, pl. 346. See also *Anon.* (1491) 1 Caryll 74, pl. 80; *Anon.* (1493) 1 Caryll 200, pl. 154; *Anon.* (1529) Spelman 30, pl. 7.

[40] *Anon.* (1491) 1 Caryll 71, pl. 76, *per* Townshend J.

[41] *Scrope* v. *Hyk* (1511) 2 Caryll 618 at p. 619. Nor could a lessee sue for a trespass before he entered: *Moots*, 142 (Inner Temple, c.1490).

[42] *Pope* v. *See* (1534) Spelman 215; 94 Selden Soc. 357 at 358. Cf. *Anon.* (1556) Dyer 134a, §10.

actions for the pleadings to turn on an alleged disseisin by the defendant, usually revealed in the replication;[43] but, since the purpose was usually to show that the title in the bar derived from the seisin gained by disseisin, some kind of re-entry was necessary in these cases to prove possession at the time of the trespass. It is difficult to distinguish between the formalities of pleading and the actual facts; but it seems likely that, as with the assize, the re-entry might have been of a formal nature rather than a complete ouster of the disseisor.[44] When the disseisee did re-enter, it was arguable that his remitter enabled him to recover damages for mesne trespasses committed while he was out of possession, even perhaps against strangers.[45] It seems to follow that, if he did not re-enter, he was not entitled to substantial damages at all.

It is only at the very end of our period that ejectment starts to be used as a new-found means of trying the lessor's title. This offered the best of both worlds, since it was a trespass action and yet it gave recovery of the land.[46] We can perhaps detect in the 1550s the first indications that ejectment might be used to try the freehold title of the lessor,[47] or a copyhold title,[48] though as yet there is no hint of fiction. Indeed, even a genuine lease made by a freeholder out of possession would at that time have been held contrary to the legislation against maintenance and buying pretended titles, and it was therefore necessary for the claimant to regain actual possession before the procedure could be set in motion.[49] It would be at least another generation before ejectment began to oust the older remedies as the freeholder's usual action of choice.[50]

---

[43] e.g. in the sample year: *Nordon v. Pyper* (1535) CP 40/1084, m. 150; *Cade v. Dawe* (1535) CP 40/1085(1), m. 352; *Chylderne v. Becher* (1535) CP 40/1085(2), m. 111 (4d. damages awarded); *Browne v. Hubbard*, ibid., m. 117; *Asshe v. Nicholles*, ibid., m. 301; *Westdene v. Warde* (1535) CP 40/1086, m. 641. See also *Bishop of London v. Kellett* (1533) Spelman 137; (1535) CP 40/1084, m. 328.

[44] So thought Sutherland, *Assize of Novel Disseisin*, 171–2.

[45] This was controversial. See *Anon.* (1490) Mich. 6 Hen. VII, fo. 7, pl. 4, at fo. 9, per Bryan CJ (damages only for initial entry, not for mesne profits); case at Frowyk's reading (Inner Temple, 1492) in *Moots*, 267 (not against strangers); *Lord Willoughby de Broke's Case* (1496) 1 Caryll 294 (only against disseisor and his agents); *Anon.* (1510/11) Spelman 11 at 12 (lies against strangers); *Pope v. See* (1534) Spelman 215, per Spelman J. and Fitzjames CJ (lies against feoffee); 94 Selden Soc. 358; *Note* (undated) Spelman 216, pl. 7 (against disseisor). See Coke's discussion of the older authorities in 11 Co. Rep. 51.

[46] See above, 635–6.

[47] *Newdigate's Case* (King's Bench, 1551) Dyer 68b; *Grotewyche v. Willoughbye* (1555) KB 27/1176, m. 37, perhaps identifiable as *Lord Clinton's Case* (1557) 110 Selden Soc. 408; *Wrottesley v. Adams* (Common Pleas, 1559) Dyer 177b; Gell's reports, I, ff. 85–92v.

[48] *Aylwyn v. Gasse* (1555) CP 40/1161, m. 639 (issue on a surrender and admittance of a copyhold in the manor of Bosham); *Anon.* (1558) Chr. Yelverton's reports, BL MS. Hargrave 388, fo. 246v (demurrer to evidence as to custom of manor; judgment to recover term).

[49] See *Partridge v. Straunge* (1553) CP 40/1151, m. 522 (debt on the statute 32 Hen. VIII, c.9); Dyer 74b; Plowd. 77 at 87. The application of the statute to leases made for the purpose of trying the title in ejectment was explicitly confirmed by *Gerard v. Worseley* (1581) Dyer 374a; 110 Selden Soc. 385, pl. 499; 1 And. 75.　　　　　[50] See Baker, *The Law's Two Bodies* (2001), 51–2.

The old real actions received a further blow, in the interests of settling 'peaceable possession of a long season', when the limitation period was shortened in 1540.[51] It was an overdue reform,[52] since—as a reader of the Inner Temple acerbically pointed out in 1531—nothing had been done to alter limitation periods since the thirteenth century.[53] The old legislation had fixed limitation periods at historical points in time, now in the remote past; but the 1540 statute adopted the more practicable solution of limiting the period over which a title could be traced. No writ of right or prescriptive claim could now be made on the basis of a seisin more than sixty years before the action; the limitation period in assizes, writs of entry, formedon, and *scire facias* to execute fines, was to be fifty years; and in actions based on the plaintiff's own seisin or possession,[54] thirty years. A doubt about the scope of the statute was resolved by an explanatory statute of 1553, which declared that it did not extend to any actions concerning advowsons or wardships—the peculiarity of which was that seisin could only be acquired at irregular intervals.[55]

---

[51] 32 Hen. VIII, c. 2. This was the subject of Robert Brooke's first reading (Middle Temple, 1542), pr. 1647. It was held that it applied to copyhold as well as freehold: *Anon.* (1552) Brooke Abr., *Limitations*, pl. 2. See also Wm Yelv. 345–6, nos. 70–1.

[52] It seems to have been first proposed by Cromwell in 1539: Elton, *Reform and Renewal*, 153–4. The first bill was defeated in the Lords.

[53] Henry White's reading on Westminster I, c. 39 (1531) BL MS. Hargrave 87(2), ff. 245v–250. He said the most recent limitation was now 270 years, and that this needed reform.   [54] e.g. trespass.

[55] 1 Mar. I, sess. 2, c. 5.

39

Property in Chattels

FITZHERBERT J. remarked in 1527 that 'common law and common reason consider goods, chattels, and money as highly as land; for many people who have no lands have goods and money of as great a value as land'.[1] However true that may have been in reality, the logic is not reflected in the level of sophistication of the substantive law.[2] The land law was at the heart of legal study and thought, dominating the work of the courts and the exercises in the inns of court, while the remainder of the law was still perceived as a law of actions rather than of discrete legal concepts. Whereas the land law was a complex intellectual structure which had become more or less independent of the forms of action, the law of chattels seems to be hidden behind the machinery of detinue, trespass, and replevin. In trespass and detinue, moreover, the routine use of the general issue kept substantive questions of property entirely hidden from sight in the majority of cases. Occasionally, in replevin and other personal actions, issue was joined on the 'ownership'[3] (*proprietas*) in chattels; but a general plea of property throws no light on what the word meant,[4] and even a special plea resulting in an issue of property may be no more illuminating.[5] Personal property did not deserve or need a Littleton, and it is not obvious where to look for the subject in Fitzherbert's abridgment. Even so, a close scrutiny of the sources shows that common lawyers were beginning to formulate a few principles of personal property. Property could not be wholly subsumed under the law of actions, because in some situations there was a right to retake chattels even where no action was

---

[1] *Marmyon* v. *Baldwyn* (1527) 120 Selden Soc. 61 at 66. Cf. *Moots*, 141 (inheritance 'worthier' than chattel).   [2] For money see below, ch. 48, 50.

[3] The English word 'owner' was commonly used for chattels: e.g. Trin. 10 Hen. VII, fo. 27, pl. 13, *per* Bryan CJ; Spelman's reading on *Quo Warranto*, 113 Selden Soc. 95, 161, 165, 166; Spelman's reading on *Prerogativa Regis* (1521) ibid. 41, 42.

[4] e.g. *Anon.* (1520) 120 Selden Soc. 45, no. 29; 94 Selden Soc. 210 n. 2. Likewise in trover: *Huttofte* v. *Thomas* (1540) KB 27/1116 m. 27 (defendant pleads property in himself and not in plaintiff).

[5] e.g. *Mynne* v. *Dusgate* (1501) KB 27/959, m. 43d (trespass to foal; pleads he bought it from E, and bailed it for safekeeping to E, who gave it to plaintiff; plaintiff replies it was his, *absque hoc* the property was in E); *Malkyn* v. *Ive* (1532) KB 27/1083 m. 31 (trespass to horse; pleads B took it and gave it to plaintiff, and defendant took it back; plaintiff replies that he possessed the horse as his own, *absque hoc* the property was in the defendant). Neither reply indicates the nature of the plaintiff's claim.

available at law,[6] and there was arguably a right to use force in defence of one's personal property.[7]

Fortescue, and probably most common lawyers of the century following, were of the opinion that—whatever may have occurred in a remote state of nature—property had become the basis of society, and that even by the laws of nature a man had the right to protect the fruits of his labour.[8] Since the greater part of the common law was predicated upon the notion of private property, the abstraction may seem rather academic; but the theory did have repercussions on the law of chattels. Unlike land, chattels were not hereditary. Neither were they endowed by nature with permanence. Property in them could therefore come and go in a manner inconceivable in the case of land. Land had to be in someone's fee, and in the absence of any claim by a subject it belonged to the king. But there was no need for chattels to belong to anyone. The law had therefore to explain how and when property arose in chattels, and the answer was found in the notion that property was founded on human industry. Industry was the principal, if not the only, way in which property could be created in an object which originally had no owner. What was, in the case of land, a mere historical explanation or an abstract speculation, was for movables a matter of living law from which principles could be deduced.

In attempting to identify these principles, it is convenient to follow *Bracton* in borrowing the Roman terminology of occupation, specification, and accession; but it should be noted that these terms do not occur in the early-modern English sources. Although there are without doubt some signs of Romanesque influence here, almost certainly by way of *Bracton*, common-law discussion was innocent of any acquaintance with purely Civilian sources and learning. The analysis of the modes of creation of movable property is a fairly natural one, once human industry is identified as the key. Only three methods spring to mind:[9] the reduction into possession (occupation) of something which was previously the property of no one (*res nullius*), the creation of a new object (specification) having a different identity from the materials from which it was made, and the severance of movable matter from (or its accession to) land.

---

[6] e.g. Yorke 222, no. 360; *Anon.* (1544) Cholmeley 450 at 451, *per* Curson.

[7] See *Philip* v. *Cobbe* (1500) KB 27/956, m. 35 (battery justified in defence of a bloodhound); Rast. Ent. 553v (611v). This was disputed at an Inner Temple moot (*c.*1530) in Caryll (Jun.) 385, no. 34. In *Bishop of London* v. *Nevell* [1521] Mich. 14 Hen. VIII, fo. 1, pl. 1 (119 Selden Soc. 90; misdated in the old edns), Brudenell CJ said that breaking a stable was not justifiable in order to repossess a horse.

[8] J. Fortescue, *De Natura Legis Naturae*, ed. Lord Clermont (1869), i. 5, i. 20, ii. 32; Rastell, prologue to Fitz. Abr. (1517); Perk. (1528), prohemium; St German, *Doctor and Student*, ed. Plucknett and Barton, 33, 35, 39. See also R. Schlatter, *Private Property: the history of an idea* (1951). For Thomas More's views see 94 Selden Soc. 210.   [9] Cf. *Bracton*, ff. 8b–10b (ii. 41–7).

OCCUPATION

The only kind of movable which normally lent itself to acquisition by occupation was the animal. Inanimate objects were either (like vegetation and minerals) part of the realty until severed,[10] or they were manufactured, or they were things in either category which had been lost by or acquired from a previous owner. Casual loss did not in itself deprive the owner of property as against a finder, as the declaration in trover testifies; nor did deliberate dereliction.[11] The finder had a good title against all but the loser. The loser, however, could sue him in detinue or trespass.[12] Animals, on the other hand, had the ability to wander off on their own and thereby divest their owners of property. And animals born out of captivity were *res nullius* from birth. The property in such animals could therefore be acquired by occupation.

The common-law theory as to the reduction of wild animals into private ownership was thus expounded by Broke J. in 1520:[13]

At the beginning of the world, all beasts were obedient to our forefather Adam, and all the four elements were obedient to him; but after he had broken the commandment of our lord God all the beasts started to rebel and to become wild, and this was a punishment for his crime. Now they are common, and belong to the first occupant (*occupanti conceduntur*), as fowls in the air, fish in the sea, and beasts upon the land. When I have taken a fowl, and by my industry have tamed it by restraining its freedom, I have a special property in it, since it has been made obedient by my own labour.

The 'special' property lasted so long as the animals remained 'obedient'. Thus, if a tamed bird of prey were let fly at a quarry, not only did the bird remain the property of its owner, but the quarry (if taken) became his also.[14] The common

---

[10] Water was a special case. According to Dudley, a grant of so many gallons a year to be drawn from my well was a grant of freehold, and yet no assize would lie upon it: reading in Gray's Inn (1496) CUL MS. Hh.3.10, at fo. 62 (no reason given). Water running in a watercourse was common property, and the right to it was an easement rather than a profit: see further below, 775-7.

[11] St German, *Doctor and Student*, ed. Plucknett and Barton, 292. Waif (goods abandoned by a thief in flight) did not belong to the Crown before inquest and seizure: Port 110, 129. See also Frowyk's reading on *Prerogativa Regis* (1495) 113 Selden Soc. 36, and Spelman's reading on the same statute (1521) ibid. 41.

[12] 94 Selden Soc. 211 n. 3; below, 805. The finder was liable for 'wilful negligence' but not for accidental loss. St German, *Doctor and Student*, ed. Plucknett and Barton, 260-1.

[13] *Fyloll v. Assheleygh* (1520) Trin. 12 Hen. VIII, fo. 4, pl. 3 (119 Selden Soc. 15); CP 40/1027, m. 433 (copied in Catlyn's precedent book, Alnwick Castle MS. 475, fo. 202); extracts pr. in *Case Law in the Making*, ed. A. Wijffels (17 CSC; 1997), ii. 17-25. There are concurring speeches by Pollard J. and Brudenell CJ. For the *occupanti ceditur* principle, cf. Justinian's *Institutes* 2. 1. 12.

[14] *Fyloll v. Assheleygh* (1520) last note, *per* Pollard J.; *Case of the Queen's Forester* (1520) Mich. 12 Hen. VIII, fo. 9, pl. 2 (119 Selden Soc. 42-3), *per* Broke J.; George Treherne's reading on the *Carta de Foresta* (Lincoln's Inn, 1520) BL MS. Stowe 414, fo. 57 (lengthy discussion); *Anon.* (1544) Trin. 36 Hen. VIII, Gell's reports, I, fo. 44, *per* Shelley J. Cf. *Shaa v. Phylpot* (1476) CP 40/860, m. 309 (justifies taking a hawk because it was killing the defendant's pigeons).

lawyers' understanding of obedience was evidently based on the Roman distinction—adopted via *Bracton*—between tamed animals which were in the habit of returning to their owner,[15] and wild animals which were the subject of ownership only so long as they were physically restrained.[16]

The young of captive animals—and presumably of tame animals at liberty — were said to belong to the owner of the mother.[17] If, however, the identity of the father was known, it seems that the owner of the father had an equal interest. In a reported case of 1484 a custom of Buckinghamshire was pleaded in relation to brooding swans.[18] This gave two chicks to the owner of the parents and one, of lesser value, to the lord of the land where they nested.[19] But an apparently un-resolved difficulty in the case was that the cock and hen belonged to different owners and it was uncertain whether they owned the chicks jointly or took one each. Underlying the discussion is an assumption that the owner of the cock had rights equal to those of the owner of the hen.[20]

Wild birds' eggs, and chicks, were considered for property purposes as part of the tree or land in which the nest was built, until such time as the chicks became fledglings and flew out of sight, when they became *res nullius*.[21] It followed that if a tree was rooted in A's land with branches overhanging B's land, the eggs in a nest on an overhanging branch belonged to A rather than B.[22] Wild animals, bees, and fish belonged to the owner of the land where they lived. If a trespasser took them, they belonged to the landowner and not the captor.[23] However, this special property which the landowner had in wild creatures was of a different character from that in tamed or captive animals and is best characterized as a right to reduce

---

[15] See *Moots*, 168 (bees and *animus revertendi*); Richard Hesketh's reading (Gray's Inn, *c.*1506/8) ff. 62–63v (beasts), 76–77 (birds); Treherne's reading, ff. 24v, 54–55v (discussion of bees and swarms, citing *Bracton*); anon. reading (probably in Gray's Inn) BL MS. Add. 35939, ff. 177–178v (discussion of bees, swarms, and hives). The source is *Bracton*, fo. 9 (ii. 43). Cf. *Crowe* v. *Barley* (1549) CP 40/1142, m. 308d (trespass for a tame goshawk; pleads it came to his possession by finding; undetermined demurrer); above, 568–9.

[16] Restraint included the fencing of a park, or (probably) putting fish in a pond: *Moots*, 83–4.

[17] Yorke 106, no. 52.

[18] *Lord Strange* v. *Forde* (1484) Mich. 2 Ric. III, fo. 15, pl. 42; KB 27/893, m. 72 (custom of Bucks. relat-ing to swans in rivers flowing into the Thames; issue whether the nest was in Bucks.).

[19] The custom was so pleaded in respect of one chick only, but the implication seems to be that the lord should have every third chick and the owner of the couple the remaining two-thirds.

[20] Cf. *Male* v. *Hole* (1472) Pas. 12 Edw. IV, fo. 4, pl.10 (owner of three brooding swans entitled to chicks, and to the chicks born to the chicks while bailed to a third party).

[21] *Anon.* (1478) Trin. 18 Edw. IV, fo. 8, pl. 7 (indictment for stealing young pigeons); *Case of the Queen's Forester* (1520) Mich. 12 Hen. VIII, fo. 9, pl. 2 (119 Selden Soc. 45), *per* Brudenell CJ; *Bishop of London* v. *Nevell* (1522) Mich. 14 Hen. VIII, fo. 1, pl. 1 (119 Selden Soc. 88), *per* Broke and Pollard JJ; St German, *Doctor and Student*, ed. Plucknett and Barton, 39.   [22] Treherne's reading (1520), fo. 53v.

[23] *Darel* v. *Yates* (1497) 1 Caryll 356; Hil. 13 Hen. VII, fo. 16, pl. 14; *Case of the Queen's Forester* (1520) Mich. 12 Hen. VIII, fo. 10, pl. 2 (119 Selden Soc. 44), *per* Elyot J. There is a discussion of bee-chasing in Treherne's reading (1520), ff. 33v–34.

them into possession. While the creatures remained wild, the landowner did not have such property that he could sell or lease them.[24] A lease could be made of the right to take them—for instance, of a warren, or even of a 'game of conies' in a certain place[25]—but not of wild rabbits themselves.[26] For a similar reason, waste could not be brought against a lessee of the land for killing game or fish.[27] The property of the landowner seems also to have been limited to animals naturally on the land; if a stranger started game on his own land, and chased it on to another's, where it was taken, the animal would belong to the captor rather than the owner of the land.[28]

Readers who chose to lecture on the law of theft were particularly fond of the finer points of law relating to the ownership of beasts and fish;[29] but their learning was focused upon the notion of a forcible taking of a thing of value, and is not necessarily a guide to the principles of personal property in general.

SPECIFICATION

The principles governing the acquisition of property by specification were clouded by the exigencies of the forms of action. Detinue would not lie for a thing which had been changed into something else, because it was founded upon a detaining of the very same thing which the plaintiff had possessed. Therefore a bailor of cloth—even of distinctively worked or decorated cloth—could not bring detinue for the clothes into which it had been made.[30] But this practical limitation did not necessarily mean that the property was changed, since the owner of the materials might be allowed to seize the object into which they had been made. In 1490 the question was fully debated in the Common Pleas, and the court adopted the practical test of identifiability.[31] If the material was still identifiable, the owner could seize it. Examples given were cloth made into a gown, wood cut into planks, iron hammered into a horse-shoe, and—the case at bar—leather made into shoes.

---

[24] *Say* v. *Dokket* (1495) Port 1 at 2; *Note* (*c.*1520/30) Yorke 136, no. 127. It was doubtful whether he could even claim damages for hunting them: *Anon.* (*c.*1529) Caryll (Jun.) 411, no. 105.

[25] Debt would lie for rent of a game of conies: *Polhill* v. *Tayller* (1521) CP 40/1031, m. 413 (judgment for plaintiff); reported in Spelman 84; *Melton* v. *Bever* (1535) CP 40/1084, m. 630d (imparlance).

[26] *Anon.* (1492) 1 Caryll 123.

[27] *Anon.* (1558) BL MS. Hargrave 4, fo. 149; MS. Harley 1624, fo. 63. On the same principle, an assize would not lie for birds or bees in a wood, but only for the wood: William Ayloffe's reading (Lincoln's Inn, 1501 or 1506) Taussig MS., fo. 152.

[28] *Case of the Queen's Forester* (1520) Mich. 12 Hen. VIII, fo. 9, pl. 2 (119 Selden Soc. 43), *per* Broke J.; Yorke 201, no. 295, *per* Pollard J.   [29] See above, 568.

[30] *The Case of Cloth of Gold*, identifiable as *Rilston* v. *Holbek* (1472) B. & M. 524, 527.

[31] *Vanellesbury* v. *Stern* (1490) CP 40/913, m. 310 (pr. 115 Selden Soc. 32–4); Hil. 5 Hen. VII, fo. 15, pl. 6; 1 Caryll 31 (on a different point); B. & M. 533 n. 20; Spelman's reading (Gray's Inn, 1519) 113 Selden Soc. 165. Cf. Port 24 (tr. 'he from whom etc. may not take them but shall have his action').

If, on the other hand, the materials were no longer identifiable, then the original owner could not seize the product. The examples given here were plate melted down and coined,[32] and barley made into malt or ale.[33] The selection of examples shows that the distinction was not very easy to understand or apply. How the owner of a tree identified his wood by inspecting planks, or why the provenance of ferrous artefacts should have been more easily ascertainable than that of silver, was not explained. It looks as though the underlying distinction rested on an alteration of composition, as by liquefying metal or fermenting malt, which prevented all possibility of identification, rather than the practicability of actual identification.[34] The question was complicated in the case of the boots by the fact that the maker had added his own thread and nails. In a contemporary case, Vavasour J. accepted that this would be a relevant factor in the case of a boat, because substantial quantities of nails and pitch were required, but said that the thread used in making a boot was of little value and *de minimis non curat lex*. This drew from Serjeant Kebell the quip that the only difference between a boot and a boat was the letter o.[35]

By 1519, according to Spelman's teaching, the identifiability test seems to have gone. The owner of the materials lost the right to retake them if their 'nature' had been changed, or if there had been some significant addition of the maker's own material.[36] The notion of 'industry' may here have played a part also. Serjeant Yorke noted that butter and cheese belonged to the maker, rather than the owner of the cow which gave the milk, because of his industry.[37] And Brudenell CJ was of the view that a bird could not be retaken if it had been baked in an oven.[38] But in both these cases there was at least a partial physical change.

The problems and the suggested solutions are strongly reminiscent of those discussed by the Romans, and in 1560 the courts would even grapple with the distinction between substance and form.[39] But there is insufficient evidence to substantiate a definite movement from a Sabinian to a Proculian position in early

---

[32] *Vanellesbury* v. *Stern* (1490) Hil. 5 Hen. VII, fo. 15, pl. 6; *Case of the Queen's Forester* (1520) Mich. 12 Hen. VIII, fo. 11, pl. 2 (119 Selden Soc. 46), *per* Brudenell CJ; Spelman's reading (1519) 113 Selden Soc. 95, 166. Thomas Marow argued in his reading (Inner Temple, 1503) that the bailor of plate was guilty of theft if he retook it after it had been refashioned, (tr.) 'and yet they were his own goods in fact, but the property was changed by the change of the fashion': Putnam, *Early Treatises*, 376.

[33] *Vanellesbury* v. *Stern* (1490) Hil. 5 Hen. VII, fo. 15, pl. 6; Spelman's reading (1519) 113 Selden Soc. 166.

[34] Cf. Fitz. Abr., *Barre*, pl. 144 (recaption permitted where (tr.) 'the same thing may be known, and the nature is not altered').   [35] *Sir William Hody's Case* (1490) 1 Caryll 45 at 47.

[36] Spelman's reading (1519) 113 Selden Soc. 166 ('if someone takes my silver and makes plate from it, or takes my malt and makes ale from it, or takes my parchment and makes a bond or other evidences, I cannot retake them because they are altered in nature and mixed with other things'). Cf. ibid. 95.

[37] Yorke 106, no. 52.

[38] *Case of the Queen's Forester* (1520) Mich. 12 Hen. VIII, fo. 11, pl. 2 (119 Selden Soc. 46).

[39] *Anon.* (1560) Moo. 19, pl. 67. See also *Anon.* (1594) Poph. 38, pl. 2.

Tudor England. Indeed, there is no demonstrable acquaintance with the Roman learning at all, except in so far as it could be gleaned from the old manuscripts of *Bracton*.[40]

SEVERANCE FROM LAND

Minerals[41] and vegetation were regarded as forming part of the land so long as they had not been reduced into possession in a movable state. They therefore passed on the death of the landowner to his heir rather than his executors. And a grant to take such things for life was itself real property, a profit à prendre, for which the assize lay.[42] Only when they had been reduced into 'manual occupation'— as distinct from possession of the land—by collection or severance, did they become chattels.[43] Much learning was devoted in the fifteenth and sixteenth centuries to deciding when chattels severed from the realty belonged to the owner of the freehold and when to the person who severed them. The question usually arose in relation to crops, and again the answer (according to some) depended on a particular application of the concept of 'industry'.

A tenant with an estate of unpredictable duration, such as a tenant at will, or his executors (if the estate determined by death), had long been permitted to take the last crop attributable to the tenant's industry before the determination of his estate, even though the possession of the land had passed to another before harvest-time. No one could now remember whether this was by common law, or by the equity of the second chapter of Merton. In 1456 it had apparently been thought to extend to disseisors, so that the disseisee who re-entered could not seize crops which the disseisor had grown from his own seed and reaped.[44] Thereafter the principle was the subject of much debate.[45] It was held that the fruits of labour were to be distinguished from the fruits of nature, and so the doctrine was limited to

[40] *Bracton*, fo. 10 (ii. 47), ascribed ownership to the maker of a new thing (*species*), without discussing the problems.

[41] Hil. 2 Hen. VII, fo. 14, pl. 20; *Bishop of London v. Nevell* (1522) Mich. 14 Hen. VIII, fo. 1, pl. 1 (119 Selden Soc. 89), *per* Broke J.; *Pope v. See* (1534) Port 22 at 23.

[42] Statute of Westminster II, c. 25. The scope of this provision was discussed by Edmund Dudley in his reading on the statute (1496), at ff. 61v–62.

[43] See the full discussion in Spelman's reading (1519) 113 Selden Soc. 165–6. Cf. Dudley's assertion that an assize lay upon a grant to take certain quarters of coal a year from a coal-mine, but not on a similar grant of coal out of a coal-stack: Dudley's reading (1496), at fo. 62.

[44] Mich. 37 Hen. VI, fo. 6, pl. 12 (Danby CJ *contra*; imparlance); Trin. 37 Hen. VI, fo. 35, pl. 22. It is not clear whether this was obiter; the plea as given in the second report concerned a tenant at will rather than a disseisor, and the opinion as to the disseisor was contrary to two earlier holdings.

[45] Fitzherbert (*Trespas*, pl. 81, 86) only abridged Danby CJ's contrary opinion in the 1456 case, though he seems later to have changed his mind (Yorke 213, no. 332). The disseisor's right to emblements was upheld by Richard Broke at Spelman's 1519 reading (113 Selden Soc. 166).

'emblements', which were crops growing by virtue of manual labour. Trees and grass, which grew naturally and not by tillage, could not be taken as emblements; nor could fruit and nuts growing on trees.[46] For this purpose it made no difference that some effort had been expended on the severance, as was inevitable in some degree, not even where wood was chopped into logs or grass made into haystacks.[47] It followed that, even though severed vegetation was a chattel, the severance alone did not alter the property. Trees, for instance, changed their nature when felled and became wood: *arbor dum crescit, lignum dum crescere nescit*.[48] But this did not alter the property, unless the timber was removed from the land and became impossible to identify.[49] Now, if severance alone did not alter the property, it was not easy to see why the disseisor should have emblements any more than he should have trees; unlike tenants for life or at will, he had no right to the land at the time of sowing. One possible argument might have been that he had merely used someone else's land to turn one form of chattel (seed) into another (grain), and if he took this back it was no loss to the disseisee of the land. But this was not legally correct, because by sowing the seed he had by his own act made it part of someone else's freehold. It was not precisely analogous to cooking his own goose in someone else's hearth.

The question was debated in a leading case of 1534, noted by three reporters.[50] In an action of trespass for taking sheaves of grain, the defendant pleaded that he had been disseised by the plaintiff, who had sown the land with his own seed, and had then re-entered and taken the grain which he found growing on the land. The plaintiff demurred. The plea does not explicitly state who reaped the grain, but since it says that the defendant found it growing on the land it must have been the defendant, the disseisee. The plea should therefore have been good: all the judges accepted that a disseisee who re-entered before reaping was entitled to emblements. But the argument in banc seems to have proceeded on the assumption that the disseisor had reaped, so that there was a conflict between freehold title and the concept of acquisition by industry. On this factual basis, Luke and Port JJ were prepared to follow the 1456 decision and hold that the disseisor was entitled to the

---

[46] Pas. 12 Edw. IV, fo. 4, pl. 10, *per* Fairfax J.; Trin. 14 Edw. IV, fo. 6, pl. 4; Trin. 15 Edw. IV, fo. 31, pl. 11; Mich. 2 Hen. VII, fo. 1, pl. 4; Hil. 5 Hen. VII, fo. 16, pl. 9; Trin. 12 Hen. VII, fo. 25, pl. 4; Spelman's reading (1519) 113 Selden Soc. 166; *Pope v. See* (1534) Port 22 at 23.

[47] Hil. 5 Hen. VII, fo. 16, pl. 9, *per* Fairfax J.; *Pope v. See* (1534) Spelman 215 at 216, *per* Port J. The first case is probably *Skerne v. Nuport* (1490) CP 40/911, m. 376, though issue was finally joined on the freehold.

[48] *Bishop of London v. Nevell* (1522) Mich. 14 Hen. VIII, fo. 2, pl. 1 (119 Selden Soc. 90), *per* Brudenell CJ. The aphorism means: 'A tree [so known] while it grows, is wood when growing it no longer knows.'

[49] Mich. 35 Hen. VI, fo. 2, pl. 3; Hil. 5 Hen. VII, fo. 16, pl. 9; *Sir William Hody's Case* (1490) 1 Caryll 45; Spelman's reading (1519) 113 Selden Soc. 165.

[50] *Pope v. See* (1534) Dyer 31b (sub nom. *Saye's Case*); Port 22; Spelman 215; KB 27/1089, m. 33 (pr. 94 Selden Soc. 357).

fruits of his own industry. Spelman J., however, held that it made no difference who brought in the grain. Upon being sown in the ground the grain acquired a vegetal form of life (*anima vegetativa*) and began to derive its being from the land, becoming part of the land itself; that being so, the disseisor could no more reap the produce of another's land than could a trespasser. Since Fitzjames CJ took the same view, the case was left undecided.[51] Another dispute which the courts failed to decide was whether emblements could be taken by the executors of a copy-holder;[52] presumably in theory it depended on the custom of each manor.

Disputes over vegetable produce also arose between landlord and tenant. The guiding principle was quite straightforward: the tenant could have the annual produce, but not the inheritance. This meant that the tenant could take grain, and the fruit of trees;[53] but he could not have the trees themselves, if they were timber, except for estovers.[54] However, when trees became chattels by act of God, through the effect of wind and weather, it was arguable that the lessee could have them.[55] It was even arguable that the lessee could have trees felled by the lessor, since the latter was not entitled to them during the term.[56]

Another kind of chattel created by 'severance' from the realty, albeit in an abstract sense, was the chattel real: for instance, a wardship severed from the seignory,[57] the next avoidance of a benefice severed from the advowson,[58] or a term of years.[59] These were chattels in the sense that they devolved on executors rather than the heir, and that they were not protected by actions which depended on seisin of the freehold.

ACCESSION

The reverse situation, the accession of chattels to the realty, whereby their nature was changed and they ceased to be chattels, also gave rise to legal difficulties. It was

---

[51] Note also *Anon.* (1526) Yorke 213, no. 332 (disseisor not entitled to emblements as against the king, though he is in the case of a common person).

[52] *Abbess of Syon* v. *Moigne* (1514) CP 40/1007, m. 441 (undetermined demurrer).

[53] *Bishop of London* v. *Nevell* (1522) Mich. 14 Hen. VIII, fo. 1, pl. 1 (119 Selden Soc. 88).

[54] *Browne* v. *Elmer* (1520) Trin. 12 Hen. VIII, fo. 1, pl. 1 (119 Selden Soc. 2); *Pasmere* v. *Beare* (1520–1) CP 40/1029, m. 547 (demurrer); *Anon.* (1550) BL MS. Hargrave 4, fo. 111v; Dal. 4, pl. 5; Moo. 9, pl. 34. For estovers see above, 643.

[55] *Abbot of Stratford* v. *Pykeryng* (1494) CP 40/930, m. 323; Mich. 10 Hen. VII, fo. 2, pl. 3, *per* Kebell sjt; *Anon.* (1533) Caryll (Jun.) 369, no. 3. (The contrary opinion later prevailed: *Harlakenden's Case* (1589) 4 Co. Rep. 62 at 63.) Dudley held that 'windfallen wood' was not part of the realty: reading (1496), at fo. 61v.

[56] *Anon.* (1533) Caryll (Jun.) 369, no. 3, *per* Shelley J. (but Fitzherbert J. *contra*).

[57] By granting it to someone else.

[58] It was common for the patron to make a grant of the next presentation only. This was properly called the next avoidance (*proxima vacatio*) but was sometimes called the next advowson (*proxima advocatio*).

[59] Above, 633.

a corollary of the emblements principle that seeds, which in the bag were chattels, became part of the land when sown. So also did transplanted trees, if they took root,[60] or timber built into a house.[61] But the problem most commonly arose in relation to artefacts attached to houses or other buildings. For the purposes of an action of trespass against a stranger, it probably did not matter whether such things were annexed to the freehold at the time or removal or not;[62] but the question could arise if someone other than the freeholder claimed a right to take them.

There was an inconclusive discussion of fixtures in 1493, when the King's Bench considered whether a church pew was part of the freehold or a chattel. Fairfax J. thought it a chattel, and likened it to an oven, vat, table-dormant (a table fixed to the ground), or a booth in a fair. Apparently the key was removability.[63] But his approach was rejected in the next decade by the Common Pleas, in what remained the leading case on the English law of fixtures for many years.[64] The tenant in fee simple had erected an oven in the middle of a house, and cemented it to the floor; the executors removed the oven; and the heir sued them in trespass. Upon demurrer by the executors, judgment was given for the heir. The oven had been annexed to the freehold, and its nature had therefore been changed from chattel into realty. It was agreed in the course of argument that the same was true of floorboards, ceilings, tables-dormant, testers (for a bed) fixed to the wall or ceiling, dyeing-vats, doors, and windows.[65] The removability test seems to have been abandoned. One reporter suggested as a test the use of a bonding material such as mortar—which had been used in the case at bar—but counsel for the heir proposed the less intelligible test of what was necessary for a 'perfect' house. On this latter test, window-casements (*fenestres*) were part of the freehold, but window-glass was not, 'for a house is sufficiently perfect even though there is no glass'.[66] The decision

---

[60] Spelman's reading (1519) 113 Selden Soc. 166. Cf. *Bracton*, fo. 10 (ii. 46).

[61] Trin. 37 Hen. VI, fo. 35, pl. 22; Hil. 5 Hen. VII, fo. 15, pl. 6; *Sir William Hody's Case* (1490) 1 Caryll 45 at 46, *per* Keble sjt; Spelman's reading (1519) 113 Selden Soc. 165.

[62] e.g. *Churchyerd* v. *Randell* (1488) CP 40/906, m. 525 (trespass to houses and taking timber, forty windows, and fifty pieces of glass); *Twisilton* v. *Carre* (1490–2) CP 40/914, m. 107 (taking a lead brewing-vat and a mashing vat); *Bettys* v. *Portlond* (1490) ibid., m. 125 (taking locks, doors, and windows); *Langham* v. *Henry* (1493) CP 40/926, m. 329 (taking joists, doors, and windows); *Brewes* v. *Totyll* (1499) KB 27/952, m. 48 (taking a gate, eight doors, sixteen windows, a lead vat, ten shelves, a quern, two 'portas caducas', and twenty timber planks; damages recovered); *Pagynton* v. *Throgood* (1502) KB 27/964, m. 93d (taking lead brewing-vats; damages recovered).

[63] *Fitzwater's Case*, Pas. 8 Hen. VII, fo. 12, pl. 3, identifiable as *Ballard* v. *Kydde* (1493) KB 27/929, m. 98 (trespass to a pew; churchwardens plead custom to assign pews at pleasure, and expulsion of plaintiff; undetermined demurrer).

[64] *Bodon* v. *Vampage* (1507) CP 40/978, m. 328; 2 Caryll 540; which is very like the case reported sub nom. *Henry's Case* (1504–5) Mich. 20 Hen. VII, fo. 13, pl. 24; Trin. 21 Hen. VII, fo. 26, pl. 4.

[65] Doors and leaded windows had been the subject of a demurrer in *Phylpot* v. *Frenche* (1480) CP 40/872, m. 429 (no judgment).

[66] Trin. 21 Hen. VII, fo. 26, pl. 4. Cf. Robert Brooke's reading (Middle Temple, 1558), pr. as *The Reading of M. Robert Brook upon Magna Charta*, 14, glossing this case (as '27 H. 7'): 'A man stealeth glass

therefore gave little clear guidance on the general principle, especially since the judges accepted obiter that a tenant for years might sometimes be entitled to remove fixtures of the nature mentioned.[67] Here the courts seem to have been influenced by the presumed purpose of annexation.[68] In other cases, the status of a fixture depended on the degree of physical annexation. In 1555 wooden floor-boards in a stable were held not be fixtures unless they could be shown to be fixed to the floor;[69] and in 1556 that window-glass was not a fixture unless it was held in place with nails which could not be removed manually.[70]

Lessees' fixtures, like emblements, were thus part of the realty for the time being even if they were removable. While they were realty, they could not be distrained. This was confirmed by the Common Pleas in 1522, when a member of Gray's Inn sued his lessor for distraining a mill-stone. He pleaded, in reply to the lessor's avowry for rent, that the stone was fixed with lathes and nails to a great piece of timber forming part of his horse-mill. The defendant rejoined that at the time of the distress the stone was not so fixed, because the miller had lifted it up to 'pick' or repair it.[71] The court held the rejoinder bad, because the stone remained a fixture even while it was temporarily removed. It was the same of windows or doors suspended from hooks, and therefore removable.[72] The removability test had evidently been completely abandoned. When it was raised in a different way in a case of 1558 it was treated with similar disdain. A writ of error was brought to reverse a judgment in forcible entry in respect of a wharf, and the error was assigned in that 'the aforesaid wharf is made from various pieces of timber joined together and removable at the will of the possessor thereof, and not established in any certain place, which pieces of timber are but a chattel and not land or tene-ment whereof any disseisin might be committed'. The judgment was nevertheless affirmed, though no report has been found.[73]

There was another, metaphysical way in which a chattel could become realty. If words were written on a piece of parchment, and a seal added, in such a way that

out of windows which be made fast with sprignails, it is felony. But contrary, if they be fastened with great nails, for then they be parcel of the franktenement.'

[67] *Mason* v. *Wytton* (1533) CP 40/1080, m. 436 (tr. 121 Selden Soc. 367); Caryll (Jun.) 366, no. 2, *per* Shelley J. (tradesman-lessee entitled at end of term to remove fixtures necessary for exercise of trade, such as a blacksmith's anvil or a brewer's vat).

[68] See *Mason* v. *Wytton* (1533) Caryll (Jun.) 366, no. 2, *per* Fitzherbert J. (oven attached to house 'only for the ease of the lessee'). However, the purpose of annexation was not pleaded; the issue was whether the vat was fixed to the freehold.

[69] *Earl of Bedford* v. *Smyth* (1554–5) Dyer 108a; CP 40/1157, m. 301 (waste).

[70] *Anon.* (1556) Chr. Yelverton's reports, fo. 241, *per* Brooke CJ (distinguishing glass fixed with 'sprigge naile', which the lessee could remove). Cf. above, n. 66.

[71] The year book uses the obscure phrases 'in pycant' and 'destre pike'.

[72] *Wistow* v. *Abbot of St Albans* (1522) Pas. 14 Hen. VIII, fo. 25, pl. 6 (119 Selden Soc. 179); 120 Selden Soc. 81. An alternative reason (*per* Fitzherbert J.) was that a mill-stone was protected from distress because of the public interest in keeping mills in operation.

[73] *Shakerley* v. *Bruer* (1558) KB 27/1187, m. 23.

it became a muniment of freehold title, the deed became part of the freehold itself.[74] What is more, the box in which the deed was put, if it was sealed up, also became part of the inheritance, and this was so even if it contained other things as well.[75] The conundrum that, so long as the box was sealed, it was impossible to see whether it contained muniments pertaining to the realty, seems to have caused little difficulty in relation to ownership.[76] But boxes and charters were only realty in the sense that they descended to the heir rather than the executor. The appropriate form of action to recover them was detinue, and they could be pawned as chattels.[77] They were perhaps the only kind of heirloom recognized at common law,[78] though under a local custom household stuff might also descend as heirlooms.[79]

Yet another way of altering property in chattels was by accession to other chattels, though there is little discussion of this situation in the books. It is implied in the case of the cobbler that, by sewing leather into boots, he made his thread accede to the product.[80] This position was adopted by Robert Brooke in his reading, when he argued that thread and lining acceded to a garment; if, therefore, the owner of the original cloth came secretly by night and took the garment from the tailor, it was not larceny of the lining.[81]

TRANSFER OF TITLE

Once human dominion was established over a thing, by one of these methods, property could be transferred from one owner to another by gift or by contract, and could be altered by a non-owner in the case of a sale in market overt,[82] or even

---

[74] Trin. 4 Hen. VII, fo. 10, pl. 4.

[75] 36 Hen. VI, fo. 27, pl. 26, *per* Prisot CJ; Pas. 22 Edw. IV, fo. 7, pl. 20; Mich. 3 Hen. VII, fo. 15, pl. 29.

[76] It did, however, prevent the formulation of an action of detinue if the contents could not be described. This was a common ground for a bill in Chancery seeking discovery.

[77] 94 Selden Soc. 217 n. 6.   [78] For attempts to create heirlooms by will see below, 747.

[79] Cf. *Anon.* (1544) Gell's reports, I, Mich. 36 Hen. VIII, fo. 36, *per* Saunders sjt (custom of Surrey *not* to allow heirlooms).

[80] *Vanellesbury* v. *Stern* (1490) Hil. 5 Hen. VII, fo. 15, pl. 6; *Sir William Hody's Case* (1490) 1 Caryll 45 at 47, *per* Vavasour J.

[81] Reading (1551) CUL MS. Gg.5.9, fo. 60 (pr. 94 Selden Soc. 217 n. 10); *The Reading of M. Robert Brook upon...Magna Charta* (1641), 10. *Bracton*, fo. 10 (ii. 46) discusses the different case where A sews B's thread into his own (A's) garment.

[82] Baker, *IELH* (4th edn), 385 (law settled in fifteenth century); *Rydnes* v. *Mille* (1486) KB 27/899, m. 32 (pleaded in trespass); *Flowre* v. *Johnson* (1523–4) CP 40/1041, m. 457d (pleaded in trespass; demurrer); *Swanton* v. *Symondys* (1549) CP 40/1140, m. 418 (pleaded in trespass); *Anon.* (1554) Dyer 99b, §66. But the passing of property could be vitiated by a successful appeal of larceny or (after 1529) conviction on indictment for larceny: 21 Hen. VIII, c. 11. It could also be vitiated by proof of collusion: anon. reading (*c.*1474) on Westminster I, c. 31, CUL MS. Ee.5.22, fo. 152. It was proposed in the 1540s that the market-overt rule be abolished in Wales: BL Cotton MS. Vitellius C.I, fo. 42v.

arguably by mere trespass.[83] But here the law lacked the kind of clarity which had been developed in the case of land. How far title to chattels could be treated as a legal abstraction, distinct from physical possession, had not been fully settled.[84] This uncertainty was reflected in legal terminology. Possession was a concept appropriated primarily to chattels real, as an equivalent to seisin,[85] but less consistently applied to movable goods.[86] On the other hand, 'property' in goods could refer to physical possession as owner or to the more abstract 'right of property' separated from possession.[87] Hence the rather esoteric debate, at the beginning of the period, as to whether a pleader should lay the 'property' in chattels as being located in a particular place.[88]

The later year books report some discussions of personal property which proceed on the basis that there were at least some common principles governing chattels and land alike. Just as someone entitled to land could not transfer title without seisin, so it was said that an owner of chattels who was out of possession could not give good title to a stranger.[89] Yet an owner of goods out of possession could arguably give them by words to the person in possession, on the analogy of a release or confirmation.[90] On the other hand, when, in 1558, it was disputed whether goods could be effectively given to someone who was not present, the difficulty seems to have arisen from the lack of an opportunity to indicate consent

[83] As to whether property was divested merely by a trespassory taking (as Bryan CJ held) see J. B. Ames, 'The Disseisin of Chattels' in *Lectures on Legal History* (1913), 172–91; *Broker's Case* (1490) Mich. 6 Hen. VII, fo. 7, pl. 4.

[84] For what follows see also Holdsworth, *HEL*, iii. 351–9. Cf. the discussion of possession in the law of larceny, above, 566–70.

[85] The standard form in pleading a leasehold title was to say that the lessee entered in the premises and was thereof possessed ('inde possessionatus').

[86] An example of the modern usage is *Broker's Case* (1490) Mich. 6 Hen. VII, fo. 8, pl. 4, *per* Vavasour J. (tr. 'although someone takes the possession from me, yet he may not take my property from me').

[87] See e.g. ibid., at ff. 8–9, *per* Bryan CJ (tr. 'the property is divested by the taking, and then he has but the right of property . . . the property, and the right of property, are not all one'). Cf. *Anon.* (1477) Pas. 17 Edw. IV, fo. 1, pl. 2, where Bryan CJ uses 'property' for the abstract right of an owner out of possession; *Anon.* (1495) Trin. 10 Hen. VII, fo. 27, pl. 13, *per* Bryan CJ ('le owner in droit').

[88] Possession was obviously a local fact, but it was arguable that if someone owned chattels he owned them everywhere: Trin. 1 Edw. V, fo. 3, pl. 5.

[89] *Broker's Case* (1490) Mich. 6 Hen. VII, fo. 9, pl. 4, *per* Bryan CJ; *Anon.* (1492) Trin. 10 Hen. VII, fo. 27, pl. 13 (misdated in print), *per* Bryan CJ; Frowyk's reading on *Prerogativa Regis* (1495) 113 Selden Soc. 37; Port 151, pl. 37; *Lyte* v. *Peny* (1541) Dyer 48; 121 Selden Soc. 447 (following Bracton). Cf. *Anon.* (1462) Mich. 2 Edw. IV, fo. 25, pl. 26, where Danby CJ apparently accepts Laken's argument to the contrary; Spelman's reading (1519) 113 Selden Soc. 160, *per* Broke.

[90] Bryan CJ held that a bailor could make an effective gift to his bailee: *Stainer* v. *Jenner* (1481) Mich. 21 Edw. IV, fo. 55, pl. 27; *Sutton* v. *Forster* (1482) Mich. 22 Edw. IV, fo. 29, pl. 10; CP 40/882, m. 349; but cf. *Mervyn* v. *Lyds* (1553) Dyer 90a at 90b. Yet he denied that he could make a gift to a trespasser: *Broker's Case* (1490), last note; *Anon.* (1492), last note (Kebell *contra*); cf. Port 151, no. 37. The latter point was affirmed by the King's Bench in *Anon.* (1530s) 121 Selden Soc. 436, no. 13.

rather than the need for a physical transfer.[91] Conversely, if the donor had possession but did not deliver it to the donee, it was arguable that title could nevertheless pass. It would pass if the possession was delivered to a third party to convey to the donee,[92] and it might pass even if there was no change of possession, in the sense that the donee was entitled to help himself.[93] But in these last cases the title was precarious, since the gift was revocable at the donor's will until the donee attained possession.[94]

There was rather more discussion in the reports concerning sale. Here there were two principal problems: first, whether title could pass by contract alone without delivery, and second, if it could, whether it passed even if no payment was made by the buyer. Although delivery to the purchaser was normally necessary to effect a transfer of title, in the later fifteenth century there were some misgivings about not acknowledging a transfer of title by bargain and sale alone. In so far as the question was whether detinue would lie against the seller, the problem could be tackled in the mind of the common-law pleader by supposing a constructive bailment.[95] This was not an outrageous fiction, since if the buyer had been present at the time of sale, and perhaps handled the goods, his leaving them in the possession of the seller until collection could well be construed as tantamount to bailment. Moreover, in the case of fungible goods there also existed a form of pleading known as debt in the *detinet*, which was the exact counterpart of debt for the price, and since it did not depend on any notion of property it did not mention a bailment.[96] In a case of 1535:[97]

a man sold someone 20,000 red herring to be delivered to him in cades at a certain day... and it was held by all the justices of both benches that he may not have a writ of detinue

---

[91] *Anon.* (1558) BL MS. Harley 1624, fo. 67; MS. Hargrave 4, fo. 124 (tr. 'If a man gives goods to some-one who is absent, it seemed to some that the property is changed and that it is in the donee until he disagrees to it; but others said that the goods do not pass before the donee consents to the gift; query'). Cf. Yorke 122, no. 88.

[92] *Stainer* v. *Jenner* (1481) Mich. 21 Edw. IV, fo. 55, pl. 27; cf. *Anon.* (1530) Pollard 270, no. 57 (delivery 'to the use of' another changes the property).

[93] *Boteler* v. *Moyle* (1485–6) CP 40/891, m. 144 (defendant in trespass pleads he was given them and so he took them as well he might; issue on gift).

[94] It was otherwise if the possession was handed to a bailee 'to the use of' a donee: *Anon.* (1530) Pollard 270, no. 57. Or if there was a 'consideration' expressed: *Lyte* v. *Peny* (1541) Dyer 49; 121 Selden Soc. 447.

[95] S. F. C. Milsom, 'Sale of Goods in the 15th Century' (1961), repr. in *SHCL* 105–32, at 122–3; D. Ibbetson, 'Sale of Goods in the 14th Century' (1991) 107 *LQR* 480 at 498 n. 74.

[96] e.g. Mich. 11 Hen. VII, fo. 5, pl. 20; *Nelson* v. *Pykerell* (1527) CP 40/1053, m. 108d (barley bought for £16 to be paid); *Wagge* v. *Auncell* (1527) CP 40/1056, m. 38 (barley bought for 5 marks paid); *Chapman* v. *Atwode*, ibid., m. 123 (malt bought at a named price, but with no averment of payment); *Echard* v. *Stede* (1529) CP 40/1060, m. 103d (barley bought for sum agreed).

[97] *Spert* v. *Abbot of Chertsey* (1534) Yorke 100; CP 40/1086, m. 523; CP 40/1087, m. 429. In 1537 there was a dispute in Gray's Inn as to whether 'detinue' would lie for grain sold from a particular granary, if not in sacks: BL MS. Hargrave 253, fo. 11v (Hales in favour, Boys against).

for the detaining in the cades, since the plaintiff never had property in them; and in a writ of detinue the plaintiff must have property at the time when the action of detinue is brought. But it was agreed that he may have a writ of debt in the *detinet*.

Given that no clear distinction was drawn in the writ or the pleadings in debt or detinue between specific and non-specific goods, this may have suggested to pleaders an analogous form of detinue for specific purchases as well. By the beginning of the sixteenth century, at any rate, the earlier reservations had vanished, and in detinue against the seller of specific goods it was no longer thought necessary to use words of bailment in the count.[98] The legal analysis by this time was that, even if the buyer did not before delivery acquire possession sufficient to maintain trespass, yet he acquired property in the sense that he could bring detinue,[99] or help himself.[100]

The more difficult question was whether a sale effected a change of property by force of the bargain alone, seen as an executory agreement, or whether it had to be executed on one side by payment.[101] Certainly payment was not necessary to the transfer of title where the goods were actually delivered.[102] But could a contract of sale change the property when there was neither delivery of possession nor payment of any money? Fortescue CJ, in *Doige's Case* (1442), had let slip a casual remark which has been taken to mean that it could.[103] In 1477, however, the Common Pleas had agreed that before payment the buyer had no right to take the goods, and indeed committed a trespass if he did so without the seller's leave. Choke and Littleton JJ took the view that property did not pass before payment, whereas Bryan CJ took the more sophisticated position that property did pass but not the right to immediate possession. On Bryan CJ's view, the unpaid seller had a defence in detinue which in effect gave him a lien.[104] There was probably no dissent from Bryan CJ's further dictum that the buyer could always take the goods if

---

[98] Milsom, 'Sale of Goods in the 15th Century', *SHCL*, 121, 131. The new form was settled in the King's Bench by 1502: e.g. *Rede* v. *Labeffe* (1502) KB 27/962, m. 60 (detinue for 10 pieces of chamlet; counts on a bargain and sale to deliver at a certain date, and payment of the £10 price; verdict and judgment for plaintiff). [99] *Anon.* (1493) 1 Caryll 193.

[100] See *Wryght* v. *Belyngham* (1497) KB 27/942, m. 26 (trespass to pipe of wine; pleads purchase for oum agreed and so took it, as well he might; issue on sale).

[101] For what follows see also Fifoot, *HSCL*, 227–9; A. W. B. Simpson, *History of the Common Law of Contract: the rise of the action of assumpsit* (1975), 164–9.

[102] *Note* (1494) Hil. 9 Hen. VII, fo. 21, pl. 21, *per* Huse CJ (and agreed by the whole King's Bench); *Anon.* (before 1506) Hil. 21 Hen. VII, fo. 6, pl. 4, *per* Tremaile J.

[103] *Shipton* v. *Dogge* (1442) B. & M. 391 at 394 (tr. 'if I buy a horse from you, the property in the horse is at once mine and therefore you shall have a writ of debt for the money and I shall have detinue for the horse upon this bargain'). Cf. Simpson, *History of Contract*, 165 ('no great signficance can be read into his remark').

[104] *Anon.* (1477) Pas. 17 Edw. IV, fo. 1, pl. 2 (tr. *HSCL*, 252–4); Milsom, 'Sale of Goods', 124. Bryan CJ's doctrine is restated in *Anon.* (1479) Hil. 18 Edw. IV, fo. 21, pl. 1; *Att.-Gen.* v. *Capel* (1494) Mich. 10 Hen. VII,

the seller expressly gave him leave to do so—either by saying 'take them, and pay when you please' or by giving him a specific date for payment[105]—but it is not recorded whether Choke and Littleton JJ would have allowed property to pass immediately in those cases.[106] The difference was not without practical consequences, because on Bryan CJ's view the seller could not dispose of the goods before payment, whereas the other view enabled him to pass them on. Bryan CJ's theory was to be influential in the nineteenth century, but it does not seem to have prevailed at the time, since it was thought that the seller should usually be free to sell elsewhere unless and until he had been paid.[107] To bind the seller to set aside the goods for the buyer it was necessary to make a token payment of earnest money, or to set a date for payment.[108] It would not have made good sense to hold a seller indefinitely bound to await a tender of payment by the buyer, perhaps years in the future. Yet the concession that title could sometimes pass without immediate payment—without even an earnest-penny, if there was a fixed period of credit—shows that there was no hard and fast rule requiring payment of money as a precondition for the passing of title.[109]

Whether title is capable of passing merely because parties intend it to pass is a question of law. Yet the reported discussions after 1475 indicate that the question of law had been tacitly answered in the affirmative, and that the decisive question had become one of fact, resting on the supposed intention of the parties.[110] Although the question in the 1477 case arose from the artificialities of pleading rather than the factual realities, we may infer from the reports of that period a general understanding that before payment of the price, or at least of earnest, the buyer had no right to possession of the goods without a special agreement to that effect. In the

fo. 7, pl. 14 (agreed by the assembled judges). Cf. the note of 1465 in Pas. 5 Edw. IV, fo. 2, pl. 20, where Heydon states the doctrine in the context of liens.

[105] Likewise *Veer* v. *York* (1470) Mich. 49 Hen. VI, fo. 18 pl. 23 (tr. '*Catesby*: if I buy a horse from you for 20s. you may detain the horse until I pay you... *Bryan* to Catesby: sir, in your case, if [he] gives [you] a day of payment, [he] may not detain the horse'); 47 Selden Soc. 163 (repr. in *HSCL*, 251).

[106] Choke J. had argued in 1470 that title passed: *Veer* v. *York*, last note (tr. 'the property is in me by the purchase, so that if a stranger takes it I shall have an action of trespass').

[107] *Southwall* v. *Huddelston* (1523) Hil. 14 Hen. VIII, fo. 22, pl. 6 (119 Selden Soc. 159), *per* Pollard J. Broke J. (119 Selden Soc. 56) allowed this, but only once the purchaser had been given time to count out his money. Cf. the shorter report in Pollard 252–3.

[108] *Att.-Gen.* v. *Capel* (1494) Mich. 10 Hen. VII, fo. 7, pl. 14; *Southwall* v. *Huddelston* (1523) Hil. 14 Hen. VIII, fo. 20, pl. 6 (119 Selden Soc. 155), and Pollard 252, *per* Fitzherbert J. It was an old principle that a sale on credit was complete when a day was set for payment: see *Staughton* v. *Love* (1397) 100 Selden Soc. 177. Cf. next note.

[109] Cf. Gregory Adgore's reading (Inner Temple, c.1490) B. & M. 483 ('A bargain where the sum and the day are expressed, but no money is paid, is void; for part must be paid as earnest...').

[110] This was the view of 'ascuns' (some of those present) in *Anon.* (1479) Hil. 18 Edw. IV, fo. 21, pl. 1, when Bryan CJ repeated his doctrine.

same vein, Serjeant Yaxley argued in a King's Bench case soon after 1500:

If I come to another to buy a piece of cloth, and ask the price, and he tells me that I may have it for 20s., I cannot then take it unless I pay the 20s.... [because] perhaps I am not worth the 20s., and therefore it is implied in the bargain that I shall pay the money for the cloth at once or else I shall not have it; but if there is a day of payment, it is a good bargain, because then [the seller has] given [me] express liberty to pay at such a day.

Tremaile J. responded that 'if someone whom I know sells me a horse for 20s., and delivers it, the property of the horse is in me straight away, even though I do not pay him and no date is set for the payment to be made, if this sale is outside a market between people who know one another; but in a market, between strangers, the money must be paid at once as well as the horse, or else it is but a negotiation (*communication*)'.[111] This was a different case, because Tremaile J. supposed a delivery of the horse; but again the solution was made to turn on the parties' intention as presumed from the circumstances. According to Fyneux CJ, if the buyer did not pay at once it was for the seller to elect whether to let him take the goods away, in which case his remedy was an action of debt if unpaid, or to retain the goods until he was paid.

The same approach was affirmed in the Common Pleas during the reign of Henry VIII. In 1523, Brudenell CJ declared that:[112]

Bargains and sales are understood in the way it has been concluded and agreed between the parties, as far as their intentions can be understood. For if I sell you my horse for £10, and we are both agreed, and I accept a penny in earnest, this is a perfect contract and you shall have the horse and I shall have an action for the money. But if I want to sell my horse to you for £10, and you say you will give £9 for him, and I say that I am content, nevertheless if you do not pay the money at once but go away, it is not a bargain...

Pollard J., likewise, said that 'bargains and sales... depend on the discussions[113] (*communication*) and words between the parties'. The question had thus become purely a matter of agreement or intention. Brudenell CJ did not in his second example mean to suggest that the parties could not, if they wished, agree to credit terms; he was evidently referring to a preliminary discussion as to price rather than a concluded sale on credit. Other speeches in the same case make it clear that title could pass without delivery or earnest payment, provided that a date was set for payment.[114]

---

[111] *Anon.* (before 1506) Hil. 21 Hen. VII, fo. 6, pl. 4 (misdated; Yaxley died in 1505). According to Yaxley, this did not apply to a bartering of goods, such as a horse for an ox, because each party could seize the chattel; but this was not so of money. For 'communication' see below, 819.

[112] *Southwall* v. *Huddelston* (1523) Hil. 14 Hen. VIII, at fo. 22, pl. 6 (119 Selden Soc. 160), *per* Brudenell CJ. Pollard and Fitzherbert JJ delivered concurring opinions. The principal case was not a sale of goods, but a conditional assignment of a term of years.   [113] Cf. the Scots word 'communing'.

[114] See fo. 20, *per* Fitzherbert J. (tr. 'if I appoint a day when the money shall be paid, and you promise and agree to it also, this is a perfect contract and I shall have possession at once and you shall have an action [of debt] at the day'); Port 110 ('if someone buys a horse for £10, the seller may refuse to

That was confirmed in 1537:[115]

And this distinction was taken, when a date was set for payment and when not; in the first case, the contract is good immediately, and an action lies on it without payment, but in the other not so; for instance, if someone buys twenty yards of cloth from a draper, the bargain is void if he does not pay the money at the agreed price immediately...

It was held in a later case that, even if earnest was paid, the seller could agree to give the buyer an option to change his mind overnight, and in this case the contract was binding but subject to a 'power to mislike'.[116] Factual details of this kind were rarely presented to the central courts. In the 1537 case, where the facts did come out, the question which arose for decision was still one of pleading: where the defendant in detinue on a sale pleaded that the sale was conditional upon the plaintiff making full payment when he came to take delivery, which party should traverse the terms of the contract?[117] Underlying such disputes was the assumption that questions of title turned not upon legal subtleties but upon the terms of bargains, express or implied. This was not necessarily a new assumption, but the general forms of pleading had managed to keep legal questions at bay until our period. Therefore, although it has been asserted that the judges of this period settled the outlines of the modern law of sale,[118] this may be too large a claim. What they established was that title to goods could be transferred without anything analogous to livery of seisin, and that the effect of gifts and sales of chattels was not governed by a physical requirement, as in the case of land,[119] but by the intention of the parties.

ESTATES IN CHATTELS

The authorities in our period took the strict view that no estates could be created in chattels,[120] because it was contrary to the nature of chattel ownership that the

receive the money, unless there is earnest, such as penny. But it is otherwise if the day of payment is expressed with certainty, for then the property is changed').

[115] *Anon.* (1537) Dyer 29b (tr.). Cf. Thomas Audley's reading (Inner Temple, 1526) CUL MS. Ee.5.19, fo. 8v (a use is changed by a sale for money to be paid at a certain day, but it is 'otherwise if no day is set, for then the use is not changed before payment').

[116] *Anon.* (1554) Dyer 99b, §66. The implication was that property would normally pass; but here the contract was outside the market, and therefore it was ineffective to pass property in stolen goods, even though the buyer confirmed his acceptance in the market.

[117] Cf. *Homerston v. Clerke* (1549) CP 40/1142, m. 456 (debt in the *detinet* for wheat sold; pleads sale on condition of completing payment on delivery, and upon the tender the plaintiff refused to pay; undetermined demurrer). [118] Holdsworth, *HEL*, iii. 354–5; Fifoot, *HSCL*, 228–9.

[119] That is, the legal title to the land. The use could pass by bargain and sale.

[120] See Yorke 228, no. 377 (tr. 'Note that if someone gives me his goods for term of my life, the remainder over, this remainder is void, and the lessee shall have them for ever'); *Anon.* (1530/1) Pollard 272,

owner for the time being of a chattel should be restrained from doing what he liked with it, even from destroying it. A gift of a chattel for an hour, as the saying went, was a gift for ever.[121] The principle was applied to chattels real as well as movables, so that a term of years could not be settled in remainder.[122]

The owner of a chattel could nevertheless grant another person the right to use it for a certain time, as where animals were leased together with land,[123] or utensils and furniture with a house,[124] or a flock of sheep (or herd of cattle) leased for years.[125] The distinction in such cases between ownership, possession, and custody, was constantly mooted in connection with the law of theft.[126] There was also a similar question in relation to distress: a distrainor had custody but not property, and if he had possession it was a 'special' possession.[127]

It was necessary in such cases to decide who could bring actions against a stranger who took the chattels away, and to understand the relationship between bailor and bailee.[128] That this was still a relatively immature branch of the law in the early sixteenth century is obvious from a discussion in 1519, at Spelman's second reading, of the nature of a pledge. There was nothing new about pledging chattels, and disputes about pledges regularly arose in litigation.[129] Indeed, large

no. 61 ('one may not make a remainder of a chattel'). For an inconclusive discussion in 1459 see Dyer 359; 94 Selden Soc. 219.

[121] Richard Broke, argument in Gray's Inn (1519), quoted below, 746; BL MS. Hargrave 253, fo. 16v, per Fitzherbert J. in Gray's Inn; Brooke Abr., Done, pl. 57; Devise, pl. 13.

[122] Litt. s. 740; Anon. (1536) Dyer 7b, §8, per Baldwin CJ and Shelley J. Cf. Perk. (1528), sig. P4v. See also above, 640–1.   [123] e.g. Taverner's Case (1543) Dyer 56a (land and flock of sheep).

[124] e.g. Browne v. Cressy (1520) CP 40/1029, m. 583; reported in 120 Selden Soc. 51; Ewarcy v. Cabot (1555) CP 40/1162, m. 908 (house in Cheapside leased to Sebastian Cabot, and long inventory of contents including 'unam mappam rotundam vocatam a round ball de discrippcione mundi').

[125] Fyneux CJ said this was common: Hil. 21 Hen. VII, fo. 15, pl. 23. Indentures leasing sheep are set out in Ben v. Knyght (1505) CP 40/976, m. 486 (debt for rent); Smyth v. Jecler (1524) CP 40/1045, m. 642 (debt on bond to perform covenants).   [126] Above, 568.

[127] William Whorwood argued at a moot that 'he had no special property but a special custody or possession, like a parker, shepherd, herdsman, or bailiff (baly), for which possession they shall have a writ of trespass': BL MS. Harley 5103, fo. 50v (tr.). In another moot, on the question whether a lord who distrained cattle was liable if the cattle escaped and trespassed, Fitzherbert said they were in the 'garde' of the lord but the property remained in the tenant: ibid., fo. 60. Richard Broke argued (ibid.) that the lord 'did not take any possession' by distraining, because the pound was 'indifferent'.

[128] See P. Bordwell, 'Property in Chattels' (1929) 29 Harvard Law Rev. 374–94, 501–20, 731–51. For the doctrine that the bailee had a 'special' property for the purpose of bringing replevin, see Hil. 21 Hen. VII, fo. 15, pl. 23, per Fyneux CJ. It was decided on demurrer in Bonathalek v. Chyton (1528) CP 40/1058A, m. 448, that the bailor of goods for safekeeping could not take them back without request. In Hyll v. Webster (1529) CP 40/1061, m. 697 (trespass), a bailee justified taking back chattels taken from him by a third party (though the jury found against him). Cf. above, 570.

[129] See Huse CJ and others (executors of Lord Dudley) v. Lord Powes (1489) Mich. 5 Hen. VII, fo. 1, pl. 1; CP 40/910, m. 340d (trespass to gold chain; pleads licence to take it as a pledge for £100); Huse v. Clyffe (1496) KB 27/940, m. 39 (detinue for jewels; pleads unredeemed pledge; issue whether goods pledged or bailed for safekeeping); Langrich v. Chambre (1501) CP 40/958, m. 355 (trespass to rings; pleads bailment in pleggiagium); Halke v. Prior of St Gregory by Canterbury (1506) CP 40/976, m. 426; pr. 116

sums were sometimes lent against valuables, such as the £2,400 lent by the city of London to Richard III on the security of a gold coronel garnished with jewels.[130] Yet the underlying theory was still unclear. Spelman propounded a conditional-gift analysis:[131]

There is a distinction between something bailed and a pledge. For if goods are bailed to another, the possession still continues in the bailor; and if a stranger takes them, either of them [bailor or bailee] may have a writ of trespass. But when goods are delivered in pledge, that is a gift upon condition... and there is no difference where the condition goes before the gift or after. Here the bailor [i.e. pledgor] has nothing but a condition, and he has no more to do with the goods than a stranger.

Serjeant Richard Broke, however, argued against the reader that conditional gifts of goods were open to the same objections as limitations of estates in goods:[132]

If I bail goods in pledge, still the property is not altered, but remains in me, and I may give them away or forfeit them; but the bailee may retain them [as security] for his duty. And, notwithstanding this pledge, the bailee may have a writ of debt for his duty, and it is no plea for the other to say that he has a pledge; but if the bailor brings a writ of detinue for his pledge the other may bar him until [he has been paid]. And it cannot be called a conditional gift for the time being, for one cannot give away goods for a time. If one gives goods for an hour it is a gift for ever, since one cannot make a reversion in goods as one can in land. It follows that the party who has the pledge has but the custody of the thing, and the property remains in the bailor.

Another kind of pledge was where chattels were mortgaged by deed of gift, apparently without possession passing; in this case the legal analysis seemed to require the concept of a shifting trust.[133] A trust or use of chattels was also recognized where a debtor made a deed of gift to trustees in order to avoid creditors.[134]

In the bailment situations there was no attempt to create a succession of owners, for the owner remained unchanged throughout. But the mechanism of a shifting trust—as in the mortgage situation—raised the possibility that the 'use and occupation' of a chattel might be settled. The question might well arise if a man granted to another that he could have certain goods on his death. It was held in the Exchequer in Henry VIII's time that such a future gift was good, and it was

---

Selden Soc. 515 (detinue for silver-gilt nut; pleads it was pledged for burial fee); *Baldwyn* v. *Marmyon* (1520) KB 27/1034, m. 27 (pleaded in trespass); *Ottyner* v. *Beurne* (1550) KB 27/1156, m. 102 (delivery *in vadium* pleaded in trover); *Merye* v. *Edges* (1555) CP 40/1164, m. 836 (case for not returning a redeemed pledge).

[130] BL Add. Ch. 73946 (transaction referred to in indenture of 22 Nov. 1485). For bills pawning plate in 1486–7 see BL Add. Ch. 73926, 74069. For a bill pawning a gold-embroidered gown in 1521 see HMC, *Report on MSS in Various Collections*, ii (1903), 231 (Buxton MS.).

[131] Spelman's reading (1519) 113 Selden Soc. 160.   [132] ibid. 160–1.

[133] See P. E. Jones, *Calendar of Plea and Memoranda Rolls 1437–57* (1954), pp. xxii–xxviii.

[134] 3 Hen. VII, c. 4 (such gifts to be void). The statute uses the words 'trust' and 'to the use of'.

reported that Fyneux CJ had been of the same opinion.[135] Still there were only two parties, the donor and the donee, but the postponement of the time when the gift was to take effect would have created something like a settlement in use with remainder to the donee.[136] The experiments did not stop there. Wills were thought to have special properties in this connection, so that—despite the principle that a gift of a chattel for an hour was a gift for ever—the ownerhip of a chattel could be 'divided' by a devise to someone for life with remainder over.[137] This may have been simply a recognition of the practice of the ecclesiastical courts, which were not restrained by any rule of canon law from enforcing such bequests. Several early-Tudor common lawyers took advantage of this testamentary power and purported to settle chattels by their wills. William Copley (d. 1490), chief prothonotary of the Common Pleas, devised chattels and heirlooms to his nephew in tail male; Henry Harman (d. 1502), clerk of the Crown in the King's Bench, bequeathed his best silver to his son and his son's heirs male; William Mordaunt (d. 1518), Copley's immediate successor, devised his books—including his books of entries—in tail male, directing that they should pass from one heir to the next without being sold; and Fitzjames CJ in 1538 entailed plate and household stuff to 'that person that shall from time to time have my house' at Redlynch, and directed his great book of statutes to 'remain to the house of Redlynch as an implement to the said house', a bequest which occasioned a lawsuit a quarter of a century later.[138] The common-law analysis of such legacies seems to have been that the use and occupation of chattels could be settled on a succession of owners by will.[139] The executors received the absolute legal title, but they were under an obligation to observe the wishes of the testator.[140] This continuing obligation

---

[135] 120 Selden Soc. 82, no. 3, referring to an undated decision of Fyneux CJ (gift of jewels to future son-in-law, to take effect on donor's death) and to *Urmeston's Case* (*c*.1522) in the Exchequer ('I will give you this gown of mine if I die before you', held good 'by several').

[136] Cf. 3 Hen. VII, c. 4, which rendered void all gifts of goods made in trust for the donor in order to defraud creditors. This measure, which was designed in particular to prevent abuses by sanctuary-men, evidently assumes that goods could effectively be granted in trust.

[137] Discussion in Gray's Inn, BL MS. Hargrave 253, fo. 16v, *per* Fitzherbert J.

[138] *Nicholas Fitzjames's Case* (1565) Owen 33. The original will, dated 23 Oct. 1538, belonged to Sir Thomas Phillipps (MS. 26723), and was sold at auction in 1997: 19 *JLH* 76, no. 571. It is registered in PCC 42 Spert; PROB 11/29, fo. 5 (whence quotations, sp. mod.). For two examples of chattels settled as heirlooms by will in the 1540s see D. English, *The Great Landowners of East Yorkshire 1530–1910* (1990), 98–9.

[139] This was the evident understanding of Sir Anthony Browne JCP (d. 1567), who left to the owners of a manor for the time being, (sp. mod.) 'the occupation and usage of all my books... without having in them any property and without any alteration, and so to continue in usage and occupation only for ever': PCC 20 Stonarde; PROB 11/49, fo. 150v. When Catlyn CJ settled the 'occupation and custody' of some tapestries, with remainders, in 1574, he directed that the life occupants should have no 'absolute property in the same otherwise to dispose of': PCC 5 Pyckering; PROB 11/57, fo. 35v.

[140] Saunders CB (d. 1576) was to employ the device of transferring all his goods and chattels real and personal, by deed of gift, to trustees to perform his last will: PCC 41 Carew (PROB 11/58, fo. 298v).

differed from their normal duty to administer the estate by handing over legacies absolutely to the legatees, and could therefore be appropriately described as a trust or use. Indeed, the beneficial property could be deemed to pass to the remainder-man, according to Fitzherbert J., even if he were not given possession by the executors.[141] If that were the case, however, the same analysis could support a settlement of chattels *inter vivos*, since the settlor retained the 'property' and the occupation could therefore be divided between successive occupants. This was apparently confirmed by the judges in the 1530s.[142] Uses of chattels—as of money[143]—were in such situations understood as subsisting independently of Chancery or ecclesiastical jurisdiction; but, as with uses of land, they were not readily accommodated within the regular common law.

The chief problem was to explain how a settlement of the occupation of chattels could be enforced. In the case of a bequest, the legal title vested in the personal representatives on death, but it was far from clear how far (if at all) they had responsibilities once they had handed possession to the first legatee. Prima facie they were bound to carry out the testator's last wishes; but if a settlement of chattels was to take effect for a long time, as in the case of heirlooms, the legal title would have to pass to successive executors of executors *ad infinitum*, which would be inconvenient because the settlor's estate would never be fully administered. In any case, movable chattels would not necessarily last for ever; and there was no law which could prevent the possessor of a chattel for the time being from destroying it. Presumably testators had no more than a hope that their wishes would be respected, for the thing might be destroyed, or sold to third parties. Brooke certainly accepted that a devisee for life could destroy the remainder by selling the chattel.[144] Perhaps the most that could be expected was that suggested by Fitzherbert elsewhere, when he said that a man could will that a named person should have his goods 'to do with them at his pleasure, and if any of them remain after his decease, [then another] should have them'.[145]

---

[141] Discussion in Gray's Inn, BL MS. Hargrave 253, fo. 16v. Fitzherbert J. and the reader both agreed that the remainderman could bring replevin, without any need for the executors to deliver possession. Neither of them, however, used the term 'use'.

[142] Brooke Abr., *Devise*, pl. 13 (pr. 94 Selden Soc. 220 n. 2); *Anon.* (1530/1) Pollard 272, no. 61 (tr. 'it was stated as law... that one may not make a remainder of a chattel in possession... it is otherwise if someone gives the occupation of a chattel for term of life or years, the remainder over; then the remainder shall be good, because the donee has no property but only the occupation').

[143] e.g. in the concept of money had and received to the use of the plaintiff.

[144] *Anon.* (1541) Brooke Abr., *Done*, pl. 57; *Chattelles*, pl. 23.

[145] Yorke 228, no. 377, *per* Fitzherbert J. Note also *Anon.* (1541) 121 Selden Soc. 444, no. 23 (perhaps the case in the last note), where Baldwin CJ held that a remainder of a lease should go 'according to the intent of the devise'.

Part IX

THE LAW OF TORTS

40

Trespass and Case

IF the law of chattels was largely subsumed under the law of actions, so to an even greater extent was the law of contract and tort. It is not wholly anachronistic to divide our material in accordance with a few convenient basic concepts such as 'torts' and 'contract', since both the concepts and the words were known in our period; but we must be careful to remember that a Tudor lawyer did not regard such divisions as fundamental, or even particularly useful.[1] What we regard as the law of contract and tort, he still regarded as the law of debt, of covenant, of trespass, and of case. Of these, it was the actions on the case which—though not numerous in comparison with trespass or debt—generated the most new legal thinking in our period. But the thinking here was unsophisticated and rudimentary in comparison with that bestowed upon the land law; practical experiments were hardly comparable with refined common learning. The new developments were outside the curriculum of the inns of court and cannot indeed be traced with any precision in the law reports: in searching for new forms of action we are dependent on the plea rolls. And when we try to understand the innovations revealed by the bare record, actions on the case seem not to observe our modern conceptual boundaries.

Actions on the case provided an escape from the formulary system, a means of developing new remedies,[2] and preferable alternatives to older remedies in which jury trial was not assured. Whatever doubts there may once have been, it was now clear that wager of law was unavailable in case, and that case could be brought in the King's Bench as well as the Common Pleas. After 1504 it was also clear that the mesne process was the same as in trespass *vi et armis*: that is, arrest and outlawry.[3] It therefore became an unwritten first principle of litigation to bring an action in trespass or case whenever possible. The difference between them was not even very sharp, since it was accepted that an action on the case could sometimes be

---

[1] Brooke Abr. has a title *Contract, Bargain, et Achate*, but it is confined to what we would call the law of sale; there are no *assumpsit* cases.

[2] See above, 324.

[3] 19 Hen. VII, c. 9 (B. & M. 342). For an erroneous attempt to use outlawry before the statute see Pas. 10 Hen. VII, fo. 21, pl. 15.

framed with a *vi et armis* clause,[4] established examples being the action for lying in wait to seize a villein[5] and the *scienter* action for damage caused by dangerous animals.[6]

Although actions on the case had been in use since the mid-fourteenth century, their scope did not widen greatly during the fifteenth century and the writs were seldom pursued beyond the interlocutory stage. For example, during the nine terms of the reign of Richard III, only 27 actions on the case were recorded in the King's Bench, all following standard forms,[7] and in only two of them did the defendant appear.[8] Not long after that came a remarkable expansion. The early sixteenth century saw the introduction of important new varieties of action—for instance, actions for defamation,[9] malicious prosecution,[10] and trover[11]—besides numerous experiments, such as the action for inducing a breach of contract, which became established as a tort,[12] and the action for an invasion of privacy, which did not.[13] We find important extensions in the availability of older actions, as in the use of *assumpsit* to recover debts, and the extended use of nuisance actions instead of the assize. There was also a marked increase in the number of such actions—especially the newest forms—which proceeded to trial and judgment.

Some familiar species of action on the case were well established before the middle of the fifteenth century, and others emerged during our period. It is almost irresistibly convenient, and not too misleading, to give names to the commonest species. We speak in terms of 'the action of *assumpsit*', or 'the action for defamation', or 'trover and conversion', as if these were distinct forms of action within the family of trespass on the case. But again a preliminary caution is required. At the same time as established categories were being developed, case still retained its essential flexibility. Thus, we find actions of *assumpsit* type in

---

[4] *Moots*, 215. See also *Boleyn v. Byron* (1513) CP 40/1003, m. 502 (impeding park-keeper; demurrer relating to title); *Wyat v. Brokas*, ibid., m. 533 (taking perquisites of napery at coronation; judgment by default). But cf. the error cases noted above, 324.

[5] e.g. *Reymond v. Lord Fitzwauter* (1521) Spelman 2 (called an action on the case); KB 27/1040, m. 40 (pr. 94 Selden Soc. 239); *Hele v. Cade* (1532) CP 40/1073, m. 509 (judgment for plaintiff).

[6] See below, 765.

[7] KB 27/888–896. The types of action were: *assumpsit* for not performing a task (9), *assumpsit* for not conveying land (7), deceit on a sale of goods (3), negligence (2), nuisance (2), failure to control fire (2), *scienter* (1), overworking a hired horse (1).

[8] *Herward v. Coton* (1485) KB 27/894, m. 37d (*assumpsit* for negligence; general issue); *Colby v. Barbour*, ibid., m. 44 (fire; imparlance). All the actions were begun by writ.

[9] See below, ch. 44.

[10] 94 Selden Soc. 247 (first noted in 1545). It was also brought in the Common Pleas: *Hert v. Serche* (1532) CP 40/1075, m. 553d (mixed with defamation); *Sparhawke v. Swanton* (1542) CP 40/1113, m. 308.

[11] See below, 804–8.　　　　　[12] See below, ch. 46.

[13] *Phyllyppes v. Hoke* (1542) CP 40/1115, m. 566d (taking secret documents from plaintiff's chamber and publishing contents, with result that plaintiff dismissed from employment).

which that word does not occur at all,[14] and we find *assumpsit* used as an ancillary element in combination with conversion[15] or deceit.[16] We may even find defamation forms used for essentially contractual purposes.[17] The variability of the forms is accompanied by a dearth of abstract principle.

GENERAL PRINCIPLES OF LIABILITY

We search the early Tudor law books in vain for any general theory governing liability for wrongs. The idea of 'wrong'—*tort* in French, *injuria* in Latin—was perhaps the broadest and least well-defined concept in the common law. Since, as we shall see, it came to encompass failures to perform undertakings or to pay debts, any exact comparison with our modern notion of tort is doomed to mislead. Our distinction between contract and tort rests on the difference between duties assumed by agreement and duties imposed by law; but even such a seemingly basic distinction was not entrenched in the law of our period. On the one hand, a breach of contract was a 'wrong',[18] remediable—one distinguished judge did not hesitate to say 'punishable'[19]—by an award of damages in an action of trespass on the case. On the other hand, negligence (falling short of a forcible trespass) was usually the subject of litigation only when it represented the neglect of a duty explicitly undertaken by the party. Indeed, almost the only actions in which we shall find negligence mentioned in pleading as part of the plaintiff's case are actions of *assumpsit*, the basis of which seems closest to what we regard as contract. Between forcible trespass and contractual negligence there was a seeming void. We shall see that the gap is to some extent an illusion caused by the opacity of pleadings in trespass. But there was nevertheless a conceptual void, and we shall have to make the most of small clues.

One principle which is explicitly discussed is that an actionable tort consists of two elements, a legal wrong (*injuria*) and consequent damage (*damnum*). For a wrong to be actionable it has to cause damage. Thus, an uninvited intervention in the affairs of another, such as a trespass on his land to save his goods, might be legally wrong and yet it was arguably not actionable if it worked good rather than harm.[20]

---

[14] e.g. actions of *bargazinasset* or *promisisset*: 94 Selden Soc. 256 n. 4. A late example of an action of *promisit* (with a plea of *Non promisit*) is *Lonner* v. *Constable* (1533) CP 40/1077, m. 535.

[15] See below, 802–3.   [16] See below, ch. 42.

[17] *Butte* v. *Stannard* (1535) CP40/1087, m. 398 (case for jilting a lover; lengthy writ, with elements of defamation but no direct *assumpsit*).

[18] *Orwell* v. *Mortoft* (1505) Mich. 20 Hen. VII, fo. 9, pl. 18 (B. & M. 406), *per* Frowyk CJ; *Pykeryng* v. *Thurgoode* (1532) Spelman 4; B. & M. 411.

[19] *Orwell* v. *Mortoft* (1505) Mich. 20 Hen. VII, fo. 9, pl. 18, *per* Frowyk CJ. For the notion of 'punishing' a tort see below, 754.

[20] *Cuny* v. *Brugewode* (1506–7) Trin. 21 Hen. VII, fo. 27, pl. 5; 2 Caryll 542 (crops saved from cattle); CP 40/978, m. 449; B. & M. 316; *Harecourt* v. *Spycer* (1520–1) Trin. 12 Hen. VIII, fo. 2, pl. 2 (119 Selden

Conversely, one might deliberately cause another damage without doing any legal wrong (*damnum absque injuria*).[21] As Broke J. explained in a case of 1520:[22]

> It is possible to damage me and yet commit no injury. For instance, if the sheriff arrests me, this is a damage because he restrains me from my liberty, but it is not an injury. Likewise if a craftsman acquires more customers for himself than another of the same craft, such as a scrivener, or a schoolmaster who has more pupils than another because he is more learned,[23] this is a *damnum* to the other but no *injuria*, because everyone ought to look after himself and it is not punishable.

According to Serjeant Yorke, there were some exceptional cases in which even a combination of damage and wrongdoing afforded no remedy; one of them was where the party caused his own misfortune.[24] These examples represent the beginnings of an attempt to find some legal principles; what we do not find stated, however, is a general principle to determine when damage was legally tortious and actionable. But a universal principle is equally elusive today. The practical approach, then as now, was to look at the precedents and to seek the policy of the law.

The common pleadings in trespass and case do not advance our understanding of these matters very far. If language were the only guide, it might be supposed that the wording of the general plea in trespass—'that the defendant is in no wise guilty (*culpabilis*) thereof'—carried the implication that fault or blame (*culpa*) was a third necessary ingredient in tort, in addition to *injuria* and *damnum*. This is, however, a somewhat circular assumption if blame is merely a synonym for legal liability. In trespass *quare clausum fregit*, the function of a plea of Not guilty was certainly not to confine attention to fault in the sense of negligence, and it is safer to assume that it did no more than put the whole of the plaintiff's case in issue. That does not mean that fault was irrelevant. An indication that it was a material factor in tortious liability may be found in the reports, in the language of punishment. The frequent talk of trespass or tort being 'punished' was usually in contexts which associated punishment with blameworthiness: it is not reasonable to punish someone in whom there is no fault.[25] Yet liability in tort had already

---

Soc. 7 at 8), *per* Newport sjt (entry to bring plaintiff a present) and Pollard J. (entry to save plaintiff from attack); Trin. 13 Hen. VIII, fo. 15, pl. 1 (119 Selden Soc. 82), *per* Norwich sjt (crops saved from cattle); *Alyn* v. *Facy* (1541) CP 40/1111, m. 616 (trespass to house; pleads house was on fire and he entered to extinguish fire and save money to use of owner; issue).

21 *Haukyns* v. *Broune* (1477) Trin. 17 Edw. IV, fo. 3, pl. 2 (B. & M. 629 at 632), *per* Nedeham J. and Billyng CJ (tr. 'there are various cases in our law where a man shall have *damnum absque injuria*, such as defamation'). Defamation subsequently became a tort: below, ch. 44.

22 *Fyloll* v. *Assheleygh* (1520) Trin. 12 Hen. VIII, fo. 3, pl. 3 (119 Selden Soc. 15).

23 An allusion to *The Case of Gloucester School* (1410) Hil. 11 Hen. IV, fo. 47, pl. 21.

24 Yorke 166 (in the context of property law).

25 *Orwell* v. *Mortoft* (1505) Mich. 20 Hen. VII, fo. 9, pl. 18, *per* Frowyk CJ (tr. 'each should be punished according to his fault'); Pas. 21 Hen. VII, fo. 22, pl. 14, *per* More sjt (tr. 'it is more right to punish

diverged from that in criminal law, since *mens rea* was not relevant in an action for damages. In a civil action, therefore, fault could not be equated with a subjective intention to cause harm.[26] Most of the dicta about blameworthiness concern what we now refer to as causation. If a defendant was not allowed to excuse an accident on the ground that he did not intend it to happen, his most obvious alternative was to show that he did not cause it. Blame could therefore be negatived by showing an act of God,[27] or of an animal behaving unpredictably, or of a stranger,[28] or of a servant exceeding his authority, or by showing that the plaintiff brought the accident upon himself.[29] Whether a defendant could excuse harm which he had physically caused, on the grounds that he had taken due care in trying to avert it, or that the plaintiff had voluntarily accepted an inherent risk, are more difficult questions which need to be tackled in the context of the different forms of action.

Discussion of these matters eludes us not because they raised questions too subtle to have occurred to the early Tudor mind, but because generally speaking they were regarded as questions of fact rather than law, or at least of fact and law inextricably mixed, and as such within the sole province of the jury. Whatever 'guilty' meant was a matter for juries, since the plea of Not guilty did not place on the record any particular facts upon which a court could rule. The vast majority of trespass entries in the rolls therefore cast no light whatever on the nature of tortious liability. The common-form phrases, with their swords, staves, and knives, do not even reveal what plaintiffs claimed to have actually happened. For our small clues we are dependent upon unusual special cases. The nature of the plaintiff's cause of action is much clearer when he uses an action on the case—as when framing a complaint of defamation or nuisance—but even in those cases the standard of liability is obscure for want of special pleading by the defendant.

---

the master, in whom the fault lies, than the servant'); anon. reading on Malefactors in Parks, CUL MS. Ee.5.22, ff. 141v–142 (tr. in 94 Selden Soc. 223: 'if he were punished it would be against all reason, inasmuch as there was no fault in him'). For other examples of the language of punishment, see 94 Selden Soc. 222 n. 8.

[26] *The Case of Thorns* (1466) Mich. 6 Edw. IV, fo. 7, pl. 18 (B. & M. 327); *Cuny* v. *Brugewode* (1506) Trin. 21 Hen. VII, fo. 27, pl. 5 (B. & M. 316); *Fyloll* v. *Assheleygh* (1522?) Trin. 12 Hen. VIII, fo. 3, pl. 3 (119 Selden Soc. 15), per Roo sjt ('the intent is the only distinction between trespass and felony').

[27] *The Case of Thorns* (1466) Mich. 6 Edw. IV, fo. 7, pl. 18, per Choke J. (gust of wind); *Pryst* v. *Belche* (1510) KB 27/994, m. 47 (fire beginning by misfortune and act of God: 'ex infortunia et actu Dei'); *Reniger* v. *Fogassa* (1550) Plowd. 1 at 10 (storms at sea). Cf. *Payne* v. *Turbutt* (1542) CP 40/1113, m. 134 (waste for burning houses leased; pleads a storm of thunder and lightning; plaintiff replies that they were burned by negligence).

[28] The act of a stranger was not a defence in the case of a bailee or innkeeper, who remained liable to the party but could sue the stranger for an indemnity: *Anon.* (1490) Mich. 6 Hen. VII, fo. 12, pl. 9; Trin. 10 Hen. VII, fo. 26, pl. 3, per Fyneux sjt; below, 761.   [29] See the examples in 94 Selden Soc. 223.

41

Negligence and Fault

THE principal actions in which negligence or incompetence was formally alleged by the plaintiff were the 'misfeasance' forms of *assumpsit*. Fault, or rather default (*defectum*), was mentioned in the two actions on the case upon the custom of the realm for the spread of fire and for the loss of goods in an inn. A modern lawyer might be tempted to see in such actions the seeds of the later tort of negligence. The historian, however, must be wary of assuming in any of these cases that the language of negligence or default necessarily betokened a regime of liability based on fault as opposed to strict liability. Conversely, it should not be assumed that, because the declaration in trespass *vi et armis* made no mention of fault or negligence, liability in trespass actions must have been strict rather than based on fault. There is no contemporary evidence that trespass and case were separated by differing standards of liability. In so far as differing standards may be discerned at all, it seems most likely that they varied according to the types of situation in which liability arose rather than the form of action through which the remedy had to be sought.

NEGLIGENT MISPERFORMANCE OF CONTRACTS

Nearly sixty *assumpsit* actions for negligence have been noted in the King's Bench rolls between 1500 and 1540, two-thirds of them *optulit se* entries in much the same form. The defendant was alleged to have undertaken to perform some specified labour or service, and then to have performed it so carelessly that some specified damage followed. It was rare for the declaration to allege an undertaking to use skill and care; the undertaking as laid was only to perform the task. To that extent the liability may have been closer to what we call tort than to contract, the undertaking being subsidiary and explanatory, and the duty of care apparently implied by law—a duty to take care in carrying out undertakings.

The adverbs used to describe the defendant's misconduct in carrying out his undertaking were (in descending order of frequency): 'negligently' (*negligenter*), 'improvidently' (*improvide*), 'in an unworkmanlike manner' (*inartificialiter*), 'unduly' (*indebite*), 'imprudently' (*indiscrete*), 'carelessly' (*incaute*), 'unwittingly' (*inscienter*), and 'unskilfully' (*absque arte*). Whatever it was that they expressed could only, it seems, be expressed negatively. The cases are all of misfeasance rather than nonfeasance; that is, there was either positive misconduct or a failure to exercise skill in performing a positive act. The actions were most commonly brought against tradesmen whose callings raised an expectation of skill: the barber whose dirty razor gave the plaintiff facial scabs;[1] the ophthalmic surgeon whose corrosive medicine resulted in blindness;[2] the veterinary surgeon or blacksmith who lamed or killed the horse entrusted to his care;[3] the scrivener who destroyed the book he was supposed to bind;[4] the fuller who damaged the cloth he undertook to full;[5] the builder whose handiwork collapsed, or threatened to do so;[6] the tiler or roofing contractor whose product leaked;[7] or the painter who used a poor quality paint which faded when exposed to air.[8] In the case of the manufacturer who met an order with defective goods,[9] or supplied goods in a defective container which occasioned their loss,[10] we cannot be sure—and we do not know

---

[1] *Bartilmewe* v. *Shragger* (1498) KB 27/949, m. 4; pr. (from Lucas's entries, fo. 98) in Rast. Ent. 2v (whence Fifoot, *HSCL*, 90).   [2] *Litilcote* v. *Capryk* (1526) KB 27/1061, m. 66.

[3] This was one of the earliest uses of case, and was still common: see e.g. *Herward* v. *Coton* (1484) KB 27/892, m. 39d (died through negligence of 'horse-leech'); *Fetiplace* v. *Amore* (1500) KB 27/956, m. 3 (blinded); *Ferrers* v. *Adam* (1506) KB 27/979, m. 19 (maimed by misplaced nail); *Parkyn* v. *Baron*, ibid., m. 49d (killed); *Hampton* v. *Harryson* (1506) KB 27/980, m. 22d (killed); *Eggecombe* v. *Wescote* (1506) KB 27/981, m. 5d (maimed by nail); *Cerry* v. *Freman* (1520) KB 27/1035, m. 2 (killed); *Warde* v. *Parker* (1521) KB 27/1040, m. 77d (sinews burned); *Betty* v. *Cutler* (1526) KB 27/1060, m. 5d (killed); *Churchill* v. *Howell* (1536) KB 27/1100, m. 51 (negligently docked and singed horse's tail whereby it died); FNB 94D.

[4] *Chudlegh* v. *Huldysse* (1499) KB 27/950, m. 16.

[5] *Kelsale* v. *Goryng* (1484) KB 27/891, m. 38 (alleges loss of profit). Cf. *Efford* v. *Alanson* (1527) CP 40/1056, m. 419 (cloth destroyed by negligence of weaver).

[6] *Alberd* v. *Rudkyn* (1491) KB 27/921, m. 44d (fallen wall); *Paston* v. *Boyse* (1500) KB 27/957, m. 46 (fallen wall); *Payne* v. *Kyng* (1505) KB 27/975, m. 44d (fallen house); *Broomholm* v. *Plomer* (1507) KB 27/982, m. 17d (fallen window); *Cory* v. *Wryght* (1507) KB 27/984, m. 47d (fallen masonry); *Maister* v. *Page* (1508) KB 27/987, m. 54 (fallen chimney); *Wodward* v. *Alen* (1508) KB 27/989, m. 70d (fallen bays); *Reynold* v. *William* (1510) KB 27/996, m. 8 (dangerous house); *Lytleton* v. *Wyllys*, ibid., m. 87d (sim.); *Hunston* v. *Wryght* (1512) KB 27/1005, m. 88d (sim.); *Bedyngfeld* v. *Paget* (1515) KB 27/1016, m. 48 (destroyed house); *Cutt* v. *Gyles* (1518) CP 40/1020B, m. 436 (collapsed barn); *Stepneth* v. *Lane* (1526) KB 27/1061, m. 22d (fallen house); *Langrege* v. *Stringer* (1535) KB 27/1094, m. 60d (decayed wall).

[7] *Skypwyth* v. *Caster* (1484) KB 27/892, m. 36d (negligent thatching by 'reeder'); *Warnet* v. *Gate* (1508) KB 27/986, m. 59; *Prior of Lewes* v. *Bottyng* (1509) KB 27/993, m. 55; *Scott* v. *Giles* (1518) CP 40/1020B, m. 436 (use of unseasoned timber); Shakelady's precedents, fo. 145v. For consequential loss see *Prior of Walsingham* v. *Trewe* (1503) KB 27/966, m. 2d (chimney built so negligently that it trapped the smoke); *Polgreyn* v. *Sergent* (1542) CP 40/1115, m. 668 (carpenter and mason built gutter of church aisle so negligently that rain damaged the timbers).

[8] *Hobart* v. *Pak* (1531) KB 27/1079, m. 46 (undertaking to paint windows with green oil paint).

[9] *Bordyour* v. *Colle* (1496) KB 27/940, m. 75 (badly made malt); *Playter* v. *Lambe* (1501) KB 27/958, m. 17 (bad tiles); *Prentyse* v. *Seman* (1503) KB 27/967, m. 42d (bad tiles); *Rede* v. *Nyghtyngale* (1505) KB 27/974, m. 7; *Fyske* v. *Andrewe* (1511) KB 27/999, m. 58 (badly cured herring); *Saunder* v. *Igolynden* (1515) KB 27/1015, m. 31 (badly fulled cloth); *Codenham* v. *Charlys* (1535) CP 40/1087, m. 501 (badly made malt); *Rychers* v. *Grome* (1537) KB 27/1103, m. 8d (bad bricks). In several of these cases a loss of profit is alleged.

[10] e.g. *Dirdo* v. *Man* (1520) CP 40/1027, m. 357 (seller of romney wine put it in a broken butt so that it leaked out).

that it mattered—whether the defendant was thought to be liable for the act of supplying an imperfect product or for his default in not supplying a perfect product; the same harm was done to the plaintiff on either analysis.[11] These professional and business cases are the common types; but there was no theoretical objection to bringing similar actions against a mere labourer who caused damage by negligent work,[12] or a nurse whose inattention caused her charge to be burned.[13] Nor does the line seem to have been drawn at physical damage.[14]

In most of the cases there was no pleading at all, because the defendant never appeared. Where the defendant did appear, he usually pleaded Not guilty or *Non assumpsit*, and so we learn no more of the substance of his defence. There does not seem to have been any uniformity of practice in choosing between these two forms of general issue;[15] and we sometimes find a more apt kind of general plea, such as that the defendant had performed his undertaking 'sufficiently' (*sufficienter*),[16] or that the damage had not been caused by his carelessness.[17] No case has been found in which a special plea in *assumpsit* throws any light on the standard of liability.[18] However, there are two cases in which surgeons sued for failing to effect cures pleaded that they had not given an undertaking to cure 'in the manner and form (*modo et forma*)' alleged by the plaintiff but had only promised to give treatment according to the best of their skill and ability.[19] These were cases of

---

11 For the difficulty of distinguishing between misfeasance and nonfeasance see below, 841–3.

12 e.g. *Lek v. Randys* (1498) KB 27/949, m. 66 (stack of wheat so negligently built that rain entered); *Wynse v. Punte*, ibid., m. 66 (hedge and ditches so negligently made that cattle entered); *Longevyle v. Abbott* (1535) CP 40/1084, m. 237 (three workmen so negligently made the head of a fishpond—*caput stagni*—that it did not hold the water back and so the fish escaped). Note also the reeder, above, 758 n. 7.

13 *Roo v. Sharlyng* (1495) KB 27/935, m. 65.

14 See *Saunderson v. Preston* (1539) CP 40/1103, m. 659 (negligent construction of window so that part of house in danger of collapse); *Halydaye v. Freme* (1540) CP 40/1106, m. 631 (negligent construction of base of watermill so that mill would not work; judgment for plaintiff); *Weldysshe v. Franklyn* (1563) CP 40/1207, m. 412 (negligent pleading by attorney, causing financial loss).

15 In 1520 we find a demurrer taken to a plea of *Non assumpsit* in an action against a carrier for losing goods by careless driving: *Elis v. Jakson* (1520) CP 40/1029, m. 554d.

16 *Woodward v. Alen* (1508) KB 27/989, m. 70d (carpenter pleads that he built 'sufficiently', *absque hoc* that the work had collapsed for want of due workmanship in the construction); *Saunder v. Igolynden* (1515) KB 27/1015, m. 31 ('well and sufficiently fulled the cloths'); *Rogers v. Holland* (1532) KB 27/1085, m. 72 (sim.); *Rychers v. Grome* (1537) KB 27/1103, m. 8d ('well and sufficiently made the bricks'). *Codenham v. Churlys* (1535) CP 40/1087, m. 501 (*protestando* that barley not good on receipt, pleads he malted it *sufficienter et artificialiter*).

17 A special plea in this form is *Joly v. Elderton* (1499) CP 40/950, m. 448 (*assumpsit* for negligently carrying a pipe of oil so that it was lost; pleads that the hoops of the pipe were defective on delivery, and traverses negligence; verdict for the defendant).

18 Cf. the unusual case of *Atwill v. Helyer* (1502) CP 40/960, m. 330, where a master sued his own servant for negligence in dying cloth; the servant pleaded the faithful exercise of his duty, and the master replied by assigning the negligence in destroying a vat of woad with quicklime (*cum callido calse*) through 'fraudulent' workmanship.

19 *Roggers v. Walssh* (1532) CP 40/1074, m. 505 (verdict for plaintiff); *Reade v. Porter* (1553) KB 27/1167, m. 118. Cf. CP 40/1079, m. 518 (pleads tender of medicine and refusal to take it).

nonfeasance rather than negligent misfeasance, though the distinction is not altogether meaningful in medical cases[20] and the pleas suggest that, in the absence of a special agreement, the liability of a surgeon was not thought to be strict. There is, however, a genuine factual difference between a contract guaranteeing a cure and a contract to do one's best for a patient. What we cannot tell is how far the supposed terms of such contracts could be implied from social usage. Generalization from these cases is therefore unwise. It would not be altogether surprising if the standard of liability in *assumpsit* for negligence turned at least in part on the construction of the contract in question.[21]

CARE OF GOODS: CARRIERS AND INNKEEPERS

Rather more information is available concerning the liability of carriers and innkeepers, probably because they were subjected to a stricter standard of care than ordinary bailees. A bailee could be made strictly liable by a contractual undertaking to that effect,[22] but if he only agreed to look after the goods with the same care as his own he might have an excuse,[23] and this latter was arguably the reasonable everyday understanding of the terms of an ordinary or non-contractual bailment.[24] He might also have been excused if the goods were stolen from him rather than merely taken by way of trespass, on the ground that the felony changed the property.[25] On the other hand, he may not have been entitled to this defence if he had deviated from the terms of the bailment by leaving the goods with a third party. In 1556, the Common Pleas entertained an action of detinue against a Norfolk esquire for a horse and bridle; the defendant had borrowed it to ride to Norwich, and was to keep it there to the plaintiff's use until the plaintiff came to

---

[20] See below, 841.   [21] Cf. the principles applied in debt on a bond, below, 827.

[22] According to St German, *Doctor and Student*, ed. Plucknett and Barton, 260, this was a contractual liability and therefore only attached if the bailee received some recompense. Cf. *Whittenson* v. *Tame* (1512) CP 40/1001, m. 614 (case against bailee on promise to return horse in as good a condition as when bailed, for so neglectfully watering and feeding it that it would not work again; issue on breach).

[23] *Anon.* (1469) Mich. 9 Edw. IV, fo. 40, pl. 22, *per* Danby CJ. The location of the risk was issuable: Hil. 3 Hen. VII, fo. 4, pl. 16 (bailment at the plaintiff's risk); CP 40/906, m. 339 (in detinue); *Denley* v. *Hooke* (1546) KB 27/1140, m. 118d (pleads sheep were delivered to him to keep in a pasture 'as he would keep his own animals', and traverses absolute promise to return them).

[24] Trin. 10 Hen. VII, fo. 26, pl. 3; also reported in Mich. 6 Hen. VII, fo. 12, pl. 9, *per* Kebell sjt; St German, *Doctor and Student*, ed. Plucknett and Barton, 260 (bailee only liable for 'default' unless he undertakes to redeliver safely at his peril).

[25] Kebell sjt so argues in Hil. 3 Hen. VII, fo. 4, pl. 16; and in *Anon.* (1492) Mich. 6 Hen. VII, fo. 12, pl. 9 (Fyneux sjt *contra*). The defence is denied by Fisher sjt (in Trin. 10 Hen. VII, fo. 26, pl. 3) on the ground that robbery did not excuse an innkeeper. J. H. Beale thought he detected a tendency to disallow the defence in the second half of the fifteenth century, but he mistakenly assumed that Fyneux was already a judge: 'The Carrier's Liability: its history' (1898) 11 *Harvard Law Rev.* 158–68, at 161.

collect it; but the defendant left it in another person's house, whence it was taken by Kett and his rebels, who rode it to death. On demurrer, this was held not to be a good defence.[26]

In the case of innkeepers, the action was founded on the 'custom of the realm', following the standard formula introduced in the fourteenth century. In later times the carrier would also be brought under a custom of the realm, but there is no mention of such a custom in the early Tudor period; the action against the negligent carrier was still *assumpsit*. The common link is that both were made responsible for the property of another as part of their business, and it seems likely that a higher standard was expected of them than of ordinary bailees. It may well have been the general understanding, in the absence of special terms, that they should insure the customer against loss or damage. Thus, in an Inner Temple discussion around 1530, it was said that a carrier or bailee for safekeeping could not plead that he was robbed of the goods, because he had undertaken the risk; it was different if a servant was robbed, because he was merely carrying out the master's orders and the risk remained with the master.[27] An innkeeper likewise was responsible for the theft of goods by strangers; indeed, this was the usual complaint in actions against innkeepers. His own remedy, in theory, was to find and sue the thieves.[28] There was therefore a chain of responsibility in which fault in the modern sense would have had no place. It is not easy to find real examples of successive actions, but there is one in the King's Bench rolls for 1555. A carrier was sued on an undertaking, in return for 12*d.*, to carry goods to Birmingham, on the grounds that through his negligence they were taken from him by persons unknown. The carrier confessed the action, but immediately sued the innkeeper of the Rose at Dunchurch for loss of the goods on the journey.[29] Both actions rested formally on an allegation of negligence or fault, but the implication of the confession may be that the carrier was considered responsible for the loss of goods whatever precautions he might have taken,[30] and that he and the innkeeper each insured his own customer. This is confirmed by an entry two years later, when an attempt by a common carrier to shift liability on to an innkeeper met with a

---

[26] *Barlee* v. *Corbett* (1556–7) CP 40/1168, m. 1005 (judgment for plaintiff).

[27] *Note* (*c.*1530) Caryll (Jun.) 391, no. 51. Cf. *Hachard* v. *Wynnals* (1511–12) CP 40/997, m. 503; Rast. Ent. 14v (account against common carrier in respect of a sack of grain; pleads theft in transit; judgment for plaintiff on demurrer).

[28] *Osbern* v. *Myller.* (1490) 1 Caryll 30, *per* Fairfax J. It was agreed that he could plead act of God, such as lightning, because he had no action over in that case. Cf. Trin. 10 Hen. VII, fo. 26, pl. 3, *per* Fisher sjt (denies that a common innkeeper has a remedy over when goods are robbed).

[29] *Colimer* v. *Arrowsmyth* (1555) KB 27/1174, m. 96 (*assumpsit*, says *non potest dedicere*); *Arrowsmyth* v. *Carter* (1555) ibid., m. 96d (innkeeper pleads Not guilty).

[30] A carrier could therefore be sued in *assumpsit* without alleging negligence: e.g. *Aylmer* v. *Dene* (1503) KB 27/969 m. 6d (*warrantizando assumpsit* to carry tun of sugar safely from London to Norwich, but wholly lost it).

demurrer.[31] The law was not finally settled in this period, because the Common Pleas judges apparently adopted the view that since the common carrier was compellable to receive goods for carriage he was not strictly liable for their loss by theft.[32]

To the extent that strict liability was regarded as the normal regime for remunerated bailees, the best means of escape was to plead a special agreement excluding or limiting liability. The normal position of a carrier was that he undertook to deliver safely; at least, that is how it was expressed in *assumpsit* declarations. But the law did not forbid a carrier, any more than a surgeon, to make other arrangements, if they were reasonable.[33] Thus, a carrier of goods by sea could plead that he had not undertaken absolutely to deliver, but had only undertaken to carry the goods safely to the best of his ability and on condition that the goods were not damaged 'by tempest of wind and sea' in the mean time.[34] In other words, he could rely on an exclusion clause which left some of the risk with the shipper.

A remarkable and revealing piece of special pleading, which must be regarded as an aberration by an inexperienced pleader, is to be seen in a King's Bench entry of 1528.[35] The plaintiff, in an unusually full declaration, complained that the defendant—for a sum of 2d. agreed—had undertaken safely to carry a butt of malmsey in his wagon from Maidstone to Sutton Valence, in Kent, that he had so carelessly loaded it on to the wagon that the wagon overturned and the hoops of the butt were broken, and that on arrival he had so carelessly unloaded the damaged butt that 100 gallons of malmsey gushed out and were lost. The defendant matched this narration of events with an even more detailed plea. Denying the undertaking by protestation, he said that he happened to be in Maidstone when the plaintiff's agent approached him and asked him to take the butt to his house in Sutton; he had agreed, and on arrival at the house the agent had directed him to unload; the defendant had declined to do so, because the weather was stormy and night was approaching, and said he would leave it till the morning; the agent had thereupon urged him to unload at the plaintiff's own risk, promising to support the tail of the wagon while he did so; then, while the butt was being unloaded, the agent

---

[31] *Hatche v. Thorne* (1557) KB 27/1183, m. 193 (trover for clothing; pleads he is a common carrier and the goods were taken from him in the Catharine Wheel in Egham through the negligence of the innkeeper; demurrer).

[32] *Anon.* (1553) Dal. 8, pl. 1 (sim. to last; held that the consignor should sue the innkeeper and not the carrier, (tr.) 'for they are not the carrier's goods, and he is not liable for them inasmuch as he is compellable by law to carry them, and it is not like where someone undertakes goods to carry generally', in which case robbery was no defence).

[33] St German, *Doctor and Student*, ed. Plucknett and Barton, 261, denied that a common carrier could exclude liability for negligence, 'for it were against reason and against good manners' (sp. mod.).

[34] *Jekeler v. Newgate* (1537) KB 27/1103, m. 9 (pleads undertaking to carry fish 'pro posse suo...si iidem pisces per ventus et maris tempestates medio tempore deteriorati non essent').

[35] *Terry v. White* (1528) KB 27/1067, m. 34d. It is not recorded that the action was ever tried.

had carelessly let go of the tail so that the butt had fallen on the ground; and finally, apparently in an attempt to hammer the hoops back into position, the agent had smashed the butt with an axe so that the wine had been spilt. The plea concluded by traversing (with an *absque hoc*) the breaking of the butt by the defendant's negligence; to which the plaintiff replied that it was broken by the defendant's negligence, through the defendant's fault. Now, it would have been more regular for the defendant in such a case to plead the general issue and tell this story to the jury, since the essence of the defence was a denial of negligent conduct rather than a justification. The core of the defence was contributory negligence, but the language of risk transference is revealing. Even if the contract for carriage was in standard form, it was open to the defendant to show that the consignor had accepted the risk of a particular mode of performance.[36] Although it is inappropriate to read too much law into such an unusual case, especially since there is no indication that it ever came before the judges, the pleadings do at least show the level of sophistication of the questions which might normally be left to juries.

The common defences in an action on the case against an alleged innkeeper were that the goods were not taken from the inn at all,[37] or that the defendant returned them to the plaintiff or at his order,[38] or that the defendant was not a common innkeeper.[39] Where goods were indisputably taken from an inn, the best line of defence was to show that the risk had not been assumed by the innkeeper. This was usually a matter of showing that the plaintiff had been given the key to his own room,[40] but it could also be achieved by showing that the plaintiff had

---

[36] Similarly, the carrier might plead that he had delivered to a third party as directed by the consignor: *Soham v. Symson* (1520) CP 40/1028, m. 309 (exigent; pr. in Herne, *Pleader*, 226); CP 40/1030, m. 504 (plea).

[37] e.g. *Bartelet v. Lawe* (1487) KB 27/902, m. 34; *Anon.* (1494) Rast. Ent. 377 (404v); *Mille v. Clerke* (1518) KB 27/1029, m. 40d; *Brigg v. Chapman* (1524) CP 40/1043, m. 567. The common formula 'Not taken from the inn in default of the defendant' was objectionable as a negative pregnant (i.e. ambiguous): 94 Selden Soc. 228. But it remained in use: *White's Case* (1558) Dyer 158b.

[38] *Monys v. Brisworth* (1493) KB 27/933, m. 85; *Cape v. Elmam* (1499) KB 27/952, m. 38d; Rast. Ent. 376v (404v); *Armestrong v. Hemmes* (1555) KB 27/1174, m. 79 (pleads plaintiff received the goods from him and for a sum agreed promised to discharge him from further keeping; demurrer). Cf. *Gebons v. Dyngley* (1514) CP 40/1008, m. 605 (pleads the goods were taken by the plaintiff's household servant living with him; demurrer).

[39] *Barker v. Burward* (1522) CP 40/1036, m. 31), Rast. Ent. 377v (405); Stubbe's entries, fo. 43v; *Parker v. Fullour* (1540) CP 40/1106, m. 407; *Gryce v. Pounde* (1550) CP 40/1145, m. 811; St German, *Doctor and Student*, ed. Plucknett and Barton, 269. In 1557 it was suggested that the test was not whether the defendant was accustomed to lodge guests but whether he had a sign at his door: *Anon.* (1557) BL MS. Hargrave 4, fo. 124v.

[40] e.g. *Kyrkeham v. Jenkyns* (1502) CP 40/959, m. 158 (pleads that goods were taken by plaintiff's own servant); *Robyns v. Dyngley* (1505) CP 40/974, m. 353 (pleads they were taken by a labourer to whom plaintiff's servant gave the key); *Hardy v. Morrys* (1552) KB 27/1162, m. 149. In the three cases where the defendant denied being a common innkeeper (last note), he also pleaded that the plaintiff had his own key. For earlier authorities, see 94 Selden Soc. 228 n. 9; B. & M. 554.

himself agreed to the method of storage which had proved defective.[41] In the 1550s the judges approved a defence that when the inn was full the innkeeper had admitted the plaintiff at his own risk to share a room with others,[42] and in another case that the plaintiff had asked for a stable for his horses, saying he would take upon himself the charge (*caperet super se onus custodiae*), and had taken the key to the stable door leaving his servant in the stable.[43] It seems, therefore, that in the absence of such a special agreement for the guest to deposit goods at his own risk, the risk of loss would have fallen on the innkeeper.

CONTROL OF HAZARDOUS FORCES

Liability for negligence was not confined to those who misperformed undertakings and bailments, but extended to those who failed to keep fire, animals, or water under proper control with the result that the person or property of another was injured. In the case of fire and animals, use was still made of special forms of action of much earlier origin, but gaps could be filled by new actions on the case.

Little is known about the standard of liability imposed by the custom of the realm in respect of fires which went out of control, because the standard plea was either the ambiguous 'Not burned for want of due custody of the fire'[44] or the general issue Not guilty.[45] There is, however, a precedent of the former plea with the inducement that the fire happened by misfortune and act of God (*ex infortunia et actu Dei*), which suggests that liability may not have been strict.[46] If a fire started by accident, so that the action on the custom of the realm was unavailable, it was possible to bring an action on the case for negligence; and this was useful to lessors who for some reason could not bring waste.[47] A special action could also be brought for an outdoor fire.[48] A less clear extension is found in a precedent of 1507,

---

[41] e.g. *Yong* v. *Rutlond* (1528) CP 40/1058A, m. 360 (plaintiff told defendant's ostler to put horse in the pasture whence it was stolen); *Hamond* v. *Hampsted* (1539) CP 40/1102, m. 543 (plaintiff declined offer to put case in locked room and assumed the risk). Cf. *Scudburne* v. *Deye* (1557) CP 40/1170, m. 1169 (horse stolen from pasture, not from inn).

[42] *Dey* v. *Ungor* (1551) KB 27/1157, m. 67; *White's Case* (1558) Dyer 158b

[43] *Hatcher* v. *Shakelforth* (1555) CP 40/1164, m. 817 (judgment for plaintiff after verdict by default).

[44] e.g. *Walker* v. *Coke* (1508) CP 40/985, m. 124d; *Prior of Norwich* v. *Drake* (1514) KB 27/1013, m. 7d; *Wyberd* v. *Heydon* (1515) KB 27/1016, m. 64; *Gravener* v. *Squyer* (1522) CP 40/1037, m. 452d (below); *Cokland* v. *Storre* (1541) CP 40/1108, m. 330.

[45] *Gore* v. *Fyle* (1528) KB 27/1066, m. 6; *Shaxton* v. *Spany* (1531) KB 27/1079, m. 14; *Bak* v. *Smyth* (1539) CP 40/1102, m. 544; *Esclyn* v. *Rychardson* (1540) KB 27/1117, m. 17d.

[46] *Pryst* v. *Belche* (1510) KB 27/994, m. 47.

[47] *Critoft* v. *Emson* (1506) CP 40/978, m. 320 (B. & M. 566 n. 13); *Anon.* (1519) Yorke 239, no. 411 (particular tenant may sue neighbour); *Gravener* v. *Squyer* (1522) CP 40/1037, m. 452d (defendant shows in evidence a lease for 40 years and possession; plaintiff demurs because he is tenant by curtesy and cannot bring waste); *Castell* v. *Browne* (1541) CP 40/1109, m. 121 (plaintiff declares on seisin of house according to custom of manor though someone else lived there). See also Fitz. Abr., *Action sur le Case*, pl. 43.   [48] *Kytt* v. *Dovell* (1522) CP 40/1037, m. 158d.

when case was brought in respect of a shooting accident; the declaration stated that the defendant had presumed to shoot with a hand-gun, and that for want of proper control of the gun a spark had flown out and burned the left eye of the plaintiff's apprentice, so that he had to abandon his apprenticeship; but another reason for framing the action in case was that it was brought by the master (for loss of services) rather than the injured apprentice.[49]

The usual action for damage done by animals was the species of trespass for knowingly retaining an animal with mischievous propensities, though at least one attorney made the understandable mistake of supposing this to be founded on another custom of the realm.[50] It was no longer certain whether the plaintiff in such an action should allege force and arms; but most plaintiffs did, unperturbed by the notion of keeping something with force.[51] Although nearly all the precedents are of dogs worrying sheep, there was no zoological limitation in respect of the biters or the bitten;[52] we find examples of dogs accustomed to biting men,[53] a boar accustomed to biting horses,[54] a tame doe accustomed to butting cows with its horns,[55] and even pigs given to knocking over beehives.[56] The *scienter* action did not expressly mention negligence, though the requirement of knowledge— held by all the justices of the Common Pleas in 1537 to be essential[57]—shows that it was not absolutely strict. Moreover, it was arguable that the owner was not liable if the animal was encouraged into mischief by a third person, such as a servant acting without authority.[58] Cattle trespass was a different legal category, since everyone knows that cattle are accustomed to munch grass; there was no need to prove knowledge of such a natural propensity, and it is likely that the owner was held liable even in the absence of fault.[59]

[49] *Clerk* v. *Terrell* (1507) KB 27/985, m. 42d.

[50] *Orenge* v. *Haywarde* (1535) CP 40/1086, m. 325 (custom of the realm to keep animals from doing harm to neighbours, and *scienter retinuit* dog accustomed to biting sheep; general issue).

[51] For exceptions, see 94 Selden Soc. 228 n. 11. Earlier declarations omit the *vi et armis* clause, and it has been suggested that confusion later arose with the action for sheep-chasing: G. L. Williams, *Liability for Animals* (1939), 280-1.

[52] It seems there never had been: Williams, *Liability for Animals*, 278-9.

[53] *Cooke* v. *Barnwell* (1496) KB 27/941, m. 13; *Gardyner* v. *Carter* (1520) KB 27/1035, m. 2 (dog accustomed to biting people walking in the street).

[54] *Baker* v. *Smyth* (1508) KB 27/989, m. 93. Cf. *Oxenbrygge* v. *Wyllerd* (1485) KB 27/896, m. 14 (dogs accustomed to biting horses). [55] *Michell* v. *Bennett* (1551) CP 40/1148, m. 609.

[56] *Lathe* v. *Mony* (1498) KB 27/946, m. 55d.

[57] *Anon.* (1537) Dyer 25b, §162; 121 Selden Soc. 438, no. 19.

[58] Hil. 13 Hen. VII, fo. 15, pl. 10 (query by reporter).

[59] See *Anon.* (1480) Mich. 20 Edw. IV, fo. 10, pl. 10, *per* Bryan CJ (owner liable even if cattle driven on to land by a third party's dogs); *Anon.* (1481) B. & M. 315, *per* Catesby J.; *Anon.* (1486) 1 Caryll 2, pl. 2 (owner liable even if cattle strayed because third party neglected to mend fence); *Anon.* (1496) ibid. 303, pl. 209; Hil. 13 Hen. VII, fo. 15, pl. 10 (owner liable for cattle which broke close of their own wrong, against his will and without his knowledge, but not if they are put in by a wife or servant acting without his knowledge).

Liability for harm caused by the negligent control of water was imposed by an action on the case, and although legal historians are wont to categorize such actions as 'nuisance', because of the damage to real property, the declarations clearly rested on negligence. In these cases it was apparently necessary to allege a duty to control the water, though the source of the duty of care is not always clear.[60] There are no indications of the standard of care.

If we may count gravity as a hazardous force, here was another area where liability was imposed for negligence in the absence of an undertaking or custom of the realm. Actions on the case were brought for such hazards as creating a dangerous structure which fell on someone,[61] or making a dangerous cavity into which someone fell.[62] Since it seems not to have occurred to anyone to impose liability on occupiers of private premises towards visitors encountering such hazards, the cases all concern highways. Examples are few and far between, and again nothing is known of the standard of liability.

ACCIDENTS BETWEEN STRANGERS

If damage was caused to a stranger[63] by an accident arising directly from some activity in which the defendant was engaged at the time, the proper remedy was not an action on the case but an action for trespass *vi et armis*, since the wrong was deemed in such a case to be forcible. But here the historian encounters a major evidential barrier. The general declaration in trespass did not disclose the true facts of the case, and the defendant by pleading Not guilty contributed nothing more. The result is that the records obscure from our view not only the very existence of accident litigation but also the legal principles on which liability was founded. What little we know of either is derived from the rare instances in which pleaders did not know or care to cloak their cases with the requisite obscurity.

---

[60] *Constable* v. *Garton* (1508) KB 27/988, m. 48 (duty of mill-keeper 'by reason of office' to control sluice); *Colles* v. *Tevy* (1514) KB 27/1013, m. 58 (accustomed to clean ditch); *Guybon* v. *Palmer* (1516) CP 40/1013, m. 106 (accustomed to repair sea-dyke to prevent flooding); *Fynamore* v. *Clyfford* (1520) CP 40/1029, m. 161 (duty of mill-keeper 'by reason of office' to control sluice; so negligently controlled it that water flooded plaintiff's land); *Abbot of Stratford* v. *Hubbulthorn* (1529) CP 40/1062, m. 521 (duty to open lock, which defendant controlled, when water rose to a high level).

[61] *Loghton* v. *Calys* (1473) B. & M. 567 (pile of logs collapsing into road); *Frankessh* v. *Bokenham* (1490) 1 Caryll 27; KB 27/915, m. 27 (millstone falling off wall onto road). Cf. B. & M. 571.

[62] Anon. reading on Westminster II, c. 13, in BL MS. Hargrave 87, fo. 375 ('If someone...digs a ditch or pit whereby a man is damaged, he shall have an action on the case and recover damages, though he may not reform it by way of presentment').

[63] i.e. if there was no privity or prior relationship between the parties. If a physical injury was caused to a customer or patient, it was not treated as forcible.

The legacy of the *Case of Thorns* (1466) was that lack of intention afforded no defence in a civil action of trespass,[64] but it was left open how far a defendant could excuse himself in respect of unintentional harm by showing that he had not been at fault. One kind of no-fault defence mentioned in the year books is what was later called inevitable accident, meaning that the defendant could not have avoided the accident by acting in a less dangerous manner.[65] Another is lack of causation, as where the plaintiff was the direct cause of his own misfortune. Despite what was said in the *Case of Thorns*, very few attempts were made to frame special pleas to excuse accidents. Two exceptional cases occurred in the 1530s. In 1531 an action of battery was brought for putting out the plaintiff's eye with an arrow twenty-two years earlier.[66] The defendant pleaded that the accident happened when she was 7 years' old and the plaintiff was 6, 'both being in their childhood and lacking the use of reason', and while they were playing they fired at each other, using little twigs drawn like bows, and the injury was an accident ('ex casu et infortunio'). The plaintiff replied *De injuria*, thereby avoiding any question of law. In the other case, a plea was entered which anticipated the celebrated case of *Weaver* v. *Ward* (1616) by eighty years but probably occasioned no legal debate.[67] A member of Clement's Inn was injured in an archery accident in St Clement's Field,[68] and brought a common action of battery. The defendant pleaded that the field contained archery butts— 'le crosse pryckes'—where the king's lieges were wont to shoot, that he fired an arrow at the target, and that while the arrow was in flight the plaintiff negligently ran across the butts and was struck, against the will of the defendant (*se invito*). The plaintiff replied *De injuria*, and a jury was summoned, though no outcome is recorded. Our injured inn of chancery student was unlikely ever to have heard such a case mooted; yet he was not advised to demur, and we can hardly doubt that the defence was considered good in substance. In 1616 the difficulty arose because the defence amounted to the general issue and should not have been pleaded in the manner of a justification; this would also been the better view in 1534 if the point had come into debate. The general issue insulated the courts in banc from questions of this kind; and it would be three centuries and more before the substantive principles of liability were removed from the province of the jury.

[64] Rede CJ is clearly referring to arguments in that case in *Cuny* v. *Brugwode* (1506) Trin. 21 Hen. VII, fo. 28, pl. 5 (tr. 'where someone shoots at the butts and wounds someone, although it is against his will he shall be called a trespasser against his intention').

[65] See *Harecourt* v. *Spycer* (1521) Trin. 13 Hen. VIII, fo. 16, pl. 1 (119 Selden Soc. 84), per Browne sjt (careless tree-felling). This is hinted at by Choke J. in the *Case of Thorns* (below, n. 67).

[66] *Coke* v. *Rendelsham* (1531) CP 40/1071, m. 313. There was no limitation period.

[67] *Ustwayt* v. *Alyngton* (1534) CP 40/1083, m. 323. Cf. *Weaver* v. *Ward* (1616) B. & M. 331 (demurrer). The *Case of Thorns* is *Hulle* v. *Orynge* (1466) B. & M. 331.

[68] The membership of Clement's Inn is not stated in the record. William Ustwayt was sued for dues by the principal of the inn in 1538: CP 40/1096, m. 662d. (He was still being sued in 1554, when he was reportedly living in Boston, Lincs.: CP 40/1159, m. 773.) John Alyngton may have been a fellow student; he was later of the Middle Temple.

42

Deceit

DECEIT (*deceptio*) seems on the face of things to have played a prominent role in actions on the case in the fifteenth and early sixteenth centuries. At any rate, the word is frequently found in the plea rolls, though—as with 'negligence'—we would be wrong to assume that it carried the same meaning as it does today. The word is found in two contexts. First, it is used as the generic name for certain kinds of action on the case—*placita de deceptione*—which may well have come to be characterized in this way for King's Bench purposes in order to ease any lingering jurisdictional doubts as to whether they were common pleas.[1] Pleas of 'deceit' included *assumpsit*,[2] conversion,[3] and procuring a breach of contract;[4] and since we sometimes find bills of *assumpsit* so entered even when no deceit is specifically alleged in the declaration,[5] we can only suppose that it denoted a broad legal category rather than a precise factual requirement. Second, however, we find that deceit or fraud is frequently pleaded as a constituent factual element in declarations upon the case. The usual phrase is 'craftily scheming to defraud' (*callide machinans defraudare*) the plaintiff, describing whatever the defendant is alleged to have done or failed to do. Sometimes the word 'defraud' gives way to 'harm', 'impoverish', or 'cause loss', and it may be that it was used in the same morally neutral sense as indicating loss caused by misleading words or conduct rather than deliberate falsehood. Admittedly that is not the primary meaning of fraud or deceit, but there is nothing in the contemporary sources to suggest that in the many actions on the case in which the allegation was made—including the majority of *assumpsit* cases—there was any need to prove an intention to deceive.[6] It was evidently expected of the pleader to use some formal exaggeration in

---

[1] See above, 152.

[2] e.g. *Bothe* v. *Kyrkeham* (1512) KB 27/1003, m. 24; *Wawen* v. *Mathewson* (1512) KB 27/1003, m. 67d, *Laverok* v. *Wygan* (1513) KB 27/1008, m. 72d (all 'deceptio super casu'); *Wright* v. *Evyngar* (1514) KB 27/1010, m. 25d ('deceptio in actione super casu', which is the usual form thereafter); below, ch. 49.

[3] e.g. 94 Selden Soc. 232.

[4] *Rector and churchwardens of St Margaret's, Bridge Street* v. *Bodefeld* (1514) KB 27/1012, m. 39.

[5] e.g. *Laverok* v. *Wygan* (1513) KB 27/1008, m. 72d (undertaking to enfeoff); *Wright* v. *Evyngar* (1514) KB 27/1010, m. 25d (undertaking by surety to save harmless); *Igulden* v. *Roberth* (1516) KB 27/1018, m. 35 (undertaking to teach grammar).

[6] Note especially *Pykeryng* v. *Thurgoode* (1532), the test-case on *assumpsit* for money, in which deceit was alleged in pleading but not mentioned at all in argument: below, 857–8.

magnifying the misconduct of a defendant, and occasionally the invective was quite imaginative;[7] but it was not taken seriously, and it cannot have been part of the issue for the jury. This obviously makes it difficult for the historian to distinguish the true cases of deceit in the plea rolls from the cases where words of deceit are no more than formal abuse of the defendant. Nevertheless, there were several species of action in which deceit appears to have been a material part of the plaintiff's case.

A writer of 1535 summarized the species of legal deceit as 'actions upon false returns of sheriffs, upon deceits in bargains, forging of deeds, and breaking of promises'.[8] The last of his four categories is *assumpsit;* but the other three are wrongs necessarily involving falsehood or misleading. The first category, false returns to writs, typified the traditional role of the action of deceit in dealing with fraud in litigation.[9] In practice, actions against sheriffs were usually for failing to return writs at all rather than for false returns;[10] similar actions could be used against attorneys who prejudiced the plaintiff by defaulting,[11] or acting in his name without authority,[12] and against litigants accused of sharp practice.[13] The disadvantage of the action was that it gave only damages, so that a party who wished to stop a suit on the grounds of malpractice by an attorney had to complain in Chancery.[14]

---

[7] e.g. *Cremour* v. *Sygeon* (1521–5) KB 27/1041, m. 33d; below, 857 (*assumpsit;* tr. 'scheming to defraud the plaintiff and not to fulfil his promise, and through his evil and impudent cunning to make him lose his goods and money'); *Boner* v. *Fellowe* (1534) CP 40/1083, m. 121 (slander; 'by pernicious and perfidious wickedness scheming maliciously to harm the plaintiff').

[8] 'Certain considerations why the spiritual jurisdiction would be abrogate', BL Cotton MS. Cleopatra F.II, fo. 250 at fo. 252 (sp. mod.).

[9] The original writ of deceit had no *cum* clause, and was in effect a special form of trespass. The extensions were actions on the case, with *cum* clauses, though Fitzherbert (FNB 95E–100D) placed them all together under the heading 'writ of deceit'. In the plea rolls, actions on the case are sometimes entered as 'deceit on the case': above, 769 n. 2.

[10] Examples of actions against sheriffs are *Lynde* v. *Corbett* (1538) CP 40/1096, m. 328 (*nihil dicit*); *Frigge* v. *Seyntlowe* (1538) CP 40/1098, m. 513 (imparlance); *Alleyn* v. *Basset* (1541) CP 40/1109, m. 605 (count only). These are actions on the case *qui tam.* See also above, 333.

[11] e.g. *Ap Rice* v. *Alden* (1555) CP 40/1164, m. 1111 (*Non est informatus*).

[12] e.g. FNB 96D; *Lord Broke* v. *Lord Latimer* (1497) Mich. 12 Hen. VII, fo. 9, pl. 5, *per* Boteler sjt; *Palmer* v. *Asketyll* (1524) CP 40/1044, m. 179; *Constable* v. *Frobusher* (1532) CP 40/1075, m. 552; (No. 2) (1534) KB 27/1092, m. 70; *Newton* v. *Belowe* (1535) CP 40/1087, m. 608d; *Hewton* v. *Forster* (1536) KB 27/1099, m. 76; *Lake* v. *Keymsey* (1539) CP 40/1100, m. 671.

[13] e.g. *Page* v. *Borowe* (1510) KB 27/995, m. 40d (bringing action in names of third parties without their notice); *Burele* v. *Lomelyn*, ibid., m. 67 (falsely claiming Exchequer privilege in London); *Huse* v. *Reyman* (1512) KB 27/998, m. 78 (deceit in procuring an Exchequer writ; plaintiff recovers £286. 13s. 4d.); *Sydnore* v. *Cosyn* (1520) CP 40/1029, m. 452 (fraudulently suing *quare impedit*); Cf. *Gylys* v. *Laurence* (1540) CP 40/1104, m. 421 (suing second writ of debt after agreement to settle; but this is framed with an *assumpsit* to withdraw the suit).

[14] e.g. *Hargyll* v. *Bosgrove* (*c*.1535) C1/824/29 (attorney accused of entering general issue when he should have pleaded a justification); *Longdon* v. *Payne* (temp. Audley) C1/844/12 (sim.). In these cases an injunction was sought against the opposing litigant.

In its wider form it could sometimes be used to falsify a common recovery,[15] though not merely on the basis of the common fiction.

The action for forgery of deeds may have developed by analogy with that for forging records, and by the sixteenth century the action on the case was as common as the action founded on the statute of Henry V.[16] Most of the actions were brought for bringing lawsuits upon forged documents, which made them in effect an extension of the first category. But the action on the case was not so limited. It could be brought in respect of documents other than deeds,[17] for forging an acquittance to destroy the effect of a genuine deed,[18] and for fraudulently annulling a genuine deed by cancellation or removal of the seal.[19]

'Deceit in bargains' comprised actions brought for selling—or more rarely hiring[20] or exchanging[21]—defective goods, either knowing them to be defective or having warranted them sound or otherwise misdescribed them. The commonest complaints were of unhealthy animals or unmerchantable goods, but there was apparently no restriction on the categories of misrepresentation, and we find actions for breach of warranty as to quantity,[22] value,[23] or title.[24] Very occasionally an analogous action might be brought on a sale of land.[25] Although Fitzherbert wrote that a warranty was essential,[26] it seems to have been more generally

---

[15] See above, 660. Likewise to falsify a recovery in ancient demesne, in which case it seems sometimes to have been collusive: *Bishop of Exeter* v. *Roo sjt* (1511) CP 40/997, m. 514 (confessed); *Queen Katharine* v. *Broke sjt* (1514) CP 40/1008, m. 733 (sim.).

[16] For examples see 94 Selden Soc. 231 n. 2. It is also found in the Common Pleas: e.g. *Cheyny* v. *Cheyny* (1507) CP 40/980, mm. 459, 535 (forging a deed); next note.

[17] e.g. *Neweton* v. *Clerke* (1504) CP 40/968, m. 470 (forging will); *Cromer* v. *Barnyng* (1510) KB 27/997, m. 62d (damages recovered against deputy customer who made a false cocket for malt shipped by the plaintiff).

[18] *Crispe* v. *Hacheman* (1526) CP 40/1051, m. 145 (judgment for plaintiff).

[19] e.g. *Cotton* v. *Buk* (1505) KB 27/974, m. 53d; *Buk* v. *Smyth* (1513) KB 27/1006, m. 75; *Turner* v. *Hall* (1528) KB 27/1067, m. 53. Cf. *Prior of Aldgate* v. *Milles* (1508) KB 27/989, m. 107 (cutting out writing on genuine deed and writing out a bond on the remaining piece of sealed parchment).

[20] The typical case is the hiring of a horse: e.g. *Watson* v. *Clere* (1499) KB 27/952, m. 63; *Grave* v. *Perysson* (1500) KB 27/954, m. 45d; *Coke* v. *Wakefeld* (1502) KB 27/963, m. 2d.

[21] Note *Suthworth* v. *Harper* (c.1502), entry copied in CUL MS. Add. 9430(3), p. 151 (warranting a ryal to be gold, when it was exchanged for 10s. in silver, it being only copper gilt).

[22] e.g. as to the length of cloth: *Crosse* v. *Pakman* (1505) KB 27/974, m. 74 (quality and length); *Seynpere* v. *Humfrey* (1519) KB 27/1033, m. 87 (quality and length); *Warden* v. *Howe* (1536) KB 27/1101, m. 28 (warranty coupled with *assumpsit*; advisement after verdict for plaintiff).

[23] *Bangyll* v. *Halle* (1483) KB 27/889, m. 13d (cloth warranted as valuable as the sample put forward 'de monstro'); *Holgyll* v. *Bernard* (1536) KB 27/1098, m. 36 (false assertion as to value of land sold).

[24] *Rorey* v. *Souter* (1491) KB 27/921, m. 91d (sale of horse knowing it to belong to a third party); *Starre* v. *Streche* (1540) KB 27/1116, m. 60 (warranty of title to horse, coupled with *assumpsit*).

[25] e.g. *Broun* v. *Goche* (1529) CP 40/1061, m. 635 (lessee falsely asserted power to sub-let; judgment for plaintiff); *Grene* v. *Howse* (1535) CP 40/1087, m. 298d (warranty on sale of messuage); *Holgyll* v. *Bernard* (1536) KB 27/1098, m. 36 (vendor of land asserted—'asserebat, dicebat et spondebat'—that it was worth a sum which was twice its true value). [26] FNB 94C (tr. B. & M. 344).

accepted that knowledge of the defect was a sufficient alternative,[27] and precedents may be found in the rolls of actions founded on knowledge without laying a warranty.[28] In form, the essence of these wrongs was not contractual in the sense that the plaintiff was complaining of a breach of promise. There was no question of either enforcing or rescinding the contract of sale,[29] unless perhaps the deceit was gross,[30] but rather the plaintiff complained of being tricked into a contract which he would not have made if he had been better informed. Hence it was permissible not only to take issue on the sale,[31] but also—and this was more common—on the making of the warranty,[32] or the deceit,[33] or the falseness of the representation.[34] It may also have been regarded as a defence that the buyer had inspected, or had had an opportunity of inspecting, the goods before the sale was concluded.[35] Representations are statements of fact, not promises; but they cause harm in a similar way, by inducing reliance, and early-modern lawyers were as capable as present-day lawyers of confusing misprepresentation with breach of promise.[36] Indeed, the confusion between warranties and promissory undertakings may have been influential in the development of *assumpsit*.[37] It also explains some oddities. For instance, in a case of 1502, the plaintiff counted on a bargain and

[27] Note (1506) 2 Caryll 552, per Frowyk CJ; James Hales's reading (Gray's Inn, 1532), fo. 38.

[28] e.g. *Snowe* v. *Fouler* (1504) KB 27/970 m. 11 (sale of boar knowing it to be leprous and unfit to eat); *Pynson* v. *Toly* (1514) CP 40/1006, m. 87d (sale of paper to a printer, knowing it to be torn and affected by damp and unsuitable for writing or printing); *Frank* v. *Quassh* (1535) CP 40/1085(1), m. 324 (sale of a cade of white herring, knowing them to be rotten, which plaintiff resold as merchantable and thereby lost credit; defendant traverses knowledge).

[29] The deceived buyer could still be sued in debt for the price: *Anon.* (1494) Hil. 9 Hen. VII, fo. 21, pl. 21, per Huse CJ.

[30] See *Audeley* v. *Sherwood* (c.1540) C1/937/36 (debt in Sheriffs' Court, London, for price of goshawk which died after two weeks; buyer says seller knew it to be sick and rotten and pulled out all the feathers and replaced them from another hawk, warranting it to be sound).

[31] e.g. *Kyrkby* v. *Dowde* (1507) KB 27/983, m. 29d; *Waller* v. *Aunger* (1520) KB 27/1036, m. 72d. Cf. *Seynpere* v. *Humfrey* (1519) KB 27/1033, m. 87 (protesting that he did not warrant the goods, pleads he did not bargain or sell them warranting their quality).

[32] e.g. *Crompton* v. *Clyffe* (1520) KB 27/1035, m. 19d (warranty on sale of sheep); *Kekewyche* v. *Broke* (1532) CP 40/1072, m. 137 (warranty on sale of horse); *Grene* v. *Howse* (1535) CP 40/1087, m. 298d (warranty on sale of messuage); *Vere* v. *Dorant* (1537) CP 40/1095, m 605 (warranty on sale of lambs).

[33] Cf. *Woode* v. *Rutter* (1538) CP 40/1096, m. 412 (sale of sick horse; pleads he sold it knowing it to be without infirmity, *absque hoc* he sold it as the plaintifff supposed; undetermined demurrer).

[34] e.g. *Fresby* v. *Fereby* (1512) CP 40/999, m. 117 (issue on merchantability of salmon); *Predyaux* v. *Tute* (1521) CP 40/1032A, m. 121 (deceit on sale of 16 pipes of beer warranted drinkable; issue on sufficiency of beer, *absque hoc* he delivered the said pipes, suggesting a confusion with contract); *Osborne* v. *Postyll* (1535) CP 40/1087, m. 320 (issue whether worsted was well woven).

[35] See *Grete* v. *Lane* (1495) KB 27/934 m. 30 (error from Bristol; deceit on sale of unmerchantable cork; pleads that warranty void because quality apparent by inspection); *Monyton* v. *Wylson* (1517) KB 27/1024, m. 23d (deceit on sale of cloth knowing it to contain flocks and to be of a different length; pleads plaintiff inspected it, and traverses warranty).

[36] For a hybrid action see *Andrew* v. *Boughey* (1552) Dyer 75a; KB 27/1160, m. 114.

[37] Kiralfy, *Action on the Case*, 90–1; Milsom, *HFCL*, 320–2.

an undertaking to fur a gown with backs of foin (beech-marten), and alleged that
the defendant had fraudulently furred the gown with bellies of foin; the defendant
pleaded that he had used fur which he had previously sold to the plaintiff, and traversed the undertaking 'in the manner and form' alleged; the plaintiff persuaded
the jury and recovered damages.[38] If the defendant's version had any colour of
truth in it, one might have expected the plaintiff to bring deceit on the sale of the
fur rather than on the contract for services; instead we have an unusual hybrid
action in which *assumpsit* and deceit on a bargain play equal parts. There are other
cases arising from sales in which warranties and promises are mixed up,[39] including for a time the form *warrantizando assumpsisset*.[40] In one such case the false
assertion which induced the purchaser to buy land was made by a party from
whom the vendor claimed to trace title, showing that the cause of action was not
contractual.[41]

Though most recorded cases fall within the four categories noted in 1535, the
analysis was not quite exhaustive. An action on the case for fraud would lie in
respect of any kind of cheating, such as the use of false dice in playing for
money,[42] or telling lies.[43] There was as yet no theoretical problem about providing
a remedy for damage caused by reliance on incorrect advice, and whether it was
fraudulent or negligent seems not yet to be a material distinction. Two inconclusive actions have been found for giving misleading character references, on which
the plaintiffs relied; but the gist of each complaint seems to have been negligence
rather than fraud.[44]

---

[38] *Frowyk v. Hurst* (1502) KB 27/965, m. 99.

[39] e.g. *Taylour v. Trevice* (1511) KB 27/999, m. 5 (sale of sweet wine with assertion of expertise; lays
undertaking in *cum* clause, and warranty in *tamen* clause); *Flight v. Harryson* (1533) CP 40/1079, m. 339
(sale of white herring with undertaking that they were merchantable; sold them knowing them to be
putrid; judgment for plaintiff). Cf. *Warden v. Howe* (1536) KB 27/1101, m. 28 (pleads *Non promisit, war-
rantizavit, nec assumpsit*).

[40] e.g. *Symondys v. Osberne* (1499) KB 27/951, m. 56d; *Rote v. Myller* (1507) KB 27/985, m. 85d; *Cokyn v.
Hopton* (1508) KB 27/986, m. 19d; *Willoughby v. Wigmore* (1522) KB 27/1043, m. 72d.

[41] *Wode v. Boveton* (1504) CP 40/970, m. 411 (deceit in undertaking that a lady could make a good
estate when land was mortgaged).

[42] FNB 95D (tr. B. & M. 344); *Povy's Case* (1505/15) C1/348/39 (action of deceit in the Sheriffs' Court,
London, for winning £10 with false dice); *Popham v. Rysley* (1535) C1/880/97 (action on the case in the
Sheriffs' Court, London, for enticing apprentice to gamble and using false dice). Cf. *Moots*, 215 (no
action for losing money at dice, but there is no reference here to deceit); C1/844/1 (almost illegible bill
in Chancery, temp. Audley C., apparently stating that there is no remedy at law for losing money
because of false dice).

[43] *Heron v. Parr* (1537) CP 40/1094, m. 439 (testator falsely persuaded by defendant that she was an
intended legatee); *Strode v. Somaster* (1549) CP 40/1139, m. 419 (pledging someone else's property as
security for loan).

[44] *Baker v. Bekett* (1531) KB 27/1079 m. 26 (referee persuaded plaintiff to employ woman as silk
thrower and promised to supervise her, but so negligently did so that silk destroyed; framed with an
assumpsit); *Maria v. Cranwell* (1556) KB 27/1178, m. 171 (plaintiff lost jewels as a result of lending key to
a stranger, relying on defendant's reference; defendant pleads Not guilty).

43

Nuisance

THE medieval concept of nuisance was so closely associated with the law of real property that it was regarded as analogous to disseisin and remedied by the assize. By 1500, however, the assize had given way for most practical purposes to the action on the case, which was both procedurally more attractive to plaintiffs and wider in scope. The takeover was not effected without conceptual difficulty. According to the year books, the fifteenth-century courts adhered to the theory that case would not lie where the assize was appropriate, and so lawyers had to set about finding and if possible enlarging lacunae in the assize.[1] The principal gaps were that the assize could not be brought by lessees for years, or between tenants in common; that it lay only between adjacent freeholders; that it did not lie for nuisances caused by nonfeasance; and that it did not lie for restricting, as opposed to completely barring, an easement such as a way or watercourse.[2] Case had been available to fill these gaps since the beginning of the fifteenth century, on the basis that a disturbance in these categories amounted to a 'personal trespass', and such actions were still common in the early Tudor period.[3] There are also, in the King's Bench rolls,[4] a good number of actions for the kinds of nuisance which were covered by the assize, such as blocking a way, diverting water, blocking a sewer or gutter, tampering with watercourses so as to cause flooding, or interfering with franchises. Here pleaders usually tried to add details in the declaration to show that the action was brought for something beyond what was remedied by the

---

[1] 94 Selden Soc. 233. For the rule against duplication of remedies see below, 840.

[2] See *Anon.* (1522) Pas. 14 Hen. VIII, fo. 31, pl. 8*bis* (119 Selden Soc. 193; B. & M. 587) (case lies for reducing a flow of water).

[3] 94 Selden Soc. 233 nn. 7–9; and 234 nn. 5–6. Examples of case for restriction of an easement are *Valans* v. *Towte* (1529) CP 40/1062, m. 415 (issue); *Adams* v. *Mountford* (No. 1) (1534) CP 40/1081, m. 435 (judgment for plaintiff); (No. 2) (1536) CP 40/1088, m. 58d (imparlance); *Dodge* v. *Myllor* (1556) CP 40/1166, m. 426 (issue).

[4] And, less commonly, in the Common Pleas: e.g. *Kayleway* v. *Baret* (1489) CP 40/909, m. 124 (diverting a watercourse); *Countess of Richmond* v. *Newhowe* (1503) CP 40/962, m. 343d (erecting a sheepfold); *Bokenham* v. *Cok* (1512) CP 40/999, m. 507 (sim.; judgment for plaintiff); *Wythe* v. *Busshop* (1515) CP 40/1010, m. 511 (diverting water; cf. King's Bench action in next note); *Willoughby* v. *Pomerey* (1515) CP 40/1011, m. 316 (obstructing a way); *Hevenyngham* v. *Odyerne* (1518) CP 40/1022, m. 627 (not allowing plaintiff to use way); *Newdegate* v. *Prior of St John's* (1520) CP 40/1028, m. 540 (interference with view of frankpledge); *Horshyll* v. *Ball* (1521) CP 40/1033, m. 748 (blocking prescriptive 'easement' of footway with a house); next note.

assize, by stressing the personal injury as opposed to the proprietary aspect of the matter. Disputes about the diversion of water were usually initiated by mill-owners—frequently religious houses—and they could claim loss of profit.[5] Blocking, damaging, or removing sewers and gutters could result in danger to health and make a house uninhabitable,[6] or could cause physical damage to the fabric.[7] Contaminating water, so as to make it undrinkable or unusable, was probably a purely personal cause of action for which the assize would not lie at all.[8] In the case of obstructing a right of way, the plaintiff would allege that he was unable to convey victuals, animals, and other necessaries to his tenement.[9] It was also usual to omit from the declaration any reference to the estates owned by the parties, so that it did not appear whether an assize lay or not. This may explain the dearth of objections to actions on the case brought for other forms of nuisance, such as diverting water or blocking rights of way, which are commonly found in the rolls.

[5] For actions by mill-owners see *Lord de Grey's Case* (1505) Mich. 21 Hen. VII, fo. 30, pl. 5 (tr. B. & M. 586); the cases noted in B. & M. 586–7; and *Blanderhasset* v. *Austyn* (1485) KB 27/896, m. 43 (with *vi et armis*); *Abbot of Pershore* v. *Barbour* (1490) KB 27/916, m. 12d; *Brewes* v. *Bateman* (1497) KB 27/942, m. 49d (issue); *Mayor of Exeter* v. *Larder* (1509) KB 27/991, m. 13 (imparlance); *Broke* v. *Budde* (1514) KB 27/1010, m. 40 (issue); *Wyth* v. *Bysshopp* (1514) KB 27/1013, m. 101 (issue); *Assheburnham* v. *Frende* (1515) KB 27/1017, m. 59d; *Prior of Chicksands* v. *Lorymer* (1517) KB 27/1022, m. 31d (imparlance); *Abbot of Buckfast* v. *Colrigge* (1522) CP 40/1034, m. 105 (imparlance); *Gardyner* v. *Saunders* (1522–3) CP 40/1039, m. 335 (issue); *Abbot of Stratford* v. *Hubbulthorn* (1529) CP 40/1062, m. 521 (imparlance); *Baker* v. *Lowe* (1535) CP 40/1086, m. 157 (issue).

[6] *Harpole* v. *Darnell* (1512) KB 27/1005, m. 85 (family made ill by dyer's refuse thrown in gutter); *Master of St Bartholomew's Hospital* v. *Pynnour* (1514) KB 27/1013, m. 60 (sewage in blocked gutter so that no one could stay in hospital without endangering life); *Broune* v. *Franceys* (1521) CP 40/1031, m. 108 (obstruction of privy next to inn so that fetid odours prevented family and guests from sleeping there); *Dean and Chapter of Exeter* v. *Hamlyn*, ibid., m. 134 ('fetores et fetida' from latrines affecting basement); *Stone* v. *West* (1534) CP 40/1083, m. 455 (piles of filth and dung near inn); *Sowthall* v. *Bagger* (1535) CP 40/1084, m. 580d (butcher's carrion); *Fitzjames* v. *Marler* (1535) CP 40/1087, m. 172d (smoke and filth from lime-kiln); Shakelady's precedents of writs, BL MS. Harley 1856, fo. 147 (dungheap near bedroom windows of inn).

[7] e.g. *Roberth* v. *Lynche* (1505) KB 27/976, m. 93 (privy erected on plaintiff's soil whereby filth and urine were projected *vi et armis* on to his land; defendant pleads freehold and justifies building a privy for necessary use); *Grendyll* v. *Pepyr* (1504) KB 27/972, m. 81 (overflow from gutter rotting timber below); *Anon.* (1508) 2 Caryll 579; Spelman 8, pl. 10 (rain descending on lower tenement through non-repair above); *Bedys* v. *Spendlove* (1522) KB 27/1044, m. 70d (sim.); *Polsted* v. *Norbryge* (1523) CP 40/1040, m. 60 (sim.); *Trefrye* v. *Burlace* (1557) KB 27/1184, m. 137 (removal of lead gutter between houses caused rain to damage walls).

[8] *Prior of Christ Church, Canterbury* v. *Hore* (1493) CP 40/922, m. 244d; Trin. 13 Hen. VII, fo. 26, pl. 4; 1 Caryll 175 (water contaminated with lime); *Busshop* v. *Scodham* (1496) KB 27/939, m. 1 (drinking water polluted by fishmonger washing salt-fish); *Stede* v. *Tele* (1510) KB 27/997, m. 53d (drinking water polluted by tanner); *Harpole* v. *Darnell* (1512) KB 27/1005, m. 85 (drinking water polluted by dyer). As for killing fish see *Cluny* v. *Horner* (1512) CP 40/998, m. 544 (with 'sordida et fetida'); *Busshell* v. *Rychardson* (1543) CP 40/1117, m. 339 (with quicklime).

[9] Cf. *Hayes* v. *Quedampton* (1485) KB 27/896, m. 54, where it is alleged merely that the way could not be passed.

The word 'nuisance'—like the even vaguer 'trespass'—is rarely found in plead-ings in actions on the case,[10] and it may be regarded as a generic term for those wrongs which hurt someone by way of annoyance or unneighbourly conduct. The interest which a nuisance infringed might be described in declarations by such terms as profit (*proficuum*), easement (*aisiamentum*), or advantage (*commodum, commoditas*), but the first two words did not yet possess the technical senses attributed to them later.[11] They were used in contract cases as well, and they were often omitted in nuisance cases. It is difficult, in fact, to find any coherent theory of nuisance liability in the early Tudor period. The action on the case undoubt-edly provided protection against a wider range of annoyances than the assize, since it was not necessary to show damage to the freehold. Thus, as was stated by Vavasour J. at an Inner Temple reading in 1494, it would lie against a neighbour who set up a dunghill too near the plaintiff's land, or against a smith who set up a forge which disturbed the plaintiff; smell and noise did not harm the freehold, but they could certainly damage the person of the plaintiff.[12] Indeed, it was because there was no injury to the freehold that case lay rather than the assize. When, in about 1500, a tenant at will sought relief in Chancery for a 'great nuis-ance' in stopping the light to his hall, placing a 'sege' with 'evill eire' near his hall, and blocking a gutter, the defendant demurred on the ground that such matters were determinable at common law—presumably by an action on the case.[13] The entitlement to freedom from such annoyance seems to have been regarded as incident to house-ownership in general, rather than a matter of prescription; and one could arguably acquire a right to a flow of light to a house merely by building first.[14] We see a concept resembling the easement of support in an action

[10] The phrase 'ad nocumentum' occurs in *Broune* v. *Franceys* (1521) CP 40/1031, m. 108.

[11] Note e.g. *Dean and Chapter of Exeter* v. *Hamlyn* (1521) CP 40/1031, m. 134 (obstructing plaintiff's lights with a new building, and erecting latrines, so that plaintiff lost the 'proficuum, commodum, et aisiamentum' of his messuage).

[12] Richard Sutton's reading (Inner Temple, 1494) BL MS. Hargrave 87, fo. 119 (tr. 105 Selden Soc. 291); Port 117, no. 64. According to Richard Littleton (in MS. Hargrave 87), the dunghill case was litigated between two neighbours in Cheapside temp. Edw. IV. See also George Treherne's reading (Lincoln's Inn, 1520) 94 Selden Soc. 235, where excessive heat is added to the list of personal nuisances. Precedents are rare, but an example of an action for noise is *Wriotesley* v. *Cobbe* (1508) KB 37/989, m. 54d (vibrations from horse-mill for grinding spices weakened foundations and shattered windows). For dunghill cases see above, 776 n. 6.

[13] *Pole* v. *Carpenter* (1500/01) C1/244/85. The plaintiff was a tenant at will, and asserted that as such he had no remedy at law, apparently overlooking the action on the case.

[14] John Hales's reading (Gray's Inn, 1514) Bodl. Lib. MS. Rawlinson C.705, fo. 51v; 94 Selden Soc. 235 n. 5 (tr. 'One may by acting first acquire an advantage against one's neighbour; for instance, if I build a house on my land adjoining someone else's land, the other may not build a house so as to stop my light coming from his land, for by building first I have the pre-eminence'); George Treherne's reading (Lincoln's Inn, 1520) BL MS. Stowe 414, fo. 79. Actions for stopping light are unusual. A rare example is *Dean and Chapter of Exeter* v. *Hamlyn* (1521) CP 40/1031, m. 134.

of 1556 for negligently pulling down an adjoining house so that the plaintiff's house collapsed; but the pleader does not yet use the language of easements and the action is essentially for negligent conduct between neighbours.[15]

There does not seem to have been any major disagreement between the two benches over the use of case instead of the assize, although some Common Pleas judges subscribed to the general principle that case should not be used where the assize lay,[16] and so occasional assizes were still brought.[17] We might indeed infer continuing opposition to case between freeholders from a refusal by the Common Pleas to enter judgment in such a case in 1526.[18] However, actions on the case for nuisance are commonly found without demur in the rolls of both benches during the early Tudor period;[19] and, although they become infrequent in the Common Pleas after the middle of Henry VIII's reign, and such writs as are found seem often to have been framed with the double-remedies principle in mind,[20] the use of case by a freeholder was sanctioned by the Common Pleas judges in 1546.[21] The only new substantive question discussed in the reports was whether case would lie for a common or public nuisance, given that such a nuisance affected the public at large and was remediable by indictment.[22] The better opinion was that case would lie, provided that the plaintiff could show some special damage

[15] Burlas v. Treffrye (1556) CP 40/1166, m. 741 (judgment for plaintiff). The defendant pleaded that the situation arose from the plaintiff's fault in not repairing his house and in fixing a gutter on the party wall, but the jury found for the plaintiff. For repair between upper and lower tenements in the same house, see Anon. (1508) 2 Caryll 579.

[16] Orwell v. Mortoft (1505) Mich. 20 Hen. VII, fo. 8, pl. 18, per Kingsmill J. (tr. B. & M. 409); Anon. (1522) Pas. 14 Hen. VIII, fo. 31, pl. 8bis (119 Selden Soc. 193; B. & M. 587). Cf. disagreements over the duplication of remedies, below, 801, 807–8, 840, 871–4.

[17] e.g. Chamberleyn v. Darry (1556) CP 40/1168, m. 1460 (judgment for plaintiff).

[18] Dod v. Nedeham (1525–6) CP 40/1048A, m. 408 (stopping a watercourse; c.a.v. for four terms after verdict for plaintiff at Shrewsbury assizes). Cf. Clerke v. Stratford (1526) CP 40/1051, m. 118 (action between adjoining freeholders for abstracting water from a fishpond by drilling in the highway running between their premises with 'penitrale vocatum an awgur'; issue).

[19] See above, 775, nn. 3–4. No demurrer to such a declaration has been found. Cf. Beaumont v. Benet (1519–25) CP 40/1024, m. 345 (case by freeholder for diverting water from mill; demurrer to prescription pleaded by defendant); issue joined in second action (1524–5) CP 40/1045, m. 546 (advisement after verdict; no judgment). The dispute concerned an alleged right to divert the water—which flowed through a sewer across the defendant's land—if the miller did not pay the defendant half the tolls.

[20] e.g. Basset v. Mannyng (1529–30) CP 40/1060, m. 445 (case by tenant in tail against stranger for diverting water and fish from fish-weir); Mychell v. Burdewood (1557) CP 40/1170, m. 937 (case for reducing flow of water to mill; plaintiff declares as a lessee for years; defendant prescribes to divert water to a meadow; plaintiff demurs).

[21] Anon. (1546) BL MS. Hargrave 4, ff. 97v–98, 121v (duplicated), per Mountagu CJ, Browne and Hynde JJ (case rather than trespass vi et armis lies for diverting a watercourse). Cf. Bevyll v. Carolles (1557) CP 40/1170, m. 957d (case by freeholder for completely stopping a watercourse; general issue).

[22] The law of public nuisance is quite fully summarized in a specimen charge for a leet (1538) BL MS. Add. 48047, fo. 71v. In connection with obstruction, it is there said that a stile is permissible so long as it is not so high that a pregnant woman cannot pass, for 'the law hath respect [for] and highly favoureth

beyond that suffered by the general public.[23] But there is no suggestion in this period that any criminal nuisance was *ipso facto* actionable on proof of special damage; indeed a common nuisance in itself was 'not a trespass to anyone'.[24] The criminal or public nature of the wrong operated only as a bar to an action, not as a foundation.

women with child' (sp. mod.). However, Baldwin CJ once explained at some length why placing a gate across a highway was a nuisance even if it could be manually opened: Wm Yelv. 327, no. 31.

[23] Mich. 27 Hen. VIII, fo. 27, pl. 10, *per* Fitzherbert J.; probably identifiable as *Hikkys* v. *More* (1535) CP 40/1085(2), m. 442 (highway obstructed so that plaintiff could not reach his pasture, though in the year book it says 'close'). Fitzherbert's view was opposed by Baldwin CJ, but is reflected in contemporary practice: e.g. *Jermyn* v. *Grote* (1505) KB 27/976, m. 19d; (No. 2) KB 27/994, m. 81d (common way); *Forde* v. *Stacy* (1511) CP 40/994, m. 344 (common way barred with gate; issue); *Austen* v. *Burgoyn* (1513) KB 27/1008, m. 75 (common pond stopped with rubbish; issue); *Cooke* v. *Brounlowe* (1557) KB 27/1183, m. 186 (lane stopped with hedges and ditches, but prescription for right of way in *que estate*; judgment for plaintiff).

[24] William Saunders's reading (Middle Temple, 1533) Pollard 267, no. 49; and cf. *Anon.* (1526) 120 Selden Soc. 57, no. 43; above, 272.

44

Defamation

AT the beginning of our period, defamation was still almost exclusively within the province of the ecclesiastical courts, where it was the subject of suits for penance but not for damages.[1] According to Fyneux CJ in 1497, it was a 'wholly spiritual offence, which may not be punished elsewhere'.[2] Calling a man a villein, or even a thief or a traitor, was therefore said to be *damnum absque injuria* in the eyes of the common law.[3]

The principal exception to this principle was the action of *scandalum magnatum*, which had become established in the fifteenth century as a statutory form of trespass warranted by earlier legislation forbidding slanderous rumours about 'great men of the realm'.[4] It enabled *magnati* to recover damages for starting or spreading such rumours. The right of action was not limited to peers and bishops, for judges deemed themselves great men,[5] and heads of religious houses were also brought within the equity.[6] Nevertheless, the origin of the remedy prevented it from having any wider application than that. Moreover, there may have been some doubt over the substantive scope of the legislation, which did not on its face contemplate a private remedy in damages. No such doubt was voiced in the first reported case, in 1497.[7] But in 1514 a plaintiff in error argued that a declaration in *scandalum magnatum* was bad if it failed to follow the statute by showing that the defamatory words led to discord between the lords and commons, whereby the realm was endangered.[8] The action was thus seen as a purely statutory creation and was not a step towards a general common-law notion of defamation. Even in

---

[1] See R. H. Helmholz, *Select Cases on Defamation to 1600* (101 Selden Soc.; 1985). There is a brief account of a defamation case argued by doctors of law *c.*1500 in *Narrative of Robert Pylkington*, 49–50.

[2] *Anon.* (1497) Trin. 12 Hen. VII, fo. 22, pl. 2 (tr. B. & M. 624 at 625).

[3] *Huukyns* v. *Drowne* (1477) Trin. 17 Edw. IV, fo. 3, pl. 2 (tr. B. & M. 629 at 632), *per* Nedeham J. and Billyng CJ.

[4] See 94 Selden Soc. 244. Earlier examples are now known. The legislation (of 1285 and 1378) was confirmed by 1 & 2 Phil. & Mar., c. 3.

[5] e.g. *Littleton* v. *Somervyle* (1473) KB 27/849, rot. warr.; *Conyngesby* v. *Sandys* (1510) KB 27/997, m. 111 (noted in 94 Selden Soc. 244 n. 8).

[6] e.g. *Prior of Coventry* v. *Coke* (1511) CP 40/995, m. 121 (extortion); *Abbot of Tavistock* v. *Whytefeld* (1531) CP 40/1069, m. 306d (perjury).   [7] *Lord Beauchamp* v. *Croft* (1497) 1 Caryll 349; below, 797.

[8] *Duke of Buckingham* v. *Lucas* (1512–16) CP 40/1001, m. 659 (recovers £40; Jenour, *Entries*, fo. 304v); KB 27/1010, m. 38 (errors assigned; nonsuit). This was the third suit by the duke against Thomas Lucas,

the first half of the sixteenth century, most recorded actions are found clustered in or just after times of political turmoil, when substantial damages could occasionally be obtained.[9]

Although there is some slight evidence that the Star Chamber had begun to take an interest in libel in the fifteenth century,[10] this again is a circumstance which indicates the lack of a regular remedy rather than the evolution of a common-law action. By 1500 the absence of a general remedy at common law was distinctly awkward. The spiritual courts were under regular attack by prohibition and *praemunire* if they entertained suits relating to accusations of temporal crime,[11] and they were unable to award monetary compensation even in respect of an allegation of spiritual misconduct.[12] Admittedly the attacks did not completely stifle the ecclesiastical jurisdiction; but they must have made suits in the Church courts at best precarious and at worst impracticable.[13] If the common-law position was accepted, it must have seemed absurd that penance could be awarded for an accusation of gluttony but not for an accusation of murder or theft, and that damages were unavailable in either case.[14] The first attempt to move the law forward occurred at the very beginning of Richard III's reign. A draper had brought an action of trespass in the Common Pleas for lying in wait to seize him as a villein so that he did not dare to go about his business; the defendant had justified by pleading villeinage, but in 1476 a jury at Royston assizes before Bryan CJ had

---

S.-G. to Hen. VII: cf. no. 1 (1510) KB 27/996, m. 63 (forgery); no. 2 (1513) CP 40/1004, m. 591 (*scandalum magnatum,* alleging embracery in the 1510 action). Cf. a fourth action, for saying he had a 'great grudge' in bringing case against Lucas: CP 40/1001, m. 653 (imparlance). And note the duke's complaint in Parliament, *HLJ,* i. 15–17.

⁹ e.g. in 1510–13: 94 Selden Soc. 244. Another group is found in 1530–5: *Earl of Northumberland* v. *Gascoigne* (1530) CP 40/1064, m. 341; *Abbot of Tavistock* v. *Whytefeld* (1531) CP 40/1069, m. 306d; *Lord Daubeney* v. *More* (1531) CP 40/1071, m. 323 (accusation of treason by Sir Thomas More of Dorset); *Earl of Cumberland* v. *Crakanthorp* (1532) CP 40/1073, m. 323; *Marquess of Exeter* v. *Coryton* (1533–4) CP 40/1077, m. 504 (verdict for 3,000 marks); *Marquess of Exeter* v. *Coryngton* (1534) KB 27/1091, m. 39 (judgment for £3,000 upon confession); *Viscount Lisle* v. *Debenham* (1535) CP 40/1085(1), m. 338 (as to which see *Lisle Letters,* ed. Byrne, ii. 459, no. 368). And another in 1554–6: *Earl of Derby* v. *Ratclyff* (1554) KB 27/1172, m. 165; *Earl of Westmoreland* v. *Lasselles* (1554) ibid., m. 169; *Lord Willoughby of Parham* v. *Thymbylbye* (1556) KB 27/1177, m. 170.   ¹⁰ 94 Selden Soc. 236.

¹¹ See above, 242; *Registrum Omnium Brevium,* fo. 42 (forgery); *Anon.* (1478) Pas. 18 Edw. IV, fo. 6, pl. 32 (trespass); *Abbot of St Albans' Case* (1482) Trin. 22 Edw. IV, fo. 20, pl. 47 (prohibition for slander); *Note* (1498) 1 Caryll 382 (prohibition lies for slander of a temporal offence); *Buscher* v. *Hegyns* (1499) KB 27/953, m. 76 (hunting offence); *Calle* v. *Stubbys* (1501) KB 27/961, m. 75 (homicide); *Penfold* v. *Facete* (1501) KB 27/961, m. 80d (theft); *Horewode* v. *Raynold* (1504) KB 27/972, m. 28 (theft); later cases in 94 Selden Soc. 67 n. 2.

¹² Nevertheless, the power to award costs in such cases was apparently upheld in *Anon.* (1497) Trin. 12 Hen. VII, fo. 22, pl. 2 (tr. B. & M. 624), *per* Fyneux CJ, Tremayle and Rede JJ.

¹³ For the decline of slander jurisdiction in the Church courts between 1500 and 1535 see Helmholz, *Select Cases on Defamation,* pp. xliv–xlv.

¹⁴ A foreign observer remarked on this around 1500: *Venetian Relation,* 34.

awarded the plaintiff £110 damages. The defendant then brought a writ of error in the King's Bench, alleging that a writ of trespass did not lie on such facts without mentioning 'some other trespass punishable by law', and that damages were not recoverable for loss of business resulting from a subjective fear of bodily harm when no actual threats had been made. The year book unfortunately reports only the initial reaction of the King's Bench when the case was opened in 1477. It seems that Billyng CJ (d. 1481) and Nedeham J. (d. 1480) were in favour of reversing the judgment on the grounds that the gravamen was merely defamation and therefore no tort recognized by law. In 1483, however, the court (now under Huse CJ) formally affirmed the Common Pleas judgment.[15] The precedent was thereafter followed in both benches until about 1512,[16] when case became available, and juries sometimes made substantal awards of damages.[17] In the absence of a report from 1483, however, it cannot be assumed that any broad principle was settled. There was certainly no intention to open up a general remedy for words. Indeed, it was made clear by the Common Pleas in 1501 that the essence of the wrong in such actions was not the spoken defamation but the putting in fear by some overt act.[18] Though described at the time as an action on the case, force and arms were a necessary ingredient in the cause of action.

The great leap forward seems to have been made around 1507, when a trickle of actions on the case for accusing people of theft begins to flow in the rolls of both benches.[19] The first case in which a defendant appeared and pleaded to issue came two years later.[20] No precise contemporary cause for this innovation has been identified, though it was a complete reversal of the previous position. The first actions are all for accusations of theft, and so there is no question of edging forward incrementally from the villeinage cases or *scandalum magnatum*: these were attempts to

[15] *Broune* v. *Haukyns* (1475–83) KB 27/862, m. 30; abr. Rast. Ent. 268v (287); Trin. 15 Edw. IV, fo. 32, pl. 15 (pleading stage); Trin. 17 Edw. IV, fo. 3, pl. 2 (tr. B. & M. 629). Before judgment was given, the defendant also brought an attaint against the jury: Pas. 21 Edw. IV, fo. 23, pl. 7; Pas. 22 Edw. IV, fo. 1, pl. 4.

[16] e.g. *Hunston* v. *Bishop of Ely* (1484) Mich. 2 Ric. III, fo. 13, pl. 35 (described as a special writ on his case, but alleging a lying in wait); KB 27/893, m. 91 (nonsuit); *Trypp* v. *Artur* (1495) KB 27/935, m. 30 (recovers 20s.); *Thomson* v. *Lee* (1498) Hil. 13 Hen. VII, fo. 17, pl. 20; 1 Caryll 369; Port 6; KB 27/949, m. 33 (pr. 102 Selden Soc. 7); above, 604; *Vyncent* v. *Drury* (1501) CP 40/955, m. 301 (19 plaintiffs found free); *Broune* v. *Hastynges* (1507) CP 40/981, m. 301; *Abbot of West Dereham* v. *Orell* (1510) KB 27/995, m. 69 (issue on villeinage); *Adam* v. *Dysshop* (1512) CP 40/1000, m. 177d (op se); *Roo* v. *Abbot of Ramsey*, ibid., m. 338 (issue); next two notes. A stray late example is *Lounde* v. *Kyme* (1525) CP 40/1048A, m. 426d.

[17] e.g. *Baude* v. *Kendale* (1489) KB 27/913, m. 32 (£10 damages); *Fox* v. *Wykam* (1495) CP 40/932, m. 338 (£120 damages); *Blake* v. *Venters* (1500) KB 27/957, m. 24d (£26 damages); *Smyth* v. *Prior of St Neots* (1509) CP 40/989, m. 419 (£340 damages).

[18] *Cartar* v. *Abbot of Malmesbury* (1501) CP 40/957, m. 320d; 2 Caryll 385.

[19] *Owughan* v. *Baker* (1507) CP 40/981, m. 596 (pr. 100 Selden Soc. 42, no. 61); *Sparow* v. *Heygrene* (1508) KB 27/986, m. 55d (pr. ibid., no. 62; tr. B. & M. 632); *Atkyns* v. *Wolaston* (1508) KB 27/988, m. 42d; *Trenouth* v. *Corton* (1508) CP 40/985, m. 64d.

[20] *Glover* v. *Wenmar* (1509–10) KB 27/991, m. 28d.

plug the jurisdictional gap and obtain a new form of remedy. However, the change was apparently established by general acceptance in practice without any major challenge in court. At any rate, no notice is taken of it in the extant reports until the 1520s, by which time it was probably too late to mount any serious resistance. A solitary demurrer in 1512 may indicate some kind of last stand; but no judgment was entered, and it seems likely that the objection was to a point of form.[21]

The earliest form of special case was that, whereas the plaintiff was of good and honest bearing and condition, and was so reputed among good and serious men (*apud bonos et graves*), the defendant—scheming to harm his name and condition—publicly accused him of theft, so that his name was harmed and he could no longer deal ('in buying, selling, and lawfully bargaining') with those honest folk with whom he had been accustomed to deal. The formula owes a good deal to the *vi et armis* writ for lying in wait to seize a villein,[22] but it has been pointed out that the recital of reputation *apud bonos et graves*, and some of the other phrases, correspond closely to the forms used in ecclesiastical courts.[23] There can be little doubt that the attorneys or clerks responsible were motivated by the desire to transfer suits from the latter to Westminster Hall, where damages were available and there was no jurisdictional threat.

The rolls show that the new action began simultaneously in both benches, and so this is one innovation which cannot safely be attributed to Fyneux CJ and his colleagues in the King's Bench. We have noted that it was Fyneux CJ who in 1497 denied the remedy, though he grew to accept it in the 1510s. Of all years, 1517 seems to be the year of final acceptance in the King's Bench: in Hilary term a judgment was entered by default; a record crop of five new actions were entered the following term; and in Trinity term a judgment was given after verdict.[24] By this time at the latest the judges must have given the new action their blessing. Judgments are found in the Common Pleas around the same time.[25] During this formative period, declarations became more sophisticated. It became usual, and before long *de rigueur*, to set out the alleged defamatory speech word for word in English.[26]

[21] *Walker* v. *Robynson* (1512) KB 27/1004, m. 77. The plaintiff did not set out the words complained of, or give details of the allegation of theft.

[22] See *Hunston* v. *Bishop of Ely* (1484) KB 27/893, m. 91 ('machinans nomen et famam predicti Thome maliciose ledere et denigrare . . . ipsumque Thomam vexare, opprimere, et totaliter destruere et exinanire').

[23] Helmholz, 100 Selden Soc., p. lxxii. The words *apud bonos et graves* were quoted directly from the constitution *Auctoritate Dei patris* which governed the English canon law of defamation.

[24] *Woode* v. *Frogge* (1517) KB 27/1022, m. 67 (judgment by default); *Lyncolne* v. *Hendy* (1517) KB 27/1024, m. 76 (pr. 100 Selden Soc. 43, no. 64; judgment after verdict, with damages increased by the court).

[25] e.g. *Vernycome* v. *Fawell* (1519) CP 40/1024, m. 352 (pr. 100 Selden Soc. 46, no. 66; judgment after verdict, for accusation of villeinage).

[26] 94 Selden Soc. 243; 100 Selden Soc., pp. lxxxii–lxxxiii. The longest quotation noted is an 84-line copy of a written bill alleging unlawful assembly: *Vaughan* v. *Gunter* (1555) CP 40/1162, m. 191.

We find experiments with special-damage clauses,[27] with more detailed allegations of general damage—including the expense of clearing the plaintiff's name (*pro declaratione sua*)[28]—and from the 1530s increasingly elaborate assertions of malice and malevolence such as devilish instigation and other kinds of counter-denigration.[29]

Although the actions began with charges of theft, they were soon extended to treason,[30] homicide,[31] and other common-law offences,[32] prominent among which are extortion, or 'polling and bribing'.[33] They were also promptly adapted for purely verbal villein-claims—that is, where there was no force and arms or lying in wait[34]—and in 1512, the year when the old *vi et armis* formula seems to

[27] 94 Selden Soc. *238 n. 7*. Note also *Haukyn* v. *Lyncoln* (1525) KB 27/1055, m. 25d (pr. in 100 Selden Soc. 49; innkeeper accused of murder, and so inn not frequented; judgment for plaintiff); *Howard* v. *Pynnes* (1537) KB 27/1105, m. 11 (loss of trade and company, and inability to buy victuals, because of accusation of heresy); and the other cases of occupational slander, below, 786-7.

[28] This becomes standard form in the 1550s: e.g. *Forman* v. *Smythe* (1555) CP 40/1161, m. 130.

[29] e.g. *Sharrowe* v. *Burdeoppe* (1534) CP 40/1080, m. 335 ('ex suo malivelo animo diabolice instigatus machinans...'); *Boner* v. *Fellowe* (1534) CP 40/1083, m. 121 ('machinans ex perniciosa nequicia ac perfida maliciose ledere...'); *Blakden* v. *Percyvall* (1536) CP 40/1088, m. 271 ('horribiliter et venenose'); *Colyford* v. *Heryat* (1536) KB 27/1099, m. 12d ('diabolice instigatione comproctus machinans...'); *Barnes* v. *Maydy* (1536) KB 27/1100, m. 44d ('ex sua perversa et nequissima cogitatione diabolice instigatus machinans...'); 100 Selden Soc., p. lxxxiv. Cf. *Methewold* v. *Beele* (1536) KB 27/1099, m. 4 ('ex suo malivolo animo diabolice instigatus machinans callide decipere et defraudare' in *assumpsit*).

[30] *Wood* v. *Frogge* (1517) KB 27/1022, m. 67 (traitor, murderer, and extortioner; judgment by default); *Streche* v. *Besceter* (1528) KB 27/1066, m. 19 (counterfeiting coin); *Willoughby* v. *Lynd* (1531) KB 27/1079, m. 8 (traitor to the king); *Thomson* v. *Preston* (1531) KB 27/1081, m. 39 (counterfeiting king's seal on writs); *Hungerford* v. *Temmys* (1534) CP 40/1083, m. 609d. Cf. *Gyttyns* v. *Fitzwilliam* (1511) KB 27/1001, m. 71 (accused of saying that Hen. VII would not live more than three years, as a result of which Edmund Dudley PC committed him to the Tower).

[31] e.g. *Hellone* v. *Tounesend* (1514) KB 27/1013, mm. 16 and 84d; *Eylnot* v. *Vytell* (1515) KB 27/1015, m. 40d; *Smyth* v. *Halle* (1515) KB 27/1017, m. 9d; *Alye* v. *Arrold* [?] (1517) KB 27/1023, m. 15d; *Webbe* v. *Dekynell*, ibid., m. 49; *Walker* v. *Robynson* (1519) KB 27/1030, m. 29 (recovers £20). Cf. *Pare* v. *Shakspere* (1511) CP 40/996, m. 314 (maliciously procuring an indictment for murder in order to disinherit him and blacken his name).

[32] e.g. *Broun* v. *Waren* (1514) KB 27/1013, m. 62 (forgery); *Southworth* v. *Bady* (1515) KB 27/1017, m. 103 (champerty); *Rudhale* v. *Whityngston* (1520) KB 27/1067, m. 37d (usury); *Grislyng* v. *Horswell* (1531) KB 27/1079, m. 28 (piracy); *Leyceter* v. *Goslyn* (1539) KB 27/1111, m. 13 (arson); *Harryngton* v. *Barnes* (1550) KB 27/1156, m. 110 (pr. 100 Selden Soc. 53; sedition); *Anon.* (1558) BL MS. Hargrave 4, fo. 143v (attempted theft). Cf. nn. 40, 41 (forgery and champerty by lawyers).

[33] e.g. *Turbervile* v. *Edmondys* (1512) KB 27/1003, m. 66d; *Prior of St Bartholomew's* v. *Alawe* (1514) KB 27/1011, m. 30; *Druell* v. *Trodys* (1515) KB 27/1016, m. 39d; *Harvy* v. *Lyster* (1517) KB 27/1023, m. 24; cf. 100 Selden Soc., p. lxxxi. This was a common category, almost as common as murder or villeinage: 94 Selden Soc. 243.

[34] e.g. *Asplyn* v. *Fox* (1511) KB 27/999, m. 73d (tr. Milsom, *HFCL*, 382); *Reynaldys* v. *Castell* (1511) KB 27/1001, m. 63d; *Spenlove* v. *Calthorp* (1512) KB 27/1005, m. 78; *Gotte* v. *Gawcell* (1514) KB 27/1012, m. 38d; *Gelget* v. *Wymbyll* (1514) CP 40/1008, m. 306d; 94 Selden Soc. 191; *Vernycome* v. *Fawell* (1519) CP 40/1024, m. 352 (pr. 100 Selden Soc. 46). See further above, 604. In all English quotations, the spelling is modernized.

have been generally given up, the Common Pleas gave judgment in such a case.[35] It became usual to set out the exact words in such cases as well.[36] The essence of the complaint was the same, namely that the plaintiff was injured in his reputation and commercial dealings, and liable to have his goods taken from him; no doubt the court could also take notice that a villein was theoretically subject to imprisonment and physical chastisement by his lord.[37] Servile status was excluded, by the canon law itself, from the scope of the ecclesiastical remedy; it was a personal defect and not a crime.[38] But the temporal loss which such an allegation caused was a sufficient justification for claiming and receiving damages. Calling someone a 'Scot' belonged in the same juristic category, since a Scot in the early sixteenth century was liable to arrest and imprisonment as an alien enemy.[39]

In 1513 a different category was opened up by a king's serjeant accused of accepting retainers against the Crown, followed soon afterwards by a notary accused of forgery and two King's Bench filazers accused of corruption and forgery.[40] Thereafter it became common for professional plaintiffs—especially lawyers[41]—to allege a loss of fees or damage to their professional standing, and (a few years later) for tradesmen to allege a loss of business,[42] or a servant a loss

[35] Perkyns v. Abbot of Combe (1512) CP 40/1001, m. 332 (£10 damages recovered upon a non potest dedicere).

[36] e.g. Newman v. Osburne (1527) KB 27/1063 m. 26 ('N. is bondman of Ralph Verney'). For other examples see above, 604 n. 61.

[37] Occasionally a plaintiff would adapt the old formula and allege threats, or a fear of going about his business, while omitting the force and arms: e.g. Coke v. Abbot of St Benet Hulme (1528) CP 40/1058A, m. 531; Nicoll v. Prioress of Rusper (1529) CP 40/1060, m. 345.

[38] Helmholz, Select Cases on Defamation, p. xxi. Nevertheless occasional cases occurred: ibid., p. xxviii (1471 and 1507).

[39] e.g. Davyson v. Broke (1514) CP 40/1008, m. 774d (threatened with imprisonment); Heron v. Nasshe (1521) CP 40/1033, m. 288 (imprisoned); Harryson v. Williams (1524) CP 40/1044, m. 510d (arrested and examined); Coxston v. Jamys (1535) CP 40/1086, m. 46d; Brightman v. Vaus (1537) KB 27/1103, m. 73 (crier of King's Bench called false Scot). For an example from a local court (c.1520) see 94 Selden Soc. 239. Cf. three cases from ecclesiastical courts (1512–15) in 100 Selden Soc., p. xxviii.

[40] Elyot v. Tofte (1513) KB 27/1006, m. 62 (king's serjeant); Broun v. Waren (1514) KB 27/1013, m. 62 (notary); Southworth v. Bady (1515) KB 27/1017, m. 103 (filazer called a 'false harlot' and accused of champerty); Hawkes v. Husee (1516) KB 27/1019, m. 68 (filazer accused of forging a deed).

[41] e.g. Wood v. Frogge (1517) KB 27/1022, m. 67 (counsel learned in the law accused of treason, murder, and extortion); Turpyn v. Clarke (1527) KB 27/1064, m. 61 (counsel accused of perjury); Arscott v. Escott (1528) CP 40/1059, m. 277; 101 Selden Soc., p. lxxxi n. 5 (counsel said to have been 'discharged of pleading' for misconduct); Bele v. Mersshe (1529) KB 27/1072, m. 77d (counsel accused of theft); See v. Hanyett (1534) KB 27/1093, m. 75 (attorney accused of receiving stolen goods); Tusser v. Bendlowes (1536) KB 27/1098, m. 22d (attorney accused of oppression); Barrowe v. Frenche, ibid., m. 73d (clerk of King's Bench, learned in the law, accused of forgery); Fowler v. Ludford (1536) KB 27/1101, m. 32 (learned in the law, accused of misconduct as steward; demurrer). See also 94 Selden Soc. 243. Cf. Gelget v. Wymbyll (1514) CP 40/1008, m. 306d (villein-claim; plaintiff an attorney, though he does not say so).

[42] Haukyn v. Lyncoln (1525) KB 27/1055, m. 25d (innkeeper). The device is not much met with before the 1530s, when it becomes regular: e.g. Barfote v. Smyth (1533) KB 27/1089, m. 79d (merchant); Wanton v. Maydewell (1536) KB 27/1099, m. 68 (mercer); Marten v. Lucas, ibid., m. 79d (brewer); Crede v. Mody

of employment,[43] as a result of defamatory words. Towards the middle of the century declarations by lawyers become more detailed, often setting out their membership of an inn of court[44] as well as their calling as 'counsel learned in the law', and if possible mentioning positions of repute such as the office of steward,[45] coroner,[46] or justice of the peace.[47] Most of the cases in this category arose from allegations of crime, but the formula enabled an action to be brought for accusations of such non-criminal behaviour or deficiencies as were either unprofessional or would in some way tend to discourage clients or customers: for instance that an attorney had been disqualified,[48] or was troublesome to his neighbours,[49] took fees from both sides,[50] or knew little law,[51] or that a justice of the peace was unfit to sit on the bench,[52] or that a merchant had become bankrupt.[53]

(1536) KB 27/1100, m. 40 (clothier); *Gay v. Steven*, ibid., m. 74d (smith); *Yaxley v. Watson* (1538) KB 27/1109, m. 46d (innkeeper).

[43] *Bosgrave v. Hargyll* (1533) CP 40/1079, m. 449 (servant of Fitzjames CJ accused of inappropriate language, for which he was dismissed); *Andrewe v. Benyngton* (1535) KB 27/1094, m. 33 (servant accused of theft, for which he was dismissed; £10 damages); *Love v. Belley* (1539) CP 40/1102, m. 407 (servant accused of failure to account for money); *Lylly v. Pygeon* (1541) KB 27/1121, m. 33 (woman servant accused of theft)   [44] Above, 427 n. 51.

[45] e.g. *Fysher v. Kyghley* (1520) KB 27/1034, m. 31d (manorial steward accused of bribery); *Fowler v. Ludford* (1536) KB 27/1101, m. 32 (manorial steward accused of mis-entering a verdict); *Jakes v. Ives* (1546) KB 27/1138, m. 137 (tr. 'not unlearned in the law of the land' and steward of Winchester College; accused of forging deeds; recovers 26s. 8d. damages); *James v. Feld* (1549) CP 40/1140, m. 429 (understeward of manors accused of deceit in not handing over money; recovers £12 damages).

[46] *Hyggons v. Botfylde* (1558) CP 40/1173, m. 644 (coroner recovers £5 for 'false perjured knave').

[47] *Wood v. Frogge* (1517) KB 27/1022, m. 67 (also counsel); *Rudhale v. Whityngston* (1520) KB 27/1067, m. 37d (also queen's receiver); *Purse v. Stepneth* (1521) CP 40/1032B, m. 293 (also 'minister' of the Common Pleas); *Danby v. Thwyng* (1532) KB 27/1083, m. 32 (also attorney); *Thymolby v. Sympson* (1535) KB 27/1095, m. 25; *Gorges v. Maundrell* (1535) CP 40/1087, m. 165; *Megges v. Kynnerdey* (1536) CP 40/1088, m. 160; *Archour v. Wescott* (1540) KB 27/1116, m. 34; *Parker v. Fitzherbert* (1540) CP 40/1105, m. 424; *Bekwyth v. Crysplyn* (1546) KB 27/1140, m. 108; *Harryngton v. Barnes* (1550) KB 27/1156, m. 110 (pr. 100 Selden Soc. 53). There are numerous examples in the 1550s.

[48] For assertions that an attorney's heels had been 'pointed upwards' see above, 439. Cf. *Markaunt v. Page* (1542) CP 40/1115, m. 538d ('Thou art a false attorney proved before all the king's justices at Westminster and art discharged of thine attorneyship there...'); *Forman v. Bellowe* (1551) KB 27/1157, m. 111 ('George Forman was by the lord chief justice of England in Easter term last thrust out of the King's Bench by the ears like a false knave as he is...'); *Colbarne v. Smyth* (1551) KB 27/1158, m. 147 ('I marvel how it is that Francis Colbarne, who is none attorney in deed...'; omits to declare that he is).   [49] *Caldwall v. Cromer* (1536) KB 27/1100, m. 50.

[50] *Kellett v. Watson* (1557) CP 40/1170, m. 1132 (declares as 'purus et immaculatus attornatus').

[51] *Swallowe v. Benberrye* (1554) KB 27/1171, m. 166 ('Thou art a false knave and...I will buy as much law for an halfpenny as thou hast in thy belly'). The defence was that he had said 'Thou art a busy, brabbling knave and a peddling lawyer, and intermeddleth in men's matters that thou hast nothing to do in, and I could buy as much law for two pennyworth of pins as thou hast in thy belly...'.

[52] *Raynesforde v. Symmes* (1551) KB 27/1158, m. 122; above, 271; *Trevanyon v. Luke* (1557) KB 27/1182, m. 20 ('a false and wicked justice and not worthy to sit on the bench').

[53] Examples have not been noted before the 1550s: *Kempe v. Reynoldes* (1552) KB 27/1163, m. 124 ('will be bankrupt within these two days'; judgment for plaintiff on demurrer to declaration); *Serle v. Stephynson* (1557) KB 27/1182, m. 81.

The third main category of defamation cases arose from accusations of socially unfortunate conditions, the classic Elizabethan example being the 'French pox'.[54] French pox cases make their debut in our period, but they are not yet frequent.[55] Leprosy is the only other medical condition noted,[56] perhaps because a suspected leper was subject to sequestration by the writ *de leproso amovendo*; but the category does not seem to have been confined to diseases.[57] Bastardy is perhaps the commonest case, though obviously an allegation of illegitimacy could affect more than merely social standing.[58]

In addition to these cases of personal defamation, the new action for words brought with it at the same time the action for slander of title,[59] and what appear to be the first traces of an action for injurious falsehood, that is, false statements which diminish the value or affect the saleability of a property or business.[60]

TEMPORAL AND SPIRITUAL DEFAMATION

The bastardy cases raised directly the question of the relationship between the new action on the case and the old ecclesiastical suit for penance, and this is doubtless why the first attempt to frame such an action (in 1523) was stopped by a demurrer.[61] We have no report of the 1523 case, nor any indication in the record that it was ever decided. Yet it is not too difficult to guess at the issue of law. It was

[54] The French pox, or *morbus gallicus* (syphilis), spread rapidly across Europe in the 1490s and was sometimes known as the great pox to distinguish it from smallpox. See J. Arrizabalaga, J. Henderson, and R. French, *The Great Pox: the French Disease in Renaissance Europe* (1997).

[55] *Outwell v. Waleys* (1535) CP 40/1085(2), m. 152 ('Thou art full of the French pox and wert laid of them at Newton Bushel'; issue); *Farnaby v. Randall* (1536) CP 40/1088, m. 484 ('cum scalis gallicis detentus'); *Smyth v. Blackburne* (1543) CP 40/1117, m. 225d ('a false knave and a stinking knave and thou hast the French pox'); *Thumworth v. Potte* (1543) KB 27/1127, m. 104d (barber-surgeon said to have 'the great pox' and so 'not meet for any honest man's daughter'). Cf. *Cowper v. Broun* (1543) CP 40/1117, m. 258 (measled whore and pocky whore); *Conack v. Cruse*, next note; *Forman v. Smythe* (1555) CP 40/1161, m. 130 (pocky knave).

[56] *Kempe v. Legatt* (1551) CP 40/1147A, m. 543 ('ye are stricken with the "leprye" and God hath laid his faggot upon you...'; recovers £8 damages). Cf. *Conack v. Cruse* (1553) KB 27/1166, m. 120 ('a naughty, pocky, and lazarous knave').

[57] Note e.g. *Reydon v. Colles* (1535) CP 40/1087, m. 172 (cuckold knave); *Rychardson v. Grey* (1548) CP 40/1138, m. 526d ('a banished man out of all countries').   [58] For bastardy cases see below, 792.

[59] *Broun v. Eylond* (1512) KB 27/1005, m. 76 (right to take toll); *Rawson v. Weston* (1514) KB 27/1011, m. 56d; *Duke of Buckingham v. Paulet* (1514) CP 40/1008, m. 158 (procuring a false inquisition *post mortem*); *Prior of Christ Church, Canterbury v. Watte* (1517) KB 27/1024, m. 40 (title to market); *Zouche v. Zouche* (1532) KB 27/1084, m. 74; *Levett v. Kynatt* (1536) CP 40/1088, m. 545d (tenant by curtesy sues someone claiming to be owner—*indubitatus hereditarius et proprietarius*—so that he cannot sell his interest).

[60] *Mordaunt v. Gedge* (1542) CP 40/1115, m. 474 (lord of manor accused of altering customs to drive away tenants, so that plaintiff could not sell his copyhold); *Rede v. Stubberd* (1557) KB 27/1182, m. 47 (defendant said miller's toll-dish was larger than it ought to be, so that people did not bring their grain to be ground).

[61] *Pulham v. Pulham* (1523) KB 27/1048, m. 30. The only other pre-1535 case noted in the rolls also resulted in a demurrer: *Hunne v. Marshall* (1513) below, 791.

all very well to permit actions at common law in respect of allegations of temporal crime, or villeinage, since those were matters outside the jurisdiction of the Church courts; but was not bastardy a spiritual matter, outside the jurisdiction of the royal courts? On the other hand, the canon law did not regard an allegation of bastardy as an imposition of 'crime' for which proceedings could be brought.[62]

Doubtless the ecclesiastical authorities saw a major sphere of jurisdiction slipping away, and there is evidence that Cardinal Wolsey tried to do something about it. A plaintiff in Chancery referred to a decree by Wolsey C. 'that upon defamation or slandering of common persons of this realm the party thereof aggrieved should have his remedy in that case by order of the spiritual law and not by any temporal action or process at the common law'.[63] This seems to mean that Wolsey C. had announced a willingness to put a stop to actions at law founded on allegations of purely spiritual offences, though no injunctions have been found to prove that he did so. The first full account of the new law of defamation, inserted in the updated edition of the *Natura Brevium* which Richard Pynson published towards the end of Wolsey's chancellorship in 1528, stated the jurisdiction division unequivocally:[64]

Note that the spiritual court should have jurisdiction in defamation cases (*in causa diffamationis*), subject to this distinction: there are two kinds of defamation, one of which is an offence by the spiritual law and the other by temporal law. Thus, if someone slanders another that he committed fornication or adultery, he may be sued for this in the spiritual court. The law is the same if he defames another of simony, or for non-payment of tithes, or for eating flesh on a fasting-day (such as Lent and others), or that he has not been confessed for a year, or that he has not received the body of our Saviour, and such like.

But it is otherwise concerning such defamations as concern merely temporal things, which are punishable by temporal law. For instance, if someone defames another of treason, murder, felony, or such like, albeit this also sounds to the displeasure of God, yet by no way and in no part is it punishable by the spiritual law... But plaintiffs who bring their actions on their case for the matters just mentioned must say that they were endamaged by the defamation: for instance, that because he defamed him of felony a merchant would not deal with him, or that through suspicion arising from the words he was arrested on suspicion of felony. Nevertheless, the issue shall not be upon the damages, but upon the speaking of the words.

This otherwise lucid account—which might have been perfectly acceptable to Wolsey—nevertheless omitted to deal with the hybrid case where an allegation of

---

[62] Helmholz, *Select Cases on Defamation*, p. xxvi, citing Lyndwood.

[63] *Stone v. Swytall* (1515/29) C1/577/43 (sp. mod.); 94 Selden Soc. 239 n. 3. The reference to 'common persons' is presumably intended to exclude *scandalum magnatum*.

[64] *Natura Brevium newly and moost trewly corrected* (1528), ff. 185v–186 (tr. from law French); repr. in Rastell's edn (1534), at 103; omitted from the English edition by Petit (*c.* 1550). Fitzherbert, surprisingly, made no mention of actions on the case for slander in FNB (1534).

spiritual misconduct resulted in temporal loss. That had been the issue in the bastardy case, since the plaintiff had emphasized the threat to his inheritance.[65] Obviously, if the jurisdiction was deemed to turn on the substance of the allegation—on the ground that if a justification were pleaded the court would have to try the substance—then the addition of temporal loss would make no difference. But if it was the consequence, the temporal damage, which justified the action on the case—on the footing that there could be no compensation for such damage in the Church courts—then there was no reason for distinguishing between temporal and spiritual words. The 1528 passage suggested that the damage was not issuable, and this proposition seems to have been accepted by the courts around this time.[66] However, the proposition that the damage was not separately issuable was not conclusive of the jurisdictional question.[67] As James Hales pointed out four years later, although the damage was not traversable, the plaintiff was nevertheless required to allege it in his writ.[68]

The matter was alluded to by St German in his *New Additions* (1531), but in the slightly guarded form of a question whether Parliament could properly introduce an action at common law for 'such words as a man hath any loss or worldly hindrance by, though they have before time been used to be sued only in the spiritual court'.[69] Clearly St German did not think the development had already occurred, though it seems that the spiritualty now feared it as a potential encroachment on the spiritual jurisdiction. The answer put in the mouth of the Student was that the hypothetical statute would be good, provided it did not prohibit the spiritual courts from using their old jurisdiction. The latter did not award recompense, and the royal courts were only concerned with 'worldly loss or hindrance'; there was therefore no overlap between the two spheres of jurisdiction. This new doctrine found its way, in a stronger form, into the response of a group of common lawyers to an attempt by canonists to define the ecclesiastical jurisdiction after the break with Rome.[70] They argued that, besides the exclusive jurisdiction over 'slander of

---

[65] Likewise in the 1513 case, Hunne had alleged damage to his temporal dealings and livelihood as a result of the assertion that he was excommunicated.

[66] *Hertrop* v. *Ryland* (1521) KB 27/1038, m. 66 (traverses damage; demurrer, but no judgment); *Russell* v. *Haward* (1536–7) Dyer 26 (tr. B. & M. 633); CP 40/1091, m. 326 (similar plea held bad on demurrer).

[67] 94 Selden Soc. 240. Cf. non-issuable allegations as to venue, which also altered jurisdiction: above, 213 n. 40.

[68] Reading in Gray's Inn (1532) B. & M. 348. Hales did not see the implications for the jurisdictional question, which he states in the same way as the 1528 treatise. Edward Hall proposed to deal with defamation in his 1540 reading on the Church, but neither manuscript reaches that point (BL MS. Hargrave 88, fo. 74; MS. Hargrave 92, fo. 57).

[69] St German, *Doctor and Student*, ed. Plucknett and Barton, 330–1 (sp. mod.).

[70] 'Certen Considerations why the Spirituell Jurisdiction wold be abrogatt and repelled or at the leest reformed' (*c*.1534), BL Cotton MS. Cleopatra F.II, at fo. 244 (sp. mod.). It is possible that St German was the author.

murder, felony, trespass, or such other whereupon actions may be taken after and tried upon the principal matter in the king's court', the royal courts already had a jurisdiction concurrent with that of the spiritual courts over all those slanders 'whereby the party defamed or reproved hath any worldly loss, as loss of goods or of service or friendship'. There was no need, it seems, for an act of Parliament to achieve this.[71] The conclusion could be deduced logically from St German's doctrine that the temporal courts could hear actions in respect of 'worldly loss', whether or not it flowed from a spiritual slander.

The jurisdictional question occasioned one of the few reported cases on defamation in the year books. An action was brought in the Common Pleas in 1535 for calling the plaintiff a heretic, and of the 'new learning',[72] an allegation which would have been exceedingly embarrassing for the lay court to try in 1535—the year of More's execution—if the defendant pleaded a justification. No doubt the judges recollected the delicate case of Richard Hunne, who had been murdered while a similar point was depending in the King's Bench.[73] Heresy prosecutions brought imprisonment and the risk of a painful death, both factors which might be thought to justify a suit for compensation at common law. But Fitzherbert and Shelley JJ ruled that the action did not lie, because the question of heresy was purely spiritual and could not be discussed in their court.[74] Their ruling accords with the statement to the same effect in 1532 by James Hales.[75] However, in the same year as the Common Pleas case, an action was brought in the King's Bench for saying that the plaintiff had broken his fast on the eve of St Thomas like a heretic. The case was tried on the general issue before Baldwin CJCP and Lyster CB, a verdict obtained for the plaintiff, and judgment entered—though not before taking advisement for four terms.[76] Since neither of the assize judges was from the King's Bench, it cannot safely be deduced that there was here a divergence between the two benches to parallel the other contemporary differences over the scope of actions on the case. It seems unlikely, indeed, that the resistance was maintained for very long. Even Fitzherbert and Shelley JJ had been prepared to allow an area of overlap where offences were punishable in both laws: for instance,

[71] They conceded, however, that 'we think it reasonable that it be prohibited than none sue in both courts'. No such legislation was passed.

[72] So says the year book. No such case has been found in the rolls, but this may be a garbled version of *Elyot* v. *Mersshe* (Trin. 1535) CP 40/1086, m. 192d ('Thou art an heretic and I will prove thee an heretic, for thou didst not receive thy maker at Easter last past'; *sicut pluries* to Mich. 1536; no appearance recorded).

[73] *Hunne* v. *Marshall* (1513) KB 27/1006, m. 36 (alleged excommunication of Richard Hunne for heresy; demurrer); Milsom, *SHCL*, 145–7; *HFCL*, 383–4; above, 241.

[74] *Anon.* (1535) Trin. 27 Hen. VIII, fo. 14, pl. 4 (tr. B. & M. 626); also in Gell's reports, I, 27 Hen. VIII, fo. 30. It was not the first attempt: cf. *Antony* v. *Gyllot* (1522) CP 40/1037, m. 763 (*optulit se* only).

[75] Reading in Gray's Inn (1532), fo. 38 (tr. B. & M. 348). Hales also denied an action for poller, shaver, fool, madman, lunatic, or vagabond.

[76] *Howard* v. *Pynnes* (1537–8) KB 27/1105, m. 11 (recovers £2 damages and £6 costs).

bawdery.[77] Another instance might be perjury, which was punishable in the Star Chamber but not generally recognized as a temporal offence before Elizabethan times.[78] In less contentious spheres than heresy, there are numerous examples from 1535 onwards of suits for spiritual matters, in both benches: for instance, bastardy,[79] drunkenness,[80] non-payment of tithes,[81] and even (in 1551) 'papism'.[82] This development is largely missed by the printed law reports. Indeed, the commonest cases in this category arose from allegations of sexual misconduct—by men and women alike[83]—a type of action not fully established in the printed reports until the 1590s. And in the 1540s we encounter three cases involving accusations of heresy in the Common Pleas rolls, all cases in which the defendant appeared but did not demur.[84] After this, there seems little doubt that an action would lie in either bench for a 'spiritual' allegation which caused temporal loss, though it might still be worth making an objection in a borderline case.[85]

By the middle of the century, plaintiffs were pushing the bounds of the action for words to the very limits. Actions were increasingly brought for words of

[77] Near-contemporary examples are *Gascoigne v. Slade* (1537) CP 40/1095, m. 149 ('you are a maintainer of bawdery'); *Yaxley v. Watson* (1538) KB 27/1109, m. 46d (innkeeper accused of keeping a bawdy house).

[78] This was a common allegation, but the subject of at least two demurrers: *Turpyn v. Clarke* (1527) KB 27/1064, m. 61; *Neyle v. Gupwyll* (1541) CP 40/1109, m. 519 (perjured churl).

[79] e.g. *Heydon v. Bokkyng* (1535) KB 27/1095, m. 65; *Stucley v. Underhyll* (1535) CP 40/1085(2), m. 105d; *Wyngfeld v. Vyncent* (1541) CP 40/1111, m. 324 (judgment by default); *Hunt v. Wyngrave* (1544) CP 40/1120, m. 624; *Dun v. Yeo* (1545) CP 40/1130, m. 103; *Hevenyngham v. Wolverston* (1546) KB 27/1138, m. 22 (20s. damages); *Stafford v. Barton* (1552) KB 27/1164, m. 183d (£200 damages for written allegation of bastardy); *Lyster v. Dalabere* (1557) CP 40/1171, m. 505.

[80] *Spaldyng v. Hoper* (1535) KB 27/1094, m. 8 (plaintiff a priest; pleads that in all the circumstances he appeared drunk and disorderly).   [81] *Hayes v. Cromboke* (1535) CP 40/1085(1), m. 153.

[82] *Hall v. Napper* (1551) KB 27/1157, m. 30 ('rank rebellion and rank papist'; justified because plaintiff denied the articles of religion). Cf., however, the mid-Elizabethan view that papism was not inherently illegal: 109 Selden Soc., p. lxxii.

[83] e.g. *Davys v. Henbery* (1536) KB 27/1100, m. 8d; 94 Selden Soc. 241 n. 4 ('played the whore'; alleges loss of marriage); *Asshe v. Wyer* (1537) KB 27/1103, m. 32 ('strong whore'; alleges loss of company); *Dunce v. Somer* (1542) CP 40/1115, m. 200 ('naught of her body and kept unlawful company with [the vicar of Selborne, and they] lived naughtily and used lechery together'); *Burdon v. Thorn* (1543) CP 40/1117, m. 203d ('Thou art a bawdy priest, for Glossop's wife was seen coming forth of thy chamber in the night time'); *Cowper v. Broun*, ibid., m. 258 ('measled whore, pocky whore, and priest's whore'; judgment for plaintiff); *Newman v. Twysylton* (1545) CP 40/1125, m. 331 ('arrant whore'); *Yeo v. Hangar* (1546) CP 40/1129, m. 591d (whore); *Andrewes v. Tompson* (1549) CP 40/1142, m. 605 ('bawdy knave': constable accused of keeping a whore in his house); *Harewell v. Jenys* (1551) CP 40/1146, m. 509 ('a common whoremaster, for he had a child by his servant Margery Best'); *Anon.* (1550) Moo. 10, pl. 38 (whoremonger).

[84] *Hercy v. Leygeet* (1542–4) CP 40/1113, m. 614 (imparlance for seven terms); *Tredenyk v. Hoblyn* (1548) CP 40/1138, m. 101 ('greatest heretic in a country'; pleads Not guilty); *Myll v. Langemede* (1549) CP 40/1142, m. 539d ('Thou art an heretic for thou didst say that God that is in heaven is not God'; pleads different words). In *Holmore v. Vycarye* (1556) CP 40/1165, m. 149, a plaintiff recovered 6s. 8d. damages for 'Thou art a thief, a rebellion, a traitor and an heretic'.

[85] e.g. *Tyrrell v. Dune* (1554) CP 40/1158, m. 709 ('Master Tyrrell doth maintain in his tenement and town of Gipping a drab, an whore, and other that keep ill rule'; undetermined demurrer).

insubstantial content, such as 'false and nasty priest',[86] 'crafty gentleman',[87] 'false harlot',[88] 'false knave',[89] 'very knave',[90] or 'renegade',[91] and this tendency no doubt explains why the judges began to react against them.[92] Even 'villein' now seems likely to mean villain, a term of vague abuse,[93] rather than bondman; and 'churl' was being used in the same way.[94] Another reason for the judicial misgivings may have been that juries were beginning to award exemplary damages around this time, although admittedly they did so only in aggravated cases.[95] The principal results of the reaction belong to the period after 1558, but before that date we already find a doctrine that words are only actionable if they specify some particular offence and are not just general abuse.[96] Vague words could not yet be explained by an *innuendo*, which was introduced into declarations in the 1540s but

[86] *Stone* v. *Hawkyns* (1545) KB 27/1135, m. 138 (recovers 13s. 4d. damages).

[87] *Bryght* v. *Heydon* (1552) KB 27/1162, m. 73 ('Master Bryght is a crafty gentleman and too crafty to dwell amongst true men'; issue).

[88] Of a man: *Clerke* v. *Grubbe* (1557) CP 40/1170, m. 908 (imparlance).

[89] *Anon.* (1549) BL MS. Add. 24845, fo. 9 (disputed whether action will lie); *Bellowe* v. *Whetston* (1550) KB 27/1154, m. 110 ('John Bellowe is a false knave...'); *Anon.* (1550/1) Moo. 10, pl. 38; BL MS. Hargrave 4, fo. 117v (false knave and wretch); *Cull* v. *Grene* (1554) KB 27/1171, m. 81 ('Thou art a false knave...'; also alleges receipt of stolen goods; demurrer). Cf. *Wall* v. *Dawkes* (1541) CP 40/1109, m. 130 ('Thou art a false fellow and a knave, and I am truer and honester than thou art'; issue); *Porter* v. *Asser* (1555) CP 40/1162, m. 342 ('thou art a very untrue and false knave and that I will prove'); *Swyfte* v. *Blythe* (1557) CP 40/1169, m. 119 ('a false knave and a packer of false matters'); *Smythe* v. *Bedulph* (1558) CP 40/1173, m. 505 ('You are a false knave and I trust to see you "tytter" in a rope'); *Chamber* v. *Stofer* (1558) CP 40/1174, m. 353 (below).

[90] *Whetcomb* v. *Whetcomb* (1555) CP 40/1163, m. 103 ('a very knave and a villain').

[91] *Budd* v. *Davye* (1555) KB 27/1175, m. 77 ('Thou art a vagabond and a "rounagate", and that I will prove').

[92] e.g. *Carpenter's Case* (1558) Gell's reports, II, fo. 49v (tr. B. & M. 637), *per* Dyer CJ. Cf. *Anon.* (1550) BL MS. Hargrave 4, fo. 105v ('knave' not traversable).

[93] See *Gale* v. *Lowe* (Guildhall, 1557) Chr. Yelverton's reports, fo. 248v (tr. 'First, whether the action lies for calling him "very villain", in as much as the words sound only in reproach, like "very knave", in which case no action on the case lies; but, notwithstanding this, it was held good...'). However, as late as 1563 it was thought desirable in such a case to declare as a free man: *Hoo* v. *Hamond* (1563) CP 40/1207, m. 327 ('Thou art a villain and a false knave and a "vastart"').

[94] *Whetcomb* v. *Whetcomb* (1555) CP 40/1163, m. 103 ('a very knave and a villain'); *Chamber* v. *Stofer* (1558) CP 40/1174, m. 353 ('a villain, a vile churl, and a false knave'); *Langwade* v. *Gressham*, ibid., m. 420 ('bond churl', declaring as a free man; defendant pleads that he said 'Thou art a very unthankful churl'). Cf. *Tusser* v. *Gardener* (1556) CP 40/1167, m. 714 ('Thou art a villein': plaintiff alleges in his declaration that he was born a free man).

[95] *Rouse* v. *Goulbold* (1551) KB 27/1157, m. 81 (£40 for treason); *Fox* v. *Antony*, ibid., m. 139 (£100 for discrediting a merchant); *Stafford* v. *Barton* (1552) KB 27/1164, m. 183d (£200 for libel alleging bastardy); *Heydon* v. *Weston* (1555) KB 27/1175, m. 158 (£1,000 damages by confession for accusing clerk of Council of treason); *Earl of Pembroke* v. *Recorde* (1556) KB 27/1180, m. 36 (£1,000 damages awarded by jury for libel). The 3,000 marks recovered by writ of inquiry in *Marquess of Exeter* v. *Coryton* (1533) CP 40/1077, m. 504 (*scandalum magnatum*) were exceptional. Damages above £20 are not otherwise encountered before 1550.

[96] James Hales's reading (Gray's Inn, 1532), fo. 38 (tr. B. & M. 348); *Hamond* v. *Cocke* (1544) Gell's reports, I, Trin. 36 Hen. VIII, fo. 39v (tr. B. & M. 634). Cf. *Anon.* (1555) Dal. 17, pl. 7 (judges say the law has changed, and that general accusations of theft and the like are actionable).

only as a means of identifying the plaintiff where the words as quoted did not name him.[97] The *innuendo* device was not much used at all in our period, and was not yet invoked to explain slang or jargon—which is quite commonly set out with no explanatory gloss.[98] Accusing a man in 1556 of 'playing Kett's part' certainly required no formal explanation.[99]

DEFENCES IN ACTIONS FOR SLANDER

Since the gist of the action on the case for slander was the speaking of false words, it was not permissible to traverse the damage and it was probably irregular to traverse the good reputation of the plaintiff.[100] Most defendants pleaded Not guilty, though issue could be joined on the speaking of the words, and in about a quarter of the cases on the issue rolls there is a special plea—either a justification or a special traverse. These special pleas deserve attention because they help to explain some of the thinking behind the action for words.

The proper way to justify a slander was to confess the words and avoid them, by pleading their truth, rather than to traverse the speaking of the words falsely. It was, however, quite common—as common as the simple confession and avoidance—for the defendant to set out a different version of what he had said and traverse the speaking of the words set out by the plaintiff. The object behind a special traverse was usually to show that the words actually spoken were undefamatory, or justifiable, though one is left to gather this from the words as they stand;[101] issue was always joined on the words spoken, not on their defamatory character or effect. Since it was not necessary for the jury to find the precise words

[97] *Wyllen* v. *Come* (1544) KB 27/1131, m. 61 ('this man, *ipsum Johannem innuendo*'); *Bryghtman* v. *Crykedorte*, ibid., m. 127 ('she, *innuendo ipsam Katerinam*'); *Hevenyngham* v. *Wolverston* (1546) KB 27/1138, m. 22 ('and the other, *predictam Mariam uxorem prefati Erasmi innuendo*, was named…'); *Tusser* v. *Gardener* (1556) CP 40/1167, m. 714 ('Thou, *innuendo ipsum Thomam*'). See 94 Selden Soc. *246* n. 5; 100 Selden Soc., p. lxxxiii n. 5. In one case an *innuendo* is pleaded in English: *Laurence* v. *Reynoldes* (1556) CP 40/1167, m. 740 ('your men, meaning the men of the said Henry Laurence').

[98] e.g. *Pegge* v. *Morgan* (1536) CP 40/1088, m. 282 ('driven out of Watford with basins', a reference to rough music); *Tytyng* v. *Bale* (1540) CP 40/1104, m. 69d ('John Tytyng the elder is a "mawment grauser"'); *Howsden* v. *Cowche* (1540) CP 40/1106, m. 580d ('Thou art a false knave and hath had twelve godfathers more than I', meaning that he had been tried by jury; cf. 1554 case, below); *Holt* v. *Clark* (1543) CP 40/1117, m. 300 ('a blind inn to maintain whores and thieves'; for blind inns, cf. above, 273); *Canterton* v. *Waglond* (1554) KB 27/1172, m. 83 ('…I will make thee hold up thy hand and put thee to thy twelve godfathers'); *Yeo* v. *Babram* (1547) CP 40/1133, m. 125 ('paper knight', meaning someone who had worn papers for perjury); *Bell* v. *Smyth* (1557) CP 40/1170, m. 529 ('such a rakehell that no man can keep anything for him'). Cf. turning up heels at Westminster: above, 439.

[99] *Cullyard* v. *Browne* (1556) CP 40/1168, m. 439 ('thou art a naughty man, for thou goest about to raise a new insurrection and camp, and playest Kett's part').

[100] For what follows, see 94 Selden Soc. *245–8*.

[101] It is made explicit in the reports of *Anon.* (1549) BL MS. Add. 24845, fo. 8v; BL MS. Hargrave 4, fo. 104v; *Brugis* v. *Warenford* (1552) Dyer 75a; and cf. *Hawley* v. *Barber* (1555) Dyer 118b.

anyway,[102] the only object of such a plea can have been to direct the attention of the jury to whether the words spoken were defamatory or not. It can be inferred from an examination of such pleas that words were not considered to be actionable if spoken in heat,[103] or if spoken conditionally,[104] or without referring specifically to the plaintiff,[105] or if they merely repeated what someone else had said.[106] A lack of directness may also have been seen as a defence, as where the words merely accused the plaintiff of behaving 'like a thief',[107] or where a defendant faced with suspicious conduct put a leading question in strong terms,[108] or where he revealed grounds for suspicion without drawing any firm conclusion.[109] Sometimes the purpose of the plea was to put the words into the context of a dialogue between the parties.[110] But in some cases the alternative words are far

---

[102] *Hamond* v. *Cocke* (1544) Gell's reports, I, Trin. 36 Hen. VIII, fo. 39v (tr. B. & M. 634), *per* Shelley J.; *Brugis* v. *Warenford* (1552) Dyer 75a; sub nom. *Bridges* v. *W.*, Dal. 9, pl. 7.

[103] *Wyberd* v. *Richardson* (1522) KB 27/1042, m. 63; 94 Selden Soc. 246 n. 2; *Strong* v. *Norres* (1546) CP 40/1127, m. 678 (plaintiff called her an old whore, and she, *irata et impatiens*, accused him of perjury; verdict for plaintiff).

[104] *Banaster* v. *Wolfe* (1533) CP 40/1078, m. 435 ('if that these things be true methinks thee a false briber and a false harlot'); *Bakar* v. *Appulton* (1533) KB 27/1079, m. 604 ('it was commonly said that ... [and] if that were true he was a wretch in his said deed'); *Lapworth* v. *Fownes* (1539) KB 27/1112, m. 27 ('thou art a false thief if carrying the king's goods from the Charterhouse of Coventry by night be theft'); *Vaus* v. *Serle* (1540) KB 27/1116, m. 110 ('if it be true that is reported ...'); *Stansby* v. *Holton* (1542) KB 27/1125, m. 22 ('if the said Steven did know her to be naught with the said Bayly and did take her into his house, that then he was a bawdy knave in so doing'). However, Shelley J. held such conditional words to be actionable, if there was no such report, since they were the cause of 'infamy and slander': *Anon.* (c.1544/5) Wm Yelv. 360, no. 101.

[105] *Fowler* v. *Kenwode* (1546) CP 40/1129, m. 315 (action for 'Thou art a traitor to the king'; pleads he said, 'He that hath taken away the church goods of Budleigh is false to the Church and a traitor to the king').

[106] *Broun* v. *Appulby* (1533) KB 27/1086, m. 63; 94 Selden Soc. 246 n. 4; *Thumworth* v. *Potte* (1543) KB 27/1127, m. 104d ('I heard say ...'); *Hevenyngham* v. *Wolverston* (1546) KB 27/1138, m. 22 ('Mr Vernam told me ...'); *Raynesforde* v. *Symmes* (1551) KB 27/1158, m. 122 ('I heard Joan Morres say ...'); *Shepperd* v. *Mason* (1556) CP 40/1168, m. 1136d ('as Drue Ward told me'). See also *Anon.* (c.1544/5) Wm Yelv. 360, no. 101.

[107] e.g. *Kyng* v. *Kyng* (1541) CP 40/1111, m. 455 ('What dost thou here, for the last time thou were here thou like a thief took away my will?'). Cf. *Strong* v. *Norres* (1546) CP 40/1127, m. 678 ('Thou liest like a false perjured knave, for thou wouldst have taken a noble to forswear thyself'); *Todde* v. *Salter* (1546) CP 40/1128, m. 111 (pleads he said the plaintiff 'did use him as a thief in taking his horse from him').

[108] *Kyng* v. *Kyng*, previous note; *Maynpace* v. *Lawley* (1549) CP 40/1141, m. 442 ('What do you mean, come you to rob me?').

[109] e.g. *Conak* v. *Pekyn* (1549) CP 40/1139, m. 449 (accused of killing children; pleads he said that plaintiff had several children by a concubine, 'yet hitherto there never came any child to light'). Cf. the conditional-speech cases above, n. 104, which draw the conclusion but do not claim the evidence to be true.

[110] e.g. *Turpyn* v. *Clarke* (1527) KB 27/1064, m. 61 (plaintiff called him a false knave and he responded); *Asshe* v. *Wyer* (1537) KB 27/1103, m. 32 (plaintiff asked defendant about a rumour and he reported what he had heard); *Heydon* v. *Suxisbyche* (1542) CP 40/1113, m. 303 (verdict for plaintiff); *Strong* v. *Norres* (1546) CP 40/1127, m. 678 (above, n. 103); *Wescott* v. *Brownyng* (1546) CP 40/1129, m. 426 (accused plaintiff of rebellion because he told tenants not to pay the subsidy).

from innocuous, for instance where they merely allege a different offence.[111] Here the point may be that the type of offence mentioned in the declaration is material and therefore issuable, even if the plea admits words which might be the subject of another action. However, in 1550 it seems to have been accepted that such a plea was bad if it merely showed that the plaintiff had been accused of a different felony.[112]

The earliest justifications were modelled on those which had become standard form in actions for conspiracy, and are closer to what we would call a defence of privilege. The defendant would plead that a crime had been committed, that he suspected the plaintiff, and that he reported his suspicion to an appropriate authority, such as a constable,[113] or justices of the peace,[114] or even the lord chancellor.[115] Some judges in this period, including Fitzjames CJ, held that slander could only be justified in a privileged situation and that truth in itself was no defence; even if an allegation were true, it could not be bandied about in an alehouse or tavern, but had to be reported in the due course of justice. This opinion may have been influenced by the canon law.[116] It was, however, refuted by the King's Bench in 1521, and by Fitzherbert JCP in 1533,[117] after which truth seems to have been generally accepted as a distinct defence.[118] Once truth was seen as an absolute justification, the plea of privilege by way of lawful prosecution could be seen as a different kind of defence in which it was not necessary for the accuser to prove the truth of what he had said. It was enough for the accuser to show that he had acted in the course of justice upon reasonable suspicion, which could be founded either on the 'common voice and fame' of the neighbourhood,[119]

[111] e.g. *Kylyowe* v. *Trehanek* (1546) CP 40/1129, m. 326 (accusation of murder; pleads he only accused him of robbery); *Swallowe* v. *Benberrye* (1554) KB 27/1171, m. 166 (above, 787 n. 51); *Hychecokkes* v. *Traunter* (1554) KB 27/1172, m. 127 (accusation of rape; pleads he said plaintiff had 'gotten [his servant] betwixt an oak and a hedge with her clothes up to her navel and his codpiece untied, and her hands bound behind her with a garter, and would have ravished her').

[112] *Anon.* (1550) BL MS. Hargrave 4, ff. 104v–105.   [113] *Bele* v. *Mersshe* (1529) KB 27/1072, m. 77d.

[114] *Prestly* v. *Reve* (1516) CP 40/1015, m. 556 (demurrer; no judgment); *Smyth* v. *Halle* (1516) KB 27/1019, m. 74; *Fysshe* v. *Kyghley* (1520) KB 27/1034, m. 31d; *Alyn* v. *Tregean* (1533) CP 40/1079, m. 455; *Rowley* v. *Roberdys* (1538) KB 27/1109, m. 68d.

[115] *Clerk* v. *Ferdinando* (1528) KB 27/1069, m. 79 (suit to Wolsey C.).

[116] Cf. Helmholz, *Select Cases on Defamation*, p. xxxi.

[117] *Reymond* v. *Lord Fitzwater* (1521) Spelman 2 (third point); *Legat* v. *Bulle* (1533) Spelman 6.

[118] Justifications then simply stated that the words were true: *Hertop* v. *Ryland* (1523) CP 40/1040, m. 402; *Pomell* v. *Cawmond* (1526) CP 40/1052, m. 508; *Belman* v. *Priour* (1532) KB 27/1084, m. 64; *Cole* v. *Render* (1533) KB 27/1089, m. 19; *Lane* v. *Grove* (1533) CP 40/1077, m. 603; *Spaldyng* v. *Hoper* (1535) KB 27/1094, m. 8; *Heydon* v. *Bokkyng* (1535) KB 27/1095, m. 65; *Pylfold* v. *Derrant* (1535) Trin. 27 Hen. VIII, fo. 22, pl. 17; CP 40/1086, m. 349. In the last case, Fitzherbert J. said the plea was 'common course'. In *Southern* v. *Prydeaux* (1537–8) KB 27/1103, m. 40, there is a demurrer to a justification.

[119] e.g. *Smyth* v. *Halle* (1516) KB 27/1019, m. 74 (first part of plea); *Baker* v. *Gresbroke* (1520) CP 40/1030, m. 428; *Feld* v. *Norton* (1533) CP 40/1077, m. 451; *Alyn* v. *Tregean* (1533) CP 40/1079, m. 455; *Thynche* v. *Farley*, ibid., m. 552; *Rowley* v. *Roberdys* (1538–9) KB 27/1109, m. 68d.

or on some particular cause specially pleaded.[120] But there was no halfway house between the two; either the words had to be true, or there had to be a formal prosecution. The Common Pleas decided in 1530 that it was no defence to plead the drawing of an information which had not been laid before a court,[121] and in 1535 that it was no plea to set out the common voice and fame as being in itself a justification for speaking untrue defamatory words, without alleging a prosecution.[122]

The canonistic view that the defendant could only justify his words, whether true or false, if he had spoken them in the public interest,[123]—though rejected by the common law where the words were in fact true—survived the fission of justifications (truth and privilege) in the diluted form of a doctrine that the privilege of a prosecutor was not absolute but could be destroyed by malice. This is shown by the appearance of a replication *de malicia* in such cases, evidently adapted from the general replication *de injuria*, to the effect that the plaintiff was motivated by malice.[124] And this, in turn, may account for experiments with a new form of action on the case in which the plaintiff anticipated a defence of lawful prosecution by alleging in his declaration the defendant's malice and the absence of reasonable cause.[125] This is the origin of the tort of malicious prosecution.

Prosecution for crime was not the only situation in which privilege might be raised. In *Lord Beauchamp* v. *Croft* (1497),[126] an action of *scandalum magnatum* brought upon an accusation of forgery, the defendant pleaded that the accusation

---

[120] e.g. *Smyth* v. *Halle* (1516) KB 27/1019, m. 74 (stolen sheep in his possession); *Bele* v. *Mersshe* (1529) KB 27/1073, m. 77d (sheep with defendant's mark found in plaintiff's flock, and he refused to explain it); *Kyng* v. *Maye* (1535–7) CP 40/1086, m. 533 (hot pursuit of armed thieves in distinctive clothes; demurrer); *Wythe* v. *Alens* (1541) KB 27/1121, m. 115 (suspected of sorcery because he had a conjuring book); *Grygg* v. *Freman* (1543) KB 27/1128, m. 74 (goods disappeared from plaintiff's keeping and she admitted taking them).

[121] *Branstell* v. *Tygo* (1530) CP 40/1065, m. 154 (demurrer; judgment for plaintiff, who was required to mitigate the damages).

[122] *Maunder* v. *Ware* (1534–5) Hil. 26 Hen. VIII, fo. 9, pl. 1; CP 40/1083, m. 409d (pr. 100 Selden Soc. 47; demurrer; judgment for plaintiff). Cf. the wider interpretation of this decision in Helmholz, *Select Cases on Defamation*, pp. lxxxiv–lxxxv.

[123] See Helmholz, *Select Cases on Defamation*, pp. xxx–xxxiv.

[124] *Hawkes* v. *Husee* (1516) KB 27/1019, m. 68 ('de malicia sua propria'); *Bele* v. *Mersshe* (1529) KB 27/1072, m. 77d ('de suis propriis precogitatis malicia, odio, mundia, et injuria, absque causis etc.'); *Bukmaster* v. *Tomlynson* (1533) CP 40/1079, m. 426d ('ex sua perversa nequicia et perfida malicia'; plaintiff recovers £6 damages).

[125] *Wryght* v. *Grove* (1533–5) CP 40/1079, m. 641 (demurrer to declaration); *Cowper* v. *Parke* (1545) KB 27/1136, m. 24 (advisement after verdict); *Pelter* v. *Derby*, ibid., m. 159d; *Bowell* v. *Baker* (1546) KB 27/1137, m. 28. Cf. the slightly different formula in *Crome* v. *Ordyng* (1556) CP 40/1166, m. 513 (imparlance); *Furlonger* v. *Chanell* (1556) CP 40/1168, m. 747 (imparlance); *Crome* v. *Ordyng* (1558) CP 40/1173, m. 526 (writ of inquiry).

[126] 1 Caryll 349; abr. Dyer 285; CP 40/940, m. 341 (imparlance). The parties (who were involved in several lawsuits) eventually submitted all their differences to arbitration: BL Add. Ch. 73699 (arbitration bond, 7 May 1498).

was made in a writ which had been duly returned. Most of the argument concerned the correct form of pleading, though the question of privilege was also raised. The defendant's counsel conceded that the law protected plaintiffs from a counter-action for defamation merely because they lost, but contended that it was unlawful to bring a false action and that it was therefore no justification for speaking false words. It must be remembered that in 1497 there was still no general action on the case for defamation, and counsel was therefore only addressing the remedy for peers. On the other side, it was argued that a plaintiff had a legal right to bring an action, and that the statute of *scandalum magnatum* could not be construed as modifying that right. The court unanimously agreed, and Bryan CJ added that a plaintiff was entitled to commit a slander 'by words during the action and while it is pending, in everything which goes in preferment of his action'.[127]

There are no firm decisions on the question whether this privilege extended to all those involved in legal proceedings, in addition to the unsuccessful plaintiff or prosecutor. In 1520 the status of a witness was considered by the King's Bench, on a demurrer to the evidence, but apparently left undecided.[128] In the 1520s and 1530s, however, the Common Pleas accepted that a witness was immune from an action of conspiracy, because the oath and the public nature of the proceedings raised a presumption that he did not act maliciously;[129] and the same logic would have barred an action for defamation. While the 1520 case was pending, the King's Bench also had to consider the case of a lawyer who justified defamatory words which he had spoken, as a duly retained counsel, in the course of recommending a settlement; the lawyer lost the verdict, but there is no indication on the face of the record that his plea caused any legal difficulty.[130] It was not clear that defamatory written pleadings in courts not of record were privileged.[131]

The majority of defamation actions were brought for words spoken to the plaintiff in the hearing of others, and it was the publication to others which caused the plaintiff's special loss. Since it was the standard practice to aver that the

---

[127] 1 Caryll at 356.

[128] *Pakeman v. Curson* (1520–5) KB 27/1034, m. 15 (demurrer to evidence showing that defendant was a witness at the quarter sessions).

[129] *Anon.* (1528/9) Wm Yelv. 317, no. 12 (by 'all the justices'); *Walker v. Collyns* (1534) Pollard 252, no. 14 ('by some members of the court'); *Anon.* (1549) BL MS. Hargrave 4, fo. 101, *per* Mountagu CJ; *Anon.* (1550/1) ibid., fo. 119v; Moo. 6, pl. 22, *per* Mountagu CJ and Hales J. For earlier precedents see *Horsyngton v. Dounton* (1511) CP 40/997, m. 450; *Pethyll v. Atwyll* (1518) CP 40/1020B, m. 439.

[130] *Audelett v. Colyns* (1522) KB 27/1045, m. 73; 94 Selden Soc. *247–8*. Wiliam Colyns pleaded that he was learned in the law, and retained of counsel; other evidence shows that he was a member of the Middle Temple (adm. 1519) and an attorney of the Common Pleas.

[131] See *Butler v. Ardeson* (1522) E13/200, m. 22 (defamatory bill exhibited before Council); *Cavendyshe v. Doddes* (1551) KB 27/1160, m. 86 (defamatory bill in Chancery, which is set out in the declaration).

defamatory words were 'related and published' concerning the plaintiff, it was probably a defence that the words were not published. The concept of publication may have been less extensive than in later times, because Brooke CJ held in 1558 that defamatory words in a private letter to a friend were not actionable, 'for it does not seem to have been done with the intention of publishing the said things'.[132] On the other hand, in 1555 the judges were not even sure that publication was essential and were prepared to countenance an action for defamatory words in a letter written to the plaintiff himself.[133]

[132] *Anon.* (1558) BL MS. Hargrave 4, fo. 127.
[133] *Thynne* v. *Sturton* (1555) Gell's reports, I, Pas. 1 & 2 Phil. & Mar., fo. 9.

45

Conversion and Detinue

THE standard medieval remedies for wrongs to chattels were trespass *de bonis asportatis*, for taking them with force, and the *praecipe* writ of detinue, for withholding them. The latter had the disadvantage of attracting wager of law, and by the beginning of our period lawyers were seeking an alternative.

Actions on the case against bailees for using or converting goods are found in the second half of the fifteenth century,[1] and are best regarded as first cousins of the well-established actions for damaging or destroying goods bailed. Since the general action against a bailee was detinue, these newer actions were open to challenge on the ground that detinue was more appropriate.[2] On the other hand, plaintiffs could contend that the action on the case provided a remedy which detinue did not. In the case of damaged goods, detinue would secure the restoration of the goods or their value but not compensation for the impairment;[3] while, in the case of complete destruction, detinue was arguably frustrated altogether because the goods no longer existed and so the plaintiff could not truthfully assert that the defendant detained them.[4] The validity of these contentions is obscured by the workings of the action of detinue. Since there could be no judicial review of a moral decision to wage of law, or of an award of damages, any substantive thinking about the scope of detinue was no more than speculation. It was no doubt reasonable to say that the bailee was estopped from pleading *Non detinet* if it amounted to a denial of the bailment; but there was no legal process which could stop the bailee's mouth if he persisted.

If an action on the case lay for damage or destruction, there was a persuasive case for extending it to conversion by spending or consumption. But the conservative view, asserted by Bryan CJ in 1479, was that any such extension would be undesirable since it would deprive the defendant of the opportunity to wage law.[5] Although the bailee was not supposed to wage his law when the loss occurred

---

[1] e.g. *Anon.* (1453) HLS MS. 156, Mich. 32 Hen. VI, unfol. (bailee of sealed box of silver alleged to have broken the seal, taken out the silver, and converted it to his own use).

[2] For the rule against duplication of remedies see above, 778 n. 16.

[3] *Hayden v. Raggelond* (1510) 2 Caryll 608 (tr. B. & M. 528); *Anon.* (*c.*1520/30) Yorke 239, no. 412; *Anon.* (*c.*1526/35) Yorke 240, no. 415 (tr. B. & M. 402).

[4] Hil. 5 Hen. VII, fo. 15, pl. 6. Cf. 94 Selden Soc. 248.

[5] *Calwodelegh v. John* (1479) Hil. 18 Edw. IV, fo. 23, pl. 5 (tr. B. & M. 526); CP 40/868, m. 428.

through his fault, the matter was left to his conscience, and allowing an action on the case would have shifted the burden of decision on to a jury. Even where the defendant in detinue chose a jury, it cannot safely be assumed that damages were never given for destruction or conversion. The later law on such matters was produced in the course of justifying the action on the case, and cannot therefore be accepted as evidence of the law prevailing before evasion was contemplated.

CONVERSION BY A BAILEE

Within sixty years, the King's Bench had sanctioned a means of escaping from Bryan CJ's orthodoxy, and the story has an exact parallel in the history of *assumpsit* as a replacement for debt.[6] One pleader in 1522 was frank enough to describe the new action as 'detinue on the case';[7] but legal propriety demanded that the new action should somehow be distinguished from the old. The escape route was that, although trespass on the case could not be brought for merely detaining or failing to return the goods bailed, it did lie for the 'misdemeanour' or tort of damaging, 'mis-keeping', or appropriating them.[8] On the same principle, a bailee who broke open a bag of jewels and converted the proceeds could be sued in trespass *vi et armis*, even though he could have waged his law if he had been sued in detinue. By 'breaking bulk' the bailee destroyed the bailment, and his misconduct was therefore a forcible wrong.[9]

The 1479 case before Bryan CJ was an action for breaking up silver cups and converting them, and it has been suggested that the earliest actions on the case for conversion were cases of complete physical alteration (*specificatio*), which is a form of destruction. The goods were 'converted' into something else; such an alteration rendered detinue inappropriate; and so there was a gap to be filled by case.[10] However, the commonest form of complaint in the plea rolls of the early sixteenth century was of opening a bag of money or goods and spending the contents.[11]

---

[6] See below, 852–62, 869–74.

[7] *Andrewe v. Fulwod* (1522) KB 27/1042, m. 32d ('de placito detentionis super casu').

[8] *Hayden v. Raggelond* (1510) 2 Caryll 608 (tr. B. & M. 528); *Anon.* (*c.*1530) Yorke 239, no. 412; *Anon.* (*c.*1526/35) Yorke 240, no. 415 (tr. B. & M. 402); *Pykeryng v. Thurgoode* (1532) Spelman 4 at 5 (tr. B. & M. 412). Case for 'misuser' is acknowledged in an Inner Temple discussion temp. Hen. VII: 105 Selden Soc. 146, *per* Fulwood.

[9] *Bourgchier v. Cheseman* (1504–8) Mich. 20 Hen. VII, fo. 4, pl. 13; KB 27/972, m. 88 (no judgment). The question as reported in the year book is only whether the conversion could be traversed, since the element of force lay in the breaking bulk rather than the conversion. But the judges in *Pykeryng v. Thurgoode* (last note) thought the case had also settled the larger question.

[10] A. W. B. Simpson, 'The Introduction of the Action on the Case for Conversion' (1959) 75 *LQR* 364–80; repr. in *Legal Theory and Legal History*, 93–109. For alteration of property by specification see above, 731.

[11] e.g. *Wynter v. Hyll* (1506) KB 27/979, m. 7d (*vi et armis* form); *Glyn v. Felyppe* (1510) KB 27/995, m. 43d (allegation of fraud); *Pert v. Starkey* (1517) KB 27/1023, m. 26 (trespass 'super casu' against executor, with *vi et armis*; judgment for plaintiff); *Leveson v. Foster* (1524) KB 27/1050, m. 61 (*assumpsit*

Putting coins back into circulation is not far removed from cutting up silver plate and spending it; in either case, the identity of the pieces of silver was lost without trace. It had also by this time become common to add to the declaration an undertaking by the bailee to look after the goods and to return them on request. One may reasonably doubt whether there really was an explicit promise in most cases. The *assumpsit* allegation embodied, in the formal language of the pleader, the common understanding of the bailee's obligation and served to distinguish the case still further from that of mere detention.[12] At any rate, the *assumpsit* was not the gist of the action.[13] The conversion in these actions was commonly alleged to be a conversion, not of the goods themselves,[14] but of the proceeds of their sale. One legal consequence of this formulation was that the action could be used both for unidentifiable property, such as silver or grain,[15] and for specific chattels.[16] And it enabled a further extension to the case of the agent who misappropriated the proceeds of sale of chattels which he was authorized to sell; here the overlap was with account rather than detinue.[17]

On the same principle as that which underlay the action for conversion, an action would lie against a bailee who simply wasted or squandered goods to no purpose. Thus, in 1515 a shopkeeper was sued by his master for giving away clothes to prodigal and ill-disposed persons and wasting money at unlawful games.[18]

but no *vi et armis*; judgment for plaintiff); *Paunt* v. *Palmer* (1524) KB 27/1051, m. 25 (similar; no verdict); *Yeo* v. *Mychell* (1525) CP 40/1049, m. 129 (no *vi et armis*); *Soler* v. *Oldeale* (1526) KB 27/1058, m. 26 (*vi et armis* form; judgment for plaintiff); *Glossop* v. *Smyth* (1528) KB 27/1069, m. 61d (similar; no verdict); *Aby* v. *Wylson* (1530) KB 27/1076, m. 28d (similar; verdict for defendant).

[12] For the bailee's liability, see above, 760–2.

[13] See *Bourgchier* v. *Cheseman* (1504–8) above (alleges *assumpsit*, breaking bulk, and conversion; defendant allowed to traverse conversion); *Wynter* v. *Hyll* (1506) KB 27/979, m. 7d (bailee traverses taking and conversion); *Rycroft* v. *Gamme* (1523) Spelman 3 (no need to allege prepayment); *Warton* v. *Ashepole* (1524) Spelman 4 ('the defendant can not traverse the undertaking, for it is immaterial, for the delivery and the conversion to his use are the cause of the action'). Cf. *Arnold* v. *Furnes* (1499) KB 27/953, m. 35d (pleads 'Did not undertake, sell, or convert'); *Wode* v. *Gamon* (1533) CP 40/1079, m. 312 (pleads *Non assumpsit*); *Fenton* v. *Nooke* (1542) KB 27/1122, m. 64 (sim.).

[14] In *Astley* v. *Fereby* (1510) CP 40/993, m. 512 (below, 805), where there was a melting down of silver, the word *convertit* was applied not to the change of form but to the subsequent appropriation.

[15] e.g. *Lincoln* v. *Sawyer* (1513–15) KB 27/1008, m. 18; 1017, m. 73 (barley); *Pratt* v. *Gybson* (1514) KB 27/1011, m. 23d (barley); *Hewys* v. *Perfrey* (1527) KB 27/1063, m. 68 (silver); *Southworth* v. *Fermour* (1529) KB 27/1071, m. 66 (silver). However, in such cases it was not absurd to allege conversion of the silver itself: *Asteley* v. *Fereby* (1510) CP 40/993, m. 512 (defendant not a bailee; see below, 805); *Williams* v. *Chalcott* (1542) KB 27/1122, m. 62.

[16] e.g. *Arnold* v. *Furnes* (1499) KB 27/953, m. 35d (hats); *Burneby* v. *Rawson* (1513) KB 27/1006, m. 27 (jewels and clothes); *Bewerley* v. *Dyngham* (1519) KB 27/1031, m. 77 (horse); *Bulkeley* v. *Cleymond* (1522) KB 27/1043, m. 68 (cameo ring); *Hartylpole* v. *Darcy* (1540) KB 27/1115, m. 23 (jewels and clothes); *Lyon* v. *Wakefeld* (1544–6) KB 27/1133, m. 73 (action against executor; demurrer to declaration).

[17] See below, 879.

[18] *Knollys* v. *Maye* (1515) KB 27/1017, m. 40. Cf. *Haltham* v. *Keles* (*c.*1535), a London suit recited in C1/834/7 (action for obtaining plaintiff's money from his servant by gaming). Apprentices commonly

And in 1532 judgment was given against a bailee who had 'wasted and consumed', without converting, the cloth which he had undertaken to look after.[19]

There is no clear evidence that the Court of Common Pleas, after the time of Bryan CJ, was hostile to actions for conversion against bailees, at any rate where they 'broke bulk', and a number of cases proceeded to issue throughout our period.[20] In a solitary reported case of 1510, the liability of a bailee for mere passive neglect was discussed but left undecided; several of the justices spoke obiter in favour of allowing an action on the case for conversion, because that was positive misconduct: not doing was a different matter.[21] The distinction seems to be a late survival of the nonfeasance–misfeasance dichotomy which had recently been abandoned in *assumpsit*.[22] Yet, even if case had become an established remedy, detinue continued to be by far the commoner form of action used against bailees, notwithstanding the risk of wager of law.[23] In the Common Pleas rolls for 1535, thirty-two detinue actions of all kinds proceeded as far as issue; law was waged successfully in three, and without success in another seven, but in the other twenty-two cases issue was joined by the country.

TROVER

The further extension of actions for conversion, to reach defendants who were not bailees, seems to have followed the same course as the development of detinue a century or so earlier: first by means of a declaration setting out how the goods came to the defendant's hands (*devenit ad manus*), and then by a declaration based on an allegation of finding (*trover*), which was or rapidly became non-traversable and therefore potentially fictitious. As with detinue, it seems that the simple *devenit ad manus* formula was chiefly used against personal representatives or others who had come by the goods of a deceased person.[24] The trover formula

covenanted not to waste their master's money in gaming: see e.g. *Hasilhert v. Fokes* (1530) 121 Selden Soc. 315 at 316.

[19] *Kynnewelmersshe v. Atkyns* (1532) KB 27/1083, m. 63d. Wasting and consuming could be coupled with conversion: e.g. *Rycroft v. Gamme* (1523) KB 27/1047, m. 21 (pr. 94 Selden Soc. 242). Or with negligence: *Sadeler v. Body* (1506) KB 27/981, m. 50d.

[20] e.g. *Tyrell v. Dervell* (1507) CP 40/981, m. 512 (bailee of chest undertook to return on request; broke bulk and converted contents); *Yeo v. Mychell* (1526) CP 40/1049, m. 129 (*assumpsit* to look after a bag of money; broke it open and converted the money); *Wode v. Gamon* (1533) CP 40/1079, m. 312 (*assumpsit* to carry barrels by boat; converted to own use and did not deliver); *Pek v. Gappe* (1551) CP 40/1147A, m. 146 (bailee of purse with money broke seals, took contents, and converted them; no *assumpsit*).

[21] *Hayden v. Raggelond* (1510) 2 Caryll 608 (tr. B. & M. 528); CP 40/992, m. 451 (demurrer; no judgment). This seems a more likely identification than that made in 94 Selden Soc. 251.

[22] See below, 841–58.

[23] e.g. *Myller v. Baynbrigg* (1554) KB 27/1170, m. 79 (detinue for long list of furniture and utensils; defendant wages law, but then waives the law and puts himself on the country).

[24] e.g. *Bourgchier v. Cheseman* (1504–8) KB 27/972, m. 88; *Andrewe v. Peryn* (1512) CP 40/1000, m. 126 (detinue of household stuff; wages law); *Byron v. Clyfton* (1512) CP 40/1001, m. 463 (detinue of

may be considered an offshoot, since it used the words 'came into the hands of [the defendant] by finding'.

The possibility of an action against a finder of goods was mooted in the later fifteenth century,[25] though the first example noticed in our period of an action on the case against a stranger is from the Common Pleas in 1510.[26] It was not a case of trover, but of buying and converting stolen goods. The plaintiff declared that his silver plate had been stolen, that he had notified the defendant, and that the defendant with this knowledge had bought the silver, melted it down, changed its shape, and converted it to his own use, refusing to compensate the plaintiff for its value. The defendant, protesting that the declaration was insufficient in law, and that he did not possess the alleged knowledge or engage in any fraudulent scheme, pleaded that he did not melt, change, or convert the silver. The issue was sent for trial at nisi prius, but no more is known. The case seems to be unique but is interesting in that it precedes by several years the first example of the trover declaration.

The trover formula, setting out an accidental loss and finding, was borrowed directly from detinue, but the combination of trover and conversion in an action on the case was not achieved until the 1520s. Like so many developments in the action on the case, it was primarily the work of the King's Bench.[27] The earliest form may be regarded as transitional between the *devenit ad manus* formula and the classical trover declaration. In a case of 1519, the plaintiff declared that he had lost the goods, that they had come into the hands of a deceased person whose widow had married the defendant, and that the defendant had sold and converted them. The defendant, protesting that the plaintiff had not possessed the goods and that they had not come into his hands, traversed the sale—and therefore, impliedly, the conversion.[28] This action was abandoned, and the plaintiff brought a second action in which he omitted to mention the loss and merely alleged that the goods had accidentally (*casualiter*) come into the hands of the deceased person. This time he won the verdict, but the court took advisement for six years and no judgment was ever entered.[29] There is no report to illuminate the nature

Canterbury Tales and other chattels; pleads *Non detinet per patriam*); *Pert v. Starkey* (1517) KB 27/1023, m. 26; *Audelet v. Latton* (No. 2) (1520–6) KB 27/1034, m. 50d (discussed below); *Southworth v. Fermour* (1529) KB 27/1071, m. 66; cf *Watson v. Woodward* (1530) KB 27/1077, m. 30 (alleges negligent keeping rather than conversion). See also *Anon.* (1542) Brooke Abr., *Accion sur le Case*, pl. 103 (*devenit ad manus* and wasting; pleads *Non devenit ad manus*).

25 *Wellys v. Robynson* (1484) Mich. 2 Ric. III, fo. 15, pl. 39 ('trespass' or detinue); identified from CP 40/890, m. 128; note at Sutton's reading in the Inner Temple (1494) 105 Selden Soc. 293, no. 40 ('trespass' lies against finder who sells, but not against one who 'behaves as a finder').

26 *Astley v. Fereby* (1510) CP 40/993, m. 512.

27 Cf. *Tothill v. Forde* (c.1522) undated writ in Jenour's entries, fo. 319v.

28 *Audelet v. Latton* (No. 1) (1519) KB 27/1030, m. 39.

29 *Audelet v. Latton* (No. 2) (1520–6) KB 27/1034, m. 50d.

of the legal difficulty presented by the case, though it may have been related to that which gave rise to the exactly contemporary debate over using *assumpsit* in place of debt.[30] Perhaps it was argued that, in the case of the finder or stranger, there was no reason to permit an alternative to debt or detinue. It might also have given an unfair second chance to a plaintiff who had been defeated by wager of law in either of those actions.[31] The inconclusive case of the widow was followed by two more inconclusive cases concerning lost purses containing money, where the plaintiff made use of the 'breaking bulk' formula against a stranger.[32] Then, in 1531—within a year, it may be noticed, of the critical decision concerning *assumpsit* for money[33]—a plaintiff in another lost-purse case framed his action in terms of an accidental loss, a coming to the hands of the defendant by finding, and a felonious sale and conversion. The words of felony would be dropped from subsequent actions, but this was otherwise the classical trover declaration. The defendant pleaded that he had bought the goods in market overt, but the jury found for the plaintiff and he recovered damages.[34] Whether or not this judgment was preceded by an argument in banc, it may be supposed that it was decisive. The action for trover and conversion soon became common form in the King's Bench, and was occasionally used even where the plaintiff was a personal representative who had no prior possession.[35] By the 1540s there were also variant declarations against finders where wrongs were alleged without speaking of conversion: for instance, actions for using or otherwise damaging the goods found so that they lost value,[36] for cancelling a bond,[37] or for detaining and misusing an indenture of lease so that the plaintiff was expelled from possession.[38]

---

[30] See below, 869–74.

[31] See *Rosendale* v. *Kelly* (1538) KB 27/1107, m. 32 (trover for two sacks of hops; pleads that he successfully waged law in an action of debt for the same hops; demurrer).

[32] *Clerke* v. *Forde* (1528) KB 27/1066, m. 33 (defendant pleads finding and a willingness to hand over); *Yong* v. *Garett* (1529) KB 27/1071, m. 63 (*devenit ad manus*; pleads finding and return). In both cases the plaintiff alleged force and arms; it was the defendant who pleaded a trover.

[33] *Pykeryng* v. *Thurgoode* (1532) below, 857.   [34] *Wysse* v. *Andrewe* (1531) KB 27/1081, m. 78.

[35] e.g. *Massy* v. *Whytefeld* (1539) KB 27/1113, m. 31 (action by executors against testator's tenant alleged to have found a bag of money on the premises demised); *Cotes* v. *Cardyn* (1540) KB 27/1117, m. 74 (action by executor alleging loss by testator); *Kent* v. *Woodcocke* (1554) KB 27/1171, m. 105 (count on a grant of chattels by the deceased, where the possession came to the defendant instead of the plaintiff).

[36] *Anon.* (1542) Brooke Abr., *Accion sur le Case*, pl. 103 (possessor of goods wasted them); *Watson* v. *Beswycke* (1545) KB 27/1137, m. 62 (finder of cup used it daily so that the weight of silver and the gilt were diminished by wear; pleads gift); *Mountstevyn* v. *Browne* (1551) KB 27/1160, m. 71 (finder of items of furniture occupied, converted, and used them so that they became decayed, torn, and of no value).

[37] *Brykenden* v. *Cosen* (No. 2) (1544) KB 27/1133, m. 39d (judgment for plaintiff).

[38] *Chaunsy* v. *Tyson* (1541) KB 27/1121, m. 135 (counts on loss and finding of indenture, a refusal to return it, a misuse of it to expel the plaintiff and take the profits to his own use, and a careless keeping so that it was taken by persons unknown; plaintiff failed to appear at trial).

The earliest actions of trover and conversion may have arisen from genuine cases of loss and finding.[39] But the wider attraction of the trover form was no doubt that, as in detinue *sur trover*, it avoided the pitfalls of the *devenit ad manus* declaration which had evidently caused trouble in the 1520s. However, this advantage could only be made generally available if the allegation of finding was not issuable. There are slight formal indications that the trover allegation was soon held not to be traversable,[40] but the prevalence of fiction is obvious enough from the items of property which became the subject of trover actions. Among the items which could not easily have been 'casually lost' and found were long lists of the contents of houses,[41] a stock of printed books,[42] and a battery of guns.[43] In the last case, a special verdict—to the effect that the guns had been seized under a royal commission—formally proves that the declaration was fictional.

In 1550 the King's Bench was asked to overturn a judgment given in the city court of Coventry on the ground that the plaintiff should have brought detinue *sur trover* rather than case.[44] But this was a case where a local pleader had alleged that the finder of a purse and money had refused to return them on request, omitting any mention of a conversion. The bare refusal to return was a detinue without more, and was never properly actionable in case in the absence of an agreement.[45] Yet there does seem to have been a short lull in the progress of trover and conversion in the mid-1550s, and a corresponding increase in the number of actions of trespass to chattels. In 1556 we even find a King's Bench defendant successfully waging law in detinue *sur trover* for a ferry-boat.[46] It can only be a matter of speculation whether this lull was the result of judicial hesitancy, since there are no reported cases. But there can have been no significant or permanent

[39] Besides the lost-purse cases, note also *Cotes* v. *Cardyn* (1540) KB 27/1117, m. 74 (defendant pleads that after finding the chattel he made proclamation for the owner to come forward, and he returned it to a goldsmith who claimed the property). [40] See 94 Selden Soc. 253.

[41] e.g. *Brykenden* v. *Cosen* (1542) KB 27/1125, m. 102 (items include a pair of clavichords); *Trotter* v. *Bretten* (1551) KB 27/1158, m. 195 (judgment for plaintiff); *Mountstevyn* v. *Browne* (1551) KB 27/1160, m. 71; *Weston* v. *Rea* (1553) KB 27/1165, m. 142 (action by administrator; defendant pleads will); *Clarke* v. *Baldwyn* (1555) KB 27/1176, m. 89. These are no doubt mostly administration disputes. Cf. *Costerd* v. *Kente* (1558) KB 27/1186, m. 123 (administrators count on loss of cow and gold coins by deceased).

[42] *Coffyn* v. *Gropall* (1551) KB 27/1160, m. 65 (long list of priced books; recovers £36). This was clearly a commercial dispute; cf. *Gropall* v. *Coffyn* (1552) KB 27/1162, m. 135 (*assumpsit* on sale of similar list of books; recovers £30).

[43] *Arundell* v. *Carye* (1549) KB 27/1149, m. 75 (11 guns 'cum uno le stock et xvii lez chambers tormentis predictis spectantibus').

[44] *Savage* v. *Morres* (1550) KB 27/1156, m. 48, first error ('protulisse debuit querelam suam sive actionem detentionis super le trover et non actionem super casum').

[45] e.g. a pledge: *Merye* v. *Edges* (1555) CP 40/1164, m. 836 (plaintiff pledged silver with defendant for a debt of £7, which he had paid, and the defendant refused to redeliver).

[46] *Style* v. *Edmundes* (1556) KB 27/1189, m. 83d (detinue for a *cimba* called the *Mary of Sandwich*).

shift of opinion in the King's Bench. Under Saunders CJ, at any rate, trover was back in regular use.[47]

The action for trover and conversion, though sanctioned by the King's Bench, nevertheless made little progress at all in the Common Pleas. Occasional writs for trover and conversion were issued by the Chancery and returned in the Common Pleas,[48] but the first known case to proceed as far as an appearance also resulted in a formal challenge noticed by two reporters. Lord Mountegle brought an action in 1554 against the countess of Worcester alleging that in 1534 he had possessed a gold chain, that he had accidentally lost it in London, that it had come into the hands and possession of the countess by finding, and that she—scheming to defraud the plaintiff of the chain—had sold it to persons unknown and converted the proceeds. Such an allegation reeks of fiction. But the countess traversed the sale of the chain—thereby impliedly confessing the trover—and to this plea the plaintiff demurred. The principal point of the demurrer was that the countess should have pleaded Not guilty. Although the reasoning is not made fully explicit,[49] the evident fear was that to allow the details to be traversed would expose the underlying fiction. But the defendant, by her counsel Serjeant Dyer, took the opportunity to challenge the action itself, on the ground that detinue was more appropriate. Dyer argued that deceit could not be alleged against a finder, since there was no privity, and that case would only lie for conversion where detinue was unavailable—for instance, if the goods were sold in market overt so that title passed to a stranger.[50] The opinion of the court on the substantive question is not fully reported but seems to have been unfavourable to the plaintiff. Judgment was never entered, but the Common Pleas continued thereafter to take a restrictive attitude towards the new form of action.

[47] *Stokes* v. *Kyrby* (1557) KB 27/1183, m. 30 (for numerous items of furniture); *Harden* v. *Rowland*, ibid., m. 114 (for plate); *Hatche* v. *Thorne*, ibid., m. 193 (for clothing; *protestando* that declaration insufficient in law); *Wyllyams* v. *Hudson* (1557) KB 27/1184, m. 177 (for jewels; judgment for plaintiff).

[48] e.g. *Bowtys* v. *Wylkynson* (1535) CP 40/1086, m. 584 (op. se).

[49] Cf. *Savage* v. *Morres* (1550), above; KB 27/1156, m. 48, third error (should not have pleaded Not guilty because no act was alleged but only nonfeasance: 'quia nullus actus supponitur fieri...sed pro non faciendo quendam actum').

[50] *Lord Mountegle* v. *Countess of Worcester* (1554–8) Dyer 121a (tr. B. & M. 532); BL MS. Harley 1691, fo. 94; Brooke Abr., *Accion sur le Case*, pl. 109; CP 40/1157, m. 284 (op. se); CP 40/1161, m. 427 (demurrer; extracted in Benl. 41, pl. 73). The demurrer was entered Hil. 1555; the last continuance was to Hil. 1558.

46

Procuring Breaches of Contract

THE action on the case for procuring a breach of contract is another example of innovation in the King's Bench under Fyneux and Fitzjames CJJ. It was usually—and has been ever since—associated with disputes over employment, its antecedent being the action on the Ordinance of Labourers for retaining or harbouring servants. The old statutory action was still common form in the early sixteenth century, but it had certain restrictions: for instance, it did not lie in respect of apprentices, professional persons, or independent contractors, and it did not lie against third parties who incited servants to transfer their services to other masters. These restrictions explain the first action on the case noticed in the rolls, which was brought by a London rector and churchwardens for procuring a parish clerk to leave their service; the defendant pleaded that he had only persuaded the clerk to return to his former parish, where he was bound by a prior retainer.[1] Here the statutory action would not have been appropriate, both because the defendant did not retain the clerk in his own service and because a clerk was probably not within the scope of the legislation.[2] In the late 1520s, actions on the case for inciting servants to leave their masters become common,[3] and variant forms are found for encouraging absenteeism,[4] and inciting an apprentice to waste his master's goods and money in gambling.[5] The only known legal challenge came in 1529, when Oliver Southworth—a filazer of the King's Bench, and a fishmonger of London—brought an action in non-standard form which may represent his own draftsmanship.[6] The complaint was that, whereas one H had been thrown out of his father's house in tattered clothes and had been wandering unemployed, as a beggar, and the plaintiff had taken pity on him and

---

[1] *Wren v. Bodefeld* (1514–15) KB 27/1012, m. 39; 2 Caryll 681.

[2] Cf. *Selers v. Cokkis* (1522) KB 27/1043, m. 33d (organist sued on the ordinance; judgment by default for 20s. 4d. damages).

[3] e.g. *Traps v. Chubbe* (1527) KB 27/1065, m. 43; *Pester v. Cobley* (1528) KB 27/1066, m. 7; *Cheryton v. Eliot* (1529) KB 27/1071, m. 5; *Polyver v. Gery* (1529) CP 40/1061, m. 562; *Goslyng v. Cokke* (1535) CP 40/1086, m. 163d (*optulit se*); *Hobert v. Cowper* (1540) KB 27/1116, m. 4; *Kelly v. Maynforth* (1545) KB 27/1134, m. 29.   [4] *Stokys v. Est* (1528) KB 27/1066, m. 10d (servant lodged with defendant).

[5] *Popham v. Rysley* (1535) in the Sheriffs' Court, London, recited in *Rysley v. Popham* (c.1536) C1/880/97. Rysley claimed the apprentice had been brought into his house by 'rufflers', unknown to himself.

[6] *Southworth v. Blake* (1529) KB 27/1072, m. 103d. For Southworth see 94 Selden Soc. 356.

retained him as an apprentice fishmonger for seven years; and whereas, in the expectation of useful service from him, he had sent him to grammar school for a year and bought him new clothes, nevertheless the defendant—scheming to deprive him of H's service and to extort and convert the profit thereof—incited and procured H to leave his service, so that the plaintiff not only lost the profit from H's service but also the wasted expenditure on clothing and educating him. Although apprentices were outside the scope of the ordinance, the allegation of special loss was intended to put the matter beyond argument. The trouble arose over the defendant's plea, for he said that the apprenticeship had not been enrolled according to the custom of London, and therefore H was free and left of his own accord, and the defendant had found him wandering at St Albans and retained him there. The plaintiff demurred to this plea, and no judgment was entered. We can only guess at the troublesome point of law, which may have been that the appropriate plea was Not guilty rather than a justification. It seems unlikely that the cause of action itself would have come into doubt.

In the same year, an attempt was made to extend the remedy to cases outside the realms of employment. A plaintiff declared that a third party (X) had promised him the first refusal if ever he should sell his copyhold lands, and that in hope of this he had set money aside and built on adjacent land; but the defendant, knowing these facts, knowing also that X was of insufficient substance to pay damages for breach of covenant, and scheming to deprive the plaintiff of his covenant with X, maliciously procured, abetted, and laboured X to break the covenant and bought the land himself. The defendant traversed the procuring, but the outcome is not recorded.[7] The case apparently stands alone and may have been forgotten. But it represents an awareness that there should be a remedy for the indirect wrong of procuring a breach of contract. If such actions were approved, it would have enabled a disappointed purchaser of land to sue not only the vendor but also a third party who bought the land with notice of the prior sale, and that would have been another instance of the common law adopting a principle of equity by means of an action on the case. Examples of actions of this kind are, however, so few that they can hardly be considered to constitute a recognized category.[8]

---

[7] *Palmer* v. *Wryght* (1529) KB 27/1067, m. 62d.

[8] Another example is *Clyfton* v. *Holford* (1555) KB 27/1176, m. 294 (instigating and soliciting a servant to break her master's trust, by persuading her to embezzle some of her master's money; issue).

Part X

THE LAW OF CONTRACT

47

Principles of Contractual Liability

PERHAPS the clearest illustration of the adaptability of the common law in the first half of the sixteenth century, and of the versatility of actions on the case, is provided by the final judicial approval of *assumpsit* for failing to fulfil promises or to pay debts.[1] Not that *assumpsit* was a common action before the middle of the century. It was numerically insignificant in comparison with debt, and even within the sphere of actions on the case it was greatly outnumbered after the 1530s by actions for slander. But its importance lay not in numbers. The experiments made by lawyers, and the decisions taken by the courts, set the English law of contract in the direction which it would follow for the next four or five centuries.

It is true that precedents of *assumpsit* for not performing promises may be found in the writ files and plea rolls from as far back as the fourteenth century.[2] Nearly all the precedents, however, indicate no more than that the plaintiff had purchased a writ in the form indicated; it does not follow that the courts had approved the underlying legal assumptions. If we are right in guessing that writs were made out by the Chancery to the order of plaintiffs,[3] these entries are no more than uncontested *ex parte* claims to a particular form of remedy. That would explain why forms are constantly found which defy the learning of the year books on liability for contractual nonfeasance. On the other hand, it can hardly be denied that a substantial current of similar forms must indicate a body of professional opinion in favour of the remedy sought. In the case of failing to perform a covenant, the lengthy interval—over a century—between the perception of a possible remedy and its sanction by the courts can be explained by the availability of an analogous remedy in many local courts; the role of the central courts was simply to remove a jurisdictional barrier which had come to seem pointless. After 1500, the extension had ceased to be controversial. And yet the further extension of *assumpsit* to enable the recovery of simple debts, though approved by the King's

---

[1] *Assumpsit* for misfeasance, on the other hand, was established by 1400. But few cases were pleaded to issue. See further above, 757–60.

[2] With the exception of actions on the case for not paying debts, which have not been found before 1500.

[3] See above, 325–7. The formulae of writs were generally matched by those of King's Bench bills, which were certainly *ex parte*; but bills were not enrolled until the defendant appeared, and so the full picture will have to await a study of the files.

Bench within thirty years of the first attempts to obtain it, was to divide the two benches for over sixty years. Differences such as these cannot be understood solely from a study of writs and bills. The creation of formulae is certainly the first stage in the process of developing a remedy, but the development cannot be regarded as complete until the remedy has been judicially sanctioned after a formal contest.

The medieval law of contract,[4] as it had developed down to the middle of the fifteenth century, was dominated by the law of evidence. If there was written evidence of a contract, in the form of a document under seal, there were few theoretical obstacles to liability. In fact most contract actions in the central courts by 1500 were founded on deeds, in the form of penal bonds.[5] On the other hand, if there was no deed, the central courts would enforce a contract only if it resulted in a debt, which could be recovered by the writ of debt, or if its breach could be classified as a trespass, either by virtue of physical damage or by virtue of deceit, in which case damages could be recovered in *assumpsit*. Moreover, in the absence of specialty, a debt could be recovered only if there was some *causa* or *quid pro quo* to bind the debtor, and if the principal debtor was still alive at the time of the action.[6]

The key question which underlies the removal of these impediments is how far they were regarded as technical requirements of the law of evidence rather than as essential prerequisites of contractual liability. This is a difficult question to answer, because the year books and reports eschew discussion of abstract principle. There was little need for principle, since the common forms fitted most cases and special pleading was discouraged where wager of law was available.[7] But some clues may be found in the tactics of plaintiffs in error seeking to reverse judgments of local courts where such technical restrictions were absent. In many local courts it was the custom to allow actions of covenant without specialty, and a cautious plaintiff was well advised to mention the custom in his declaration as a safeguard against a writ of error.[8] If the custom was not so averred, it might be contended that the common law governed the matter by default, and then the absence of specialty might be assigned as error.[9] However, when an attempt was made in 1533 to overturn the

---

[4] The word 'contract' is here used in its modern sense, and not in the more confined medieval sense.

[5] For bonds see below, ch. 48.

[6] See W. M. McGovern, 'Contract in Medieval England: the need for quid pro quo and a sum certain' (1968) 54 *Iowa Law Rev.* 19–62; 'The Enforcement of Oral Contracts prior to Assumpsit' (1970) 65 *Northwestern Univ. Law Rev.* 576–614; Simpson, *History of Contract: the action of assumpsit*, 53–88.

[7] Yorke 221, no. 356 ('Note as a maxim that one shall never traverse the cause of a contract where one could wage one's law').

[8] e.g. *Bonyfaunte* v. *Hackewill* (1516) KB 27/1020, m. 26 (alleged custom to sue in Provost Court of Exeter on covenants 'per nuda verba absque scriptis'); *Bodman* v. *Carwardyn* (1555) KB 27/1174, m. 86 (alleged custom to sue in Hereford court of piepowder on 'covenants made orally and without specialty', *ore tenus et absque specialitate facte*).

[9] e.g. *Colman* v. *Thomas* (1530) KB 27/1075, m. 62; *Webbe* v. *Colston* (1552) KB 27/1164, m. 128; *Hunte* v. *Cotton* (1554) KB 27/1172, m. 132 (covenant on a lease; reversed); *Tolpatt* v. *Grovet* (1557) KB 27/1182, m. 35 (Chichester; covenant on a lease). The first three were all from Exeter.

judgment of a borough court on the ground that by the law and custom of England no action of covenant was maintainable without specialty, the King's Bench rejected the submission and affirmed the judgment.[10] The only sensible interpretation of this decision is that the rule requiring proof of covenant by specialty was not a substantive rule governing contracts everywhere but merely a customary rule of practice in the central courts of common law. That was St German's view of the matter.[11] A similar challenge was made to actions of debt upon *concessit solvere*—that is, a mere grant to pay, or concession of indebtedness[12]—on the explicit ground that it was necessary to show some *quid pro quo* for the debt, since *ex nudo pacto non oritur actio*. In 1519 a judgment was reversed on this ground,[13] though in two later cases the court took advisement and no decision was reached.[14] This was therefore a more problematic case. It may be that the need for *quid pro quo* in debt was seen as more substantive than the need for a deed in covenant,[15] with the consequence that it could only be displaced by local custom, as in London; and yet, if the forms of action were dissolved away, a grant to pay was difficult to distinguish from a covenant. Then again, the rule that executors could not be made liable at common law for debts without specialty could be regarded as a substantive principle, so that it was unacceptable to impose such liability even in local courts without a custom,[16] and the executors could not waive the need for specialty by pleading the general issue.[17]

[10] *Welsshe* v. *Hoper* (1533) KB 27/1088, m. 26 (from Hereford; pr. in 94 Selden Soc. 324); reported on another point in Spelman 120.

[11] He held that it did not extend to the Chancery either: *A Little Treatise*, ed. Guy, 111–12.

[12] See above, 283 n. 49 (London), 308 n. 160 (local courts).

[13] *Tofte* v. *Clerke* (1519) KB 27/1033, m. 67 (Shrewsbury; error assigned because the declaration did not show *quid pro quo*—'non ostendit in narratione pro quo predictus D ei fuit indebitatus, etiam non apparet quod predictus defendens habuit quid pro quo'). Cf. *Welsshe* v. *Hoper* (1533) KB 27/1088, m. 26 (pr. 94 Selden Soc. 324), where it is apparently assigned as error that since no *quid pro quo* was alleged, covenant would not lie without specialty but rather debt on a grant (*concessio*).

[14] *Blyke* v. *Barston* (1530) KB 27/1075, m. 26 (Worcester; error assigned because the plaintiff did not allege 'pro qua causa aut aliqua re certa idem T. concessit se debere...'); *Blathewit* v. *Lobbe* (1535) KB 27/1097, m. 31 (New Sarum; error assigned 'in hoc quod ex nudo pacto illo per legem terre Anglie non oritur aliqua actio'). The maxim was also cited in *Marler* v. *Wilmer* (1539) KB 27/1111, m. 64; 41 CLJ 143 (Coventry; *assumpsit* against an executor).

[15] See *Executors of Dudley* v. *Lord Powes* (1488) Mich. 4 Hen. VII, fo. 1, pl. 1 (pledge pleaded in trespass: whether *quid pro quo* must be shown for the debt); CP 40/910, m. 340d; *Mervyn* v. *Lyds* (1553) Dyer 96a at 96b (tr. 'a quid pro quo, which is necessary to every contract').

[16] The clearest case is *Slech* v. *Reynerd* (1531) CP 40/1071, m. 501 (manor court; reversed on a writ of false judgment). Cf. *Asteley* v. *Thurkell* (1502) KB 27/963, m. 62 (Bedford; reversed, but this point not assigned as error); *Serle* v. *Bolyn* (1524) KB 27/1051, m. 28 (Oxford; assigns as first of six errors that no action of debt on a simple contract lies against executors by the laws of England; reversed); *Nasshe* v. *Boket* (1532) CP 40/1074, m. 552 (vill of Maldon; demurrer there on this point; reversed, but other errors assigned); *Busshell* v. *Norman* (1534) KB 27/1092, m. 20 (Hull; reversed, but probably on another ground). The only case in which a local custom was expressly alleged is *Lowth* v. *Wellys* (1520) KB 27/1037, m. 28 (Colchester; plaintiff in error assigns that no such custom was ever used in Colchester before).

[17] *Anon.* (c.1516/19) Chaloner 281, no. 7.

On the other hand, some may have seen this as a rule of evidence rather than of contract, as in the case of covenant. At any rate, such a rule of positive law was not necessarily binding in conscience;[18] and even at common law debts could survive on death where there was specialty, so that executors or heirs were liable if the plaintiff had a deed.[19]

Where the plaintiff counted in debt but failed to show specialty or *causa*, or to follow (where available) the customary *concessit solvere* formula, the supposed debtor could protest that the very notion of debt without *causa* was 'unbelievable and incomprehensible'.[20] In 1532, a judgment was reversed where the plaintiff 'did not declare upon any deed, specialty, contract, loan, or other sufficient cause whereupon an action might accrue'.[21] To dispense with written evidence was one thing, but to dispense with the basis of contractual liability for a debt was another. The most difficult area was the informal covenant without recompense. If the only obstacle to liability was the evidential requirement, it might be thought that when that was removed a bare covenant would be enforceable without more. It was a moral principle that every one should keep his word.[22] On the other hand, it might be argued on the analogy of debt that when the specialty requirement was removed it became necessary to show some *quid pro quo* to support the promise.[23]

The impression given by the error cases is that the rule requiring formality was generally evidential, and could be dispensed with, whereas the essence of contract was reciprocity and—in the absence of a formal acknowledgment of indebtedness by deed or *concessit solvere*, which bound the debtor by way of estoppel rather than contract—the requirement of *quid pro quo* could not be dispensed with. These turn out to be the guiding principles behind the extension of *assumpsit* and the emergence of the doctrine of consideration. The delay between the invention of actions on the case upon promises, in the mid-fourteenth

[18] In *Anon.* (1524) Yorke 203, no. 300, it was held that a subpoena lay against the executors in Chancery, if they had assets, (tr.) 'for by the common law the party has no remedy against executors upon contracts made by their testator'. This is supported by the lord chancellor's remark in Pas. 7 Hen. VII, fo. 12, pl. 2.

[19] For debt against an heir (who was only liable if expressly mentioned) see Yorke 107, no. 53; *Warcop v. Musgrave* (1555) Dyer 111b; *Warcop v. Laton* (1556) CP 40/1166, m. 365 (demurrer to declaration, followed by nonsuit).

[20] *Fyssher v. Warner* (1526) KB 27/1059, m. 28 (from Rochester; error assigned because it appeared by the declaration that the plaintiff had bought 200 quarters of grain for nothing, 'quod credi sive intelligi non potest'). Judgment was reversed, but other errors were assigned.

[21] *Whittymer v. Collyng* (1532) KB 27/1082, m. 28 (from Bridgnorth; error assigned because 'non narravit super aliquo facto seu specialitate nec aliquo contractu seu mutuatione nec super aliqua sufficiente causa unde actio accresceret'). Judgment was reversed, but other errors were assigned.

[22] For contemporary indications of this notion see 94 Selden Soc. 258.

[23] Cf. *Reniger v. Fogassa* (1550) Plowd. 1 at 5, where Griffith S.-G. argues that a 'recompense' is necessary to distinguish a perfect agreement from a bare communication.

century, and the developments of the early Tudor period is therefore not explicable in intellectual terms alone. It may be accounted for partly by the availability of reasonably efficacious local courts for commercial as well as consumer litigation, but more probably by the very widespread use of deeds.

48

Debt and Formal Contracts

FOR a contract to bind the parties it had to be settled and complete, rather than a 'bare communication'—which seems to have meant an inchoate discussion.[1] And the best way of establishing a settled agreement was by showing that it was embodied in a deed. Original written contracts have not survived in such large quantities as muniments of title, because after performance the documents served no purpose. A great deal may nevertheless be discovered about contracts which were contested. Many thousands of bonds and indentures were the subject of litigation, and in nearly every case the exact terms were set out in the record. In the case of a covenant, the terms were usually recited in what seems to be a fairly exact paraphrase, but in the more common case of a conditional bond the condition was read and set out verbatim.[2] We therefore possess, in the plea rolls, a vast repository of contracts from all over the country. And it is obvious from this abundant evidence that deeds were used by many people for their more important transactions. The commonest use by far was to secure payment of a debt or delivery of grain; other common contexts were leases, sales of land, and submissions to arbitration. But the variety of subject-matter was limitless.

Contracts made by indenture were common, and, as Fitzherbert pointed out,[3] they were not confined to the world of conveyancing. We find parchment and wax used for building contracts,[4] covenants by tradesmen to repair

---

[1] *Anon.* (before 1506) Hil. 21 Hen. VII, fo. 6, pl. 4 (above, 743); *Southwall* v. *Huddelston* (1523) Hil. 14 Hen. VIII, fo. 17, pl. 6; 119 Selden Soc. 150 at 153, 155, 156, 158, 161; above, 743; *Reniger* v. *Fogassa* (1550) Plowd. 1 at 5, *per* Griffith S.-G. Cf. *Anon.* (1535/45) Yelv. 333, no. 44, where it seems to mean an informal agreement. And in *Anon.* (1550) BL MS. Hargrave 4, fo. 111v; Dal. 7, pl. 2 (abr. Moo. 8), it was held that where, 'upon a communication between them', one party said he would lease land to the other, this was a valid lease before the deed was sealed.

[2] The bond had to be produced in court. The defendant prayed oyer of the bond, which was read but not entered, and then prayed oyer of the condition, which was entered 'in hec verba'.   [3] FNB 145A.

[4] See L. F. Salzman, *Building in England down to 1540* (1952), 546–83 (examples from 1485–1538); *Prior of Taunton* v. *Byrt* (1522) CP 40/1037, m. 323 (covenant; detailed masonry specifications for a chancel); *Kyngston* v. *Cobbe* (1548) CP 40/1137, m. 515 (covenant; detailed specifications for a gatehouse). For examples of debt on an indenture, and debt on a bond to perform an indenture, for building work, see 94 Selden Soc. 260 n. 1–2; *Cryve* v. *Yerham* (1490) CP 40/912, m. 106 (bond to perform indenture for roofing chapel of Thorpland next Snoring, Norfolk); *A Down* v. *Bowreman, same* v. *Belamy* (1526) CP

goods,[5] a covenant by a scrivener to make an illuminated antiphoner,[6] a covenant by a married woman practitioner to teach 'the science and mystery of surgery',[7] an agreement to serve an esquire on a pilgrimage to Jerusalem 'in the land of Judea',[8] a solus agreement for skins,[9] a charterparty,[10] and even contracts for rustic labour.[11] Apprenticeships were usually secured by indenture,[12] and besides the common-form covenants on both sides these might contain special provisions: for example, in 1499 a Canterbury dyer covenanted to provide for an apprentice to be schooled in reading, writing, and singing.[13] Indentures were also commonly used for marriage agreements, with covenants by the parents to provide land and money.[14] Whether the remedy for breach of such an agreement was an action of covenant or of debt depended on whether a monetary penalty was provided for, either in the indenture[15] or—as was more usual—in a separate performance bond. The preponderance of debt actions testifies to the prevalence of penalties, which had obvious advantages whether or not the full sum was exacted.[16] Besides securing a better remedy in the event of breach, the written contract had the further advantage of setting down the precise details not only of what was agreed but of how disputes should be resolved. For example, in a series of bell-founding contracts we find provisions for a panel of musical experts to assess the tuning, and the harmony with the existing bells, and covenants to remove the bells and recast them

40/1051, mm. 155, 160 (bond; covenant to ceil roof of church and make two windows patterned on those in another church); *Lomnor* v. *Birde* (1527) CP 40/1056, m. 628 (bond; agreement to build three-storied tenement according to a plan—'platt'—containing four sheets of royal paper; cf. 94 Selden Soc. *307*); *Browne* v. *Holgill* (1536) CP 40/1091, m. 420 (debt by carpenter's executrix against master of Savoy Hospital; detailed specifications for a new infirmary).

[5] e.g. *Skerne* v. *Decon* (1506) KB 27/981, m. 104 (cooper covenants to repair a mashing-tun).

[6] *Berney* v. *Flowyrdewe* (1502) CP 40/959, m. 113 (issue on performance).

[7] *Adams* v. *Gosse* (1554) CP 40/1158, m. 605.

[8] *Hutchynson* v. *Restwold* (1556) CP 40/1167, m. 711 (issue on whether they ever embarked on the journey). The servant was to be kept in necessaries and paid £40 on return. Cf. *Allyn* v. *Jenkynson* (1556) CP 40/1168, m. 858, where the contract looks more like a wager that the plaintiff would not reach Jerusalem, 'then being under the dominion of the Great Turk'; but he came back with a certificate from one Brother Boniface de Aragusio, keeper of the convent of Mount Syon.

[9] *Bray* v. *White* (1528) CP 40/1058A, m. 638 (butcher covenants to supply skins to skinner).

[10] *Barker* v. *Coppyng* (1558) CP 40/1174, m. 925 (lease of ship, boat, and tackle, with detailed terms).

[11] e.g. *Kene* v. *Feld* (1522) CP 40/1035, m. 550 (digging and ploughing, and removing clay); *Mayor of Exeter* v. *Damsell* (1537) CP 40/1094, m. 412 (repairing hedges and ditches).

[12] These are common. At least three examples of indentures of apprenticeship are found in the rolls for 1510–11: CP 40/990, m. 296; CP 40/995, m. 320; CP 40/996, m. 416. The apprentice bound himself to learn with diligence and to avoid misbehaviour—fornication is often specifically forbidden—while the master undertook a reciprocal duty to give instruction.

[13] *Balle* v. *Cornewell* (1504) CP 40/968, m. 337.   [14] See above, 688.

[15] Note *Saunders* v. *Rokysley* (1530) CP 40/1066, m. 329, where debt was brought on a covenant in a bill of sale of sheep that if any of the sheep should die of the pox or the rot the defendant would return 3s. per wether and 2s. per ewe, averring that 50 wethers died of the rot.   [16] See below, 822.

at the founder's expense if they did not pass the examination.[17] Churchwardens who omitted such precautions could easily find themselves in trouble.[18]

It has been suggested that *assumpsit* was developed to provide remedies in those cases where the precaution of formality had been omitted 'because of the insignificance of the sums involved or the inexperience of the parties'.[19] No doubt many cases may be so explained. But it seems that the precaution was often omitted for building contracts and other significant situations similar to those mentioned above.[20] Professional advisers such as doctors and lawyers avoided making contracts by deed, doubtless because they took their fees in advance and preferred not to be bound themselves; deeds would be used only when annuities were granted for services rendered.[21] When such a grant was solely for past advice (*pro consilio impenso*), the deed imposed no positive obligation on the part of the recipient; but if it was also 'for advice to be given' (*pro consilio impendendo*) the failure to provide it could be pleaded in defeasance of the annuity.[22] The mercantile community seem also to have been particularly reluctant to use deeds, even when very substantial sums of money were involved.[23] They relied on each other's word, or on commercial paper which according to the international usage of merchants did not need to be sealed.[24] No doubt it would have been a sensible reform to treat

[17] 94 Selden Soc. 260–1. To the cases there cited may be added *Fyssher* v. *Harryson* (1489) CP 40/907, m. 103 (bells for Pavenham, Beds.); *Colyer* v. *Hasylwode* (1508) CP 40/986, m. 348 (bells for Pirbright, Surrey); *Hastynges* v. *Mellour* (1525) CP 40/1048A, m. 106 (Nottingham founder); *Curson* v. *Skotte* (1527) CP 40/1056, m. 408; *Glasyn* v. *Russell* (1530) CP 40/1067(1), m. 521 (bells for a Cornish church cast in Exeter); *Gray* v. *Ellis* (1535) CP 40/1087, m. 337 (bell for Askerswell, Dorset); *Pylston* v. *Grene* (1539) CP 40/1103, m. 655 (bells for a Shropshire church cast in Worcester); *Churchwardens of Happisburgh, Norfolk* v. *Pope* (1546) CP 40/1129, m. 420d (bell to be cast by Thomas Laurens); *Muscote* v. *Newton* (1549) CP 40/1141, m. 359 (bells for Earls Barton, Northants). For a demurrer to a plea of harmony see *Gryffyth* v. *Selyok* (1512) CP 40/1001, m. 614.

[18] e.g. *Lovell* v. *Ford* (temp. Audley C.) C1/839/47 (bellfounder's executors claim payment under single bond and refuse to return bell).

[19] Thorne, 'Tudor Social Transformation and Legal Change', 20.

[20] e.g. the cases of building work in parish churches cited in 94 Selden Soc. 261.

[21] e.g. *Yakesley* v. *Say* (1521) CP 40/1032B, m. 270, where a Cambridge medical scholar ('in medicinis studens') extracted a deed of annuity from his patient's husband as a reward for advice given; the defendant pleaded that he delivered the deed as an escrow on condition that the plaintiff cured his wife, which he did not. There are numerous examples of lawyers granted annuities for counsel.

[22] *Frenshe* v. *Viscount Berkeley* (1482) CP 40/880, m. 456; *Swetenham* v. *Illingworth* (1491) CP 40/918, m. 110; *Hexte* v. *Chambernon* (1496) CP 40/938, m. 360; *Gawecell* v. *Prior of Bynham* (1504) CP 40/968, m. 463; *Glover* v. *Empson* (1514) CP 40/1006, m. 553; reported in Dyer 1b; Plowd. 382; 109 Selden Soc. 150; *Smyth* v. *Downe* (1518) CP 40/1020B, m. 348; *Rudhale* v. *Conneway* (1520) CP 40/1029, m. 541; *Haldesworth* v. *Prior of Lewes* (1537) CP 40/1093, m. 456 (canon lawyer refusing to give counsel in common-law action).

[23] e.g. *Mowenslowe* v. *Crowche* (1531) KB 27/1080, m. 38 (£400 recovered on informal exchange of money); *Bonvise* v. *De la Sala* (1543) KB 27/1126, m. 80 (£110. 18s. 4d. claimed on an informal exchange agreement); *Saxcy* v. *Hudson* (1553) KB 27/1167, m. 145 (£852 recovered on informal factoring agreement). For the second case see below, 859.

[24] Cf. *Haken* v. *Helle* (1491) KB 27/919, m. 78d (debt on sealed bill payable at the Barrow Mart in Brabant; money paid into court); *Draymews* v. *Bailly* (1502) C1/239/17 (debt on sealed bill for Flemish

certain categories of paper, such as bills of exchange, as amounting to specialty for the purposes of the actions of debt and covenant. But the common law was too firmly settled to permit of so radical an adjustment. Deeds were defined partly by their physical characteristics. They required not only seals, which had to be still in place at the time of the action,[25] but also—on the view which prevailed—formal words of sealing in the attestation clause.[26] Nothing else could be recognized. Merchants and tradesmen were therefore left with no better remedies to enforce weighty transactions than were available to humble countrymen disputing the sale of firewood or piglets. The needs of the former were more likely to have induced reform than the less significant affairs of the lowly.

PENALTIES AND CONSCIENCE

The principal advantage of the conditioned bond over the simple covenant was that it fixed the sum of money recoverable in the event of breach, whereas in an action of covenant the damages were left to the decision of a jury. It may also have cast the burden of proof of performance on to the defendant, since the procedure was for the plaintiff merely to proffer the bond and for the defendant to pray oyer of the condition and plead its performance. A third advantage was that if the sum

money, payable to plaintiff or bearer; brought in Chancery because drawn in Bruges and so no remedy at law); *Albert* v. *Goodwyn* (1503) CP 40/963, m. 471; Rast. Ent. 157 (159) (debt on sealed bill of exchange for Flemish money payable in the Cold Mart; issue on the exchange rate); *Dormer* v. *Wethers* (1528) CP 40/1057, m. 328 (debt on sealed bill of exchange payable to plaintiff or bearer; judgment on confession); *Brodmore* v. *Seller* (1528) CP 40/1059, m. 505 (debt on sealed bill payable to bearer, without words of sealing; demurrer); *Walker* v. *Myddylton* (1542) KB 27/1122, m. 105 (debt on sealed bill of exchange payable to bearer on arrival of ship from Danzig).

[25] *Nichols* v. *Haywood* (1545) Dyer 59a (special verdict as to loss of seal after issue joined); *Bassett* v. *Tourney* (1553) CP 40/1155, m. 109 (pleads the seal was broken and the plaintiff 'novum sigillum fictum apposuit et annexit', *et sic non est factum*; verdict for plaintiff). A common way of cancelling a bond was to pull off the seal. See *Husey* v. *Gybbes* (1532) CP 40/1074, m. 429d (defendant pleads payment and return of bond, and that he broke off the seal, and the plaintiff found the bond in his house with the seal broken off, *et sic non est factum*; undetermined demurrer). If two sealed a bond, the loss of one seal would avoid it: *Anon.* (1488) Hil. 3 Hen. VII, fo. 5, pl. 20.

[26] For fluctuating opinions on the need for the 'sigillum meum apposui' clause, see *Anon.* (1482) Hil. 21 Edw. IV, fo. 81, pl. 30 (*meum* not essential, implying that the rest is); *Anon.* (1505) 2 Caryll 471, pl. 332, per Frowyk CJ (not essential), doubted by reporter; *Anon.* (1525) Spelman 132 (*signum* for *sigillum*); *Brodmore* v. *Seller* (1528–9) CP 40/1059, m. 505 ('as my deed I write this bill with my hand and put thereto my sign'; demurrer); sim. Spelman 134, pl. 9; *Ap Holl* v. *Moyle* (1529) KB 27/1070, m. 64d ('in witness whereof I . . . have written this bill with mine own hand'; demurrer); *Fortescue* v. *Nevell* (1531) CP 40/1070, m. 319 ('to this bill I have put my seal sign manual'; demurrer); *Anon.* (1536) Dyer 19a, §113, and fo. 22b; *Day* v. *Brodbank* (1540) CP 40/1105, m. 555 (held unnecessary on demurrer); cited 109 Selden Soc. 115–18; *Anon.* (1546) and *Anon.* (1551) BL MS. Hargrave 4, ff. 98v (pr. Dal. 1), 121v–122 ('In witness whereof I have set my hand' held sufficient); *Sheldon* v. *Horton* (1555) CP 40/1164, m. 959 (held necessary on demurrer); 109 Selden Soc. 119; discussed in *Dodge* v. *Bedingfield* (1565) 109 Selden Soc. 115. There was no need for a date: *Anon.* (*c.*1544/5) Wm Yelv. 360, no. 99.

in the bond was fixed at a level which greatly exceeded the loss likely to flow from breach, the fear of incurring the penalty put additional pressure on the obligor to perform. This last advantage was regarded as morally dubious, though it is not certain how far relief was given against penalties in our period. The conclusion has been drawn from surviving Chancery records that there was no settled practice of granting relief against penalties until the second half of the sixteenth century.[27] On the other hand, Cardinal Moreton C. declared in 1494 that, 'When someone is beholden to another in a principal debt, the debtee cannot in conscience take anything in respect of this indebtedness except the principal, even if the debtor is bound to him in twenty penalties'.[28] The case concerned a creditor who had taken a number of different kinds of security for the same debt, though the remark was made in response to Serjeant Kebell's submission that a penalty of £100 for non-payment of a penny could be taken in good conscience. That penalties were unconscionable therefore seems to have been a familiar notion long before relief came to be routinely granted. This is hardly surprising, since it may already have been informally recognized in courts of law. In the city of London there was a custom to relieve against penalties by allowing the defendant in an action of debt on a money-bond to confess the bond but request a jury to assess the true debt.[29] And there is a strong likelihood that a similar result was achieved in the common-law courts less formally through the *remittitur* procedure.[30]

Rather slighter evidence suggests that the Chancery also noticed the principle of conscience now embodied in the doctrine of equitable estoppel. A petition was laid before Sir Thomas More C. by a party who had been sued in the Common Pleas on a bond which he was supposed to have forfeited for not repairing premises. The petitioner claimed that the parties made a later agreement that the lessor would not take advantage of non-repair if the lessee would cause a mill to be built. Since this matter was not pleadable at common law, in the absence of specialty, the petitioner sought an injunction to stay the action of debt.[31] It will be noted that the alleged deficiency in the common law is not that it declined in principle to take account of such facts, but only that the facts could not be asserted by parol evidence against a deed. Nevertheless, the clear assumption was that a forfeiture should not be enforced when the obligee had himself condoned or acquiesced in the breach of condition.

[27] Henderson, 'Relief from Bonds in the English Chancery', 298–306.

[28] *Sir William Capell's Case* (1494) Port 13 at 14. Note also *Willes v. Warham* (1528) CP 40/1059, m. 734 (pr. 94 Selden Soc. 346), where it seems to be assumed that the Chancery would not enforce the penalty in a recognizance.

[29] St German, *Little Treatise*, ed. Guy, 111; *Anon.* (1557/8) BL MS. Harley 1624, fo. 69; MS. Hargrave 4, fo. 126v. The custom is set out in *Platte v. Aylyfe* (1553) CP 40/1153, m. 101 (bond for £200, jury assesses true debt as £93, 13s. 4d.).   [30] See above, 381–3.

[31] *Abell v. Green* (1529/32) C1/601/52. The outcome is not known.

These were, however, marginal problems. What is obvious from the plea rolls is that the possibility of mitigating the harshness of a penalty did nothing to diminish the popularity of penal bonds. If anything, the number of bonds made—and the size of the penalties in them[32]—increased steadily towards the end of our period.

THE COMMON LAW OF BONDS

Very little substantive law emerged in actions of debt on bonds, despite their importance, because the procedure for their enforcement was very straightforward. It is true that there were more demurrers in such actions than in any other category of action, but the point of law was usually a narrow question of construction raised by a plea of performance of the condition.[33] Rarely is it possible to discern the exact point in dispute, which may sometimes have been purely technical: for instance, that performance was pleaded too generally,[34] or that 'Not harmed' (in debt on a bond to perform a condition to save harmless) was pleaded too generally,[35] or that 'windows' were left in the plea.[36] General pleading was a constant problem, presumably because the profession never fully accepted the necessity of drawing lengthy pleas to match the wording of a series of conditions when most of them were irrelevant to the issue. Since the plaintiff had to assign a particular breach in any case, he gained nothing from a special plea of performance other than the opportunity to catch the defendant out in some discrepancy.[37] At the end of the fifteenth century the logic of pleading seemed to permit general pleas of performance where the covenants were affirmative, but not where they

---

[32] A penalty of £2,100 was recovered in *Compton* v. *Yorke* (1526) CP 40/1051, m. 455 (concerning London customs duties), and in *Newenham* v. *Assheton* (1553) KB 27/1165, m. 61, a penalty of £1,500. Both were judgments upon confession (*nihil dicit*). £200 is not an unusual sum in the 1550s.

[33] Thirty-three examples of demurrers to pleas of performance were noted in the Common Pleas (CP 40) between 1530 and 1550: 1078, m. 413; 1082, mm. 107, 416; 1084, m. 332; 1089, m. 459; 1096, mm. 110d, 413; 1098, m. 514; 1099, m. 107; 1101, mm. 335, 642; 1103, mm. 402, 523, 655; 1105, m. 508; 1107, m. 337; 1111, m. 726; 1112, m. 519; 1113, m. 518; 1115, mm. 109, 403; 1117, m. 309; 1122, m. 350; 1124, m. 454; 1130, m. 413; 1135, mm. 529d, 610; 1136, m. 514; 1140, mm. 427, 534; 1142, mm. 709, 710, 723.

[34] Numerous examples might be so explained: CP 40/962, m. 488; CP 40/1082, m. 416; 1101, m. 642; 1103, m. 523; 1105, m. 508; 1112, m. 519; 1113, m. 518; 1115, mm. 109, 403; 1142, mm. 709, 710, 723; 1164, m. 1254; 1165, mm. 130, 336.

[35] There were repeated demurrers to general pleas of *Non damnificatus*: e.g. *Abbot of Fountains* v. *Mellers* (1516) CP 40/1013, m. 438; *Kendall* v. *Bardesey* (1538) CP 40/1099, m. 122; *Hadley* v. *Hawtrey* (1542) CP 40/1112, m. 728; *Magdalen College, Oxford* v. *Arderne* (1549) CP 40/1139, m. 417d (held bad); *Cervyngton* v. *Buller* (1555) CP 40/1163, m. 723d (held bad); *Monnengys* v. *Frothyngham* (1558) CP 40/1175, m. 638d. Nevertheless, Brooke Abr., *Conditions*, pl. 93, says that in 38 Hen. VIII (1546/7) it was decided that a general plea was good.

[36] This may have been the point in at least three cases: CP 40/1135, m. 695; 1136, m. 457; 1143, m. 541.

[37] See *Combe* v. *Elryngton* (1493) 1 Caryll 145; CP 40/924, m. 290 (undetermined demurrer); *Moleyns* v. *Cooke* (1512) CP 40/1000, m. 415d (judgment for plaintiff on demurrer).

were negative.[38] In the later 1520s, however, the Common Pleas apparently announced that general pleas of performance were acceptable,[39] though Fitzherbert J. spoke angrily against the innovation in 1534 and said that such 'corrupt pleas' should be 'utterly abolished'.[40] Although Fitzherbert's view seems to have attached more weight to formalism than to practical sense, it nevertheless prevailed for the rest of the period.[41] Indeed, in 1549, when a general plea of performance was challenged in the King's Bench, Serjeant Pollard challenged his opponent to produce 'any book adjudged since the time of Edward I' in support of it, adding that, 'as Aristotle said, there is no disputing with anyone who will deny a maxim or principle'.[42]

The reports give the impression that pleading caused more difficulty in these cases than questions of substantive law. The courts did, however, develop some basic principles governing the discharge of debts. In understanding them, it is necessary to distinguish clearly between the discharge of the penalty, by payment, and the avoidance or 'defeasance' of the bond itself by performance of the condition on which its validity was dependent. The parol evidence rule prevented the former from being pleaded without a deed of release or acquittance,[43] whereas discharge of the condition could be pleaded by matter in pais.[44] The reason for the distinction depended on the form of the money bond rather than on the law of deeds in general. A bond contained an acknowledgement under seal that the obligor was 'firmly bound' to the creditor in a stated sum of money; this was taken

---

[38] *Anon.* (1484) Mich. 2 Ric. III, fo. 17, pl. 44, *per* Huse CJ; *Maryon* v. *Lacy* (1494) 1 Caryll 237; Hil. 10 Hen. VII, fo. 13, pl. 3; CP 40/927, m. 323.

[39] *Anon.* (1527/8) Wm Yelv. 318, no. 13 (general plea upheld, so that plaintiff must assign particular breach; but difference of opinion noted); perhaps identifiable as *Wellys* v. *Mompesson* (1528–9) CP 40/1058A, m. 455 (undetermined demurrer); Yorke 244, no. 426 (general plea now acceptable); Brooke Abr., *Conditions*, pl. 2 (prothonotaries say general plea unacceptable).

[40] Trin. 26 Hen. VIII, fo. 5, pl. 26 (tr. 'Fitzherbert said this same term that this manner of pleading was worthless, and was angry with Browne because he pleaded in such a way, and said that this pleading was never seen until these last two years, and if anyone would demur upon such pleas he would give judgment against them, so that such corrupt pleas should be utterly abolished in time to come').

[41] *Anon.* (1541/2) Brooke Abr., *Conditions*, pl. 198; *Covenants*, pl. 35; *Anon.* (c.1546) Wm Yelv. 337, no. 53 (noted as 'experience' in the Common Pleas that general pleas were invalid); *Anon.* (1549) next note (King's Bench); *Rolf* v. *Alday* (1553) CP 40/1154, m. 876 (successful demurrer to general plea that he had performed 'all and singular the covenants'); *Bolte* v. *Cragge* (1554) CP 40/1159, m. 418 (undetermined demurrer); *Searle* v. *Pace*, ibid., m. 606 (judgment for plaintiff on demurrer); *Killingworth* v. *Askewe* (1555) CP 40/1164, m. 1306d (sim.).   [42] *Anon.* (1549) BL MS. Hargrave 4, fo. 103 (tr.).

[43] *Halys* v. *Iden* (1521) CP 40/1032A, m. 652 (demurrer to parol acquittance); *Parmenter* v. *Hartcastle* (1555) CP 40/1161, m. 607 (sim.). The rule applied even in the harsh case where the debtor took back his bond in lieu of an acquittance, and the creditor improperly took it from him and sued on it: *Donne* v. *Cornwall* (1486) Pas. 1 Hen. VII, fo. 14, pl. 2; B. & M. 255; *Gryffyth* v. *Treheyron* (1539–40) CP 40/1103, m. 427d (undetermined demurrer); *Waberley* v. *Cockerel* (1541) Dyer 51a; B. & M. 257; *Partryche* v. *Harryson* (1546) CP 40/1128, m. 517 (judgment for plaintiff on demurrer).   [44] Yorke 160, no. 186.

to be formal evidence of a debt,[45] and therefore a plea of payment, or of discharge by agreement, in relation to that sum of money was a contradiction of the very words of the deed. On the other hand, if (for example) the condition of the bond was to pay a lesser sum of money, there was no contradiction in showing that the lesser sum had been paid because that was an event contemplated by the condition; the payment prevented the bond from taking effect. Following the same principle, there could be no objection to a plea of payment in an action of debt on a sealed bill witnessing a loan, since it was no contradiction of a loan to show that it had been repaid.[46] Likewise, it was logically consistent to allow payment to be pleaded in respect of a covenant to pay money, since it did not contradict a covenant to show that it had been fulfilled.[47]

   The condition of a bond could be discharged by performance, by frustration, by agreement, and perhaps by fundamental breach.[48] The stock examples of frustration were acts of God,[49] or of enemies,[50] or of the obligee himself,[51] which rendered performance impossible; and the underlying principles were fully

   [45] It was said that a bond could be made in words such as 'I promise to pay' or 'I shall pay': *Hatley's Case* (1482) Mich. 22 Edw. IV, fo. 21, pl. 1, at fo. 22. But this was very unusual. An example is set out in *Bumpstede* v. *Pount* (1555) CP 40/1164, m. 845 ('*concessit debere... et promisisset solvere*' at a certain day).
   [46] *Persy* v. *Lant* (1535) CP 40/1087, m. 111 (issue joined on repayment).
   [47] *Gregory* v. *Rokys* (1535) CP 40/1087, m. 345 (issue); *Palmer* v. *Byllyngton* (1537–8) KB 27/1104, m. 74 (covenant to pay money in a marriage agreement; undetermined demurrer to plea). It was said to be otherwise if debt was brought upon a covenant to pay money: *Anon.* (1534) Dyer 6, pl. 3 (questioned); *Anon.* (Hil. 1537) Dyer 25, pl. 160; 121 Selden Soc. 437, no. 17. But no good reason was given.
   [48] e.g. *Mathew* v. *Barley* (1556–7) CP 40/1168, m. 1308 (apprentice sued for penalty for leaving his master pleads that the master ill-treated him by imprisoning him; the plaintiff does not deny that this could be a defence, but relies on a custom of London whereby an apprentice could appeal to the masters of his craft for a transfer of his articles, which he did; demurrer).
   [49] The usual case is death before the time set for performance: *Moots,* 256; *Anon.* (1489) Hil. 4 Hen. VII, fo. 4, pl. 7; *Vavasour* v. *Polend* (1494) Hil. 9 Hen. VII, fo. 17, pl. 11, *per* Rede sjt, and fo. 20, pl. 16, *per* Fyneux J.; *Cowper* v. *Abbot of Thornton* (1495) Pas. 10 Hen. VII, fo. 18, pl. 4, *per* Kebell and Mordaunt sjts; *Anon.* (1495) Port 16, *per* Fyneux J.; *Blyke's Case* (1499) Hil. 15 Hen. VII, fo. 2, pl. 5; Trin. 15 Hen. VII, fo. 13, pl. 24; *Barnard* v. *Hyll* (1515) CP 40/1011, m. 531 (condition for G to make release before coming of age, and G died before coming of age; plea upheld on demurrer). Cf. *Browne* v. *Elmer* (1520) Trin. 12 Hen. VIII, fo. 1, pl. 1 (119 Selden Soc. 3), per Broke J. (lightning, or act of the king's enemies, as defences in waste); *Anon.* (1537) Dyer 33, noted below, 827 n. 57 (effect of heavy storm); *Anon.* (1557) BL MS. Harley 1624, fo. 57; B. & M. 258 (heavy flooding). Cf. *Anon.* (1499) Trin. 14 Hen. VII, fo. 32, pl. 8, *per* Bryan CJ (frustration by death no different from initial impossibility).
   [50] e.g. *Lincolne's Case* (1482) Hil. 21 Edw. IV, fo. 17, pl. 4; Pas. 22 Edw. IV, fo. 6, pl. 17; *Saunder* v. *Maruffo* (1529) KB 27/1072, m. 62d (condition to obtain dispensation from Rome for Irish bishop-elect; pleads he obtained the bull but delivery was hindered by enemies; undetermined demurrer). However, a covenant by a lessee to repair was not discharged by act of God or the king's enemies, presumably because repair was not impossible: *Sherborne's Case* (1522) Spelman 85. See also St German, *Little Treatise,* ed. Guy, 119.
   [51] *Moots,* 161 (A is bound to marry B and the obligee marries B; or C is bound to an abbot that D will enfeoff him and D becomes the abbot's monk); Gray's Inn moot in BL MS. Harley 5103, fo. 46 (A is bound to B never to marry; then B marries A; and then they divorce); *Anon.* (1482) Mich. 22

discussed in relation to the third case in 1494.[52] A prior was bound to find a chantry priest in the plaintiff's chapel, and the question was whether he was discharged if the plaintiff allowed the chapel to collapse.[53] Serjeant Kebell argued that it was a strict liability. If someone was bound to pay money in St Paul's, and the church fell down, he would be obliged to make a tender on the ground where the church stood. Moreover, if someone bound himself to pay a debt in Sir Thomas Bryan's parlour, and Bryan would not let the debtor in, the debtor would forfeit his bond because he had bound himself at his peril.[54] The judges, however, approached the question as one of construction.[55] Bryan CJ said that if one was bound to find a chantry priest he was also by implication bound to supply book and candle; but he could hardly be expected to find the chapel as well, and it was not fitting to say mass in an open field. Fyneux J. agreed. If the obligor bound himself to find a chaplain to sing in St Paul's, and the church fell down, he was not bound by necessary implication to rebuild St Paul's.[56] All deeds, he said, should have a reasonable construction. What the judges could not agree upon was whether the obligation would revive if the chapel was in fact rebuilt: in other words, whether this was a case of discharge properly so called or of a suspensory condition.[57]

Presumably the effect of any frustrating event depended ultimately on the interpretation of the contract, since there might be an acceptance of risk by either party. Thus, on a lease of animals for profit, the contract might continue to bind even if some of them died through natural causes; this was decided upon demurrer in a case of 1527 concerning a lease of four bears.[58] If on a true

Edw. IV, fo. 25, pl. 6; *Anon.* (1489) Hil. 4 Hen. VII, fo. 4, pl. 7, *per* Bryan CJ (same cases); Yorke 165, no. 199; *Anon.* (1537) Dyer 30b.

[52] *Ferrers* v. *Prior of Newark* (1494) 1 Caryll 230; Hil. 10 Hen. VII, fo. 13, pl. 4; CP 40/926, m. 427. The obligation here arose from a grant by final concord, but all the discussion concerned bonds. For an earlier full discussion see *Harrington's Case* (1482) Mich. 22 Edw. IV, fo. 25, pl. 6.

[53] Cf. *Brudenell* v. *Abbot of Woburn* (1504) CP 40/968, m. 490 (action on the case for failing in a prescriptive duty to find a chaplain; defendant pleads that the chapel was so weak and ruinous that it was unsafe to celebrate mass there).

[54] Whether the debtor could plead that, when he came to tender, the creditor hid himself ('secrete se abscondit in mansione sua'), was the subject of a demurrer in *Fortescue* v. *Arkysworthy* (1525-6) CP 40/1048A, m. 587 (no judgment).

[55] For a similar analysis of the cases, see D. Ibbetson, 'Fault and Absolute Liability in pre-Modern Contract Law' (1997) 18 *JLH* 1 at 8-9.

[56] Cf. *Dounyng* v. *Hobbey* (1554) CP 40/1158, m. 504 (in *assumpsit* for not roofing a chancel, the defendant pleads that the plaintiff pulled down the walls).

[57] Cf. *Anon.* (1537) Dyer 33a (heavy storm discharges penalty for not repairing river banks, in respect of recent damage, but not the covenant itself). This is another example of reasonable construction. The lessee is not liable for the immediate effect of a storm, because time is needed to carry out the repairs; but he must repair within a reasonable time.

[58] *Foord* v. *Chaundeler* (1527-8) CP 40/1056, m. 798 (debt on bond against surety; lease of four bears called Tom, Harry, George, and Meg, to have and hold and take profits for one year; pleads that Tom

construction of the bond the obligor was to act 'at his peril', that is, under a strict liability, he could not escape the penalty merely by showing that the breach of condition was not his fault. Thus, if a man bound himself to be in two places on the same day, there was no defence.[59] Likewise initial impossibility did not discharge the obligation.[60] Even impossibility caused by the intervention or non-cooperation of a third party afforded no defence.[61]

Another mode of discharge was accord and satisfaction,[62] where the creditor accepted a chattel—such as a horse,[63] a piece of plate, or conger eels[64]—or an estate in land,[65] or payment in a different place,[66] or whatever, in lieu of the original duty.[67] The principle was first established in relation to simple contracts. It could not apply to a debt acknowledged by deed, such as the penalty in a bond, because the acknowledgement under seal was incontrovertible,[68] but it did apply to a collateral debt secured by a bond, so that a condition to pay a sum of money could be discharged by accord and satisfaction, and the relevant facts could be proved by parol evidence.[69] The logic behind the plea applied also to agreements to render chattels, so that a condition to supply grain or a horse could be satisfied by money.[70] On the

and Meg died; plea held bad on demurrer; writ of error brought). This is a remarkable instance of animals being named in the record.

[59] Case at Marow's reading (Inner Temple, 1503) Port 157. The principal case was whether a recognizance to appear in court was discharged by subsequent imprisonment for felony.

[60] *The Trinity* (1495) Pas. 10 Hen. VII, fo. 22, pl. 21, *per* Bryan CJ (but cf. the report in Hil. 11 Hen. VII, fo. 16, pl. 13, where he seems to say the opposite); *Anon.* (1499) Trin. 14 Hen. VII, fo. 32, pl. 8, *per* Bryan CJ; *Speke* v. *Flemyng* (1522) Pas. 14 Hen. VIII, fo. 25, pl. 7, at fo. 28 (119 Selden Soc. 186), *per* Pollard J.; *Anon.* (1523) 120 Selden Soc. 81, pl. 1; *Browning* v. *Beston* (1555) Plowd. 131v at 133 (condition to go to Paris in two hours); *Anon.* (1550) BL MS. Hargrave 4, fo. 112, *per* Hales J. For earlier authorities, see D. Ibbetson, 18 *JLH* 26 n. 41.

[61] *Anon.* (1489) Hil. 4 Hen. VII, fo. 3, pl. 7 (condition to enfeoff A, a woman, who subsequently marries); *Vavasour* v. *Polend* (1494) Hil. 9 Hen. VII, fo. 20, pl. 16, *per* Fyneux J. (condition to enfeoff B, who refuses to accept it); *Sherborne's Case* (1522) Spelman 18, 85 (condition to perform award, and arbitrators decline to inform him what they have awarded). This was a case for equitable relief: see *Mortimer* v. *Rastell* (1562) 18 *AJLH* 304 (house pulled down by commissioners for rebuilding St Paul's).

[62] A bare accord without satisfaction, i.e. execution of the accord, was not sufficient: below, 864.

[63] *Anon.* (1496) Pas. 11 Hen. VII, fo. 21, pl. 6, *per* Jay sjt; *Anon.* (1543) Dyer 56b.

[64] *Anon.* (undated) Rast. Ent. 202 (205v).   [65] *Anon.* (1496) Pas. 11 Hen. VII, fo. 21, pl. 6.

[66] Hales's reading (Gray's Inn, 1532) BL MS. Hargrave 92, fo. 29.

[67] *Moots*, 256; *Anon.* (1484) Mich. 2 Ric. III, fo. 22, pl. 52; *Anon.* (1488/9) 1 Caryll 19–20, pl. 27; *Vavasour* v. *Polend* (1494) Hil. 9 Hen. VII, fo. 20, pl. 16, *per* Fyneux and Vavasour JJ; *Anon.* (1495) Hil. 10 Hen. VII, fo. 14, pl. 11, *per* Bryan CJ; 1 Caryll 289, pl. 198; Port 15; *Anon.* (1505) 2 Caryll 482, *per* Frowyk CJ; *Anon.* (1512) Dyer 1a.

[68] *Anon.* (1495) Mich. 10 Hen. VII, fo. 4, pl. 4 (by all the justices present); *Browne* v. *Rede* (1523) CP 40/1040, m. 541d (pleads delivery of cloth in satisfaction of penalty in bond; judgment for plaintiff on demurrer); *Bushe* v. *Tame* (1535–7) CP 40/1084, m. 633 (plea that plaintiff accepted horse in satisfaction of bill; held bad on demurrer); *Machell* v. *Wolsey* (1542) CP 40/1112, m. 644 (plea that testator accepted worsted in satisfaction of bill; judgment for plaintiff on demurrer).   [69] Yorke 160, no. 186.

[70] *Vavasour* v. *Polend* (1494) Hil. 9 Hen. VII, fo. 18, pl. 11, *per* Vavasour J.; *Anon.* (1495) Port 15; *Anon.* (1505) 2 Caryll 482, *per* Frowyk CJ.

other hand, a lesser sum could not be satisfaction for a larger because it was demonstrably less than what was due,[71] and on the same principle payment of the same sum at a later day could not be satisfaction since it could not be as valuable as prompt payment.[72] Nor could a condition to make a feoffment of land be satisfied by a substituted performance, apparently because land was of a higher nature.[73] It was also held that a condition to perform some bodily service had to be performed strictly and could not be varied, or discharged by a payment of money.[74] No explanation is offered for this last distinction.

Although parol evidence could not be given to contradict a deed, the defendant in debt on a bond could deny the force of the deed, by pleading either duress or *non est factum*, and prove the facts by parol evidence. Duress was not a case of *non est factum*,[75] perhaps because it made the bond voidable rather than void; and there was no halfway house, such as saying that a bond was made under protest to avoid inconvenience.[76] In 1527 a defendant in debt on a bond pleaded that the plaintiff had taken from him a pardon which he (the defendant) had obtained for his own sister, and threatened to beat him if he took it back unless he executed the bond; since the threat was only conditional, this might have been considered a case of duress of goods, but the bond was nevertheless held void.[77] Most pleas of *non est factum* were general, but there were three special cases regularly encountered.[78] The first was where the bond was delivered as an escrow,[79] to take effect on the fulfilment of some condition—such as the payment of money or delivery of goods—and the condition had never been fulfilled.[80] The second was where the

---

[71] *Anon.* (1494) Mich. 10 Hen. VII, fo. 4, pl. 4, *per* Bryan CJ (but denied by Fyneux J.); Hales's reading (1532) BL MS. Hargrave 92, fo. 29. Cf. *Bugg* v. *Sorell* (1538–9) CP 40/1099, m. 435d (debt for £16; pleads arbitration award to pay £9, which he did; undetermined demurrer).

[72] Hales's reading (1532) BL MS. Hargrave 92, fo. 29.

[73] *Vavasour* v. *Polend* (1494) Hil. 9 Hen. VII, fo. 18, pl. 11, and fo. 20, pl. 16, *per* Vavasour J.; ibid., fo. 21, *per* Bryan CJ; *Anon.* (1495) Port 15; *Anon.* (1495) Hil. 10 Hen. VII, fo. 15, pl. 11, *per* Bryan CJ; *Anon.* (1505) 2 Caryll 482, *per* Frowyk CJ (because it is an inheritance). Cf. *Wyllyams* v. *Vyncent* (1522) CP 40/1037, m. 819 (bond to perform covenant to give an acre of wood yearly; pleads payment of 20s. a year in satisfaction; held bad on demurrer).

[74] *Anon.* (1488/9) 1 Caryll 19, pl. 27; *Anon.* (1495) 1 Caryll 289, pl. 198; *Anon.* (1512) Dyer 1a; *Bedell's Case* (1514) Spelman 84 (decided on demurrer).

[75] Hales's reading (1532) BL MS. Hargrave 92, fo. 30.

[76] *Wilson* v. *Parcy* (1535) CP 40/1087, m. 343 (pleads bill sent to him with wrong sum inserted, and he sealed it because it was more trouble than it was worth not to; plea held bad on demurrer).

[77] *Hasebury* v. *Toy* (1527) CP 40/1055, m. 353d (judgment on demurrer).

[78] The list is not exhaustive: see *Pawlet's Case* (1501) Pas. 16 Hen. VII, fo. 7, pl. 10 (pleads bond sealed and delivered to John Pawlet senior, not his son, the plaintiff).

[79] As to whether a deed could be delivered as an escrow to the obligee himself see *Anon.* (1527) Wm Yelv. 365, no. 104; Pas. 19 Hen. VIII, fo. 8, pl. 12; *Anon.* (1544) Gell's reports, i, Mich. 36 Hen. VIII, fo. 23v.

[80] e.g. *Lee* v. *Wodcrove* (1504) CP 40/970, m. 143; *Meredith* v. *Somer* (1506) CP 40/978, m. 427; *Quarles* v. *Gale* (1518) CP 40/1022, m. 530 (performance of covenants); *Grome* v. *Pers* (1537) CP 40/1093, m. 617

bond had been altered in some way after execution,[81] for instance by adding a numeral;[82] adding a condition to a single bond—though it could only make it less onerous than it was—had the same effect.[83] And the third was where the defendant was a layman and unlettered (*homo laicus et minime litteratus*)[84] and the bond,[85] or the condition, or the indenture referred to in the condition, had been misread to him before execution. Illiteracy here must often have meant an inability to read or understand Latin.[86] And it is possible that the allegation of illiteracy was sometimes fictional,[87] the real issue being—as in later law—the deception. But the allegation was material, presumably because a person was supposed to look after his own interests when executing a deed.[88] The principal discussion of the law during our period concerned the effect of partial misreading.[89] An action was brought by the executor of Sir John Speke, sheriff of Devon, upon a bond

(delivery of wool); *Assheley* v. *Newenham* (1539) CP 40/1100, m. 317d (delivery of salt); *Reynolde* v. *Hole* (1539) CP 40/1102, m. 126 (payment of money); *Danyell* v. *Danyell* (1542) CP 40/1112, m. 434 (delivery of diamond ring to third party). Cf. *Herrys* v. *Pechye* (1537) CP 40/1094, m. 315 (condition to prove delivery of grain to plaintiffs first husband).

[81] e.g. *Anon.* (1488) Hil. 3 Hen. VII, fo. 5, pl. 20; *Donne* v. *Cornwall* (1486) Pas. 1 Hen. VII, fo. 14, pl. 2, *per* Kebell sjt; *Swyllyngton* v. *Lucok* (1504) CP 40/970, m. 448 (erasure and interlineation, 'et sic non est factum'); *Speke* v. *Flemyng* (1523) Spelman 86, *per* Pollard J.; *Monoux* v. *Fairfax* (1531) Spelman 329; Yorke 198; CP 40/1069, m. 532 (demurrer to declaration where plaintiff's name altered in bond); *Alen* v. *Hygden* (1541) CP 40/1109, m. 156 (words struck through 'et sic non est factum'); *Anon.* (1550) BL MS. Hargrave 4, fo. 109; Moo. 10, pl. 37 (erasure); and cf. *Anon.* (1556) Chr. Yelverton's reports, fo. 240v (erasure by consent of both parties makes a deed void). According to Hales's reading (1532) BL MS. Hargrave 92, fo. 30, this was not technically a case of *non est factum*. Yorke 213, no. 330, says the principle applied even if the erasure or interlining was made before delivery. Erasing the *condition* made the bond single: *Anon.* (1556) Chr. Yelverton's reports, fo. 240v.

[82] *Clarell* v. *Haselwode* (1501) CP 40/958, m. 150 ('l' added before 'xx' to make 'lxx').

[83] *Millys* v. *Guldeford* (1507–35) CP 40/986, m. 617; KB 27/1005, m. 26 (94 Selden Soc. *344*); Spelman 167; 2 Caryll 616, 625; Yorke 205, no. 307; Chaloner 281, no. 8; Hil. 26 Hen. VIII, fo. 10, pl. 4. The case was not, however, formally resolved: above, 392.

[84] A woman might plead that she was *mulier laica* (e.g. CP 40/912, m. 359; CP 40/997, m. 329; CP 40/1019, m. 326), but *homo laica* is encountered in CP 40/1026, m. 556; CP 40/1102, m. 448.

[85] e.g. *Pulteney* v. *Perwyche* (1502) KB 27/964, m. 63 (single bond misread as conditional; assigned as error that he should have pleaded *non est factum* generally); *Raynton* v. *Wyttby* (1540) CP 40/1104, m. 145 (single bill misread as conditional); *Assheley* v. *Orpyn* (1541) CP 40/1108, m. 131d (sim.); *Ayra* v. *Goodale* (1541) CP 40/1109, m. 118 (bond misread as a receipt).

[86] One defendant preferred to plead that he did not understand Latin ('homo laicus non intelligens Latinum') rather than that he was illiterate: *Russo* v. *Hubberd* (1503) CP 40/964, m. 413.

[87] Some surprising claims were made to illiteracy: e.g. *Speke* v. *Flemyng* (1523) CP 40/1032B, m. 306 (Nicholas Flemyng, gent., sometime sheriff's clerk; discussed below); *Skewys* v. *Trewynnard* (1535) CP 40/1085(2), m. 109d (William Trewynnard, gent., who became an MP in 1542 and was a member of Clement's Inn: CP 40/1033, m. 392d).

[88] *Martyn* v. *Chetwyn* (1558–9) CP 40/1176(1), m. 333d (demurrer to plea of misreading which omitted the allegation of illiteracy).

[89] *Speke* v. *Flemyng* (1521–3) Pas. 14 Hen. VIII, fo. 25, pl. 7 (119 Selden Soc. 180); Spelman 84–6; Port 80, 108; CP 40/1032B, m. 30d (pr. 119 Selden Soc. 189; demurrer); second action in CP 40/1039, m. 539 (pr. 94 Selden Soc. 284; issue); above, 387 (Chancery suit). Flemyng had been appointed jointly with others.

conditioned to perform an indenture of 1516 whereby the defendant was appointed sheriff's clerk. The defendant pleaded that he was a layman and unlettered, that the indenture was read to him in English as containing only one of the six covenants which were actually set down in it,[90] that he was told by Sir John that if he performed that covenant the bond would be void, that he had executed the bond in reliance on the reading and the assurance, and that he had performed the covenant read out to him. To this plea the plaintiff demurred, and argued that the plea should have concluded 'and so not his deed' (*non est factum*). The lengthy year-book report reveals an equal division of judicial opinion as to whether the bond was wholly void, in which case the plea should indeed have concluded *non est factum*, or whether the obligor was bound to observe the one covenant which had been read out, in which case his plea was good without the conclusion. It seems that the latter position, supported by Brudenell CJ and Fitzherbert J., was accepted by the parties, because after the argument in banc the plaintiff brought a second action in the same form and issue was joined on the performance. There was no reason why a man should not be bound to perform part of an indenture, provided that the part could sensibly be severed from the rest. Partial misreading was therefore not strictly a case of *non est factum*.[91]

The general plea *non est factum* was remarkably frequent. For example, in over 360 actions on bonds which were pleaded to issue in the Common Pleas in 1535, there were almost as many pleas of *non est factum* (124) as of payment (132), and indeed a higher proportion of *non est factum* cases went to trial.[92] It stretches credulity to suppose that a third of all bonds were suspected forgeries, and so the suspicion must arise that debtors' attorneys were entering the plea simply as a kind of general issue which placed the matter at large before the jury.[93] This had turned out to be the only real weakness of bonds; for, however careful a man was with his pen and his sealing wax, he could not escape the perils of jury trial. Sir Thomas Elyot, a lawyer with practical experience as a clerk of assize, thought this a serious defect in the law:[94]

And not only sealing... is insufficient, but also it is now come into such a general contempt that all the learned men in the laws of this realm, which be also men of great wisdom, can

---

[90] This was the covenant to pay £48 at the Exchequer for the proffers of the sheriff. The other covenants related to the collection of revenues, and the preparation and presentation of accounts at the Exchequer in discharge of the sheriff.

[91] See *Anon.* (1530) Pollard 277, no. 75, *per* Fitzjames CJ (conclusion *non est factum* held to waive a special plea of misreading).

[92] Figures from CP 40/1084–1087. The commonest issues were: payment of money in condition, 132 (7 tried); *non est factum*, 124 (16 tried); performance of condition (including delivery of grain), 57 (9 tried); duress, 21 (7 tried); fully administered, 18 (1 tried).

[93] In *Stanton* v. *Lambe* (temp. Audley C.) C1/886/42, it was complained that the plaintiff's attorney had pleaded *non est factum* without the plaintiff's consent, when he should have pleaded *nil debet*.

[94] Elyot. *The Governour* (1531), fo. 195v (sp. mod.).

not with all their study devise so sufficient an instrument to bind a man to his promise or covenant, but that there shall be some thing therein espied to bring it in argument, if it be denied. And in case that both the parties be equal in estimation or credence, or else he that denieth [be] superior to the other, and his witnesses depose on knowledge of the thing in demand, the promise or covenant is utterly frustrate, which is one of the principal decays of the public weal.

USURY

Penalties were not the only moral concern to affect legal debate about the law of contract in the early Tudor period. The expansion of moneylending and dealing on credit gave rise to a renewed concern about usury. The prohibition was originally canonical, and punishment continued to be imposed by the ecclesiastical courts in our period;[95] but we are here concerned with its place in secular law. Although the Statute of Merton, c. 5, prohibited usury in the case of minors, it had not laid down any means of enforcement; and it was clear law in the fifteenth century that usury did not invalidate penal bonds.[96] So the matter rested until 1487, when concerns about the practice of moneylending influenced Parliament to take punitive measures.[97]

According to the preamble to the statute of 1487, 'importable damages, losses and impoverishing of this realm is had by damnable bargains grounded on usury coloured by the name of new chevisance, contrary to the law of natural justice'. It was therefore enacted that usurious bargains by way of dry exchange or fictitious transactions should be void, and that some of them should attract a penalty recoverable by any informer. Since it was feared that juries in towns might frustrate the legislation by perjury, it was further provided that the Chancery should have the same jurisdiction as the common-law courts.[98] The common informers went to work,[99] but the 1487 legislation did not define new chevisance or dry exchange, and was 'so obscure, dark, and diffuse' that it had to be replaced by a much simpler statute in 1496. There is some evidence that the principal reason

[95] Helmholz, *Canon Law and the Law of England*, ch. 17. See also J. T. Noonan, *The Scholastic Analysis of Usury* (1957); N. Jones, *God and the Moneylenders: usury and the law in early modern England* (1989); E. Kerridge, *Usury, Interest, and the Reformation* (2002). Jones is mainly concerned with a later period.

[96] Two anon. readings in BL MS. Hargrave 87, ff. 385v–386v, 393r–v. It had been settled in 1352: Mich. 26 Edw. III, fo. 17, pl. 9; Fitz. Abr., *Det*, pl. 181. Cf. Noonan, *Scholastic Analysis of Usury*, 107–8.

[97] The statute may have been influenced by a long-established custom of London: as to which see G. Seabourne, 19 *JLH* 116.

[98] 3 Hen. VII, c. 5. For the meaning of dry exchange, see R. de Roover, *Gresham on Foreign Exchange* (1949), 161–5.

[99] e.g. *Wale v. Mason* (1492) KB 27/925, m. 70. Cf. Jones, *God and the Moneylenders*, 48, who suggests that the statute was little enforced.

for the reformulation was the confusion resulting from litigation over the moneylending activities of Sir William Capell.[100]

The new statute identified three categories of usury which would give rise to a penalty: lending money for a fixed time and taking more in return, under a contract made at the time of the loan ('saving lawful penalties for non-payment of the same money lent'); selling goods to persons in necessity, and buying them back within three months at a lower price; and, third, taking the profits of land assigned during the period of a loan 'without any condition or adventure'.[101] A lecture on this statute, attributed to George Treherne (1520), thought it merely a confirmation of the common law, the canon law, and the law of nature, and discussed a number of examples taken from historical and canonical sources.[102] The reader pointed out that the law not only forbade taking interest on loans but also an investment without risk, as where a merchant lent money to another who was going abroad to trade on the footing that he should be repaid together with all the profits. It was the element of risk which made financial investments lawful.[103] But he thought that depositing money in a bank was not usurious, because 'the use of the thing is separated from the ownership' (quia usus rei separatur a dominio).

The courts had occasion to consider the effect of the statute on bonds and mortgages, but declined to give it an expansive interpretation. When an obligor in 1526 attempted to plead that his bond was given to secure a usurious transaction, entered into when he was in great necessity for want of money, the plea was held bad on demurrer.[104] It does not appear from the record whether the plea failed on technical grounds or on principle, but no further challenges to bonds have been found. There seems likewise to be no judicial pronouncement on informal usurious contracts, though St German in 1530 stated them to be void.[105] In the case of mortgages, where the mortgagee took the profits of land, the conclusion was that if land was sold or leased to a creditor on condition that the debtor would have the land back if he repaid at any time before a certain day, this was not usurious, because

[100] This was Edward Hall's recollection in 1541: reading in Gray's Inn, BL MS. Hargrave 92, fo. 61v. For Capell see above, 823; Toft v. Capel (1505) Hil. 21 Hen. VII, fo. 14, pl. 20; KB 27/975, m. 66.

[101] 11 Hen. VII, c. 8.

[102] HEHL MS. 2537. The lecture is expressly attributed to Treherne and is said to have followed his reading on the forest law (Lincoln's Inn, 1520); but none of the numerous other versions of his 1520 reading include this lecture on usury. There is also an exposition of usury in Edward Hall's reading (1541) BL MS. Hargrave 92, ff. 61v–62; and a few brief remarks in William Staunford's reading (Gray's Inn, 1545) ibid., fo. 103.

[103] Cf. Core v. May (1536) Dyer 20; Spelman 132; KB 27/1097, m. 33 (printed 94 Selden Soc. 327); B. & M. 243 (debt for £20 paid to the defendant to invest in French prunes, one party to 'bear the adventure' of the exchange at Rouen and the other of shipping the prunes to London).

[104] Danyell v. Pawne (1526) KB 27/1061, m. 22. The alleged transaction was a sale of cloth by way of 'chevancia', which enabled the plaintiff to gain £5. 15s. for a two-month loan of £20. The defendant pleaded that both the pact and the making of the bond were void by reason of the statute of 1487.

[105] St German, Doctor and Student, ed. Plucknett and Barton, 228 ('money usual is no contract').

there was no certain period of gain; but if the condition was to return the land if the money was repaid on a certain day, this was usury.[106] The statute therefore seems to have had little or no effect on the validity of the most commonplace transactions, even though it could be enforced by way of an action of debt for the penalty.

Within its sphere of operation, however, the legislation was indeed actively enforced at the end of Henry VII's reign, not only by common informers[107] but also by Henry Toft—a clerk to the attorney-general, James Hobart—who achieved some notoriety as a 'promoter'.[108] It was still being actively enforced on the eve of the reforming statute of Henry VIII: in 1545, five informations on the 1496 statute are to be found in the Exchequer remembrance rolls, one of them alleging the receipt of 50 per cent interest *per annum*.[109] A curious omission in the legislation is that there was no provision for compelling the repayment to the debtor of what he had paid by way of usury. It was agreed in a case of 1488 that, although a usurious payment was refundable in conscience, it was improper for an executor to make such a refund by way of administration since he was concerned only with legal claims; and there was no means of recovering the money at common law.[110] Occasional petitions were presented to the chancellor seeking relief against usurious bonds, on the grounds that there was no remedy at law, though it is far from clear how far the Chancery responded.[111]

The main defect in the law, of course, was that it penalized what were presumably everyday practices and were not universally regarded as immoral. No doubt it was wrong to take unfair advantage of those in desperate straits, but the fine scholastic distinctions adopted from the medieval canonists were as remote from common perceptions of morality as they were from commercial and social reality. Why should wild financial speculation by the gullible be tolerated,

---

[106] Brooke Abr., *Usurie*, pl. 1 (1537) and pl. 2 (1539).

[107] e.g. *Anon. (erased)* (1500) CP 40/951, m. 460 (still on 3 Hen. VII); *Rede* v. *Wyskard* (1501) CP 40/956, m. 376 (still on 3 Hen. VII); *Rede* v. *Fuller* (1502) CP 40/962, m. 502; *Hawes* v. *Chester* (1506) CP 40/976, m. 490 (debt on 11 Hen. VII in respect of a mortgage); *Cantelowe* v. *Harsenap* (1506) CP 40/978, m. 318 (debt on 11 Hen. VII in respect of a sale and resale of wool); *Broke* v. *Wylbrom* (1508) CP 40/986, m. 656; *Awdewyn* v. *Over* (1508) ibid., m. 682.

[108] e.g. *Toft* v. *Hylton* (1500) CP 40/952, m. 304 (issue); (No. 2) CP 40/956, m. 427; CP 40/958, m. 315; *Toft* v. *Johnson* (1501) CP 40/956, m. 314 (judgment for defendant); CP 40/970, m. 117 (attaint); *Toft* v. *Wattys* (1503) CP 40/965, m. 303; cf. *R.* v. *Copynger* (1507) CP 40/981, m. 520. Inexplicably, most of these actions are on the repealed 1487 statute. For Toft see 94 Selden Soc. 49; 102 Selden Soc. 14 n. 1.

[109] *Bocher* v. *Newcome* (1545) E159/204, Pas., m. 21 (lent £5 for six months, taking a bond as surety, and taking 33s. 4d. by way of usury); *Ildam* v. *Elyott*, ibid., m. 40 (lent £40 for a year, taking £6 profits of land by way of usury); *Hasylwod* v. *Mathewe*, Trin. m. 17 (lent £10 for seven months, taking jewellery as surety, and taking 10s. by way of usury); *Att.-Gen.* v. *Hunt*, Mich. m. 32 (lent £100 for a year, taking a bond as surety, and taking 20 marks by way of usury); *Wallys* v. *Walker*, Mich. m. 33 (lent £80 to Lord Daubeney for a year, taking a bond as surety, and taking £40 by way of usury).

[110] *Sonde* v. *Pekham* (1488) Trin. 4 Hen. VII, fo. 13, pl. 12; KB 27/909, m. 76.

[111] e.g. *Hyckes* v. *Fewter* (temp. Audley C.) C1/813/56 (advocate of the Arches lent client £40 to pursue appeal to Rome, taking £3. 6s. 8d.); *Maddokes* v. *Aleyn* (temp. Audley C.) C1/852/1.

because of the saving power of risk, when a loan at moderate interest to a commercial equal was not? In 1546 came a modest and short-lived reform, which had first been considered by Cromwell ten years earlier.[112] Under the guise of a further reinterpretation of the existing law, and its reinforcement with even heavier penalties, Parliament sanctioned the taking of interest up to a limit of 10 per cent *per annum*.[113] The statute made no mention of the law of God, and was thought by the unworldly to show an undue deference to growing immorality.[114] Indeed, even a learned man of law held that it had merely removed the temporal penalty and left the moral offence in place;[115] while others thought Parliament should deprive usurers of their principal if they acted immorally, for instance by taking more than 5 per cent.[116] After seven years, the statute of 1546 was repealed as too permissive, and the repealing statute emphasized that usury was 'by the word of God utterly prohibited'. Although the new penalties of 1546 were removed, the punishment for usury was now to be forfeiture of the principal as well as the interest, together with fine and imprisonment at the king's pleasure.[117] The judges held in 1552 that the repealing statute did not apply retrospectively to loans lawfully made between 1546 and 1552.[118] However, a possibly unintended consequence of the new formulation was that the offence could now be committed merely by contracting for a usurious gain, whether or not anything was actually received.[119]

DEBT AND WAGER OF LAW

The defendant in debt on a contract was in most cases allowed an election to wage his law or to ask for a jury.[120] The principal exceptions, where wager of law was

---

[112] Elton, *Reform and Renewal*, 150, 166.

[113] 37 Hen. VIII, c. 9. An example of an action on the statute is *Rypton v. Davyson* (1551) KB 27/1158, m. 145 (loan of £80, for which he took £17 and six yards of damask by way of usury).

[114] See Jones, *God and the Moneylenders*, 49. Jones reports (ibid.) that he could trace only fifteen Exchequer informations on the 1545 Act.

[115] Wm Yelv. 350, no. 76 (dictum by William Staunford, *c*.1549). Staunford admitted that the spiritual remedy was 'but a bare remedy', but 'the great matter is the offence which is committed against almighty God'.

[116] According to D. Lloyd, *State-Worthies* (1670), 388–9, this had been the view of Sir David Broke (CB 1553–8).

[117] 5 & 6 Edw. VI, c. 20. When this was repealed in 1571, the statute of 1546 was revived: 13 Eliz. I, c. 8.

[118] *Anon.* (1552) Dalison's reports, BL MS. Harley 5141, fo. 1; Dal. 12, pl. 17 (by all the justices of the Common Bench and Portman JKB).

[119] *Wytton v. Morgan* (1551–3) CP 40/1153, m. 428d; sub nom. *Whitton v. Marine*, Dyer 95a; probably the case in Dal. 12, pl. 16 (which propounds a subjective test of usury). The statute was also enforced in the King's Bench: *Worland v. Fettyplace* (1556) KB 27/1178, m. 173.

[120] In *Hatcum v. Bromefeld* (1530) CP 40/1066, m. 519, a defendant waged his law in debt on an arbitration award to pay 40s. in satisfaction for wrongs done.

forbidden, were debt on a bond, statutory actions,[121] debt for rent,[122] debt for arrears of an account taken before auditors,[123] and debt for an attorney's fees.[124] It was probably not allowed in the case of a corporation unless the head had personal knowledge of the contract, though because of earlier authorities to the contrary this was repeatedly disputed in cases concerning religious houses.[125] The Common Pleas showed no hostility to the procedure, and in 1492 overturned earlier decisions so as to allow it in debt upon a sale of land.[126] But the acceptability of wager of law was to become a point of difference with the King's Bench.[127]

The procedure was for the defendant to swear that he did not owe the sum in demand, or any penny thereof, and for his eleven compurgators to take an oath in support.[128] Almost certainly the court did not require all the compurgators to be neighbours of the defendant, and by 1515 we hear of 'knights of the post' being employed as professional swearers.[129] Wager of law was still very much in regular use in the central and local courts throughout our period, but it was not the automatic bar which is sometimes assumed. In fact, a majority of defendants in the Common Pleas who had an election to wage law asked for jury trial instead, and relatively few successful wagers are recorded. In 1535, for example, only 10 per cent of defendants who appeared in actions of debt on a contract avoided liability by performing their law.[130] There are several possible reasons for this. No doubt some debtors and compurgators were too honest to risk damnation by a false oath. Others were unable to be present in court.[131] And perhaps there was still some check on the residence of the compurgators, which would have made it difficult to produce all twelve hands at the bar.[132] As a matter of strategy, moreover, a debtor with no money might with no expense gain time by asking for a jury,

---

[121] *Martyn* v. *Kyme* (1495) Hil. 10 Hen. VII, fo. 18, pl. 18; CP 40/935, m. 347.

[122] J. Rastell, *Exposiciones Terminorum* (1527 edn), fo. 70; St German, *Doctor and Student*, ed. Plucknett and Barton, 109.   [123] Rastell, *Exposiciones Terminorum* (1527 edn), fo. 70.

[124] *Buxton* v. *Chapman* (1485) CP 40/892, m. 330 (demurrer to wager of law). This was because the fee was fixed by law. Cf. *Homwode* v. *Homwode* (1506) CP 40/975, m. 349 (wager of law in debt for money laid out on legal fees and costs).   [125] Above, 624.

[126] *Anon.* (1492) 1 Caryll 91, pl. 100 (held by all the judges, on demurrer).   [127] See below, 871–4.

[128] Rastell, *Exposiciones Terminorum* (1527 edn), fo. 70; *Diversite de Courtz* (1533), sig. C2v. The number of hands was often less than twelve in local courts. In his first edition (*c*.1523), Rastell said the defendant should bring six, eight, or twelve, as the court should assign (sig. E5).

[129] *Wylson* v. *Archer* (*c*.1514/15) C1/369/92 ('the said John waged his lawe forsweryng hymself upon a bok with xii [*sic*] other untrue men called knightis of the post'). Cf. 'paper knight', above, 794 n. 98.

[130] In 1535, of 169 defendants who appeared in actions of debt on a contract, 73 pleaded *Nil debet per patriam* and 54 pleaded *Nil debet per legem*; of these 54, 17 were recorded as having performed their law and 13 as having defaulted. On the other hand, only 6 verdicts (all for the plaintiff) are recorded in the sample. These figures are from an analysis of CP 40/1084–1087.

[131] e.g. *Vyvalde* v. *Norrey* (*c*.1536) C1/914/31 (merchant living in Genoa unable to wage law).

[132] Law could not be performed at nisi prius.

whereas if he waged law he would have to lay out money promptly in procuring the attendance of compurgators. Nevertheless, from the plaintiff's point of view, wager of law was an unsatisfactory method of resolving disputes and was sometimes complained of in Chancery[133]—though it is far from certain that there was any remedy there.[134] Even if the risk was only one in ten, the possibility that a defendant might perjure himself out of a debt was—as we shall see—the principal reason for the development of *assumpsit* for money in the early sixteenth century.[135]

[133] e.g. *Wylson* v. *Archer* (*c*.1514/15) C1/369/92 (above, note 129); *Parrys* v. *Snowe* (temp. More C.) C1/666/28-9 (plaintiff nonsuited because defendant by 'wilful perjury' proposed to do his law); *Mynshull* v. *Archer* (temp. Audley C.) C1/850/44 (perjured compurgation in borough court; demurrer); *Rosyngdale* v. *Kellett* (temp. Audley C.) C1/880/64 (defendant 'not regarding the punishment of God, nor regarding his truth, honesty, nor conscience', waged his law against a merchant stranger ignorant of the common law).

[134] St German, *Doctor and Student*, ed. Plucknett and Barton, 109, says there was not. Nor was there in the ecclesiastical courts: 'Certen Considerations why the Spirituell Jurisdiction wold be abrogatt and repelled or at the leest reformed' (*c*.1534) BL Cotton MS. Cleopatra F. II, at fo. 243.

[135] Below, 852-62.

49

Assumpsit for Nonfeasance

BEFORE *assumpsit* could be used to recover debts, a major conceptual obstacle had to be removed. The fifteenth-century law of *assumpsit* as revealed in the year books was based on the distinction between misfeasance, which was actionable in trespass on the case, and nonfeasance, which was not. By 1532, however, Spelman J. could observe with satisfaction that this distinction was irrational and had been rejected.[1] The nonfeasance doctrine, if so it may be called, was certainly by that time in tatters, if not entirely destroyed; but to understand its demise we must first understand why it prevailed for as long as it did.

The difficulty was once thought to be that trespass was perceived to be a tort in which positive conduct was an essential element, so that not doing something was not merely an irremediable trespass but no trespass at all. Yet this can never have been wholly true,[2] because outside the sphere of contract there had always been actions on the case for nonfeasance which were free from objection—based on failures to perform public duties,[3] customary duties to repair or to find chaplains,[4] or to remove tithe-sheaves from the land.[5] Nor was there any difficulty over maintaining a conceptual boundary between contract and tort, because there was no reason why a breach of promise should not be regarded as a 'tort' for the purposes of trespass on the case.[6] The legal difficulty was to accommodate within trespass that which was not a wrongful act causing physical damage, but the disappointment of an expectation raised by words. Nonfeasance could only be a legal

---

[1] *Pykeryng* v. *Thurgoode* (1532) Spelman 4 at 5 ('nul diversite en reson'); below, 857–8.

[2] There are indeed precedents—from the fourteenth century onwards—of *assumpsit* for nonfeasance, and these continue to be found as *optulit se* entries in the rolls. But the year books are against it until the end of the fifteenth century.

[3] e.g. the duty of common innkeepers and blacksmiths to accommodate and serve travellers: Pas. 14 Hen. VII, fo. 22, pl. 4, *per* Heigham sjt; *Anon.* (1503) 2 Caryll 417, no. 29; *White's Case* (1558) Dyer 158b. For qualifications of the duty see John Grene's reading (Inner Temple, 1499) Port 168, no. 76; James Hales's reading (Gray's Inn, 1532) Wm Yelv. 310, no. 4; *Anon.* (1557/8) BL MS. Hargrave 4, fo. 124v (does not extend to lodging house).

[4] For the last see Baker, *IELH*, 409 n. 41; *Fuljambe* v. *Knyfton* (1556) CP 40/1165, m. 931 (prescriptive duty to find chaplain to say mass on certain days of the week).

[5] e.g. *Bydwell* v. *Sage* (1530) CP 40/1067, m. 707.

[6] See *Pykeryng* v. *Thurgoode* (1532) Spelman 4 at 5, *per* Spelman J. ('this action is founded on another *tort*, namely the breaking of the promise'). The word *tort* did not then carry any technical connotation, and is perhaps best translated as 'wrong': above, 753. See also 94 Selden Soc. 257.

wrong if there was a legal duty to act. If the duty was imposed by custom or pre-scription, there was no difficulty; but if it was imposed solely by words of promise or bargain, the appropriate remedy was covenant or debt. The true principle, there-fore, was not so much that not doing was no trespass, but that actions on the case were not available in situations where there was an older or more 'general' writ pro-vided in the Register.[7] This rule against double remedies became common currency, if not by that name, in the early sixteenth century,[8] and either then or soon after-wards acquired the persuasive if erroneous explanation that the statute *In Consimili Casu* only sanctioned actions on the case where there was no pre-existing remedy.[9] The proponents of the rule did not object to a choice of two different remedies aris-ing from the same factual situation, which often occurred,[10] but to two forms of action being founded on the same cause of action.[11] Here there is another parallel between the action on the case and the Chancery subpoena: neither was available except where the established remedies of the common law failed. Contractual nonfeasance was caught by this principle, because not performing promises was governed by the action of covenant and not paying money by that of debt.

A second problem, not much to the fore in the reports but perhaps of continu-ing force, was that which had restricted covenant to written promises in the first place. Words were evanescent—'naked breath'[12]—and therefore difficult to prove to a jury, since the parties could not give evidence.[13] Moreover, they were not as obviously harmful as deeds; whatever damage they caused was indirect. Damage caused by defamatory words was treated as *damnum absque injuria* until the beginning of the sixteenth century,[14] while a threat to knock a house down, if unaccompanied by overt action, was never actionable.[15] If, then, the law provided no remedy in the case of a malevolent promise to demolish a house, followed by

---

[7] See S. F. C. Milsom, 'Not Doing is No Trespass' (1954) 12 *CLJ* 105; reprinted in *SHCL*, ch. 2.

[8] *Orwell v. Mortoft* (1504) Trin. 20 Hen. VII, fo. 9, pl. 18, *per* Kingsmill J.; *Lord Grey's Case* (1505) Mich. 21 Hen. VII, fo. 30, pl. 5, *per* Pygot sjt (denied); Pas. 14 Hen. VIII, fo. 31, pl. 8*bis* (119 Selden Soc. 193), *per* Broke J.; *Jordan's Case* (1535) Mich. 27 Hen. VIII, fo. 24, pl. 3, *per* Knightley sjt (denied); *Anon.* (1543) Gell's reports, I, Pas. 34 Hen. VIII, fo. 15; B. & M. 415, *per* Shelley J.

[9] This may be the implication of a passage in Yorke 240, no. 415, more fully quoted in note 11, below ('...where he can have an original writ *at common law* he shall not have an action on the case...'). Cf. [1972] *CLJ* at 217. For the attribution of case to the statute, see *Carvanell* v. *Mower* (1533) 121 Selden Soc. 425 at 426.

[10] See the discussion in *Pykeryng* v. *Thurgoode* (1532) Spelman 4; *Jordan's Case* (1535) Mich. 27 Hen. VIII, fo. 24, pl. 3.

[11] *Anon.* (1526/35) Yorke 240, no. 415 (tr. 'as to the [supposed] maxim that where he can have an ori-ginal writ at common law he shall not have an action on the case, that is not so; for he may have either, but not upon the same point for which he could have the action at common law'). See 94 Selden Soc. 263 n. 5.

[12] *Waberley* v. *Cockerel* (1541) Dyer 51a ('nude vent').

[13] For some indications of how informal contracts could be proved see above, 364.   [14] Above, 781.

[15] *Haukyns* v. *Broune* (1477) Trin. 17 Edw. IV, fo. 3, pl. 2; B. & M. 629–30, *per* Wode. Yet when a threat to burn a house was put into writing it could actually turn arson into treason: 8 Hen. VI, c. 6.

inaction, it was not obvious that it should provide a remedy in the case of a bene-
volent promise to erect a house, followed by inaction. In either case there were
words, but empty words without deeds did not change anything. The problem was
partly evidential: how did one satisfy a jury that a carpenter had promised to build
a house when there was no writing and he had not started to build?[16] And it was
partly substantive: damage resulting from mere words was *damnum absque
injuria*,[17] because 'doing nothing cannot make life worse'.[18]

NONFEASANCE AND NEGLIGENCE

Actions on the case for 'misfeasance', where a task had been undertaken and then
done badly, so that damage resulted, had been sanctioned by the courts since the
fourteenth century.[19] They were obviously free from the difficulties outlined above,
both because there was physical damage and because that damage made the breach
of promise visible to the jury. The underlying agreement was still a matter of invisible words, but the words were less significant here because an action of trespass
would have lain for the same damage even if there had been no agreement. If a
careless surgeon injured a patient unnecessarily with his knife, it was actionable in
case; whereas if a stranger inflicted a knife-wound it was a battery. Nonfeasance was
quite another matter, because a mere stranger was not liable in tort for failing to do
something for another. But here it must have been obvious from the beginning that
a line between acts of negligence and negligent omissions, where the consequences
were similar, was elusive and not very helpful. Take the case of the negligent
doctor again. The classical formulation of the writ was that he applied his cure so
unskilfully that the patient was made worse, which looks like misfeasance. But it
would be strange if the formula only covered the case of a positive injury inflicted
by the doctor. Suppose the medicine applied was an inert placebo, and the illness
became worse for lack of due treatment, or suppose the cure was applied to the
wrong part of the body, or even that the doctor failed to do anything at all.[20] In all
these cases the patient deteriorated through the doctor's carelessness, and it seems
probable that they could all have been included under the notion of 'applying a
cure unskilfully', even when there was no act which made things worse.

[16] This seems to be the sense of the older year-book cases, such as Mich. 2 Hen. IV, fo. 3, pl. 9; Mich.
11 Hen. IV, fo. 33, pl. 60; B. & M. 378–80. Cf. Pas. 32 Edw. III, Fitz. Abr., *Barre*, pl. 262, *per* Finchden sjt
(tr. 'agreement cannot be tried, for it depends on a man's will').

[17] *Haukyns v. Broune* (1477) Hil. 17 Edw. IV, fo. 3, pl. 2; B. & M. 632, *per* Billyng CJ and Nedeham J.

[18] Simpson, *History of Contract*, 227.   [19] See also above, 757–60.

[20] e.g. *Carre v. Gonetour* (1508) KB 27/989, m. 46 (surgeon left patient uncured); *Reynold v. Humfrey*
(1514) KB 27/1011, m. 11d (wound left uncured, so that patient sustained greater damage than before);
Roggers v. Walssh (1532) CP 40/1074, m. 505 (surgeons left a leg uncured); *Bonacre v. Worthe* (1533) CP
40/1079, m. 518 (surgeon administered undue medicines so that leg not cured). See also 94 Selden
Soc. 264–5.

Similar difficulties of analysis are suggested by the common case of the bailee who looked after goods so carelessly that they were lost or damaged. Sometimes, no doubt, a bailee might be guilty of positive misconduct. But equally common must have been the case of simple failure to take proper precautions to ensure that the goods did not deteriorate from natural causes,[21] or to prevent them from being stolen by third parties.[22] This was undeniably nonfeasance, and a situation where detinue lay; yet by 1487 at the latest an action on the case was judicially approved, on the footing that a decrease in value was not remediable in detinue.[23] A variation on this theme occurred in the case of carriers. The complaint could be of positive misconduct, such as overloading or dangerous driving; but more often a vehicle ran into difficulties against the forces of nature, and any fault lay in failing to exercise proper control. Again in that case the distinction between act and omission is not very meaningful. When in 1493 a barge-master was sued for the loss of a cargo for want of proper steering, and the defendant argued that this was merely nonfeasance, the court declared it a 'great misfeasance' and ruled that the point was not worth arguing.[24] There was a failure to deliver the cargo, which resembles nonfeasance, and a failure of control; but both failures resulted from a negligent course of conduct.

In these cases it might be said that the trusting of the doctor or the bailee with the physical care of person or property resulted in a continuing relationship in which an omission was not mere nonfeasance. An omission in the context of such a relationship could fairly be described as misconduct. Such a distinction would be more difficult to apply to the carpenter who failed to build, or the vendor who failed to convey, since here the parties were dealing with a future design rather than with bodies or things which needed care. That is why a person who promised to look after goods, but never took delivery of them, could not be sued in *assumpsit* for that kind of nonfeasance.[25] Yet even in the case of the inactive

---

[21] e.g. *Anon.* (1487) Hil. 2 Hen. VII, fo. 11, pl. 9; tr. B. & M. 398 (sheep died); *Athowe* v. *Wake* (1506) KB 27/980, m. 55 (sheep died); *Sadeler* v. *Body* (1506) KB 27/981, m. 50d (goods wasted and consumed); Shakelady's precedents, fo. 141 (armour rusted); Yorke 239, no. 412 (robe eaten by moths); *Pykeryng* v. *Thurgoode* (1532) Spelman 4 at 5 (robe eaten by moths); Hales's reading (1532) Wm Yelv. 310, no. 4.

[22] *Shelton* v. *Prior of Norwich* (1498) KB 27/948, m. 5d.

[23] *Anon.* (1487) Hil. 2 Hen. VII, fo. 11, pl. 9; tr. B. & M. 398 (shepherd); and see *Hayden* v. *Raggelond* (1510) 2 Caryll 608 (B. & M. 528); Yorke 239, no. 412; 94 Selden Soc. 265. It may not even have been necessary to allege an undertaking in such cases: B. & M. 398 n. 18; *Bluet* v. *Bouland* (1472) ibid. 563.

[24] *Johnson* v. *Baker* (1493) 1 Caryll 135 (pr. B. & M. 400). The record (CP 40/914, m. 104) says 'negligently and improvidently steered', so it seems the argument must have been directed to the absence of a negligent act rather than the failure to deliver the cargo. Cf. other unreported cases in 94 Selden Soc. 265–6; *Gryce* v. *Longebak* (1535) CP 40/1086, m. 163 (carrier of wine by sea left it open to the sun's rays so that it become sour); *Wode* v. *Hunt* (1544) CP 40/1120, m. 419; (No. 2, 1547) CP 40/1132, m. 302 (carrier left cargo unattended on quay, whence it was put on the wrong ship and lost at sea).

[25] *Anon.* (1487) Hil. 2 Hen. VII, fo. 11, pl. 9, *per* Townshend J.; James Hales's reading (Gray's Inn, 1532) BL MS. Hargrave 92, fo. 37v (B. & M. 346).

builder there could be physical damage. For instance, if he was engaged to build or repair a roof, his failure might result in damage by rain to the timbers or contents.[26] Or suppose he agreed to ceil with timber wainscotting but instead used ash and poplar; this was misconduct, but was it not essentially a total failure to do what was promised?[27] Suppose also that a carrier utterly neglected to transport a cargo of wine from Bordeaux, so that it turned sour.[28] In all these cases there was physical damage, and in most of them the distinction between nonfeasance and misfeasance could easily be reduced to a semantic quibble about the words used to describe the default: for example, an omission to take proper precautions while performing an activity could with careful draftsmanship be presented as negligent misconduct. And then there is the question of damage. A mere loss of expectation or profit might not be the kind of damage recoverable in trespass. But the failure to perform a promise might well cause the promisee more particular harm by reason of reliance, as where a doctor failed to treat a patient, or a seller or carrier failed to deliver goods or materials required for manufacture or resale, or where actors failed to perform a village play so that the churchwardens lost the food and drink which they had laid in for the spectators.[29]

It need not surprise us that the rather scholastic distinction between nonfeasance and misfeasance did not stand the test of time. But the rule against overlapping remedies continued. To see how it was avoided in the realm of what might be termed mere nonfeasance—where there was no physical custody, care, or control—we should examine in turn the three principal cases in which the law seems to have changed in our period, ending with the establishment of *assumpsit* for money.

PROMISES TO CONVEY LAND

One of the commonest forms of nonfeasance writ in the fifteenth-century plea rolls was that alleging a failure to deliver seisin of land previously sold to the plaintiff. The number of such writs reflects the importance of land and the temptation for sellers to withdraw when faced with a better offer. Yet the doctrine of the year books, throughout the century, was almost constantly against the use of the

[26] 94 Selden Soc. 266, 274; *Lovell* v. *Moore* (1508) CP 40/985, m. 267 (failure by builder to rebuild hall, so that timbers rotted by rain); *Bretton* v. *Hampton* (1508) KB 27/986, m. 47d (failure to repair house, so that it fell down); *Southworth* v. *Apowell* (1535) CP 40/1089, m. 614 (failure by tenant to maintain house 'bene, competenter, et tenantlyke, videlicet wyndetyght et watertyght', so that the timber was rotted by rain); Shakelady's precedents, BL MS. Harley 1856, fo. 145v.

[27] *Gaudy* v. *Rede* (1521) CP 40/1031, m. 328 (alleging fraud rather than negligence). Shakelady gives a form of writ against an artist for painting a portrait of the plaintiff so negligently that the colours faded: BL MS. Harley 1856, fo. 143.   [28] *Lyster* v. *Sygons* (1509) CP 40/987, m. 405.

[29] *Churchwardens of Halesworth, Suffolk* v. *Hethe* (1543) CP 40/1117, m. 276 (undertaking 'ad quoddam spectaculum sive ludum apud ecclesiam . . . ludere'). The defendants were all from Yarmouth.

writ for a mere passive failure to convey. The legacy of *Doige's Case* (1442),[30] decided by all the judges of England, was that *assumpsit* would lie against a vendor who deceitfully disabled herself from performance by conveying to a third party; and it seems that until the end of the century the remedy was only available where title had passed to a third party.[31] It is true that the Chancery continued to issue writs for mere failure to complete the contract by delivering seisin, but none of them proceeded very far.[32]

The new learning which allowed an action against the vendor, even where there was no intervening third party, was apparently accepted by 1499. The statement occurs, not in a reported case, but at the end of a remark by Fyneux CJ which Fitzherbert heard in Gray's Inn, presumably at a reading.[33] According to Fitzherbert's note, if a man bargained to sell land for money, and promised[34] that he would convey if the money was paid, but then failed to convey according to the covenant, an action on the case would lie and there was 'no need to sue a *subpoena*'. The final aside is telling. The Chancery had been active in this field,[35] and it was beginning to become standard doctrine that a bargain and sale of land raised an implied use in favour of the purchaser, provided there was consideration in the form of an actual or promised payment.[36] The early King's Bench declarations follow this notion closely, by alleging first that the plaintiff had bought land for a sum paid, or to be paid, next that the defendant had undertaken to deliver seisin or make an estate within a certain time, and finally that he had failed to do so. The doctrine of conscience was thus received into the common law.

In the twenty years following the 1499 statement there are over thirty examples of this kind of action in the King's Bench rolls, but in only a handful of them did

---

[30] *Shipton* v. *Dogge* (1442) Trin. 20 Hen. VI, fo. 34, pl. 41 (B. & M. 391); KB 27/717, m. 111. Followed by the Common Pleas in the fifteenth century: B. & M. 395.

[31] See *Anon.* (1487) Hil. 2 Hen. VII, fo. 12, pl. 15 (feoffment of third party is cause of action and traversable); *Karre* v. *Kyng* (1487) Mich. 3 Hen. VII, fo. 14, pl. 20, *per* Bryan CJ (it is a 'great misfeasance'); CP 40/898, m. 124; *Weldysshe* v. *Godhewe* (1489) CP 40/907, m. 907 (pleads infancy); *Byngham* v. *Walden* (1505) CP 40/970, m. 619 (issue on sale to third party).

[32] e.g. *Gunter* v. *Page* (1484) KB 27/890, m. 8d; *Tynton* v. *Jurnet*, ibid., m. 15d; *Stonham* v. *Martyn*, ibid., m. 17d; *Goche* v. *Meke* (1484) KB 27/893, m. 11; *Frankessh* v. *Hunte*, ibid., m. 65 (*barganizasset*); *Paxman* v. *Mannyng* (1485) KB 27/896, m. 12 (undertaking to make feoffment); *Porter* v. *Osberne*, ibid., m. 8d. These are all op. se entries.

[33] Trin. 14 Hen. VII, Fitz. Abr., *Action sur le Case*, pl. 45; repr. in Mich. 21 Hen. VII, fo. 41, pl. 66; tr. B. & M. 401; below, 847. The words 'in greis Inne' appear in the first edition of Fitz. Abr., but are omitted in the later editions and in the year book. Simpson, *History of Contract*, 261, questions whether this part of the note is even attributable to Fyneux: it could conceivably have been an addition by Fitzherbert himself.

[34] This word is missing, but the sense calls for it.

[35] Barbour, *History of Contract in Early English Equity*, 116–23.

[36] *Duke of Buckingham's Case* (1505) Mich. 20 Hen. VII, fo. 10, pl. 20; *Anon.* (1507) Hil. 21 Hen. VII, fo. 6, pl. 4; Yorke 135, no. 125 (use changed when first instalment of price paid); *Southwall* v. *Huddelston* (1523) Pollard 253, nos. 16–17; *Anon.* (1532) Brooke Abr., *Feffementes al Uses*, pl. 40; Simpson, *History of Contract*, 258–9, 346–8.

the defendant appear. In a case of 1507, the defendant sought to show that an agreement to sell was conditional upon the payment of money, and not a bargain for ready money paid,[37] which seems to rest on the assumption that the cause of action depended on an executed bargain. The same conclusion may be drawn from the next case, in 1509, when a plea of *Non assumpsit* was accompanied by a protestation that the defendant did not bargain in the way alleged and that the plaintiff did not pay any money for the bargain.[38] In the third case, the defendant simply pleaded *Non assumpsit*; the issue was tried before Fyneux CJ in London in 1514, and a verdict and judgment given for the plaintiff. This is the first judgment found in a nonfeasance case in the absence of a disablement. Curiously enough, the bill was described in the roll as one of deceit on the case (*deceptio super casu*), though no deceit was formally alleged. It is also worth noting that, although the plaintiff alleged an advance payment of £5, he only recovered £4. 10s. in damages.[39] Nevertheless, the remedy seems thereafter to be firmly in place in the King's Bench. The Common Pleas followed suit in the same decade, and judgments there are likewise found in nonfeasance cases without mention of disablement.[40]

Since Fyneux CJ seems to bear a major share of the responsibility for this development, it is valuable to find in 1518 an action which he brought himself by bill of privilege in his own court and which appears to carry the law of contract a stage further. The form is unorthodox, and it is difficult to suppose that the chief justice did not settle it himself. The legal problem was that Fyneux had not paid any money in advance, but had merely tendered payment at the time set for completion. The bill begins with a long inducement setting out a final concord and a bargain—in the perfect tense—to sell the land to Fyneux, the vendors undertaking and faithfully promising (*super se assumentes et fideliter promittentes*) that he should have the land, and Fyneux in return undertaking to pay, followed by an assertion that he tendered the money and requested performance, but the defendants schemed to deprive him of his bargain by covin and sold the land to another, 'against the form of the bargain and undertaking'.[41] This was a case of disablement by deceit, but the plaintiff had not—as in *Doige's Case*—paid any money in advance. The action did not proceed beyond imparlance, and the precedent was not followed; but the form is theoretically important as showing the significance attached, presumably by Fyneux himself, to what will soon be called consideration. An allegation of payment, or some other alteration of position, became routine in

---

[37] *Samson* v. *Raddysshe* (1507) KB 27/985, m. 69.   [38] *Erlewyn* v. *Erlewyn* (1509) KB 27/992, m. 23.
[39] *Laverok* v. *Wygan* (1513–14) KB 27/1008, m. 72d.
[40] e.g. *Badnour* v. *Downe* (1511) CP 40/996, m. 361 (judgment on *non est informatus*); *Blyke* v. *Eyns* (1512) CP 40/999, m. 436 (judgment after verdict); *Abbot of Pershore* v. *Keys* (1523) CP 40/1041, m. 620 (judgment for plaintiff on *nihil dicit*). Cf. *Wentworth* v. *Crayford* (1543) CP 40/1117, m. 158 (action for not leasing land as promised for £20 paid; *non est informatus*; inquest awards £28; court takes advisement).
[41] *Fyneux* v. *Clyfford* (1518) KB 27/1026, m. 76; 94 Selden Soc. 268.

standard cases of *assumpsit* for not conveying land,[42] and we shall return to its importance when revisiting Fyneux CJ's dictum of 1499.[43] But the 1518 action shows that Fyneux was prepared to countenance actions of *assumpsit* founded on mutual promises, and therefore places the emergence of a consensual view of contract quite close to the first establishment of *assumpsit* for nonfeasance.

The use of *assumpsit* for not conveying land to a purchaser for value was never seriously questioned in either of the benches after 1499, and yet there was no dramatic flood of judgments in such cases. Specific performance in Chancery was no doubt a preferable remedy where there had been no disablement. But it must also have been the case that most bargains and sales were embodied in deeds or records, and secured by bonds. The actions on the case were therefore typically brought to enforce transactions at the bottom end of the land market, including a high proportion of agreements to surrender copyholds.[44]

PROMISES TO PERFORM ACTS OR SERVICES

The history of actions on the case for failing to perform personal services followed exactly the same course as that of the actions for failing to convey land, except that here the 'disablement' doctrine had no place. Throughout the fifteenth century the plea rolls are full of *optulit se* entries of writs in which the defendant is alleged to have undertaken—usually in return for money paid—to do something, and then failed to do it (*minime fecit*, or *facere non curavit*).[45] The year books during the same period are full of dicta that such actions do not lie, because a deed is required.[46] As early as 1440, however, one of the prothonotaries of the Common Pleas had been heard to say that a builder could be sued for nonfeasance if he had

---

[42] For considerations other than money, see *Hubbert v. Gough* (1524) KB 27/1050, m. 27 (land promised in marriage agreement; judgment for plaintiff); *Coo v. Grene* (1529) KB 27/1073, m. 52 (land bought with grain).   [43] Below, 847.

[44] Examples are: *Palmer v. Togood* (1514) CP 40/1008, m. 318; *Gosnold v. Laundy* (1518) CP 40/1022, m. 730d (judgment for plaintiff); *Wode v. Legat* (1527) CP 40/1056, m. 518; *Ames v. Kechyn* (1529) CP 40/1061, m. 402; *Showbrugh v. Launcey* (1535) CP 40/1085(1), m. 168; *Sheldon v. Flemyng* (1536) CP 40/1088, m. 52d; *Heron v. Jekell* (1537) CP 40/1093, m. 95; *Pygryn v. Baker* (1539) CP 40/1102, m. 586d; *Uston v. Hunte* (1549) KB 27/1152, m. 23 (judgment for plaintiff); *Went v. Went* (1550) CP 40/1144A, m. 439d; *Cooke v. Keymer* (1551) KB 27/1158, m. 115; *Calver v. Calver* (1555) CP 40/1164, m. 1105 (judgment for plaintiff); *Whelowes v. Whelowes* (1557) CP 40/1169, m. 422d.

[45] King's Bench examples temp. Ric. III are: *Swethale v. Ecclys* (1484) KB 27/891, m. [59]d (failure by 'thaxster' to thatch roof); *Cornburgh v. Shorday* (1484) KB 27/892, m. 17d (failure by mason to rebuild houses); *Paston v. Godered*, ibid., m. 39 (failure to rebuild house); *Laweson v. Webster* (1484) KB 27/893, m. 42 (failure to build house); *Brygge v. Yarham*, ibid., m. 43 (sim.); *Dobbes v. Yarham* (1485) KB 27/894, m. 49d (sim.); *Dowesyng v. Kent*, ibid. (failure to plaster house); *Chaumbyr v. Game* (1485) KB 27/895, m. 10 (failure to build chimney).

[46] 94 Selden Soc. 269 n. 6. It was still arguable in the 1480s and 1490s that case would not lie for nonfeasance: *Anon.* (1487) Hil. 2 Hen. VII, fo. 11, pl. 9; tr. B. & M. 398 (shepherd); *Karre v. Kyng* (1487)

been paid in advance, because there was *quid pro quo* and because the plaintiff had been damaged.[47] This was refuted by his contemporaries, and omitted from the printed year books, but it shows that the later doctrine was canvassed long before the time of Fyneux—and indeed just before the judges in *Doige's Case* accepted the *quid pro quo* argument in the case of disablement from performance. Nevertheless, the final change of mind is established by Fyneux CJ's dictum in Gray's Inn in 1499:[48]

Note that if a man makes a covenant to build me a house by a certain date, and does nothing about it, I shall have an action on my case for this nonfeasance as well as if he had done it badly, because I am damaged by it: by Fyneux. And he said that it had been so adjudged, and he held it to be law.

The report of this remark has given some difficulty, because it makes no mention of prepayment; but the passage makes little sense without it, especially since the next sentence—discussed above—stresses the need for prepayment in the case of not conveying land sold. It is not otherwise clear in what sense the customer is 'damaged' (*en damages*) by the nonfeasance. If Fyneux CJ really did not think prepayment necessary—and his action in 1518 encourages us to think that he may not have done—then his views did not prevail at the time. Only six years later, Frowyk CJ emphasized that the prepayment was an essential ingredient in the cause of action in such cases, and this was also the view of Fitzherbert, St German, James Hales, and others.[49]

Although Fyneux CJ stated that the point had been adjudged, no one has yet found the judgment in the King's Bench rolls. There is an action against a carpenter for nonfeasance in the very year 1499, in a form which was by then quite common, and unusually it proceeds as far as declaration and imparlance; but this does not necessarily mean that the case was judicially before the court.[50] The case

---

Mich. 3 Hen. VII, fo. 14, pl. 20, *per* Vavasour sjt (agent); *Johnson* v. *Baker* (1493) 1 Caryll 135 (carrier); above, 842; but none of these turned out to be cases of nonfeasance.

[47] *Anon.* (1440) B. & M. 389 at 390, *per* Browne.

[48] Trin. 14 Hen. VII, Fitz. Abr., *Action sur le Case*, pl. 45 (tr.). For the date, see above, 844 n. 33.

[49] *Orwell* v. *Mortoft* (1504–5) Trin. 20 Hen. VII, fo. 9, pl. 18 (tr. B. & M. 408–9); 2 Caryll 465, 493 at 495, *per* Frowyk CJ (tr. 'If I covenant with a carpenter to make a house, and pay him £20 to make the house by a certain day, and he does not make the house by the day, I shall now have a good action on my case by reason of the payment of my money; and yet it sounds only in covenant, and without payment of money in this case there is no remedy'); FNB 145G (who says that the money makes it a 'bargain between them'); St German, *Doctor and Student*, ed. Plucknett and Barton, 228–9; *Anon.* (1526/35) Yorke 240, no. 415, at 241 (tr. 94 Selden Soc. 296–7; B. & M. 402–3); Hales's reading (Gray's Inn, 1532) BL MS. Hargrave 253, fo. 12 (but cf. Wm Yelv. 310, where he held that a lease to the promisor had the same effect).

[50] *Warner* v. *Canfeld* (1499) KB 27/951, m. 54d (op. se); KB 27/953, m. 85d (imparlance in Michaelmas term). The declaration mentions a prepayment of 18s. For seven other precedents around this time (all op. se entries), see 94 Selden Soc. 270 n. 8.

of the carpenter was the stock example of nonfeasance in the year books, perhaps because writs in this form were so common, and it seems possible that the innovation was first made in the case of independent contractors in order to fill a gap in the remedy provided by the Ordinance of Labourers.[51] Actions were also brought on parol retainers of professional people, such as surgeons,[52] teachers,[53] and clerical officials,[54] who would likewise have fallen outside the statute. It is true that there are even more instances of actions against labourers, for failing to perform menial tasks,[55] but these are always framed in terms of particular tasks undertaken for a specific payment, so that there was arguably no general retainer in service to which the statute could attach. There was no obvious advantage in using *assumpsit* rather than the statutory action; but the former had fewer restrictions, and required cases to be viewed in terms of contract rather than status.

The first recorded sixteenth-century King's Bench judgment in an action of this kind was in 1516, which places it—significantly, we might think—within five years of the first judgment for not delivering seisin and of the first judgment in slander.[56] It was also, perhaps no less significantly, a case tried before Fyneux CJ. The wording of the bill is far removed from the brief standard forms of writ which had been used throughout the fifteenth century, for it is unusually detailed and has obviously been drawn to fit the particular circumstances. Indeed, the use of a special bill, drawn by counsel, and the fact that judgment was obtained within a year, suggest a new-found resolution lacking in the stream of inconclusive actions over the previous hundred years. The complaint was that the defendant had undertaken, for £4 paid by the plaintiff, to teach the plaintiff's son grammar and other sciences so that he could go to Oxford, and to maintain the son at board for four years, and yet, little regarding his promise or the fact that the boy was at the best age for learning, but scheming to make him forget what he had already learned and to prevent him learning any more, for one and a half years went about his own business, giving him no direction, and for the last two years left him wandering and untaught, as a result of which the boy lost the knowledge of grammar and all that would have followed from it, and irrevocably wasted three and a half years of his life, to his damage of £100. Despite the ingenious elaborations of consequential loss—loss which a modern lawyer would regard as the son's rather than the father's—the complaint was essentially of not doing what was promised and paid for. The defendant pleaded Not guilty, and after a trial before Fyneux CJ in

---

[51] Simpson, *History of Contract*, 261–2; Baker, *IELH*, 333–4.   [52] See above, 759.

[53] e.g. *Cokyn* v. *Hopton* (1508) KB 27/986, m. 19d (organ-player paid to teach plaintiff's son *scienciam suam in musica organiste*); *Igulden* v. *Roberth* (1516) below.

[54] e.g. *Bothe* v. *Kyrkeham* (1509–11) KB 27/999, m. 71 (Chancery clerk undertook for 30s. 4d. to enrol pardon; pleads privilege); *Ewer* v. *Elys* (1521) CP 40/1033, m. 304; Spelman 3 (clerk of manorial court undertook for 10s. to enter record of real action).

[55] See 94 Selden Soc. 271 n. 4.   [56] See above, 784, 845.

banc the jury found him 'guilty of the deceit' and awarded £7 damages, considerably less than the plaintiff had asked for, but more than he had laid out.[57] Even after this, however, judgments were not frequent. The first we have noted for not performing a particular job of work was as late as 1532.[58]

The paucity of judgments, and therefore presumably of arguments in court, may explain the slowness of the profession at large to notice that anything significant had been decided. A few months after the judgment of 1516—though no connection is likely—the case of the carpenter was discussed in Gray's Inn at Peter Dillon's autumn reading. It is almost the only contract case to have come to light in the reports of learning exercises, and is remarkable for its apparent conservatism.[59] The previous Gray's Inn discussion of 1499 seems to have been completely forgotten, even though the first volume of Fitzherbert's *Abridgement* had just been printed and both Fyneux and Fitzherbert were still in touch with the inn. The report conveys the impression that the law was still unsettled. The reader, and one fellow bencher, argued in favour of allowing an action on the case. Two other benchers argued that actions on the case lay only for misfeasance, while a fifth argued that physical damage was necessary.[60] The reader did not put up a very strong argument to counter the old learning, but merely the circular assertion that 'every law is based on reason, and reason wills that if a man has an injury he should have an action'. However, there was no mention of prepayment in the case as put, or in the arguments, and so it may be that the question was tacitly limited to what we should call a promise without consideration. Certainly when we next hear of such a discussion in Gray's Inn, at James Hales's reading of 1532, the new learning has become accepted: *assumpsit* will lie for nonfeasance, provided there is either physical damage or prepayment.[61] This was the position from which the classical common law of contract developed. In the case of physical damage, it would not be necessary to show prepayment or any other

---

[57] *Igulden* v. *Roberth* (1516) KB 27/1018, m. 35.

[58] *Diconson* v. *Campe* (1532) KB 27/1082, m. 34 (undertaking by lessee, for 24s. paid, to enclose the demised land with hedges). No judgments at all have been noted in the Common Pleas, but note *Donnyng* v. *Hobbey* (1554) CP 40/1158, m. 504 (undertaking to roof a chancel; issue on plea that plaintiff had demolished the walls).

[59] Reading (Gray's Inn, 1516) LI MS. Misc. 486(2), fo. 7v (tr. 94 Selden Soc. 272; B. & M. 401). It is not obvious how the case arose from the text, which was the Statute of Ireland *De Coheredibus*.

[60] The clarity of Tingleden's argument is marred by the apparent loss of the word 'not' in the report. He followed his own doctrine when bringing an action in the same year for failing to build a wharf, alleging that land was flooded in consequence: *Tyngylden* v. *Mauncye* (1516) KB 27/1019, m. 59.

[61] BL MS. Hargrave 92, at fo. 37v (tr. 94 Selden Soc. 273; B. & M. 345). Cf. a shorter report in BL MS. Hargrave 253, fo. 12 (tr. 'Mr Reader said, if a man comes to me and says, "Give me £10 and I will make you a barn of such and such length", and does not do so, I shall have an action on my case. It is otherwise where no money is given, for then it is but *nudum pactum*. And this here is nonfeasance, but because I have no remedy for my money this is the reason why I shall have this action'). There is another extract (from MS. Hargrave 253) in Wm Yelv. 310, no. 4.

consideration, or even an undertaking;[62] but in order to sue for economic loss, or loss of expectation, it would be necessary to show that the plaintiff had entered into a reciprocal bargain.[63]

It is unfortunate from the historian's point of view that the establishment of the action on the case for not doing things was accompanied by so little reported discussion or explanation. Neither in the cases of failing to convey land nor in those of failing to perform a service or task was much substance usually at stake, and the development may not have been fought very hard. But some clues as to the legal thinking may be gleaned from the wording of the writs and bills, which underwent some changes between the beginning of Henry VII's reign and the middle of Henry VIII's. The original formula set out an undertaking (in the pluperfect tense) to perform the act, in return for a certain sum of money, and a failure (in the perfect tense). By 1500 a more elaborate form had begun to creep into use, and it became standard form within a few decades. It divided the underlying contract or bargain from the undertaking: whereas the defendant had bargained (*barganizasset*) or agreed (*convenisset*) to do something, and had undertaken (*assumpsisset*) to do it within a certain time, he did not do it. Later in the century the separation between the bargain and the promise would be made still more explicit by shifting the undertaking into the perfect tense (*assumpsit*); but already, in the earlier form, pleaders had seen merit in presenting the undertaking in a separate clause and coupling it with some additional responsibility not embodied in the bargain, usually a time-limit. This formulation emphasized that the action was not brought on the bargain or covenant, for which older actions were available, but on something more specific. A time-limit might have been seen as providing also an element of disablement; no matter that the party might still do the thing promised, he could no longer do it on time.

Another elaboration, which became more common in the first decades of the sixteenth century, was to allege wherever possible some consequential loss flowing from the failure to act. The archetypal case, mentioned in the year books and registers of writs, was damage to the timber or contents of houses as a result of failing to repair or roof them. Other examples were loss of profits,[64] the loss of a promotion through failure to obtain a papal bull,[65] the loss of food and drink bought for the expected audience at a village play which was cancelled,[66] the inability to plead a pardon because of a clerk's failure to enrol it,[67] and—in the

---

[62] Baker, *IELH*, 395.   [63] For consideration see below, 862–8.

[64] e.g. *Martyn v. Warner* (1516) KB 27/1020, m. 45d (refusal to accept lease of mill); Shakelady's precedents, BL MS. Harley 1856, ff. 150v (failure to build a mill), 152v (not carrying goods needed for resale); FNB 94A (not making a carriage).

[65] *Howe v. Maruffo* (1520) KB 27/1037, m. 38d. Raphael Maruffo was the principal broker in papal bulls for many years, and was involved in numerous suits, usually debt on bonds.

[66] *Churchwardens of Halesworth v. Hethe* (1543) CP 40/1117, m. 276; above, 843 n. 29.

[67] *Bothe v. Kyrkeham* (1509–11) KB 27/993, m. 35d; KB 27/999, m. 71.

schoolmaster case of 1516—the irrevocability of misspent youth and the loss of learning through lack of exercise.[68] By 1557 it would even be possible to think of bringing *assumpsit* for breach of promise of marriage, by relying on the loss of gifts and moneys laid out in contemplation of marriage, though the promisor demurred to that part of the declaration which rested on his refusal to marry, doubtless because it was a spiritual matter.[69]

The final stage in the evolution of the typical declaration in our period was the elaboration of the breach-clause to include a general allegation of deceit and injurious reliance on the undertaking. The element of injurious reliance is more often met with in the money cases to be considered presently, but the 'craftily scheming to defraud' (*callide machinans defraudare*) clause became common form in *assumpsit* generally and indeed in all other actions on the case.[70] The inspiration no doubt was *Doige's Case*, and in the context of sales of land it was occasionally used even in the late fifteenth century.[71] But it is difficult to believe that this clause, at any rate when it became standard form, was intended as a serious charge of fraud in anything like the modern sense. The notion of fraud does not seem obviously appropriate to the case of the craftsman who did not meet an order; his contract did not exclude other employment, and so he had not (like Mrs Doige) disabled himself by turning his contractual allegiance elsewhere. Deceit is not mentioned by Fyneux, Fitzherbert, or Spelman, or in the other reports, as an essential prerequisite to liability for nonfeasance, and still in the 1530s a few cases may be found where the allegation was entirely omitted. In the action on the case for deceit properly so called, the action on a warranty,[72] the general issue was *Non decepit*; but in *assumpsit* for nonfeasance—also summarily referred to in the plea rolls as 'a plea of deceit'[73]—the deceit was never traversed, even by protestation. It is difficult to avoid the conclusion that this common-form deceit, though regarded as a helpful embellishment, was not altogether vital to the cause of action.[74] In any case, it was not in most cases formally attached to the prepayment;

---

[68] *Igulden* v. *Roberth* (1516) KB 27/1018, m. 35; above, 848–9.

[69] *Curtes* v. *Chersey* (1557–9) CP 40/1170, m. 730 (imparlance); CP 40/1176(1), m. 636 (plea as to the diamond ring, chattels, and money; demurrer to residue). The plaintiff was an alderman of London. Cf. *Lewes* v. *Style* (1506) below, 855–6, where no undertaking was alleged.

[70] Before *machinans defraudare* becomes *de rigueur*, we occasionally find the more neutral 'scheming to harm (*pejorare*)' or 'scheming to endamage (*dampnum incurrere*)'. For other varieties see further 94 Selden Soc. 274.

[71] e.g. *Entwysell* v. *Clerk* (1489) KB 27/912, m. 46. It was, nevertheless, unusual. It does not occur in any of the 27 writs on the case recorded in the King's Bench temp. Ric. III (7 of which are for failing to convey land): KB 27/888–896. [72] See above, 771–3.

[73] J. Rastell, *Exposiciones Terminorum* [*c.*1523], sig. C1, likewise called the action 'deceit' (sp. mod. 'Deceit . . . lieth where any deceit is done to a man by another so that he hath not sufficiently performed his bargain or not performed his promise'). Cf. above, 769.

[74] This is confirmed by *Andrew* v. *Boughey* (1551–2) Dyer 75a at 75b; KB 27/1160, m. 114 (demurrer but no judgment).

the defendant was not necessarily being sued for tricking the plaintiff out of his money, but perhaps for cheating the plaintiff of his bargain.[75] This is a rather ambiguous kind of deceit, hovering between contract and tort.

What emerges from these developments in the forms of declaration is that pleaders were desirous to emphasize that the action on the case was founded on a cause of action other than a mere failure to perform a covenant. If it could be labelled 'deceit', so much the better, so long as the deceit was not put in issue. However, the safest course for the plaintiff was not to sue on an agreement without more—since that was actionable by writ of covenant—but to sue for breach of a collateral promise to perform the agreement by a date now past, and allege consequential loss flowing from reliance on the promise, since it was arguable that neither was remediable in the action of covenant.[76] Similar thinking lay behind the third and most important category of nonfeasance, the failure to discharge a debt.

PROMISES TO PAY MONEY OR DELIVER FUNGIBLES

When Fyneux CJ made his pronouncement on nonfeasance in 1499, no one seems yet to have thought of using *assumpsit* to recover a debt. This was the one case not found in the fifteenth-century plea rolls,[77] and it was to prove a much more contentious area of development than that of covenant.[78] The root of the difference, presumably, was that the action of debt—unlike covenant—lay without specialty, and therefore there was another policy in play. The developments previously outlined enabled covenants to be enforced without the need for written evidence under seal, and thus brought Westminster Hall into line with most local courts throughout the country. The evidential requirement had come to seem outmoded and unnecessary. On the other hand, extending *assumpsit* into the field of debt would threaten the right of most debtors to wage their law,[79] and, as we have seen, this was a right by no means universally despised in 1500. Still, the logic of *assumpsit* for nonfeasance pointed inexorably towards allowing *assumpsit* for not delivering fungible goods and for not paying debts. If it was possible to

[75] Cf. the hybrid assertion in *Skipwith* v. *Rowlett* (1555) KB 27/1176, m. 229, where in *assumpsit* for non-delivery of grain the plaintiff alleged that the defendant had schemed to defraud him of the grain and to convert the purchase money to his own use without good conscience ('absque omnia bona consciencia').

[76] As a result of dicta in *Doige's Case*, which to some extent reinterpreted the earlier law: Milsom, 81 *LQR* 510; Baker, 94 Selden Soc. 264; *IELH*, 321.

[77] Note, however, the entry in Brooke Abr., *Action sur le Case*, pl. 110, purporting to abridge a case of 1484 which is not in print: as to which see Simpson, *History of Contract*, 286–7.

[78] The disagreement between the King's Bench and Common Pleas (below, 869–74) did not extend to the covenant cases.

[79] Cf. the similar problem facing the action on the case for conversion as a substitute for detinue: above, ch. 45.

avoid the objection that not performing a covenant sounded only in covenant, it ought by analogy to be possible to avoid the objection that not paying a debt sounded only in debt. It was only a matter of identifying the appropriate formula for presenting non-payment as a trespass.

The analogy probably first suggested itself in the case of unspecified goods. Although the duty to render or yield them up (*reddere*) was enforced by the action of debt in the *detinet*,[80] such a duty was often difficult to distinguish from that arising from a covenant to deliver unspecified goods, especially if the vendor and the carrier were one and the same person by reason of a promise to deliver. The fifteenth century already knew the action on the case for not delivering goods, which was modelled on that for not delivering seisin of land,[81] though in a case of 1443—the only reported challenge before 1500—opinion had been against it.[82] No doubt an undertaking to deliver specific goods would have been indistinguishable in principle from the undertaking in *Doige's Case*, and if the goods were then sold to a third party or destroyed there would be the requisite element of disablement. The only analogous situation in the case of unspecified goods would be where the vendor had entered into a solus agreement, because he would then disable himself by making any sale to a third party; but we have not as yet noticed any examples of this before the early sixteenth century.[83] Nevertheless, the writ and count in *assumpsit* for chattels normally drew no distinction between specific goods and fungibles,[84] and this ambiguity may have assisted the next step.

In a leading Common Pleas case of 1504-5—sometimes known as the *Case of Barley*—the plaintiff went a step too far in overlooking the distinction between

[80] The true action was debt in the *detinet* (without the word *debet*), because the value of the fungibles might change and therefore the value had to be assessed: *Anon.* (1495) Mich. 11 Hen. VII, fo. 5, pl. 20, *per* Bryan CJ; *Spert* v. *Abbot of Chertsey* (1536) CP 40/1088, m. 429; Yorke 100, no. 36 (debt in *detinet* on a sale of red herring; pleads *Non detinet*). Cf. the loose remarks in *Pykeryng* v. *Thurgoode* (1532) Spelman 4 at 5, *per* Spelman J. (debt in the *debet et detinet*) and Port J. (detinue); *Anon.* (1543) below, 871-2, *per* Shelley J. (detinue).

[81] e.g. from the end of the century, *Burnell* v. *Wylkyn* (1490) KB 27/916, m. 55 (non-delivery of household goods sold); *Tanner* v. *Weller* (1496) KB 27/941, m. 49d (non-delivery of wool sold). For slightly later examples see 94 Selden Soc. 276 n. 3. On the same principle, an action could be framed for not delivering money to a third-party creditor: *Gybbes* v. *Wolston* (1483) CP 40/883, m. 355 (judgment for plaintiff).

[82] *Tailboys* v. *Sherman* (1443) B. & M. 395 (failing to deliver wine; there seems to have been an implied contract of carriage, since the contract was made in Lincoln and delivery was to be in Guldilo).

[83] They become fairly common, especially in connection with the wool trade: e.g. *Makeley* v. *Ferrant* (1511) KB 27/1001, m. 68 (wool); *Wykys* v. *Hyder* (1512) CP 40/1000, m. 543 (wool); *Kentyng* v. *Doket* (1514) KB 27/1001, m. 56d (cheese); *Muklowe* v. *Wright* (1517) CP 40/1018, m. 326 (wool); *Ferne* v. *Miller* (1518) CP 40/1022, m. 728 (wool); *Baker* v. *Hartyng* (1521) CP 40/1032B, m. 337 (crops); *Audelett* v. *Osburne* (1524) CP 40/1045, m. 529 (wool); *Baker* v. *Laynston* (1529) CP 40/1062, m. 132d (wool); *Reynold* v. *Croppe* (1533) CP 40/1079, m. 556 (wool); *Stansby* v. *Branstell* (1534) CP 40/1083, m. 504d (wool; agreement in a sealed bill).

[84] See e.g. *Maget* v. *Hykkys* (1504) CP 40/969, m. 437 (*assumpsit* for non-delivery of 20 cades of red herring).

specific and unspecified goods, and thereby occasioned a major debate which was reported in the year books and also by Caryll.[85] This was an action against a seller of barley who had undertaken not only to render but to deliver. Mindful, perhaps, of the 1443 decision, or perhaps following precedents from the city of London,[86] the plaintiff's lawyer[87] decided not to rely on the old covenant type of declaration but to try to fit his case into the form used against bailees for conversion of specific goods. He declared that, whereas he had bought sixty quarters of barley from the defendant for £6 agreed, and the defendant had 'undertaken, covenanted, and bargained' to deliver them by a date now past, the defendant—'scheming fraudulently and craftily to defraud' him—converted the barley to his own use and did not deliver it. The defendant took an equally unusual course by not traversing the undertaking or the conversion but pleading that the plaintiff did not buy the barley from him in the manner alleged. An even more unusual course was taken at Norwich assizes, where the presiding judge happened to be Fyneux CJ. The plaintiff produced evidence that he bought the sixty quarters of barley for £6 as he had alleged, and to this evidence the defendant demurred. It is difficult to see what question could possibly have been raised by such a demurrer which could not just as well have been taken on a motion in arrest of judgment. The effect, nevertheless, was to place before the judges in banc the question whether such an action was maintainable.[88] No doubt the plaintiff's counsel tried to argue that the defendant was in effect a bailee for safekeeping of the barley which he had bought,[89] but the argument was doomed to fail in the absence of an assertion that any specific sacks of barley had been appropriated to him at the time of sale. If he could not show that the property in any identifiable sacks had passed to him, then the defendant could not be said to have converted his barley. And yet, if the element of conversion was disregarded, the only remaining complaint was of the bare failure to deliver at the appointed day, which was actionable in debt.[90] All the judges of the Common Pleas except Frowyk CJ thought this was a fatal objection,

[85] *Orwell* v. *Mortoft* (1504–5) CP 40/972, m. 123 (pr. 116 Selden Soc. 466; tr. B. & M. 406); Mich. 20 Hen. VII, fo. 8, pl. 18 (tr. B. & M. 408); 2 Caryll 465, 493; BL MS. Hargrave 105, ff. 233, 236; MS. Add. 35938, fo. 195v.

[86] See *Asshe* v. *Hayle* (1485) C244/139/100, a plaint from the Sheriffs' Court (H sold 53 bales of woad to A, who left them with H until they could be delivered, and H promised/undertook [word lost] to do this; H never delivered them, but converted them to his own use). The bales appear to be treated as specific goods.

[87] The attorney was William Knyghtley of Norfolk (Coke's grandfather). Neither the reports nor the demurrer to the evidence mention the plaintiff's counsel.

[88] This question had already been argued at the pleading stage (Mich. 1504): YB.

[89] See 2 Caryll 493 (tr. 'In an action of trespass on the case, the plaintiff counted that he had bought twenty quarters of malt from the defendant for a certain sum of money paid beforehand, which malt he left with the defendant for safekeeping to the use of the plaintiff himself until a certain day now past . . .'). That is not how the count is entered on the roll: B. & M. 406.

[90] Even though the word *convenisset* was used, it does not seem to have been argued that there was a covenant to deliver rather than a passive debt. Probably this was because the agreement was to deliver at the place where the bargain was made, and so there was no element of carriage.

and it is reported that even Fyneux CJ shared the majority view. No judgment was entered,[91] the experiment was not repeated, and so the case was hardly a precedent for anything. Yet it was an important case, both for the well-reported discussion of the general problem of remedies, and for Frowyk CJ's influential dissenting judgment. To Frowyk CJ's way of thinking, the conversion was just an irrelevance, and therefore it did not matter that property had not passed. The buyer had paid his money[92] and had not received his barley; and an action on the case was available to 'punish' this 'misdemeanour', since it went beyond mere detention. Looking back, it is hard to understand how those who disagreed could have distinguished this from the case of the paid carpenter who failed to build, except on the unstated premise that the desire to escape from wager of law was not yet regarded with sympathy. As it happens, Frowyk CJ's position was to take firm root in the King's Bench, whereas the more reticent view of his brethren—and of Fyneux CJ at that time—was to remain the orthodox Common Pleas position until the end of the century.[93]

The one money case which the Common Pleas accepted without demur was that of the undertaking to 'save harmless' (to indemnify a surety).[94] Prototype actions were already known in local courts,[95] and this was also the context of the first known King's Bench judgment in *assumpsit* for money.[96] But this kind of action, though brought for a specific sum of money, had not been accommodated within the action of debt and therefore did not raise the question of overlapping remedies and wager of law.[97]

Several other early experiments with actions on the case for money were likewise just outside the proper territory of debt. In 1506 a jilted lover sued his former fiancée for money which he had laid out to counsel in maintenance of her lawsuits, and for the return of rings and jewels. He carefully avoided any mention of a promise to marry, which would have raised jurisdictional problems, and relied instead on words of comfort implying the prospect of marriage; but there is a strong hint of *Doige's Case* in the assertion that the defendant, scheming to defraud the plaintiff of his money and goods, had neither reimbursed him nor married him but had

---

[91] Fitzjames CJ said in 1536 that judgment was given for the plaintiff (Dyer 22b), but this is not borne out by the record. However, the year book apparently reports the argument at the pleading stage (Mich. 1504), and so the case could only have gone to the trial if the court had given its preliminary approval.

[92] This is assumed as a fact in all the reports, but there is no mention in the record that the £6 was paid.   [93] See further below, 869–74.

[94] *Blakburn* v. *Walker* (1506) CP 40/976, m. 312; Stubbe's entries, fo. 47; *Blakburn* v. *Fournes* (1507) CP 40/980, m. 416; *Blakburn* v. *Lokwode* (1508) CP 40/986, m. 307. For later cases (with judgments) see below, 869.

[95] See *Fenby* v. *Baly* (1485) KB 27/896, m. 40 (error from Norwich; plea of trespass and deceit; *assumpsit* to save a pledge harmless and refusal to do so; no errors assigned).

[96] *Wright* v. *Evyngar* (1514) KB 27/1010, m. 25d (action by factor against principal on a promise to save him harmless against the king in respect of a bond not to leave Calais or go into Burgundy, alleging that he was compelled to pay 20 marks to Dudley; recovers £8).

[97] Note, however, the obsolete viscontiel action *de plegiis acquietandis*: below, 870.

fraudulently become engaged to another. The action was tried before Fyneux CJ, and the jury gave the plaintiff damages for the money laid out.[98] Like the *Case of Barley*, this precedent stood alone and was not built upon; but it represented an important leap. An obligation to refund money could now be enforced by an action on the case.

A trickle of miscellaneous actions for money and fungibles followed, none of which squarely raised the problem of double remedies.[99] Actions by and against sureties became well established by 1520,[100] as were soon afterwards actions on promises to pay pro rata for goods delivered over a period.[101] The year 1520 saw three important experiments with far-reaching consequences. First, in *assumpsit* against an Italian merchant, damages were recovered for the value of foreign currency due to the plaintiff in exchange for English money.[102] Second, an important precedent was set for bringing *assumpsit* against executors to recover a simple debt guaranteed by their testator,[103] another case where the action of debt was unavailable. This case was reported, and the year-book reporter added a query whether the action would have lain against the testator himself. In fact, just such a judgment—against a guarantor—was given the same term.[104] A remark made by More J. shows that the court was influenced, in extending these remedies, by the existence of remedies in the city of London courts.[105]

---

[98] *Lewes* v. *Style* (1506) KB 27/979, m. 71d. It influenced the first known declaration for breach of promise of marriage: *Curtes* v. *Chersey* (1557–8) above, 851. And it was still remembered temp. Eliz. I: Cro. Eliz. 79; HLS MS. 1192, fo. 13; CUL MS. Hh.2.9, fo. 26v, *per* Catlyn CJ.

[99] See 94 Selden Soc. 277–9, 282–3. The case of *Wawen* v. *Mathewson* (1512–13) KB 27/1005, m. 67d, discussed ibid. *279*, seems to have arisen from a sale of specific goods (barrels of salmon) rather than fungibles as there suggested. However, actions for non-delivery of fungibles are found, more or less in the old form: e.g. *Paston* v. *Butler* (1506) KB 27/981, m. 16 (railings); *Traps* v. *Richardson* (1507) KB 27/983, m. 27 (cloth sold by sample); *Abraham* v. *Prior of Royston* (1512) KB 27/1005, m. 56 (malt); *Campe* v. *Mason* (1519) KB 27/1033, m. 31 (wheat required for baking bread); *Tuttelsham* v. *None* (1520) KB 27/1034, m. 38 (wheat).

[100] e.g. *Soham* v. *Codlyng* (1516) KB 27/1021, m. 42; *Fraunces* v. *Tate* (1518) KB 27/1026, m. 39d ('de placito debiti super casu'); *Machell* v. *Sawell* (1519) KB 27/1030, m. 63; *Deryng* v. *Snowe* (1519) KB 27/1033, m. 15 (against surety); *Grafton* v. *Bold* (1520) KB 27/1037, m. 88d (judgment against surety); *Blaknall* v. *Pawne* (1522) KB 27/1045, m. 96 (judgment for surety). Nineteen examples were noted between 1520 and 1535, and formal approval was given in *Squyer* v. *Barkeley* (1532) KB 27/1085, m. 32d (pr. 94 Selden Soc. 253); Spelman 7 (reserved judgment against surety); *Holygrave* v. *Knyghtysbrygge* (1535) KB 27/1094, m. 30d (pr. 94 Selden Soc. 256); Mich. 27 Hen. VIII, fo. 24, pl. 3; Spelman 7 (reserved judgment for surety).

[101] *Barbour* v. *White* (1527) KB 27/1064, m. 35d; *Haymond* v. *Lenthorp* (1528–31) KB 27/1065, m. 77d (demurrer); *Stevens* v. *Herde* (1530) KB 27/1075, m. 75; *Turner* v. *Nelethorpp* (1531) KB 27/1078, m. 66 (noted in *LPCL*, 400 n. 43); *Jones* v. *Darrell* (1534) KB 27/1091, m. 24d; *Fressher* v. *Deacon* (1535) KB 27/1097, m. 39. This was not a case where debt lay: Pas. 12 Edw. IV, fo. 9, pl. 22, *per* Bryan CJ.

[102] *Blanke* v. *Spinula* (1520) KB 27/1036, m. 75 (£104 recovered; noted in *LPCL*, 400 n. 42).

[103] *Cleymond* v. *Vyncent* (1520–1) Mich. 12 Hen. VIII, fo. 11, pl. 3 (119 Selden Soc. 46; B. & M. 446); Port 10; KB 27/1037, m. 40 (copied in Maycote's entries, fo. 37; and in Catlyn's precedent book, Alnwick Castle MS. 475, ff. 52v–53v; pr. 102 Selden Soc. 10; judgment for plaintiff). See also below, 870.

[104] *Grafton* v. *Bold* (1520) KB 27/1037, m. 88d.

[105] Port 10 (B. & M. 447). There had also been a remedy in the ecclesiastical courts, but it was vulnerable to prohibition and *praemunire*: above, 242.

The third precedent seemed to provide an interim answer to the still more important question whether *assumpsit* could be used as an alternative to debt on a contract, though the matter was not fully settled during Fyneux CJ's tenure of the chief justiceship. In the very same roll as the executor and surety judgments, in 1520, there is a judgment entered in *assumpsit* in favour of a vendor of wheat who had not been paid the purchase price. The plaintiff counted on a bargain to buy the wheat, an undertaking to pay the price, and delivery of the wheat by the plaintiff, and then alleged that the defendant—'scheming wickedly and maliciously to deceive the plaintiff'—refused to pay.[106] The record does not reveal whether this case prompted any legal challenge, but the new extension was certainly challenged the following year when a slightly more elaborate declaration was made in a similar case. A vintner complained that he had discussed the sale of some wine with the defendant's wife, that the defendant (knowing of this) requested the plaintiff to sell and deliver the wine, promising to pay £23. 6s. 8d. within six months; the plaintiff, trusting in the promise, delivered the wine and received 30s. in part payment; but the defendant, scheming to defraud the plaintiff and not to fulfil his promise, and scheming of his evil and impudent cunning (*ex ejus mala et proterva solercia*) to make him lose his goods and money, refused to pay, sold the wine to others, and converted the proceeds. The defendant demurred to the bill, and the court took advisement until Easter term 1525, when the action was discontinued.[107] Despite the imaginative display of invective, this was effectively an action to recover a simple debt for goods sold, and even without a report we can guess at the ground of the demurrer. The great issue was whether *assumpsit* could properly be used as a substitute for debt. Further experiments were doubtless deterred during the 1520s because of this undetermined demurrer,[108] and the matter was not resolved by the King's Bench until 1532, in the leading case of *Pykeryng* v. *Thurgoode*.

Richard Pykeryng was a London brewer with some experience of Common Pleas litigation against defaulting suppliers of malt in the years of dearth,[109] and it is tempting to guess that he had found the action of debt unsatisfactory. In 1532, having taken the advice of Robert Maycote, clerk of the papers in the King's

---

[106] *Snothe* v. *Vowell* (1520) KB 27/1037, m. 63. The defendant pleaded that there was an indenture of sale, and traversed the informal bargain. Although the plaintiff alleged a promise to pay £42, he recovered only £9. 10s. 4d.

[107] *Cremour* v. *Sygeon* (1521–5) KB 27/1041, m. 33d.

[108] Note also the demurrer in *Haymond* v. *Lenthorp* (1528–31) KB 27/1065, m. 77d (solus agreement), which kept the issue before the court in the interim; though it seems to have been a case where debt did not lie (since the quantity of fungibles was not fixed at the outset), and the demurrer was to the plea in bar rather than the declaration. See 94 Selden Soc. 283, which omits to mention the plea.

[109] See *Pekeryng* v. *Mathewe* (1529) CP 40/1063, m. 600d (writ of debt in the *detinet* for non-delivery of malt).

Bench,[110] he brought a bill in the King's Bench for non-delivery of forty quarters of malt. He declared that, whereas for £5. 13s. 4d. paid in advance and another £5. 13s. 4d. to be paid on delivery, the defendant had in October 1531 bargained and sold forty quarters of malt to be delivered to the plaintiff by 25 February 1532, and had there and then promised and undertaken to deliver it accordingly, and the plaintiff (hoping for faithful delivery) made less provision of malt for his brewery, nevertheless the defendant, scheming to run him into loss, did not deliver any malt, so that the plaintiff was short of malt for his brewing and was constrained to buy from elsewhere after 25 February at a far dearer price. The plaintiff won a verdict before Fitzjames CJ at the Guildhall, and the defendant moved in the King's Bench to arrest the judgment on the ground that the proper remedy in such a case was an action of debt. The only judge who succumbed to this argument was Port J., who observed that it was a case of nonfeasance: 'there is no act done by the defendant, but only the non-delivery, for which detinue[111] [sic] lies'. The rest of the court (Fitzjames CJ, Conyngesby and Spelman JJ) agreed to enter judgment for the plaintiff. Their reasoning may be summarized by saying that there was both *injuria* and *damnum*—a wrong in the breach of promise, and damage flowing from the non-delivery—and that where the two concurred an action was available. Spelman J. said that Port J.'s distinction between nonfeasance and misfeasance had been exploded by the earlier decisions about bailees, carpenters, and sellers of land. And the fact that another form of action was available on the facts was immaterial, since the causes of action were different; in such cases the plaintiff could elect which action to bring.[112] Thus the King's Bench declined to follow the majority in the *Case of Barley*, and accepted the logic of Fyneux CJ (in 1499) and Frowyk CJ (in 1505) as justifying an action on the case for debt.

After this decisive judgment, *assumpsit* for money blossomed in the King's Bench and soon became common form. From being unheard of in 1500, it became by the 1530s the only kind of *assumpsit* action regularly proceeding to judgment,[113] though it should be noted that it was not even then a significant threat to the Common Pleas debt business which it paralleled.[114] The action made possible the beginnings of a commercial jurisdiction in the King's Bench, chiefly in

[110] He was the plaintiff's attorney: 94 Selden Soc. 247. Maycote may also have drawn the bill in *Cleymond* v. *Vyncent*, which is copied in his book of entries (above, 856 n. 103).

[111] Presumably debt in the *detinet*, since no specific malt was set aside: cf. Shelley J. in the same sense, below, 872, text at n. 203.

[112] *Pykeryng* v. *Thurgoode* (1532) KB 27/1083, m. 65 (pr. 94 Selden Soc. 247); Spelman 4. A similar judgment is found in *Hudson* v. *Webbe* (1539) KB 27/1112, m. 73 (non-delivery of wheat, so that plaintiff lost profit and had to buy elsewhere at a greater price to feed his household).

[113] In 1538 as many as six judgments were entered: 94 Selden Soc. 279.

[114] e.g. in 1535 there were 58 judgments for the plaintiff in Common Pleas actions of debt on a contract.

London cases tried before the chief justice at the Guildhall. At the end of the 1530s, and especially under the chief justiceships of Sir Edward Mountagu (1538–45) and Sir Richard Lyster (1545–53), there was a noticeable expansion in the scope of remedies extended to commercial litigants, perhaps drawing them away from the city courts:[115] *assumpsit* could now be used to enforce contracts for carriage by sea,[116] marine insurance contracts,[117] factoring arrangements,[118] partnership and joint-venture agreements,[119] and bills of exchange.[120] Nevertheless, the expansion of *assumpsit* was not limited to the commercial sphere, and we may note new remedies for marriage-money,[121] to enforce wagers,[122] and to recover legacies.[123] The action was free from some of the technicalities of debt, and thus could be brought for sums of money which were not fixed at the outset—using precursors of the *quantum meruit* and *quantum valebant* formulae[124]—and also, arguably, for

[115] For marine insurance litigation in London in the 1530s see above, 284 n. 65.

[116] *Sabyn* v. *Toly* (1541) KB 27/1121, m. 111 (promise to pay freight; defendant refused to load ship on arrival at Bordeaux; pleads late arrival of ship); *Closter* v. *Cannesby* (1550) KB 27/1154, m. 126 (freight).

[117] *Mayne* v. *De Gozi* (1538) KB 27/1107 m. 37; above, 215 n. 51.

[118] *Cordell* v. *Crystyan* (1538) KB 27/1109, m. 24d (35s. recovered); *Saxcy* v. *Hudson* (1553) KB 27/1167, m. 145 (trading in Danzig; £852 recovered).

[119] *Beale* v. *Barnes* (1542) KB 27/1125, m. 24 (mercer and grocer; £105 recovered at the Guildhall); *Bowyer* v. *Rawlyns* (1544) KB 27/1132, m. 111 (grocers); *Massy* v. *Marten* (1544) KB 27/1133, m. 123 (grocers).

[120] *Dolphyn* v. *Barne* (1540) KB 27/1116, m. 35d (judgment by default); *Maynard* v. *Dyce* (1542) KB 27/1125, m. 110 (nonsuit); *Long* v. *Hunt* (1544) KB 27/1131, m. 136 (judgment for plaintiff); *Towll* v. *Hawkyns* (1549) KB 27/1152, m. 143; *Moreany* v. *Basyng* (1551) KB 27/1157, m. 40. For exchange contracts not mentioning bills see *De Grady* v. *De Benexia* (1539) KB 27/1113, m. 65 (*assumpsit* to pay for ducats received at Micena by way of exchange); *Bonvise* v. *De la Sala* (1543) KB 27/1126, m. 80 (*assumpsit* that debt would be paid in gold ducats at Medina del Campo, or defendant would repay in English money).

[121] *Andrews* v. *Hosyer* (1549) KB 27/1151, m. 83; *Howes* v. *Wolley* (1550) KB 27/1153, m. 60; *Kaye* v. *Kocson* (1551) KB 27/1157, m. 107; *Rokes* v. *Godsalve* (1555) KB 27/1174, m. 97; *Atwell* v. *Smyth* (1557) KB 27/1182, m. 110. Cf. Rast. Ent. 4 (promise to pay for wedding feast); *Clifton* v. *Molyneux* (1555) KB 27/1176, m. 74 (action for return of money under marriage agreement). It was previously thought that an action might lie for marriage-money in the church courts: above, 242 n. 79.

[122] *Cokerell* v. *Tolowrge* (1538) KB 27/1109, m. 61 (as to plight of Emperor Charles V); *Strong* v. *Smyth* (1543) KB 27/1126, m. 67 (whether plaintiff could shoot an arrow 300 yards against the wind; issue as to whether he was confined to one shot); *Holte* v. *Prycke* (1553–4) KB 27/1167, m. 134 (demurrer to declaration).

[123] *Whyte* v. *Batysford* (1538) KB 27/1108, m. 27d (pr. 94 Selden Soc. 259); Spelman 8. The action seems to gain ground in 1555: *Morgayn* v. *Mompesson* (1555) KB 27/1173, m. 27; *Nollothe* v. *Eyott* (1555) KB 27/1174, m. 63; *Holmes* v. *Warren* (1555) KB 27/1176, m. 235 (promise by executrix's husband).

[124] e.g. *Dyxson* v. *Bulson* (1533) KB 27/1086, m. 73d (promise to satisfy and content plaintiff for his labour); *Salwey* v. *Abbot of Pershore* (1539) CP 40/1102, m. 324 (promise to pay clerk of peace all fees due for the indictments of 120 defendants at quarter sessions); *Curttes* v. *Baron* (1551) KB 27/1157, m. 150 (promise by surety to pay English equivalent of debt in Flemish pounds if principal defaults); *Chanons* v. *Somer* (1555) KB 27/1173, m. 32 (promise to pay 'quecunque onera et custagia' for board and tuition); *Barley* v. *Brett* (1555) KB 27/1175, m. 89 (promise to pay the market-price for malt at the time of delivery—'tantum pecunie quantum dicte deliberationis tempore ejusdem vendi potuerit in marcato apud Rayston'). For promises to pay pro rata for goods supplied over a period, see above, 853 n. 83.

instalments of a debt before the last was due.[125] By 1555 there were over fifty cases a year, in the King's Bench, of *assumpsit* to recover money.[126] The Common Pleas, as we shall see, did not follow suit.

Those who drew the money counts during the formative years used similar devices to those being developed in the other forms of *assumpsit* for nonfeasance, including usually a formal but non-issuable allegation of deceit,[127] and taking care always to show some loss over and above the mere non-receipt of the money owed. One kind of loss was that incurred by the plaintiff's performance of his side of the contract in reliance on the defendant's promise (*fidem adhibens promissioni*), and this was first suggested in the actions by sureties who had been made to pay a third party.[128] The other kind was consequential loss flowing from the failure to have the money on time: for instance, a loss of an investment opportunity, an inability to pay creditors,[129] and—usually consequent on the last— a loss of creditworthiness. These elements were often combined, and the last bears some resemblance to the averments of damage in declarations for slander.[130] Similar loss could be shown in contracts for fungibles, such as the inability to fulfil a contract for their resale. But here there was more scope for variation, since the plaintiff could allege a rise in the market-price, a hindering of trade for want of raw materials, or even an inability to keep his apprentices fully employed.[131] These additional elements were clearly thought to justify or strengthen the case for using *assumpsit*, but—so far as one can tell from the verdicts—the damages recovered were more or less equal to the full debts due and were not limited to the special factors.[132]

---

[125] *Pecke* v. *Redman* (1555) KB 27/1171, m. 106; Dyer 113a (instalments of grain; undetermined motion in arrest of judgment); *Lord Zouche* v. *Digby* (1557) 110 Selden Soc. 416 (Rutland assizes).

[126] Fifty-six cases were counted in the King's Bench rolls for 1555 (KB 27/1173–1176). Eighteen of them proceeded to judgment, and another twenty-seven reached the general issue (*Non assumpsit*).

[127] There was no such allegation in *Pykeryng* v. *Thurgoode*, and it is clear from the other reported cases that the concept of deceit played no significant role in the arguments.

[128] 94 Selden Soc. 280.

[129] Usually unnamed, but sometimes identified: e.g. *De la Sala* v. *De la Sala* (1537) KB 27/1105, m. 89d (four named creditors). Plaintiffs sometimes alleged that they were in danger of imprisonment for debt by reason of failing to pay third parties: e.g. *Feke* v. *Pecke* (1555) KB 27/1175, m. 3.

[130] See above, 784. Note the detailed additional clause in *Stokell* v. *Bastard* (1541) KB 27/1121, m. 75 (tr. 'whereby he not only lost his good credit, reputation, and opinion among all subjects of the said lord king with whom he was accustomed to deal, by reason of the due and just performance of his promises, especially with Nicholas Hoo and John Wyatt, to whom he was indebted in the aforesaid £14. o. 4d. which he had promised and pledged himself to pay at a certain day and time now past, but also various profits...').

[131] For examples see 94 Selden Soc. 280. Note also *Middelton* v. *Bedford* (1552) KB 27/1163, m. 91 (non-delivery of barley whereby baker lost credit with customers, lost profits from selling bread, and was less able to support his household and servants; judgment for plaintiff).

[132] See 94 Selden Soc. 284.

THE 'INDEBITATUS' COUNT

The action of *assumpsit* for money has sometimes been referred to generically as *indebitatus assumpsit*, though this is strictly the name of a particular species of count which was relatively uncommon in our period.[133] Instead of setting out the transaction which gave rise to the debt, or a *colloquium*,[134] a plaintiff sometimes declared on a state of indebtedness and a promise on a particular day to discharge the debt. The formula began in actions against sureties and personal representatives, where it referred to another person's indebtedness to the plaintiff, and then in the 1530s and early 1540s some other cases were discovered in which it proved a convenient way of stating the plaintiff's case: for instance, where the defendant had borrowed money from the plaintiff,[135] or where the defendant acknowledged that a total sum was due in respect of a string of past transactions and in return for a relatively small sum—perhaps fictitious—promised to settle the account.[136] In these early examples the reason for the indebtedness was always stated, and therefore there was no substantive difference from the common form of declaration. The account cases are related to the declaration upon an account stated (*insimul computassent*), in which the plaintiff alleged that the parties accounted together and upon the account the defendant acknowledged his indebtedness and promised—usually in return for a small sum—to discharge it;[137] the *indebitatus* formula here looks like an attempt to combine the *insimul computassent* count in debt with the *concessit solvere* formula used in London and other local courts.[138]

The next step was the 'general' *indebitatus* formula, in which the reason for the indebtedness was not set out at all. This was sanctioned by the King's Bench in 1540,[139] after which—often with a small payment alleged in return for the promise[140]—it is found occasionally in the rolls of that court, though it never

---

[133] See D. J. Ibbetson, 'Assumpsit and Debt in the Early Sixteenth Century: the origins of the indebitatus count' (1982) 41 *CLJ* 142–61.

[134] i.e. a 'communication', or discussion, explaining the context of the promise.

[135] e.g. *Molens* v. *Champyon* (1542) KB 27/1123, m. 61; *Hylbrond* v. *Pyerson* (1542) KB 27/1125, m. 93d.

[136] *De la Sala* v. *De la Sala* (1537) KB 27/1105, m. 89d (40s. paid for promise); *Morres* v. *Ive* (1555) KB 27/1176, m. 256 (2s. paid for promise). See also 94 Selden Soc. 281.

[137] e.g. *Skypwith* v. *Hawkys* (1535) KB 27/1095, m. 39; *Worsley* v. *Maskrey* (1547) KB 27/1144, m. 63 (judgment upon *nihil dicit*); *Parker* v. *Rychardes* (1548) KB 27/1146, m. 80 (judgment after verdict). In these cases it was usual to allege a small payment for the *assumpsit*.

[138] For *concessit solvere* see above, 283 n. 49, 308, 815.

[139] *Robynson* v. *Wynter* (1540) KB 27/1117, m. 73d (judgment on *non est informatus*). In *Bromage* v. *Cokkett* (1543) KB 27/1129, m. 117, this formula is entered as 'debt on the case' (*placitum debiti super casum*). Cf. *Byllyngesley* v. *Bowne* (1541) KB 27/1121, m. 35d (tr. 'for various sums agreed'); *Laundys* v. *Hatcher* (1552) E13/235, m. 37 ('indebitatus pro diversis causis et considerationibus').

[140] *Grene* v. *Pychard* (1545) KB 27/1135, m. 40d (*assumpsit* for 12d.; writ of inquiry); *Byddell* v. *Wyrley* (1546) KB 27/1140, m. 70 (*assumpsit* for 12d.); *Welbecke* v. *Osnard*, ibid., m. 78 (*assumpsit* for 12d.); *Carvanyell* v. *Harvey* (1550) KB 27/1156, m. 119 (*assumpsit* for 12d.); *Bowles* v. *Whalley* (1553) KB 27/1168,

overtakes in frequency the more particular declaration. It had the advantage that the plaintiff did not need to disclose his case in detail. For instance, an action could be brought on a promise to pay the debts of a deceased person without setting out the causes or the details of the administration.[141] At the end of our period we also find a few examples of what would become the classical common counts, where the reason for the indebtedness is stated—albeit in general terms only—such as 'money had and received'[142] or 'goods sold'.[143] There may, therefore, have already been some misgivings about the wholly general formula, which would be outlawed early in the seventeenth century; but neither formulation was very common in the 1540s and 1550s,[144] and the story may be regarded as belonging to the next chapter in the history of contract.

CONSIDERATION

The classical doctrine of consideration was formulated during the Elizabethan period, though its origins may be traced to our period.[145] Its story has given considerable trouble, because it seems to fulfil two different functions.[146] On the one hand, it describes the elements required, in addition to a mere agreement, to warrant an action on the case instead of an older action, and these elements—the prepayment, and the detriment or consequential loss—are not of the same kind. In this role it has more to do with tort, or with the legal theory underlying trespass on the case, than with contract. On the other hand, consideration represents the nearest the Tudor common lawyers came to contractual theory, the notion that a parol promise was only binding if it was part of a reciprocal bargain. In this sense

m. 152 (*assumpsit* in consideration of 10s. paid); *Granado v. Sherman and others* (1555) KB 27/1175, mm. 121, 127, 133 (*assumpsit* for 10s.); *Partryche v. Flyngant* (1558) KB 27/1185, m. 31 (*assumpsit* for 12d.).

[141] e.g. *Sowthill v. Pygott* (1546) KB 27/1139, m. 33 (promise by administrator for 12d.); *Dygby v. Lady Zouche* (1557) KB 27/1183, m. 73 (whereas Lord Zouche was indebted to the plaintiff, afterwards for 12d. Lady Zouche promised to pay; judgment for plaintiff).

[142] e.g. *Taylor v. Uvedall* (1557) KB 27/1182, m. 172 ('indebitatus... pro diversis denariorum summis ... prius habitis et receptis'); *Newall v. Huett* (1557) KB 27/1183, m. 68 (sim.). Cf. *Tylston v. Harwell* (1557) KB 27/1181, m. 170 ('indebitatus... pro diversis pecuniarum summis prius debitis'). For doubts about this form, which clashed with the old action of account, see below, 879–80.

[143] e.g. *Hardye v. Bantyng* (1557) KB 27/1184, m. 127 ('indebitatus... pro diversis marchandisis... preantea emptis').

[144] Only 5 of the 53 cases of *assumpsit* for money noted in the King's Bench rolls for 1555 were in the *indebitatus* form; and none of them in the general form.

[145] For further detail, and differing analyses, see J. L. Barton, 'The Early History of Consideration' (1969) 85 *LQR* 372–91; Simpson, *History of Contract*, 316–488; Baker, 'Consideration' (1977) 94 Selden Soc. 286–97; 'Origins of the "Doctrine" of Consideration 1535–85' (1981), repr. in *LPCL*, 369–91; D. J. Ibbetson, 'Consideration and the Theory of Contract in Sixteenth Century Common Law', in *Towards a General Law of Contract*, ed. J. L. Barton (1990), 67–123 (which is chiefly concerned with the Elizabethan period). [146] See also 94 Selden Soc. 292–7.

it first appeared as an anonymous principle in the law of sale, where it was used to explain the passing of title.[147] Its first appearance by name, however, was in the law of uses. Consideration, in the sense of the valuable recompense which distinguishes a bargain from a mere covenant,[148] could impose a use upon the owner of land,[149] whereas a mere declaration of intention without conveyance, consideration, or recompense, could not.[150] In both these cases, the creation of intangible rights of ownership is made to depend on reciprocity. To work the feat of generating or changing property, without a transfer of physical possession, something had to be given or promised in exchange. That might be regarded as a theory of property rather than of contract, using those terms in their modern senses. But, if an exchange of property was to be effective, it had to be embodied in a mutually binding contract; and so it was not a large step from the reasoning in the cases on sale to the broader proposition that only an agreement with recompense was legally binding, whereas a 'bare communication' was not.[151] St German, writing in 1530, was able to put in the mouth of his Student a principle which applied equally to sales and to promises in general:[152]

And a nude contract is where a man maketh a bargain or a sale of his goods or lands without any recompense appointed for it. As, if I say to another, 'I sell thee all my land (or all my goods)', and nothing is assigned that the other shall give or pay for it, that is a nude contract; and, as I take it, it is void in the law and conscience. And a nude or naked promise is where a man promiseth another to give him certain money such a day, or to build him an house, or to do him such certain service, and nothing is assigned for the money, for the building, nor for the service; these be called naked promises, because there is nothing assigned why they should be made. And I think no action lieth in those cases though they be not performed.

He also argued that 'if he to whom the promise is made have a charge by reason of the promise, which he hath also performed, then in that case he shall have an action for that thing that was promised, though he that made the promise have no

---

147 See above, 741. Likewise on a sale of land: *Docwra's Case* (1535) Mich. 27 Hen. VIII, fo. 28, pl. 16 (tr. 'upon payment of the money this is a perfect bargain and contract, for the parties have *quid pro quo*').

148 See Thomas Audley's reading (Inner Temple, 1526) CUL MS. Ee.5.19, fo. 8v (tr. 'to every bargain is requisite … a consideration in fact or in law'); *Docwra's Case* (1535) Mich. 27 Hen. VIII, fo. 28, pl. 16 (tr. 'here is no consideration to make a bargain or contract, but only a bare covenant'); *Reniger v. Fogassa* (1550) Plowd. 1 at 5, *per* Griffith S.-G. (recompense).

149 See Gregory Adgore's reading (Inner Temple, c.1490) CUL MS. Hh.3.10, fo. 22v (tr. 'a consideration may change the use'). See also Simpson, *History of Contract*, 327–74.

150 St German, *Doctor and Student*, ed. Plucknett and Barton, 124, 142, 225.

151 See the argument, probably by Plowden, in *Reniger v. Fogassa* (1550) Plowd. 1 at 5 (tr. 'an agreement concerning personal things is a mutual assent of the parties, and ought to be executed with a recompense, or otherwise ought to be so certain and sufficient that it may give an action or other remedy for the recompense; if it is not so, then it shall not be called an agreement but rather a bare communication without effect').

152 St German, *Doctor and Student*, ed. Plucknett and Barton, 228–9 (sp. mod.).

worldly profit by it'. On the other hand, 'a thing past' could not be recompense: 'if the thing be promised for a cause that is past, by way of a recompense, then it is rather an accord than a contract; but then the law is that upon such accord the thing that is promised in recompense must be paid or delivered in hand, for upon an accord there lieth no action'.[153]

St German may have seen this as an application of substantive principles of morality, not directly related to lawyers' notions of property, contract, or tort. It is not made clear whether the Student is talking about debt or *assumpsit*, or both, and perhaps it did not matter; the point was to show how the common-law principles were consistent with morality and conscience. Though it is noteworthy that the Student did not use the word 'consideration' in these passages,[154] the principle was soon to be baptized by the pleader, who may have settled on a vague word because of its helpful ambiguity. Consideration, like the Romanistic 'cause', could mean both the factual reason for making the promise (*causa promissionis*)[155] and also the legal reason why the promise was actionable (*causa actionis*). It could therefore encompass both recompense, which explained the promise, and the detrimental reliance which justified an action for nonfeasance. This was a broader notion than the *quid pro quo* of debt and of the law of sale, because recompense was not the only acceptable cause of action in *assumpsit*.[156] It remains to show how the broad principle which had emerged by 1530 was translated into the language of pleading.

By 1539 the King's Bench was prepared to say that an undertaking was only actionable if it was supported by some 'cause' (*causa*).[157] This should not be taken as marking the arrival of the classical doctrine, since the sparse references to the words 'cause' and 'consideration' in the reports show that it was sometimes used in the alternative sense of a justification for using an action on the case.[158] In this sense, any action on the case, even the action for defamatory words, required

---

[153] ibid. 230, 231–2 (sp. mod.). For accord and satisfaction see above, 828. For the doctrine that an executory accord was ineffective, see also Hales's reading (Gray's Inn, 1532) BL MS. Hargrave 92, fo. 29; *Gybson* v. *Abraham* (1545) KB 27/1136 m. 156 (judgment on demurrer).

[154] The word is used by the Doctor on p. 229 ('he is bounden in conscience ... though there be no consideration of worldly profit').

[155] See e.g. the elaborate declaration in *Brice* v. *Amydas* (1526) CP 40/1051, m. 316 (the defendant, considering that a use would pass to his wife on the death of B, persuaded B not to clog it with a jointure by promising B and his wife to assure other premises instead). The phrase *considerans quod* indicates a subjective sense of consideration. (No other examples have been noticed.)

[156] In *Cleymond* v. *Vyncent* (1520–1), above, 856, as reported in Port 10, it was argued that the surety had no recompense; but he was liable because the plaintiff had relied on the undertaking in entering into the sale.

[157] *Marler* v. *Wilmer* (1539) KB 27/1111, m. 64; below, 866. Cf. *Isack* v. *Barbour* (1563) KB 27/1207, m. 55 (must be supported by 'consideration').

[158] e.g. *Anon.* (1526/35) Yorke 240, no. 415, at 241 (prepayment is 'a consideration why I should have an action on my case for the nonfeasance').

consideration.[159] Nevertheless, it is from around 1539 that the *in consideratione* clause makes its appearance in King's Bench *assumpsit* declarations, and this technical change in pleading may tell us more about contemporary contractual theory than the rather unhelpful abstractions found in the reports.

The occasion for the change in pleading practice was probably a difficulty caused by the evolution of the standard *assumpsit* declaration into a bipartite formula in which the undertaking was deliberately separated from the underlying agreement.[160] The nonfeasance declaration was in the form: whereas, in return for (*pro*) a certain sum, D had agreed to do something, and D has undertaken to do it within a certain time, or in a workmanlike manner, D has nevertheless failed to do it. The declaration in *Pykeryng* v. *Thurgoode* was in essentially the same form: whereas, in return for a certain sum, D had bargained and sold malt to P, and D has undertaken to deliver the malt by a certain date, D has failed to do so. The bipartite declaration emphasized that the action was brought on the specific promise rather than on the underlying bargain, in order to avoid the double-remedy objection, but the result was that the undertaking—whether or not it was genuine[161]—now appeared to be gratuitous and detached from the reciprocal bargain. The prepayment, on which so much stress had been laid, was shown as a constituent element in the precedent bargain but was not directly linked to the separate promise to perform the bargain. One solution which became common in the time of Henry VIII was to avoid all mention of a precedent bargain or contract, and to allege a delivery rather than a sale of goods, or a discussion (*colloquium*) rather than a bargain. Another was to give the undertaking an explanation of its own. Here the commonest device—dating from 1515 at the latest[162]—was to say that the undertaking had been given in return for (*pro*) a small sum of money, such as 4*d*. or 1*s*. No doubt this was often fictional;[163] but the need to use a fiction demonstrates the pleader's dilemma, and his uneasiness about alleging an undertaking without a supporting cause.[164]

---

[159] *Lucy* v. *Walwyn* (1561) B. & M. 485 at 486, *per* Nicholls.   [160] See above, 850.

[161] By the end of our period we encounter the doctrine that 'every contract executory is an undertaking in itself', i.e. that an *assumpsit* is implied in any debt: *Norwood* v. *Norwood and Rede* (1557) Plowd. 180v at 181v (tr.).

[162] *Manby* v. *Barton* (1515) KB 27/1016, m. 61 (in return for $1\frac{1}{2}d$., promised to return horse). Cf. *Lemyng* v. *Beverley* (1526) KB 27/1061, m. 68d (lessor promised, in return for 12*d*., that he had a good interest to demise); *Tayllor* v. *Kyme* (1533) KB 27/1088, m. 24 (in return for 12*d*., promised to look after horse); *Wyvell* v. *Frenche* (1534) KB 27/1092, m. 72 (executors promise, for 2*s*., to pay testator's debt).

[163] It was sometimes denied by protestation: e.g. *Tayllor* v. *Kyme* (1533) KB 27/1088, m. 24; *Wyvell* v. *Frenche* (1534) KB 27/1092, m. 72; *Pynnok* v. *Fyndern* (1539) KB 27/1112, m. 32; *Annesley* v. *Kytley* (1539) KB 27/1113, m. 62. In *Lord Grey's Case* (1567) HLS MS. 2071, fo. 18v (tr. B. & M. 492 at 493) it was said to be alleged as a matter of course and to be non-traversable.

[164] The fiction also conveniently suppressed for a time problems which emerged later, such as privity: e.g. *Dolphyn* v. *Barne* (1540) KB 27/1116, m. 35d; *LPCL*, 354–5 (action by acceptor against drawer of

This brings us to the case of 1539, *Marler* v. *Wilmer*, which came before the King's Bench on a writ of error from Coventry.[165] The plaintiff complained in the mayor's court that he had sold goods to the defendant's testator for a sum to be paid on request, and that after the testator's death the defendant executor took upon himself and faithfully promised to pay the sum but had not done so. The local court gave judgment for the plaintiff, upon demurrer, and the defendant brought a writ of error in the King's Bench. One of the points assigned for error was 'that it does not appear in the declaration for what cause (*ob quam causam*) he made the aforesaid undertaking, whether for money paid beforehand or receipt of part of the aforesaid goods, and so *ex nudo pacto non oritur actio*'. Other objections were that the action should have been debt rather than 'deceit on the case', and that to bind the executor the plaintiff should have produced a deed. Unfortunately, the suit ends with the *scire facias* to summon the defendant in error; but the main objection is interesting enough regardless of the outcome. The declaration had to explain the undertaking, and it was not enough merely to mention a precedent bargain without a linking clause. The objection would have applied with equal force to the common declaration in *assumpsit* for the price of goods, and it can hardly be a mere coincidence that within a year or two of *Marler* v. *Wilmer* several new linking formulae had been invented in the context of *assumpsit* for money. The commonest of the new devices can best be described as a *quid pro quo* clause. It was used mainly in actions to recover the price of goods, which was the commonest use of *assumpsit* by 1540. The plaintiff alleged a sale of the goods for a certain sum, or (more neutrally) a delivery of goods worth a certain sum, 'for which goods (*pro quibusquidem bonis*)' the defendant undertook to pay the sum.[166] Thus the goods were treated as the *quid* 'pro quo' the undertaking was given. The buyer could adapt the same formula by making the prepayment the *quid* 'pro quo' the promise was made to deliver the goods.[167] For over twenty years the *quid pro quo* formula dominated *assumpsit* declarations and bid fair to jostle the consideration formula out of use.

a bill of exchange). And it enabled *assumpsit* to be brought for non-contractual debts: e.g. *Treffrye* v. *Buys and another* (1545) CP 40/1125, mm. 145 and 158 (customs duties promised to customer of Fowey).

[165] KB 27/1111, m. 64. See *LPCL*, 372 n. 11; Ibbetson, 'Assumpsit and Debt', at 144, 152–9.

[166] e.g. *Flynt* v. *Phylpott* (1540) KB 27/1117, m. 31 (goods delivered); *Courte* v. *Hatche* (1540) ibid. m. 37 (goods resold); *Curtes* v. *Middelmore* (1541) KB 27/1118, m. 40 (goods sold); *Whyttyngstall* v. *Fytzherbert* (1541) KB 27/1119, m. 39 (goods delivered); *Balnett* v. *Ingoldesby* (1541) KB 27/1120, m. 31 (sim.); *Ede* v. *Decon* (1541) KB 27/1121, m. 29 (money paid and goods delivered); *Kene* v. *Style* (1541) ibid., m. 63 (goods delivered); *Stokell* v. *Bastard* (1541) ibid., m. 75 (goods sold and delivered); *Ap Robert* v. *De Grado* (1542) KB 27/1125, m. 39 (services). Thereafter the formula is common form.

[167] e.g. *Grey* v. *Bate* (1544) KB 27/1133, m. 105 (judgment for plaintiff).

The consideration clause which appeared in 1539 performed exactly the same linking function as the *quid pro quo* clause. At first it was simply an alternative, chosen whenever it seemed more apt or elegant than the word *pro*. The first recorded case illustrates this well. The plaintiff complained that, whereas the defendant's wife had before the marriage been indebted to the plaintiff for board, lodging, and a loan, the defendant in full knowledge of this, afterwards, in consideration of his impending marriage and for (*pro*) 12*d.* paid to him, undertook to pay off the debt, but had not done so.[168] The plaintiff's counsel had seen fit to make use of the fictional shilling in addition to the true cause, and so the *in consideratione* clause was used to avoid the repetition of *pro*, a word in any case more appropriate to introduce a payment than a marriage.[169] In the next instance in the King's Bench rolls, the undertaking to pay was in consideration of wrongs done and for (*pro*) 12*d.* paid; again *in consideratione* is a companion to *pro*, both to avoid inelegant repetition and because it is more apt to describe a motive founded on something past.[170] In a third early case, the two phrases occur together as past and present moving causes, where a woman had asked a man to ride on a journey with her, and in return for (*pro*) his company and in consideration that he had lent her money, she promised to give him a ring.[171] Sometimes the two phrases were combined to form *pro et in consideratione*.[172]

In the decade after 1540 there are at least thirty-two instances of consideration clauses in the King's Bench plea rolls, but there is little uniformity in their form or function. In one back-to-front case the *assumpsit* was the consideration for the plaintiff's performance.[173] In nearly all the cases, however, the consideration was used to explain a promise to pay money. It might be a past act[174]—such as the

---

[168] *Harvy* v. *Stone* (1539) KB 27/1112, m. 65.

[169] Marriage had often been treated as a 'consideration' to raise a use, and it was more accurate to describe it as such than as *quid pro quo* because usually there were other reasons for the marriage. For this usage see *Brice* v. *Amydas* (1526) CP 40/1051, m. 316 ('in consideratione maritagii'); *Anon.* (1530) Yorke 146, no. 154; *Anon.* (1532) Pollard. 276, no. 72; *Bolde* v. *Molyneux* (1536) Dyer 17b, §100; *Lyte* v. *Peny* (1541) Dyer 49b, §11.

[170] *Phyllyp* v. *Heeth* (1540) KB 27/1116, m. 23d. For the early association of consideration with causes past, or 'precedent', see Dyer 49a–b; St German, *Doctor and Student*, ed. Plucknett and Barton, 229. The first noticed mention of consideration in an *assumpsit* action occurs not in a declaration but in a plea of accord: *Hewton* v. *Foster* (1536) KB 27/1099, m. 76.

[171] *Turfote* v. *Pycher* (1543) KB 27/1130, m. 104.

[172] *Rent* v. *Danyell* (1549) KB 27/1150, m. 104; *Mychelborne* v. *West* (1558) CP 40/1176(1), m. 847 ('pro et in consideratione solutionum', undertook to save harmless). Cf. *Pyrry* v. *Appowell* (1545) KB 27/1134, m. 67d ('in consideratione et recompensatione').

[173] *Owtrede* v. *Whyte* (1546) KB 27/1138, m. 24d (judgment for plaintiff).

[174] e.g. *Phyllyp* v. *Heeth* (1540) KB 27/1116, m. 23d (injuries done); *Tyll* v. *Brockhouse* (1548) KB 27/1147, m. 103d (goods taken).

delivery of goods[175] or money[176]—or a bargain,[177] or a continuing state,[178] or a promise of a future act.[179] It might be highly vague, as in the 'for various considerations' (*pro diversis considerationibus*) sometimes tacked onto the fictional small sum paid to bind the promise,[180] or 'in consideration of the foregoing' and for (*pro*) a small sum paid.[181] Even in the 1550s the mention of consideration was optional,[182] and—being still used chiefly in *assumpsit* for money—it was altogether unknown in the Common Pleas until Mary I's reign.[183] For all these reasons, the emergence of the classical doctrine must be located in the next generation.

[175] e.g. *Conyers v. Spekeman* (1549) KB 27/1151, m. 63 (judgment by default); *Hodgeson v. Fenwyk* (1550) KB 27/1153, m. 75 (judgment for plaintiff); *Newman v. Harvy* (1555) KB 27/1175, m. 94 (judgment for plaintiff).

[176] e.g. *Busshewell v. Bye* (1546) KB 27/1138, m. 67d (in consideration that D had previously received £10. 3s. 4d. from P's testator, and for 2s. paid, D promised to pay P £10. 3s. 4d.); *Kyndersley v. Tull* (1555) KB 27/1175, m. 151d (in consideration that P delivered £107. 8s. 4d. to D to D's use, D promised to pay £107. 8s. 4d. to P); *Andrewe v. Clerke* (1555) KB 27/1176, m. 221 (P at request of D delivered £10 in half-sovereigns to D, in consideration of which delivery D promised to pay £10 in gold to P).

[177] e.g. *Gell v. Gell* (1547) KB 27/1144, m. 78 (P and D discussed a sale of bark, and thereupon P bargained and sold bark of 1,200 trees to D, in consideration of which bargain and sale, and for 12d. paid, D promised to pay £3; judgment for plaintiff); *Bradshawe v. Glosse* (1555) KB 27/1175, m. 184d (in consideration that P at D's request bargained and sold to D cattle worth £36. 0. 12d., D promised to pay £36. 0. 12d.); *Draper v. Patten* (1555) KB 27/1176, m. 201 (P agreed to sell freehold to D, and D in consideration of the sale promised to pay various unspecified sums of money and a hogshead of claret every year); *Eyer v. Gery* (1555) ibid., m. 60 (P bargained and sold lease to D, and D in consideration of the bargain promised to pay £400).

[178] e.g. marriage: *Harvy v. Stone* (1539) KB 27/1112, m. 65; *Holt v. Oxenden* (1542) KB 27/1125, m. 38 (judgment for plaintiff); *Kaye v. Kocson* (1551) KB 27/1157, m. 107 (money promised 'in consideratione maritagii'); *Byrde v. Lovett* (1551) KB 27/1158, m. 88 (bed and utensils promised 'in consideratione matrimonii'); *Rokes v. Godsalve* (1555) KB 27/1174, m. 97. Friendship and goodwill: *Rent v. Danyell* (1549) KB 27/1150, m. 104 ('pro et in consideratione amicitie et benevolencie'). Having goods as an administrator: *Hudson's Case* (1558) cited in HLS MS. 16, fo. 423v (1588).

[179] e.g. *Holt v. Oxenden* (1542) KB 27/1125, m. 38 (impending marriage; judgment for plaintiff); *Staunton v. Smythyman* (1544) KB 27/1133, mm. 119, 119d, 121 (permission to pasture); *Tyrenden v. Hewes* (1545) KB 27/1135, m. 109d (building a house); *Cooke v. Sutton* (1547) KB 27/1143, m. 103 (provision of board and washing for sick lodger); *Pynnok v. Clopton* (1548) KB 27/1145, m. 60 (permitting defendant to obtain administration); *Annell v. Brande* (1549) KB 27/1151, m. 34 (delivery of malt); *Uston v. Hunte* (1549) KB 27/1152, m. 23 (surrender of copyhold; judgment for plaintiff); *Josselyn v. Shelton* (1558) CP 40/1173, m. 532 (impending marriage).

[180] e.g. *Cawenfeld v. Elder* (1546) KB 27/1137, m. 113d (*pro* 4d. 'et pro aliis subsequentibus considerationibus'); *Pynnok v. Clopton* (1547) KB 27/1141, m. 79 (*pro* 5s. 'et pro aliis considerationibus inter ipsos concordatis'); *Holmes v. Harrison* (1549) KB 27/1149, m. 32 (*pro* 2s. 'et pro diversis aliis causis et considerationibus'); *Norman v. Moore* (1549) ibid., m. 117 (sim.); *Newman v. Gybbe* (1549) KB 27/1152, m. 135 (sim.).

[181] e.g. *Gyles v. Duffeld* (1555) KB 27/1174, m. 98 (sale and delivery of sheep for £14; afterwards *in consideratione premissorum* and *pro* 4d. paid, undertook to pay £14); *Snell v. Dauncey*, ibid., m. 136 (delivery of £5 to use of defendant; afterwards *in consderatione premissorum* and *pro* 5s. paid, undertook to pay £5); *Fraunces v. Smyth* (1558) CP 40/1173 (rent of house and fishing rights).

[182] Of the 53 cases of *assumpsit* for money noted in the King's Bench rolls for 1555, only 19 mentioned consideration.

[183] The earliest examples noted on the prothonotaries' rolls are *Dyve v. Chanon* (1556) CP 40/1165, m. 531 (in consideration of a grant of an office, promised to pay annuity); *Bradford v. Duffeld*, ibid.,

THE COURTS BEGIN TO DIFFER

As a result of the vagaries of law-reporting, a chief justice of the Common Pleas—Sir Thomas Frowyk—has appeared to posterity as the principal author of *assumpsit* for money. Although there is no reason to doubt that his opinion was accurately reported, the impression given by this isolated piece of evidence is misleading. We have already noticed that his opinion was a dissent, and that it was fifteen years before it began to prevail. What is more, the establishment of the action, when it came, was chiefly a King's Bench phenomenon. The development seems to have been accepted by mid-century in the Exchequer.[184] But it was not, in our period, accepted in the Common Pleas.

In the covenant cases there was probably general agreement between the courts that case should lie, provided some prepayment had been made—and provided there was no deed.[185] Fitzherbert J. himself accepted that,[186] and it was clearly laid down by the court in his time.[187] This is probably the reason why *assumpsit* was generally accepted in surety cases in the Common Pleas,[188] since these were seen to depend on covenants to pay money rather than debts. There was likewise no overt objection to any other kind of money claim which lay outside the scope of debt.[189]

---

m. 932 (in consideration of 1*d.* paid, promised to return coins bailed); *Grene* v. *Hedde* (1557) CP 40/1169, m. 544 (in consideration of money delivered to use of defendant, he undertook to pay it back); *Curtes* v. *Chersey* (1557) CP 40/1170, m. 730 ('in consideratione premissorum ac ob alias certas, bonas, et rationabiles considerationes', promised to consummate marriage).

[184] e.g. *Fennell* v. *Newyngton* (1550) E 13/232, mm. 7d, 8d (*assumpsit* for the price of goods; verdict and judgment for plaintiff).

[185] It remained necessary to bring covenant if there was an indenture under seal. Cf. *Heron* v. *Robson* (1532) CP 40/1074, m. 543 (*assumpsit* on a lease; defendant pleads in abatement that the demise was by indenture, which he set out, 'and therefore he ought to have brought an action of covenant and not an action on the case'; demurrer). If a party agreed to make an indenture, and then refused to execute the deed, *assumpsit* might be brought on the underlying agreement: *Strete* v. *Yardley* (1528) Wm Yelv. 313, no. 8.   [186] FNB 145G (94 Selden Soc. 270 n. 3).

[187] *Ewer* v. *Elys* (1522) Spelman 3; cited, Yorke 241, no. 415; CP 40/1033, m. 304 (pr. 94 Selden Soc. 241); *Anon.* (1526/35) Yorke 240, no. 415, at 241 (tr. 94 Selden Soc. 296–7; B. & M. 402 at 403); *Strete* v. *Yardley* (1528) Wm Yelv. 313, no. 8.

[188] e.g. *Smyth* v. *Hylton* (1528) CP 40/1058A, m. 635 (action by surety for loan to buy wares in Iceland; judgment on *non potest dedicere*); *Tylney* v. *Palmer* (1535) CP 40/1085(1), m. 301 (action by surety for debt; judgment on *non potest dedicere*); *Norres* v. *Clerke* (1536) CP 40/1091, m. 431 (action by surety for defendant's appearance; judgment for plaintiff after verdict); *Dawson* v. *Smyth* (1542) CP 40/1115, m. 418d (action against surety; judgment for plaintiff after verdict); *Fulmerston* v. *Hussey* (1547) CP 40/1133, m. 403 (action on promise, given in return for 7*s.* 6*d.*, to pay existing debt of £24 which third party owed to plaintiff; recovers £20).

[189] Note the odd cases of *Wylliams* v. *Jenkyn* (1547) CP 40/1134, m. 126 (undertaking to pay 4 marks in satisfaction of wrongs done; pleads *Non assumpsit*); *Dyve* v. *Chanon* (1556) CP 40/1165, m. 531 (in consideration of grant of office, undertook to pay annuity); *Bradford* v. *Duffeld*, ibid., m. 932 (in consideration of 1*d.* paid, undertook to redeliver coins bailed; verdict and judgment for plaintiff; writ of error, 1558); *Josselyn* v. *Shelton* (1558) CP 40/1173, m. 532; Benl. 57 (in consideration of an impending marriage, bride's father promised to pay 400 marks to groom's father).

Actions for the non-delivery of fungibles were also thought safe by some practitioners,[190] presumably on the footing that these were essentially brought to enforce covenants to deliver goods rather than to recover debts,[191] though doubts had been stirred before the end of the 1520s.[192]

The first reported signs of dissent come from 1535, when Fitzherbert J.—who evidently led Common Pleas opinion at that time—declared that the case of *Cleymond* v. *Vincent* (1520), the case in which *assumpsit* for money was first judicially approved, was not only wrong but should be taken out of the books.[193] That was an action against the executrix of a surety, and so it was doubly proof against the problem of duplication with debt. But Fitzherbert J. had doubts about the surety cases as well; at any rate, in the converse case of the surety seeking an indemnity, he favoured the resurrection of the old viscontiel action *de plegiis acquietandis*, which—if indeed it was still available—would have raised the double-remedy objection to *assumpsit* in that case.[194] A promised indemnity was the subject of another reported Common Pleas case in 1542. This was an action of *assumpsit* on a promise to indemnify a serjeant-at-mace in carrying out his duties. The plaintiff was a serjeant of one of the sheriffs of London, who had been asked to arrest one George Ferrers MP upon a King's Bench *scire facias* by a creditor who asserted that Ferrers was not a member of the present parliament and promised the serjeant an indemnity for the consequences. Ferrers was in fact member for Plymouth, and his arrest caused a stir over parliamentary privilege.[195] In the event, the serjeant was removed from office and imprisoned in the Tower by order of the House of Commons, and he complained that the defendant had not indemnified him. This was not an action for a fixed sum of money; but the governing principles were the same as where a surety promised an indemnity for another's debt, since such promises were in either case covenants. Serjeant Bromley objected that the action was 'based on a naked promise, and no specialty nor any money is

---

[190] e.g. *Fermour* v. *Hochyns* (1520) CP 40/1030, m. 353 (writ of inquiry upon *nihil dicit*); *Cressall* v. *Wylson* (1521) CP 40/1032A, m. 322 (pleads arbitration); *Salter* v. *Walpole* (1522) CP 40/1035, m. 116d (writ of inquiry upon *non potest dedicere*); *Halle* v. *Bensted* (1526) CP 40/1049, m. 307 (imparlance); *Jeckelove* v. *Meryell* (1536) CP 40/1091, m. 327 (sim.); *Swetman* v. *Meyre* (1540) CP 40/1104, m. 237 (op. se); *Byrkett* v. *Sturton*, ibid., m. 370 (sim.). Most of these were for non-delivery of grain. For solus agreements see above, 853 n. 83.

[191] Some examples are clearly contracts for carriage as well as delivery: e.g. *Tuttesham* v. *None* (1523) CP 40/1040, m. 408 (undertaking to deliver grain sold; action against executrix); *Johnson* v. *Bramston* (1524) CP 40/1044, m. 267d (covenant to carry tallow from Ipswich to Bordeaux and to deliver at Bordeaux); *Wode* v. *Gamon* (1533) CP 40/1079, m. 312 (undertaking to carry cargo by sea, alleging conversion as well as non-delivery); *Borne* v. *Grene* (1538) CP 40/1097, m. 419d (undertaking to carry and deliver successive cargoes of grain, coal, and salt; pleads condition).

[192] *Colman* v. *Grene* (1528) CP 40/1057, m. 338 (demurrer); below, 871.

[193] *Anon.* (1535) Trin. 27 Hen. VIII, fo. 23, pl. 21 (B. & M. 447 at 448).

[194] FNB 137C; and see 94 Selden Soc. 282. No example of the action has been found from our period; but see *Coxe* v. *Thornes* (1566) Dyer 257a; Coke, *Entries*, fo. 434v.   [195] See above, 84.

given in covenant, but it is simply a promise'. Serjeant Hales for the plaintiff, though equipped by his Gray's Inn reading with examples of case for nonfeasance, is reported as making a rather pedestrian reply. Willoughby J. thought the action would lie; but Shelley J., having remarked that it was 'a good case, from which much learning may arise', said that he preferred to be advised. He would 'not say precisely that the action does not lie' but only that it was 'a doubtful case'.[196] The doubt, however, related not to the use of *assumpsit* in lieu of covenant, but to what we would identify as a consideration question: whether an indemnity could be given to someone for performing his legal duty. Although the report does not say so, this obviously led to the more delicate question of jurisdiction over questions of parliamentary privilege. But there was nothing in the report,[197] or in any other case from this period, to suggest Common Pleas hostility to actions on informal covenants.

The replacement of debt was another matter entirely. Here wager at law was at stake, and there was a view—shared even by those with liberal attitudes towards law and conscience[198]—that wager of law afforded a proper protection to the individual and should be defended against circumvention. In 1528 a Common Pleas action for non-delivery of grain was stopped by demurrer;[199] and in 1533, when another such action proceeded as far as a verdict for the plaintiff, the court took advisement and no judgment was entered.[200] In the second case there was probably a successful motion in arrest of judgment, in which case we may deduce that the court deliberately declined to accept the King's Bench decision in *Pykeryng* v. *Thurgoode* from the very beginning. We do know as a fact that when another such action was brought in 1543,[201] although apparently no objection to the use of *assumpsit* was made by counsel for the defendant, Shelley J. intervened to stop the suit:[202]

[196] *Taylour* v. *Whyte* (Hil. 1543) CP 40/1116, m. 108 (general issue; no judgment); reported sub nom. *Sukley* v. *Wyte* (Pas. 1543) Gell's reports, I, Pas. 34 Hen. VIII, fo. 12v (B. & M. 404). Robert Taylour was serjeant-at-mace to Henry Suckeley, sheriff of London. Ferrers was a mainpernor of John Weldon, who owed Thomas Whyte £166. 13s. 4d.

[197] Save that Bromley sjt thought it arguable.

[198] e.g. St German, *A Little Treatise*, ed. Guy, 117 (referring to the liability of executors).

[199] *Colman* v. *Grene* (1528) CP 40/1057, m. 338 (defendant bargained and sold grain to plaintiff for £19 agreed, and promised to deliver at Whitsun, but scheming to defraud him of the bargain did not do so; demurrer to declaration). No judgment was entered.

[200] *Baron* v. *Wilson* (1533) CP 40/1079, m. 344 (plaintiff bought barley and beans for £24 and defendant promised to deliver by Lady Day 1532 but did not do so; no deceit is alleged). Cf. *Dalton* v. *Baker* (1534–5) CP 40/1083, m. 453 (promise to pay in two instalments for wool sold and delivered; confessed at assizes, and damages assessed by writ of inquiry; court takes advisement).

[201] If, as seems likely, it is identifiable as *Thwaytes* v. *Bealles* (Pas. 1543) CP 40/1117, m. 306, it was a less straightforward parallel than Gell's report suggests. The plaintiff declared on a delivery of malt to the defendant, who promised to sell it and pay the plaintiff 4s. 4d. for every quarter sold; the defendant pleaded a variation of the agreement, and issue was joined on the terms. This seems too uncertain to support an action of debt. No doubt that explains the absence of a demurrer by the defendant.

[202] *Anon.* (1543) Gell's reports, I, Pas. 34 Hen. VIII, fo. 15 (tr. B. & M. 415). Willoughby J. concurred.

It seems to me that there is another point in the case, for I believe that the action does not lie here. An action on the case does not lie in any case except where the plaintiff is without other action. But here he could have an action of detinue.[203] I perceive your purpose, however. You brought this action because he cannot wage his law in this action, as he could in an action of detinue.

No doubt he did; and the implied rebuke shows that evading wager of law was considered by Shelley J. an unworthy end. This was evidently the general view of the Common Pleas at least until the middle of the century, because no judgments for money in cases of simple contract are found in the plea rolls.[204] Indeed, when an attempt was made to recover the price of goods in 1550, it was firmly met by a demurrer to the declaration.[205] As a consequence, debt and wager of law remained in regular use in the Common Pleas,[206] and even an attorney might find himself barred by this means.[207] Moreover, it was not beyond the legal imagination in the 1540s for a plaintiff who had been barred by wager of law in the Common Pleas to start again by bringing *assumpsit* in the King's Bench.[208]

    The same objection did not reach actions of *assumpsit* against executors or administrators, even in the absence of a separate promise by the latter for a fresh consideration,[209] since there was no older action in such a case and no question of waging law. Yet Shelley J. was against these actions as well,[210] and according to Brooke that had always been the Common Pleas position.[211] The reason was presumably that given by Fitzherbert J. in 1535. Debts due by reason of a simple contract die with the person, because a personal action dies with the person: *actio*

---

[203] More correctly debt in the *detinet*, assuming the facts as stated in the report. Cf. Port J., above, 858 n. 111.

[204] A judgment for £20 on a *nihil dicit* is found in *Duplake* v. *Glover* (1549) CP 40/1140, m. 411, but this was an action for marriage-money and therefore arguably not for a debt. Occasional op. se entries are also found, and a few appearances: e.g. *Homerston* v. *Rikkys* (1541) CP 40/1110, m. 318 (action for price of iron sold and delivered; imparlance); *Rous* v. *Wychyngham* (1542) CP 40/1113, m. 331 (action for price of land sold; imparlance).

[205] *Bayly* v. *Davye* (1550) CP 40/1144A, m. 425 (no judgment). For an apparent change in the 1550s see below, 873.   [206] There are even a few stray examples in the King's Bench in the 1550s.

[207] *Predyaux* v. *Doble* (1558) CP 40/1176(1), m. 745 (client wages law successfully in debt for an attorney's fees and expenses). If the action had been for fees alone, wager of law would not have been available.

[208] *Smyth* v. *Brayne* (c.1544/7) C1/1156/44.

[209] Such promises are occasionally alleged: e.g. *Sandeford* v. *Byddell* (1555) KB 27/1174, m. 84 (promise by administrators to pay debt, in return for 20s. paid; judgment for plaintiff); *Cheyney* v. *Tusser* (1556) CP 40/1165, m. 627d (promise by testatrix when single to pay debt for goods delivered; op. se only).

[210] *Sukley* v. *Wyte* (1543) Gell's reports, I, Pas. 34 Hen. VIII, fo. 12v (tr. B. & M. 404 at 405: 'it seems to me that the action on the case does not lie against executors on a promise made by their testator. This was in effect affirmed by the whole court; but query'). See also *Anon.* (1545) Brooke Abr., *Action sur le Case*, pl. 4.

[211] Brooke Abr., *Action sur le Case*, pl. 106 (abridging the 1535 case). Cf. *Tuttesham* v. *None* (1523) CP 40/1040, m. 408 (action against executrix on testator's undertaking to deliver grain sold; issue on the terms).

personalis moritur cum persona.[212] Fitzherbert J. had castigated the King's Bench decision of 1520, in which he had himself (as counsel) persuaded the court to arrive at the wrong conclusion, saying that the court had acted unilaterally without consulting the Common Pleas judges; the decision was 'not law without doubt'. According to a later recollection by Dyer CJ, the Common Pleas relented when Mountagu CJ was translated to the Common Pleas from the King's Bench in 1545 and brought with him the practice of making executors liable in *assumpsit.*[213] However, this is not borne out by the plea rolls, in which no judgments in such cases have come to light. By 1558, the two benches had agreed to differ on these issues, though there was not yet open conflict. In 1557 the King's Bench was invited to reverse the decision of 1520 concerning executors, given the 'great reputation' of Fitzherbert J., whose 1535 remarks had now been published in print. But in support of the decision it was argued that personal representatives ought not to keep the assets for themselves when there were debts unpaid, and that it was for the good of the testator's soul to pay off his debts. The court, 'without solemn argument', affirmed its decision of 1520 and gave judgment for the plaintiff.[214]

During the mid-1550s, the Common Pleas may have relaxed its general position somewhat, and a number of actions on the case for money are found in the rolls.[215] But full acceptance there was not. The conflict between the two courts was ultimately to become intolerable because of their different views as to how actions of *assumpsit* for money should be left to the jury. A short but revealing note by Dyer shows that the difference of approach had already taken root by the end of our period. The King's Bench were willing to imply a promise to pay a debt, and therefore it was necessary only to prove an indebtedness, whereas the Common Pleas required proof of an express promise to pay the money at a later day.[216] Since most actions were tried on circuit by assize commissioners, who were not necessarily judges of the court where the suit was commenced, the country litigant

---

[212] *Anon.* (1535) Trin. 27 Hen. VIII, fo. 23, pl. 21 (tr. B. & M. 448). The maxim had been quoted by Fyneux CJ in the 1520 case, but he said it did not apply to debts.

[213] *Anon.* (1571) BL MS. Add. 25211, fo. 100 (tr. B. & M. 450). Cf. the note written by Gilbert Gerrard in Hil. 1545 to the effect that the King's Bench allowed case against executors but the Common Pleas did not: 121 Selden Soc. 471.

[214] *Norwood v. Norwood and Rede* (1557) Plowd. 180v; KB 27/1182, m. 188 (abr. B. & M. 448). Cf. *Derneley v. Rawlynson* (1555) KB 27/1176, m. 265 (judgment against an administrator); *Dyxson v. Cove*, ibid., m. 271 (judgment against an executrix).

[215] *Harrys v. Estwyke* (1555) CP 40/1164, m. 451 (£4 awarded as the price of a gelding bargained and sold; an unsophisticated declaration, with no mention of deceit or consequential loss, and an ungrammatical *assumpsit* inserted in the *cum* clause); *Assheton v. Drewe* (1558–9) CP 40/1176(1), m. 556 (action for £36. 15s. as price of sheep; recovers £28. 11s. 8d.). Cases pleaded to issue (*Non assumpsit*) are: *Rogers v. Bennett* (1556) CP 40/1166, m. 1051 (action for rent of sheep); *Toller v. Walter* (1558) CP 40/1175, m. 156 (action for price of malt sold); *Bachecrofte v. Roo*, ibid., m. 411 (action for price of wool sold).

[216] *Anon.* (1559) 110 Selden Soc. 420 (Northampton assizes, before Dyer and Bendlowes JJ Ass., Griffin concurring). See also *Edwards v. Burre* (1573) Dal. 104 (tr. B. & M. 416).

was thereby placed in considerable uncertainty. This may account for the prevalence of London suits at the beginning of the King's Bench development.[217] But the general unpredictability of country cases would in the end result in a major clash. Already by 1559, therefore, the scene was neatly set for the conflict to come at the end of the century.

[217] M. J. Prichard has pointed out that, since King's Bench cases from London were usually tried at the Guildhall by the CJKB, the city plaintiff could be confident of a jury direction in accordance with the King's Bench philosophy.

50

Accountability and Quasi-Contract

THE ACTION OF ACCOUNT

THE action of account had come to perform two quite different functions by the end of the fifteenth century.[1] Against a bailiff,[2] guardian in socage,[3] common receiver, or other agent, it was intended primarily to secure an enquiry by way of audit into a series of transactions outside the plaintiff's direct knowledge. The court appointed auditors, who might be either professional auditors[4] or officers of the court,[5] and the results of their work were sometimes annexed to the record.[6] On the other hand, account could also be brought in respect of a particular sum of money received to the use of the plaintiff, where there was a trust or a restitutionary duty and the object was to recover the specific sum.[7]

In neither mode did the action work very well, and it was no longer as common as it had been in earlier centuries. The auditing procedure was cumbersome,

---

[1] There are notes of lectures on the action by William Wadham (Lincoln's Inn, 1505) and Thomas Lane (Lincoln's Inn, 1534) in Taussig MS., ff. 182–190, 230v–237; by James Hales (Gray's Inn, 1532) in BL MS. Hargrave 92, ff. 35v–37; and by Francis Morgan (Middle Temple, Lent 1553) in BL Harley 5156, ff. 35v–38.

[2] Note *Abbot of Buckfast v. Horswyll* (1505) 2 Caryll 485 (port-reeve of borough sued as bailiff; demurrer to evidence); *Rokewode v. Parker* (1518) CP 40/1022, m. 835 (pleads he managed land as executor and not as bailiff; demurrer to the evidence); *Earl of Rutland v. Uvedale* (1557) CP 40/1170, m. 818 (account against receiver; pleads the payments were from tenants and so he should have been sued as bailiff; demurrer).

[3] Such actions were rare, but not unknown: e.g. *Kyrkeby v. Bowman* (1518) CP 40/1058A, m. 307; *Dogett v. Merchant Taylors Company* (1544) CP 40/1121, m. 725 (demurrer to declaration); *Eresye v. Dobson* (1555) CP 40/1164, m. 1123.

[4] See *Earl of Northumberland v. Wedall* (1523–7) CP 40/1039, m. 109; 94 Selden Soc. 263 (Thomas Tomworth, auditor of the Exchequer, and Guthlac Overton of Lincoln's Inn, a professional auditor).

[5] e.g. *Queen Katharine v. Benton* (1515) KB 27/1016, m. 24 (two filazers conduct audit at Westminster); *Anon.* (1515) Rast. Ent. 14 (filazer and attorney conduct audit in Temple Church); *Michell v. Atwyll* (1537) CP 40/1095, m. 558 (John Jenour, second prothonotary, and Alan Hord, clerk of the warrants). Cf. *Mower v. Carvanell* (1526) KB 27/1061, m. 74 (John Palmer, filazer, and Edmund Page of the Inner Temple).

[6] e.g. *Anon.* (1505) Rast. Ent. 15v; *Goodwyn v. Hamerton* (1492) CP 40/921, m. 171; *Hachard v. Wynnals* (1511) CP 40/997, m. 503; Rast. Ent. 14v; *Michell v. Atwyll* (1537) CP 40/1095, m. 558.

[7] e.g. if A delivered money to X to pay to B, and he did not, either A or B could bring account against X: *Orwell v. Mortoft* (1505) 2 Caryll 493 at 494, *per* Frowyk CJ (see below, n. 33).

potentially oppressive,[8] and not very effective.[9] In one embarrassing year-book case, also reported by Spelman, a defendant was incarcerated for five years without an account being taken.[10] The unfortunate defendant had been a servant of the earl of Northumberland for twenty-three years—during a period when the earl's fortunes had declined rapidly—and was supposed to have handled several thousand pounds of the earl's receipts, but his difficulty appears to have been that the books were in the hands of one of the duke's auditors.[11] It is not clear that the earl achieved anything by these protracted proceedings,[12] except no doubt to set his servants in turmoil. A voluntary accounting, or an arbitration, must have been a more attractive alternative to a judicial audit, and it could be enforced by bonds or by an action of debt upon an account stated (*sur insimul computassent*).[13] In an action for a single sum, there was no point in holding an audit at all, since the object was to determine whether the plaintiff was entitled to the sum and to levy it. Actions of this kind are found as late as the 1550s, in which the true dispute, though hidden from sight, is clearly not about the proper settling of accounts.[14] A major problem with these actions was that, at the first stage, the defendant was only allowed to plead in bar of the account—that is, to challenge the accountability—and not in bar of particular items of debt,[15] though he could present his case at large before the auditors and if an item of account then resulted in a demurrer this had to be referred back to the court.[16] The auditors themselves, however, were not confined to strict law, and could charge a commercial receiver with the profits he could have made from money received even when through indolence he had not put it to best use.[17]

In addition to the procedural drawbacks, there were recurrent difficulties over the scope of the action. It was settled, after dispute in the 1480s, that it lay against a

---

[8] Though a defendant could be released on mainprise: *Canon* v. *Crowe* (1530) CP 40/1065, m. 101d; Spelman 10.   [9] It could not be used against clergy: *Blythe* v. *Holford* (*c.*1500) C1/247/40.

[10] *Earl of Northumberland* v. *Wedall* (1523–7) Spelman 9; Mich. 18 Hen. VIII, fo. 2, pl. 13; CP 40/1039, m. 109 (abstracted in 94 Selden Soc. 262). He also sued Wedall on a bond concerning the repair of a manor place: CP 40/1038, m. 449.

[11] This emerges from the bill in Chancery in *Wedall* v. *Edgar* (*c.*1523/5) C1/593/79 (pr. 94 Selden Soc. 264).

[12] He also sued other receivers: CP 40/1037, m. 282.

[13] For the distinction between a formal accounting and an informal 'reckoning' see *Baynard* v. *Maltby* (1525–31) KB 27/1054, m. 23d (pr. 94 Selden Soc. 267); Spelman 10 (demurrer to the evidence; judgment for plaintiff). For *assumpsit sur insimul computassent* see above, 861.

[14] e.g. *Knyght* v. *Chamberlayn* (1555) KB 27/1175, m. 35d (receipt of £25 by hand of Sir William Herbert); *Beldon* v. *Chamberlayn*, ibid., m. 198d (receipt of £33. 4s. 6d. by hand of Sir William Herbert); *Ellyott* v. *Turvervyle* (1555) KB 27/1176, m. 26 (receipt of £14 by hand of Edward Dymocke, treasurer of Henry VIII, in 1544; verdict for plaintiff and judgment *quod computet*). In each case the plea was 'Never receiver'.

[15] *Welford* v. *Sambroke* (1482–5) Trin. 1 Edw. V, fo. 2, pl. 2; below, n. 26; *Duchess of Norfolk* v. *Aleyn* (1497) Port 3, no. 3; CP 40/942, m. 333 (pr. 102 Selden Soc. 5–6); *Anon.* (1557/8) BL MS. Hargrave 4, fo. 123.

[16] e.g. *Queen Katharine* v. *Benton* (1515) KB 27/1016, m. 24 (demurrer to plea before auditors).

[17] James Hales's reading in Gray's Inn (1532) BL MS. Hargrave 92, fo. 37.

'bailiff' (*ballivus*) of goods;[18] but it was unclear whether it would lie against the bailiff of a park,[19] or against a tenant in common of goods who bailed them to his partner to trade with,[20] or in respect of a tortious taking.[21] The inappropriate word *ballivus* was used only because of Chancery conservatism in refusing to extend the writ formulae.[22] It did not here mean bailee, because account could not be brought against a bailee or finder of goods who would not return them to the owner. There had to be a relationship of accountability, such as that imposed by an agency to sell the goods and account for the proceeds; and such a relationship presupposed that property passed to the accountant.[23] On the same principle, account was unavailable against a bailee or servant charged with a specific task.[24] Thus, in an action of account against a supposed 'bailiff' (*ballivus*) of cloth, it was a good plea to say that the defendant was a common carrier who was handed the goods to take from Exeter to London and deliver to a named person, which he did.[25] A receiver of money could likewise bar the account by pleading that he had received the money from the plaintiff for a specific purpose which had been fulfilled, such as a payment over to a third party, in which case the issue would be whether the money had been received in an accountable way (*ad computandum*).[26] Even in a restitutionary claim to recover back an overpayment, the use of account could be challenged if there

[18] The precedents were against bailiffs of manors, shops, or houses, and their stock: see *Wellys* v. *Robynson* (1484) Mich. 2 Ric. III, fo. 14, pl. 39; CP 40/890, m. 128 (bailiff of house, with 'care and administration' of cloth); and cf. Rast. Ent. 17. For a dispute about goods in gross see Keil. 114; *Moots*, 80.

[19] *Say* v. *Dokket* (1495) Mich. 10 Hen. VII, fo. 6, pl. 12; Trin. 10 Hen. VII, fo. 30, pl. 28; Port 1, pl. 2; CP 40/930, m. 410 (pr. 102 Selden Soc. 2–3).

[20] *Anon.* (1495) Hil. 10 Hen. VII, fo. 16, pl. 14; probably the same as Rast. Ent. 17v, pl. 5. Serjeant Kebell, ibid., said account did not lie between joint owners; but the question of tenants in common was left undetermined. There was a special form of account between merchants 'per legem mercatoriam': e.g. *Audeley* v. *Marham* (1501) CP 40/957, m. 36 (op. se).

[21] Bryan CJ said account would lie for a tortious taking of the plaintiff's rent: *Dean of St Paul's Case* (1489) Pas. 4 Hen. VII, fo. 6, pl. 2. But this was denied in *Anon.* (1554) Brooke Abr., *Accompt*, pl. 89, because there was (tr.) 'no privity in law or in fact'. Likewise *Moots*, 287; James Hales's reading (Gray's Inn, 1532) BL MS. Hargrave 92, ff. 35v (profits of land taken by intruder), 36 (wrongful taking of money). Cf. Pas. 22 Edw. IV, fo. 5, pl. 15.

[22] *Wellys* v. *Robynson* (1484) Mich. 2 Ric. III, fo. 14, pl. 39, *per* Catesby J. (tr. 'the [clerks] of the Chancery will not these days make any writ of account unless it is as receiver of money or else as bailiff'); *Moots*, 80, no. 51 ('that which he supposes in his writ about being his bailiff is only words of form').

[23] *Wellys* v. *Robynson* (1484) Mich. 2 Ric. III, fo. 14, pl. 39 (contrasted with detinue, which affirms property in the plaintiff); CP 40/830, m. 128 (verdict and judgment for defendant); undated note in Port 80, no. 7, perhaps based on same case.

[24] The lack of accountability meant that a bailee or servant was also excused by robbery: *Note* (*c.*1530) Caryll (Jun.) 391–2, no. 51.

[25] *Hamlyn* v. *Hawell* (1518) CP 40/1022, m. 446. Cf. Rast. Ent. 17v, pl. 5, where an alleged *ballivus* of cloth pleaded that he was joint occupier with the plaintiff.

[26] *Welford* v. *Sambroke* (1482–5) Trin. 1 Edw. V, fo. 2, pl. 2; Mich. 1 Hen. VII, fo. 2, pl. 1; CP 40/882, m. 356 (discontinued); *Anon.* (*c.*1511) 120 Selden Soc. 19; *Anon.* (*c.*1533/4) Caryll (Jun.) 371, no. 9; *May* v. *Anger* (1535) CP 40/1085(2), m. 412 (stopped by protection). The plaintiff in the 1535 case, suing as administrator of George Wody, was the defendant in *Core* v. *May*, below.

was an agreement concerning the effect of overpayment.[27] These issues—'Never his bailiff' or 'Never his receiver for rendering account'—were far from being straightforward questions of fact, and might well divert serious litigation into the realms of high abstraction.

A means of escape from some of these difficulties was suggested by the action of debt, since debt would lie where money was paid for a purpose which failed.[28] The propriety of using debt in lieu of account was challenged in the King's Bench in a case reported by both Dyer and Spelman.[29] The plaintiff, a London grocer, claimed that he had paid £20 to a deceased painter-stainer to exchange at Rouen and invest in French prunes; but the payee had died before purchasing any prunes, and so the plaintiff had claimed the return of the £20 from his administrator by writ of debt. The plaintiff obtained judgment by default in the Common Pleas, and the administrator brought a writ of error, assigning the single error that 'by the law of the land a writ of account could have been conceived and maintained' but not debt. The judgment was nevertheless affirmed, with one dissentient. According to the majority, following a decision of 1367, the plaintiff had an election between the two actions. The court emphasized that the reasoning applied only where the plaintiff himself had paid money to the defendant. A third-party payee could not bring debt, because 'the money was never his and he was not privy to the contract'.[30] Therefore it seemed, contrary to earlier precedents,[31] that debt could not be brought against a receiver of money from a third party to the use of the plaintiff.[32]

ACTIONS ON THE CASE

The deficiencies of the actions of account and debt explain why thoughts turned to actions on the case as the potential source of an alternative remedy. Although an action of trespass could only lead to damages, and not to an account before auditors, both the question of accountability and the establishment of what was due could be dealt with at the trial. This must have been a preferable mode of proceeding, provided that the situation to be unravelled was not too complex for a jury.

---

[27] *More* v. *Laskey* (1557) CP 40/1170, m. 907d (pleads he sold tin to plaintiff for £4 per cwt and agreed that if at the next coinage any of the tin was valued below £4 per cwt he would repay the difference, and traversed that he was a receiver).

[28] This is suggested in *Orwell* v. *Mortoft* (1505) B. & M. 410, *per* Frowyk CJ.

[29] *Core* v. *May* (1535–7) CP 40/1083, m. 154 (judgment at first instance); KB 27/1097, m. 33 (affirmed on a writ of error; pr. 94 Selden Soc. 327); Dyer 20a; Spelman 132. Core may have learned from May's difficulties the previous year: above, 877 n. 26.

[30] Cf. Fitzherbert's dictum at a Gray's Inn moot (*c.*1500) BL MS. Harley 5103, fo. 60v (tr. 'A. F. said that . . . if I bail £20 to J. S. to deliver to T. etc., T. shall not have an action of debt against J. S. for there was no contract between them; but an action of account lies').

[31] Cf. Rast. Ent. 157v (159) (1486); Brooke Abr., *Dette*, pl. 129.

[32] Account lay in this case: *Anon.* (1557/8) BL MS. Hargrave 4, fo. 127v, *per* Brooke CJ.

The formula most frequently used was adapted from the action against a bailee for conversion.[33] It will be recalled that in such actions it was common to allege a conversion not of the goods bailed but of the proceeds of their sale,[34] and so it was but a short step to using the same action against an agent who converted the proceeds of sale of goods which he was authorized to sell. It was usual to add an *assumpsit* to perform the agency agreement. Such actions appear in the King's Bench in the 1520s,[35] and are occasionally found in the Common Pleas.[36] Probably the reason why no serious objection was raised by the latter is that wager of law was not generally available in account.[37]

By the middle of the sixteenth century, *assumpsit* could also be brought against a partner or agent, alleging a simple promise to account and a failure to do so.[38] A remarkable instance of such an action is found in the King's Bench rolls for 1553, when *assumpsit* was brought against a factor (*serviens*) who had promised to sell merchandise in Danzig and account to the plaintiff. The defendant pleaded that he was an apprentice, and traversed the *assumpsit* in the manner and form alleged; but the jury found for the plaintiff with £852 damages. The defendant tried to reverse the judgment by a writ of error *coram nobis*, but was told that his only remedy was in Parliament.[39]

Another development of the mid-sixteenth century was to use *assumpsit* in the single-sum situations where the 'receiver' was not a retained agent—for instance to obtain rescission of a conditional contract, or to enforce a trust of money. Examples are actions to recover deposits paid by purchasers of copyhold land, where the vendor failed to secure the admittance of the purchaser,[40] and actions against receivers of single sums of money which they failed to pay to the

[33] As to money, see *Orwell* v. *Mortoft* (1505) 2 Caryll 493 at 494, *per* Frowyk CJ (tr. 'if I deliver money to someone to deliver over, and he does not do so but converts the money to his own use, I may elect whether to have an action of account against him or an action on my case').   [34] See above, 803.

[35] e.g. *Snowden* v. *Fulwode* (1523) KB 27/1047, m. 22; *Pyfford* v. *Byrde* (1524) KB 27/1052, m. 61 (defendant alleged to be a servant); *Miller* v. *Dymok* (1530) KB 27/1077, m. 72A (judgment for plaintiff).

[36] *Weston* v. *Dymmok* (1521) CP 27/1032A, m. 403 (judgment on *non potest dedicere*; the plaintiff was an attorney for whom the defendant had undertaken to sell four tuns of wine); *Thwaytes* v. *Bealles* (1543) CP 40/1117, m. 306 (see above, 871 n. 201).

[37] See *Huntley* v. *Fraunsham* (1560) Dyer 183; Coke, *Entries*, fo. 47v.

[38] e.g. *Beale* v. *Barnes* (1542) KB 27/1125, m. 24 (*assumpsit* by joint occupier of merchandise to behave well and to account; plaintiff recovers £105); *Massy* v. *Marten* (1544) KB 27/1133, m. 123 (sim.; imparlance); *Graver* v. *Brewton* (1550) CP 40/1143, m. 153 (action by executors against testator's factor *in partibus transmarinis*, who promised to render an account and failed to do so). A precursor of this form is *Parker* v. *Bisshoppe* (1518) KB 27/1029, m. 91 (*assumpsit* against joint owner of sheep on promise not to sell any without consent and to answer for a moiety of the profit; pleads he did not buy jointly).

[39] *Saxcy* v. *Hudson* (1553) KB 27/1167, m. 145 (judgment at first instance); KB 27/1173, m. 163 (writ of error).

[40] *Howse* v. *Bert* (1540–1) CP 40/1104, m. 319 (demurrer); (No. 2) CP 40/1108, m. 404 (imparlance). Cf. *Sedley* v. *Fyppys* (1540) CP 40/1105, m. 505 (alleged promise to return deposit of £6 if sale not completed; pleads he sold unconditionally for £6).

plaintiff,[41] or to pay over to a third party as required.[42] There was, in such cases, an election between account, debt, and case.[43] And in 1542 the King's Bench approved an *indebitatus* action to enforce a duty to pay arising from a receipt of money due to the plaintiff by reason of a benefice;[44] this may be considered an antecedent of some of the restitutionary forms of *assumpsit* developed in the following century. Nevertheless the action on the case rested formally on an undertaking to pay the plaintiff, and it is a matter of conjecture whether the undertaking could at this date be fictional. Certainly the development of *assumpsit* stopped short in this period of allowing the payee to enforce a trust of money created by a third-party payer,[45] which usually needed a fiction. Therefore the replacement of account was incomplete, and would not be completed until the approval in the seventeenth century of the count for money had and received.[46]

[41] *Grene* v. *Hedde* (1557) CP 40/1169, m. 544 (in consideration of sum paid to defendant's wife to his use, defendant promised to repay; pleads *Non assumpsit*).

[42] *Joachym* v. *Kelke* (1527) KB 27/1065, m. 27d; *Kellett* v. *Heton* (1540) CP 40/1107, m. 558d (with allegation of conversion to own use); *Wade* v. *Kent* (1555) KB 27/1173, m. 21 (sim.; judgment for plaintiff); *B.* v. *B.* (undated) Rast. Ent. 10. A stray earlier precedent is *Gybbes* v. *Wolston* (1483) CP 40/883, m. 355 (judgment for plaintiff).

[43] *Pykeryng* v. *Thurgoode* (1532) Spelman 4 at 5, *per* Conyngesby J. and Fitzjames CJ. For account in these cases, see James Hales's reading (Gray's Inn, 1532) BL MS Hargrave 92, fo. 35v.

[44] *Guynell* v. *Ap Robert* (1542) KB 27/1122, m. 132d (*indebitatus* for tithes, oblations, and emoluments received by the defendant out of the plaintiff's provostship; verdict and judgment for plaintiff).

[45] Dyer J. said in *Anon.* (1558) BL MS. Harley 1624, fo. 58v, that the proper action was account, or detinue if the money was in a bag.

[46] Even the King's Bench at first denied an action on the case for money had and received, on the ground that the proper action was account: *Anon.* (1573) 3 Leo. 38, pl. 62. For earlier precedents in the rolls, however, see above, 862 n. 142.

BIBLIOGRAPHY[1]

1. CONTEMPORARY SOURCES

(1) Legal records in print

Since for this period there are about 200 miles of Common Pleas plea rolls alone (reckoning both sides of each membrane),[2] it is not surprising that only a tiny proportion of the surviving record material is in print. No term-bundle of plea rolls for the Tudor period has been published or even calendared in its entirety, and indeed only a few single cases have been printed verbatim, mostly in Selden Society volumes. The records of the central courts and government departments are held by the Public Record Office, Kew. There is a calendar of the common-law records in M. Giuseppi, *Guide to the Contents of the Public Record Office*, i (1963); and a more detailed list in the Public Record Office online catalogue at http//: catalogue.pro.gov.uk. Records of the Great Sessions of Wales are now in the National Library of Wales, Aberystwyth. Records of local courts are mostly in county and municipal record offices.

Acts of the Privy Council, new series, ed. J. R. Dasent (1890–1907), 32 vols. Vols. 1–6 (1890–3) cover the period 1542 to 1558.

Beddington (Surrey): *Courts of the Manors of Beddington and Bandon 1498–1552*, tr. H. M. Gowans, ed. M. Wilks and J. Bray (Sutton, 1983).

Bromsgrove (Warwickshire): *The Court Rolls of the Manor of Bromsgrove and King's Norton 1494–1504*, ed. A. F. C. Baber (Warwick, 1963).

Buckingham (archdeaconry): *Courts of the Archdeaconry of Buckingham 1483–1523*, ed. E. M. Elvey (19 Buckinghamshire Record Society, Aylesbury, 1975).

Caernarvonshire: *Calendar of the Caernarvonshire Quarter Sessions Records 1541–58*, ed. W. O. Williams (Caernarvonshire Historical Society, Caernarvon, 1956).

Guildford (Surrey): *Guildford Borough Records 1514–46*, ed. F. M. Dance (Surrey Record Society, 1958).

Journals of the House of Commons, vol. i (1547–1628), ed. T. Vardon and T. E. May (1803).

Journals of the House of Lords beginning Anno Primo Henrici Octavi, vol. i [1846]. Begins with the memoranda (1510–15) of Dr John Taylor, clerk of the parliaments, which are also found

---

[1] Unless otherwise stated, printed books were published in London.

[2] H. R. Plomer estimated in 1910 that there were 57,400 membranes in CP 40 temp. Hen. VII, and 102,566 membranes temp. Hen. VIII: 1 *The Library* (3rd ser.) 290. The number increases in the 1540s and 1550s.

in a seventeenth-century copy in BL MS. Harley 2235, ff. 34–129; both texts are corrupt, but each sometimes corrects the other. There is no journal between 1515 and 1533.

Lincoln (diocese of): *An Episcopal Court Book for the Diocese of Lincoln 1514–20*, ed. M. Bowker (61 Lincoln Record Society, Lincoln, 1967).

New Forest: *A Calendar of New Forest Documents*, ed. D. J. Stagg (5 Hampshire Record Series, Winchester, 1983).

Orders of the High Court of Chancery, ed. G. W. Sanders (1845), 2 vols.

Prescot (Lancs.): *A Selection from the Prescot Court Leet Records 1447–1600*, ed. F. A. Bailey (89 Record Society of Lancashire and Cheshire; 1937).

Proceedings and Ordinances of the Privy Council of England, ed. H. Nicolas, vii (1837). Contains the contents of PC 2/1 from 1540 to 1542; continued in *APC*.

Ramsey (Hunts.): *The Court Rolls of Ramsey, Hepmangrove and Bury, 1268–1600*, ed. E. B. de Windt (Pontifical Institute of Medieval Studies, 17 Susbidia Mediaevalia, Toronto, 1990). Published on microfiche.

Select Cases before the King's Council in the Star Chamber, ed. I. S. Leadam (16 Selden Soc.; 1902; 25 Selden Soc.; 1910), 2 vols. The cases date from 1477 to 1544.

Select Cases concerning the Law Merchant, ed. C. Gross (23 Selden Soc.; 1908), 129–33. Most of the volume relates to an earlier period.

Select Cases in Manorial Courts 1250–1550, ed. L. R. Poos and L. Bonfield (114 Selden Soc.; 1998).

Select Cases in the Council of Henry VII, ed. C. G. Bayne and W. H. Dunham (75 Selden Soc.; 1958).

Select Cases in the Court of Requests 1497–1569, ed. I. S. Leadam (12 Selden Soc.; 1898).

Select Pleas in the Court of Admiralty, ed. R. G. Marsden (6 Selden Soc.; 1892; 11 Selden Soc.; 1897), 2 vols. Includes records from 1527.

Witney (Oxon.): *Calendar of the Court Books of the Borough of Witney 1538–1610*, ed. J. L. Bolton and M. M. Maslen (54 Oxfordshire Record Society, Oxford, 1981–2).

York (City): *Sheriffs' Court Books of the City of York 1471–1500*, tr. P. M. Stell (York, 1999).

(2) Reports of cases

Anon., year books Edw. V to Hen. VIII (1591; repr. 1679). The 1591 edition by Tottell was the first collected edition, but all the contents had appeared earlier in various editions. For a complete bibliography see *STC*[2] i. 436–48. The years 12–14 Hen. VIII were published in a new edition, with translation and apparatus, in 119 Selden Soc. (2002).

Anon., unprinted reports temp. Hen. VII, in an abridgment of year books, Philadelphia Free Library, H. L. Carson Collection, MS. LC 14.35. The original reports are very sparse.

Anon., reports temp. Hen. VIII, BL MS. Hargrave 388, ff. 273–295v ('En temps H. 8'), a collection of 63 cases (1509–35), mostly from the 1530s. There are other copies in BL MS. Hargrave 3 and MS. Lansdowne 1072. In all three manuscripts the reports are found in conjunction with Yorke's reports (q.v.), but the style seems different, and they may have been taken by two or three different reporters in Lincoln's Inn. All three texts continue 'En temps Phillip et Mary', though these are probably additions by Christopher Yelverton (q.v.), who compiled MS. Hargrave 388. Edited in 120 Selden Soc. (2003), 8–80.

Anon., reports (*c.*1530–42), BL MS. Harley 1691, ff. 57r–v, 113–115, 123–145. Edited in 121 Selden Soc. (2004), 421–48.

Anon., *Select Cases in the Exchequer Chamber before all the Justices of England*, ii (1461–1509), ed. M. Hemmant (64 Selden Soc.; 1948). These are selections from the year books, printed and manuscript.

Baker, J. H. (ed.), *Reports of Cases from the time of King Henry VIII* (120–1 Selden Soc.; 2003–4). An edition of previously unpublished reports from various sources, as noted elsewhere in this section.

Bendlowes, W., *Les Reports de William Benloe*, ed. J. Rowe (1689). Sometimes called Old Benloe (cases 1532–79). The reports are by William Bendlowes (d. 1584) of Lincoln's Inn (adm. 1534, bencher 1549), serjeant at law 1555. They may be corrected from Bodl. Lib. MS. Rawlinson C.728 (copy by his son, apparently prepared for publication in 1601). For the numerous manuscripts, see Abbott, *Law Reporting*, 92–4.

—— *Les Reports des divers Resolutions... avecque autres Select Cases* (1661). The 1661 edn, sometimes called New Benloe (cases 1530–75, with additions), is inferior to that of 1689.

Brooke, R., *La Graunde Abridgement* (1573). The compiler (Sir Robert Brooke, CJCP) died in 1558, and the volume includes some original reports down to that year. Note also *Ascun Novel Cases de les Ans et Tempz le Roy H. 8, Edw. 6 et la Roygne Mary* (1576), which were abstracted from the abridgment by Richard Bellewe; tr. English by J. March (1651).

Caryll, J. (I), *Reports of Cases by John Caryll*, ed. J. H. Baker (115–16 Selden Soc.; 1999, 2000). The reports are by John Caryll (d. 1523), of the Inner Temple, prothonotary of the Common Pleas 1493–1510, serjeant at law 1510, king's serjeant 1514–23. They extend from 1485 to 1522. Partly pr. in *Relationes quorundam Casuum selectorum ex Libris Roberti Keilwey*, ed. J. Croke (1602), a work sometimes cited as 'Keilwey', though he was merely the owner of the copy.

Caryll, J. (II), reports (*c.*1527–37), BL MS. Harley 1691, ff. 98–133; IT MS. Petyt 511.13, ff. 1–6v. These notes are by John Caryll (d. 1566), son of Serjeant Caryll, a barrister (and later a bencher) of the Inner Temple; the Westminster cases are interspersed with Inner Temple material. Edited in 121 Selden Soc. (2004), 366–416.

Chaloner, R., reports, GI MS. 25, ff. 19v, 172, 288v–289v. Roughly written reports (*c.*1515–19) by Robert Chaloner (d. 1555) of Gray's Inn, later a bencher. Edited in 121 Selden Soc. (2004), 248–89.

Cholmeley, R., reports, LI MS. Hale 189, ff. 249–256. Three cases (1544) reported by Randle Cholmeley (d. 1563), barrister of Lincoln's Inn (called 1543), later serjeant at law. Edited in 121 Selden Soc. (2004), 450–68.

Dalison, W., reports, BL MS. Harley 5141. Unprinted reports (Mich. 1552 to Pas. 1558) by William Dalison (d. 1559) as JKB. This copy was made in 1569 for William Lambarde, who married the widow of Dalison's eldest son.

—— *Les Reports des divers Special Cases... colligees par Gulielme Dalison*, ed. J. Rowe (1689). This edn includes cases after Dalison's death and the attribution is doubtful; they are probably by Richard Harpur (q.v.).

Dyer, J., *Ascuns Novel Cases* (1585/6). Reports published posthumously from the notebooks of Sir James Dyer (d. 1582) of the Middle Temple, JCP 1557–9, and later CJCP. Dyer's own reports begin in the 1530s, but the volume begins with a few of earlier date.

—— *Cases from the lost Notebooks of Sir James Dyer*, ed. J. H. Baker (109–10 Selden Soc.; 1994). A supplement to the 1585/6 edn, containing cases excluded by the Elizabethan editors but copied in manuscript by others.

Fitzherbert, A., *Magnum Abbreviamentum* (1514–17). A compilation by Anthony Fitzherbert (d. 1538), serjeant at law 1510, later JCP, which includes some 39 brief original reports from 14 to 19 Hen. VII (1499–1504), probably by Fitzherbert himself when a member of Gray's Inn. Twenty of these cases were reprinted in the year book 15 Hen. VII, ff. 8–11, pl. 2–21; and nineteen more in 21 Hen. VII, ff. 39–41, pl. 49–67.

Gell, A., unprinted reports, in 2 vols: (i) (*c.*1541–55), Library of Congress (Law Div.) MS. 15; (ii) (continued *c.*1557–62), MS. from Hopton Hall now in the Derbyshire Record Office, Matlock (part of D3287). These are by Anthony Gell (d. 1583) of the Inner Temple (adm. 1547, bencher 1558), though the earliest terms are similar in style to the printed year books and may have been by another hand.

Hare's reports. Fragments only remain of some reports (*c.*1516–45) in BL MS. Lansdowne 1084 and HLS MS. 1058, extracted and probably abridged from 'Liber Hare'. This is almost certainly Sir Nicholas Hare (d. 1557), of the Inner Temple (adm. 1515, bencher 1532), recorder of Norwich in 1536, knighted 1539, later MR 1553–7. Edited in 120 Selden Soc. (2003), 84–8.

Harpur, R., reports. Unprinted reports (beginning Mich. 1546) by Richard Harpur (d. 1577) of the Inner Temple (adm. 1537, bencher 1554), later serjeant at law and JCP. For the numerous manuscripts, see Abbott, *Law Reporting*, 114–15, 122–6. Cf. Dalison's reports, above.

Keilwey, R., *see* Caryll (I).

More, J., abridgment (*c.*1505), BL Royal MS. 17 E. VI. Cases from Edw. III to Hen. VI, with additions down to 21 Hen. VII, probably by John More (d. 1530) of Lincoln's Inn, serjeant at law 1503, later JKB.

Plowden, E., *Les Comentaries, ou les Reportes de dyvers Cases* (1571, 1579); tr. English 1659. Reports by Edmund Plowden (d. 1585) of the Middle Temple (bencher 1557). The first volume covers the period 1550–71.

Pollard's reports. A series of alphabetically arranged reports (*c.*1514–34) in BL MS. Hargrave 388, the only known text, where 75 cases from a source called 'Pollarde' are inserted in a rearranged copy of Spelman. The reporter is almost certainly Richard Pollard (d. 1542) of the Middle Temple (adm. 1519, bencher 1535), later king's remembrancer of the Exchequer (1535–42): see 93 Selden Soc., pp. xxv–xxvi; 120 Selden Soc., p. xxxviii. Edited in 121 Selden Soc. (2004), 246–77.

Port, J., *The Notebook of Sir John Port*, ed. J. H. Baker (102 Selden Soc.; 1986). Reports (*c.*1493–1536) by John Port (d. 1540) of the Inner Temple (bencher 1507), serjeant at law 1521, JKB 1525–40. Pr. from a unique autograph manuscript in HEHL MS. HM 46980, unknown to scholars before it was sold at Sotheby's in 1979.

Porter's notebook, HLS MS. 47. Reports of dicta in Gray's Inn, in a volume bearing the name 'W. Porter', including a few reports of cases at Westminster from 1522–3 (ff. 36v, 46v, 55, 67–68v), which are edited in 120 Selden Soc. (2003), 81–3. Porter may not have been the compiler; but cf. the clerk of the Crown of that name, below, 887.

Spelman, J., *The Reports of Sir John Spelman*, ed. J. H. Baker (93 Selden Soc.; 1977; introd., records and apparatus in 94 Selden Soc., 1978). Reports (*c*.1500–40) by John Spelman (d. 1546) of Gray's Inn (bencher 1514), serjeant at law 1521, JKB 1531–46.

State Trials: *Cobbett's Complete Collection of State Trials* [ed. F. Hargrave and others], vol. i: 1163–1600 (1809). Repr. from chronicles and other sources.

Yelverton, C., reports, BL MS. Hargrave 388, ff. 243v–255v; MS. Lansdowne 1072, ff. 50v–55. Unpublished reports (Trin. 1556 to Mich. 1562) by Christopher Yelverton (d. 1612) of Gray's Inn (adm. 1552), subsequently JKB. References here are to MS. Hargrave 388.

Yelverton, W., reports, BL MS. Hargrave 253. Reports of cases (1526–40) probably by William Yelverton (d. 1586), bencher of Gray's Inn (read 1534), interspersed with readings and moots in Gray's Inn. Edited in 121 Selden Soc. (2004), 290–365.

Yorke, R., reports, BL MS. Hargrave 388, ff. 211–272; MS. Hargrave 3, ff. 3–23; MS. Lansdowne 1072, ff. 4–35; Gonville and Caius College, Cambridge, MS. 601 ('De abrig. Rogeri Yorke servientis ad legem'). Notes of cases (mostly *c*.1520–35, but with a few from the first decade of Hen. VIII) by Roger Yorke (d. 1536) of Gray's Inn (bencher 1523), serjeant at law 1531: see 93 Selden Soc., p. xxvii. The notes include cases from the Western circuit and Serjeants' Inn, and exercises in Gray's Inn. Edited in 120 Selden Soc. (2003), 89–245.

(3) Formularies, precedents, and books of entries

Anon., precedents of indictments from Kent (*c*.1480–5, perhaps copied slightly later), with some additions from Kent and other counties on the Home circuit down to the 1530s, BL MS. Add. 42077. Several of the additions mention John Hales JP (named on fo. 27 as steward of the liberty of the prior of Christ Church, Canterbury, in 1501).

Anon., Common Pleas entries (*c*.1480/90), BL MS. Harley 5157. Cases mostly from Hen. VI and Edw. IV, with a case of 5 Hen. VII (apparently added) on fo. 272. Belonged to Richard Colnett of Lincoln's Inn, probably the Hampshire attorney of the Common Pleas (d. 1505/6); a namesake of the same inn, doubtless his son, was exigenter of the same court 1534–40.

Anon., Crown Office precedent roll (*c*.1487), BL MS. Add. 35205. Begun temp. Hen. VI but continued down to 1487.

Anon., King's Bench Crown Office entries (*c*.1500, with additions), PRO, KB 15/42. The first 200 ff. date from *c*.1465–95, after which there are a few entries in the same hand *c*.1495–1500, then (from fo. 232) additions temp. Hen. VIII and (from fo. 255) additions temp. Eliz. I. Written on paper, with a limp vellum cover marked 'Oli: Cook E. iiii <& Hen. vii>'; Cook has not been identified. 'Liber Milonis Sandys clerici corone': i.e. belonged to Miles Sandys (d. 1601), clerk of the Crown 1559–97. In 1974 this was in the Supreme Court Library: see 94 Selden Soc. *338* n. 3, *362* n. 3. Cited here as 'Crown Office entries'.

Anon., King's Bench Crown Office entries, BL MS. Add. 25168. This is largely a copy of KB 15/42, or of a similar text, together with some notes from the controlment rolls temp. Hen. VIII, made c.1595. There is an entry of 1594, copied in the same hand, on fo. 445. The directions of writs on fo. 544 include Lord Burghley as lord treasurer (i.e. 1572/98).

Anon., *La Forme d'Office d'un Clerk de Peas* (c.1500), BL MS. Harley 1777, ff. 33v–48 (with precedents added); also in London Guildhall Lib. MS. 3035, ff. 59–64; Derbs. Record Office MS. D2440; Oslo/London, The Schøyen Collection, MS. 1641. (A fifth text was given to New York University School of Law in 1929, but it is no longer there.) The name of Sir Robert Drury (JP Suffolk 1488–1535) occurs in the precedents, which range in date from 1494 to 1501.

Anon., Common Pleas entries (c.1500), BL MS. Lansdowne 1074. Cases to Hen. VII.

Anon., Common Pleas entries (c.1510), BL MS. Add. 37488. Cases from Hen. VI to 1510, apparently collected by a prothonotary, probably William Mordaunt (d. 1518), chief prothonotary 1490–1518. See above, 345. Some of the cases were incorporated in Jenour and Rastell.

Anon., *Modus tenendi Curiam coram Justiciariis ad Assisas* (c.1518), in JHB MS. 39, ff. 29–39; also in Newberry Library, Chicago, Case MS. fK 545.3575, ff. 26–35v. These are both later copies, but the earlier precedents name Elyot and Pollard JJ (Western circuit 1509–22), and some are dated Feb. 1518; there are added some precedents from the fifteenth century, and some from later in Henry VIII's reign.

Anon., *Modus tenendi Curiam ad Gaolam Deliberandam* (temp. Hen. VIII), following the previous item in both manuscripts (but ending abruptly in the second paragraph in the first); Newberry MS., ff. 36–38v. This contains three notes of cases on the Midland circuit in 1544–5 (Newberry MS., fo. 37; pr. in 121 Selden Soc. 469–70), though the main text may be contemporaneous with the assize manual. The commission begins 'Henricus etc.' The text relates to the gaol delivery at assizes rather than quarter sessions.

Anon., Common Pleas entries (c.1530), BL MS. Harley 1715. Cases from Hen. VII and Hen. VIII, including a few related reports in law French (pr. in 120 Selden Soc. 1–7). Perhaps associated with Richard Cupper (see 109 Selden Soc. 41).

Anon., Chancery Crown Office precedents (c.1540), Essex Record Office, MS. D/DP L32. Belonged c.1550 to Richard Garth (d. 1598) of Lincoln's Inn, probably clerk of the petty bag, and Nicholas Metcalff (d. 1581) of Lincoln's Inn, six clerk. Apparently from the library of Sir William Petre (d. 1572).

Anon., Chancery Crown Office precedents (1536 to Eliz. I), consisting chiefly of patents and proclamations, PRO 30/26/116. Formerly Egremont MS. 154; presented to the PRO in 1950.

Anon. (perhaps Caunton, N.), precedents of indictments from Kent (c.1542/5), Kent Archives Office, MS. U4 and MS. U419.01. Two fragments of the same book, containing 42 indictments. Probably compiled by or for Nicholas Caunton, clerk of the peace for Kent 1542–68. Tr. by R. E. A. Poole in *A Kentish Miscellany*, ed. F. Hull (11 *Kent Records*; Chichester, 1979), 128, at 138–57.

Anon., *Regule atque Ordines nonnulle Observande tam in Sessione Pacis quam in Sessione Gaole Deliberationis* (temp. Edw. VI), Bodl. Lib. MS. è Mus. 57, ff. 87v–89 (with the separate section 'Modus intrandi deliberationem gaole' beginning on fo. 88). The gaol delivery here referred to is at the assizes. The commission begins 'Edwardus'.

Catlyn, R., collection of precedents and legal notes, partly in the hand of Sir Robert Catlyn (d. 1574), Alnwick Castle MS. 475. Signed 'Liber Roberti Catlyn' on fo. 1. Most of the precedents (apart from extracts from the medieval rolls of Parliament) are from the reigns of Hen. VIII and Mary I.

Coke, E., *A Booke of Entries* (1614).

Hales, J., collection of precedents and documents relating to the Chancery, especially the hanaper office (1545–72), BL MS. Add. 38136. Evidently compiled by or for John Hales (d. 1572), clerk of the hanaper (for whom see below, 895).

Hebylthwayte, J., *Liber Presidencie diversorum Instrumentorum tam Spiritualium quam Temporalium* (1547), BL MS. Stowe 856. A slight collection, written calligraphically with red and violet rubrication; includes some precedents of pleading in the cinque ports.

Hudson, William, collection of Star Chamber precedents, copied from the lost register books, known from a copy made in 1636: BL MS. Lansdowne 639.

Intrationum excellentissimus Liber (1510).

Intrationum Liber (1546). A different text from the foregoing. It has some affinity with Jenour's entries.

Jenney, W., *Modus formulandi Billarum in Banco Domini Regis quando Defendens est in Custodia Mariscalli* (temp. Edw. IV), CUL MS. Add. 7912, ff. 294–302. A collection of precedents rather than a narrative. Belonged to William Jenney (d. 1483), JKB, and perhaps compiled by him. Ed. C. A. F. Meekings, 'A King's Bench Bill Formulary' (1985) 6 *JLH* 86–104.

Jenour, J., Common Pleas entries, Library of Congress (MSS Division), MS. Phillipps 26752. Belonged to John Jenour (d. 1542), of the Middle Temple, second prothonotary 1513–42, but probably of earlier origin. See above, 345–6.

Levyns, C., collection of precedents relating to Canterbury and the business of an attorney there (*c.*1535), BL MS. Stowe 850. Christopher Levyns, whose signature in red ink occurs several times throughout the book, was of Gray's Inn (adm. 1526) and was of Canterbury in 1539 (CP 40/1102, m. 558). The book subsequently belonged to Thomas Rolfe (d. 1566), also of Gray's Inn (adm. 1543), a Kentish MP (signature on fo. 210v).

Lucas, J., King's Bench entries (temp. Hen. VII–VIII), Library of Congress (MSS Division), MS. Phillipps 11910. There are several ownership inscriptions of John Lucas (d. 1525), filazer of the court 1503–25, including a note of his admission to New Inn in 1501. Many of the contents were incorporated in Rastell.

Madox, T., *Formulare Anglicanum* (1702). Precedents of conveyancing, including several from this period.

Maycote, R., King's Bench entries (temp. Hen. VIII), Library of Congress (MSS Division), MS. Phillips 9071. Robert Maycote (d. 1533) was clerk of the papers of the court.

Phaer, T. (ed.), *A Newe Boke of Presidentes* (1543). Precedents of conveyancing. The preface is signed by Thomas Phaer, though the contents seem be of earlier origin.

Porter, W., precedent book relating to the Crown Office in Chancery (*c.*1505–21), PRO, C193/142. William Porter was clerk of the Crown in Chancery from 1504 until his death on 4 March 1522.

Rastell, W., *A Colleccion of Entrees* (1566; repr. 1574). For the constituent contents, see above, 345–6. Some additions were made in the 1596 edn (repr. 1670), with the result that (after fo. 83) the numbering of the folios is different. Citations here are to the 1566 edn, with the corresponding pages of the 1670 edn in parentheses.

Registrum Omnium Brevium (1531). The text is of fifteenth-century origin, with minimal updating.

Ricart, R. *The Maire of Bristowe is Kalendar* (1479), ed. L. T. Smith (5 Camden Soc., 2nd ser., 1872). Notes and precedents relating to mayoral business.

Stubbe, E., Common Pleas entries (temp. Hen. VIII), BL MS. Add. 24078. Edward Stubbe (d. 1533), of Lincoln's Inn, was chief prothonotary 1518–33.

Shakelady, R., precedents of writs (*c.*1550–60), BL MS. Harley 1856. Rowland Shakelady was a cursitor of the Chancery, adm. Lincoln's Inn 1527.

(4) Readings in the inns of court[3]

Bibliography: J. H. Baker, *Readers and Readings in the Inns of Court and Chancery* (13 Selden Soc. Suppl. Ser.; 2001).

Collection: *Readings and Moots in the Inns of Court in the Fifteenth Century*, i, Readings, ed. S. E. Thorne (71 Selden Soc.; 1954).

Anon., reading on Magna Carta (early 1530s), BL MS. Harley 4990, ff. 146–171. A date before 1536 is suggested by the treatment of religious houses and monks without any hint of the Dissolution; moreover, the treatment of benefit of clergy does not mention the major statutory restrictions of 1531. On the other hand, the reader's contention that the king was supreme governor of the spiritualty at common law, and that 'ceo authoritie que le pape avoit gayne en cest terre fuit per usurpation et nemy de jure', does not seem likely to have been made in a public lecture long before 1534. The rhetorical style of the preface is close to that of the speeches to new serjeants at law in 1521 and 1531.

Adgore, Gregory, on 1 Ric. III, c. 1 (uses), Inner Temple (*c.*1489), CUL MS. Hh.3.10, ff. 19–28; Univ. Coll. Oxford, MS. 162, ff. 102–109; LI MS. Maynard 3, ff. 191–210; Kansas Univ. MS. D. 127.

Audley, Thomas, on 4 Hen. VII, c. 17 (uses), Inner Temple (Autumn 1526), BL MS. Hargrave 87, ff. 427–457; CUL MS. Ee.5.19, ff. 1–17v; Univ. Illinois at Urbana-Champaign MS. 27, ff. 68–98v.

Ayloffe, William, on Westminster II, c. 25 (assizes), Lincoln's Inn (Autumn 1501), LI MS. Hale 189, ff. 304–341.

Bromley, George, on Gloucester, cc. 9–14, and Marlborough, cc. 1–8, Inner Temple (Lent 1509), CUL MS. Ee.3.46, ff. 10–23v.

Bromley, Thomas, on 11 Hen. VII, c. 20 (jointure), Inner Temple (Autumn 1533), BL MS. Lansdowne 1119, ff. 86–94; MS. Lansdowne 1133, ff. 30–54v.

Browne, Anthony, on 34 & 35 Hen. VIII, c. 20 (recoveries), Middle Temple (Lent 1554), BL MS. Harley 5156, ff. 38v–40.

---

[3] This list is limited to principal texts, including those cited above.

——on 32 Hen. VIII, c. 30 (jeofails), Middle Temple (Autumn 1555 as serjeant-elect), BL MS. Hargrave 199, ff. 2–21.

Browne, George, on 32 Hen. VIII, c. 34 (leases on condition), Gray's Inn (Lent 1547), BL MS. Hargrave 92, ff. 108–118v.

Brooke, Robert, on 32 Hen. VIII, c. 2 (limitations), Middle Temple (Autumn 1542), pr. as *The Reading of Sir Robert Brooke upon the Statute of Limitations* (1647).

——on Magna Carta, c. 18 (pleas of the Crown), Middle Temple (Lent 1551), CUL MS. Gg.5.9, ff. 56–97; BL MS. Harley 5225, ff. 22–34; MS. Lansdowne 1134, ff. 82v–99; Bodl. Lib. MS. Rawlinson C.644, ff. 1–53v.

Carus, Thomas, on Westminster II, c. 6 (voucher), Middle Temple (Lent 1548), HLS MS. 5054, ff. 54–79v.

Caryll, John, on Marlborough, cc. 27–9, Inner Temple (Autumn 1510 as serjeant-elect), CUL MS. Ee.3.46, ff. 50–55.

Catlyn, Robert, on 32 Hen. VIII, c. 36 (fines), Middle Temple (Autumn 1547), BL MS. Lansdowne 1133, ff. 2–29; Exeter Coll. Oxford MS. 108, ff. 84–104v.

Chaloner, John, reading on Westminster II, cc. 8–12, 34–5, Gray's Inn (1493 or 1494), GI MS. 25, ff. 263–276.

Coke, William, on 32 Hen. VIII, c. 7 (tithes), Gray's Inn (Autumn 1546), BL MS. Hargrave 92, ff. 104–107.

Constable, Robert, on Westminster II, cc. 1–2, Lincoln's Inn (Autumn 1489), pr. in 71 Selden Soc. 171–237.

——on *Quo Warranto*, Lincoln's Inn (Lent 1494), BL MS. Lansdowne 1119, ff. 68v–73. This was heavily influenced by Dudley's reading on the same text.

——on *Prerogativa Regis*, Lincoln's Inn (Autumn 1495 as serjeant-elect), partly pr. (cc. 1–7 only) as *Prerogativa Regis: tertia lectura Roberti Constable de Lyncolnis Inne anno 11 H. 7*, ed. S. E. Thorne (New Haven, 1949). Texts of portions omitted from the printed edition are in LI MS. Maynard 3 and Univ. Coll. Oxford, MS. 162.

Corbet, Reynold, on 2 & 3 Edw. VI, c. 8 (inquisitions *post mortem*), Middle Temple (Lent 1552), BL MS. Harley 5156, ff. 15–22; East Sussex Record Office MS. QCP/5, ff. 42v–47.

Densill, John, on 4 Hen. VII, c. 24 (fines), pr. as *Le Reading del Monsieur Denshall sur l'Estatute de Finibus fait Anno 4 H. 7* (1662); and found in numerous manuscripts.

Dudley, Edmund, on *Quo Warranto*, Gray's Inn (c. 1485/90), CUL MS. Hh.3.10, ff. 1–18v.

——on Westminster II, c. 25 (assizes), Gray's Inn (Lent 1496), CUL MS. Hh.3.10, ff. 59–93v.

Dyer, James, on 32 Hen. VIII, c. 1, and 34 & 35 Hen. VIII, c. 5 (wills), Middle Temple (Autumn 1552), pr. in *Three Learned Readings* (1648); also found in manuscript.

Englefield, Thomas, on Westminster II, cc. 39–40, Middle Temple (Autumn 1520), CUL MS. Hh.3.9, ff. 82v–90v.

Fitzherbert, Anthony, on Marlborough, c. 11, or 36 Edw. III, c. 15 (treason), concerning pleading, Gray's Inn (*c.*1507), LI MS. Maynard 3, ff. 1–42v; Exeter Coll. Oxford MS. 108, ff. 42–83; BL MS. Add. 36079; repeated in 1510 as serjeant-elect, Spelman 75.

Frost, William, on *Quia Emptores*, Lincoln's Inn (Lent 1491), BL MS. Harley 1336, ff. 138v–140.

Frowyk, Thomas, on Westminster II, cc. 6–11, Inner Temple (Autumn 1492), CUL MS. Dd.3.41, ff. 82–99; LI MS. Maynard 70, ff. 67v–89.

—— on *Prerogativa Regis*, Inner Temple (Autumn 1495), numerous manuscripts.

Gawdy, Thomas, on Westminster II, c. 14 (waste), Inner Temple (Autumn 1553), BL MS. Add. 25195, ff. 5–6.

Gilbert, Ambrose, on 32 Hen. VIII, c. 1, and 34 & 35 Hen. VIII, c. 5 (wills), Lincoln's Inn (Lent 1556), numerous manuscripts.

Gosnold, John, on 32 Hen. VIII, c. 28 (leases), Gray's Inn (Lent 1542), BL MS. Hargrave 92, ff. 63–85.

Hales, Edward, on Magna Carta, c. 11 (common pleas), Inner Temple (Lent 1512), CUL MS. Ee.3.46, ff. 66–73.

Hales, James, on 23 Hen. VIII, c. 15 (costs), Gray's Inn (Autumn 1532), BL MS. Hargrave 92, ff. 21–40. The portion dealing with actions on the case is printed in B. & M. 345–51. In *Readers and Readings* this was tentatively dated 1537; but it is mentioned in Moyle's reading of 1533, which immediately followed it: BL MS. Hargrave 92, fo. 47.

—— on Westminster II, c. 45 (executions), Gray's Inn (Lent 1540 as serjeant-elect), BL MS. Hargrave 253, ff. 62–68.

Hales, John, on Westminster II, c. 39 (sheriffs), Gray's Inn (Autumn 1514), GI MS. 25, ff. 290–300v.

Hall, Edward, on Magna Carta, c. 1, of Holy Church, Gray's Inn (Lent 1541), BL MS. Hargrave 92, ff. 57–62v.

Harlakenden, Thomas, on Magna Carta, c. 35 (sheriffs' courts), Gray's Inn (Lent 1525), BL MS. Harley 1210, ff. 146v–151.

Hendley, Walter, on 21 Hen. VIII, c. 3 (abridgment of plaints), Gray's Inn (Lent 1530), BL MS. Hargrave 92, ff. 6–17v.

—— on 21 Hen. VIII, c. 19 (avowries), Gray's Inn (Lent 1535), BL MS. Hargrave 92, ff. 18–20v (incomplete).

Hesketh, Richard, on the *Carta de Foresta*, Gray's Inn (*c.*1506/8), numerous manuscripts. The text used here is BL MS. Lansdowne 1145.

Hutton, John, on Westminster II, c. 12 (felony), Inner Temple (*c.*1490), CUL MS. Hh.3.10, ff. 28v–36.

Kydwelly, Morgan, on Magna Carta, c. 11 (common pleas), Inner Temple (Lent 1483), CUL MS. Ee.5.18, ff. 26–41.

Littleton, Richard, on Westminster II, c. 12 (felony), Inner Temple (Lent 1493), CUL MS. Hh.3.6, ff. 1–22; BL MS. Harley 1691, ff. 188–193v.

Luke, Walter, on *De Religiosis*, Middle Temple (Autumn 1520), CUL MS. Hh.3.9, ff. 72–81.

Malet, Baldwin, on Magna Carta, cc. 18–23, Inner Temple (Autumn 1512), CUL MS. Ee.3.46, ff. 74–81.

Marow, Thomas, on Westminster I, c. 1 (peace of the realm), Inner Temple (Lent 1503 as serjeant-elect), numerous manuscripts; edn by B. H. Putnam, *Early Treatises on Justices of the Peace* (Oxford, 1924), 289–414.

Marshall, William, on *Quo Warranto*, Lincoln's Inn (Lent 1516), LI MS. Maynard 70, ff. 90–115v; BL MS. Lansdowne 1122, ff. 35–81; Taussig MS., ff. 7–24. This was largely derived from Dudley's reading on the same text.

Morgan, Francis, on Westminster II, c. 11 (account), Middle Temple (Lent 1553), BL MS. Harley 5156, ff. 35v–38.

Mountford, Francis, on Westminster II, c. 13 (felony), Inner Temple (Lent 1527), CUL MS. Ee.5.19, ff.113–123; BL MS. Hargrave 87, ff. 177–186.

Moyle, Thomas, on 21 Hen. VIII, c. 15 (recoveries), Gray's Inn (Lent 1533), BL MS. Hargrave 92, ff. 41–56v.

Plowden, Edmund, probably on Merton, c. 4 (dower), Middle Temple (Lent 1558), Exeter Coll. Oxford MS. 108.

Prideaux, John, on 1 & 2 Phil. & Mar., c. 12 (distresses), Inner Temple (Autumn 1555 as serjeant-elect), BL MS. Lansdowne 1134, ff. 99v–104; Taussig MS., ff. 1–6.

Pygot, Thomas, on Marlborough, cc. 14–25, Inner Temple (Lent 1510), CUL MS. Ee.3.46, ff. 34–49.

Ramsey, John, on 2 & 3 Edw. VI, c. 8 (copyholds), Gray's Inn (Autumn 1556), LI MS. Maynard 60, pp. 305–15.

Smith, John, on 27 Hen. VIII, c. 10 (uses), Taussig MS.; BL MS. Harley 1691, ff. 163–165.

Snede, Richard, on Magna Carta, c. 1 (liberties of the Church), Inner Temple (Lent 1511), CUL MS. Ee.3.46, ff. 56–65v.

Spelman, John, on *Quo Warranto*, Gray's Inn (Lent 1519), Gray's Inn MS. 25, ff. 277–289; Nottingham Univ. Lib. MS. Middleton L.18b, ff. 46–60v; Bodl. Lib. MS. Rawlinson B.432, ff. 40–51; Exeter Coll., Oxford MS. 116, ff. 75–81; St John's Coll., Cambridge MS. S.28, ff. 147–160v; pr. as *John Spelman's Reading on Quo Warranto delivered in Gray's Inn (Lent, 1519)*, ed. J. H. Baker (113 Selden Soc.; 1997). This was largely derived from Dudley's reading on the same text.

—— on *Prerogativa Regis*, Gray's Inn (Lent 1521 as serjeant-elect), GI MS. 25, ff. 302–323.

Stanley, Thomas, on 32 Hen. VIII, c. 5 (debts), Gray's Inn (Autumn 1550), BL MS. Hargrave 199, ff. 22–62.

Staunford, William, on 34 Edw. III, c. 12 (treason), Gray's Inn (Lent 1545), BL MS. Hargrave 92, ff. 86–103v.

Stoughton, Gilbert, on Magna Carta, cc. 2–10, Inner Temple (Autumn 1511), CUL MS. Ee.3.46, ff. 1–9.

Symonds, William, on 32 Hen. VIII, c. 28 (leases), Inner Temple (Autumn 1549), CUL MS. Gg. 3.26, ff. 349–352v; MS. Ll.3.12, ff. 1–15v; BL MS. Harley 1691, ff. 202–207; Devon Record Office MS. 189/M/add. 3.

—— (Lent 1554) on 3 & 4 Edw. VI, c. 3 (commons), BL MS. Harley 1691, ff. 134–139.

Tichborne, Nicholas, on Marlborough, cc. 9–13, Inner Temple (Autumn 1509), CUL MS. Ee.3.46, ff. 61–90.

Treherne, George, on the Carta de Foresta, Lincoln's Inn (Autumn 1520), numerous manuscripts. The original text is in French. An English translation which enjoyed a wide circulation is stated in BL MS. Stowe 414, fo. 203v, to have been made by Henry Stafford (d. 1562), Lord Stafford, in 1 & 2 Phil. & Mar. (1554/5).

Wadham, William, on Westminster II, cc. 11–17, Lincoln's Inn (Lent 1505), Taussig MS., ff. 182–212; BL MS. Hargrave 87, ff. 309–325v.

—— on Westminster II, cc. 3–5, Lincoln's Inn (Lent 1520), LI MS. Maynard 70, ff. 1–47; HLS MS. 13, pp. 67–116.

White, Henry, on Westminster I, cc. 34–9, Inner Temple (Lent 1531), BL MS. Hargrave 87, ff. 234–261.

Williams, Thomas, on 35 Hen. VIII, c. 6 (juries), Inner Temple (Lent 1558), pr. as *The Excellency and Praeheminence of the Law of England asserted* (1680), pt i, pp. 1–170.

Willoughby, George, on *Prerogativa Regis*, Inner Temple (Lent 1549), BL MS. Harley 1691, ff. 197–201. This was largely derived from Frowyk's reading on the same text.

Wood, Anthony, on Westminster II, c. 1 (*De Donis*), Middle Temple (Lent 1549), CUL MS. Gg.5.9, ff. 19–48v.

Yorke, Roger, on *Prerogativa Regis*, Gray's Inn (Lent 1531 as serjeant-elect), BL MS. Hargrave 253, fo. 77v.

For moots see also *Readings and Moots in the Inns of Court in the Fifteenth Century*, ii, Moots, ed. J. H. Baker and S. E. Thorne (105 Selden Soc.; 1990).

(5) Records of the inns of court and chancery

General: Denton, T., Bacon, N., and Cary, R., report to Henry VIII on the inns of court (1539), pr. in E. Waterhous, *Fortescutus Illustratus* (1663), 543–6; repr. in *English Historical Documents*, ed. C. H. Williams (1971), 563–73; and in D. S. Bland, 'Henry VIII's Royal Commission on the Inns of Court' (1969) 10 *JSPTL* 178–94. For the date and composition see R. M. Fisher, 14 *JSPTL* 108–9.

General: 'Orders Made and Agreed upon to be Observed and Kept in all the Four Houses of Court' (22 June 1557), *BBLI*, i. 320–1; *MTR*, i. 111–12; *CITR*, i. 192–3; W. Dugdale, *Origines Juridiciales* (3rd edn, 1680), 310–11.

Clement's Inn constitutions: 'Le liver des constitutions et orders del hospic. de Clements Inne', Public Record Office, PRO 30/26/74/4 (transcript dated 1635); tr. only in *Pension Book of Clement's Inn*, ed. C. Carr (78 Selden Soc.; 1960), 218–26. The MS. was presented to the PRO by Richard Stephens Taylor (d. 1950), son of one of the last members of the Inn. An inaccurate transcript was privately printed, with parallel translation, as: *The Book of Constitutions and Orders of the Honble. Society of Clement's Inn and Translations thereof* ('Printed for the Society A.D. 1880. C. J. Mander, Principal').

Clifford's Inn statutes: 'Ceux sount lez estatutz et ordinauncez pur le bon et honorable gov...le Chancellor...faitz pur estre tener et garder et...Clyffordes Inne lan du reigne le Roy Henry...Holland donquez le Principall et...Et escriptez lan du...Roy Henry le v[i]ij xx° Hugh Goodman esteant Principall', IT MS. Misc. 189 (formerly in the hall of Clifford's Inn). Vellum triptych, with the royal arms supported by a lion and bull sejant at the head of the central panel, the initials in blue and gold. See S. Ireland, *The Inns of Court* (1800), 76–8 (woodcut of the triptych on p. 78); C. M. Hay-Edwards, *A History of Clifford's Inn* (1912), facing p. 58 (reproduction of the woodcut, dated 1381), 59–66 (extracts from a transcript). Ireland wrote in 1800 (p. 78) that 'the writing is at present scarcely legible', while Hay-Edwards in 1912 (p. 59) wrote that 'nothing remains of the writing today'; nevertheless, though faint, most of it is still quite legible. It may be corrected from a seventeenth-century transcript recently acquired by the Inner Temple archives (CLI 4/1).

Furnival's Inn: *Early Records of Furnival's Inn edited from a Middle Temple manuscript*, ed. D. S. Bland (Newcastle upon Tyne, 1957). These are extracts from the lost records, made c.1636 by a member of Lincoln's Inn. The manuscript was one of three presented to the Middle Temple by Lord Reading in 1910, and there is a transcript by W. P. Baildon in LI MS. Misc. 720.

Gray's Inn: *The Register of Admissions to Gray's Inn, 1521–1881* [A–C only, arranged alphabetically], ed. J. Foster (privately pr., 1887).

—— *The Register of Admissions to Gray's Inn, 1521–1889*, ed. J. Foster (privately pr., 1889).

Inner Temple: *Students admitted to the Inner Temple 1547–1660* (1877).

—— *Masters of the Bench of the Hon. Society of the Inner Temple, 1450–1883*, ed. J. E. Martin (privately pr., 1883).

—— *The Inner Temple: its early history, as illustrated by its records, 1505–1603*, ed. F. A. Inderwick (1896). This is cited as *CITR*, being the first volume of the series subsequently entitled *Calendar of Inner Temple Records*.

Lincoln's Inn: *Records of the Honorable Society of Lincoln's Inn. Vol. I. Admissions from A.D. 1420 to A.D. 1799*, ed. W. P. Baildon (1896).

—— *Records of the Honorable Society of Lincoln's Inn: the Black Books. Vol. I. From A.D. 1422 to A.D. 1586*, ed. W. P. Baildon, with introd. by R. D. Walker (1897).

Middle Temple: '[sp. mod.] A description of the form and manner how and by what orders and customs the state of the fellowship of the Middle Temple . . . is maintained, and what ways they have to attain unto learning', BL Cotton MS. Vitellius C. IX, ff. 319–323v (now badly damaged); pr. in Dugdale, *Origines Juridiciales*, 193–7 (including words now lost), and repr. from thence in W. Herbert, *History of the Inns of Court* (1804), 211–22; new edn in R. M. Fisher, 'Thomas Cromwell, Dissolution of the Monasteries, and the Inns of Court, 1534–1540' (1973) 14 *JSPTL* 103 at 111–17.

—— *A Calendar of the Middle Temple Records*, ed. C. H. Hopwood (1903).

—— *Minutes of Parliament of the Middle Temple. Vol. I. 1501–1603*, ed. C. T. Martin (1 Middle Temple Records, gen. ed. C. H. Hopwood, 1904).

—— *Register of Admissions to the Honourable Society of the Middle Temple from the Fifteenth Century to the year 1944*, ed. H. A. C. Sturgess (1949). Vol. I covers the period 1501–1781.

New Inn constitutions: 'Constitutiones Novi Hospicii', 6 pp. in a booklet inscribed on the cover, 'New Inn Orders translated anno 1668', MT archives, MT 12/MIS17. There is also an eighteenth-century copy, inscribed on the cover, 'New Inn Constitutions Translated from the French in the Year 1668', 7 pp., in MT 12/CON1. The French text, which has not been found, was said in 1662 to be 'fixed with a chayne in the common hall of this house, and made tyme out of mynde': MT 12/MIS16. It seems to have been more or less coeval with the constitutions of Clement's Inn and Clifford's Inn.

(6) Tracts, letters, legislation, and other documents

The Boke of Justices of Peas (c.1505/6); repr. in facsimile, with an introduction by P. R. Glazebrook (Menston, 1972); and again, without introduction (808 The English Experience; Amsterdam, 1976). The text dates from the mid-fifteenth century, and was only slightly updated when first printed.

Book of Thinges inquirable in all inferior Courtes [1537?], BL MS. Add. 48047, ff. 59–79v. This is a draft charge to a court leet. (See Elton, *Policy and Police*, 336–9.)

A Breviat of the Effectes devised for Wales [c.1540/1] ed. P. R. Roberts (26 Camden Miscellany, 1975), 31–47, from BL Cotton MS. Vitellius C. 1, ff. 39–43. A partly unfulfilled scheme for remodelling the courts in Wales, with a Welsh Chancery.

Brinklow, H., *Henry Brinklow's Complaynt of Roderyck Mors* [c.1542], ed. J. M. Cowper (Early English Text Soc., 1874).

Cavendish, G., *The Life and Death of Cardinal Wolsey*, ed. R. S. Sylvester (243 Early English Text Society, Norwich, 1959). The text of this edition was based on the autograph in BL MS. Egerton 2402. A less scholarly edition from the same manuscript was published in a limited edition of 325 copies by the Alcuin Press as *The Life and Death of Thomas Wolsey the Great Cardinal of England* (Chipping Camden, 1930).

'Certen Considerations why the Spirituell Jurisdiction wold be abrogatt and repelled or at the leest reformed' [c.1534]. BL Cotton MS. Cleopatra F. II, ff. 241–245. Written in response to a 'bill' (which does not survive) containing an assertion of various heads of spiritual jurisdiction; there are internal references to three different statutes of 1533. It is in a very similar style to St German's tracts.

A Discourse of the Common Weal of this Realm of England [1549], ed. E. Lamond (Cambridge, 1929). First pr. in 1581 as by W. S. (unidentified).

Diversite de Courtz et lour Jurisdictions (1526); tr. into English by W. Hughes (1646, repr. 1903, 1968). The date 1523 in one edn is a misprint for 1532, and so the 1526 edn is the first. The introduction to the 1903 reprint (Legal Classics Series, Washington), p. xii, contains the crass error of supposing that it was an 'original monograph' by Hughes. It has been attributed (e.g. in the old *DNB*) to Sir Anthony Fitzherbert, but without good evidence. Putnam (*Early Treatises on Justices of the Peace*, 178–9 n. 3) suggested a connection with Morgan Kydwelly's reading of 1483 on the courts (above, 890), but there is less resemblance between the texts than she supposed: see *CELMC*, 209–11, arts. 7 and 15. The tract was probably written temp. Hen. VII, though the form of writ appointing a chief justice has had the name of Fitzjames (CJKB in 1526) inserted.

Dudley, E., *The Tree of Commonwealth* (1509); ed. D. M. Brodie (Cambridge, 1948).

'Ecclesiastical lawes devised in Kyng Henry the viijth dayes' (1535), BL MS. Add. 48040, ff. 13–104v. A draft outline revision of the canon law, probably produced by the working committee of canonists chaired by Dr Richard Gwent, dean of Arches, in 1535. See F. D. Logan, 'The Henrician Canons' (1974) 47 *BIHR* 99–103. Pr. with translation in *Tudor Church Reform: the Henrician canons of 1535 and the Reformatio Legum Ecclesiasticarum*, ed. G. Bray (8 Church of England Record Soc., Woodbridge, 2000), 1–143.

Elyot, T., *The Boke named the Governour* (1531).

—— *The Book named the Governor*, new edn by S. E. Lehmberg (227 Everyman's Library; 1962). Version in modern spelling.

Ferrers, G., *The Great Charter . . . with divers Olde Statutes* (1542), preface.

Fitzherbert, A., *La Novel Natura Brevium* (1534). 1st edn printed anonymously.

—— *The Newe Boke of Justices of the Peas* (1538); repr. in facsimile (109 The English Experience, Amsterdam, 1969); also repr. in facsimile, with introduction by P. R. Glazebrook (1972; reissued, Abingdon, 1982).

Fitzherbert, J., *The Boke of Surveyeng and Improumentes* (1523); repr. in facsimile (657 The English Experience, Amsterdam, 1974). The 1534 edn identifies the author as 'Master' Fitzherbert. The identificaton is not entirely free from doubt, but the most likely candidate is John Fitzherbert (d. 1531), Sir Anthony's elder brother: see F. Boersma, *Sir Antony Fitzherbert* (1978), 226–32.

[Gardiner, S.], *The Letters of Stephen Gardiner*, ed. J. A. Muller (Cambridge, 1933).

Hales, J., *Oration in Commendation of Lawes [of England]* [*c*.1540/2]. Free Library of Philadelphia MS. LC 14.32(1); copy in BL MS. Harley 4990, ff. 1–48. Dedicated to Sir Anthony Browne. The author was John Hales (d. 1572) of Coventry, later clerk of the hanaper, MP, and controversialist: *DNB*; 94 Selden Soc. *367*; 109 Selden Soc., pp, xlviii, 92–7. He is to be distinguished from John Hales (d. 1540) of Canterbury, bencher of Gray's Inn and baron of the Exchequer.

Hall, E., *Hall's Chronicle: containing the history of England . . . to the end of the reign of Henry the Eighth . . . carefully collated with the editions of 1548 and 1550* [ed. H. Ellis] (1809). Edward Hall was a bencher of Gray's Inn (above, 890).

[Ireland] Quinn, D. B. (ed.), 'The Bills and Statutes of the Irish Parliaments of Henry VII and Henry VIII' (1941) 10 *Analecta Hibernica* 71–169 (a calendar, with texts of those not printed elsewhere).

[Ireland] *The Statutes at Large passed in the Parliaments held in Ireland* (Dublin, 1786–1801), 20 vols. First pr. in 1762, a revised edn was pr. in 1885 (repr. Dublin, 1995).

Letters and Papers of Henry VIII, ed. J. S. Brewer, J. Gairdner, and R. H. Brodie (1862–1932), 21 vols in 33 (repr. 1965 as 23 vols. in 38).

The Lisle Letters, ed. M. S. Byrne (Chicago, 1981), 6 vols. An edition in modern spelling of the correspondence (1532–40) of Arthur Plantagenet, Viscount Lisle, preserved in the PRO.

Materials for a History of the Reign of King Henry VII, ed. W. Campbell (RS, 1873), 2 vols.

More, T., *The Debellation of Salem and Bizance*, ed. J. Guy, R. Keen, C. H. Miller, and R. McGugan, in *The Complete Works of St Thomas More*, vol. x (New Haven, Ct, 1987).

Morison, R., *A Perswasion to the Kyng that the Law of his Realme shulde be in Latin* [*c*.1536]. BL Royal MS. 18 A. 50 (royal presentation copy, with arms and monogram HR). There is a corrected draft in BL Cotton MS. Faustina C. II, ff. 5–22.

—— *Humanist Scholarship and Public Order: two tracts against the pilgrimage of grace by Sir Richard Morison*, ed. D. S. Berkowitz (Washington, 1984).

Perkins, J., *Perutilis Tractatus Magistri Johannis Parkins Interioris Templi Socii* (1528); tr. English 1555. Later known as Perkins's *Profitable Book*.

Pilkington, R., 'The tytyll of Pylkyngton to Anesworth landes', commonly known as *The Narrative of Robert Pilkington*, manuscript formerly at Newburgh Priory, Yorks. (Sir George Wombwell) now in the North Yorkshire Record Office, Northallerton, ZDV (Mic 1002); calendared and partly pr. in HMC, *Report on Manuscripts in Various Collections*, ii (1903), 28–56. A first-hand description of prolonged litigation (1478–1511) between the Pilkington and Aynesworth families over the manor of Mellor, Derbs. The paper is badly damaged in the top left corner, with the loss of several lines of text on each page.

The Plumpton Letters and Papers, ed. J. Kirby (8 Camden Soc. 5th ser.; Cambridge, 1996). This supersedes *Plumpton Correspondence*, ed. T. Stapleton (1839; repr. with an introduction by K. Dockray, Gloucester, 1989). A collection of 252 letters concerning the Plumpton family of Plumpton, Yorks., many of them concerned with litigation. Sir Robert Plumpton (d. 1525) was heavily involved in lawsuits throughout his life.

Rae, J., *see Statutes of Henry VII.*

Rastell, J., *Liber Assisarum* [*c.*1514], preface.

—— *Exposiciones Terminorum Legum Anglorum* [1523?] (repr. 1527). Later known as *Les Termes de la Ley.* See J. H. Baker, 'John Rastell and the Terms of the Law' (forthcoming).

Rastell, W., *A Colleccion of all the Statutes* (1557). An alphabetical rearrangement.

Reformatio Legum Ecclesiasticarum [1551/2]. Draft code of canon law (in Latin) prepared by the Cranmer commission in the name of King Edward VI but never approved by the king, Parliament, or Convocation. It was first printed in 1571; and a new edn from that text by E. Cardwell was printed at Oxford in 1850. An edn from BL MS. Harley 426 appeared as *The Reformation of the Ecclesiastical Laws of England, 1552*, ed. J. C. Spalding (19 *Sixteenth Century Essays and Studies*, Kirksville, Mo., 1992). The editor considered this to be the final version of the code, but it seems rather to be an incomplete working draft: see the review by D. MacCulloch in 44 *Jnl Eccles. History* at 309–10. The best edn, with translation in parallel, is now *Tudor Church Reform: the Henrician canons of 1535 and the Reformatio Legum Ecclesiasticarum*, ed. G. Bray (8 Church of England Record Society, Woodbridge, 2000), 145–743.

Replication of a Serjeant at the Laws of England [*c.*1531], BL MS. Harley 829, ff. 53–59v (St German's copy); whence the other known manuscripts derive. The first printed edn in *Law Tracts*, ed. F. Hargrave (1787), has now been superseded by the edn in J. Guy, *St German on Chancery and Statute*, 99–105. The tract is cast in the form of a dialogue, in the manner of St German's *Doctor and Student*, parts of which it criticizes. It is possible that St German wrote it himself, so that he could pen his *Litle Treatise* in response. Sir Thomas Audley has also been suggested as a possible author, in view of the strong criticism of the jurisdiction over uses in his reading of 1526 (above, 43, 667).

Roper, W., *The Lyfe of Sir Thomas Moore*, ed. E. V. Hitchcock (Early English Text Soc., 1935).

St German, C., *The Fyrste Dyaloge… The secunde Dyalogue in Englysshe* (1531); repr. in facsimile (Menston, 1970).

—— *St German's Doctor and Student*, ed. T. F. T. Plucknett and J. L. Barton (91 Selden Soc.; 1974).

—— *A Litle Treatise concerning Writs of Subpena* [*c.*1531], BL MS. Harley 829, ff. 60–81v (mostly autograph). The first printed edn in *Law Tracts*, ed. F. Hargrave (1787), 332–5, has now been superseded by J. Guy, *Christopher St German on Chancery and Statute* (1985), at 106–26. For the authorship see Yale, 'St German's Little Treatise concerning Writs of Subpoena' (1975) 10 *Irish Jurist* (new ser.) 324–33; and Guy, *St German on Chancery and Statute*, 56–62.

Scott, J., treatise on tenures, dated 8 Hen. VII ('omnia et singula prerecitata in predictoque impressata apud Dorney in comitatu Buk. per me Johannem Scott de Greys Yn pennata atque composita fuerunt tempore … Regis Henrici septimi videlicet anno octavo nobilissimi regni sui'). Univ. Coll. Oxford MS. 160. Nothing else is known about John Scott of Gray's Inn.

Smith, T., *A Discourse of the Commonweal of this Realm of England*, ed. M. Dewar (Charlottesville, Va., 1969)

—— *De Republica Anglorum* (1583), ed. M. Dewar (Cambridge, 1982). A new edn of the same book.

Starkey, T., *Dialogue between Cardinal Pole and Roger Lupset* [*c.*1532/5]. The readable version by S. J. Herrtage, *England in the Reign of Henry VIII*, pt i (Early English Text Soc.; 1878), has now been superseded by a more scholarly edition: *Thomas Starkey: a dialogue between Pole and Lupset*, ed. T. F. Mayer (37 Camden Soc. 4th ser.; 1989).

Statutes of Ireland, see Ireland.

The Statutes of Henry VII: in exact facsimile from the very rare original, printed by Caxton in 1489, ed. with an introd. and end notes by J. Rae (1869).

Statutes of the Realm. Vols i to iv (1810–19) contain the statutes from Magna Carta to the end of Mary I's reign.

Staunford, W., *Les Plees del Coron* (1557). Repr. in facsimile, with an introd. by P. R. Glazebrook (Guildford, 1971).

—— *An Exposition of the Kinges Prerogative* [preface dated 6 Nov. 1548] (1st edn 1567). A near contemporary manuscript version, which belonged to Sir Robert Catlyn, is now Alnwick Castle MS. 475, ff. 136–171v. Another (lacking the first three folios) is in Bodl. Lib. MS. Ashmole 1149(4).

Taverner, R., *Institutions in the Lawes of Englande* [1538?]. The 1540 edn has a preface by Richard Taverner, though his authorship is open to question.

Testamenta Vetusta, ed. N. H. Nicolas (1826). 2 vols of wills from PCC.

Tudor Royal Proclamations, ed. P. L. Hughes and J. F. Larkin (New Haven, 1964–9), 3 vols.

Venetian relation: *A Relation, or rather a True Account of the Island of England about the Year 1500*, ed. C. A. Sneyd (37 Camden Soc.; 1847); tr. from Italian.

Vergil, P., *Anglica Historia* (Basle, 1534; enlarged edn 1546).

—— *Polydore Vergil's English History*, ed. H. Ellis (Camden Soc.; 1846).

—— *The Anglica Historia of Polydore Vergil 1485–1537*, ed. D. Hay (74 Camden Soc. 3rd ser.; 1950). Parallel text and tr. of the Tudor portion only.

Wingfield, R., *Vita Mariae Reginae*, ed. D. McCulloch (29 Camden Soc. 4th ser.; 1984).

2. SECONDARY MATERIAL

Abbott, L. W., *Law Reporting in England 1485–1585* (1973).

—— 'Public Office and Private Right: the legal establishment in the reign of Mary Tudor' in *The Mid-Tudor Polity, c.*1540–1560, ed. J. Loach and R. Tittler (1980), 137–58.

Adair, E. R., 'The Statute of Proclamations' (1917) 32 *EHR* 34–46.

Allen, J. W., *A History of Political Thought in the Sixteenth Century* (1928).

Alsop, J. D., 'The Theory and Practice of Tudor Taxation' (1982) 97 *EHR* 1–30.

—— 'Innovation in Tudor Taxation' (1984) 99 *EHR* 83–93.

—— 'The Act for the Queen's Regal Power 1554' (1994) 13 *Parliamentary History* 261–76.

Ames, J. B., *Lectures on Legal History* (Harvard, Mass., 1913).

Arnold, C., 'The Commission of the Peace for the West Riding of Yorkshire 1437–1509' in *Property and Politics: essays in late medieval English history*, ed. T. Pollard (Gloucester, 1984), 116–38.

Arnold, M. S., 'The Medieval Rules of Pleading' (1985), 100 Selden Soc., pp. x–xx.

——Green, T. A., Scully, S. A., and White, S. D. (eds), *On the Laws and Customs of England: essays in honor of S. E. Thorne* (Chapel Hill, NC, 1981).

Arrizabalaga, J., Henderson, J., and French, R., *The Great Pox: the French Disease in Renaissance Europe* (New Haven and London, 1997).

Bacon, F., *The History of the Reign of King Henry VII*, ed. J. Weinberger (Ithaca, NY, 1996).

Baker, J. H., 'The Dark Age of English Legal History' in *Legal History Studies 1972*, ed. D. Jenkins (Cardiff, 1975), 1–27.

——*English Legal Manuscripts* (Zug, 1975–8), 2 vols.

——'The Old Constitution of Gray's Inn' (1977) 81 *Graya* 15–19; repr. in *LPCL*, 39–43.

——'The Law Merchant and the Common Law before 1700' (1979) 38 *CLJ* 295–322; repr. in *LPCL*, 341–68.

——'The Attorneys and Officers of the Common Law in 1480' (1980) 1 *JLH* 182–203.

——'The English Legal Profession 1450–1550' in *Lawyers in Early Modern Europe and America*, ed. W. Prest (1981), 16–41; repr. in *LPCL*, 75–98.

——'The Refinement of English Criminal Jurisprudence 1500–1848' in *Crime and Criminal Justice in Europe and Canada*, ed. L. A. Knafla (Calgary, 1981), 17–42; repr. in *LPCL*, 303–24.

——'Origins of the "Doctrine" of Consideration 1535–85' in *On the Laws and Customs of England*, ed. Arnold *et al.* (1981), 336–58; repr. in *LPCL*, 369–91.

——'The Inns of Court and Chancery as Voluntary Associations' (1983) 11–12 *Quaderni Fiorentini*, pt i, 9–38; repr. in *LPCL*, 45–74.

——'Lawyers Practising in Chancery 1474–1486' (1983) 4 *JLH* 54–76.

——'The Legal Education of Richard Empson' (1984) 57 *BIHR* 98–9.

——*The Order of Serjeants at Law* (5 Selden Soc. Suppl. Ser.; 1984).

——*English Legal Manuscripts in the United States of America* (Selden Soc.; 1985, 1990), 2 pts.

——'English Law and the Renaissance' (1985) 44 *CLJ* 46–61; repr. in *LPCL*, 461–76.

——*The Legal Profession and the Common Law: historical essays* (London and Ronceverte, 1986). Collected papers.

——'The Inns of Court and Legal Doctrine' in *Lawyers and Laymen*, ed. T. M. Charles-Edwards, M. E. Owen, and D. B. Walters (Cardiff, 1986), 274–86; repr. in *CLT*, 37–51.

——'Early Tudor Reports and the Plea Rolls' (1987) 18 *Cambrian Law Jnl* 25–33.

——'Introduction' to Legal Classics Library reprint of *Doctor and Student* (Birmingham, Alabama, 1988), 1–26.

——'Records, Reports, and the Origins of Case-law in England' in *Judicial Records, Law Reports, and the Growth of Case Law*, ed. J. H. Baker (5 CSC, Berlin, 1989), 15–46; repr. in *CLT*, 133–64.

——'Personal Actions in the High Court of Battle Abbey 1450–1602' (1992) 51 *CLJ* 508–29; repr. in *CLT*, 263–85.

—— 'Personal Liberty under the Common Law of England, 1200–1600' in *The Origins of Modern Freedom in the West*, ed. R. W. Davis (Stanford, Calif., 1995), 178–202 (with notes at 343–54); repr. in *CLT*, 319–47.

—— 'Sir John Melton's Case (1535): Cockermouth Castle and the three silver luces' (1996) 55 *CLJ* 249–64; repr. in *CLT*, 365–82.

—— *Catalogue of English Legal Manuscripts in Cambridge University Library* (Woodbridge, 1996).

—— 'The Books of the Common Law' in *The Book in Britain: Volume III, 1400–1557*, ed. L. Hellinga and J. B. Trapp (Cambridge, 1999), 411–32.

—— *The Common Law Tradition: lawyers, books and the law* (London and Rio Grande, 2000). Collected papers.

—— 'Due Process and Wager of Law: Judicial Conservatism in the Tudor Common Pleas' in *Human Rights and Legal History: essays in honour of Brian Simpson*, ed. K. O'Donovan and G. R. Rubin (Oxford, 2000), 271–84.

—— *The Law's Two Bodies: some evidential problems in English legal history* (Oxford, 2001).

—— *Readers and Readings in the Inns of Court and Chancery* (13 Selden Soc. Suppl. Ser.; 2001).

—— *An Introduction to English Legal History* (4th edn, 2002).

—— 'Benefit of Clergy in England and its Secularization 1450–1550' in *Ins Wasser geworfen und Ozeane durchquert? Festschrift für Knut Wolfgang Nörr*, ed. M. Ascheri, F. Ebel, M. Heckel, A. Padoa-Schioppa, W. Pöggeler, F. Ranieri, and W. Rütten (Cologne 2003), 27–37.

—— 'John Rastell and the Terms of the Law' (forthcoming).

—— and Milsom, S. F. C., *Sources of English Legal History: private law to 1750* (1986).

Ball, R. E., 'Exchequer of Pleas, Bills and Writs' (1988) 9 *JLH* 308–23.

Barbour, W. T., *The History of Contract in Early English Equity* (Oxford, 1914).

Barton, J. L., 'The Statute of Uses and the Trust of Freeholds' (1966) 82 *LQR* 215–25.

—— 'The Early History of Consideration' (1969) 85 *LQR* 372–91.

—— *Roman Law in England* (5 Ius Romanum Medii Aevi, pt 13a; 1971).

—— 'Future Interests and Royal Revenues in the Sixteenth Century' in *On the Laws and Customs of England*, ed. Arnold *et al.* (1981), 359–82.

Bassett, M., 'The Fleet Prison in the Middle Ages' (1944) 5 *Univ. Toronto Law Jnl* 383–402.

Bayne, C. G., *The Council of King Henry VII* [*c.*1935], vols iii and iv (ff. 400–788) only, JHB MS. 96. These contain the end of Bayne's account of the Star Chamber, followed (from fo. 498) by his account of the Court of Requests. The treatment consists largely of summaries of selected cases from the manuscript records. Some of this material was used in 75 Selden Soc., but abridged and reworked by Dunham: *see* Dunham, introd. to *Select Cases in the Council of Henry VII*.

Beale, J. H., *A Bibliography of Early English Law Books* (Cambridge, Mass., 1926); with suppl. by R. B. Anderson (1943).

Bean, J. M. W., *The Estates of the Percy Family, 1416–1537* (Oxford, 1958).

—— *The Decline of English Feudalism, 1215–1540* (Manchester, 1968).

Bedonelle, G., and le Gal, P., *Le 'Divorce' du Roi Henry VIII: études et documents* (Geneva, 1987).

Behrens, G., 'An Early Tudor Debate on the Relation between Law and Equity' (1998) 19 *JLH* 143–61.

—— 'Equity in the *Commentaries* of Edmund Plowden' (1999) 20 *JLH* 25–50.

Bell, H. E., *An Introduction to the History and Records of the Court of Ward and Liveries* (Cambridge, 1953).

—— *Maitland: a critical examination and assessment* (1965).

Bellamy, J., *The Tudor Law of Treason an introduction* (1979).

—— *Criminal Law and Society in Late Medieval and Tudor England* (Gloucester, 1984).

—— *The Criminal Trial in Later Medieval England* (Toronto, 1998).

Bender, P., *Die Rezeption des römischen Rechts im Urteil der deutschen Rechtswissenschaft* (Frankfurt, 1979).

Benson, J., *Village Borough Courts* (79 Transactions of the Devonshire Association; 1948).

Beresford, M. W., 'The Common Informer, the Penal Statutes, and Economic Regulation' (1958) 10 *Econ. Hist. Rev.* (2nd Ser.) 221–37.

Berkowitz, D. S. (ed.), *Humanist Scholarship and Public Order: two tracts against the Pilgrimage of Grace by Sir Richard Morison* (Washington, 1984).

Bernard, G. W., *War, Taxation and Rebellion in Early Tudor England: Henry VIII, Wolsey, and the Amicable Grant of 1525* (Brighton, 1986).

—— 'The Tyranny of Henry VIII' in *Authority and Consent in Tudor England: essays presented to C. S. L. Davies*, ed. G. W. Bernard and S. J. Gunn (Aldershot, 2002), 113–29.

—— and Guy, J. A., 'The Pardon of the Clergy Reconsidered' (1986) 37 *Jnl Ecclesiastical History* 258–87.

Bevan, A., 'The Role of the Judiciary in Tudor Government, 1509–47', Ph.D. diss. (Cambridge, 1985).

—— 'The Henrician Assizes and the Enforcement of the Reformation' in *The Political Context of Law*, ed. R. Eales and D. Sullivan (1987), 61–76.

Biancalana, J., *The Fee Tail and the Common Recovery in England 1176–1502* (Cambridge, 2001).

Bindoff, S. T., *The History of Parliament: the House of Commons 1509–58* (1982), 3 vols.

Blanchard, I., 'Population Change, Enclosure and the Early Tudor Economy' (1970) 23 *Economic History Rev.* 427–45.

Bland, D. S., 'Rhetoric and the Law Student in Sixteenth Century England' (1957) 54 *Studies in Philology* 498–508.

—— 'Henry VIII's Royal Commission on the Inns of Court' (1969) 10 *JSPTL* 178–94.

—— 'Learning Exercises and Readers at the Inns of Court and Chancery in the Fifteenth and Sixteenth Centuries' (1979) 95 *LQR* 244–52.

Blatcher, M., 'Touching the Writ of Latitat: an act "of no great moment"' in *Elizabethan Government and Society: essays presented to Sir John Neale*, ed. S. T. Bindoff, J. Hurstfield, and C. H. Williams (1961), 188–212.

—— *The Court of King's Bench 1450–1550: a study in self-help* (1978).

Boersma, F. L., 'Sir Antony Fitzherbert and *La Graunde Abridgement*', Ph.D. thesis (Michigan, 1977; publ. Ann Arbor, 1978).

—— 'Sir Antony Fitzherbert: a biographical sketch and short bibliography' (1978) 71 *Law Library Jnl* 387–400.

——'Fitzherbert's *Natura Brevium*: a bibliographic study' (1978) 71 *Law Library Jnl* 257–65.

——*An Introduction to Fitzherbert's Abridgement* (Abingdon, 1981).

Bordwell, P., 'Property in Chattels' (1929) 29 *Harvard Law Rev.* 374–94, 501–20, 731–51.

Bowker, M. (ed.), 'Some Archdeacons' Court Books and the Commons' Supplication against the Ordinaries of 1532' in *The Study of Medieval Records: essays in honour of Kathleen Major*, ed. D. A. Bullough and R. L. Storey (Oxford, 1971), 282–316.

Boynton, L., 'The Tudor Provost–Marshal' (1962) 77 *EHR* 437–55.

Bradshaw, B., *The Irish Constitutional Revolution of the Sixteenth Century* (Cambridge, 1979).

——'The Controversial Sir Thomas More' (1985) 36 *Jnl Eccles. Hist.* 535–69.

Brand, P., 'Irish Law Students and Lawyers in Late Medieval England' (2000) 32 *Irish Historical Studies* 161–73.

Brentnall, H. C., 'Venison Trespasses in the Reign of Henry VII' (1949) 53 *Wilts. Archaeological and Natural History Magazine* 191–212.

Britnell, R. H., *Growth and Decline in Colchester 1300–1525* (Cambridge, 1986).

Brodie, D. M., 'Edmund Dudley: minister of Henry VII' (1932) 15 *TRHS* (4th ser.) 133–61.

Brooks, C. W., *Pettyfoggers and Vipers of the Commonwealth: the 'lower branch' of the legal profession in early modern England* (Cambridge, 1986).

——*Lawyers, Litigation and English Society since 1450* (1998).

——and Sharpe, K., 'History, English Law and the Renaissance: a comment' (1976) 72 *Past and Present* 133–42.

Brown, D. H., 'Historical Perspectives on the Statute of Uses' (1979) 9 *Manitoba Law Jnl* 409–33.

Brown, R. S., 'The Cheshire Writs of Quo Warranto in 1499' (1934) 49 *EHR* 676–84.

Bryson, W. H., *The Equity Side of the Exchequer* (Cambridge, 1975).

Buck, A. R., 'The Politics of Land Law in Tudor England 1529–40' (1990) 11 *JLH* 200–17.

——'Rhetoric and Real Property in Tudor England: Thomas Starkey's *Dialogue between Pole and Lupset*' (1992) 4 *Cardozo Studies in Law and Literature* 27–43.

Bush, D., *The Renaissance and English Humanism* (1939).

Bush, M. L., 'Protector Somerset and Requests' (1974) 17 *Historical Jnl* 45–64.

——*The Government Policy of Protector Somerset* (1975).

——'The Act of Proclamations: a reinterpretation' (1983) 27 *AJLH* 33–53.

——'Tax Reform and Rebellion in Early Tudor England' (1991) 76 *History* 379–400.

——' "Up for the Commonweal": the significance of tax grievances in the English rebellions of 1536' (1991) 106 *EHR* 299–318.

Byrom, H. J., 'Richard Tottell: his life and work' (1927) 8 *The Library* (4th ser.) 195–232.

Caesar, J., *The Ancient State, Authoritie and Proceedings of the Court of Requests*, ed. L. M. Hill (Cambridge, 1975).

Cameron, A., 'A Nottinghamshire Quarrel in the Reign of Henry VII' (1972) 45 *BIHR* 27–32.

——'Complaint and Reform in Henry VII's Reign: the origins of the statute of 3 Hen. VII, c. 2?' (1978) 51 *BIHR* 83–9.

Campbell, B. M. S., 'The Population of Early Tudor England: a re-evaluation of the 1522 Muster Returns and 1524 and 1525 Lay Subsidies' (1981) 7 *Jnl Historical Geography* 145–54.

Capua, J. V., 'The Early History of Martial Law in England' (1977) 36 *CLJ* 152–73.

Carlton, C., *The Court of Orphans* (Leicester, 1974).

Carpenter, C., 'Law, Justice and Landowners in Late Medieval England' (1983) 1 *LHR* 205–37.

—— *Locality and Polity: a study of Warwickshire landed society 1401–99* (Cambridge, 1992).

Carter, P., 'The Records of the Court of First Fruits and Tenths 1540–1554' (1994) 21 *Archives* 57–66.

Caspari, F., *Humanism and the Social Order in Tudor England* (Chicago, 1954).

Champion, W. A., 'Litigation in the Boroughs: the Shrewsbury *Curia Parva* 1480–1730' (1994) 15 *JLH* 201–22.

Chibi, A. A., 'Henry VIII and his Marriage to his Brother's Wife: the sermon of Bishop John Stokesley' (1994) 67 *Historical Rev.* 40–56.

Chrimes, S. B., *English Constitutional Ideas in the Fifteenth Century* (Cambridge, 1936; repr. New York, 1965).

—— *Henry VII* (1972).

—— Ross, C. D., and Griffiths, R. A. (eds), *Fifteenth Century England 1399–1509* (2nd edn, Stroud, 1995).

Clayton, D. J., 'Peace Bonds and the Maintenance of Law and Order in Late Medieval England: the example of Cheshire' (1985) 58 *BIHR* 133–48.

Coing, H., *Die Rezeption des römischen Rechts in Frankfurt am Main* (Frankfurt am Main, 1939).

—— *Römisches Recht in Deutschland* (6 Ius Romanum Medii Aevi, pars v, Milan, 1964).

—— (ed.), *Handbuch der Quellen und Literatur des neueren europäischen Privatrechtsgeschichte*, ii, pt 2 (Munich, 1976).

Coke, E., *Institutes of the Laws of England* (1628–44), 4 pts.

Coleman, C., and Starkey, D. R., *Revolution Reassessed: revisions in the history of Tudor government and administration* (Oxford, 1986).

Coleman, D. C., *The Economy of England 1450–1750* (Oxford, 1977).

Condon, M. M., 'Ruling Elites in the Reign of Henry VII' in *Patronage, Pedigree and Power in Late Medieval England*, ed. C. Ross (Gloucester, 1979), 109–37.

—— 'An Anachronism with Intent? Henry VII's Council Ordinance of 1491/2' in *Kings and Nobles in the Later Middle Ages*, ed. R. A. Griffiths and J. Sherborne (Gloucester, 1986), 228–53.

—— 'From Caitiff and Villein to Pater Patriae: Reynold Bray and the profits of office' in *Profit, Piety and the Professions in Later Medieval England*, ed. M. Hicks (1990), 137–68.

Cooper, J. P., 'The Supplication against the Ordinaries Reconsidered' (1957) 72 *EHR* 616–41.

—— 'Henry VII's Last Years Reconsidered' (1959) 2 *Historical Jnl* 103–29.

—— 'Patterns of Inheritance and Settlement by Great Landowners from the Fifteenth to the Eighteenth Centuries' in *Family and Inheritance*, ed. J. Goody, J. Thirsk, and E. P. Thompson (Cambridge, 1978), 192–327.

Cornwall, J., *The Revolt of the Peasantry, 1549* (1977).

—— *Wealth and Society in Early Sixteenth Century England* (1988).

Cowley, J. D., *A Bibliography of Abridgments* (Selden Soc.; 1932).

Cross, C., Loades, D., and Scarisbrick, J. J. (eds), *Law and Government under the Tudors* (Cambridge, 1988).

Cruickshank, C. G., *The English Occupation of Tournai, 1513–19* (Oxford, 1971).

Dahm, G., 'On the Reception of Roman and Italian Law in Germany' in *Pre-Reformation Germany*, ed. E. Strauss (London and Basingstoke, 1972), 282–315.

Davenport, F. G., 'The Decay of Villeinage in East Anglia' (1900) 14 *TRHS* (2nd ser.) 125–41.

Davies, C. S. L., 'Slavery and Protector Somerset: the Vagrancy Act of 1547' (1966) 19 *Econ. Hist. Rev.* (2nd ser.) 533–49.

—— 'The Cromwellian Decade: authority and consent' (1997) 7 *TRHS* (6th ser.) 177–95.

—— 'Tournai and the English Crown, 1513–19' (1998) 41 *Historical Jnl* 1–26.

—— 'Tournai MPs at Westminster?' (2001) 20 *Parliamentary History* 233–5.

Davies, R. R., 'The Twilight of Welsh Law 1284–1536' (1966) 51 *History* 143–64.

Davis, E. J., 'The Beginning of the Reformation: Christchurch, Aldgate, 1532' (1925) 8 *TRHS* (4th ser.) 127–50.

Davis, J., 'The Authorities for the Case of Richard Hunne (1514–15)' (1915) 30 *EHR* 477–88.

Dawson, J. P., *A History of Lay Judges* (Cambridge, Mass., 1960).

—— *Oracles of the Law* (Ann Arbor, 1968).

Derrett, J. M., 'Neglected Versions of the Contemporary Account of the Trial of Sir Thomas More' (1960) 33 *BIHR* 202–23.

—— 'The Trial of Sir Thomas More' (1964) 79 *EHR* 449–77; repr. with revisions in *Essential Articles for the Study of Thomas More*, ed. R. S. Sylvester and G. P. Marc'hadour (1977), 49–78.

—— 'The Affairs of Richard Hunne and Friar Standish' (1979) in *Complete Works of Sir Thomas More*, ix. 213–46.

DeVine, S. W., 'The Concept of Epieikeia in the Chancery of England's Enforcement of Uses before 1535' (1987) 21 *Univ. British Columbia Law Rev.* 323–50.

Dickens, A. G., *The English Reformation* (2nd edn, 1989).

Dietz, F. C., *English Government Finance 1485–1558* (1921; 2nd edn, 1964, as vol. i of *English Public Finance*, 2 vols.).

Dodds, M. H., and Dodds, R., *The Pilgrimage of Grace 1536–7 and the Exeter Conspiracy 1538* (Cambridge, 1915), 2 vols.

Doe, N., *Fundamental Authority in Medieval English Law* (Cambridge, 1990).

—— 'Legal Reasoning and Sir Roger Townsend' (1990) 11 *JLH* 191–9.

Donahue, C. (ed.), *The Records of the Medieval Ecclesiastical Courts. Part II: England* (7 CSC, Berlin, 1994).

Drobac, J., 'The "Perfect" Jointure: its formulation after the Statute of Uses' [1988] *Cambrian Law Rev.* 26–44.

Du Boulay, F. R. H., 'Who were Farming the English Demesnes at the End of the Middle Ages?' (1965) 47 *Econ. Hist. Rev.* (2nd ser.) 443–55.

Dugdale, W., *Origines Juridiciales* (3rd edn, 1680).

Dunham, W. H., introduction to *Select Cases in the Council of Henry VII*, ed. C. G. Bayne and W. H. Dunham (75 Selden Soc.; 1958). *See also* Bayne, C. G.

Dunham, W. H., 'Regal Power and the Rule of Law: a Tudor paradox' (1964) 3 *Jnl British Studies*, pt ii, 24–56.

——and Wood, C. T., 'The Right to Rule in England: depositions and the kingdom's authority 1327–1485' (1976) 81 *Amer. Hist. Rev.* 748–52.

Dyer, C., *Lords and Peasants in a Changing Society: the estates of the bishopric of Worcester, 680–1540* (Cambridge, 1980).

Eagleston, A. J., *The Channel Islands under Tudor Government, 1485–1642: a study in administrative history* (Cambridge, 1949).

Edwards, J. G., *The Principality of Wales 1267–1967: a study in constitutional history* (Caernarvon, 1969).

Edwards, P., *The Horse Trade of Tudor and Stuart England* (1988).

Eising, K., *Aspekte des englischen 'de facto'-Gesetzes vom 14. Oktober 1495* (Munich, 1995).

Ellis, S. G., 'The Destruction of the Liberties: some further evidence' (1981) 54 *BIHR* 150–61.

——'The Common Bench Plea Roll of 19 Edw. IV' (1984) 31 *Analecta Hibernica* 21–60.

——*Reform and Revival: English government in Ireland, 1470–1534* (Royal Historical Soc., 1986).

——*Tudor Frontiers and Noble Power: the making of the British state* (Oxford, 1995).

Elton, G. R., 'The Evolution of a Reformation Statute' (1949) 64 *EHR* 174–97; repr. in *Studies*, ii. 82–106.

——*The Tudor Revolution in Government: administrative changes in the reign of Henry VIII* (Cambridge, 1953).

——'An Early Tudor Poor Law' (1953) 6 *Econ. Hist. Rev.* (2nd ser.) 55–67.

——*Star Chamber Stories* (1958).

——'Henry VII's Council' (1959) 74 *EHR* 686–90; repr. in *Studies*, i. 294–9.

——'Henry VIII's Act of Proclamations' (1960) 75 *EHR* 208–22; repr. in *Studies*, i. 339–54.

——'Why the History of the Early-Tudor Council remains Unwritten' in *Annali della Fondazione Italiana per la Storia Amministrativa*, i. (1964), 268–96; repr. in *Studies*, i. 308–38.

——'Government by Edict' (1965) 8 *Historical Jnl* 266–71; repr. in *Studies*, i. 300–7.

——'The Law of Treason in the Early Reformation' (1968) 11 *Historical Jnl* 211–36.

——'The Rule of Law in Renaissance England' in *Tudor Men and Institutions*, ed. A. J. Slavin (Baton Rouge, La, 1972), 265–94, repr. in *Studies*, i. 260–84.

——*Policy and Police: the enforcement of the Reformation in the age of Thomas Cromwell* (Cambridge, 1972).

——*Reform and Renewal: Thomas Cromwell and the common weal* (Cambridge, 1973).

——*Studies in Tudor and Stuart Politics and Government* (Cambridge, 1974–83). 3 vols. of collected papers.

——*Reform and Reformation: England 1509–1558* (Cambridge, Mass., 1977).

——'The Sessional Printing of Statutes, 1484–1547' in *Wealth and Power in Tudor England*, ed. Ives *et al.* (1978), 68–86; repr. in *Studies*, iii. 92–109.

——*English Law in the Sixteenth Century: reform in an age of change* (Selden Soc. lecture, 1979).

——*The Tudor Constitution* (2nd edn, Cambridge, 1982).

—— *England under the Tudors* (3rd edn, 1991).

Emsley, K., and Fraser, C. M., *The Courts of the County Palatine of Durham from earliest times to 1971* (Durham, 1984).

Endicott, T. A. D., 'The Conscience of the King: Christopher St German and Thomas More and the development of English equity' (1989) 47 *Univ. Toronto Faculty of Law Rev.* 549–70.

Ernst, D. R., 'The Moribund Appeal of Death: compensating survivors and controlling jurors in early modern England' (1984) 28 *AJLH* 164–88.

Evans-Jones, R. L. (ed.), *The Civil Law Tradition in Scotland* (Stair Soc., Edinburgh, 1995).

Feenstra, R., 'The Development of European Private Law: a Romanist watershed?' in *The Civilian Tradition and Scots Law*, ed. D. L. C. Miller and R. Zimmermann (Berlin, 1997), 103–15.

Ferguson, A. B., 'The Tudor Commonwealth and the Sense of Change' (1963) 3 *Jnl British Studies*, pt i, 11–35.

—— *The Articulate Citizen and the English Renaissance* (1965).

—— *Clio Unbound: perception of the social and cultural past in Renaissance England* (Durham, NC, 1979).

Fideler, P. A., and Mayer, T. F., (eds), *Political Thought and the Tudor Commonwealth* (1992).

Fifoot, C. H. S., *History and Sources of the Common Law: tort and contract* (1949).

Fisher, R. M., 'The Inns of Court and the Reformation 1530–80', Ph.D. diss. (Cambridge, 1974).

—— 'Thomas Cromwell, Dissolution of the Monasteries, and the Inns of Court, 1534–1540' (1977) 14 *JSPTL* 103–17.

—— 'Thomas Cromwell, Humanism and Educational Reform, 1530–1540' (1977) 50 *BIHR* 151–63.

Fox, A., and Guy, J. A., *Reassessing the Henrician Age: humanism, politics and reformation, 1500–50* (Oxford, 1986).

Fox, K. O., 'An Edited Calendar of the First Brecknockshire Plea Roll of the Courts of the King's Great Sessions in Wales, July 1542' (1965) 14 *National Library of Wales Jnl* 469–84.

Garrett-Goodyear, H., 'The Tudor Revival of *Quo Warranto* and Local Contributions to State Building' in *On the Laws and Customs of England*, ed. Arnold *et al.* (1981), 231–95.

Geritz, A. J., and Laine, A. L., *John Rastell* (Boston, 1983).

Gilmore, M. P., *Humanists and Jurists: six studies in the Renaissance* (Cambridge, Mass., 1963).

Glazebrook, P. R., 'The Making of English Criminal Law: the reign of Mary Tudor' (1977) *Criminal Law Rev.* 582–97.

Goldsworthy, J., *The Sovereignty of Parliament: history and philosophy* (Oxford, 1999), chs 4–5.

Goodman, A., *The New Monarchy: England, 1471–1534* (Oxford, 1988).

Gorla, G., and Moccia, L., 'A Revisiting of the Comparison between Continental Law and English Law' (1981) 2 *JLH* 143–56.

Graham, H. J., 'The Rastells and the Printed English Law Book of the Renaissance' (1954) 47 *Law Library Jnl* 6–25.

—— ' "Our Tong Maternall Marvellously Amendyd and Augmentyd": the first Englishing and printing of the medieval statutes at large, 1530–8' (1965) 13 *UCLA Law Rev.* 58–98.

Graham, H. J., and Heckel, J. W., 'The Book that "Made" the Common Law: the first printing of Fitzherbert's *La Graunde Abridgment*, 1514–16' (1958) 51 *Law Library Jnl* 100–16.

Graves, M. A. R., 'Freedom of Peers from Arrest' (1977) 21 *AJLH* 1–14.

Gray, C. M., *Copyhold, Equity, and the Common Law* (Cambridge, Mass., 1963).

Green, T. A., 'The Tudor Transformation of the Law of Homicide' in 'The Jury and the
English Law of Homicide, 1200–1600' (1976) 74 *Michigan Law Rev.* 413, at 472–99.

—— *Verdict according to Conscience: perspectives on the English criminal jury 1200–1800*
(Chicago, 1985).

Griffiths, M., 'Kirtlington Manor Court 1500–1650' (1980) 45 *Oxoniensia* 260–83.

Griffiths, R. A., 'Wales and the Marches' in *Fifteenth Century England 1399–1509*,
ed. S. B. Chrimes *et al.* (2nd edn, Stroud, 1995), 145–72.

Grummitt, D., 'Henry VII, Chamber Finance and the "New Monarchy": some new
evidence' (1999) 72 *BIHR* 229–43.

—— '"One of the mooste pryncipall treasours belongyng to his Realme of Englande":
Calais and the Crown, *c.*1450–1558' in *The English Experience of France, c.1450–1558*, ed. D.
Grummitt (Aldershot, 2002), 46–62.

Gunn, S. J., 'The Act of Resumption of 1515' in *Early Tudor England*, ed. D. Williams
(Woodbridge, 1989), 87–106.

—— *Early Tudor Government, 1485–1558* (Basingstoke and London, 1995).

Guth, D. J., 'Notes on the Early Tudor Exchequer of Pleas' in *Tudor Men and Institutions*,
ed. Slavin (1972), 101–22.

—— 'Enforcing Late-Medieval Law: patterns of litigation during Henry VII's reign' in *Legal
Records and the Historian*, ed. J. H. Baker (1978), 80–96.

—— and McKenna, J. W. (eds), *Tudor Rule and Revolution: essays for G. R. Elton from his
American friends* (Cambridge, 1982).

Guy, J. A., 'Wolsey, the Council and the Council Courts' (1976) 91 *EHR* 481–505; repr. in
Politics, Law and Counsel, ch. 4.

—— 'A Conciliar Court of Audit at Work in the Last Months of the Reign of Henry VII'
(1976) 47 *BIHR* 289–95; repr. in *Politics, Law and Counsel*, ch. 2.

—— 'Thomas More as Successor to Wolsey' (1977) 52 *Thought: Fordham University
Quarterly* 272–92.

—— *The Cardinal's Court: the impact of Thomas Wolsey in Star Chamber* (Hassocks, 1977).

—— *The Public Career of Sir Thomas More* (Brighton, 1980).

—— 'Henry VIII and the Praemunire Manoeuvres of 1530–31' (1982) 97 *EHR* 481–503; repr.
in *Politics, Law and Counsel*, ch. 7.

—— 'The Development of Equitable Jurisdiction 1450–1550' in *Law, Litigants and the
Legal Profession*, ed. A. H. Manchester and E. W. Ives (1983), 80–6; repr. in *Politics, Law
and Counsel*, ch. 1.

—— (ed.), *Christopher St German on Chancery and Statute* (6 Selden Soc. Suppl. Ser.; 1985).

—— *The Court of Star Chamber and its Records to the Reign of Elizabeth I* (1985).

—— 'Thomas More and St German: the battle of the books' and 'Law, Equity and
Conscience in Henrician Juristic Thought' in *Reassessing the Henrician Age*, ed. Fox and
Guy (1986), 95–120, 179–98; repr. in *Politics, Law and Counsel*, ch. 8.

—— 'The Privy Council: revolution or evolution?' in *Revolution Reassessed*, ed. C. Coleman and D. Starkey (1986), 59–85; repr. in *Politics, Law and Counsel*, ch. 10.

—— Introduction and Appendix C (concerning St German) to *The Complete Works of St. Thomas More*, vol. x (New Haven, 1987).

—— *Tudor England* (Oxford, 1988).

—— 'Law, Equity and Conscience in Henrician Juristic Thought' in *Reformation, Humanism and 'Revolution'*, ed. G. J. Schochet (Proceedings of the Folger Institute Center for the History of British Political Thought, Washington, 1990), 1–15.

—— *Politics, Law and Counsel in Tudor and Early Stuart England* (Variorum Collected Studies Series, Aldershot, 2000). Collected papers.

—— *Thomas More* (2000).

—— *See also* Bernard, G. W.; Fox, A.

Gwyn, P., ' "Where Conscience hath the most Force": Wolsey and the law' in *The King's Cardinal* (1990), 101–43.

Haigh, C., 'Church Courts and English Law' in *English Reformations* (Oxford, 1999), 72–87.

Hale, M., *Prerogatives of the King*, ed. D. E. C. Yale (92 Selden Soc.; 1975).

Hamilton, D. L., 'The Learned Councils of the Tudor Queens Consort' in *State, Sovereigns and Society in Early Modern England: essays in honour of A. J. Slavin*, ed. C. Carlton (Stroud, 1998), 87–101.

Hanbury, H. G., 'The Legislation of Richard III' (1962) 6 *AJLH* 95–113.

Harding, A., *A Social History of English Law* (1966).

Harris, B. J., 'Aristocratic Women in Early Modern England' in *State, Sovereigns and Society in Early Modern England: essays in honour of A. J. Slavin*, ed. C. Carlton (Stroud, 1998), 3–24.

Harriss, G. L., 'Thomas Cromwell's New Principle of Taxation' (1978) 93 *EHR* 721–38.

—— 'Theory and Practice in Royal Taxation: some observations' (1982) 97 *EHR* 811–19.

Harrison, C., 'Manor Courts and the Governance of Tudor England' in *Communities and Courts in Britain, 1150–1900*, ed. C. Brooks and M. Lobban (1997), 43–59.

Harrison, C. J., 'The Petition of Edmund Dudley' (1972) 87 *EHR* 82–99.

Harvey, P. D. A. (ed.), *The Peasant Land Market in Medieval England* (Oxford, 1984).

Haskett, T. S., 'The Medieval English Court of Chancery' (1996) 14 *LHR* 245–313.

Hastings, M., *The Court of Common Pleas in Fifteenth-Century England* (Ithaca, NY, 1947).

Hatcher, J., *Plague, Population and the English Economy 1348–1530* (1977).

Hawkes, E., 'Women's Knowledge of Common Law and Equity Courts in late-Medieval England' in *Medieval Women and the Law*, ed. N. J. Menuge (Woodbridge, 2000), 145–61.

Hayes, R. C. E., ' "Ancient Indictments" for the North of England, 1461–1509' in *The North of England in the Age of Richard III*, ed. A. J. Pollard (Stroud, 1996), 19–45.

Hazeltine, H. D., 'The Renaissance and the Laws of Europe' in *Cambridge Legal Essays* (Cambridge, 1926), 139–71.

Hearnshaw, F. J. C., *Leet Jurisdiction in England* (Southampton Record Society; 1908).

Heinze, R. W., *The Proclamations of the Tudor Kings* (Cambridge, 1976).

Helmholz, R. H., 'Assumpsit and *Fidei Laesio*' (1975) 91 *LQR* 406–32; repr. in *Canon Law and the Law of England*, 263–89.

Helmholz, R. H., 'Debt Claims and Probate Jurisdiction in Historical Perspective' (1979) 23 *AJLH* 68–82; repr. in *Canon Law and the Law of England*, 307–21.

—— *Select Cases on Defamation to 1600* (101 Selden Soc.; 1985).

—— 'Usury and the Medieval English Church Courts' (1986) 61 *Speculum* 364–80; repr. in *Canon Law and the Law of England*, 323–39.

—— *Canon Law and the Law of England* (London and Ronceverte, 1987). Collected papers.

—— *Roman Canon Law in Reformation England* (Cambridge, 1990).

—— 'Ecclesiastical Lawyers and the English Reformation' (1995) 3 *ELJ* 360–70.

—— 'Trusts in the English Ecclesiastical Courts 1300–1640' in *Itinera Fiduciae*, ed. R. H. Helmholz and R. Zimmermann (19 CSC, Berlin, 1998), 153–72.

—— *The* ius commune *in England: four studies* (Oxford, 2001).

Henderson, E. G., 'Relief from Bonds in the English Chancery: mid-sixteenth century' (1974) 18 *AJLH* 298–306.

—— 'Legal Literature and the Impact of Printing on the English Legal Profession' (1975) 68 *Law Library Jnl* 288–93.

—— 'Legal Rights to Land in the Early Chancery' (1982) 26 *AJLH* 97–122.

Herbruggen, H. S., 'The Process against Sir Thomas More' (1983) 99 *LQR* 113–36.

Hicks, M. A., 'Attainder, Resumption and Coercion 1461–1529' (1984) 3 *Parliamentary Hist.* 14–31.

—— (ed.), *Profit, Piety and the Professions in Later Medieval England* (Gloucester, 1990).

Hill, L. M., 'The Two-Witness Rule in High Treason Trials: some comments on the emergence of procedural law' (1968) 12 *AJLH* 95–111.

—— See also Caesar, J.

Hilton, R. H., 'Swanimote Rolls of Feckenham Forest' in *Miscellany*, i (1 Worcs. Hist. Soc., new ser.; 1960), 37–52.

History of Parliament: see Bindoff, S. T.; Wedgwood, J. C.

Hoak, D., *The King's Council in the Reign of Edward VI* (Cambridge, 1976).

—— 'The Iconography of the Crown Imperial' in *Tudor Political Culture*, ed. D. Hoak (Cambridge, 1995), 54–103.

Hogrefe, P., 'The Life of Saint Germain' (1937) 13 *Rev. English Studies* 398–404.

—— *The Sir Thomas More Circle* (Urbana, Ill., 1959).

—— 'Sir Thomas More and Doctors' Commons' (1967) 4 *Moreana*, pt xiv, 15–21.

—— *The Life and Times of Sir Thomas Elyot* (Ames, Ia, 1967).

—— *Tudor Women: commoners and queens* (Ames, Ia, 1975).

Holdsworth, W. S., *A History of English Law* (1903–66), 16 vols.

—— 'The Prerogative in the Sixteenth Century' (1921) 21 *Columbia Law Rev.* 554–71.

Holmes, C., 'G. R. Elton as a Legal Historian' (1997) 7 *TRHS* (6th ser.) 267–79.

Holmes, P. J., 'The Great Council in the Reign of Henry VII' (1986) 101 *EHR* 840–62.

—— 'The Last Tudor Great Councils' (1990) 33 *Historical Jnl* 1–22.

Horowitz, M. R., 'An Early Tudor Teller's Book' (1981) 96 *EHR* 103–16.

—— 'Richard Empson, Minister of Henry VII' (1982) 55 *BIHR* 35–49.

Horrox, R., *Richard III: a study of service* (Cambridge, 1989).

Hoskins, W. G., *The Age of Plunder* (1976).

Houlbrooke, R., 'The Decline of Ecclesiastical Jurisdiction under the Tudors' in *Continuity and Change*, ed. R. O'Day and F. Heal (Leicester, 1976), 239–57.

—— *Church Courts and People during the English Reformation 1520–70* (Cambridge, 1979).

—— 'The Making of Marriage in mid-Tudor England' (1985) 10 *Jnl Family History* 339–52.

Hoyle, R. W., 'An Ancient and Laudable Custom: the definition and development of tenant right in north-western England in the sixteenth century' (1987) 116 *Past & Present* 24–55.

—— 'Tenure and the Land Market in Early Modern England' (1990) 43 *Econ. Hist. Rev.* (2nd ser.) 1–20.

—— 'Resistance and Manipulation in Early Tudor Taxation: some evidence from the North' (1993) 20 *Archives* 158–76.

—— 'Crown, Parliament and Taxation in Sixteenth-Century England' (1994) 109 *EHR* 1174–96.

—— 'The Origins of the Dissolution of the Monasteries' (1995) 38 *Historical Jnl* 287–305.

—— *The Pilgrimage of Grace and the Politics of the 1530s* (Oxford, 2001).

Hunnisett, R. F., *The Medieval Coroner* (Cambridge, 1961).

—— 'The Last Sussex Abjurations' (1964) 102 *Sussex Archaeological Collections* 39–51; (1965) 103 *Sussex Archaeological Collections* 49–52.

—— *Calendar of Nottinghamshire Coroners' Inquests 1485–1558* (25 Thoroton Soc. Record Series, Nottingham, 1969).

—— *Sussex Coroners' Inquests 1485–1558* (74 Sussex Record Soc., Lewes, 1985).

Hurstfield, J., 'The Greenwich Tenures of the Reign of Edward VI' (1949) 65 *LQR* 76–81.

—— 'The Revival of Feudalism in Early Tudor England' (1952) 37 *History* 131–45.

—— 'Was there a Tudor Despotism after all?' (1967) 17 *TRHS* (5th ser.) 83–108.

Ibbetson, D. J., 'Assumpsit and Debt in the Early Sixteenth Century: the origins of the indebitatus count' (1982) 41 *CLJ* 142–61.

—— 'Consideration and the Theory of Contract in the Sixteenth Century Common Law' in *Towards a General Law of Contract*, ed. J. L. Barton (8 CSC; Berlin, 1990), 67–123.

—— 'Fault and Absolute Liability in pre-Modern Contract Law' (1997) 18 *JLH* 1–31.

—— 'Case Law and Judicial Precedents in Medieval and Early-Modern England' in *Auctoritates: xenia R. C. van Caenegem oblata*, ed. S. Dauchy, J. Monballyu, and A. Wijffels (Brussels, 1997), 55–68.

—— *A Historical Introduction to the Law of Obligations* (Oxford, 1999).

—— 'Legal Printing and Legal Doctrine' (2000) 35 *Irish Jurist* 345–54.

Ives, E. W., 'The Reputation of the Common Lawyer in English Society, 1450–1550' (1960) 7 *Univ. Birmingham Historical Jnl* 130–61.

—— 'The Genesis of the Statute of Uses' (1967) 82 *EHR* 673–97.

—— 'The Common Lawyers in pre-Reformation England' (1968) 18 *TRHS* (7th ser.) 145–73.

—— 'A Lawyer's Library in 1500' (1969) 85 *LQR* 104–16.

—— 'The Purpose and Making of the Later Year Books' (1972) 89 *LQR* 64–86.

—— ' "Ayenst taking awaye of Women": the inception and operation of the abduction act of 1487' in *Wealth and Power in Tudor England*, ed. Ives *et al.* (1978), 21–44.

—— 'Crime, Sanctuary, and Royal Authority under Henry VIII: the exemplary sufferings of the Savage family' in *On the Laws and Customs of England*, ed. Arnold *et al.* (1981), 296–320.

Ives, E. W., *The Common Lawyers in pre-Reformation England* (Cambridge, 1983).

—— *Anne Boleyn* (Oxford, 1986).

—— Knecht, R. J., and Scarisbrick, J. J. (eds), *Wealth and Power in Tudor England: essays presented to S. T. Bindoff* (1978).

Jack, S., and Schofield, R. S. (eds), 'Four Early Tudor Financial Memoranda' (1963) 36 *BIHR* 189–206.

Jack, S. M., 'The Conflict of Common Law and Canon Law in Early Sixteenth Century England: Richard Hunne revisited' (1985) 3 *Parergon* (new ser.) 131–45.

Jansen, S. L., *Political Protest and Prophecy under Henry VIII* (Woodbridge, 1991).

Jenkins, D., 'English Law and the Renaissance Eighty Years On: in defence of Maitland' (1981) 2 *JLH* 107–42.

Jones, G. H., *History of the Law of Charity 1532–1827* (Cambridge, 1969).

Jones, Neil G., 'Tyrrel's Case and the Use upon a Use' (1993) 14 *JLH* 75–93.

—— 'Trusts, Practice and Doctrine: 1536–1660', Ph.D. diss. (Cambridge, 1994).

—— 'Uses, Trusts, and a Path to Privity' (1997) 56 *CLJ* 175–200.

—— 'The Influence of Revenue Considerations upon the Remedial Practice of Chancery in Trust Cases, 1536–1660' in *Communities and Courts in Britain, 1150–1900*, ed. C. Brooks and M. Lobban (1997), 99–113.

—— 'Trusts in England after the Statute of Uses: a view from the 16th century' in *Itinera Fiduciae*, ed. R. Helmholz and R. Zimmermann (19 CSC, Berlin, 1998), 173–205.

Jones, Norman, *God and the Moneylenders: usury and law in early modern England* (Oxford, 1989).

Jones, P. E., 'The City Courts of Law' (1943) 93 *Law Jnl* 285–302.

Jones, W. J., *The Elizabethan Court of Chancery* (Oxford, 1967).

Jones, W. R. D., *The Tudor Commonwealth 1529–59* (1970).

—— *The Tree of Commonwealth 1450–1793* (Madison, 2000).

Jordan, W. K., *Edward VI* (Cambridge, Mass., 1968–70), 2 vols.

Kaufman, P. I., 'Henry VII and Sanctuary' (1984) 53 *Church History* 465–76.

Kaye, J. M., 'Early History of Murder and Manslaughter' (1967) 83 *LQR* 365–95, 569–601.

—— 'A Note on the Statute of Enrolments 1536' (1988) 104 *LQR* 617–34.

Kelley, D. R., *Foundations of Modern Historical Scholarship: language, law and history in the French Renaissance* (New York, 1970).

—— 'History, English Law and the Renaissance' (1974) 65 *Past & Present* 24–51; repr. in *History, Law and the Social Sciences* (1984), pt xi.

—— *The Human Measure: social thought in the western legal tradition* (Cambridge, Mass., 1990).

—— 'Law' in *The Cambridge History of Political Thought 1450–1700*, ed. J. H. Burns and M. Goldie (Cambridge, 1991), 66–94.

Kelly, H. A., *The Matrimonial Trials of Henry VIII* (Stanford, Calif., 1976).

Kelly, J. M., *A Short History of Western Legal Theory* (Oxford, 1992), ch. 5 (1350–1600), 159–202.

Kelly, M. J., 'Canterbury Jurisdiction and Influence during the Episcopate of William Warham 1503–32', Ph.D. diss. (Cambridge, 1963).

—— 'The Submission of the Clergy' (1965) 15 *TRHS* (5th ser.) 97–119.

Kenny, C., *King's Inns and the Kingdom of Ireland* (Dublin, 1992).

Kermode, J. (ed.), *Enterprise and Individuals in Fifteenth-Century England* (Stroud, 1991).

Kerridge, E., *Agrarian Problems in the Sixteenth Century and After* (1969).

—— *Usury, Interest, and the Reformation* (Aldershot, 2002).

Kesselring, K., 'A Draft of the 1531 "Acte for Poysoning" ' (2001) 116 *EHR* 894–9.

Kiralfy, A. K. R., *The Action on the Case* (1951).

—— *A Source Book of English Law* (1957).

Kirby, J. W., 'A Fifteenth-Century Family: the Plumptons of Plumpton and their lawyers, 1461–1515' (1989) 25 *Northern History* 106–19.

Kisch, G., 'Humanistic Jurisprudence' (1961) 8 *Studies in the Renaissance* 71–87.

Kitching, C., 'The Prerogative Court of Canterbury from Warham to Whitgift' in *Continuity and Change*, ed. R. O'Day and F. Heal (Leicester, 1976), 191–214.

—— 'The Durham Palatinate and the Courts of Westminster under the Tudors' in *The Last Principality*, ed. D. Marcombe (Nottingham, 1987), 49–70.

Knafla, L. A., 'The Matriculation Revolution at the Inns of Court in Renaissance England' in *Tudor Men and Institutions*, ed. Slavin (1972), 232–64.

Knowles, D., *The Religious Orders in England*, iii: *the Tudor Age* (Cambridge, 1959); repr. in *Bare Ruined Choirs: the dissolution of the English monasteries* (Cambridge, 1976).

Koschaker, P., *Europa und das römische Recht* (Munich and Berlin, 1947; 4th edn, 1966).

Krause, H., *Kaiserrecht und Rezeption* (Heidelberg, 1952).

Kreider, A., *English Chantries: the road to dissolution* (97 Harvard Historical Studies, Cambridge, Mass., 1979).

Kunkel, W., 'The Reception of Roman Law in Germany: an interpretation' in *Pre-Reformation Germany*, ed. E. Strauss (1972), 263–81.

Lachmann, R., *From Manor to Market: structural change in England* (Madison, 1987).

Lambert, J., *Les Year Books de Langue Française* (Paris, 1928).

Lander, J. R., 'Bonds, Coercion and Fear: Henry VII and the peerage' in *Florilegium Historiale*, ed. J. F. Rowe and W. H. Stockdale (Toronto, 1971), 327–67.

—— *English Justices of the Peace 1461–1509* (Gloucester, 1989).

Lander, S., 'Church Courts and the Reformation in the Diocese of Chichester, 1500–58' in *Continuity and Change*, ed. R. O'Day and F. Heal (Leicester, 1976), 215–37; and in *The English Reformation Revisited*, ed. C. Haigh (Cambridge, 1987), 34–55.

Lang, R. G. (ed.), *Two Tudor Subsidy Assessment Rolls for the City of London: 1541 and 1582* (London Record Soc., 1993).

Langbein, J. H., *Prosecuting Crime in the Renaissance: England, Germany, France* (Cambridge, Mass., 1974).

Lapsley, G. T., *The County Palatine of Durham* (8 Harvard Historical Studies, Cambridge, Mass., 1900).

Leadam, I. S., 'The Security of Copyholders in the Fifteenth and Sixteenth Centuries' (1893) 8 *EHR* 684–96.

—— 'The Last Days of Bondage in England' (1893) 9 *LQR* 348–65.

—— *The Domesday of Inclosures, 1517–18* (1897), 2 vols.

—— Introduction to *Select Cases in the Court of Requests 1497–1569* (12 Selden Soc.; 1898).

—— Introductions to *Select Cases before the King's Council in the Star Chamber*, i (16 Selden Soc.; 1902) and ii (25 Selden Soc.; 1911).

Lehmberg, S. E., 'Star Chamber 1485–1509' (1961) 24 *Huntington Quarterly* 189–214.

—— *The Reformation Parliament 1529–36* (Cambridge, 1970).

—— 'Early Tudor Parliamentary Procedure: provisos in the legislation of the Reformation Parliament' (1970) 85 *EHR* 1–11.

—— 'Sir Thomas Audley: a soul as black as marble?' in *Tudor Men and Institutions*, ed. Slavin (1972), 1–31.

—— 'Parliamentary Attainder in the Reign of Henry VIII' (1975) 18 *Historical Jnl* 675–702.

—— *The Later Parliaments of Henry VIII, 1536–47* (Cambridge, 1977).

—— *The Reformation of Cathedrals* (Princeton, 1988).

Le Van Baumer *see* Van Baumer, F. le.

Levine, M., *Tudor Dynastic Problems 1460–1571* (1973).

—— 'The Place of Women in Tudor Government' in *Tudor Rule and Revolution*, ed. D. J. Guth and J. W. McKenna (Cambridge, 1982), 109–23.

Lewis, T. E., 'The History of Judicial Precedent III' (1931) 47 *LQR* 411–27.

Lidington, D. R., 'The Enforcement of Penal Statutes at the Court of Exchequer', Ph.D. diss. (Cambridge, 1988).

Loach, J., *Parliament and the Crown in the Reign of Mary Tudor* (Oxford, 1986).

—— *Parliament under the Tudors* (Oxford, 1991).

—— *Edward VI* (New Haven and London, 1999).

Loades, D., *Power in Tudor England* (Basingstoke and London, 1997).

Lockwood, S., 'Marsilius of Padua and the Case for the Royal Ecclesiastical Supremacy' (1991) 1 *TRHS* (6th ser.) 89–119.

Logan, F. D., 'The Henrician Canons' (1974) 47 *BIHR* 99–103.

—— 'Doctors' Commons in the Early Sixteenth Century: a society of many talents' (1988) 61 *BIHR* 151–65.

Lubasz, H., 'The Corporate Borough in the Common Law of the late Year-Book Period' (1964) 80 *LQR* 228–43.

Luckett, D., 'Henry VII and the South-Western Escheators' in *The Reign of Henry VII: proceedings of the 1993 Harlaxton symposium*, ed. B. Thompson (Stamford, Lincs., 1995), 54–64.

—— 'Crown Office and Licensed Retinues in the Reign of Henry VII' in *Rulers and Ruled in Late Medieval England: essays presented to Gerald Harriss*, ed. R. E. Archer and S. Walker (1995), 223–38.

McCauliff, C. M. A., 'Parliament and the Supreme Headship: Church–State relations according to Thomas More' (1999) 48 *Catholic University Law Rev.* 653–84.

MacCulloch, D., 'Bondmen under the Tudors' in *Law and Government under the Tudors*, ed. C. Cross *et al.* (1988), 91–109.

McGlynn, M., 'The King and the Law: Prerogativa Regis in early Tudor England', Ph.D. thesis (Centre for Medieval Studies, University of Toronto, 1997).

—— 'Teaching the Law in a Time of Change: the Royal Prerogative and the Statute of Uses' in *Learning the Law: Teaching and the Transmission of English Law, 1150–1900*, ed. J. A. Bush and A. Wijffels (London and Rio Grande, 1999), 211–25.

—— *The Royal Prerogative and the Learning of the Inns of Court* (Cambridge, forthcoming in 2003).

McGovern, W. M., 'The Enforcement of Informal Contracts in the Later Middle Ages' (1971) 59 *California Law Rev.* 1145–93.

McIntosh, M. K., 'Social Change and Tudor Manorial Leets' (1984) in *Law and Social Change*, ed. Guy and Beale, 73–85.

—— *Autonomy and Community: the royal manor of Havering 1200–1500* (Cambridge, 1986).

—— 'Money Lending on the Periphery of London, 1300–1600' (1988) 20 *Albion* 557–71.

—— *Controlling Misbehaviour in England, 1370–1600* (Cambridge, 1998).

McKenna, J. W., 'The Myth of Parliamentary Sovereignty in Late-Medieval England' (1979) 94 *EHR* 481–506.

Maffei, D., *Gli Inizi dell'Umanesimo Giuridico* (Milan, 1956).

Maitland, F. W., *English Law and the Renaissance* (Cambridge, 1901); repr. in *Selected Historical Essays of F. W. Maitland*, ed. H. M. Cam (1957).

—— *Collected Papers of Frederic William Maitland*, ed. H. A. L. Fisher (Cambridge, 1911), 3 vols.

Marsden, R. G., 'The Vice-Admirals of the Coast' (1907) 22 *EHR* 468–77.

Mayer, T. F., *Thomas Starkey and the Commonweal: humanist politics and religion in the reign of Henry VIII* (Cambridge, 1989).

—— 'Tournai and Tyranny' (1991) 34 *Historical Jnl* 257–77.

Meekings, C. A. F., 'King's Bench Files' in *Legal Records and the Historian*, ed. Baker (1978), 97–139.

Mehren, von, *see* Von Mehren

Merriman, R. B., *Letters and Life of Thomas Cromwell* (1902), 2 vols.

Metzger, F., 'Das Englische Kanzleigericht unter Kardinal Wolsey', Ph.D. diss. (Erlangen, 1976).

—— 'The Last Phase of the Medieval Chancery' in *Law-Making and Law-Makers in British History*, ed. A. Harding (1980), 79–89.

Miklovich, J. I., 'The Significance of the Royal Sign Manual in Early Tudor Legislative Procedure' (1979) 52 *BIHR* 23–36.

Miller, D. L. C., and Zimmermann, R., *The Civilian Tradition and Scots Law* (20 Schriften zur Europäischen Rechts- und Verfassungsgeschichte, Berlin, 1997).

Milsom, S. F. C., 'Not Doing is no Trespass: a view of the boundaries of Case' (1954) *CLJ* 105–17; repr. in *Studies in the History of the Common Law*, 91–103.

—— 'Richard Hunne's "Praemunire"' (1961) 76 *EHR* 80–2; repr. in *Studies in the History of the Common Law*, 145–7.

—— 'Reason in the Development of the Common Law' (1965) 81 *LQR* 496–517; repr. in *Studies in the History of the Common Law*, 149–70.

—— 'Law and Fact in Legal Development' (1967) 17 *Univ. Toronto Law Jnl* 1–19; repr. in *Studies in the History of the Common Law*, 171–89.

—— *Historical Foundations of the Common Law* (2nd edn, 1981).

—— *Studies in the History of the Common Law* (London and Ronceverte, 1985). Collected papers.

—— *See also* Baker, J. H., and Milsom, S. F. C.

Mirow, M. C., 'Readings on Wills in the Inns of Court, 1552–1631', Ph.D. diss. (Cambridge, 1993).

Mirow, M. C. 'Monks and Married Women: the use of the yearbooks in defining testamentary capacity in sixteenth- and seventeenth-century readings on wills' (1997) 65 *RHD* 19–39.

Moore, P. R., 'The Heraldic Charge against the Earl of Surrey 1546–7' (2001) 116 *EHR* 557–83.

Moreton, C., 'A "best betrustyd frende": a late medieval lawyer and his clients' (1990) 11 *JLH* 183–90.

—— 'The "Library" of a Late-Fifteenth-century Lawyer' (1991) 13 *The Library* (6th ser.) 338–46.

—— *The Townshends and their World: gentry, law, and land in Norfolk c.1450–1551* (Oxford, 1992).

Muldrew, C., *The Economy of Obligation: the culture of credit and social relations in early modern England* (Basingstoke, 1998).

Murphy, V. M., 'The Debate over Henry VIII's First Divorce: an analysis of the contemporary treatises', Ph.D. diss. (Cambridge, 1984).

—— *see also* Surtz, E., and Murphy, V.

Newman, C. M., 'Local Court Administration within the Liberty of Allertonshire, 1470–1540' (1995) 22 *Archives* 13–24.

—— 'Order and Community in the North: the liberty of Allertonshire in the later fifteenth century' in *The North of England in the Age of Richard III*, ed. A. J. Pollard (Stroud, 1996), 47–66.

Nicholls, K., *Land, Law and Society in Sixteenth Century Ireland* (1976).

Nicholson, G., 'The Act of Appeals and the English Reformation' in *Law and Government under the Tudors*, ed. C. Cross *et al.* (Cambridge, 1988), 19–30.

O'Day, R., 'The Law of Patronage in Early Modern England' (1975) 26 *Jnl Eccles. Hist.* 247–60.

Oestmann, C., *Lordship and Community: the Lestrange family and the village of Hunstanton, Norfolk, in the first half of the sixteenth century* (Woodbridge, 1994).

Ogle, A., *The Tragedy of the Lollards' Tower* (Oxford, 1949).

Osler, D., 'The Myth of European Legal History' (1997) 16 *Rechtshistorische Jnl* 393–410.

Palgrave, F., 'Inventory and Calendar of the Baga de Secretis' (1842) 3 *DKR*, app. ii, 210–68; (1843) 4 *DKR*, app. ii, 213–97.

Pantzer, K., 'Printing the English Statutes 1484–1640: some historical implications' in *Books and Society in History*, ed. K. E. Carpenter (New York, 1983), 61–102.

Parmiter, G. de C., 'Tudor Indictments, Illustrated by the Indictment of Sir Thomas More' (1961) 6 *Recusant Hist.* 140–56.

Parry, G., *A Guide to the Records of the Great Sessions in Wales* (Aberystwyth, 1995).

Patterson, N., 'Gaelic Law and the Tudor Conquest of Ireland' (1991) 27 *Irish Historical Studies* 193–215.

Payling, S. J., 'Arbitration, Perpetual Entails and Collateral Warranties in Late-Medieval England' (1992) 13 *JLH* 32–62.

—— 'Social Mobility, Demographic Change and Landed Society in Late Medieval England' (1992) 45 *Econ. Hist. Rev.* 51–73.

—— 'The Politics of Family: late medieval marriage contracts' in *The McFarlane Legacy*, ed. R. H. Britnell and A. J. Pollard (New York, 1995), 21–47.

Pettegree, A., *Foreign Protestant Communities in Sixteenth-Century London* (Oxford, 1986).

Phythian-Adams, C. V., 'Rituals of Personal Confrontation in Late Medieval England' (1991) 73 *Bull. John Rylands Lib.* 65–90.

Pickthorn, K., *Early Tudor Government* (1934; repr. 1949), 2 vols.

Pierce, T. J., 'The Law of Wales: the last phase' (1963) *Trans. Honorable Soc. of Cymmrodorion* 7–32.

Plomer, M. R., 'Two Lawsuits of Richard Pynson' (1909) 10 *The Library* (2nd ser.) 115–33.

—— 'An Inventory of Wynkyn de Worde's House "The Sun in Fleet Street" in 1553' (1915) 6 *The Library* (3rd ser.) 228–34.

—— 'Richard Pynson, Glover and Printer' (1922) 3 *The Library* (4th ser.) 49–51.

Plucknett, T. F. T., 'Some Proposed Legislation of Henry VIII' (1936) 19 *TRHS* (4th ser.) 119–44.

—— *Concise History of the Common Law* (5th edn, 1956).

Pollard, A. F., *England under Protector Somerset: an essay* (1900).

—— 'Council, Star Chamber and Privy Council under the Tudors' (1922–4) 37 *EHR* 337–60, 516–39; 38 *EHR* 42–60.

—— *Wolsey* (1929; repr. with notes and corrections, 1953; repr. with an introd. by G. R. Elton, 1965).

Poole, R. E. A., 'A Sixteenth-Century MS of Precedents of Indictments' in *A Kentish Miscellany*, ed. F. Hull (11 Kent Records, Chichester, 1979), 128–62.

Prall, S. E., 'The Development of Equity in Tudor England' (1964) 8 *AJLH* 1–19.

Pronay, N. 'The Chancellor, the Chancery and the Council at the End of the Fifteenth Century' in *British Government and Administration*, ed. H. Hearder and H. R. Loyn (Cardiff, 1974), 87–103.

Pugh, T. B. (ed.), *The Marcher Lordships of South Wales 1415–1536: select documents* (Cardiff, 1963).

—— and Robinson, W. R. B., *Sessions in Eyre in a Marcher Lordship: a dispute between the earl of Worcester and his tenants in Gower and Kilvey in 1524* (4 South Wales and Monmouth Record Society Publications, Newport, 1957).

Putnam, B. H., *Early Treatises on the Practice of Justices of the Peace in the Fifteenth and Sixteenth Centuries* (Oxford, 1924).

—— 'Sixteenth-Century Treatises for Justices of the Peace' (1947) 7 *Univ. Toronto Law Jnl* 137–61.

Quinn, D. B., 'Anglo-Irish Local Government 1485–1534' (1939) 1 *Irish Historical Studies* 354–81.

Ramsay, N. L., 'What was the Legal Profession?' in *Profit, Piety and the Professions in later Medieval England*, ed. M. Hicks (1990), 62–71.

—— 'Scriveners and Notaries as Intermediaries in Later Medieval England' in *Enterprise and Individuals in Fifteenth-Century England*, ed. J. I. Kermode (Stroud, 1991), 118–31.

Rawcliffe, C., *The Staffords: earls of Stafford and dukes of Buckingham* (Cambridge, 1978).

Reed, A. W., *Early Tudor Drama: Medwall, the Rastells, Heywood, and the More circle* (1926; repr. 1969).

Reeves, A. C., 'The Great Sessions in the Lordship of Newport 1503' (1975) 26 *Bulletin of the Board of Celtic Studies* 323–41.

Reeves, J., *A History of English Law from the Time of the Saxons to the End of the Reign of Philip and Mary* (1787), 4 vols.

Reid, R. R., *The King's Council in the North* (1921; repr. Wakefield, 1975).

Reynolds, S., 'The History of the Idea of Incorporation or Legal Personality' in *Ideas and Solidarities* (1995), pt vi, 1–20.

Rhodes, E. H., 'Calendar of Decrees of the Court of General Surveyors 34 to 38 Hen. 8' (1869) 30 *DKR* 166–96.

Richardson, H. G., 'The Early History of the Commissions of Sewers' (1919) 34 *EHR* 385–93.

Richardson, W. C., 'The Surveyor of the King's Prerogative' (1941) 56 *EHR* 52–75.

—— *Tudor Chamber Administration, 1485–1547* (Baton Rouge, La., 1952).

—— *History of the Court of Augmentations, 1536–54* (Baton Rouge, La., 1961).

Roberts, P. R., 'The Welsh Language, English Law and Tudor Legislation' (1989) *Trans. Hon. Soc. of Cymmrodorion* 19–75.

—— 'The "Henry VIII Clause": delegated legislation and the Tudor principality of Wales' in *Legal Record and Historical Reality*, ed. T. G. Watkin (1989), 37–49.

—— 'The English Crown, the Principality of Wales and the Council in the Marches 1534–1641' in *The British Problem c.1534–1707*, ed. B. Bradshaw and J. Morrill (Basingstoke, 1996), 118–47.

Roberts, R. J., 'John Rastell's Inventory of 1538' (1979) 1 *The Library* (6th ser.) 34–42.

Robinson, O. F., Fergus, T. D., and Gordon, W. M., *European Legal History* (3rd edn, 2000).

Robinson, W. R. B., 'The Tudor Revolution in Welsh Government 1536–43: its effect on gentry participation' (1988) 103 *BIHR* 1–20.

—— 'The County Court of the Englishry of Gower 1498–1500: a preliminary study' (1995–6) 29 *National Library of Wales Jnl* 357–89.

—— 'Princess Mary's Itinerary in the Marches of Wales, 1525–27' (1998) 71 *BIHR* 233–52.

—— see also Pugh, T. B., and Robinson, W. R. B.

Rodgers, C. P., 'Humanism, History and the Common Law' (1985) 6 *JLH* 129–56.

Ross, R. J., 'The Commoning of the Common Law: the Renaissance debate over printing English law, 1520–1640' (1998) 146 *Univ. Pennsylvania Law Rev.* 323–461.

Rowan, S., *Ulrich Zasius: a jurist of the German Renaissance* (Frankfurt, 1987).

Ruddock, A. A., 'The Earliest Records of the High Court of Admiralty, 1515–58' (1949) 22 *BIHR* 139–51.

Rueger, Z., 'Gerson's Concept of Equity and Christopher St Germain' (1982) 3 *Hist. Pol. Thought* 1–30.

Sainty, J., *List of English Law Officers, King's Counsel and Holders of Patents of Precedence* (7 Selden Soc. Supp. Ser.; 1987).

—— *The Judges of England 1272–1990* (10 Selden Soc. Supp. Ser.; 1993).

Savine, A., 'Copyhold Cases in Early Chancery Proceedings' (1902) 17 *EHR* 296–303.

—— 'Bondmen under the Tudors' (1902) 17 *TRHS* (2nd ser.) 235–89.

—— 'English Customary Tenure in the Tudor Period' (1905) 19 *Quarterly Jnl Economics* 33–80.

Scarisbrick, J., 'The Pardon of the Clergy' (1956) 12 *Historical Jnl* 22–39.

—— 'Cardinal Wolsey and the Common Weal' in *Wealth and Power in Tudor England*, ed. Ives *et al.* (1978), 45–67.

—— 'Henry VIII and the Dissolution of the Secular Colleges' in *Law and Government under the Tudors*, ed. C. Cross *et al.* (1988), 51–66.

Schneider, M. H., 'Thomas More as Viewed by two French Jurists' (1970) 27 *Moreana* 107–10.

Schoeck, R. J., 'Rhetoric and Law in Sixteenth Century England' (1953) 50 *Studies in Philology* 110–27.

—— 'The Date of the Replication' (1960) 76 *LQR* 500–3.

—— 'The Libraries of Common Lawyers in the Renaissance' (1962) 6 *Manuscripta* 155–67.

—— 'Sir Thomas More, Humanist and Lawyer' (1964) 34 *Univ. Toronto Quarterly* 1–14.

—— 'The Place of Sir Thomas More in Legal History and Tradition' (1978) 23 *American Jnl of Jurisprudence* 212–23.

Schofield, R., *Parliamentary Lay Taxation 1485–1547*, Ph.D. diss. (Cambridge, 1963).

—— 'Taxation and the Political Limits of the Tudor State' in *Law and Government under the Tudors*, ed. C. Cross *et al.* (1988), 227–55.

Scott, K. L., 'Additions to the Oeuvre of the English Border Artist: the *Nova Statuta*' in *The Mirrour of the Worlde* (Roxburghe Club; Oxford, 1980), 45–68.

Seipp, D., 'Jurors, Evidences, and the Tempest of 1499' in *The Jury in the History of the Common Law*, ed. J. W. Cairns and G. McLeod (2002), 75–92.

Sellar, W. D. H., 'Forethocht Felony, Malice Aforethought and the Classification of Homicide' in *Legal History in the Making*, ed. W. M. Gordon and T. D. Fergus (1991), 43–59.

Shaller, T. K., 'English Law and the Renaissance: the common law and humanism in the sixteenth century', Ph.D. thesis (Harvard, 1979).

Sharpe, J. A., 'The History of Crime in Late Medieval and Early Modern England: a review of the field' (1982) 7 *Social History* 187–203.

Sheail, J., 'The Distribution of Taxable Population and Wealth in England during the Early Sixteenth Century' (1972) 55 *Trans. Institute of British Geographers* 111–26.

Sherrington, E. J., 'The Plea-Rolls of the Courts of Great Sessions 1541–75' (1964) 13 *National Library of Wales Jnl* 363–73.

Siegel, J. A., 'The Aristotelian Basis of English Law 1450–1800' (1981) 56 *New York Univ. Law Rev.* 18–59.

Simpson, A. W. B., 'Keilwey's Reports' (1957) 73 *LQR* 89–105.

—— 'The Reports of John Spelman' (1957) 73 *LQR* 334–8.

—— 'The Introduction of the Action on the Case for Conversion' (1959) 75 *LQR* 364–80; repr. in *Legal Theory and Legal History*, 93–109.

—— 'The Early Constitution of the Inns of Court' (1970) 28 *CLJ* 241–56; repr. in *Legal Theory and Legal History*, 17–32.

—— 'The Source and Function of the Later Year Books' (1971) 87 *LQR* 94–118; repr. in *Legal Theory and Legal History*, 67–91.

—— *History of the Common Law of Contract: the rise of the action of assumpsit* (Oxford, 1975).

—— 'The Early Constitution of Gray's Inn' (1975) 34 *CLJ* 131–50; repr. in *Legal Theory and Legal History*, 33–52.

—— *A History of the Land Law* (2nd edn, Oxford, 1986).

Simpson, A. W. B., *Legal Theory and Legal History: essays on the common law* (London and Ronceverte, 1987). Collected papers.

Skeel, C. A. J., *The Council in the Marches of Wales* (1904).

Skyrme, T., *History of the Justices of the Peace, i: England to 1689* (Chichester, 1991).

Slack, P., *Poverty and Policy in Tudor and Stuart England* (1988).

Slavin, A. J. (ed.), *Tudor Men and Institutions* (Baton Rouge, La, 1972).

——— 'The Fall of Lord Chancellor Wriothesley: a study in the politics of conspiracy' (1975) 7 *Albion* 265–86.

Smart, S. J., 'John Foxe and "The Story of Richard Hun, Martyr" ' (1986) 37 *Jnl Eccles. Hist.* 1–14.

Smith, J. B., 'Crown and Community: the principality of Wales in the reign of Henry Tudor' (1966) 3 *Welsh History Rev.* 145–71.

Smith, J. H., *Appeals to the Privy Council from the American Plantations* (New York, 1950).

Smith, R. B., *Land and Politics in the England of Henry VIII: the West Riding of Yorkshire 1530–46* (Oxford, 1970).

Somerville, R., 'Henry VII's "Council Learned in the Law" ' (1939) 54 *EHR* 427–42.

——— 'The Duchy of Lancaster Council and the Court of Duchy Chamber' (1940) 23 *TRHS* (4th ser.) 159–77.

——— *History of the Duchy of Lancaster, i* (1953).

——— 'The Palatine Courts in Lancashire' in *Law-Making and Law-Makers in British History*, ed. A. Harding (1980), 54–63.

Squibb, G. D., *The High Court of Chivalry* (Oxford, 1959).

——— *Doctors' Commons: a history of the college of advocates and doctors of law* (Oxford, 1977).

Stacy, W. R., 'Richard Roose and the Use of Parliamentary Attainder in the Reign of Henry VIII' (1986) 29 *Historical Jnl* 1–15.

Stein, P. G., 'Legal Humanism and Legal Science' (1986) 54 *RHD* 297–306.

Stephen, J. F., *A History of the Criminal Law of England* (1883), 3 vols.

Stevens, L. C., 'The Contribution of French Jurists to the Humanism of the Renaissance' (1953) 1 *Studies in the Renaissance* 92–105.

Stoljar, S. J., *History of Contract at Common Law* (Canberra, 1975).

Storey, R. L., *Diocesan Administration in 15th Century England* (2nd edn, York, 1972).

Strauss, G., *Law, Resistance and the State: the opposition to Roman Law in Reformation Germany* (Princeton, 1986).

Stuckey, M., 'A Consideration of the Emergence and Exercise of Judicial Functions in the Star Chamber' (1993) 19 *Monash Law Rev.* 117–64.

Surtz, E., and Murphy, V., *The Divorce Tracts of Henry VIII* (Anger, 1988).

Sutherland, D. W., *The Assize of Novel Disseisin* (Oxford, 1973).

Tawney, R. H., *The Agrarian Problem in the Sixteenth Century* (1912); repr. with introd. by L. Stone (1967).

Teeven, K. M., 'The Emergence of Modern Contract Law in the Tudor Period' (1983) 10 *Ohio Northern Univ. Law Rev.* 441–61.

Thirsk, J. (ed.), *Agrarian History of England and Wales, iv. 1500–1640* (Cambridge, 1967). New editions of each chapter were included in *Chapters from the Agrarian History of England and Wales* (Cambridge, 1990), 5 vols.

—— *Tudor Enclosures* (1958); repr. in *The Rural Economy of England* (1984), 65–83.

—— *Economic Policy and Projects* (1978).

Thompson, F., *Magna Carta: its role in the making of the English constitution 1300–1629* (1948).

Thorne, S. E., 'Tudor Social Transformation and Legal Change' (1951) 26 *New York Univ. Law Rev.* 10–23; repr. in *Essays in English Legal History*, 197–210.

—— 'English Law and the Renaissance' in *La Storia del Diritto nel Quadro delle Scienze Storiche* (Milan, 1966), 437–45; repr. in *Essays in English Legal History*, 187–95.

—— *Essays in English Legal History* (London and Ronceverte, 1985). Collected papers.

Thornley, I. D., 'The Treason Legislation of Henry VIII' (1917) 11 *TRHS* (3rd ser.) 87–123.

—— 'The Destruction of Sanctuary' in *Tudor Studies: Presented to A. F. Pollard*, ed. R. W. Seton-Watson (1924), 182–207.

Thornton, T., 'Local Equity Jurisdictions in the Territories of the English Crown: the Palatinate of Chester, 1450–1540' in *Courts, Counties and the Capital in the Later Middle Ages*, ed. D. E. S. Dunn (Stroud, 1996), 27–52.

—— *Cheshire and the Tudor State, 1480–1560* (Woodbridge, 2000).

—— 'Fifteenth-Century Durham' (2001) 11 *TRHS* (5th ser.) 83–100.

—— 'The English King's French Islands: Jersey and Guernsey in English politics and administration, 1485–1642' in *Authority and Consent in Tudor England: essays presented to C. S. L. Davies*, ed. G. W. Bernard and S. J. Gunn (Aldershot, 2002), 197–217.

Tittler, R., 'The Incorporation of Boroughs, 1540–58' (1977) 62 *History* 24–42.

Tubbs, J. W., *The Common Law Mind: medieval and early modern conceptions* (Baltimore, 2000).

Tucker, P., 'Relationships between London's Courts and the Westminster Courts in the Reign of Edward IV' in *Courts, Counties and the Capital in the later Middle Ages*, ed. D. E. S. Dunn (Stroud, 1996), 117–37.

—— 'London's Courts of Law in the Fifteenth Century: the litigants' perspective' in *Communities and Courts in Britain, 1150–1900*, ed. C. Brooks and M. Lobban (1997), 25–41.

Turpin, C. C., 'The Reception of Roman Law' (1968) 3 *Irish Jurist* (new ser.) 162–74.

Ullmann, W., 'This Realm of England is an Empire' (1979) 30 *Jnl Eccles. Hist.* 175–203; facsimile repr. in W. Ullmann, *Jurisprudence in the Middle Ages* (1980).

Van Baumer, F. le, 'St German: the political philosophy of a Tudor lawyer' (1937) 42 *American Historical Rev.* 631–51.

Van Caenegem, R. C., 'The "Reception" of Roman Law: a meeting of northern and Mediterranean traditions' (1972) 1 *Medievalia Lovaniensia* 195–204.

Van Patten, J. K., 'Magic, Prophecy and the Law of Treason in Reformation England' (1983) 27 *AJLH* 1–32.

Vines, P., 'Land and Royal Revenue: the Statute for the Explanation of the Statute of Wills, 1542–1543' (1997) 3 *Australian Jnl of Legal History* 113–30.

Vinogradoff, P., 'Reason and Conscience in Sixteenth Century Jurisprudence' (1908) 24 *LQR* 373–84; repr. in *The Collected Papers of Sir Paul Vinogradoff*, ii (Oxford, 1928), 190–204.

Virgoe, R., 'The Benevolence of 1481' (1989) 104 *EHR* 25–45.

—— 'Inheritance and Litigation in the Fifteenth Century: the Buckenham disputes' (1994) 15 *JLH* 23–40.

Vogt, W., *Franciscus Duarenus 1509–59* (Stuttgart, 1971).

Von Mehren, A., 'The Judicial Conception of Legislation in Tudor England' in *Interpretations of Modern Legal Philosophies*, ed. P. Sayre (New York, 1947), 751–66.

Walker, D. M., *The Legal History of Scotland: the sixteenth century* [1488–1603] (Edinburgh, 1995).

Warnicke, R. M., 'Sexual Heresy at the Court of Henry VIII' (1987) 30 *Historical Jnl* 247–68.

—— *The Rise and Fall of Anne Boleyn: family politics at the court of Henry VIII* (Cambridge, 1989).

Watkin, T. G., 'Legal Cultures in Mediaeval Wales' in *Legal Wales*, ed. T. G. Watkin (Cardiff, 2001), 21–39.

Waugh, W. J., 'The Great Statute of *Praemunire*' (1922) 37 *EHR* 173–205.

Wedgwood, J. C., with Holt, A. D., *History of Parliament: biographies of members of the Commons House 1439–1509* (1936).

Wegemer, G. B., *Thomas More on Statesmanship* (Washington, 1996).

Weinberger, J., *see* Bacon, F.

Weir, J. A., *see* Wieacker, F.

Whittick, C., 'The Role of the Criminal Appeal in the Fifteenth Century' in *Law and Social Change in British History*, ed. J. A. Guy and H. G. Beale (1984), 55–72.

Whittle, J., *The Development of Agrarian Capitalism: land and labour in Norfolk 1440–1580* (Oxford, 2000).

—— and Yates, M., '*Pays réel* or *pays légal*? Contrasting patterns of land tenure and social structure in eastern Norfolk and western Berkshire, 1450–1600' (2000) 48 *Agricultural History Rev.* 1–26.

Wieacker, F., *Privatrechtsgeschichte der Neuzeit* (Göttingen, 1952; 2nd edn, 1967); tr. by T. [= J. A.] Weir as *A History of Private Law in Europe* (Oxford, 1995).

Wijffels, A., 'Law Books at Cambridge 1500–1640' in *The Life of the Law*, ed. P. Birks (1993), 59–87.

Williams, C. H., 'The So-Called Star Chamber Act' (1930) 15 *History* 129–35.

Williams, P., *The Tudor Regime* (1979).

Williams, W. L., 'The Union of England and Wales' (1907–8) *Trans. Honourable Soc. of Cymmrodorion* 47–117.

Williams, W. R., *The History of the Great Sessions in Wales 1542–1830* (Brecknock, 1899).

Winfield, P. H., 'Abridgments of the Year Books' (1923) 37 *Harvard Law Rev.* 214–44.

Wolffe, B. P., *The Crown Lands 1461 to 1536: an aspect of Yorkist and early Tudor government* (1970).

Wood, C. T., *see* Dunham, W. H.

Woolfson, J., *Padua and the Tudors: English students in Italy, 1485–1603* (Cambridge, 1998).

Wright, S. M., *The Derbyshire Gentry in the Fifteenth Century* (8 Derbyshire Record Soc., Chesterfield, 1983).

Wunderli, R., *London Church Courts and Society on the Eve of the Reformation* (1981).

Yale, D. E. C., 'St German's Little Treatise concerning Writs of Subpoena' (1975) 10 *Irish Jurist* (new ser.) 324–33.

Yeazell, S. C., *From Medieval Group Litigation to the Modern Class Action* (New Haven and London, 1987).

Youings, J., 'The Terms of Disposal of the Devon Monastic Lands' (1954) 69 *EHR* 18–38.

—— 'The Council in the West' (1960) 10 *TRHS* (5th ser.) 41–60.

—— 'The Monasteries' in *Agrarian History of England and Wales, iv: 1540*, ed. J. Thirsk (Cambridge, 1967), 306–55.

—— *The Dissolution of the Monasteries* (1971).

Youngs, F. A., 'Towards Petty Sessions: Tudor JPs and the divisions of counties' in *Tudor Rule and Revolution*, ed. D. J. Guth and J. W. McKenna (Cambridge, 1982), 201–16.

Zell, M. L., 'Early Tudor Justices of the Peace at Work' (1978) 93 *Archaeologia Cantiana* 125–43.

Zimmermann, R., *see* Miller, D. L. C.

INDEX OF NAMES

INDEX OF SUBJECTS